King's Treasury
of **Dynamic**
PREACHING

King's Treasury
of Dynamic
PREACHING
Cycles A-B-C

KING DUNCAN

RESOURCE PUBLISHERS

TABLE OF CONTENTS

Cycle A

Cycle B

Cycle C

Introduction

I hate dull, lifeless preaching. How's that for a positive beginning? But I do! I don't just yawn when I hear dull preaching, I get angry. How dare that pastor waste my time! Even more importantly, how dare that pastor take the greatest privilege given to any man or any woman, the privilege of standing before God's people and proclaiming God's message, and waste it by being boring! The purpose of Dynamic Preaching as well as the workshops on preaching that I have had the privilege of conducting for pastors from a multitude of different traditions over the past 30 years have had one goal in mind: helping pastors have a dramatic impact on their congregations.

This means helping pastors make their messages entertaining—yes, I did say entertaining. You will find lots of humor in Dynamic Preaching. It is better to have people laughing than to have them sleeping.

This also means helping pastors make their sermons more visual. Dynamic Preaching seeks not so much to move from point to point as from picture to picture—mental pictures, that is. We were making the Gospel visual long before the first pastor introduced PowerPoint to his or her congregation. Why? We have become a visually-oriented people. Any time the pastor is rambling on in abstract theological language, the minds of the people in the congregation are taking a stroll to the lunch table or to the office or to a host of other concrete destinations.

The six most important words in the preacher's vocabulary are "Let me give you an example." This is the role, of course, of illustrations. Don't talk to me abstractly about love—give me examples of love in action. Don't talk to me of salvation—give me examples of people who have had their lives turned around by the Good News of Jesus Christ. Dynamic Preaching has always been a treasure trove of illustrations.

Ultimately this means helping pastors move people to action. Whether you regard yourself as an evangelical preacher, a liturgical preacher or a prophet seeking God's justice for the oppressed—the ultimate call of Christ is to get people moving—inviting their neighbors, sharing their resources, helping usher in the Kingdom of God.

I am so grateful to two men who have allowed me to make Dynamic Preaching available to a growing body of pastors—Jim Colaianni of Resource Publishers and Dr. Brett Blair of Sermons.com. I am also grateful to my wife Selina who has handled the business end of our work over these many years. Our work has truly been one of love and we are most grateful.

– King Duncan, Dynamic Preaching

Cycle A

When The Messiah Comes:
There Will Be Light
Isaiah 2:1-5

Dr. Rob Boyd tells about a man whose name was Charlie Stink. People constantly picked on Charlie Stink because of his name. His friends encouraged Charlie Stink to have his name changed. Finally he agreed and went to court to take care of the legal requirements to have his name formally changed.

The next day his friends asked him, "What did you have your name changed to?"

And Charlie Stink replied, "I changed my name to George Stink, but for the life of me, I can't see what difference it will make." (1)

Well, I believe old Charlie Stink missed the point of having his name changed, don't you?

People often miss the point when it comes to Advent and Christmas. For some, this season of the year is simply an opportunity to throw parties and to exchange gifts. They see it simply as an opportunity to eat, drink and be merry. For merchants it is a time to salvage a lackluster year of retail sales. For consumers it is a period of dread as we contemplate the crowded stores and the crowded calendar. All of this misses the point of Advent and Christmas, of course. Advent and Christmas are the coming of Light and Love.

Little Joey asked his mother at Christmas time: "Mom, why do people put lights on their houses?"

"They are celebrating Jesus' birthday," she replied.

"When is Jesus' birthday?" asked Joey.

"He was born on Christmas," his mother replied.

"Jesus was born on Christmas?" Joey exclaimed. "What a coincidence!"

Little Joey is the reason we have all those signs that say, "Jesus is the reason for the season." And, of course it's true. He is the reason for the season. He brought light and love into the world. Because of his coming we have fellowship with the Father. To help us get the real point of the Advent season, I want to take us back about 750 years before Christ to a prophet named Isaiah. Isaiah was both a prophet of judgment and a prophet of hope.

Over the next four weeks we are going to deal with some of Isaiah's most memorable writings concerning the coming Messiah—what it will mean for the world when the Messiah comes. But we will also remind ourselves that the manger of Bethlehem was only the beginning of messianic history. The kingdom of God came into the world with the birth of Jesus, but the fulfillment of that kingdom will only come when the love of Christ reigns over all the earth. So, Advent is a two-fold celebration, a celebration of the birth of the prince of peace, and a celebration of the coming age when the peace, joy and love of Christ will dwell in every heart. Today our emphasis is on the light of Christmas.

In today's lesson Isaiah writes, "He will judge between the nations and will settle disputes for many peoples. They will beat their swords into plowshares and their spears into pruning hooks. Nation will not take up sword against nation, nor will they train for war anymore. Come, O house of Jacob, let us walk in the light of the LORD."

Isaiah spoke of a world of peace and light. Next week we will deal with peace. Today, we want to talk about light.

Nearly eight hundred years after the time of Isaiah, the Apostle Paul would write, "The hour has come for you to wake up from your slumber, because our salvation is nearer now than when we first believed. The night is nearly over; the day is almost here. So let us put aside the deeds of darkness and put on the armor of light."

If there is one theme that is appropriate for this season of the year it is light. Some of you have already gotten out the lights for your Christmas tree. Some of you will perhaps light up the entire inside and outside of your house. A few people go hog-wild—as they say in the South—when it comes to Christmas lights. They will strain every utility plant for miles around with their addiction to brightening up their homes. That's all right, as long as we understand what Isaiah meant when he said, "Let us walk in the light of the LORD." And what Paul meant when he wrote: "The night is nearly over; the day is almost here. So let us put aside the deeds of darkness and put on the armor of light."

Come back with me to the night of May 5, 1942. Europe is mired in the brutal violence of World War II. The Nazis are slaughtering millions of Jews throughout Europe. On the night of May 5, 1942, a small band of Ukrainian Jews from the town of Korolówka decided to hide out from the Nazis in an underground cave. Thirty-eight people, ranging in age from a toddler to a seventy-five year-old woman, created a home underground. They had no advanced equipment, only some lanterns, cooking pots, firewood, and food. For 344 days, almost one full year, none of these cave-dwellers saw the light of day. Some of the men would emerge from the cave at night to search for food or firewood, but no one came out during the daylight hours. Finally, on April 12, 1943, after receiving news that the Germans had retreated, the cave dwellers emerged from underground to see the sun for the first time in almost a year. (2)

How eagerly those cave dwellers awaited being able to leave the darkness and walk in the light. When Isaiah writes in chapter nine, verse two: "The people walking in darkness have seen a great light; on those living in the land of the shadow of death a light has dawned," he is describing that kind of anticipation about seeing the light which the Messiah will bring.

One writer has said that, if you want to really appreciate the contrast between darkness and light today, all you have to do is view nighttime satellite images of North and South Korea. South Korea is bathed in light, with its cities gleaming in the blackness, while North Korea, still primitive in so many ways, is dark.

But it's more than just the lack of visible light that makes North Korea a place of darkness. The North Korean government is one of the most repressive governments on earth. Radio and television sets are hardwired to receive only government propaganda. In 2004, the government banned cell phones. North Koreans still have no access to the Internet—a source of information readily available in almost every other country.

There is another significant contrast, however, between the two: the North is officially atheist—the last remaining "Stalinist" communist society. The South, on the other hand, has known Christian influence for more than a century. (3) In fact, one of the largest Christian churches in the world is in South Korea.

Darkness is a very potent symbol of sin and estrangement. Author Bruce Larson tells of driving on a highway near Scranton, Pennsylvania years ago in the middle of the night. As he was driving along, he took the wrapper off some candy. Finding the ashtrays in the car full, he absentmindedly opened the car window and threw the wrapper out onto the ground. Suddenly he realized what he had done. He also realized that he would never have done this in the daylight. Somehow, the very darkness encouraged him to litter, a thing he deplores. There is something about light that reminds us of our responsibility to other people and helps us to do the responsible thing.

"People who do not live in fellowship with others," writes Larson, "live in perpetual darkness and continually do things of which they are ashamed. But people who live in a fellowship where they know and are known live in the light and are encouraged to be and to do those things of which they can be proud." (4)

Just as darkness symbolizes sin and estrangement, light represents grace and love.

In 1973, Margaret Craven wrote a book titled I Heard the Owl Call My Name. It is a book where the central character, Mark Brian, is a young priest who has only three years to live. His doctor and his bishop have not told him of his prognosis. The bishop sends Mark to a remote Native-American village called Kingcome. He believes that in this small community Mark will be able to find enough of the meaning of life, so that when the time comes he will be ready to die.

It is his first Christmas Eve in the village. Mark is in the church. Everything is ready. He is alone, waiting in the hushed silence with the candlelight shining on the statue that stands in the front of the church, a statue of Christ holding a little lamb. The young priest walks slowly down the center aisle. Not wanting to open the door until the very last minute for fear of losing the precious heat, he walks to the window at the left of the door and looks outside.

The snow lays thick on the ground. He sees the lights of the houses go out, one by one, and the lanterns begin to flicker as the members of the local tribe come slowly, single file, along the path to the church. How many times had the people of his parish traveled this path, he wonders. He goes to the door and opens it, and then steps out into the soft white night, the snow whispering now under the footfalls.

For the first time he feels he knows the people making their way to his church and he feels a deep sense of commitment to them. When the first of the tribe reaches the steps, he holds out his hand to greet each of them by name. (5)

In this story Margaret Craven captures the meaning of this season of the year. The darkness of winter and the faithful villagers lighting their lanterns and walking to the little church where light will flood every heart and they will be united in the love of the Bethlehem babe is a picture of Advent. Darkness is a potent symbol of sin and estrangement. Light is an even more potent symbol of grace and love.

Walking in the light means walking in fellowship with God and one another. That's what we need to see. Walking in the light is a summons to community and peace. We live in a contentious and conflict-filled world. Sometimes even some of our most treasured traditions are sources of conflict.

I was amused to read that in Fort Collins, CO, sometime back a civic task force recommended that red and green lights be banned from the city's holiday display. Why? It was deemed that red and green lights are too religious, so they should not be part of a civic celebration. Later cooler heads on the City Council prevailed and the lights were allowed to remain.

I doubt that most of us would think of Christmas lights as being too religious. Especially when we see them adorning the homes of people who verge on being outright pagans. But it reminds us of how potent a symbol light can be. "The light shines in the darkness, and the darkness can never extinguish it," writes John in the prologue to his Gospel. And it's true. Light is more powerful than dark. Love is more powerful than hate. Faith is more powerful than fear.

The month of December is one of the darkest months of the year. When we put up our Christmas lights we are affirming that the darkness shall never overcome the light. We are affirming those positive values of peace and justice and love and hope. Most of all we are affirming the presence of God in our world.

As people of the light, our job is to make sure the light of Christ shines ever more brightly in this world of darkness. How do we do that? By continually walking in the light ourselves. By living a life of integrity and love.

There is a story that has been circulating on the web about a church Christmas pageant. The day of the presentation finally arrived. A young girl named Jana was so excited about her part that her parents thought she was to be one of the main characters, though she had not told them what she was to do.

The parents of the children in the pageant were all there and one by one the children took their places. Jana's parents could see the shepherds fidgeting in one corner of the stage which was evidently intended to be a field. Mary and Joseph stood solemnly behind the manger. In the back three young wise men waited impatiently. But still little Jana sat quietly and confidently.

Then the teacher began: "A long time ago, Mary and Joseph had a baby and they named Him Jesus," she said. "And when Jesus was born, a bright star appeared over the stable."

At that cue, Jana got up from her chair, picked up a large tin-foil star, walked behind Mary and Joseph and held the star up high for everyone to see.

When the teacher told about the shepherds coming to see the baby, the three young shepherds came forward and Jana jiggled the star up and down excitedly to show them where to come. When the wise men responded to their cue, she went forward a little to meet them and to lead the way, her face as alight as the real star might have been.

The playlet ended. They had refreshments. On the way home Jana said, with great satisfaction, "I had the main part!"

"You did?" her Mom asked, wondering why she thought that.

"Yes," she said, "'cause I showed everybody how to find Jesus!" (6)

And ultimately that is what it means to walk in the light. It is to show the world how to find Jesus. It is to so live that people see in us year round the love of the Bethlehem babe. That is our part and it is the main part—to show the world how to find Jesus.

1. The Timothy Report, http://www.timothyreport.com.

2. "The Cave Dwellers" by Peter Lane Taylor from National Geographic Adventure, published in Reader's Digest, January 2005, pp. 134-141.

3. Charles R. Boatman, editor, The NIV Standard Lesson Commentary, 2009-2010 (Cincinnati: Standard Publishing, 2009), pg. 379.

4. Ask Me To Dance (Waco, TX: Word Books, 1972), pg. 52.

5. Cited at Drema's Sermon, http://www.fairlingtonumc.org/sermons_2002/sermon12242002.htm.

6. Author unknown. Cited in Sermon Fodder, Sermon_Fodder-subscribe@yahoogroups.com.

When The Messiah Comes:
There Will Be Peace
Isaiah 11:1-10

Some of you will remember an old comedy team from the early part of the twentieth century named Laurel and Hardy. They produced some marvelous work. Their comedy was slapstick, but it also showed a deep understanding of human nature.

Conrad Hyers, in his book And God Created Laughter tells about an early Laurel and Hardy film from 1925 titled Big Business. Stan and Ollie are Christmas-tree salesmen in California—going from house to house in a Model T truck loaded with trees.

The story begins innocently enough—with a touch of the Christmas spirit and good cheer. Before long, however, things deteriorate considerably.

Stan and Ollie come to the door of one homeowner who has a somewhat salty disposition and is in no mood to put up with door-to-door salesmen. He is not interested in a tree.

When he shuts the door after declining Stan and Ollie's offer, a tree branch gets caught in the door jamb. Ollie rings for the irritated homeowner to open the door and release the branch. Then as Stan is explaining the reason for this second intrusion, the man slams the door and catches Stan's coat in the door. Again the doorbell is rung, and as Stan is apologizing, the incensed homeowner slams the door and once more catches the tree in the jamb. When the irate homeowner comes to the door for a fifth time, he brings along clippers, with which he cuts up the tree and tosses it on the lawn. Stan concludes, "I don't think he wants a tree."

By this time, however, Ollie is furious. He pulls the man's doorbell off the wall. When the dismayed homeowner picks up the phone to call the police, Ollie cuts the wire to the phone as well. The film then records a gradually escalating conflict in which the homeowner destroys Stan and Ollie's truck and trees, piece by piece, while Stan and Ollie destroy his house and shrubbery, piece by piece. "An eye for an eye and a tooth for a tooth" wins the day. What had started out with a "Merry Christmas" ends up with two piles of rubble. (1)

Sometimes what happens between individuals also happens between nations. Today's words from the prophet Isaiah are some of the most beautiful words ever written about humanity's longing for peace. Listen to some selected words from Isaiah's writing: "A shoot will come up from the stump of Jesse . . . The Spirit of the LORD will rest on him—the Spirit of wisdom and of understanding, the Spirit of counsel and of power, the Spirit of knowledge and of the fear of the LORD . . . with righteousness he will judge the needy, with justice he will give decisions for the poor of the earth . . . The wolf will live with the lamb, the leopard will lie down with the goat, the calf and the lion and the yearling together; and a little child will lead them . . . The infant will play near the hole of the cobra, and the young child put his hand into the viper's nest. They will neither harm nor destroy on all my holy mountain, for the earth will be full of the knowledge of the LORD as the waters cover the sea."

In other words, Isaiah says, when the Messiah comes in all of his fullness, all people will live in peace and dignity and love together. This is where the world is headed. The birth of Jesus was the beginning of a grand and glorious invasion of divine love. In the language of war, a beachhead has been established. The seed of the kingdom of peace and love has been planted. The love of a tiny infant will some-day overcome all the anger and hostility and hatred that reside in human hearts, and we shall know that we are all brothers and sisters in Christ. And all people across this globe will live in peace and dignity together.

That's Isaiah's message to us today. Even though young men and women are still giving their lives in faraway places like Iraq and Afghanistan, there will come a time when war will be no more.

War is a terrible thing. Some of you have been there. You know. Sherman was right. War is hell. Someone once said, "War never decides who's right . . . only who's left."

A few years ago there was a movie titled War Games which some of you un-doubtedly saw. In this movie some young kids hack a government computer and set off a simulated thermonuclear war that moves within inches of becoming a real world war. In the end, one of the teenagers and a scientist who invented the simu-lated war game for the government try to beat the computer at its own game and end the threat of war. In a final move, they ask the computer how to win this war. The computer answers, "The only way to win is not to play the game." (2)

That is the only way to win the game of war, not to play the game. Or as they used to say in the 1960s, "What if they threw a war and nobody came?"

An elderly man saw some six and seven-year-old children at play, and asked, "What are you playing?"

"War," responded the kids.

"Why don't you play peace instead," said the man.

The children stopped, put their heads together, discussed something among themselves, then looked puzzled and finally ran out of words. One of them went to the elderly man and asked, "Grandpa, how do we play peace? We don't know the game." (3)

I fear that this is all too often true. We've been at war so often that we don't even know how to play peace.

I picked up another piece of trivia. Did you know that between five and ten people are killed or injured in Guatemala every Christmas by falling bullets? Each December police call on revelers not to fire pistols into the air to celebrate. "Lots of people die when bullets fall on their heads," a police spokesman said. "This tra-dition of shooting in the air is a very dangerous practice." (4)

I don't want to be critical, but to me there is something very unsettling about firing guns in the air to celebrate the birth of the Prince of Peace. War is a terrible thing.

When the Messiah comes war will be no more. That has always been the hope and the prayer of the people called Christians. The testimony of Scriptures is that there will come a time when all of God's children will come to the realization that, in Christ, we are all brothers and sisters. Artificial boundaries will cease to exist. We will all belong to one kingdom, the Kingdom of God.

The early Christians did not bear arms. They believed that God would soon straighten out the world and that they should follow their Master's example and lay down their lives for the world. However as time passed and Christ did not come as quickly as they had expected, they began to moderate their views on war. Sometimes it is necessary to don armor and fight in order to keep evil people from forcing their will on the weak and innocent. At such times it is permissible to take up arms, but this should be the last resort. War should always be the last option available. And we should always look for ways to be peacemakers. Further, we should always look for that day when the Messiah comes for the final time and the "wolf will live with the lamb, the leopard will lie down with the goat, the calf and the lion and the yearling together; and a little child will lead them . . ." That's a beautiful scene, isn't it?

Rector Judith Davis tells about Christmas at her house. Her young son Jamie, a toddler, had a baby doll (they try to have gender inclusive toys, says Davis). Jamie mostly ignored his doll. The doll was a girl all dressed in pink in a pink bassinet.

They had been reading Jamie the Christmas story from a board book. The book showed baby Jesus in the manger at the stable and the familiar animal characters, the ox and donkey and cow and sheep gathered there. Jamie was at an age when he probably didn't have a clue who baby Jesus is, but he knew the story on some level.

One day, a few days after they had been reading the story and showing him the pictures in the book, they found Jamie over by his baby doll with all his Little People farm animals and his Noah's ark animals all lined up around the bassinet. The most wonderful part was that all God's animals were there—not just the donkey and sheep and cow, but giraffes, zebras, horses, pigs, lions, tigers, alligators, elephants, hippos and others. He was so proud of his scene, his recreation of the Christmas story in the book.

The next night his Mom went into Jamie's room to tell him goodnight, and he had arranged his animals once again. Only this time, along with the turtles and the alligator and the horse and cow and sheep, were Pooh bear and Eeoyre and Barney.

"Out of the mouths and actions of babes we usually find the best theology," says Judith Davis. And the theology today is that Isaiah prophesied the peaceable kingdom when all the animals would live in peace together and the lion would eat straw with the ox and the wolf and the lamb would lie down together . . ." (5)

What a perfect picture of Christmas. War is a terrible thing. When the Messiah comes there will be no more war. Until the day comes when Christ reigns over this world, let us do all within our power to bring peace to our little corner of the world.

An unknown author wrote something which I believe is important. He called it a letter from Jesus about Christmas. I hope you will listen carefully:

"It has come to my attention," Jesus begins, "that many of you are upset because some folks are taking my name out of the season . . . How I personally feel about this celebration can probably be most easily understood by those of you who have been blessed with children of your own. I don't care what you call the day. If you want to celebrate my birth, just get along and love one another!

"Now, having said that, let me go on. If it bothers you that the town in which you live doesn't allow a scene depicting my birth, then just get rid of a couple of Santas and snowmen and put in a small Nativity scene on your own front lawn. If all my followers did that there wouldn't be any need for such a scene on the town square because there would be many of them all around town.

"Stop worrying about the fact that people are calling the tree a holiday tree, instead of a Christmas tree. It was I who made all trees. You can remember me anytime you see any tree. Decorate a grape vine if you wish: I actually spoke of that one in a teaching, explaining who I am in relation to you and what each of our tasks were. If you have forgotten that one, look up John 15: 1-8.

"If you want to give me a present in remembrance of my birth here is my wish list. Choose something from it:

1. Instead of writing protest letters objecting to the way my birthday is being celebrated, write letters of love and hope to soldiers away from home. They are terribly afraid and lonely this time of year. I know, they tell me all the time.

2. Visit someone in a nursing home. You don't have to know them personally. They just need to know that someone cares about them.

3. Instead of writing to the President complaining about the wording on the cards his staff sent out this year, why don't you write and tell him that you'll be praying for him and his family this year. Then follow up. It will be nice hearing from you again.

4. Instead of giving your children a lot of gifts you can't afford and they don't need, spend time with them. Tell them the story of my birth, and why I came to live with you down here. Hold them in your arms and remind them that I love them.

5. Pick someone that has hurt you in the past and forgive him or her.

6. Did you know that someone in your town will attempt to take their own life this season because they feel so alone and hopeless? Since you don't know who that person is, try giving everyone you meet a warm smile; it could make the difference.

7. Instead of nit-picking about what the retailer in your town calls the holiday, be patient with the people who work there. Give them a warm smile and a kind word. Even if they aren't allowed to wish you a "Merry Christmas" that doesn't keep

you from wishing them one. Then stop shopping there on Sunday. If the store didn't make so much money on that day they'd close and let their employees spend the day at home with their families.

8. If you really want to make a difference, support a missionary—especially one who takes my love and Good News to those who have never heard my name.

9. Here's a good one. There are individuals and whole families in your town who not only will have no "Christmas" tree, but neither will they have any presents to give or receive. If you don't know them, buy some food and a few gifts and give them to the Salvation Army or some other Christian charity, and they will make the delivery for you.

10. Finally, if you want to make a statement about your belief in and loyalty to me, then behave like a Christian. Don't do things in secret that you wouldn't do in my presence. Let people know by your actions that you are one of mine.

Don't forget; I am God and can take care of myself. Just love me and do what I have told you to do. I'll take care of all the rest. Check out the list above and get to work; time is short. I'll help you, but the ball is now in your court.

And do have a most blessed Christmas with all those you love and remember . . . I LOVE YOU, JESUS." (6)

Stan and Ollie escalated a simple attempt at a sale of a Christmas tree into a horribly insane and destructive conflict. Christ wants us to do just the opposite. He wants us to escalate the peace and love of Christmas until it leads to a world of tranquility for all God's children. Will you do your part?

1. (Atlanta: John Knox Press, 1987).
2. Cited in Randy Rowland, Get A Life! (New York: Harper Collins Publishers, 1992), pp. 160-161.
3. Dr. Eleazar Fernandez, http://www.peaceucc.org/sermons/sermon_030506_fernandez.htm.
4. William Hartston, The Encyclopedia of Useless Information (Naperville, IL: Sourcebooks, Inc., 2007), p. 165.
5. http://www.washingtonparish.org/christmas%202004%20sermon.htm.
6. Carol Richardson, MONDAY FODDER, http://www.fishermansnet.com/monday-fodder/.\

When The Messiah Comes:
There Will Be Singing
Isaiah 35:1-10

Our theme for this third Sunday in Advent is music. "When the Messiah comes there will be singing." I think most of us love the music of Christmas. Of course, I realize that not all of us are musicians.

A man and his wife were browsing in a crafts store one day when the man noticed a display of country-style musical instruments. After looking over the flutes, dulcimers and recorders, he picked up a shiny, one-stringed instrument he took to be a mouth harp. He put it to his lips and, much to the amusement of other shoppers, twanged a few notes on it. After watching from a distance, his wife came up and whispered in his ear, "I hate to tell you this, honey, but you're trying to play a cheese slicer." (1)

Not all of us are musicians.

One woman was talking about her parents who had recently retired. Her mom had always wanted to learn to play the piano, so her dad bought her mom a piano for her birthday. A few weeks later, the woman asked how her mom was doing with it.

"Oh, we returned the piano," said her dad, "I persuaded her to switch to a clarinet instead."

"How come?" the woman asked.

"Well," he answered, "because with a clarinet, she can't sing while she plays."

We're not all great singers. That's all right. We can still make a joyful noise.

I'm reminded of the story of a Roman Catholic Church in which the choir director had gone to a great deal of trouble preparing an excellent soprano for a solo for Sunday Mass. As the soloist's beautiful voice soared through the church, she was suddenly joined by a bedraggled "street person" who had wandered in and taken a seat near the choir. The newcomer's voice had seen better days, and it quavered along, slightly off-key, through the entire song. The choir members kept looking frantically at the director, who made no move to interrupt the intruder.

Afterward, some of the members of the choir asked the director why he hadn't stopped her.

"Because," he replied, "I wasn't sure which song God would like better." (2)

I would hate to think of this season of the year without the great Christmas hymns and carols. Of course, times are a-changing. Have you noticed that the Christmas tradition of caroling seems to be disappearing? There was a time when small groups would go around in neighborhoods and people would sing carols to their neighbors. That tradition is almost extinct. However I did read about a new twist to this old tradition. Now we have what might be called, "virtual caroling."

A Radio Shack ad a couple of years ago showed how it's done: A little old lady opens her door to find a video iPod on her front stoop. Out of the small, sleek iPod comes the tinny sounds and tiny pictures of children singing "Hark, the Herald Angels Sing." Next door the kids are waving from a window.

According to Maria Puente of USA Today, it's an appealing notion: Spread cheer without leaving the warmth (and the giant-screen TV) of your own home. Virtual caroling. Must be why YouTube boasts more than 300 caroling videos. We can enjoy the carolers without even going to the trouble of opening our front door. (3)

Today's prophecy from Isaiah tells us that when the Messiah comes, there will be singing. There are few passages as joyful as Isaiah 35. Isaiah writes, "The desert and the parched land will be glad; the wilderness will rejoice and blossom. Like the crocus, it will burst into bloom; it will rejoice greatly and shout for joy. The glory of Lebanon will be given to it, the splendor of Carmel and Sharon; they will see the glory of the LORD,   the splendor of our God. Strengthen the feeble hands, steady the knees that give way; say to those with fearful hearts, 'Be strong, do not fear; your God will come . . . Then will the eyes of the blind be opened and the ears of the deaf unstopped. Then will the lame leap like a deer, and the mute tongue shout for joy. Water will gush forth in the wilderness and streams in the desert. The burning sand will become a pool, the thirsty ground bubbling springs . . . and the ransomed of the LORD will return. They will enter Zion with singing; everlasting joy will crown their heads. Gladness and joy will overtake them, and sorrow and sighing will flee away.'"

It would be difficult to paint a picture in which the joy of the Lord is portrayed more vividly than that. "They will enter Zion with singing . . ." Music is very important to us at Christmas time.

The Gospel of Luke doesn't actually tell us that the angels were singing in the heavens when Christ was born, but we would like to think they were. Here's how the verse from Luke's Gospel actually reads: Suddenly a great company of the heavenly host appeared with the angel, praising God and SAYING, "Glory to God in the highest, and on earth peace to men on whom his favor rests." (Luke 2:13-14, emphasis added) Luke tells us they were saying, not singing. I like to think they were singing.

Someone defined the difference between rap music and opera like this: Opera is people singing when they should be talking, and rap is people talking when they should be singing. Maybe the angels were rapping out the message to the shepherds. Probably not. I still would like to think they were singing, singing in beautiful harmony. If they weren't singing, they should have been. Music is a wonderful gift from God.

There is a quote attributed to Victor Hugo, "Music attempts to express what cannot be said about something on which it is impossible to remain silent." I like that. It helps explain why music is such an integral part of Christmas.

Music gives us the opportunity to express our joy and thanksgiving.

The famous preacher of another generation C.H. Spurgeon once said, "I used to know an old Methodist; and the first thing in the morning, when he got up, he began singing a bit of a Methodist hymn; and if I met the old man during the day, he was always singing. I have seen him in his little workshop, with his lapstone on his knee, and he was always singing, and beating with his hammer. When I said to him once, 'Why do you always sing, dear brother?' he replied, 'Because I always have something to sing about.'" (4)

That's a good enough reason to sing. In Isaiah's prophecy Isaiah promises the people that they will one day return to Zion. Zion is symbolic of Jerusalem, of the Promised Land. Isaiah was writing during the times of the divided kingdom. The land had been overrun numerous times by their enemies. Prisoners of war had been carried off to become slaves in distant lands. Isaiah promises that one day they will be able to return home to Zion, the city of God. For them this will be a time of great joy and so they sing.

For Christians, Zion is that city of God which is heaven. And again, when we enter that place of eternal promise, there will be singing. For those of us who know Christ's love in our hearts, there is a need to say thank you to God for what God has done for us.

Charles Duke, a former astronaut, came to Christ some years after walking on the moon. After his time with NASA he had lacked purpose and meaning in his life. His wife, Dottie, was also troubled. In fact, she contemplated suicide. But then she began to attend church where she gave her life to Christ. Sometime later at his wife's Bible study Charles Duke gave his life to Jesus as well. He found a new and compelling purpose for his life. Today he offers this comment on his conversion, "Walking on the moon cannot compare with walking on earth with Jesus." (5)

When you feel like that you want to sing. Music allows us to express our joy and thanksgiving.

There's a second thing music does for us: it draws us closer together as the family of Christ. In my mind, I can see that band of refugees Isaiah envisions returning to their homeland, singing as they travel together. I love to be part of a congregation that is singing the great hymns of the church. I love to be at a Christmas party when someone suggests that we sing carols. It's one of the touchy-feely moments that is almost sacramental. We sing together and we feel like an extended family. That's the way Christmas ought to be.

Rich Mullins was a beloved artist and songwriter in the world of contemporary Christian music. Before he was tragically killed in a jeep accident on September 19, 1997, he had written many beautiful praise songs that have touched the hearts of many people.

Eric Hauck, a close friend of Rich, recalled being with him in a worship service just a few days before he died. Some friends wanted to gather together and praise God, and everyone had brought instruments to play together. The music sounded awful—even the leaders were singing out of tune. Rich later went up to the microphone and said, "I love to be in church. I love to listen to people sing and play from their heart. In my profession we worry about being in tune and sounding good, but this music tonight is the most pleasing to God, because it is so real, and it comes from the hearts of the children of God." That was the last time Eric ever saw Rich Mullins cry. (6)

Some of us know what he was talking about and why he was crying. We know about the power of music to draw people together in worship. It reaches across the boundaries of social status, and gender and race.

Under a cultural exchange program a rabbi from Russia was visiting with a Christian family in Texas. Since it was Christmas the family wanted to take him to some of the finest places in Houston, so they all went to a favorite Chinese restaurant. Throughout the meal the rabbi extolled the wonders of America in comparison to the bleak conditions of his homeland. When they had finished eating the waiter brought the check, a fortune cookie, and a small brass Christmas tree ornament as a present for the rabbi. They all laughed when the rabbi pointed out that the ornaments were stamped "made in India."

But the laughter soon subsided when they saw that the rabbi was quietly crying. They all thought that the rabbi must have been offended by receiving a Christmas tree as a gift. But no, he smiled and shook his head and said, "Nyet, I was shedding tears of joy to be in a wonderful country, in a Chinese restaurant in which a Buddhist gives a Jew a Christmas gift made by a Hindu!" (7)

Christmas reminds us that Christ came to shine his light into the heart of everyone on this earth, of whatever race or creed. When we sing, we sing as the family of God. I have often wondered why God created us with voices that are so different. The soprano can hit such high notes; the bass can get so low. But then we blend our voices into one glorious sound. To me, it easily qualifies as proof of God's existence. Why would blind evolution give us such a gift? It makes no sense. Music calls us together into one beautiful family. Especially at Christmas. We sing "Joy to the World" and "Hark the Herald Angels Sing" and "What Child Is This" and I believe the angels sing with us. When the Messiah comes there will be singing. Singing allows us to express our joy and thanksgiving. Singing draws us closer together.

And most importantly of all, music speaks to us of God.

Several years ago there was an article in a church journal about a church in Jackson, Tennessee that used music to help what are called at-risk children. They used volunteer piano teachers who gave lessons to under-privileged kids. The idea worked. Pride, self-esteem, and academic performance among these kids from disadvantaged backgrounds were all enhanced. Not only that, but the program caught the attention of the Rockefeller Foundation for Fine Arts in New York. The foundation thought the program might be developed nationally. So they sent world-renowned pianist Lorin Hollander to go to Jackson and take a look.

While Hollander was there he shared something significant with his audience. He shared with them his own experience of being a battered child. He said that there are a lot of children out there who are mortally wounded in the soul. These are children who are battered spiritually and creatively. And then Hollander said this. He said that music can bring the spirit of love into the lives of these children who have become lost. By allowing them to discover creativity in music, they can begin to express the divine love of God. Finally, Mr. Hollander had this to say: "When I was a little child and first heard Bach, I told my sister we didn't have to be afraid of the dark anymore; someone is watching over us. I heard it in the music." (8)

Music speaks to us of God. That is why music has always been part of the church. And, of course, that is why music is such a big part of Christmas. So, let us prepare for the birth of Christ with songs of joy and thanksgiving. Let us sing as God's people with one unified voice. And let us pray that in the music we will sense the Holy Spirit at work in our lives drawing us closer to one another and to God. Isaiah writes about the coming messianic age, "They will enter Zion with singing; everlasting joy will crown their heads. Gladness and joy will overtake them, and sorrow and sighing will flee away." That's the promise of Christmas. That's worth singing about.

1. Ed Preacher's Laughter for a Saturday.
2. Kate Kellogg, The Catholic Digest, September 1992, p. 65.
3. USA Today, 12-17-07, pp. 1-2D. Contributed by Dr. John Bardsley.
4. http://www.spurgeon.org/sermons/2260.htm.
5. Jerry Ruff, http://www.sumcnj.com/sermons/srm2003/Sermon07.13.03.htm.
6. Daily Grace: Devotional Reflections to Nourish Your Soul (Colorado Springs, Co: Cook Communications Ministries, 2005), p. 112.
7. C. Robert Allred, Th.D., http://www.bobssermons.com/sermons/archive/041212.htm.
8. Charles Hoffman, "A Thing of Beauty," in The United Methodist Review, 3/24/94. Cited by Rev. San Dieguito, http://www.sdumc.org/sr083103.

When The Messiah Comes: God Will Be With Us
Isaiah 7:10-16; Matthew 1:18-25

Some unknown wit has published an essay on the Internet on the joys of being a male of the species. He says, "Men are just happier people." Then he explains why. Here are some of the advantages he lists with regard to being male: "Your last name stays put. Wedding plans take care of themselves. Chocolate is just another snack. You can never be pregnant. Same work, more pay. (Uh, oh . . . I'm going to start a brawl with that one.) Wrinkles add character. Wedding dress $5000. Tux rental-$100. New shoes don't cut, blister, or mangle your feet.

"Phone conversations are over in 30 seconds flat. A five-day vacation requires only one suitcase. You can open all your own jars. You get extra credit for the slightest act of thoughtfulness. If someone forgets to invite you, he or she can still be your friend.

"Your underwear is $8.95 for a three-pack. Three pairs of shoes are more than enough. You are unable to see wrinkles in your clothes. Everything on your face stays its original color. The same hairstyle lasts for years, maybe decades. You only have to shave your face and neck.

"You can play with toys all your life. One wallet and one color for all seasons. You can wear shorts no matter how your legs look. You can "do" your nails with a pocket knife."

And here's the clincher, "You can do Christmas shopping for 25 relatives on December 24 in 25 minutes. No wonder," he says, "men are happier." (1)

Well, I hope you men will do a better job this year. You still have a few days left to get prepared.

Someone else published a list of "Things Wives Don't Want To Hear Their Husbands Say On Christmas Day." Here's a few, just as fair warning:

"You like it, hon? Almost look like real diamonds, don't they?"

"That's right, hon. Your own subscription to 'Guns & Ammo.'"

"It's two sizes smaller, darling—you know, for motivation."

And the final thing wives don't want to hear: "Well, if it isn't Roy and Angela and their seven kids—with suitcases! What a pleasant surprise!" (2)

Isaiah the prophet is preparing us for the coming Messiah. Today we read these words: "Therefore the Lord himself will give you a sign: The virgin will be with child and will give birth to a son, and will call him Immanuel."

In today's lesson from the Gospel of Matthew we read how this prophecy is fulfilled. An angel appears to Joseph in a dream and says to him: "Joseph son of David, do not be afraid to take Mary home as your wife, because what is conceived in her is from the Holy Spirit. She will give birth to a son, and you are to give him the name Jesus, because he will save his people from their sins." All this took place to fulfill what the Lord had said through the prophet: "The virgin will be with child and will give birth to a son, and they will call him Immanuel"—which means, "God with us."

Here is why we celebrate Christmas—God came to dwell with us. "They will call him Immanuel—God with us."

The magazine, The Week, carried a story about Newark, New Jersey. I don't know what you see when you try to visualize Newark, NJ. Many people see darkness and decay. In fact, Newark has been called America's most troubled city.

Newark lost most of its employers decades ago, says this article in The Week. Today, more than a quarter of Newark's population lives below the poverty line. Located just 10 miles from New York City, Newark used to be a thriving manufacturing center. At its peak, around World War II, the city had a population of 450,000.

However, in the 1960s, affluent citizens began to flee the city, and the federal government constructed giant housing projects there. In 1967 there were terrible riots, resulting in 26 deaths and hundreds of torched businesses. Eight years later, Harper's magazine called Newark America's "worst city." By 2007, Newark had been reduced from 450,000 people to 280,000 people. It had one supermarket, and a single movie theater.

And yet, today something is happening in Newark thanks to a tireless mayor named Cory Booker. Nearly everything about Booker is unique. Unlike previous mayors, he is not only a product of the suburbs but of Stanford, Yale Law School, and Oxford, which he attended as a Rhodes Scholar. A 6-foot-3, 250-pound vegetarian, Booker could have lived a life of comfort and affluence. Instead he opted to live for eight years in one of Newark's most crime-ridden public-housing projects, from which he won a seat on the city council. In 2007, he was elected mayor.

What has Booker achieved as mayor? Well, for one thing he's attracted more than $100 million in private philanthropy, including city programs funded by the likes of Oprah Winfrey, Jon Bon Jovi, and Brad Pitt. Booker tapped the Gates Foundation and others to fund charter schools, and raised millions to renovate and expand 20 city parks. He's struck deals with employers in the region, such as Continental Airlines, to hire more Newark residents. And he has begun to remove the stench of corruption that enveloped Newark for decades. And while achieving all this, he has maintained a relentless focus on his top priority: fighting crime.

Has crime been reduced? Dramatically. During Booker's term, homicides have declined 28 percent, shootings are down 46 percent. March of 2010 was Newark's first month without a murder since 1966. Booker has personalized the fight against crime by personally traveling the city late into the night, challenging drug dealers to get off the street and complacent cops to get out of their squad cars. "He is fearless," said a member of Booker's security detail. (3)

Now, it's always risky to praise a politician or any celebrity in a sermon. Invariably, sooner or later, they will do something to embarrass themselves and you. I don't know anything about Cory Booker's personal life or values, but I do know this: When a graduate of Stanford, Yale and Oxford—a Rhodes Scholar, nonetheless—voluntarily moves into one of Newark's most crime-ridden public-housing projects, somebody ought to pay attention.

Here's the good news for the day: St. Paul said about Jesus, "For you know the grace of our Lord Jesus Christ, that though he was rich, yet for your sakes he became poor, so that you through his poverty might become rich." (II Cor. 8:9)

Jesus didn't leave Stanford, Yale and Oxford. He left the throne of glory to become the babe of Bethlehem, born in a stable because there was no room in the inn. Why did he do it? Because the world sat in darkness, to use Isaiah's rich metaphor. Christmas is not simply the celebration of the birthday of a good man, but of light penetrating darkness, hope penetrating despair, life overcoming death, salvation delivering fallen humanity. "They will call him Immanuel"—which means, "God with us."

What does it mean to say that God is with us? It means, first of all, that God cares enough for us individually that He seeks to invade the chaos of our lives.

Author Max Lucado tells a remarkable story of the son of a rabbi who battled severe emotional problems. One day the boy went into his backyard, removed all his clothing, assumed a crouched position, and began to gobble like a turkey. He did this, not just for hours or days, but for weeks. No pleading would dissuade him. No psychotherapist could help him.

A friend of the rabbi, having watched the boy and shared the father's grief, offered to help. He, too, went into the backyard and removed his clothes. He crouched beside the boy and began gobbling, turkey-like. For days, nothing changed. Finally the friend spoke to the son. "Do you think it would be all right for turkeys to wear shirts?" After some thought and many gobbles, the son agreed. So they put on their shirts.

Days later the friend asked the boy if it would be acceptable for turkeys to wear trousers. The boy nodded. In time, the friend redressed the boy. And, in time, the boy returned to normal. (4)

What an amazing story. What amazing love. Do you understand that this is what Christmas is all about? It's more than the birth of a special baby, it is more than an angel's song. It is God invading our world, stripping himself of all His power and dignity that he might die naked on a cross in our behalf.

A pastor tells about a big Christmas dinner at one of his denomination's children's homes. As preparations were being made for the dinner and the unwrapping of presents under the tree, one of the littlest boys hid under his bed and refused to come out.

Rev. Henry Carter went to Tommy hiding under the bed and told him about the lights on the Christmas tree and the gifts awaiting him. There was no answer. Rev. Carter kneeled beside the bed and pulled back the spread. There were two big wet crying eyes looking out at him. Tommy was eight but looked five because of early malnourishment. He could have easily been pulled out from under the bed, but it was not pulling that Tommy needed; it was trust and a sense of belonging. Because he could not think of anything else to do, Rev. Carter got down on his stomach and squeezed under the bed beside Tommy. He lay there with his cheek pressed against the floor talking about the big wreath above the roaring fireplace and the filled stocking that hung with Tommy's name on it. He talked about the carols they would sing and the turkey almost ready to serve. And he talked about the baby Jesus who was born in a stable and laid in a manger because there was no room for him in the inn. Then running out of anything else to say he simply lay there beside Tommy. After a bit, a small child's hand slipped into Rev. Carter's hand. Rev. Carter said, "You know Tommy it's kind of close quarters under here, let's you and I crawl out where we can stand up." As they slid out from under the bed he realized that he had been given a glimpse of the wonder of Christmas. Had not God come down to where we are to sidle up close to us? Was it not God's Spirit that wooed us out of our lonely hiding place into a world of light and life and belonging? (5)

This is what Christmas is all about. God invades our world, crawls under the bed, as it were, comforts us and draws us out into the light.

And what is our response to God's coming into our world? It is to take the love of Christ to everyone we meet. Our response is not to be a matter of simply passive receiving. We are to pass on to others what has been given us.

Tony Campolo tells about a friend who pretends to go shopping each Christmas season in the Nordstrom department store located in her wealthy Los Angeles suburb. Campolo says that she "pretends to go shopping" at Nordstrom because the store is so upscale that she rarely purchases anything there. But she goes there during the Christmas shopping days because the ambience is spectacular.

He says his friend gets herself a Nordstrom shopping bag, fills it with tissue paper, and meanders around the store, enjoying the decorations and listening to the live music playing in each department.

On one of these Christmas visits to Nordstrom, this friend was on the top floor, where the most expensive dresses were for sale, when the doors of the elevator opened and a bag lady from off the streets stepped out. When his friend saw this woman, she fully expected that a couple of security guards would show up momentarily to usher the woman out of the store. After all, this woman, whose raggedy clothes were covered with dirt from the streets, was not the kind of person who could afford to buy much of anything at Nordstrom, let alone one of the expensive dresses for sale on the top floor. But instead of security guards, a tall, stately saleswoman appeared and went up to the homeless woman. She asked, "Can I help you, Madam?"

"Yeah!" said the homeless woman in a gruff voice. "I want a dress!"

"What kind of dress?" inquired the saleswoman. "A party dress," was the answer.

"You've come to the right place," the saleswoman replied. "We have the finest dresses in the world."

Indeed they did! The least expensive dress on the rack of evening gowns cost just under a thousand dollars.

The two women looked over the dresses as they talked about which color would be best, given the homeless woman's coloring. After a discussion that went on for more than ten minutes, they picked two dresses off the rack. Then the saleswoman said, "Follow me, Madam. I want you to try on these dresses to see how you look in each of them."

Campolo's friend was flabbergasted. She knew the saleswoman must have realized that this homeless woman didn't have the means to buy any of the dresses for sale in the store.

When the two women went into the dressing room to try on the dresses, Campolo's friend went into the dressing room next to theirs and put her ear against the wall so she could listen to what they said. After a while, she heard the homeless woman say, "I've changed my mind. I'm not going to buy a dress today."

The saleswoman answered, "That's quite all right, Madam, but I'd like you to take my card. Should you come back to Nordstrom, I would consider it both a privilege and a pleasure to wait on you again."

Campolo's friend was more than surprised by the kind and respectful way in which this saleswoman treated a woman who obviously had not the means to buy anything in that upscale store. "This saleswoman did what a Christian should do," says Tony Campolo. In all probability, she treated everyone she met in her everyday encounters in the work place as Jesus would treat them." (6)

Do I need to say anything more about the meaning of Christmas? Isaiah said it all nearly three thousand years ago: "The virgin will be with child and will give birth to a son, and they will call him Immanuel"—which means, "God with us." When God is with us, we are empowered to live in extraordinary ways.

1. MONDAY FODDER, To subscribe http://family-safe-mail.com/magiclist/.
2. The Timothy Report, http://www.timothyreport.com.
3. "Newark's Big Dreams," The Week, April 30, 2010.
4. Originally told by Joseph Shulam. Cited in Cure For The Common Life (Nashville: W Publishing Group, 2005).
5. A sermon synopsis by C. Robert Allred, Th.D.,
http://www.bobssermons.com/sermons/archive/031221.htm.
6. letters to a young evangelical (New York, NY: Perseus Books Group, 2006), pp. 243-245.

When The Messiah Comes:
A Child Will Be Born
Isaiah 9:2-7, Luke 2:1-14, (15-20)
Christmas Eve

It was a cold December afternoon. Rain mixed with snow splashed against the windshield. Overhead dark clouds hovered seemingly just above the treetops. All day long two men, a pastor named Jerry and a layman named Jim, had been delivering Christmas boxes. Many of the families who would receive these boxes would get nothing else for Christmas that year. The pickup truck had been loaded when the two men started out on their journey but now, only one box remained. It was covered with an old piece of tarp to protect it against the rain.

The address on the card meant a drive of several miles beyond the city limit. "What do you think?" Jim asked. He was the driver and it was his truck. Pastor Jerry knew what Jim was thinking. Why drive way out in the country when we could give this last box to someone close by and be home in thirty minutes? It was a tempting thought. Pastor Jerry had a Christmas Eve Communion Service scheduled for 8 p.m. and he could use the time to prepare.

Jim, however, answered his own question, "Well, let's give it a try. If we can't find the place, we can always come back and give the box to someone else."

The rain was pouring down by the time they reached the address on the card. The old white framed house stood on a hillside overlooking the valley. It had once been an elegant place, the centerpiece of a large farm. Now, the farm was gone and the house had deteriorated over the years.

The two men slipped and slid, huffed and puffed as they carried the box up the hill. The red clay offered no foothold and the box, wet from the rain, was beginning to come apart. They climbed the high steps to the porch, set the box down and slid it across the floor. They straightened up just in time to glimpse the face of a small boy at the window. He had been watching them coming up the hill. Now, he announced their arrival with shouts of excitement, "They're here, Grandma, they're here!"

The door opened and an older woman greeted them. Her gray hair was pulled back in a bun at the back of her neck. She had on a dark, plain dress with a white apron. She was drying her hands with a dishtowel and explained to them that she had been doing the supper dishes. "I told you, they would come," a child's voice said from behind her. A little boy with black hair and bright dark eyes rushed to the box and began pulling at the goodies inside.

The woman told them that she and her grandson were all that was left of her family. The father and mother had divorced and gone their separate ways. The little boy had been left behind for Grandma to raise. She said, "Oh, I am so glad you are here. He was up early this morning looking for you. He sat by that window all day. I wasn't sure you would come and I tried to prepare him in case of a disappointment. But he just said, 'Don't worry, Grandma, I know they will come.'" (1)

That young boy didn't know it, but, in a sense, he was speaking for all Christianity. A thankful people, more than one billion of us around the world, pause for a few moments this night and pray, "We knew he would come."

The prophet Isaiah, speaking in behalf of God, had promised it hundreds of years before, "For to us a child is born, to us a son is given, and the government will be on his shoulders. And he will be called Wonderful Counselor, Mighty God, Everlasting Father, Prince of Peace." And he has come, just as promised.

Those are magnificent descriptions of the long-awaited Messiah, are they not? "Wonderful Counselor, Mighty God, Everlasting Father, Prince of Peace."

I'm glad that modern writers are not trying to find a word descriptive of Christ. We've become so lacking in imagination in this high tech age that any effort we might make would be pitiful in comparison to Isaiah. Nowadays the language of business and computers dominates our daily speech. No frills, just information. And new words are being created, words that we sometimes call technospeak.

In an interview in the online edition of Newsweek magazine, author Don Watson expresses his futility with our language because it has changed due to the popularity of a business culture. He describes how his granddaughter's elementary school requires that kids write "personal mission statements" and identify their "core values" before they graduate on to middle school.

But the strangest instance of the business mentality spreading beyond reasonable boundaries is a hospital that classifies newborn babies as—are you ready for this?— "obstetric products." (2) Let me say that again, babies are now "obstetric products." Can you imagine the angels announcing at Jesus' birth, "This day there is born to you an 'obstetric product,' which is Christ the Lord!" Or Isaiah proclaiming, "For to us an 'obstetric product' is born . . ."

No, we will settle for the traditional language: "to us a child is born, to us a son is given, and the government will be on his shoulders."

Can there be a more perfect place to be on Christmas Eve than God's house? Can there be a more perfect story than the story of the first Christmas?

God entered the world as a tiny babe. That's impossible for us to get our minds around—yet I can't imagine any better news in all the world. The Creator of the universe loved us enough to come into our world, and he did it not in power, but in the most helpless guise possible, that of an infant. There's something about a baby, isn't there, or even a young child?

During the first year and a half of World War II, London was under heavy bombing from German airplanes. Churchill knew that Hitler would win, and

England would be destroyed, if he could not unite America as an ally with Britain in the war. Then, on December 7, 1941, Hitler's ally Japan attacked the United States at Pearl Harbor. Churchill left London and rushed to Washington to meet with President Roosevelt and speak to Congress, to try to get America to help England fight the war.

It was Christmas Eve, 1941. Churchill was a guest of President Roosevelt at the White House.

It had been a very busy day for Churchill. That morning he had given an important speech, broadcast live on radio, before a combined meeting of the House of Representatives and the United States Senate. He had spent the rest of that busy day in private interviews and meetings. That evening he had given another speech when he helped the President light the National Christmas Tree. Afterwards Churchill went to his room in the White House to prepare for a much needed night of rest.

Also staying in the White House that Christmas Eve was the President's special assistant, Harry Hopkins, and his nine-year-old daughter Diana. Late in the evening there was a knock on the child's door. She rose from her bed and opened it. There was the White House butler, standing stiffly in his formal dress. He looked down at the little girl and said in a very serious voice, "Miss Hopkins, the Prime Minister wants to see you." The little girl was frightened as she pulled on her robe and followed the stately butler down a long, dark corridor to the Monroe Bedroom. The butler knocked on the door, and the girl heard a gruff indistinguishable response from inside. When the door opened the child saw the penetrating eyes of the Prime Minister, Winston Churchill, staring down at her. She was shocked when Churchill reached out his arms and embraced her. He paused, and then said, "I'm a lonely old father and grandfather on Christmas Eve who wanted a little girl to hug." Then he glanced bashfully at the butler and sent her back to bed.

One of Churchill's many biographers said, "This is a side of Winston Churchill few people know. Images of Churchill the war leader, the award-winning author, the master speechmaker, or the astute politician come easily; but not images of Churchill the devoted father and grandfather—not the kind of man who might need a little girl's hug on a lonely Christmas Eve. (3)

I guess all of us need a hug on Christmas Eve, particularly from a child. There's something about a baby or a young child. That's one reason Christmas Eve is so wonderful—the joy of anticipation that we see in our children's eyes. God entered the world as a babe in a manger.

Here's the second thing we need to see: That babe became our Savior.

"And he will be called Wonderful Counselor, Mighty God, Everlasting Father, Prince of Peace." He didn't stay a baby, did he? He became "the man for others." There are no adjectives lofty enough to describe our feelings about the man from

Nazareth. I like the way Dan Owens put it:

Just ask the angels what they think of Jesus, they'll tell you, "A Savior has been born unto you, He is Christ the Lord."

Ask John the Baptist and he'll tell you, "Behold the Lamb of God who takes away the sins of the world."

Ask the demons what they think of Jesus, they will tell you. "What do you want with us, Son of the most high God?"

Ask Judas what he thinks about Jesus, he will tell you, "I have betrayed innocent blood."

Ask the apostle Paul, what do you think about Jesus? He will tell you, "that nothing compares to the surpassing greatness of knowing Christ Jesus my Lord."

Ask Pilate what he thinks, he will tell you, "I find no fault in this just man."

Ask the Roman centurion what he thinks of Jesus, he will tell you. "Surely this is the Son of God."

Ask Thomas what he thinks about Jesus, he'll fall down prostrate before him and cry out, "My Lord and my God."

Ask Peter, what do you think about Jesus and he will tell you. "God has made this same Jesus, whom you crucified, both Lord and Christ." (4)

We celebrate the fact that God became a tiny babe, but we also celebrate that this tiny babe became our Savior.

To me, one of the charms of Christmas in the popular culture is that it is the season of misfits—misfits like "The Littlest Angel" who couldn't get his halo on properly—or "The Charlie Brown Christmas Special" about that loveable loser, Charlie Brown—And how about Rudolph, the reindeer with the bright shiny nose?

"Rudolph, the Red-Nosed Reindeer" is said to be the only 20th century addition to the Santa Claus story. He was first introduced as an advertising gimmick. However, he has become more famous and loved among children than Dasher, Dancer, Prancer, Vixen, Comet, Cupid, Donner and Blitzen. Rudolph turned 71 this year.

You know his story: There once was a reindeer who was teased by other reindeer because of his big bright, red nose, but he saved Christmas one foggy night when his nose became a beacon that guided Santa's sled.

Seventy-one years ago Montgomery Ward—remember them?—gave copies of a poem, "Rudolph, the Red-Nosed Reindeer," to customers for their children. It was an enormous success—the store gave away more than six million copies over the years. In 1946 Montgomery Ward transferred the copyright of the poem back to Robert May, who worked for the department store when he wrote it in 1939. May, who had a sick wife and 6 children to put through school, sold the rights to a children's book publisher within a month. The book sold more than 100,000 copies.

Then, in 1949, a New York songwriter, Johnny Marks, a friend of May's wrote a 113 word song based on the poem. It took months to convince anyone to record the song, and when he pitched it to cowboy actor Gene Autry—anybody remember him?—he was turned down, politely but firmly. It was Autry's wife who talked him into recording the song.

Autry said he would record Rudolph only as the B-side on what he thought would be a hit Christmas tune titled "If It Doesn't Snow on Christmas." That song has long been forgotten.

"Rudolph the Red-Nosed Reindeer" was introduced by Autry at a Madison Square Garden concert in September 1949. By Christmas, record sales were near 2 million. It has now sold more than 100 million copies, making it second only to "White Christmas" on the all-time seasonal hit parade. (5)

Now, why would I spend so much time on this little song about a red-nosed reindeer? Christmas is a time for celebrating misfits because Christ became a misfit in our behalf. He who lived in glory gave it all up to become a tiny babe—and then he became a grown man who suffered and died for the sins of the world. God entered the world as a babe in a manger. That babe became our Savior.

And there was only one reason Christ came—he came because he loved us so much. "God so loved the world that he gave His only begotten son . . ."

In an old Peanuts comic strip, that other popular misfit Charlie Brown cracks open his piggy bank. He says, "Look, I've got $9.11 to spend on Christmas."

Lucy is not impressed. "You can't buy something for everyone with $9.11, Charlie Brown," she responds.

Charlie Brown retorts, "Oh yeah? Well, I'm gonna try!"

"Then," Lucy continues, "they're sure gonna be cheap presents."

"But," Charlie Brown says with absolute conviction, "nothing is cheap if it costs all that you have." (6)

That tiny babe gave his all when he became a man, and it was for us. And for only one reason. God loves us every one. So have a grand Christmas Eve and a wonderful Christmas Day, and give God thanks. "For to us a child is born, to us a son is given . . ." He came. He loved us so much, he came. We knew he would.

1. Jerry Anderson, Hummingbirds & Hollyhocks, (Knoxville: Seven Worlds Corp., 2000), pp. 99-100.
2. Newsweek, July, 18, 2005, p. 4.
3. Stephen Mansfield, Never Give In (Highland Books, 1995), p. 127. Cited by Dr. R. L. Hymers, Jr., http://www.rlhymersjr.com/Online_Sermons/2007/122307PM_PresentForJesus.html.
4. Contributed. Source: Whirlwind Resources/Help 4 Sunday.
5. New York Daily News, 12/23/95, p. 19, "As a Hit-Maker, Rudolph Reigns." Contributed by Dr. John Bardsley.
6. Martin R. Bartel, Parables, etc.

Surprised By Christmas
Luke 2:1-14
(Christmas Day)

If we took a poll of the most boring places on earth, a significant number of votes would probably go to doctors' offices. But it was in a boring doctor's office that Robert Fulghum was surprised, and even reminded of God.

Fulghum had been under the weather for a while, so on a bleak February day he went to the doctor. As he sat in the waiting room, he noticed an attractive elderly couple waiting, too. The woman wore holly berries and poinsettia leaves in her hair. The man leaned toward Fulghum, smiled, and announced, "Merry Christmas!"

Fulghum replied in same before he realized what he was saying. It wasn't Christmas. It was February. Then the man began singing Christmas carols. The receptionist addressed the old man as Uncle Ed, bidding him Merry Christmas and asking him to come on back for his appointment. After the old man left, his wife moved over next to Fulghum to explain his strange behavior.

The woman had noticed that, after a couple of strokes some years back, her husband's behavior was changing. Then, one March morning quite unexpectedly, he had come down the stairs announcing that he had forgotten it was Christmas. He urged his wife to help him put up decorations and wrap gifts. The bewildered woman called up their daughters, and the whole family got together and celebrated Christmas that day. It was actually a warm, enjoyable experience.

After their daughters left, the man asked his wife to tell him about his childhood Christmases. Maybe it was merciful that he didn't remember his abusive childhood, when his family never celebrated Christmas. His wife, who had never lied to him, loved him too much to tell him the truth. So she spun tales of wonderful holidays, full of love, and family traditions, and memorable gifts. Her husband was pleased. Now every few months, the woman explained, her husband will suddenly announce that it is Christmas, and the family will once again gather to celebrate the occasion. The daughters think of these celebrations as Father's Day, their time to make him happy. No one ever knows when the Christmas conviction will strike, but they are ready and willing to participate in it whenever it does. The woman remarked, "It's kind of refreshing to have Christmas come as a surprise." (1)

IF THERE IS ONE THING WE CAN SAY ABOUT CHRISTMAS, IT IS THAT IT IS A SURPRISE. There have been few events in history that were quite as surprising.

The shepherds out on the hillside were certainly surprised. In fact, the whole thing so unnerved them that they were "filled with fear." This was no ordinary night. I wonder, if later, as they tried to tell their story to their neighbors about what they saw that night, if people didn't look at them like some of us do those people in

Roswell, New Mexico who claim to have seen UFOs. Can't you hear their friends and neighbors: You saw what? Angels? They did what? They sang? The shepherds were surprised by Christmas.

Mary and Joseph were surprised. The whole affair put a terrible strain on their relationship, as you can imagine. It took the intervention of an angel first to Mary and then to Joseph to put their hearts at peace. The birth of the Son of God is not something that happens every day to just anyone. Mary and Joseph were surprised.

Certainly Herod was surprised. "Go find the child that is to be born king of the Jews that I may come and worship him, too." We know better than that. Herod was so shocked by the whole situation that he had a whole generation of baby boys wiped out. Herod was surprised.

Even more importantly, the people of Israel were surprised. The Messiah was to come, they were convinced of it, but not like this. The Messiah was to come with power and might. To be sure, Isaiah had written, "For unto us a child is born, unto us a son is given . . ." But Isaiah wrote that several hundred years before the birth of the Christ child. Besides, the Messianic passages of the Hebrew Bible are a bit obscure. You can read lots of things into them . . . but a babe? God in a manger? Surprise!

The point has been made by many authors, but it is still a good one.

The year was 1809. A war-weary world was anxiously watching the march of Napoleon across Europe. People were discouraged. Hope for the future was frail. All the while, however, babies were being born. Alfred Lord Tennyson, Edgar Allen Poe, Oliver Wendell Holmes, Felix Mendelssohn, William E. Gladstone, destined to become one of England's finest statesman, Charles Darwin, and a young unpromising boy named Abraham Lincoln were all born in that very same year. While one age was dying, another was being born. That is the way God works. Quietly, steadily. It really should not surprise us. We want to look for God in the whirlwind and storm; God speaks in quiet whispers. Carl Sandburg put it best: "A baby is God's opinion that life should go on." If there is one thing you can say about Christmas, though, it is a surprise.

IF YOU HAVE EVER EXPERIENCED THE TRUE MESSAGE OF CHRISTMAS, THEN YOU KNOW WHAT IT IS TO BE SURPRISED. That's the second thing we need to see. Experiencing the love of Christmas is still a surprise.

How many times have you heard it said, "Oh, if we could keep the Christmas spirit all year long." Why do we say that? Isn't it because it is a surprise when people actually are charitable to one another? Isn't it a surprise when somebody actually goes out of their way to help somebody else?

Fred V. Alias wrote a book several years ago about people in his corporation. Fred is with Holiday Inn hotels. One of the people Fred wrote about was a man named Rick. Fred wrote that Rick was one of those people who make you proud to be a member of the human race. Rick was a shift leader at the Front Desk at one of their hotels. One blustery November day, Rick was enjoying a day off, browsing through garage sales and thrift stores. At one stop, he caught bits of conversation between a lady and her little girl. The child was begging her mother to buy an old, dilapidated doll house for $15.

The mother, struggling to maintain some dignity, reminded the little girl that they only had money for a coat. But the little girl kept begging. She promised she wouldn't even let herself feel the cold if she could only have the doll house. The mother's eyes welled with tears, but she hastily paid for the stained, rag tag coat and left.

Rick, totally on impulse, hopped into his car and discreetly followed them to a run-down house. He noted their address and quickly drove back to the thrift shop to buy the doll house.

He gathered paint and fabric and tools and proceeded to "renovate" the beat-up doll house. He even wallpapered the kitchen. Six weeks later, the doll house sparkled. It was now a colorful dream home, complete with miniature furnishings. Something even Santa could not improve upon.

In the cold, gray dawn of Christmas Day, Rick loaded his treasure into his car and drove over to the little girl's house. He gently cleared the snow from the front steps and carefully placed the doll house (wrapped only with a big red bow and letter from Santa) at the front door.

Not wanting to embarrass the family, he quietly drove away and spent the rest of his Christmas morning as Manager on Duty at the Hotel. (2)

Can't you imagine the look of wonder and joy on one little girl's face on Christmas morning? Surprise!

Such self-giving love always comes as a surprise in this cold, cruel world. It's not something we expect. It's a bonus that we find here and there an aberration. We don't know why it is so surprising. We've heard a million times that it is more blessed to give than to receive. And somehow we suspect that is true. But we see it so rarely lived out. And when it is lived out, we are surprised. Christmas comes as a reminder of a spark of goodness that lies, often uncultivated, in every soul. And that brings us to our last thought for this very special time of the year.

CHRISTMAS IS INTENDED TO BE GOD'S SURPRISE FOR THE WORLD. God looked down upon creation in profound sorrow. Humanity, God's highest creation, had been a disappointment. Instead of embracing peace, humanity embraced war; instead of embracing generosity and love, humanity embraced greed and hate. So God had a baby born in the little town of Bethlehem as a shining star to lead toward a new humanity. This was God's surprise for God's world.

A familiar story tells us that, on Christmas Eve in 1870, during the Franco-Prussian War, when Paris was besieged, the French and Germans faced each other in trenches before the city. Suddenly, a young Frenchman jumped out of his trench, and in a beautiful singing voice astonished the Germans with Adolphe Adam's incomparable "Cantique de Noel" ("O Holy Night"). The men on the opposite side seemed awestruck by his performance; and not a shot was fired in his direction. When the French singer had finished the carol, a tall German responded. He came out of his trench to sing, in his own language, Luther's beloved Christmas hymn, "Von Himmel Hoch" ("From Heaven Above I Come to You") (3)

For one brief moment in the midst of the insanity of war, there came a message of God's love and God's hope. That is what Christmas is all about. God sent a babe into the world. And that babe grew to adulthood and he gathered around him men and women that he called out to be his Christmas light to the world. And friends, you and I are those men and women today. We are the ones Christ has called to love the world as he loved the world. We are to be God's Christmas surprise to our families, to our friends, to our community, to our world. Can't you imagine how surprised our community would be if each person in this room determined to live out the love and joy of Christmas throughout the year? That's God's plan; that's God's gift to humanity.

Do you remember the bishop's speech in the vintage motion picture, The Bishop's Wife? Composed by Cary Grant and spoken by David Niven, this speech carries an important message for this event we celebrate. I quote:

[Today] I want to tell you the story of an empty stocking.

Once upon a midnight clear there was a Child's cry, a blazing star hung over a stable, and wise men came with birthday gifts.

We haven't forgotten that night down the centuries. We celebrate it with stars hung on the Christmas tree and the cry of bells and gifts. Especially with gifts.

We buy them and wrap them and put them under the tree. You give me a tie, I give you a book, Cousin Martha always wanted an orange squeezer, Uncle Harry can use a new pipe. Oh, we forget nobody. Adult or child. All the stockings are filled. All, that is, except one. We have even forgotten to hang it up. A stocking for that Child born in a manger. It's His birthday we're celebrating. Don't let us forget that. Let us ask ourselves what He would wish for most, then let each put in his share: lovingkindness, warm hearts, and the stretched-out hand of tolerance all the shining gifts which make up peace on earth. Unquote. (4)

That's God's surprise gift for the world: it is when you and I fill Christ's stocking with lovingkindness, warm hearts, and the stretched-out hand of tolerance all the shining gifts which make up peace on earth.

1. Robert Fulghum, Maybe (Maybe Not) (New York: Villard Books, 1993) p. 57-63.
2. Without Reservations (Pennsylvania: Haddon Craftsmen, Inc., 1992), pp. 73-75.
3. Maymie Richardson Krythe, All About Christmas (New York: Harper & Brothers, 1954).
4. James F. Bender, How to Talk Well (New York: McGraw-Hill Book).

Back To Real Life
Matthew 2:13-23

It's hard not to feel a little let down on the day after Christmas.

A few days after Christmas one year Presbyterian pastor Jon M. Walton was noticing that all the Christmas decorations at one of the local pharmacies had been removed. These decorations already had been replaced with Valentine's Day trinkets and cards. Red boxes of candy, teddy bears with big hearts on them, red candles for romantic lighting.

The clerk behind the counter was complaining to another of her co-workers, "I hate Valentine's Day," she said. "I never have a boyfriend and I hate Valentine's Day."

Then Walton goes on to comment with these words, "Nothing is as over as Christmas when it's over. The empty boxes, the pretty paper on the floor, the stray tinsel from the tree with which the cat has played and left abandoned on the sofa, the empty cartons of eggnog stuffed into the trash bag. Life has come back to normal, whatever that is, and it means that the diversion of the past few weeks, the frenzy and fuss, the lights and glitter are packed away once again like the star at the top of the tree; taken down and carefully wrapped, padded and protected in its ample box. And what is left? A war in Iraq [and Afghanistan], homeless people sleeping in door stoops, hungry people begging for food, worries about health, kids that concern us, jobs that wear us down. We're back to where we left off before the holidays . . . Like the folks who were left in town after the Lone Ranger had been for a visit, we may ask out loud, "Who was that masked man?" Or better said, "Who was that babe wrapped in swaddling clothes, left lying in a manger?" (1)

Well, we haven't moved that far from Christmas yet. We're just one day away from celebrating Christ's birth. But there is the inevitable letdown. So much was packed into the four weeks of Advent. We can talk about keeping Christmas all year long, but who could handle it? We don't want the clogged streets around the mall all year. And who could maintain the pace of eating? In fact, many of us are already planning our diets to begin January 2.

Actually, we need a little respite from all the busyness, don't we? Mary and Joseph weren't allowed to reside permanently in Bethlehem and neither can we. It's back to the real world.

You know what happened to Mary and Joseph and the babe after Christ's birth. After the wise men were gone, an angel of the Lord appeared to Joseph in a dream. "Get up," he said, "take the child and his mother and escape to Egypt. Stay there until I tell you, for Herod is going to search for the child to kill him." So Joseph got up, took the child and his mother during the night and left for Egypt, where he stayed until the death of Herod.

The holy family left just in time, for when Herod realized that he had been outwitted by the wise men, he was furious, and he gave orders to kill all the boys in Bethlehem and its vicinity who were two years old or younger. Such was the cruelty of the king of Judea.

After Herod died, an angel of the Lord appeared in a dream to Joseph in Egypt and said, "Get up, take the child and his mother and go to the land of Israel, for those who were trying to take the child's life are dead." So Joseph got up, took Mary and the child and went to the land of Israel as he was told. But when he heard that Archelaus was reigning in Judea in place of his father Herod, he was afraid to go there. Having been warned in a dream, Joseph withdrew to the district of Galilee. And there he raised his family in a town called Nazareth.

We complain because we have to go back to the real world after Christmas, but our world does not compare to the world of this young family we have been celebrating these past four weeks. They lived in a world where a cruel tyrant could order all infants and toddlers to be put to death. They lived in a world where there were no jets to take them comfortably down to Egypt. The back of a donkey would have to suffice, or perhaps they made the journey on foot. Whatever the means of transportation, it was a hard, tiring journey. They lived in a world where, even after Herod's death, they could not be certain they would be safe. Herod's sons were as cruel as he.

So, Christmas is over. Where does that leave us? Over the weeks of Advent we celebrated the prophecies of Isaiah. When the Messiah comes, Isaiah said, the world will have light and love and peace and joy. The faithful will sing in delight, for Immanuel, God with us, will be born. And he was born. And the world was forever changed. But what now? Where is all the light, love, peace and joy when Christmas is over?

As we noted the first Sunday in Advent, the kingdom of God only established a beachhead at the birth of Christ. The manger was just the beginning of God's plan. There is much yet to be done. The babe must become a man. He must teach us his ways. Then we must teach the world. Then in the fullness of God's time, the age of the Messiah will be ushered in. What are we to do in the meantime?

We do what Joseph did during those dark days following Christ's birth. First of all, we trust God. When Joseph was warned in a dream to flee Herod's wrath, he acted promptly. Joseph trusted God then just as he trusted God when the angel told him that the child within Mary was conceived by the Holy Spirit. This was the kind of man Joseph was. He was a man of character who trusted God. When God spoke, he obeyed.

Ray Pritchard tells of visiting a graveyard with his brother in a rural area near Florence, Alabama. He says they drove along a remote country road and finally stopped near the ruins of an antebellum plantation. They got out and walked into the forest about a quarter of a mile. There they found the family cemetery for the owners of the 19th-century plantation. They climbed over a low wall and began inspecting the gravestones, most of them 150 years old. Most of the markers contained phrases like, "Loving father," "Beloved mother," "Darling son," "Rest in Peace," "Asleep in Jesus," and so on. Eventually they came to the grave of the man who had owned the plantation for many years. Under his name there was the date of his birth and the date of his death. Then there was a five-word statement that summed up his whole life: "A man of unquestioned integrity." Just five words. Nothing more, nothing less. (2)

Those words could have been etched on Joseph's grave. "A man of unquestioned integrity." Also, we could add, a man of faith. What is faith?

The writer of Hebrews tells us what faith is. He uses Abraham as an example of a man of faith. What was special about Abraham? God came to Abraham and said, "Go from your country and your kindred and your father's house to the land that I will show you . . ." And a few verses later we read, "So Abram went, as the Lord had told him . . ." (Genesis 11:26-23:1). No argument. No delay. God spoke, Abraham obeyed.

Later God comes to Abraham and tells him to go to the region of Moriah and sacrifice his son as a burnt offering on a mountain there. Imagine what a terrible command this was, "Sacrifice your son, your only son, whom you love . . ." It is the most horrifying nightmare a parent could have. But then the Scripture says, "Early the next morning Abraham got up and saddled his donkey . . ." No hesitation on Abraham's part. God speaks, Abraham obeys. That, according to Hebrews, is faith. It is not intellectual assent to an abstract idea. It is complete obedience to the will of God.

An angel comes to Joseph in a dream and tells him not to be afraid of taking Mary as his wife even though she is with child. Then Matthew tells us, "When Joseph woke up, he did what the angel of the Lord had commanded him and took Mary home as his wife." And, as we've already noted, when an angel came and told him to take Mary and the child and to flee into Egypt, Matthew tells us, "So Joseph got up, took the child and his mother during the night and left for Egypt . . ."

That was Joseph. A man of integrity; a man of faith. Do you think it might make a difference if all the people who call Jesus Lord had that kind of integrity, that kind of complete trust in God's will and God's way? My guess is that it would change the world overnight. The first thing we need to do after Christmas is to keep trusting God.

The second thing we need to do is to take care of those we love. That was Joseph's primary concern. He loved Mary and he loved their son Jesus and he was committed to doing whatever was necessary to keep them safe and to provide for them—not only to provide for them materially, but emotionally and spiritually. That is what we do when Christmas has passed. We keep trusting God and we take care of those we love—not only materially, but emotionally and spiritually. We love them, listen to them, encourage them. We understand that they are God's gift to us and we treat them with love and dignity.

Jesse Jackson tells the story of a visit he made to the University of Southern Mississippi. While touring the campus with the university president, he saw a towering male student, six-feet, eight-inches tall, holding hands with a fidgety coed barely three-feet tall. What a contrast, six feet eight inches tall and only three feet tall. His curiosity piqued, Jackson watched as the young man, dressed in a warm-up suit, tenderly kissed the tiny coed, and sent her off to class.

The president said that the student was a star basketball player. Both parents had passed away when he was a teenager, and he made a vow to look after his sister. Many scholarships came his way, but only Southern Mississippi offered one to his sister, too.

Jackson went over to the basketball star, introduced himself, and said he appreciated the way he was looking out for his sister. The athlete shrugged and said, "Those of us who God makes six-eight have to look out for those he makes three-three." (3) Don't you wish every young person could have that kind of love for his or her siblings? We live lives of faith and we look out for those we love.

And that brings us to the last thing. What do we do when Christmas has passed? We remember the world to whom Christ came and for which he died.

Why did Christ come into the world? One reason and one reason alone: Because, "God so loved the world." That's it. Christmas is centered in love. We want to keep the Christmas spirit all year long, because the Christmas spirit consists of loving our neighbor and loving God not just one day of the year, but all the year round.

I want to close with a haunting story told by author W. B. Freeman.

A man was walking down a dimly lit street late one evening when he heard muffled screams coming from behind a clump of bushes. "Alarmed, he slowed down to listen and panicked when he realized that what he was hearing was the unmistakable sounds of a struggle—heavy grunting, frantic scuffling, and tearing of fabric.

"Only yards from where he stood, a woman was being attacked. He froze in his steps, hardly daring to breathe lest the attacker should notice his presence. But then a strange thought occurred to him: Should he get involved?

"Frightened for his own safety, he cursed himself for having suddenly decided to take a new route home that night. He had family responsibilities; what if he became another statistic? He instantly had the urge to run to a safe place and use his cell phone to call the police. But he could hear the struggle becoming more desperate.

"An eternity seemed to pass as he argued with himself. The deliberations in his head had taken only seconds, but already the girl's cries were growing weaker. He had to decide—and fast. How could he sleep at night if he walked away from this?

"So he finally resolved that he could not turn his back on the fate of this unknown woman, even if it meant risking his life.

"Known neither for his bravery nor for his athletic abilities, he nonetheless summoned up all the moral courage and physical strength he could muster. And once he had finally determined to help the girl, he became strangely transformed. He ran behind the bushes and pulled the assailant off the woman and wrestled with the attacker for a few minutes until the man fled.

"Panting hard, he scrambled upright and approached the girl, who was crouched behind a tree, sobbing. In the darkness, he could barely see her outline, but he could certainly sense her trembling shock. Not wanting to frighten her further, he first spoke to her from a distance. 'It's okay,' he said soothingly. 'The man ran away. You're safe now.'

"There was a long pause, and then he heard these words, uttered in wonder, in amazement. 'Dad, is that you?' Out from behind the tree stepped his youngest daughter." (4)

What if he had passed by that night? What if he had decided not to get involved?

What I want to say to you on this Sunday after Christmas is this: We will only have the true spirit of Christmas when we understand that every child on this earth is ultimately our son, our daughter, our brother, our sister. It's good that we take care of those we love. However, as people of faith, the babe in Bethlehem's manger calls us to expand those borders, to understand that the good of every person on this earth is our concern.

So, Christmas is over, but living for Jesus may just be getting started for some of us. Trust God. Take care of those you love. Expand your love to all for whom God sent His son into the world.

1. http://www.fpcnyc.org/sermons/2007/pdfs/070107.pdf
2. http://www.keepbelieving.com/sermon/2003-08-24-Finishing-Well/.
3. Philip Yancey, Rumors of Another World (Grand Rapids, MI: Zondervan, 2003), pp. 203-204.
4. The Longer-Lasting Inspirational Bathroom Book (New York: FaithWords Hatchette Book Group, 2007), pp. 28-29.

Adopted! Thank God!
Ephesians 1:3-14

James King, a former missionary to Africa, once told a true story about a woman in one of the churches under his care. What caught Rev. King's attention was that this lady would not only come to every service on Sunday morning and Wednesday evening, but that she would be accompanied by her scruffy, mangy looking dog.

The dog would enter with the woman and sit beside her during the service. At the conclusion of the service, when the invitation was given by the pastor to come for forward for prayer, the dog would come along and take his place beside her at the altar.

Tragically this woman's husband was a wife-beater who resented her Christian faith. One day he beat her so severely for her Christian life-style that she died. Without a sign of contrition he even forbade the pastor to conduct a Christian funeral for her.

After the woman's death her hard and cruel husband took over the care of her dog. Soon he noticed something quite interesting about the dog. He noticed that the dog would disappear on Wednesday evenings about 7:00 and didn't reappear for about two hours. It happened again on Sundays—about 9:00 a.m. the dog was gone and returned about 12:30. The dog did the same thing every week.

Eventually, the man's curiosity was so aroused that he decided to follow the dog and see what it was up to. He soon followed the dog to the humble little church his wife had attended. The dog went in and took his seat on the aisle next to the seat that this faithful woman had always occupied. He sat there quite still while the service went on.

At the close of the service, the man was surprised and a little taken-back to see that as soon as the pastor gave the call to come forward for prayer, the dog got up and shuffled forward to take a place at the altar where this man's wife had prayed.

The man was so touched that eventually he too went forward and gave his life to Christ. Now the dog, says James King, comes to church with a new master. (1)

We're beginning a new year. Wouldn't it be great if we could also begin a new life with a new Master like the owner of that dog?

Some of us are undoubtedly making resolutions for this New Year. Some wag has suggested that this year we make resolutions that we can actually keep.

For example, gain weight. At least 30 pounds. Or stop exercising. Waste of time. Or read less. After all, it just makes you think. And watch more television. Then you won't have to think at all. Or procrastinate more . . . starting tomorrow.

I think you will agree these are resolutions we can all keep.

But what if, instead of a resolution, we were to experience a revolution? Suppose we turned completely around with a new set of attitudes, a new set of motivations, a new set of feelings about life and about others?

Our text for the day from Ephesians offers that kind of possibility. St. Paul writes, "Praise be to the God and Father of our Lord Jesus Christ, who has blessed us in the heavenly realms with every spiritual blessing in Christ. For he chose us in him before the creation of the world to be holy and blameless in his sight. In love he predestined us to be adopted as his sons [and daughters] through Jesus Christ, in accordance with his pleasure and will—to the praise of his glorious grace, which he has freely given us in the One he loves."

I believe the key word in this passage is the word, "adopted." Imagine you are a third world child, an orphan, living in poverty and squalor. A wealthy couple from the developed world, a loving couple with resources untold—who desperately long for a child—comes to your sad orphanage and through the filth and the flies they see a small face and it is your face and they say to the person in charge, we want that child, and they take you to their home and they dress you in new clothes and give you new opportunities. But most of all they give you a new identity. You are no longer an orphan, no longer a nobody. Now you are their child, heir to everything they own. You have a place in the world. You are no longer a child of poverty, but a child of privilege. What a beautiful thing this would be to happen to any child, particularly one who lives in want. Do you understand that this is our story—your story and mine? This is what St. Paul meant when he wrote in Romans 5:8: "But God demonstrates his own love for us in this: While we were still sinners, Christ died for us." And in today's lesson, "In love he predestined us to be adopted as his sons through Jesus Christ, in accordance with his pleasure and will . . ."

Unless you understand what God has done for you, you can never be all God has called you to be.

Do you understand what God has done for you in Jesus Christ? Do you know what it is to be lost, and then be found? Do you know what it is to be blind, then suddenly able to see? Do you understand what it means to be a child in an orphanage—unwanted, unloved—and then to be adopted by a loving parent?

It may sound ironic, but the greatest barrier to our truly embracing a new life in Christ is that we already have it so good. Oh, to be sure, there are challenges that each of us face. But let's admit it—there are people who would give anything to be in our shoes. It is hard to be a Christian when you are surrounded by so much affluence. Why do we need God? We can get all our daily needs met by mammon—at least that is how it appears to the casual mind.

And it may be that growing up in a Christian culture may even work against us to a certain extent. Some of us have been in the church all our lives. And we have had loving families who supported us and nurtured us in healthy values. How can we be lost? How can we need saving? If we had struggled more with life, we would understand what good news the Gospel really is.

Pastor Edward Markquart, a Lutheran pastor in Seattle tells about a young man who approached him following an activity at their church on a Wednesday night. The young man came to Markquart to show him his progress in school. The young man pulled his grades out of his black, leather jacket and laid them on the altar for Markquart to see. The young man was not a child or even a teenager. He was thirty-three years old, going to a technical school, and he was studying to become a licensed practical nurse.

Markquart looked at the grade card. The young man had an A in pharmacology. He had an A in practicum; the on-the-floor practical nursing which is so important. He was proud of his achievement. Then the young man reminded Markquart of his story: Twenty years ago he had dropped out of school as well as life . . . at the age of thirteen. "It was twenty years since he had been in school. He used drugs—marijuana, cocaine, alcohol, and everything else the world had to offer in those years. For more than a decade, he had been a prisoner, a captive. And slowly, ever so slowly, he found himself. Slowly he was healed, and slowly he was liberated, and now he [was] getting A's in school. He was so proud as he laid his report on the altar . . ." (2)

That young man would certainly understand the metaphor of adoption. He now had a new life. He had been pulled from darkness into the light. He had been brought from spiritual poverty to spiritual plenty. In a sense, he had been blind, but now he could see.

Some of us, on the other hand, just don't get it. We've been in church all our lives. The Christian life is just a synonym for respectability, decency, fitting in.

We don't quite get it when British evangelist Michael Green says, "Jesus did not come to make bad men good, but to make dead men live." We don't think of ourselves as dead in our sins. And yet, if Christ does not live in our hearts—that is exactly what we are.

Jesus called us white-washed tombs. "You are like whitewashed tombs," he once said, "which appear beautiful on the outside, but inside are full of dead men's bones . . ." (Matthew 23:15). He was speaking to the Pharisees, but he is also speaking to anyone who has the form of godliness but not its spirit.

Some of you will head to the gym in the weeks ahead and seek a new body. Others will go back to school and try to improve your mind. Still others may seek out some kind of on-the-job training in order to advance professionally. But what Christ offers you this year is an opportunity for an entirely new life. A new attitude, a new sense of identity, a new heart as it were—all this Christ offers. But that is unlikely to happen unless we understand what God has done for us. We must understand our need before we can understand God's provision.

Christ died for us that we might live for him. Paul calls us a chosen people. Israel was a chosen people, chosen to be a light unto the world. In the same way we are a chosen people, chosen to be God's people.

Do you remember the first time you were chosen for anything?

Author Bruce Larson says his first memory of being chosen came in the third grade when he was chosen to be a blackboard monitor. He was chosen not because he was a model student, but because his parents wined and dined his teacher. When he got the privilege of cleaning the blackboards, he thought he had arrived . . . until his classmates began to call him "teacher's pet." His new status was a mixed blessing.

His next triumph came in sixth grade when he was chosen to be a member of the safety patrol. He could wear that white belt and a badge and order his fellow fifth and sixth graders to stop and start at will at street crossings. However, he says, he also bore, with the other patrol members, the stigma of being part of "the establishment." At recess they were often teased and avoided. Being chosen, again, had its bitter side.

Later, as a member of his high school football team, he dreamed of someday being chosen for the starting lineup. The day finally came when the coach read off the names of the starting team and said, "Larson, right tackle." This was his glorious moment, except, he says, he was well aware that he was chosen because the first and second string right tackles were both out with injuries. Furthermore, his team was soundly defeated.

Then there was the junior prom. Of all the girls he knew, he wanted most of all to go with a young lady named Marjorie. Marjorie said, "Yes," and this was a triumph. She had chosen him to be her date—except he learned later that she really wanted to go with his best friend, who had asked somebody else. She was going with him in order to be near his friend.

He says he felt like that young man who said to his girlfriend, "Darling, I don't have a sailboat and a sports car like Jerome, but I love you with all my heart."

"I love you too, dear," she replied, "but tell me more about Jerome." (3)

Each time Bruce Larson was chosen, he found it to be a mixed blessing. Being chosen by God can be a mixed blessing, too, for those who go into it without understanding what God desires of us.

The prophets tried to remind Israel that God chose it to be blessed, but also that God chose it to be a blessing to others. That is why God chose us as well. God has blessed us; we are to be a blessing to others.

Pastor Hugh Cox tells the story of a couple named Bob and Mary. Bob was a successful entrepreneur in his thirties who fancied himself a self-made man. He lived in a large house in the country and had a beautiful wife and thought he had his whole world put together. One day his wife Mary came home and announced that she had found the answer to the nagging emptiness in her life. She said that a friend had led her to Jesus Christ and that she was sure this was what had been missing.

Bob reacted negatively, indicating that he wasn't pleased and didn't share her enthusiasm for this new discovery. He pointed out to Mary that religion was for the blind, the lame and the weak—not for people like them. They already had everything they needed.

Through the following weeks Bob gave Mary a hard time about her new-found faith. He ridiculed her for her commitment. He was caustic, sarcastic and cynical. Yet he noticed that in the days that followed, Mary's life became more secure and confident, and, in fact, she was becoming a more beautiful person. Her growing sense of meaning and purpose only served to highlight his sense of emptiness which led him to even consider suicide, on three separate occasions.

Finally, the power of Mary's life so struck Bob's heart that he fell on his knees alone in a hotel room while on a business trip away from home. He lifted his eyes toward heaven and prayed, "Lord, this is Bob. If you can take me the way I am, I need what you've given to Mary." (4)

Bob did not realize that at that moment he had become chosen—chosen to be blessed and chosen to be a blessing to others. Bob discovered what it is to be adopted as God's own child. But, first of all, he needed to become aware of his need. And so do we.

But there's one thing more to be said. We have been adopted that we might grow into the likeness of Christ. Some children who have been adopted torture themselves that they have never known their real parents. They do not understand that when people have loved you, and raised you, and nurtured you in every good way, they are your real parents. Anybody can be a biological parent. It takes no brains and no character to produce a child biologically. It is a lifetime commitment, however, to be an adoptive parent—one who chooses to love and be responsible for another human being.

God is our adoptive parent. God is also our real parent whose love is beyond measure. But here is what we need to understand: the purpose of our adoption is that someday we shall reflect the nature of God's Son, Jesus Christ.

San Diego pastor Mark Trotter, a few years ago, told a beautiful story about a boy whose parents were missionaries to India. When the boy was 12 years old, his parents left him and his younger brother to go to India and take up their tour of duty there. Their intention was that once they got settled they would send for the boys. But shortly after they left America, World War II broke out. They couldn't get to the boys, and they couldn't get the boys to them. So the separation between the missionaries and their sons went on for something like eight years.

When the war was over, the parents returned to America. Their oldest son was 20 years old and in college. He recalled how excited he was when he got the word that his parents would soon arrive in their hometown by train. The son got to the train depot early, even before the sun came up. When the train finally pulled in, the mother and father were the only ones who got off the train. The son wrote these words:

"I could barely see them in the haze, and they could hardly see me. We embraced in the semi-darkness. Then my mother took my hand and led me into the light of the waiting room. There were tears running down her cheeks as she looked at me. She kept looking at my face, staring hard. Then she turned to my dad and called him by name, 'Arnett,' she cried, 'he's gone and looked just like you! He looks just like you!'" (5)

That's what God desires out of each of us—that we reflect the nature of God's Son, Jesus Christ. How about you? Are you there yet? Or are you still on the outside looking in? Do you understand what God has done for you? Do you understand how much God loves you? Are you ready to go beyond resolutions this New Year to a revolution—a new life, a new purpose, a new identity as one who belongs to God?

1. Cited by Charles Mallory, http://www.sermoncentral.com/sermons/delegated-expectations-charles-mallory-sermon-on-evangelism-urgency-133036.asp.
2. http://www.sermonsfromseattle.com/christmas_the_liberator.htm.
3. Bruce Larson, Living Out the Book of Acts (Dallas: Word Publishing, 1984), p. 73.
4. http://stpaulstervuren.be/nurture/sermons/15dec02.htm.
5. The Rev. Dr. James W. Moore, http://day1.org/595-grit_grace_and_gratitude.

Lift Up Your Eyes
Isaiah 60:1-6

Americans have traditionally been thought of as a positive, hopeful people—perhaps the most positive, hopeful people on earth.

Anthony Jay in his book Management and Machiavelli tells an interesting story about a British friend of his who was on a trip to America years ago. When he was in the lounge at Idlewild airport, a stranger rushed up to him.

"You're from England?" noted the stranger. "Yes," his friend answered, "are you?"

"Used to be," the stranger answered. "Living over here now. Where do you come from?"

"Cobham," answered Jay's friend.

"How marvelous," said the stranger. "I used to live on Epson Downs. Loveliest place in the world."

"But presumably you like it better here?" his friend asked.

"I loathe it here," replied the stranger.

"Then your wife likes it better?" asked the friend.

"She hates it," said the stranger.

"Then [surely] you're earning a lot more than you were?" asked the friend.

"The [heck] I am. I'm working harder and earning less," said the stranger.

"Well, why stay here?" asked Jay's friend. "Why not come back with us?"

"I'll tell you why," answered the stranger. "Because I've got a feeling here," and he started slapping the back of his head violently, "that tomorrow I'm going to hit the jackpot. I haven't hit it in eleven years, but I still feel I could hit it tomorrow. And it's a feeling you can't get in Britain. That's why I'm not coming back." (1)

For this man, America represented hope, opportunity. That has been true for many generations. We call it the "American dream." It is the dream of a better life, and historically it has kept the people of the U.S. a hopeful, positive people. Even a terrible depression and two world wars could not dampen American optimism. Our music and our motion pictures have reinforced this positive spirit.

A British sailor recalls when World War II was ending. Allied servicemen and women were returning home by the hundreds of thousands. He was about to be discharged from the Royal Navy. He decided to enjoy an evening out, and bought a ticket to a play in London. It was opening night of some American musical. He didn't know what the show was about. All he wanted was to celebrate the fact that he had lived through a war, and would soon be going home.

The first thing he noticed entering the theater was the brilliance of the lights. For years, he and his companions in battle had to get used to muted lighting— sometimes, none at all. Now, the world was suddenly bright again. And the mood, he noticed, was festive and electric. But nothing prepared him for what happened when the curtain rose. The stage blazed with a sunlit world stretching infinitely—or so it seemed. The dancers and actors positively leaped upon the stage. The music joined them. The opening words transformed everyone. They went like this: "There's a bright golden haze on the meadow, There's a bright golden haze on the meadow, The corn is as high as an elephant's eye, And it looks like it's climbin' clear up to the sky."

Many of you know the rest:

"O what a beautiful morning! / O what a beautiful day!

I've got a wonderful feeling / Everything's going my way."

Oklahoma! was the musical. And it brought a sudden blaze of energy, hope and a feeling of possibility for a decimated Europe and for America itself. (2)

The musicals of the 1940s and 50s—particularly those of Rogers and Hammerstein—are a uniquely American phenomenon. Europeans make fun of the somewhat Pollyanna enthusiasm that these productions represent. Only in America, European cynics complain, must every movie have a happy ending. That has been our tradition. Hope, optimism, energy for the future—that is our heritage.

Do you sense that we may be losing that hopeful glow? Perhaps it's the slow recovery from the recession, but people seem more hopeless, they seem angrier, more dogmatic—or is it just my imagination? Even though we are still a very affluent people with strong corporations, a military second to none, world class schools and hospitals and a standard of living that is still the envy of the world—many of our people have reached the conclusion that we have lost our way—that the days ahead will not be as bright as our former days.

The prophet Isaiah lived in a time when the people had nearly lost all hope. But they had good reason. Many of Israel's best and brightest were slowly returning from living as slaves in Babylon. The city of Jerusalem and its temple lay in ruins. The once proud empire of David and Solomon was now a small colony on the fringe of the Persian Empire. Doom and gloom were everywhere, when suddenly Isaiah, sounding somewhat like Rogers and Hammerstein, bursts on the scene proclaiming, "Arise, shine, for your light has come, and the glory of the Lord rises upon you. See, darkness covers the earth and thick darkness is over the peoples, but the LORD rises upon you and his glory appears over you. Nations will come to your light, and kings to the brightness of your dawn. Lift up your eyes and look about you: All assemble and come to you; your sons come from afar, and your daughters are carried on the arm. Then you will look and be radiant, your heart will throb and swell with joy . . ."

It is appropriate at the darkest time of the year that we celebrate Epiphany. One of the great themes of Epiphany is that of hope and light. "A light shines in the darkness . . ." And "Arise, shine, for your light has come, and the glory of the Lord rises upon you . . ." I believe it is particularly significant that Isaiah proclaims, "Lift up your eyes . . ."

There is an interesting relationship between downcast eyes and depression. People who are feeling down express that emotion by continually gazing down. Conversely, it makes sense that you can make yourself feel better by intentionally seeking to look up. At this dark gloomy time of the year, you can do yourself a favor by lifting up your eyes. The Psalmist wrote, "I lift up my eyes to the hills—where does my help come from? My help comes from the LORD, the Maker of heaven and earth." (Psalm 121:1-2) This is our hope.

Why should we lift up our eyes this day? Let's begin here: You may think you are forgotten. You are not. That was Isaiah's message to his people. They thought God had forsaken them.

Todd Stanton, a youth pastor in Clarksdale, Mississippi, tells a wonderful story about the Sydney Swans—a team in the Australian Rules football league. The Swans had the worst record, the worst players, the worst coach, and the worst fans in the league. Most of their home games were played in front of empty seats.

But a strange thing happened. The team got a new coach and a few new players, and started winning. Before long, the team that had been the laughing-stock of the league was a power-house. And since everybody likes a winning team, you can imagine what happened next. The stands began to fill. Thousands of people who had no interest in the team before began to attend games religiously. The Swans became the talk of the town. Everyone wanted to be identified with them. Downtown Sydney was awash in the team's colors, and people could be seen wearing Swans merchandise everywhere! Soon it became almost impossible to get a ticket to a Swans game.

One Sunday afternoon the Swans were playing a rival team in front of a capacity crowd. As the TV cameras zoomed in on the revelry and joy in the stands, one focused on a single man who was cheering and waving a sign that he had obviously made himself. Grinning proudly, he held up his sign for all the world to see. Here is what the sign said: I WAS HERE WHEN NOBODY ELSE WAS!"

Todd Stanton goes on to write: "That's Jesus! When you're not winning, when all the odds are stacked against you, when you've become the laughing-stock of your school or family, when you feel like the biggest loser of all time, Jesus is cheering you on! He's there when nobody else is." (3) You may think you're forgotten. You are not.

Here's the second thing we need to see: You may think you are on your own. You are not. Someone is with you.

Dr. Steve Stephens tells about a Russian poet and composer named Nicolaie Moldova. Nicolaie experienced firsthand the brutality of the prison system in Russia under communism. "Lie on your belly!" a guard yelled to Nicolaie.

Nicolaie dropped to the icy cold floor, knowing that the torture would be excruciating. The guards then marched on his back, legs, and feet with their heavy boots for the next hour. They left Nicolaie badly bruised and bleeding.

His fellow prisoners rushed to his side, deeply concerned about his condition. Nicolaie raised his head. "I have written a new hymn while I was being walked upon," he said. Then he began to sing, "May I not only speak about future heavens," his song began, "but let me have heaven and a holy feast here."

After Nicolaie was released from prison, the communist police went through his home and confiscated manuscripts that he had been working on for several years. Much of his lifework was gone, but Nicolaie would not let this loss stop him. He composed another hymn, "I worship you with gratitude for all you ever gave me, but also for everything beloved you took from me. You do all things well, and I will trust you."

"Nicolaie Moldova could have been a victim," says Steve Stephens, but he learned an important lesson: "Life is an attitude. He had a battle plan. He chose to look up, instead of being pulled down. He decided to cry out to God. Now his songs are sung throughout Russia." (4)

You may think you've been forgotten. You may think you're on your own. You may think you'll never make it through. Who says it's up to you?

A dad tells about taking his four-year-old daughter on her first trip to Disneyland. She couldn't wait to get on Mr. Toad's Wild Ride. As the car zoomed through the crazy rooms, into the path of a speeding train, and through walls that fell away at the last second, the tiny girl clutched the little steering wheel in front of her. When the ride was over, she turned to her dad a little shakily and said, "Next time, you drive. I didn't know where I was going." She didn't realize that she really was not in control the entire time.

I'm not sure that you and I have that much control over our lives, either. Life happens. Sometimes we feel like we are forgotten. Sometimes it feels like we are on our own. Sometimes it seems that we will not make it through. But friends, here's the good news. We are not in control. A loving God is in control. Life shall not defeat us.

"Arise, shine, for your light has come ... Lift up your eyes and look about you ... Then you will look and be radiant, your heart will throb and swell with joy ..." Amen.

1. An Inquiry into the Politics of Corporate Life (New York: Bantam, 1967), pp. 194-195.
2. Herbert O'Driscoll, Christian Century, November 29, 2003, p. 19. Cited by The Rev. Charles Booker-Hirsch, http://www.northsidepres.org/worship/sermons/sermon/85.
3. "The Beacon," Vol. 22, Number 29, August 7, 2006, p. 2. Cited in Monday Fodder, http://www.fishermansnet.com/monday-fodder/.
4. The Wounded Warrior (Sisters, OR: Multnomah Publishers, Inc., 2006), pp. 100-101.

Aha! An Epiphany!
Matthew 3:13-17 or Luke 3:15-16, 21-22

There is a wonderful story about a young man who was dating a very attractive girl. One Sunday after church the two went for a picnic. The young man had made arrangements to rent a row boat. His plan was to row to a small island on their favorite lake and enjoy a lunch which he himself had prepared.

Since he had been unaccustomed to making lunches, he had forgotten to pack a number of things. His attractive friend said, "It might be nice if we had some salt, ketchup and napkins." Without hesitation the young man got into the boat and rowed back to shore to get these missing items.

This routine occurred twice more that afternoon—he rowed back to shore to retrieve items that she requested. By the end of the extremely warm day, he had perspired so much that his good suit was soaked.

But he realized something that afternoon. He realized there had to be a better way. The young man's name, by the way, was Clarence Evinrude. Later that very evening he designed the world's first outboard motor. An industry was born because a young man had fallen head over heels for a young woman who kept making requests of him. I will add that she later became his wife. (1)

We call the "Aha!" moment Clarence Evinrude had that hot afternoon that led to the invention of the outboard motor an epiphany, a moment of sometimes life changing realization.

Let me tell you another story—about little Benny, an African-American lad who grew up in a single parent home. Benny's mother Sonya had been raised in foster homes. She had a third grade education and was married by the time she was 13. After getting married, Sonya discovered much to her dismay that her husband, a Baptist preacher, was already married and had five children. So much for having a life partner.

Now what was she to do? She now had two little boys, Benny and his younger brother, to rear. I'll tell you what she did. Sonya worked at two, sometimes three jobs at a time to provide for her two boys. Not too surprisingly, Benny experienced difficulty in school, eventually falling to the bottom of his class. In fact, until he got into Junior High, Benny was convinced he was stupid; his nickname was "Dummy." To complicate things further, Benny developed a violent, uncontrollable temper.

But Sonya did not give up on her son. Determined to help him turn his life around, she required him to read two books a week and write reports on the books. He didn't realize at the time that his mother herself could barely read. Sonya's disability did not keep her from putting marks on her son's papers. She also limited his TV viewing. Soon Benny amazed his instructors and classmates with his improvement. "It was at that moment that I realized I wasn't stupid," he recalled later.

Within a year he was at the top of his class.

After this epiphany in Junior High School that he was not stupid, Benny went on to Yale and the University of Michigan Medical School. And at the age of 32, Dr. Benjamin Carson became the youngest surgeon in the nation to hold the position of Director of Pediatric Neurosurgery at Johns Hopkins University. As a surgeon he was chosen to separate several sets of what are popularly known as Siamese twins. (2)

Clarence Evinrude one afternoon saw the need for a motor for a rowboat. At age 11, Benjamin Carson realized that he was no dummy.

One more quick story. In 1927, at age thirty-two, a young man named Buckminster Fuller was standing on the shores of Lake Michigan. He was intent on committing suicide by throwing himself into the freezing waters of that great lake. His first child had died. He was bankrupt. He was discredited. He was jobless. He had a wife and a newborn daughter, yet he felt hopeless.

But suddenly he had a realization, an epiphany if you will. He realized that his life belonged not to himself but to others. He chose that moment to embark upon an experiment to discover what a little, penniless, unknown individual might be able to do on behalf of humanity. He thought, if my life belongs not to myself but to others, then what can I do for others? Over the next fifty-four years, he became one of America's best known architects, designers, and inventors.

Imagine! A man who is bankrupt, discredited, jobless, and about to commit suicide, and he has an epiphany: my life doesn't belong to me; it belongs to others. (3)

Clarence Evinrude realized that there must be a better way. Benjamin Carson realized he wasn't stupid. Buckminster Fuller realized he existed to serve humanity.

This is the first Sunday in the church season of Epiphany. This should be a time of new understandings, new beginnings, new ideas about what it means to follow Christ.

Aha! moments are a common experience in human lives. We often ask of people who have made extraordinary accomplishments or who have overcome difficult circumstances, "When was it that you first realized . . . ?" For example, "When was it that you first realized that help was on its way?" asks the television reporter of the person who has just been rescued. Or perhaps in a different setting, "When was it that you first realized that your life was empty and without meaning?" Or again, "When was it that you first realized that the game was won?"

It is a familiar question. "When was it that you first realized . . . that you were growing up . . . that your marriage was in trouble . . . that it was time to allow your daughter to make her own decisions?" The moment of realization—the Aha! Experience—the time of epiphany—what a powerful moment it is.

One morning in 1888, Alfred Nobel, the inventor of dynamite, the man who had spent his life amassing a fortune from the manufacture and sale of weapons of destruction, awoke to read his own obituary. The obituary was printed as a result of a simple journalistic error—Alfred's brother had died, and a French reporter carelessly reported the death of the wrong brother. Alfred Nobel was shocked by what the newspaper had to say about him. He saw himself for the first time as the world saw him—"the dynamite King," the great industrialist who had made an immense fortune from explosives. This—as far as the general public was concerned—was the entire purpose of his life.

None of his true ideals were recognized or given serious consideration. He was quite simply a merchant of death, and for that alone would he be remembered . . . As he read his obituary with horror, Nobel resolved to make clear to the world the true meaning and purpose of his life. This could be done through the final disposition of his fortune. His last will and testament would be the expression of his life's ideals . . . The result was the most valued of prizes given to those who have done most for the cause of world peace. (4)

What a dramatic breakthrough that moment of realization was for the man for whom the Nobel peace prize was named.

There are some Biblical scholars who contend that our Scripture lesson for today contains a moment of realization—an epiphany—in the life of Jesus. He had gone out to hear the fiery evangelist John the Baptist preach in the wilderness. When the invitation was given for baptism, Jesus stepped forward. We don't know what that baptism represented in Jesus' mind. Obviously it was not a cleansing from sin. Perhaps it was an act of identification with the summons to righteousness that John was proclaiming. Whatever the reason, Jesus stepped down into the water and was baptized of John. At that moment something came over Jesus. While he was praying, says Luke, "the heaven was opened and the Holy Spirit descended upon him in bodily form, as a dove, and a voice came from heaven, 'You are my Son, whom I love; with you I am well pleased.'"

A dramatic moment in the life of Jesus—a time of realization, if you will—an Aha! experience. How important those moments are in our lives. Let me ask you about some epiphanies that may have occurred in your life.

For example, when was it that you first realized the majesty of God? Was it the beauty and grandeur of creation that first evoked that realization?

Roy L. Smith tells about an aged and scholarly minister with a flair for astronomy who spent the night on a California mountaintop with a group of young men from his church. It so happened that a little after midnight two great stars came into conjunction, and the dear old man went from sleeping bag to sleeping bag, shaking them and shouting, "Get up! Get up! Don't miss it! Don't let God Almighty put on such a show as this for just this old mule and me!"

Anyone who is sensitive to the beauty of nature sees God daily. When was it that you first realized the majesty of God? Perhaps it was at the birth of your first child. What greater miracle in all of creation is there than this—the birth of a new human being. As we watch that child learn to smile and to make sounds—then to talk and to walk and finally to grow into a mature person, we are led to the dramatic realization that there is more to life than mere physics and chemistry. Behind creation stands a Creator. When was it that you first realized the majesty of God? Here's a second question.

When was it that you first realized your own inadequacy to deal with life's critical issues? We are inadequate, you know. There is much in life that we are unable to control.

Dick Emmons wrote a humorous but somewhat plaintive little poem that was published years ago in Golf Digest. It went like this:

I bought a set of brand-new clubs
And rushed out to the tee;
The brand-new clubs are really great—
But I'm the same old me.

"I'm the same old me . . . ." Each of us could sing that sad refrain, could we not? We've a world of good intentions, but very little ever really changes. It's not that we don't want to do better. It's not that we don't have the natural gifts to do better. But somewhere in our own makeup some vital element is missing. When was it that you first realized your own personal inadequacy? Perhaps it was in a time of crisis or great disappointment. They come to us all.

Sometimes we feel like the deep sea diver who had scarcely reached the bottom when a message came from the surface. "Come up quick," the message said, "The ship is sinking."

"Between a rock and a hard place," we call it. "On the horns of a dilemma." We have all been there. And a cry has come unconsciously from our lips, "Oh, God!"

When was it that you first realized your own personal inadequacy? Perhaps it was while someone you loved lay critically ill. Remember all of those promises you made . . . all the good things that you resolved you would do . . . if only God would intervene. Many years ago actor Burt Reynolds was in a movie titled, "The End." In a humorous scene at the conclusion of the movie Reynolds' character decides to commit suicide. He attempts to drown himself in the ocean, but then, far off from shore, he changes his mind. Swimming toward the distant shoreline, he makes all kinds of extravagant promises to God—if only God will let him get back to shore safely. As he creeps closer and closer to shore, however, the promises get less and less extravagant until finally when he reaches shore safely, he cancels the whole agreement. He's safe. Why make promises to God now. We have been guilty of that, have we not?

When was it that you first realized the majesty of God? When was it that you first realized your own personal inadequacy? Final question.

When was it that you first realized that you are God's own child? Oh, not in the same way that Jesus heard the voice from heaven saying, "You are my Son, whom I love . . ." His relationship with God was unique. He was the Son of God. And yet he taught us to pray "Our Father . . . ." I, too, am a child of the King and so are you. Last week our theme was "adopted"—adopted to be God's own child—children of the King.

C.S. Lewis, the great British writer, was fearful of giving in to the demands of God, but finally there came that moment of realization, that epiphany. He writes, "That which I greatly feared had at last come upon me. In the Trinity Term of 1929 I gave in and admitted God was God, and knelt and prayed." C. S. Lewis, who has influenced so many people around the world with his writings about God, came reluctantly to God, but the world was greatly blessed when he did.

Henri Frederic Amiel has written: "We dream alone, we suffer alone, we die alone, we inhabit the last resting-place alone. But there is nothing to prevent us from opening our solitude to God. And so what was an austere monologue becomes dialogue."

How is it with your life? Is it still an austere monologue? It need not be. It can be a rich and beautiful dialogue between yourself and God.

Many years ago some doctors in an Ohio penitentiary performed an experiment. They believed that an operation on a man's brain would change him and rid him of criminal tendencies.

A prisoner in that prison submitted to the operation. But the operation was a failure. The man was released from prison, but soon he was back in again for forgery. In order for a person to be changed, he or she must have a changed heart.

When was it that you first realized the majesty of God? When was it that you first realized your own personal inadequacy to deal with the critical issues of life— that you needed a changed heart? And then, when was it that you first realized you are God's own child? Perhaps, for someone, it has happened just now. If so, pray this prayer: "Lord, you are God. I need You. I can't make it on my own. I need for You to change my heart, change my priorities, change my purpose for living. Help me to bear the image of your Son in whose name I pray. Amen."

1. Rev. Richard E. Stetler, http://dickstetler.com/1998_The%20Power%20Of%20Humility.htm.
2. Jim Barnes, http://www.christcov.org/sermons/06-05-14%20Sermon%20Notes.doc.
3. Buckminster Fuller Institute Web site: http://www.Bfi.org/. Cited in Andy Andrews, Mastering The Seven Decisions . . . (Nashville: Thomas Nelson, 2008).
4. Nicholas Halasz, author of Nobel.

Love Lifted Me
Psalm 40:1-11

In the television drama, "The Sopranos" there is a scene that takes place at a funeral. The guests receive prayer cards with a picture of Jesus on them along with a prayer.

One of the guests at the funeral remarks that as a kid he always wondered about the value of these cards. He collected baseball cards, he said, and they increased in value. Why not the prayer cards? "I don't get it," says the guest. "Ten thousand dollars for Mickey Mantle and zip for Jesus . . ." (1)

I suspect that says something about the values of our culture.

When the rock group of the nineteen-sixties said they were more popular than Jesus Christ, they hit the nail squarely on the thumb. They WERE more popular than Jesus. Our values as a culture are all out of whack.

Fortunately the Psalmist had a better set of values. We read in today's lesson, "I waited patiently for the Lord; he turned to me and heard my cry. He lifted me out of the slimy pit, out of the mud and mire; he set my feet on a rock and gave me a firm place to stand. He put a new song in my mouth, a hymn of praise to our God . . ."

What a beautiful picture of the life of faith. "He lifted me out of the slimy pit, out of the mud and mire; he set my feet on a rock and gave me a firm place to stand. He put a new song in my mouth, a hymn of praise to our God . . ." It reminds me of the old Gospel hymn, "Love lifted me." Surely the composer had the psalmist's words in mind. "Love lifted me. Love lifted me. When nothing else would help love lifted me . . ."

Have you ever been in a slimy pit?

A cartoon appeared sometime back in the New Yorker magazine. The cartoon shows Moses carrying the two tablets of the Law down from the mountain. He enters the camp of the Hebrew people, the people he has been faithfully leading. He discovers they are having a rousing good time: dice games, dancing girls, tobacco, alcoholic drink. The cartoon has the people greeting Moses, holding the Ten Commandments, with these words: "Well and good, [Moses]. [We] hope this isn't meant to be a criticism of our current life style." (2)

Well, maybe it was intended to be a little criticism . . . Have you ever been in a slimy pit? The slimy pit could refer to our morals. Morals are important.

A priest in the Church of England tells of attending a soccer match a few years back. He was there because his eight-year-old son was a member of one of the teams. A friend of his named Andy was supposed to referee the game. Unfortunately, by 2:30 PM Andy had not arrived. The boys could wait no longer, and this young priest was pressured into being the substitute referee. There were a number of difficulties with this: he had no whistle; there were no markings for the boundaries; he didn't know any of the boy's names; they didn't have uniforms; and, worst of all, he barely knew the rules of soccer and he was to be the referee.

As you might imagine, the game soon descended into utter chaos. Some shouted the ball was in, others that it was out. The young priest had no idea one way or the other. Then the fouls started. Again, some boys cried out, foul, others yelled that it wasn't a foul. Again, he had no idea one way or the other. So, he let them play on. Then people began to get hurt. Thankfully, before anyone was seriously injured, his friend Andy arrived. Andy blew his whistle, passed out the uniforms, marked the boundaries with cones, called the ball in and out, also called the fouls correctly, and the boys had the game and the time of their lives." (3)

Life needs a referee. Rules and boundaries have a purpose. They help us live our lives in a wholesome and affirming way. They keep people from getting hurt. They keep people from getting exploited. They keep us safe.

The Rev. Charles Cook of Fayetteville, North Carolina served with the US Army. He tells the story of the day he arrived in Vietnam. The soldier showing him around pointed to a minefield. It was not what he expected. What he saw looked like a beautiful soccer field. The field was as green and flat as the top of a billiard table . . . The only problem was that it contained hundreds of deadly mines.

One afternoon much to his horror, Cook saw a group of kids playing stickball right in the middle of that minefield. The MP's who were supposed to be watching the field went colorless, then started yelling, screaming, and waving their arms at the kids, who did not understand a word of English. It would have been funny, had it not been so dangerous. One sweating MP quickly found a map of the field that gave the location of the mines, and his squad beat a careful route to the children. Grabbing the children, who were writhing and screaming in terror, they carefully began to retrace their steps back to the end of the minefield.

At about the same time the children's parents arrived to see their kids flailing insanely and being hauled off the field by a squad of hefty American GI's. You can imagine the terror of these children and their mothers, who were gesticulating in helpless anguish. The mothers tried to run toward the children, but they were held back at the edge of the minefield by another squad of MP's. These mothers probably believed their children were being killed. Actually, exactly the opposite was happening. They were being protected. They could not realize that the MP's prohibition against playing soccer on that minefield was infinitely more merciful than a thoughtless permission would ever have been.

Cook writes, "That night, as I lay on my cot, I wondered what would have happened if, in the name of a shallow and indulgent love, the company commander had listened to the cries of those children. I tried to imagine him saying, 'Oh, I'm sorry. We really did not mean to inconvenience you. Go ahead and finish your game of ball.' Would it have been loving for the commander to relax the rules against playing in the minefield? As I lay awake on my cot, listening to explosions in the distance, I could not help wondering if the God of the Ten Commandments is less interested in spoiling his children's fun than in telling them that they are in a minefield." (4)

The slimy pit may refer to our morals. Morals are important. They keep us safe. They keep our families safe. There is someone in this room today who may be sliding down the slope right now of a slimy pit. That person could make a tragic mistake if he or she doesn't get their act together.

The slimy pit may refer to our morals. Or it may simply mean that somehow in life we have lost our way. We have lost our sense of purpose. We no longer feel that life has meaning or value.

The New York Times printed a news story from Rome several years ago about a woman named Concetta Brigante. Mrs. Brigante was spotted climbing out of a seventh-floor window of her apartment building. Soon she was balancing precariously on the ledge of the building far above the ground. The neighbors, naturally frantic, called the police. Firemen put up a ladder and forcibly rescued Mrs. Brigante. Nobody listened to her protests, and she was taken to a mental clinic as a would-be suicide.

At the clinic Mrs. Brigante finally got to tell her story. She was housecleaning and accidentally locked herself in her room. She was merely trying to get into the room next door via the ledge. (5)

She was hardly in a slimy pit. She was teetering on the ledge of a tall building. Nevertheless, she certainly was at risk of taking a tragic fall—not because she was a bad person, not because she was an uncaring person, but because, quite by accident or poor judgment, she had somehow gotten herself into a bad situation.

I run into people all the time who are really good people, but somehow they've missed the true meaning of life. And because of this, they lack joy, they lack purpose. They may even be filled with feelings of anger and bitterness. They don't know why. Yet it's affecting their sense of well-being. It's affecting their faith. Like the psalmist, they are in the slimy pit.

So what do you do when you find yourself in a slimy pit? The best thing we can do is to call out to God. "I waited patiently for the Lord; he turned to me and heard my cry . . ."

Have you ever cried out to God? My guess is that most of us have at some time in our lives, for one reason or another. Perhaps it was in a time of personal need. Like Mrs. Brigante you found yourself teetering on the edge of disaster. Perhaps this impending disaster was a medical emergency, a business failure, a moral lapse. Where can you turn at such times but to the Lord?

People amaze me. We think if we just work hard enough, if we just have a positive attitude, if we redouble our efforts and run really fast, we will be able to distance ourselves from all our problems. We're like a woman that Barbara Brown Taylor tells about.

Mrs. Taylor moved out to the country. This woman, a friend of hers, came out for a visit. But, on the way, she got seriously lost. These were the days before cell phones, so she was on her own with nothing but some confusing directions and a badly out-of-date map. Already an hour later than she wanted to be, she was speeding through the little town of Mount Airy when she saw blue lights in her rearview mirror. Busted, she pulled over on the shoulder of the road and had her license ready when the officer arrived at her window.

"I am so sorry," she said, handing it to him along with her registration. "I know I was speeding, but I've been lost for the last forty minutes and I cannot find Tower Terrace anywhere on this map."

"Well, I'm sorry about that too, ma'am," the officer said, writing up her citation, "but what made you think that hurrying would help you find your way?" (6)

Good question. We think if we work hard enough, if we redouble our efforts and just run fast enough, or if we have a positive attitude about everything, we can lift ourselves out of the slimy pit. Instead, we often dig a hole, deeper and more difficult to escape.

But it doesn't have to be that way. God is a God who rescues people from slimy pits. The Psalmist writes, "I waited patiently for the Lord; he turned to me and heard my cry. He lifted me out of the slimy pit, out of the mud and mire; he set my feet on a rock and gave me a firm place to stand. He put a new song in my mouth, a hymn of praise to our God . . ."

What great good news that is. God rescues people from slimy pits. We are not helpless. We matter to God. God's chief obsession is our best good. Our baptism is a reminder to us of that.

Dr. Fred Craddock tells of serving as a chaplain for a week at a rural hospital in Georgia. It was a small hospital. During that week a baby was born. Craddock noticed a crowd of people looking through the glass to the room where the tiny infant lay. He asked one of them about the child's gender and its name. He was told it was a girl, Elizabeth.

Then he found the young father leaning against a wall. Craddock congratulated him on a beautiful baby. They could see Elizabeth through the glass, squirming, and red faced. She was so red-faced Craddock was concerned that the young father might think that something was the matter. He explained to the young man that Elizabeth wasn't sick. "It's good for babies to scream and do all that," he said. "It clears out their lungs and gets their voices going."

The young father said, "Oh, I know she's not sick." Then he added, "But she's mad as hell." When he realized who he was talking to, the young man said, "Pardon me, Reverend."

Craddock said, "That's all right. Why's she mad?"

The father said, "Well, wouldn't you be mad? One minute you're with God in heaven and the next minute you're in Georgia!"

Craddock said, "You believe she was with God before she came here?"

The young father said, "Oh, yeah."

Craddock said, "You think she'll remember?"

This young father said, "Well, that's up to her mother and me. It's up to the church. We've got to see that she remembers, 'cause if she forgets, she's a goner." (7)

When we baptize a child, we are saying that this child matters to God and it is our responsibility to remind this child that he or she matters to God and that God will always be there to listen and to lift.

On our own you and I have a tendency to foul up our lives, sometimes quite miserably. Sometimes we may end up in a slimy pit. But there's good news. There is One who loves us, and listens to us, and if need be, lifts us out of the slimy pit and sets our feet on solid ground again.

1. Brent J. Eelman, http://www.apcusa.org/s051106eelman_Did_We_Forget.html.

2. From a sermon by the Rev. Carolyn Estrada, Episcopal Church of the Messiah, Santa Ana.

3. http://www.utepiscopal.org/Sermons/sermon17B.htm.

4. Rev. Richard J. Fairchild, http://www.spirit-net.ca/sermons/b-le03su.php.

5. Bruce Larson, Ask Me To Dance (Waco, TX: Word Books, 1972), pp. 9-10.

6. Leaving Church (New York, NY: HarperOne, 2006), pp. 133-134.

7. Fred B. Craddock, Craddock Stories (St. Louis, MO: Chalice Press, 2001).

The Great Physician
Matthew 4: 12-23

It was rumored that the owner of a certain hardware store had discovered a cure for arthritis. As you might imagine, this stirred a great deal of interest in the small town where the hardware store was located.

One day, the locals saw a little old lady, bent over on her cane, enter the store for a visit. A little later this same lady came out walking almost perfectly straight with her head held high. The crowd cheered. "It's a miracle!" they declared. Then they wondered. What did the owner of the hardware store do that allowed this poor lady to overcome her affliction?

The little old lady explained the so-called miracle. "He sold me," she said, "a longer cane." (1)

I will admit, it's not a great joke. But it does frame our topic for the day. Here's a question I want you to consider—does Jesus heal people today? There is no doubt that in many instances in the New Testament, Jesus performed works of healing. He healed bodies as well as minds. We read these important words at the end of today's lesson from Matthew's Gospel: "Jesus went throughout Galilee, teaching in their synagogues, preaching the good news of the kingdom, and healing every disease and sickness among the people." So, healing bodies played a big role in Jesus' ministry. The question is, does Jesus still heal people today?

I must tell you that there are many conscientious Christians who believe Jesus healed people during New Testament times, but does not heal people today.

Don't get me wrong. These people are not agnostics or atheists. They are very orthodox in all of their beliefs. Yet they cannot bring themselves to believe that Jesus still heals today. There are many well thought out reasons for this.

For one thing, many of these people have become disenchanted by some so-called Christian healers who have taken advantage of people at their moment of greatest need. They have seen these unscrupulous charlatans exploit the yearnings of people who are hurting. And it's turned them off. You and I can appreciate their feelings. There is nothing worse than those who take advantage of weaker people in the name of Christ.

Philip Yancey tells the story of a young theological student who years ago went to a service conducted by a well-known faith healer. In this meeting a doctor was carried in on a stretcher. This doctor had been diagnosed with incurable cancer.

There in the meeting this doctor got up and walked around and everyone cheered wildly. He was told he had six months to live, but tonight he believed that God had healed him. The young man told Yancey, "I had never known such certainty of faith before. My search was over; I had seen proof of a living God in those people on the stage." So impressed was he with this proof that God healed this man that he tried to follow up and talk with this doctor. A week later he listened excitedly as the phone rang in the doctor's home. When the phone was answered, the young man explained the reason for the call. There was a long silence.

"Who are you," a woman's voice finally came back over the phone line. Another long silence. Then she spoke in a flat voice, pronouncing each word slowly. "My . . . husband . . . is . . . dead." Just that one sentence, nothing more, and she hung up. That's when the young theology student gave up on God. (2)

What a sad, sad story. But that is one reason some people don't believe that Jesus heals today, the actions of a few who have abused their calling as servants of God.

But there's another more compelling reason for them to question whether Jesus heals today. Many of them have seen people they love suffer terribly from a disease. They have prayed for these loved ones and they have seen no change in their condition. So these believers have grown calloused, disenchanted. And who can blame them? The silence of God can sometimes be quite dispiriting.

Some of these followers of Christ who question whether Christ heals today have come to the conclusion that God has placed us in a lawful universe that precludes specific healing acts. They believe that, in place of miraculous acts of healing, God has given us the wonders of medical science. God works today through great doctors, and through wondrous technology, and through amazing drugs rather than through any supernatural miracles. And who can doubt the wonders of modern medical technology? So these believers make a compelling case for their lack of faith in healing miracles.

And finally and most convincingly, many of these conscientious Christians have concluded that it would be unfair if God healed some people today, but not others. Why would God heal one person's arthritis, but not another's cancer—particularly if both were righteous persons? Above all things, says scripture, God is just.

Thus these conscientious followers of our Lord believe with all their heart that Jesus did heal people two thousand years ago, but not today. They believe that Jesus healed people in the New Testament only for the purpose of bringing people to faith. Healing was not his primary purpose, teaching and preaching were. He healed only to help people understand who he was and why he was sent. And certainly many did believe in him because they saw his power to heal.

Have you ever thought about what it would have been like to live in Jesus' time when medicine was so primitive? Obviously there were no antibiotics nor were there any FDA approved drug therapies.

Pliny the Elder, a Roman historian, published an encyclopedia around 70 A.D., just after the time of Jesus. Pliny called his work, Natural History. In his Natural History Pliny revealed the generally low condition of medical science in the world during Jesus' time. He told how physicians prescribed curious concoctions for their patients. These concoctions were made from ashes of such things as a burnt wolf's skull, stags' horns, heads of mice, the eyes of crabs, owl's brains, the livers of frogs and other like elements. For dysentery these doctors administered powdered horses' teeth. A cold in the head was cured by kissing a mule's nose. (3) Remember that, any of you who have the sniffles. Don't reach for the Allerest®. Just look for a friendly mule.

Now imagine, if you will, that into this primitive world where people had little hope of being cured by any other means came a man who could but speak a word and the blind could see and the lame walk. No wonder people believed that he was from God. Jesus healed people. We all believe that. The question is—does he still heal people today?

I want to say to you that, yes, there is evidence that Christ still heals people today.

The world famous Mayo Clinic was founded by Dr. Will Mayo and his brother, Charles. Dr. Will Mayo once spoke these encouraging words: "I have seen patients that were dead by all standards. We knew they could not live. But I have seen a minister come to the bedside and do something for [a patient] that I could not do, although I have done everything in my professional power. But something touched some immortal spark in [that patient] and in defiance of medical sense, that patient lived."

Thus spoke Dr. Will Mayo. There is evidence that Christ still heals people today.

C.S. Lewis once told of a woman he knew whose thighbone was eaten through with cancer. It took three people to move her into a bed. The doctors predicted she had only a few months of life. The nurses, who knew better, predicted a few weeks. A minister came to her bedside, laid hands on her and prayed. A year later the patient was walking and the man who took the last X-ray photos of her thigh was saying: "It's miraculous."

Some of you could undoubtedly share with me stories of people you know whom doctors had given up on, but somehow people prayed, and the doctors were proved wrong. It does happen. Not always—not even most of the time—but it does happen.

Sociologist and respected evangelist Tony Campolo tells of being at a Midwest church-related liberal arts college, and being in the chapel on a particular evening.

As he was delivering his lecture, a woman walked down the aisle, accompanied by a young boy whose legs were in braces. She asked for prayer for her son, that he might be healed.

So Campolo delayed his lecture and some people gathered with him to pray for this boy with bad legs. Nothing happened. They all left.

Several years later Campolo was back in that same area, and a woman came up to him and spoke to him.

"Do you remember me?" she asked.

"No," said Campolo. "Have we met before?"

"Yes," she answered. "I came to the college for your lecture, and I interrupted and asked if you would pray for my son, who was in leg braces."

"Oh yes," Campolo said. "I remember. How is he?"

"He is healed," the woman answered. "This is my son, standing right next to me."

"That's wonderful," said Campolo. "How did that happen?"

"We prayed," she said. "That night when we got home and he went to bed, he started crying. His legs hurt against the braces. Over a period of time his legs grew straighter, and the doctor said he didn't understand it but my son was healed."

Of course Campolo was thrilled to see the power of God at work in such a way. He went to a group back home and told them this story, and most were thrilled to hear it. But one of the folks said, "I don't think it could happen that way; it doesn't fit my thinking." (4)

Don't be surprised that someone responded like that. There may be someone in this congregation today who would respond in much the same way. You may be asking in your heart, "If Christ healed that boy's legs, why doesn't he heal my nephew? Why doesn't he heal my mother of her cancer? Why did he allow my Dad to have that heart attack?"

It is a complicated question with no satisfactory answer. Again, please understand that it is the exception and not the rule. But there have been too many people who have reported that the doctors told them they did not have a chance, and yet they made what can only be called a miraculous recovery. We simply cannot dismiss their testimonies.

We know that some miracles could be explained if we knew all the facts. We're not naive. We know that some healings may grow out of the strong connection between the mind and the body. Some people make themselves sick because of what Zig Ziglar calls "stinking thinking." Why shouldn't other people use healthy thoughts to think themselves to wellness.

Back in 1974 Robert Ader, a psychologist at the University of Rochester, did a brilliant study discovering for the first time the role of the mind in relation to the immune system. He demonstrated what most of us have always felt, that the condition of the mind and the emotions can have a profound effect on the condition of the body. A new science came into our vocabulary: Psychoneuroimmunology—the mind's effect on the immune system. And we know there is truth to this science.

Some people would contend that this mind-body connection is the explanation of all such healing. They point to how often Jesus said, "Your faith has made you well." And certainly, that was part of it. When people believe in Jesus, it might very well unlock streams of healing within the body.

But that brings us to the real question: What about those people who believe in Christ whose bodies are not healed? The truth of the matter is that this is more often the case than not. More than simple belief must be at work in cases where healing does occur.

Of course, every good doctor will tell you that there are simply things with regard to healing that they do not understand. They have seen people whom they would never expect to leave the hospital do so, and some of these people have no religion at all. Some of them are miserable human beings—but still, they got well.

Others were people of glowing optimism with many friends praying for them and caring for them, yet they remained in pain and eventually they died. There is no simple explanation no matter what anyone says.

But this needs to be said this day: Many good people have experienced healing that was genuine and they have no explanation except the power of prayer.

There is much about healing and faith we do not understand, but here is what I believe. Whenever you have a need whatever it might be—for healing, for a loved one who is going through a difficult time, for guidance in a time of deep uncertainty. Whatever your need is—take it to God in prayer. If it is truly life shattering, ask others to pray for you as well. And then trust God. God does answer prayer. Sometimes it's not exactly how we hoped, sometimes it's not on our timetable, but God does answer prayer. The important thing is to trust God's love for you. If you trust God, everything ultimately will work according to God's plan, and God's plan is always for his children's good.

"Jesus went throughout Galilee, teaching in their synagogues, preaching the good news of the kingdom, and healing every disease and sickness among the people." I believe he still heals people today. Trust him. And believe that in all things, even when we may not discern how, God works for our best good.

1. THE JOKESMITH
2. Hugh Cox, http://www.stpaulstervuren.be/nurture/sermons/new/16may04.htm.
3. J. W. Shepard, The Christ of the Gospels (Grand Rapids: Eerdmans, 1939), p. 240.
4. http://www.foresthillspres.org/MyWayOfThinking.htm.

Hey, Foolish Thing!
I Corinthians 1:26-31

Have you ever noticed that some bright people can say really dumb things? My favorite example is singer Mariah Carey. It was, allegedly, from her lips that we heard these sensitive words: "Whenever I watch TV and see those poor starving kids all over the world, I can't help but cry. I mean I'd love to be skinny like that, but not with all those flies and death and stuff." Some bright people can say dumb things.

When the American baseball player Bill Gullickson signed a phenomenal contract to play baseball in Japan, he was asked what daily life was like in Japan. He replied that the language was the most difficult and different feature. "It's crazy," he said. "The only American words I saw were Sony and Mitsubishi." (1)

Well, I guess those are American words.

There is no limit to the foolish things people do and say—particularly our legislators.

A few years back a man named Robert W. Pelton did some research on laws that have been passed with regard to behavior in churches. Some of them are quite interesting.

For example, young girls are never allowed to walk a tightrope in Wheeler, Mississippi, unless it's in a church. I'm sure there's a good reason why this law was put on the books. I simply can't imagine what it could be.

In Blackwater, Kentucky, tickling a woman under her chin with a feather duster while she's in church service carries a penalty of $10.00 and one day in jail.

In Honey Creek, Iowa, no one is permitted to carry a slingshot to church except police. (Obviously the NRA has not heard about Honey Creek or they would be carrying assault rifles.)

No citizen in Leecreek, Arkansas, is allowed to attend church in any red-colored garment.

Swinging a yo-yo in church or anywhere in public on the Sabbath is prohibited in Studley, Virginia.

And, finally, turtle races are not permitted within 100 yards of a local church at any time in Slaughter, Louisiana. (2)

There is a lot of foolishness in the world—and that foolishness includes you and me. That's right. St. Paul calls us foolish. He writes in I Corinthians 1: 26-29, "Brothers, think of what you were when you were called. Not many of you were wise by human standards; not many were influential; not many were of noble birth. But God chose the foolish things of the world to shame the wise; God chose the weak things of the world to shame the strong. He chose the lowly things of this world and the despised things—and the things that are not—to nullify the things that are, so that no one may boast before him."

He's talking about us. We are the foolish things he's referring to. He's talking about people who make up the church. Let me read it again, "Brothers think of what you were when you were called. Not many of you were wise by human standards; not many were influential; not many were of noble birth. But God chose the foolish things of the world . . ."

Paul is saying, "Look, God hasn't chosen celebrities or rocket scientists to proclaim His word. He's chosen people like us—farmers, fishermen, tax-collectors, housewives . . ." Today we might say, "God's chosen electricians and plumbers and sales people and teachers . . ." That's who God depends on. God uses everyday people to do His work.

We worship celebrities in our culture. Actor David Niven once told a wonderful story about actress Loretta Young. Some of you will remember Loretta from her television show, at least those of you who remember black-and-white television.

When she was young, Loretta Young was quite pretty. It was her looks, says Niven, not her talent that got her cast in film after film.

Cecil B. DeMille was once directing Loretta Young in a movie titled, The Crusades. She was doing a scene urging Richard the Lion-Hearted to fight on behalf of the Christian nations in the crusades. Loretta read the line: "Richard, you gotta save Christianity!" She wasn't very convincing. So DeMille took Loretta aside and asked her to put some AWE into her line. They reshot the scene, and Loretta Young said: "Aw, Richard, you gotta save Christianity!" (3)

We are a culture that worships celebrities. But it is not celebrities that God is depending on to change the world . . . or rocket scientists or the rich and powerful. God depends on Sunday school teachers, greeters, people singing in the choir, people filling out pledge cards . . . good people . . . not superstars, but solid responsible church people. That is who God is depending on. God uses common, everyday people to do his work. That is what Paul is saying when he writes, "Brothers, think of what you were when you were called. Not many of you were wise by human standards; not many were influential; not many were of noble birth. But God chose the foolish things of the world . . ."

Now to tell you the truth, I wouldn't have done it that way if I had been God. I wouldn't have started at the bottom of society and worked my way up. I wouldn't have had my Son be born to Mary and Joseph in the stable of Bethlehem. I would have had him born in Caesar's household. Then one day he could stroll out on his balcony and wave his hand and said, "From now on everyone will be Christians." But that was not how God did it. God started at the very bottom of society with very ordinary people and that is still how God is working today. Through ordinary folk like you and me. We are God's plan for saving the world. God is counting on us. "Who? Us?" Yes, us. God is counting on us to turn the world upside down. You can see why Paul says it sounds like foolishness to the world.

God chose the church to do His work in the world. This is the primary reason Christ came into the world.

If you ask most Christians why Christ came into the world, they will say he came to die for our sins. And that's true, of course, but there is another reason Christ came into the world: it was to train an ordinary group of people to take his message to the world. Who was that group of people? Why us, the church. The key reason Christ came into the world was to found the church. We are to be his body doing his saving work in a world that is lost.

Christ started with only 12 men and an unknown number of women. By the time he died, the company was still very small. Then, after Pentecost, that number exploded. By the time Paul was preaching to the Corinthians, there were tiny churches planted in towns all along the Mediterranean. Still, it seemed like a mighty stretch when St. Paul said that God was going to use this motley group of generally powerless people to turn the world upside down. Of course, it was not long, relatively, before that tiny group of believers took over the whole Roman Empire, but at the time Paul was preaching it probably did sound like so much foolishness that God was going to do anything significant with the church.

Do you know that there are still people today who think it is foolishness that God is going to do anything significant with the church? And the sad thing is that some of these people are in the church. Some people still don't understand that the church is at the center of God's plan.

Now I know that silly things happen in the church. I've seen them. Sometimes tragic things happen in churches. Some of the most unchristian people in the world are found on church rolls—bigots, snobs, uncaring people—people who are an embarrassment to God. I'm very aware of that.

But I also know this and you know it too, the best people in this [city] are in the church. I run into them all the time. They are people who care about their families, care about their neighbors, care about their communities—and the reason they care is that once upon a time they stood at the altar of a church like this one and gave their heart to Jesus. There is really only one way to make this community a better community, one way to make this city a better city, one way to make this a better world and that is to bring everyone we meet to Jesus. There is nothing else that will work. That is how God has chosen to turn this world upside down. The work of the church is serious work, important work, life changing work. It's work that God is calling you and me to do.

Now this means something quite obvious: If the church is the means that God has chosen to turn this world upside down, each of us has a part to play. If this is God's plan—not to work through celebrities and rocket scientists but through ordinary folks like you and me—it means that there is something for each of us to do.

Arthur Gordon once told about a man named Charlie who joined a prayer group to which Gordon belonged. Charlie wasn't a joiner. So the next time Gordon saw Charlie he asked him why he had joined this prayer group.

"Well," said Charlie, "I had problems and I was praying about them, but I didn't seem to be getting anywhere. Then one day I read an article about bees. When it gets too hot in a hive, a group of worker bees all face in one direction, anchor themselves to the floor, and fan their wings rapidly. One bee alone wouldn't make much of a difference, but a lot of bees can produce an air current strong enough to draw fresh, cool air into the hive and blow the stale air out.

"So, I said to myself, 'If a group of bees working together can activate a healing current that changes everything for the better, maybe a group of people can do the same thing.'" (4)

That's a pretty good description of what the church is all about. We're like those bees. On our own we can't get much done, but flapping our wings in unison we can blow out the stale air of sin and oppression. But each of us must do our part.

Once there was a young Methodist pastor serving a two-point circuit in the hills of East Tennessee. [In other words he preached each Sunday morning to two congregations.] The larger church which had their service at 10:00 a.m. had an average attendance of 70. The smaller church which had the 11:00 hour for their service had an average attendance of 4. The young pastor resented preaching to 4 people. Particularly at 11:00. He had already preached his sermon once. He had it down pat, and now he was preaching it to 4 people, basically 2 elderly couples. It was depressing.

He felt it would make much more sense if the four people at that service would hop in his car and go with him down to the other church. Four people. There was another elderly couple that came sporadically. So sometimes there were 6. There was one old gentleman who came on Christmas and Easter. So on those Sundays they had 7, but he rarely came any other time.

One Sunday, however, this old gentleman named Claude showed up on a regular Sunday. And at the conclusion of the service the young pastor could see that something in the service had touched Claude quite dramatically. He went back to him and asked, "Claude, is there a problem?"

Claude squinted his eyes and looked up at his young pastor. "Preacher," he said, "things aren't going to be like this around here anymore."

"I didn't know if he meant he was going to burn down the church or what," the young pastor said later. "I didn't know any other way that church could be changed."

But the next Sunday morning when the pastor drove up to that little church, there were cars everywhere. He went inside and there were children and teenagers and older people. And on the little board where they posted the attendance for Sunday School, it said 58. Fifty-eight! Now, that's not a big crowd at most churches, thought the young pastor, but when you've been averaging 4, it's all the people in the world.

He looked for Claude. "Where did all these people come from?" He asked.

"Well, preacher," Claude said, "I know these hollows up in here better than you do. I went to old folks and shut-ins I knew who weren't going to church and I said, 'If I come and get you Sunday in my station wagon would you come to our church Sunday morning?' and every once in a while someone would say, 'Why Claude you don't have to come for me. My daughter could bring me down there.' And I would go to a family that had young children and say, 'If my son or I came to pick up your children Sunday morning would you let them come to our church?' And every once in a while someone would say, 'Why you don't have to come after my children. I could bring them.' And this is what happened."

Fifty-eight people! Well, the young pastor knew it wouldn't last. And it didn't. The next Sunday they were down to 56. The following Sunday, though, they had 60. And for a decade after that, that small church which had once averaged 4 on Sunday mornings averaged about 50 people—most of whom would never have been in church except that a 75-year-old man named Claude was determined that his church wasn't going to be like that anymore. And that's all it takes. (5)

Why? Because God chose to do something foolish. God chose ordinary people like you and me, and God set out to change the world one person at a time. Was God foolish—to count on such as us? Only you and I and God know the answer.

1. Roger E. Axtell, Do's and Taboos of Humor Around the World (New York: John Wiley & Sons, Inc., 1999), p. 183.
2. The Door. Christian Reader, Vol. 33, no. 5. Cited in SermonCentral Weekly Newsletter.
3. Gene Shalit, Great Hollywood Wit (New York: St. Martin's Press, 2002), p. 78.
4. Daily Guideposts, http://www.ourprayer.org/dailyguideposts.
5. The young pastor was King Duncan, writer, Dynamic Preaching.

K. I. S. S.
I Corinthians 2:1-5

A woman tells about her five-year-old son playing in his first neighborhood softball game. The little guy named Frankie stepped up to the plate while his Dad shouted instructions from the sidelines. Mom and Dad both cheered excitedly when Frankie clouted the ball well out into right field. Charged with excitement, the youngster scampered around first base and rounded second. Then, confused by so much shouting, he hesitated on third base and seemed not to know what to do next.

"Run HOME, Frankie!" his dad screamed, wanting desperately to see him score. "Run HOME!"

With that, Frankie turned, scooted across left field, squeezed through the fence and disappeared. They found him later sitting in the kitchen of the family home. (1)

Well, he did just as his Dad instructed him to do. His father yelled, "Run home," and that's exactly what he did. His father needed to be a little clearer in what he was directing him to do.

Most of you are familiar with the little acronym, K.I.S.S. "Keep it simple, stupid." I suspect that there are two inscriptions that ought to be on every pulpit. The first is from John 12:20: "Sir, [or Madam], we would see Jesus." The second is K.I.S.S., "Keep it simple, stupid."

Writer and Presbyterian pastor Bruce Larson gives us an interesting perspective on the development of two denominational groups in the U.S.

He says that in the early years of our country's history, there were two different approaches to evangelism by two of our great denominations. The Methodist Church felt the West was expanding so fast that there wasn't time to thoroughly equip and train preachers and lay evangelists. They sent out anyone who had the call, and the West was evangelized by Methodist circuit riders. The Presbyterians on the other hand felt the gospel was so important it could be entrusted only to seminary graduates with a background in Greek and Hebrew. And so they took their time in sending out pastors who were better educated. That is why, says Larson, there are more Methodists in America than Presbyterians. (2)

Here's something that is even more revealing. A study sometime back showed that of the 100 largest churches in America, the overwhelming percentage of them are served by pastors who are NOT seminary graduates. Think about the implications of that for a moment. Is it possible that going to seminary might actually make a pastor less effective? I don't think so. However, this might say something to us about what happens in the pulpit. It might be a reminder to pastors to keep our preaching accessible to all.

If you think that the K.I.S.S. approach to preaching is a little too unsophisticated for a learned church like ours, let me hasten to say to you that the idea is not my own. Listen as the Apostle Paul describes his own efforts at communicating the Gospel. He says to the Corinthians, "When I came to you, brothers, I did not come with eloquence or superior wisdom as I proclaimed to you the testimony about God. For I resolved to know nothing while I was with you except Jesus Christ and him crucified. I came to you in weakness and fear, and with much trembling. My message and my preaching were not with wise and persuasive words, but with a demonstration of the Spirit's power, so that your faith might not rest on men's wisdom, but on God's power."

Now, St. Paul is not saying he "dumbed down" the Gospel. Anyone who has spent much time deciphering the Apostle Paul's theology knows that his theology can be quite challenging at times. But he is saying that he tried to communicate the Gospel to the churches in which he ministered as simply and as directly as he could. He was not trying to impress people with his knowledge but with God's love and God's power. Indeed, I believe that, from these words, he too would encourage those two inscriptions on every pulpit: "We would see Jesus" and K.I.S.S., "keep it simple, stupid."

"For I resolved to know nothing while I was with you except Jesus Christ and him crucified. I came to you in weakness and fear, and with much trembling. My message and my preaching were not with wise and persuasive words, but with a demonstration of the Spirit's power . . ."

If you have experienced the power of God in your life, you don't have to hide behind pretty language. Author King Duncan tells of hearing a well-known pastor in his part of the country preach on one of Jesus' healing miracles. "This pastor was a somewhat liberal pastor who had many reservations about the plain teachings of scripture," says Duncan. "I'm not sure he believed that Jesus ever really healed anyone or not. Now I'm a person of at least average intelligence," he continues, "but when this pastor finished his sermon I had absolutely no idea what he said. Not really. He had used fine sounding words to hide his reservations about his own beliefs."

St. Paul had no reason to hide behind pretty language. He had experienced Christ's power in his own life. All he had to do was to testify to that experience.

It is like a humble couple who had only recently dedicated themselves to Christ. They were good people with one weakness. They were illiterate. They could not read. However, they did not allow this limitation to keep them from being involved in a Christian community.

They met on a regular basis with a group of other believers all of whom dressed alike while engaged in a certain project. The men all wore red shirts when working on this project, so the woman made a red shirt for her husband. He came home after the meeting, however, with a look of disappointment on his face because the other men had a message printed on their shirts but he did not. Of course, he had no idea what the message said since he could not read, but it bothered him that his shirt bore no message.

His wife, undaunted by her inability to read, decided to sew a message on his shirt as well. She chose three words which she copied from a sign in a store window across the street. Neither she nor her husband knew what the words meant but he wore his new lettered shirt to the next meeting. Afterwards he came home bubbling with joy. He said all of the men really liked the inscription because it so aptly described the wonderful change they had seen in his life. It turned out that his wife had sewn these words that she had seen on a store on her husband's shirt, "UNDER NEW MANAGEMENT." (3)

I guess that said it all. Since they had met Christ, their lives were under new management.

You don't have to be a rocket scientist to testify to the power of God in your life. If Christ has touched you, healed you, given you a reason to go on, if you are under new management, tell the story to others. Tell it plainly. Tell it simply so no one can misunderstand.

In May 2001, a young man in New York City went to the top of a building and threatened to jump off. He had a problem with his girlfriend and thought life wasn't worth living. However, something was different about this young man. He was deaf.

Police tried using a bullhorn to send a loud message to him but to no avail because he couldn't hear it. Fortunately, one policeman tried a different tactic. He had been a volunteer teacher of sign language in a deaf school. He went to the top of the building and by using sign language, talked the boy out of jumping. How was he able to reach him when the other policemen failed? He knew how to speak his language.

This is what the apostle Paul meant says author Kent Crockett when he said, "To the weak I became weak, that I might win the weak. I have become all things to all men, that I may by all means save some." (1 Cor. 9:22). "He wasn't talking about compromising his beliefs," says Crockett, "but he had learned to communicate the saving power of Jesus to others by speaking on their wavelength." (4)

"For I resolved to know nothing while I was with you except Jesus Christ and him crucified. I came to you in weakness and fear, and with much trembling. My message and my preaching were not with wise and persuasive words, but with a demonstration of the Spirit's power . . ."

We all know that communication is difficult. Not only communication from the pulpit, but communication in marriage, communication in the workplace, communication between cultures.

Liz Curtis Higgs tells a humorous story about a woman named Eilene from Maine. Eilene longed for a little relief from the embarrassment she felt while visiting a school and orphanage in Kenya. Dozens of children who spoke only Swahili pressed around her, trying to see if the white of her skin would rub off. What took her back was that they were all yelling, "Jumbo!" and "Super!"

Eilene grumbled to her interpreter, "I know I need to lose weight, but I didn't think I was [so] fat and large [that they would yell 'jumbo' and 'super']."

The interpreter burst out laughing, then explained, "In Swahili, jumbo means 'hello' and super means 'hello very much. '" (5)

Communication is a difficult art even under the best of circumstances. We're told that during World War II, a misunderstanding over just one word—the verb "to table"—created great debate and ill will. According to the memoirs of Sir Winston Churchill, he and his staff were discussing with their American allies whether they should "table" a certain issue. However, when Americans "table" an issue, it means they set it aside for consideration at a later time; when the British "table" an issue it means to place it on the table for immediate discussion. "A long and acrimonious argument ensued," Churchill wrote, until finally the two sides discovered their respective cultures had contrasting definitions for the same term. (6)

Communication is difficult. During court one day, the judge quietly passed the clerk a note reading: "Blind on right side, may be falling. Please call someone."

Understandably alarmed, the clerk called for help. While waiting for the help to come he reassuringly whispered to the judge that paramedics were on their way and would arrive shortly.

Puzzled, the judge pointed to a sagging Venetian blind on the right side of the court room and explained, "I was thinking maybe someone from maintenance!"

Communication is difficult. However, effective communication is critical. How many marriages fail because couples lose the ability to communicate? How many families are in distress because parents and offspring fail to communicate? How many hurting people could be helped if someone would simply take the time to communicate with them?

Dr. Steve Stephens tells about a man named Paul who owned a little deli next door to his office. Stephens says Paul served the best hot pastrami sandwich he'd ever had. Stephens would go in and they'd chat about their kids. They were friendly, but they never talked about deep matters. They would run into each other on occasion. They would smile; they would make small talk and say they ought to get together sometime and get to know each other better.

The last time Stephens saw Paul, Paul told him life was tough. His deli was losing money and things weren't going well at home. He said, "Dr. Steve, I ought to make an appointment and talk to you about some things that are really bothering me." Stephens told him that he could call anytime.

Paul never called. Two days later Stephens dropped into his deli, but Paul wasn't there. The deli was unusually quiet and the help looked downcast. "Where's

Paul?" Stephens asked cheerfully.

"Oh, you haven't heard?" said the young lady behind the counter. "Paul shot himself last night. He died instantly."

Stephens couldn't believe it. Why would he kill himself? Why didn't he talk to someone? And then Stephens thought the really hard question, "Why hadn't I asked more questions when he mentioned his hardships?" (7)

Communication is difficult, but communication is also critical in living together in families and as communities. Here's the final thing to be said: Communication of the Gospel is our primary responsibility as Christians. What was Christ's final instruction to his disciples? "Go and make disciples of all nations, baptizing them in the name of the Father and of the Son and of the Holy Spirit, and teaching them to obey everything I have commanded you."

This is our primary task as believers in Jesus the Christ. We are to communicate the good news. There are many ways of communicating. We can preach and we can teach. But the best ways to communicate require very few words. Listening is probably the most powerful form of communication—listening to your spouse, listening to your kids, listening to the concerns of your neighbor, the way Steve Stephens wishes he had listened to his neighbor Paul. We communicate by listening, and we communicate by the way we live. As the old ditty goes, "I'd rather see a sermon than hear one any day."

The important thing to realize is that you don't have to be a scholar to tell the good news of Jesus Christ. You don't have to be a person of great eloquence, education or even intelligence. If you have experienced Christ's power in your life, tell it. If you have Christ's love in your heart, live it. K.I.S.S.—Keep it simple, saint!

1. Lillian Gonsalves, Reader's Digest, May, 1984.
2. Bruce Larson, The Communicator's Commentary (Luke) (Word, Inc. 1983), p. 162.
3. Illusaurus.
4. www.kentcrockett.blogspot.com.
5. Help! I'm Laughing and I Can't Get Up (Nashville: Thomas Nelson, 1998), p. 49.
6. Roger E. Axtell, Do's and Taboos of Humor Around the World (New York: John Wiley & Sons, Inc., 1999), p. 8.
7. The Wounded Warrior (Sisters, OR: Multnomah Publishers, Inc., 2006), pp. 117-118.

Act Quickly—Catch It Early
Matthew 5:21-37

Some of you may be familiar with the Darwin Awards. People are nominated for the Darwin Awards when they do something really stupid that costs them their lives. The reason that they are called the Darwin Awards is that by offing themselves in such an absurd way, it is suggested that these misguided folks have inadvertently improved the gene pool for rest of humanity. It's a cynical view of life, but it has led to a collection of stories that are both true and bizarre.

For example, there is the story of a Darwin Award winner named Christopher, a nineteen-year-old man in Missaukee County, Michigan. Christopher spent an evening sometime back partaking of a large quantity of alcoholic beverages when he noticed a shortage in his liquor supply. He concluded that his neighbor had stolen a bottle of his booze! With a knife he went to his neighbor's home, to no avail, whereupon he retired to his own apartment to brood about revenge. And he continued to drink.

Finally, when he was thoroughly sloshed, he figured out the perfect way to get back at his liquor-thieving neighbor. He would stab himself and blame the neighbor!

A witness testified that he saw Christopher enter the bathroom while he was calling 9-1-1. Christopher calmly informed the 9-1-1 dispatcher that his neighbor had stabbed him. Witnesses said Christopher looked fine when he emerged from the bathroom, but a moment later spurts of blood emanated from his chest. Suddenly he began screaming, begging for help. The dispatcher heard a woman shout, "Why did you do this?" He collapsed at the door of his apartment.

Deputies arrived quickly, but Christopher had already bled to death from self-inflicted stab wounds to his chest. An autopsy determined that he had stabbed himself twice. The first wound apparently didn't look dangerous enough, so he tried again. The second time, the knife plunged into his left ventricle. This wound did the trick. He was dead in two minutes.

The ironic thing is that his plan to frame his neighbor for his stabbing was a complete failure. A witness confirmed that the neighbor was not even in the apartment. All Christopher got for his attempt at revenge was an accidental death sentence. (1)

Could anybody actually be that dumb? Well, yes. Notice that he had been drinking a significant amount of liquor. Drinking has that kind of effect on many otherwise intelligent people—it makes them do some really stupid things.

A better question is whether anyone could get that angry over a missing bottle of liquor that they would hurt themselves in order to gain revenge? The answer seems again to be in the affirmative. People make mistakes like that every day. Note how many people, after a divorce, carry around feelings of intense anger and desire for revenge for years. And, generally, the only person they hurt is themselves.

Jesus, as usual, hit the nail squarely on the head. "You have heard that it was said to the people long ago, 'Do not murder, and anyone who murders will be subject to judgment.' But I tell you that anyone who is angry with his brother will be subject to judgment . . . anyone who says, 'You fool!' will be in danger of the fire of hell.

"Therefore, if you are offering your gift at the altar and there remember that your brother has something against you, leave your gift there in front of the altar. First go and be reconciled to your brother; then come and offer your gift.

"Settle matters quickly with your adversary who is taking you to court. Do it while you are still with him on the way, or he may hand you over to the judge, and the judge may hand you over to the officer, and you may be thrown into prison. I tell you the truth, you will not get out until you have paid the last penny."

Obviously this text refers to some legal niceties from Jesus' time with which we are not familiar. His point however is clear. Don't let your anger fester and grow. Act quickly. Get rid of it. It will do you no good.

Author Kent Crockett tells about Sam and Jacqueline Pritchard, a British couple, who started receiving mysterious phone calls to their home in the middle of the night. The person on the other end never said anything. After a long pause, he would hang up.

The Pritchards changed their phone number to stop the harassing night calls. The stalker changed his tactic. He started sending them obscene and threatening anonymous letters in the mail. Then the problems escalated. The couple discovered their house had been daubed with paint, and their tires were slashed. The Pritchards became prisoners in their own home and spent a small fortune on a security system. Here's what was puzzling—they had no idea what they had done to deserve such cruel treatment.

After four months of unexplained terrorism, they finally met the perpetrator. Mr. Pritchard caught James McGhee, a 53-year-old man, while he was damaging their car.

As they looked at each other, Pritchard asked McGhee, "Why are you doing this to us?"

McGhee responded, "Oh, no—I've got the wrong man!"

McGhee thought he was terrorizing a different man named Pritchard, who had been spreading rumors about him. He found the Pritchards in the telephone directory and assumed the husband was the person responsible for slandering him. He got the wrong Pritchard. (2)

What an absurd turn of events, but anger has a tendency to do funny things to us. It blinds us to reality. It blinds us to consequences. It blinds us to the irrational harm that may come from our rage. For your own best interest, if you are angry with someone, let it go. Act quickly before you cause yourself and them any harm.

The same thing is true when it comes to temptation. Jesus continues, "You have heard that it was said, 'Do not commit adultery.' But I tell you that anyone who looks at a woman lustfully has already committed adultery with her in his heart. If your right eye causes you to sin, gouge it out and throw it away. It is better for you to lose one part of your body than for your whole body to be thrown into hell. And if your right hand causes you to sin, cut it off and throw it away. It is better for you to lose one part of your body than for your whole body to go into hell."

I suspect the Master is indulging in a little hyperbole here. He doesn't really expect us to gouge out an eye or cut off a hand. At least I hope not. But the principle is the same. Do not let sin take root in your heart. The consequences can be tragic.

Andy Andrews in his book Mastering the Seven Decisions that Determine Personal Success tells a revealing story about a well-known, wealthy industrialist in the 1920s. This man was said to have single-handedly controlled a vast portion of our country's prosperity.

With his wealth, this wealthy industrialist purchased a zoo. It wasn't a public zoo. He had no desire to benefit the public. No, it was his personal zoo, located on his estate, for the pleasure of this one man and his family. National dignitaries were occasionally invited to visit his zoo, but the rest of the population was shut out.

This man collected animals from all over the world, and it was not long before his zoo was one of the most complete collections the zoological world had ever known. One day, the man heard about a rare and beautiful type of gazelle from Africa. No zoo in the world had yet obtained this animal for their collection. So, naturally he became obsessed with the idea of becoming the first to own one of these amazing creatures.

He mounted an expedition to Africa where he contacted the natives to learn about this animal and its whereabouts. Over and over he was told, "You'll never catch one. They're too fast and too strong. You can shoot and kill them from a distance—but you'll never get close enough to take one alive."

This made the endeavor even more appealing to him. He told a reporter who was on the safari with him, "Don't listen to them; I'll get as many of them as I want! And it won't be a problem." And he did. Here is how he went about it.

When his men located a herd of these gazelles, he would pour sweet feed—a blend of oats and barley rolled in molasses—on the ground in an open area in the middle of the night and then leave. The next night, he would scatter the feed again. For two weeks, he spread the feed, night after night.

The animals, of course, came in and ate this delicious concoction. On the first night of the third week, he scattered the feed and sank an eight-foot post into the ground twenty feet away. The next night, he scattered the feed and sank another post into the ground twenty feet in the opposite direction. Every night, he added a post. Then he started putting boards between the posts while scattering the feed.

Six weeks rolled by. He continued adding posts and boards until he had a corral built around the feed. Every night the gazelles would find the gaps between the posts and would come into the corral and feed. They seemed to be impervious to the fact that they were gradually being closed in. Finally, he watched one night as the entire herd squeezed through the final gap. He moved in behind them and nailed the last board into place. The animals were trapped inside the corral. He then proceeded to choose the animals he wanted to take back to his zoo. He let the others go.

When he was asked how he knew how to catch them, he said: "I treat animals the same way I treat people: I give them what they want. I give them food and shelter. In exchange, they give me their beauty and their freedom." (3)

This is the way temptation works. We are drawn in little by little until a fence is built around us. It may begin with a glance . . . a casual remark . . . a phone call . . . and eventually heartbreak. Do not let sin take root in your heart whether it be anger or lust or whatever it may be. Get rid of it. Act quickly. Let it go.

But how do you do that? The best way to let go of negative, hurtful emotions or desires is to turn to God. Don't try to handle it alone.

Leslie Dunkin once told about a dog he had when he was a boy. His father would occasionally test the dog's obedience. He would place a tempting piece of meat on the floor and give the command, "No!" The dog was not to touch the meat. The dog, which must have had a strong urge to go for the meat, was placed in a most difficult situation—to obey or disobey his master's command.

Dunkin said, "The dog never looked at the meat. He seemed to feel that if he did, the temptation to disobey would be too great. So he looked steadily at my father's face." Dunkin then made this spiritual application: "There is a lesson for us all. Always look up to the Master's face." (4)

That may sound a little simplistic, but it is also true. The best thing you can do when you are tempted by anger or lust or any other hurtful emotion or desire is to keep your gaze fixed on your faith. If you have committed yourself to Christ, you know what is right and what is wrong. You know that which is life-affirming and that which is destructive. Do not even allow yourself a glance in the direction of that which would pull you down. And pray with all your might that God will help you deal with your anger, deal with your lust, deal with your spiteful tongue or whatever there is in your life that could bring a blemish to your reputation or cause you to hurt someone else.

And if you have already gotten yourself in a bad situation, remember that God is a God of healing and reconciliation. There is still hope if you are willing to yield to God's control.

Years ago, Dr. Charles Sheldon sat on the side of a hill at Winona Lake with a thousand other men and listened to the life story of the speaker on the platform. Here is what that speaker had to say, "Twenty-five years ago, I was in a saloon in Chicago. I was not dead drunk, but I had been drinking all the evening and I was pretty well under the influence. The barkeeper came out from behind the bar and threw me out into the street. I got up and started for Lake Michigan to drown myself. I said as I went along, 'I am of no use. I have spent my last cent for drink. I am separated from my wife. I have committed nearly every crime in the State of Illinois except murder. I haven't a friend in the world, and I might as well end it.'

The speaker continued: "I passed an open door on Clark Street, and without knowing to this day why. I went up the steps and into a hall filled with men and women. It was the Pacific Garden Mission, and I went stumbling down the wide aisle clear down to the platform on which a tall man was talking. I fell down right in front of the platform and lay there in a drunken stupor. The man who was talking kept right on, speaking over my fallen body. When he was through and the people in the hall had gone out, he came down, lifted me up, took me into a room, put me into a clean bed, and I slept off my drunk and woke up the next morning sober. I had a bath and a good breakfast, and—I haven't time to tell the whole story, but in that Pacific Garden Mission under the ministration of Col. Clark and his devoted wife I was soundly converted by the Lord Jesus Christ, was baptized, and became a new man."

The man up on the platform paused a moment, then he said: "Tonight I plan to take the evening train to Chicago, and tomorrow night I shall be speaking on that same platform in front of which I lay drunk that night 25 years ago, and preach the same gospel to fallen men and women that Col. Clark preached to my salvation. I am reconciled to my wife and we are living happily together. I have a good job, money in my pocket, and more friends than I can count. And I am one of the happiest men in the world, because by the power of Jesus Christ I have been born again."

The man up there on that platform was named Harry Monroe and when he died 10 years later it took all day for the men and women he had helped bring to Christ pass by his casket. He was one of the most useful men that Chicago ever knew, says Charles Sheldon. Yet if any of us had seen him that night he was drunk in that saloon we might have said, "Let him drown himself. He is of no use to anyone." But the Divine power laid hold on Harry Monroe and created him anew. (5)

My friends, when sin has us it its grip, the worse thing we can do is to depend on our own willpower, our own ingenuity, our own strength to extricate us. At such times we need the power of God to come into our lives and make us new people. The important thing is to act quickly before you cause yourself and anyone else any hurt or harm. Too much is at stake. Ask God's help today.

1. Cadillac News in Wendy Northcutt, The Darwin Awards 4 (New York: Penguin Group Inc., 2006), pp. 159 & 161.
2. I Once Was Blind, But Now I Squint (Chattanooga, TN: AMG Publishers, 2004), p. 71.
3. (Nashville: Thomas Nelson, 2008).
4. Richard De Haan, http://preceptaustin.org/hebrews_12_sermon_illustrations.htm
5. Diogenes Allen, Between Two Worlds (Atlanta: John Knox Press, 1971), p. 25.

You Are God's Temple
I Corinthians 3:16-23

Since tomorrow is Presidents' Day, I thought I would begin with a favorite story about Abraham Lincoln. One of the endearing traits that Lincoln displayed was his ability to laugh at himself, and especially at his rather plain appearance. He said that sometimes he felt like the ugly man who met an old woman traveling through a forest. The old woman said, "You're the ugliest man I ever saw."

"I can't help it," the ugly man said.

"No, I guess not," the woman admitted, "but the least you could do is stay home."

One reason Lincoln was a great man was his ability to laugh at himself.

One of the most popular films of recent years was a movie about a mentally challenged man named Forrest Gump. In the book by Winston Groom upon which the movie was based, there is a scene in which Forrest and his roommate at the University of Alabama have a serious problem. The friend's car has a flat tire, and while the friend is changing it he drops the lug nuts into the sewer. The friend is very upset because the two of them are late for football practice. Their legendary coach, Bear Bryant of the Alabama Crimson Tide, would not tolerate this. Forrest makes a suggestion, "Well, why don't you take one nut off the other three tires, and then all four wheels will have three nuts. That should at least get us to practice."

The friend looks at him. His face turns beet red with anger and embarrassment at the simplicity of Forrest's suggestion. At the top of his lungs his friend screams, "I don't understand how could you think of that. You're an idiot!"

Forrest replies, "I may be an idiot, but at least I'm not stupid." (1)

How do you feel about yourself? Abraham Lincoln knew that he was homely in his appearance, but that did not keep him from becoming our greatest president. Forrest Gump understood his limitations, but that did not keep him from seeing things other people missed.

How do you feel about yourself?

A few years back, The Rev. Jesse Jackson energized many young people, particularly many African-American young people with his chant, "I am somebody! I may be poor but I am somebody! I may be in prison but I am somebody. I maybe uneducated but I am somebody!"

How do you feel about yourself? Here's what the Bible says about you: "Don't you know that you yourselves are God's temple and that God's Spirit lives in you?"

Did you hear that? You are God's temple. How do you feel about yourself now? This is why you are somebody: you are the dwelling place of God.

Here is where we begin: God's dwelling place is within God's people. When Paul used these words, "Don't you know that you yourselves are God's temple . . ." he was referring to the church. God's dwelling place is the church.

But not our building. There are two words in Greek for "temple." The one used here denotes not so much a building but the true dwelling-place of God. Paul is saying that as individual members of Christ's body and as a church body, we are God's dwelling place.

Do you remember when Jesus had his encounter with the Samaritan woman at the well? Remember how she said to him, "Our fathers worshiped on this mountain, but you Jews claim that the place where we must worship is in Jerusalem."

How did Jesus answer this woman's statement? He said, "A time is coming and has now come when the true worshipers will worship the Father in spirit and truth, for they are the kind of worshipers the Father seeks. God is spirit, and his worshipers must worship in spirit and in truth." (John 4:22-23)

God is Spirit. That means that God does not have a physical dwelling place. God is not on a mountain or in a building. God dwells within the hearts and minds of God's people. The dwelling place of God is God's people.

Now we have to be careful. Some of our New Age friends would declare that because we are the dwelling place of God, therefore we are God. At least that was actress Shirley MacLaine's famous contention a few years back—that we are God.

Nothing could be further from the truth. We are all too human. That is why in a later chapter St. Paul warns us, "Flee from sexual immorality." We are all too human, but listen as Paul continues this interesting thought: "All other sins a man commits are outside his body, but he who sins sexually sins against his own body." Then he adds these comforting words that resemble today's text, "Do you not know that your body is a temple of the Holy Spirit, who is in you, whom you have received from God? You are not your own; you were bought at a price. Therefore honor God with your body." (6:18-20)

It could not be clearer. We are not God, but we are the dwelling place of God if we belong to Christ. This is why we are somebody. Not because of our intelligence, not because of our looks, not because of our athletic ability—but because the Holy Spirit of God lives within us.

Flannery O'Connor once wrote a short story titled, "A Temple of the Holy Ghost." In it O'Connor tells of a precocious twelve-year-old girl. This girl has two teenage cousins who have come to visit her. Well, teenage girls have a way of attracting teenage boys. Two country boys have come to visit her cousins. The girl overhears her cousins mock a certain nun, Sister Perpetua. This good Sister has suggested a formula for young ladies to use in fending off fresh young men in the back seats of cars. "Stop sir!" the nun taught the girls to say. "I am a Temple of the Holy Ghost!"

The cousins think such advice is hilarious. The twelve-year-old girl, however, is moved by it. The news that she is the dwelling place of God makes her feel as if somebody has given her a present. She takes it seriously. (2)

We should take it seriously, too. We are the dwelling place of God. We are the temple of the living God. What does that mean? Let me suggest some things.

First of all, when God dwells within us, we know who we are. That's important. Many people wander around saying they need to find themselves. No, they need to find Christ—then they will find themselves.

Tommy Nelson in his book, The 12 Essentials of Godly Success, tells about a man named Robert Howard. Robert Howard was from Cross Plains, Texas. A small man, says Tommy Nelson, Robert Howard was a borderline schizophrenic. He lived in his own world. Howard had few friends, didn't marry and lived with his mother. Howard earned his living by doing odd jobs. He didn't relate well to people.

Then his mother fell ill and went into a coma. His mother was the only friend Robert ever had. When the nurse told him she would never recover, Robert went home and fired a bullet into his brain. He was thirty years old.

When relatives went through Robert's meager possessions, they discovered great bundles of writing that Robert had never submitted to a publisher—writing which showed a brilliant imagination. In his writing Robert had erected his own personal world. In this world which he imagined, he was not a frightened young man from Cross Plains, Texas, who lived with his mother. Rather he was a bold, strong, handsome adventurer who conquered kings and warriors. This daring adventurer knew no fear. He was loved by women and revered by men. In his imagination, Robert Howard had created a popular hero which he named Conan the Barbarian. Yes, it is the same Conan which we know not only from Robert Howard's writings but from a most popular movie starring Arnold Schwarzenegger. Millions and millions of dollars worth of Robert Howard's works about Conan the Barbarian have sold, all of which came after his tragic death. (3)

What a sad, sad story. Robert Howard had no sense of personal identity. He did not know who he was. He tried to live his life through the fictional Conan. In the real world, he was a man who couldn't cope.

Contrast Robert Howard with the twelve-year-old girl in Flannery O'Connor's short story. This girl is moved by the idea that she is the dwelling place of God. What a healthy idea to grab a young woman's brain. This idea gave her a heightened sense of her own worth. St. Paul writes, "Don't you know that you yourselves are God's temple and that God's Spirit lives in you?" That's who we are. So that's the first thing it means to have God dwelling with us. We have the presence of the Holy Spirit in our lives to give us a sense of identity. We know who we are.

In the second place, when God dwells within us, we know how we are to live. Our sense of identity—our sense of self-esteem as it is sometimes called—cannot be divorced from our behavior.

In Sy Montgomery's book, Journey of the Pink Dolphins, the character Necca speaks these unforgettable words, "When people forget who they are, they forget how to act."

Steve Farrar tells about a young man named Adam Clarke who was a sales-clerk in a store that sold fine silk to people of the upper classes in London. One day his employer showed young Adam how he could increase sales and profits. As he measured the silk out he was to subtly stretch it, thereby giving the customer less for his or her money.

Young Adam Clarke looked his employer straight in the eye and said, "Sir, your silk may stretch but my conscience won't." (4)

Adam Clarke knew who he was and therefore he knew how to live. Our sense of identity—our sense of self-esteem—cannot be divorced from our behavior.

Psychiatrist Theodore Dalrymple wrote an article for the September 1995 issue of Psychology Today magazine. He wrote that twenty years earlier, when he first began to practice, no one ever complained of a lack of self-esteem. Now, hardly a week goes by, he writes, without a patient making that complaint as if they expected him, the doctor, to fix it.

One young man came to visit him concerned about his low self-image. He felt this was the cause of most of his problems. His mother agreed. She, too, felt he suffered from low self-esteem. It was this condition, the patient and his mother said, that caused him to beat up his pregnant girlfriend, which resulted in a miscarriage.

The doctor was not convinced. "It couldn't be the other way around, could it?" the doctor asked.

The young man asked, "What do you mean?"

The doctor said, "Could it be that your behavior caused you to have a poor opinion of yourself?"

This possibility, of course, was rejected out of hand by the patient, and probably by his mother as well. (5)

Our schools and many self-styled self-help gurus have done an excellent job of helping people, particularly many young people, develop high self-esteem. This will only serve them well if they also develop good character, for identity and behavior cannot be separated.

As Joseph Telushkin says in his book The Ten Commandments of Character, "Self-esteem . . . derives in part from knowing that one has done the right thing." (6)

When God dwells within us, we know who we are and we know how we are to live. We are to live like Jesus. We are to live with integrity and with love.

But one thing more needs to be said. When God dwells in us, we have a Friend who will be with us in any situation. When God dwells in us, we not only have an internal guide, but also an internal comforter. When God dwells in us, we are never on our own, and neither are those we love.

The Right Reverend Charles G. von Rosenberg tells an important story involving his son John. At age two and a half, John was found to have a kidney problem that required surgery. Their family lived in a rather remote area of North Carolina at that time, without good medical facilities, and so they traveled to Duke University Hospital for the surgery.

On the night prior to the trip to Durham, von Rosenberg spent hours pacing in John's room. He was afraid, upset, and angry—angry at the circumstances, angry at God, and, in truth, angry at himself. After all, he was John's father, and he was supposed to be able to protect his son from this kind of experience. And so, he paced and paced and paced.

At some point—about 2:00 in the morning—an amazing thing happened. Charles von Rosenberg says he suddenly became aware of something new, as though something had been spoken to him. And the message was this. The child in that bed, his child, was in truth, first of all, God's child. As his dad, von Rosenberg had only a temporary responsibility, on God's behalf. But the child belonged to God. Therefore, whatever happened at Duke—even the worse that can happen—would not change the most important thing that could be said about John. He is—and always will be—God's child.

At 2:00 in the morning, says von Rosenberg, a tremendous burden was lifted off his shoulders. He knew that he still had a responsibility for his son—but not the ultimate responsibility. Further, he knew that neither the absolute best nor the absolute worst for John was in his hands. Rather, that it was—and is—in God's hands. (7)

That's what it means to be a temple of the Holy Spirit. We belong to God, and so do those we love. When God dwells in us, we know who we are. We know what we are to do—be Christ's disciple. And we know who goes with us—a Friend who can meet our every need. "Don't you know that you yourselves are God's temple and that God's Spirit lives in you?"

1. Cited by Ron Brugler, http://www.swedenborg.org/odb/sermon_detail.cfm?sermonID=2543.
2. Flannery O'Connor: The Complete Stories (New York: Farrar, Straus Ft Giroux, 1983), p. 238. Cited by Philip Yancey, Rumors of Another World (Grand Rapids: Zondervan, 2003), p. 85.
3. (Nashville: Broadman & Holman Publishers, 2005), pp. 101-102.
4. Finishing Strong Going the Distance for Your Family (Sisters, OR: Multnomah Publishers, Inc., 1995), pp. 93-94.
5. Http://www.medicinenet.com/script/main/art.asp?articlekey=35176. Cited by Stephen Arterburn, The Secrets Men Keep (Nashville: Integrity Publishers, 2006), p. 136.
6. (New York: Random House, Inc., 2003), p. 25.
7. http://www.etdiocese.net/sermons/2005/1-30-St-Francis-Ooltewah.htm.

Worry Not
Isaiah 49:14-15; Matthew 6:24-34

Do you have a worrier in your family? Kais Rayes writes that he and his wife found their whole life turned upside down when their first child was born. Every night, the baby seemed to be fussy, and many nights it seemed that their baby cried far more than he slept. Says Rayes, "My wife would wake me up, saying, 'Get up, honey! Go see why the baby is crying!'" As a result, Rayes found himself suffering from severe sleep deprivation.

While complaining to his coworkers about his problem one day, one of his colleagues suggested a book on infant massage. Rayes immediately went in search of the book and that night, he tried the technique, gently rubbing his baby's back, arms, head, and legs until the baby was completely relaxed and obviously had fallen into a deep sleep. Quietly tiptoeing from the darkened room so as not to disturb the rhythmic breathing of the baby, he made his way directly to his own bed in hopes of enjoying a well-deserved full night of sleep.

No such luck. In the middle of the night, his wife awoke him in a panic. "Get up, honey!" she said as she jostled him awake. "Go see why the baby is not crying!" (1)

Do you know anybody like that? Some people are just worriers. Even when things go well—they worry, they fret, they fume. They worry that something bad will happen.

Dr. Rachel Naomi Remen tells many memorable stories in her book, Kitchen Table Wisdom: Stories That Heal.

In one of her stories she asked one of her patients to describe her husband. The woman laughed and told a story about a visit they made to Hawaii. An organized and frugal man, her husband had reserved compact rental cars on each of the four islands months in advance. On arriving on the Big Island and presenting their reservation to the car rental desk, they were told that the economy car they had reserved was not available. Alarmed, she watched her husband's face redden as he prepared to do battle. The clerk didn't seem to notice. "I am so sorry, sir," he said. "Will you accept a substitute for the same price? We have a Mustang convertible." Barely mollified, her husband put their bags in this beautiful white sports car and they drove off.

The same thing happened throughout their holiday. They would turn in their car and fly to the next island, only to be told that the car they had been promised was not available. They offered a substitute for the same price and each time the substituted car was an upgrade—far nicer than the car they had expected. It was amazing, she said. After the Mustang, they had been given a Mazda MR-10, a Lincoln Town Car, and finally, a Mercedes, all with the most sincere apologies. The vacation was absolutely wonderful and on the plane back, she turned to her husband, thanking him for all he had done to arrange such a memorable time. "Yes," he said, pleased, "it was really nice." Then, much to her amazement he added, "Too bad they never had the right car for us." She said he was absolutely serious. (2)

What do you do with people like that? Some people can see the dark side of any cloud, even one with a silver lining. They are worriers. They fume, they fret, they stay stressed out.

Do they ever read the words of Jesus? "Therefore I tell you, do not worry about your life, what you will eat or drink; or about your body, what you will wear. Is not life more important than food, and the body more important than clothes? Look at the birds of the air; they do not sow or reap or store away in barns, and yet your heavenly Father feeds them. Are you not much more valuable than they? Who of you by worrying can add a single hour to his life?

"And why do you worry about clothes? See how the lilies of the field grow. They do not labor or spin. Yet I tell you that not even Solomon in all his splendor was dressed like one of these. If that is how God clothes the grass of the field, which is here today and tomorrow is thrown into the fire, will he not much more clothe you, O you of little faith? So do not worry, saying, 'What shall we eat?' or 'What shall we drink?' or 'What shall we wear?' For the pagans run after all these things, and your heavenly Father knows that you need them. But seek first his kingdom and his righteousness, and all these things will be given to you as well . . ."

From reading this I'm tempted to declare that it is a sin to worry. However, if I did that, I would just give some of you one more thing to worry about. I will say this: you put a terrible burden upon yourself when you cannot relax and trust in God.

A word that is often used in our society is not worry, but its sister emotion, stress. A lecturer was explaining stress management to an audience. He raised a glass of water and asked, "How heavy is this glass of water?"

Answers called out ranged from 10 oz. to 16 oz. The lecturer replied, "The absolute weight doesn't matter. It depends on how long you try to hold it.

"If I hold it for a minute, that's not a problem. If I hold it for an hour, I'll have an ache in my right arm. If I hold it for a day, you'll have to call an ambulance.

"In each case, it's the same weight, but the longer I hold it, the heavier it becomes."

He continued, "And that's the way it is with stress management. If we carry our burdens all the time, sooner or later, as the burden becomes increasingly heavy, we won't be able to carry on. As with the glass of water, you have to put it down for a while and rest before holding it again. When we're refreshed, we can carry on with the burden.

"So, before you return home tonight," said the lecturer, "put the burden of work down. Don't carry it home. You can pick it up tomorrow. Whatever burdens you're carrying now, let them down for a moment if you can. Relax; pick them up later after you've rested. Life is short. Enjoy it!" (3)

You put a terrible burden upon yourself when you cannot relax and trust in God. Dr. Steve Jackson tells about a seaplane back in December, 2005 that lifted out of the warm waters just off South Beach in Miami carrying 18 passengers and a crew of 2 to the Bahamas. Seconds later a wing fell off the plane. The aircraft plummeted into the ocean killing all onboard. The NTSB determined that a catastrophic failure had occurred in the wing caused by a tiny stress fracture between the wing and fuselage; a crack that was undetectable to the human eye. The plane had endured the stresses and strains of thousands of take-offs, landings, and hours in the air. But finally, after all the stresses a wing must endure, the part failed.

Dr. Jackson says, "In our hurry-up, pressure-cooker world, such stress in terms of our human lives is common. And sometimes, even in the good times like those folks were probably enjoying on that tropical day in paradise in Miami, those stresses threaten to pull us apart unless we do something about them; unless we find a remedy." (4)

Before we seek a remedy for worry and stress, however, there are some things we need to understand about these powerful and destructive forces.

First of all, many of us have a susceptibility to stress and worry built into our personalities. Many of us "inherited" a susceptibility to worry. We got it from our parents. I don't mean that it is genetic necessarily—though there might indeed be a genetic component to it. I mean that some of us had parents who were not able for one reason or another to give us an emotionally secure environment during our formative years.

This is what we learned from the highly respected psychologist Erik Erikson. He taught that during the first stages of our lives, we either developed a sense of trust or a sense of mistrust about our environment. And throughout our lives, how we respond to life will be affected by which of these emotions dominates our life—trust or mistrust.

Erikson held that the conflict between trust and mistrust arises in the very first stage of a child's development. Successful resolution of this conflict depends largely on the infant's relationship with the primary caregiver. Let's say, for example, that our caregiver is by nature a person who is not able to express warmth and nurture. Many parents are not able to express unconditional love, because they did not receive unconditional love when they were young. We are not blaming anybody. We're simply stating a fact. Some parents are emotionally limited themselves. So they could not provide us with a secure sense of the world. If we encounter trust during our infancy, says Erikson, the stage is set for a lifelong perception of the world as a good and pleasant place. But if our caregiver wasn't emotionally adept at expressing warmth and love, then it's likely we grew up to be mistrustful and insecure. (5) Many of us have a susceptibility to stress and worry built into our very personalities.

On top of that, modern life has many built-in stressors.

Some of us have very stressful jobs. Some of us have family situations that are stressful. Some of us may have medical conditions that we worry about. Life has many built-in stressors. Stress, anxiety, depression, insomnia, suicide, and other signs of insecurity, tension, and hopelessness have become shockingly commonplace in modern society. According to pollster Louis Harris, "fully 90 percent of all adult Americans, a substantial 158 million people, report experiencing high stress, with as many as six in every ten reporting 'great stress' at least once or twice every week." (6)

I was reading an interesting study by the American Medical Association about the stress put on young doctors because of excessive work hours. This study says that such stress is not safe for young doctors or their patients. (7)

Doctors are not the only people who are working longer hours nowadays. One reason corporations are not hiring like they once were is that corporations have grown accustomed to getting more and more work out of employees they already have. And this takes a toll on their employees.

Of course, many people wish that working too hard was their problem. Many families are under much stress due to one or both providers being completely out of work. A devoted Christian sales manager, aged 57 with two daughters in college, found himself laid off in favor of a younger, more aggressive manager. He wonders how he will be able to continue to provide his family with anything like the comfortable lifestyle they have grown accustomed to. He says to his pastor, "I'm trusting God, but I'm also facing some very difficult decisions." He's not destitute by any means, but that does not mean he is not under enormous stress. Meanwhile door after door keeps shutting in his face.

We've never seen housing collapse as it has these past few years. Owning your own home has always been considered a key element of the American dream but not anymore. It's tough.

Some of us are especially susceptible to stress. And modern life has many built-in stressors. But here's the good news for the day: The best cure for worry and stress is to trust God completely. Jesus reminds us that God provides for the birds of the air. "They do not sow or reap or store away in barns," said the Master, "and yet your heavenly Father feeds them." Then he asked a very powerful question: "Are you not much more valuable than they?" And the answer is, yes, you are much more valuable than they.

Marion Rawson Vuilleumier in her book Meditations by the Sea gives several examples of how God has provided for His creation.

She notes that some birds migrate thousands of miles across empty oceans. Some of these birds, like gulls and sea ducks, can rest on the ocean surface, storing up energy for further flights. Their feathers contain an ointment that protects them from the wet and cold. But there are other winged creatures that fly over vast stretches of the ocean with seemingly no place to break their journey.

One example is the Monarch butterfly. The monarch is the only butterfly known to make a two-way migration as birds do. In the summer you can find Monarchs in northeastern climes like Newfoundland and New England. However, Monarchs cannot survive cold winters. Somehow God has made it possible for them to know when it is time to travel south for the winter. Some fly as far as 3,000 miles to reach their winter home in Mexico. In this astonishing annual pilgrimage they fly around city buildings and over coastal waters. They stop briefly to feed on flowers when available, and they cluster at night in trees when they are over land. At sea Monarch butterflies rest on the masts of fishing boats. Only God knows how they make this extraordinary journey safely.

According to The National Geographic tall ships are often a haven for birds in flight. Kenneth Garrett, who sailed from Poland to America during the Bicentennial rendezvous of tall ships, wrote that a pair of doves came aboard briefly. Later a tiny wren alighted on his ankle and scurried up his trouser leg. The wren warmed and rested itself in his trouser leg for about 45 minutes and then emerged and took off for shore. (8)

The birds of the air "do not sow or reap or store away in barns, and yet your heavenly Father feeds them. Are you not much more valuable than they?"

Do you understand how much God loves you? Our lesson from Isaiah today contains some beautiful words. Listen closely, "But Zion said, 'The LORD has forsaken me, the Lord has forgotten me.'" Then God answers this plaintive cry: "Can a mother forget the baby at her breast and have no compassion on the child she has borne?" Then God adds, "Though she may forget, I will not forget you!"

Friend, if you are one of those people who has difficulty with trust, today is the day to turn around. God loves you like a mother loves the child at her breast. Relax. By the grace of God, you're going to make it. "Look at the birds of the air . . ."

1. God's Devotional Book for Mothers (Colorado Springs: Cook Communications Ministries, 2005), p. 269.
2. (New York: The Berkley Publishing Group, 1996), pp. 176-177.
3. From the Internet. Source unknown.
4. http://www.newsongweb.org/Sermons/2006%20Sermons/11-12-06.htm.
5. Erik H. Erikson, Childhood and Society (New York: W. W. Norton), p. 339. Cited in Howard E. Butt Jr., Who Can You Trust? Overcoming Betrayal and Fear (Colorado Springs: Waterbrook Press, 2004).
6. Burt Nanus, The Leader's Edge (Chicago: Contemporary Books, Inc., 1989), p. 3.
7. "Excessive Work Hours Are Not Safe," wwwania-assn.org/ama/pub/article/1 61 6-5665. html.
8. Marion Rawson Vuilleumier, Meditations by the Sea (Nashville: Abingdon Press, 1980), p. 96.

Come With Me To The Mountain
Exodus 24:12-18; 2 Peter 1:16-21; Matthew 17:1-9

Charles Swindoll in his book Day By Day tells the story of a mysterious event that occurred several years ago to a group of young guys from the church he pastored in Southern California. They were on a mountain climbing excursion, along with their youth leader. While taking in the breathtaking sights, the leader realized he had lost the trail. A heavy snowfall had completely covered the path, and he didn't have a clue where they were or how they could get back to the main camp. Sundown was not far away, and they were not equipped to spend the night on the craggy windblown slopes where the temperature would soon drop even lower.

While trudging through the snow, entertaining thoughts just this side of panic, they suddenly heard someone on the slopes above them yell down: "Hey—the trail is up here!" They glanced up and to their relief saw another climber in the distance. Without hesitation, they began to make their way up to the large boulder where the man was sitting. The climb was exhausting, but their relief in finding the way gave their adrenaline a rush.

Finally they arrived . . . but to their surprise the man who had yelled at them was nowhere to be found. Furthermore, there were no traces in the snow that anyone had been sitting on the boulder, nor were there footprints around the rock. The trail, however, stretched out before them, leading them to safety. (1)

To this day, they do not know the identity of the stranger who led them to safety. Swindoll thinks he may have been an angel.

Mysterious things happen on mountains.

In our lesson from Exodus, the Lord says to Moses, "Come up to me on the mountain and stay here, and I will give you the tablets of stone, with the law and commands I have written for their instruction." Then Moses set out with Joshua his aide, and Moses went up on the mountain of God. This turned out to be one of the most pivotal events in human history. For there he received the Ten Commandments.

In Matthew 17 we read about another pivotal and mysterious event that occurred on a mountain. Jesus is on the mountain with his three closest disciples—Peter, James and John. On this mountain these three disciples saw their Master transfigured. His face shone like the sun, and his clothes became as white as the light. Just then there appeared before them Moses and Elijah, talking with Jesus. Peter said to Jesus, "Lord, it is good for us to be here. If you wish, I will put up three shelters—one for you, one for Moses and one for Elijah."

While he was still speaking, a bright cloud enveloped them, and a voice from the cloud said, "This is my Son, whom I love; with him I am well pleased. Listen to him!"

When the disciples heard this, they fell face down to the ground, terrified. But Jesus came and touched them. "Get up," he said. "Don't be afraid." When they looked up, they saw no one except Jesus.

In our reading from the epistle, Peter testifies to that startling event. He writes, "We did not follow cleverly invented stories when we told you about the power and coming of our Lord Jesus Christ, but we were eyewitnesses of his majesty. For he received honor and glory from God the Father when the voice came to him from the Majestic Glory, saying, 'This is my Son, whom I love; with him I am well pleased.' We ourselves heard this voice that came from heaven when we were with him on the sacred mountain."

I want to give you an invitation this morning to come with me to the mountain. In a figurative sense, let's leave the everyday world behind for a few moments and stand with those three disciples on that mountain.

In the first place, we also need to see who Jesus is. Listen to the words of the great author and pastor Leslie Weatherhead:

"Some years ago I had a strange dream. I am not making this up for the purpose of the sermon. I was passing through a time of great difficulty and unhappiness, and in my dream I was to be offered a personal interview with Christ, and I thought, 'Ah, I will ask Him this. I will ask Him that. Now I shall get an answer to all my questions and the key to all my problems.' Believe it or not, in the glory of His presence it was not that I forgot to ask Him anything. It seemed utterly unnecessary and meaningless. Somehow I had an overwhelming feeling that even He would not be able to explain to me because my mental grasp was so tiny, but there came an overwhelming feeling of supreme joy that questions no longer needed to be answered. It was sufficient to know there was an answer. I knew that all was well and somehow I knew that all was well for everybody. Another text came to my memory: 'In that day ye shall ask me nothing.'" (John 16). (2)

Leslie Weatherhead found himself in the presence of Christ and he found himself speechless. But he never forgot that experience. Who could? We all need to see Jesus.

In one of his first books, titled Night Flight, Antoine de Saint-Exupery, the late French aviator and philosopher, described what it's like to lose your way piloting a plane in the darkness of the night sky, flying without instruments. He described the feeling of helplessness of one such flight. Finally catching the whisper of a radio control operator, he frantically asks him to flash the signal at the air field so he can know whether or not the light he sees on the horizon is safety or a star. When the man replies that he has flashed the light, but the flier sees nothing happen, the pilot knows that he has not yet found the light which will guide him home. (3)

We all need to find the light that will guide us home. That light, of course, is

Jesus Christ. Or as John Newton has put it:

How sweet the name of Jesus sounds/ In a believer's ear;
It soothes his sorrows, heals his wounds/ And drives away his fear.
It makes the wounded spirit whole/ And calms the troubled breast;
'Tis manna to the hungry soul/ And to the weary rest.

Yes, come to the mountain. See who Jesus is. He is more than Moses and Elijah, more than the Law and the Prophets. See His face shine with the love of God. Come with me to the mountain. Catch a glimpse of Who He is.

Perhaps, on that mountain, we will catch a glimpse of what we too can be.

Those disciples saw Christ transfigured. They could not know that a transfiguration was also taking place within them. To be sure, that transfiguration would not be apparent until Pentecost. But it was happening. You cannot come into the presence of Jesus without becoming conscious of what, by his grace, you might one day be. As Disraeli put it: "To believe in the heroic makes heroes."

Nehru wrote: "The mere act of aiming at something big makes you big. Strive for great accomplishments, and you will accomplish much."

Or as Teddy Roosevelt once wrote: "Far better it is to dare mighty things, to win glorious triumphs, even though checkered by failure, than to rank with those poor spirits who neither enjoy much nor suffer much because they live in the grey twilight that knows neither victory nor defeat."

The disciples stayed in the company of greatness and thus they became great as well. Even to believe that greatness is possible has extraordinary merit.

Augustus Caesar was barely five feet seven inches tall, pale and delicate, with a weak throat and poor circulation, who all his life had to live on a strict diet and constantly struggle against bodily frailty. Yet see what Augustus Caesar did!

One element in his amazing career is undoubtedly the fact that in his youth he visited Theogenes, a famous astrologer, to have his horoscope cast. When Theogenes saw the young man's horoscope, so runs the story, he was so impressed with the marvel of it that he fell on his face and worshiped him.

You and I do not believe in astrology but, you see, Augustus did. It was a superstition, but, being believed, it worked. All his later life through difficulty, peril, burden-bearing, and inner struggle for self-conquest, he kept an undiscourageable faith in his destiny, which the stars had foretold. (4)

It was this undiscourageable faith that the disciples discovered that helped transform their lives. There is something about a mountaintop experience that can help you be more than you have ever been before.

John A. Redhead, Jr. tells of a father and son who have a really good relationship. Among their many good times together, one stands out above all the rest: It was a hike up a particular mountain where they seemed to reach the height of a beautiful friendship. After they returned home, there came a day when things did not seem to run as smoothly. The father rebuked the son, and the son spoke sharply in return. An hour later the air had cleared.

"Dad," said the son, "whenever it starts to get like that again, let's one of us say 'The Mountain.'" So it was agreed. In a few weeks another misunderstanding occurred. The boy was sent to his room in tears. After a while, the father decided to go up and see the boy. He was still angry until he saw a piece of paper pinned to the door. The boy had penciled two words in large letters, "The Mountain." That symbol was powerful enough to restore the relationship of father and son. (5)

Come with me to the mountain. It is there that relationships can be made right. Come with me to the mountain. See who Jesus is. See what by his grace you and I can yet become. Perhaps on that mountain we will gain new confidence in God's presence in our lives. All of us believe in an intellectual way that God is with us. But sometimes we need a mountain-top experience to make that intellectual belief a divine reality in our lives.

Rev. Kip Gilts tells of hearing author Philip Yancey speak on prayer. One of the stories Yancey told was about climbing Mt. Wilson in Colorado with his wife, Janet. Yancey said that, just as he and Janet got to the top of Mt. Wilson, a thunderstorm rolled in. They were at an elevation over 14,000 feet, far beyond the timberline, which made them walking lightning rods. He said the metal climbing rods in his hands and the ice ax on his back were tingling from all the electricity in the air. They were both scared, and they had good reason to be. They reviewed their lessons on what to do if caught above the timberline in a lightning storm. They couldn't lie down. Rocks conduct electricity. It was important that they separate so if one of them got struck by lightning, the other one could report what happened. They were to keep their feet together, crouch down and walk down the mountain.

Philip Yancey said as they started down that mountain he received a marvelous insight into his life—and the insight was this: he, Philip Yancey, was not in control. That's an insight that many of us need. Control is an illusion. We fool ourselves when things are going our way that we are the masters of our destiny. Nothing could be further from the truth. Yancey went on to say that neither he nor we are any more in control of our lives here and now, than he and his wife, Janet, were on top of that mountain. (6)

We are not in control but we can trust the One who is in control. That's the good news for the day. The One who is in control can be trusted.

In 1351, the Earl of Wickham decided to found a college called New College in Oxford, England. The times were grim. The bubonic plague had taken a terrible toll on the population. People were angry and frightened. Nevertheless, Wickham trusted God with all his heart and he was determined to make his new college succeed. Wickham paid for the building of the college and the college flourished.

Centuries later, it was time to replace the oak beams in the main hall of New

College, Oxford. The authorities approached the Earl of Wickham's descendants to ask for a donation to cover the cost of the new beams. To their surprise, the Earl's descendants were ready for them. "We have been waiting for you," they said. "The oak beams are ready for you." It turned out that the Earl of Wickham, over 500 years earlier, had foreseen the need of replacing the beams, and had planted a grove of oaks specifically for that purpose during his lifetime! (7)

My friend, that's faith. That's the kind of faith we need for the living of our lives. Where do we find it? Where do we obtain the confidence in the future so that we might invest in that which is lasting?

We are already in the right place.

Carl Jung, the great psychoanalyst, was counseling a man who had been in therapy for six months and was getting no better. Finally Jung said, "Friend, I can't do any more for you. What you need is God."

"How do I find God, Dr. Jung?" the man asked.

"I don't know," said Jung, "but I suspect if you will find a group of people some place that believe in Him passionately and just spend time with them, you will find God." The man did just that and he was healed.

This sanctuary is our mountaintop. We are together with others who believe in God passionately. In our own minds and hearts, let us see who Jesus really is. Let us see ourselves as we might be by God's grace. Let us gain confidence—confidence in God's presence and providence that we might be strong for the living of this hour.

It's like a song that Barbra Streisand sang years ago in the musical, "On A Clear Day You Can See Forever." Streisand sang, "On a clear day rise and look around you And you'll see who you are. On a clear day how it will astound you that the glow of your being outshines every star . . ." (8)

The being of Christ outshone every star, and as we fix our gaze on him we can glow, too, because we learn from him who we really are. On that mountain in his presence we gain confidence in his purpose for our lives. As she sang in the last two lines of the chorus,

"You can hear, from far and near, A world you've never, never heard before. And on a clear day on a clear day You can see forever And ever and ever more."

1. (Nashville: W Publishing Group, 2000), p. 216.
2. Leslie D. Weatherhead, Key Next Door (Nashville: Abingdon Press, 1959).
3. Gerald Kennedy, The Lion and the Lamb (Nashville: Abingdon Press, 1950), p. 188.
4. Harry Emerson Fosdick, Riverside Sermons (New York: Harper and Brothers, 1958).
5. Robert A. Beringer, Lectionary Homiletics, Mar. 92, p. 8.
6. http://www.am-umc.org/sermons/2006/sermon061119.htm.
7. Bruce Larson, The Relational Revolution (Waco: Word Books, 1976), p. 62.
8. Beth Johnston, http://www.geocities.com/Athens/Styx/4291/greena396.html#Feb18.

Rock Solid
Matthew 7:21-27

I read a quirky little item sometime back. It seems that the Main Library at the University of Indiana sinks over an inch every year. It seems that when it was built, engineers failed to take into account the weight of all the books that would occupy the building. And so the library is sinking. Obviously some heavy reading takes place at the University of Indiana.

It is a foolish person who does not take into account both the weight of a structure, and its contents, as well as the foundation on which it will stand before beginning construction.

On more than one occasion Jesus used the example of constructing a building to make a serious point. Here's what he had to say on this occasion: "Everyone who hears these words of mine and puts them into practice is like a wise man who built his house on the rock. The rain came down, the streams rose, and the winds blew and beat against that house; yet it did not fall, because it had its foundation on the rock. But everyone who hears these words of mine and does not put them into practice is like a foolish man who built his house on sand. The rain came down, the streams rose, and the winds blew and beat against that house, and it fell with a great crash."

The point of this parable is clear: Wise people build their lives on a solid foundation. Every architect knows that, but still, it happens from time to time. The principle of a solid foundation is ignored . . . with disastrous consequences.

Joe Emerson in his book I Wanted the Elevator, But I Got the Shaft tells about a skyscraper called the Columbus Building that was erected nearly a hundred years ago in Chicago. Chicago sits on the sandy shores of Lake Michigan.

When the Columbus Building was erected it soared above the city, but slowly it began to sink into the sand upon which it was constructed. When it was shored up on one side, it would sink on the other. Finally it had to be torn down. It was impossible to find any way to save it from the shifting sands.

Fortunately, by the time the next skyscraper, the Prudential Building, was erected geologists knew what it took to build a skyscraper in Chicago. Pilings were driven 108 feet into the ground. In fact, 187 such pillars were driven down that way until they came to rest on a sheet of solid rock called the Niagara Shelf, which runs all the way to Niagara Falls. Then, and only then, did the Prudential Building rise. It is still standing today. (1)

It's one of the self-evident truths of life: it's important to build on a solid foundation.

Dr. Norman Vincent Peale once noted that New York City's Manhattan Island is solid bedrock. Because of that foundation, scores of towering skyscrapers have been built on Manhattan. But builders were not always successful even in Manhattan.

When they started digging the foundation for the Chase Manhattan Bank, for example, they ran into trouble. Unlike much of the area, the excavators knew before they started digging that the site was not solid rock. But they were not prepared for what they found. The location where the bank was to be built was oozy quicksand.

Knowing that no building could be erected on such a squishy foundation, the bankers called in experts. One suggested driving pilings deep into the quicksand until a solid base was hit—like the Prudential building in Chicago. Another suggested another approach. But the cost of using either method was prohibitive.

They called in some geologists. "How long will it take to turn this quicksand into solid rock?" they asked. The geologists responded, about a million years. The bankers felt they couldn't wait that long!

The solution was finally found when some experts who understood the properties of quicksand were consulted. Sinking pipes into the quicksand, they pumped in sodium salicylate and calcium chloride. In only a few days with these chemicals added to its composition the quicksand hardened. Soon the foundation was laid and the sixty-floor bank building was erected on a solid foundation. (2) The lesson is clear: want to build something great and lasting? Begin with a solid foundation.

The Greek mathematician Archimedes understood that principle. In fact, he asked for only one fixed and immovable point and he said he could move the whole earth. As he put it, "I may have great hopes if I find even the least thing that is unshakably certain."

Ah, that is the problem, isn't it? Where do we find that which is unshakably certain? Even the most solid bedrock can be shaken if subjected to an earthquake of sufficient force.

Of course, Jesus wasn't talking about building skyscrapers in Matthew 7, but building lives. Where do you find that point that is unshakably certain upon which to build a life?

You find it, of course, in Christ's teachings. Jesus said, "Everyone who hears these words of mine and puts them into practice is like a wise man who built his house on the rock . . ." The Word of God is the foundation on which we build our lives. Jesus is the Word which became flesh. Both Old Testament and New testify to him. Fill yourself full with the teachings of scripture. That is the first step in building a firm foundation.

In one of the Chicken Soup for the Soul books there is a beautiful story told by a medical doctor, Dr. James C. Brown, about a patient of his. The patient was a five-year-old boy named Bobby. Bobby had been diagnosed with leukemia at age four. His cancer was now in remission. Still he had come to the hospital for a series of diagnostic tests that were a routine part of his treatment plan.

Bobby had bright blue eyes and a shy smile, says Dr. Brown, that at first glance didn't reveal the wisdom gained through his one-year struggle against cancer. Bobby had lost all of his hair while undergoing chemotherapy. Chemo often left him nauseous and unable to eat. Bobby had experienced numerous painful procedures and this day was to be no exception. Bobby would undergo a procedure that was extremely painful. He had been through it before, so he knew what to expect.

Dr. Brown explained to him what they were going to do, and why, and the importance of him remaining very still. Bobby assured his doctor that he would be very still, and he promised that the nurses and technologists in attendance would not need to hold him down.

As they began, Bobby asked, "Dr. Brown, would it be okay if I say the Twenty-third Psalm while you stick me?"

"Of course, that would be fine," Dr. Brown said, and they began the procedure.

Bobby recited beautifully. There were no tears and he stayed perfectly still. The procedure went well. Afterward Bobby said, "Dr. Brown, that really didn't hurt much." The doctor and the nurses knew better.

Then Bobby caught the doctor by surprise. He asked, "Dr. Brown, do you know the Twenty-third Psalm?"

"Well, sure," Dr. Brown answered.

"Can you recite it like me?" Bobby asked.

"Well, I don't know. I think so," Dr. Brown said, realizing that he was going out on a limb.

"Let's hear you," said Bobby.

So Dr. Brown proceeded to stumble through the Twenty-third Psalm. His performance was quite shabby in comparison to Bobby's, and he didn't have a needle sticking in his back like Bobby did. As he recited the Psalm, Dr. Brown noticed all the other white-coated professionals in the room trying to disappear as they feared being called on next.

Then beautiful and bald Bobby said to all of them, "You know, you really should learn the Twenty-third Psalm by heart. Because when you say it out loud, God hears you and he lets you know inside your heart that He is being strong for you when you can't be strong for yourself." (3)

Wow! There's a young man whose life is built on a strong foundation. The first step is to fill yourself full of the Word of God. Many people have found great strength in that Word.

Secondly, you build a strong foundation when you put Christ's teachings into practice. "Everyone who hears these words of mine and puts them into practice is like a wise man who built his house on the rock . . ."

We all know it's true. You can attend Bible studies six days a week and twice on Sunday, but if you do not practice Christ's teachings, you are building on shifting sand.

This is a word you and I need to hear time and time again. We live in a world of shifting sand. Our situation is like the young man who was taking an exam.

"Ken," the teacher asked him during an exam, "how close are you to the right answer?"

"About two seats," Ken replied.

We laugh, but deep down we wonder if we are becoming a society of cheaters. We are people who prefer the easy way. Values like honesty and fidelity that use to be fixed are now sliding into the pit of relativity. It may be that the biggest challenge we face as a society, more than our fading economy or the threat of terrorism, is our loss of personal and corporate integrity.

Allen C. Emery was a successful businessman and committed churchman. He credits his father for his values.

Once his father lost a pair of expensive binoculars. He filed an insurance claim and received a considerable amount of compensation for his loss. Later he found the binoculars. Immediately he wrote the insurance company and returned the money—much to the surprise of the executives at the insurance company. They informed him that not many people have that kind of integrity. This made an impact on his son.

In his book A Turtle on a Fencepost, Emery writes, "Today I find myself still asking, 'What would daddy do?' when confronted with those decisions in business and in life that are so often not black and white, but gray. I am in debt to the memory-making efforts that my father made to imprint indelibly upon my mind the meaning of integrity." (4)

What values are your children learning? Are you helping them build on a solid foundation? Do they see a commitment to integrity and right living on your part? "Everyone who hears these words of mine," our Savior said, "and puts them into practice is like a wise man who built his house on the rock . . ."

In a sense, all of society depends on people who put Christ's teaching into practice. Society needs people who can be depended on. Our church needs people who can be depended on. Little children need parents who can be depended on. We need people who not only hear the Word, but people who live by that Word.

Dr. Wesley Shotwell tells a wonderful story about a U.S. Naval Academy graduate named Charles Plumb. Plumb was a jetfighter pilot in Vietnam. After 75 combat missions, Plumb's plane was shot down by a surface-to-air missile. Plumb ejected and parachuted into enemy hands. He was captured, and then spent six years in a Communist prison. He survived that ordeal, and then began to lecture about lessons he learned from that experience.

One day, Plumb and his wife were sitting in a restaurant and a man at another table came up and said, "You're Charles Plumb! You flew jetfighters in Vietnam from the aircraft carrier Kitty Hawk, You were shot down!"

"How in the world do you know that?" asked Plumb.

"I packed your parachute," the man replied.

Plumb was surprised and thankful. The man pumped his hand and said, "I guess it worked!"

Plumb assured him, "It sure did. If your chute hadn't worked I wouldn't be here today."

Plumb couldn't sleep that night thinking about that man. He says, "I kept wondering what he might have looked like it [in] uniform. I wondered how many times I might have seen him and not even said "good morning" or anything else, because you see, I was a fighter pilot, and he was just a mere sailor."

He thought about the many hours that sailor had spent on a long wooden table in the bowels of the ship unseen by everyone carefully weaving the shrouds and folding the silks of each chute, holding in his hands the fate of someone he did not know. That lowly sailor was unseen and unsung, and yet, because he did his job men lived who would have otherwise died. What would have happened if that lowly sailor had decided that he didn't want to do his job anymore? What if he said, "If I can't be a fighter pilot then I just won't do anything?" It would have been a disaster . . . (5)

You see, it doesn't matter if you are a fighter pilot or a lowly sailor packing parachutes, the question is, are you doing it with integrity? Are you faithful in your task? Are you living according to the teachings of Jesus? If so, then all of us are better for it. "Everyone who hears these words of mine," Jesus said, "and puts them into practice is like a wise man who built his house on the rock . . ."

What kind of foundation are you building for your life and for those you love? Fill yourself up with God's Word, then put that Word into action.

1. (Nashville: Dimensions for Living, 1993).
2. Norman Vincent Peale, The Amazing Results of Positive Thinking (Englewood Cliffs, N.J.: Prentice-Hall, Inc. 1959), p. 10. Cited in J. B. Fowler, Jr., Illustrating Great Words Of The New Testament (Nashville: Broadman Press, 1991).
3. Jack Canfield and Mark Victor Hansen, Chicken Soup for The Christian Soul 101 Stories to Open the Heart and Rekindle the Spirit (Deerfield Beach, FL: Health Communications, Inc, 1997), pp. 305-306.
4. (Waco: Word Books, 1979).
5. http://www.ashcreekbaptistchurch.com/sermons/allonebody.pdf.

The Case Of The Dancing Men
Psalm 51:1-17

Some of you may be fans of the PBS show, Mystery. Pastor Richard Slater tells about a scene in one of those PBS presentations, a Sherlock Holmes mystery, "The Case of the Dancing Men." As the story opens, a young woman is gathering flowers in her garden. Suddenly, her face is transformed into terror by something she sees. She drops her basket of flowers and runs panic stricken toward her home. Once inside, she bolts the windows and doors, draws the drapes tight, and falls sobbing and trembling into a chair. Her alarmed husband and maid both rush to her aid. She is both unable and unwilling to tell them what has frightened her so.

A long time passes before she is finally able to take her husband to the garden and show him the cause of her terror. Someone has painted small figures of dancing men on the wall of her garden. These dancing men are symbols of a troubled past that she has tried to forget. From this moment on, she walks about half dazed, with terror always lurking in her eyes. She could not leave her past behind. (1)

David, King of Israel, had an experience that struck terror into his heart. It wasn't a painting on a wall that awakened the past for him. Rather it was a simple story told to him by the prophet Nathan. "There were two men in a certain town," Nathan began, "one rich and the other poor." The rich man had an immense herd of sheep and cattle, but the poor man had nothing except one small lamb. The poor man raised the lamb as a pet. It grew up with his children. It shared his food, drank from his cup and even slept in his arms. It was like a daughter to him.

Now a traveler came to visit the rich man. The rich man was obligated to provide a meal for his visitor. However, instead taking one of his own sheep or cattle to sacrifice for the meal, he took the small lamb that belonged to the poor man, slaughtered it and had it prepared for his visitor.

When Nathan finished his story, David was filled with righteous indignation toward the rich man and said to Nathan, "As surely as the Lord lives, the man who did this deserves to die! He must pay for that lamb four times over, because he did such a thing and had no pity."

Then Nathan said to David, "You are the man! . . . You struck down Uriah the Hittite with the sword and took his wife to be your own." (2 Samuel 12: 1-9)

It's one of the most powerful scenes in all of literature. "You are the man!"

David had sinned. He knew it. The entire nation knew it. The prophet Nathan confronted him with it. Adulterer. Murderer. David had abused his power as the divinely appointed ruler of his nation. A man after God's own heart, but he had failed God and he had failed his nation. Ultimately he had failed himself. In the quiet of the night, the guilt and the shame weighed heavily upon him, and he began to pray. We have his words in Psalm 51, "Have mercy on me, O God, according to your unfailing love; according to your great compassion blot out my transgressions. Wash away all my iniquity and cleanse me from my sin. For I know my transgressions, and my sin is always before me. Against you, you only, have I sinned and done what is evil in your sight . . ."

As you and I come to this sacred place on this special night, we probably do not feel the weight of our sins like David did. That is not because we have not sinned. It's just that as a culture we have developed a highly effective ability to rationalize and justify our behavior. We don't even use the word sin anymore. We "make mistakes." We "mess up." We shrug our shoulders and declare, "Oh, well, nobody's perfect"—as if somehow that is an acceptable excuse for our misdeeds. Something has happened to us as a people that has caused us to shrug off responsibility for doing wrong.

The story's told about a man who visited Niagara Falls. As part of his excursion he traveled down into "the cave of the winds." This is a place behind the falls where you can look out on the tumbling waters. The noise is deafening.

This man asked the guide how he stood such noise.

The guide replied. "I never hear it."

"What do you mean?" asked the visitor.

The guide said, "When I first started to work here I couldn't stand the noise, but now I am used to it and I never hear it."

We're like that with regard to much of the sinfulness of our culture. We've acclimated ourselves to it. Behaviors that used to bother us, we now accept.

David had sinned and he knew it. The guilt lay heavily upon him.

David was not only sorry for his sins, but he was determined to change. He prays that God will not only forgive him, but also make him a new person. He prays, "Cleanse me with hyssop, and I will be clean; wash me, and I will be whiter than snow . . . Hide your face from my sins and blot out all my iniquity." Then he adds some of the most beautiful words in scripture: "Create in me a pure heart, O God, and renew a steadfast spirit within me. Do not cast me from your presence or take your Holy Spirit from me. Restore to me the joy of your salvation and grant me a willing spirit, to sustain me."

David knew that he could not achieve the kind of change he needed on his own. Only by the grace and love of God could he really become the kind of man his family and his nation needed—the kind of man God intended him to be.

A conference on comparative religions was held in Great Britain. One of the questions being debated was the uniqueness of the Christian faith. One expert said that what makes Christianity unique is the incarnation: "The Word became flesh and dwelt among us." (John 1:14) But someone pointed out that other religions also claim that their gods visited earth in human form. Another expert said the resurrection made Christianity unique. But again, other great religious figures are said to have returned from the dead.

The debate was raging on when the great Christian writer C. S. Lewis entered the room. When he learned that they were discussing the unique contribution of Christianity to world religions, Lewis responded, "Oh, that's easy. It's grace." Grace—God's unconditional love for human beings. After some discussion, everyone had to agree. (2)

David was heartsick over his sin and he wanted to change. "Create in me a pure heart, O God . . ." He knew that his only hope was God's grace. Fortunately, David was a recipient of God's grace.

David experienced God's grace and became Israel's greatest king. This did not mean that David escaped the consequences of his misdoing. David's family life is one tragedy after another following his sin with Bathsheba. He paid for his sin for the rest of his life. We cannot sow wild oats, to use the old expression, and pray for a crop failure. There are consequences every time we break God's laws. But there is also forgiveness and the opportunity to make a new beginning. God's grace does not depend on our actions, but God's action in Jesus Christ who died that we might live. God's grace grows out of God's unconditional love for every one of us.

Jerry Jenkins wrote a bizarre true story many years ago about a man awakened in the middle of the night by a phone call. He was groggy. The girl on the other end was weeping. "Daddy," she said, "I'm pregnant." Though stunned beyond belief, he forgave her and prayed with her. The next day he and his wife wrote her two letters of counsel and love. Three days later the man received another phone call. His daughter was shocked by the letters. She was not the one who had called earlier . . . Apparently some other girl had dialed a wrong number.

However, his daughter was overwhelmed by her father's letters. "These letters are my treasure," she said later. [These are] "real love letters written by a godly father who never imagined he would have to write them to his own daughter."

Here are some of the things her father said in those letters when he thought his daughter was pregnant out of wedlock:

"Part of me seemed to die last night. Not because of what it means to me as much as what it means to you. You were free to make all kinds of choices. Now you are shut up to a few, and none of them to your liking. But God will see you—and us—through.

"Though I weep inside, I can't condemn you, because I sin too. Your transgression here is no worse than mine. It's just different. Even if my heart did not shout out to love and defend and protect you—as it does—the New Testament tells me I can't take forgiveness myself and withhold it from others.

"We think of sin as acts. But sin is a package, an attitude that expresses itself in different ways and to different degrees. But it all comes from the same sin package you inherited through us. Christ is the only difference.

"God forgives this sin as well as others—really forgives and cleanses. David was a man of God when he went into his experience with Bathsheba and in the grace of God he came out a man of God. And his sin included murder!

"Satan has no doubt tried to tell you that this affects your standing before God. It doesn't, but it will affect your relationship till you bring the whole matter to Him. There will be a coolness, a separation, an estrangement, until you open the problem by confessing and asking forgiveness.

"I will not reproach you or [your boyfriend]. I will not even dare to look down at you in my innermost heart, but it is not because the issue doesn't matter. The responsibility is his no less than yours. This is not an ideal basis for marriage. You want a husband who takes you by choice. But if you face the issue and God so leads, He could build a solid marriage. We stand ready to do whatever we can.

"We're praying much. We love you more than I can say. And respect you, too, as always.

"Saturday I was very downcast. I tried to sing as I worked outside, and then, increasingly, I seemed to see a calm and loving face I knew was Jesus. It was no vision—I didn't see details—but it was a strong reminder that He is with us and waiting for us to remember this. He loves us and will help us through, especially you. It's great to know Jesus is walking with you.

"While we can't say that God causes failures, He does permit them, and I think it's clear He uses them to build character and beauty that we'd never have without them. Remember, God's love is in even this, maybe especially in this.

"We're glad that in a measure, at least, we can help the daughter we love so much. This is a day of testing, but hold our ground we must. God will give us the victory. That's wonderful. We're looking forward to your being at home. Love, Dad." (3)

Friends, that's grace. David experienced that grace and so may we. Do you carry around a secret sin in your heart? I hope you don't have to have your own "dancing men" experience before you bring that secret to God. He loves. He forgives. Come, experience God's grace this night.

[Tonight the symbol we will leave here with will not be a drawing of a dancing man reminding us of our sin. Rather we will leave with a cross marked on our forehead as a reminder of God's grace. We wear this mark not as a sign of our superiority but as a mark of humility and thanksgiving for what God has done for us. Thanks be to God for His unconditional acceptance of sinners like you and me.]

1. http://www.fccleb.org/sermons/Slater.4.20.03.html.
2. I'm sorry. I have misplaced the source of this illustration.
3. Jerry B. Jenkins, "Treasure By Mistake," Moody Magazine, September 1991, 6. Cited at http://www.joshfranklin.org/2/post/2013/12/a-treasure-by-mistake.html.

The Garden Of Temptation
Genesis 3:1-7; Romans 5:12-19; Matthew 4:1-11

A woman tells of joining a weight-loss organization. At one meeting the instructor held up an apple and a candy bar.

"What are the attributes of this apple," she asked, "and how do they relate to our diet?"

Among the answers that came from the group: "Low in calories" and "lots of fiber."

She then detailed what was wrong with eating candy, and concluded, "Apples are not only more healthful but also less expensive. Do you know I paid seventy-five cents for this candy bar?"

The group stared as she held aloft the forbidden treat. From the back of the room a small voice spoke up, "I'll give you a dollar for it."

That's human nature, isn't it? To prefer the candy bar to the apple? Of course, some say it was the apple that got us in trouble in the first place.

It's one of the world's best-known stories. Everything in the garden was beautiful and good. Adam and Eve were forbidden only one thing. There was a tree in the center of the garden—the tree of the knowledge of good and evil. The scriptures do not say it was an apple tree, but it doesn't hurt to visualize the forbidden fruit as a big, juicy Golden Delicious. God told Adam and Eve that they could eat the fruit of any tree in the garden except that one. Of course, you know what people are like. Mark Twain once said that God's mistake was not making the snake forbidden—for then Adam would have eaten it.

But one day Eve is walking in the garden. And she sees the forbidden fruit and, at the urging of the serpent, she takes one little bite. And then, to compound her error, she gave a bite to Adam. And so Eve has been blamed since time immemorial for leading Adam into sin.

But note how the story reads: "When the woman saw that the fruit of the tree was good for food and pleasing to the eye, and also desirable for gaining wisdom, she took some and ate it. She also gave some to her husband, who was with her, and he ate it." (Gen. 3:6, emphasis added).

Adam was with Eve when she ate the forbidden fruit. Bear in mind that Eve was not present when God told Adam not to eat of the Tree of Knowledge of Good and Evil. Yet, when the serpent tempts Eve, Adam does not speak up. But that's not all. He remains silent and then watches Eve as she takes the forbidden fruit and eats it. Remember that God told them they would die if they ate the forbidden fruit. Only after Adam sees that Eve is still alive does he take some from her and eat himself. What a man. Instead of loving his wife, Adam uses her as a guinea pig to test God's command.

So, Adam was at least an accessory to the crime. When God confronts Adam about his misdeed, Adam, being a typical husband, tries to put the blame on Eve, but God knows better. They both violated God's command, and now they must pay.

Nancy Leigh DeMoss has this to say about this first couple's sin: "When we find something we like at the store, one of the first things we do is look at the price tag . . . Wouldn't it be nice . . . if we understood the cost of sin right up front? If the forbidden fruit had been rotten and crawling with worms, do you think Eve would have taken any? But Genesis tells us, 'When the woman saw that the fruit of the tree was good for food and pleasing to the eye, and also desirable for gaining wisdom, she took some and ate it.' She acted on her immediate desires without looking at the price tag." (1)

That's the most common error people make. Would any young person experiment with drugs or alcohol if they could see where the journey may end? Would any spouse be unfaithful to his or her mate if the heartache and pain were evident up front?

Adam and Eve ate of the forbidden fruit.

The first casualty of Adam and Eve's misdoing is loss of innocence. The Bible tells us the eyes of both of them were opened, and they knew that they were naked. They sewed fig leaves together and made themselves loincloths.

Joey Adams quipped, "They argued over who would wear the plants in the family." The innocent Adam and Eve discover what it means to be naked. Exposed. Ashamed.

And with the loss of innocence came a loss of intimacy. Nothing would ever be the same for this couple, and subsequently for all people. We simply cannot overemphasize the brokenness that comes into human relations from this day forward—particularly with regard to family life.

Consider, for example, relationships between siblings in the book of Genesis alone: Cain versus Abel, Isaac versus Ishmael, Esau versus Jacob, Joseph versus his brothers—every one of these stories is a disaster! In a fallen world, people are estranged from one another—husbands are estranged from their wives, parents are estranged from their children, neighbors are estranged from one another.

In his bestselling book titled Blink, author Malcolm Gladwell tells the story of something that happened on the night of February 3, 1999. A 22-year-old black immigrant from Guinea was standing in the doorway of his South Bronx apartment when four plainclothes policemen, all white, drove up. These policemen dressed in civilian clothes jumped out of their vehicle and approached the man with their weapons drawn asking for a word with him. The man matched the description of a serial rapist that had been active in the neighborhood a year earlier.

The immigrant, meanwhile, knew someone who had recently been robbed by a group of armed men. He was terrified: there he was in the middle of a bad neighborhood after midnight and some very large men were striding toward him. The immigrant panicked and ran up the stairs toward his apartment and reached for the doorknob, while, the officers would testify later, turning his body sideways and digging into his pocket for something. Then the immigrant, who spoke very little English, pulled a black object from his pocket and pointed it toward the officers in the dim light of the stairwell. You can probably guess the rest of the story. Forty-two gunshots later the officers found themselves leaning over the immigrant's bullet riddled body. They found the object that was in his hand was his wallet which he was trying to show them. (2)

That's the way things are in a fallen world. It simply cannot be exaggerated how much the loss of innocence and intimacy cost humankind.

Ignoring God's command changes everything in Adam and Eve's life. Even the serpent is caught up in the aftermath of their misdeed. God decrees that it will crawl on its belly and eat dust all the days of its life.

The serpent pays for its crime. And Adam and Eve pay for their crimes. To Eve, God says, "I will greatly increase your pains in childbearing; with pain you will give birth to children. Your desire will be for your husband, and he will rule over you."

Here's an interesting question for you to ponder: Are these truly curses which God placed upon the woman or are these merely a description of how life will be in a fallen world? For example, suppose modern science were to eliminate all pain in childbirth? Would that mean that we have eliminated God's curse?

And how about women's subjection to men? Is that a curse or is it simply a description of the way things are in a fallen world?

Actually, this question is academic because Christ has removed the curse from Eve, as well as from all humanity. St. Paul, not exactly regarded as a feminist, writes in Galatians 3:28, "There is neither Jew nor Greek, slave nor free, male nor female, for you are all one in Christ Jesus." So, women, if you are living in subjection to your husband, don't say this is the biblical way to live. Christ removed that burden from your shoulders. According to this ancient story, Eve paid a high price for her disobedience.

Adam paid, too. To Adam, God says, "Cursed is the ground because of you; through painful toil you will eat of it all the days of your life. It will produce thorns and thistles for you, and you will eat the plants of the field. By the sweat of your brow you will eat your food until you return to the ground, since from it you were taken; for dust you are and to dust you will return."

Notice that it is not the man who is cursed, but the ground. Man already had been given dominion over the garden. He was already responsible for its upkeep. But now it will no longer be a joy to maintain. The loss of intimacy not only extended to Eve, but even to the earth from which Adam had come. Now life would be "toil."

The Hebrew word for toil is the same word as that used for the pain that the woman will experience in childbearing.

Here again, is this a curse or a description? Many men love their work, as do many women. Other things are actually much more like the pain of childbirth than going to the office each day. (Then again—I don't know your boss.)

There is a fourth punishment, the most deadly of them all, which is visited on both Adam and Eve. They are banished from the Garden of Eden: "So the Lord God banished him from the Garden of Eden to work the ground from which he had been taken. After he drove the man out, he placed on the east side of the Garden of Eden cherubim and a flaming sword flashing back and forth to guard the way to the tree of life." (Gen. 3:24)

And that's where many people live today—East of Eden, in a state of brokenness, estrangement and shame. None of this was God's original intent. Don't blame God for broken homes, broken bodies, broken neighborhoods and a broken world. This is the result of humanity expressing its free will.

Why did Adam and Eve disobey God? Well, why do you and I disobey God? There's something within us that is in rebellion. Why did the first man and woman sin? Why do you and I sin?

Well, somebody says, "The devil made me do it." Wrong answer, unless you are Flip Wilson's "Geraldine." Remember that time-honored routine.

Geraldine's husband asks, "Why did you buy the new dress?"

"Well, honey, the devil made me do it."

"Didn't you say, 'Get thee behind me Satan?'"

"Yeah, but he said it looked good in back, too."

Bad theology. All throughout scripture we see that the devil does one thing. He tempts. You and I make the choice whether to give in or not. So, don't blame the devil. You and I are responsible for our own actions.

A better question is, did God know that Adam and Eve would sin? And the answer would have to be yes, God knew. God gives us freedom, but God knows our hearts. If God did not give us freedom and allow us to experience the consequences of that freedom, we would remain forever infantile. Freedom and failure seem to be essential to emotional and spiritual growth.

In Romans 5 we find the best explanation that I know of for why God created a world in which the possibility of sin exists: Paul says that "suffering produces endurance, and endurance produces character, and character produces hope, and hope does not disappoint us." In other words, God wants to build people of character, people suitable to inhabit eternity with God, and that is why God gives us freedom—even the freedom to disobey.

It is significant that God put an angel with a flaming sword at the entrance to the Garden of Eden. This is the Bible's way of saying that never again on this earth will people live in a perfect paradise. Never again on this earth will people live in perfect innocence and intimacy. We had our chance, and we blew it.

But wait, there is hope. That is what the Gospel is all about. There are three gardens of note in scripture. One, of course, is Eden, where humanity first cried out, "Not your will, but mine be done."

The second is Gethsemane, where a lonely figure cries out, "Not my will but thine be done." Later, on a hill nearby, Jesus hangs on a cross. And like the original Adam, he is naked but not ashamed. He is suffering on our behalf so that the curse of death may be removed. St. Paul put it like this in today's epistle: "For if the many died by the trespass of the one man, how much more did God's grace and the gift that came by the grace of the one man, Jesus Christ, overflow to the many . . . just as the result of one trespass was condemnation for all men, so also the result of one act of righteousness was justification that brings life for all men. For just as through the disobedience of the one man the many were made sinners, so also through the obedience of the one man the many will be made righteous."

In other words, through one man, Adam, sin entered the world. However, through another solitary individual, Jesus of Nazareth, came victory over sin and death. Jesus faced the Tempter in the wilderness and did not sin. But, on the cross, he gave himself as a sin offering for us all.

There is a final garden of importance to us. It is at end of the Bible, in the very last chapter of Revelation: "Then the angel showed me the river of the water of life, as clear as crystal, flowing from the throne of God and of the Lamb down the middle of the great street of the city. On each side of the river stood the tree of life, bearing twelve crops of fruit, yielding its fruit every month. And the leaves of the tree are for the healing of the nations. No longer will there be any curse. The throne of God and of the Lamb will be in the city, and his servants will serve him."

In Christ, the curse of death has been removed. Christ has made it possible for innocence and intimacy to be restored. The tree of the knowledge of good and evil will one day be transformed into the tree of life.

And that is our hope. This broken world is not God's final word because one man kneeled in a garden and prayed, "Not my will, but thine be done," then he allowed himself to be sacrificed upon a cruel cross. But that is all it took, and sin and death no longer had dominion over us. Thanks be to God for God's great gift in Jesus Christ.

1. Found on the Internet. Source unknown.
2. Dr. Steve Jackson, http://www.newsongweb.org/Sermons/2006%20Sermons/11-12-06.htm.

This sermon was adapted from King Duncan's book, The Great . . . and Not So Great . . . Love Stories of the Bible.

Leaving Home
Genesis 12:1-4a

There was an article about two Irishmen who set up a company in order to sell dirt—genuine Irish dirt—to Americans. The two men say the demand for this "official Irish dirt" has been phenomenal. They sold one million dollars worth of their product in a very short time. One elderly New York businessman placed a $100,000 order so he could be fully buried in genuine Irish soil. (1) Obviously that gentleman was very, very homesick. His body was in the US, but his heart was still in his homeland.

That happens to many people who are transplanted to another culture. You miss the sights and sounds and perhaps even the dirt of home.

A woman named Janet Ross, a native of Texas, joined her Navy husband on his tour of duty in Japan. The first thing Janet did was look for a job to supplement their income.

She was pleased when her first interview netted a secretarial position at the nearby Army facility. She was sure her typing skills had landed her the post. But a few weeks later her boss, a full colonel, called her into his office. He proceeded to admonish her that she was too quiet. "The reason I hired you," he explained, "was your delightful Texas accent. I'm homesick for someone who can talk right." (2)

Well, not everybody agrees that Texans "talk right," but if you've ever lived in a culture other than your own, you understand. We have an expression, don't we, that says it all? "There's no place like home."

Author Max Lucado tells about a parakeet in Green Bay, Wisconsin named Pootsie that evidently suffered from homesickness. Pootsie escaped from her owner and came into the keeping of the humane society of Green Bay. When no one else claimed Pootsie, a woman named Sue Gleason did. Sue and Pootsie hit it off. They talked and even bathed together, becoming fast friends.

But one day the little bird did something incredible. It flew over to Mrs. Gleason, put its beak in Sue's ear, and whispered, "Fifteen hundred South Oneida Street, Green Bay."

Gleason was dumbfounded. She researched and found that the address which Pootsie recited actually did exist. She went to the house and found a seventy-nine-year-old man named John Stroobants.

"Do you have a parakeet?" she asked.

"I used to," said the elderly gentleman. "I miss him terribly."

When he saw his Pootsie, he was thrilled. "You know," he said with delight, "Pootsie even knows his phone number." (3)

That sounds far-fetched to many of us, but there is something about home.

We often describe our country as being very mobile, but did you realize that fifty per cent of Americans live within 50 miles of their birthplace? Most people, given a choice, like to stay anchored close to home. Not everybody, of course, but most people are more comfortable in familiar surroundings.

For many of us, home gives us a sense of identity. Janet Ross may have gone to Japan to be with her Navy husband, but in a sense she was still a Texan. People move to this country, but at heart they are still Italian, Irish, Scottish, African. They move to another state but they're still Hoosiers, Gators, Yanks.

This is why sports teams have such a following. People define themselves as Southern Californian Trojans or Tennessee Volunteers or Minnesota Golden Gophers. This explains why people can be so fanatical about their sports team. This is part of who they are.

The Associated Press carried an article about a dentist in North Canton, Ohio who came up with a way for sports fans to show off their loyalty to their the home team. When he fits his patients with a porcelain crown, they can have it decorated with their favorite athletic team's logo.

One Cleveland Indians fan had a crown with Chief Wahoo placed over a lower left molar. For those of you who aren't baseball fans, Chief Wahoo is the Indians' team symbol.

The dentist, Dr. Fred Scott, said he normally puts the logos on lower back molars, where it doesn't show when people smile.

A decoration can add $50 to $100 to the cost of a crown. One of Scott's dental designs was for his son, John. "John is studying mortuary science in school," Scott said. "He wants a casket [on his crown]."

Well, it takes all kinds, but many people like to carry home with them. Home gives us our identity. We have deep emotional ties there.

Bishop William Willimon tells about a man who was in a Japanese prisoner of war camp during World War II. It was a place of unbearable torture and degradation. The prisoners were treated horribly.

One of the prisoners, a man from Illinois, would sometimes hum songs to himself as the prisoners were being led out to the fields to work each day. Walking along in the sweltering heat, miserable, unfed, unwashed, he often hummed "America, the Beautiful." The Japanese guards did not know the tune, so the song meant nothing to them. But to the prisoners, the tune, evoking the "amber waves of grain" and "the purple mountain majesties," reminded them of home. This simple tune filled them with hope and courage. Soon, the whole camp was humming the tune each day on the way out to work. The guards seemed oblivious to the revolutionary significance of this defiant gesture. (4)

Many people get homesick when they are far from home. Sir Walter Scott said: "Breathes there the man with soul so dead / who never to himself hath said, / 'This is my own, My native land.' / Whose heart hath n'er within him burned, / as home, his footsteps he has turned / from wandering on a foreign strand."

Our story from the book of Genesis is about a couple who were called to leave home. Their names were Abram and Sarai. We know them, of course, as Abraham and Sarah.

More than 1,700 years before the time of Jesus, God came to Abram and gave him a command and a promise: "Go from your country and your kindred and your father's house to the land that I will show you. I will make of you a great nation, and I will bless you, and make your name great, so that you will be a blessing. I will bless those who bless you, and the one who curses you I will curse; and in you all the families of the earth shall be blessed."

Abram was a wealthy landowner living in Ur, in Mesopotamia, in the north of what is now Iraq. He had family, friends, an honored place in the community. This was no small demand that God was laying on him.

It certainly could not have been easy for Sarai, his wife, either. Sometimes moving is more difficult for the spouse, or for the children, than it is for the one who has been called to leave to go to a new place.

A Philadelphia schoolteacher tells about a fourth grader who came to her and said, "Miss, I won't be coming back to this school anymore. I don't know where I'm going. But I won't be coming back here. And this is my dolly; I'm going to give her to you because I know that you will give her a wonderful home." (5)

Children sometimes understand things in a way that adults never can.

It's not an easy thing to leave home. Home is where the heart is, says the old platitude. And it is true. God told Abram to leave his home. That must have been difficult for both Abram and Sarai.

However, God spoke and Abram obeyed. It is one of the most important statements in all sacred literature: "So Abram went, as the Lord had told him . . ."

It would be impossible to overstate the significance of Abram's step of faith for the subsequent history of the world. Three great world religions—Judaism, Christianity and Islam trace—their roots back to Abram's act of obedience. "So Abram went, as the Lord had told him . . ."

This, by the way, is what faith is. God speaks, we obey. We don't say, "I've got to bury my father"; we don't say, "I can't afford it"; we don't say, "My friends in Sunday School won't approve." God speaks. We obey. Faith is much, much more than belief. Jesus said even the demons believe. Faith is action. Faith is obedience to God.

When Hitler and the Nazi Party took control of Germany in the 1930s, many German Christians refused to cooperate. One of these was Martin Niemoeller, a Lutheran pastor. He was put in prison for his disobedience.

Someone said to his father, "Mr. Niemoeller, it must be a terrible thing to have your son put in prison by the Nazis."

Mr. Niemoeller answered, "Yes, but it would be a much more terrible thing if

God wanted someone to do it and my Martin was not willing." (6)

We really should talk more about the cost of committing ourselves to Jesus. So many people today think they can follow Jesus and it not make any difference in the way they live their lives. That's absurd.

At a meeting of the Fellowship of Christian Athletes years ago, Bobby Richardson, former New York Yankee second baseman, offered a prayer that says it all: "Dear God, Your will, nothing more, nothing less, nothing else. Amen."

God told Abram to leave his home and go to a new country. God spoke and Abram obeyed. And God made Abram a promise: "I will make of you a great nation, and I will bless you, and make your name great, so that you will be a blessing. I will bless those who bless you, and the one who curses you I will curse; and in you all the families of the earth shall be blessed." God and Abram enter a covenant relationship. Abram and his descendants sometimes forgot their part in that covenant, but God never forgets His.

Some of you will remember when Roger Staubach was the quarterback of the Dallas Cowboys. He helped bring Dallas an NFL championship in 1971.

Staubach admitted that his position as a quarterback who didn't call his own plays was a source of trial. Coach Tom Landry sent in every play. He told Roger when to pass, when to run and only in emergency situations could he change the play (and he had better be right!). Even though Roger considered coach Landry a "genius" when it came to football strategy, pride said that he should be able to run his own team. Roger later said, "I faced up to the issue of obedience. Once I learned to obey there was harmony, fulfillment, and victory." (7)

Abram obeyed God and God fulfilled His promise to make of Abram a great nation. But one thing more needs to be said. God called Abram to be a blessing to others. Whenever Abram's descendants—whether they be Jews, Muslims or Christians—cease to be a blessing to others, they are ultimately disobedient to God.

Now we have to be careful. This thing of being obedient to God can be tragically abused. There are people who have done terrible things in this world and they have explained it like this: God told me to do it. Friends, mark this down and never forget it: If you hear a voice and it tells you to do something hateful, something violent, something that brings pain to others—that is not the voice of God. That is the voice of Satan. God calls us to be a blessing—to our family, to our neighbors, to the world as a whole. As St. Paul writes in II Corinthians 5:19, "God was reconciling the world to himself in Christ . . . And he has committed to us the message of reconciliation." That's who we are and what we are about: God has blessed us and we are to be a blessing to others.

A story from Yugoslavia tells of four angels who witnessed creation.

The first angel observed God's handiwork in awe and said: "Lord, your creation is beautiful! How did you do it?" That's the worldview of a scientist.

The second angel observed in awe and said: "Lord, your creation is beautiful! Why did you do it?" That's the worldview of a philosopher.

The third angel observed in awe and said: "Lord, your creation is beautiful! Can I have it?" That's the worldview of a materialist.

Finally, the fourth angel observed in awe and said: "Lord, your creation is beautiful! Can I help?" That's the worldview of God's faithful. (8)

That is the kind of obedience that God honors. God told Abram to leave his home and God made Abram a promise and an assignment—that he would be blessed and that he would be a blessing. May we be blessed and may we be a blessing to others as well.

1. Ananova (10-30-06) http://www.ananova.com
2. "Humor In Uniform."
3. Traveling Light (Nashville: W Publishing Group 2001), p. 153.
4. http://www.chapel.duke.edu/worship/sunday/viewsermon.aspx?id=70.
5. William H. Cosby Jr. and Alvin F. Poussaint, MD, Come On, People (Nashville: Thomas Nelson, 2007), p. 91.
6. Karl D. Babb, editor, Adult Life And Work Lesson Annual 1993-94, (Nashville: Convention Press, 1993).
7. Keith Buice, http://www.sermoncentral.com/sermon.asp?SermonID=87020&ContributorID=13996.
8. Windows to Truth, April/May/June 1992). Cited in James W. Moore, Some Things Are Too Good Not To Be True (Nashville: Dimensions for Living, 1994).

The Evangelist Has A Shady Past
John 4:5-42

After listening to a prominent evangelist on the radio, eight-year-old Debbie asked her six-year-old brother David, "Do you know about Jesus?"

Expecting a new slant on the old story, David replied, "No."

Sister said, "Sit still because this is really scary." After explaining the gospel as only an eight-year-old could, she popped the question.

"Now, David, when you die, do you want to go to heaven to be with Jesus, God, your Mommy and Daddy, and big sister, or do you want to go to the lake of fire to be with the Devil and bank robbers?"

David thought a moment, then replied, "I want to stay right here." (1)

Sounds like a smart little fellow. Maybe little Debbie was not the ideal evangelist. But her heart was in the right place. It's a wonderful thing to help people find Jesus.

The highly esteemed theologian Karl Barth had a painting of the crucifixion on the wall of his study that was painted by the artist Matthias Grunewald. In the painting there is an image of John the Baptist. The artist portrayed John the Baptist pointing his finger to the cross of Jesus in the center of the painting. It's said that when Barth would talk with a visitor about his work, he would direct them to John the Baptist in the painting, and he would say, "I want to be that finger." Barth wanted to point people to Christ. (2)

Pointing people to Christ is our most important task as his people. This is properly referred to as evangelism, sharing with others the love of Jesus Christ.

German evangelist Reinhard Bonnke says this about sharing the gospel: "I actually believe with all of my heart that the ministry of evangelism is the most important [ministry] of all because [God] is out to rescue the perishing and to save the drowning. This is the heart of God. Salvation cost Him everything—His only begotten Son.

"When God created the world, He didn't sweat—not one drop of perspiration. But God was sweating blood at the cross. That's what it cost Him to save us. That's not a small thing. So proclaiming the cross is not a side thought, an afterthought. It's not on the back burner; it must be the front burner . . ."

Rev. Bonnke is right. Christ calls his followers to be evangelists. Today's message is about one of the most effective evangelists who ever lived. But this evangelist had a shady past.

Now, when I say "a shady past," some of you who are over 40 may have a picture in your mind of Sinclair Lewis' Elmer Gantry, or of Jimmy Swaggart or Jim Bakker or some other well-known modern evangelist with a blemished past. Modern TV evangelism is more like show business than it is about church. As such it often draws personalities with enormous egos who may start out with good intentions, but sometimes falter along the way.

And it is not always sex that is their weakness as some of you might think. Some of our best known religious figures have been snared by another deadly temptress— greed—materialism—mammon. "God has blessed them really good," in their own eyes. And God wants their followers to keep supporting them in the manner to which they have grown accustomed. If they do, say these slick performers—God will give them every good thing. They conveniently forget Jesus' words, "You cannot serve God and mammon."

But nobody's ever thrown out of a pulpit for greed, unless outright fraud can be proved. But sex is an issue that gets people's attention. So sexual sin can stain a religious figure forever. It may be unfair, but it is true.

And thus we come to today's evangelist with the shady past. Her sin was sexual. She was a woman of questionable reputation. But rather than detracting from her role as an evangelist, it actually enhanced it. Because people who knew her could see the change that Jesus had made in her life. They knew that her testimony rang true. She is best known to us, of course, as the woman at the well.

Our story takes place in a Samaritan town called Sychar, near the plot of ground Jacob gave to his son Joseph. Jacob's well was there, and Jesus, tired as he was from the journey, sat down by the well. It was about the sixth hour.

His disciples had gone into the town to buy food. A Samaritan woman came to draw water. Jesus asked her, "Will you give me a drink?"

The Samaritan woman said to him, "You are a Jew and I am a Samaritan woman. How can you ask me for a drink?" For Jews do not associate with Samaritans. And righteous Jewish men did not speak to women they did not know.

Jesus answered her, "If you knew the gift of God and who it is that asks you for a drink, you would have asked him and he would have given you living water."

The woman was surprised. "Sir," she said, "you have nothing to draw with and the well is deep. Where can you get this living water? Are you greater than our father Jacob, who gave us the well and drank from it himself, as did also his sons and his flocks and herds?"

And, of course, Jesus was greater than Jacob. She simply could not realize how much greater he was.

Jesus answered, "Everyone who drinks this water will be thirsty again, but whoever drinks the water I give him will never thirst. Indeed, the water I give him will become in him a spring of water welling up to eternal life."

The woman didn't have a clue what Jesus was talking about but she was tired of carrying a heavy water jug back from the well each day. This Jew was promising her a source of water that would never cease flowing and that sounded good.

The woman said to him, "Sir, give me this water so that I won't get thirsty and have to keep coming here to draw water."

Then Jesus surprised her again. He told her, "Go, call your husband and come back."

Whoa, he hit a nerve. "I have no husband," she replied.

Jesus said to her, "You are right when you say you have no husband. The fact is, you have had five husbands, and the man you now have is not your husband. What you have just said is quite true."

Do you understand that biblical people are really not any different than people today? You and I know couples who are cohabitating without the benefit of wedlock. Does it surprise you that they did so in Jesus' time as well?

The woman was impressed. "Sir," she said, "I can see that you are a prophet. Our fathers worshiped on this mountain, but you Jews claim that the place where we must worship is in Jerusalem."

Jesus declared, "Believe me, woman, a time is coming when you will worship the Father neither on this mountain nor in Jerusalem. You Samaritans worship what you do not know; we worship what we do know, for salvation is from the Jews. Yet a time is coming and has now come when the true worshipers will worship the Father in spirit and truth, for they are the kind of worshipers the Father seeks. God is spirit, and his worshipers must worship in spirit and in truth."

The woman said, "I know that Messiah is coming. When he comes, he will explain everything to us."

Then Jesus declared, "I who speak to you am he."

Just then his disciples returned and were surprised to find Jesus talking with a woman. But no one asked why he was doing this.

Then, leaving her water jar, the woman went back to the town and said to the people, "Come, see a man who told me everything I ever did. Could this be the Christ?" The people of the town made their way toward Jesus. And many of these Samaritans believed in him, says John, because of the woman's testimony. They urged him to stay with them, and he stayed two days. And because of his words many more became believers. They said to the woman, "We no longer believe just because of what you said; now we have heard for ourselves, and we know that this man really is the Savior of the world." What a wonderful story of redemption. Jesus reached out to this Samaritan woman; then she reached out to the people in her village.

One reason Jesus may have had such an effect on this woman was the respect he showed her. Arnold Prater in his book The Presence makes an interesting point. He says that in verse 21 when Jesus called this woman with a checkered past, "woman," the Greek word gune, which he used, is not a term used for scolding or contempt but is used lovingly as a term of great endearment. He says that it should be better translated as "special lady."

Think of it: this woman is a village outcast. She cannot associate with the other women. She has been divorced several times, and is now living with a man who is not her husband. Yet Jesus, seeing the possibilities in her, calls her "special lady." He used the same word for this woman that he used for his mother at the wedding in Cana and on the cross. (3)

Perhaps that is what struck this woman the most. He treated her with dignity and respect, the way we all should treat others. That is where effective evangelism begins. He treated her as a person who really mattered, and she could not wait to tell her friends.

Here is something we need to see. The most effective messengers of the Gospel are real people who have had their lives transformed.

Now, obviously, people who are phony in their witness to Christ are not going to be effective. None of us will tolerate for long someone who is an outright phony.

There was an interesting item in Harper's Magazine sometime back. It was about a popular book that was out at the time the magazine was printed. The book was titled Staying Married and Loving It. It was written by Dr. Patricia Allen and Sandra Harmon. Sounds good, doesn't it? Staying Married and Loving It. Maybe so, but consider this fact: the co-authors of this book have been married a total of five different times. (4) That happens, even with nice people, but it's not a very good testimony to the joys of matrimony.

Reader's Digest told a story a few years ago about a company that glued a tiny seed to a brochure that was advertising their product. The brochure said, "If you have the faith as a mustard seed in our product, it will produce profound results for you." Several months later, a customer wrote back saying, "You will be very interested to know that I planted your mustard seed and now I have a beautiful plant covered with tomatoes!" Obviously, it was a tomato seed, not a mustard seed. (5) Bad witness!

It's true, outright phonies will not gain a hearing for long. But I believe this truth has more general application.

Many people today are growing disenchanted with what might be termed "celebrity evangelism." Certainly, TV evangelists are no longer enjoying the following that they once did.

Some of you will remember when evangelist and faith healer Oral Roberts headed a vast TV empire. He became so famous that he became the target of comedians.

According to one joke Simon Peter knocks on the door to God's office in heaven and says, "You'll never guess who just arrived. It's the Oral Roberts."

"Show him in," God says.

As Roberts enters the office, God asks, "Are you the Oral Roberts?"

"Yes," he admits.

"Well," God says, "I've got this aching shoulder. . . ." (6)

Pastor Roberts undoubtedly has made his contribution to the faith, but it is telling that when one newspaper carried a news item recently about a stay that Roberts had in a hospital after undergoing tests for chest pains, the item appeared in the newspaper's column called, "Show Biz Shorts." (7)

Well, TV evangelism is show biz. That's also true when we treasure the witness of famous athletes or Hollywood stars or singers above the witness of the ordinary believer. The most effective messengers of the Gospel are real people who have had their lives transformed.

This applies not only to celebrity Christians but also what we might call super saints. Some of you may think that your witness for Christ might not be very effective because at some time in your life you messed up. Actually, the exact opposite may be true. Most people today are turned off by what we may call super saints. Most people want to hear from somebody whose faith has been tested . . . who knows what it is to experience grace.

Pastor Jay Kesler once told about a boy who had been arrested for armed robbery. The boy's parents, who were professing Christians and very active in their church, were so ashamed that they didn't leave their home for several days. They didn't know if they could face people again, particularly those in their church.

The parents finally went to church, and their shame and fear made them stick together like burrs. But something wonderful happened. A stream of people came to them. And the chief reason they came to them was not so much to console them as to ask for help for their own spiritual problems.

The father said later, "It seems to me that when people take a super-spiritual pose in church, pretending to have no problems, the other church people are afraid to be honest about their own problems for fear that they will look like failures. It's strange that when we tried our best and, at least on the surface, succeeded in our Christian lives, we didn't touch other lives. Now that we are having problems with our son, other people ask for our help—they want to know how God is working out our problems." (8)

If, like the Pharisees, we parade our superior righteousness or spirituality, we will do more to turn people off than we will do to attract them to Christ. The only man who has ever lived who was without sin was Jesus of Nazareth, and yet, many of the religious people could not accept him as the Messiah, because he associated with sinners and did not appear very saintly. In fact, aside from his love and his miracles, he seemed very much like a real person.

And that is who Jesus wants to share their faith: real people who have had their lives transformed by his power.

Are you among that number? Have you had a deep failure at some time in your life and found that God's promises are real? If so, share your story with others. And if you are going through a time of failure and pain right now, don't shrink back from Christ. He is saying to you, "Special lady, special gentleman, my grace is sufficient for you. I died that you might live. Accept my gift of love this day."

The evangelist had a shady past, but her friends knew that her testimony was real. Christ had brought her from darkness into the light.

1. Jim Abrahamson in Edward K. Rowell, 1001 Quotes, Illustrations, and Humorous Stories (Grand Rapids: Baker Publishing Group, 2008), p. 322.
2. Jeremy Troxler, http://faithandleadership.com/sermons/coming-soon
3. (Nashville: Thomas Nelson Publishers, 1993).
4. "Harper's Index," August 1998, p.13.
5. http://www.kentcrockett.blogspot.com/.
6. "Positive Paternalism" by Dr. Robert R. Kopp, Jan. 23, 2000, p. 3.
7. Ernest W. Ranly, "Shaky reforms," Christian Century, March 3, 1993.
8. Billy Graham, "The Healer of Our Broken Hearts," Decision, Feb. 2003, pg. 5.

Playing The Blame Game
John 9:1-41

A little girl was riding along on her bike when she bumped her head on a low hanging branch of a tree. She ran into the house crying, "Mommy! Mommy, Joey hurt me!"

Her mom looked up from what she was doing. She said patiently, "Sissy, Joey didn't hurt you. Joey's not even here. He went to the grocery store with your Dad."

The little girl got a startled look on her face. Then in a bewildered voice the little girl asked, "Does that mean stuff like this can happen on its own at any time [with no one being at fault]?" Then she added, "Whoa, bummer!" (1)

Well, it is a bummer. Bad things can happen at any time to anyone—and sometimes there's no one to blame.

In today's lesson from John's Gospel, Jesus' disciples encounter a man blind from birth. The disciples ask Jesus, "Rabbi, who sinned, this man or his parents, that he was born blind?"

There it is, that question: who is to blame for this man's misfortune? Somehow if we can just affix blame, we think it will make the situation better. There will at least be some meaning to the event—maybe even a solution. If there's somebody to blame, it means there is a way of gaining control over life. If bad things just happen, with no one to blame, then there's no control, and that is scary.

Pastor Joan Dennehy tells about a girl in the 8th grade who came home one day to find a yard sale sign in front of her home. Her neighbors were picking through her family's belongings. Her bitter mother tells her that her father has ruined the family business the same way he has ruined her. When they move to Florida a month later, everything they own fits neatly into the trunk of the car.

The first thing the girl notices at her new school is that everyone smokes cigarettes. She picks up the same habit; then comes pot, then the loss of her virginity, and, down the road, a miscarriage.

When she tells her mother she is quitting high school, her mother slaps her across the face. Her father lights a cigarette and begins to talk with it between his lips. "Freedom—she wants her freedom," he says. "Now that we're down, she's going to kick us with her freedom."

Her mother digs her fingers into her stomach and cries, "We've lost her, we've lost her"—as if she were dead.

Fast forward a few years. Now the girl is 31 and she still doesn't have a high school diploma. Her mother blames her father. Her father blames former president Ronald Reagan. She doesn't know who to blame first, maybe her parents, who sold her dog for $15 the day they moved. (2) All she knows is that she is desperately unhappy and she needs someone to blame.

The blame game. It's been around since the Garden of Eden. "Rabbi, who sinned, this man or his parents, that he was born blind?"

It's an absurd question, of course. How could a man BORN blind be responsible for his predicament? Did he sin in his mother's womb? Kick his mother a little too hard perhaps?

If you follow this line of thinking, you're left with only one viable conclusion—it must be his parent's fault. Can you imagine how hurtful this explanation would be to this man's parents? Not only would their precious son never be able to see, but it was somehow their fault. They had offended God sometime in the past—maybe without even realizing it—and this was their punishment.

For most of us, this is an absurd line of thinking. It really makes God look like a second-rate deity. And yet, there are many sincere Christian people who, when something tragic happens in their life ask, did I somehow cause this? Is God punishing me for some transgression of which I am not even aware?

Of course, it depends on how you think about God. Does God punish people for the merest transgression—even one that might be unconscious? Does God make little children suffer because their parents have somehow offended Him?

Jesus' answer to his disciples' question is intriguing: "Neither this man nor his parents sinned," said Jesus, "but this happened so that the work of God might be displayed in his life."

What does that mean? How can an affliction—particularly one as debilitating as blindness—display the work of God? Well, let's look for a few moments at the story.

First of all, we see Christ heal this man born blind. That's important. It is not God's will that this man—or any man or woman whoever they may be—be blind. Blindness comes from many sources. It might be the result of trauma or disease. In a man born blind, maybe damage to a gene was responsible. We don't know. However, we do know this: if you are blind, physically blind, you are not that way because God willed it. If you have cancer, or some other adverse condition, it is not because God willed it. If you are going through a devastating time financially, it is not because God willed it. God's will is always for wholeness and health. God's will is for your needs to be met. That is why Christ healed this man. Healing is God's will.

This is so important for us to understand. If, when we are going through a time of extreme heartache and we insist on playing the blame game, we may be cutting ourselves off from the very power that can heal us.

Notice how Christ heals this man. According to our lesson, he spits on the ground, makes some mud with the saliva, and puts it on the man's eyes. Then he tells the blind man to go wash in the Pool of Siloam.

Now the blind man might have responded to Jesus' actions in many ways. He could have said, "This is dumb. How in the world could putting mud on my eyes heal me? I'm not going to move one inch. It's ridiculous." That is how many of us might have responded—particularly if we had let our blindness defeat us, make us bitter, cause us to give up on God. That's how this man could have responded.

I can't help but believe that this man's healing was connected to the positive way he responded to Jesus' command. John indicates to us that the man immediately went to the pool, washed in the pool, and came home seeing. He responded in faith and his faith was rewarded.

We don't know why Jesus used this particular method of healing on this man. I have no doubt Jesus could have simply spoken and the same result would have been accomplished. Maybe it was important to Jesus to see this man do his part by washing in the pool.

However, here's what the man's healing says to me: if you have some tragedy in your life or in the life of someone you love, believe that God's will is for healing. Look for that healing. Work for that healing. Never give up hope. Just as Christ healed the man blind from birth, God's will is for all God's children to be well, to be strong.

That's true of all of life. If you have a hurt of any kind, or a need of any kind, whether it is physical or mental or emotional or financial or whatever it may be—don't sit around wondering who is to blame. Don't sit around feeling sorry for yourself. Focus on God's desire for healing. Do what you can to bring healing. Focus on it, expect it. At, least believe that God wants to heal your heart, your attitude, your feelings about your hurt or need. Put yourself in a frame of mind to receive whatever healing God may have for you.

Remember, God can use even the most adverse circumstances to our best good. That's what St. Paul says to us in Romans 8:28, "And we know that in all things God works for the good of those who love him, who have been called according to his purpose." God can use even the most adverse circumstances to bring a blessing into our life.

Pastor Kirk Greenfield tells a powerful story about a friend of his who is a Korean War veteran. Soon after his friend joined the army he decided to enter airborne training. He entered this particular branch of the army because he learned that soldiers willing to parachute received higher pay. Was he in for a surprise!

Greenfield says his friend soon realized higher pay was not an adequate reason for parachuting from a plane. He requested a transfer. The army did not take well to his request. In fact, he was punished for requesting the transfer. He was put on "grunt patrol." Every day he was forced to march many miles. To make matters worse, at the end of the day, he and the other soldiers on grunt patrol were ordered to dig elaborate foxholes. This continued for several weeks until he was deployed to Korea.

He says his friend becomes emotional when he relates the next part of the story.

His friend and his detachment of twenty men were ordered to hold a line one night during a fierce battle. He dug in with the other men. Many of the men could not dig a decent foxhole. Well, because of his time on grunt patrol, his friend already had much practice digging foxholes, so he helped them. That night they came under multiple attacks. When the sun came up, there were over thirty dead enemy soldiers lying in front of their position. He and his friend and two others were the only American survivors. The situation had been so desperate that when British Royal Marines arrived soon after they nearly shot the four survivors because they didn't see how any allied soldiers could have survived.

Later, when they were being moved behind the lines, it was brutally cold. Many of the soldiers rode in the troop trucks and suffered the loss of toes and fingers due to frostbite. Greenfield's friend chose to walk. When darkness fell, they came under air attack. The lights on the trucks made them easy targets. His friend survived because he was walking behind.

At this point in the story, Kirk Greenfield says his friend looks at him with tears in his eyes and says, "People wonder why I love the Lord." Twice in 24 hours he came close to death. He survived because he knew how to dig good foxholes and was in good enough shape to walk instead of ride. These abilities came from the punishment he had received earlier on grunt patrol. (3)

"In all things God works for the good of those who love him . . ." That's a hard thing to remember when you are going through difficult times, but it's true. God can use any circumstance. When you are going through a difficult time, look for some way this can be used to God's glory. Let it make you better rather than make you bitter. And that brings us to the final thing to be said.

The most tragic blindness is blindness of the heart. It's interesting. This should have been the most joyful day in this man's life. He had been blind all his life. Then this man Jesus came by and did something quite remarkable. He took some dirt and some of his own saliva and made mud. Then he put the mud on this man's eyes and told him to wash in the Pool of Siloam. So the man did as he was told and then he came home able to see.

This is an extraordinary miracle. A man who had never seen anything before now had his vision! Shouldn't someone throw him a party? Well, his neighbors didn't. Some of them refused to believe this was the same man they had known. It didn't fit their theology. They had never known a blind man who was healed and they refused to accept him. Neither did the leaders of the synagogue. In fact, they threatened to throw him out of the synagogue if he didn't recant his testimony that Jesus had healed him. You see, his neighbors and the leaders in his synagogue were blinder than this man had ever been. They were blind to who Christ was. They were blind to what God was doing in their midst. They let their own petty interests and experiences blind them to a richer understanding of the blessings God had in store for them. They weren't bad people. They were simply locked in to a certain way of thinking about life and about God. They didn't see the bigger picture.

It's like a story that Dave Bosewell tells in his book, How Life Imitates the World Series. He tells a story about Earl Weaver, former manager of the Baltimore Orioles. Sports fans will enjoy how Weaver handled superstar Reggie Jackson who was on that team.

Weaver had a rule that no one could steal a base unless he was given the steal sign by one of the coaches. This upset Jackson because he felt he knew the pitchers and catchers well enough to judge himself who he could and could not steal off of. So one game he decided to steal without a sign.

He got a good jump off the pitcher and easily beat the throw to second base. As he shook the dirt off his uniform, Jackson smugly smiled with delight, feeling he had vindicated his judgment to his manager.

Later Weaver took Jackson aside and explained why he hadn't given him the steal sign. First, the next batter was Lee May, his best power hitter other than Jackson. When Jackson stole second, first base was left open, so the other team simply walked May intentionally, taking the bat out of his hands.

Second, the following batter hadn't been strong against that particular pitcher, so Weaver felt he had to send up a pinch hitter to try to drive in the men on base. That left Weaver without bench strength later in the game when he needed it.

The problem was, Jackson saw only his relationship to the pitcher and catcher. His manager, Earl Weaver, was watching the whole game. (4)

You and I need to expand our thinking about our lives to seek God's perspective on the things that happen to us. Rather than trying to find someone to blame when something bad occurs in our life, we need to affirm that God's will is always for our best good. God wants us to be well. God wants to see that our needs are provided. In times of suffering, remind yourself, first of all, of that truth: God wants me to be well.

Second, remind yourself that all things work to the good for those who love God. Look for ways that God can use your present adversity for the good. Perhaps this experience will make you stronger. Maybe this experience will make you more compassionate toward the struggles of others. Maybe this experience will draw you closer to God.

Finally, pray that God will help you see the bigger picture. Pray that you will sense God's will for your life. It may be that up to this point you, too, have been blind. Pray that God will help you see God's hand, God's plan, and your place in it.

1. Pastors Story File, May 1994, 10.7.1 Saratoga Press, Box 8, 311 Elizabeth Avenue, Suite B, Platteville, CO.
2. http://www.olypen.com/rose/Findlay/services2002/sermon2002-0310.htm.
3. http://www.lifeway.com/lwc/article_main_page/0%2C1703%2CA%253D154689%2526M%253D200272%2C00.html.
4. Cited in Dennis Swanberg, ManCode: Keys to Unlocking a Balanced Life (Nashville: Freeman-Smith, 2009), p. 106.

Daring Thomas
John 11:1-16

Pirates have been in the news over the past few years. Not the romanticized pirates of the Caribbean, but real life pirates in places like Somalia—desperate, violent men who have garnered ransoms of millions of dollars by taking hostages from ships.

If I were to ask you to name a famous pirate from history, who would it be? My guess is that many of you would come up with the name Blackbeard. Blackbeard was a notorious English pirate who operated around the West Indies and the eastern coast of the American colonies during the early 18th century.

There was an article in the magazine American History Illustrated, however, that punched a few holes in the reputation of this well-known buccaneer.

As pirates go, Blackbeard (the alias for Edward Teach) was actually nothing special, according to this article. He amassed little treasure and showed little daring. He tended to prey only on small defenseless boats where the plunder was puny but risk almost nil. He was neither invincible nor difficult to capture. The truth is that there was little effort to bother with him. A corrupt North Carolina governor fenced much of his stolen cargo for him, and the English didn't seem to have any real reason to chase after him. Compared to more accomplished pirates, it could be fairly said that Blackbeard was a joke.

However, Blackbeard was a great cultivator of his own fame. He spread stories and composed "press releases" about his exploits that made him seem grander than he was. Hence, his name survives when greater pirates have been forgotten. (1)

Blackbeard worked very hard, not at pirating, but at publicity. And so we remember him to this day. He knew what many celebrities today also know. You can manipulate your image. You can be famous for being famous—think Paris Hilton and Kevin Federline. You don't really have to accomplish anything. You only need to find a way to keep your name in the headlines.

I wish the disciple Thomas had a better press agent. Thomas, as you will remember became well known in history because of one tiny episode in his life. He gained a reputation, a tarnished reputation if you will, that has stayed with him now for 2100 years. In scripture he is called Thomas, or Didymus which means "the twin." Thomas undoubtedly had a twin brother. However, whenever we think of him, what name immediately comes to mind? That's right, "Doubting Thomas."

Each year on the Sunday after Easter pastors who follow the lectionary tell the story of Doubting Thomas. Three weeks from now, we will do so ourselves. But this poor disciple's reputation extends beyond the church. Even in our secular culture, if someone is dubious about claims of any kind, they are apt to be called a Doubting Thomas.

Has anyone in scripture been so universally—and in my mind, so unjustly maligned than Thomas? Oh, we think of Judas the betrayer and Pilate washing his hands of his responsibility for Jesus' death. But they stand justly accused. But Thomas?

Would you permit me the opportunity today to seek to reverse the reputation of this unjustly accused young man? I will attempt to do so now and I will seek to do so again on the Sunday after Easter.

Today I would like to rename him "Daring Thomas." After all, his reputation for doubting is based on a very brief mention toward the end of John's Gospel. Today's lesson takes place earlier in that same Gospel. It has only a brief mention of him as well, but this passage clearly shows Thomas as more daring rather than doubting.

I suppose the reason we so rarely notice this more positive picture of Thomas' character is because it is contained in the story of the raising of Lazarus, a story that is so powerful that a brief mention of the disciple Thomas is barely worth noting.

When our story opens Jesus has just learned that his close friend Lazarus is sick. Lazarus lived in the village of Bethany with his sisters Mary and Martha. Bethany was a small village about two miles from Jerusalem. At this moment Jesus is a considerable distance from Bethany. It is evident, however, that Mary and Martha hoped that Jesus, their close friend who had healed so many other people, would do something to help their brother Lazarus. Yet when he heard that Lazarus was sick, Jesus stayed where he was two more days, a fact that greatly troubled Mary and Martha. Finally, however, he said to his disciples, "Let us go back to Judea."

This time it was his disciples who were troubled. Earlier Jesus' enemies in Judea had tried to stone him. There were people in Judea who would not rest until Jesus was forever silenced. "But Rabbi," his disciples protested, "a short while ago they tried to stone you, and yet you are going back there?"

Jesus answered that their friend Lazarus had fallen asleep and he was making this dangerous journey to wake Lazarus up. When they expressed puzzlement at this, he explained that Lazarus was actually dead, but he was going there to be with him. At this, one of his disciples stepped forward and challenged the rest of the disciples, "Let us also go, that we may die with him."

It was our friend Thomas who spoke out with so much boldness. This is the very same Thomas who would later get the reputation as a doubter. And yet, in this passage Thomas was willing to die for Christ—and this was before he and the other disciples were even certain who Christ was. "Let us also go, that we may die with him." Why do we insist on calling him Doubting Thomas? Well, we'll deal with that after Easter. But today let's exult in our new friend, Daring Thomas.

It is always thrilling to meet someone who is genuinely committed to Christ. There are so many people who bear Christ's name, but would never really think of dying for him.

There is a cartoon character named PONTIUS' PUDDLE. In one cartoon Pontius is in church. Pontius Puddle is very much like you and me—he has good intentions, but he's not exactly ready to set the world on fire. The cartoonist depicts Pontius' style of worshipping with a take-off on the lead-in to the old Superman TV show:

"Able to drop a quarter in the offering plate without embarrassment . . .

Capable of waking from a dead sleep and finding the right song in seconds . . .

Look! Out in the sanctuary—it's a teacher! . . . It's an usher! . . . No! . . . It's a PEW POTATO." And Pontius is snoring away!

You're familiar with couch potatoes. This is how one observer described a pew potato:

"A Pew Potato wants to be cared for but doesn't know how to care.

A Pew Potato wants to be visited but never visits.

A Pew Potato wants the benefits of Bible study but leaves the [work] to someone else.

A Pew Potato catalogs the mistakes of others but misses his/her own.

A Pew Potato has not only forgotten what he/she used to be but has also lost sight of what he/she could become.

New Potatoes become Pew Potatoes, says this observer, when they stop growing and just vegetate. (2)

I've known a few Pew Potatoes in my day.

A story is told of a pastor years ago whose daughter came to him and announced that she wanted to go to Uganda as a missionary. He told her that he would not allow her to go to such a dangerous place. After explaining that Christians were often persecuted in Uganda, he suggested that she would have no problem finding missionary work in their own city.

Two years later she was still resolved to go to Uganda. Although he was quite upset about her decision, he went to the airport to see her off. As he watched her plane exit the runway, he commented that he had wanted her to be a respectable Christian— not a real one. (3)

Many of us, if we were honest, would confess that we come closer to the profile of a respectable Christian than a real one. Sacrifice and commitment are really not part of our vocabulary.

A few years ago, Rabbi Jan Goldstein had the opportunity to meet Mrs. Jihan Sadat, widow of the former Egyptian president, Anwar Sadat.

You may not know, but in the beginning of Sadat's presidency, the Egyptian president had championed war against Israel. He was part of the destructive cycle of hatred and bloodshed that has stalked the Middle East for decades. But then one day, Sadat determined to become a peacemaker. He wanted to break down the walls of violence and misunderstanding between the Egyptians and Israelis. He knew that members of his own political party would try to kill him to stop the peace process.

Mrs. Sadat recalled the day that Anwar told her he was going to Jerusalem to negotiate a peace settlement. She protested that his enemies would kill him. He replied, "Then I would have died for peace."

His trip to Jerusalem was an historic moment, and it opened President Sadat's eyes to the possibilities of a peaceful future between the two countries. Mrs. Sadat reports that he came back from the trip energized, full of joy. Not long afterwards, he was assassinated. (4)

It's sad, but that sort of thing happens in the real world even today. It takes people who are really committed to peace, really committed to justice, and, with regard to Thomas, really committed to the Lordship of Jesus Christ to make any real difference at all.

Let me ask you what it is that you are truly committed to? For what or for whom would you be willing to die? That's not an easy question. Those of you who are parents would answer, your children. You would give your life for your children.

You can identify with a woman named Paula Chican of Tempe, Arizona. A few years ago Paula was on board Northwest Airlines flight 225 which crashed just after taking off from the Detroit airport, killing 155 people. Only one person survived that crash, Paula's four-year-old daughter, Cecelia.

News accounts say when rescuers found Cecelia they did not believe she had been on the plane. Investigators first assumed Cecelia had been a passenger in one of the cars on the highway onto which the airliner crashed. But when the passenger register for the flight was checked, there was Cecelia's name.

Cecelia survived because, even as the plane was falling, her mother Paula, un-buckled her own seat belt, got down on her knees in front of her daughter, wrapped her arms and body around Cecelia, and would not let her go. (5)

Cecelia survived because of her mother's love for her. You and I understand that. You who are parents would gladly trade your life for the lives of your children.

But besides your children, for what or for whom would you be willing to give your life? Some of you would answer, your country. There are men and women who this day are offering up their lives for their country in far-off places like Afghanistan and Iraq. We salute them and pray that they will return to us safely.

Patriotism is a powerful emotion in many lives. Evangelical researcher George Barna says that more people in this country are willing to die for their country than for their faith. They view themselves as Americans first and Christians second. That is a disturbing thought to those of us who believe that nothing is ever to come before God, but it is a noble thing to die for one's country.

What is it, or who is it for whom you would give up your life? Does Christ come first in your life? Would you die for Christ? Be honest. Some people who bear Christ's name won't even get out of bed on Sunday morning to worship him much less die for him. How about you?

Here is the Good News for the day: you and I will probably never be asked to die for Christ. We are, however, asked to live for him.

You can relax. Chances are you will never be asked to give up your life for your faith. It's not going to happen. What we are asked to do, rather, is to make our lives a living sacrifice for him. Will you go that far? Will you put Christ first in your everyday life?

A man joined the Navy and soon after had to attend a wedding. He asked an officer for a pass. He was told he had to be back by 7 p.m. Sunday.

"You don't understand, sir," the man said. "I'm in the wedding."

"No, YOU don't understand," the officer replied. "You're in the Navy."

When you make a commitment to the armed services, it takes priority over the rest of your commitments. So it is when you make an authentic commitment to Christ—every area of your life will be affected by that commitment. Thomas had that kind of commitment. I see Thomas as an enthusiastic, willing young man who was passionate about serving Christ. Jesus was returning to an area where people were threatening his life and Thomas responded, "Let us also go, that we may die with him." That's not the response of a doubter.

Soren Kierkegaard once said this age will die, not from sin, but from a lack of passion. Thomas had passion. Three weeks from now we will revisit Thomas and try to determine if there was something that robbed him of his passion. Stay tuned for that. But on this occasion when Christ was going back to Judea where his life was being threatened, Thomas was more daring than doubting.

Would you like to know how Thomas' life ended? Thomas became a leader of the early church. Just like Peter and Paul went to Greece and Rome, and Mark went to Egypt and Syria, Thomas made his way as far as India. There are burial remains and churches in India named after St. Thomas and inscribed with his 52 A. D. landing and missionary work there before he was later martyred. The oldest of India's churches ascribe their faith to the missionary work of daring Thomas. (6)

I hope there's a bit of Daring Thomas in you. I hope there's a bit of Daring Thomas in me. Faith is not to be taken for granted. We would not be in this room today if earlier generations of Christ's followers had taken their faith for granted. We probably will never be asked to die for Christ, but we are asked to go forth from this room living for him. That is our challenge. Can Christ count on you?

1. Rosenthal, Leon S., "Blackbeard: Cardboard Corsair," American History Illustrated (June, 1968), pp. 5-9, 46-47.
2. George White in The United Methodist Reporter, 1-15-88, p. 2.
3. Robert H. Spain, How to Stay Alive (Nashville: Dimensions, 1992), p. 13.
4. Jan Goldstein, Life Can Be This Good (Berkeley: Conari Press, 2002), pp. 139-142.
5. Bryan Chapell, In the Grip of Grace (Grand Rapids: Baker, 1992). Cited in Perfect Illustrations (Wheaton: Tyndale House Publishers, 2002).
6. Rev. James Mueller,
http://www.predigten.uni goettingen.de/predigt.php?id=163&kennung=20070415en.

The Triumph And The Tragedy
Matthew 21:1-11
(Palm/Passion Sunday)

On Palm Sunday April 9, 1865, Confederate General Robert E. Lee surrendered to Ulysses S. Grant, General of the Union Army, at the village of Appomattox Court House, Virginia. This surrender ended the bloodiest war ever fought on American soil. State against state, brother against brother; it was a conflict that literally tore our nation apart.

Five days later—Good Friday, April 14, 1865—America's most revered president, Abraham Lincoln, was shot and mortally wounded by John Wilkes Booth in Ford's Theatre.

It was Lincoln who wrote the Emancipation Proclamation that ended slavery in the U.S. forever. It was Lincoln who wrote and gave The Gettysburg Address. Lincoln hated war, but he was drawn into this one because he believed it was the only way to save the nation. On Palm Sunday the war ended. Triumph. On Good Friday, Abraham Lincoln became the first U.S. president to be assassinated. Tragedy.

Welcome to Holy Week. Welcome to the triumph and the tragedy of the six days preceding Easter. That's the kind of world we live in—the triumphant end to a terrible war on Sunday, and the tragic slaying of the great leader who brought us through that war on Friday. One moment we are on top of the world, believing that nothing can go wrong. And then suddenly, literally, all hell breaks loose. That, as they say, is life.

Go with me now to the year 1942. The first American troops are marching into London. We are entering the conflict known as World War II. The people of London are cheering the American soldiers. The friendly reception exhilarates the young soldiers. They sing as they march. Suddenly the troops turn into a main street and a strange hush falls over the scene. The happy songs die on their lips. They are looking for the first time upon an area in London that has been blown to bits. They see the great wounds on the city inflicted by falling bombs. They suddenly realize the city has suffered terribly. In these young soldiers' hearts, one moment celebration; the next, great sadness. (1)

Life is like that. Celebration and sadness; triumph and tragedy.

Do some of you remember the days when we said that the best investment you can make is owning your own home? Remember when banks were begging people to take out home loans, because property values seemed destined to rise forever? Remember how you could look at the equity in your home and feel rich? How foolish we were to forget the lesson of the stock market scarcely a decade ago. In a free market bubbles have a tendency to burst. All it takes is one little pin prick. It's happened over and over through history, but we have short memories. It's easy to forget, for example, that the stock market crash of 2000-2002 caused the loss of $5 trillion in the market value of companies. It can happen so quickly.

The triumph and the tragedy. Palm Sunday. Good Friday. Life happens.

The amazing thing is that it happened to the Son of God. Acclaimed on Sunday, crucified on Friday—it's incredible. Didn't they realize who he was? Sure, he gave up his divinity when he entered the world as a tiny baby, but couldn't they see his miracles? Didn't he raise Lazarus from the dead? Couldn't they sense he was no ordinary man? He was Messiah, Savior, Redeemer, sent into the world by the Father to save the world from its sins. How could they miss it? How could they not know?

Maybe it was because he came riding into town on a donkey. How's that for lowering expectations? Kings ride on magnificent horses, not lowly donkeys. They ride in limos, not in Yugos. Would we vote for a President who rode around in a rusted out 1970 Ford Pinto? In our world, image is everything.

The Greek author Plutarch describes how kings are supposed to enter a city. He tells about one Roman general, Aemilius Paulus, who won a decisive victory over the Macedonians. When Aemilius returned to Rome, his triumphant procession lasted three days. The first day was dedicated to displaying all the artwork that Aemilius and his army had plundered. The second day was devoted to all the weapons of the Macedonians they had captured. The third day began with the rest of the plunder— borne by 250 oxen, whose horns were covered in gold. This included more than 17,000 pounds of gold coins. Then came the captured and humiliated king of Macedonia and his extended family. Finally, Aemilius himself entered Rome, mounted on a magnificent chariot. Aemilius wore a purple robe, interwoven with gold. He carried his laurels in his right hand. He was accompanied by a large choir singing hymns, praising the military accomplishments of the great Aemilius. (2) That, my friends, is how a king enters a city.

But the King of Kings? He entered riding on a lowly donkey. If he had consulted his political advisors, they would have been aghast. What was he up to? Leaders are supposed to project strength and power. Think Ronald Reagan, not Jimmy Carter.

Jesus wasn't listening to his political advisors when he made his entrance into Jerusalem that day. Instead, he was listening to the prophet Zechariah. Zechariah envisioned the King of Kings, the Messiah, coming not on a great stallion, but riding on a humble donkey.

Zechariah also foretold what this Messiah on a donkey would do: he would "cut off the chariot from Ephraim and the war horse from Jerusalem." Zechariah also foretold what this Messiah would say: "peace to the nations."

Zechariah foresaw it. Jesus fulfilled it. (3)

No wonder holy week moves from triumph to tragedy. The expectations of the people had been dashed. They had voted for change, but change was nowhere in view. Besides, who can live with "peace to the nations"? Bring the troops home?

Not when you have enemies who want to destroy you. Even Jesus' disciples expected him to exercise his kingship by vanquishing their enemies. The two disciples on the Emmaus road tell the resurrected Jesus, who walks along with them, yet whom they do not recognize, that they had hoped that this Jesus was the one to redeem Israel (Luke 24:21). When Jesus appears to his disciples before his ascension, the disciples are still asking, "Lord, is this the time when you will restore the kingdom to Israel?" (Acts 1:6). They wanted Jesus to establish an earthly kingdom and to make them his lieutenants. Gee, were they disappointed. They wanted Churchill and they got Gandhi. And so some of the crowd turned away from him and much of the crowd turned against him. It should not be surprising that some of those who sang their sweet hosannas on Palm Sunday were shouting "Crucify him! Crucify him! Crucify him!" on Good Friday. Triumph and tragedy. Palm Sunday, Good Friday—the crowds turned their backs on the Son of God.

The obvious question is, would it be any different today? Would we welcome Christ into our community, into our family, even into our church? It is an unsettling question, but it needs to be asked.

Fleming Rutledge in her book, The Bible and the New York Times, tells the story of a woman in her church who would not come to church on Palm Sunday. [Evidently, in their church they enacted the scene in Pilate's court yard on Palm Sunday.]

This woman couldn't stand being asked to shout "Crucify him! Crucify him!"

"I just can't do it," the woman explained.

Rutledge says, "I always felt very sad for her. She had missed the whole point. She could have come to church every other Sunday of the year and she still would have missed the whole point . . . It was very important to her to think of herself as one of the righteous. She could not confront her own darkness. How sad this is. If she but knew it, there is great power in the act of repentance." (4)

Can we confront our own darkness? Can we confront our need for repentance? Would we welcome Christ into our world? For you see Christ, the real Christ, comes as a disturber, an unsettler, almost as an anarchist. Think of the things we value. Status. Power. Money. Image. How does it all square with this humble figure riding on a donkey? Not very well, does it? Look at our popular heroes. I'm thinking about the action-type movies preferred by most males. How do the heroes of these movies spend their time? Blowing things up. Avenging past wrongs. Asserting their dominance over their foes. Again, reconcile these images with that humble figure riding on a donkey.

Do you understand what it means to say Jesus is Lord? It means that we need to examine our lives, examine our goals, examine what it is that we are living for and ask ourselves is it enough? Is this really the meaning of life? Or is there more? Is there an eternal dimension of life that calls us toward the heroic? Holy week should be the time for increased reflection and subsequent repentance as we measure our lives by our Lord's life and death.

The triumph and the tragedy. Palm Sunday. Good Friday. Life happens. The amazing thing is that it happened to the Son of God. Would it be any different today? Of course not.

A few years ago Pastor Javier Viera and his wife Marianne wandered into the New York Historical Society to see an exhibit that had been recommended to them by a friend. The exhibit was titled "Without Sanctuary." It was an array of photographs and postcards which had been collected by a collector, James Allen.

These photographs and postcards were of lynchings that had taken place throughout the United States. The exhibit is hard to talk about on Palm Sunday—picture after picture of a limp body hanging from the end of a rope. The images were grotesque and disturbing says Viera.

"However, what was most disturbing about these photographs," says Viera, "was not the bodies of the victims. In each picture was a gathering of ordinary people who came to watch the atrocities take place. The lynching was a social event. People dressed up for the occasion . . .

"It was clear that these lynchings were a cultural phenomenon. They were events not be missed. In [one] picture, as a body is hanging from the noose . . . you can see in the background a man smoking a cigar with a broad smile on his face. Others are sipping beer, gossiping, smiling and laughing. A couple flirts and enjoys a romantic moment. Little boys beam with broad smiles, seemingly filled with pride to be part of such an auspicious gathering . . . Something else was more troublesome yet than the fine, upstanding people in these pictures. The images of these events had not only been documented on film," says Viera, "they were also turned into postcards. They were cherished mementos to be mailed to family and friends . . ." (5)

O. K., you and I are repulsed by these images. What I want to remind you is that these are not images from Rome 2,000 years ago. These are images from America 100 years ago. And friends, the same dark heart that beat in the hearts of our ancestors beats within us.

As much as we would like to think differently, human nature has not changed in these past 100 years. That is why any appeal to discrimination, prejudice, hatred—whether against people of another race or another religion, or whatever that prejudice might be—cannot be tolerated, not by people whose Lord was hung on a tree while mocking soldiers gambled for his garments below.

Palm Sunday. Good Friday. Life happens. It happened to the Son of God. It still happens in our world today.

But here is what we must see: while the cross of Christ reveals the evil humanity is capable of, it also reveals the love of which God is capable. Ultimately the story of Holy Week is one of triumph and tragedy, then triumph once again, not only because of Easter Sunday, but because of Christ's victory over sin and death on Calvary.

This is why the cross is so precious to believers. It calls us to repentance, but it also represents God's grace which covers all our sins, even our most grievous sins.

Edward Grinnan tells a moving story about his mother. His mother moved into an assisted living home after Alzheimer s made it impossible for her to live alone.

She'd only been there a week when he got a call from the supervisor. "I hate to tell you this," said the supervisor, "but your mom's been swiping things from other people's rooms. Socks, candy bars, T-shirts. Nothing big—except that one lady's cross is missing."

Grinnan could scarcely believe this. His mom was the most honest person he knew. She once drove twenty miles back to a store where the clerk had given her too much change.

The next time he visited her, he gently chided her for the pilfering. "You've got to cut that out, Mom," he said, sitting with her in the lunchroom. "Did you take that cross?"

She shook her head, her curly gray hair bouncing. "Sure about that?" he pressed.

His mother turned away, then reached into her purse and pulled out the small silver cross. She set it down on the table and stared at it.

"I wasn't trying to steal," was all the explanation she gave.

Later he turned over the cross to the supervisor, apologizing. "Don't, don't," she said. "Your mom's a charmer. She's just trying to hang on to the things that mean the most to her."

The next time Grinnan came to the assisted living center he brought his mom a small silver cross. She stopped stealing after that.

Eventually they had to move Grinnan's mom to a facility where she could receive more care and where, of course, she charmed everyone. "She even led prayers on Friday morning. She had forgotten almost everything else, yet the prayers came to her lips as if she had freshly committed them to memory. And when she died, the saddest people of all were the people she prayed with on Friday morning with that little silver cross he gave her clutched in her hand." (6)

Her story gives new meaning to that line in the old Gospel song, "I will cling to the old rugged cross and exchange it someday for a crown."

The triumph and the tragedy. They cheered Jesus on Sunday and on Friday they hung him on a tree. But God had the last word. God took that tree and made it a symbol of our salvation from the forces of sin and death. Triumph and tragedy, then triumph once again. Thank God for that final triumph—the triumph over sin and death.

1. Dr. C.A. McClain.
2. Sigurd Grindheim, http://www.sigurdgrindheim.com/sermons/king.html.
3. Pastor Jim Rand, http://www.tosapres.com/sermons.php?sermon=96
4. (Grand Rapids: William B. Eerdsmans Publishing, 1998), pp. 126, 129. Cited by Javier Viera, http://www.mamaroneckumc.org/2003sermons/0413.htm.
5. Ibid.
6. Daily Guideposts (Nashville: Ideals Publications, 2006), p. 73.

Why Are You Here?
1 Corinthians 11:23-26
(Maundy Thursday)

Dr. William P. Barker once told a beautiful story about the isle of Iona. Iona is off the west coast of Scotland. It seems that in the sixth century A.D. St. Columba sailed from Ireland to the Isle of Iona. Ever since then Iona has been considered a holy place by many Christians.

The focal point of Iona, says Barker, is the magnificent Abbey Church. The foundation of this gem of early Christian architecture is over 1,400 years old. The church has been lovingly rebuilt, stone by stone. Once the exterior was restored, volunteers refurbished the interior and installed a new pulpit, lectern, and altar. Now worshipers fill the ancient Abbey Church once again.

"In the refurbishment project, it came time to prepare the bread plates to be used for Communion. There were to be eight bread plates in all, made of wood. The artisans intended to carve a verse from Scripture into the rim of each plate.

"Seven verses were quickly selected. Only one verse remained. The committee in charge asked the supervising architect to make the final selection. His choice was from the Gospel of Matthew, chapter 26. He used the words of the Revised Standard Version of the Bible in which Jesus says to Judas, 'Friend, why are you here?'" (vs. 50). (1)

You remember the setting for this question. Jesus was with his disciples at a place called Gethsemane. He had gone there to pray. Afterward he had a word with his disciples. While he was still speaking, Judas, one of the Twelve, arrived. With him was a large crowd armed with swords and clubs, sent from the chief priests and the elders of the people. Judas had arranged a signal with them: "The one I kiss is the man; arrest him."

Going at once to Jesus, Judas said, "Greetings, Rabbi!" and kissed him.

And Jesus replied, "Friend, why are you here?" Then the men stepped forward, seized Jesus and arrested him. It is a very dramatic scene and the question is a dramatic question: "Friend, why are you here?"

Tonight we have come to this place as part of our Holy Week remembrance. We certainly have not come because we are planning to betray Christ. Indeed, we have come to declare that Jesus is our Lord. Still, we might look into our hearts and hear the Lord ask us this night that same dramatic question, "Friend, why are you here?"

This night is intended as a night of reflection, repentance and renewal. As we examine our hearts in these next few moments, let me explain why we have come to Christ's holy table.

We are here, first of all, because the Master told us to be here. St. Paul writes,

"For I received from the Lord what I also passed on to you: The Lord Jesus, on the night he was betrayed, took bread, and when he had given thanks, he broke it and said, 'This is my body, which is for you; do this in remembrance of me.' In the same way, after supper he took the cup, saying, 'This cup is the new covenant in my blood; do this, whenever you drink it, in remembrance of me.' For whenever you eat this bread and drink this cup, you proclaim the Lord's death until he comes."

We are here this night because the Lord instructed us to be here.

For the next few moments I would like to take you back a few years to that day when Buzz Aldrin and Neil Armstrong first landed on the moon. It was July of 1969. Buzz Aldrin had decided that as soon as the module set down on the moon, he would celebrate the Lord's Supper. Listen as he describes that event:

"We awoke at 5:30 a.m. Houston time. Neil and I separated from Mike Collins in the command module. Our powered descent was right on schedule. With only seconds worth of fuel left, we touched down at 3:30 p.m. Now was the moment for Communion. So I un-stowed the elements in their flight packets. I put them and the Scripture reading on the little table in front of the abort-guidance-system computer. Then I called back to Houston. 'Houston, this is Eagle. This is LM Pilot speaking. I would like to request a few moments of silence. I would like to invite each person listening in, wherever and whoever he may be, to contemplate for a moment the events of the past few hours and to give thanks in his own individual way.'"

For Aldrin, his way of giving thanks was to observe the sacrament of Holy Communion. He describes the moment like this, "In the blackout I opened the little plastic packages, which contained bread and wine. I poured wine into the chalice my parish had given me. In the one-sixth gravity of the moon, the wine curled slowly and gracefully up the cup. It was interesting to think that the very first liquid ever poured on the moon, and the first food eaten there, were (communion) elements. Just before I partook of the elements I read the words, which I had chosen to indicate our trust that as (human beings) probe into space, we are in fact acting in Christ. I sensed especially strongly my unity with our church back home, and with the Church everywhere. I read: 'I am the vine, you are the branches. Whoever remains in me and I in him, will bear much fruit; for without me you do nothing.'" (2)

I'm sure there were those who protested Aldrin's actions. That's the kind of world we live in. But the sacrament of the Lord's Supper is at the very heart of life in the Christian community. Why are we here? We are here because the Master told us to be here.

We are also here because we know the Lord is here with us. Jesus says to us in Matthew 18:20, "For where two or three gather in my name, there am I with them." Especially is that true in the sacrament of the Lord's Supper. Christ is here in a very real way seeking to make himself known to each of us.

There is a most unusual website on the Internet at www.johnspirko.com. The heading on the site is "Free John Spirko." For more than twenty years there has been a most controversial case in the state of Ohio. It is the case of John Spirko. Spirko has spent twenty-seven years in prison, twenty-three of them on death row, for a crime he allegedly never committed. Spirko is not a sympathetic figure. He has committed other crimes, but there are many knowledgeable people who believe he did not commit this particular crime. Just before he was to be executed, the Governor of Ohio commuted Spirko's sentence to life without parole lest an innocent man be executed.

On the "Free John Spirko" website is a message from David Van Dyke, pastor of Broad St. Presbyterian Church, in Columbus, Ohio. Van Dyke reached out to Spirko and ministered to him in the time before he thought Spirko was going to be executed. He was with him when Spirko's final appeal was rejected by the U. S. Supreme Court and it appeared certain that he was be executed the next day. Van Dyke describes his experience with Spirko. He says that each time he visited Spirko, the institution's rules seemed to change. Sometimes they wouldn't allow him to take his wallet inside, other times they would. At first he took Spirko communion, but then one day they wouldn't let him take his little baggie of bread and small bottle of juice inside. So the last few times he visited John, he didn't even attempt to bring the communion elements.

When Van Dyke visited Spirko on the day after the Supreme Court refused to hear his final appeal, a guard asked him, "Where's your communion stuff at?"

Van Dyke said he didn't have it with him because in the past they wouldn't let him take it inside.

Another guard said, "If you don't got the communion stuff, you ain't goin' back!"

"Listen," Van Dyke said, "I've driven up here from Columbus and if I have to, I'll go get some communion stuff." This was agreeable to the prison staff, so he headed out in search of some stuff that could serve as an impromptu holy meal. The first place he came to was a BP gas station and convenience store. No grape juice, but he did find something called "Goofy Grape Soda" in the pop section of the store, but when he couldn't find anything that resembled bread—just peanuts, chips, and doughnuts—with his theological mind racing, he noticed the service station also housed a Subway Sandwich shop. So, he negotiated for a plain bun and headed back to the prison.

Once back on death row, he took out the plain bun, placed it on the table between Spirko and himself, and then he poured some Goofy Grape into two coffee cups. Van Dyke notes that Presbyterians aren't big on winging things, especially things like communion liturgy, but the bread at least smelled good—fresh. Sitting across the table from each other, he reminded Spirko that it was called the Last Supper because it would be the last time Jesus and his friends would break bread together. Then the two of them held hands, bowed their heads and prayed together.

They prayed, says Van Dyke, for peace in the world, for an end to corrupt systems, for the powers that be—one of Spirko's favorite expressions—and for justice. And then Pastor David Van Dyke prayed this prayer, "Pour out your Holy Spirit, O God, upon us and upon these gifts of bread and cup"—these gifts of plain bun and Goofy Grape soda, Van Dyke thought to himself, "that they may be to us the communion of the body and blood of Christ."

When the prayer was over, Van Dyke picked up the bread and before tearing it in half, heard himself saying words both familiar and yet alive with poignant new meaning, "On the night of his arrest—before he would be unfairly tried and executed by the state, whose chief legal officer admittedly found no fault in him—Jesus took bread and broke it."

In a small room on Ohio's death row, and with his clock about to start ticking, John Spirko and Pastor David Van Dyke "sat together silently, and took their time chewing on large pieces of the bread of life," and then they "drank salvation out of Styrofoam cups." Van Dyke closes his testimony with these words, "It was quiet, we were alone—just the three of us." (3)

I like the way he ended that little narrative, "we were alone—just the three of us." In a very real way Christians believe that anytime we eat the loaf which is his body and drink from the cup which is his blood, Christ is present.

Why are we here? We are here because the Master told us to be here, and we are here because we know the Lord is here with us.

Finally we are here so we will not forget what Christ has done for us. "Do this," said the Master, "in remembrance of me." And so we are here remembering the life, death and resurrection of Jesus Christ.

There is a time-honored story about the novelist Somerset Maugham. We're told that Maugham kept a cracked earthenware cup on the mantel of his plush London home. When someone asked him about that ugly, broken centerpiece among all of the beautiful objects of art there in his home, he explained that during the First World War he had been on a troop ship crossing the Atlantic Ocean. During that crossing the soldiers' rations of water were reduced to just one cup a day. He said it was that very cup now gracing his mantel from which he drank that daily ration of water. He said, "I keep [the cup] on the mantel as a reminder that I can never take my blessings for granted."

We come here this night to ensure that we never take for granted what the Lord has done for us. Why are we here? We are here because the Master told us to be here, because we know the Lord is here with us and so we will never, never forget.

1. Tarbell's Teacher's Guide, Sept. 1997-Aug. 1998 (Colorado Springs: David C. Cook. Publishing Co., 1997).
2. From an internet preaching listserv. Cited by Beth W. Johnston, http://www.geocities.com/Athens/Styx/4291/purple0401.html.
3. http://www.johnspirko.com/links/communionstuff.html.

Was There No Other Way?

Isaiah 52:13-53:12

(Good Friday)

Are you familiar with the legend of the robin? According to this tale the robin was originally a little brown bird. That is, until Good Friday—the first Good Friday. On that dark day this little brown bird saw a man nailed to a cross, slowly dying. He was all by himself . . . and there was no one to help him. The little brown bird began trying to free the man from the cross. The bird flew around and around until he found a way to remove a thorn from the crown of thorns that circled the man's head, and in removing the thorn the little robin stuck himself. And then, diving back and forth to the nails and to the thorns on the man's head, the little brown robin got his little breast all red with blood, and since then he has been known as the bird with the red breast.

It's just a legend, of course. But it reminds us of the seriousness of this day.

The prophet Isaiah tried to prepare us for Good Friday. Hundreds of years before Christ's birth Isaiah wrote, "He was despised and rejected . . . a man of suffering, and familiar with pain. Like one from whom people hide their faces he was despised, and we held him in low esteem. Surely he took up our pain and bore our suffering . . . he was pierced for our transgressions, he was crushed for our iniquities; the punishment that brought us peace was on him, and by his wounds we are healed. We all, like sheep, have gone astray, each of us has turned to our own way; and the Lord has laid on him the iniquity of us all." (53:3-6)

Welcome to this commemoration of Good Friday—a day when we focus our minds and hearts on Christ's suffering and death for the sins of the world.

Sir John Bowring understood the meaning of the cross. Bowring was a leading man of his time. He was twice elected to Parliament. He spoke five languages. He was knighted by the queen. He was governor of Hong Kong. He wrote thirty-six books ranging from religion to politics. Yet all that we have from his pen is a poem he wrote—a poem set to music—a poem that has become a hymn. He wrote it as he sailed along the China Coast. He passed Macao, where an earthquake had leveled the city. He saw the ruins of a mission church. The cross which had stood atop the chapel now stuck out of the ruins of the city. Musing on that mental image, Bowring wrote these lasting words:

"In the cross of Christ I glory/ Tow'ring o'er the wrecks of time." (1)

The cross does tower over the wrecks of time.

George Buttrick once wrote, "The magnetism of the Cross so strangely persists as to indicate a miracle. For why should anyone today trouble himself about a peasant hung in an obscure land many centuries gone?" It is because we see and we understand that Christ died in our behalf. The very Son of God gave his life for us.

But was it really necessary? Was there no other way? Theologians have pondered that question through the centuries with few satisfying answers. However, a few moments of calm reflection will reveal that, indeed, there was no other way.

For one thing, Jesus could not ask his disciples to pay a greater price than he was willing to pay. Think of Stephen as the stones rip his flesh, and Peter as he dies crucified upside down. Many of the followers of Jesus were burned as torches in Nero's gardens or torn apart by wild animals in the gladiator's arena. Only a soft, sentimental unrealistic faith would conjure the supposition that there was any other way for Jesus but the way of the cross. This is a hard world. The affluence and security of our land shelter us from that truth. Many people through the ages have given their lives for what they believe.

Melvin L. Cheatham, a medical missionary, tells an extraordinary story from his service a few years back during the war in Bosnia. He was assisted by a local doctor, Dr. Josip Jurisic, as he operated on a soldier of the Bosnian Muslim Army. The soldier had been shot through the neck and was paralyzed from the neck down. In removing the bullet that had shattered his spine, Dr. Cheatham found it had blown his spinal cord in two and knew he would remain paralyzed for the rest of his life. The soldier had not been breathing very well when he arrived at the hospital. Knowing that because of paralysis of his chest muscles he would continue to have difficulty breathing after the surgery, they left the tube in his airway, placing him on a ventilator to help him breathe. The ventilator was powered with an electrical generator using diesel fuel because the hospital had electric power only intermittently.

The next morning as they made their rounds, Dr. Jurisic took Cheatham aside to a quiet corner where it was safe to talk and told him the bad news about the paralyzed soldier. "During the night the supply of diesel fuel ran out," he said, "the generator quit working, his ventilator stopped, and he could not breathe on his own, so he died."

Naturally Cheatham was sad, but what Dr. Jurisic said next stunned him and caused him to tremble all over. "Professor," Josip said, "Because it was you who operated on the soldier and he died, I fear his people will come for you and will kill you. Therefore, I have changed the medical record. I have erased your name as the surgeon, and I have written my name in place of yours."

For a long moment Cheatham says he looked into the eyes of this compassionate man. His throat became dry and he could feel a large lump forming. Finally he said to Dr. Jurisic, "But surely, my friend, that means they will come for you and will kill you."

Dr. Jurisic said quietly, "You can leave this place of war, and I cannot. I am prepared to die in your place, if I must, in order that you might live."

Dr. Melvin Cheatham says, "When I looked at this physician, holding the report with his name in place of mine, I thought of the Great Physician, Jesus Christ, who was willing to take my place and die for me on the cross." (2)

It may be the scandal and tragedy of our land and our times is that there is nothing for which people will give their lives. We are so accustomed to comfort and convenience that it would be very difficult for many of us to pay the ultimate penalty for our faith. This may be the first reason that Jesus had to die. He could not ask his disciples to pay a greater price than he was willing to pay.

There is a second reason why there was no other way. Without the cross you and I could not see the destructiveness of sin. Sin hurts. Sin destroys. The word sin has almost disappeared from our vocabulary, but the consequences of sin will forever haunt our world.

During the Franco-German War two shells fell close to a house near the scene of a major conflict. The owner decided to keep them as a curiosity. After polishing them, he put them near his fireplace. One day he showed these interesting objects to a visiting acquaintance. His friend was suddenly struck by a horrible thought. "What if they're still loaded?" he inquired in alarm. Being an expert in such matters, he quickly examined the shells. "Get them away from the heat of the fire immediately!" he suddenly exclaimed. "They're as deadly as the day they were made!" (3)

So it is with sin. It is deadly. It can kill bodies, it can kill marriages, it can kill a church, it can kill a soul. An unknown author put it like this: "Sin steals joy. Sin removes confidence. Sin brings guilt . . . Sin quenches God's Spirit. Sin brings physical damage . . . Sin causes an ache in the soul. Sin breaks God's heart. Sin opens the door to other sins. Sin produces fear. Sin makes me its slave. Ask yourself, 'Is this a price I really want to pay? Is this a price I can afford to pay?'" (4)

Sin took God's only Son and crushed his body. Jesus was only 33 when he died upon Calvary. Think of that . . . 33—a very young man! Falsely accused, bitterly reviled and yet guilty of no wrong. A healer and helper, a lover of little children, a liberator of people imprisoned by their own sin and guilt, a man who knew God intimately enough to address him as "Abba," Daddy, and yet never lost his concern for the least and the lowest. Yet there he hangs on the cross of Calvary, and it was sin that put him there—your sin and my sin. That's what sin is. That's what sin does.

Would I be wrong if I said that many of us are like Celia, the young society leader in T.S. Eliot's play The Cocktail Party? Celia is talking to a psychiatrist named Reilly. She is confessing that she has discovered a sense of sin in her life. Sin is not a familiar word to her. She explains that her upbringing had been "pretty conventional." She had always been taught to disbelieve in sin. "Oh," she says, "I don't mean that it was never mentioned! But anything wrong, from our point of view, was either bad form, or was psychological." (5)

That's true of many of us. For far too many, sin is a meaningless term—it is merely bad form or a petty peccadillo. We do not perceive that there is an enemy within our gates, a betrayer in our hearts, a demon within our consciousness that can bring inconceivable tragedy into our lives. We chuckle when someone sings, "I was sinking deep in sin, 'Whoopee!'"

The cross shows us that sin is no casual matter. Sin is the enemy of our bodies, of our marriages, of our relations with one another and with God. There was no other way for God to show us that except on Calvary.

But there is one more reason why there was no other way but the cross. There was no other way for God to show the depth and the width of His love except by the gift of His Son. John puts it like this, "In this is love—not that we loved God, but that he loved us and gave his Son to be the expiation for our sins." (I John 4:10)

Corrie Ten Boom put it like this: "In the forest fire, there is always one place where the fire cannot reach. It is the place where the fire has already burned itself out. Calvary is the place where the fire of God's judgment against sin burned itself out completely. It is there that we are safe."

Wayne E. Ward described it like this: "All heaven and earth converge upon that central cross. The drama of redemption reached its amazing climax when human sin rose up and divine love reached down to that cross on Calvary! No words could possibly catch the despair which overwhelmed the disciples as they took the body down from the cross and laid it in Joseph's tomb. The drama was over. The king had come, but he was a king that nobody wanted. With wicked hands men had brutally tortured him and his dead body was already in the grave, from which no traveler ever returned." (6)

"What wondrous love is this, O my soul," writes the poet. "That caused the Lord of bliss to lay aside his crown for my soul, for my soul, to lay aside his crown for my soul."

That is why it had to be. Jesus could not ask his disciples to make a sacrifice he was not willing to make himself. There was no other way to reveal the awfulness of man's sin and the awesomeness of God's love.

Of course, the challenge to each of us is to respond in faith to that love, to cast off the sin that so easily besets us, and to give our lives to Him as He gave His life for us.

1. Source unknown.
2. Make a Difference: Responding to God's Call to Love the World (Nashville: Thomas Nelson, Inc., 2004), pp. 87-88.
3. Rev. Adrian Dieleman, http://www.trinityurcvisalia.com/sermons/1ki13.html.
4. MONDAY FODDER.
5. Billy Graham, How To Be Born Again (Waco: Word Books, 1977).
6. Wayne E. Ward, The Drama Of Redemption (Nashville: Broadman Press, 1966).

Eyewitness News

Acts 10:34-43; John 20:1-9

(Resurrection of the Lord)

Country music star Kenny Chesney sings a song that contains this refrain, Everybody wanna go to heaven; Hallelujah, let me hear you shout; Everybody wanna go to heaven; But nobody wanna go now.

Deep in our hearts we know it's true. We talk about heaven, but regardless of how wonderful we have heard it described, most of us are not eager to make the journey.

We're like the man who was sentenced to death. He was asked if he had any last requests. He said that he loved to sing and wanted to sing his favorite song one more time. He was asked what his favorite song was. He replied, "One Billion Bottles of Beer on the Wall."

We don't know how long it would take to sing all the choruses to "One Billion Bottles of Beer on the Wall," but suffice it to say, he wasn't eager to face death.

And that's the way most of us are. And the question is, why? Isn't the grave simply a passageway to eternity? Isn't that which awaits us far superior to what we have now? Could it be that in spite of our protests to the contrary, we have a subtle fear down in our hearts that the Gospel is simply too good to be true?

Author Ron Mehl writes about a bridge in his home town of Portland, Oregon that goes nowhere. When the bridge was built back in the mid-1960s, it was designed to accommodate a freeway running east, but the freeway was never completed. "The result is an exit that drops off into empty space. You can see where the road was supposed to go. It juts out just a bit from the bridge structure, then it is cut off as though sliced by a giant knife. The entrance ramp permanently blocked, the exit now goes nowhere— except into the waters of the Willamette River far below." (1)

That's how some people view the grave—an exit off the freeway of life that goes nowhere. That is our fear—but our hopes reside elsewhere. Deep in our hearts is the longing that the bridge of life has been completed. That life goes on. That those we have lost in this world will be reclaimed in the world beyond.

It's like a story that pastor Edward Markquart tells about a young American author who had written a short story that was a masterpiece. Like so many young authors, he borrowed a plot from a more famous, older author. He borrowed this plot but wanted to improve it and change it. The young author was a realist, not a romantic at all like the older author. He took the plot of the older author and he wrote it more realistically, so he thought.

One day, the older author, a college professor, invited the younger author to come and read his new, revised story to him. The plot was this: It was a story of a son of a poor widow who lived in a village in Pennsylvania. One day, the young boy set out for New York to seek his fortune, and as he left home, his mother said to him:

"Johnny, you are going to New York but I want you to remember one thing. If life ever really gets bad for you in the big city, I want you to know you can come home and there will always be a light on in our house for you. There will always be a light in the window of our house to remind you that you are always welcome home."

According to both versions of the story, Johnny went to New York and he had a very horrible experience. Life went from bad to worse, and the bottom dropped out and he ended up penniless and friendless. He finally remembered: "I'll go home. There will be a light in the window for me." But . . . in the new version of the story, the young man returned to his village in Pennsylvania and he came up over the crest of the hill, and his house was dark. There was no light in the window.

Slowly, the old professor rose quietly to his feet and spoke softly but firmly to the young author: "You put that light back into the window. I don't like your story the way it is." (2)

That is why we make our way to church on Easter Sunday—to be reassured that the light still burns in the window. We come to this place to be reminded that Jesus really did rise from the grave and that, because he lives, we too shall live.

But how do we know? How do we know the resurrection is true? To answer this question author Kent Crockett points us to a more recent dramatic event.

On April 15, 1912 The RMS Titanic, the largest passenger steamship in the world at that time, sank in the Atlantic Ocean. The Titanic was on her maiden voyage from Southampton, England to New York City.

The Titanic was designed by some of the most experienced engineers of its time. These engineers used the most advanced technologies available to make it allegedly the safest ship ever built to that time. Many thought it to be virtually invincible. Thus the world was shocked with news of its sinking. Aboard the ship for her maiden voyage were many celebrities. Among them were Leonardo DiCaprio and Kate Winslet. Well, not really. But they certainly brought the tragedy to life on the silver screen. The sinking of the Titanic is one of the best-known events of the twentieth century.

But how do we know for sure that the Titanic really sank? Lillian Asplund, the last US survivor of the Titanic, and the last living person to remember its sinking, died in May 2006. Therefore, no one alive today can give us an eye witness account. So does that mean it never happened?

Of course not. Approximately 1,500 passengers drowned in the sea that terrible day, but 700 passengers survived. Those survivors were eyewitnesses to the accident and even though none of them are alive now, newspapers recorded their comments about what they saw. No one living today questions whether or not the Titanic sank because we have a record of the eyewitness reports. (3)

Now, how do we know that Jesus rose from the dead? How do we know it's real? Just like we know about the sinking of the Titanic, through eyewitness reports.

There were people who were there. They saw him. They saw the nail prints in his hands and the mark of the sword in the side that was pierced. Their eyewitness testimonies have been preserved for us in Scripture.

The Apostle Peter was one of those eyewitnesses. We have his testimony in Acts 10. He was preaching in Caesarea to a Gentile audience at the home of Cornelius, a Roman army officer. Listen to his words: "You know the message God sent to the people of Israel, telling the good news of peace through Jesus Christ, who is Lord of all. You know what has happened throughout Judea, beginning in Galilee after the baptism that John preached—how God anointed Jesus of Nazareth with the Holy Spirit and power, and how he went around doing good and healing all who were under the power of the devil, because God was with him. We are witnesses of everything he did in the country of the Jews and in Jerusalem. They killed him by hanging him on a tree, but God raised him from the dead on the third day and caused him to be seen. He was not seen by all the people, but by witnesses whom God had already chosen—by us who ate and drank with him after he rose from the dead."

Simon Peter was there! He was there in the courtyard when Jesus was falsely accused. He was there when they nailed Jesus to the ugly cross. He was there when the women went to the tomb and found it empty. He was there when Christ appeared after his resurrection to his disciples. He was there. The words from Acts are an eyewitness report. Paul tells us in I Corinthians 15:6-8 that there were 500 such eyewitness to Christ's resurrection.

Eyewitness testimony—just as convincing as the eyewitnesses to the sinking of the Titanic. No, these witnesses are even more convincing than those of the Titanic. Here's the real proof. These eyewitnesses were so insistent that Jesus rose from the dead that they were willing to die rather than recant their testimony. When they were threatened with death and offered their release if they would deny Christ, they refused. And for that reason most of them died cruel deaths. Peter was crucified upside down. Paul was beheaded. Thomas was killed with a spear. James was executed with a sword. Philip was crucified. (4)

It's hard to dispute the testimony of an eyewitness, particularly one who will die rather than recant his testimony. And why would we want to dispute their testimony? All of creation testifies to the wonder of the resurrection.

Pastor Billy D. Strayhorn tells about a visit he made to a woman whose husband had died and whose funeral he'd held about two months before.

It was one of those dark, drizzly days. Pastor Strayhorn wasn't even sure if Emma was home. The house was dark and all closed up; all the blinds and curtains were drawn. He rang the doorbell, nothing. He knocked and then heard a quiet voice say, "I'll be with you in a minute."

Emma finally came to the door. As they walked down the hall to the living room, Strayhorn couldn't help but notice the whole house was dark. It was all sealed up like a tomb. They sat down and went through all those first few minutes of formalities that you go through when you have guests. And then all of a sudden Emma burst out with a question for her pastor. "Is the resurrection real?" she asked.

Strayhorn answered, "Yes."

She asked, "Well, how do you know?"

They talked about the passages of scripture that dealt with the resurrection. They talked about those where Jesus foretold his own death and gave us the promise of the resurrection. They talked about how they had to accept it on faith. It was all very Biblical and theologically correct.

Evidently, it was not enough. With a deep sigh Emma said, "I want a sign."

Strayhorn told her the only sign he knew of was the empty tomb.

Emma said, "That's not enough. I want more than that."

As they talked, the rain had been coming down harder and harder. It had gotten even darker. The day seemed to match their moods. Strayhorn himself was depressed. He'd come to help and hadn't done a very good job. Before he left, they prayed and he prayed for a sign for Emma. Something to ease her grief and to help her know the truth of the resurrection. As they walked down the hall, he felt sort of useless because he hadn't been able to reach her.

When he opened the door, the first thing Pastor Strayhorn noticed was that it had stopped raining and the sun was starting to peek out of the clouds. The sky off in the east was still dark and stormy but the western sky was beginning to lighten up. About the same time that he heard the door close, he looked up. And he immediately turned around and rang the doorbell.

The door opened and he took Emma's hand. He pulled her outside and pointed. They both stood there in stunned silence as they looked at one of the most beautiful rainbows either one of them had ever seen. It was a full horizon to horizon rainbow. The colors were brilliant. Emma started crying. And then she started laughing. She looked at her pastor and through her tears and laughter said, "He's alive!!!" She gave him a hug and immediately ran inside and started opening curtains and blinds. (5)

I am glad that rainbow appeared in the sky for Emma, but really all of creation testifies to the resurrection. The rhythms of winter and springtime. The beauty of a sunset and the certainty of sunrise. You don't have to be a poet or a painter to recognize that it is all too wondrous to have happened with no design. He's alive! The birds returning from their winter homes and the tiny buds of the flowers that peek out from the earth so recently cold and lifeless testify to all who will listen, He's alive. All of creation bears eyewitness testimony to the truth of Christ's resurrection.

But there is one more eyewitness that we need to take into account. It is the testimony of the Holy Spirit within the hearts of those who believe. Paul writes in Romans 8, "And if the Spirit of him who raised Jesus from the dead is living in you, he who raised Christ from the dead will also give life to your mortal bodies because of his Spirit who lives in you . . . The Spirit himself testifies with our spirit that we are God's children (11, 16)."

This is the ultimate witness to the truth of the resurrection—the Holy Spirit of God alive within us. Years ago a songwriter named Alfred Ackley put it in a simple Gospel song that expressed it for many Christians, "You ask me how I know he lives? He lives within my heart."

I love the way Pastor Rick Calhoun has put it. He writes, "The Resurrection of Jesus Christ from the dead was never meant to be proved but experienced. As a matter of fact it cannot be proved, as no one of us was there. We have to take the word of others who were. Those early witnesses were very passionate about their testimonies. Many were to be martyred in defense of their convictions. But ultimately the resurrection is to be experienced not proved. The most convincing evidence of the Resurrection of Christ is the transformation of the people who know Jesus and believe in Him. I decided long ago, the only proof of Easter I will ever need is memory. I remember what my life was like before I met the living Christ and I know what my life is now, as I share it with Him. I would not stand here and tell you I am always the man I should be. But thanks to the living Christ, I am not the man I used to be either. The risen Jesus Christ has made all the difference." (6) Christ living within us does make all the difference. And so we come this Easter Sunday to reaffirm what the Bible, creation and our own hearts tell us is true: Jesus Christ is alive!

Author Jim Moore tells about a woman who was a member of the choir in his church. One day she was diagnosed with a terminal illness. She lived only a few weeks after that. When he visited her in the hospital she told him that she wanted to be buried in her choir robe. She said, "I've heard that in heaven all God's children have robes, and I want to take mine, just in case." (7)

That's how a saint of God faces death. With humor and anticipation—with joy and expectation. The light still burns in the window. A bridge is completed between earth and eternity. Rather than singing with terror, "One billion bottles of beer on the wall, one billion bottles of beer," we sing triumphantly, "I got a robe, you got a robe, All of God's children got a robe; When I get to heaven Gonna put on my robe, I'm gonna shout all over God's heaven . . ." He is alive!

1. Ron Mehl, Love Found a Way (Waterbrook, 1999), pp. 20-21.
2. http://www.sermonsfromseattle.com/easter_fountain.htm.
3. Written by Jim Collins and Marty Dodson.
http://www.lyricsyoulove.com/k/kenny_chesney/everybody_wants_to_go_to_heaven/
4. Thanks to pastor and author Kent Crockett for this illustration.
http://www.kentcrockett.blogspot.com/.
5. http://www.epulpit.net/billy100.htm.
6. http://www.firstumcpueblo.org/php/see_sermon.php?sid=10295.
7. Mark Trotter, http://clergyresources.net/Trotter/Trotter%20Easter%20Sunday.htm.

Disillusioned Thomas
John 20:19-31

Pastor Paula Womack made a "Top Ten" list (aka David Letterman) of ways you can tell it's the Sunday after Easter. Not all the items on her list fit us, but some of them are very clever. So, here are six ways you tell it's the Sunday after Easter:

Number six: There's not a lily available for purchase anywhere.

Five: Wal-Mart has rotated the Easter candy to the clearance table and brought out the Mother's Day cards and gift ideas.

Four: The stores have removed the stuffed bunnies from the shelves and replaced them with the newest line of Harry Potter action figures.

Three: You had no trouble finding a seat at church (even if you were late for worship).

Two: The number of visitors in the worship service has dropped dramatically.

And the number one way you can tell it's the Sunday after Easter: The number of people who look like visitors but are actually church members who haven't been here for a while has dropped dramatically. (1)

Welcome on this Sunday after Easter, which is known in some churches as Low Sunday. (Really)

As we noted three weeks ago, on the Sunday after Easter we normally tell the story of Doubting Thomas and his response to the resurrected Christ. On this day many pastors will talk about the nature of doubt and how doubt is a healthy emotion. All of us doubt at some times in our lives.

However, doubt is a somewhat intellectual exercise. Very cerebral. It's possible to have doubts about some aspect of Christian faith and still continue serving Christ as if you have no doubt at all. We now know that, to a certain extent, this was true of Mother Teresa, one of the great saints who ever lived. But it's been true of many saints through the ages. All of us doubt from time to time. That goes with having a brain. But my purpose this day is not to focus on doubt, but on an experience and an emotion that grips many saints of God much more deeply than doubt. That emotion is disillusionment.

And that brings us back to Thomas. A few weeks ago we called him Daring Thomas. We felt it was a more appropriate name than Doubting Thomas. The reason we said that was that on one occasion Jesus was returning to Judea where his life was in danger. The disciples, almost to a man, urged him not to go. But it was Thomas, Daring Thomas, who declared, "Let us also go, that we may die with him." It was a heart-felt declaration of Thomas' loyalty to Christ. He was willing to give his life for the man he believed to be the anointed one of God.

But today we are dealing not with Daring Thomas. Today we are dealing with "Disillusioned Thomas." I believe this is a more accurate description than Doubting Thomas. After Christ's crucifixion, Thomas is thoroughly disillusioned. In his mind, Jesus has let him down. You see, Thomas is a very intense young man, as we have already noted. He was willing to drop everything and die for the Master. But like all the other disciples, he thought Jesus fit the common expectation of a Messiah—someone who would restore the glory of Israel—someone who would throw off the yoke of the despised Romans. He believed that right up until the time the soldiers drove nails into Jesus' hands and feet.

How could the Messiah possibly be put to death? Thomas wondered with horror. The Messiah should wear a crown of gold, not a crown of thorns. Had it all been a pipe dream? Had he sold them a bill of goods? Now the other disciples were saying Jesus was raised from the dead. Yeah, right! thinks Thomas to himself. Fool me once, shame on you. Fool me twice, shame on me. And so, just for today, we are going to call him Disillusioned Thomas.

Have you ever been disillusioned? With a marriage, perhaps. Or a career? Maybe with a pastor or someone you looked up to? It happens and it hurts.

Most of you are familiar with the great psychiatrist Sigmund Freud. Freud was one of the most influential men who ever lived. That's why it's disturbing that Freud ruled out almost any role for God in human life. Disillusionment may have played a role in Freud's attitude toward faith.

When Freud was two years old, a nursemaid was employed in the Freud household. This nursemaid made a profound impression on young Sigmund. He was very much attracted to her. She took him to church with her, told him stories from the Bible and indoctrinated him in the beliefs of the church. So impressed was the young lad that on returning home from a church service he would pretend he was the preacher.

Unfortunately this nursemaid was convicted of a theft in a local store and consequently was dismissed. "It would be fair to surmise," suggests one psychiatrist, "that Freud's hostility to religion and religious ceremonies goes back to his disappointment with the very person who first introduced him to religion." (2)

That happens. Someone lets us down—someone we have looked up to—and we set up defenses so it never happens again. That's a difficult situation.

Thomas was disillusioned because he misunderstood why Christ came into the world. He was not alone. Right up until he ascended into heaven, Christ was surrounded by people who loved him but did not understand him. They expected him to redeem Israel and throw off the yoke of Rome. Of course, he would redeem Israel, and all of humankind, though not in the way that they expected.

So, all of the disciples were disillusioned, disappointed, dejected. If Thomas was slower to accept the resurrection than the others, it may have been because he had been more intense in his devotion than the others. He was willing to die for Jesus. Peter had denied Christ. Judas had betrayed him. But Thomas was willing to die for him. Thomas' expectations had been higher—so perhaps his fall from faith had been farther. He simply did not realize that Christ's suffering and death had been a necessary part of God's plan.

Every once in a while I run into a person who has grown disillusioned with God.

Usually at the heart of that disillusionment is a misunderstanding of the way God works in the world. They expect God to work according to their plans, but God works in His own way and according to His own timetable. Some people can't deal with that.

Let's face it: there is much in life none of us understands. We've dealt with this many times before, of course, but many people are deeply concerned when God works in a different way from what we expect.

For many years, pastor and author Dr. Gerald Mann had a weekly television ministry. He tells of one occasion when the director of that ministry came out during a break and said, "We have a call from Florida. It is a child nine years old."

The child's name was Sarah. She had a question. This was live, interactive television, remember. Mann never knew what was coming. He says he'll never forget Sarah's quavering, haunting, small voice. She said, "Dr. Mann, why does God allow grown-ups to kill kids?" How would you handle that question?

Sara continued, "They told me at Sunday School that if I prayed, God would protect us, but God didn't protect my cousin, Suzanne. She was seven years old and someone killed her."

Gerald Mann says he was absolutely stumped. Live television. How do you talk about such things to a nine year old? And yet she had asked the question that every one of us who dares to believe will ask sooner or later. If God is great and God is good, why do the innocent suffer? (3) There is much in life we do not understand, and if something terrible happens to us or to someone we love, disillusionment is apt to follow.

A few years ago, a fascinating book by Mitch Albom hit the bestseller lists. You may have read it. It was titled, Tuesdays with Morrie. Here's the story. The author learns that his old teacher is slowly dying of Lou Gehrig's disease. After an absence of many years, the two reconnect and begin to get together every Tuesday. The book shares some of the great lessons that emerge from those weekly conversations. For example, here is a sample exchange that blends humor and pathos:

"Okay, question," Mitch says to Morrie. Morrie's bony fingers hold his glasses across his chest, which rises and falls with each labored breath.

"What's the question?" Morrie asks.

"Remember the book of Job?" says Mitch. "Job is a good man, but God makes him suffer."

"To test his faith, I remember," says Morrie.

"Takes away everything he has," Mitch continues, "his house, his money, his family . . . Makes him sick."

"To test his faith," Morrie says again.

"Right," Mitch says. "To test his faith. So I'm wondering . . . What do you think about that?"

Morrie coughs violently, his hands quiver as he drops them to his side. "I think," he says, smiling, "God overdid it." (4)

Well, in our estimation, God does overdo it sometimes, though, technically, the story of Job says that God allowed Job to suffer, not that God made him suffer. However, some people with a weak faith can't even handle that—that God sometimes allows suffering. They become bitter. They blame God when adversity comes. And disillusionment sets in—a disillusionment very much like that of Thomas. Some of you have been there. At least for a while. If you haven't yet, give yourself time.

Fortunately, this is not the end of the story. Thomas was dejected, disappointed, disillusioned. A friend that he loved was dead. More than that, a teacher he revered, looked up to, would given his life for, had let him down.

But Thomas didn't drop out of the fellowship. This is so important. Thomas was there with the other disciples when they met together after Jesus' resurrection. He could have made excuses. He could have stayed home and wrapped himself in gloom and despair. Who would have blamed him? Why should he have to listen to a fairy tale about his dead friend being raised from the dead?

"Unless I see the nail marks in his hands," Thomas said adamantly, "and put my finger where the nails were, and put my hand into his side, I will not believe it." But still he went to be with the other disciples. He still went to church.

I see it happen all the time. A person goes through a difficult time when they feel God has let them down and the first thing they do is drop out of the fellowship. They miss one Sunday, then a second, and before very long, going to church takes far more effort than staying home. Friends, that's always a mistake. This is where the people are who care about you.

A Presbyterian pastor once told Tony Campolo about his early days of ministry at a small country church. One day, a young woman came to the church to present her child for baptism. She had given birth to the child out of wedlock. This was in a small rural community. This occurred in a time and place where a young woman in this situation was often shunned.

The day of the baptism, the young woman and her baby stood alone before the congregation. The pastor hadn't recognized the awkwardness of the situation until he asked, as part of the baptismal service, "Who stands with this child to assure the commitments and promises herewith made will be carried out? Who will be there for this child in times of need and assure that this child is brought up in the nurture and admonition of the Lord?"

At that moment, he realized that there was no godmother or godfather on hand to answer the question. But, as though on cue, the entire congregation stood and with one voice said, "We will!" (5)

Thank God for that congregation. A young woman and her child could have been rejected. That rejection could have led to a very real disillusionment with anything religious. This mother had the courage to bring her child to the community of faith. Fortunately, she found a group of people who would stand with her and support her.

Thomas was hurt but he still went to church. He still didn't have the answers he was seeking. He still didn't understand why his Master was dead, but at least he didn't cut himself off from the fellowship of faith.

And in that fellowship of faith the risen Christ appeared to Thomas.

You know the story. Though the doors were locked, Jesus came and stood among them and said, "Peace be with you!" Then he turned to Thomas and said to him, "Put your finger here; see my hands. Reach out your hand and put it into my side. Stop doubting and believe."

Thomas said to him, "My Lord and my God!" And Thomas went on to become a great Christian missionary leader. My guess is that his time of disillusionment and doubt actually left him stronger than he was before. It happens more often than you can imagine. People go through a time of testing and they come out better rather than bitter. In their time of need they feel the comforting presence of Christ, and something wonderful happens in their life. In their hearts they cry out, "My Lord and my God!" and the darkness that has enveloped them becomes as bright as day.

Dr. Steve Jackson tells about a man of his acquaintance who has dealt with disappointments that would have killed someone without the kind of faith he has. He had one daughter killed in a motorcycle accident on her high school senior trip. A second daughter died of cancer in her early thirties. A son died of a sudden heart attack at age forty. And his last remaining daughter was killed instantly in her early forties when her husband cut down a tree and she walked outside at just the wrong moment and was struck by the tree. On top of that a few years later this man buried his wife. But, says Jackson, this man has incredible faith, and the suffering he has faced, the disappointments life has dealt him, have left him stronger and more Christ-like than you can imagine. (6)

It happens. Here's how—maintain your connection to the fellowship of saints. Let the people in the church love you and pray for you. Maintain an openness to the comforting and healing power of the Holy Spirit. Give Christ a chance to come to you and show you his hands and his feet—for he has been where you are. He wants to help you, like Thomas, to move from being disillusioned to being dynamic. It can happen. Don't give up. Trust in the risen Christ and your Christian friends and you will endure.

1. http://www.northraleighunited.org/Sermons/ontheroad.htm.
2. A. Dudley Dennison M.D., Shock It To Me Doctor! (Grand Rapids: Zondervan Publishing House, 1970), pp. 74-75
3. http://www.csec.org/csec/sermon/mann_3615.htm
4. (New York: Doubleday, 1997), pp.150-151. Cited by Rev. Dr. David E. Leininger, http://www.presbyterianwarren.com/overdoes.html.
5. Tony Campolo, Letters to a Young Evangelical (New York: Perseus Books Group, 2006), pp. 78-79.
6. http://www.newsongweb.org/Sermons/2006%20Sermons/11-05-06.htm.

Loving Deeply

1 Peter 1:17-23

(Mother's Day)

Since today is Mother's Day, I thought I would begin with a list someone has made which they have called "Murphy's Laws of Parenting." See if you can identify with any of these:

1. The later you stay up, the earlier your child will wake up the next morning.

2. The gooier the food, the more likely it is to end up on the carpet.

3. The longer it takes you to make a meal, the less your child will like it.

4. A sure way to get something done is to tell a child not to do it.

5. For a child to become clean, something else must become dirty.

6. Toys multiply to fill any space available.

7. Yours is always the only child who doesn't behave.

8. If the shoe fits . . . it's expensive.

9. Backing the car out of the driveway causes your child to have to go to the bathroom.

Do any of these strike home?

It isn't easy being a Mom. I chuckled when I read a story by a Mom named Mary Jane Kurtz. Mary Jane says that when she was a young, single mom with four children, it was difficult to get them all ready for church on Sunday. One particular Sunday morning as the children started to complain and squabble, Mary Jane stomped from one room to the other, saying out loud why it was important they go to church as a family and have a good attitude. Suddenly, she noticed all four children huddled together and laughing.

"What's so funny?" Mary Jane asked.

"Mom," they said, "every time you slam down your foot, smoke comes out. It must be the wrath of God!"

In reality, it was some powder Mary Jane had sprinkled in her shoes. But it worked. She says they made it to church on time that morning and practically every Sunday thereafter. (1)

I'm not suggesting that any of you busy Moms sprinkle powder in your shoes. I'm just reporting on Mary Jane's experience.

What we don't want to do on this Mother's Day, 2011 is take our Moms for granted. I've cited it before, but the best example I know of that is the Mother's Day card that reads like this: "Forget the housework, Mom. It's your day. Besides, you can always do double duty and catch up on Monday!" (2)

I suspect some of you Moms can relate to that. Since this is Mother's Day, I want to draw your attention to our lesson from the Epistle, particularly the twenty-second verse, where we read these words, "Now that you have purified yourselves by obeying the truth so that you have sincere love for your brothers, love one another deeply, from the heart." What a perfect text for a day when we honor our Moms. "Love one another deeply, from the heart."

Note that these words are directed at the community of faith. They are not being written for the secular community. The writer of this passage uses phrases like, "Since you call on a Father who judges each man's work impartially . . ." And a little further he writes, "For you know that it was not with perishable things . . . you were redeemed . . . . but with the precious blood of Christ . . ." And then, still further he writes, "Now that you have purified yourselves by obeying the truth so that you have sincere love for your brothers, love one another deeply, from the heart." Then he adds, "For you have been born again, not of perishable seed, but of imperishable, through the living and enduring word of God."

These are not words that the secular world would even understand. These are words written for the community of faith. It is Christians to whom he is saying, "Love one another deeply, from the heart."

Love is the glorious burden of the Christian.

Christians disagree about all kinds of things. We disagree on social issues. For example, some Christians are teetotalers when it comes to alcoholic beverages; others see no problem with drinking in moderation. We argue over how people are to be baptized and whether Christ is present in the Eucharist. Christians subscribe to both liberal and conservative political philosophies. We have all kinds of differing interpretations of Scripture. But one thing we cannot remove from the Christian community and still call ourselves followers of Christ is love—deep, persistent, sacrificial love. We are a people who claim that God is love and we are a people who are called to model love in the world.

This is not to say that love does not exist in the secular world. It does.

Dr. Thomas Lane Butts tells a wonderful story about Larry Doby, the first African American baseball player in the American League. Doby played for the Cleveland Indians in the nineteen forties and fifties.

Doby was in his rookie season. He was reputed to be a good player, and an excellent hitter. He came to bat in his first game, and the fans waited to see what he could do. It was a disaster. He swung at the first three pitches and missed them all by a least a foot. He struck out. The fans "booed" him off the field.

Larry Doby stared at the ground as he walked back to the dugout. He went to the end of the bench, sat down, and put his head in his hands. The next batter was second baseman Joe Gordon, an All Star hitter, who had always hit this particular pitcher well. Everyone knew he could not only hit the ball, he could put it out of the park. Joe Gordon stepped up to the plate, swung at the first three pitches and missed each pitch by at least a foot. The fans could not believe it. A huge silence fell over the crowd.

Joe Gordon stared at the ground as he walked back to the dugout. He went to the end of the bench, sat down by Larry Doby, and put his head in his hands.

That is the stuff of which baseball legends are made. Even today people wonder, did he strike out on purpose? Of course, nobody knows for sure, except Joe Gordon. But, here is what is interesting: It is reported that from that day on, Larry Doby never went on the baseball field but that he did not reach down and pick up the glove of his teammate, Joe Gordon, and hand it to him. (3)

We see love lived out in many areas of our secular world.

A man tells a delightful story about an occasion when his cell phone quit working. This occurred just as he was trying to let his wife know that he was caught in a freeway gridlock and would be late for their anniversary dinner. He wrote a message on his laptop asking other motorists to call her. He printed it on a portable ink-jet that he had in the car and taped it to his rear windshield.

When he finally arrived home, his wife gave him the longest kiss ever. "I really think you love me," she said. "At least 70 people called and told me so."

We see love lived out in many areas of our secular world. The difference is that for the world, love is the exception, not the rule.

For the 70 who called this woman to tell her that her husband was caught in traffic, another 500-600 probably passed by indifferently. Another 70 probably cursed the man for trying to burden them with his dilemma. That's the way the world operates. Love is the exception, not the rule.

There was a column in the Denver Post sometime back about an 85-year-old Denver woman, Ellie Lindecrantz, who was flying to Florida to stay there for a few months. She was to be met in Florida by her husband, who had driven the family car there. After arriving at Denver International Airport, 85-year-old Ellie had asked for a wheelchair to take her to the gate. She was waiting under the departure/arrival screens. Suddenly, she started to feel chest pains. She is quoted as saying, "I hurt a lot. I knew I needed help." A young man stopped to look at the screens above her. She told the man she had severe chest pains and really needed some help. He said, "I hope you feel better," and walked away.

She called to another person nearby, asking for help. She just needed to get to the airport's urgent care facility. The woman kept walking.

By this time, Ellie had taken two nitroglycerin tablets. The wheelchair still hadn't arrived. She took a few steps toward a uniformed woman monitoring lines at the ticket counter, and said she really needed someone to help her. The woman looked at her ticket and said, "You should ask American Airlines to help you." The American Airlines counter was nowhere in sight.

Ellie sat down, took another nitro. In severe pain, she called her daughter, Greta, on her cell phone. Greta was in her car in Golden, Colorado but called 9-1-1 immediately. The dispatcher there patched it through to Denver, which transferred her to the Denver International Airport dispatch. Greta relayed all the information about her mother, and the man on the phone said, "We haven't had any emergency calls."

"This is an emergency call," Greta said. "My mother needs help."

"What do you want me to do about it?" said the man at DIA.

Finally, after four nitro tablets, and after almost 30 minutes had passed, the wheelchair attendant arrived. Ellie told him she needed to go to the medical part of the airport right away. But the attendant didn't understand English. He could tell that something was wrong, though, so he took her to a friend, another airport worker, who translated for them. As soon as he figured out what was wrong, the attendant sped her through the crowds to the infirmary, where Ellie was stabilized and taken to the hospital by ambulance. "It was not a good experience," Ellie said later from her bed at Exempla St. Joseph Hospital. The writer of this article in the Denver Post, Diane Carman, notes that the worst part for Ellie was the sense of abandonment. (4)

Ask for help in the secular world when you are drowning and someone is as apt to throw you an anchor as a lifejacket. Not always, of course. We see love lived out in many areas of our secular world. The difference is that for the world, love is the exception, not the rule.

For Christians love is to be the rule. There can be no exceptions. Jesus says in John 13:35, "By this everyone will know that you are my disciples, if you love one another." Jesus said we are to even love people who are mean to us. No exceptions. Obviously we would like for there to be exceptions: people who offend us, for example, or people who bully us.

Barbara Brown Taylor tells the story of her nephew Will's first birthday party. Little Will was the center of everyone's attention, and so he happily did a little dance—until a jealous 7-year-old named Jason charged over, put both of his hands on Will's chest and shoved. Will fell hard. His rear end hit first, then his head, with a crack.

He looked utterly surprised at first. No one had ever hurt him before, and he did not know what to make of it. Then he opened up his mouth and howled, but not for long. His mother hugged him and helped him to his feet, and the first thing Will did was to totter over to Jason. He knew Jason was at the bottom of this thing, but since such meanness was new to him he didn't know what to do. So he did what he had always done. He put his arms around Jason and laid his head against that mean little boy's body.

"What Will did to Jason put an end to the meanness in that room," observes Barbara Brown Taylor. "That is what love is . . . not a warm feeling between like-minded friends but plain old imitation of Christ, who took all the meanness of the world and ran it through the filter of his own body, repaying evil with good, blame with pardon, death with life. Call it divine reverse psychology. It worked once, and it can work again, whenever God can find someone else willing to give it a try." (5)

For Christians love is to be the rule. There are to be no exceptions. Why? Because we are loved by one who makes no exceptions. Our Master put it like this in John 15:12, "My command is this: Love each other as I have loved you." Christ makes no exceptions. Neither can we.

Some of you may be familiar with Brennan Manning, a speaker and author who has inspired many, many people through his books. Actually Brennan was not the name Manning was given at birth.

To discover how he got his name you have to go back to 1952 to a place named Pusan, Korea. At midnight two best friends, Richard Manning (as he was known then) and Ray Brennan were side by side in a Korean foxhole, awaiting their orders. They were casually eating chocolate bars. Suddenly the unthinkable happened. A deadly hand grenade landed next to Ray Brennan. Then Ray Brennan did something quite extraordinary. Brennan casually tossed aside his candy wrapper, threw his body on the grenade, glanced a loving wink at Manning, his best friend, and allowed the grenade to explode under him. He gave his life for Richard Manning.

Eight years later, when it came time for Manning to enter the Franciscan priesthood, he adopted a new name, as was the custom at ordination. Because of the sacrifice of his friend he took the name Brennan as his first name, thus he became Brennan Manning. Now you know the rest of the story. Brennan Manning hoped to live sacrificially in the same way his friend had modeled for him. (6)

Of course, this is the love that Christ modeled for us. It is the very love of God. We see love lived out in many areas of our secular world. The difference is that for the world, love is the exception, not the rule. For Christians love is to be the rule. There are to be no exceptions. Why? Because we are loved by One who makes no exceptions.

1. Edward K. Rowell, 1001 Quotes, Illustrations, and Humorous Stories (Grand Rapids: Baker Publishing, 2008), p. 330.

2. Charles Swindoll, Day By Day (Nashville, TN: W Publishing Group, 2000), p. 130.

3. http://www.day1.net/index.php5?view=transcripts&tid=406.

4. 27 January 2006. Cited by The Rev. Peter Munson, Boulder, Colorado, http://www.saintambrosechurch.net/sermons/mainThingLove1_29.html.

5. Christianity Today, January 11, 1999, P. 74. Cited by Tony Grant, http://yarpc.tripod.com/parachut.htm.

6. Greg Ogden, http://www.cc-ob.tv/search.php?series_id=95&category=Sermon.

It's Not Fair!

1 Peter 2:19-25

Strange things happen in this world. Surely you've noticed that.

There was a news report about two motorists who had a head-on collision—and I do mean a head-on collision. It happened in heavy fog near the small town of Guetersloh, Germany. The two motorists were guiding their cars at a snail's pace near the center of the road in the dense fog. Each of them had his head out of the car window trying to see. And yes, before they realized it, they smacked their heads together. Both men were hospitalized with severe head injuries. Their cars weren't even scratched. (1)

Strange things happen. And sometimes these events don't seem quite fair.

Actress Helen Hayes used to tell of walking down the Champs Elysees in Paris with former Broadway star Mary Martin, who was wearing a new designer outfit.

A bird came down, went swoosh, and made a mess on Mary's expensive outfit. Helen expected Mary to blow her top. Instead Mary simply said, "For some people, they sing."

That brings us to our theme for the day. Sometimes life isn't fair. That's what Mary Martin was saying. For some people birds sing. For others, they simply make a mess. It isn't fair.

Futurist Faith Popcorn approaches this subject from a different angle. She writes about the "Right, But" Club. The "Right, But" Club has as its members all the people who did the right thing, BUT life still didn't work out for them as they had planned.

"I exercised BUT got heart disease"; "I took antioxidants BUT got cancer"; "I spent quality time with my kids BUT their SAT scores stink"; "I went to an Ivy League school BUT I'm stuck in middle management quicksand."

Ms. Popcorn says, "It shouldn't be surprising that life isn't predictable, but our consumer society, the self-help industry and the media have all conspired to have us believe that we can actually micromanage our destinies." (2)

What a profound statement. We think we ought to have absolute control of our lives, and then comes a little bird, and plop! Or, in a fog, we bump heads with our neighbor.

Someone who has experienced life's strange twists and turns has turned it into a radio weather forecast: "Fair today—grossly unfair tomorrow."

Even if you are serving God, life can treat you unfairly.

Philip Yancey, one of our very best Christian writers, devoted an entire book to this problem. He called it quite simply, Disappointment with God. When something grossly unfair happens in our lives, many Christians blame God.

For example, there was an interesting tidbit in The Week magazine last fall.

The magazine reports that after a football game, Buffalo Bills receiver Steve Johnson blamed God for letting him drop what would have been a game-winning touchdown pass. This is what he tweeted afterward in capital letters with lots of exclamation points and question marks: I PRAISE YOU 24/7!!!!!! AND THIS IS HOW YOU DO ME!!!! YOU EXPECT ME TO LEARN FROM THIS??? HOW???!!! I'LL NEVER FORGET THIS!! EVER!! It was just a dropped pass, but Steve Johnson unloaded on God. Johnson, of course, is not alone.

In the mid-16th century, a group of 50 Spanish nuns led by Sister Teresa of Avila traveled on foot to a neighboring convent in a rugged storm. Crossing a rickety bridge over a swollen stream, the sisters prayed that the bridge would hold up until they were safely across. It didn't. Near the center it collapsed, spilling all of the nuns into the water. As they managed to swim safely to shore, Sister Teresa raised her eyes toward heaven and said, "Lord, if this is the way you treat your friends, it is little wonder you have so many foes."

Sister Teresa was known for her wit and her sense of humor. She was actually having a little fun with this incident. She was sainted by the Catholic Church, but she also knew that the God in whom she believed didn't prevent bad things from happening to good people. (3)

We've all been there. Not with a dropped pass, perhaps, or a collapsed bridge, but there has been some time in our lives when we, too, have felt that life has treated us unfairly. And we, too, have blamed God.

Philip Yancey studied this problem at great length and this is what he found. Some people caved in when they felt God let them down while others used their time of adversity as a stepping stone to a richer, fuller relationship with God. I was especially impressed by Yancey's description of a man named Douglas.

Yancey says that when he got to the portion of Disappointment with God that dealt with the Book of Job, he decided to look around and find the person he knew who was most like Job. He found such a person. This man, he felt, was a righteous man in the same sense that Job was righteous.

The man, named Douglas, was a good man. He had been trained as a psychotherapist, but he gave up his lucrative practice working primarily with the rich and well-connected and started to work in the inner-city among poor people. Most of us would agree that this was a noble endeavor. Yet after he did this, his life started to fall apart.

The first thing that happened was that his wife came down with breast cancer. She started taking chemotherapy treatments and that affected his whole family. She was always tired and often felt sick. Douglas had to pick up a lot of work around the house. The spot of cancer spread and appeared on her lungs. His wife's life was seriously threatened and a new series of treatment started.

Douglas had to deal with that new situation. Then, on top of this, his family was involved in a serious traffic accident. A drunk driver crossed the median, and smashed into their car head on. Douglas's twelve-year-old daughter went through the windshield and was badly lacerated in the face. His wife was also hurt. The worst injuries were to Douglas himself. Douglas hit his head on the dashboard. First, he had trouble with his vision. One of his eyes wouldn't cooperate and he saw double. He couldn't even walk down a set of stairs without stumbling. The worst thing to him was that he could no longer read. Douglas loved to read.

Yancey knew Douglas. He knew his story. So, when he started to write about the Book of Job, he decided to interview Douglas. He called him up and scheduled an appointment. They met for breakfast. Douglas told him some of the story. They sat and chatted for a while. After breakfast had been served, Yancey said, "Well, Douglas, I'm writing a book about disappointment with God. I thought of all the people I know who have the right to be disappointed with God, you're right at the top of the list. Tell me, what would you say to people who are disappointed with God?"

Douglas thought for a minute and stroked his beard. Finally he looked at Yancey and said, "You know, Philip, I don't think I've ever been disappointed with God."

This shocked Yancey. He was amazed. He had specifically chosen Douglas because he thought of all the people he knew, he was the one most likely to be disappointed, even angry at God, because of the unfairness he had seen.

Yancey asked, "How can this be?"

Douglas said, "You know, Philip, I learned a long time ago and especially through this accident not to confuse God with life. Is life unfair? You bet. My life has been unfair. What has happened to my wife, what has happened to my daughter, what has happened to me, it's unfair. But I think God feels exactly the same way. I think He is grieved and hurt by what that drunk driver did as much as I am. Don't confuse God with life." He said, "As I read the Bible, especially the Old Testament, I notice that those people were able to separate the physical reality of their lives from the spiritual reality of their relationship with God."

Yancey says that as they sat there together, they went through some of those people in the Bible. They turned to a passage, for example, in Ezekiel where God tells about three of His very favorite people: Daniel, Noah and Job. "Think about those three people," says Yancey. "One of them spent the night with a bunch of lions; one of them lived through a huge flood that killed thousands of people and then, of course, there's Job, the greatest example of unfairness in the Bible. Yet when God looks at those people, He says these are three of my favorites. All three of them— Daniel, Noah, Job—and many others—Abraham, David . . . learned to have a relationship with God that didn't depend on how healthy they were and how well their lives were going."

Yancey says he and Douglas sat there together going through so many of these stories from the Bible. Suddenly Douglas glanced down at his watch and said, "I've got to go. I'll leave you with one last thought and that's this. If you are ever tempted to confuse God with life, go back and read the story of Jesus, the story of God on Earth. Ask yourself how Jesus would have answered the question, is life unfair." Just before he left, Douglas said, "For me, the cross of Christ demolished for all time the idea that life is supposed to be fair." (4)

Wow! All I can say is that I hope when you and I are treated unfairly by life we can have both the wisdom and the faith in God that Douglas has. Just because you are seeking to do the right thing doesn't mean that life will treat you fairly. Indeed, you could be treated unfairly simply and solely because you are trying to do the right thing. In our letter from I Peter, we read these words: "For it is commendable if a man bears up under the pain of unjust suffering because he is conscious of God. But how is it to your credit if you receive a beating for doing wrong and endure it? But if you suffer for doing good and you endure it, this is commendable before God."

The implication is that you can suffer ill because you are doing wrong and you can suffer ill because you are doing right. Life happens. As Douglas had learned, we must separate life from God. Life can treat us unfairly. God only seeks that which is good for us. God wasn't trying to teach Steve Johnson a lesson when he dropped that pass. Steve made a miscue. He dropped a pass. It may have been simply bad luck or bad hands, but it wasn't God's fault. However, God can help Steve put that mishap into perspective and help him to be a more mature Christian, maybe even a mature believer like Douglas.

Douglas was certainly right about one thing. The best example that life isn't fair is the crucifixion of Christ. The writer of I Peter continues: "To this you were called, because Christ suffered for you, leaving you an example, that you should follow in his steps. 'He committed no sin, and no deceit was found in his mouth.' When they hurled their insults at him, he did not retaliate; when he suffered, he made no threats. Instead, he entrusted himself to him who judges justly. He himself bore our sins in his body on the tree, so that we might die to sins and live for righteousness; by his wounds you have been healed."

That brings us to the good news for the day. We live on the other side of Easter. Resurrection faith is about living faithfully in an unfair world. Christ conquered death. What does that mean for us? Two things.

First of all when life treats you unfairly, focus on God's promises. Remember particularly these words of scripture: "And we know that in all things God works for the good of those who love him, who have been called according to his purpose." (Romans 8:28) God doesn't cause bad things to happen to us, but God can take everything that happens and use it to our good.

When complimented on her homemade biscuits, the cook at a popular Christian conference center said: "Just consider what goes into the making of these biscuits. The flour itself doesn't taste good, neither does the baking powder, nor the shortening, nor the other ingredients. However, when I mix them all together and put them in the oven, they come out just right." (5) That's the first thing, trust that God can use all things to our best good.

In the second place, look for ways an unfair event can be turned to something beneficial.

Dr. Ray Pritchard tells about a friend of his named Jim Warren who was the longtime host of Primetime America on the Moody Broadcasting Network. Warren passed along this bit of advice to Pritchard: "Ray, when hard times come, be a student, not a victim."

The more Pritchard pondered those simple words, the more profound they seemed to be. Many people, he says, are professional victims, always talking about how unfair life is. "A victim says, 'Why did this happen to me?' A student says, 'I don't care why it happened. I want to learn what God is trying to teach me.' A victim looks at everyone else and cries out, 'Life isn't fair.' A student looks at life and says, 'What happened to me could have happened to anybody.' A victim feels so sorry for himself that he has no time for others. A student focuses on helping others so that he has no time to feel sorry for himself. A victim begs God to remove the problems of life so that he might be happy. A student has learned through the problems of life that God alone is the source of all true happiness." (6)

That's wise advice. Be a student, not a victim. Look for ways an unfair event can be turned to something beneficial. Turn your mess into a ministry.

Mother Teresa once wrote about a situation she said she would never forget. One day in Venezuela she went to visit a family who had donated a lamb to her order of nuns. She went to thank them and there she found out that they had a badly handicapped child. She asked the mother, "What is the child's name?" The mother gave her a most beautiful answer. "We call him 'Teacher of Love,'" said the mother, "because he keeps on teaching us how to love. Everything we do for him is our love for God in action." (7) There was a family that had learned to be students, not victims.

Life can be unfair, but don't confuse life with God. Trust in God's promises. Look for ways you can turn a mess into a ministry. The most unfair act in history was the crucifixion when the innocent Son of God was slain. But we live on the other side of the resurrection. We can see God's power over life's unfairness. God can help us deal with the unfair events that happen to us.

1. http://www.mustsharejokes.com/page/Funny+True+Stories
2. Faith Popcorn and Adam Hanft, Dictionary of the Future (New York: Hyperion, 2001), p. 156.
3. The Rev. Dr. George B. Wirth, http://day1.org/944-trust_at_28000_feet.
4. Philip Yancey, Disappointment with God, http://www.csec.org/csec/sermon/yancey_3302.htm.
5. http://funnysermons.com/
6. http://www.keepbelieving.com/sermon/2002-04-07-The-Sixth-Law-There-is-No-Growth-Without-Struggle/.
7. No Greater Love (Novato, CA: New World Library California, 1989), pp. 24-25.

Family Resemblance
John 14:1-14

There was a story on the Internet recently that proves rednecks aren't confined to the southern part of the United States. According to this story a man in Australia was fined after police discovered that he had used a seat belt to buckle in a case of beer while his five-year-old son was consigned to playing in the car's floor—totally unprotected.

Constable Wayne Burnett said he was "shocked and appalled" when he pulled over the car one Friday in the Australian town of Alice Springs. A 30-can beer case was strapped safely in between two adults while the child sat on the floor. (1)

We definitely know where that father's priorities were. Here's the question for the day: Will his son someday have the same skewed values? Have you heard the expression, "Like father, like son?" Our topic today is "Family Resemblance."

Once, years ago, there was a band of pirates who swept through a village in China. These pirates captured all the men of the town and carried them away. One of these captured men was a Mr. Li. Mr. Li left behind him a wife and small son.

Mrs. Li worked hard to provide for her son, but times were tough for a single mom. And years passed with no word of her captured husband.

Meanwhile, the little boy was always asking of his mother, "What did father look like!"

Her answer always was the same, "When you were little everyone said you looked like your father."

As the boy grew older, he ran with the wrong crowd, and took to opium, smoking, and heavy drinking. His rough life gradually affected his appearance.

One day Mrs. Li got word that someone had seen her husband alive in Singapore. She immediately sent the boy, now a young man, to look for him. Upon arriving in Singapore the young man bought a stool and a mirror and seated himself at a street corner. That was the only way to know if his father came by. He would look for someone who looked like the face he saw in the mirror.

One day a man came by claiming to be his father. The young man didn't believe this man. He said, "My mother told me to look for someone who looked exactly like me. This mirror is the only way I can compare faces. You don't look at all like me."

However, he accepted this man as his friend. The man even gave him a job. For six months they stayed together while he worked in his new friend's shop.

One day the young man realized he had been so busy and so happy that his promise to his mother had been forgotten. He again took his mirror and stool to search for his father. Before he left the shop, however, he held up the mirror for one more look. In the mirror staring back at him this time he saw not only his own face, but the face of his friend. It was amazing—in the six months of association and the desire to please his new-found friend—he had grown to look like his friend, who was indeed his father. (2)

Jesus says in our lesson for today, "When you have seen me, you have seen my father." And that is often true, isn't it? Children often resemble their parents.

In the South someone might say, "He's the spittin' image of his Daddy." I don't know where that expression came from. An Internet search comes up fruitless. However, the expression means that there's a close resemblance between father and son. Same color hair, perhaps. Same contour of the face. Maybe even the same swagger. Of course, we could say just as easily that a child resembles his or her mother.

It always amuses me with a newborn how people will say, "Why he looks just like his father." Well, if Dad is bald and wrinkled, I suppose that is true. We could say that the newborn looks like its mother. However, according to research on this subject, usually people will say of a newborn, he or she looks like his or her father. Go figure.

An objective observer might question whether a newborn resembles anybody at all. But who wants to spoil the moment? Nevertheless, it is common as children grow toward adulthood that they do take on many characteristics of their parents. There is nothing unusual about that. People in the same family resemble each other.

Indeed, there have been studies that show that husbands and wives after many years of living together begin to resemble one another. I'll let some of you married couples decided whether that is good news or bad news.

Of course, there are also recent studies that suggest that some people look like their pet dogs. We'll ignore those studies for today.

The really scary thing about children is that they often not only look like us, but they act like us too.

Many years ago, a television ad campaign featured a little boy imitating his father in various everyday activities. The father sprayed the car with a water hose, then the son sprayed it with his water pistol. A voice-over then said, "Like father, like son."

Similar scenes followed to drive home this point. Then the final scene showed the father reaching into his pocket and pulling out a pack of cigarettes, lighting one up, then laying the pack on the ground beside him. The son then picked up the pack of cigarettes as if to take one. The voice-over then asked ominously, "Like father, like son?" (3)

It is a frightening responsibility to each of us as parents to realize that our children may reflect not only our appearance but also our values, our habits, as well as our strongest and weakest points.

A minister tells of a time he went to counsel a family about their son's drug use. The father was distraught as he described the impact of drugs upon his relationship with his son. He said, "The thing that bothers me most about his being into drugs is the fact that drugs have made him a liar."

Moments later the phone rang and the boy's mother went to answer it. She came back into the room with the message that the call was for the father. The father replied, "Tell him I am not at home."

The minister commented that drugs had not made this boy a liar; his father had. (4)

"When you have seen me, you have seen my father." Family resemblance—it doesn't always happen, but to a certain extent, children reflect their parents. Not only do children sometimes look like their parents, they also act like their parents.

Unfortunately, some children are emotionally scarred by their parents. Some of you have experienced this.

A subtle piece of Jewish humor makes a good point about child-rearing. Three Jewish mothers were bragging about their sons.

"My son is a wealthy lawyer," said one. "For my birthday he gave me this fur coat."

Said the second: "My son is a medical doctor and last winter he gave me a vacation in Miami Beach."

The third thought for a moment then blurted out, "My son sees a fancy psychiatrist each week. He pays the psychiatrist $100 an hour. And guess who he spends his time talking about—ME!"

She did not realize that the fact that her son was talking to a psychiatrist about her was not a compliment.

All of us reflect our upbringing. Many of us bear scars from our relations with our parents. Many of the emotional problems we are experiencing today had their genesis in the earliest days of our childhood experiences.

Perhaps our parents were overly protective. You have heard about the mother who sent a note to her son's teacher: "Austin is very sensitive. If he needs disciplining, please do not slap him. Slap the boy next to him and this will frighten Austin into doing right."

Some parents are overly protective. Helicopter parents they're called nowadays, always hovering, overly involved in their children's lives. Some of these children will have a difficult time coping when they are on their own.

Other parents hurt their young simply because they, the parents, are unable to adequately express their love. When that happens a child will often go through life looking for acceptance and approval. Even if they know deep in their hearts that their parents really do love them—these children will always have a subtle feeling that they never quite measured up to their parents' expectations.

There was a prominent psychologist in the early part of the twentieth century who influenced the child-rearing practices of some parents. Incredibly, this psychologist was strictly opposed to any displays of affection between parents and their children. He advised parents like this:

"Mothers just don't know, when they kiss their children and pick them up and rock them, caress them and juggle them upon their knee, that they are slowly building up a human being totally unable to cope with the world it must later live in . . . There is a sensible way of treating children. Treat them as though they were young adults . . . Never hug or kiss them, never let them sit on your lap. If you must, kiss them once on the forehead when they say goodnight . . . Can't a mother train herself to substitute a kindly word, a smile, in all of her dealings with the child, for the kiss and the hug, the pickup and the coddling? . . . If you haven't a nurse and cannot leave the child, put it out in the backyard a large part of the day. Build a fence around the yard so that you are sure no harm can come to it. Do this from the time it is born . . . If your heart is too tender and you must watch the child, make yourself a peephole so that you can see it without being seen, or use a periscope . . . Finally, learn not to talk in endearing and coddling terms." (5)

That sounds like a spoof of parental advice, but I understand that Dr. J. B. Watson, the well-known psychologist, actually said that! What utter and complete nonsense. But there were some parents who took Watson seriously. God help their children.

Even more common, however, are parents who are not able to express open, unconditional love because they never experienced such love themselves. If your parents were not able to express unconditional love, chances are you have difficulty expressing such love yourself.

To a great extent children do reflect the nature of their parents. Certainly all of us reflect the homes in which we were raised. And to a certain extent each of us can affirm the words of scripture: "When you have seen me, you have seen my father." "When you have seen me, you have seen my mother—or my grandmother" or whoever was most responsible for raising us.

Now here is the good news for the day. Jesus reflected his Father. He reflected God's character and God's nature. The writer of the Gospel of John is saying something very important here in reporting these words of our Master: "When you have seen me, you have seen my father." He is saying that we don't have to wonder what God is like. All we have to do is look at Jesus.

The Internet carried a beautiful story recently by a man named Jim Newman. Newman was taking the train home from downtown Chicago. He was seated in the same car with a young lady and her mother and grandmother. The three women had apparently been downtown for a day of shopping, and perhaps sightseeing.

The grandmother was in a wheelchair, and obviously had some diminished faculties. Her hearing was not so good, and the mother (her daughter) often had to explain things to her several times before Grandma seemed to understand.

The daughter had Down syndrome. During the train ride, her mother made a game with her of finding the temperatures in different cities, as listed in the newspaper, and then figuring out which city was warmer or colder than another city.

Through it all, Mother never wavered. It had to have been a long day, and she was surely tired. It would have been easy for her to decide that Grandma didn't really need to understand something instead of explaining it to her patiently for the fourth time. It would have been easy for her to give her daughter some mindless diversion to keep her occupied for the hour long train ride home. But she spoke with them, and laughed with them, and they talked about their day, and they explored useless weather facts from far away places long after it must have stopped being interesting.

As fate would have it, they were getting off at the same stop as Newman. They had backpacks and shopping bags, and Grandma in a wheelchair of course, so as they neared the station, Newman asked if they would like some help. The mother looked up at him and smiled, and said, "No, thank you, we're doing fine." (6)

They were doing fine, wouldn't you say? A grandmother with diminished mental capacity—a daughter with special needs—and yet this Mom gave them her full attention and love. I would call that sacrificial love. I would call it very close to agape love.

That's the kind of love I see in Jesus—compassionate love, self-giving love, love with no limits. Jesus reached out to those who hurt, those who were filled with sorrow, even those who treated him with contempt. And here is that good news: God is exactly like Jesus. The God of all the universe, the God who created everything that is, was, or ever will be—that God is a God of unlimited love. That is what this verse says, "When you have seen me, you have seen my father."

Some of those who purport to be followers of Jesus have given God a bad name. They spew out hatred toward others of God's children. Sometimes they even do it in Jesus' name. May God have mercy on their souls. Can you even imagine Jesus hurling cruel taunts at others? No way. He even forgave the soldiers who drove nails through his hands and feet and nailed him to a tree and hurled cruel taunts at him. There was no hatred in Christ. And there is no hatred in God. John, in his Epistle, suggests that God is not capable of hatred. He writes, "Whoever does not love does not know God, because God is love" (1 John 4:8). God is love. That says it all. Jesus is the perfect reflection of God.

And that is the message we take to the world. Our Master said, "When you have seen me, you have seen my father." May others be able to say about us, "When we've seen [John, Mary, Tyler, etc], we've seen Jesus." May they see, even in us, a family resemblance to God.

1. http://www.funnysermons.com/sermons/laughingstock/2-corinthians-13-11-13-may-15-08.html.
2. Source unknown.
3. The NIV Standard Lesson Commentary, 2009-2010 (Cincinnati: Standard Publishing, 2009), p. 187.
4. Raymond McHenry, Something to Think About ((Hendrickson Publishers, 1998).
5. J. B. Watson, Psychological Care of Infant and Child (Norton, N.Y., 1928).
6. (David C. Cook Publishing Company, 1992).

Because I Live
John 14:15-21
(Memorial Day Weekend)

Actor Martin Sheen is known for his deep religious and social convictions. Some of you will remember him best for his role as President Bartlett in the television show "The West Wing."

Sheen shared with motivational speaker Tony Robbins an interesting story about something that happened to him while he was making the movie Apocalypse Now.

The cast had been filming under a grueling schedule deep in the jungles of the Philippines. After a restless night, Sheen woke up the next morning and realized he was suffering a massive heart attack. Portions of his body were numb and paralyzed. He fell to the ground and, through nothing but sheer will power, crawled to the door and managed to get help.

Through the efforts of the film crew, doctors, and even a stunt pilot, he was flown to a hospital for emergency care. His wife Janet rushed to his side. He was becoming weaker with each moment. Janet refused to accept the graveness of his condition—she knew that Martin needed strength—so she smiled brightly at him and said, "It's just a movie, babe! It's only a movie."

Sheen told Robbins that at that moment, he knew he was going to make it. He couldn't laugh, but he began to smile, and with the smile, he began to heal. After all, in movies, people don't really die, do they? (1) For an actor, what could you say that would bring more comfort than that? "It's just a movie, babe! It's only a movie."

There are times we wish life was only a movie, don't we? Things would be so much easier. When you're young, you want a fast forward button. Fast forward to Christmas, fast forward to getting your driver's license, fast forward to getting out from under your parents' strict rules.

As an adult, when times are good, you would like a pause button. As the disciples suggested to Jesus on the Mount of Transfiguration, wouldn't it be nice to build three booths and just remain where we are? Why can't our children just remain adorable infants? Why can't our marriage remain forever like those early years of passion and discovery? If we just had a pause button . . . .

Some of us would like a rewind button and, perhaps, a delete button. If we could just go back and undo some of the things we've said and some of the things we've done.

And then some of us, in the later years of life, would like to hit a button that would simply slow down the film. Life is getting away from us so fast.

And then there are those times of crisis, when we would like to pretend it is not really happening at all. Wouldn't it be great if we could say, "It's only a movie, babe. It's only a movie. In a little while we'll be able to walk out of the theater and things will be all right." But life isn't a movie. It's real. And sometimes life hurts. Where then do we turn for encouragement?

I believe there is no better place to turn than our lesson for the day from John's Gospel where Christ says to us, "Because I live, you also will live."

That's it! That's the heart of Christian faith. Christ is alive and because he is alive, we can live lives that overcome every obstacle.

Some of you are familiar with the Gospel song written many years ago by Bill and Gloria Gaither. The refrain goes, "Because He lives, I can face tomorrow. Because He lives, All fear is gone. Because I know He holds the future, And life is worth the living just because He lives." The story behind that song is inspiring.

In the late 1960s, while expecting their third child, the Gaithers were going through a traumatic time. Their firstborn child, Suzanne, was four, and her sister Amy was three months old. The timing for another baby wasn't ideal. On top of that, Bill was recovering from a bout with mononucleosis.

The breakup of the marriage of Bill's sister, Mary Ann, had left his family devastated. What's more, a close friend had accused Bill and Gloria of using their ministry just to make a few bucks. All this plunged Bill into a deep depression.

Gloria remembers this also as a time of fear and sadness in society. This was the time of the "God is dead" movement. Drug abuse and racial tension were increasing. The thought of bringing another child into such a world was taking its toll.

But after a simple prayer by one of Bill's close friends, the strength of the Holy Spirit seemed to come to their aid. Christ's resurrection, in all its power, was reaffirmed in their hearts. They were assured that the future, left in God's hands, would be just fine.

In July 1970 a healthy baby, Benjamin, was born. Inspired by the miracle of their son's birth, "Because He Lives" poured out of the Gaithers' grateful hearts. The song clearly affirms the hope believers have in Christ. We can face tomorrow, with all its uncertainty, as we realize that God holds the future and makes life worth living. (2)

"Because I live, you also will live . . ." said Christ to his disciples. What does that say to you and me about our lives?

Christ's words remind us, first of all, that we are loved. Listen, now, to the rest of this passage: "Because I live, you also will live. On that day you will realize that I am in my Father, and you are in me, and I am in you. Whoever has my commands and obeys them, he is the one who loves me. He who loves me will be loved by my Father, and I too will love him and show myself to him." Christ is saying to us that we are loved.

In a world as immense as ours and as complicated, it is easy to think of ourselves as having no value. Cogs in a machine, numbers in a computer, faceless, nameless, unnoticed by the universe at large. No wonder we feel powerless.

Sometime back there was a speech by Tom Kalinske, Chairman of LeapFrog, the maker of creative educational games for children. Kalinske began with a story, a true story which originates from a friend of his who was hired to shoot a documentary film about computers and education.

The film was about an experiment in a Southern California junior high school, a test of a new computer system which was programmed with learning games that reinforced the fundamentals of math and reading and writing. This particular school was chosen in order to make the computer's job as tough as possible—because year after year, its students scored in the lowest statewide percentiles in every subject.

The experiment took place ten years ago, when computers were still pretty exotic contraptions to find in a public school. Naturally, the principal wanted to minimize the risk that the computers would be damaged in any way. And so he made a decision to exclude the special education class from the experiment.

You see, the special ed kids were always a bit out of control.

That would have been the end of the story if it weren't for a very dedicated special ed teacher. When she heard that her kids were going to sit on the sidelines while everyone else got time on the computers, she made such a fuss that the principal gave in.

And so, the special ed kids got their four hours a week at the computers. And when, in just one semester, some of these kids learned more than in the preceding ten years, the administration realized that something very special and very unexpected had happened.

There was a Hispanic girl who was placed in special ed because she just never learned to read. And she was terribly intimidated in class, so she never was able to communicate that she simply didn't get the basic phonic concepts. But the computer didn't intimidate her, and in one semester, she'd begun to read at her proper grade level.

The most touching story, however, was a kid named Raymond, who had every problem in the book. A dysfunctional home, acute shyness, bad eyesight and zero academic performance. But in the one semester he had with the computer, Raymond caught up seven years of math.

They got him in front of the camera for an interview and asked how it was that he blossomed so magnificently.

"Well," he replied, "you see, all the kids here call me retard. The computer calls me Raymond." (3)

Did you get that? "The kids ... call me retard. The computer calls me Raymond." What in the world could be more de-motivating, more dispiriting, more discouraging than to think that nobody believes in you? How could you ever believe in yourself?

Christ reminds us that Somebody in this universe not only notices us, but loves us and believes in us. What many people need to know is not only that they can believe in God, but God believes in them. We're not merely a nameless, faceless blob of protoplasm taking up space in the universe. The God of all the universe sees us, notices us, listens to us, believes in us.

Not only does Christ love us, Christ is always with us. "I am in my Father, says Christ to us, "and you are in me, and I am in you." Did you hear that? Christ is within us. We don't have to go to a mountaintop to find God. We don't have to peer through the Hubble telescope. All we have to do is to listen for the Divine whisper from within ourselves. "Find a place in your heart," said an ancient sage named Theophan the Recluse, "and speak there with the Lord. It is the Lord's reception room."

Some people seem to find this room easily. Others have more difficulty.

Pastor John Ortberg tells about some friends of his who have a daughter. When she was five years old, this girl told her parents, "I know Jesus lives in my heart, because when I put my hand on it I can feel him walking around in there." (4)

Out of the mouths of babes come words of wisdom. Christ lives within us. That's good news because, as the writer of I John reminds us, "Greater is he that is in you, than he that is in the world." (4:4, KJV)

A teenager named James Dungy committed suicide a few years ago. It was a terrible blow to his father Tony, who at the time was the much-respected coach of the Indianapolis Colts. Many prayers were lifted up as the Dungy family mourned this loss. In an interview after his return to his position as head coach, Dungy thanked the Colts organization for its support, and then he said words that surprised no one who knew him. "My faith in Christ," said Tony Dungy, "is what's gotten me through this." (5)

How many of you parents have asked yourselves how you could ever cope if something tragic were to happen to one of your children? Here's how—by faith in Christ. "Greater is he that is in you, than he that is in the world." Christ not only loves us. Christ also lives within us and Christ will help us endure any crisis if we will trust him.

Most people believe in God. But many people have only a God "out there." They have never opened themselves to the God who dwells within. To people with this problem, God seems somehow remote, unconcerned about their everyday cares and concerns. They have never seen God as a living presence in their lives.

A story is told of a mother who, rather than asking her children the question: "How was your day?" did something much more helpful. As she tucked her children into bed each night, she asked them this question: "Where did you meet God today?"

In answer to her question about where they met God, they would answer, one by one: "A teacher helped me; there was a homeless person in the park; I saw a tree with lots of flowers on it." After they finished telling her where they had met God that day, she would tell them where she met God, too. (6)

What a grand exercise! We meet Christ everywhere when Christ dwells within us. We can face tomorrow because Christ loves us and Christ is with us.

But note one thing more. Christ says, "Because I live, you also will live. On that day you will realize that I am in my Father, and you are in me, and I am in you. Whoever has my commands and obeys them, he is the one who loves me . . ." (emphasis added).

The love we have in Christ is not a sentimental, mushy feel-good experience that says we are free to do our own thing. Love for Christ is expressed through obeying his commands. We are soldiers in Christ's army in the war against every form of sin and injustice. That is what gives our lives meaning and purpose.

Tomorrow is Memorial Day. On that day we honor those men and women who have given their lives in service to our country. The obedience that the soldier gives to those in command often puts our obedience to Christ to shame.

In 2005, Capt. James Key, US Army Chaplain, wrote some words which were carried in USA Today:

"This past year," Capt. Key writes, "I served as chaplain for a 600 soldier logistics battalion in Baghdad . . . These soldiers had to deliver supplies along the most dangerous routes in Iraq. When bombs exploded, the reality of war forced many to do some serious soul searching . . .

"I am back home in the states now, a safe distance away from the death and war that challenge many servicemen and women in ways most people in our country will never fully understand.

"One evening, a casualty officer and I drove down the road on our way to inform a soldier's spouse that her husband had died in Iraq. As an Army chaplain, I thought about how difficult it would be for this young mother and how empty the two children's lives would be without their dad . . .

"This year, as we celebrate Memorial Day, we should pause as a nation . . . and think about the men and women who continue to fight and die in such places as Iraq and Afghanistan. It is true," writes Capt. Key, "War is hell, freedom is expensive, death is painful and faith still matters—especially to those in the foxhole." (7)

Jesus put it like this, "Greater love has no one than this: to lay down one's life for one's friends" (John 15:13). Jesus is our friend. He lay down his life for us. Because he lives, we can face tomorrow. He loves us. He dwells within us. Can we not live for him?

1. Anthony Robbins, Notes from a Friend (New York: Fireside, 1995), pp. 76-77.
2. http://www.hymnlyrics.org/mostpopularhymns/because_he_lives.html.
3. Vital Speeches of the Day, November 1, 1994, p. 37.
4. God Is Closer than You Think (Grand Rapids: Zondervan, 2005).
5. Cited by Tony Grant, http://yarpc.tripod.com/avgjoe.htm.
6. Dorothy C. Bass, http://funnysermons.com/.
7. May 26, 2006, p. 11 A, "Remember the Guys in the Foxholes." Contributed by John Bardsley.

When Christians Pray
Acts 1:12-14

There is a story by Hugh Price Hughes titled, "The City of Everywhere." In this story a man arrives in a city one cold morning. As he gets off the train, he sees that the station is like any other station except for one thing—everyone is barefoot. No one wears shoes.

He notices a barefoot cab driver. "Pardon me," he asks the driver, "I was just wondering why you don't wear shoes. Don't you believe in shoes?"

"Sure we do," says the driver.

"Why don't you wear them?" asks the man.

"Ah, that's the question," the driver replies. "Why don't we wear shoes? Why don't we?"

At the hotel it is the same. The clerk, bell boys, everybody is barefoot. In the coffee shop he notices a nice looking gentleman at a table opposite him. He says, "I notice you aren't wearing any shoes. I wonder why? Don't you know about shoes?"

The man replies, "Of course I know about shoes."

"Then why don't you wear them?" asks the stranger.

"Ah, that's the question," says the man. "Why don't we? Why don't we?"

After breakfast he walks out on the street in the snow but every person he sees is barefoot. He asks another man about it, and points out how shoes protect the feet from cold. The man says, "We know about shoes. See that building yonder? That is a shoe manufacturing plant. We are proud of that plant and every week we gather there to hear the man in charge tell about shoes and how wonderful they are."

"Then why don't you wear shoes?" asks the stranger.

"Ah, that's the question," says the man.

Dr. Robert E. Goodrich told this story in his book, What's It All About? Then he asks, "Don't we believe in prayer? Don't we know what it could mean to our lives? . . . Of course we do; we know about prayer. Then, why don't we pray? Ah, that's the question. Why don't we pray? . . . Why don't we?" (1)

Powerful things happen when people pray.

Our lesson from the book of Acts takes place immediately after Christ's ascension into heaven. The disciples are in a period of waiting. Remember that Christ said to them just before he ascended, "Do not leave Jerusalem, but wait for the gift my Father promised, which you have heard me speak about. For John baptized with water, but in a few days you will be baptized with the Holy Spirit." Now they were in that period of waiting.

The writer of Acts tells us, "They returned to Jerusalem from the hill called the Mount of Olives, a Sabbath day's walk from the city. When they arrived, they went upstairs to the room where they were staying. Those present were Peter, John,

James and Andrew; Philip and Thomas, Bartholomew and Matthew; James son of Alphaeus and Simon the Zealot, and Judas son of James. They all joined together constantly in prayer, along with the women and Mary the mother of Jesus, and with his brothers."

Notice how they prepared themselves for the gift of the Holy Spirit, "They all joined together constantly in prayer . . ."

Why do you suppose that was? What is there about prayer that they knew, but we've forgotten?

Let's begin here: they prayed to receive God's power.

Jesus had given them an impossible task. They were to go to all the nations of the world and make disciples of all people. They knew there was no way this could possibly be accomplished without God's help.

Years ago, speaker Mark Sanborn was on a cruise with his wife. This was a new experience for them and he was curious about the workings of this great ocean-going vessel. He visited the bridge of the ocean liner and spoke with the captain. Mark asked the captain about the biggest seas he had ever sailed in that ship. The captain told Mark that he had been in seas with ninety foot waves. Impressed, Mark inquired about how he had managed to keep the ship intact. The captain told him that while ninety foot waves were daunting, the ship could negotiate them quite handily as long as the ship didn't lose power. "If you lose power in big seas in any boat," he explained, "you're in serious trouble. Under power, the boat can stay perpendicular to the waves. Without power, the boat would drift parallel to the waves and be capsized or swamped." (2)

Obviously you don't want to be in an ocean liner in a great storm without power. Neither did the disciples want to be in a situation where they were witnessing about Christ to the sometimes hostile nations of the world without God's power.

Leadership expert John Maxwell tells of a sailor stationed in Pearl Harbor in 1941. On December 7, Japanese aircraft attacked the naval base, and this man took his position at one of the ship's guns.

He fired round after round at the attacking planes, but none went down. That's when it occurred to him that his ship was prepped for naval exercises but not for real battle. He was firing blanks. To look at him standing on deck, machine gun blazing, it would appear that he was doing battle, but the truth was, he lacked the important tools to do the job. (3)

I wonder if both these stories don't illustrate the problem with the church today. We seem to have lost power. We seem to be drifting rather than making an impact on the world around us. We may be manning our positions, but we seem to be firing blanks. We're becoming more like the world than the world is becoming like the kingdom of God. Could the problem be that we have quit depending on prayer?

A kindergarten class went to a fire station for a tour and some instruction in fire safety. The fireman was explaining what to do in case of a fire.

He said, "First, go to the door and feel the door to see if it's hot." Then he said, "Next, fall to your knees. Does anyone know why you ought to fall to your knees?" the fireman asked.

One of the little tykes said, "Sure, to start praying to ask God to get you out of there!" In a sense the little tyke was right. There's a time when prayer is the most appropriate response to a difficult situation.

Why do Christians pray? We pray for power to do what God has called us to do. We pray for power to be what God has called us to be. We ask not for power for our own selfish desires, but so we can fulfill God's desires for us.

Joanie Yoder in the devotional, Our Daily Bread, tells about a friend of hers who understands why we are to pray. She notes that most people own a calendar or an appointment book in which they record details of future commitments. She says this friend of hers uses one in the opposite way. He doesn't record key activities until after they've taken place. Here's his approach:

Each morning he prays, "Lord, I go forth in Your strength alone. Please use me as You wish." Then, whenever he accomplishes something unusual or difficult, he records it in his diary in the evening.

For example, he may write, "Today I was enabled to share my testimony with a friend." Or, "Today God enabled me to overcome my fear through faith." One day, he wrote, "Today I was enabled to help and encourage a troubled person."

Her friend uses the word enabled because he knows he couldn't do these things without God's help. By recording each "enabling," he is giving God all the glory. Relying constantly on God's strength, he can testify with the apostle Paul, "I can do all things through Christ who strengthens me" (Philippians 4:13).

"As you enter each new day," says Joanie Yoder, "ask God to strengthen and use you. You can be sure that as you look back on your day, you'll praise and glorify the Lord as you realize what He has enabled you to do."

That's a beautiful approach to prayer. The followers of Jesus after his ascension prayed to receive God's power.

Mother Teresa was once crossing the border into Israel when a guard asked her if she was carrying any weapons. That was a pretty strange question for a nun wearing a habit, but she looked the guard in the eyes and defiantly said, "Yes, I have my prayer books." (4)

The early followers of our Lord prayed for God's power. They also prayed to receive God's presence. Jesus had promised them a gift. He had promised them they would be baptized with the Holy Spirit. They did not know yet what this meant. They would discover what it meant at Pentecost. It meant that God would be a daily presence in their lives and would give them wisdom and comfort and the ability to do what needed to be done in every situation. Do I need to say that each of us needs God's presence in our lives for the very same reason?

It reminds me of a couple that I read about recently. Rachel and Jim owned a commercial building, half of which Jim used for his dental practice. For fifteen years, they had experienced no difficulty in renting out the other half of the building. They counted on the extra money to pay their bills. Then they lost their renter. A real estate agent told them, "Forget about advertising for a while. Absolutely nobody is renting."

To ease her financial worries, Rachel started swimming laps at her local YMCA pool.

One day when she was feeling especially anxious, she decided to pray as she swam, using the alphabet to keep track of the number of laps. She focused on adjectives to describe God, starting with the letter A. "You are the almighty God," she prayed on lap one. "A benevolent God, a beautiful God," she prayed on the next lap, and then, "You are a caring, creative, can do God." By the time she had completed twenty six laps, an hour had passed, and her fears were gone. She knew God would provide.

A short time later, a physical therapist called to say she had seen the "For Rent" sign in the window and asked to see the office. It was what she wanted. So, she and her partner rented the space. Rachel still prays while swimming laps.

"After all," she says, "I've discovered God's goodness stretches from A to Z!" (5)

In my estimation, the miracle was not that Rachel and Jim found a renter. The miracle was that, as she swam those laps and affirmed the goodness of God using the letters of the alphabet, she experienced God's closeness and God's love. If we are awash in God's presence we can handle any situation in life.

The disciples of Jesus experienced God's power in a magnificent way. It did not take the early church very long to become a major force in the Roman Empire. But individually, the leaders of the church often experienced torture and death because of their faith in Christ. If they had not felt that God was with them through the power of the Holy Spirit, they would not have been able to persevere. So, after Christ's ascension, his disciples prayed constantly. They prayed for God's power. They prayed for God's presence.

And they prayed that they would stay centered in God's purpose.

Here is where we may fall short as the people of God today. We need to pray mightily that God will keep us in the center of God's purpose.

Most of you are familiar with Chuck Colson, former hatchet man for Richard Nixon and now a born again and thoroughly committed spokesman for Christ.

Colson tells of being in a coffee shop once with his associate, Fred Rhodes.

"Two cheese omelets, one milk, and one iced tea," Fred said to the waitress.

After she left, Chuck and Fred reviewed the next day's schedule. Then they had a rather long blessing. When they finished, the waitress was standing nearby with their food.

"Hey, were you guys praying?" she asked.

"Yes, we were," said Colson.

"Hey, that's neat," said the waitress. "I've never seen anybody do that in here before. Are you preachers?"

They said no, but added that they worked in the same business.

She said, "I'm Christian. At least I was once."

"What happened?" the men asked.

A sad, nostalgic look crossed her face. "I accepted Jesus as my Savior at a rally when I was a teenager," she said. "Then I went to live in Hawaii. Well, I just lost interest, I guess. Forgot about it."

"I don't think you lost it," Colson said gently. "You just put it aside for a while."

The waitress seemed thoughtful. "It's funny," she said, "but the moment I saw you guys praying I felt excited all over again."

"Once you accept the Lord," said Fred, "He becomes part of your life. You can try to turn away from him ... but he's still there. He loves you, and like the prodigal son, will take you back."

The next day they saw the waitress again. She told them she was joining a Bible study the next day and that she was going to find a church, too. She said, "I've come back."

"Until that night," writes Colson, "I had felt awkward at times praying over meals in crowded restaurants. Never again." (6)

At that moment in the coffee shop, as he prayed, Chuck Colson was in the center of God's purpose. He was doing what God wanted him to do. That's what happens when Christians pray.

Some people think of prayer as simply begging God to fulfill their selfish desires. That could not be further from the kind of prayers that were being offered up by those disciples after Christ's ascension. They were praying for God's power. They were praying for God's presence. And they were praying that they might stay centered in God's purpose.

What happens when Christian pray? Great things happen. Why? Because we have God's power, God's presence and God's purpose. What more could you ask for?

1. Cited in Charles L. Allen, All Things are Possible through Prayer (Westwood, NJ: Fleming H. Revell Co., 1963), pp. 52- 53.
2. You Don't Need a Title to Be a Leader (Colorado Springs: Waterbrook Press, 2006), p. 45.
3. What really counts (Nashville: Thomas Nelson Inc., 2005), p. 163.
4. Taken from www.benwitherington.blogspot.com; November 11, 2005. Cited by Gary Yates, http://www.preaching.com/sermons/11547123/.
5. God's Devotional Book: Inspiration and Motivation for the Seasons of Life (Colorado Springs: Cook Communications Ministries, 1984), p. 211.
6. Charles W. Colson, Life Sentence (Grand Rapids: Fleming H. Revell, 1979), pp. 105-106.

In Our Own Language

Acts 2:1-11

(Pentecost)

A man was lecturing in Latin America. He was going to use a translator, but to identify with his audience, he decided to begin his talk by saying in Spanish, "Good evening, ladies and gentleman."

He arrived at the auditorium a little early and realized he did not know the Spanish words for ladies and gentlemen. Being rather resourceful, he went to the part of the building where the restrooms were located, looked at the signs on the two doors, and memorized those two words.

When the audience arrived and he was introduced, he stood up and said in Spanish, "Good evening, ladies and gentlemen." The audience was shocked. The people seemed stunned. He didn't know whether he had offended them or if perhaps they hadn't heard him or understood him. So he decided to repeat it. Again in Spanish he said, "Good evening, ladies and gentlemen."

One person in the audience began to snicker. Pretty soon the entire audience was roaring in laughter. Finally, someone told him that he had said, "Good evening, bathrooms and broom closets!" (1)

I guess it pays to know the language of the people to whom you're speaking. Of course it works both ways. Those who come here from other lands have the same difficulty with our language.

A Latin American minister was touring the U.S. in an effort to boost financial support for missionaries and ministries in his home country. At a church luncheon, he was telling the guests about his home country, his family, and the important work being supported there.

As he concluded, he said, "And I have a charming and understanding wife but, alas, no children." After a pause, he said, haltingly, "You see, my wife is unbearable."

Puzzled glances in the audience prompted him to try to clarify by saying: "What I mean is, my wife is inconceivable."

Observing the laughter in the audience, he realized his mistake, but floundered deeper into the intricacies of the English language by correcting triumphantly, "That is, my wife, she is impregnable!" (2)

Of course, with our many dialects, even within this land it is sometimes difficult to understand people of different regions.

A New Yorker visited the home of a Kentucky business colleague. The wife introduced him to their lovely little daughter. "Her name is Marlon," said the proud mom, "after ma favorite movie star."

The New Yorker asked, "You named your daughter after Marlon Brando?"

"No silly," said the mom, "ah named her after Marlon Monroe." (3)

It helps if you can speak the language of the person with whom you are speaking. That's one of the things that I love about the story of the first Pentecost.

You know the story well. "When the day of Pentecost came, they were all together in one place. Suddenly a sound like the blowing of a violent wind came from heaven and filled the whole house where they were sitting. They saw what seemed to be tongues of fire that separated and came to rest on each of them. All of them were filled with the Holy Spirit and began to speak in other tongues as the Spirit enabled them.

"Now there were staying in Jerusalem God-fearing Jews from every nation under heaven. When they heard this sound, a crowd came together in bewilderment, because each one heard them speaking in his own language. Utterly amazed, they asked: 'Are not all these men who are speaking Galileans? Then how is it that each of us hears them in his own native language?'" Then follows a partial list of the nations which were represented that day—fifteen of them in all.

What an amazing event! I've often wondered whether this was a miracle of speaking or a miracle of hearing. Did these uneducated Galileans speak in all these different languages or did they speak their own language and those listening, by the guidance of the Holy Spirit, simply hear the words in their own language? Either way it was a marvelous miracle.

Ron Mehl, in his beautiful little book, Love Found a Way, tells about one of his favorite movie scenes. It takes place in the classic Christmas movie Miracle on 34th Street. A little girl is brought into a department store to visit Santa Claus. The girl's guardian isn't sure they should have come, for the girl speaks only Dutch. The worried woman doesn't want the girl's tender heart to be disappointed by a Santa who understands only English. But as Santa takes the little one onto his lap, he looks into her eyes and begins gently speaking to her ... in Dutch! The little girl's face lights up like a lamp, because Santa knows her language. (4)

I wonder if the writers of this movie even knew that once upon a time such a thing really did happen. On the day of Pentecost a group of Galileans were testifying and people from at least 15 countries heard them speak in their own native tongue!

Think about that for a moment. Think how difficult communication is, even among those who speak the same language. Communication is difficult even among people who share the same experiences. How many couples in counseling say, "We've lost the ability to communicate." And here on the day of Pentecost we have people across the spectrum of languages and nationalities and experiences understanding these humble messengers of God. There is much we can learn from the first Pentecost.

First of all, we see that the Christian faith is a universal faith. People from differing nations understood the Gospel message. Why? Because, for one thing, the message was meant for all nations and all peoples.

Like all the people on earth, we in this land are somewhat ethnocentric. Ethnocentric is a fifty-cent word that means we think everybody on earth ought to be like us—look like us, talk like us, think like us. And we think God ought to favor us. After all, we are a Christian nation. At least in our own minds we are. I wonder what God thinks of us . . . really.

It shocks us when we realize that God is a universal God. Intellectually we understand that it's true, but at a more basic level we want a God who is very like us. Surely God speaks English as His native tongue. Surely God has western values. And then we meet a Christian from Africa, or Asia, or Europe who has very different ideas about God, and it is disturbing. We thought we had God in a box. No wonder J. B. Phillips said to us a few decades back that Our God is Too Small.

There are wonderful Christian people in almost every nation in the world. Naturally they see the world through the lens of their own culture and they think their way is best as well. We all surely give God a good laugh at our provincialism.

God is a universal God. God is the God of the Chinese and the Congolese, of the Iraqis and the Afghans, as well as the Canadians and the Americans. God has no favorites. What God favors is justice and righteousness and compassion and love— wherever those characteristics are found. What God is seeking is the day when all of the world's people will know God's love and God's peace—and will know themselves to be brothers and sisters in Christ. The Christian faith is a universal faith. That's the first thing this passage says to us.

The second thing it says is that God comes to us just as we are. People from these many nations heard the Gospel spoken directly to them in their own language. That is critically important.

Ron Mehl tells another story that speaks directly to this truth. He tells of a time when the children's choir of his church (all six hundred of them) sang for a service. After they sang, Mehl learned that a certain little red-headed boy was in the audience. The youngster was deaf. As the concert progressed, the lad was at least mildly interested in watching the singing children but there was no message there for him. How could there be? He couldn't hear any of the words.

Suddenly everything changed, says Mehl. The choir began to sing in this little guy's language, signing the words with their hands as well as singing with their voices. They were singing and signing the beautiful Lanny Wolfe chorus:

Jesus we crown You with praise, Jesus we crown You with praise,

We love and adore You, bow down before You, Jesus we crown You with praise.

"The boy suddenly stood up in his seat. His eyes lit up, big as saucers. They were singing to him! He could hardly contain his joy. His little hands began to sing as he signed along with the choir. When the choir finished, that excited little redhead thought the evening had been planned just for him." Mehl adds this comment: "And I believe in my heart that he was right." (5)

He was right. Whoever we are, God speaks our language. We don't have to have a college degree to hear God speak to us. We don't have to speak English. We don't even have to speak or hear at all. God's language is the language of the heart. In fact, according to St. Paul, simple people may hear God more clearly than those who are encumbered with many degrees.

In First Corinthians we read, "Where is the wise person? Where is the teacher of the law? Where is the philosopher of this age? Has not God made foolish the wisdom of the world? For since in the wisdom of God the world through its wisdom did not know him, God was pleased through the foolishness of what was preached to save those who believe." Then a little further he writes, "Brothers and sisters, think of what you were when you were called. Not many of you were wise by human standards; not many were influential; not many were of noble birth. But God chose the foolish things of the world to shame the wise; God chose the weak things of the world to shame the strong."

Now, I am not anti-intellectual. I believe in the value of education. But we dare not think that God speaks only to the sophisticated. God speaks to even the simplest among us. God speaks to us where we are. That's not only true of our intellectual differences, but it is true of our personality as well.

Have you ever noticed that people are different? Some people are quite easy going. They seem to get along with everybody they meet. Nothing ever seems to ruffle them. Some other people are very precise. They want everything done just right. Some people are party animals. They are energized by being around other people. They like being in the limelight and they make every event they participate in more enjoyable.

Then there are some people who like being in control. They are rather impatient with those who are not as action oriented as they are.

I heard about a woman who was in this latter category. She liked being in control. She made life difficult for her husband, Tom. The scary part was that she was becoming more domineering all the time—even to the point of Tom insisting she see a psychiatrist.

After much pleading, she finally agreed to go, much to Tom's surprise. After she came out of the office, following an hour with the psychiatrist, Tom asked, "How did it go, dear. Was it helpful?"

"I'm not sure," she replied. "It took most of the hour to convince the doctor that the couch would look a whole lot better on the right instead of the left side of the door." (6)

People are different. To a certain extent, that is the way God created us. It's in our genetic code. Some of us are somewhat emotional; some of us are more intellectual. I am convinced God speaks to engineers differently than God speaks to artists. Engineers need all the nuts and bolts of faith. Artists sense a bigger canvas. The point is that God comes to us where we are. God speaks our language. God speaks to us according to our own needs. And God uses different means to speak to us according to those needs.

In worship, some people respond to scripture, others to the liturgy, still others to the music and even a few to the sermon. People are different. Christ came to St. Paul in a different way than he did to Simon Peter. The point is that God comes to us individually as well as corporately. God speaks to us according to our needs. God comes to us where we are.

That is the meaning of the incarnation. We cannot separate Pentecost from the entire Christ event. In Christ God entered the world. Why? To draw close to humankind ... to reveal to us God's nature ... to help us prepare for the coming kingdom. God came to us at Christmas in Jesus Christ, and God came to us at Pentecost in the form of the Holy Spirit. God came speaking our language that we might know God and have life through Him. Now it is our mission to translate the Gospel into language that our friends and neighbors can understand as well.

Dr. Daniel Lioy tells a story about Marilyn Laszlo, a Bible translator in the jungles of Papua, New Guinea. In the small village of Hauna Marilyn teaches the people to read and write their own language and has aided in the formation of a strong church.

One day, a canoe loaded with 15 people from a distant village arrived to receive medical help. They stayed for a week in Marilyn's village and attended services where they heard the Gospel for the first time. Before they returned home, the visitors asked, "Could you come to our village so that we might know about God, too?"

Several weeks later, some Christians set out for the village. They arrived to find a new building, very different from the surrounding houses, standing in the center of the village. When the missionaries asked about the structure, they were told, "That's God's house! That's our church!"

The missionaries were puzzled, knowing there had not been any Christian work in that part of the country. "What's the building for?" they asked. "Well, we saw that church in your village, and our people decided to build a church, too. Now we are waiting for someone to tell us about God in our language." (7)

I believe there are people in this community who are waiting to hear the Gospel in a language they can understand. We dare not wait for them to learn our language, the language of words like incarnation and transfiguration. Those words mean nothing to lost souls. We need to translate the Gospel into words and acts that no one can misunderstand—words like love, compassion, forgiveness and acceptance. God speaks to us according to our needs. Let us speak to the world according to its needs as well.

1. Rusty Wright & Linda Raney Wright, 500 Clean Jokes and Humorous Stories (Uhrichsville, OH: Barbour & Co.), p. 87.

2. Mikey's Funnies, http://www.agathongroup.com/.

3. The Jokesmith (Marlborough, MA: www.Jokesmith.com, Volume XXIV number 4, 2008), p. 2.

4. (Colorado Springs: Waterbrook Press, 1999), p. 69.

5. Ibid., pp. 70-71.

6. James E. Myers, A Treasury of Husband and Wife Humor (Springfield, IL: Lincoln Herndon Press, Inc, 1994).

7. International Bible Lesson Commentary (Colorado Springs: David C. Cook, 2008), p. 62.

Kissing Cousins

2 Corinthians 13:11-13

(Trinity Sunday; Father's Day)

If you happened to look at a church calendar for today, the first Sunday after Pentecost, you may have seen that today is called Trinity Sunday. That might have given you cause for alarm. You may have thought to yourself, "Oh, no, a deep, dull sermon is coming on the mystery of the Trinity." That would be a perfectly natural reaction. So, to keep you awake, I'm going to address an entirely different subject—that of kissing. And I'm going to begin with the worst joke about kissing that I know.

It seems a new weight-loss clinic opened for business. This clinic promised a brand new method of reducing. An overweight man named Harry decided to give it a try. Upon entering, Harry saw a sign that offered the following rates: Ten-pound loss: $10.00; Twenty-pound loss: $20.00; Fifty-pound loss: $100.00.

Harry decided on the ten-pound program. Paying $10.00, he was directed to a room. When he entered, he saw a gorgeous woman with a sign around her neck that read: "If you catch me, you may kiss me." Harry took off in hot pursuit, huffing and puffing, heaving and sweating, but the woman continued to out run Harry until he lost ten pounds. He finally caught her and was given a kiss as a reward.

Pleased with the experience and the results, Harry decided to try the twenty-pound program. Paying $20.00, he was directed to another room. There he met an even more beautiful woman. However she was even faster than the first woman. She also wore a sign around her neck that read, "If you catch me, you may kiss me." Harry began the chase. It ended with him losing twenty pounds but he gained a kiss.

Now Harry is really pleased with this experience and the results. He can't wait to find out about the $100.00 program. That program promised him a weight loss of fifty pounds. He had already lost thirty pounds and he would be really svelte if he could drop another fifty pounds.

Harry pays the $100.00 and is directed to still another room. Upon entering, to his horror, he finds a huge, hulking, ugly gorilla with a sign around its neck. The sign said, "If I catch you, I'm going to kiss you!" (1)

I told you it was a bad joke. Here's some information that is more helpful.

Sometime back, psychologists working with a group of German insurance companies found a positive correlation between husbands kissing their wives and their performance on the job. Their studies showed that men who kiss their wives goodbye before going to work each morning are affected in a positive way for the rest of their day. They drive to work more efficiently and more safely. And listen to this, men, kissing husbands live five years longer than their less romantic counterparts. The studies showed that men who do not kiss their wives goodbye are apt to be moody, depressed and disinterested in their jobs. Hey, I didn't make this up. I'm simply reporting the facts. However, to be fair, kissing may be more a consequence than a cause of a happy life situation. This subject, says one researcher, warrants continued investigation by every husband and wife. (2) So men, get with it.

Now, since this is Father's Day, you can see how kissing might be an appropriate subject. We kiss one another within families to show our love. That is a beautiful thing. But you may be asking yourself how on Trinity Sunday I can justify a sermon on kissing? Well, in our Epistle for the day, St. Paul talks about kissing . . . and he is for it! Surprise, surprise!

Of course, this was a very special kind of kissing. In our lesson for the day we find Paul's final words to the church at Corinth. He writes at the conclusion of this important letter, "Greet one another with a holy kiss." Then he adds, "All the saints send their greetings."

So, there it is, "Greet one another with a holy kiss." Here's what's even more interesting. This instruction is repeated several times in the New Testament. Paul also wrote to the church in Rome, "Greet one another with a holy kiss" (Romans 16:16). He said it twice to the believers in Corinth (1 Corinthians 16:20, 2 Corinthians 13:12), and also to the church in Thessalonika (1 Thessalonians 5:26). And Paul wasn't the only one to talk about people in church kissing. In his first letter, Peter wrote, "Greet one another with a kiss of love" (1 Peter 5:14).

Now, before you get too excited about this text, you need to understand that this style of kissing had nothing at all to do with romance. Actually, in the early church, men kissed men and women kissed women.

Now, if that makes you a little queasy, let me remind you that there are many cultures today in which it is perfectly acceptable for men to kiss men and women to kiss women. In our culture we see parents kissing their children and women kissing women on the cheek, but it is very rare to see men kiss one another. And yet, this is exactly what St. Paul is referring to. "Greet one another with a holy kiss." In that culture, men kissing men, as a sign of affection and respect, was acceptable and quite common. When the early Christians came to church and met each another, and when they parted, they kissed. This holy kiss was not given on the mouth, of course, but on the cheek, or the forehead, and often on the hand. You remember how Judas betrayed Christ with a kiss.

Of course, this kind of kissing was strictly non-sexual. It was a sign of the love and the fellowship that existed within congregations. What may surprise you is that until 1528, the holy kiss was part of the Catholic mass. The Protestant Reformation in the 1500s removed the kiss from Protestant services entirely. Protestants have always been a little stuffier than Roman Catholics.

Now why is this important to us today?

The holy kiss reminds us what the church was meant to be. The early church understood itself to be a family. They were brothers and sisters in Christ. They took that literally. They took care of one another. They made sure the widows and orphans were provided for. One person's problem became the problem of them all. We sing, "They'll know we are Christians by our love." But they lived it out.

Pastor Steven M. Conger tells about a question that the head coach at Gilman High School in Baltimore often asks his players. The coach will ask the players, referring to himself and his assistants, "What is our job?"

That seems like a strange thing for a football coach to ask his players concerning himself and his assistants: "What is our job?" But that is the question.

And the answer?

"To love us!" the players yell back.

Then the coach shouts, "And what is your job!"

"To love each other!" the boys respond. (3)

I wonder what would happen if we tried that in our service. Suppose I were to ask you, "What is my job?" And you answered, "To love us." And then I asked, "What is your job?" And you were to answer, "To love each other." Could it be that athletic teams understand something that churches do not?

Business legend Lee Iacocca once asked legendary football coach Vince Lombardi what it took to make a winning football team. Here is how Lombardi answered, "There are a lot of coaches with good ball clubs who know the fundamentals and have plenty of discipline but still don't win the game. Then you come to the third ingredient: If you're going to play together as a team, you've got to care for one another," said Lombardi. "You've got to love each other. Each player has to be thinking about the next guy and saying to himself: If I don't block that man, Paul is going to get his legs broken. I have to do my job well in order that he can do his. The difference between mediocrity and greatness," Lombardi said, "is the feeling these guys have for each other." (4)

Again I ask, is there something athletic teams know that churches do not? We used to know it, but we have forgotten it. If we love Christ, our next job is to love one another, and then we are to love the world for which Christ died. The holy kiss reminds us what the church was meant to be. We are the family of Jesus Christ—brothers and sisters in him.

The holy kiss also reminds us of how we are to be different from the world. Put the emphasis here on the word "holy."

Holy means separate, distinct, and set apart. We are called to be a holy people, a holy nation, and, therefore, the way we kiss (as well as everything we do in life) should be holy too.

Am I the only one in this room who is concerned about the sexualization of our culture? Am I the only one who is disturbed by seeing some young teens dressed like hookers? And in some cases, acting like hookers? Am I the only one who is disturbed to see so many actors on primetime television—even during the so-called family hour between 8:00 and 9:00—hopping from bed to bed as if casual sex has displaced baseball as America's favorite pastime? And what disturbs me most is that surveys show that people who call themselves Christians are not that much different in their moral practices than the world outside in this respect.

Let me hasten to add, as I have many times before, that on this matter there is a clear divide between those who take their faith seriously and those who simply have their names on a church roll. Still, we are part of a culture that shows some very unhealthy trends.

A man sent a letter to Ann Landers. He wrote, "This is for the woman who was distressed about her son. I would like to ask her some questions about the boy. Is he disrespectful? Has he been arrested for drunk driving? Has he been kicked out of college for cheating? Has he made his girlfriend pregnant? Does he get failing grades? Does he steal money from your purse? . . . If you can answer 'No' to all these questions," says this writer, "stop complaining. You have a great kid." It was signed, "Ralph N., Oakland, CA."

Here is how Ann Landers answered him. "Your letter showed just how much times have changed. You said that if a kid today isn't on drugs, doesn't get failing grades, hasn't been arrested for drunk driving, or kicked out of college for cheating, hasn't made his girl friend pregnant, or stolen from your purse, that he's great. But you make no mention of achievement. There's not a word about integrity, a sense of responsibility, decency, morality or service to others." Then she went on to add, "What a sad commentary on our times. Good Lord, where is our nation headed," asks Ann Landers, "and who is going to lead us there?" (5)

Our country is headed in the wrong direction with regard to sexual morality. And who is going to lead us out? It should be those who understand what it is to be set aside for God's service. It ought to be those who understand the principle of the Holy Kiss. The holy kiss reminds us what the church was meant to be. We are the family of Jesus Christ—brothers and sisters in him. And the holy kiss reminds us of how we are to be different from the world.

Finally the holy kiss reminds us what Christ has done for us. Back in the 1960s there was an expression that went like this: commit an unnatural act—love somebody. It sounds lascivious, but not necessarily.

Where does love come from? Love is an unnatural act. We are born self-centered. The natural thing is not to love other people—even those closest to us—but to use other people to meet our own needs. We come into this world utterly self-centered. If you have any question about that, spend time with a newborn baby. It will let you know very quickly that you are there to meet his or her needs.

Love is a very unnatural act. We have to learn to love by being loved. If someone does not show us love, we will not have the capacity to love someone else. But where did love come from in the first place? It came from the heart of God. In I John 4 we read, "Dear friends, let us love one another, for love comes from God. Everyone who loves has been born of God and knows God. Whoever does not love does not know God, because God is love. This is how God showed his love among us: He sent his one and only Son into the world that we might live through him. This is love: not that we loved God, but that he loved us and sent his Son as an atoning sacrifice for our sins. Dear friends, since God so loved us, we also ought to love one another. No one has ever seen God; but if we love one another, God lives in us and his love is made complete in us" (7-12).

The first Holy Kiss was when God sent Christ into the world. The second Holy Kiss was when God sent His Holy Spirit into the world. What has kissing got to do with the Trinity? Love is what the Trinity is all about.

There is an ancient legend that, as the aged Apostle John lay dying, his brokenhearted community gathered round him and begged him to impart one last word. He mustered his final breath and said, "Love one another."

He fell silent.

"Is there more?" they asked.

"That is enough," he said. (6)

It is enough. The holy kiss reminds us what the church was meant to be. We are the family of Jesus Christ—brothers and sisters in Christ. And the holy kiss reminds us of how we are to be different from the world. We are set aside to show the world what real love is. Finally the holy kiss reminds us what Christ has done in our behalf. "This is love: not that we loved God, but that he loved us and sent his Son as an atoning sacrifice for our sins."

I'm not going to tell you to give each other a holy kiss before you leave here today. Men, you can relax. But I am going to ask you to make every kiss that you do give a holy kiss. Do not hold back from showing affection to those you genuinely care for, but do not be like the world. We live in a world of cheap kisses, tawdry kisses— kisses whose aim is to use people, not love them. We are those who have been set apart to engage in holy kissing, kisses of genuine love and respect. In the name of the Father and the Son and the Holy Spirit from whom all true love comes. Amen.

1. Russ Fisher, In Search of the Funny Bone (Houston: Rich Publishing Co., 1988), pp. 35-36.
2. Homemade, April, 1990.
3. "What The World Needs Now," www.ridgeumc.org/files/Nov_18.pdf.
4. Christopher Stinnett, http://funnysermons.com/
5. Melvin M. Newland, TX, http://www.sermoncentral.com/sermon.asp?SermonID=33953.
6. A. J. Conyer, The Eclipse of Heaven (Intervarsity Press, 1992), 185. Cited in
Mark Buchanan, Hidden In Plain Sight (Nashville: Thomas Nelson, Inc., 2002), p. 178.

A Lesson From Dr. Seuss

Romans 6:12-23

"Congratulations, today's your day. You're off to great places and away. You have brains in your head. You have feet in your shoes. You can steer yourself any direction you choose." Those rhythmic words of advice come from the delightful little book by Dr. Seuss titled Oh, the Places You'll Go! (1)

"You're on your own," he continues. "And you know what you know. And YOU are the one who'll decide where to go."

It's up to us, says Dr. Seuss. The world is ours and we are free to choose what kind of life we will have. He even provides a warning: "You'll look up and down streets. Look 'em over with care. About some you will say, 'I don't choose to go there.'" With your head full of brains and your shoes full of feet, you're too smart to go down a not-so-good street."

I wish that were true, don't you? I wish we only went places our brains told us to go—that we always made rational choices.

A. Philip Parham tells about a minister who asked a person he was counseling if he had any trouble making decisions. The man answered, "Well, yes and no."

Parham notes that the word intelligence comes from two words—inter, meaning "between," and legere, meaning "to choose." An intelligent person is one who has learned to choose between good and evil, truth and falsehood, love and hate, gentleness and cruelty, humility and arrogance, and life and death. (2)

In other words, "You'll look up and down streets. Look 'em over with care. About some you will say, 'I don't choose to go there.'" As one preacher in the Southern U.S says, "God always votes yes, the devil votes no, and your vote decides the election."

Life is about choices. That's where we want to begin today.

Professional speaker Phillip Wexler notes that the human being is the only creature on earth that is not the prisoner of its programming, but is the master of it. Birds are programmed to fly south in the winter. They don't suddenly decide that because of the bad economy they had better stay home this year. Beavers build dams. Fish swim in schools. Only humans decide to build a dam or to go back to school. We have the power to decide. That doesn't mean, of course, that we always make good decisions.

Some of you will remember an episode of Seinfeld in which George Costanza is frustrated because every decision he makes turns out to be wrong. Jerry says, "Here's your chance to do the opposite. If every instinct you have is wrong, then the opposite would have to be right."

George realizes that Jerry is on to something. If he would act and react completely opposite of his normal actions and reactions, he might have better results. George makes a decision to alter his behavior. "Yes! I will do the opposite!" he declares.

It turns out that Jerry was right. Whenever George does the opposite of his normal reactions, the situation always turns out in his favor. (3)

You really have to have a perverse view of the world to make such an approach to life work for you, but that is why the comedy on Seinfeld worked.

And yet, many of us will have to confess that there is something within us that invariably draws us toward making bad choices.

A customer in a bakery was observed carefully examining all the rich-looking pastries displayed on trays in the glass cases.

A clerk approached him and asked, "What would you like?"

The customer answered, "I'd like that chocolate-covered, cream-filled doughnut, that jelly-filled doughnut and that cheese Danish."

Then with a sigh he added, "But I'll take an oat-bran muffin."

Why is it that we are drawn to that which is bad for us—especially when we know that making bad choices can sometimes be disastrous?

When Pompeii was being excavated, they found a woman's body. Her body had been preserved by the ashes from Mount Vesuvius as it swept over the city. This woman's feet were turned toward the city gate, toward safety—but her face was turned backward. She was looking back toward something that was just beyond her outstretched hands. The archeologists wondered what she was looking for. As they dug, they found a bag of pearls. Maybe she dropped this bag of pearls as she ran for her life. Maybe someone else dropped them, and this lady saw the chance for instant wealth. But, one way or another, with her life on the line, she thought it was worthwhile to stop and pick up some pearls. She turned to pick them up and the volcanic ash swept over her. (4)

What a terrible choice. It was a very human thing to do—to reach out for the bag of pearls, but it cost her her life.

There are many choices that people make that end up costing them their lives, or their families, or their health, or their peace of mind. Anything that causes you to hurt yourself or to hurt someone else is going to be a bad choice.

Some of you will remember the story of a teenage girl who was out on a date one night. Her boyfriend suggested they go to a party where there was going to be alcohol and drugs and all kinds of illicit activity.

This particularly responsible young woman said, "No, I'm not going to do that. And if you're going to do that, you can take me home."

Her boyfriend said, "What's the matter? Are you afraid your Daddy will hurt you?"

She said, "No, I'm afraid that I will hurt my Daddy."

She knew that what her boyfriend was suggesting was a bad choice. "You'll look up and down streets. Look 'em over with care. About some you will say, 'I don't choose to go there.'"

The Bible says that we are drawn to bad choices because of our sinful nature. In today's lesson from the Epistle, St. Paul writes, "When you were slaves to sin, you were free from the control of righteousness. What benefit did you reap at that time from the things you are now ashamed of? Those things result in death! But now that you have been set free from sin and have become slaves to God, the benefit you reap leads to holiness, and the result is eternal life. For the wages of sin is death, but the gift of God is eternal life in Christ Jesus our Lord" (20-23).

St. Paul contrasts people who are enslaved to sin and those who are servants of God. We need to understand what he is saying.

First of all, let's acknowledge that we are sinners. Even the best of us are sinners. W. E. Sangster is generally regarded as one to the ten greatest preachers of the twentieth century, but he knew he was a sinner. In a painfully honest look at his own life, W. E. Sangster wrote in his journal that he had many shortcomings in his spiritual life. He confessed that he was sometimes irritable and easily put out. He was impatient with his wife and children. He acknowledged that most of his study had been crudely ambitious; that he wanted degrees more than knowledge and praise rather than equipment for service.

Even in his preaching he feared that he was more often wondering what the people thought of him, than what they thought about Christ and His word.

He said he had long felt in a vague way, that something was hindering the effectiveness of his ministry and he had concluded that the "something" was his failure in living the truly Christian life. It troubled him that the girl who had lived as a maid in his house for more than three years had not felt drawn to the Christian life because of him. He said he found slight envies in his heart at the greater success of other young ministers. He felt vaguely jealous when they attracted more notice than he did. (5)

You get the idea. W. E. Sangster was one of the great Christian leaders of his time, but he knew deep in his heart that he was not everything that Christ meant for him to be. He was a sinner, just as you and I are sinners. He made bad choices just as you and I make bad choices. He needed God's help daily just as you and I need God's help daily.

W. E. Sangster was a sinner, yet he still made better choices than perhaps ninety-nine per cent of humanity. That is because he not only knew of God's grace, he knew of God's power to help us choose rightly. W.E. Sangster chose to be a servant of God rather than a slave to sin.

Please don't let the first-century imagery of being a slave or a servant get in the way of your understanding. We could use the imagery that Christ used of "taking up his yoke" (Mt 11:29), and we would be on the same road.

Let's use another example. Thirty years ago a psychologist named William Glasser wrote a very helpful book titled, Positive Addiction. Think about that term for a moment, positive addiction. Usually when we think of addiction we think in negative terms—drugs, alcohol, online porn, violent video games—anything we can become so obsessed with that it will be destructive to us—mentally, physically or spiritually. We know how many lives have been damaged by negative addictions.

Glasser noted that there are some activities, however, that we can become addicted to that will result in positive benefits for ourselves and others. One of the most obvious is physical exercise. Glasser came to understand the power of positive addiction from his experience as a runner. Running or almost any physical exercise can become addictive. Not only can you get to the point where you actually look forward to slogging down the street in the wind and the cold, but you are irritable and disoriented when something interferes with your daily run. It becomes an addiction—a positive addiction. On the other hand, the benefits of a positive addiction can be amazing. Weight loss, decline in blood pressure, regulation of blood sugar, improvement in your cardio-vascular condition, etc.—the list of possible health benefits is amazing.

You can become addicted to all kinds of positive activities. Glasser listed such things as gardening, juggling, swinging a bat, bathing, creative but non-critical writing, and knitting. Just about anything can become a positive addiction if it is something you do religiously, if it benefits you and those around you, and if it does not cause you to neglect other positive activities you ought to be involved in. (6)

Positive addiction is like being a servant of God. It means daily making choices that are in keeping with God's will for wholeness and health. It means choosing daily, with God's help, attitudes and actions that bring God glory.

Olympic swim coach Daniel F. Chambliss put it like this: "Great accomplishments, we often assume, require heroic motivation: an intense desire to be the best, an inner strength beyond all measure, some special love of school, of family, of country. Some one of these must, we think, drive the superlative athlete . . . In fact," he says, "world class athletes get to the top level by making a thousand little decisions every morning and night. If you make the right choice on each of these—decide to get up and go to practice, decide to work hard today, decide to volunteer to do an extra event to help your team—then others will say you 'have' dedication. But it is only the doing of those little things, all taken together, that makes that dedication. Great [athletes] aren't made in the long run; they are made every day." (7)

Positive addiction. Servants of God. Or, as Dr. Seuss says, "You'll look up and down streets. Look 'em over with care. About some you will say, 'I don't choose to go there.' With your head full of brains and your shoes full of feet, you're too smart to go down a not-so-good street."

Life consists of making choices. The Bible says that we are drawn to bad choices because of our sinful nature. But it doesn't have to be that way. We can train ourselves, by God's grace, to daily make good choices.

Pastor Tommy Barnett tells a revealing story of an encounter he had with singer Elvis Presley many years ago. Elvis was in the congregation at a church where Barnett was preaching. Elvis seemed moved by the sermon, and wanted to talk to Barnett afterwards. Elvis knew that he needed to repent of his lifestyle and return to his Christian faith. But the allure of show business was so strong that he felt like he had no choice but to keep going in the same direction. With tears rolling down his face, Elvis asked, ". . . what if I renounce show business and find that serving God won't bring joy to my heart?" (8)

Sounds like a sensible question, doesn't it? Of course, we all know what show business did to this talented man. Elvis had it all but became a poster child for, and ultimately a victim of, bad choices.

Choosing Christ invariably helps us make better choices. That's one reason the Christian faith has stood the test of time. When people give their lives to Christ they become better parents, they become better citizens, they live happier, more fulfilled lives. We all know it's true.

But let me say this. It happens only if you make your faith the most important part of your life. It works only if you take your faith seriously. I'm not being judgmental here. Studies show that people who only show up at church occasionally—who have only a casual relationship with God—are as clueless as everyone else about what it takes to have a fulfilling life. They make the same bad choices, they have the same emptiness, as the world outside.

Only when Christ becomes a real presence in our lives do the benefits of faith show themselves. The words "servants of God" may rub us the wrong way, but they emphasize the completeness of the commitment that is required.

The choice is put squarely to us by St. Paul. He writes, "The wages of sin is death, but the gift of God is eternal life in Christ Jesus our Lord." The choice couldn't be any plainer than that.

Or, as Dr. Seuss puts it, "Congratulations, today's your day. You're off to great places. You're off and away. You have brains in your head. You have feet in your shoes. You can steer yourself any direction you choose." With God's help, you can!

1. Random House (January 22, 1990).
2. Letting God: Christian Meditations for Recovering Persons (Harper San Francisco, 1987).
3. http://www.kentcrockett.blogspot.com/
4. John Gerike, http://www.goodshepherdlutheran.com/files/sermons/2006/sermon060827.pdf.
5. Gordon MacDonald, Restoring Your Spiritual Passion (Nashville: Thomas Nelson Publishers, 1986).
6. (Harper & Row, 1976).
7. W. B. Freeman, The Little Book of Olympic Inspiration (Tulsa: Trade Life, 1996, p. 139).
8. Tommy Barnett, Adventure Yourself (Lake Mary, FL.: Creation House, 2000), p. 126.

An Invitation To Tired Souls
Matthew 11: 25-30

Welcome, on this July 4 weekend. Tomorrow we will be celebrating one of the most remarkable documents ever created, the Declaration of Independence. We give God thanks for our freedom. And we pray that in our own small way we will contribute to the coming of the day when all the world's people will be free.

There is a delightful story about an elderly lady who had always wanted to travel abroad. She'd never even been out of the country, so she started the process by getting her passport.

She went to the passport office and asked how long it would take to have a passport issued. The clerk told her that she would have to take the loyalty oath first. "Raise your right hand, please," he said.

The lady did as she was told.

"Do you swear to defend the Constitution of the United States against all its enemies, domestic or foreign?" was the first question.

Her face paled and her voice trembled as she asked in a very small voice, "Uhhh . . . all by myself?" (1)

Well, that would be a big responsibility for any one person to bear.

Our lesson for today is from Matthew: "Come to me, all you who are weary and burdened, and I will give you rest. Take my yoke upon you and learn from me, for I am gentle and humble in heart, and you will find rest for your souls. For my yoke is easy and my burden is light."

What an interesting lesson for this particular weekend. I say it is interesting because there is a statue that stands in New York Harbor welcoming immigrants from almost every land on earth. We know her as the Statue of Liberty. Within the pedestal on which this great statue stands is a poem by Emma Lazarus graven on a tablet with these immortal words that describe the highest ideals of this nation of immigrants, "Give me your tired, your poor, Your huddled masses yearning to breathe free, The wretched refuse of your teeming shore. Send these, the homeless, tempest-tossed to me, I lift my lamp beside the golden door!"

Today, we as a nation may not be quite as willing to extend that invitation as we once were, but thankfully Christ still extends his invitation to all who would heed it, "Come to me, all you who are weary and burdened, and I will give you rest . . ."

Is there anyone in this room who knows what it is to be tired?

I was amused to read about an incident that occurred at Yosemite National Park. Some of you are perhaps familiar with a gigantic granite dome in that park called Half Dome. Half Dome rises more than 4,737 feet above the valley floor. It is a popular hiking destination. In 1993 a woman called 911 from the top of Half Dome using her cell phone. According to dispatch, she said: "Well, I'm at the top and I'm really tired."

The answering ranger asked if she felt sick.

"No," she said, "I'm just really tired and I want my friends to drive to the base and pick me up."

The dispatcher explained that she would have to hike down the trail she had ascended.

The visitor replied, "But you don't understand, I'm really tired."

What happened next? "It turned out we got really lucky," the ranger said, "her cell phone battery died." (2)

Anyone who has ever gone on a long hike can sympathize. A person can get "bone-tired" on such a hike.

Do you know what it is to be really tired?

I heard of a mom who was playing cops and robbers in the backyard on a summer evening. One of her boys pointed a toy gun and shouted, "Bang, you're dead." She slumped to the ground, and when she didn't get up, a neighbor ran over to see what was wrong.

As the neighbor bent over, Mom opened one eye and whispered, "Shhhh . . . don't blow my cover. It's the only chance I get to rest." (3)

Hikers and busy moms are not the only ones who are tired, of course. Fatigue can take a toll on the best of us.

Popular author Gordon MacDonald says that his father taught him to ski when he was a young boy. MacDonald still remembers one of the first pieces of advice his father gave him on the slope: "Remember, son," said his dad, "more accidents happen in the final hour of the day than at any other time." MacDonald says he now knows that his father was correct.

"Trying to get one more downhill run in before the ski row closes, some skiers will rush down the slope forgetting that their bodies are tired and that their reflexes are no longer sharp. Shadows are long; icy and bare spots are hidden. The combination of a depleted body and obstacles not easily seen creates conditions . . . in which accidents are far more likely to happen."

His dad was right. At the end of the day it is wise to ski much more cautiously. You can be more tired than you realize . . . plus you can't always trust the terrain. (4)

Fatigue has been a factor in many tragic accidents, not only with skiers but also with the operators of automobiles. I won't ask you if any of you have ever fallen asleep driving. Fortunately you lived to tell about it, but it happens more than any of us would like to think.

Fatigue produces slow reflexes and poor decision making. There is evidence that some of the best known tragedies of the past several decades—the Exxon Valdez spill, the Challenger rocket explosion, the Chernobyl nuclear reactor meltdown and the Three Mile Island near-disaster—were all caused in part by decisions made by people in critical positions who were suffering from fatigue, often caused by sleep deprivation.

Here again, I'm tempted to have you raise your hands if you have trouble sleeping at night. According to the Sleep Foundation, more than 60 percent of Americans get less than the eight hours of sleep. This is rest the average adult requires. Forty-three percent of Americans report that several days each month they are too sleepy to perform efficiently at work or at home. (5) On a less dramatic scale, how many of us are grouchy and short-tempered with our loved ones, simply and solely because we are tired?

It's almost as if Christ had us in mind when he spoke those beautiful words, "Come to me, all you who are weary and burdened, and I will give you rest. Take my yoke upon you and learn from me, for I am gentle and humble in heart, and you will find rest for your souls. For my yoke is easy and my burden is light."

You realize, of course, that a tired body is preceded by a tired mind. Not always, of course. Some people are tired because they do hard physical labor. Others are tired because of strenuous recreational exercise, though not as many as you might think. Many people who are into running or swimming or basketball or some other strenuous sport will tell you that, over time, exercise actually produces more energy than it depletes. Sitting around doing nothing is the fastest way to grow tired and out of sorts. A tired body is preceded by a tired mind.

Of course I realize that exercise isn't for everybody.

One man said his doctor told him that jogging would add years to his life. The man says, "I think he was right. I feel ten years older already."

Another poor guy said he finished 50 push-ups this morning! But he adds that he started those 50 pushups back in 2005.

Another man says he is also into exercise. He says, "Every morning I awaken to the alarm, jump from bed, and run around the block six times . . . Then I kick that little block under the bed and go back to sleep."

Most of us are not tired from straining our muscles. Most of our fatigue is mental. It takes energy to deal with customers all day long. It is draining to sit in front of a computer screen. Many of us have jobs that are repetitive or that require precision, and so we drag ourselves into our homes barely able to put one foot in front of the other. We're tired! We're beat!

Then sometimes something quite interesting happens. The phone rings and a friend asks us to go shopping or dancing or bowling or something else we enjoy, and suddenly we have a burst of energy that belies our exclamations of fatigue. Have you noticed? Where does that new energy come from? It comes from our mind.

It is amazing how much energy people have who are driven by a sense of purpose. Ralph Waldo Emerson once said that the power of the Gulf Stream will flow through an ordinary drinking straw, if the straw is placed parallel to the flow of the stream. The same is true of our lives. Align them with some great purpose and it is amazing how much power, how much energy they can produce.

These words of Jesus speak of the source of that energy: "Come to me, all you who are weary and burdened, and I will give you rest. Take my yoke upon you and learn from me, for I am gentle and humble in heart, and you will find rest for your souls. For my yoke is easy and my burden is light." The yoke suggests that we are getting prepared to work in concert with him. The rest that Jesus gives is not the rest of lying around doing nothing. The rest that Jesus gives is the rest of a renewed mind and a refreshed spirit. It is the rest of a new purpose for life.

One of the great missionaries of the twentieth century was a man named E. Stanley Jones. Jones was a man of amazing energy who wrote several best-selling books. It is hard to imagine that his career was once threatened and nearly cut short by chronic worry.

When he first arrived in India, Jones wore himself out, working and worrying. "I was suffering so severely from brain fatigue and nervous exhaustion," he later wrote, "that I collapsed, not once but several times." Aboard a ship returning to America, Jones collapsed again and the doctor put him to bed. After a year's rest, he attempted to return to India, but became a bundle of nerves on the return trip and arrived in Bombay a broken man. His colleagues warned him that any attempt to continue ministering in such a state of anxious care could be fatal.

While praying one night, groping in emotional darkness, Jones seemed to hear a Voice ask him, "Are you yourself ready for this work to which I have called you?"

"No, Lord," replied Jones. "I am done for. I have reached the end of my resources."

"If you will turn that over to Me and not worry about it," the Voice seemed to say, "I will take care of it."

Jones answered, "Lord, I close the bargain right here."

A great sense of peace closed in over Stanley Jones. He felt a rush of abundant life that seemed to sweep him off his feet. His energy returned, his enthusiasm bubbled over, and he plunged back into his work with a vitality he had never before known. Jones went on to spend a lifetime of ministry in India, writing numerous books, and ministering to multitudes around the world.

He later wrote, "This one thing I know: my life was completely transformed and uplifted that night . . . when at the depth of my weakness and depression, a voice said to me: 'If you will turn that over to Me and not worry about it, I will take care of it,' and I replied, 'Lord, I close the bargain right here.'" (6)

Maybe you and I need to close a bargain with God. Do you have that sense of peace that Stanley Jones found in his encounter with God? So many of us are tired because of mental and emotional conflicts that are draining us of our energy. We need to turn our worries, our concerns, our doubts and fears over to God.

Then we need to be yoked to Christ.

The elderly lady who went to the passport office didn't want to feel the weight of protecting the constitution of the United States on her shoulders alone. That is a common mistake. Many of us are trying to shoulder burdens alone, burdens that Christ would like to shoulder with us.

Jesus said, "My yoke is easy and my burden is light." A "yoke" is most commonly associated with oxen and other animals that are harnessed together so they can help farmers plow. To be yoked with Christ is to allow him to share the burden of our daily lives, to allow him to take off our shoulders the weight of trying to solve our problems alone. Being yoked with Christ is one of the secrets of a productive life.

Dr. Herb True tells about a conversation he had with a trainer of Clydesdale horses. According to this trainer the average Clydesdale is able to pull about 7,000 pounds. Put two Clydesdales together, however, and their combined pull should equal 18,000 pounds. However, working as a team, with proper training the same two Clydesdales are capable of pulling 25,000 pounds—more than 3 times as much as one Clydesdale.

In business this is called synergy. Get two people complementing one another to work in tandem, and much more can be produced than by either one working alone. Imagine then how effective our lives could be if we worked in tandem with the One who is the source of all ideas, the source of all energy, the source of all that has ever been created.

The English theologian F. B. Meyer once visited the American evangelist Dwight L. Moody in Northfield, Massachusetts. Moody showed Meyer a team of oxen and said that whenever one of those oxen was being yoked in, the other, which might be on the far side of the farmyard, would come trotting up and stand beside the other one until it was yoked in also. Meyer then made this encouraging application to us in our relationship to Christ: "Jesus stands today with the yoke upon His shoulder. He calls to each one and says, 'Come and share my yoke, and let us plow together the long furrow of your life. I will be a true yokefellow to you. The burden shall be on me.'" (7)

How about you? Are you tired of being sick and tired? Are you ready to trust him with your worries and emotional conflicts? "Take my yoke upon you and learn from me," says the Master, "for I am gentle and humble in heart, and you will find rest for your souls. For my yoke is easy and my burden is light."

1. "Kitty's Daily Mews" <kittysdailymews-subscribe@topica.com.
2. "Stories from records of the National Park System." From the Internet,
3. Mort Crim, Second Thoughts—One Hundred Upbeat Messages (Deerfield Beach, FL: Health Communication, 1997).
4. Rebuilding Your Broken World (Nashville: Oliver-Nelson Books, 1988).
5. Ruth La Ferla, "Sleep, the Final Luxury," New York Times, December 11, 2000.
6. Robert J. Morgan, Preacher's Sourcebook Creative Sermon Illustrations (Nashville: Thomas Nelson, Inc., 2007), p. 807.
7. Biblical Illustrator.

The Receptive Heart
Matthew 13:1-9, 18-23

Life is a matter of attitude. All the great motivational speakers tell us that. To succeed in life, attitude is critical. Of course, not everyone has a great attitude. In fact, some people have a downright rotten attitude. The Internet carried an item recently that reflects a rotten attitude. It is called the "Cynic's Guide to Life." It's a clever take-off on some of life's familiar clichés. See if you recognize any of these:

A journey of a thousand miles . . . begins with . . . a broken fan belt and a leaky tire.

I believe for every drop of rain that falls, a flower grows . . . and a foundation leaks and a ball game gets rained out and a car rusts and . . . [You get the idea.]

Follow your dream! . . . Unless it's the one where you're at work in your underwear during a fire drill.

Do not walk behind me, for I may not lead. Do not walk ahead of me, for I may not follow . . . Do not walk beside me, either, just leave me alone.

If you don't like my driving . . . don't call anyone . . . Just take another road. That's why the highway department made so many of them.

It's always darkest before the dawn . . . So if you're going to steal the neighbor's newspaper, that's the time to do it.

Keep your nose to the grindstone and your shoulder to the wheel . . . it's cheaper than plastic surgery. And finally:

This land is your land . . . This land is my land . . . So stay on your land. (1)

Not everybody has a great attitude, but a great attitude is important to all of life. In fact, our attitude can determine whether or not we respond to the Gospel.

Jesus is teaching by the Sea of Galilee. Such large crowds have gathered around him that he gets into a boat and sits in it to teach, while all the people stand on the shore. He begins his teaching with a parable: "A farmer went out to sow his seed. As he was scattering the seed, some fell along the path, and the birds came and ate it up. Some fell on rocky places, where it did not have much soil. It sprang up quickly, because the soil was shallow. But when the sun came up, the plants were scorched, and they withered because they had no root. Other seed fell among thorns, which grew up and choked the plants. Still other seed fell on good soil, where it produced a crop—a hundred, sixty or thirty times what was sown." Then Jesus says, "Whoever has ears, let them hear."

Jesus explains this simple parable later in this chapter. The soil, he says, is anyone who hears the message of the Gospel. Now think about that for a moment. You and I are the soil in this parable. I could have said we are dirt, but that sounds a little negative. Jesus is trying to make a positive statement here. We are soil, potentially rich soil, productive soil.

Of course, on one level we are soil. We are dirt. The writer of Genesis tells us that we were created out of the dust of the ground. Genesis 2:7, "Then the LORD God formed a man from the dust of the ground and breathed into his nostrils the breath of life, and the man became a living being." So Jesus begins his explanation by saying "The soil is anyone who hears the message of the Gospel."

"The seed sown along the path," explains the Master, "is anyone who hears the message about the kingdom and does not understand it. The evil one comes and snatches away what was sown in their heart."

Why don't these people understand the message of the kingdom? One reason might be that they have been culturally conditioned to think in a very small box.

Mahatma Gandhi led the nation of India through the process of gaining independence from Great Britain. Gandhi believed one of the biggest challenges to the independence movement in India was not the British but the mindset of most Indians themselves. He recognized that most Indians had such a low opinion of themselves that many believed they deserved to be ruled by the British. Unfortunately for these humble people, the British knew how they felt, and used their attitudes against them.

The British presence was not all that large in India. It amounted to a few governors scattered around that immense country of hundreds of millions of people and small pockets of military troops. Describing Britain's power over his people, Gandhi said that never were so many ruled by so few. So he set out to show India a different way of thinking, one that spoke into their souls and called them to greatness. The outcome was India's successful move to national independence in 1948. (2)

In the same way, we have people in our culture who may not respond to the Gospel because they have been conditioned against it. They may sit in a church pew week after week, but they have been so beaten down by their upbringing, by the negative expectations of others—they have such a low opinion of themselves—they cannot even hear the message of grace. They want to believe, but their low attitude of themselves makes it nearly impossible. Every time a little seed of hope is planted in their hearts, the evil one comes and snatches it away from them with lies about their self-worth. That, says Jesus, is the seed sown by the path.

"The seed falling on rocky ground," he explains, "refers to someone who hears the word and at once receives it with joy. But since they have no root, they last only a short time. When trouble or persecution comes because of the word, they quickly fall away."

In Palestine much of the land is a thin two- or three-inch veneer of soil over limestone bedrock. Seed falls on this thin layer of soil, the warm sun quickly heats the seed, and it sprouts in feverish growth. But then the sun beats down, the plant's roots meet the bedrock, and it withers and dies. (3) It dies because the soil is rocky ground.

Who does the rocky ground refer to? How about the complacent church member with one foot inside the church and one foot out? More concerned with respectability than with righteousness, this is the half-hearted saint who never makes a full commitment to Christ and his kingdom.

Evangelist Donald Grey Barnhouse once told a story about a man who bought a bottle of perfume in Paris at a very good price and brought it home. It was a very expensive perfume in a very beautiful bottle. His wife was proud of it, and used the perfume until it was all gone. Even then she kept the bottle on her boudoir table so that her friends, in coming into her room, would say, "Oh, that was such and such perfume."

There came an occasion when the woman wanted to wear this expensive scent, but the bottle was empty, so she put a handkerchief into the bottle and closed it. After a day there was enough of the perfume on the handkerchief to give a faint fragrance, but after that it was all gone. However, there was still enough odor around the bottle so that someone could say, "Oh, that was such and such."

Barnhouse would tell that story and say, "There are many people in our churches who are like that. If you come near them and listen to their conversation you may be able to say, 'Oh, grandfather was a Christian.' The fragrance of his commitment still lingered in their lives, but as far as they themselves are concerned, the bottle is empty. They have no life and fragrance of Christ of their own."

He said that once he told the story that way and afterward was walking down the street to his hotel. He nearly overtook three people who had evidently been at the church service. One of them was saying, "I liked that story that he told about the perfume bottle because it reminded me of a very expensive perfume that Frank brought me from Paris. It is a beautiful bottle, but I have never broken the seal. It sits right there on my dresser and the light shines through it. It is a beautiful amber."

Barnhouse broke into the conversation. They recognized him and laughed that he should have overheard them. "But," he said, "don't you see that the perfume was given to you for use? And what an illustration that is."

Barnhouse went on to say that so many Christians who have been given so much, keep it tightly sealed in themselves. No one passing near would know for a moment that they have the life of God in them. And the wonderful thing about God's perfume is that as we share it with others, God keeps filling the bottle. (4)

"The seed falling on rocky ground," explains the Master, "refers to someone who hears the word and at once receives it with joy. But since they have no root, they last only a short time." These are shallow, complacent church people, still getting by on their grandfather's faith, or their mother's faith. They have no root. The bottle is empty.

There is a third group who is exposed to the Gospel message. "The seed falling among the thorns," says the Master, "refers to someone who hears the word, but the worries of this life and the deceitfulness of wealth choke the word, making it unfruitful."

Now this group is easy to identify. They're already checking their watches to see when this service will be over so that they can get on to their real interests and concerns. They've got to get to the restaurant before the other churches let out. Company is coming tomorrow. Got to make sure the house is just so. The market's bounced around a lot this year. Got to go over all my investments. "The seed falling among the thorns, refers to someone who hears the word, but the worries of this life and the deceitfulness of wealth choke the word, making it unfruitful." These are not bad people. They just never really focus on God and what God expects out of them. God is basically irrelevant to their world.

Dr. Greg Herrick tells about a writer who married his secretary. The writer was a stern and difficult person. Herrick recounts that the man dearly loved his wife, "but he was thoughtless and absorbed in his own interests and activities, treating his wife as if she were still his employee.

"Stricken with cancer she was confined to bed for a long time before she died. After her funeral, the writer went back to his empty house. Disconsolate and grieving deeply, he wandered around aimlessly downstairs, engrossed in thinking about the woman he had loved. After a while he went upstairs to her room and sat down in the chair beside the bed on which she had been lying for months. He realized with painful regret that he had not sat there very often during her long illness.

"He noticed her diary. While she was alive, he never would have read it, but now that she was gone he felt free to pick it up and thumb through its pages. One entry caught his eye: 'Yesterday he spent an hour with me. And it was like being in heaven. I love him so much.' He turned a few more pages and read, 'I listened all day to hear his steps in the hallway. And now it's late. I guess he won't come to see me.' He read a few more entries and then threw the book on the floor and ran out into the rain back to the cemetery. He fell on his wife's grave in the mud, sobbing, 'If only I had known . . . if only I had known.'"

Dr. Herrick adds, "I wonder how many of us will stand before the Father someday, saying, 'If only I'd known, if only I'd known . . . how much you loved me.' In contrast to the writer's wife who apparently said little or nothing about her love, God on the other hand has made it abundantly known how he feels about a relationship with us." (5) But we're too busy, too concerned about all the things that are important to us. We are like the seed that fell among the thorns.

But there is a final group of people in Jesus' parable. "The seed falling on good soil refers to someone who hears the word and understands it. This is the one who produces a crop, yielding a hundred, sixty or thirty times what was sown."

That is the wonderful thing about seed sown on fertile soil. It can lead to a harvest bountiful beyond imagination. As someone has said, you can count the seed in any apple, but you can't count the apples in any one seed.

French author Jean Giono tells the story of a young man who was undertaking a lone hiking trip through Provence, France, and into the Alps in the year 1913. The young man runs out of water in a treeless, desolate valley where only wild lavender grows and there is no trace of civilization except old, empty crumbling buildings. Lacking water he encounters a shepherd who shows him a spring where he can drink.

Curious about this man and why he has chosen such a lonely life, the young man stays with him for a time.

The shepherd, Elzéard Bouffier, after being widowed, has decided to restore the ruined landscape of the isolated and largely abandoned valley by single-handedly cultivating a forest, tree by tree. He has made thousands of holes in the ground with his curling pole dropping into the holes acorns that he has collected.

The young man leaves the shepherd and returns home, and later fights in the First World War. In 1920, shell-shocked and depressed after the war, he returns. He is surprised to see young saplings of all forms taking root in the valley, and new streams running through it where the shepherd has made dams higher up in the mountain. The young soldier makes a full recovery in the peace and beauty of the re-growing valley, and continues to visit the Bouffier the shepherd.

Over four decades, Bouffier continues to plant trees, and the valley is turned into a kind of Garden of Eden. Giono writes: "On the site of the ruins I had seen in 1913 now stand neat farms . . . The old streams, fed by the rains and snows that the forest conserves, are flowing again . . . Little by little, the villages have been rebuilt. People from the plains, where land is costly, have settled here, bringing youth, motion, the spirit of adventure." (6) Good seed sown on good soil brought forth a bountiful harvest due to the dedication of one man.

Four kinds of soil, says Jesus. Four kinds of people—those who have been culturally conditioned to resist the message of God's grace; those who have heard the message, but have never given themselves completely to it; those who have heard it, but have too many other concerns to focus on God, and finally those who hear the Word, apply it to their lives, and become fruitful disciples of Jesus Christ. Which kind are you?

1. Monday Fodder, http://family-safe-mail.com/.
2. Mike Barrett, The Danger Habit (Colorado Springs: Multnomah Publishers, 2006), pp. 61-62.
3. R. Kent Hughes, "Mark: Jesus, Servant and Savior" in Preaching the Word, volume 1 (Westchester, IL: Crossway Books, 1989), 107.
4. Timeless Illustrations for Preaching and Teaching (Peabody, MA: Hendrickson Publishers, Inc., 2004), pp. 432-433.
5. Cited by Dr. Bruce Havens,
http://home.comcast.net/~accucc/Sermons/sermon_2005_06_12.htm.
6. http://en.wikipedia.org/wiki/The_Man_Who_Planted_Trees.

What To Do With The Weeds
Matthew 13:24-30, 36-43

Those of you who are gardeners are familiar with Murphy's First Law of Gardening: When weeding, the best way to make sure you are removing a weed and not a valuable plant is to pull on it. If it comes out of the ground easily, it is a valuable plant.

And, of course, there is a corollary to that law: To distinguish flowers from weeds, simply pull up everything. What grows back is weeds.

Last week we dealt with the parable of the sower and we learned that different kinds of soil produce differing levels of results. Today we are confronted with the question: what do you do with the weeds? Because we know, those who have ever tried to plant a flower garden, or a vegetable garden or even a plain ordinary lawn, the weeds are going to come.

So listen to Jesus' parable: "The kingdom of heaven is like a man who sowed good seed in his field. But while everyone was sleeping, his enemy came and sowed weeds among the wheat, and went away. When the wheat sprouted and formed heads, then the weeds also appeared.

"The owner's servants came to him and said, 'Sir, didn't you sow good seed in your field? Where then did the weeds come from?'

"'An enemy did this,' he replied.

"The servants asked him, 'Do you want us to go and pull them up?'

"'No,' he answered, 'because while you are pulling the weeds, you may uproot the wheat with them. Let both grow together until the harvest. At that time I will tell the harvesters: First collect the weeds and tie them in bundles to be burned; then gather the wheat and bring it into my barn.'"

If you take Jesus literally, this is a scary parable. The weeds are going to be thrown on a fire and burned. Jesus isn't actually giving us a guide to growing good wheat, of course. He's talking about human behavior. But one thing's for sure, in this scenario, you do not want to be a weed.

It's like a story our Roman Catholic friends tell. In the Roman Church, seven is traditionally the age of reason. When children reach seven they are expected to attend Mass regularly and go to confession. Why? Because when they are seven they are accountable for their sins.

One five-year-old girl was impressed when she learned about the age of reason. When her older brother turned seven she greeted him like this, "Happy birthday, Matthew. Now you can go to hell." (1)

What an honor. You've finally arrived. Now you can go to Satan's domain. It's scary. But let's be clear on one thing, judgment is an important fact of life.

Someone was commenting on the often heard remark, "Everything happens for a reason." "Yes," said this observer, "and the reason is found in Galatians 6:7, 'Whatever a man sows, that he will also reap . . .'"

The reason some things happen to us is that we are reaping what we have sown.

Judgment is a fact of life. You play, you pay—as we say in the common vernacular. Not always of course, but often that is the case.

In the movie The Last Emperor, the young child anointed as the last emperor of China lives a magical life of luxury with a thousand eunuch servants at his command.

"What happens when you do wrong?" his brother asks him.

"When I do wrong, someone else is punished," the boy emperor replies.

To demonstrate, he breaks a jar, and one of the servants is beaten. (2)

What a neat system if you are the emperor. You do the crime, someone else does the time.

We can say that doesn't happen in real life, but in a sense it does. How often are innocent people punished for the sins of a drunk driver, for example? How many innocent children suffer because of the sins of abusive parents? How many spouses suffer because of the waywardness of their partner?

Usually, however, we reap what we ourselves have sown. There is a bumper sticker with this message: "Honk if you love Jesus! Text while driving if you want to meet Him."

That's an example of reaping what we have sown. However, if we get hit by that texting driver, we have reaped what another has sown.

You and I may look at this parable and say it is horrible that the weeds get thrown in the fire, but that's the way life is. It is absurd to sugarcoat reality. If you plant bad seed, no use praying for a good harvest. Most of the time you're going to get what you sow. Or, as someone has said, "If the grass looks greener on the other side of the fence, it may mean they take better care of their lawn."

What is dangerous is trying to figure out what other people are going to reap. Some people, I'm sorry to say, delight in separating people into acceptable and unacceptable, worthy and unworthy, good and bad, wheat and weeds.

Notice what happens in this parable. The landowner's servants come to him to tell him that there are weeds in his wheat and ask him if he wants them to pull the weeds up? The landowner tells them no, wait until the harvest and then separate them.

Harvesting the wheat in Jesus' time was arduous work. The harvesters would use sickles. They would bend over and cut the wheat just above the ground. But what happens if weeds are growing midst the wheat? We're told that the weeds in Jesus' parable were a poisonous variety called "bearded darnel." In the early stages of growth this bearded darnel so closely resembles wheat that it is not possible to distinguish one from the other. Later when it is possible to distinguish between them, the roots of the wheat and weeds are so intertwined that one could not be pulled without also tearing up the other. To rip up the weeds would also be to destroy the growth of the wheat. So the landowner was being wise when he said, "No . . . let both grow together until the harvest." So, the harvesters were not allowed to try to separate the weeds from the wheat until the final harvest.

Now what does that mean for us? A constant theme in Jesus' teaching is that his followers were not to pass judgment on others. This is very important. Traditionally the primary sin of highly religious people is being self-righteous and judgmental. We have a tendency to judge for ourselves who is fit for the kingdom and who is not, who is spiritual and who is worldly. This is a dangerous tendency. I want to suggest to you three key reasons why we cannot be the ones to decide who is wheat and who is a weed.

First of all, we should not judge others because we ourselves are not totally acceptable.

Writer Kent Crockett tells about a married couple who pulled into a full service gas station to refuel their car. As the tank was being filled, the station attendant washed the windshield. When he finished, the husband stuck his head out the window and said, "It's still dirty. Wash it again."

"Yes, sir," the attendant replied.

After he cleaned it a second time, the husband said, "Don't you know how to wash a windshield? It's still filthy. Now do it again!"

The attendant scrubbed the windshield a third time, carefully looking for any messy spots he might have missed. By now the husband was fuming. "I can't believe you are so incompetent that you can't even do a simple job like cleaning a windshield! I'm going to report you to your boss!"

Just then, his wife reached over and removed his glasses. She wiped them clean with a tissue, then put them back on his face. And it was amazing how clean the windshield was! (3)

"Do not judge, or you too will be judged," said the Master. "For in the same way you judge others, you will be judged, and with the measure you use, it will be measured to you" (Matthew 7:1).

We forget when we judge others that we are looking through a smudged lens. Sometimes we criticize others unfairly. We don't know all their circumstances, or their motives. Only God, who is aware of all the facts, is able to judge people rightly.

Even a saint like John Wesley made this mistake. Wesley once told of a man he had little respect for because he considered him to be miserly and covetous. One day when this person contributed only a small gift to a worthy charity, Wesley openly criticized him.

After the incident, the man went to Wesley privately and told him he had been living on parsnips, a kind of carrot, and water for several weeks. He explained that before his conversion, he had run up many bills. Now, by skimping on everything and buying nothing for himself, he was paying off his creditors one by one.

"Christ has made me an honest man," he said, "and so with all these debts to pay, I can give only a few offerings above my tithe. I must settle up with my worldly neighbors and show them what the grace of God can do in the heart of a man who was once dishonest." Wesley then apologized to the man and asked his forgiveness. (4)

Jesus said that we have enough to do to look to our own acceptability to spend time evaluating the acceptability of others. We are not to judge others, first of all, because we are not perfect ourselves. Leave it to God to judge who is wheat and who is a weed.

But there is a second and even more important reason we are not to judge others. When we pass judgment on others, we distance ourselves from them.

Pastor Jason Freyer says that when he was in college, he was walking to class with a few friends who were asking him how he could be a Christian when so many of the Christians they saw on TV were judgmental, nasty self-centered people. He told them that he really thought that Christian people as a whole were doing much better.

As those words left his mouth, he said, they rounded the corner and were met by a group of students, carrying huge 30 foot banners that said things like "Turn or Burn" and "Gays will die in hell" and "I know what you did last night, and God doesn't like it."

Young Freyer was furious. He walked up to one of the women who was carrying a sign and asked her if she thought she was really being effective. In his estimation it seemed as though many people were just walking away mad, rather than walking away in the love of Christ.

The woman told him that in Matthew 5 Christians are told they would face all kinds of persecution. Freyer says he wanted to shake her and scream, "BUT HE DOESN'T ASK US TO LOOK FOR IT!"

Later he realized why he was so angry with her methods. She wasn't engaging anyone. "It's easy to stand on the sidelines, says Freyer, "with a sign or a bullhorn and tell other people how wrong they are. It's much different though to actually engage with people, learn their stories, learn their hurts, learn their lives." (5)

We all are familiar with John 3: 16, "For God so loved the world that he gave his one and only Son, that whoever believes in him shall not perish but have eternal life." Do you remember John 3:17? "For God did not send his Son into the world to condemn the world, but to save the world through him." Christ did not come to condemn people but to save them. And so it is with us. We are not here to judge other people—whether it's our friend who sleeps around, or who drinks too much, or even who themselves are too critical or judgmental. Our task is to love people and to witness to them of a God who loves them.

You see the real problem with passing judgment on others is that it does not allow us to be vehicles of God's grace. Our central task is to help other people experience God's grace just as we have experienced that grace. We cannot do that if we come across as one with a condemning attitude. Besides, we simply don't know what kind of hurts other people may have experienced.

Ken Collins, a pastor in Kentucky, was working one day near a barn. Suddenly he realized that he wasn't alone. A squirrel scurried by him into the barn. The squirrel was squeaking as he ran. Then the squirrel emerged from the barn and began running alongside the barn. Collins realized he was coming again in his direction. The thought came to him that this animal perhaps had rabies. He armed himself with a club. However, the squirrel again passed him and went to a huge tree. There it stopped, unable to climb. Then Collins saw the problem. As the squirrel turned to face him it spread its front legs and he could see the area where a bullet had entered the squirrel's chest. Unable to climb the tree, the squirrel finally disappeared into the woods.

Pastor Collins whispered, "Lord what message is there in this scene?" Then, in the quietness of his own heart, the Lord spoke to Ken Collins and here is what God said, "Ken, you just witnessed a squirrel that was unable to climb because it was wounded. I have a lot of children who have been wounded by Satan . . . but they are still my children. Do not condemn because you don't understand but do all you can to help them now that you do understand." There is much wisdom in those words.

F.B. Meyer once said that when we see a brother or sister in sin, there are two things we do not know: First, we do not know how hard he or she tried not to sin. And second, we do not know the power of the forces that assailed him or her. We also do not know what we would have done in the same circumstances. (6)

The teaching of the parable is clear: there will come a time when the wheat is separated from the weeds. But only God is in a position to judge which is which. In the meantime let's focus on what God has called us to do—to love all people and to witness to the amazing grace of God as shown in Jesus Christ.

1. Alexander Humez, Nicholas Humez and Joseph Maguire, Zero to Lazy Eight (Simon & Schuster), Reader's Digest, Dec. 1994, p. 154.
2. Philip Yancey in What's So Amazing About Grace? Leadership, Vol. 19, no. 3.
Cited by Rev. Adrian Dieleman. http://www.trinitycrc.org/sermons/1tim2v05-06.html.
3. http://www.kentcrockett.blogspot.com/.
4. Daily Bread, July 20, 1992. http://www.sermonillustrations.com/a-z/j/judging.htm.
5. http://www.westminster-church.org/pdfs_2008/sermons/My_Revolution.pdf
6. Stephen Brown, Christianity Today, April 5, 1993, p. 17.

God's Most Troubling Promise
Romans 8:28

Have you ever noticed that life is full of challenges? Have you noticed that, sooner or later, all of us are going to have some pretty steep mountains to climb?

I heard about a woman named Jill whose car was unreliable. She called her friend John for a ride every time her car broke down. One day John got yet another one of those calls.

"What happened this time?" he asked.

"My brakes went out," Jill said. "Can you come and get me?"

"Where are you?" John asked.

"I'm in the drugstore," Jill responded.

"And where's the car?" John asked.

Jill replied, "It's in here with me." (1)

That's life, we say. Sometimes you're the bug; sometimes you're the windshield, but life is one series of challenges after another. Some of these challenges are routine everyday headaches and irritations. The car breaks down; you're late for work. The heavens unleash rain on your daughter's wedding. You have lunch with someone you want to impress; afterward you discover that the whole time you were with them, you had a piece of spinach firmly entrenched in one of your front teeth. These kinds of events drive you crazy, but they are just passing flights of bad luck.

However, some other challenges are nothing short of heart-wrenching tragedies. The death of a loved one. An ominous diagnosis in the doctor's office. The loss of a job or the breakup of a family. Some of the challenges we encounter can be handled quite easily; others, though, threaten to crush us. And then we come to this verse, Romans 8:28, "And we know that in all things God works for the good of those who love him, who have been called according to his purpose."

Think about that for a moment: "In all things God works for the good of those who love him." What does that mean? Does it mean that faith is a blanket that we can toss over ourselves and nothing really bad will happen to us? "In all things God works for the good . . ." I wish we had that kind of security blanket.

Do you remember a television show from a few years ago called "Early Edition"? Set in Chicago, "Early Edition" followed the adventures of a young man named Gary Hobson who mysteriously received a newspaper, the Chicago Sun-Times, each morning. Except, there was something different about this particular Sun-Times.

For one thing, you may remember, it was delivered by a cat. But even more mysteriously, it was the newspaper for the NEXT day. In other words, it was a newspaper that carried stories about events that hadn't happened yet. So, the plot was that the newspaper would alert Gary Hobson to some tragedy that was going to happen within the next 24 hours. He, in turn, would attempt to keep this tragedy from occurring.

Pastor Susan Langhauser tells about one episode, which she calls her favorite. It begins with a morning newspaper with a headline that screams, "150 DIE AS PLANE CRASHES ON TAKE OFF." Also, at the bottom of the page was a tiny story about a little girl, hit by a car, who dies in the street awaiting transport to the hospital.

Determining that he must help the 150 who would die in the plane crash rather than the one little girl, Hobson drives frantically to the airport. However, he gets hopelessly delayed in gridlock on the freeway. While he agonizes over his inability to get to the airport, the little girl cycles past him on a nearby street. He decides he had better help her, and veers off the highway, reaching her just after she has been hit. He scoops her up and races to the nearest hospital, where, of course, she survives due to his timely assistance. As he sits dejectedly wishing he could have made it to the airport, the doors fly open and the girl's parents rush in, the father dressed in an airline pilot's uniform. He had been pulled from his flight just before take off with the news of his daughter's accident, and the delay diverted the tragedy reported in the early edition. (2)

Wouldn't it be great if God worked that way?—a plane doesn't crash because a pilot gets diverted by his little girl's accident? Perhaps sometimes God does work that way.

Christian writer Lindsay Parkhill says, "God brings about the good by weaving together our daily decisions." I believe there is something to that, but what about the planes that do crash? What about the children who do get hit by cars? Where is God then? What does it mean to say that "in all things God works for the good of those who love him"? Does it mean that God magically protects His children from harm? You and I know from experience that is not true. Some of the best people in the world have tragic things happen to them.

Does it mean, then, that perhaps God sends challenges to us in order to test us and to make us stronger? If it is true that in all things God is working to our best good, does that mean that God sometimes sends us difficult circumstances for our best good? I have to tell you some wonderful people believe that.

In his book Please Don't Tell My Parents, Dawson McAllister tells the story of an incredible teenager he calls JoAnn. Early in JoAnn's life her mother's boyfriend abused her sexually. The state placed her in a foster group home. She was separated from her mother and both her brothers.

To make matters worse, JoAnn had scoliosis, which caused a hump to grow in her back. Doctors surgically inserted a rod which helped some but her back remained crooked. You can imagine what a test this was for a teenage girl, at a time in her life when her appearance was so important to her.

Even worse was how she was treated by other young people. She wrote a letter to Dawson explaining the incredible amount of razzing she took every day from the kids at school. They actually punched her, laughed at her, and talked down to her as if she were mentally challenged.

But this was JoAnn's response to the situation. She said that God must be planning one heck of a ministry for her. How does she know that? She says because God "has already given me an excellent testimony." (3)

Does that explain why tragedies occur in our lives—so that God can give us an excellent testimony? That is how many believers interpret life. Everything in life is from God. Everything happens for a reason.

It is an appealing theology in some ways. There is comfort for many people in believing that in any tragedy, no matter how awful, a loving God is somehow working to their good. And many scriptures lend themselves to that interpretation. But not all. And it would be very difficult to believe that God would cause something like sexual abuse or a terrible, debilitating illness or the tragic death of an innocent child in order to somehow teach us a lesson. What kind of God would do that? No, God has put us in a world where bad things do happen to good people, but He does not pick us out specifically for some kind of trial by fire. Life happens, but God is always good.

So, do we ditch these words altogether: "And we know that in all things God works for the good of those who love him, who have been called according to his purpose"? Not at all. They are words of encouragement and faith. But we must deal with them in terms of the whole Bible and our own experience.

First of all, we need to affirm that we live in a world of natural law. This is how creation functions as well as it does. For example, we can always count on the law of gravity to keep us from floating off into space. That law will never fail us. At the same time we can also count on the law of gravity to kick in when we step off the roof of a high building. The law of gravity will pull us very painfully and probably fatally to the ground below. It is a painful lesson to learn, but we could not live one day on the earth if the laws of nature were suspended even for a moment.

God has created us and placed us in a wonderful, lawful universe. We should celebrate that truth every day of our lives. That's why we have air to breathe and food to eat. That is why we are able to drive our cars along highways. That is why the sun comes up each morning and sets in the evening.

Many of the tragedies that occur in life are a simple consequence of the natural order. Someone is driving too fast in a car and tries to negotiate a curve and there is a tree and the law of nature says there is going to be a crash. God didn't cause that.

Sometimes tragedies occur because people do dumb things, like driving a car too fast. Sometimes bad things happen because the laws of nature were somehow broken in ways we don't understand and cannot control. How many deaths occur each year because of defective genes in the human body for which there is no accounting? But this does not mean that God or the universe picked us out specifically to be punished.

Jesus affirmed this principle in Luke 13. Listen to these words, "Now there were some present at that time who told Jesus about the Galileans whose blood Pilate had mixed with their sacrifices. Jesus answered, "Do you think that these Galileans were worse sinners than all the other Galileans because they suffered this way? I tell you, no! . . . Or those eighteen who died when the tower in Siloam fell on them—do you think they were more guilty than all the others living in Jerusalem? I tell you, no! . . ." (1-5)

In other words, just because someone suffers, does not mean that they have somehow sinned. We live in a wonderful world, a beautiful, abundant world. But sometimes things happen. Sometimes we can figure out why they happened; sometimes we cannot. They just happen.

Here's the second thing we need to see: our perspective on these events will determine how successful we are in handling them. In other words, our faith will determine how well we deal with the sometimes tragic events that occur in everyone's life. Notice that St. Paul says, "And we know that in all things God works for the good OF THOSE WHO LOVE HIM . . ."

Theologian R. C. Sproul notes that it doesn't say, "for those who BELIEVE IN HIM." It says, "those who love Him." When you love God, you look at life differently than do those who only believe in Him.

Pastor Richard Stetler tells of a 9-year-old boy named Billy in his congregation who died of leukemia a few years ago. As Pastor Stetler was approaching the boy's house to comfort Billy's parents, he wasn't sure that he would be able to answer all the questions those parents would undoubtedly have. Questions like: "If God is a God of love, why this? Why didn't God answer our prayers? What more could we have done? Why would God give us such a beautiful son and either allow him to die or take him away from us?" What Pastor Stetler didn't know was that he would receive a lesson in mature Christian faith from these grieving parents.

As he approached the front door, Stetler was greeted by Billy's dad. All he could think to say was, "I'm terribly sorry."

The father said, "Thank you Dick, but don't be. We are sad, of course, but Jean and I are so profoundly grateful that we had Billy for the nine years that we did!"

There were no questions, Stetler continues. There was no anger. Stetler explains it this way: "Both of them were standing in another place. You see, they knew God." (4)

Those parents WERE standing in a different place. They not only knew God, they loved God. That made all the difference in the world. They didn't believe that God had cruelly given their son leukemia in order to somehow punish them or to test them. They didn't have a God like that. Instead, they gave God thanks for allowing them to have their son as long as they did. Friends, that's faith.

The secret to a successful life is to love God. Many people believe in God. Few people love God. When you move from believing in God to loving God, you discover that life works. There is a peace, a joy that undergirds all of life. It doesn't mean you have all the answers, but you learn to trust in a loving God who will help you withstand the most severe storm and will place your feet on solid ground once again.

In Decision magazine years ago there was a story of a young couple who were quite successful: three children in private schools, a mansion, two luxury cars, a vacation house on the lake, etc. Life was sweet, and money made their world go round.

Then one day the bottom dropped out of this couple's life. A partner in their business embezzled nearly half a million dollars, and their business collapsed. In the midst of this, their oldest son was killed in a car accident.

At this point their relationship with each other and with life itself could have taken a very bad turn. That has happened to other couples in similar circumstances. But something positive happened at this juncture in the lives of this particular couple. A neighbor invited them to church.

Thinking that they had nothing to lose by going, the couple started attending church, eventually becoming regular members. To their amazement, they found they enjoyed Bible study. They enjoyed making lots of genuine friends and feeling accepted for who they were—not for what they had in the way of material possessions. Their children also found a place to belong where they weren't judged by the clothes they wore or what kind of car their parents drove. (5)

Wow! Wouldn't you like to have this kind of impact on someone's life—just by inviting them to church? This couple's relationship with God grew. They went beyond believing in God to loving God, and they discovered a richness in life they had never known before. That can happen to us as well. We need not wait until a tragedy strikes. In all things God works to the good for those who love Him. That doesn't mean God causes all things. We live in a lawful universe. Most of the time, those laws work to our benefit. But every once in a while those laws can be quite cruel. One thing they cannot do, however, is separate us from God's love. If we love God as God loves us, God has promised us that, in the long term, together we can handle our lives in such a way that we will be able to praise God for His goodness at all times and in all circumstances and give thanks for His many blessings.

1. Doc's Daily Chuckles - go here http://family-safe-mail.com/lists/?p=subscribe&id=55.
2. http://www.adventlutheranchurch.com/sermontexts/sermon060122.shtml
3. Dawson McAllister, Please Don't Tell My Parents: (Dallas: Word Publishing, 1992), p. 154. Cited in Gwendolyn Mitchell Diaz, Sticking Up For Who I Am (Colorado Springs: NavPress, 2003), p. 46.
4. http://www.stmatthews bowie.org/Worship/Sermons/1997/sermon_7_27_97.asp.
5. March 1996, p. 33. Cited in David C. Cook, Good Night, God! (Colorado Springs: Cook Communications Ministries, 2004), pp. 162-163.

When The Caterers Weren't Available
Matthew 14:13-21

Today's lesson is on one of Jesus' best known miracles, the feeding of the 5,000. Of course, as someone has noted, if Jesus were alive today, he wouldn't be allowed to get away with half the miracles he performed. It's not just that we live in such a skeptical, rationalist age. It's all the red tape as well. Here are a few examples.

Turning water into wine. This would provoke immediate protests from the alcoholic beverage industry, who would argue that it was unfair competition, amounting to a monopoly. It would also be denounced by various Christian bodies as irresponsible and likely to lead to drunkenness.

Feeding the multitude. Serving bread and fish to thousands of people at an outdoor event would require the approval of government health inspectors to ensure that the food had been prepared by qualified food handlers in a hygienic environment. Baskets of leftovers would also need to be disposed of properly.

Walking on water. This could only be done if it were preceded by a disclaimer that nobody should try this at home, particularly not children or young people.

The miraculous catch of fish. Fish stocks are now rigorously conserved to protect against over-fishing, and such large catches would undoubtedly exceed the fishermen's quotas, leading to stiff penalties.

Healing a man born blind. This apparent act of kindness would lead to all sorts of problems with Medicare or Medicaid. All disability benefits would immediately be stopped, and the man in question would probably face an investigation into whether his previous claims had been genuine.

Raising the dead. Environmental health officers wouldn't be happy about this one, either, as there are stringent rules governing the proper disposal of bodies. There would also be major difficulties when the recently deceased tried to use their credit cards. (1) Imagine the difficulties Jesus would face if he tried to perform such miracles in today's world.

Pastor Walter Harms says that in his early years at seminary, he worked for an upscale catering company. He says this company once served 3,000 people for an 11:00 p.m. meal. The meal included shrimp, sliced turkey, filet, rich meat spaghetti, salad, bread, and brownies. It was a monumental task. It took a full week to prepare 1,000 pounds of shrimp, 70 turkeys, 35 electric roasters of spaghetti, 700 pounds of fillet, dozens of 3 by 5 feet sheets of brownies, and many large baby-bathtubs of salad! (2)

Can you imagine such an operation—serving a meal to three thousand people? Makes me tired thinking about it. Now imagine feeding five thousand people . . . no, double that. The scripture says there were five thousand MEN, plus women and children. I believe that five thousand hungry men would be enough to feed, but women and children, too? Quite an undertaking, and it had to be done right away. They didn't have a week to prepare. But we're getting ahead of our story.

A crowd had followed Jesus out into the wilderness, and evening was approaching. Concerned, the disciples came to the Master and said, "This is a remote place, and it's already getting late. Send the crowds away, so they can go to the villages and buy themselves some food."

Jesus replied, "They do not need to go away. You give them something to eat."

Well, you can imagine the disciples' surprise when Jesus said that. He wants them to feed maybe ten thousand people on the spot?

"We have here only five loaves of bread and two fish," they answered.

"Bring them here to me," he said. And he directed the people to sit down. It is obvious that Jesus is in charge of the situation. "Have the people sit down," he said.

Dr. John Claypool tells about a missionary to China in the late nineteenth century during a time when a terrible famine swept over that country. This missionary had connections back in the states, so he arranged to have a whole boat load of foodstuff shipped over and sent to the mainland of China.

The people waited for many, many weeks for this shipment of food. When word came that the ship had landed and the food was being unloaded, there was great excitement all around the mission compound. Word was sent out that the next Tuesday at eight o'clock people could come and food would be distributed.

You can imagine what happened. Before dawn that day, thousands of hungry Chinese gathered in hope. When the distribution began, there was such a frenzy on the part of all of these people to get some food that a riot broke out. Several people wound up being injured, a few people were actually killed. The police finally had to come in and bring order again through force. The missionary was absolutely broken-hearted. What he had intended to be part of the answer had turned into another problem.

That night he was so distraught he could not sleep. As was his custom, he found himself going to the Bible for consolation. Late that night, he opened to this passage where Jesus encountered a multitude of hungry people. Then a detail of the story leaped out at the missionary that he had never noticed before. Jesus had the people sit down. It suddenly dawned on the missionary that that is a wonderful form of crowd control. If people are seated, they cannot riot. He couldn't wait until the next morning to announce that once again they would try to distribute food, only this time everyone was made to sit down. The second distribution went as well as the first had gone badly. The missionary wrote back home that he had a renewed appreciation for the common sense of Jesus. (3)

Jesus had the people sit down. Taking the five loaves and the two fish and looking up to heaven, he gave thanks and broke the loaves. Then he gave them to the disciples, and the disciples gave them to the people. They all ate and were satisfied, and the disciples picked up twelve baskets full of broken pieces that were left over.

This is an amazing story, one we would do well to study more carefully.

Notice, first of all, Christ's concern for the multitude. Matthew begins this story by saying, "When Jesus landed and saw a large crowd, he had compassion on them and healed their sick..." Nothing new in that. Throughout the Gospels he shows compassion to the least and the lowest.

Jesus came with one purpose and desire—to seek and to save the lost. When he gazed out over Jerusalem, he wept. He knew the heartaches, the headaches, and the hungers that go with being human. Bring the masses from the ends of the earth. The compassionate Christ cares for each and every one.

Someone tells of being in the bathroom at a popular coffee chain. Someone wrote on the bathroom wall, "What Would Jesus Do?"

One person answered the question by writing, "Wash His hands."

Then a third person wrote, "And your feet."

What a wonderful perspective on the nature of Jesus. He would wash our feet. Jesus cares about people. He had compassion for the multitude.

Actually, to really appreciate Christ's love for people, we need to go back a verse further. The story actually begins like this: "When Jesus heard what had happened, he withdrew by boat privately to a solitary place. Hearing of this, the crowds followed him on foot from the towns..." Did you catch that? "When Jesus heard what had happened and withdrew to a solitary place..."

What was it that happened? If we go back a few verses we discover that Christ's beloved cousin John the Baptist had been beheaded by King Herod. How do you think Jesus felt when he got this news? How would you feel? A family member that you were very close to has been the victim of an atrocious crime. No wonder Matthew said that Jesus withdrew to a solitary place. Don't you think that maybe Jesus wanted to be alone to grieve the death of his cousin? But then Matthew adds, "Hearing of this, the crowds followed him on foot from the towns..."

Jesus can't even have a few moments to grieve. If this had happened to me, the last thing I would feel like is seeing a mob of people coming to me for help. But that's me... and perhaps that's you... but that's not Jesus. Jesus had compassion for the crowd. And he still gazes upon us with that same compassion today.

But there is a second thing we need to see: not only does he have compassion, but he is also capable. He is not only compassionate, he is capable, he is competent to do for us more than we are able to imagine.

Many people have tried to give a rational explanation for the miracle of the fishes and loaves. Early in the twentieth century, it became fashionable to find natural explanations for miracles. Albert Schweitzer wrote that each of the 5,000 people was so completely impressed in the presence of Jesus that they felt satisfied even though they were not actually filled. Another theory was that the crowd brought food with them. When a small boy offered to share his lunch, this shamed others into offering theirs as well—and the first church covered-dish supper was born. [Now you know why there was so much food left over.]

These explanations miss the point, however. The important point of this story is that Christ is able to supply our needs, no matter how he does it. Our needs may be physical or emotional or spiritual, but Christ is sufficient.

This may be the point at which a lot of us are missing the joy of our faith. We believe that God cares about us and our need, but we don't really believe that God is able to help us. And thus we lead joyless, powerless lives. But what good is compassion without capability? He is able!

Some of you will remember the amazing story of explorer Richard E. Byrd who spent the winter of 1934 at Bolling Advance Weather Base in Antarctica. The temperature at this base ranged from 58 to 76 below zero. By the time he was rescued, he was suffering from frostbite and carbon monoxide poisoning.

Afterward he wrote about his experience in a book which he titled, Alone. Here is how he described his experience: "I had hardly strength to move. I clung to the sleeping bag, which was the only source of comfort and warmth left to me and mournfully debated the little that might be done. Two facts stood clear. One was that my chances of recovering were slim. The other was that in my weakness I was incapable of taking care of myself. But you must have faith—you must have faith in the outcome, I whispered to myself. It is like a flight . . . into another unknown. You start and you cannot turn back. You must go on . . . trusting your instruments, the course you have plotted." (4)

That sounds very much like the life of faith. You must go on trusting the One who has brought you this far. Christ is not only compassionate, but he is capable.

But there is one more thing that needs to be said: Christ depends on the community of faith; Christ uses what we give him to work with.

You may have noticed that in Matthew's telling of the feeding of the five thousand, he does not mention the young boy who had with him the five loaves and two fish. We have to go to John's Gospel for that small detail.

But what if that young boy had not been willing to share his five loaves and two fish? Surely Christ would still have found a way to feed the multitude, but it does seem to be a clear principle of faith that God works best when God has something to work with. It might be fish and bread—it might be a tiny baby hidden in the bulrushes—it might be a shepherd boy guarding his father's sheep—but God needs something or somebody with which to work.

There was an article in People years ago about a nine-year-old girl named Kassandra. Young Kassandra read a story one time about some foster children who were forced to drag their belongings in a garbage bag from home to home every time they moved. "These kids, they have nothing," she thought to herself, and she got upset and decided to do something about it.

And so Kassandra organized a barbecue and, with a group of friends, decorated 100 pillowcases with fabric markers so that these foster children would have something pretty to carry their belongings in. She and her friends also included in each pillowcase an address book—so that the children could keep in touch with family and friends. The pillowcases also held a journal, pens and a stuffed animal. Over a three-year-period Kassandra donated more than 1,000 of her Good Night, Sleep Tight pillowcases to foster kids throughout her state. One of those children is Amy, age 12. "I use the journal every night and I love the stuffed horse—he is so cuddly," says Amy. (5) Like the boy with the fishes and loaves, Kassandra is using what she has to bring happiness to children who have so little.

In 2 Kings 4, there is a woman whose husband had died, and the creditors were coming to take away her sons as slaves for payment. She cries out to the prophet Elisha for help. Elisha's response is to ask her a question, "What do you have in your house?"

All she had in the cupboard was a little oil—but when she took it and put it in the hands of God, a miracle happened, and her needs were met. Whenever we have a need, or someone we care about has a need, the first question we need to ask is, "What do I have in my house?" Are there some fishes and loaves or some oil that God could use in a miraculous way? Before you answer, think about what you have for a moment. It might be some material possession. It might be some talent. But is there something that you have—however small—that God might use to meet someone else's need?

A man's wife had died. He was inconsolable. He took flowers to her grave every day. He consulted a priest who counseled him for three months. One day the priest saw the flowers the man had brought to his session and the priest said, "Today, I don't want you to go to place those flowers on your wife's grave. I want you to go to St. John's Hospital down the block and go into each room and give a flower to each patient."

The next week the man came to his session in an elated state. "I had a wonderful time giving those flowers away," he said. "Those people appreciated them so much and I made so many friends. I can't stay today for my session since I'm going back to visit the new friends I met." (6)

Are there some fishes and loaves or pillowcases or flowers in your life that you can use to bring joy into someone else's life?

Christ has compassion for our needs. And he is able to meet our needs. And sometimes he uses us to meet the needs of others. He is able to use us in a wonderful way, if we are willing to take the little we have and let Him use it as He will.

1. Simon Coupland, Spicing Up Your Speaking, #75 p187f. Cited by Dave Faulkner, http://dave-faulkner.typepad.com/dave_faulkner_life_spirit/2006/08/sermon_john_651.html.
2. http://www.predigten.uni-goettingen.de/archiv-7/050731-5-e.html.
3. http://www.csec.org/csec/sermon/claypool_3716.htm.
4. God's Little Devotional Book (Tulsa, OK: Honor Books, Inc., 1973), p. 201.
5. "Precious Cargo" People, May 8, 2006, p. 196
6. Cited by Fr. Jerry Fuller, o.m.i., http://www.spirit-net.ca/sermons/a-or18-fuller.php.

Don't Be Afraid
Matthew 14:22-33

Have you ever noticed that fear can cause people to do some really stupid things?

When that terrible earthquake and tsunami hit Japan a few years back, it reminded me of a Serbian man named Lucas who was a victim of a giant tsunami that devastated countries around the Indian Ocean a couple of years ago. Lucas, aged 30, was nowhere near where the tsunami hit. He was safely at home in Serbia at the time. However, he was watching television and he was so shocked when he saw the tsunami footage on TV that he jumped out his apartment window. As he fell from the second floor, it occurred to him that the tsunami was not actually a threat to southern Serbia, but it was too late to avoid impact: he suffered two broken legs and a damaged spine.

Recovering later from his tsunami injuries, Lucas threatened to sue the local television station for announcing that "the tsunami is coming our way," and people should "immediately evacuate." A spokesperson for the television station said Lucas must have misunderstood the reporter's words. (1)

Well, I've heard things on TV that made me feel like jumping out of a window, but fortunately I've restrained myself. However, fear makes people do outrageous things.

Historians tell us that King Charles VIII of France, who ascended to the throne in 1483, became paranoid with the thought that someone was trying to poison his food. As a result, he began eating less and less. Tragically, the less he ate, the more suspicious he became. He finally died in 1498—not from poisoning, but from malnutrition. (2) Fear had done him in.

Many years ago, Dr. Norman Vincent Peale told of a young woman who was destroyed by her fears. At the time, this woman was a world-class tennis star. However, as a small girl thirty years before, she had watched in terror as her mother died suddenly of a heart attack while being treated by a dentist. The traumatic experience so profoundly affected this young woman that in the thirty years that followed, she absolutely refused any dental treatment. The mere suggestion of going to a dentist terrified her. And this despite her realization that the dentist to whom her mother had gone had no responsibility for her mother's death. It was just a coincidence that the heart attack which caused her death occurred at the dentist's office.

But finally dental work became so necessary that the woman was compelled to have it done in spite of her terror. She insisted, however, that her physician accompany her to the dentist's office. But it was to no avail. As she sat in the dentist's chair, just like her mother had thirty years before, she was suddenly seized by a heart attack and died.

The London newspaper which reported the story headlined it with the words "Killed by thirty years of thought!" (3)

Fear is a powerful force in our lives.

Lee Iacocca, the former head of Chrysler Corporation asks in a recent book why the SUV has been such a success. What is its purpose? Very few people go off road, so it's not because they need a rugged all-terrain vehicle. The SUV doesn't have the passenger or storage capacity of a minivan, or the good ride and handling of a car. So, what is the motivation for buying an SUV? Why are people lugging around all that extra weight? Bigger engines (usually V8s) are not known for fuel economy and low emissions.

Iacocca attributes it to fear. He writes, "I think the SUV feeds a strong desire for security and control on the road. In this day and age, people want to put as much steel and iron around them as they can. They equate weight with safety. It's a factor, but in no way compares to solid structural design and the use of multiple air bags . . . With thousands of other SUVs speeding past them, not to mention eighteen wheelers and cement mixers, drivers just feel more secure. It's a perception and Detroit promoted it. One SUV brand advertised itself with the headline, "Look upon it as a 4,000 pound security blanket . . ."

Iacocca adds, "If you want guaranteed safety on the road, why not drive a tank!" (4) Oops. I better not give some of you, ideas.

All of us know what it is to be afraid.

It was Dave Barry, that great humorist, who said, "All of us are born with a set of instinctive fears—of falling, of the dark, of lobsters, of falling on lobsters in the dark, or speaking before a Rotary Club . . . and of the words 'Some Assembly Required.'" (5)

Famed pastor Dr. Carlyle Marney used to say that we play hard to forget that we live in a haunted house. In a sense we do. Fear is a powerful force in our lives, particularly as we continue to struggle to overcome a steep economic downturn, and as many of us struggle with the difficulties of aging. That is why today's lesson from Matthew's Gospel is so important to us.

In the story we dwelt with last week, Jesus had fed five thousand men, and their wives and children, with just five small loaves of bread and two fish. Now the Master needed some time alone. He sent the crowds home and he sent the disciples out in a boat on the Sea of Galilee while he went to a mountain to pray.

The Sea of Galilee is a large body of water, eight miles wide by thirteen miles long. Of the twelve disciples, Peter, Andrew, James and John were all fishermen. They knew the Sea of Galilee very well. They knew that, at that time of year (probably around mid-spring), the Sea of Galilee was subject to strong gusts of wind. The late afternoon and evening was not a good time to be out in the middle of the lake.

(6) Maybe that is why Matthew tells us that Jesus "made the disciples" get into the boat. Perhaps the four fishermen could already tell that a storm was brewing.

The boat was a considerable distance from land and was being buffeted by the waves, says Matthew, because the wind was against it. Shortly before dawn Jesus went out to the boat, walking on the lake. It is difficult enough for us to imagine someone walking on a sea when it is calm, but try to imagine someone walking on the water when the wind is whipping the surface and large waves are forming. The disciples were already uneasy in the storm. Now when they saw Jesus walking on the lake, they were terrified.

"It's a ghost," they cried out in fear.

But Jesus immediately said to them: "Take courage! It is I. Don't be afraid."

And that's Christ word for us this day. "Take courage. It is I. Don't be afraid." In the face of difficult economic times, in the face of declining health, in the face of concern about a loved one dealing with illness or a teenager dealing with an assortment of issues, don't be afraid. Christ is with you.

Marilyn Hedgpeth was brought up in the Moravian Church. She says that it was the custom in that church for members to post daily watchwords, verses of scripture to give them strength, guidance, and encouragement for the day.

She chose an unusual verse, Isaiah 42:3, as her self-appointed "watchword." This verse reads like this: "A bruised reed he will not break, a smoldering wick he will not snuff out." Ms. Hedgpeth says she memorized this verse early on and she has pulled it out, mulled it over, rolled it around in her mouth and repeated it as a sentence prayer, whenever she felt overwhelmed by life, which, she says, is frequently and often.

"A bruised reed, he will not break . . . a bruised reed, he will not break . . . a bruised reed, he will not break."

Even as a child, "when calamity would present itself: when she would wake, sweating, from a nightmare; when a bicycle fall would result in skinned elbows and knees; when the preacher's kid next door would beat her up; when she would draw the 'wild man of Borneo card' from the Old Maids' deck and freak out; when she would watch the Wizard of Oz; when her behavior would press her mother to threaten, 'you are cruisin' for a bruisin'; she would counter internally with her watchword: 'a bruised reed he will not break; a bruised reed he will not break; a bruised reed he will not break.'"

And likewise, even today, she says she has not deviated far from her childhood pattern: when one of her children is hospitalized; when her workload overwhelms; when someone close dies; when she and her beloved spouse are at loggerheads; when someone in her congregation suffers an unspeakable tragedy; she still counters internally with that watchword: "a bruised reed he will not break, a smoldering wick he will not snuff out." (7)

That rather obscure verse from Isaiah 42 reminds Marilyn Hedgpeth that she is not alone, that God is watching over her. That might work for some of us who are going through troubled times. "A bruised reed he will not break, a smoldering wick he will not snuff out." Don't be afraid. Christ is with you just as he was with his disciples that day on the Sea of Galilee. Jesus said to them, "Take courage. It is I. Don't be afraid."

Then, in the midst of this inspiring story, Simon Peter provides us with a little comic relief.

"Lord, if it's you," Peter called to Jesus, "tell me to come to you on the water."

"Come on," Jesus said. Then Peter got down out of the boat, walked on the water and came toward Jesus. But when he saw the wind, Peter was afraid and, beginning to sink, he cried out, "Lord, save me!"

Simon Peter discovered very quickly that he wasn't Jesus. He also discovered the danger in focusing on his situation and not the Savior. He was afraid and began to sink. Immediately, says Matthew, Jesus reached out his hand and caught him. "You of little faith," Jesus said to him, "why did you doubt?"

The worst thing we can do in a storm is to let go of our faith. That's the most important thing we need to see. If we let go of our faith, we will surely sink. However, if we will just hold on to our faith and look for Christ's hand reaching out to us, we can make it through any storm.

Pastor Ted Miller tells about a very active woman in his church named Jeanne. Jeanne was an officer in the church. She was involved in everything that had to do with the life of that church. However, Jeanne had cancer. At one point, she had an eye removed due to cancer. That did not slow her down a bit. But when her breast cancer reoccurred, it came back with a vengeance. Very quickly, she was laid low by extensive chemo-therapy. She lost her hair and a lot of weight. She looked terrible and she knew it, and so she shut herself away in her home and requested no visitors.

Members of the congregation respected that request. Some accepted it with relief, in fact, because it is hard to be with someone you care about and to see them in such agony, so most people stayed away. The problem was that Jeanne was lonely. This gregarious, involved, energetic woman was lonely and afraid.

When her birthday came . . . on Mother's Day . . . Pastor Miller's congregation decided to take a risk. Having briefed her daughter-in-law about their plan, just about the whole congregation packed into cars after the Sunday service and made their way to Jeanne's home. She was lying on the couch in her living room, and they all marched through there blowing kisses or touching her hand. Then about 100 of them gathered on the front lawn and sang "Happy Birthday."

Writes Pastor Miller, "We stormed the barrier of her fear and of our own . . . from then on, visitors were welcomed . . . and able to come whenever she felt able.

For the six weeks that remained of her life, Jeanne was never alone again." (8)

The worst thing we can do in the midst of a storm is to lose our faith, to look down at the waves, to lose our confidence in our Master. We need to keep our eyes upon Jesus. We need to see his hand extended to us, reaching out to catch us just as it was extended to Simon Peter. Sometimes that hand is extended through our church family and other Christian friends.

The point is, Christ is able to deliver us from the storm. Christ can save us. As Paul wrote in Ephesians 3:20-21: "Now to him who is able to do immeasurably more than all we ask or imagine, according to his power that is at work within us, to him be glory in the church and in Christ Jesus throughout all generations, for ever and ever!"

Matthew concludes this passage by writing: "when they climbed into the boat, the wind died down. Then those who were in the boat worshiped him, saying, 'Truly you are the Son of God.'" Here is one of the true keys to life: it is in the storms of life we are most likely to discover who Christ is.

Most of you know the story of Helen Keller, the little deaf and blind girl who, thanks to a loving and dedicated teacher became a world-famous speaker and author. Helen Keller met every U.S. President from Grover Cleveland to Lyndon B. Johnson and was friends with many famous figures, including Alexander Graham Bell, Charlie Chaplin and Mark Twain. Not bad for someone who could not hear or see.

Do you know the most remarkable thing about Helen Keller? In the midst of her limited interaction with the world, she was able to say these words, "I thank God for my handicaps, for through them I have found myself, my work and my God." (9)

Now that's the way to handle a storm! That can happen for any of us, regardless of the storm in which we find ourselves. Hear Christ's words, "Take courage. It is I. Don't be afraid." The worst thing we can do in a storm is to let go of our faith. Christ is able to deliver us from the storm. Trust him. Believe in him. See him reach out to you to lift you from the angry waves. He is the Lord of heaven and earth. Don't be afraid.

1. Wendy Northcutt, The Darwin Awards 4: Intelligent Design (New York: Penguin Group (USA) Inc., 2006), p. 268.
2. Leland Gregory, Stupid History: Tales of Stupidity, Strangeness, and Mythconceptions Throughout the Ages (Kansas City: Andrews McMeel Publishing, LLC, 2007), p. 113.
3. Norman Vincent Peale, Enthusiasm Makes The Difference (Englewood Cliffs, N.J.: Prentice-Hall, Inc. 1967), p. 60.
4. Lee Iacocca With Catherine Whitney, Where Have All the Leaders Gone? (New York: Simon & Schuster, Inc, 2007), pp. 176-177.
5. http://www.phobialist.com/fears.html?sa=X.
6. John A. Boadus, A Commentary on The Gospel of Matthew (Philadelphia: American Baptist Publication Society, 1888), p. 327.
7. Marilyn T. Hedgpeth, http://www.firstpres-durham.org/Sermons/011308.pdf.
8. Thomas E.S. (Ted) Miller, http://www.fpccr.org/sermons/sermon_09-17-06.htm.
9. Contributed. Source unknown.

Send Her Away!
Matthew 15: 21-28

Those of you who are of a certain age might remember a little song from the 1960s. It was a tune by the Kingston Trio with the misleading title, "Merry Minuet." It was anything but merry, but it was a satirical song that describes some of the turmoil in the world today. It went like this:

They're rioting in Africa. They're starving in Spain.

There's hurricanes in Florida and Texas needs rain.

The whole world is festering with unhappy souls.

The French hate the Germans; the Germans hate the Poles.

Italians hate Yugoslavs; South Africans hate the Dutch,

And I don't like anybody very much.

But we can be tranquil and thankful and proud,

For man's been endowed with a mushroom shaped cloud.

And we know for certain that some lovely day

Someone will set the spark off and we will all be blown away.

They're rioting in Africa. There's strife in Iran.

What nature doesn't do to us, will be done by our fellow man. (1)

It's satire, but it also is a pretty apt description of the human condition. Situations change, but human nature doesn't. There is something about us all that causes us to brand people who are not like us as unlikable, inferior, undeserving—to reject them and shut them out—even to go to war with them. So it was in Galilee 2100 years ago.

Matthew tells us that "leaving that place, Jesus withdrew to the region of Tyre and Sidon." Tyre and Sidon lay outside the land of Palestine to the north of Galilee. It was a land occupied by people of various religions. None of these religions was more detestable to the Jews than the Canaanite religion. So it is significant that Matthew, writing primarily for a Jewish audience, reports that a Canaanite woman from that vicinity came to Jesus and was crying out to him, "Lord, Son of David, have mercy on me! My daughter is demon-possessed and suffering terribly."

Certainly it was nothing new for someone to come to Jesus crying out for healing—either for themselves or for someone they loved. News was traveling fast about Jesus' ability to heal. The feeding of the 5000 that we dealt with two weeks ago came about because of the crush of people coming to the Master to be healed. But a Canaanite? They were "religious scum" as far as the Jews were concerned.

And it didn't help that this particular Canaanite was a woman. As you well know, in the time of Jesus, women had very little status in Jewish society. They were considered the property of their husbands or their fathers. They had very few rights. This inferior status was reinforced by the religious customs of the day.

Bible scholar Walter Shurden points out that in the Temple there was a literal wall that separated Jewish women from Jewish men. There was another wall that separated the laity from the priests . . . On the one hand, these separations were meant to honor God, says Shurden. On the other hand, those walls bore the message, "This is special. We are special. You, you're not quite so special." (2)

In that culture men were special; women were not. Is that still true in our culture today? You will need to ask a woman seated near you.

In Jesus' time it was not kosher for a Jewish man to interact with a strange woman, particularly a Canaanite woman. She surely knew this. Who did this woman think she was, crying after this Jewish teacher like this?

It is interesting, don't you think, that she called him, "Lord, Son of David"? This is a messianic title. Outside of Simon Peter, who else was ready to proclaim Jesus as the Messiah? No one in Matthew's Gospel. There's more to this woman than meets the eye.

Matthew tells us that when this woman confronted Jesus with this appeal to heal her daughter, "Jesus did not answer a word." My guess is that for a moment Jesus was taken off-guard. We sometimes forget that Jesus was both fully human and fully divine. There were times when he was more human than others.

There were times when he grew weary. There were times when he grew angry. The Bible tells us that Jesus was "without sin," but that doesn't mean that he never stubbed his toe. A woman of a despised religion has appealed to him as the Messiah. This is something new. He is processing this in his mind, and at first he doesn't answer her.

His disciples can see that she is troubling the Master. "Send her away," they urge him, "for she keeps crying out after us."

He answers quietly, "I was sent only to the lost sheep of Israel."

This is an important statement. There is no evidence in the Gospels that Jesus even so much as entered a Gentile home. His mission was to bring salvation to the world through the historical framework of the Jewish faith. This did not mean that he was anti-gentile. He was not anti-anybody. But he was here for a specific task—to usher in a new kingdom—the kingdom of God—specifically built on the moral and theological foundation of Judaism. This woman's situation and her earnest plea were forcing him to think about his announced mission outside the box, and he seems uncertain about how to deal with her.

The woman came and knelt before him. "Lord, help me!" she said. And Jesus replied with words that have troubled his followers through the ages. Jesus used the d-word. "It is not right," he said, "to take the children's bread and toss it to the dogs."

It sounds very much like Jesus is calling this woman a dog. Bible scholars have tried to soften Jesus' response by pointing out that the word he used for dog refers to a household pet, not to a mongrel chained up in the backyard. Some of you have pets that are like family members. Some of you have pets that you feel closer to than family members. Still, this seems uncharacteristic of Jesus. Maybe this is just a test of this woman's faith.

Maybe Jesus had a smile on his face and the woman could see in his eyes that he was not meaning to be offensive. As William Barclay has noted, "The tone and the look with which a thing is said make all the difference. Even a thing which seems hard can be said with a disarming smile. We can call a friend . . . 'a rascal' with a smile and a tone which takes all the sting out of it and which fills it with affection. We can be quite sure that the smile on Jesus' face and the compassion in his eyes," says Barclay, "robbed the words of all insult and bitterness."

Maybe so. Or maybe he was just absentmindedly citing a common saying of the time. "It is not right to take the children's bread and toss it to the dogs."

Or maybe, just maybe, this story was included as a reminder of how pervasive prejudice is in every culture and how hurtful it can be to use a derogatory term for another human being. Maybe it was intended to shock us. Remember, Matthew was writing for a Jewish audience. They themselves had probably referred to Canaanites as dogs, if not overtly, at least within their hearts.

At any rate, this caustic phrase hangs out there causing us discomfort, "It is not right to take the children's bread and toss it to the dogs."

And then this woman gives a wonderful response, "Yes it is, Lord," she said. "Even the dogs eat the crumbs that fall from their master's table."

Touché! You weren't going to dismiss this worried mother with a casual offhanded remark. She knew who she was. She might be a Canaanite . . . she might be a woman . . . but she had a place in the world. She had rights as a child of God. And besides, she knew she was in the presence of the Messiah. If she knew anything at all about the messianic age prophesied by the Jews, she knew it would usher in an age of peace and justice. If Jesus was who he said he was, he could not turn her away. It would be unjust. And, of course, he didn't. Jesus said to her, "Woman, you have great faith! Your request is granted." And her daughter was healed at that moment.

"Send her away," the disciples had urged. "She's not of the right faith. Send her away. She's a woman. Send her way. She's a nuisance." But this woman knew what many people don't even seem to grasp today—even some who bear the name Christian. Thanks to the grace of God, everyone deserves his or her place in the sun. It doesn't matter who they are.

The Rev. Francis A. Hubbard describes an incident that occurred between her second and third years of seminary. Hubbard did an eight-week stint of Clinical Pastoral Education at New England Deaconess Hospital in Boston. She and her classmates were student hospital chaplains, under the supervision of professional hospital chaplains. They learned about pastoral care for the sick while seeing, in the course of eight weeks, as many extremely sick patients as a typical parish priest would see in eight years.

Two of the patients who remain vivid in Hubbard's memory were women who had cancer. Both of these women described themselves to Hubbard as lapsed Roman Catholics. Both told Hubbard that they pictured God as powerful but very remote. Moreover, they pictured Him as male, cold and uncaring. Their impression of Jesus was just the same. Both told her that in their hours of suffering and great need they thought it was useless to pray to God the Father or to Jesus so, each said, "I pray to Mary, because she's a woman and she understands."

Francis Hubbard is a Protestant. Inwardly she cringed at the idea of praying to Mary. Still she wanted to minister to these two women. She prayed with them, trying to emphasize God's love and compassion. Then, after she left their bedsides, it hit her: what if they had been Protestant and had the same image of God as male, remote and uncaring—but had no Mary to whom to pray? Francis Hubbard pauses and then she adds, "And then I thanked God for Mary." (3)

That's a powerful insight, isn't it? Sometimes a culture can harbor prejudices—prejudice between the genders, prejudice between racial groups and prejudice between religious groups. These prejudices serve as barriers to fully accepting one another. Some of these prejudices may affect even how we see God. We may not even be aware that we share those prejudices until something happens that wakes us up, that shocks us as this story of the Canaanite woman shocks us, and suddenly we see that among those who acknowledge that Jesus is the Lord, the son of David, the son of God, Messiah, such prejudices are unacceptable.

Prejudice comes in many forms. It can be racial, it can be economic, it can have to do with gender. Prejudice displays itself in many ways.

Pastor Chuck Currie says that before going to seminary he worked for about 17 years with programs that addressed issues of homelessness.

The first shelter he worked at once conducted an experiment to chronicle the different ways homeless people are treated compared to those of greater means.

On a downtown city side street they parked a van that contained a hidden camera. One of the residents of their shelter, dressed in donated clothing from their clothing room, got out of the van and collapsed on the sidewalk. Chuck Currie reports that people literally stepped over this homeless man. People walked past. People averted their eyes. This man became invisible to people—many of whom you would suspect are Christians—because of his poverty.

Perhaps you can guess how the story ends. The man got up and returned to the van and changed into a business suit. He got back out of the van and once again collapsed on the sidewalk. People rushed to his aid. He was no longer invisible.

He was no longer a stranger. He was no longer the despised Canaanite. (4)

Prejudice comes in many forms. Prejudice can keep us from seeing other people and their needs. Prejudice can cause us to ignore and even avoid people who are not like us. However, understand this: when the Kingdom comes all prejudice will be expelled. The Canaanite woman saw that. She knew that Jesus was the Messiah and she knew, therefore, he could not turn her away.

I read a story recently about how one community dealt with prejudice in their community. After a lengthy court battle, the Missouri Ku Klux Klan was granted permission, in March 2000, to participate in the state's Adopt a Highway program. This victory would force the state to use taxpayer money to place Adopt a Highway road signs on a one mile stretch of road advertising the KKK.

The Klan's victory was crossed out the following month when their organization was removed from the program. The reason? The state legislature decided to name the Klan's designated portion of road (I-55 south of St. Louis) after civil rights activist Rosa Parks—and the Klan never showed up to clean. I suppose the only cleansing the Klan is interested in is racial cleansing. (5)

I think that is a delightful story. It's almost as delightful as this story of the Canaanite woman. By the way, did you realize that this woman is the only person in the Gospel of Matthew, male or female, who is commended for having great faith? Others are commended for their faith, but only she for her GREAT faith. Certainly she was a lady with great determination. The prejudices of the society in which she lived did not get her down. She attacked them head on. Of course, she was a mother who was concerned about her daughter. Love gives a person courage. She was pushy, perhaps. She was a nuisance. But she was a hero of the New Testament. It's clear she was a hero to Jesus . . . Jesus said to her, "Woman, you have great faith! Your request is granted." And her daughter was healed at that moment.

1. Lyrics by Sheldon Harnick. Cited by Rev. Ken Kesselus,
http://www.ecusa.anglican.org/6087_27601_ENG_HTM.htm.
2. Cited by the Rev. M. Christopher Boyer, http://gsbchurch.com/Sermons/2006_07_23_Tear-DownTheWall.pdf.
3. http://www.stbarnabas sbnj.org/sermons/070304s.htm.
4. http://chuckcurrie.blogs.com/Luke17.pdf.
5. Leland Gregory, Stupid History: Tales of Stupidity, Strangeness, and Mythconceptions Throughout the Ages (Kansas City: Andrews McMeel Publishing, LLC, 2007), p. 260.

I Will Build My Church
Matthew 16:13-20

There is an old, old story—a real classic—that some of you may remember. It's about a cowboy who went to church for the very first time. He was really enthusiastic about the experience.

He was telling a friend what had happened. He said, "I rode right up to the church on my horse and tied her to a tree in the corral."

The friend said, "You don't mean the corral, you mean the parking lot."

"I don't know, maybe that is what they called it," the cowboy said. "Anyway, I tied my horse up and then went in through the main gate."

"You mean the front door of the church," said the friend.

"Well, I guess that's right," the cowboy continued. "Anyway, a couple of fellows took me down the long chute."

"You mean down the center aisle," his friend corrected once again.

"Yeah, then they put me in one of those little box stalls!"

"You mean a pew," suggested his friend.

"Yeah, now I remember!" said the cowboy, "That's just what the lady said when I sat down beside her!"

Silly things happen sometimes in churches—ridiculous things. Sometimes sad things happen in churches.

There is no such thing as a perfect church. You will agree with me on that. Just as there is no perfect pastor, there are no perfect churches. Sometimes we do great things for God; sometimes we spend endless hours arguing over matters of no consequence at all. Churches are as apt to take sides as we are to take up a cross.

You're familiar with the little verse, "For where two or three gather in my name, there am I with them" (Matthew 18:20). Someone named Joseph Garlington paraphrased that verse to read like this: "If two or three of you will ever get together on anything, I'll show up to see it for myself." (1)

That's hilarious . . . but it's also sad. Churches have sometimes been downright destructive to the spiritual lives of those who turn to them for guidance.

Matthew Fox tells the story of a priest who ran a parish in Manhattan. He was dismayed by the empty seats in his church. Where had the people gone? Would advertising help? That would be very expensive in Manhattan. Some churches advertise. But they spend an enormous amount for each new person they attract. Then this priest had an idea. He put an ad in the New York Times inviting Christians who felt wounded by the Christian church to come on a Tuesday night to talk about it. He hoped at least thirty would show up. Instead, 450 showed up. (2)

That's disturbing. But people are hurt sometimes in church. You have probably heard the church accused of being the only army that shoots its wounded. And sometimes it's true. No force from the outside can defeat the church. Most of the damage comes from within. People, even church people, can say and do cruel things.

I am convinced that we do silly and sometimes hurtful things in church because we are not aware of how important the church is to the plan of God. If we knew who we are and how much depends on us, we would be transformed into a different kind of body altogether. We are those who are called to be light and salt to the world. We are those who are called to be the living embodiment of Christ in the world. We are those for whom Christ gave his life. We are the church of Jesus Christ. Consider our Gospel lesson for today.

When Jesus came to the region of Caesarea Philippi, he asked his disciples, "Who do people say the Son of Man is?"

They replied, "Some say John the Baptist; others say Elijah; and still others, Jeremiah or one of the prophets."

Let's pause for a moment. Don't you think it is interesting that some people thought Jesus was John the Baptist? Herod had recently beheaded John the Baptist. And yet some of the people thought that Jesus was none other than John the Baptist come back to life. Why would they think that?

Origin, one of the great early church fathers, said that, since Jesus and John the Baptist were cousins, perhaps they looked alike. Herod himself, who ordered the beheading of John the Baptist, was confused by Jesus' appearance and wondered if Jesus was John the Baptist raised from the dead (Mark 6:16). (3) We must move on, but I think it is interesting that they confused Jesus with his cousin.

The disciples report to Jesus that some of the people are saying he is John the Baptist or Elijah or Jeremiah or one of the prophets.

"But what about you?" he asked. "Who do you say I am?"

Simon Peter answered, "You are the Messiah, the Son of the living God."

Jesus replied, "Blessed are you, Simon son of Jonah, for this was not revealed to you by flesh and blood, but by my Father in heaven. And I tell you that you are Peter, and on this rock I will build my church, and the gates of Hades will not overcome it."

This passage is one of the pivotal passages in scripture. And there is so much that could be said about it. But I have so little time that I want to focus only on a few words, particularly these words: Jesus says, "On this rock, I will build my church."

Do you understand that one of the primary reasons Jesus came into the world was to build the church? If I were to ask you, "Why did Jesus come into the world?" some of you would answer, "to die for our sins" or "to show us what God is like" or to "teach us a better way." And all of that is true. But consider what his first action was after his baptism by John and his temptation in the wilderness. He called the first disciples. In other words he started a church. Then he spent three years training those disciples in what they were to do after he would no longer be with them.

From the beginning Christ devoted the major part of his ministry to building a church—not a church building but a church community. He could have built a building, of course. After all, he was a carpenter.

In a recent book, Professor Reynolds Price suggests a different perspective on Jesus' early years. He suggests that "Jesus seems to have spent his youth working with his brothers in Joseph's construction business. The Greek word so famously translated 'carpenter' can mean, more broadly, a builder." In other words, Jesus could have been in the construction business. That's a new concept to me: Jesus the builder.

Commenting on this insight, Pastor John M. Buchanan writes, "What a nice new thought. Maybe what Jesus actually did for thirty years was not only make tables and stools and bowls and spoons in a tidy carpentry shop, as I was taught in Sunday school. Maybe he and Joseph built houses, dug the forms for the footing, and built the frame for the walls and the supporting beams for the ceiling. Maybe Jesus built homes in which people lived. Maybe he and Joseph traveled to Sepphoris each day and worked on the Roman amphitheater. Maybe he built synagogues." (4)

It is interesting to think of Jesus not only as a carpenter, but also as a home builder or perhaps the builder of synagogues. In our lesson for today, however, he is not talking about building a physical structure, but a spiritual structure. He tells his disciples that he will build his church, "and the gates of Hades will not overcome it." What a strong metaphor. Imagine the church as a mighty army storming the very ramparts of hell and smashing down the gates of the last vestiges of Satan's dominion.

It's important for us to see that this is one of the primary reasons Christ came into the world—to build his church. What is the church? It's us—you and me. As Christ's church, we are the people set apart by God to transform the kingdoms of this world into the kingdom of God.

If that is true, and I believe it is, we cannot afford the time to be silly or petty. We need to keep our eyes focused on what Christ has called us to be and to do. And what are we called to be and do?

First of all, we are to provide a witness to God in the world. One way we do that is by modeling for the world how people are to live in relationship to one another. We are to model for the world the love of Jesus Christ.

In 1964, Dr. Jim Standiford's father chewed out the Administrative Board of their home congregation. This was not the first time. Standiford's father was a frequent and severe critic of those with whom he disagreed on church matters. Then Standiford's grandmother died. His grandmother was one of the matriarchs of the congregation. She was affectionately known to all as "Mother Standiford."

At the end of her funeral service, as Standiford's dad was beginning to walk down the aisle out of the church behind her casket, he collapsed. Then something dramatic happened. Two of the very persons his father had so recently publicly criticized came to his side, lifted him, and walked down the aisle one on each side supporting him. It was in that moment, as a high school junior, Standiford says, that he saw the church in a whole new light. It was at that moment that he knew the main course of life is our relationship with Christ, and with each other in Christ. Those two men's demonstration of their love for his father became Jim Standiford's call to ministry. (5) If the church is the hope of the world, we need to witness to Christ's love within our own fellowship. We need to show the world how Christians can love.

Second, we need to witness to God's love for the world.

Bishop William Willimon tells about a church in Florida. This church had once been a great congregation in the heart of the city. But the city changed, the neighborhood declined, and now the congregation was made up mostly of those who commuted in on Sundays from the suburbs. Like many such congregations, they had a problem with vagrants, homeless men around the church. They put locks on the doors. At night, the homeless people broke the locks. A meeting was held to discuss further security measures, bigger locks, better doors. What could be done to keep these vagrants from damaging their precious building?

"I'm bothered," said one woman on the board, "by the church locking out, and shutting doors, particularly to those in need."

"Well what do you want us to do?" asked one of the members of the board, "just throw open the doors and tell 'em, 'come on in, help yourself'?"

"Why not?" piped up a voice at the back of the room.

What? "Why not?" It was one of the oldest members of the congregation. "We've been having a tough time attracting folk to this church. Here are people who are so eager to get into the church they break the doors down. Let's let 'em in."

"I move the question!" said someone else. They took a vote. That night, they left the doors unlocked, wide open. Twenty homeless men showed up. There were problems, she said, but gradually the church did what was necessary to accommodate them.

"Those men have given new life to our church," she said. "They helped us be a real church." (6)

One observer has noted, "A church can either be a cruise ship or a battleship. On a cruise ship, everyone expects to be waited on and entertained. On a battleship, everyone is trained for a specific job and works with others as a team." (7)

How about our church? Are we a cruise ship or a battleship?

There was an item carried by the Associated Press about a church that has gone missing. I don't mean it is neglected, or abandoned. I mean missing.

A 200-year-old church in Russia has simply disappeared. The Church of the Resurrection, a Russian Orthodox Church had been abandoned when the communists were in firm control of the country. Officials now, however, were considering reopening it. It appears, though, that villagers from a nearby village dismantled the church and sold it off brick by brick. A local businessman apparently paid one ruble (4 cents) per brick.

In poorer, rural regions, vandals or petty thieves regularly steal gilded icons or donations from churches and sell them for alcohol or drugs. However, this may be the first reported case of stealing an entire church building. (8)

When I read this, I thought about all the churches that are missing from the field of action when it comes to battering down the gates of Hades. Those gates represent all that is cruel, all that is debasing, all that is unjust in our world. The gates of Hades, Bible scholar Tom Long says, are "a symbol for everything that opposes God's will: the powers of death and destruction that ravage human life." (10)

That is the calling of the church—to dismantle those gates. It is our reason for being. Christ has called us into being to be his body in the world—healing the sick, casting out demons, reconciling the world unto God. We are to witness to God's presence in the world by loving one another and by loving the world for whom Christ died. It's time we help Jesus with his biggest construction job of all . . . building the church and helping him build the Kingdom of God on Earth.

1. Monday Fodder, http://family-safe-mail.com/.
2 Cited by Susan Jeffers, Ph.D., Embracing Uncertainty (New York: St. Martin's Press, 2003), pp. 211-212.
3. Edward Markquart,
http://www.sermonsfromseattle.com/series_a_the_keys_of_the_kingdom.htm.
4. Price, A Serious Way of Wandering, p. 13. Cited at http://covenantnetwork.org/sermon&papers/buchanan9.html.
5. http://www.fumcsd.org/sermons/sr080606.html.
6. http://www.chapel.duke.edu/worship/sunday/viewsermon.aspx?id=89.
7. Kent Crockett's Sermon Illustrations. www.kentcrockett.com.
8. The Associated Press, November 13, 2008.
9. Westminster Bible Companion: Matthew (John Knox Press), p. 186.

Oops! I Did It Again
Matthew 16:21-27

Have you ever had a setback, a defeat, a screw-up? Have you ever snatched failure from the jaws of success?

Playwright Oscar Wilde once commented after a disastrous opening night that his play was a great success but the audience was a failure. That's one way of handling defeat, I guess.

Winston Churchill had that same ability to spin a setback a setback into something else. He was once asked, "What most prepared you to lead England through World War II?"

His reply? "It was the time I repeated a class in grade school."

His questioner then asked: "You mean you flunked a grade?"

Winston Churchill straightened himself up to his full height and replied: "I never flunked in my life. I was given a second opportunity to get it right!" (1)

That's the way to handle a defeat—look at it as a second chance to get it right.

Simon Peter knew about second chances. You will remember from last week that Jesus and his disciples were in the region of Caesarea Philippi, when Jesus asked them, "Who do people say the Son of Man is?" They replied, "Some say John the Baptist; others say Elijah; and still others, Jeremiah or one of the prophets."

"But what about you?" Jesus asked. "Who do you say I am?"

It was Simon Peter who answered, "You are the Messiah, the Son of the living God." And Jesus heaped on Simon Peter words of profound praise for his answer: "Blessed are you, Simon son of Jonah, for this was not revealed to you by flesh and blood, but by my Father in heaven. And I tell you that you are Peter, and on this rock I will build my church . . . ."

Today's lesson follows that rapturous scene. Matthew tells us that from that time on Jesus began to explain to his disciples that he must go to Jerusalem and suffer many things at the hands of the elders, the chief priests and the teachers of the law, and that he must be killed and on the third day be raised to life. At this, says Matthew, Simon Peter took Christ aside and began to rebuke him. Can you imagine anyone rebuking the Messiah, the Son of the Living God? Simon Peter has proclaimed Jesus as the Messiah. Now he is rebuking him. "Never, Lord!" he said. "This shall never happen to you!"

Well, you know what happens next. Jesus turns and says to Peter, "Get behind me, Satan! You are a stumbling block to me; you do not have in mind the concerns of God, but merely human concerns."

What a turnaround! It takes Simon Peter only seven verses to go from being the rock upon which Christ will build his church to being the voice of Satan tempting Christ to avoid the cross. That is one of the reasons I love the Bible. There is no effort to sanitize these stories. There is no attempt to make biblical characters more holy than they were.

One moment Peter proclaims Christ as the Messiah and the next moment he is telling Christ how to go about his work. One moment he is in the garden defending Christ with a sword against a Roman legion, and the next he is standing outside the palace where Jesus is being tried and denies with an oath that he ever knew Jesus. One moment he is in hiding as his Master is being crucified, and the next he is proudly proclaiming Christ's message to thousands of listeners on the Day of Pentecost. This is Simon Peter.

Even more important, however, is this truth: we are Simon Peter. Up and down, in and out, defending and denying—that's us. We can identify with this fickle disciple. When he looked back on it later, Simon Peter probably regretted trying to correct Jesus. But we all say dumb things from time to time. We all take our feet and shove them—toes first—into our mouths. Maybe I'm just speaking for myself, but I suspect it is part of the human condition.

In her memoirs, Barbara Bush described one of her most embarrassing moments. Along with her husband, then the Vice President, Mrs. Bush was lunching with Emperor Hirohito at Tokyo's Imperial Palace. Sitting next to the Emperor, Mrs. Bush found conversation an uphill task. To all her efforts at verbal engagement, the Emperor would smile and simply answer "Yes" or "No," with an occasional "Thank you" tossed in.

Looking around at her elegant surroundings, Mrs. Bush complimented Hirohito on his official residence.

"Thank you," he said.

"Is it new?" pressed Mrs. Bush.

"Yes." Hirohito replied.

"Was the old palace just so old that it was falling down?" asked Mrs. Bush.

In his most charming, yet regal, manner, Hirohito replied, "No, I'm afraid that you bombed it." (2)

Oops! Mrs. Bush doesn't regard that as one of her finest hours. But we've all done it—at the least appropriate moment, we've blurted out something dumb.

It's like a tour group of college students in Italy. They were standing just inside St. Peter's Basilica, the second largest church in the world. The tour guide explained, "This church is so large that no man on earth could hit a baseball from one end to the other—not Lou Gehrig, not Babe Ruth, not even Mark McGuire."

The group stared in silence at the beautiful marble sculptures, intricate paintings, and glorious mosaics all around the enormous building. Then a certain college girl interrupted the silence with an astonished question: "You mean, they actually let them hit baseballs in here?" (3) Okay, we might think she's a few fries short of a Happy Meal, but all of us have blurted out remarks just as clueless.

Simon Peter rebuked Jesus. The truth is that Peter cared about his Master. He didn't want him to suffer and die. But something else vexed Peter. How could the Messiah be put to death? That didn't make sense. Peter was impetuous and a little impertinent in his rebuke of Jesus, but he was being quite honest. "Never, Lord!" he said. "This shall never happen to you!" As usual Peter was probably saying what the other disciples were thinking.

If we were honest about it, there is a lot about our faith that bothers all of us. If that is not so, why are we not turning this community upside down with our zeal for the Gospel? Why are we so anemic in our witness for Christ?

Soren Kirkegaard once told a parable about a town where all the citizens loved and admired the fire chief and his crew. One day the alarm went off at the fire house and so the chief and his crew hurried to get into their wagon to race toward the burning building. But part of the way there the road was blocked. Hundreds of citizens were standing in the street holding squirt guns! Occasionally the people would turn in the direction of the fire and shoot off their tiny guns. The fire chief yelled at them, "What are you doing? Why do you have water pistols? What are you trying to accomplish?"

The citizens replied, "We've all gathered here to support your efforts! We all believe in the good work you do in this community, and each of us has come to make a humble contribution."

The people in the crowd then once again smiled at each other, looked in the direction of the raging inferno and squirted some more water from their pistols. In disbelief, the fire chief looked at them and said, "Get out of here! Fires like this are not for well-meaning people who want to make limited contributions! Such situations demand firemen who are ready to risk their lives in putting out the flames!" (4)

Rather than fire hoses, we so often stand around squirting our water pistols, don't we? Why? Because we are like Simon Peter before he was confronted by the risen Christ. Sometimes we're up, sometimes we're down. Sometimes we are convinced; other times we are confused. Sometimes we are soldiers in Christ's army; at other times we are missing in action. Thank God for grace. Surely none of us merit salvation.

After Christ confronts Peter about his impetuous comments, Christ spells out what is facing those who would give their lives to him completely. Jesus says to his disciples, "Whoever wants to be my disciple must deny themselves and take up their cross and follow me. For whoever wants to save their life will lose it, but whoever loses their life for me will find it . . ."

This is heavy stuff. Jesus says if we want to follow him, we must take up his cross.

In August of 2003, the Church of the Holy Cross in New York City was broken into twice. In the first event, thieves made away with a metal moneybox. Three weeks later, vandals escaped with something much more puzzling. Being a Catholic church, there was a large crucifix in the church. The thieves had unbolted the 4-foot long, 200-pound plaster Jesus from the crucifix, but left behind the wooden cross to which it was attached.

The church caretaker, David St. James, confessed his bewilderment at this. "They just decided, 'We're going to leave the cross and take Jesus,'" he said. "We don't know why they took just him. We figure if you want the crucifix, you take the whole crucifix." (5)

We know why, don't we? Many people would like to have Jesus and leave his cross behind. Jesus represents forgiveness and grace. Jesus is a divine Friend who accepts us as we are, hears our prayers and helps us in times of need. Who wouldn't want Jesus? But his cross, on the other hand, represents discipline and self-denial. The cross represents service and sacrifice. The cross represents taking our eyes off of ourselves and putting them on those for whom Christ died. That's an entirely different matter altogether. We want Jesus; we're uncertain about taking up his cross.

A seminary student served part time as pastor of a church. He led his church to do what he believed Christ calls all Christians to do—to reach out to all people including those who are different—socially, ethnically, economically. And some of those people began to attend his church. But then some of the more influential church members began to be "concerned" because of these people who were attending "their" church. So the pastor said, "Well, folks, this is what The Great Commission says that we are to do." He was saying to them, "This is our mission. This is our responsibility." Jesus told us to go out and makes disciples of all people.

This pastor received such opposition to the whole idea of reaching out to all people that he put The Great Commission to a vote in his church! Do we support it or not? That sounds a little comical to us—voting on Jesus' direct command to his church to go out and make disciples of all people. It sounds like Simon Peter admonishing Jesus in our lesson for the day, but that's what they did. And guess what? The church actually voted against The Great Commission! Can you imagine?

One pastor says he heard this pastor tell this and he just shook his head in disbelief. But then he realized that there are churches all across our land who have already voted against The Great Commission by their inactivity, by their apathy, by their nonchalant attitude toward anything spiritual. There are people who call themselves "Christian" around the world, starting right here in our own community, who have already voted against The Great Commission by their don't-care attitude regarding our responsibilities for service in the Kingdom of God. (6)

Yes, those thieves are not the only ones who want to take Jesus, but not his cross. That is our temptation as well.

Peter backslid in a hurry when he was first confronted with the message of the cross. Often we will, too. But fortunately that is not the end of the story. Peter had an encounter with the risen Christ, and the man who had been a fickle reed became a solid rock of faith and service. That can also happen to us.

Allan Emery in his book A Turtle on a Fencepost tells a moving story from his childhood. He was taking a train trip with his parents. On this trip he noticed a porter moving about with a decided limp. The porter told young Emery that he had an ingrown toenail. A chiropodist had worked on it the previous day, and it had become infected. Obviously he was in great pain. They talked about other subjects and Emery went to bed. During breakfast the next morning Emery's father commented upon the way the porter appeared to be in pain. Emery filled him in on the reason. After the meal, Emery went back to the observation car, returning to their car a half hour later to see the porter coming out of his parents' drawing room. As the porter walked toward him, Emery saw that the porter was distressed, great tears were cascading down his cheeks onto his white jacket. He went into the men's lounge, sat down upon the leather bench, put his hands over his face and cried. Emery sat beside him. He was particularly concerned because the porter had just left his parent's accommodations. He asked, "Are you crying because your toe hurts?"

The porter replied, "No, it is because of your daddy." He went on to tell Emery that his father had approached him, to ask about his toe. His father told the porter that he was not a doctor, but he felt he might be able to help him. The porter was reluctant but, at his father's insistence, he went into the drawing room and exposed his toe, terribly inflamed and swollen. Emery's father suggested he lance it, clean it out, and bandage it to relieve the pain and expedite healing. The porter agreed and, as he told Emery of it, he burst out crying again. Emery asked, "Did it hurt that much?" He said, "It didn't hurt at all, and it feels fine now." "Then, why are you crying?" Emery asked.

"Well," said the porter, "while he was dressing my toe, your daddy asked me if I loved the Lord Jesus. I told him my mother did but that I did not believe as she did. Then he told me that Jesus loved me and had died for me. As I saw your daddy carefully bandaging my foot, I saw a love that was Jesus' love and I knew I could believe it. We got down on our knees and we prayed and, now, I know I am important to Jesus and that he loves me."

With that he started crying again, happy and unashamed. When his sobs subsided, he earnestly burst out, "You know, boy, kindness can make you cry." (7)

Well, kindness can make you cry. But that is part of what taking up the cross of Jesus is all about. We love as he loved. We don't try to repeal the Great Commandment or the Great Commission. We try to live them out. Oh, we backslide sometimes, just as Peter did, but by God's grace we pick ourselves up, dust ourselves off, and even more importantly, we hoist the cross back on our shoulder, and we seek to live as Jesus lived. That's who we are. That's what we do. And in all things, we give God the glory.

1. Daily Grace Devotional Reflections to Nourish Your Soul (Colorado Springs: Cook Communications Ministries, 2005), p. 189.
2. Bob Dole, Great Political Wit: Laughing (Almost) All the Way to the White House (New York: Doubleday, 1998), p. 135.
3. Laughter for a Saturday. Subscribe @ http://family-safe-mail.com/magiclist/.
4. Tony Campolo, Let Me Tell You a Story (Nashville: Word Publishing, 2000), pp. 82-83.
5. Andrea Elliott, "Thieves Take Figure of Jesus, but Not the Cross," New York Times (8-25-03). Cited by Greg Asimakoupoulos in Leadership.
6. Rocky Henriques, from a sermon titled "Living the Resurrection Life," MONDAY FODDER http://family-safe-mail.com/.
7. (Waco, Texas: Word Books, 1979), pp. 44-46.

Reconciliation Day
Matthew 18:15-20

Some of you may be fans of "Click and Clack, the Tappet brothers," the mechanics on NPR's Car Talk. Click and Clack are the radio names for the hosts of Car Talk, Tom and Ray Magliozzi. Someone wrote Tom and Ray a letter sometime back.

Dear Tom and Ray:

Today I was involved in an accident. I was happily cruising along at the speed limit . . . in the right lane, when someone came up behind me. He was clearly very upset that I was doing just the speed limit, and he could not stand being unable to get around me because of a line of cars in the other lane. He began to follow me very closely.

Now, this situation activated some kind of psychological trigger for me, and I responded by tapping my brakes, causing him to swerve into the other lane (fortunately, there was a gap in the line of cars there). He didn't stay there, though. He swerved back into my lane, and followed me even more closely. I responded by applying my brakes gently, and he proceeded to hit my car—four times before we came to a stop! I got out of the car and started yelling at him, which he reacted to by leaving the scene . . .

Now, legally, I know that the accident is entirely his fault. But ethically, I feel that I could have avoided the accident if I had not reacted in such a rash way . . . My question is, can you suggest an alternate, less self-destructive but equally satisfying response other than hitting the brakes when I am being tailgated? – [signed] Cliff

Click and Clack answer like this:

You want something equally as satisfying as having him crash into your car four times and then take off? Well, you could drive into a tree to make him feel bad. Unfortunately, the only reasonable thing to do in that situation is ignore the guy, Cliff. That's difficult to do when somebody is being an unmitigated jerk . . . But if you're doing the speed limit and driving legally, that's the only good solution. Anything else is escalation—and, as you realized, that makes you equally responsible for the results. He does one thing; you retaliate by doing something else. Then he retaliates, and pretty soon . . . nobody even remembers, or cares, who started it.

It's very tempting to "teach the other guy a lesson." But that's not your job. My brother tried that for years. When someone would tailgate him, he'd stop the car in the middle of the road, get out, walk around and ask if there was a problem. After being punched in the nose five or six times, and paying off the vacation homes of several local plastic surgeons, he finally gave up and now leaves the lessons to the police.

That's what you need to do, too, Cliff . . . When something like this happens, remember that people ultimately get what they deserve, even if it isn't at that exact moment. If you're a nice person, good things will happen to you. If you're a jerk, the police will eventually pull you over, you'll get a $200 ticket, [and] your insurance rates will go up $400 a year. (1)

Interesting situation, don't you think? Have you ever been in this situation or one like it? Have you ever been in a situation where you were right, but you knew an expression of anger would cause the situation to escalate?

Nearly twenty years ago there was another interesting letter—this time to advice columnist Ann Landers. It also dealt with handling anger and resentment. It reads like this:

Dear Ann Landers, I've suddenly become aware that the years are flying by. Time somehow seems more precious. My parents suddenly seem old. My aunts and uncles are sick. I haven't seen some of my cousins for several years. I love my family Ann, but we've grown apart. Then my thoughts turn to the dark side. I remember the feelings I've hurt, and I recall my own hurt feelings—the misunderstandings and unmended fences that separated us and set up barriers.

I think of my mother and her sister, who haven't spoken to each other in five years. As a result of that argument my cousin and I haven't spoken either. What a waste of precious time.

Wouldn't it be terrific if a special day could be set aside to reach out and make amends? We could call it "Reconciliation Day." Everyone would vow to write a letter or make a phone call and mend a strained or broken relationship. It could also be the day on which we would all agree to accept the olive branch extended by a former friend. This day could be the starting place. We could go on from here to heal the wounds in our hearts and rejoice in a brand new beginning. Signed, Van Nuys.

Ann's response was this: "This is a great idea. I propose that every year at this time we do just that—that we celebrate "Reconciliation Day" and pick up the phone or write a letter that will bring joy to someone who might be in pain." (2)

I don't know if Reconciliation Day ever got off the ground, but it is certainly a great idea. Particularly with regard to our lesson for today. Jesus says in Matthew 18:15, "If your brother or sister sins [against you], go and point out their fault, just between the two of you. If they listen to you, you have won them over . . ." (3)

Many of you remember Tim Russert who died of a heart attack in 2008 at the young age of 58. Russert was the much respected moderator for the weekly news show Meet the Press. A few years ago he published a book titled Big Russ and Me: Lessons of a Father and Son. As a result of that book, Russert received thousands of letters and e-mails. He read them all. It took him about a year and a half to do that.

The end result of all the letters and e-mails was another book, Wisdom of Our Fathers: Lessons and Letters from Daughters and Sons.

Of all that correspondence the vast majority came from people who, like Tim

Russert, had nothing but praise to offer on behalf of their fathers. There was only one person who asked to remain anonymous. It came from a woman who was estranged from her father. She asked to remain anonymous because of the progress she had made at reconciliation. Inspired by Russert's first book she writes about her struggle to find a way to open the door to her father, even a crack. She remembered how, as a child, she and her father would open a bag of pistachios, and carefully place all of the empty shells back in the bag so it looked as though none were eaten. It was their shared joke to see who would reach into the bag next for the surprise. So, in an attempt to heal the breach between them, she sent her father a bag of pistachios. It came back a few days later, nothing but empty shells. It was a beginning. (4) Such beginnings are important.

Reconciliation is at the heart of Christian faith. Paul writes in II Corinthians 5:18, "All this is from God, who reconciled us to himself through Christ and gave us the ministry of reconciliation . . ." That is who we are. We are a reconciling community. Christ has reconciled us with God. We, then, are to be reconciled with one another. So, if someone has something against us, or if someone has done something to us, rather than striking out in anger we are to go to that person and seek to be reconciled.

Dr. Daniel Lioy tells about an incident involving former major league first baseman, J. T. Snow when he was with the San Francisco Giants. Snow was at bat during a spring training game when Pitcher Randy Johnson threw a 100 MPH pitch that hit Snow's left wrist, ricocheted into his left eye and broke his left eye orbit.

The following day, Snow called his mother—not to talk about himself but to see how she was doing. Snow had not spoken with his parents for nearly three years. We don't know why, but Snow's relationship with his parents had been fractured. An ocean of silence kept them apart. Snow learned in this conversation that his mother had cancer. Twenty five percent of her scapula had been removed because of a growing tumor. She also had undergone 35 days of radiation and was preparing for chemotherapy. Snow regretted that time of not speaking. Ultimately, it did not matter who was right or wrong. They needed each other. As a result of Snow's call, the family reconciled. (5)

To think what might have happened if Snow had not called home. His mother might have died without him even knowing about it.

Warren Wiersbe tells about a handsome elderly man who stopped by his study one day. The man asked Wiersbe if he would perform a wedding for him. Wiersbe suggested that the man bring his intended bride in so that they might chat together and get better acquainted, since he hesitated to marry strangers.

"Before she comes in," the man said, "let me explain this wedding to you. Both of us have been married before—to each other! Over thirty years ago, we got into an argument, I got mad, and we separated. Then we did a stupid thing and got a divorce. I guess we were both too proud to apologize. Well, all these years we've lived alone, and now we see how foolish we've been. Our bitterness has robbed us of the joys of life, and now we want to remarry and see if the Lord won't give us a few years of happiness before we die." (6)

That sometimes happens to a couple, doesn't it? Somebody does something dumb, or says something dumb, then pride gets involved, and a relationship that could have worked out beautifully gets broken. What a beautiful thing it is, however, to see such a relationship restored.

Of course, for a relationship to be restored someone has got to take the first step. "If your brother or sister sins [against you], go and point out their fault, just between the two of you . . ." In other words, taking the first step is usually the business of the one who is closer to Christ. Reconciliation is tied to the cross. Paul writes, "All this is from God, who reconciled us to himself through Christ and gave us the ministry of reconciliation . . ." It is because Christ reconciled us through his death on Calvary that we are able to take the first step to be reconciled with those who have hurt us. God took the first step to heal the rupture with humanity; now we are to take the first step in healing any ruptures in relationships with others.

You may know the story of the famous feud between John Adams and Thomas Jefferson. The feud began when Jefferson defeated Adams in his bid for a second term as President. On the eve of his inauguration, Jefferson went to the White House to tell Adams he hoped they could still be friends. Before Jefferson could say a word, Adams began ranting, "You have turned me out! You have turned me out!"

For eleven years, they did not talk. Then some of Jefferson's neighbors visited Adams. The old man burst out; "I always loved Jefferson and I still love him."

The neighbors brought that message to Jefferson, who urged a mutual friend to let Adams know of his "affections." Adams responded with a letter, and so began a correspondence that is among the greatest in American history. The relationship was healed, but somebody had to take the first step. (7)

Pastor Harold Oliver tells about the mother of a friend of his who hadn't talked to her sister for years (in fact for almost as long as his friend could remember). But one day as he was visiting her, there was a friendly phone conversation. When his mother hung up, he asked, amazed, "Was that Aunt Martha?"

"Yup," his mother said.

"Well, I've never heard you talk to her before," he said. "That's great! What happened?"

His mother said, "I realized I don't have a lot of years left and I didn't want to carry this thing for the rest of my life. So I prayed to Jesus and I called Martha up."

That's what must be done if relationships are to be restored: "I prayed to Jesus and I called Martha up." Reconciliation is what Christian faith is all about. Who's going to take the first step? It will normally be the one who lives closest to Christ.

Of course, some wrongs are so grievous that they can only be forgiven by the grace of God.

C. Wayne Hilliker tells about a television program which showed a group of young people about to receive their driver's license. They were sitting in a court-room and listening to two speakers who appeared to be a father and his teenage son. The teenager spoke first. With eyes never looking up, he slowly and quietly told his story about something that had happened to him less than a year ago. He had been driving too fast, he said, and had lost control, with the car going off the road, and colliding with a tree. He managed to survive, but his passenger, his best friend, died instantly of a broken neck. He went on to describe, quite graphically what his buddy looked like, and how he felt, and how he would never be able to forgive himself for what he had done.

And then he sat down.

Next to speak was the man beside him who turned out to be, not his father, but the father of the boy whom this driver had killed. The father spoke quietly, with difficulty, but also with dignity. He went on to share with a room full of soon to be licensed teenage drivers what it meant for him as the father, and for the boy's mother to lose their only child. He described in quite a bit of detail the kind of young man their son was. He went on to imagine some of the possible contributions their son could have made to the community, had he lived. His comments clearly demon-strated that in his mind, there was no greater sacrifice than the sacrifice of an un-finished life. The father pointed out how proud he had been of his son and how proud he now was of this young man beside him who was willing to testify in this manner, to other drivers, in such a painful and costly, but powerful way.

The reconciliation between this father and this teenage driver was born out of their mutual desire to see some kind of "saving possibility" arise out of the death of a precious loved one. (8) I don't know about you, but when I hear of an act like this, I have to believe God is at work.

All of us are tempted to strike back at the offensive driver. All of us are tempted to hold on to resentments even to the point of allowing precious relationships to be severed. But what would Jesus have us do? It's clear in this passage. He would have us take the first step. Let's make today our Reconciliation Day.

1. www.cartalk.com/content/columns/Archive/2006/June/06.html. Cited by Pastor Susan Barnes, http://www.firstpresbaker.org/Sermons/Sermons_2006/August_13_06.htm.
2. Cited by Rev. Richard J. Fairchild, http://www.rockies.net/~spirit/sermons/a le06sesn.php.
3. Some translations (including the NIV) omit "against you." These words appear in some manu-scripts, but not others.
4. Cited by Rev. Thomas A. Roan,
http://www.wtcongregationalchurch.org/sermondetail.php?sermon_id=80.
5. Tarbell's Lesson Commentary, Sept. 2004-August 2005 (Colorado Springs: Cook Communications).
6. Be Rich (Wheaton, IL: Victor Books, 1976), pp. 117-118.
7. Contributed. Source unknown.
8. http://www.chalmersunitedchurch.com/sermons/sep12s99.htm

A Difficult Day To Follow Jesus
Matthew 18:21-35

It's hard to believe this is the tenth anniversary of the tragic event we know simply by its date, 9-11. On September 11, 2001 nineteen members of the terrorist group al-Qaeda hijacked four commercial passenger jet airliners.

The hijackers intentionally crashed two of the airliners into the Twin Towers of the World Trade Center in New York City, killing everyone on board. Both buildings collapsed within two hours, destroying nearby buildings and claiming nearly 3,000 lives.

The hijackers crashed a third airliner into the Pentagon in Arlington, Virginia, just outside Washington, D.C. The fourth plane crashed into a field near Shanksville, Pennsylvania after some of its passengers and flight crew attempted to retake control of the plane, which the hijackers had redirected toward Washington, D.C to target the White House.

There were no survivors from any of the flights. Many of you were glued to your television screens and saw the collapse of the World Trade Center as it happened. It is a sight many of us will never forget.

This is a day that is very difficult for citizens of our country. Not only were 3,000 precious lives lost on that horrific day, but, included in that number were 836 responders, firefighters and police personnel, who had come to rescue people from the terrorist attacks. The overwhelming majority of casualties in all four attacks were civilians, including nationals of more than 70 countries. (1)

There were many, many stories of incredible courage that came out of that tragic event. One of the most touching was the story of Jeremy Glick, a passenger on United Flight 93. Jeremy was the Sales and Marketing executive of a hot internet company.

A former national collegiate judo champion in college, Glick was recently married and the proud father of a beautiful three-month-old daughter. He didn't want to go on Flight 93. It was his first business trip in months. Since the birth of his daughter, Emmy, he had been reluctant to leave home. However, there was an important conference in San Francisco and his wife Lyzbeth urged him to go, and stop worrying about her and the baby.

Jeremy planned to fly out on the previous day, but got stuck in traffic on his way to the Newark Airport. He rebooked for the following morning. Not long after the flight was underway, Jeremy called Lyzbeth on his cell phone to report that five hijackers had taken over the plane. She was able to tell him about the plane crashes into the World Trade Center and later the Pentagon. Jeremy and several other passengers on that flight determined that they had to do something.

We presume that the passengers managed to carry out their intention because Flight 93 was the only one of the four hijacked planes that took no casualties on the ground. A group of men literally gave their lives to save the lives of people they did not even know.

I am impressed with what Jeremy told Lyz during the twenty minutes they were able to talk before the plane went down. Interviewed on "Dateline," Lyzbeth Glick shared the essence of that conversation:

"We said I love you a thousand times over and over again, and it just brought so much peace to us," says Lyzbeth ... "He told me, `I love Emmy'—who is our daughter—and to take care of her. Then he said, 'Whatever decisions you make in your life, I need you to be happy, and I will respect any decisions that you make.' That's what he said and that gives me the most comfort. He sounded strong. He didn't sound panicked, very clear headed. I told him to put a picture of me and Emmy in his head to be strong."

A widow at 31, Lyz says she is not angry and she has no regrets. "I don't feel like there are things left undone with my relationship with Jeremy," says Lyz. "We did it all, and I don't feel like I've left anything unsaid to him, and I don't feel like he's left anything unsaid to me. And I don't think many people who are so young can say that." (2)

No, they can't. But it is sad that any young family in the world should be put through that ordeal.

I said 9-11 is difficult for our country. September 11 is particularly difficult for Christians. It is either ironic or providential, depending on your theology, that our lesson from the Gospel for this day begins like this: "Then Peter came to Jesus and asked, 'Lord, how many times shall I forgive my brother or sister who sins against me? Up to seven times?'"

Jesus answered, "I tell you, not seven times, but seventy times seven."

Don't you think that is an interesting lesson for this day? After all, this is the ultimate lesson in all of scripture on the subject of forgiveness and, when it comes to 9-11, forgiveness is the last thing many Americans plan to do.

The day after September 11, Bishop William H. Willimon saw a couple being interviewed on the news. They were standing on the street, before the wreckage of ground zero, obviously in great grief. Their beloved daughter had perished in the cataclysm. Through tears, they shared their grief with the reporter.

The reporter, stammering, said to them, "Well, I know that you will be able to go to your place of worship this weekend and there maybe you'll find some consolation in your faith ..."

And the grieving mother replied, "No, we won't be going to our place of worship this weekend 'cause we're Christians, and we know what Jesus commands about forgiveness, and frankly, we're just not yet ready for that. It'll be some time before we'll want to be with Jesus." (3)

What a powerful story—and how we can sympathize with that mother. Jesus tells us to forgive our enemies, and of course—being human—the people who are responsible for this terrible crime are the last people on earth most of us want to forgive. Many

Christians would prefer to blow these terrorists off the face of the earth and then forgive them. But we who follow Jesus do not have that luxury.

There is an epitaph in a cemetery in Atlanta that a woman had inscribed on the tomb of her adulterous husband. The epitaph said, "Gone, but not forgiven." Some of you can relate to that emotion.

C.S. Lewis made an important distinction between excusing and forgiving. If somebody jostles me accidentally and I drop my books, I excuse that—it didn't hurt me that much, and it was unintended. But if a person does something to injure me or my family and the hurt will go on hurting for years, I can't excuse it. I have only the option of forgiving or not forgiving. (4)

Forgiveness is not easy. And yet not forgiving can take an even greater toll on us than forgiving ever could.

David Zersen, writing on the Internet, tells about a movie that some of you may have seen—The Upside of Anger, starring Joan Allen and Kevin Kostner.

Joan Allen plays the role of Terry, an angry housewife, with four daughters. Terry is angry because her husband has run off with his secretary to live in Sweden. As the plot unfolds, the viewer becomes involved in her relationships with her four daughters. These relationships are all complicated and dysfunctional because of the rage that Terry holds against her former husband. She takes some satisfaction in finally hearing at least some of her daughters say about her husband and their father, "we hate him too."

The story gets more complicated as Terry becomes involved with Denny, a neighbor, who finally moves in with her and the girls, and who also experiences the brunt of her anger at being jilted by her husband . . .

At the end of the movie, Denny is exploring acreage in back of the house for a new subdivision that is to be built. The workers uncover an old well, and what do they find when they look inside?! Terry's husband, the one who was supposed to have run off to Sweden with the secretary, but who apparently fell in a well and drowned while walking the dog. So the infidelity never happened except in Terry's mind. But because she imagined that it did happen, Terry lived with immense feelings of abandonment. She adopts a lifestyle of alcoholism and jealous rage, of vituperative anger. And she almost ruins the lives of those closest to her in the process. (5)

It is a sad, sad story. Even if her husband betrayed her and abandoned her, surely forgiveness would have been a healthier response for all concerned than a lifetime of anger and resentment. Anger and resentment take an enormous toll.

Dr. M. Scott Peck, a psychiatrist, says in his book The Road Less Traveled, that unless we are able to at least move toward the work of forgiving the person who hurt us, even the person who does not deserve our forgiveness, there will not be mental health. Forgiveness is not easy. And yet, not forgiving can take a greater toll on us than forgiving ever could.

Kenneth Hart, a psychology professor at the University of Windsor in Ontario,

Canada studied sixty-six recovering alcoholics. The individuals had one thing in common: They were all angry with someone. Teaching forgiveness, Hart found, is one way to break the cycle that causes recovering alcoholics to relapse. If they release their anger through forgiveness, they no longer have a reason to use alcohol as an escape.

One of the former addicts said, "Forgiveness is more for yourself than for the person you're forgiving. For me to forgive that person sets me free." (6)

I wonder if there is anyone here in this room today who needs to be set free?

Forgiveness is not easy. Ask God. Forgiveness is what the cross is all about. On Golgotha, God forgave the sins of the world through the suffering of His Son. The forgiveness we grant others is built on what God has done for us.

After Jesus tells Peter to forgive his brother seventy times seven, he tells Peter a fascinating parable about a king who decides to settle his accounts with his servants. There is one servant who owes the king a massive amount of money—the equivalent of ten thousand bags of gold. Since the servant is not able to repay the money, the king orders that the servant and his wife and children and all that he has be sold to repay the debt. The man pleads to the king, "Be patient with me and I will pay back everything." Incredibly the king takes pity on the man, cancels the debt and lets him go.

Now what does this forgiven servant do? Well, there is another servant who owes him money. It's not a large amount, about a hundred silver coins. Nevertheless he goes to his fellow servant who owes him money and grabs him and begins to choke him. His fellow servant falls to his knees and begs him, "Be patient with me, and I will pay it back." But he refuses. Instead, he has the man thrown into prison.

When the other servants see what happened, they are outraged and go and tell the king everything. Then the king calls the servant in. "You wicked servant," he said, "I canceled all that debt of yours because you begged me to. Shouldn't you have had mercy on your fellow servant just as I had on you?" In anger the king hands him over to the jailers to be tortured, until he pays back all he owes.

Having told this parable, Jesus said, "This is how my heavenly Father will treat each of you unless you forgive your brother or sister from your heart."

This is the one teaching of our faith that separates us from all others faiths—we are to forgive as we have been forgiven. We are even to forgive our enemies. Why? Because God has forgiven us. God gave His only Son in order that we might be forgiven. We in turn are to forgive those who have transgressed against us. Do you see now why I say that Sept. 11 is particularly difficult for Christians? The couple who said they would not be in worship after Sept. 11 because they knew Jesus would be requiring forgiveness out of them was making one of the most honest professions of faith that I can imagine. Forgiveness is hard. Forgiveness cost God His Son.

This brings us to the final thing to be said: forgiveness is only possible by God's grace. If someone has hurt you, deeply hurt you, forgiveness IS possible only if you offer your hurt to God.

It may be that there are circumstances where forgiveness is not humanly possible.

One theologian puts it this way: "We who follow Christ are always being commanded to do things we cannot do. We are commanded to love those who are not loveable. We're called to serve without counting the cost. But the hardest commandment is the commandment to forgive. We are bidden to do it, not because it is humanly possible, but because as we try to do what God commands us to do, the ability to do it is given to us by the God of Grace."

A man who has shown us the capacity to forgive is Nelson Mandela of South Africa. Pastor Tony Campolo has a friend who knows Mandela quite well. One day this friend asked Mandela about his ability to forgive. He said, "Mr. Mandela, when you were released from prison, when you were let out of that cellblock, you marched across the yard to the gates of the prison. I got my daughter up in the middle of the night to see the scene. As you were marching across the courtyard, the camera zeroed in on your face and I'll never forget your face. It was full of anger and hatred, animosity. I have never seen so much anger and so much hatred written on a man's face. That's not the Nelson Mandela I know today."

Mandela said, "It's interesting you should say that because as I left the prison block and marched across the courtyard, I thought to myself, 'They're letting me go, but everything that was important is taken from me. My cause is dead.'" He did not know that it was not dead. He had been kept in solitary confinement. He did not know he had become a folk hero. "My cause is dead," he said. "My wife, they have taken her from me. My friends have been put to death. Everything and everybody that means anything to me, they've taken away. It's all gone and I hated them for it. Then I remembered," said Nelson Mandela, "what Jesus said about forgiveness, and God spoke to me and said, 'Nelson, for twenty-seven years you were their prisoner but you were always a free man. Don't let them turn you into a free man only to make you into their prisoner.' And I realized the importance of forgiveness." (7)

He's right, of course. We must forgive, not only because of what anger and resentment will do to us, but because forgiveness comes from the heart of God. We forgive because of the immensity of God's forgiveness in our behalf. So this is a difficult day. And this is a difficult commandment. What it requires of us is nothing less than a new heart of God's love. Will you pray for that new heart today?

1. http://en.wikipedia.org/wiki/September_11_attacks.
2. From a sermon by Donel McClellan, http://fccbucc.pair.com/lot_for_sale.htm.
3. Bishop William H. Willimon, http://day1.org/950-how_you_will_know_if_its_jesus.
4. Gary D. Stratman, http://www.preaching.com/sermons/11565669/.
5. http://www.predigten.uni-goettingen.de/archiv-7/050911-1-e.html.
6. Turning Point Daily Devotional,
http://www.turningpointonline.org/site/PageServer?pagename=index.
7. http://www.csec.org/csec/sermon/campolo_4313.htm.

A Four-Word Memoir
Philippians 1:21-27a

Human beings are a terrific source of creativity. Even at the time of death. For example, consider this epitaph on a grave from the 1880s in Nantucket, Massachusetts:

Under the sod and under the trees . . . Lies the body of Jonathan Pease.

He is not here, there's only the pod . . . Pease shelled out and went to God.

Or this one from a more recent burial:

Here lies my wife . . . Here let her lie.

Now she's at rest . . . And so am I.

Or this one from the grave of a dentist named John Brown:

Stranger! Approach this spot with gravity!

John Brown is filling his last cavity.

Epitaphs normally seek to sum up a person's life in just a few words.

If you had to sum up your life in just a few words, how would you do it?

Author Ernest Hemingway was once challenged to prove his skill as an author by writing a story in only six words. Hemingway responded with these six ingenuous words: "For sale: baby shoes. Never worn." It would be difficult to tell a heart-breaking story more succinctly than that.

In the tradition of Hemingway, an online literary magazine known as Smith challenged its readers a few years ago to write the story of their own lives—their memoirs—using just six words. The editors published the best responses to their challenge in a little volume. The title, of course, was six words: Not Quite What I Was Planning, subtitled, Six-Word Memoirs by Famous and Obscure Writers. One famous author, Joyce Carol Oates, submitted these six words: "Revenge is living well without you." Comic Stephen Colbert submitted this one: "Well, I thought it was funny." Singer Aimee Mann summed up her life like this: "Couldn't cope so I wrote songs." Best-selling author Sebastian Junger submitted this: "I asked. They answered. I wrote."

The book contains submissions by obscure writers, too. I like this one from someone named John Kurtz: "Kentucky trash heap yields unexpected flower." And this plaintive plea from an unknown person: "Applied at Target. World is ending." And this one from a 27-year-old man after a breakup: "I still make coffee for two." How about this one? "70 years, few tears, hairy ears." And the best one of all? Here's my choice: "Cursed with cancer. Blessed with friends." (1)

St. Paul is writing to the church at Philippi from a prison cell. Even in prison his ministry has been fruitful. He wants the Christians at Philippi to know that what has happened to him—his imprisonment and persecution—has actually helped to spread the gospel. His steadfast witness has won converts even in jail. Still, he knows that his situation is precarious. He knows that he could be facing martyrdom and so he begins to ponder what this might mean. And here is his conclusion—it's a win/win situation.

In fact, he sums up his situation in what could easily be two four-word memoirs: "to live is Christ; to die is gain."

Let's begin with that first memoir: "To live is Christ." What a wonderful way to sum up Paul's life. At first, he had been a persecutor of Christians. However, when Paul met Christ on the Damascus Road and gave his life to Christ, he gave himself to Christ completely. That is why he had such a profound effect on the development of the early church. That is why we carry so many of his writings in our New Testaments. For Paul it could easily be said, "To live is Christ."

Josh McDowell tells about the time he was visiting with a "head-hunter"—an executive recruiter who seeks new corporate executives for companies. The man told McDowell about a recent experience he had with a man he interviewed. "When I get an executive that I'm trying to hire for someone else," said the head-hunter, "I like to disarm him. I offer him a drink, take my coat off, then my vest, undo my tie, throw up my feet and talk about baseball, football, family, whatever, until he's all relaxed. Then, when I think I've got him relaxed, I lean over, look him square in the eye and say, 'What's your purpose in life?' It's amazing how top executives fall apart at that question.

"Well," he continued, "I was interviewing this fellow the other day, had him all disarmed, with my feet up on his desk, talking about football. Then I leaned up and said, 'What's your purpose in life, Bob?' And he said, without blinking an eye, 'To go to heaven and take as many people with me as I can.' For the first time in my career," said this corporate head-hunter, "I was speechless." (2)

You and I would probably use different language, but could we state our life purpose that succinctly and would our life purpose contain a reference to Christ? For example we might say, "To leave this world a better place and to glorify Christ in all I do." Or we might say, "To live a life of love following the example of Jesus Christ." The question is, is our faith the pre-eminent decider in choosing our life purpose?

Maybe you read about Wesley Britt, a 6-foot-8-inch, offensive lineman formerly with the New England Patriots. It's an interesting story. Britt is a graduate of the University of Alabama and played for the Crimson Tide. In his senior year he was one of 22 players nationwide chosen to the Playboy All-American team.

With the honor comes a free week at the Playboy Mansion in California, the opportunity to meet Hugh Hefner himself, and a chance to be pampered by real-life Playboy bunnies. What football player wouldn't jump at an opportunity like that? For one, Wesley Britt. He said it didn't sound like the sort of thing he should do.

Britt takes his faith seriously. He spends a lot of time visiting churches and speaking to young people about the importance of embracing and living faith. Without sounding prudish or self-righteous, he said visiting the Playboy Mansion wasn't the thing for him to do.

"Initially, I was like, 'Yeah, I'm going to take it. It's a great honor,'" he said. "But after thinking about it for a while, I decided this is not one of my goals. I put God first and I set my goals for Him. I talked to God about it—and I felt it just wasn't the right thing to do."

As you might expect, he has taken some ribbing from college buddies. A few just outright told him he was crazy. One or two offered to wear a disguise and take his place. Many more, however, have spoken of how they respect him for his decision. (3)

I don't know about you, but I am encouraged that there are still young people like Wesley Britt who are that serious about their faith in Christ. It's a challenge to each of us.

"To live is Christ." That's a four-word memoir that sums up the abundant life. What would you substitute in its place? "To live is work?" "To live is football?" "To live is my iPod?" Surely you can see how pathetic that is. I suspect some of you would substitute "To live is my family." And certainly our family is important. But here is the truth of the matter, there are many people with good jobs, nice families and fun hobbies, who when they come to the end of the day realize that none of it is enough to satisfy their deepest hunger.

Maybe you remember the scene in the movie City Slickers in which the character played by comedian Billy Crystal is visiting his son's school to tell about his work. He's a salesman, but obviously he doesn't find any fulfillment in it or in his life in general. Listen as he unloads on the bewildered students:

"Value this time in your life, kids, because this is the time in your life when you still have your choices. It goes by fast.

"When you're a teenager, you think you can do anything and you do. Your twenties are a blur.

"Thirties you raise your family, you make a little money, and you think to yourself, 'What happened to my twenties?'

"Forties, you grow a little pot belly, you grow another chin. The music starts to get too loud, one of your old girlfriends from high school becomes a grandmother.

"Fifties, you have a minor surgery—you'll call it a procedure, but it's a surgery.

"Sixties, you'll have a major surgery, the music is still loud, but it doesn't matter because you can't hear it anyway.

"Seventies, you and the wife retire to Fort Lauderdale. You start eating dinner at 2:00 in the afternoon, you have lunch around 10:00, breakfast the night before, spend most of your time wandering around malls looking for the ultimate soft yogurt and muttering, 'How come the kids don't call? How come the kids don't call?'

"The eighties, you'll have a major stroke, and you end up babbling with some Jamaican nurse who your wife can't stand, but who you call mama."

Then he turns to the children and asks, "Any questions?" (4)

And the real question is, "Is that all there is?" Is that it? And the answer is that without Christ, that really is all there is.

Ralph Barton was an outstanding cartoonist who discovered that even fame and fortune were not enough. He left this note pinned to his pillow before taking his own life: "I have had few difficulties, many friends, great successes; I have gone from wife to wife, from house to house, visited great countries of the world, but I am fed up with inventing devices to fill up twenty-four hours of the day." (5)

Even writer Ernest Hemingway who truly had it all could not cope with the meaninglessness of his own life. He could write the beautiful six-word memoir that we began this message with, but he could not face life. On July 2, 1961 at 5:00 in the morning, he died as a result of a self-inflicted shotgun blast to the head.

"Is that all there is?" And the answer is that without Christ, that really is all there is. No wonder people seek to lose themselves in their work, lose themselves in mean-ingless recreation, lose themselves in drugs and alcohol. If that is all there is, life is hardly worth the effort. But that is not all there is. "To live is Christ," said St. Paul. As someone has said, "Life without Christ is a hopeless end, but with Christ, it's an endless hope."

In his book, The Pursuit of Happiness, David Myers surveys all the research that's been done on happiness. He looks at money, power, fame and all the other things the world calls us to follow. In the end, he concludes that the happiest people are those who are active in their church and some form of social ministry serving others. (6)

That doesn't surprise me at all. "To live is Christ."

But what about that second four-word memoir: "To die is gain"? That requires a greater faith. We rarely talk about the eternal dimension of our faith, about heaven and life after death, except at Easter. Yet it is an integral part of what it means to follow Jesus.

Here St. Paul's faith shines through once again. Listen to his words, "For to me, to live is Christ and to die is gain. If I am to go on living in the body, this will mean fruitful labor for me. Yet what shall I choose? I do not know! I am torn between the two: I desire to depart and be with Christ, which is better by far; but it is more neces-sary for you that I remain in the body. Convinced of this, I know that I will remain, and I will continue with all of you for your progress and joy in the faith, so that through my being with you again your boasting in Christ Jesus will abound on account of me."

St. Paul couldn't lose. If he lived, he could continue sharing his faith in Christ. If he died, he knew he would be going home to be with Christ—win/win.

It's like a story that is told about the great evangelist Dwight L. Moody. Moody was traveling by boat on one of the Great Lakes when a really bad storm developed. The other passengers on the boat cowered in fear. They even started an impromptu prayer meeting asking God to deliver them from the storm. Moody didn't join in this prayer meeting. When asked why not, he answered with these words, "I have a sister in Chicago and one in heaven and I don't care which I see tonight." (7)

That is basically what St. Paul is saying. "To live is Christ . . . there is much yet to be done." However, "to die is gain . . . I'm going home to be with Christ."

Pastor Dan Mangler tells an old fable from Holland about three tulip bulbs. These bulbs were named NO, MAYBE, and YES. Someone had placed them in the bottom of a tin to save them until planting time. One day they were discussing their future as tulip bulbs.

NO said, "As far as I am concerned, this is it. We have come as far as we are going to come as bulbs. That's all right. I'm content. I don't need anything else."

MAYBE said, "Well, maybe there is something more. Perhaps if we try real hard good things will happen to us." And MAYBE tried hard to be all that he could be but little changed and soon he gave up in frustration.

YES, on the other hand said, "I believe there is something more, but I don't believe that it is up to us. I have heard that there is One who can help us be more than we are if we simply trust him."

One day a hand reached down into the tin to select bulbs for planting. NO and MAYBE shrank back but YES gladly gave himself into the hand of the gardener. He could scarcely believe what was happening when he was buried underneath a mound of dirt. But when the springtime came YES burst forth in radiant color. He was now a beautiful flower. (8)

In my mind, that little fable deals with both dimensions of our faith. When we surrender our lives to the Master Gardener or, using the language of St. Paul, when we die to the world and are made alive to the Spirit, our lives become a beautiful flower in this world. On the other hand, even when this life is over and our bodies join the dust of the earth, we shall be even more beautiful than before. "To live is Christ and to die is gain."

If you were to sum up your life in a six or eight-word memoir, how would it read?

One writer suggests that our memoirs would be quite different from St. Paul's. "To live is to be entertained, to die is to miss all the fun."

"To live is all of the things I want, to die is to lose it all."

"To live is to be in the best of health, to die is to lose my life, what now?" (9)

It is a sobering thought. It sort of sums up what we said earlier, Without Christ, why bother? Could we sum up our lives in the way St. Paul summed up his? "To live is Christ; to die is gain."

1. Adapted from a sermon by Reverend Richard E. Allen, Jr., http://www.mamaroneckumc.org/11142010.htm.
2. http://www.friendshipunitedchurch.org/sermons/2006-03-05%20Ambition%20is%20not%20a%20dirty%20word.shtml
3. Steve Shepherd, http://www.sermoncentral.com/sermons/expectation-and-hope-steve-shepherd-sermon-on-faith-general-61890.asp?Page=1.
4. Charles W. Colson, The Body (Word Publishing, 1992), pp. 168-169. Cited at http://www.sermonillustrations.com/a-z/m/meaning.htm.
5. Morning Glory, May 29, 1993. Cited at http://www.sermonillustrations.com/a-z/m/meaning.htm.
6. ez.sermons blog, http://ezsermons.typepad.com/ezsermons/2005/05/mark_63034.html.
7. Patrick Doherty, sermoncentral.com.
8. Contributed. Source unknown.
9. Kevin Pierpont, http://kevinpierpont.com/229/to-live-is-christ-philippians-121/.

Jesus Would Do What?
Philippians 2:1-11

A woman named Naomi Magdanz in Lodi, California tells about her 6-year-old grandson, Joshua. Joshua attended a Vacation Bible School with the theme, "What Would Jesus Do?" To remind the children of the theme, they made little armbands with WWJD on the band.

One evening Joshua's mother asked him to change his clothes. Joshua looked at his armband and said, "WWJD - What would Jesus do?"

His mother replied that she thought Jesus would do what his mother asked him to do and change his clothes.

Joshua thought for a moment, then remarked, "I don't know; [Jesus] seems to be wearing the same clothes in every picture I see of him." (1)

Well, maybe so. There's a lot about Jesus we do not know. Of course, children are always going to see something in a story that you and I do not.

On Saturdays the custom at the Erickson house in Peoria, IL, is for Ken Erickson's wife to clean out leftovers from the refrigerator. One Saturday, she gave the one remaining portion of tortellini to their 6-year-old son, Jeremy. However, their 8-year-old son, Matthew, also wanted some of the tortellini, so bickering ensued.

After several unsuccessful attempts to mediate the dispute, Ken decided on a theological approach. Hoping to convince Jeremy to share his portion with Matthew, he said, "Jeremy, what would Jesus do in this situation?"

Jeremy, perhaps thinking about the feeding of the 5,000 immediately responded, "Oh, Dad, He would just make more!" (2)

Maybe Jeremy's right. Theologians warn us against trying to speculate too glibly about what Christ would do in any given situation. After studying Jesus' parables in depth, one scholar said that the only reliable answer to the question, "What would Jesus do?" can be summed up in two words: "Something unexpected."

That is probably true as well. And yet the question is an important one. St. Paul writing in Philippians almost requires us to ask the WWJD question. He writes, "Therefore if you have any encouragement from being united with Christ, if any comfort from his love, if any common sharing in the Spirit, if any tenderness and compassion, then make my joy complete by being like-minded, having the same love, being one in spirit and of one mind. Do nothing out of selfish ambition or vain conceit. Rather, in humility value others above yourselves, not looking to your own interests but each of you to the interests of the others. In your relationships with one another, HAVE THE SAME MINDSET AS CHRIST JESUS . . ."

In other words, think and act like Jesus. "Have the same mindset as Christ Jesus . . ." We are to do as Christ would do. Now, what WOULD Jesus do?

Paul gives us some definite clues. He begins with Christ's humility. "Do nothing out of selfish ambition or vain conceit," he writes. "Rather, in humility value others above yourselves, not looking to your own interests but each of you to the interests of the others."

Obviously, St. Paul didn't take any self-esteem training. "Value others above yourselves?" That flies in the face of everything we are teaching our kids today. What is it that Whitney Houston sang a few years ago? "I found the greatest love of all inside of me . . . The greatest love of all is easy to achieve . . . Learning to love yourself, it is the greatest love of all." Even in church we say, "You have to love yourself before you can love others." Doesn't St. Paul understand that? Of course he does. But he also understands that human beings are by nature self-centered. Nobody really has to tell us to love ourselves.

Of course there are some people who need to learn to stand up for themselves. Some people allow themselves to be subjected to all kinds of abuse because of their unwillingness to assert themselves. But do not confuse this with humility.

News columnist Bill Farmer tells about J. Upton Dickson, a fun-loving person who announced he was writing a book about people who let others run all over them. The book is titled Cower Power. He also was forming a group for these insecure, submissive people which he called the Doormats. It's an acronym for "Dependent Order of Really Meek and Timid Souls." Their motto is: "The meek shall inherit the earth—if that's okay with everybody." The national symbol for these folks, says Dickson, is the yellow traffic light. (3)

Humility is not the same thing as cowardice. Some of the most courageous people who have ever lived have been motivated by their concern for others. They were humble but they were not doormats. And reason has to be applied to this teaching just as to every text of Scripture.

In the book, God's Little Lessons for Leaders there is a story about a man who was driving down a country road, when he came to a narrow bridge. In front of the bridge was a sign that read, "Yield." Seeing no oncoming cars, the man continued across the bridge and on to his destination. On his way back along this same route, the man came to the same one-lane bridge from the opposite direction. To his surprise, he saw another "Yield" sign posted there.

Curious, he thought. I'm sure there was a sign posted on the other side. Sure enough, when he reached the other side of the bridge and looked back, he saw the sign. Yield signs had been placed at both ends of the bridge so that the drivers from both directions would give each other the right of way. (4)

Now that appears to be a reasonable way to prevent a head-on collision, but what it really is, is a recipe for paralysis. Suppose two cars approached the bridge at the same time? If they both obeyed the law, neither of them would move forward. There would be a perpetual stalemate.

We need to apply our reason here, but we also ought to recognize the danger if both cars try to cross the bridge at the same time. Somebody has to yield.

It's like a story that Max Lucado tells about the reformer Ulrich Zwingli. Zwingli promoted unity during the time of the Protestant Reformation. At one point he found himself at odds with the father of the Reformation, Martin Luther. Zwingli did not know what to do. He found his answer one morning on the side of a Swiss mountain. He watched two goats traversing a narrow path from opposite directions, one ascending, the other descending. At one point the narrow trail prevented them from passing each other. When they saw each other, they backed up and lowered their heads, as though ready to lunge. But then a wonderful thing happened. The ascending goat lay down on the path. The other stepped over his back. The first animal then arose and continued his climb to the top. Zwingli observed that the goat made it higher because he was willing to bend lower. (5) The goat who lay down humbled himself in order that a higher good could be attained.

In his ground breaking book, Good to Great, business writer Jim Collins explored the difference between some companies he defined as "good" companies, and other companies he defined as "great" companies. His question was "what are the differences between good companies and great companies?"

One of the startling answers turned out to be that in all the great companies, the leaders shared at least one trait—humility. To use his language, when things were going well, the great leaders looked out the window and saw the "team" succeeding, when things were not going well, the great leader would look in the mirror and see himself or herself, and ask "what am I missing?" (6)

When St. Paul looked at Jesus, the first thing he saw was Christ's humility. Do you understand how important humility is to anyone who would do something of lasting value? Christian thinkers have always rated Pride, or hubris, to be the original and most serious of the seven deadly sins, and the source of the other sins. Why? Because pride leads invariably not only to the swelling of one's own ego, but also to the loathing of others. Dictators rule from pride; leaders lead from humility.

Annette Simmons in her book The Story Factor tells a wonderful story about a young executive named Skip. "Skip looked into the sea of suspicious stockholders," she writes, "and wondered what might convince them to follow his leadership. He was thirty-five, looked thirteen, and was third-generation rich. He could tell they assumed he would be an unholy disaster as a leader. He decided to tell them a story. [He said,] 'My first job was drawing the electrical engineering plans for a boat building company. The drawings had to be perfect because if the wires were not accurately placed before the fiberglass form was poured, a mistake might cost a million dollars, easy. At twenty-five, I already had two masters' degrees. I had been on boats all my life and frankly, I found drawing these plans a bit . . . mindless. One morning I got a call at home from a $6-an hour worker asking me, "Are you sure this is right?" I was incensed. Of course I was sure—"just pour the [blankety-blank] thing." When his supervisor called me an hour later and woke me up again and asked, "Are you sure this is right?" I had even less patience. "I said I was sure an hour ago and I'm still sure."

"'It was the phone call from the president of the company that finally got me out of bed and down to the site," this young executive continued. "If I had to hold these guys by the hand, so be it. I sought out the worker who had called me first. He sat looking at my plans with his head cocked to one side. With exaggerated patience I began to explain the drawing. But after a few words my voice got weaker and my head started to cock to the side as well. It seems that I had (being left-handed) transposed starboard and port so that the drawing was an exact mirror image of what it should have been. Thank God this $6-an-hour worker had caught my mistake before it was too late. The next day I found this box on my desk. The crew bought me a remedial pair of tennis shoes for future reference. Just in case I got mixed up again—a red left shoe for port, and a green right one for starboard. These shoes don't just help me remember port and starboard. They help me remember to listen even when I think I know what's going on.'

"As he held up the shoebox with one red and one green shoe, there were smiles and smirks. The stockholders relaxed a bit. If this young upstart had already learned this lesson about arrogance, then he might have learned a few things about running companies, too." (7)

Humility is an essential characteristic of a leader. Now imagine the power of humility in the Son of God.

It surely took Paul's breath away to realize that the Messiah, the very Son of the Most High God, had humbled himself in behalf of sinful humanity. He writes about it in the rest of this passage: "Do nothing out of selfish ambition or vain conceit. Rather, in humility value others above yourselves, not looking to your own interests but each of you to the interests of the others. In your relationships with one another, have the same mindset as Christ Jesus: Who, being in very nature God, did not consider equality with God something to be used to his own advantage; rather, he made himself nothing by taking the very nature of a servant, being made in human likeness. And being found in appearance as a man, he humbled himself by becoming obedient to death—even death on a cross! Therefore God exalted him to the highest place and gave him the name that is above every name, that at the name of Jesus every knee should bow, in heaven and on earth and under the earth, and every tongue acknowledge that Jesus Christ is Lord, to the glory of God the Father."

What a magnificent passage! The Son of God humbled himself in our behalf. What would Jesus do? To answer that question, you must begin with his humility.

If you want to live as Jesus lived, you must be willing to look beyond you own needs to the needs of others.

This does not mean you loathe yourself. Do you think Jesus loathed himself? Of course not. But, in contrast to most of the rest of humanity he did not live just for himself. He lived and died for you and me.

Jack Kelley, a reporter for USA Today once told the story of the ravaging famine in Somalia, East Africa. In a village decimated by starvation, a photographer noticed a little boy suffering from malnutrition. When the photographer handed a grapefruit to the little boy, he was so weak that he couldn't even handle the grapefruit. A member of the crew cut it in half and gave it to him. He picked it up, looked as if to say thanks, and walked back toward his village. There on the ground was another little boy, the first boy's younger brother, who appeared to be dead, his eyes completely glazed over. His older brother knelt down, bit off a piece of the grapefruit and chewed it for a moment. He then opened up his younger brother's mouth, put the chewed piece in, and worked his brother's jaws up and down.

Later, the news crew learned that the older brother had done that same routine for about two weeks until he, himself, finally died of malnutrition. The younger brother survived. (8)

Friend, wouldn't you love to have a brother like that? You do.

Theologian Leonard Sweet talks of the four "rules" by which we live: The Iron rule—Do to others before they do to you; The Silver rule—Do to others as they do to you; The Golden rule—Do to others as you would have them do to you; and, The Titanium rule—Do to others as Jesus has done to you. (9) There's the rule that we should strive for.

This does not mean living your life as a doormat. It simply means valuing the welfare of others at least as much as you value your own life. I believe that is the definition of courage. I believe that is what it means to be a hero. I believe that is what it means to have the mindset of Christ Jesus who "made himself nothing by taking the very nature of a servant, being made in human likeness. And being found in appearance as a man, he humbled himself by becoming obedient to death—even death on a cross! Therefore God exalted him to the highest place and gave him the name that is above every name, that at the name of Jesus every knee should bow, in heaven and on earth and under the earth, and every tongue acknowledge that Jesus Christ is Lord, to the glory of God the Father."

What would Jesus do? He would do what was good for everyone concerned, not just himself. Go and do likewise.

1. Adventist Review, ISSN 0161-1119, (c) April 5, 2001, http://www.adventistreview.org/.
2. Paul Decker in "Do We Have Enough for Dinner?" on SermonCentral.
3. Glenn Van Ekeren, Speaker's Sourcebook II Quotes, Stories, & Anecdotes for Every Occasion (Englewood Cliffs, NY: Prentice Hall, Inc., 1994), p. 340.
4. Colorado Springs: Cook Communications Ministries, 2005), p. 143.
5. Max Lucado, Cure For The Common Life (Nashville: W Publishing Group 2005).
6. Reverend Alisdair Smith, http://www.cathedral.vancouver.bc.ca/news_info/sermons/2005_0925.htm.
7. Secrets of Influence from the Art of Storytelling (New York: Basic Books, 2001).
8. Tom Mullins, The Confidence Factor (Nashville: Thomas Nelson Publishers, 2006), pp. 126-127.
9. Jeeva Sam, <http://our.homewithgod.com/sermonsbyjeevasam/YearC/Epi- phany/serm_feb18_01.htm>.

Cheering For The Underdog
Matthew 21:33-46

Since this is football season, I want to begin with a couple of football stories.

The first is about a place kicker who was so angry with himself after missing a field goal that when he got to the sidelines, he literally kicked himself. Yes, he missed there, too.

The second story concerns a game between traditional football powers Michigan State and UCLA.

The score was tied at 14 with only seconds to play. Duffy Daugherty, Michigan State's coach, sent in place-kicker Dave Kaiser who booted a field goal that won the game.

When Kaiser returned to the bench, Coach Daugherty said, "Nice going." Then Daugherty noted with some surprise, "But you didn't watch the ball after you kicked it."

"That's right, Coach," Kaiser replied, "I was watching the referee instead to see how he'd signal it. I forgot my contact lenses, and I couldn't see the goal posts. (1)

Whoa, that's what every team needs—a vision impaired field goal kicker.

Football, and indeed all sports, are a wonderful part of our culture—particularly college football. College-aged young people are so creative.

Newspaper columnist Neil Steinberg, author of a book about pranks college students play, tells about a prank that the students at Auburn once played on the Georgia Tech football team.

The year was 1896. The game was at Auburn. The Tech team was due to arrive by train. Prior to their arrival, Auburn students went down to the railway station and coated the tracks with grease. When the Georgia Tech team finally did arrive, it took their train 10 miles to come to a stop. The players had to hike all that distance back to the field to play. Subsequently, Georgia Tech lost 45-0. (2)

Football is a wonderful sport. What is interesting about all sports is that there are some people who always cheer for the underdog. Have you noticed that? These people are masochists. Cheering for the underdog is the surest way possible to be disappointed most of the time. I mean, let's face it, some teams would have a difficult time against the cheerleading squad.

I love what Orlando Magic general manager Pat Williams said about his team's record back in 1992, before the Magic learned to win games. Williams said, "We can't win at home. We can't win on the road. As general manager, I just can't figure out where else to play."

Coach Lou Holtz made a similar comment when he was coaching at South Carolina. He said, "Someone wrote a great football song for us that could be sung only after a winning game. By the time we won a game, everybody had forgotten the words."

"The race is not [always] to the swift," says the writer of Ecclesiastes, "nor the battle to the strong." (9:11) But, says one cynic, "that's the smart place to put your money." In every game there is an underdog, a team that is overmatched, a team not expected to win. And many of us can't help cheering for that underdog.

Our text for today suggests that Jesus knew what it was to be an underdog. Jesus was not expected to win. The writer of Matthew puts it this way, quoting two verses from Psalm 118: "Have you never read in the Scriptures?" he asked. "The stone the builders rejected has become the cornerstone; the Lord has done this, and it is marvelous in our eyes." (22-23).

These words have brought inspiration to millions of believers through the ages: "The stone the builders rejected has become the cornerstone . . ."

Jesus knows what it is to be rejected. It says of him, "The stone the builders rejected . . ." That is a clear reference to Christ. Jesus was rejected by his own people. That's the first thing we need to see. Jesus knows what it is to battle overwhelming odds. He knows what it is to be disrespected, to be in great pain, and ultimately, to confront death. He knows what it is to be the underdog.

Remember that the next time you are in a tight spot. Remember that when you are rejected, when you lose the big contract, when you get bad news from the doctor, even when the final door—the door of death—is closing in your face—Jesus has faced it all, too. He knows what it is to be on the losing end.

This is important. Sometimes all of us are underdogs. If you look at yourself as a top dog and you think that you will never be on the losing side, just wait. Life happens and all of us, sooner or later, will draw the short straw.

We live, for example, in a time of soaring divorce rates. It rarely happens that two people walk away from a divorce both feeling that they have won. Usually at least one partner loses in a big way.

Writer Philip Yancey tells a heartbreaking story about a European immigrant suffering from leukemia who was telling Yancey and some other visitors about her loneliness.

The group asked if she had any family. She replied that her only son was trying to get emergency leave from the Air Force in Germany so he could be with her. "And her husband?" they asked. She swallowed hard a few times and then said, "He came to see me just once. I was in the hospital. He brought me my bathrobe and a few things," she continued. "The doctor stood in the hallway and told him about my leukemia." Her voice started to crack and she dabbed at her eyes before continuing. "[My husband] went home that night, packed up all his things, and left. I never saw him again."

"How long had you been married?" Yancey asked after a pause. The group gasped aloud at her answer: "Thirty-seven years." Thirty-seven years of marriage and her husband walks out on her when she contracts a fatal disease.

Here is what is really disturbing. Yancey notes that some researchers report a seventy percent breakup rate in marriages in which one of the partners has a terminal illness. In one group of thirty people which was studied, no marriages remained intact longer than two years. (3) Talk about kicking you while you're down. Life can sometimes be very cruel. People we love and depend on for support can sometimes be very cruel.

There are times when all of us are underdogs. Few of us will go through our lives unscathed by disappointment and sometimes outright despair. It may be marital discord, it may be professional failure, it may be physical impairment. And, of course, all of us die sooner or later from something. Life is hard. Most of us will cope with the deep valleys we encounter. Most of us will move on. But still all of us will suffer a few body blows.

I like the story of C. D. "Bigboy" Blalock, a boxer back in the 1930s. Blalock once fought against an unnamed boxer from Mississippi. The only reason we remember Bigboy is because of a dubious distinction that he earned in that fight.

Bigboy was a powerful man with a devastating roundhouse swing. He decided to try this move against this boxer from Mississippi. Unfortunately, when Bigboy swung his famous roundhouse blow, at that very moment his opponent stepped too close. Bigboy's arm swung all the way around the man's head and Bigboy ended up hitting himself in the face instead of his opponent. Bigboy fell back and was down for the count. He is the only boxer in the history of boxing known to have knocked himself out.

Thankfully, most of us are not like Bigboy. We win a few in life, we lose a few, but we hang in there and keep fighting. Still, sometimes it gets discouraging.

That's why it's important to know that Jesus not only was the underdog and understands what it is to lose, but that Jesus was also victorious and teaches us that we can be victorious, too.

Notice these words again, "The stone the builders rejected has become the cornerstone . . ." These are important words. Jesus is speaking to a crowd that included scribes and Pharisees. That was the very religious establishment that would be responsible for his death on the cross.

To them, writes theologian Hans Kung, Jesus was "a skandalon, a small stone over which one might stumble. He was attacked on all sides. He had not played any of the expected roles: for those who supported law and order he turned out to be a provocateur, dangerous to the system. He disappointed the activist revolutionaries by his nonviolent love of peace. He offended passive, world forsaking ascetics by his worldliness. And for those who adapted themselves to the world, he was too uncompromising. For the silent majority he was too noisy and for the noisy minority he was too quiet, too gentle for the strict and too strict for the gentle." (4)

And thus he was rejected by the religious establishment and eventually by the crowds that had once hailed him. For the moment those who persecuted him looked like the winners. They had their way with Jesus. They had him scourged. They whipped up the crowd to yell, "Crucify him, crucify him, crucify him." They planted his cross in the ground and hung him there naked in utter shame and humiliation. They won . . . at least that is how it would seem . . . but only for a while.

Do you remember the words to the Dallas Holm song that was so popular a few decades back? "Go ahead, Drive the nails in my hands; Laugh at me where you stand; Go ahead, and say it isn't me; The day will come when you will see! 'Cause I'll rise again; Ain't no pow'r on earth Can tie me down; Yes, I'll rise again . . . Death can't keep me in the ground!" (5)

"The stone the builders rejected has become the cornerstone . . ." Jesus was saying to the scribes and Pharisees that he was the stone that would be rejected. Their way, however, was fated to fail. They would reject him but that he would become the cornerstone of a new approach to faith, to life, to God.

You need to understand about cornerstones. A cornerstone is everything when building a structure. A cornerstone is laid at the beginning, in the foundation. Everything else is built upon this one cornerstone. If the cornerstone is straight and square, the rest of the building will be straight and square. A building that leans will not endure. Jesus, the stone that was rejected, became the cornerstone, the most important stone in the new Temple which God alone was constructing.

The underdog would become the victor. And so it is with everyone who follows Jesus. The Christian faith is a positive faith, a hopeful faith. It is a faith of overcoming obstacles, a faith of believing that no mountain is too high, no valley is too deep. As Rocky Balboa said in the latest movie of the Rocky series, "You, me, or nobody is gonna hit as hard as life. But it ain't about how hard you hit; it's about how hard you can get hit and keep moving forward." That's who we want to be—people who, by the grace of God, keep moving forward regardless of what life may send.

But it is not in our own strength that we conquer. Read those two verses from the Psalm again, "The stone the builders rejected has become the cornerstone; the Lord has done this, and it is marvelous in our eyes . . ." It is the Lord who is our strength. It is God who gives us the victory. Here is the good news for the day—if you trust in God, you will ultimately win with God.

John Killinger tells a wonderful story about a former student of his named Barry Howard who's a pastor in Pensacola, Florida. Barry is writing a book about his experiences with people who were dying. One story that will be in this book is about a man in his late seventies who had been in the hospital several days awaiting death. In the middle of the night, Barry's phone rang. It was the man's wife. They had just called her from the hospital to say that the end was near. Would he please come by and pick her up and go with her?

"In the hospital room, her son and daughter were already by the bedside. Her husband lay there, his eyes shut and an oxygen mask on his face. Once or twice, he seemed to be struggling with the mask, and his son reached out and straightened it and moved his hand away. The third or fourth time, Barry said, 'Wait a minute. Maybe he wants it off so he can say something.'

"He did want to say something. 'Hold my hand,' he murmured huskily to his wife. She took his hand and stood by the bed. The mask was restored, and this time he lay quietly, content to be holding his wife's hand. Then, very gently and soothingly, the wife began to sing. It was an old hymn called 'Victory in Jesus.' Before she had sung very much, her daughter joined in and sang alto. And then the son, who had been crying, began to sing tenor. When they finished that song, they sang 'Great Is Thy Faithfulness.' And when they finished that, they began singing 'Amazing Grace.'

"They were on the last verse of 'Amazing Grace'—'when we've been there ten thousand years, bright shining as the sun'—when the life line on the bedside monitor went flat and the man was gone. It was an amazing experience, said Barry. When they entered the room, there had been pain and suffering and tension. But now, when the man died to the strains of those familiar old hymns, there was joy and composure and even thanksgiving. Everything was good—life, death, everything." (6)

It is good. All of us, no matter how charmed our life has been until now, will sometime know what it is to be an underdog. At such times it is good to know that Jesus was an underdog, too. "The stone the builders rejected has become the cornerstone; the Lord has done this, and it is marvelous in our eyes . . ." It is marvelous in our eyes. As Christ was victorious, through him we can be victorious, too.

1. Bits & Pieces, September 15, 1994. http://www2.ragan.com/html/main.isx.sub=226.
2. If at All Possible, Involve a Cow: The Book of College Pranks. Cited by Peninsula Daily News, April 25, 2005, http://peninsuladailynews.com.
3. Where Is God When It Hurts? (Grand Rapids: Zondervan, 1990).
4. http://www.kuc.org/sermons/073006.htm.
5. © EMI Music Publishing, http://www.lyricsmode.com/lyrics/d/dallas_holm_praise/rise_again.html.
6. http://www.csec.org/csec/sermon/killinger_5112.htm.

At The Banquet . . . In Your Pajamas
Matthew 22:1-14

The Rev. John Thomas tells about a week he once spent at a Benedictine monastery with a group of other seminary students. At noon each day he and the other students joined the Benedictine monks, along with a number of people from the local community, to celebrate the Eucharist.

One day Rev. Thomas watched a couple of retirement age make their way to receive the bread and the cup. The man wore a sweatshirt that said, "I can only be nice to one person a day, and today is not your day. Tomorrow doesn't look too good either."

The Rev. Thomas had a negative reaction to the man's shirt. What was this man thinking? Thomas wondered. And why did his wife let him get out of the house dressed that way? Why would he receive Christ's broken body with a message emblazoned across his chest that read, "I can only be nice to one person a day, and today is not your day. Tomorrow doesn't look too good either"?

The next day the couple was back. This time the retired man's sweatshirt read, "What don't you understand about the word 'no'?"

Obviously, Thomas admits, he knew nothing about this man. But it bothered him that he would want to participate in the sacrament of communion while wearing slogans indicating that he wanted nothing to do with other people. (1)

That's an interesting perspective. I have to confess that I have never paid much attention to what people wear in worship—even to receive the Lord's Supper. I suspect the retired man who wore the offending T-shirts never connected his apparel with what was happening in church. Most pastors nowadays are just grateful lay people show up for worship. What people wear is of little consequence.

But it reminded me of a parable that Jesus told about a king who prepared a wedding banquet for his son. He sent his servants to bring those who had been invited to the banquet, but they refused to come.

Then the king sent some more servants. "Tell those who have been invited that I have prepared my dinner: My oxen and fattened cattle have been butchered, and everything is ready. Come to the wedding banquet."

But those invited paid no attention. They went off to take care of their own concerns—one to his field, another to his business. Here's the remarkable thing—the rest of the invited citizens not only refused the king's invitation, they went so far as to seize the king's servants, mistreat them and kill them . . . This was quite a remarkable response to a simple wedding invitation. Quite rightly, the king was enraged. He sent his army and destroyed those who had killed his servants and burned their city.

Then the king said to his servants, "The wedding banquet is ready, but those

I invited did not deserve to come. So go to the street corners and invite to the banquet anyone you find." So the servants went out into the streets and gathered all the people they could find, bad people as well as good, and the wedding hall was filled with guests.

Now, up to this point, the meaning of Jesus' parable is pretty clear. He is expressing his disappointment with the scribes and Pharisees who are rejecting him and on the verge of murdering him, and he is saying that they will be left out of the kingdom. Meanwhile, those who respond to his invitation to the banquet, bad people as well as good, will be let in.

But then Jesus adds a little addendum to this parable, another parable if you will. When the king came in to see the guests who had come to the banquet, he noticed a man who was not wearing wedding clothes.

One commentator suggests that special wedding clothes may have been provided at the door by the host, free to all who came to the banquet. This may reflect a tradition in Jesus' time. Providing the guests with a wedding garment would have been particularly important in Jesus' parable because many of the guests were drawn from common walks of life, their clothing was dirty or ragged. So, in order to maintain the dignity of the occasion these special garments would be available at no cost. To reject them would be to reject the host's generosity. It would be an insult.

This man had no such garment on. And when the king saw him, he said, "Friend, how did you come in here without a wedding garment?" The man was speechless.

Then the king told the attendants, "Tie him hand and foot, and throw him outside, into the darkness, where there will be weeping and gnashing of teeth."

Then Jesus adds these cryptic words: "For many are invited, but few are chosen."

Who is this poor man who failed to dress appropriately for the wedding and what's he got to tell us? Surely he was aware of the solemn nature of the occasion. He reminds me of dreams some of us may have had where we find ourselves at a party and everyone else is nicely dressed, but we are in our pajamas . . . or less. It's an uncomfortable position.

Some of you may remember a comedian from the early days of television named George Gobel. Gobel's most famous line was, "Well, I'll be a dirty bird." Anyone admit that you remember George Gobel? Gobel was a master of self-deprecating humor. At one festive affair he was asked how he felt to be among so many well-known celebrities. He described himself in his typically humble way. "I feel," he said, "like a pair of brown shoes in a room full of tuxedos." Well, obviously, you don't wear brown shoes with a black tuxedo, not at a fancy, dress-up affair.

Of course, people are not as concerned about their dress as they used to be, but most of us conform when it is a formal occasion, particularly a wedding. This man did not and the king was enraged. What was there that caused the king to react so negatively toward this man's lack of wedding apparel?

It couldn't have been his worthiness or unworthiness to be at the wedding. In the parable Jesus made the point that both good and bad were accepted at the king's table. This is what grace is about, God's amazing grace. Both good and bad people are invited by God to receive the gift of God's love. It sometimes bothers us that the riff-raff of society have as much claim on the kingdom as we do, but Jesus stated that fact several times. God loves sinners, which is good since we all qualify.

It's like a minor fad that swept our land back in the 1980s. Do you remember that, for a while, it became fashionable for people to own potbellied pigs? Buyers shelled out thousands of dollars to own these exotic house pets imported from Vietnam. Their breeders claimed these mini-pigs were quite smart and would grow to only 40 pounds. Well, they were half right, says author Jim Nicodem. The pigs were smart. But they had a tendency to grow to about 150 pounds and become quite aggressive. And soon people started falling out of love with potbellied pigs.

Fortunately, a man named Dale Riffle came to the rescue. "Someone had given Riffle one of these pigs, and he fell in love with it. The pig, Rufus, never learned to use its litter box and developed this craving for carpets and wallpaper and drywall. Yet Riffle sold his suburban home and moved with Rufus to a five-acre farm in West Virginia. He started taking in other unwanted pigs, and before long, the guy was living in hog heaven.

"There are currently 180 [pot-bellied] residents on his farm. According to an article in U.S. News & World Report, they snooze on beds of pine shavings. They wallow in mud puddles. They soak in plastic swimming pools and listen to piped-in classical music. And they never need fear that one day they'll become bacon or pork chops. There's actually a waiting list of unwanted pigs trying to get a hoof in the door at Riffle's farm.

"Dale Riffle told the reporter, 'We're all put on earth for some reason, and I guess pigs are my lot in life.' How could anybody in his right mind fall in love with pigs?" asked Nicodem. "I'll tell you something even more amazing. An infinite, perfectly holy, majestic, awesome God is passionately in love with insignificant, sinful, sometimes openly rebellious, frequently indifferent people. God loves people like you and me." (2)

What was the problem that this man's dress was not appropriate? It couldn't have been his worthiness or unworthiness to be there. God's offer of grace is available to all, no matter how sordid our background may be.

And it couldn't be because the man couldn't afford the right apparel. His bank account would have been irrelevant to Jesus. In similar parables that Jesus told, it is obvious that God wants His house filled . . . with the poor, the maimed, the blind and the lame. In this world we may cater to the wealthy, the athletic, the well-connected—but in the kingdom, according to the teachings of Jesus, the well-to-do, the so-called beautiful people, are at the bottom of the totem pole.

It is a tragic mistake to equate wealth with worth. When somebody dies someone may ask, how much was he worth? They mean, of course, how much money did he leave behind? Get real! There are many people who have huge bank accounts who are very close to worthless as human beings. Conversely there are many people who will never accumulate much of anything of material value, but their passing will be greatly mourned by those who knew them and loved them.

Did you know that the artist Rembrandt was declared bankrupt in 1656? He had to sell his wife's grave in order to survive. Things didn't improve from there. He died penniless in 1669. How much was Rembrandt worth? Not much in monetary terms at the time of his passing—but, to the art world, few people have been worth as much. The man who did not have on the wedding garment—it couldn't have been because he couldn't afford better clothes. Jesus was clearly biased in favor of those who couldn't afford fancy garments.

There is a story about John Wesley, the founder of Methodism. The story may be apocryphal, but it reveal's Wesley's heart. In Wesley's time the churches in England were only for the rich. You had to have fine clothes and be clean to attend church in the 1700s. To make sure that the poor could not ruin their fine places of worship the churches were built up high in a rectangle without any steps to enter them. You could only get into them from a carriage. It is said that John Wesley had steps put in his churches so the poor could enter to worship God. A seemingly small thing, perhaps, to you and me but what an enormous step for the poor. (3) Like John Wesley, Christ was biased in favor of the poor.

So, what was it? What caused the king to be so furious at the guest who was not appropriately dressed? If it was not that his background had been questionable or that his bank account had been lacking, what was it, then, that got him into so much trouble with the king? Could it be that this man represents all those who accept the free gift of grace—who call themselves Christians but who in their personal lives show none of the signs of actually being Christian? As someone has said, grace is free, but there are standards. It is expected if you accept Christ's free gift of eternal life, that from that day forward, you will seek to adopt Christ's character as well. Or, to put it another way, you are invited to be a guest at Christ's banquet table, but you are not allowed to spit in his face with unacceptable behavior after you are there.

We're not talking about legalism here or what is sometimes called, works righteousness. It is true that we are not saved by our good works, but good works are the fruit of being saved.

In one of his books, author James Moore tells an old Japanese legend of a man who died and went to heaven. As he was shown around, he was much impressed with the sights—beautiful gardens where lotus flowers bloomed, mansions built of marble and gold and precious stones. It was all so beautiful, even more wonderful than he had imagined!

But then the man came to a very large room that looked like a merchant's shop. Lining the walls were shelves on which were piled and labeled what looked very much like dead mushrooms. On closer examination, however, the newcomer to heaven saw that they were not mushrooms at all. Actually, they were human ears! His guide explained that these were the ears of people on earth who went diligently to their places of worship and listened with pleasure to the teachings of faith, yet did nothing about what they heard; so after death, they themselves went somewhere else and only their ears reached heaven! (4)

That's a little grotesque, but it makes a point. While it is true that we are saved by our faith in Christ and our faith alone, a reading of the Gospels contains convincing evidence that there are expectations of those who eat at Christ's table. We are to live by Christ's teachings.

Augustine, one our early church fathers, writing in about the year four hundred, commented about the wedding garments that the bride and groom wear for the wedding, the wedding garment that all people are to wear. Augustine said that garment is charitable love. "Charitable love for your neighbor. No, not just family love for your spouse and children." Augustine, in his sermon on this text, said that even the sparrows love their own family. That is no big deal. You love your family? Big deal. So do the sparrows. But you are not a sparrow. You are a human being. You are made in the image of God. You are made to make this world a better place . . . And you have all kinds of excuses not to do this: "I can't. I am busy. Taking care of my family. Taking care of my job. Taking care of my home. I have a thousand and one excuses so as to avoid helping the world be a better place." (5) But this is the garment Christ asks us each to put on when we come to his banquet table. Charitable love. The love of God.

This poor man who did not have on the proper wedding attire earned the wrath of the king, but don't feel sorry for him. He received the same invitation everyone else received. He was to be the king's guest, at no cost to himself, at a magnificent wedding feast thrown for the king's son and his bride. But when they handed out the free wedding garments, when they asked him to dress appropriate to the event to which he had been invited, he refused. This was his choice, just as it is our choice when we accept Christ's invitation to come to the banquet table. Will we put on the garment of Christ's love? The choice is ours and ours alone to make.

1. http://www.day1.net/index.php5.

2. Preaching Today. Cited in Edward K. Rowell, 1001 Quotes, Illustrations, and Humorous Stories (Grand Rapids: Baker Publishing Group, 2008), pp. 328-329.

3. Helen Almanza, http://www.tarrytownumc.org/sermons/sr20070715.html.

4. God Was Here, and I was Out to Lunch (Nashville: 2001).

5. Edward F. Markquart, http://www.sermonsfromseattle.com/series_a_excuses_to_avoid_a_wedding.htm.

Don't Mess With The IRS
Matthew 22:15-22

It is a familiar saying, even to non-believers—particularly in the King James translation: "Render therefore unto Caesar the things which are Caesar's; and unto God the things that are God's."

There are only two things which are inevitable goes the old expression, death and taxes. At least death doesn't increase, someone has opined, every time Congress meets.

The Eiffel Tower, someone else has said, is the Empire State Building after taxes.

Have you ever noticed that when you combine the two words, "THE" and "IRS," it spells "THEIRS"?

Some of you may remember the story of Lady Godiva, a real person, who allegedly rode through the streets of her town without benefit of clothing. What you may not know is why she behaved in such a scandalous way. She was the wife of Leofric, Earl of Mercia, and supposedly she made her famous ride through the town of Coventry in exchange for her husband promising to cut taxes. (1)

Let's hope that our representatives in congress, who make extravagant claims about cutting taxes, don't follow Lady Godiva's example.

One of my favorite IRS stories is told by Donna Bell, an IRS employee. She says that she was working at her desk close to tax day, April 15, one year when an elderly woman approached her. The lady said she needed a thick stack of tax forms.

"Why so many?" asked Ms. Bell.

"My son is stationed overseas," she said. "He asked me to pick up forms for the soldiers on his base."

"You shouldn't have to do this," Ms. Bell told her. "It's the base commander's job to make sure that his troops have access to the forms they need."

"I know," said the woman. "I'm the base commander's mother." (2)

Even a base commander needs his mother's help when it comes to dealing with the IRS.

I suppose that most of us are smart enough, or intimidated enough, not to mess with the IRS. There are mafia bosses in jail—not for murder or other mayhem—but for failure to pay taxes on their ill-gotten gains. Not only can the IRS come after us when we fail to pay our taxes but the penalties that they add on can be horrendous. As someone else has said, "Don't cheat the government unless you look really good in stripes."

I know it's a long time until April 15 and perhaps you would prefer not to think about it. After all, April 15 is not only income tax day, it is also the day the Titanic sunk and the day Lincoln was shot. It's not a good day regardless of how you look at it.

And yet, taxes seem to be on everyone's mind nowadays. Should we add more taxes for the very wealthy? How can we cut the national debt without raising taxes?

Actually taxes were on the mind of people in Jesus' time as well. However, taxation carried an even more sinister connotation in biblical times, because when you paid taxes you were helping prop up Israel's oppressors, the Romans. Taxes were not paid to Israel or Judah. Most of the tax dollars went directly to Rome. To most Jews, this was offensive. The people of Israel were no different than any other occupied land. They resented their hard earned money going to the treasury of the people who ruled over them.

To add insult to injury, the Roman tax could only be paid with a Roman coin. This coin had stamped on it the image of Caesar himself. The inscription on it read: "Tiberius Caesar, august son of the divine Augustus, high priest." This coin with Caesar's image on it violated the second commandment as far as the Jews were concerned, the commandment regarding the creation of graven images.

So the Pharisees and the Herodians, that is, those in league with Herod, thought they had a winning hand when they posed a question to Jesus about paying taxes to Rome. "Teacher," they said hypocritically, "we know that you are a man of integrity and that you teach the way of God in accordance with the truth. You aren't swayed by others, because you pay no attention to who they are. Tell us then, what is your opinion? Is it right to pay the imperial tax to Caesar or not?"

It was a no-win situation for Jesus, or so they thought. If he counseled against paying taxes, he would be in trouble with the Romans; if he spoke in favor of paying the tax, the common people would be enraged. His enemies would have him just where they wanted him.

But Jesus knew their evil intent. He said, "You hypocrites, why are you trying to trap me? Show me the coin used for paying the tax." They brought him a denarius, and he asked them, "Whose image is this? And whose inscription?"

"Caesar's," they replied.

Then he said to them, "So give back to Caesar what is Caesar's, and to God what is God's."

When his enemies heard this, Matthew tells us, they were amazed. So they left him and went away. "Render . . . unto Caesar the things which are Caesar's; and unto God the things that are God's."

We know what belongs to Caesar, don't we? We get information from the IRS each year reminding us what we owe to Caesar. But what about God? WHAT DO WE OWE GOD? Let's talk about that for a few moments.

First of all, of course, we owe God our money. This church would not be here if you did not believe in giving God your money. Whether you give God a tithe, 10 percent, or even a fraction of that, you and I understand that giving is part of our responsibility as followers of Christ.

We owe money to our country because we drive on its roads. Somebody has to pay for those roads. Somebody has to pay for our schools, our military and all the benefits of a free and affluent land. In much the same way we give to God in order that the Gospel may be proclaimed and that future generations may have the same spiritual benefits that we enjoy.

Mark Sanborn is a well-known writer and motivational speaker. In one of his books, he tells about a friend of his, now deceased, who was well-known in business circles. His name was Charlie "Tremendous" Jones. Some of you know about this dynamic sales personality. Charlie "Tremendous" Jones died in October of 2009 and there was quite a remarkable "Homecoming Celebration" held in his behalf. You can view that moving service in full on the Internet.

Charlie Jones had a "tremendous" attitude about life. Mark Sanborn called Charlie "Tremendous" Jones one of the most philanthropic people he knew. Throughout his life, Sanborn says, Charlie Jones gave lavishly of his time and money. So Mark Sanborn was surprised when Charlie Jones announced to him and his other friends, "I've given up on giving." Says Sanborn, "There had to be more to the story, we knew." What would cause one of the most giving people on earth to give up on giving?

Charlie "Tremendous" Jones explained why he had given up on giving like this: "Everything I have," he said, "my life, my potential, my time—was given to me. I've decided to spend the rest of my life returning." (3)

Charlie was giving up on giving because he realized he hadn't been truly giving in the first place. How can you give what you do not own? He realized that he wasn't really GIVING to God. He was RETURNING to God was what was God's already.

I believe most of us understand that, but it is good to be reminded. A church like ours couldn't survive very long if people just gave to God when they felt inspired to do so. There are some people who give according to whether they like the pastor or whether they approve or disapprove of what the denomination is doing. They have their reward. The church, however, depends on more mature followers of Christ who give because they recognize that all of life is a gift from a loving God, and we are simply returning a portion of what God has bestowed on us.

Sometime back ABC TV news carried a brief story about Louise Hauser of Houston, Texas who won $50,000 on the game show, "Who Wants to Be a Millionaire." Here is the remarkable thing about Louise. Her home had sustained significant damage in Hurricane "Ike" a few months before. She is not a wealthy woman. She could certainly have used all of the $50,000. Yet Louise Hauser gave $10,000 of her prize winnings—that's 20% or two "tithes" of that money—to the West Houston Assistance Ministries, a food pantry where she works. She plans to give to her church as well. By way of explaining her generosity to an astonished reporter, Hauser said, "My husband Nick and I have a very simple life and we don't require much in the way of 'stuff' to be happy. I'm very blessed." (4)

She is blessed. Beyond the blessing of material goods, Louise is blessed with spiritual maturity. She understands that happiness does not consist in having stuff. Happiness comes from being in a right relationship with God and our neighbor. The first thing we owe God is our money.

The second thing we owe God is our joyful service. I say joyful service because the people who serve God best don't think of it as a duty, but as a privilege. For them service is a natural response to God's goodness.

The editorial staff of a Sunday magazine at one time created a "Faith in Life" award. This was their way of increasing their readership and at the same time recognizing those who best demonstrated their faith in daily living. The readers were encouraged to submit letters of nomination to the paper telling stories of those persons who best lived their faith in their daily lives.

A large number of the nominating letters that came in mentioned people who either (1) had attended church regularly for years; (2) had given a sizable amount of money to their church or favorite charity; or (3) had done both. Many of the letters included newspaper clippings that showed the dedication of the person who was being nominated for the award.

Some folks were surprised when the winner was announced. His letter of nomination had arrived at the paper written in crayon—with no newspaper clippings attached. The letter read like this: "Anthony is a plumber. He helped some people fix up a house for my friend's family because their first house burned down. He also visits my grandmother in the nursing home and makes her happy with his stories and his harmonica playing. He is a lot like Jesus. I hope he wins. But if he doesn't it won't matter. He will still be the same good old Anthony." And it was signed, "Love, Anne." (5)

I like that. He "makes [my grandmother] happy with his stories and his harmonica playing. He is a lot like Jesus." There are people I've known through the years like Anthony the plumber. Some are members of this church. They take being a good neighbor seriously. They are continually doing good things for others.

Anthony is like another man I heard about recently named Arnold Billie. For more than a quarter of a century, Billie was a rural mail carrier in southern New Jersey. His daily route took him sixty-three miles through two counties and five municipalities. Mr. Billie, as he was affectionately known, did more than deliver the mail. He provided "personal service." Anything a person might need to purchase from the post office, Mr. Billie provided—stamps, money orders, pickup service. All a customer needed to do was leave the flag up on their mailbox.

One elderly woman had trouble starting her lawn mower, so whenever she wanted to use it, she would simply leave it by her mailbox, raise the flag, and when Mr. Billie came by, he would start it for her! Mr. Billie gave a new definition to the phrase "public servant." (6)

There ought to be a special place in heaven for people like Anthony the plumber and Arnold Billie. There probably is. These are people who live out their faith in a wonderful way. Thank God for them. What do we owe God? We owe Him our money. We own Him our joyful service.

But the most important thing we owe God is, of course, ourselves. We need to understand this. More important than our material possessions, more important than our acts of neighborliness, is that we have dedicated ourselves whole-heartedly to God.

Whose image was engraved on the Roman coins? That's easy to answer— Caesar's. In whose image were we created? God's. Render unto Caesar that which is Caesar and unto God that which is God's. In other words, as ones created in the image of God, we owe God everything we are and everything we hope to be.

Many years ago an American church leader named Wilber Chapman asked the founder of The Salvation Army, General William Booth, if he could explain why his work had prospered so. "He hesitated for a second," Dr. Chapman said, "and . . . I saw the tears come into his eyes and steal down his cheeks, and then [General Booth] said, 'Sir, I will tell you the secret. God has had all of me. There have been men with greater brains, men with greater opportunities, but from the day I got the poor of London on my heart and a vision of what Jesus Christ could do with the poor of London, I made up my mind that God would have all of William Booth that there was. And if there is any power in The Salvation Army today,' he said, 'it is because God has all the adoration of my heart, all the power of my will, and all the influence of my life.'"

What did William Booth give to God?—"all the adoration of my heart, all the power of my will, and all the influence of my life."

I like the way a retired pastor, Walter Harms, sums this lesson up. He says that we cannot do anything for God. "You cannot hug God. You can't give God a dime. You can't demonstrate in concrete form love for God. But you can love all those made in the image and likeness of God. You can hug them. You can give to them in their need. You can demonstrate to them you are vitally interested. You can give them your attention and time. And in loving them you love our Lord Jesus who in flesh and blood has shown us the image and likeness of God!" (7)

And he's right. Whose image was engraved on the Roman coins? Caesar's. In whose image were we created? God's. "Render unto Caesar that which is Caesar and unto God that which is God's."

1. William Hartston, The Encyclopedia of Useless Information (Naperville, IL: Sourcebooks, Inc.. 2007), p. 159.
2. America In Uniform, http://www.beliefnet.com.
3. You Don't Need a Title to Be a Leader (Colorado Springs: Waterbrook Press, 2006), p. 85.
4. Pastor Richard Allen, http://www.mamaroneckumc.org/2008sermons/20081116.htm.
5. Rev. Richard J. Fairchild, http://www.rockies.net/~spirit/sermons/c-or32sesn.php.
6. God's Little Devotional Book (Tulsa: Honor Books, Inc., 1973), p. 229.
7. Walter W. Harms, http://www.predigten.uni-goettingen.de/archiv-7/051016-4-e.html.

Living To Please God
1 Thessalonians 2:1-8

A surgeon says that one night during his residency he was called out of a sound sleep to the emergency room. Unshaven and with tousled hair, he showed up accompanied by an equally unpresentable medical student.

In the ER they encountered the on-call medical resident and his student, both neatly attired in clean white lab coats. The medical resident said to his student, "You can always tell the surgeons by their absolute disregard for appearance."

Two evenings later, the same young surgical resident was at a banquet when called to the ER for yet another emergency. He was stitching away on his patient—this time wearing a tuxedo from the banquet—when he encountered that same medical resident with his student. The medical resident looked at the surgical resident now wearing the tuxedo, then said to his student, "Sure is sensitive to criticism, isn't he?"

Have you ever been unfairly criticized by someone else—a family member, perhaps—or a colleague—or a customer? It happens . . . to all of us. No one is exempt.

The Gettysburg Address is considered the most eloquent oration in U.S. history. And yet, the editor of the Chicago Times, a prominent newspaper of its day, ridiculed that address which had been delivered, of course, by President Lincoln. On November 20, 1863, the day after Lincoln delivered his famous speech, the editor of the Times wrote: "The cheek of every American must tingle with shame as he reads the silly, flat and dish-watery utterances of the man who has been pointed out to intelligent foreigners as the President of the United States." (1)

Sooner or later all of us have to deal with criticism. Let me ask you a second question: Has anyone ever tried to flatter you? That is, have they ever tried to praise you extravagantly? Let me guess—we are not nearly as sensitive to flattery as we are to criticism, are we?

I chuckled when I read a story about the late, great motivational speaker Cavett Robert. Robert was a humble, kind man who was also a successful lawyer, salesman, and founder of the National Speakers Association.

Robert once told of looking out his window one morning and seeing a skinny twelve-year-old boy going door to door selling books. Robert further noticed that the boy was headed for his house. Robert turned to his wife and said, "Just watch me teach this kid a lesson about selling. After all these years of writing books about communication, lecturing all over the country," Robert continued, "I might as well share some of my wisdom with him. I don't want to hurt his feelings, but I'll get rid of him before he knows what's happened. I've used this technique for years, and it works every time. Then I'll go back and teach him how to deal with people like me."

Mrs. Robert watched as the twelve-year-old boy knocked on the door. Cavett Robert opened the door and quickly explained that he was a very busy man. He had no interest in buying any books. But he said, "I'll give you one minute, but then I have to leave. I have a plane to catch."

The young salesman was not daunted by Robert's brush-off. He simply stared at the tall, gray-haired, distinguished-looking man, a man that he knew was fairly well known and quite wealthy. The boy said with a sound of awe in his voice, "Sir, could you be the FAMOUS Cavett Robert?"

To which Robert replied, "Come on in, son." Mr. Robert bought several books from the youngster—books that he admitted he might never read. The boy had mastered one principle—the principle of making the other person feel important—and it worked. (2)

Sometimes we are criticized. People say unfair, negative things. Sometimes we are flattered. People puff us up and make us feel better about ourselves than is good for us. How do you get to the point that neither praise nor criticism affects your day?

St. Paul knew what it was to be criticized. In the New Testament church there was a group of people known as the Judaizers who wanted to keep Christianity as a Jewish sect. Since Paul was determined to take the faith to the Gentiles, these Judaizers looked for every opportunity to find fault with him. They accused him of being in the ministry just for the money. That was a joke. Paul continued to support himself as a tent maker after he began his ministry so he wouldn't be a financial burden on young, struggling Christian congregations. Those who knew Paul best knew that he did nothing for his own gain.

These Judaizers also accused him of spreading lies and untruths. Again, they were way off-target. St. Paul didn't soft-pedal the Gospel or use flattery upon his hearers. He told it as it was, as we used to say. Still, they criticized. And so Paul was forced to defend himself. He writes, beginning with verse 5: "You know we never used flattery, nor did we put on a mask to cover up greed—God is our witness. We were not looking for praise from people, not from you or anyone else . . ." Then what was Paul looking for? The answer lies in the second half of verse 4: "We are not trying to please people but God, who tests our hearts." St. Paul had no interest in pleasing people. St. Paul lived to please God.

Would you like to live your life impervious to the hurtful or unhelpful opinions of other people? Would you like to live so that you are not fazed either by criticism or flattery? Here is the answer: live to please God. It's a simple thing. If your primary audience is God, if your primary goal is to have God say at the end of your life, "Well done, thou good and faithful servant," then what difference would it make what other people say about you? It would make no difference whatsoever.

Now, how do you live to please God? St. Paul gave us the answer both in his words and in his life.

First of all, to please God, live with integrity. That's what St. Paul did. He says to the church at Thessalonica, "For the appeal we make does not spring from error or impure motives, nor are we trying to trick you. On the contrary, we speak as those approved by God to be entrusted with the gospel . . . You know we never used flattery, nor did we put on a mask to cover up greed—God is our witness."

Paul lived a life of integrity. Living a life of integrity is more than simply keeping the commandments. There are many people of whom it could be said that they have never killed, never stolen, never committed adultery. That doesn't mean they live a life of integrity. Keeping the commandments is an outward act. Living a life of integrity comes from within.

Dr. Haddon Robinson once told the story of a writer for a newspaper in Toronto, Canada who undertook an investigation into the ethical practices of auto repair shops in his town. He took a spark-plug wire off of his engine, making the car run unevenly. He took the car in to different shops and asked them to fix it. Time after time people sold him unnecessary repairs or charged him for repairs that were not done. Finally, he went to a small garage. A fellow named Fred came out, popped open the hood, and said, "Let me listen to that thing." After a few seconds, he told the reporter, "I think I know what's wrong." He reached down and grabbed the wire, announcing, "Your spark-plug wire came off." And he put it back on.

The reporter asked, "What do I owe you?"

"I'm not gonna charge you anything," Fred replied. "I didn't have to fix anything; I just reattached the wire."

The writer then told Fred what he was doing and that he had been charged all kinds of money by mechanics looking at that same wire. He asked Fred, "Why didn't you charge me anything?"

Fred said, "Are you sure you want to know? I happen to be a Christian and believe that everything we do should be done to glorify God. I'm not a preacher and I'm not a missionary, but I am a mechanic and so I do it honestly. I do it skillfully and I do it to the glory of God."

The next day in the newspaper was a headline that read, "Christian Mechanic, Honest to the Glory of God." (3)

Integrity is honesty. It is an uncompromising commitment to be truthful and trustworthy.

In the fourth round of a national spelling bee in Washington, eleven-year-old Rosalie Elliot, a champion from South Carolina, was asked to spell the word "avowal." Her soft Southern accent made it difficult for the judges to determine if she had used an a or an e as the next to last letter of the word. The judges deliberated for several minutes and also listened to tape recording playbacks, but still they couldn't determine which letter had been pronounced.

Finally the chief judge, John Lloyd, put the question to the only person who knew the answer. He asked Rosalie, "Was the letter an a or an e?"

Rosalie, surrounded by whispering young spellers, knew by now the correct spelling of the word. But without hesitation, she replied that she had misspelled the word and had used an e.

As she walked from the stage, the entire audience stood and applauded her honesty and integrity, including dozens of newspaper reporters covering the event. While Rosalie had not won the contest, she had definitely emerged a winner that day. (4)

Do you want to please God? Live a life of integrity. That's hard to do in a world like ours. We live in Spin City, when prominent and influential people from every walk of life hedge the truth. They don't steal, not in the classic understanding of the word, they don't kill, they don't overtly disobey God's law. They simply shade the truth. They use flattery and deceit. Often they are motivated by greed. It's not good business to be completely honest about your wares. Advertisers would be unemployed overnight. A life of integrity won't make you popular. However, it will make you respected. Even more importantly, there is an audience of One who will be applauding. Want to live a life pleasing to God? Here's the first ingredient: live with integrity.

Here is the second: live a life of love. St. Paul writes, "We are not trying to please people but God, who tests our hearts. Even though as apostles of Christ we could have asserted our authority. Instead, we were like young children among you. Just as a nursing mother cares for her children, so we cared for you. Because we loved you so much, we were delighted to share with you not only the gospel of God but our lives as well."

The reason Paul had such impact on the churches he served was that the people knew he genuinely cared about them. As has been often said, "People don't care how much you know until they know how much you care." St. Paul cared.

In 1821, a young lawyer named Thaddeus Stevens took on the case of a slave owner whose slave, Charity Butler, had run away. Stevens argued successfully for the prosecution, and Butler was returned to her slave owner. Case won. According to the standards of his profession, Stevens should have been elated. Exactly the opposite was true, however. Historians believe that this case affected Stevens deeply. He knew that he had been successful in an unjust cause. This didn't cause him elation, but shame. As a result, he became a passionate advocate against slavery. He went on to serve seven terms in U.S. Congress, and was the driving force behind the 14th and 15th Amendments to the Constitution, guaranteeing equal protection under the law and giving slaves who had been set free the right to vote. In 2002, while excavating parts of Stevens' property, archeologists discovered that Stevens also had beneath his home a hidden passageway, most likely used to hide runaway slaves escaping by way of the Underground Railroad. (5)

Thaddeus Stevens went beyond being a man who was simply honest and upright. He became a man with a cause, the cause of the abolition of slavery. He became a man intent on pleasing God.

It's like something Tony Campolo, a professor of Sociology at Eastern College in Pennsylvania, and a dynamic preacher of the Gospel once said, "What you commit yourself to be will change what you are and make you into a completely different person. Let me repeat that. Not the past but the future conditions you, because what you commit yourself to become determines what you are more than anything that ever happened to you yesterday or the day before. Therefore I ask you a very simple question: What are your commitments? Where are you going? What are you going to be? You show me somebody who hasn't decided, and I'll show you somebody who has no identity, no personality, no direction." (6)

St. Paul had a direction for his life. And neither his critics nor those who tried to veer him off-course with flattery or lies could make a dent in his contribution. He knew what it took to live a life pleasing to God—living a life of integrity and living a life of love.

Another preacher named Tony, Tony Evans said it beautifully as well: "When your passion upon getting up each morning is to say, 'How can I make God look good today?'; when the passion of your life is to someday open your eyes in eternity and hear Jesus say, 'Well done, My good and faithful servant'; when that becomes the consuming passion of your existence, it absolutely transforms your everyday experience."

Does that describe how you live your life? Isn't it about time it did? How can I make God look good today? How can I live to please God? The answer is simple— by the grace of God live a life of integrity. Live a life of love.

1. Leland Gregory, Stupid History Tales of Stupidity, Strangeness, and Mythconceptions Throughout the Ages (Kansas City: Andrews McMeel Publishing, LLC, 2007), p. 117.

2. Dr. Alan Zimmerman, www.drzimmerman.com. Cited by John C. Maxwell, Winning With People (Nashville: Nelson Books, 2004).

3. Tommy Nelson, The 12 Essentials of Godly Success (Nashville: Broadman & Holman Publishers, 2005), p. 148.

4. God's Little Devotional Book for Graduates (Tulsa: Honor Books, Inc., 1995), p. 159.

5. "Digging into a Historic Rivalry" by Fergus M. Bordewich, Smithsonian, February 2004, pp. 96-107.

6. Cited in Glenn Van Ekeren, Speaker's Sourcebook II—Quotes, Stories, & Anecdotes for Every Occasion (Englewood Cliffs, NY: Prentice Hall, Inc., 1994), p. 67.

Written On Our Hearts

Jeremiah 31:31-34

(Reformation Day)

"We all live in a box," the biggest kid said.

"A what?" asked Sister Mary Rose McGeady of Covenant House, a shelter for abused and runaway children.

"A box," he said.

And right there on a city street Sister Rose learned of six children fleeing from abusive homes who lived in a cement box. The six kids huddled closer together and stared at Sister McGeady, trying not to look too ashamed or embarrassed about how they looked and how they sounded. They were dirty, and bedraggled, and unkempt, and dressed in rags. Sister McGeady wanted to hug them all. Six beautiful kids . . . runaways . . . living inside a box.

"Do you think I could see this box?" asked the Sister. "I mean, is that O.K.?"

The kids looked at each other, waiting for the oldest boy to make the decision. But the youngest couldn't wait. "Sure, Sister," he said. "It's not far from here."

When they got there, the kids scrambled over a chain link fence surrounding a sort of concrete cavern. Sister McGeady didn't even try to follow them. The idea of a 65 year old nun trying to climb a fence was just too ridiculous.

The kids stood in front of their box beaming. "It's great," the biggest kid said. He was obviously the leader. "It's dry and warm and even has a fence for protection. So don't worry about us," he said. The others nodded.

Sister McGeady wanted to point out how little protection it really was. "You know," she said, "we've got a great place for you to stay tonight, if you don't want to sleep in this box. We've got warm, clean beds, and good food, and clean clothes, and you can take a hot shower. Would you like to come back to our shelter with me?"

"Well, thanks, but not now," the oldest said. "We got it all figured out," he said. "We're like a family. We all take care of each other."

Sister McGeady resisted the temptation to lecture them about their dream world. She wanted to yell. "You call this a family! A family is supposed to protect kids and help them prepare for life! Not one of you is over 18. You don't know anything about life yet! But you're going to learn. You're going to learn about pimps and pushers. You're going to learn about pneumonia and even worse diseases. You're going to learn about hunger and how quickly you can die. Have you thought about that?

"Have you thought about the rest of your lives? Do you really want to live in a cement box forever? And if not, how will you ever get out of here? I'll tell you how, because there are only three ways—drugs, prostitution . . . or death. That's it, kids. That's your future." She didn't say any of those things. She looked at those bright, hopeful—and hopelessly naïve—faces and asked God to watch over them. (1)

She didn't scream at those desperate kids, but I want you to imagine that she did. Then I want you to visualize the prophets of Israel and Judah trying to get the attention of their people. God made a covenant with the people of Israel when he brought them out of Egypt. God gave them the Law inscribed on stone tablets. If they would keep God's Law and walk in God's way, then God would bless them and make them a great people. However, almost immediately the people broke that covenant by engaging in all sorts of pagan immorality.

It was not because the prophets had a bad disposition that they sometimes preached doom and gloom. Like Sister McGeady, they simply wanted to warn the people what lay ahead if they continued on their current path. But the people refused to listen. They stoned the prophets and turned their backs as the prophets tried to warn them. By the sixth century B.C., when Jeremiah was attempting to speak to the people on behalf of God, the kingdom had been divided, Jerusalem had been destroyed, and most of the leaders and key citizens of the nation had been deported. It is a nation in total disarray that Jeremiah is addressing. And in the midst of seeking to dissuade them of their apostasy, Jeremiah offers a word of hope: "The days are coming," declares the LORD, "when I will make a new covenant with the people of Israel and with the people of Judah. It will not be like the covenant I made with their ancestors when I took them by the hand to lead them out of Egypt, because they broke my covenant, though I was a husband to them," declares the LORD. "This is the covenant I will make with the people of Israel after that time," declares the LORD. "I will put my law in their minds and write it on their hearts. I will be their God, and they will be my people. No longer will they teach their neighbor, or say to one another, 'Know the LORD,' because they will all know me, from the least of them to the greatest," declares the LORD. "For I will forgive their wickedness and will remember their sins no more."

Welcome on this day when we celebrate the New Covenant. For isn't that what Christ was all about? Christ turned religion upside down. What distinguishes the New Covenant from the Old? Let's consider three ways in which they differ.

First of all, with the New Covenant, faith moved from external to internal. In place of external commandments that were impossible to keep, God gave us the indwelling presence of the Holy Spirit to guide us into righteous living. Christ did not come to destroy the law. He simply internalized that law, thus fulfilling Jeremiah's prophecy: "I will put my law in their minds and write it on their hearts . . ."

I heard a silly story about two men who had been floating in a raft at sea for weeks. Finally they scribbled a message—"HELP"—corked it in a bottle, and tossed it into the waves. Next day a bottle floated up to the raft and one of the men eagerly opened it to find a message inside. "Hey," he said to his friend, "it's from a doctor who found our bottle."

"Well," asked the eager sailor, "what does it say?"

"It says," read his friend, "get plenty of rest, drink lots of liquid and send me another message in the morning."

Well, someone answered their summons for help, but what good did it do them? In the same way, the Jewish people had the Law, but what good did it do them? It prescribed how they should live, but it did not give them the power to live that way. They didn't need an external prescription. They needed internal power. With the New Covenant faith moved from external to internal.

In the second place, with the New Covenant, faith moved from formal and distant to personal and intimate. No longer would the Law stand between humanity and God. "No longer will they teach their neighbor," writes Jeremiah, "or say to one another, 'Know the LORD,' because they will all know me, from the least of them to the greatest."

There is a difference between the God of Mount Sinai and the God who walked the dusty hills of Galilee. It is the difference between religion that is remote and distant and religion that is warm and personal.

Erma Bombeck, before her death, shared an incident in one of her columns that demonstrated this difference. She tells about a really bad day she had once, a day when she was in a bad mood and didn't want to see anybody. She really would have liked to run away. Yet it seemed that everyone needed to talk with her. Even on her way to the airport, a taxi driver talked the entire way about his son who was away at college.

Finally, she was about to board her plane. She thought, at last, a few beautiful moments with my own thoughts. It was then that the voice next to her, belonging to an elderly woman, said: "I'll bet it's cold in Chicago."

Stone-faced, Erma Bombeck replied, "It's likely."

The woman persisted: "I have not been in Chicago for nearly three years. My son lives there, you know."

"That's nice," Erma said, her eyes intent on her book.

Again the elderly woman spoke: "My husband's body is on this plane. We have been married for 53 years. I do not drive, you know, and when he died, a nun drove me home from the hospital . . . the funeral director let me come to the airport with him."

Erma Bombeck said, "I do not think I have ever detested myself more than I did at that moment. Another human being was screaming to be heard, and, in desperation, had turned to a cold stranger who was more interested in a novel than she was in the real-life drama at her elbow. She needed no advice, money, assistance, expertise, or even compassion. All she needed was someone to listen. She talked numbly and steadily until we boarded the plane, and she took her seat. As I put my things in the overhead compartment, I heard the woman's plaintive voice say to her seat companion, 'I'll bet it's cold in Chicago,' and I prayed, 'Please, God, let her listen.'" (2)

That is the difference between the God of Sinai and the God who showed Himself on the shores of Galilee. It is the difference between a God who is remote and distant and a God who is personal and intimate.

Finally, with the New Covenant, faith moved from conditional to unconditional. Through the work of Christ, the promise was fulfilled: "I will forgive their wickedness and will remember their sins no more."

This faith is available to all who will receive it—with no strings attached. This is the difference between a contract and a covenant.

All of us know what a contract is. A contract between two parties spells out both parties' obligations and includes penalties if these conditions are not met. Contracts are broken when one of the parties fails to keep his promise.

Someone has compared it to an appointment with a doctor. If you miss your appointment, the doctor is not obligated to call the house and inquire, "Where were you? Why didn't you show up for your appointment?" He simply goes on to his next patient. However, you may find it harder the next time to see the doctor. You broke an informal contract. According to the Bible, however, the Lord asks: "Can a mother forget the baby at her breast and have no compassion on the child she has borne? Though she may forget, I will not forget you!" (Isa. 49:15)

The Bible indicates the covenant is more like the ties of a parent to her child than it is a doctor's appointment. If a child fails to show up for dinner, the parent's obligation, unlike the doctor's, isn't canceled. The parent finds out where the child is and makes sure he's cared for. One party's failure does not destroy the relationship. Our children will always be our children. We will always be their parent. And God will always be our God. That is the nature of grace. It is unconditional. It is personal. It is internal. And it is eternal. It never fails. Perhaps it is time for some of us to come out of the cement boxes in which we have been living and let the God of the New Covenant love us.

1. Sr. Mary Rose McGeady, Does God Still Love Me? Letters from the Street (Covenant House, 1995), pp. 81-85.
2. Dr. Thomas Lane Butts, http://day1.org/1522-dr_thomas_lane_butts_just_listen.

Which Mask Will You Wear?
Matthew 23:1-12

Tomorrow night is Halloween. In spite of the practice nowadays of thinking of Halloween as the Devil's night, Halloween is actually a holiday with rich religious origins. The "Hallow" in Halloween comes from the same root as "Hallowed be Thy Name." Halloween is the day before the traditional Christian celebration known as All Saints' Day. It was intended to be a "hallow(ed) e'en."

Our tradition in which we think of ghosts and trick-or-treating comes from Celtic beliefs. The Celts believed that the souls of the departed roamed the earth one night in the fall. Since it was a time of harvest, the people would huddle together in front of fires, eating, and telling stories. And thus Halloween evolved into a celebration of witches and ghouls and fiends—far removed from All Saints' Day.

I trust that all of our children will be careful if they go trick or treating tomorrow night. You parents will make certain of that. At least, trick or treating in our community will be nothing like trick or treating in Churchill, Manitoba.

Churchill is a small town on the shore of Hudson Bay in Manitoba, Canada. Manitoba is most famous for being populated by polar bears. In fact, Manitoba is known as the "Polar Bear Capital of the World." That is why children trick or treating in Churchill have to be really careful. The rules for trick or treating in Churchill, Manitoba are quite strict—no polar bear costumes and no white costumes at all—including ghost, nurse and bride costumes. And definitely no seal costumes. The reason? Polar bears may show up at any time.

To protect children going door to door on Halloween night, conservation officers and game wardens are out on patrol in Churchill armed with dart guns to tranquilize any bears wandering into town. A helicopter does surveillance over the area. Local volunteers with two-way radios patrol in cars. Police constables carry shotguns to frighten away furry white marauders. And while noise may help, authorities agree that the most effective deterrent against prowling bears is light. Each year more than a dozen fire trucks, ambulances and police cruisers are positioned around the perimeter of Churchill, their bright lights flashing into the night. (1)

So, you thought you were concerned about your child going out on Halloween night. We have it made. At least we don't have to worry about polar bears.

But, since tomorrow is Halloween, some of us may be thinking about what kind of costume to wear, or at least what kind of mask to put on. Jesus was thinking about the same thing in our lesson for the day from Matthew's Gospel, though he was not thinking about Halloween. He was thinking about the costumes and masks that people put on in everyday life, especially the Pharisees. Listen carefully to his words:

Then Jesus said to the crowds and to his disciples: "The teachers of the law and the Pharisees sit in Moses' seat. So you must be careful to do everything they tell you. But do not do what they do, for they do not practice what they preach. They tie up heavy, cumbersome loads and put them on other people's shoulders, but they themselves are not willing to lift a finger to move them.

"Everything they do is done for people to see: They make their phylacteries wide and the tassels on their garments long; they love the place of honor at banquets and the most important seats in the synagogues; they love to be greeted with respect in the marketplaces and to be called 'Rabbi' by others . . ."

Let's stop there. You get the idea. Jesus said about the teachers of the law and the Pharisees, "They do not practice what they preach." Have you ever run into someone like that—who does not practice what they preach?

Do you remember the famous outlaw Jesse James? It is said that Jesse James killed a man in a bank robbery and shortly thereafter was baptized in a nearby Baptist Church as if nothing had happened. Then he killed another man, a bank cashier, and immediately joined the church choir and taught hymn singing. As one commentator reported, "He liked Sundays, Jesse did, but he couldn't always show up at church. On . . . Sundays, he robbed trains." (2)

I believe you could say about Jesse James that he did not practice what he preached. I've been told that some politicians also suffer from this same affliction.

There is a story told of former president Theodore Roosevelt. During one of his election campaigns a delegation of citizens came to Roosevelt's home. Roosevelt met them with his coat off and his sleeves rolled up. He said, "Why don't you come down to the barn with me, and we can talk while I do some work."

The delegation followed him to the barn. Roosevelt picked up a pitchfork and looked around for the hay to pitch up into the hayloft. There was none there. He called out to his assistant, "John, where's all the hay?"

"Sorry, sir," John called down from the hayloft. "I ain't had time to toss it back down again after you pitched it up while the Iowa delegation was here." (3)

Well, that's politics, as we say. Politicians wear masks.

Having said that, I must add this rejoinder. The truth of the matter is that all of us wear masks from time to time. On occasion we all play the hypocrite. Certainly I'm conscious of that. Every time I talk about taking up the cross and following Christ, I am confronted with the question of how much my faith costs me and whether I am giving my all to serve the Master. You understand that. It's true of you as well. The critics are right. The church is full of hypocrites. The more conscious you are of Christ's call, the more you are aware of how inadequate your own witness is.

In an interview in the magazine The Door, famed psychiatrist M. Scott Peck tells about the first time he went to hear the Swiss physician Paul Tournier, one of the most influential Christians in the world.

Following Tournier's lecture there was a time of questions and dialogue, at which point a man stood up and asked, "Dr. Tournier, what do you think about all the hypocrites in the churches of America?"

Stumbling over the English words, Tournier apologized and said he did not understand the meaning of the word "hypocrite." Several people offered definitions. "Phony, pretending to be something that they're not, unauthentic, false."

Suddenly the doctor's eyes lit up. "Ah, hypocrites, now I understand . . . C'est moi! C'est moi. I am the hypocrite." (4)

The closer you are to Jesus, the more you measure your life by his life, the more aware you are of your shortcomings. We cry out with Paul Tournier, "C'est moi! It's me! I am the hypocrite."

I guess that is why I like the expression, "If a hypocrite is standing between you and God, it just means the hypocrite is closer to God than you are."

There is some truth to this expression. We are all hypocrites. We all wear masks. Some people, however, take it to the extreme. This is what Jesus disliked about the Pharisees. We talk about "wearing your religion on your sleeve." The Pharisees literally wore their religion on their foreheads and arms for everyone to see. They wore phylacteries, little leather boxes on their foreheads. These boxes contained verses from the Old Testament. They also liked to wear long tassels. Both of these actions are based on obscure references in the Old Testament. Their only practical purpose, however, was to show how religious and devout the Pharisees were. Common people like shepherds and fishermen did not wear them. Meanwhile the Pharisees oppressed the common people with their interpretations of the Law. The Pharisees counted 613 laws from the Old Testament that the people were to do in order to live lives that were pleasing to God. By focusing on these 613 religious rules and regulations, the Pharisees neglected the weightier issues of love and justice. (5) This is what Christ meant when he said, "They tie up heavy, cumbersome loads and put them on other people's shoulders, but they themselves are not willing to lift a finger to move them."

We all wear masks. But the Pharisees took the wearing of masks to the extreme. If you work at looking more religious than you really are, then Jesus has some harsh words for you as well.

However, there is something else that needs to be said on this Sunday before Halloween. Be careful about judging other people by the masks they wear. This is a different perspective on wearing masks.

Marilyn Morgan Hellenberg tells about a creature that appeared at her door one Halloween. She called it the scariest creature she's ever seen. The rubber mask, covering the young man's face and head, had twisted features, a pulled-down mouth and a bright red "wound" on the cheek. Quickly, Marilyn dropped a couple of home-baked cookies into the young man's sack and he hurried away.

A couple of days later, when the paper boy came to collect, he said, "Those sure were good cookies you gave out on Halloween!" You guessed it. He was the young man behind that mask. Marilyn could hardly believe it! Darren's a real sweetheart, she says—good-natured, polite, working to become an Eagle Scout.

It made Marilyn wonder: "Could there be a lovable child of God behind some of the ugly masks we wear? That woman with the stringy, unwashed hair who sat near [us] in church last week. Might there be a sweet-natured child with little self-esteem behind her unkempt disguise? That opinionated man who seems so cocky. Is it possible there's a little boy behind his blustery camouflage, hoping his fear won't show? The pushy woman crowding in front of [us] at the post office. I wonder if the little girl in her has felt ignored too long.

"There's a child in me, too," says Marilyn Hellenberg, "and she sometimes hurts. Thank God for those special people who care enough to look beyond the false faces I sometimes wear!" (6)

Those are wise words. Be careful about judging people by the masks they wear. For example, young people often try on many masks as they seek to determine an authentic identity. Goth dress, piercings, tattoos—all of these are masks. Of course, so is the double-breasted suit, and the Coach handbag. Be careful of judging people on their outward appearance. We all wear masks of one kind of another.

The Pharisees were wearing masks. They were pretending a piety they did not possess. Who among us has not done the same thing?

Here's the important thing we need to see: regardless of the mask we wear, we cannot fool God. Regardless of what kind of mask we choose to put on, God knows us as we really are. God see our hearts. God knows our real priorities.

According to Dr. Kenneth Gangel, each year in Basel, Switzerland the good Protestant townspeople have a festival in which they all don masks and go through the city doing things and going places they would never consider doing or going under normal circumstances. The mask, which veils their identity, emboldens them to do these things. One year, the Salvation Army, concerned about the abandonment of moral standards, put up signs all over the city, which read, "God sees behind the mask."

God does see behind the mask. It troubled Jesus that the Pharisees taught one thing and did something else. Here's why that bothered Jesus so much. The Pharisees were in places of responsibility. They were the spiritual leaders of their community. If they taught one thing and did something else, what would that say to those who were looking to them for guidance?

The same thing is true of us. If we have given our lives to Christ, we have a responsibility. That responsibility is, with God's help, to make our deeds match our words. We are not only to talk the talk, we are to walk the walk.

An amusing story is told about a high school concert a few years ago. It seems the band was to give its spring concert. A couple of days before the concert, the director took sick and a substitute was brought in who didn't know the students. One of the trombone players came to a friend and asked, "Hey, Joe, fill in for me on the trombone at the concert. I've got a big date for that night."

The friend protested, "Well sure, but I can't play the trombone. I've never touched one in my life."

"No problem," replied the trombonist. "Just watch the other trombone players. Do what they do. Nobody will ever know."

Joe tried to explain that he was nervous about faking it on the trombone, but his buddy finally persuaded him that all he had to do was just pretend to play. Joe reluctantly agreed. The night of the concert came, and Joe put on his friend's band uniform and carried the trombone to the stage with the other trombonists and band members. Joe watched the others, and picked up his instrument when they picked up theirs. When the other trombonists seemed to extend their slides, Joe extended his. Joe began to relax. Later in the program, however, he noticed that a piece of music called for all four trombones to play a brief trombone quartet. Joe waited until that part came, and rose with the other trombonists when the substitute director pointed his baton toward them. Looking out the corner of his eye, Joe raised his trombone to his lips simultaneously with the others. All four took a breath and with a united motion pulled their sliding trombones in a gesture that indicated proud harmony. But not a sound came forth. It turned out that all four were filling in for friends who were trombonists! They were all pretenders, and so there was no trombone quartet that night. (7)

This is a reminder of the one thing that cannot be faked. It is service—service to Christ and to other people. How will other people know we are truly disciples of Jesus Christ? By our love, by our service to others. After Jesus points out the grievous behavior of the Pharisees, Jesus concludes with what is really important in showing our devotion to God. He said, "The greatest among you will be your servant. For those who exalt themselves will be humbled, and those who humble themselves will be exalted."

Loving service to others is something that can't be faked. If you're tired of wearing a mask, then ditch it. Live a life of authentic Christian service. Give yourself to God. Give yourself to serving God's children.

1. Alma Barkman, Daily Guideposts (Nashville: Ideals Publications, 2006), p. 308.
2. Biblical Illustrator.
3. Don Friesen, http://www.ottawamennonite.ca/sermons/examine.htm.
4. John F. Westfall, Enough Is Enough (New York: Zondervan Publishing House, 1993), p. 104.
5. Edward F. Markquart, http://www.sermonsfromseattle.com/series_a_hypocricy_of_the_pharisees.htm.
6. Daily Guideposts, 1991 (Carmel, New York: Guideposts, 1990), p. 285.
7. Dr. William P. Barker, Ed., Tarbell's Teacher's Guide (Elgin, IL: David C. Cook Co., 1990).

Being Prepared
Matthew 25:1-13

Hurricane Bob was bearing down on the Atlantic coast. Safe in his home on that same coast, a man named J. R. thought he was well prepared. The power failed, but that didn't faze him. As night fell, he simply fired up some oil lamps and placed his Coleman camping stove on top of the electric range in his kitchen to cook his dinner. So what if he had no electricity? He was able to enjoy a delicious meal thanks to his Coleman stove. He commended himself on his foresight. He went to bed secure in the knowledge that Mother Nature could not beat him.

Meanwhile, outside diligent linemen worked through the night to restore power. Before dawn, all the appliances in J. R.'s house were again working, including the electric range. But J. R., as prepared as he was, had overlooked one important detail . . .

He had forgotten that he had been using the electric range when the power went off. And since there was no power . . . he had not thought to turn off the burner that he had been cooking on. Unfortunately that was the burner on which he had placed the Coleman gas stove. You've already guessed it. The power returned, the burner on the electric stove came on, and the Coleman gas stove sitting on the electric range went off—literally. The stove's gas canister exploded, blowing the kitchen wall two feet off the foundation, snapping several floor joists, and smashing every window in the house. The explosion caused $65,000 in damage. Don't worry. J. R. was safe. Fortunately, he had closed his bedroom door. (1)

Can somebody tell me the Scout motto? That's right . . . be prepared . . . in this case, thoroughly prepared. If you skip one little detail . . . well . . . you're in trouble.

A 36-year-old carpenter in Vancouver, British Columbia named William will testify to that. William hoped to become a stunt man. William knew that movie people were jetting in from all over the world that year for the Vancouver Film Festival. He decided to catch their attention by bungee jumping off Vancouver's Lions Gate Bridge. He could see himself gracefully descending to the deck of a passing cruise ship, and disengaging himself from the bungee cable as smoothly as James Bond, to the awe of the ship's passengers. When word got around, producers would marvel at his work, and discuss over cocktails who would hire him for their next film.

William planned his stunt for over two years, checking the height of the tides, boat schedules, and deck layouts. He even lined up sponsors and recruited assistants.

The stunt began perfectly. William took a swan dive off the bridge, trailing the bungee cord behind him. He felt it grow taut as it stretched and began to slow his descent. The tennis court of the cruise ship drew nearer. And nearer. And nearer . . .

Somehow William had miscalculated the length of his bungee cord. Subsequently, he slammed into the tennis court, hurtled into a volleyball net, bounced against a deck railing, and found himself flying once more into the air, watching the cruise ship sail away.

Don't worry. William survived. Although he had failed to make his James Bond entrance, "People on the boat loved it," he told a reporter. "They were screaming, yelling, waving." A witness, however, described the reaction as "shrieks of horror."

When the stunt was over, William dangled above the water for a few minutes, confirming that no bones were broken, and making a mental note to use a shorter bungee cord next time. William is still waiting to hear from the movie producers. (2)

The scout motto is correct. Be prepared—be thoroughly prepared.

Jesus told a parable about the kingdom of God. It concerned some young women who were part of a wedding party. Ten bridesmaids, he said, took their lamps and went to meet the bridegroom. But only five of the bridesmaids were wise enough to fill their lamps with oil. Only five of them were prepared. So when the bridegroom was delayed, five of the ten bridesmaids ran out of oil and had to go buy some more.

The bridegroom came, of course, while they were gone, and the bridesmaids who were prepared went in with him to the wedding feast. When the five who had gone to buy more oil returned, they found the door to the wedding feast locked. They had missed the feast because they were not prepared. "Therefore keep watch," the Master said, "because you do not know the day or the hour." That is not simply a good idea. It is a direct command from our Lord. Keep watch. Be prepared.

Life is full of the unexpected. Sometimes, no matter how carefully we've planned ahead, life sneaks up behind us and smacks us on the head.

In one of Bill Waterson's cartoon series, Calvin and Hobbes, Calvin enters the living room one morning dressed in a large space helmet, a long cape, a flashlight in one hand and a baseball bat in the other.

"What's up today?" asks his mother looking at his extraordinary costume.

"Nothing so far," Calvin answers.

"So far?" she questions.

"Well, you never know," replies Calvin. "Something could happen today."

As Calvin leaves—his mother starts thinking about Calvin's helmet, the cape, the flashlight and the baseball bat. The final caption shows her thinking, "I need a suit like that!" (3)

We all need a suit like that. Life sends us challenges. We often call these "learning experiences." That doesn't mean they don't hurt. We learn all right, but we take our lumps. That's life. You better be prepared.

One of the best examples of a mother preparing her young for the ups and downs of life comes from Gary Richmond's book, A View from the Zoo. In chapter one Richmond gives us an amazing look at the birth of a baby giraffe.

Now here's the first thing you need to recognize—giraffes have long legs—very long legs. The body of a mother giraffe is some ten feet from the ground and she does not lower her body when she gives birth. When a calf is born, he immediately falls ten feet to the ground and lands on his back. Ten feet is a long way to fall. What a way to come into the world. Then after falling on its back, the newborn calf rolls over on his stomach with his legs tucked under him. At this point the mother giraffe does something extraordinary. She waits about a minute and then she kicks the newborn calf head over heels and sends it sprawling. Talk about tough love. If the baby giraffe doesn't immediately get up on its legs, she kicks it again, and again. Finally, the little giraffe stands for the first time on its very wobbly legs. He's now ready to follow her and the rest of the herd.

Please understand. The mother giraffe is not being cruel to her baby. Quite the contrary! She knows that lions and hyenas and leopards would love to make a meal of a baby giraffe. So, she needs her baby calf to get to its feet as quickly as possible so that it can keep up with the herd. Kicking him is her way of protecting her young one from predators.

Sometimes we may also feel as though life has no sooner gotten us to our feet when it turns around and suddenly knocks us back down. The next time that happens to you, think about the newborn giraffe. Life may simply be strengthening us for an unknown future. (4)

Life is full of the unexpected. None of us is totally prepared, but it is important that we do all we can. We live in a very fragile world. Life itself is very fragile. The parent of every teenager with a driver's license is aware of the risk involved. Many of us in the middle and later years of life are becoming aware of friends who are dying untimely deaths because of cancer and heart attacks. And we wonder, could I be next?

Life is fragile. Nowadays, family relationships are fragile. One out of every two marriages ends in divorce. About one-half of our nation's children live in homes with one biological parent absent. Life is fragile. Family life is fragile. There are no guarantees of success or happiness for any of us. We need to be prepared for whatever life may send us. "Keep watch," the Master said, "because you do not know the day or the hour."

We are certainly not prepared for Christ's return. That is what our lesson is about—Christ's return to earth at the end of time. We have no idea when that may be, of course. It may be thousands of years away, or it may be today. Still, Christ tells us to be prepared. Be prepared to give an account of your life.

I heard of one man who was prepared, at least in one respect. His name was Jan Christian Smuts. He was a statesman in the early days of the Republic of South Africa.

Smuts was nearing retirement when a French journalist approached him about writing the story of his life. Smuts agreed.

At the interview Smuts stood up, looked at the journalist, and said, "Here is my library, my files, my records, my diary. It is all for you to examine."

Startled, the writer said, "But, sir, you don't really mean that I can go through all of your records. Surely you have some secrets."

"No," General Smuts replied, "there are no secrets." (5)

Wouldn't that be a wonderful thing to be able to say about your life? "No secrets." We would all sleep better at night; we would have healthier marriages, healthier hearts, healthier lives—if only we could say with Jan Christian Smuts, "There are no secrets."

Of course there will be a time when all secrets will be revealed.

Author Peter Graystone recalls a conversation that he had with a friend on a subway when he was 16. He and his friend were bored and started whispering to one another about their fellow passengers—trying to guess what each one did for a living based entirely on their appearance. As the train drew into the station a middle aged woman walked the length of the train and came directly to where they were sitting. "You are wrong," she said as she passed. "I actually teach children who are deaf how to lip read." (6)

Whoa. They learned a lesson in a hurry. They thought no one would guess what they were doing, but one woman did. She read lips. Better be careful who's listening— even if they are not within range of the sound of your voice. There will be a time when all secrets will be revealed. Of course, there is One before whom no secrets are ever hidden. Are you prepared to give an accounting to the One before Whom the secrets of all hearts are disclosed?

Be prepared. Watch and be ready. Life is fragile. Ultimately there are no secrets. But there is another perspective concerning watching and waiting—we are to watch with a positive anticipation.

Soon our children will be waiting and watching with great expectancy for Santa. They are not waiting with fear and dread. They are waiting with joyful hearts.

It troubles me that so many Christians look toward the future with doubt and dread. Of course, Christians are not unique in this respect.

There was an item in The Washington Post years ago that I found amusing. It seems a religious campaign was being waged in Jerusalem at that time by very conservative Jews against women's wigs. "Ultra-Orthodox" Jews declared that a wig is an insufficient covering for the head of a married woman and that a woman wearing a wig is "preparing herself for hell," in the words of one public slogan. Another wall message announced, "When the Messiah comes, the first thing he will do is eliminate the wig."

That's absurd, but we need to understand that Christians can be just as silly. In fact, there is so much silliness and so many scare tactics surrounding portrayals of the Second Coming of Christ that it is difficult to take them seriously. Many of the books and films that purportedly picture Christ's return are clearly intended to scare believers into repentance. Well, we do need to repent. We do need to clean up our lives, but the coming of the Lord, whether at Christmas or at Christ's return on the last day ought to be something Christ's followers look forward to. We ought to be like little children whose father loves them very much, but has gone on a long business trip. Now they can't wait for their Daddy to come home. We wait not with fear, but with faith.

The point is to be prepared. Be prepared so that if you dropped dead this moment, you would have nothing to apologize for. Be prepared so if you were offered the biggest promotion in your life, you would be ready to step into your new role. Be prepared so that if some tragedy entered your life, you would be able to ride out the storm, because your prayer life was rich and you knew you had a Friend. Be prepared.

Harold Ivan Smith in his book No Fear of Trying tells a fascinating story about how battleships from World War II like the Iowa, and the New Jersey, and the Wisconsin, were put into mothballs. These ships, weighing 58,000 tons, with seventeen inches of armor and superior speed, helped America win that war.

"In an era of the modern navy, the ships were deemed out-dated and were drydocked. As the boilers cooled, the network of hundreds of miles of pipes were drained. Fuel and all flammable liquids were siphoned out. Motors were cleaned thoroughly; pumps were filled with preservative chemicals.

"All openings were covered with sealants or metal hatches to prevent moisture from entering. Winches, machinery, and any moving parts were covered in airtight igloos. Dehumidifiers were installed throughout the ships. Some critics fumed that it would have been cheaper to have sunk them.

"For twenty-five years these mothballed relics were monitored by the U.S. Navy's Ship Maintenance Facility staff, specialists in the art of preserving ships.

"Then the Reagan administration called for an immediate increase in the size of the Navy, and the ships were recommissioned. Immediately these ships that had been dry-docked had to be made sea-worthy. But listen, the specialists who had been looking after them knew what they were doing. When senior staff boarded the Iowa, they said it was as if the ship's crew had merely gone on weekend leave. Duty schedules, posted twenty-five years earlier, had not even yellowed in the dark, cool air." (7)

The ships were ready to go about their business. Are you that prepared for both the challenges and the opportunities that life will send you? Are you ready to stand before God and give an account of your life? "Therefore keep watch, because you do not know the day or the hour . . ." Be prepared. It's the smart thing to do.

1. Wendy Northcutt, The Darwin Awards 4 (New York: Penguin Group, 2006), pp. 213-214.

2. DarwinAwards.com © 1994 – 2005. AP, cnn.com. Cited by WITandWISDOM.

3. Dr. Dan L. Flanagan, http://www.asiweb.com/community/churches/stpaulsumc-sermons/Nor-12-5-99.asp.

4. (Dallas: Word Publishing, 1987), pp. 15-17.

5. Wilson O. Weldon, Not Afraid! (Nashville: The Upper Room, 1984).

6. Jim Pye, http://www.sermonsplus.co.uk/Ephesians%205.15 20.htm.

7. Jim Stewart, "Navy's Sleeping Giants Awaken to a New World," Atlanta Constitution, May 26, 1987, 1-A. Cited in Harold Ivan Smith, No Fear of Trying (Nashville: Thomas Nelson Publishers, 1988), pp. 8-9.

How Big Of A Risk Would You Take?
Matthew 25:14-30

Are you a risk taker? Do you know someone who is?

A young man enlisted in the 82nd Airborne Division. He was assigned to their jump school. He eagerly asked his recruiter what he could expect at jump school.

"Well," the recruiter said, "it's three weeks long."

"What else?" asked the young soldier.

"The first week they separate the men from the boys," the recruiter said. "The second week, they separate the men from the fools."

"And the third week?" the soldier asked.

"The third week," the recruiter said with a grin, "the fools jump." (1)

Does jumping from an airplane appeal to you? Are you one of the fools?

Or are you more like the six-foot eight-inch young man who applied for a job as a lifeguard? He stepped to the counter and announced, "I'm here about the lifeguard job."

The recruiter asked, "Can you swim?"

The six-foot-eight applicant replied, "No, but I can wade pretty far out!" (2)

At six-foot-eight he might be able to do that without taking too much of a risk.

I'm amazed at some of the risks young people are taking nowadays with so-called extreme sports. There was a young guy not too long ago, a skateboarder, who jumped over the Great Wall of China. He became the first person in history to clear the wall without motorized aid.

Thirty-year-old Danny Way missed his first try, but then completed the jump across the 61-foot gap four times. On his last three attempts, he added 360-degree spins. His effort was made possible by the "mega ramp," a gigantic structure that he built near his home in Southern California.

"I was aware of the dangers," Way said, "and my heart was pumping in my chest the whole time." Several thousand people, including China's minister of extreme sports, gathered to witness the spectacle at the wall's Ju Yong Guan Gate near Beijing. (3)

That's amazing to me . . . first of all that he was successful ...and secondly, that he would take such a risk in the first place. How about you? How big of a risk are you willing to take?

Jesus once told a parable about a man who was going on a journey. Before going on that journey, the man . . . obviously a very wealthy man . . . called his servants and entrusted his wealth to them. To one servant he gave five bags of gold. Let's see, at the current price of gold that would be a considerable amount of money. Someone has estimated it would total about two and one-half million dollars. To another servant he gave two bags of gold, worth about one million dollars, and to another servant he gave one bag, worth a half-million dollars. He gave to each of the servants, says Jesus, according to his ability. Then the wealthy man went on his journey.

Well, you know the story. The man who received five bags of gold went at once and put his money to work and gained five bags more. I don't know where he got that kind of return. We need to find out who his financial advisor was.

So also, the one with two bags of gold gained two more. But the man who had received one bag, dug a hole in the ground and hid his master's money . . . in the ground! This was quite a common practice, by the way, in that part of the world for people who did not trust banks. Remember the man in another of Jesus' parables who is digging in a field and finds a treasure buried there. This may well have been some person's life savings that they had buried in that field and never retrieved.

After some time, the master of the servants returned to settle accounts. The man who had received five bags went first. "Master," he said, "you entrusted me with five bags of gold. See, I have gained five more."

His master was delighted. "Well done, good and faithful servant!" he said. "You have been faithful with a few things; I will put you in charge of many things. Come and share your master's happiness!"

The man with two bags came. "Master," he said, "you entrusted me with two bags of gold; see, I have gained two more."

Again his master replied, "Well done, good and faithful servant! You have been faithful with a few things; I will put you in charge of many things. Come and share your master's happiness!"

Then the man who had received one bag came. Can't you see him shuffling forward with his eyes downcast, afraid to look his master in the eye?

"Master," he sort of mumbles, "I knew that you are a hard man, harvesting where you have not sown and gathering where you have not scattered seed. So I was afraid and went out and hid your gold in the ground. See, here is what belongs to you."

Let me pause here. If you had never heard this parable before, how would you expect the master to feel? He had entrusted his wealth to his three servants. Two of them had not only protected that with which they had been entrusted, but they had doubled it. Now this third servant is asked to account for his stewardship. And he is forced to announce that he had buried his master's wealth in the ground and had not added an ounce to what he had been given. If you had been his boss, how would you feel? Disappointed? Frustrated? Perhaps even angry? Well, you got that right!

His master replied, "You wicked, lazy servant! So you knew that I harvest where I have not sown and gather where I have not scattered seed? Well then, you should have put my money on deposit with the bankers, so that when I returned I would have received it back with interest.

"So take the bag of gold from him and give it to the one who has ten bags. For whoever has will be given more, and they will have an abundance. Whoever does not have, even what they have will be taken from them. And throw that worthless servant outside, into the darkness, where there will be weeping and gnashing of teeth."

This is quite a remarkable parable. So many of Jesus' parables come from real life situations. They are designed to make us think.

Notice, first of all, that the third servant who took his master's gold and buried it in the ground did so because he was afraid. That's a common experience—fear. I wonder how many of us fail to be the people God has called us to be because we are afraid. Some of us are afraid of what other people will think of us. That often happens to us when we're young. We may do things we know we shouldn't do because we want to fit it, we want to be cool.

But it doesn't stop with our teen years. As we get older, we may give an anemic witness to our faith because we don't want our friends to think we're some kind of religious nut. Someone cracks a racist joke. We put on a social smile. We may even give a pleasant chuckle, even though it makes us uncomfortable. We don't want to offend our friends by expressing indignation. We're afraid of what others think. For some people this is the dominating fear in their lives. Some of us are cowards for Jesus.

Mark Twain once said, "It is curious that physical courage should be so common in the world and moral courage so rare."

A rap singer has an interesting way of expressing it. He has "updated" some of the advice given by the book of Ecclesiastes to add these lines: "There's a time to speak up . . . and a time to shut up . . . There's a time to hunker down . . . and a time to go downtown . . . There's a time to talk . . . and a time to walk . . . There's a time to be mellow . . . and a time not to be yellow." (4) Well, he's right. There is a time not to be yellow. The third servant who took his master's gold and buried it in the ground was yellow. He was a coward. He buried his master's wealth because he was afraid.

Notice, in the second place, who the man was afraid of—he was afraid of his master. "I knew that you are a hard man, harvesting where you have not sown and gathering where you have not scattered seed. So I was afraid and went out and hid your gold in the ground. See, here is what belongs to you."

Is there any place in this parable that indicates his master was a hard man? He appears to be a very generous man to me. He entrusted his servants with a considerable amount of money, about four million dollars. When two of the servants doubled their money he praised them lavishly, "Well done, good and faithful servant! You have been faithful with a few things; I will put you in charge of many things. Come and share your master's happiness!"

But this servant was afraid of his master. Why? We don't know, but it happens. I've met people who for some reason or another are afraid of God. They serve a God of vengeance and punishment. They distrust God and because they distrust God, they don't trust other people or life in general. They don't even trust themselves.

I am convinced that the kind of God people have determines how willing they are to risk great things for God. If you are here this morning out of fear, you probably don't enjoy worship very much. You're here because you're afraid that God will punish you if you stay home. No wonder there is so little joy and power to your faith. God is looking for people who love Him and enjoy Him and are willing to do great things for Him.

It's like a story that author Mike Barrett tells. Mike is a dedicated surfer. In his book The Danger Habit Mike tells of taking his six-year-old son, Caleb, surfing for the first time. After months of planning the trip and talking to Caleb about how to surf, and how warm the water is in Hawaii, and how "cool" surfers are in Hawaii, Mike and his son rented a long board off the beach in Waikiki and walked into the water.

They started by lying together on the deck of the ten-foot-long board and paddling out one hundred yards in the ocean. On the way out, Caleb had some questions: "What if I fall? What if we can't catch a wave?" But once they were in position, Caleb was ready. They slowly turned the board around and waited.

When a wave came, Mike started paddling as hard as he could while Caleb got ready to stand up in front of him and surf. Caleb caught on pretty fast. Sometimes he would jump up before they even caught the wave. But when his timing was right, and the wave propelled them toward shore, joy poured out of Caleb's body. It was the most wonderful experience imaginable.

Here's the interesting thing, says Mike—Caleb can't swim. This made Mike's wife a bit nervous. Of course, Mike felt the high stakes were somehow part of what made the experience so thrilling for both of them. Mike is careful to note that the water was crystal clear and only about four feet deep, so if Caleb had slipped off the board, Mike could have easily grabbed him and lifted him to safety. This was not, he says, a Michael Jackson-dangling-his-son-over-the-balcony scene.

The point is that this was a turning point for Caleb. He had ventured into a place of danger with his loving and protective father and emerged from the water alive and changed. From that day on, Caleb has called himself a surfer. (5)

Caleb knew he could trust his Dad and so he could relax and enjoy the experience. Do you trust your Heavenly Father? Do you see God as a loving and protective Parent who will not let you go under? Then why do you have that worried expression on your face? How we see God will determine how vitally we will live out our faith. The third servant hid his gold in the ground because he was afraid. The person of whom he was afraid was his master.

Finally, notice how angry the master was at the man who buried his gold rather than invested it. "Throw that worthless servant outside," said the master, "into the darkness, where there will be weeping and gnashing of teeth."

It's important for us to realize this is a parable and not an allegory. Jesus is not telling us that God is exactly like the wealthy man in this story. I personally don't believe that God is going to toss us into outer darkness for spiritual and moral cowardice. But this parable does make its point quite emphatically—it is a terrible thing to bury the gifts God has given us and not to use them. It is a terrible thing to give in to fear and timidity when God is calling us to stand up against evil. It is a terrible thing to live your life cowering in fear rather than trusting in your Heavenly father. One does not light a lamp and put it under a bushel. Followers of Jesus are to live by faith and not fear.

We get the same message about courage from the movie series, Lord of the Rings. In the first saga of this series titled The Fellowship of the Ring, Frodo and Sam are leaving their beloved shire, a land of streams and valleys and meadows and forests. They are on a journey that will take them to the very ends of the earth, only they don't know that yet. They think they're simply traveling to the next county.

As they cross a field, Sam stops. Frodo stops as well.

"What's the matter, Sam?" asks Frodo.

"If I take one more step," Sam says, "I'll have gone further than I've been before."

Frodo smiles, walks back to him, puts his arm around him and reminds him that it's a dangerous thing, just going out your front door. "And, together, they take the next step, and the next, and the next, into dangers and wonders beyond imagining, into a life that transforms them both. Into life to the fullest." (6) Followers of Jesus live by faith, not by fear. Sometimes that means they go farther than they've ever gone before.

I read recently about a priest in Africa who faked a crime he did not commit and got himself imprisoned so that he could minister to those who needed him most. Do you have that kind of faith? How much are you willing to risk for Jesus?

A former police officer with the Los Angeles Police Department tells how the department would demonstrate to rookie officers the value of the bullet-proof vests they'd been issued. The vests were placed on mannequins and then the officers would fire round after round into the vests. The rookies were asked to check to see if any of the rounds had penetrated the vests. Invariably the vests would pass the test with flying colors. Then the instructor in charge of the demonstration would turn to the rookie officers and ask, "So who wants to wear a vest and let us test how it works on you?" (7)

That's the real test of faith, isn't it? It's one thing to see a mannequin get shot in the chest wearing a vest, it's another when you have to put your life on the line, trusting that same vest. Following Jesus means walking by faith not fear. Following Jesus means trusting God. Following Jesus means seeking to hear the Master say, "Well, done thou good and faithful servant," because we've attempted great things for God. Sure, it involves risk. Every great advance in life does. But the rewards are incredible. How about you? How big of a risk are you willing to take for God?

1. ArcaMax - Jokes, http://tinyurl.com/9kf44.
2. Stan Toler, Lead to Succeed (Kansas City: Beacon Hill Press, 2003).
3. The Week, July 22, 2005.
4. God's Little Devotional Book for Graduates (Tulsa: Honor Books, Inc., 1995), p. 41.
5. Mark Buchanan, Hidden In Plain Sight (Nashville: Thomas Nelson, Inc., 2002), pp. 207-208.
6. (Colorado Springs: Multnomah Publishers, 2006), pp. 33-34.
7. The Very Rev. Sherry Crompton, http://sermons.trinitycoatesville.org/.

The Love Of The Shepherd
Ezekiel 34:11-16

Sheep sometimes have a reputation for being passive and helpless. "Gentle as a lamb," we say. Well, maybe . . . maybe not.

Reuters News Service told of an Egyptian man who had been pushed to his death from a three-story building by a sheep that he was preparing for slaughter. The report noted that many Egyptian city dwellers keep livestock on their rooftops. This particular city dweller had been fattening the sheep in question for months getting it ready for a ritual sacrifice. Before that could happen, however, for some unknown reason the sheep butted the man, knocking him off the roof. Neighbors found him lying bleeding on the ground below. He died soon after reaching the hospital.

It is a tragic story, of course, but it is still odd. A sacrificial sheep mortally wounding the man who was going to sacrifice him. It is ironic, but not entirely unique.

About that same time, a Bedouin shepherd also in Egypt was shot in the chest and killed when one of his flock jogged his loaded shotgun as he slept. Afterward, police seized the gun, which was not licensed. I believe the moral here has more to do with keeping your eye on a loaded weapon than it has to do with the nature of sheep. Still, it's rather odd.

Research in New Zealand, which is famous for having more sheep than people, has shown that one-third of farmers there have been seriously injured in attacks by sheep, often being charged from behind and receiving damaged knees and broken vertebrae.

Meanwhile, in England a twenty-eight year old parachutist named Alison Pearson made a 13,500-foot drop from an airplane without incident—except that she landed in a field full of sheep. A ewe in that field panicked at Alison's sudden arrival and attacked her. Allison received serious chest injuries from being charged by a sheep.

Finally, in Wales, gangs of sheep from the local hills have taken to hanging out in the car-park of the ASDA supermarket. I'm not making this up. According to news reports, these sheep menace customers in order to get fed. Flocks of them follow people to their cars and nose about in the trunk as groceries are being loaded. They are particularly fond of fresh cakes and French bread, although ice cream is also popular. (1)

I'll bet you didn't know that sheep like ice cream. Here's something that is important—not only aren't sheep as passive and helpless as we have supposed, sheep also have an undeserved reputation for being dumb, says a British behavioral scientist named Keith Kendrick.

Kendrick's team found that sheep can recognize as many as 50 other sheep for up to two years. This means that sheep have a reasonable amount of intelligence. Kendrick suggests that they may have similar abilities in many ways to humans. (2)

These thoughts about sheep might help us focus our attention today on these words from our Old Testament lesson from Ezekiel. Ezekiel writes, "For this is what the Sovereign Lord says: 'I myself will search for my sheep and look after them. As a shepherd looks after his scattered flock when he is with them, so will I look after my sheep. I will rescue them from all the places where they were scattered on a day of clouds and darkness. I will bring them out from the nations and gather them from the countries, and I will bring them into their own land. I will pasture them on the mountains of Israel, in the ravines and in all the settlements in the land. I will tend them in a good pasture, and the mountain heights of Israel will be their grazing land. There they will lie down in good grazing land, and there they will feed in a rich pasture on the mountains of Israel. I myself will tend my sheep and have them lie down, declares the Sovereign Lord. I will search for the lost and bring back the strays. I will bind up the injured and strengthen the weak . . .'"

Notice how intimate the relationship is between sheep and the Shepherd in this passage. "I myself will search for my sheep and look after them. As a shepherd looks after his scattered flock when he is with them, so will I look after my sheep." Here the sheep is Israel and the Shepherd is, of course, God.

Notice how devoted the shepherd is to his sheep. God really cares about His people. That's a good thing to know. God really does care.

A national church executive, The Rev. Ronald Glusenkamp, tells what it means to him that the Shepherd cares for His sheep. He says he can remember standing in the hallway of the church that he and his family were members of during his childhood.

At one particular place in the hallway of that church, there was a large picture of Jesus as the Good Shepherd. In the picture Jesus carried a little lamb and connected to Jesus, the Good Shepherd, by flowing ribbons were lots of other little lambs. In fact, the picture carried all the names of this particular congregation who were under the age of three years. It was a cradle roll. The little boy lambs were connected by blue ribbons, and the little girl lambs were connected by pink ribbons. As a little boy, this church executive remembers standing there, finding his name and knowing that he belonged, that he was loved because he was one of Jesus' little lambs, that all of them were connected to Jesus and connected to each other. They belonged. They were loved. (3)

Some of you can relate to that. You remember in your childhood seeing a picture like that, too . . . the Good Shepherd holding a little lamb in his arms . . . and you knew that you were that lamb. What a picture of security and well-being!

The scriptures are full of images of the Good Shepherd. "The Lord is my Shepherd, I shall not want . . ." Psalm 23 has given comfort to millions of believers through the ages, through good times and bad. In John 10, Jesus uses that same imagery. He says, "I am the good shepherd. The good shepherd lays down his life for the sheep . . ." (v. 11) Then later in that same chapter we read, "My sheep listen to my voice; I know them, and they follow me . . ." (v. 27)

Author Os Hillman tells about a friend of his who was visiting Israel with some other Christian friends. They were in an agricultural area visiting some of the famous Biblical sites when they came near a group of sheepherders. There was a round pen used to bring the sheep in for the night. They watched toward the end of the day as a shepherd brought his flock into the pen. Then, a few minutes later, another shepherd brought his flock into the same pen. Then, a few minutes later, yet another shepherd brought his sheep into the pen.

Now there were three groups of sheep in the same pen with no identifying marks on any of them. His friend wondered how in the world they would separate their sheep the next day.

The next morning a shepherd came over to the pen and made a sound to his sheep. One by one the sheep filed out to follow him. Only his sheep followed his voice. The other sheep waited patiently. Hillman's friend said it was an amazing scene to see—the sheep recognized their shepherd's voice and followed him while the other sheep remained in the pen. (4) "My sheep listen to my voice," said Jesus. "I know them, and they follow me . . ."

That's like an experience that Dennis Covington tells about. He recalls what it was like as a child being called home. He describes it this way, "It's late afternoon at the lake. The turtles are moving closer to shore. The surface of the water is undisturbed. Most of the children in my neighborhood are called home by their mothers. They open the back doors, wipe their hands on their aprons and yell 'Willie!' or 'Joe!' or 'Ray!' Either that or they use a bell, bolted to the door frame and loud enough to start the dogs barking in backyards all along the street.

"But," says Dennis Covington, "I was always called home by my father and he didn't do it in the customary way. He walked down the alley all the way to the lake. If I was close, I could hear his shoes on the gravel before he came in sight. If I was far, I would see him across the surface of the water, emerging out of the shadows and into the gray light. He would stand with his hands in the pockets of his windbreaker while he looked for me. This is how he got me to come home. He always came to the place where I was before he called my name." (5) Isn't that a beautiful picture? "He always came to the place where I was before he called my name."

Most of us can think back to our childhood when someone called our name and we knew we were loved. We knew that someone cared about us, that we were important to them. That very fact gave our lives meaning. It still gives us a sense of identity even today.

The picture of God in the Old Testament, particularly in the prophets vacillates between warnings and promises. But here in the book of Ezekiel, we find this beautiful picture of God's love. "I myself will tend my sheep and have them lie down, declares the Sovereign Lord. I will search for the lost and bring back the strays. I will bind up the injured and strengthen the weak . . ."

This is who God is, Ezekiel is saying to us—God loves us in an intimate and personal way. We can find that kind of God a few places in the Hebrew Scriptures, most notably in the prophets. However, it took the coming of Jesus to show just how much God loves us, not only as a Good Shepherd, but also as a loving Parent. It took the coming of Jesus for us to know that we could call God, "Abba—Daddy." This is really who God is. God cares for us more than we can imagine. This is the unique message of the Christian faith.

A young American woman was visiting China for the first time. She stood one morning in Canton in the midst of a Buddhist temple. The guide had told the party that this was the "House of 10,000 Buddhas," and it was easy to believe he had not exaggerated.

The girl stared at the countless carved wooden faces, some of which were hideous and most of which were grotesque. Finally she asked, "I have been looking for one that looks like the 'good shepherd,' but I don't see any. Don't they have one that cares?" (6)

This is no disrespect to Buddhism. Buddhism is at heart a philosophy—not a living faith. Theoretically it is possible to be a Buddhist and a Christian. Here is the important thing—do not look to Buddhism to tell you what God is like. It does not pretend to do that. Only Jesus can show us what God is like.

And here is what we learn from Jesus—God loves His sheep so much that He will lay down His life for them. That is what we read in John 10:11: "I am the good shepherd. The good shepherd lays down his life for the sheep . . ." On the surface of it, that sounds absurd. As someone has said, "If it seems foolish to think of a man being willing to die for mere animals, however great his affection for them, remember this. There is a far greater gap between God and human beings than there is between human beings and sheep." (7) It's an extraordinary idea, but this is what Christians believe: The Divine Shepherd lay down his life for His sheep. If that doesn't take your breath away, what will?

I like the way writer Ron Hutchcraft puts it in one of his devotionals. He tells the story of one of the most famous race horses of all time, Seabiscuit. It is set against the backdrop of the Great Depression.

Seabiscuit was the son of a champion but he was not like his father. Seabiscuit had been forced to run with better horses so they would gain confidence by beating him. When he raced, he did what he was trained to do—lose. Because of the poor treatment Seabiscuit received, he became an angry, almost uncontrollable horse. Finally he was given a chance by a trainer many considered to be too old and a jockey many thought to be too big. But Seabiscuit thrived in the care of people who believed in him and became one of the greatest horses of all time. The trainer sees in the horse something others have missed. When Seabiscuit's eventual owner is deciding whether to buy this apparent loser, his trainer says, "You don't throw a life away just because it's been banged up a little." And when the trainer wants to fire the jockey, the owner reminds him, "You don't throw a life away just because it's been banged up a little."

After telling Seabiscuit's story Ron Hutchcraft says, "Maybe you're one of those 'banged up lives.' You've been treated poorly, you've been made to feel that you never measure up, that you're a loser, people have undervalued you ... But there is someone who has never thrown away a banged up life, who sees beyond what's on the outside to the wounds on the inside and the potential He built into you when He made you. Jesus is your hope of a new beginning where the future does not have to be just an extension of a broken past. In Isaiah 61:1 ... the Bible says of Jesus, 'The Lord ... has sent Me to bind up the brokenhearted, to proclaim freedom for the captives and release from darkness for the prisoners ... to provide for those who grieve in Zion—to bestow on them a crown of beauty instead of ashes—a garment of praise instead of a spirit of despair.' Jesus has done that for millions of banged up people for two thousand years. He can do it for you ... The Bible says of his death on the cross: 'He carried our sorrows ... He was pierced for our transgressions, He was crushed for our iniquities ... and by His wounds we are healed' (Isaiah 53:4-5). With someone who loves you so unconditionally, so completely, you don't ever again have to trash yourself, trash other people, or trash your future. You can tear up that name tag that identifies you as 'victim' and replace it with the new identity Jesus gives you—'child of the King.' ... Jesus, God's one and only Son, sacrificed Himself to become the ultimate banged up life for you. However much you have been betrayed, you can trust Him. However much you have been hurt and rejected, you can count on His 'never leave you' love. And your new beginning can start this very day." (8)

What a wonderful description of God's love. We began this message with a story of a shepherd being sent to his death by a sacrificial lamb. What defies all logic is to imagine a Shepherd willingly and knowingly becoming a sacrificial lamb. And as the writer said, "There is a far greater gap between God and human beings than there is between human beings and sheep." But that is the good news for the day: God really does love you that much. The Shepherd lay down his life for His sheep.

1. Exploding Pigs compiled by Ian Simmons, Barnes & Noble Books, New York, 1997, pp. 9-10.
2. Reuters.
3. http://www.day1.net/index.php5?view=transcripts&tid=126.
4. One Flock, One Shepherd. Cited by Monday Fodder, dgaufaaa@iohk.com.
5. Salvation On Sand Mountain, Cited by in a sermon on the Internet by Steve Hyde.
6. A Treasury of Bible Illustrations, compiled by Ted Kyle and John Todd, AMG Publishers, Chattanooga, 1995, p. 231.
7. Richards, Lawrence O. The 365-Day Devotional Commentary (Colorado Springs: ChariotVictor, 1990), pp. 784-785.
8. Ron Hutchcraft Ministries, Inc., "A Word With You." Subscribe at http://hutchcraft.us1.list-manage.com/subscribe?u=4982b673c348d54cfae116dbb&id=0029706fc2.

Cycle B

Waiting For A Savior
Isaiah 64:1-9 Mark 13: 32-37

Margaret was all ready for her date. She was wearing her best outfit, her hair was fixed, her makeup was perfect. Imagine her disappointment when her date didn't show up! After an hour of waiting, Margaret decided that he wasn't going to come. She changed into her pajamas, washed off her makeup, gathered up a bunch of junk food, and parked herself in front of the television for the evening. As soon as she got involved in her favorite show, there was a knock on the door. She opened it to find her handsome date standing on the doorstep. He stared at her in shock, then said in disbelief, "I'm two hours late, and you're still not ready?" (1)

Welcome on this First Sunday of Advent. This is the Sunday we begin getting ready to celebrate Christ's birth. [The choir is preparing its music, we're in the process of decorating the church, special services have been planned . . .]

It's always amazing to watch our society gear up for the celebration of Christmas. The placement of lights. The playing of carols—even before Thanksgiving. The holiday sales. Even the post office is affected. I remember an old David Letterman line. "Here's some good news out of Washington, D.C.," said Letterman. "The post office says it is ready for the big holiday Christmas crush of mail. They have already placed an order for 10 million new signs that will read: 'This Window Closed.'"

Well, our friends at the U. S. Postal Service do their best, but it's an enormous job to get ready for Christmas. It's an enormous job getting ready for Christmas for many of us. One poor guy says, "I started my Christmas shopping. I shopped at three banks for a loan." Some of you can relate to that. We've barely finished with Thanksgiving and we're already getting ready for Christmas.

Of course, our Jewish friends have spent hundreds, even thousands of years waiting to celebrate the coming of the Messiah. In fact, they're still waiting. They do not believe, as we do, that the Messiah has come in the person of Jesus Christ.

Leo Rosten tells an amusing story that comes out of the Jewish tradition. There was a man in a small Russian village who, because of a disabling condition, could not find employment. The community council wanted to help him but they also wanted to protect his pride. They decided to give him a job. They paid him two rubles a week to sit at the town's entrance and be the first to greet the Messiah when he arrives. "Just sit on the hill outside our village every day from dawn to sunset," they tell him. "You will be our watchman for the approach of the Messiah. And when you see him, run back to the village as fast as you can, shouting, 'The Messiah! The Messiah! He is coming!'"

The man's face lit up just thinking of the glory of his new position.

Every morning he greeted the dawn from the hill and not until sunset every day, did he leave his treasured post.

A year went by, and a traveler, approaching the village, noticed the figure sitting on a hill. "Sholem," called the traveler. "What are you doing here?"

"I am waiting for the Messiah!" the man replied. "It's my job."

The traveler was somewhat amused. "How do you like this job?" he asked, suppressing a smile.

"Frankly, it doesn't pay much," said the poor man, "but it's steady work." (2)

That would be steady work if you did not believe that Jesus was the Messiah—twenty-five hundred years of waiting and watching for the coming of the Lord.

The prophet Isaiah was waiting on the Messiah. He writes these words as he begins the 64th chapter, "Oh, that you would rend the heavens and come down, that the mountains would tremble before you! As when fire sets twigs ablaze and causes water to boil, come down to make your name known to your enemies and cause the nations to quake before you!" (1, 2)

Isaiah lived in a time when the people of Israel were suffering because of their infidelity to God. Isaiah knew that the people could not save themselves. It was too late for that. He cries out, "All of us have become like one who is unclean, and all our righteous acts are like filthy rags; we all shrivel up like a leaf, and like the wind our sins sweep us away. No one calls on your name or strives to lay hold of you; for you have hidden your face from us and have given us over to our sins . . ." (6,7)

He paints a rather stark picture of Israel's current situation. Then, on a gentler note he writes, "Yet you, Lord, are our Father. We are the clay, you are the potter; we are all the work of your hand. Do not be angry beyond measure, Lord; do not remember our sins forever. Oh, look on us, we pray, for we are all your people." (8, 9) Isaiah was waiting for a Savior.

Many people today are waiting for a Savior. Did you know that? And some of them are our neighbors.

Rev. Curt Anderson in a sermon on the Internet compares the plight of these people to the two young lovers in the Broadway musical, West Side Story. As you may remember, West Side Story is based on Shakespeare's classic drama, Romeo and Juliet.

In West Side Story the lovers are Tony, a former member and leader of the street gang, The Jets, and Maria, who has recently arrived in this country from Puerto Rico. Her brother is Bernardo, present leader of the street gang, The Sharks.

Like most recent immigrants to this country, the Puerto Ricans are not accepted by those who already live here; and that animosity is intensified in the conflict between The Jets and The Sharks.

In the midst of that animosity and hatred, Tony and Maria meet and fall in love. Fairly soon after realizing they are in love, they also realize there is no place for their love in the world they live in. And they sing: "There's a place for us, Somewhere a place for us, Peace and quiet and open air, Wait for us, Somewhere. There's a time for us, Someday a time for us, Time together with time to spare, Time to learn, time to care, Someday . . . Somewhere. There's a place for us, A time and place for us. Hold my hand and we're halfway there. Hold my hand and I'll take you there. Somehow . . . Someday . . . Somewhere."

Of course, we all know that in that world, there was not a place for them. Tony is shot by a member of The Sharks as he is running to Maria. He dies in her arms.

And as all this is happening, the music of that song, Somewhere, is playing underneath the action. It gives added poignancy to know that there is no place, no time, no world where their love can exist. Right then, for them, Somewhere is, literally, Nowhere.

But the power of that scene, that movie, is that although that world does not yet exist for them—it could someday, and it will, and we know it. (3)

Somehow . . . Someday . . . Somewhere. The world awaits a Savior. In the same way that Isaiah cried out, "Oh, that you would rend the heavens and come down . . ." many in our world still cry out for a Savior.

The Savior came in the babe of Bethlehem, but still the world waits. That is the meaning of Advent. Advent is the celebration of what has been and what is yet to be. The Savior of all the world came to us in the babe of Bethlehem, but this was simply the beginning of God's redeeming work. A beachhead was established, but the war over evil and darkness still has not been won. That victory will only be complete when the Savior returns and the kingdom of God is established in this world even as it is in heaven.

It is so easy with our comfortable lives to focus on the beauty and the joy of Christmas. It is much more difficult for us to focus on Advent, that season when the world groans with birth pangs as it awaits God's final victory over sin and suffering.

A couple from the United States spent some time serving as missionaries in one of the former Soviet republics. They were caring for children in an orphanage and, like anyone who has been involved in ministry with such kids, they were simply overwhelmed by the tragedy of so many children who'd been abandoned.

On one occasion this missionary couple was teaching the children about Christmas. They told them all about Mary and Joseph, the shepherds and wise men, and about the baby Jesus. They told them all about the stable, the manger, and the star in the sky. They told them all about God's love for the world embodied in the birth of Jesus. And after teaching the children the Christmas story, this couple invited them to draw some pictures of the manger scene.

All of the pictures were wonderful! But one in particular caught their attention. It was drawn by a little boy named Misha. And what made Misha's drawing distinctive was that there was not one, but two babies lying in the manger.

"Misha, what a wonderful picture!" said the woman missionary. "But who is the other baby in the manger with the baby Jesus?"

Misha looked up with a lovely expression on his face. "The other baby is Misha," he smiled.

"Oh? How is it that you added yourself to the manger scene?" she asked.

And this is what Misha said. "When I was drawing the picture of the baby Jesus, Jesus looked at me and said, 'Misha, where is YOUR family?' I said to Jesus, 'I have no family.' Then Jesus said to me, 'Misha, where is your home?' And I said to Jesus, 'I have no home.' And then Jesus said to me, 'Misha, you can come and be in my family and live in my home.'" (4)

That's a lovely story, and we are so thankful that Misha was introduced to Jesus. But do you understand that two thousand years after the coming of Christ, millions of children come from situations like Misha's? They are still awaiting a Savior. You'll find them in the former Soviet Union. You'll find them in Afghanistan. You'll find them in Africa. You'll find them in the gang-ridden neighborhoods of our inner cities. You'll find them right here in our own community.

Of course, it is our responsibility to reach out to these little ones, to show them the love of Jesus, but the truth of the matter is that, for the most part, they are forgotten this Advent season. Their only hope is that Christ will return and usher in the kingdom promised in Scripture, a world where there will be no more suffering, no more pain; where people will live in peace and harmony, where in Isaiah's beautiful imagery, "The wolf will live with the lamb, the leopard will lie down with the goat, the calf and the lion and the yearling together; and a little child will lead them (Isaiah 11:6-9)." Do you not hear the cry of these little ones? "Oh, that you would rend the heavens and come down . . ." The Savior has come, but much of the world still awaits a Savior.

Here is the promise of scripture: Christ will return and truly the day will come when no child will be left behind. There will someday be peace and justice in this world. Sin and suffering shall cease. It is the promise of Scripture that one day the nations of the world will beat their "swords into plowshares and their spears into pruning hooks" (Isaiah 2:4).

Dr. Tom Long tells about the congregation he is a part of in Atlanta, GA. It is a Presbyterian church across the street from the state Capitol. Homeless people mill around outside the doors of the beautiful gothic structure that houses this congregation. Fortunately, this is a caring church and some of the homeless have found a spiritual home in the church. They have become a part of the worshipping community.

But others living on the streets will not come inside. They distrust any institution. They prefer their current circumstances. So, when these homeless would not come to them, the church decided to go to the homeless. One of the associate pastors took her guitar and moved out on the sidewalk to have worship services on the street for the people who would not come inside. And the homeless responded to this unique outdoor ministry.

It was just before Lent when this pastor to the homeless announced that on the upcoming Wednesday in the small chapel of their church they were going to have a very special service. In this service, she explained, the pastor would be taking the ashes of some palm branches and making a cross on the forehead of people in the service and they would, in turn, make the cross on the forehead of their fellow worshippers, until everyone was marked with the cross of Jesus on their face. Remember, she was speaking to people who had resisted coming inside the church, but something about how she explained this Ash Wednesday service evidently struck a positive chord with her homeless congregation. When the Ash Wednesday service came about sixty of them crowded inside the little chapel for the service.

Coincidentally, a member of the Georgia legislature across the street invited his colleagues to participate in the church's Ash Wednesday service as well, and about forty of them showed up. Can you see the scene? Forty men and women from the State legislature and other members of this prominent church crowded into this small chapel, rubbing shoulders with sixty homeless people. Can you see them taking the palm ashes and placing them on one another's foreheads in the name of Christ? To Tom Long, this was a preview of how things will be in the Kingdom of God. (5)

This is what Advent is really about. It's not about lights and carols, and buying presents. True, it is about preparing ourselves to celebrate the birth of the Savior more than two thousand years ago, but it is also about preparing ourselves and our world for the Savior's return at the end of days when things in this world will be set right. No one knows when that day will be, but I do know this, the cries of God's children will not forever be unanswered. "Oh, that you would rend the heavens and come down . . ." Our Savior has come down in the manger of Bethlehem, and he is coming again to answer the cries of his children for peace and justice and the end of all suffering and pain.

1. Steve Barry, "Life in these United States," Reader's Digest, Oct. 1992, p. 82. Contributed by Dr. John Bardsley.
2. Leo Rosten, The Joys of Yinglish (New York: McGraw Hill Publishing Company, 1992).
3. http://www.firstcongmadison.org/sites/firstcongmadison.org/files/uploads/sermons/pdf/srm112810_0.pdf.
4. Martin C. Singley, III, http://www.tellicochurch.org/Year%20B%20Sermons/ 021224.html.
5. I had the privilege of hearing Tom Long tell this story in a worship service

The Missing Figure In The Nativity Scene
Mark 1: 1-8

A three-year-old was helping his mother unpack their nativity set. He announced each piece as he unwrapped it from the tissue paper. "Here's the donkey!" he said. "Here's a king and a camel!"

When he finally got to the tiny infant lying in a manger he proclaimed, "Here's baby Jesus in his car seat!"

Well, it wasn't a car seat, but that would be an easy mistake to make, wouldn't it?

We all love nativity scenes. Baby Jesus in the manger . . . Mary and Joseph hovering reverently over the holy child . . . shepherds, wise men, assorted cattle, sheep and camels . . . and, of course, a donkey.

But, as someone has noted, there is always one person missing from these nativity scenes. "Correct me if I am wrong," writes the Rev. Darrik Acre, "for I imagine that collectively we have seen a tremendous amount of Christmas displays. So if you have found him somewhere, please let me know. But have you ever seen John the Baptist in any of the nativity scenes? He would be this hairy, unkempt, wild-looking guy wearing camel's hair. There would be a piece of locust caught between his teeth and dried honey in his beard. Louder than any Santa says, 'Ho, ho, ho,' you would hear the automated voice of John the Baptist screaming, 'The kingdom of heaven is near.' Has anyone noticed a figure like that in any of the nativity scenes that are traditional to our celebration of Christmas?" (1)

Well, no. At least, I've never seen a nativity scene featuring John the Baptist. Yet, on the second Sunday of Advent, we always encounter this strange lonely figure sounding his message out in the wilderness, "Prepare the way for the Lord."

The Gospels give us a rough outline of John's life. According to Luke, John was Jesus' second cousin. John also was the product of a miraculous birth. His parents were both quite elderly when John was born.

According to Luke's account, before the angel Gabriel was dispatched to the Virgin Mary, he first appeared to an elderly priest named Zachariah. At the time, Zachariah was in the temple performing his priestly functions. Gabriel told Zachariah that he and his wife Elizabeth would have a son, even though she was far past normal child-bearing age. Zachariah became literally speechless at this announcement. His speech did not return until he named his newborn son, John.

John the Baptist came from good stock. Both Zachariah and Elizabeth were of priestly lineage. Elizabeth was about six months pregnant, when her much younger cousin Mary came to her and announced that she also had conceived a child, but this child was of the Holy Spirit. Elizabeth's unborn child "jumped for joy" in her womb at Mary's announcement. So John the Baptist's birth was a very special event just as Jesus' birth was very special.

We know nothing of John's childhood, but we have a very vivid picture of him as an adult. He was a preacher of justice and righteousness, who called people to a baptism of repentance. And people poured out of Jerusalem to hear John preach his austere message. Among those who came to John to be baptized was his cousin Jesus. The Gospel of Matthew tells us that John was reluctant to baptize Jesus. "I need to be baptized by you," he said. Jesus persuaded John to baptize him nonetheless (Matthew 3:13-15).

The scriptures are also very clear about John's role in the drama of the nativity. John was to prepare the way for the coming of Christ. According to Luke 1:17 John's role was "to turn the hearts of the fathers to the children, and the disobedient to the wisdom of the just; to make ready a people prepared for the Lord."

There are several passages within the Old Testament which are prophetic of John the Baptist in this role. These include Malachi 3:1 that refers to a prophet who would prepare the way of the Lord: "Behold, I will send my messenger, and he shall prepare the way before me . . ."

The Jews of Jesus' day expected Elijah to come before the Messiah; indeed, some modern Jews continue to await Elijah's coming. This is why the disciples asked Jesus in Matthew 17:10, "Why then do the teachers of the law say that Elijah must come first?" Jesus tells his disciples that Elijah has already come in the person of John the Baptist. This was John's role—to prepare the way.

Some of you are old enough to remember when President Nixon made his historic visit to the People's Republic of China in 1972. Up until the 1970s, few major nations recognized the legitimacy of that nation's communist government. Nixon's visit had considerable political peril for the United States, since it risked straining relations with the Soviet Union, Japan, and Taiwan which thought of itself as the real government of China.

Someone had to go before Nixon to lay the groundwork for his visit. That someone was U.S. Secretary of State Henry Kissinger. In 1971 Kissinger held secret talks with China and he visited there in October 1971 and February 1972 to continue laying the groundwork for Nixon's visit. The details to be worked out were staggering. Kissinger did his job well and history was made. (2) Today China is one of our most important business partners, and while China is not as open and progressive as we would like it to be, it is not nearly as threatening militarily as we thought it might be.In much the same way that Henry Kissinger prepared the way for President Nixon, John the Baptist prepared the way for Christ.

John's message was one of righteousness and justice. John's message was much more austere than that of Christ, but it was necessary. People needed to know what was at stake before they could be receptive to the work of a Redeemer.

One writer compares the work of John the Baptist to that of a doctor named

Ignaz Phillip Semmelweis, today known as the "savior of mothers."

In 1818, Semmelweis was born into a world of dying women—particularly women dying in the act of childbirth. The finest hospitals lost one out of six young mothers to a scourge known as "childbed fever." And here's why.

A doctor's daily routine began in the dissecting room where he performed autopsies. From there he made his way to the hospital to examine expectant mothers . . . without ever pausing to wash his hands. Semmelweis was the first man in history to associate such examinations with resultant infection and death in maternity wards. His own practice was to wash with a chlorine solution, and after eleven years and the delivery of 8,357 babies, he lost only 184 mothers—about one in fifty which was a miniscule number in that day of primitive medical practices.

Semmelweis spent the vigor of his life lecturing and debating with his colleagues. Once he argued, "The fever is caused by decomposed material conveyed to a wound . . . I have shown how it can be prevented. I have proved all that I have said. But while we talk, talk, talk, gentlemen, women are dying. I am not asking anything world shaking. I am asking you only to wash . . . For God's sake, wash your hands."

But virtually no one believed him—in spite of the fact that various studies showed that hand-washing reduced mortality to below 1%. Doctors and midwives had been delivering babies for thousands of years without washing, and no outspoken Hungarian was going to change them now! Semmelweis's practice earned widespread acceptance only years after his death, when Louis Pasteur confirmed the germ theory. In 1865, a nervous breakdown (or possibly Alzheimer's) landed Semmelweis in an asylum, where ironically he died of septicemia, at age 47. (3)

Incredible, but that's how we treat our prophets. All he asked people to do was to wash their hands. John the Baptist came telling people to wash themselves as well. He didn't know of ways to protect the physical health of people, but he knew what you must do to protect your spiritual health—wash away your sins. That's what his baptism was all about. You can't prepare the way for the Lord unless you rid yourself of sin.

That's true for us as well as it was for the people who heard John preach. If you have difficulty getting into the Christmas Spirit, look into your heart and see if the problem could be greed, or lust, or anger, or resentment, or guilt. Sin always robs us of our joy regardless of the season.

Evangelist Franklin Graham tells about a woman named Tia Ana who discovered the joy that comes to those who have been washed of their sins. Ana grew up in the capital city of El Salvador. As a young girl, Ana was abused by close family members. She ran away from home at the age of seven. Once on the streets, she had to fight to survive. Eventually she fell into prostitution.

The result of those tragic years as a prostitute made it impossible for Ana to bear a child. As her lifestyle took its toll on her, she became desperate and cried out to God, asking Him to save her from the life she was living. He did, and Tia Ana turned her life over to the Lord and began serving Him.

Ana desperately wanted to have a child, but she knew that would never happen. Again, she sought the Lord and laid her burden before Him. "Lord," she said, "if You will just give me a child, I will raise that child to serve You faithfully." Through the support and encouragement of her church, she began to minister to the people on the streets, in particular the children of prostitutes. In the process, the Lord did bring into her life a little orphan girl, and Ana began raising the child as her very own.

As time passed, Ana realized that there were so many children without parents. She noticed that the daycare centers downtown were closing, especially those that cared for the children of prostitutes, leaving these children to fend for themselves. Ana opened the doors of her home to feed and love these children.

Tia Ana now runs a daycare center that ministers to approximately seventy-five children. Ana told Graham, "I try to give them the most important value of life: To have faith in the Name that is above all names—the Son of the Living God." (4)

Ana had discovered the true joy of Christmas—the love of Jesus Christ reaching out from her heart to others. But first she had to repent from her sin.

You and I need to repent of our sins as well. Our situation is not as desperate as Tia's, but we also have our issues with sin. Perhaps it is the sin of being obsessed with our own needs and concerns. Perhaps it is the sin of being obsessed with materialism and greed. It may consist simply of a blindness to the needs of others.

A Peanuts cartoon strip featured Linus writing a letter to Santa Claus: "Dear Santa, Please don't bother to come to my house this year. I realize that there are many children who will not have a Christmas at all. Go to someone more needy."

Lucy walks by and happens to read the letter. In exasperation she says, "What kind of letter is that?"

Linus responds, "I'm hoping he'll find my attitude particularly refreshing." (5)

Well, I suspect Santa would find it refreshing. That is not where most of us are. And I'm not talking about just children. It's true of adults, too. The more we have, the more we feel we need. And the more we feel we need, the less we feel we have to share with others. And Christmas, ironically, brings out the worst in us. In Jesus' name we go on a hedonistic binge that mocks the Savior born in a stable among the least and the lowest.

I was amused to read a review of a Christmas song that pop singer Cliff Richard released in England a few years back. The song reached the top 10 charts in Great Britain. The lyrics of the song titled, "Savior's Day," reflected Cliff Richard's Christian faith and included lines such as "Life can be yours on Savior's Day—Don't look back or turn away."

A pop magazine reviewed the song. The reviewer wrote these words about

"Savior's Day": "The song is ok," the reviewer said, but "there is no holly, no mistletoe, no wine, no presents around a tree, no Santa. In fact," wrote the reviewer, "this song hasn't got anything to do with Christmas at all." (6)

If that doesn't make you laugh, it will make you cry. What have we done to Christ's birthday? John the Baptist would probably have a few choice words to say about that. In essence, he would tell us to repent. He would tell us to open our hearts to the real meaning of Christmas. He would help us look beyond our own needs to the needs of those less fortunate. "Prepare ye the way of the Lord."

We're all too much like a proud mother, interestingly enough, named Mary. Mary was trying to get her son ready for the church's annual Christmas program. Certain that the whole church clamored for her six-year-old Billy's great talent, she looked forward to teaching him Joseph's part. When he was only selected to play a wise man in the program, she decided he would be the best looking wise man in the program.

Though she had an impossible holiday schedule, Mary frantically finished making the costume, complete with bushy, fake-fur beard.

The pageant was magnificent, especially Billy, and especially all the beautiful carols the children sang. Mary praised Billy to the stars for singing them all.

Then the director announced they were trying to establish a new wardrobe closet where costumes could be accumulated for future pageants. Would the children donate their costume? Mary urged Billy to donate his, which he did. Except for the beard, which he continued to wear. Pressing him to hurry so they could go on to the next thing on their schedule, he refused to give it up. "Why, Billy?" Mary asked.

"Mom," said Billy, "you know those songs in the pageant? I never learned them. With this beard on, I could just move my mouth and nobody knew."

Mary said, thinking of her busy meaningless schedule, "That was when it hit me. I was going through the motions of Christmas when I didn't know the song." (7)

Do you know the real song of Christmas? John the Baptist did. Tia Ana did. Billy's mother Mary did when she stopped long enough to reflect. It's about preparing the way of the Lord by repenting of our sins and opening our hearts to the Lord of love. Are you ready for Christmas? Or do you need to hear the voice of John crying, "Repent"?

1. Preacher's Magazine, http://www.nph.com/nphweb/html/pmol/pastissues/2005%20Advent/webdec4.htm.
2. Ronald L. Nickelson, The NIV Standard Lesson Commentary, 2009-2010. Cincinnati: Standard Publishing, 2009, S. 161.
3. Rev. Adrian Dieleman, http://www.trinitycrc.org/sermons/lk19v42f.html.
4. The Name (Nashville: Thomas Nelson, Inc., 2002), pp. 141-142.
5. "Guilt-Free Praying," by Robert Jeffress, MOODY, September 1995, p. 29.
6. Bud Precise, http://www.blueroof.org/Sermons/sermon122604.htm.
7. Davis Carothers.

Jingle Bells At A Funeral
I Thessalonians 5: 16-18

Dennis Wilson is a backup singer in the country music's unofficial capital, Nashville, Tennessee. In the book Real Country Humor Wilson tells a true story about a friend of his who sings professionally at funerals and weddings.

Sometime back this friend got a call from a lady whose husband had died of a heart attack. She said, "I heard you sing at my cousin's funeral, and I wondered if you'd sing at my husband's funeral. He just died."

Wilson's friend said, "Yes, ma'am, that's what I do. Did you have anything particular in mind?"

She said, "Well, it was so sudden and I'm so upset, I haven't been able to think straight."

"What was something he really liked?" his friend asked, and she finally thought long enough about it to come up with "Jingle Bells."

"Yes, that's it," she said. "He really liked 'Jingle Bells.' Maybe you could sing that one."

His friend thought for a moment and said, "'Jingle Bells' wouldn't be appropriate for a funeral, would it?"

"But that was his favorite song," the woman insisted.

"Okay, then," he said, "I'll do it."

When his friend got there for the funeral, everybody was crying and carrying on—it had been such a sudden death. But he got up and started singing, "Dashing through the snow . . ." People started frowning and giving him dirty looks. He says he could feel the hostility in the air. But he managed to finish the song and sit back down.

After the funeral, the lady came over with the money to pay him for singing. As she handed him the envelope she said in a scolding voice, "I meant the song 'Glory Bells!'—not 'Jingle Bells.'" (1)

"Jingle Bells" at a funeral? Well, maybe. Keep that thought in mind for a few moments.

Christmas is a joyous celebration. You would agree with that, wouldn't you? The Christmas season is a time of great joy. Well, our lesson from the Epistle tells us that all of life should be a joyous celebration. Because the Lord of life has come into our world, every day should be a time of joy. That says to me that we should even be able to sing "Jingle Bells" at a funeral if we understand the Gospel rightly.

I Thessalonians 5, verse 16, only contains two words . . . making it one of the shortest verses in the Bible, but what a perfect verse for the third Sunday in Advent. The words of this short verse are, "Rejoice always." That's clear enough, isn't it? It doesn't say, "Rejoice sometimes." It doesn't say, "Rejoice when times are good and the economy is strong." It doesn't even say, "Rejoice during the Advent-Christmas season." It says simply, "Rejoice always." It could say, "Sing 'Jingle Bells' at a funeral."

In many churches the third Sunday in Advent is known as Gaudete Sunday, from the Latin word for "rejoice." In churches that celebrate Gaudete Sunday, a pink candle in the Advent wreath is lit. It is a reminder in the midst of the otherwise somber season of Advent, that the coming of the Lord which we are preparing to celebrate is a season of great joy. "Joy to the world," we sing, "the Lord has come."

Certainly the Christmas season gives us many opportunities for joy. We are surrounded by reminders that this is to be a season for being glad.

One woman, Wendy Wright, discovered the joy of the Christmas season in one of the most unlikely of places—a homeless shelter in her city. Wendy and some others from her church visit homeless shelters each year to sing Christmas carols. The people living in homeless shelters have had their childhood dreams shattered, says Wendy. They live with very little hope. "In that setting," Wendy says, "songs of snowmen and Christmas wish lists and hearty good cheer ring hollow." What does ring true is the good news of a Savior.

At one of the shelters at which they were singing, Wendy met a man she says she will never forget. The group had been singing their Christmas carols in a smoke-filled, noisy room. They were ready to wind it all up when a homeless man about fifty in a soiled jacket approached Wendy. She recalls that this man's "perceptions of things, due either to ill health or some chemical substance, seemed doubtful." But he asked Wendy if she would sing his favorite Christmas song with him. The song was, "O Holy Night."

Wendy agreed and they began singing. The crowded room gradually grew silent as the two of them raised up their voices together. "O Holy Night! The stars are brightly shining, / It is the night of the dear Savior's birth . . ."

The man in the soiled jacket leaned on the edge of a tattered sofa about three feet from Wendy singing with his eyes closed. As he sang Wendy noticed a change come over the man. "The tired creases of his street-weary face softened as he [sang]," she recalls.

As he continued to sing, his face shone and tears fell gently from his lowered eyes. "I knew, at that moment," Wendy says, "that his longing and mine were one . . . it is etched on the human heart." (2) That longing is for a Savior.

There are many opportunities during the Christmas season to experience joy. But the writer of Thessalonians would have us experience joy all year long. He would have us experience joy when the carols and the lights and the nativity scenes have all been put away. How do we do that? We do that by reading the rest of the sentence from I Thessalonians. The two words, "Rejoice always," are only the first phrase in a sentence with three parts. The entire sentence reads like this: "Rejoice always, pray continually, give thanks in all circumstances; for this is God's will for you in Christ Jesus."

These are the keys to having the Christmas spirit in your life at all times—"Rejoice always, pray continually," and "give thanks in all circumstances." That really makes sense if you think about it.

Verse sixteen reads, "Rejoice always." Paul is saying to us, first of all, that joy is a primary characteristic of a Christian. If you do not have a sense of joy in your life, you need to examine your Christian faith and see if perhaps you have a problem that you are not acknowledging.

Theologian Marcus Borg notes that in English, the words "joy" and "jewel" come from the same root words. Like a jewel, joy is of great value and beauty, and greatly prized. But unlike a jewel, it can neither be purchased nor possessed. It is a gift. We cannot make joy happen and we cannot own it. As the Apostle Paul says, it is one of the primary gifts of the Spirit. Joy comes from God. Joy is God's will for us.

Joy does not come from having life figured out. Joy comes from relaxing oneself in the knowledge that we are loved.

There is a charming story in Boswell's life of Johnson. Johnson met a man called Edwards who had been at college with him and whom he had not seen for forty years. They went to Johnson's rooms and talked of many things. Telling of what he had done since they had been to college together Edwards said: "You are a philosopher, Dr. Johnson. I have tried too in my time to be a philosopher; but, I don't know how, cheerfulness was always breaking in." (3)

There are many people who rob themselves of joy because they think that they have to be able to fully understand life. Let me assure you that will never happen. That's what it means to live by faith. We don't understand everything that happens in life, but we know the Creator of the universe loves us. Bethlehem's babe reminds us of that.

Joy does not come from having life figured out. Neither does it come from always living in the sunshine. C. S. Lewis used to talk about the difference between joy and pleasure. Joy comes from within. It is steady and abiding. Pleasure, on the other hand, comes and goes with whatever is happening in our environment. It is extrinsic because it arises from the outside. When the circumstances change in one direction, pleasure comes. When fortune reverses, pleasure leaves.

We have our small pleasures, and that's fine. But one day they will fail us. Joy will never fail us. Joy resides within us and undergirds us regardless of what is happening on the outside. It is the free gift of God that comes with faith in Jesus Christ.

If you believe in Jesus Christ and your heart is not filled with joy, ask God for it. It is your birthright as one who has given your life to Jesus. Christmas is a perfect time for doing that. Joy is not only the privilege, but also the responsibility of a Christian. It is our witness to the world that God is alive.

A French philosopher once said, "I look at the Christians or those who call themselves such. They look so morbid and sad. If that's Christianity, I'll have no part of it."

I say to you that something is wrong with the Christians he is encountering. If you know that Christ is your Savior, if you know that God loves you, if you know that your life has meaning and purpose and that you have a Friend who will stand with you through eternity, how can you not feel a sense of joy? "Rejoice always." That's verse sixteen. Then verse seventeen tells us, "Pray continually . . ."

Paul is telling us, in the second place, to cultivate a sense of God's presence within us—a presence that we carry with us always. If we have a sense of God's presence in our lives at all times, we will be able to rejoice. That's what it means to pray continually.

Prayer is not a mere ritual in which we repeat the same words over and over, "Forgive me of my sins, take care of my family, God is great, God is good, now we thank God for our food." Paul doesn't mean for us to mouth formulaic prayers all the time. He certainly doesn't mean for us to bow our heads and close our eyes while we're driving. When he says "pray continually," he is telling us to get to the very heart of prayer. Live in God's presence. Let God's Spirit so fill us that every moment is touched by God's glory and love.

Years ago, Journalist Skip Thurman told of meeting a remarkable Washington, D.C. cab driver named Percival Bryan. Bryan came to the United States in 1924, as a stowaway on a banana boat from Jamaica. For decades after his arrival in Washington Bryan drove people—both ordinary people and famous people—in his cab. While driving them, Bryan had the quirky habit of asking each passenger to sign a guest book. After more than 50 years, eight cabs and carrying hundreds of thousands of passengers, Percival Bryan's autograph collection has been put on display at the Smithsonian Institute. It contains the names of presidents, jazz greats, senators, scientists, and everyday people; mostly everyday people. The 312 books that make up this collection chronicle one man's journey through some of America's most volatile times.

In a story Thurman wrote about Bryan, Thurman reports that Bryan was remarkable for his friendliness and poise. One night, his passengers, two young white men, robbed him. But before the ride was over, not only had they given back the money, they had both signed his book.

"What keeps you going?" asked Thurman. "My priorities," Bryan said, "friends. Most of all, God. Every morning I get down on my knees and I have my little prayers. I ask God to go with me, protect me, ride with me, and take my eyesight, my nose, my mouth—especially my mouth—and share it with others. And I tell you, sometimes I feel very rich. Don't have nothin', not much money in my pocket, but inside I feel like I have done my best and God has given me the wisdom and the strength to keep going." (4)

Cabby Percival Bryan is with God now, but those autograph collections in the Smithsonian speak of a man who knew how to rejoice always and to pray continually.

God rode with him in his cab. God was the major influence in how he conducted his life. His life was a continuous prayer, and joy was his constant companion. God was with him always. That's the second key for keeping the Christmas spirit all year long. Cultivate a sense of God's presence and carry it with you everywhere you go. "Rejoice always, pray continually, give thanks in all circumstances . . ."

Here is the final key: "Give thanks in all circumstances . . ." Develop a profound sense of gratitude in your life that you can hold on to regardless of your circumstances.

During World War II, American soldier David Read spent many years as a prisoner of war in a Bavarian prison camp. For the first few years in that camp, says Read, the prisoners were able to keep their spirits up. They even found a way to celebrate the major holidays, like Christmas. But one Christmas, near the war's end, the men in the camp were beginning to lose hope. They didn't even have the heart to plan anything for Christmas. Read wrote a poem encouraging the men to celebrate Jesus no matter what the circumstances. He recalled the apostle Paul's words in Philippians 2: 1-11, where he wrote about being shipwrecked, beaten, and imprisoned for his preaching. But he never lost the joy of proclaiming the good news of Jesus Christ.

After his return from war, David Read entered the ministry. Many years later, he recalled that final Christmas in a prison camp, and he wrote, "The Gospel is no less true when circumstances are most terrible. If we soak ourselves in this truth we shall never find ourselves making excuses for our lack of desire to celebrate . . . May Christmas joy be real and radiant for us all—no matter what our circumstances." (5)

"Count your many blessings . . ." says an old Gospel tune. Do it daily, even when things are not going well and it will transform your life.

"Rejoice always, pray continually, give thanks in all circumstances; for this is God's will for you in Christ Jesus." Ask God for joy if you do not have it in your life already. Joy is your privilege and responsibility as a follower of Jesus Christ. Cultivate a sense of God's presence and carry it with you always. That's what it means to "pray continually." And develop a profound sense of gratitude in your life that you can hold on to regardless of your circumstances—a gratitude attitude. This is God's will for you, says St. Paul. Listen to the message of these three short verses and I promise you that you will become a new person. The spirit of Christmas will be with you throughout the year. You might even request "Jingle Bells" to be sung at your funeral.

1. Bobby Braddock, Real Country Humor collected and edited by Billy Edd Wheeler, August House, Little Rock, 2002.

2. Wendy M. Wright, The Vigil (Nashville: Upper Room Books, 1992), pp. 45-46.

3. James Boswell, Life of Dr. Johnson, entry for 17 April 1778. William Barclay, And He Had Compassion (Valley Forge, PA: Judson Press, 1976), p. 162.

4, Cited by the Very Rev. Sherry Crompton, http://sermons.trinitycoatesville.org/.

5. I'll Be Home for Christmas (New York: The Stonesong Press, Inc., 1999), pp. 115-117.

Christmas Is A God-Thing
Luke 1:26-38

There was a story years ago in the Canadian version of the Reader's Digest of a large moose that wandered into a residential area in Calgary, Canada. The moose ended up on the lawn of a lady named Lorna Cade. A Fish and Wildlife officer was dispatched to try to coax the magnificent animal back into the wild. After two hours of absolutely no progress, the officer finally shot the moose with a tranquilizer dart. The moose bolted down a lane and eventually collapsed on another nearby lawn.

The reporters who had been following this event interviewed the lady at the house where the moose collapsed. They asked her what she thought about the moose which had passed out on her lawn. "I'm surprised," she answered, "but not as surprised as my husband will be. He's out moose hunting." (1)

Her husband had gone out looking for moose and a large moose had come to him.

That is the message of Christmas. While humanity spends its time seeking after God, God comes to us in the babe of Bethlehem. Christmas is a God-thing. The angel Gabriel was sent to Nazareth, a town in Galilee, to a virgin pledged to be married to a man named Joseph, a descendant of David. The virgin's name was Mary. The angel said to Mary, "Greetings, you who are highly favored! The Lord is with you."

Mary was greatly troubled at his words and wondered what kind of greeting this might be. The angel said to her, "Do not be afraid, Mary; you have found favor with God. You will conceive and give birth to a son, and you are to call him Jesus. He will be great and will be called the Son of the Most High. The Lord God will give him the throne of his father David, and he will reign over Jacob's descendants forever; his kingdom will never end."

"How will this be," Mary asked the angel, "since I am a virgin?"

The angel answered, "The Holy Spirit will come on you, and the power of the Most High will overshadow you. So the holy one to be born will be called the Son of God ..." Christmas is a God-thing.

We could not reach up to God, so God came down to us. That's the good news for today.

Michael Hendrix tells about a dinner party he once attended during the Christmas season. The house was properly decorated, including an electric train set up around the base of the tree. One of the children was running the train too fast and it derailed. She was bent over the train trying to put it back on the track. The host noticed what she was doing and went over to help. He said to her, "You can't do that from above; you have to get down beside it." Then he lay down on the floor beside the train where he could see to place the train back on the track.

"What a wonderful way to think about the incarnation," Hendrix says. "The human race had derailed and needed to be put back on the track of life. It couldn't be done from above; God had to come down beside us in order to put us on track. That's what God did in Jesus Christ. God came and lived among us in the person of His Son Jesus to show us His love and to put us back on the track of life."

Some of you have undoubtedly seen the 1962 film Lawrence of Arabia, which was loosely based on the life of T.E. Lawrence, a flamboyant and controversial British military figure. Lawrence was a British citizen who led an army of Arabs against the Turks in the First World War. Lawrence once said this concerning his service in that conflict: "No man could lead Arabs except he ate the rank's food, wore their clothes, lived level with them, yet appeared better in himself." (2)

That's what God did for us. When we could not reach up to God, God came down to eat our food, wear our clothes, live level with us. We call that Incarnation—God took on human flesh in the manger of Bethlehem.

Now you may be wondering what it means to say that we could not reach up to God. It means many things.

For example, it means we could not reach up to God intellectually. That is, our little brains are not sufficient to understand God.

Christian faith is not a philosophy that someone thought up. Christian faith is revelation. God revealed His purpose and plan, His love and His grace, in the person of Jesus of Nazareth. If there are some things about our faith you do not understand, join the crowd. If we could understand everything there is about God, God would not be God. We do not have the mental capacity to reach up to God intellectually. Let's use an example—a metaphor, if you will—of the intellectual gulf that separates us from God.

Remember Humphrey the humpback whale? Humphrey became a national celebrity in 1985 when he made his way into the San Francisco Bay and headed up the Sacramento River into fresh water—which, of course, could have been fatal for him. Each evening a large local television audience would tune in for the latest update on Humphrey's plight. Then national media coverage began and the whole country watched the ensuing story.

Many experts and well-meaning lay people attempted to get Humphrey to turn around and go back to the saltwater environment of the ocean, but nothing worked. Several weeks of being trapped in the fresh water of the Sacramento Delta began taking a toll on Humphrey. His skin was graying and he was becoming more and more listless. None of the traditional herding techniques were working and the world held its breath as Humphrey appeared to be dying.

As a last ditch effort, Dr. Bernie Krause, who had recorded the sounds humpback whales made while feeding suggested using them as a possible way to lure Humphrey out. No one knew if this would work, but it was their last shot at saving him. A speaker was lowered over the side of a boat, the sounds of other humpback whales were played, and everyone stood quietly while the eerie songs reverberated through the hull. Suddenly, Humphrey emerged from the water at the bow of the ship right where the speaker was playing, and gazed at the startled crew. The Captain quickly started down the river with Humphrey following close behind.

As they approached the San Francisco Bay, and the water gained in salinity, Humphrey was visibly excited and began diving deeply to everyone's delight and amazement. It was like the climax to a Hollywood film. The air was filled with helicopters and the river banks were lined with thousands of spectators all cheering Humphrey on to freedom. Though the crew lost sight of him that night, they picked him back up in the morning and led him out through the Golden Gate Bridge, to the freedom of the Pacific Ocean where he promptly headed south to parts unknown. (3)

Don't you think that's interesting? They failed using various methods to lure Humphrey to turn around. Nothing worked until he heard the recorded sounds of other humpback whales. I guess it takes a whale to talk to whales!

Now imagine God's dilemma. God sought to communicate His love and His purpose for humanity through the Law and through the prophets, through Scripture, and through the worship of the Hebrew people in the Temple of Jerusalem. But still the people did not get it. We did not know how much God loves us and that God's ultimate plan was for us to love one another. So God did the only thing left. God became one of us in the babe in the manger. God came to us when, intellectually, we could not reach up to Him.

But that was not the only way we could not reach up to God. We also could not reach up to God morally. That is, before the coming of Jesus the Jewish people believed that the way to God is through right living. If you could just follow the Law and keep all its ordinances, then you could be saved. But salvation by righteousness did not work. For some, their devotion to the Law deteriorated into an odious legalism. They looked down their noses at others who were not as righteous as they. While others, feeling that they had no hope of fulfilling the Law, simply threw up their hands in despair and did not bother to try.

They were like the little girl who was Christmas shopping with her mom. The little girl, about three years old, was obviously beginning to get tired. The long line at the register was moving slowly. Her mother's patience also was stretched to the breaking point, and her voice sounded irritable.

"Straighten up and be nice," the mother said as the child began to cry and whine.

"Mommy, I'm all out of nice," came the response. (4)

Well, sometimes adults run out of nice, too, and it is not a pretty sight to see.

"Nobody's perfect," we say at such times. And, of course, it's true. But sometimes when we give in to our imperfections, sad things happen.

Dr. Samuel Massey tells of watching a World War II movie once. In this particular movie one character is giving lessons to another character about how to destroy a dam. The pupil anticipated that, if you packed the dam with enough dynamite you could send the entire dam skyward. But the teacher explained that far less explosive power was needed. "Place a few sticks in critically vulnerable places, blow them up, and then wait patiently," he said. "Silently, but certainly, the pent-up water would do the rest of the job washing the dam downstream." (5)

What's true of a dam can also be true of a family or a reputation. One time of "running out of nice," can sink us. One seemingly minor indiscretion can blow a hole in a life. Who will help us? Who will save us when we've blown up our life? We know the answer to that, don't we?—the Savior of the world.

I love something that author Max Lucado said in one of his books. "It is unfortunate that most of us see ourselves as a composite of all our failures," writes Lucado. "When we look in the mirror we may only see our failures. Even though many of us can't see beyond the failures, this is not the way God views us. As a loving God, he looks past our failures. Can you imagine a loving parent introducing their children by saying, 'This is my daughter Meagan, who stained the carpet with grape juice when she was two,' or 'This is my son Myles, who broke a valuable vase last week.' If loving parents don't have a need to memorize their children's failures, you can rest assured our loving heavenly Father has no use for such memories either." (6)

Jesus showed us God's amazing grace. He helped us by understanding that grace is not something you earn, but is a free gift. We could not reach up to God intellectually . . . or morally . . .

We could not even reach up to God with our good deeds or good works. Even now, 2100 years after the birth of Christ, we know what God wants of us. God wants us to love one another. God wants us to take care of the least and the lowest. God wants us to lay down our lives for others, even as He lay down his life for us. But time after time we fail the test of love and compassion, just as we failed the test of keeping all the ceremonial and moral laws. We don't have it in us to love as Christ loved us.

Robert Morris tells a somewhat amusing and also telling story about a disheveled Hispanic man who showed up at the rear of a church after midnight service on Christmas Eve. The pastor of this particular inner city congregation, named Mark, was a friend of Robert Morris. Mark was a man who was devoted to serving the homeless, but he was getting weary and this final Hispanic gentleman was almost "one homeless person too many" for him. Mark knew that his commitment to being a "caring" pastor had put him in this position, but he was starting to feel sorry for himself. On the way to the shelter, he stewed in his own anger at himself, at the man, and ultimately at God.

Finally, realizing he didn't know the stranger's name, he asked. The man answered, "Hayzoos," which is, of course, the Spanish pronunciation for "Jesus." The ironic humor of the whole situation suddenly washed over Mark's mind and heart. Here he was griping to God about taking a man named Jesus to a shelter on Christmas Eve! He felt as if it were a huge cosmic trick. The comic aspect of it both judged his anger and redeemed him out of it. "Leave it to God to beat us at our own game," he thought to himself. (7) And so, gratefully, that Christmas Eve he provided shelter to a homeless man named "Hayzoos," Jesus.

Anyone who seeks to do good burns out at some time or another. It's inevitable. We're not Christ. There are many loving and devoted people in this congregation. I know that you serve God in our community. I am so thankful for each of you. But none of us, no matter how much good we do, can keep it up forever. We cannot love as Christ loved. Our love is a drop in the ocean compared to the love Christ showed for us on Calvary.

We cannot reach up to God . . . intellectually . . . morally . . . or even in terms of our good works. And that is why the world needed Christmas. Christmas is the celebration of God reaching down to us when we could not reach up to Him.

Rowan Williams, the Archbishop of Canterbury, tells of watching a video showing the work of one of the most experienced therapists in Great Britain. In the video this therapist seeks to explain what she is trying to do with her methods to treat a young man suffering from extreme autism.

In the video you see, first of all, this young man, severely disturbed, beating his head against a wall and then walking fast up and down the room, twisting and flicking a piece of string. The therapist's first response is strange: she begins to twist and flick a piece of string as well. When the young man makes a noise, so does she; when he begins to do something different, like banging his hand on a table, she does the same.

The video shows what happens over two days. By the end of the two days, the boy has begun to smile at the therapist and to respond when touched. A relationship has been created. Here is what the therapist said about it: "Autism arises when the brain senses too much material coming in, too much information. There's a feeling of panic; the mind has to regain control. And the best way of doing this is to close up on yourself and repeat actions that are familiar; do nothing new, and don't acknowledge anything coming from outside. But when the therapist gently echoes the actions and rhythms, the anxious and wounded mind of the autistic person sees that there is, after all, a link with the outside world that isn't threatening. Here is someone doing what I do; the world isn't just an unfamiliar place of terror and uncertainty, and when I do this, I can draw out an answer, an echo; I'm not powerless. And so relationship begins."

Archbishop Williams says, "To see this sort of thing in action is intensely moving. This is real mental and spiritual healing at work. But it gives us a powerful image of what it is we remember at Christmas," that at Christmas God broke down the barriers between ourselves and God by becoming one of us, one with us, one alongside us." (8)

And that is the good news for this final Sunday of Advent. When we could not reach up to God, God reached down to us. God became as we are that we might know God's love and be led to love one another as Christ has loved us.

1. Calgary. MerryHearts@xc.org. Tue, 26 May, 1998.

2. Chevis F. Horne, Basic Bible Sermons (Nashville: Broadman Press, 1992), p. 40.

3. http://en.wikipedia.org/wiki/Humphrey_the_Whale.

4. Debra Klingsporn, "For Women Only," Marriage Partnership, Winter 1994, p. 28.

5. http://day1.org/540-youve_got_to_be_kidding.

6. The Timothy Report, http://www.timothyreport.com.

7. Salt of the Earth, January/February 1995, p. 32.

8. Cited by Ned Provost, http://www.christchurchwinnetka.org/SermonsESP12-24-04.htm.

The Light Of Christmas
Isaiah 9: 2-6; Luke 2:1-14
(Christmas Eve)

Welcome on this holiest of nights. I want to begin with a story about a young man named Marty. Marty was a bright, lively eight-year-old who suffered from a minor disability—he was deaf in one ear. He lived in a rural community of farms and fences. Marty's mom, Diane, was proud of her son. She knew he had a kind and loving heart.

Several weeks before Christmas one year, Marty shared a secret with his mother. He had been doing extra chores and saving up his allowance in order to buy a Christmas present, a pocket compass, for his best friend, Kenny. Kenny was being raised by a single mom and life for their family was a daily struggle just to acquire the most basic of needs of food and clothing.

Diane knew that Kenny's mom was a very proud woman. Diane doubted that Kenny's mom would allow Kenny to accept a gift if he couldn't give one in return. Marty argued with his mother and finally said, "But what if it was a secret? What if they never found out who gave it?" Diane finally relented. If somehow Marty could give Kenny the gift without anyone knowing who gave it, that would be acceptable. So, on Christmas Eve Diane watched her son walk out the door, cross the wet pasture and slip beneath the electric fence on his mission of kindness.

Marty raced up to Kenny's door and pressed the doorbell. Then he ran down the steps and across the yard so he wouldn't be seen. Suddenly, the electric fence loomed in front of him. He could not avoid it. The shock knocked him to the ground and he gasped for breath. Slowly, he got up and stumbled home.

When he arrived home Diane treated the blister on Marty's face cause by the electric fence, then put him to bed. That night as Diane tucked Marty in, she silently complained to God for allowing her son to be hurt when he was performing a good deed. The next day, however, Kenny came to the front door excitedly talking about his new compass. Amazingly, Marty—who, you'll remember, was deaf in one ear—seemed to hear Kenny talking—with both of his ears.

A few weeks later, a school nurse confirmed what Diane suspected: Marty's hearing in his deaf ear had been completely restored. Though doctors said it might have been the shock from the electric fence, Diane believed it was a Christmas miracle. (1)

Christmas is a night for miracles. It is a magical night of wonder and faith. The children are excited. Moms and Dads are excited, too, as they remember the joy and anticipation they felt as youngsters as Christmas approached, and they see that same joy in the eyes of their children.

How good it is to hear the prophetic words of Isaiah, "The people walking in darkness have seen a great light; on those living in the land of deep darkness a light has dawned . . . For to us a child is born, to us a son is given, and the government will be on his shoulders. And he will be called Wonderful Counselor, Mighty God, Everlasting Father, Prince of Peace."

All of us know what it is to walk in darkness at some time in our lives. Darkness comes in many forms—loneliness, pain, grief, confusion, heartache. All these emotions seem to be intensified at Christmas.

It is no accident that Christmas falls just after the shortest day of our year. December 21st, known as the winter solstice, is usually the shortest day of the year because the sun is shining directly on the Tropic of Capricorn, meaning that it is the day that we receive the least amount of direct sunlight. Many of you are familiar with the term Seasonal Affective Disorder—S. A. D. Periods of physical darkness can breed depression, melancholy, sadness. But, at the darkest time of the year, our world turns a corner. From today on, our days will get longer. There will be a little more sunlight each day. Christmas reminds us that light is coming into our world, in a physical sense as well as a spiritual one!

The shepherds out on a Judean hillside knew about darkness in a way that city dwellers, particularly modern city dwellers cannot. There was no artificial lighting in their world. The only light came from the stars above. So you can imagine how startled they were to be suddenly surrounded by a great light. Luke tells us an angel appeared to them and the glory of the Lord shone around them. The glory of the Lord is a wonderful thing, but when you are not expecting it, it must have seemed like an alien invasion.

Luke tells us the shepherds were terrified. They had never experienced light like this. But the angel reassured them. "Do not be afraid. I bring you good news that will cause great joy for all the people. Today in the town of David a Savior has been born to you; he is the Messiah, the Lord. This will be a sign to you: You will find a baby wrapped in cloths and lying in a manger." And suddenly, Luke tells us, a great company of the heavenly host appeared with the angel, praising God and saying, "Glory to God in the highest heaven, and on earth peace to those on whom his favor rests."

In the darkness there is a light that shines . . . And that light is a babe born in Bethlehem. That's the good news for this night. In John 8:12 Jesus says to us, "I am the light of the world. Whoever follows me will never walk in darkness, but will have the light of life." If you are experiencing any darkness in your life right now, there is a light dawning, and that light is an infant born to be our Savior.

On The Protestant Hour sometime back, the Rev. Harry H. Pritchett, Jr., told about the worst nativity pageant he could ever remember. It was at the church where he grew up. The youth group was staging a manger scene. Pritchett was chosen to play Joseph and his future wife, Allison, was chosen to play Mary. They did their parts with seriousness and commitment, looking as pious as possible. And then it came time for the shepherds to enter. The choir was singing "While Shepherds Watched Their Flocks by Night," and some of their fellow young people dressed in flannel bathrobes and toweled head gear proceeded to the altar steps. Young Pritchett and Allison both managed to gaze solemnly at the straw which contained a naked light bulb. But then one of the shepherds broke the sacred spell. With his back to the congregation, he said in a very loud whisper for all the cast to hear, "Well, Joe, when you gonna pass out cigars?"

The spell of that occasion was not simply broken by his remark, it exploded. The Mary and Joseph cover was completely destroyed as it became impossible to hold back the bursts of laughter. The chief angel, standing on a chair behind them was the worst. She shook so hard that she fell off her chair and simply rolled over on the floor, holding her stomach. The strains of "Silent Night" and "0 Little Town of Bethlehem" were hardly sufficient to cover the uncontrolled snorts of the main characters. Their much upset but good-sported youth advisor said, "The only thing that didn't go to pieces was the light bulb in the manger, it never went out." Harry Pritchett thought to himself later, that's a nice image—the light in the manger never goes out regardless of any mess we may make of things. (2)

That light never goes out. If you are experiencing a time of darkness in your life, there is hope, and that hope has to do with a small babe lying in a manger. That babe has brought light into the world. He has changed our world. Those of you who are parents know how a baby can do that.

The year was 1953, and the Korean War was drawing to a close. U.S. soldiers stationed around Korea didn't have much to do as they waited for the armistice negotiations to wrap up. Hugh Keenan was a young sailor assigned to the U.S.S. Consolation, a medical ship. Morale was low on the ship, and like many of his buddies, Hugh was homesick. He had a wife and daughter back in the States, and he was desperate to return to them. Someone suggested that Hugh might get a lift from visiting a local Korean orphanage run by Catholic nuns.

As Hugh toured the orphanage, eager little faces peered at him. The nuns ran the place with very little money, but a lot of faith and resourcefulness. Apple crates served as cribs for many of the babies. One baby in particular caught Hugh's eye. He was a biracial baby, part American and part Korean; such a child would surely face prejudice in Korean society. A lieutenant and the skipper from Hugh's ship were visiting the orphanage, too, and they decided to find a good home for the child in America.

But until the Consolation could return to the States, the baby boy would have to live on the ship. Instantly, morale on the ship shot up. The sailors set up babysitting shifts, so that all the men would get a chance to feed, change, bathe, or watch after the little boy. Some of the men fashioned homemade toys for the child. They hung his cloth diapers out to dry with the ship's signal flags, which proved confusing to a number of passing ships. Everyone took an interest in this new child and his well-being.

When Hugh Keenan finally stepped forward and offered to adopt the child, the ship's crew burst into cheers. But there was still the matter of getting his official papers signed, and the Korean bureaucracy moved extremely slowly. So the ship's chaplain, Father Riley, took matters into his own hands. He set up a poker game between himself and an official of the Korean government. The Father put up $200 of his own money for the game. The ship's doctor donated his watch, a precious family heirloom, to sweeten the pot. And the Korean official brought a passport for the baby. Whoever won the game would get everything in the pot. Father Riley won.

Hugh Keenan took his son home and named him Daniel Edward Keenan. The Daniel comes from Hugh's father's name. Edward is the first name of Father Riley. Daniel grew up a happy child, in a stable and loving home. When Daniel was seven, Hugh told him the story of his adoption. In 1993, veterans from Hugh's ship came together for a reunion, and Daniel was brought in as a "surprise guest." The men were thrilled to see him, thrilled that their little boy—the child they had cared for— had grown to be a fine man. They all felt they had a part in raising him. (3)

It's amazing how a baby can change your life. But one baby changed all our lives. "A light shines in the darkness . . ."

It is the darkest part of the night that we are most prone to see the light of God. When the world needed him most, Christ was born in Bethlehem of Judea. But it is also true in our lives, when we need the light of God the most, is when we are most likely to see that light.

James W. Moore tells a wonderful story about a man who was experiencing darkness in his life. The man had suffered from a stroke which affected both his legs, one arm, and most of his speech. He was frustrated because he was unable to communicate with other people, especially his wife. His life was filled with loneliness and some anger. One day his pastor came to visit him. The pastor found it difficult to communicate with the man for very long. The pastor was tempted to ignore the man and talk to his wife, or to ask him simple questions, much as people do when talking to a baby.

As the pastor was getting ready to leave he remembered reading that some stroke victims can sing, even though they cannot talk. The pastor began singing, "Silent night, holy night, all is calm, all is bright." It seemed like a miracle, but the man who suffered the stroke, the man who had such difficulty communicating with anyone, also began singing. There was no stuttering, no breakdown in forming words. He just sang: "Round yon virgin mother and child. Holy infant, so tender and mild." As the man reached for his pastor's hand to hold, his wife joined in the singing, "Sleep in heavenly peace, sleep in heavenly peace." "We finished," the pastor said. The man smiled, and "God was there." (4)

If that seems like a miracle, remember that Christmas is a time for miracles. A light shines in the darkness. The glory of the Lord shone around Shepherds on a bleak Judean hillside. A babe is born in a manger in Bethlehem. Rejoice, your light has come.

1. Diane Rayner in Christmas Memories compiled by Terry Meeuwsen (Nashville: Thomas Nelson, 1996), pp. 95-100.
2. http://www.sermonmall.com/SampleMall/98/dec98/122498b.html.
3. "Baby on Board," by Michael A. Lipton and Paula Yoo, People, December 8, 1997, pp. 137- 140.
4. Is There Life After Stress? (Nashville: Dimensions in Living, 1992), pp. 72- 73.

Thank You For Coming

Hebrews 1:1-4

(Christmas Day)

It was Christmas Eve—the one night in the year when 7-year-old Bobby was in a hurry to go to bed. His stocking was tacked to the mantel; the beautiful tree stood in the corner. He kissed his mother and father good night. Then he raced upstairs and leaped into bed.

It seemed to Bobby that he hadn't been asleep any time when a harsh voice shouted "Get up!" He opened his eyes, blinking in the bright sunlight. Then he remembered what day it was. With a joyful shout he hurried into his clothes and bounded down the stairs. On the bottom step he stopped. No stocking hung from the mantel. The Christmas tree was gone too. "But . . . but I put the angel on myself," Bobby began, when the shrill whistle from the factory made him jump.

"The factory can't be open on Christmas!" Bobby thought, as he put on his coat and ran out of the house. The gateman at the factory was his friend. He would tell Bobby why . . .

"Clear out of here, you!" The gateman jerked his thumb at him. "No kids allowed!"

As Bobby slowly turned to go, he saw to his amazement that up and down the street all the stores were open. "Why are they open on Christmas?" he asked a woman coming out of the supermarket.

"Christmas?" The woman asked. "What's that?"

The hardware store, the bakery, the five-and-ten—everywhere it was the same. People were busy. They were cross. They'd never heard of Christmas.

"I know one place where they've heard of Christmas!" Bobby cried. "At my church! There's a special service this morning!"

He started to run. Here was the street! At least he thought it was. But there was only a weed-grown vacant lot. The tower with the carillon bells, the Sunday School windows where Bobby had pasted snowflakes–there was nothing here.

Just then, from the tall grass near the side of the road, Bobby heard a moan. A man was lying on the ground.

"A car struck me!" he gasped. "Never even stopped!"

"Help!" called Bobby to a lady walking past. "This man is hurt!"

The lady jerked Bobby away. "Don't touch him! He doesn't live here. We don't know anything about him."

"I'll run to the hospital, mister," Bobby promised. "They will send an ambulance." And he tore off down the street.

"Hospital of the Good Samaritan," Bobby had often read the name over the archway in the great stone wall. But now the stone wall ran around an empty field. Where the name of the hospital had been, was carved instead, "If He Had Only Come."

Suddenly Bobby was running home as if his life depended on it. Last night his father had read from the Bible! Maybe the Bible would tell him why everything was changed. The Bible was still lying on the table in the living room. Bobby snatched it up, ran upstairs to his room. But where the New Testament should have started, there were only blank pages. There was no Christmas story—no Jesus at all.

Bobby flung himself on his bed and began to cry . . .

"Merry Christmas, Bobby!" It was his mother's voice from downstairs. "Aren't you getting up on Christmas morning?"

Bobby sprang out of bed and ran to the window. It had only been a nightmare. There was a Christmas wreath on the house across the street. And suddenly the carillon bells from the church tower began to ring: Joy to the World! The Lord is Come!

"Here I come, Mother!" Bobby called. But he paused at the door and shut his eyes. "You came!" he whispered. "Thank you for coming!" (1)

That is our prayer to the Lord Jesus this Christmas Day . . . Thank you for coming.

Comedian Bob Hope used to joke about how poor his family was when he was growing up.

They were so poor, he said, they didn't get presents, but on Christmas Eve they would hang up their stockings before they went to bed and sure enough, the next morning when they woke up they'd be nice and dry.

Hope also said that since his folks couldn't afford to buy them any toys for Christmas . . . every Christmas Eve after everyone went to bed, his father would tear an extra page off the calendar; and when the kids came downstairs the next morning, He'd point to the calendar and say, Look, it's December 26th. Where were you kids yesterday? You MISSED CHRISTMAS! (2)

We don't know if Bob Hope was joking or not, but we're glad we didn't miss Christmas. We're here, and life is good, and we are thankful.

One of my favorite Peanuts cartoons has Lucy coming to Charlie Brown and saying, "Merry Christmas, Charlie Brown. Since it's this time of the season, I think we ought to bury past differences and try to be kind."

Charlie Brown asks, "Why does it just have to be 'this time of the season'? Why can't it be all year long?"

Lucy looks at him and exclaims, "What are you, some kind of fanatic?"

That, of course, is the challenge of Christmas . . . and the dream. Why can't we preserve feelings of peace and goodwill all through the year? Maybe if we fully grasped what happened at Christmas, it would make a difference.

The writer of Hebrews tried to express the true meaning of Christmas in our lesson for today from the Epistle: "In the past God spoke to our ancestors through the prophets at many times and in various ways, but in these last days he has spoken to us by his Son, whom he appointed heir of all things, and through whom also he made the universe. The Son is the radiance of God's glory and the exact representation of his being, sustaining all things by his powerful word. After he had provided purification for sins, he sat down at the right hand of the Majesty in heaven. So he became as much superior to the angels as the name he has inherited is superior to theirs."

There are at least three stunning claims about Christ that the writer makes in this passage. First of all, he tells us, the babe in the manger is the fulfillment of the plan of God. The birth of Christ was no accident. Since the beginning of time God has tried to express God's plan and God's purpose for humankind without impinging upon our freedom of choice. Most recently before the coming of Jesus, God spoke through the prophets who called for righteousness and justice and who tried to express to Israel how important Israel was to God's plan. But the people misunderstood the message. Or they refused to listen. That happens even today.

Luis Palau tells the story of a wealthy European family who decided to have their newborn baby baptized in their enormous mansion. Dozens of guests were invited to the event, and they all arrived in the latest of fashions. After depositing their elegant coats on a bed in an upstairs room, the guests were entertained like royalty. Soon the time came for the main purpose of the evening, the infant's baptism. When they asked for the child, no one seemed to know of his whereabouts. Panic ensued as they desperately searched for the baby. In a few minutes the child was found—buried underneath all of the coats, jackets, and furs. The very object of the day's celebration had been forgotten, neglected, and nearly smothered. (3)

We are often reminded to remember "the reason for the season." The materialism, the hedonistic partying that takes place in our society before Christmas can smother the call for righteousness and justice today just as it did during the times of the prophets. The coming of Christ is the fulfillment of the plan of God. Christ came to call us again to righteousness and justice and to demonstrate once and for all how important we are to God's purpose for the world.

The second thing the writer says to us is that Christ is the perfect reflection of the character of God. He writes, "The Son is the radiance of God's glory and the exact representation of his being . . ."

One woman tells about her niece Samantha who was a teacher at a Christian elementary school. She had the job of producing the Christmas play one year.

She stressed to her students that if they forgot their lines, they should ad-lib something instead of just standing there.

On the big night, all went well until the Three Wise Men made their entrance. The first was perfect. "Baby Jesus, here is your gold," the boy said.

The second boy was perfect, too. "Baby Jesus, here is your frankincense," he said.

The boy playing the third Wise Man said, "Baby Jesus, here is your . . ." and froze, having forgotten the name of his gift.

After a tense few seconds had passed, the teacher whispered out to him, "Say anything!"

The boy then peered into the manger and exclaimed, "Oh, doesn't he look just like his dad!" (4)

Well, he does look just like his Dad, says the writer of Hebrews. Christ "is the radiance of God's glory and the exact representation of his being . . ." That doesn't mean that Jesus looked like God, of course, but it does mean that Jesus showed us everything we need to know about God—God's self-giving love for all people.

There is one thing more that the writer of Hebrews tells us. Christ now reigns with the Father. "After he had provided purification for sins," says the writer, "he sat down at the right hand of the Majesty in heaven . . ."

The humble carpenter who worked with his hands, who held little children in his arms, who reached out to the lepers and the lame, the least and the lowest, this humble carpenter now occupies the throne with the Father. An old spiritual says it like this: "Oh, Mary, where is your baby?" Mary answers, "They done took Him from the manger and done carried him to a throne."

Why is that Good News? Here's why. In I John 2:1 we read these words, "My dear children, I write this to you so that you will not sin. But if anybody does sin, we have an advocate with the Father—Jesus Christ, the Righteous One . . ." That's amazing good news. Jesus sits at the right hand of God. He knows what we're going through. He's been here, and now he is an advocate in our behalf. "They done took Him from the manger and done carried him to a throne." This is the meaning of Christmas day. God's plan for humankind has been fulfilled. The Savior of the world has come. He is the perfect representation of God, and now he reigns with God, world without end, forever and ever.

1. A story from Norman Vincent Peale, Author Unknown.
2. Mark Adams, http://www.redlandbaptist.org/sermons/sermon20001224.php.
3. Luis Palau, Where Is the Child? Luis Palau, 142. 1988, p. 1-2 Cited by Raymond McHenry, Something to Think About (Peabody, MA: Hendrickson Publishers, Inc., 1998).
4. Mark Mail, http://mrhumor.net/l.

Two Inches Of Faith
Luke 2:22-40

First of all, I want to congratulate you on making it to church on this first Sunday of the New Year. That means you have kept at least one of your New Year's resolutions. Well done! I won't ask how you are doing with your other resolutions.

One man I heard about went to a wishing well as his first act of the New Year.

"Dear Wishing Well," he wrote, "My personal wish in 2012 is a big fat bank account and a slim body. PLEASE don't mix these two up like you did last year!" (1)

We all hope for a better New Year, don't we? For ourselves and for those we love.

Our lesson today from the Gospel of Luke represents a significant time in the life of a young family. It is about a young couple who present their child to God. [Most of you who have children have done that at one time or another and you know what a significant event that is.]

Luke tells us that when the time came for the purification rites required by the Law of Moses, Joseph and Mary took Jesus to Jerusalem to present him to the Lord. This was one of the primary duties of first century Jewish families. In the book of Exodus appear these words: "Every firstborn male is to be consecrated to the Lord" (13:2). That's interesting, don't you think? No mention of little girls, just firstborn males. We are doing a little better today.

According to Leviticus 12 while they were presenting their son before God the family was also supposed to offer a sacrifice of a year-old lamb. In Leviticus 12:8, however, there is a disclaimer and little girls make it in this time. Speaking about the mother of a newborn we read these words: "When the days of her purification for a son or daughter are over, she is to bring to the priest at the entrance to the tent of meeting a year-old lamb for a burnt offering . . . But if [the mother] cannot afford a lamb, she is to bring two doves or two young pigeons . . ."

So, if you can afford it, you are to offer a lamb. However, if you can't afford a lamb, you are to offer two doves or two pigeons. That, of course, is exactly the sacrifice that Mary and Joseph made when they presented Jesus to God—two doves. We'll come back to that in a few moments.

But Luke's story continues. "Now there was a man in Jerusalem called Simeon, who was righteous and devout. He was waiting for the consolation of Israel, and the Holy Spirit was on him. It had been revealed to him by the Holy Spirit that he would not die before he had seen the Lord's Messiah. Moved by the Spirit, he went into the temple courts. When the parents brought in the child Jesus to do for him what the custom of the Law required, Simeon took [the child] in his arms and praised God, saying: 'Sovereign Lord, as you have promised, you may now dismiss your servant in peace. For my eyes have seen your salvation, which you have prepared in the sight of all nations: a light for revelation to the Gentiles, and the glory of your people Israel.'

"The child's father and mother marveled at what was said about him. Then Simeon blessed them and said to Mary, his mother: 'This child is destined to cause the falling and rising of many in Israel, and to be a sign that will be spoken against, so that the thoughts of many hearts will be revealed. And a sword will pierce your own soul too.'"

There are some very important lessons that we can take away from this reading, especially those of us with families.

It's challenging having a family nowadays. I read an amusing story recently of a father and his eight-year-old son who were lying on the grass by the riverbank, looking up at the sky and watching the wisps of cloud float gently overhead.

After a few minutes of silence, the boy turned to the father and asked, "Dad, why are we here?"

The father waxed philosophical. "That's a good question, Son. I think we're here to enjoy days such as this, to experience nature in all its glory, the vastness of the sky, the beauty of the trees, the song of the birds, the rippling flow of the water. We're here to help make the world a better place, to pass on our wisdom to future generations who will hopefully profit from our achievements and learn from our mistakes. We're here to savor the small triumphs of life—passing your school exams, the birth of a new member of the family, promotion at work, a win for the home team! And we're here to comfort those dearest to us in times of distress, to provide kindness and compassion, support and strength, to let them know that, no matter how bad a situation may seem, they are not alone. Does that answer your question, Son?"

"Not really, Dad," the boy answered.

"No?" asked his father.

"No," replied the son. "What I meant was, why are we here when Mom said to pick her up forty minutes ago?" (2)

It's not easy having a family. It wasn't easy for Mary and Joseph.

Let's begin with Mary and Joseph's social and economic status. Don't you think it is quite fascinating that they couldn't afford to buy a small lamb to present at the Temple for Jesus' presentation? They had to settle for a pair of turtledoves. They really must have been quite poor. Do you know any young family that is struggling to make it in this tough economic environment? Assure them they are not alone. The parents of our Lord struggled just as surely.

You're asking why God doesn't make it easier for you financially? If God was going to help anyone with their finances, it certainly would have been Mary and Joseph. Maybe there are some things God leaves to us. Or maybe God wants us to see that there are things much more important that we can give our children than material wealth—like our time, our attention, our spiritual guidance and moral example.

One day a family of four, a typical, all-American family with a mother, father, a son and a daughter, showed up at the door of a family counselor. The session quickly became a shouting match, with everyone competing for attention and demanding that their plight was worse than the rest.

"My family demands that I do everything for them," the mother moaned. "They never take responsibility for themselves!"

The father complained about the lack of respect he felt. "When I speak, no one listens to me, so it's just useless to keep talking!"

"Stop yelling," the nine-year old son interjected. "All you ever do is yell!"

The teenage daughter sat quietly in a corner, looking sad and dejected, without saying a word.

"Everyone, please be quiet!" the counselor finally shouted loud enough to be heard over the din of the complaining and whining. Everyone stopped talking in mid-sentence.

"Your family is missing something and I will tell you what it is. Tonight, and every night until I see you again, I want you to eat supper together at the dinner table, holding hands and saying grace before you eat."

"That's preposterous," the mother complained, "that would mean missing practices and lessons and we don't even like the same things for dinner!"

"I'm too busy working," the father said. "I have to work all the time, sometimes late in the night so this ungrateful family can have the best money can buy," he sneered.

"I don't want to hold hands! We don't even go to church." cried the son.

Still the teenager said nothing, just hung her head in silence.

They were still fighting as they went out the door and continued to argue all the way home. But, that night they said grace and ate dinner together. It was uncomfortable, but they got through it with only a little fighting. And each day it became more natural. They even invented their own prayers.

When they saw the counselor a couple of weeks later, he remarked on the smiles he saw all the way around the room—including the teenager, who finally spoke.

"That's the best advice we've ever gotten," she said. "I get the chance to see my Mom and Dad and brother every day for at least a few minutes." They all agreed, and shared a family hug.

That family found that, over time, they were able to become a real family that was able to show that they cared for each other. (3)

Mary and Joseph couldn't surround their child with material goods, but they could surround him with love. They could give him time and attention and spiritual and moral guidance. Even though he was the Son of God remember he was a real boy. He emptied himself when he became a human being. He needed the love and the nurture of a family. Every child does. Many parents feel guilty that they cannot give their children nice toys and expensive playthings. They shouldn't. Only feel guilty if you're letting them grow up feeling unloved. A good way to start the New Year would be to take stock of the time you take as a family remembering God.

The first lesson that we learn from this story is that Mary and Joseph had few material resources. That is how God began His redemption of humankind—at the bottom of society—with a borrowed manger and the most humble of homes. Jesus never did get into accumulating treasure on earth. His friends even had to borrow a grave to bury him in.

But notice a second thing: Mary and Joseph had no idea what lay ahead of them. You would think, when we read the Christmas story that Mary and Joseph could look forward to a charmed life. After all, their son was the Messiah. Their life should be easy. Their child was in God's care. Little did they know what lay ahead.

As Mary and Joseph offered up the pair of turtledoves for the sacrifice, could they possibly have imagined that their son would one day be offered up as the sacrifice to end all sacrifices? Could they in their wildest dreams have seen where this happiest of occasions would one day lead—that the son they dedicated to God in the temple would kneel in a garden and confirm that dedication with drops of sweat like great drops of blood falling to the ground around him as he prayed, "Not my will, but yours be done?"

The Biblical record is clear that Mary and Joseph could not see where God was leading their son. Neither could the rest of their family. Only after his resurrection did they comprehend.

Luke tells us that Simeon recognized immediately that this was the Christ child. The Holy Spirit had revealed this to Simeon. And he announced it to Jesus' parents. How did they react? Luke writes, "The child's father and mother marveled at what was said about him. Then Simeon blessed them and said to Mary, his mother: 'This child is destined to cause the falling and rising of many in Israel, and to be a sign that will be spoken against, so that the thoughts of many hearts will be revealed. And a sword will pierce your own soul too.'"

Prophetic words to be spoken to Jesus' mother—"And a sword will pierce your . . . soul too." Could there be a more terrible sword than watching your son die on a cross?

When we bring a child into the world we have no idea what the future may hold. Do any of you with children ever worry about them? Get ready for a lifetime of that.

One man writes that he and his wife found their whole life turned upside down when their first child was born. Every night, the baby seemed to be fussy, and many nights, it seemed to the young couple that their baby cried far more than he slept.

Says this father, "My wife would wake me up, saying, 'Get up, honey! Go see why the baby is crying!'" As a result, the father found himself suffering from severe sleep deprivation.

While complaining to his coworkers about his problem one day, one of his colleagues suggested a book on infant massage. The desperate father immediately went in search of this book and that night, he tried the technique, gently rubbing his baby's back, arms, head, and legs until the baby was completely relaxed and obviously had fallen into a deep sleep. Quietly tiptoeing from the darkened room so as not to disturb the rhythmic breathing of the baby, he made his way directly to his own bed in hopes of enjoying a well-deserved full night of sleep.

In the middle of the night, however, his wife woke him in a panic. "Get up, honey!" she said as she jostled him awake. "Go see why the baby is NOT crying!" (4)

There's plenty to worry about when you're a parent, regardless of how old your child is. Even late in life, you worry about their health, their financial status, whether they are happy and their home life is secure. None of us knows what the future holds for ourselves or for those we love.

There is only one thing we know as we enter a New Year. It was the same thing Mary and Joseph knew: both we and those we love are in God's hands. That doesn't mean life will always be a smooth road for us. Everyone encounters bumps along the way. We get discouraged, sometimes even bitter, but we do not give up, for we trust that an Unseen Hand is leading us.

It's like a church that the Rev. Suzanne E. Watson tells about, Saint David's Episcopal Church in San Diego, California. From the parking lot, she notes, a long, winding path leads to the sanctuary, landscaped with trees and plants indigenous to the Holy Land. Walking through the olive trees and fragrant flowers, the first thing that a visitor sees is a solid, even cracked, unfinished concrete portico extending from the worship space. The stark brokenness of the entry is startling. Even more shocking is the support, or lack thereof; it appears to be held up by two massive concrete pillars, but when one looks closely, the pillars stop two inches below the overhang. It appears that there is nothing supporting the massive, cracked concrete structure.

A wary guest asked, "Is it structurally sound?"

"The answer is yes; it was constructed in full compliance with the state's building codes. But the architects intentionally designed the real support to be invisible. The entry to that sanctuary represents all people as we come to Christ broken and unfinished," says Rev. Watson, "and although we have many visible and tangible supports on our Christian path, such as scripture, worship, the sacraments, and our faith community, that last 'two inches' of our Christian journey is built on faith. Faith in things that we cannot see." (5)

Mary and Joseph trusted in that which they did not see. They were like most families. They struggled with their finances. They tried their best to raise their son, but there is much evidence that they did not quite understand him. They lived by faith—that invisible "two inches" that we all embrace. They made it. So can we.

1. Doc's Daily Chuckles. To subscribe: http://family-safe-mail.com/lists/?p=subscribe&id=55.
2. MONDAY FODDER.
3. Therapy for the Human Family by Bill Fulton, Grace and Trinity Episcopal Churches, Winfield and Arkansas City, Kansas. Adapted. "One Lord, One Table," Rev. Billy D. Strayhorn, http://www.epulpit.net/051002.htm.
4. Kais Rayes. Cited in God's Devotional Book for Mothers (Colorado Springs: Cook Communications, 2005), p. 269.
5. http://www.episcopalchurch.org/sermons_that_work_127261_ENG_HTM.htm.

We Saw His Star
Matthew 2:1-12

Have you ever seen a UFO? Don't laugh. Former president Ronald Reagan did. During a routine flight while he was governor of California, Reagan reported seeing a bright white light zigzagging through the sky. After having his plane give chase for a few minutes, Reagan told the Wall Street Journal that "all of a sudden to our utter amazement it went straight up into the heavens."

Former President Jimmy Carter had a similar experience in 1969, 7 years before he was elected president. "It was the darndest thing I've ever seen," Carter said during the 1976 campaign. "It was big; it was very bright. It changed colors and it was about the size of the moon. We watched it for 10 minutes, but none of us could figure out what it was. One thing's for sure. I'll never make fun of people who say they've seen unidentified objects in the sky." (1)

Welcome to this celebration of Epiphany. Epiphany celebrates an event in which a group of magi saw something bright and mysterious in the heavens—not a UFO, but a star, a very bright star. They followed it until it came to rest over the house where Mary and Joseph were staying along with their infant son. Once inside they fell down and worshiped Jesus and offered him gifts of gold, frankincense and myrrh. "We have seen his star in the east," they explained. These magi are celebrated as the first gentiles to acknowledge Jesus as the king of kings.

The gospel of Matthew tells their story. Little is known about who these men really were, where they came from, or even how many of them there were. Early scholars inferred that there were three of them because three different gifts were named, but we do not know for sure. Neither do we know the nation from which they came. Some scholars argue that the group probably came from Babylon, since Babylon is directly east of Jerusalem and the Babylonians were astute astronomers with records dating back to 2000 BC. Indeed, since the Jews were once captives in Babylon, it makes sense that the wise men would have known of the expected King and the Old Testament prophecies surrounding his arrival. They could even have been descendants of Jews who did not leave Babylon after their forced captivity, though that would throw into uncertainty the idea that they were the first gentiles to acknowledge Christ.

What was the nature of the light that guided them? It is called a "star," but, if so, it was an unusual one. It was exceedingly bright and it seemed to move before them.

The favored theory is that the star may have been a nova or an extremely rare supernova—a white dwarf star that has blown off its upper layers in a violent explosion, making it as much as fifty thousand times brighter than our sun and viewable as a bright star in the night sky, lasting perhaps for several months to more than a year. (2)

Another favorite theory is that it was Halley's Comet. This would explain its movement in the sky.

Nativity sets always include the three magi as if they were present in the stable at Jesus' birth. However, it is plain that these men did not arrive until possibly two years after Christ's birth, certainly some time after his presentation in the Temple (Luke 2:22- 39). Immediately after their visit, you'll remember, Mary and Joseph fled with Jesus to Egypt, where they probably stayed till after Herod's death in 4 B.C.

We could go on, of course, with much historical speculation about these men who occupy such an interesting place in our faith. It's all part of the magic of the birth of our Lord.

I like humorous columnist Dave Barry's take on the wise men. He writes, "This is the time of year when we think back to the very first Christmas, when the Three Wise Men—Gaspar, Balthazar and Herb, went to see the baby Jesus and, according to the Book of Matthew, 'presented unto Him gifts: gold, frankincense, and myrrh.'

"These are simple words, but if we analyze them carefully," says Dave Barry, "we discover an important, yet often overlooked, theological fact . . . that there is no mention of wrapping paper.

"If there had been wrapping paper," Barry continues, "Matthew would have said so. 'And lo, the gifts were inside 60 square cubits of paper. And the paper was festooned with pictures of Frosty the Snowman. And Joseph thinketh to throw it away, but Mary saith unto him, she saith, "Holdeth it! Verily I say unto thee, thou art not looking, yonder in thine hand is nice paper! Saveth thou it for next year!" And Joseph did roll his eyes. And the babe was more interested in the paper than the frankincense.'

"But these words do not appear in the Bible, which means that the very first Christmas gifts were NOT wrapped. This is because the people giving those gifts had two important characteristics: 1. They were wise. 2. They were men. And of course, the Gift Bag wouldn't be discovered for thousands of years." (3)

Well, I suspect most men don't like wrapping gifts, and we can assume that the gold, frankincense, and myrrh were unwrapped. But, seriously, what does this ancient story say to us? There are three elements that stand out to me.

First, we see the genuine searching of these men from the east. The magi traveled many miles without maps, or even GPS systems . . . trusting only in some ancient and somewhat obscure biblical writings that their search would yield this king whom they sought. Surely friends and family back home tried to dissuade them. Surely they became discouraged as they trod mile after fruitless mile. Obviously they had a great yearning to bow down before one who was greater than themselves.

You and I have that yearning. It is the earnest searching of the heart of every man and woman for God.

Many years ago, writes an unknown author, a little boy lay on his small bed, having just retired for the night. Before going to sleep, he moved in the direction of the large bed on which his father lay, and said: "Father, are you there?"

"Yes, my son," was the answer. The little boy turned over and went to sleep, without a thought of harm.

Tonight the little boy is an old man of seventy, and every night before going to sleep, he looks up into the face of his Heavenly Father and says, "Father, are you there?"

And the answer comes back, clear and strong: "Yes, my son." (4)

You don't have to be a pagan from a far off land to seek God. I don't know about you. Every time I come into this room, there is part of me that is still seeking God. I continually need to be reminded that I am not dependent on my own resources. There is One far greater than I who is in control of this universe. We see in this simple story the genuine searching of these men from the east.

We also see the cruel, self-seeking attitude of Herod. We can almost see the sneer on his face as he says deceitfully, "Go and search carefully for the child. As soon as you find him, report to me, so that I too may go and worship him."

Herod was a cruel man. Secular historians tell us that as well as the Bible narrative. But he is not alone. The world has always been inhabited by cruel men and so often, it is the innocent who have suffered in their hands.

Have you ever heard of the so-called Candelaria Massacre? This heinous crime took place one night in 1993 in Rio de Janeiro, Brazil. The tragedy involved the murder of 8 street children who were sleeping in a church doorway. In the trial 3 years later, 2 former policemen were convicted. One was sentenced to 309 years in prison, reduced to 89 years after retrial (even though Brazil has a 30-year limit on incarceration).

Some suspected the crime was part of a plot by police officers to earn extra money from shopkeepers by getting rid of street children who commit petty crimes against the merchants. However, the defendant testified the killings happened because some children had thrown stones at a police car the previous day—as if that made the reaction excusable.

History is full of cruel ironies, and here's the one in this story: the name of the defendant given the 309-year sentence for killing the eight children was Marcus Emanuel! A man whose surname means "God with us" (Matthew 1:23) repeated the crime Herod had sought to commit against the true Immanuel—the baby Jesus.

We may not know the true reason for Marcus Emanuel's crime, but Herod's motive was clear. He was so intent on eliminating threats to his kingship that he was willing to kill innocent infants to ensure his continued rule. Such is the power of sin that Jesus came to destroy. (5) We see the earnest yearning of the magi to worship the new- born king. We see the cruelty of Herod's response.

And, finally, we see the adoration of the magi for the child as they give him their gifts. It's a beautiful scene. The magi offer him gifts of gold, frankincense and myrrh.

William Barker tells a legend regarding the three gifts that the magi brought. According to this legend the famed explorer Marco Polo, while traveling through ancient Persia, found the village where the wise men had lived. The legend says that there were three Magi named Caspar, Melchior, and Balthasar. Caspar was young and beardless; Melchior was older, with a long beard and white hair; and Balthasar was a swarthy, middle-aged man.

The story claims that the Magi brought several gifts with them so that they could offer whatever tribute would be most appropriate. They had gold in case the baby was royalty—a king. The frankincense was in the event that the baby had an aura of divinity. Last, they included myrrh in case they determined that he would be a physician.

This legend has them coming to the manger in Bethlehem. When they arrived they entered the cave one at a time to visit the baby. Melchior, the old man, went first to visit the child. Next, Balthasar crouched and entered the stable, and Caspar visited last. Then the three wise men compared notes. They felt that all of their gifts should be left. They believed that the baby Jesus was a king, was possessed with divinity, and would also be a healer. (6) And, of course, they were right.

It's just a legend. But again it is part of the magic of the story of Christ's coming. History takes a back-seat to theology. Who was this babe of Bethlehem? He was royalty, divinity, healer. And the world still yearns for him today.

1. Augusta Chronicle, 1/28/01. Cited in Paul Grobman, Vital Statistics (New York: Penguin Group, 2005), p. 317.
2. W. B. Freeman, The Longer-Lasting Inspirational Bathroom Book (New York: FaithWords Hatchette, 2007), pp. 53-54.
3. http://www.thatsrich.com/wrapping.htm.
4. Gary Bowell, Stones with Fair Colors. Cited by Ronald George, http://www.wvcis.net/~george1/sermons/001008pm.htm
5. Ronald Nickelson, The NIV Standard Lesson Commentary, 2009-2010 (Cincinnati: Standard Publishing, 2009), p. 155.
6. Dr. William P. Barker, Tarbell's Teacher's Manual (Elgin, IL: David C. Cook Church Ministries, 1994).

I Am Baptized!
Mark 1:7-11

Because of their age and relative inexperience, children and young people rarely get asked for advice by adults. This is sad, since the young tend to have amazing powers of observation, as well as the free time to ponder the strangeness of human nature.

In his book Wit and Wisdom from the Peanut Butter Gang, H. Jackson Brown, Jr. interviews children and young teens to get their ideas on subjects like families and school. Here is a sample of their wisdom:

"You can't trust dogs to watch your food." — Patrick, age 10

"'Casserole' is just another word for 'leftovers.'" — Emily, age 14

"You can't hide mashed potatoes in your hat." — Chris, age 9 (You have to wonder how he knows that.)

"You should not be the first one to fall asleep at a slumber party." — Katie, age 12

And this final thought from Laura, age 13: "No matter how hard you try, you can't baptize a cat!" (1)

I can't speak from experience, but I imagine that is true. Of course, it is not always easy to baptize humans, either. Our Baptist friends who baptize by total immersion tell hilarious stories about some of the problems they face.

For example, Dr. Drexel Rayford tells about his experiences baptizing young people at his first church, the Muldraugh Baptist Church in Muldraugh, Kentucky.

Their church baptistery, says Dr. Rayford, was fed by weak plumbing and normally took over 36 hours to fill. However, due to some quirk of the plumbing, sometimes the water would suddenly start gushing out rather than trickling as it normally did, and if you weren't regularly checking back on the level of the water, it could overflow into the choir loft.

Unfortunately they couldn't trust their custodian, Homer, to make certain things worked right. Homer often slipped off and spent his hours at the local tavern.

One time Rayford told Homer to fill the baptistery on Thursday before a Sunday service in which they were planning to baptize nine young persons—eight girls and one 13-year-old boy. Rayford then went out of town and came back on Saturday night. He didn't think to check the baptistery.

Sunday morning came and Rayford discovered that the baptistery was bone dry. Nine kids were getting baptized in just three hours. This was a big day for their families. There was no way to cancel the baptisms for lack of water. So Rayford literally ran to the parsonage next door, grabbed a garden hose, ran it across the driveway, up the front steps, down the center aisle and into the baptistery. In one hour, the baptistery was full of water, right out of a Kentucky limestone well. And it was cold, really cold, Rayford reports. It must have been all of 50 degrees, which might as well have been freezing for the young people who were being baptized.

He says he himself was shaking as he looked up at the baptismal candidates gathered in their thin, little white robes at the top of the ladder. They were excited. He warned them that the water wasn't all that warm. Later, he says, as each descended into the pool, their little eyes bugged out, they became stiff as boards, and he had a rather difficult time getting them to bend enough to get them under the water.

The girls took it well, but the boy was more difficult. The moment his bare foot hit the water, he let out a shocked noise. Getting him under the water turned into a wrestling match. Water sloshed over the glass at the front of the baptistery, soaking the basses in the last row of the choir loft. As he emerged from the water the young man shouted loudly, "Oh GOD, that's cold!!!"

By this time the entire congregation was rocking with laughter. Later, the chairman of the deacons, who was one of the basses on the back row of the choir loft said, "Well pastor, that's one baptism we all participated in!"

Dr. Drexel Rayford says he laughs every time he thinks about that incident. But on later reflection he realized that deacon had it right. We all do participate in the sacrament of baptism. (2)

Baptism is a sacrament of the church. That is the first thing we need to see. Baptism belongs to the church. No matter how it is performed, baptism is at the heart of our faith. Every religious tradition has its own approach to baptism, but every major Christian body recognizes the importance of baptism. It is a holy rite even in the humblest of circumstances. And, if at all possible, it is a celebration of the whole body of Christ. We all participate in it. There are circumstances which may require a person to be baptized in a private setting, but this should be an unusual circumstance. This is a celebration of the entire church. That's the first thing to be said about baptism.

Here's the second: baptism is a sacrament. Jesus himself was baptized. That's one thing that makes it a sacrament. He was baptized at the hand of John the Baptist. John's baptism was a baptism of repentance. The water was a symbol of the washing away of sin. Jesus, of course, had no sin. We believe that in submitting to baptism he was setting an example for us. He was also identifying with the message of repentance that John preached. Jesus knew and later preached that repentance was necessary in order to live the kingdom life.

Jesus was baptized by John, but John knew that really he should be baptized by Jesus. He was baptizing the Son of God. Just as Jesus was coming up out of the water, he saw heaven being torn open and the Spirit descending on him like a dove. And a voice came from heaven: "You are my Son, whom I love; with you I am well pleased."

The other people on the banks of the Jordan River that day had no idea of the significance of this event. Christ's true identity was still hidden from them. But John knew, and even more important, God knew: "You are my Son, whom I love . . . ."

And so we count baptism as a sacrament of the church. Jesus was baptized and we who follow Christ understand baptism to be central to the Christian life.

But there is something else we need to see: baptism is a sign that we belong to Christ. In a sense there is a voice that comes from heaven whenever anyone is baptized that says: "You are my child, whom I love; with you I am well pleased." It doesn't matter that we are not sinless as Christ was, but because of what God has done in Christ, we are accepted as if we were. We are God's beloved. No matter how the water is applied, baptism is sign and seal that we are no longer our own. We belong to Christ.

Episcopal Priest Doug Bailey tells about going to Atlanta to officiate at the baptism of his grandson. At the parish where the baptism was occurring they had a custom. Someone in the church would create a banner for each of the children who were being baptized. On the banner was the child's name, the date of the baptism and the phrase "Christ's Own Forever" on it. It's a nice custom.

After the baptismal liturgy was over, Rev. Bailey, his family and friends of the newly baptized child went to a party at the parents' home. As the child's mother entered the house, she took the baptismal banner and put it on a tack outside the front door of their home.

That same afternoon, some of their friends who lived nearby and who had been out of town for the week drove by the house. They saw the banner bearing the child's name. The banner also bore the date and the phrase "Christ's Own Forever." They were mystified. What does the banner mean? "Christ's Own Forever."

An hour later in the middle of the party; the phone rang. It was the voice of the neighbor who had driven by and seen the banner outside the house. "I'm so sorry to trouble you," she said. "I feel awful asking you this, but has something terrible happened while we've been out of town? (This was followed by an awkward silence).

Then the voice on the other end of the line asked, "Did your son die?" (3)

Well, no, though we could understand how they might have gotten that impression. Their son had not died. They just wanted the world to know that their son belonged to God: "Christ's Own Forever." Baptism means we belong to Christ.

It is said that whenever Martin Luther found himself ready to give up, whenever worry for his own life and the life of the Church he loved overwhelmed him, he would touch his forehead and say to himself: "Remember Martin, you have been baptized."

Baptism is a sacrament. Baptism is a sign that we belong to God.

Baptism is also a statement of where our ultimate allegiance lies. The reason we present ourselves or our children for baptism is that we are making a statement about who we are and what is important in our lives.

Robert McAfee Brown tells of a time in 1960, when he participated in a Lutheran worship service in East Berlin, only a short time before the Berlin Wall was constructed. There were not many people present for the worship service, because church attendance was viewed with suspicion by the state. The East German Republic had developed secular alternatives to replace all of the rituals of the church. Nonetheless, a young couple came to the worship service and presented their child for baptism. Brown was amazed, and wondered why this couple would jeopardize their future and that of their child by insisting on this ancient ritual of baptism when a secular alternative was available?

Brown writes, "The couple does not have to answer my question. Their very act of bringing their baby to the church is a public statement of their priorities. They engage in significant risk because of their faith. In the face of their quiet, public courage I feel unworthy." (4)

This couple wanted to make a statement: our child belongs to God, and nothing—even the power of the state—was going to deter them from making that statement.

There was a cartoon in Leadership Journal sometime back that had a subtle message. It showed a church secretary buzzing the pastor and announcing, "It's Monty Williams. He wants to know if he can audit your discipleship class on 'Total Commitment.'" (5)

The joke is, of course, that a lot of people would like to simply audit the course on total commitment rather than doing the real thing. When we understand the significance of Christian baptism, however, we see the folly in that. Christ did not audit the course that took him to the cross. He took the real thing. When we live out our baptism we live out his purpose for our life. Baptism is a sacrament of the church. It is sign and seal that we belong to God. It is a statement of where our ultimate allegiance lies.

And one thing more: Baptism is a sign of our new life in Christ.

There is a delightful story about a precocious three-year-old named Joey, who did not enjoy baths. Seeking to overcome his objections, his mother said, "Don't you want to be nice and clean?"

Joey replied, "Yes, but can't you just dust me off?"

That's what a lot of us would like when it comes to baptism—a simple dusting.

One man said that at a certain point in his life he considered joining a Baptist Church. He was even willing to be totally immersed in order to make this move. Luckily, he knew a minister in that faith, having dated the minister's daughter. He asked him if he would consider performing the service.

The Baptist pastor paused a minute or two, gave him a long thoughtful look and said, "If you're serious about this, a mere dipping just won't do for you. We'll have to find a place to anchor you overnight."

I suspect that a lot of us would need to be anchored for a while to get rid of all our sins. We need to understand that baptism isn't a ritual by which we are washed clean. Neither is it a sign that we are going to try our best to quit sinning, as noble and as necessary as that might be. Baptism is a symbol that we have already been accepted by God and that in God's eyes we have already been made clean by Christ's sacrifice on the cross. Therefore, since this has happened, we respond by taking on a new life in Christ.

Pastor Thomas Pinckney uses a wonderful analogy of this truth. He says that one summer his boys discovered large clay deposits in the swimming hole he and they had built in the Green River. The boys discovered that this clay made great body paint! They would get all wet, then smear clay over their entire body, head to foot.

One day he noticed the two boys covered with clay, with a gleam in their eyes, whispering among themselves. Then they turned toward their mother and declared, "We love you, Mommy!"—and ran toward her covered with mud with the intention of giving her a big hug. She naturally ran in the opposite direction. Who wants to be hugged by two boys covered with yucky clay?

But Mothers don't always run from dirty children, even though they may get covered with filth themselves, do they? asks Pinckney. Imagine this, he says: "You hear the distressed cry of your child and look up: Your precious daughter has fallen face first in the mud, and now runs toward you, tears streaming through the dirt. Here she comes, with mud on her clothes, her face, in her hair, her eyes, her ears, her mouth. What do you mothers do? Do you say, 'Don't come near!' Do you say, 'You made your mess—now clean it up!' To an older, responsible child, you might say that. But not to one who can't clean herself. You take her in your arms, soiling your own clothes; you comfort her, then gently clean all the sand and dirt and refuse from her eyes, ears, nostrils, mouth. You love her, clean her, and comfort her. That child has come to you, in effect saying through her tears: 'I am a mess. I can't clean myself. If you are willing, you can make me clean.' And you are willing." (6)

That is what God has done for us in Christ Jesus. Baptism doesn't make that possible for us. Baptism is an acknowledgement that it has already been done in our behalf. We belong to God. Baptism is our response of faith. It shows where our allegiance lies. It acknowledges that we are seeking to live a new life in Christ.

Before you leave this room, you might want to pause for a moment, touch your forehead, and say gratefully, "I am baptized!"

1. (Nashville: Rutledge Hill Press, 1994).
2. http://www.walnutgrovebaptist.com/Sermons/2007/2007 01 07.htm.
3. http://www.stpaulseattle.org/sermons/Lent1_06.html.
4. Rev. Daniel W. Matthews, http://www.finleypres.org/worship/sermons/20030112.htm.
5. Jim Hammond, http://www.vvchristianchurch.net/Sermons/CR2.htm.
6. Thomas C. Pinckney, http://tcpiii.tripod.com/mark1c.htm.

Doing Your Own Thing
1 Corinthians 6:12-20

Have you ever had the urge to simply do your own thing without any regard to how the world may view your actions? If you have ever had that urge, you would not be the first to feel that longing . . . or to act on it.

In the late 1960s, a group of hippies—remember them?—living in the Haight Ashbury District of San Francisco decided that personal hygiene—taking baths and showers and washing your hair, etc.—was a middle class hang up they could do without. So, they quit indulging in these bourgeois activities. Baths and showers, while not actually banned, were discouraged. In the words of author Tom Wolfe, these hippies "sought nothing less than to sweep aside all codes and restraints of the past and start out from zero."

Before long, the hippies' aversion to modern hygiene had consequences that were as unpleasant as they were unforeseen. Wolfe describes them: "At the Haight Ashbury Free clinic there were doctors who were treating diseases no living doctor had ever encountered before, diseases that had disappeared so long ago they had never even picked up Latin names; diseases with contemporary names such as the mange, the grunge, the itch, the twitch, the thrush, the scroff, the rot."

The itching and the manginess eventually began to vex even the hippies, leading them to seek help from the local free clinics. They had to rediscover for themselves the rudiments of personal hygiene. Wolfe refers to this as the "Great Relearning." (1)

Hippies are no longer in vogue, but their guiding attitude in life is still very much with us. Even though we don't hear the phrase much anymore, people still want to do their own thing . . . make their own rules . . . serve as their own moral guide. "This is my body. I will do with it as I please." Ever hear that one before? "This is my money. I will spend it as I please. This is my life. If I want to squander it, that is my right."

Have you ever encountered someone with that kind of attitude? Perhaps a few of you did when you got up this morning and looked in the mirror.

This is the spirit of our time. We're a little more sophisticated about it than the young people of the 60s, but still that is basically how we live. People want to be free to do their own thing.

After captivating an audience at Yale University, the late novelist Ayn [pronounced Ine] Rand was asked by a reporter, "What's wrong with the modern world?"

Without a moment's hesitation Rand replied, "Never before has the world been so desperately asking for answers to crucial questions, and never before has the world been so frantically committed to the idea that no answers are possible." Then Ayn Rand added this thought, "To paraphrase the Bible, the modern attitude is, 'Father, forgive us, for we know not what we are doing—and please don't tell us!'" (2)

In this instance Ayn Rand was right. Behavior that would have been shocking to previous generations is accepted now with a shrug.

Obviously, this is not the biblical understanding of life. In fact, in the story of Adam and Eve in the very beginning of our Bible, this is the attitude that got humanity in trouble in the first place. To state things even more emphatically, you could make a case that this is the very definition of sin—doing your own thing with total disregard for God's purpose for your life.

St. Paul ran into this sort of attitude more than two thousand years ago. Conversion to Christianity was a great liberation to many who had felt enslaved by the Jewish Law. They felt gloriously free when they became Christians, and they exulted in their new freedom. But soon that freedom turned to license. St. Paul writes, "'I have the right to do anything,' you say . . ." and that is indeed what many of the Corinthians were saying. But St. Paul counters, you may have a right to do anything, "but not everything is beneficial . . ." And he focuses on two examples: food and sex. Interesting choices!

Now, food's easy to deal with—and maybe we should since America is in the midst of an obesity epidemic. And why should we be surprised?

One woman says that after her husband asked her to help him shed some unwanted pounds, she stopped serving fattening TV snacks and substituted instead crisp celery, the perfect diet food.

While her husband was unenthusiastically munching on a stalk one night, a commercial caught his attention. As he watched longingly, a woman spread gooey chocolate frosting over a freshly baked cake. When it was over, her husband turned to her. "Did you ever notice," he asked dejectedly, "that they never advertise celery on TV?" (3)

That's true, even if celery is the perfect snack as far as calories are concerned. If we want to lose weight, we're not going to get any help from Madison Avenue. That's one reason it's hard for some of us to keep our weight under control.

I heard a hilarious story recently about a man who started a new diet, The Purina Diet—named, of course, for Purina dog food. Well, he didn't really eat dog food, but have you noticed how some people can ask silly questions?

Well, this guy is standing in line at Wal-Mart with a large bag of Purina. A woman behind him asked if he had a dog. There he is standing in line with a large bag of Purina . . . "Well, duh . . . ." So he decided to have some fun.

He told her no, he didn't have any dogs. He went on to explain that he was starting The Purina Diet . . . again . . . although he probably shouldn't because . . . the last time he'd ended up in the hospital . . . However, he had lost 50 pounds on the diet . . . before he awakened in an intensive care unit with tubes coming out all over the place and IVs in both arms.

He told her that it was essentially a perfect diet and that the way that it works is to load your pants pockets with Purina nuggets and simply eat one or two every time you feel hungry. He went on to say that the food is nutritionally complete so he was going to try it again.

He says that by this time practically everyone in the line was enthralled with his story, particularly a guy who was behind the lady who asked the question. Horrified, she asked if he'd ended up in the hospital in that condition because he had been poisoned by eating all that dog food. With a serious expression on his face he told her no; he said it was because he'd been barking in the street and a car hit him.

At this, he said, the guy behind this lady was about to have a heart attack, he was laughing so hard. (4) Well, so much for dumb questions . . .

I don't guess any diet is perfect, even the Purina Diet. Losing weight is hard. But at least it is easy to see what happens to you if you eat excessively. We may be free, as St. Paul says, to do anything, but not everything is beneficial. With regard to food, it usually becomes self-evident.

The dangers of sexual freedom may not be quite as obvious.

There was a time when the greatest fear of unrestrained sexual freedom among "nice" young people was pregnancy. Then came the fear of sexually-transmitted disease, especially the HIV virus. These risks are still with us, of course. Still, even if you are able to perfectly control these adverse consequences, there are still risks to practicing unrestrained sexual freedom—spiritual risks, emotional risks.

There was a sad story recently in the magazine The Week. It was titled, "Not Your Parents' Divorce." It was written by Susan Gregory Thomas. Ms. Thomas is a member of Generation X, that group of young people born between 1965 and 1980. Census data show that almost half of Generation Xers come from split families; 40 percent of Generation Xers were latchkey kids. Ms. Thomas and her husband both came from split families and she describes in stark detail just how devastating divorce can be for children. She cites a 2004 study which described Generation X as "the least parented, least nurtured generation in U.S. history." She says that both she and her husband were determined that once they were married, they would never, never divorce, especially after they had kids of their own. But they did. Even though, according to Ms. Thomas, they really, really tried to hold their marriage together, it did not work out.

What interests me is that she admits that she and her husband knew the statistics and knew the risks of how to prepare for marriage. For example, they thought their marriage would be stronger if they lived together before they married. In her own words, "We were together for nearly eight years before we got married, and even though statistics show that divorce rates are 48 percent higher for cohabitants, we paid no heed."

That's sad. Living together before marriage has been shown scientifically to be detrimental to the marriage relationship. Why does every generation of young people think things will somehow be different for them? Why do we continually have to relearn the lessons of the past? Some things never change. Ms. Thomas writes, "We also paid no heed to his Catholic parents . . . when they warned us that we should wait until we were married to live together. As they put it, being pals and roommates is different from being husband and wife." Then she adds, "How bizarrely old-fashioned and sexist!" (5)

Well, maybe it is old-fashioned and sexist, but that doesn't keep it from being true. I'm not passing judgment on this couple, nor on Generation X, nor on Boomers for the high rate of divorce that so badly affected Generation X, nor on any other generation or group. I'm simply appealing to all of us to recognize that the wisdom of the Bible has been established over hundreds of generations. The only safe sex is sex practiced within the marriage relationship. And that relationship is to be exclusive. People make mistakes of course, even the best intended of us, but the ideal remains. As Paul cites from Genesis, "The two are to become one flesh."

Humanity has experimented for thousands of years with various other approaches to the question of sexual morality. And no approach yet has come even close to the Christian ideal of a young woman and a young man enjoying a romantic, even passionate courtship but delaying sexual relations until after marriage—a marriage to which they dedicate themselves before God and their faith community, "until death us do part." Usually if a couple devote themselves to one another, and to God, it works. They find fulfillment and a lifetime of happiness.

And there is a reason it works: we do not belong to ourselves. We belong to Christ. St. Paul writes, "Do you not know that your bodies are temples of the Holy Spirit, who is in you, whom you have received from God? You are not your own; you were bought at a price. Therefore honor God with your bodies."

Here is the crux of the matter, our bodies are not our own and we dishonor God when we do anything with our body that harms it or that could bring us shame.

Some of you who are basketball fans may know the name A.C. Green. At the 2011 All Star Breakfast, A.C. Green was awarded the Bobby Jones Award for character, leadership, and faith in the world of basketball in the home and the community.

A. C. Green is a man who takes care of his body. A former NBA all-star and three time World Champion Los Angeles Laker, Green played in more consecutive games than any other player in NBA and ABA history. He played in 1,192 straight games. If you know anything about the toll professional basketball takes on the body, you will be impressed with A.C. Green's record. He earned the nickname "Iron Man."

Here is something you may not know, Green is a deeply religious man who, before his marriage a few years back, was well-known in the NBA for his commitment for delaying sex until he was married. If you know about some of the sexual activities of many NBA players, that will impress you even more. During his playing days, according to a report on CNN, his teammates would frequently send women to tempt Green to compromise his morals. Instead, he would respond by calmly quoting scripture. He even established a foundation—The A. C. Green Youth Foundation—that works with underprivileged youth and encourages sexual abstinence. Green says, with regard to sexual abstinence, "If I can do it in the role that God took me on, traveling throughout the NBA, there's not a teenager that can tell me it's tougher on them."

No one can argue with A. C. Green about that. "When you have a vision, a purpose, and understand your calling," says Green, "you can do extraordinary things for God, even in the midst of a peculiar situation. Living in the NBA for twenty years was very peculiar. But at the same time, it did not separate me from the goal I had— the burning passion that God put in my heart: to instill some kind of hope into our future generation, our kids." (6)

Honor God with your body, says St. Paul. Certainly A. C. Green has done that. He has disciplined his body both to make himself an outstanding athlete and to make himself into an outstanding husband for his wife. When it came to making a choice between doing his own thing and doing God's thing, A. C. Green chose God. Every study I've seen, even by secular authors and researchers say he made the right choice.

Every generation goes through the process of relearning what humanity has already discovered. There are not only physical laws, but moral laws and spiritual laws that govern this universe. The hippies had to relearn them about hygiene. They were stupid you say? Perhaps no more stupid than we are by the ways we dishonor the body and dishonor God today.

There is an old story about several large signs posted on a piece of property that said "No Trespassing." But that didn't stop young boys from climbing the fence in order to reach the apples that grew on a large tree in the forbidden territory.

One day, a small boy slipped while he was climbing the apple tree, and fell onto a pile of sharp branches, cutting himself badly, and breaking his ankle. Alone and afraid, the young boy lay crying for hours.

Finally, the owner of the property happened by. He came over and lifted the boy from the ground. The child was afraid of the farmer. After all, he had posted all these "No Trespassing" signs. But the old gentleman merely smiled at the boy and said, "I didn't put the signs up to be mean. I put them there to try to keep things like this from happening. It was kindness which caused me to want to protect little boys just like you."

So it is with God. God's "No Trespassing" signs are not placed around certain areas of our lives to be mean, but for our benefit. God wants only the best for us.

Remember these all-important words from scripture: "Do you not know that your bodies are temples of the Holy Spirit, who is in you, whom you have received from God? You are not your own; you were bought at a price. Therefore honor God with your bodies."

1. Christina Hoff Sommers. Cited by Barry Robinson, http://www.rockies.net/~spirit/sermons/b or20 keeping.php.

2. Howard G. Hendricks and William D. Hendricks, Living By The Book (Chicago, IL: Moody Press, 1991).

3. Kathy Zellers, "Life In These United States."

4. Marty's Joke of the Day. To subscribe, send a blank email to: martysjotd-subscribe@ya-hooGroups.com.

5. From In Spite of Everything by Susan Gregory Thomas. Random House, 2011. The Week August 5, 2011.

6. Robert H. Schuller, Don't Throw Away Tomorrow (New York: HarperCollins Publishers, Inc., 2005), pp. 89-91.

A Cantankerous Prophet
Jonah 3:1-5; 10-11

There are some jokes that are so bad they bear retelling. [So, if any of you remember me telling this story, keep that in mind.] (1)

It seems there was once a fisherman ... you already know it's going to be bad, don't you? This fisherman and his wife were blessed with twin sons. They loved the children very much, but couldn't think of what to name them. Finally, after several days, the fisherman said, "Let's not decide on names right now. If we wait a little while, the names will simply occur to us."

After several weeks had passed, the fisherman and his wife noticed a peculiar fact. When left alone, one of the boys would turn toward the sea, while the other boy would face inland. It didn't matter which way the parents positioned the children, the same child always faced the same direction—one faced toward the sea and the other faced away. "That's it," said the fisherman. "Let's name the boys Towards and Away since one boy is always looking TOWARDS the sea and the other is always looking AWAY." His wife agreed, and from that point on, the boys were simply known as TOWARDS and AWAY.

The years passed and the lads grew tall and strong. The day came when the fisherman said to his sons, "Boys, it is time that you learned how to make a living from the sea." They provisioned their ship, said their goodbyes, and set sail for a three-month voyage.

But something happened. Three whole years passed by. The fisherman's wife feared that all three of her men had been lost at sea. One day, however, the grieving woman saw a lone man walking toward her house. She recognized him as her husband.

"My goodness! What has happened to my darling boys?" she cried.

The ragged fisherman began to tell his story: "We were just barely one whole day out to sea when Towards hooked into a great fish. Towards fought long and hard, but the fish was more than his equal. For a whole week they wrestled upon the waves without either of them letting up. Eventually the great fish started to win the battle, and Towards was pulled over the side of our ship. He was swallowed whole, and we never saw either of them again."

"Oh dear, that must have been terrible!" said his wife. "What a huge fish that must of been!"

"Yes, it was," said the fisherman, "but you should have seen the one that GOT AWAY. . . ."

O.K., it's bad. But what a great story to prepare us to hear, once again, the old story of Jonah and the big fish.

God came to a man named Jonah and told him to go to Nineveh, a wicked city, and "preach against it because its wickedness has come up before me." In other words, his assigned task was to proclaim God's judgment on Nineveh's sins.

But Jonah didn't want to go to Nineveh. Nineveh was the capital of Assyria, the historic enemy of Israel. In the eighth and seventh centuries B.C., the Assyrians plundered Palestine, looted and burned its cities and deported its inhabitants. In 722-721 B.C., it was Assyria that destroyed the Northern Kingdom.

Jonah hated the Assyrians, and so when God came to him and told him to preach to the people of Nineveh, Jonah went in the opposite direction. He boarded a ship traveling westward, bound for Tarshish on the coast of Spain, at the opposite end of the known world. He was fleeing from his calling; he was fleeing from the Lord. Of course, Jonah did not understand that Jehovah is a universal God from whom there is no escape.

You have probably heard sermons before from the book of Jonah on the futility of running from God. Yet we all do it at some time in our lives. We don't board ships. We do it with our minds and hearts. We tune God out. We ignore the voice that calls us to serve our neighbor, serve our church, serve our God.

The immortal philosopher Soren Kierkegaard put it like this, "At each man's birth there comes into being an eternal vocation for him, expressly for him. To be true to himself in relation to this eternal vocation is the highest thing a man can practice."

Well put! Have you discovered your calling from God?

Bishop William Willimon tells an amusing story about a young man named Sam who was quite troubled. Totally irresponsible, he made many mistakes, including flunking out of college. Forced to find a job, he met a woman there and married. They began attending a small church.

As time went on Sam felt a tugging on his heart, as if God were calling him toward the ministry. He dreaded telling his parents. Finally however he did. He explained that even though his life had taken uncertain twist and turns, he now felt he had found his calling.

When he had finished saying this, his mother burst into tears. Then she cried, "I'm so ashamed! I can't believe this has happened!"

The young man was baffled by her response. "What do you mean?" he asked.

"I can't believe this has happened," she said. "Didn't I tell you that before you were born I had had a couple of miscarriages? I didn't think we would ever have a child. So I promised God that if he would let me have a baby, that I could bring to term, if it were a boy I would name him Samuel and would dedicate him to God, just like Hannah did back in the Old Testament."

Sam couldn't believe what he was hearing. "Why didn't you ever tell me?" he asked. "You could have saved me a whole lot of trouble if you would have told me about this."

"We're Methodists," the mother replied. "How was I to know something like this would work? I didn't even know that we even believed in this kind of thing. How was I to know that it would work?" (2)

I suspect many of us would be surprised at how many prayers we've prayed over the years that have been answered. Sam was destined for the ministry. He would not be content anywhere else.

Jonah tried to flee from his calling and from God. But what happened? You know the story. The ship that he was on encountered a vicious storm and was tossed about on the waves like a toy. The winds and the waves were so fierce that seasoned sailors begged to their gods for mercy. Finally they cast lots in order to determine who the gods were angry with. "Tell us, who is responsible for making all this trouble for us?" they prayed.

The lot, of course, fell upon Jonah. Jonah confessed that he had displeased his God by seeking to flee from God's presence. So they asked him, "What should we do to you to make the sea calm down for us?"

"Pick me up and throw me into the sea," Jonah replied, "and it will become calm. I know that it is my fault that this great storm has come."

To their credit, these men did not want to throw Jonah overboard. They did their best to row back to land. But they could not, for the sea grew even wilder than before. Then they cried out to the Lord, "Please, Lord, do not let us die for taking this man's life. Do not hold us accountable for killing an innocent man, for you, Lord, have done as you pleased."

Then they took Jonah and threw him overboard, and the raging sea grew calm.

And the Bible tells us that the Lord appointed a great fish to swallow up Jonah, and Jonah was in the belly of that fish for three days and three nights. I believe it was Dwight L. Moody who said that it was perfectly easy for a great fish to swallow Jonah whole. After all, Jonah is only one of the minor prophets.

Anyway, it is interesting to note that Jesus once referred to the story of Jonah. Remember how he told skeptics that the only sign that they would receive would be the sign of Jonah? Christ would emerge from the ground on the third day after his crucifixion just as Jonah had emerged from the belly of the fish.

Now we all should know the story up to this point. The big fish can no longer stomach Jonah after three days and coughs him up on dry land—alive and well, and probably well chastened. Here is how one teacher visualizes the prophet Jonah. "I can just picture Jonah sitting on the beach, with a sign hanging around his neck stating, 'If swallowed, induce vomiting.'"

At this point the Lord came to Jonah a second time and told him again to go preach to Nineveh. And this time Jonah was in no mood to argue. So he went to Nineveh and preached like he had never preached before.

"Forty days," he cried, "and the Lord will destroy this city. Forty days is all you have to repent." And something amazing occurred. Says the scripture, "The people of Nineveh believed God." They proclaimed a fast and put on sackcloth—all of them, from the greatest to the least. Even the king of Nineveh repented. He dressed in sackcloth and issued a decree of total surrender to the will of God. The revival was an astounding success. Every sinner repented. Every heart was changed. You would think that a preacher would rejoice in such a great victory being given to him. But not Jonah. And then the very thing Jonah feared most occurred. God changed His mind and decided not to destroy Nineveh.

Then we come to some of the most fascinating sentences in all of the Bible: "But to Jonah this seemed very wrong, and he became angry. He prayed to the Lord, 'Isn't this what I said, Lord, when I was still at home? That is what I tried to forestall by fleeing to Tarshish. I knew that you are a gracious and compassionate God, slow to anger and abounding in love, a God who relents from sending calamity. Now, Lord, take away my life, for it is better for me to die than to live.'"

Can you believe that? Jonah had preached to the Ninevites. They had repented. Because they had repented, God had changed His mind about destroying them. Jonah should have been thrilled. Instead Jonah was so upset that God had changed his mind about destroying these people—he was so angry that he asked God to take his life. He was so angry that he literally wanted to die.

Then Jonah went out on a hill overlooking the city to see what would happen to Nineveh—to see if God would acknowledge Jonah's displeasure. And, at this point, God decides to have a little fun with His cantankerous prophet. God makes a plant grow up near Jonah to shade him while he sits and pouts. And the plant pleases Jonah immensely. It's one thing to have a temper tantrum. It's another thing to sit all day in the hot sun. If he's going to sit there until he dies, at least he will do it in comfort.

But then dawn comes the next morning and the Lord sends a worm to attack the plant that is shading Jonah so that it withers and dies. Then God sends a hot east wind, and the sun beats down on Jonah's head. The heat is so intense Jonah faints. The heat makes Jonah so uncomfortable and so angry that again he asks God to let him die.

But then God speaks to Jonah. God asks Jonah if he is angry over the plant dying. Jonah answered that of course he is, angry enough to die. And then God teaches Jonah a lesson. In two of the most important verses in the Bible, God says to Jonah, "You have been concerned about this plant, though you did not tend it or make it grow. It sprang up overnight and died overnight. And should I not have concern for the great city of Nineveh, in which there are more than a hundred and twenty thousand people who cannot tell their right hand from their left—and also many animals?"

And that is how the book of Jonah ends. One scholar suggests that the figure "120,000 persons who do not know their right hand from their left" is referring to young children in the city which suggests a total population of 1 million or more.

This is the lesson Jonah learned that day: God's love is a universal love. God's love is as certain for the people of Nineveh as it is for the people of Jerusalem or New York or San Francisco or Phoenix or Birmingham or [our town].

God does not respect nations or races or even religions. God loves all people— white people, black people, rich people, poor people, old people, young people— God isn't interested in labels, professions or even philosophies. God is only interested in people. "God so loved the world," states John 3:16. It doesn't say, God so loved North America, or English speaking people, or capitalists, or liberals, or anything like that. "God so loved the world"—that's the gospel.

We have to learn to live together. We must learn to respect each other as members of a single family of God.

I don't want to drive this point into the ground. But this is what the book of Jonah is about. God loves everybody: Jews and gentiles, Arabs and Africans, the people of Nineveh and the people of Israel. There is no place in the kingdom of God for any kind of hatred—racial, religious, or national. We all belong to one great family, and Christ died for everyone's sins. Your sins, my sins, but also the sins of our worst enemies.

Robert W. Youngs tells of having lunch at a small inn. Across the bottom of the menu was this notice: ONLY CHRISTIANS SERVED HERE. Being quite naive in those days, he remarked to his table companions that it was refreshing to find a hotel so interested in the Christian life.

"You miss the point," one of his friends replied. "The hotel means that Jews are not welcome here." (3)

That means that Jesus wouldn't have been welcome there. Which of course is the idea. Anyplace where any of God's children are not welcome, Jesus is not welcome. Thank God we do not see signs like that nowadays. Things have improved a little in our land. But the demand for us to love all people is still with us.

The little children's song says it best, "Jesus loves the little children, all the children of the world. Red and yellow, black and white, they are precious in his sight. Jesus loves the children of the world."

1. From Dynamic Preaching, 2001. Source: Merry-Hearts@xc.org, Monday, July 13, 1998.
2. http://www.chapel.duke.edu/worship/sunday/viewsermon.aspx?id=96.
3. Robert W. Youngs, What It Means To Be a Christian (New York: Farrar, Straus & Cudahy, 1960).

When The Service Was Interrupted
Mark 1:21-28

"I don't know why I remember the episode so vividly," writes author King Duncan. "I remember so few instances from my childhood. But this one stands out. I couldn't have been more than five. We were members of a tiny rural church. Our hymns came from a small paperback hymnal of Gospel songs [the Upper Room hymnal].

"Worship was a bit emotional; the preacher a little loud. There was no formal liturgy. The pews were hard. There was no air conditioning. The windows were open. It was a hot summer morning. A couple of dogs lazed out on the front porch of the church. From time to time a portion of the message would be drowned out by a farm truck rattling by or a motorcycle.

"Then suddenly our worship was interrupted. A woman who lived near the church but was not a member of the church was standing at the door sobbing hysterically.

"'Somebody, please help,' she cried from just outside the door. 'There's been an accident,' she said, 'a man's hurt bad. He's layin' in a ditch.'

"Some of the men rushed out to see what they could do. One of the women of the church rushed to this woman's side and tried to console her. 'Come inside,' the woman said calmly.

"'Oh, no,' the distraught woman wailed, 'I can't come in. I can't come in.' And she rushed down the steps of the church and disappeared. And as far as I know, she never came in that church or any other church for the rest of her life.

"I don't know what that woman's story was," says Duncan. "She was not a bad person as far as I know. But there was some reason she could not so much as place a foot inside a church."

It's fascinating some of the things we remember from our childhood.

One Sabbath day Jesus was teaching in the synagogue in Capernaum. The people were amazed at his teaching, because he taught them as one who had authority not as the teachers of the law. That's an interesting phrase: "as one who had authority . . ."

Where does authority come from? If you've ever been in the military or in a highly structured business environment, you know where it comes from. It comes from rank or position in a hierarchy.

James Fixx published a book of games which he called, More Games for the Super-Intelligent. In that collection he offers this wonderfully challenging puzzle from a military setting:

You are a captain in charge of one sergeant and four men. Your task is to raise a 100-foot flagpole and slide it into a hole 10-feet deep. You have two ropes—one

22-feet long and one 26-feet long—two shovels, and two buckets. How do you accomplish your task?

The answer is this: Since you're a captain, you turn to the sergeant and say, "Sergeant, get the flagpole up!" That's positional authority. You command those who are under you, and they obey.

Walter Anderson tells how as a young Marine, his fingers were crushed in an accident. They were swollen and immobile for a few days. As the swelling went down, the doctor ran some tests to measure the extent of his injuries. The doctor said, "Try to move the first finger of your right hand." Walter tried, but couldn't move it. The doctor suggested that they wait another day and try again. But Walter's platoon sergeant, who was standing nearby, stepped forward. He looked at Walter and commanded loudly, "move the first finger of your right hand now!" And Walter moved that finger. (1)

Maybe you've had a sergeant or a boss like that at some time. Of course, this type of authority has its limits.

You've probably heard the story of a second lieutenant at Fort Bragg, N.C. who discovered that he had no change when he was about to buy a soft drink from a vending machine. He flagged down a passing private and asked him, "Soldier, do you have change for a dollar?"

"I think so," the private said cheerfully. "Let me take a look."

The second lieutenant drew himself up stiffly. "Soldier," he said, "that's no way to address an officer. We'll start all over again. Do you have change for a dollar?"

The private saluted smartly, looked straight ahead, and said, "No, sir!"

In that situation, pulling rank backfired.

Some people have authority because of their rank or position. Others have authority because of their personality, or their knowledge or their extreme competence.

As a carpenter, Jesus had no positional authority in the community. His authority came from his wisdom and knowledge and his competence at interpreting God's Word. Even as a boy Jesus wowed people with his wisdom and his grasp of scripture. Of course the people in Capernaum could not know that his authority came from a more important source. All they knew is that they had never heard an individual teach like Jesus taught. They said to one another, "He teaches as one who has authority, not as the teachers of the law."

But even Jesus got interrupted from time to time. This time it wasn't a woman standing outside the door pleading for help, but rather it was a man in the synagogue who disrupted Jesus' teaching.

That's significant. Don't think that all the needy people in this world are on the outside of the church. There are many people on the inside of the church who have very deep needs. Indeed, sometimes needy people are attracted to the church.

Mark tells us this man was "possessed by an impure spirit." We don't know what Mark meant by this. Most modern people dismiss the idea of demons and unclean spirits. We assume this is pre-scientific language for mental illness, but who knows? Whatever the origin of his problem, obviously the man was deeply distressed. He cried out, "What do you want with us, Jesus of Nazareth? Have you come to destroy us? I know who you are—the Holy One of God!"

It's interesting. The impure spirits recognized who Jesus was long before the people of Capernaum.

"Be quiet!" said Jesus sternly. "Come out of him!"

And then something remarkable happened. The impure spirit shook the man violently and came out of him with a shriek.

The people were all so amazed that they asked each other, "What is this? A new teaching and with authority! He even gives orders to impure spirits and they obey him." And Mark tells us, "News about him spread quickly over the whole region of Galilee."

"What is this?" the people asked, "A new teaching—and with authority! He even gives orders to impure spirits and they obey him."

So, Jesus had authority because of his teachings. But he also had authority because of his power over what Mark calls "impure spirits." In other places we see his authority over disease, and over nature, and even over death.

This brings us to something obvious we need to affirm about Jesus: he was unique. There was no one quite like him.

There were other fine teachers in Galilee, but they could not cast out impure spirits, or turn water into wine or heal the leper or multiply the fishes and the loaves or forgive sins. There was something about Jesus which could not be said about his contemporaries. He had authority—physical authority, spiritual authority, moral authority. Even after his death and resurrection, he had authority. When confronted by someone who was demon-possessed or who was blind or physically-challenged, all the disciples had to do was evoke Jesus' name and demons were cast out and the physically-challenged were made whole and the blind could see. That's authority.

Singer and songwriter Gloria Gaither put it this way as part of a musical that she and her husband Bill composed several years ago: "Jesus. The mere mention of His name can calm the storm, heal the broken, raise the dead … I've heard a mother softly breathe His name at the bedside of a child delirious with fever, and I've watched that little body grow quiet and the fevered brow cool. I've sat beside a dying saint, her body racked with pain, who in those final fleeting seconds summoned her last ounce of ebbing strength to whisper earth's sweetest name—Jesus, Jesus … Emperors have tried to destroy it; philosophers have tried to stamp it out.

Tyrants have tried to wash it from the face of the earth with the very blood of those who claim it. Yet still it stands . . . Jesus . . ." (2) Friends, that's authority.

The distinguished British intellectual Malcolm Muggeridge put it like this: "I may," he once said, "I suppose . . . pass for being a relatively successful man. People occasionally stare at me in the streets—that's fame. I can fairly easily earn enough to qualify for admission to the higher slopes of the Internal Revenue—that's success. Furnished with money and a little fame even the elderly, if they care to, may partake of trendy diversions—that's pleasure. It might happen once in a while that something I said or wrote was sufficiently heeded for me to persuade myself that it represented a serious impact on our time—that's fulfillment. Yet, I say to you—and I beg you to believe me—multiply these tiny triumphs by a million, add them all together, and they are nothing—less than nothing, a positive impediment measured against one drink of that living water Christ offers to the spiritually thirsty, irrespective of who or what they are." (3) That's authority.

Jesus was a wonderful teacher, but no mere teacher has the authority to raise the dead. Jesus was a leader, a prophet, a moral visionary—but none of these explain his impact on civilization. As some unknown writer expressed it a generation ago:

"Socrates taught for 40 years, Plato for 50, Aristotle for 40 and Jesus for only 3 years. Yet the influence of Christ's ministry infinitely transcends the impact left by the combined years of teaching from these greatest of philosophers.

"Jesus painted no pictures, yet some of the finest artists such as Raphael, Michelangelo, and Leonardo da Vinci received their inspiration from Him.

"Jesus wrote no poetry, but Dante, Milton and scores of the world's greatest poets were inspired by Him.

"Jesus composed no music; still Haydn, Handel, Beethoven, Bach and Mendelssohn reached their highest perfection of melody in the music they composed in His praise.

"Every sphere of human greatness has been enriched by this humble Carpenter of Nazareth."

It took a Roman centurion, stationed at the foot of the cross who watched him die, to sum it all up, "Surely this man," the centurion testified, "was the Son of God!" (Mt. 27-54)

No one else who has ever lived spoke with the authority with which Christ spoke. He was unique. There has never been another like him. This brings us to an obvious question: If Jesus is the Son of God, shouldn't we reflect his influence more in our lives? If he is the Son of the most high God and if his teachings are the foundation upon which our lives are built, shouldn't that fact be reflected in how we live?

Donald Grey Barnhouse tells a story of something that happened to him many years ago during the Korean War. Barnhouse was aboard a flight from New York to

Los Angeles. The flight attendant seated a girl in her early twenties beside him.

Obviously this girl had never flown before. Over the loudspeaker, the flight attendant said, "Fasten your seatbelts." The girl didn't even know what a seatbelt was.

Pastor Barnhouse helped her and asked, "You've never flown before?"

She said, "No, this is my first time." As he spoke to her, she opened her pocketbook, and there was a picture of a handsome young GI.

Barnhouse said, "You're going out to see him?"

"Yes," she said, "he's coming home. I'm going to see him."

She went on to explain that they had gotten married a year and a half before. They had a honeymoon of just a few days, then he had gone to the coast and left for Korea. Now he was coming back home; she was going to see him.

Barnhouse could tell that going to see her husband meant more to this young woman than anything else. He was her bridegroom; she was his bride and she was going to see him.

Then Donald Grey Barnhouse says something important. He says, "You wonder sometimes why Christians live as they do and make the choices they make. They are on their way to see their bridegroom, yet they go right out and live in the world as though it made no effect in their life at all..." (4)

And that's true, isn't it? One day we are going to see the Bridegroom, our Lord and Master, and it doesn't seem to matter in how we live our lives. Do you believe Jesus is who he says he is? If so, does his influence show on your life, or does your life more accurately reflect simply the community in which you live and the people with whom you associate? He spoke with authority.

And this brings us to a final question: If Jesus is who he says he is, shouldn't we tell the good news to others?

A young boy from a non-Christian family named Palmer Ofuoku was placed in a mission school by his Nigerian parents because they knew he would receive a good education there. He attended the school for years, yet he did not convert to Christianity. He remained an adherent of a traditional African religion.

One year a new missionary came to the school who began to develop close relationships with the students, including Palmer. Eventually the missionary led this young Nigerian to Christ. Palmer Ofuoku explained the missionary's influence like this: "He built a bridge of friendship to me, and Jesus walked across." (5)

That is the best definition of evangelism that I have ever heard. "He built a bridge of friendship to me, and Jesus walked across." That's what you and I should be doing each day of our lives—building bridges of friendship to the people around us so that Jesus may walk across.

Jesus spoke with authority. There has never been another like him. He is the

Son of God. That ought to make a difference in how we live our lives. We ought to be telling others about him. We ought to be building bridges to others so that Christ may walk across.

1. Walter Anderson, The Confidence Course (New York: HarperPerennial).
2. Mike Trout, Off the Air (Nashville: Thomas Nelson Publishers, 1995), pp. 177-178.
3. Jesus Rediscovered (Doubleday, 1969).
4. Timeless Illustrations for Preaching and Teaching (Peabody, MA: Hendrickson Publishers, Inc., 2004), pp.214-215.
5. Brian Harbour, 2 Corinthians (Convention Press, 1989).

Seeking Christ
Mark 1:29-39

Sometime back Dr. Phil Berry took a picture outside a roadside convenience store. The store was on the Texas border on the highway leading to Colorado. It was one of those portable advertising signs with flashing lights along the top meant to lure in passersby.

At the top of the sign it read, "Last chance Lotto Texas, clean restrooms, snacks." Then, at the bottom of the sign, almost like an afterthought, it read, "Jesus is Lord."

"It's like, on the way out of Texas, whatever you need, they have it," says pastor Glen Schmucker referring to Berry's picture. "A little snack? A place to freshen up? A place to do a little gambling? A little bit of Jesus? Whatever you need, they've got it." (1)

Perhaps we shouldn't be too cynical. At least, they're making an effort to share Jesus, even if he doesn't have top billing over clean restrooms or the Texas Lotto.

I heard recently of someone else who sought to share Jesus in a somewhat unconventional way. A couple in Canton, Ohio thought they saw the image of Jesus in the wood grain of a door in their house. This image was so striking that they cut it out of the door and carried it with them when they moved to another house. They kept it because the thought of it gave them encouragement. When the devastating tsunami hit Japan last March, they chose to share this striking image with the world. They thought it might encourage others as it had encouraged them.

The interesting thing is that 41% of the people who responded to an NBC online poll concerning the image claimed that they saw Jesus too. However, the wife claims that it could also be the Virgin Mary, and 6% of the people who responded to the poll did see Mary and not Jesus. It makes sense that Jesus' image should appear in a door, says one commentator. After all, Jesus did say, "I am the door." (John 10:7) And he was a carpenter.

Of course, we see this kind of thing all the time. One lady in St. Petersburg Florida claims seeing Jesus' image in a potato chip! (2)

My guess is that we see what we want to see, and our deepest yearning of all is to see Jesus. Our deepest yearning is to encounter God. And so, in our search for meaning our eyes pick up patterns that, while random, seem to reveal God's presence. And that gives us peace and . . . hope. And we want the world to know what we've seen.

It is also a reminder to us of how popular Jesus still remains in the secular world in which we live.

Have you ever noticed how often Jesus appears on the cover of Time and Newsweek? Someone once asked the religion reporter for the Washington Post why that was. His answer was that every time Jesus is on the cover of these magazines, they see a spike in their sales. Jesus is commercially attractive. He is still popular with lots of folks—people like you and me.

He was also popular when he first began his ministry two thousand years ago. The scene we have in our lesson from the gospel of Mark takes place at the house of Simon Peter where Jesus heals Simon's mother-in-law.

I don't know if you have thought about the disciples of Jesus having families or not. Here is evidence that they did. Jesus heals Simon Peter's mother-in-law. As impetuous and outspoken as Simon Peter was, some of you might wonder what kind of son-in-law he was. Nevertheless, after reporting the healing of Peter's mother-in-law the writer of the Gospel of Mark says this: "That evening after sunset the people brought to Jesus all the sick and demon-possessed. The whole town gathered at the door . . ."

Think of that, "The whole town was gathered at the door . . ." I guess this was the first-century equivalent of the flash mob. They didn't communicate by cell phones or Twitter. They had to do it the old-fashioned way, person to person. But it worked. The whole town gathered at the door. Everyone wanted to see Jesus.

A little further on we read, "Very early in the morning, while it was still dark, Jesus got up, left the house and went off to a solitary place, where he prayed. Simon and his companions went to look for him, and when they found him, they exclaimed: 'Everyone is looking for you!'"

In the vernacular of today, Jesus was a rock star. Everyone was looking for him.

I don't know how to say it without it sounding like a platitude or a cliché, but I believe that even today people everywhere are still looking for Christ. They may not know his name, and they might use religious symbols and terminology that is different from what you and I would ever use, but they are searching for Christ all the same.

After all, he is the way, the truth, and the life. And all people, everywhere, need what only Christ can offer them.

Everyone needs a sense of direction for his or her life. In a sense everyone is, to one degree or another, lost. Where are they going to find direction for their lives except in Jesus?

It's like something that Dr. Lee F. Tuttle once told about that almost affected the course of the Second World War. In December 1944 the U.S. Army and its Allies were on the offensive. For six months they had rolled with relentless precision across Western Europe. But suddenly, one December day, a major portion of the mighty Allied juggernaut ground to a halt. A counter offensive had been launched by the Germans. If that counter offensive had succeeded, the end of the war might have been indefinitely delayed. As it was, the German drive almost did succeed, and a part of that was due to some brilliant strategy devised by the defenders of the Third Reich.

A few days before the Allied operation, German soldiers dressed in American uniforms, together with American jeeps, were parachuted behind American lines. These "soldiers from the sky" carried no weapons. Their single mission was to discover the roads over which reinforcing Allied armies might travel and change all the signs which pointed to strategic towns and villages. And this simple task of turning the signposts to give wrong directions had deadly consequences. When the defenders in the "Battle of the Bulge" called for help as the Germans attacked, many of the reinforcements never arrived. Whole battalions were lost while trying to find their way across a countryside where the signposts were either down or wrong. (3)

Dr. Tuttle's point in relating these events was to say to us that we live in a time when many of the signposts have been torn down: moral signposts, ethical signposts, theological signposts. Because of this, many of us lose our way in life.

Have you ever been lost while traveling? It is a terrible experience. Maps no longer seem to make sense. When other people try to help, it often only makes matters worse. Well, the same thing can happen on the road of life. When we are lost, life no longer makes sense to us.

In Great Britain, there is an epitaph on a tombstone of a three-week-old child that says it for all of us, regardless of our age. The epitaph reads like this:

It is so soon that I am done for,

I wonder what I was begun for.

The years pass so quickly. And many of us have no idea what we're here for. We feel lost. Where can we turn for direction for our lives? There is only one place that is reliable. We can turn to Jesus and find in him that for which we are so desperately searching. We see in him what we were created to be—sons and daughters of the Divine. We are precious people who have been bought with Christ's blood. When we turn to Jesus, we rediscover our purpose, our sense of direction.

But there is a second thing we find in Jesus—we find someone we can follow. Christ not only points the way, but he goes with us and leads the way for us. Indeed, he is the way.

There is another true story that comes out of World War II. A platoon of American soldiers was stranded on one side of a mine field they had to cross. The commander of the platoon came up with a plan: one man would walk across the mine field, leaving clear footprints for others to follow. If this first man hit a mine, then another man would take his place and would also walk across the field in his footsteps . . . until he fell as well, and so on . . . until finally someone had cleared a path for all the soldiers. It was a great plan, but it seemed guaranteed to leave some casualties.

The young soldiers, with their hearts in their throats, agreed to the plan. However, they wondered, which one of them would be chosen to walk the field first? To their surprise, it was their commander who began walking first across the field. As their leader, he insisted on risking his life for the sake of his men. The commander crossed the field safely. Following closely in his footsteps, all the soldiers made it across the field as well. (4)

That's leadership. That's courage. That's being willing to lay down one's life for one's friends. And, of course, that is what Christ did for us on Golgotha. Not only does Christ point to the direction we are to go, he goes before us, giving his life that ours might be saved.

The writer of Hebrews in the New International Version of the scriptures calls Christ "the pioneer and perfecter" of our faith. Some translations of that verse call him the "author and finisher," but I prefer the NIV. The Greek word translated "author" is archçgos and that word means "one [who] takes the lead in anything and thus affords an example, a predecessor in a matter, pioneer" (Thayer's Greek English Lexicon).

Jesus is a pioneer in the same way that the company commander in WW II was a pioneer. He takes the dangerous path and clears the way for us. Jesus does not ask us to go anywhere that he has not gone before himself.

The writer of Hebrews tells us that we are to fix our eyes upon him, in the same way that those soldiers fixed their eyes on the company commander in order to make it through the mine field of life and death. Christ gives us a sense of purpose and direction for our lives. Christ leads the way and beckons us to follow.

But there's one more reason the world longs to see Jesus. When we follow him, he leads us to a specific destination—life with the Father. When we follow Jesus we discover abundant life . . . not because we deserve it, but because of what Christ has done on Calvary.

Sometime back, The Christian Century magazine carried a story by Lillian Daniel. Ms. Daniel told the story of a large collection of Southeast Asian pottery that her parents owned. Daniel says her parents had collected this pottery on several trips to that part of the world over the years, and carefully kept it in their home.

However, there was always one piece in this beautiful collection that always seemed out of place. This piece had once been a fine antique vase with a cream glaze and blue Japanese design, but now it was damaged. And yet her parents kept it amid their finer pieces, even though it was a mass of cracks, crudely glued together with what was obviously the wrong type of adhesive. Ms. Daniels notes that everywhere the 20 or so pieces of that vase met one another, glue had bubbled out yellow as it dried, leaving the vase grotesquely scarred.

She says that she once suggested to her mother that she get rid of that one ugly piece of pottery. And so her mother told her the story behind the vase and why they could not part with it.

Her father had bought that vase when he was a journalist covering the Vietnam War. Returning home, he had wrapped and hand carried the vase as he traveled the long journey back in taxis, on several airlines, and several buses. He protected it through all of the journey back before walking up his driveway with this special vase in his hands.

At that very moment, as her father walked up the driveway, his two year old daughter rushed toward him with her arms outstretched for an embrace. Surprised and elated, her father tried to hold on to the vase and yet also open his arms to his beloved daughter. When he did that, the vase fell and broke into pieces. Ms. Daniel, of course, was that two-year-old. She ends her story like this: "Thus it was that night, my mother pulled out the glue, she repaired the vase, and she pronounced it precious." (5)

That cracked vase was almost as precious to her mother as we cracked and imperfect vessels are to God. Those who trust in Jesus and seek to walk in his steps are the recipients of abounding and overflowing love and grace. And even though we are imperfect in our service to Christ and humanity, God's love for us and acceptance of us never ceases.

It's like a story that Tony Campolo tells. The story is set in Heaven. St. Peter handles admissions at the pearly gates according to the story and the Apostle Paul acts as the administrator of the celestial kingdom, taking a monthly census of Heaven's inhabitants.

But something doesn't add up. Each time Paul counts the number of people in Heaven, his number far exceeds the number of admittances that Peter has registered. This discrepancy mystifies them both for quite a while.

Then, one day, Paul runs up to Peter and excitedly shouts, "Peter! Peter! I figured out why our numbers don't match. I figured out why there are so many more people in Heaven than you're letting in at the pearly gates. It's Jesus! It's Jesus! He keeps sneaking people over the wall." (6)

Jesus offers unlimited grace to all who would trust their lives to him. You may say as I do, I don't deserve God's grace. That's all right. You and I are among those whom Christ will sneak over somehow. That's what grace is all about.

No wonder people advertise Jesus on signs for clean rest rooms and the Texas Lotto. No wonder people see Jesus on doors, and even on potato chips. Everyone deep down wants what only Jesus can provide.

"Everyone is looking for you. . ." said the disciples to Jesus. It was truer than they knew. And it is still true today. He is the answer to every man's, every woman's, every young person's deepest need. He gives us direction and purpose for our lives. We never need fear what lies ahead for he goes with us. He never takes us anywhere he has not been himself. He is the pioneer and the perfecter of our faith. And the destination is sure—abundant life with the Father. Isn't that what you are looking for today?

1. Rev. Alex Stevenson, http://www.clifftemple.org/sermons/2001 02 04.html.

2. http://www.geocities.com/Athens/Ithaca/1506/east3a.htm

3. Dr. Earnest A. Fitzgerald, God Writes With Crooked Lines (New York: Atheneum, 1981).

4. William Beausay II, The Leadership Genius of Jesus (Nashville: Thomas Nelson Publishers, 1997), pp. 16-17.

5. Rev. Steven R. Jones, http://www.gbgm umc.org/williamsburgumc/Sermons/August%2013,%202006.htm.

6. Tony Campolo, letters to a young evangelical (New York: Perseus Books Group, 2006), pp. 49-50.

The Reluctant Celebrity
Mark 1:40-45

We live in a world that canonizes celebrity. It no longer matters how much a person has accomplished or how much they have contributed to society. All you have to do to become famous in today's world is to keep yourself in front of the media.

We have people, it's often noted, who are famous simply for being famous. People like Paris Hilton and Nicole Ritchie, for example. They became so famous that they starred in their own reality show "The Simple Life." Before that, says one critic, Paris Hilton did pretty much nothing except be the heiress to the Hilton Hotel fortune. Also on the list are other names ripped from Hollywood's gossip columns, such as Brandon Davis, Kim Kardashian, Jack and Kelly Osborne (Ozzy's kids) and Kevin Federline—Britney Spears' ex for those of you don't keep up with such matters. People who are famous simply for being famous. (1)

I suspect that most of us would have mixed feelings about being celebrities. Fred Allen once quipped that a celebrity is one who works to be known, then wears dark glasses so as not to be recognized. Well, most of us can relate. After all, who wants to live under a magnifying glass?

When the late Walt Disney was asked what he thought about being famous, he replied, "It feels fine when you get a choice reservation at a football game, but it's never helped me make a good picture or command the obedience of my daughter. It doesn't even seem to keep fleas off our dog, and if being a celebrity doesn't give one an advantage over fleas, then I guess there can't be much in it after all." Disney was a sensible man who was able to put life into perspective, but I suppose celebrities serve their purpose. They make life more interesting for those who identify with them.

A few years ago there was a 310-pound defensive tackle for the Chicago Bears who suddenly became a national celebrity. He was known as William "The Refrigerator" Perry. You football fans remember Perry. In a four-week period, he did the unthinkable. He stepped out of his role as a lineman and ran the ball successfully for yardage. He even caught a pass for a touchdown. Then he ran for another touchdown. It was the first time a defensive tackle had ever, in the history of football, been given the ball to carry to make a touchdown. Sports fans were captivated by this extraordinary event—which, for many people, put the fun back in football. Perry became a television star, appearing on the "Tonight" show, the "Today" show, and the nightly network news shows. There were as many as one hundred requests per day for endorsements, and an extra $750,000 in fees came his way.

Meanwhile his mother said, "I know he was good, but I don't think he's that good." And his wife said, "This was great for a while, but now it's ridiculous. It's gotten out of hand." [It's hard to impress the women in your life.]

Perry himself said, "As fast as it comes, that's how fast it goes." He was right. (2) William "The Refrigerator" Perry is quickly being forgotten. But he had more than his fifteen minutes of fame. For a while, he was a genuine celebrity.

One thing Jesus did not want to be was a celebrity. You can see that in our lesson for today. A man with leprosy came to him. The man got down on his knees in front of Jesus and said, "If you are willing, you can make me clean."

It's interesting. The NIV says that Jesus was "indignant" at this request. Other versions say he was "filled with compassion." Perhaps he felt a little of both. He wanted the man with leprosy to be healed. Jesus wants everyone who is physically sick or emotionally sick, to be healed. He wants everyone who is hurting in any area of life to be released from that hurt. Maybe you're hurting financially as you watch the equity in your house drop, or hurting emotionally as you watch your children turn their back on you. People hurt in a multitude of ways, and none of it is what Christ desires for his people. Believe that. Is it God's will for anyone to have leprosy, or cancer, or heart problems, or whatever pain we may have? No, it is not God's will for anyone to suffer. That's why God gave us the gift of medical science. God wants us to live free from disease.

But Christ did not come into the world to be a medical doctor or a psychologist. There was no way for Christ, while he was confined in a physical body, to heal everyone who needed him. There were not enough hours in a day or a week or a lifetime. That does not mean that he was not willing. It was simply a practical impossibility. Besides, healing individuals was not his primary mission. He didn't want people to suffer, but neither did he want to be lured away from his primary purpose. His primary mission was to establish the kingdom of God in our midst. His primary mission was to preach and to teach and to instruct his disciples so that they might carry on his work when he was gone.

But notice what happens in this encounter with the man with the disease of leprosy. The man says, "If you are willing, you can make me clean."

And Jesus reaches out his hand and touches the man. "I am willing," he said. "Be clean!"

Immediately the leprosy left the man and he was cleansed. Now, notice what happens. Jesus sent him away at once with a strong warning: "See that you don't tell this to anyone. But go, show yourself to the priest and offer the sacrifices that Moses commanded for your cleansing, as a testimony to them."

So, what does the man do? He does the exact opposite of what Jesus asks him to do. "Instead," Mark tells us, "he went out and began to talk freely, spreading the news." Now notice what follows, "As a result, Jesus could no longer enter a town openly but stayed outside in lonely places. Yet the people still came to him from everywhere."

Jesus could no longer enter a town openly! Here was his real mission—to spread the good news of the coming kingdom, but his success as a healer stood in the way of what he was sent to do. Perhaps that is the reason that nine times in the Gospels—particularly in the Gospel of Mark—Jesus tells people to keep quiet about who he is or what he's done for them.

For example, Jesus raised Jairus' daughter from the dead—one of the most amazing miracles in history. Then what does he do? Mark says he gave strict orders not to let anyone know about it (5:35-43).

He healed a man who could not speak or hear. Then he tells the man not to tell anyone. Think about that for a moment. Here is a man who had been deaf and mute, perhaps all his life, who is now able to hear and talk, and Jesus tells him not to tell anyone how it happened. That might be a little unrealistic.

But it wasn't just the people he healed. In Matthew 16:20 we read, "Then he warned his disciples not to tell anyone that he was the Christ." And again, in Mark 9:9—following that spectacular event on the Mount of the Transfiguration—we read, "As they were coming down the mountain, Jesus gave them orders not to tell anyone what they had seen until the Son of Man had risen from the dead."

The last thing Jesus wanted was to be a celebrity. Unfortunately, celebrity came to him. And in one sense, celebrity killed him. The more the authorities knew about him the more they feared him. He was a threat to all the powers that be. It would have been best for him if he had kept a low profile. Don't rock the boat. Go with the flow. He had not come into the world to be a physician but to tell the world about God's love.

Still, when he was confronted with someone who was hurting he could not help but heal. Why? Because he cared. He himself embodied the love of the Father . . . so when the man with leprosy said, "If you will, you can make me clean," Jesus could not help but say, "I am willing."

Writer James Hume tells about a friend of his in Washington who woke up one morning to find his left arm paralyzed. He couldn't feel a thing in his left hand. He rushed to the office of a neurosurgeon in Bethesda who ministered to Presidents as well as Navy brass in a nearby hospital. He told the doctor about his arm. The doctor, in a heavy German accent, replied, "Do not fear. You haf come to the right place. See that certificate on the wall. I vas graduated from the University of Vienna. "

Humes' friend said, "Doctor, my hand, I can't feel a thing!"

"It is nothing," said the doctor. "I am expert in the field. See that other certificate. I vas elected to the Royal Academy of Neurosurgeons.

"But, Doctor," his friend asked, "did I have a stroke? I can't feel . . ."

"Be patient," the doctor interrupted. "You are in goot hands. See that other certificate. That's for ven I addressed the Vorld Institute of . . ."

With that, Humes' friend left and went to his neighborhood doctor, who told him, "Trevor, you just slept on your arm. If the feeling doesn't come back by dinnertime, give me a call."

Humes says the moral of this little story for him was this: "People don't care how much you know unless they know how much you care!" The neurosurgeon his friend consulted mostly cared about displaying his accomplishments. His patients were secondary. The neighborhood physician cared about his patients. (3)

Jesus cared about people. Even if it gave him less time for preaching and teaching. Even if it ultimately cost him his life, he could not pass by someone who was hurting.

Jesus could not pass by people who were hurting, and they in turn could not help talking about the wonderful things he had done for them. And the more they talked, the more of their friends came to Jesus as well. And the less time he had for his ministry. We could say it was a "vicious" cycle, but it was anything but vicious. Jesus simply cared too much for his own good and people who encountered him were so touched by him they simply could not keep it to themselves even when he told them to be quiet.

We can understand, can't we? If Christ has touched your life, how can you be quiet about it? When people have something important happen in their lives they want to share it. Besides, they were but following Christ's example. He responded to them with love and healed them, and they wanted to pass the news of his power to their friends so that they could be healed, too. It was the caring thing to do.

Rev. Richard J. Fairchild tells about a 92-year-old woman whom he calls one of the most beautiful people he has ever met. Unfortunately, this elderly woman was not only advanced in years; she was a paraplegic. She was confined to a hospital's extended care ward . . . and there she lived all her days splitting time between her bed and her wheel chair.

This dear lady had diabetes and several other problems—and over the previous five years she had first one foot, then the other, then a leg, and then another, amputated so that she might be able to go on living. She had considerable pain, most days she was very uncomfortable—and she had no family or close friends to come in and visit—she had simply outlived most of them.

What this lady did during her days, however, was quite wonderful, Rev. Fairchild reports. When she was able, she wheeled her chair up and down the corridors of the extended care ward where she would pop in and visit all the other folks in the place. She learned their birthdays and sent them cards. She noticed when they seemed depressed and listened to them talk about their problems and gave their hand a squeeze and prayed with them if they were willing. She went to the recreation room and took part in the games—often helping the staff help others. She was a light in a dark place—full of joy and peace despite her own troubles and woes.

Rev. Fairchild writes, "I always prayed with her on my visits—I would pray for her and she would pray for those around her and she would always give thanks to God at the end of each prayer for his goodness and his love—for how He worked His will—and helped her each day—even in the days of pain." (4)

Do you think this wonderful woman was doing those good works and spreading all that cheer to draw attention to herself? Not at all. People who continually seek to draw attention to themselves are the unhappiest people on earth. Haven't you noticed that? No, her desire was to draw people's attention to her Lord and Savior. Christ had touched her life and she wanted to share his love with others. She had a story to tell and she told it. That's the way things ought to happen.

I wish we were more like the people Jesus healed, as well as this elderly woman. I wish we felt so much joy from what Jesus has done in our lives that we couldn't help telling our story to others. But there's one thing more to be said.

Jesus' acts of healing validated the message he came to proclaim. Jesus came to proclaim a kingdom in which people would live in peace and love with God as their King. The response of the people to his acts of healing was inconvenient but ultimately it helped drive home what he was about—people came to see that God loved them as individuals and that their needs and concerns mattered to God.

There was a tragic event that happened not too long ago in Chicago. A 15-year-old boy was shot by gang members while he was playing basketball. He lay bleeding to death in an alley just steps away from a hospital emergency room. The emergency room personnel refused to treat him, saying it was against hospital policy to go outside. They would have to call 911 instead. After waiting about 20 minutes, a frustrated police officer finally commandeered a wheelchair and brought the boy in himself, but it was too late and the boy died. (5)

Now, we don't know all the facts of this case and we would not presume to pass judgment on the hospital personnel, but each of us knows what Jesus would have done. He would have given up his life if it were necessary in order to save this boy. Of course, he has already given up his life to save not only this boy, but each of us as well. His actions of healing, his actions of sacrificial love validate the kingdom he proclaimed. His message was not of a God who is remote from our needs and concerns. His message was of a God who has come near and is working in the hearts of those who are open to him to establish in this world a new way of living—a new way of loving and helping and serving. As we seek to be his people may our lives also validate the message we proclaim that, in the words of that little chorus of the sixties, "the Lord of us love has come to us, we want to pass it on."

1. http://www.glamorati.com/celebrity/2008/10-examples-of-people-who-are-famous-for-being-famous/
2. Gilbert Brim, Ambition (New York: Basic Books, 1992).
3, The Sir Winston Method (New York: William Morrow and Company, Inc. , 1991), pp. 24-25.
4. http://www.rockies.net/~spirit/sermons/c-thansesn.php.
5. Rev. Jeren Rowell,
http://www.nph.com/nphweb/html/pmol/pastissues/Lent%202009/webmay24.htm.

Do You Know How To Listen?
Mark 9:2-9

Do you have anyone in your family who has a listening problem? Notice I did not say a hearing problem. Many people have ears that work quite well; nevertheless, they are very selective in what they hear.

The story is told of King Edward VII. His grandson, Prince David, had a good relationship with his grandfather. Still David was a child, and adults in England during this period, particularly royalty, were not known to listen to children.

At dinner on one occasion little David tried to get his grandfather's attention. He was reprimanded immediately for interrupting the king's conversation at table. So the young prince sat in silence until given permission to speak. When he was allowed finally to address his grandfather, he said, "It's too late now, grandpapa. It was a caterpillar on your lettuce but you've eaten it." (1)

The king should have listened to his grandson. It pays to listen—to children, to friends, to co-workers, to other family members. Yet, authentic listening is rare.

Former President Bill Clinton once compared it to running a cemetery. "Being President," he said, "is like running a cemetery: you've got a lot of people under you . . . and nobody's listening."

You've heard the old aphorism that God gave us two ears but only one mouth indicating that God wanted us to spend twice as much time listening as talking. However, it could be that God gave us two ears and one mouth because listening is twice as hard as talking.

As someone has said, "Most conversations are simply monologues delivered in the presence of witnesses."

Sometimes, for one reason or another, we deliberately do not listen. Either we are not interested or something else has our attention.

Dr. Robert R. Kopp tells about an old Mutt and Jeff routine. A few of you more "experienced" members may remember the Mutt and Jeff cartoon series. It hasn't been published in thirty years, but it had a loyal following in days gone by.

Mutt and Jeff built a soundproof room. To test it, Mutt went into the room and closed the door. Jeff yelled from the outside, "Can you hear me?"

And Mutt answered, "No."

It's an absurd routine, of course, but sometimes we may deliberately tune out someone else.

Pastor John Kramp reports that his grandmother had a unique way of ending arguments with her spouse. When Grandma got tired of listening to her husband, she would just turn off her hearing aid. As he said, "Grandmother refused to hear anything she didn't want to hear." Grandmother's not the only one. Sometimes we do not want to listen.

Sometimes we may not listen because what is being said is too threatening, too painful.

In one of her books Joyce Landorf tells of a friend of hers who had just been told that she had breast cancer, and her only hope was to have a mastectomy, removing both breasts. She was crushed by the news, and turned to her mother, who had not always been there for her, for some support in her time of crisis. She called her mother and asked to have lunch with her.

After they had lunch together, Joyce's friend said, "Mother, I have just received some terrible news. I have just come from the doctor's office; I have been told that I have cancer, and it is necessary for me to have a mastectomy."

Her mother replied, "Your sister has the most wonderful recipe for making chicken enchiladas."

Joyce's friend tried again, "Mother! You didn't hear me. I told you that I have just come from the doctor's office, and I have cancer. I am going to have surgery on Tuesday. I am scared!"

Her mother replied, "Please don't raise your voice when you talk to me."

By then the daughter was getting desperate and shouted, "Mother! Please listen to me! I have cancer! I might die! I might die!"

The mother replied, "Don't talk to your mother in that tone of voice. I won't have it! And if you leave the enchiladas in the oven too long, they will dry out!" (2)

It's evident that this piece of information was too painful for this mother to process, and so she simply tuned it out.

Paul Tillich, noted theologian of a past generation, once wrote these important words, "The first duty of love is to listen." And that's true. The first duty of love is to listen.

Listening is particularly important in families. That should be self-evident, but evidently it is not.

There was a study sometime back in San Francisco of teenage prostitutes. These young women were asked about their home life growing up. "Is there anything you needed most and couldn't get?" the researchers asked.

Invariably their answer, which was accompanied by sadness and tears was, "What I needed most was someone to listen to me. Someone who cared enough to listen." (3)

How many children and teenagers would echo that same cry? How many spouses? We all need someone who will listen.

Robert Herron says that good listening is like tuning in a radio station. For good results, you can listen to only one station at a time. He says that trying to listen to his wife while looking over an office report is like trying to receive two radio stations at the same time. He ends up with distortion and frustration. Listening requires a choice of where to place your attention. To tune in to your spouse or your children, you must first choose to put away all that will divide your attention. That might mean laying down the newspaper, moving away from the dishes in the sink, putting down the book you're reading, setting aside your projects . . . (4)

Studies show that most of us are not as good at multitasking as we think we are. When it comes to listening, there is really no such thing as multitasking.

A mother named Star Paterson tells of standing at the kitchen sink, working diligently on dinner preparations, her mind totally committed to the task at hand—peeling potatoes. In the army, she notes, they call it "KP" duty. Star thinks that's a good title for the task, but in her home KP stands for "Kid Pleasing." Mashed potatoes are one of her kids' favorite foods. So, when she is doing KP duty, in her mind she is doing something that will please her kids.

One day as she was busy with her "KP" duty, her middle son, three-year-old Steven, was playing nearby. Being a conscientious mother, Star's ears were tuned to her son while her eyes focused on the pile of potatoes. Within a few moments she felt a tug on her skirt proceeded by the words, "Mommy . . ." She nodded in agreement, giving some brief verbal acknowledgments as well. There were more tugs on her skirt and more little sounds, "Mommy . . ." Again, she'd give a brief verbal comment and yet stay right on task at her "KP" duty. After all, she was working so hard to perform that all important, kid-pleasing task.

Five minutes passed. Steven continued to chatter and then she felt those tugs on her skirt again. This time the tugs seemed harder and more persistent. She finally put her potatoes down in the sink and bent down to her son. Steven took her face in his two little chubby hands, turning her directly to his line of vision and said, "Mommy, will you listen to me with your eyes?"

"Fourteen years later," says Star Paterson, "I am still learning to listen with my eyes . . ." (5)

It's like something that Pastor Warren once noted in an issue of Rick Warren's Ministry Toolbox. He said that we spend about 40 percent of our waking hours listening, yet most of the time we're only listening at 25 percent efficiency, and that creates many of our problems. He goes on to offer three, what he calls, "hearing aids":

The first one he lists is, listen with your eyes. Approximately 80% of communication is non-verbal. Facial expressions and body language usually tell the real story. Look at people when you listen to them!

2. Listen with your heart. Be sympathetic. Tune in to the emotions behind the words.

And finally, he advises, make [it a habit to take] time to listen to the people around you. (6)

This is to say that listening is hard work. It has to be something you are committed to. Listening to your family, listening to your coworkers, listening to those you come into contact with as you go about your daily business. The first duty of love is to listen.

Of course, our primary responsibility is to listen to Christ. If we are poor listening to others, think how poor we are at listening to him.

Our lesson for the day is that magnificent scene on the Mount of Transfiguration. Our Master took Peter, James and John with him up a high mountain where they were all alone. There Christ was transfigured before them. His clothes became dazzling white. And there appeared before them Elijah and Moses, who were talking with Jesus.

Peter said to the Master, "Rabbi, it is good for us to be here. Let us put up three shelters—one for you, one for Moses and one for Elijah." Mark tells us that he did not know what to say, they were so frightened.

Then a cloud appeared and covered them, and a voice came from the cloud: "This is my Son, whom I love. Listen to him!"

That has always been the Christian's primary task—to listen to Christ, for he is the one who can guide us toward better relationships and a more fulfilling life.

It is like a man named Ron Mehl who tells about playing golf one time at the prestigious Cypress Point Golf Course in California. At this club each golfer is assigned a caddy. Ron's caddy was an elderly gentleman by the name of Ed. At each hole, Ron asked Ed for advice. Surprisingly, each time Ed's advice seemed to Ron to be way off. So, Ron ignored Ed's advice and went with his own knowledge, experience and instincts. Consequently, his golf game that day was lousy!

When it became obvious to Ed that his advice was being ignored, he confronted Mehl. Ed made it clear that he had only one job and that was to caddy this course day after day. Every inch of the fairways, rough and greens was etched permanently on his brain. Ed, the caddy, told Ron Mehl, "If you want to play this course well, you have to trust what I say." (7)

Well said. In the game of life, you and I need to listen to Christ and we need to trust what he says. To apply Rick Warren's Hearing Aids, we need to turn our eyes toward Jesus, we need to listen to him with our hearts, and we need to take time each day for the sole task of listening. What does Christ have to say to us that we need to hear?

He may want to talk with us about how we are treating family members or co-workers or friends. He may want to talk to us about our discipleship, about our faithfulness to the church. He may want to talk to us about some undesirable behavior that has crept into our life. Or he may simply want to offer us encouragement as we live our lives.

Of course, some of the things he would say to us are not things we might want to hear. Like the grandmother who turned off her hearing aid, some of us might work very hard at not listening to Christ. But we need to listen and we need to trust him. Today's lesson is for us in particular, "This is my Son, whom I love. Listen to him!"

Are you willing to take that step? Are you willing to fulfill the first duty of love—to listen with your eyes, listen with your heart, to take time to really listen to your family, your friends, your co-workers, and particularly to Christ? I read a story recently that will put all of us to shame when it comes to being willing to listen.

Dr. Noah Gilson, a medical doctor tells about an eighteen-year-old patient of his named Mark who developed an autoimmune reaction that left him almost completely paralyzed. He wasn't even able to speak. His parents insisted that he was a fighter, that somehow he'd get through this, but meanwhile, immobile and on a ventilator, Dr. Gilson wondered how Mark was even going to be able to ask questions or be involved in any way in his own care.

The solution was simple and at the same time quite remarkable: Mark's parents, the Orsinis, would sit at Mark's side each day and recite the alphabet. When they got to a letter Mark needed to spell a word, he'd nod "yes." They'd write it down, then start over and wait for him to nod again. This went on hour after hour, day after day.

Can you imagine a more laborious task? And yet, the Orsisnis never lost patience, and Mark was involved with every decision regarding his care.

Unfortunately, standard therapy wasn't helping, so Dr. Gilson proposed a risky procedure to filter Mark's blood. Mark agreed. After the treatment Mark showed decided improvement, and soon he could move his toes, his legs, and his arms. In fact, Mark made a full recovery, went on to college and is doing well now.

Looking back Dr. Gilson says that he is still in awe of Mark and his parents. He calls the parents some of the most amazing people he's ever met, sitting by Mark's bed for hours, patiently listening to their child speak, letter by letter. Dr. Gilson says when he saw Mark after his recovery, "I wanted to tell him of my shame when my children tried to talk to me, and I brushed them off because I didn't have time to listen. I wanted to say I'd never forget him or his parents . . ." (8)

In her book called The Listeners, Taylor Caldwell says, "Man does not need to go to the moon or other solar systems. He does not require bigger and better bombs and missiles. His basic needs are few, and it takes little to acquire them . . .

he can survive on a small amount of bread in the meanest shelter. But his real need, his most terrible need, is for someone to listen to him . . ."

We all need someone to listen to us. But we also need to listen. We need to listen to one another and we need to listen to Christ. A voice came from the cloud: "This is my Son, whom I love. Listen to him!" That is not simply good advice. That is a command from God.

1. John Kramp, Getting Ahead by Staying Behind (Nashville: Broadman & Holman Publishers, 1997), p. 137.
2. Source unknown.
3. Jim Reapsome, Homemade.
4. Homemade, June, 1987.
5. Kathy Collard Miller and D. Larry Miller, God's Vitamin "C" for the Spirit (Lancaster, PA: Starburst Publishers, 1996).
6. PreachingNow, Vol. 3, No. 7, February 17, 2004.
7. Jerry Ruff, http://www.sumcnj.com/sermons/srm2003/Sermon07.13.03.htm.
8. Medical Economics (March 22, 2002). Cited in Stephen R. Covey, Everyday Greatness (Nashville: Rutledge Hill Press, 2006), p. 271.

Crashing The Party . . . Literally
Mark 2:1 12

There was an unusual story that came out of Russia not too long ago. A Russian teenager—unable to get a ticket to see his favorite rock group "Agatha Christie" perform—shocked those who did have tickets by falling through the roof of the auditorium in the middle of the concert. In his fall, he broke both legs. But that did not deter him from staying until the end of the concert. The unidentified 16-year-old had attempted to climb into the concert through a rooftop ventilation hatch. However, the hatch collapsed, and he fell into the concert hall. Doctors wanted to hospitalize him immediately, but he refused to be moved until the rock show was over. (1)

Interesting story. Does that in any way remind you of a story in the New Testament? How about the man who was lowered through the roof in order that he might see Jesus?

As we've noted before, in today's vernacular, Jesus was a rock star when he first began his ministry. Today's lesson contains another example of his popularity. Our story is set in Capernaum, which was now Jesus' hometown. When the people of Capernaum discovered he had come back home, they gathered in such large numbers at the house in which he was staying that there was no room left, not even outside the door. And so, there in that house he preached the word to them.

While he was preaching four men came to the house. They were carrying a mat on which lay a friend of theirs, a paralyzed man. Since they could not get him to Jesus because of the crowd, they made an opening in the roof above. Now that's determination, isn't it?

It's really quite an amusing scene, if you think about it. Jesus was preaching . . . and overhead these four men were digging through the roof. How distracting would that be? We're told that houses in that day were usually constructed with flat roofs, accessible by a staircase on the outside of the home. The roofs were used for work as well as sleep.

The roofs were designed to be quite sturdy, but this particular roof was no match for the determination of these four men. They were determined to get their friend to Jesus. Can you imagine the chaos that must have ensued from these men frantically digging through the roof while a service is going on below? Surely sticks, tiles, straw— all sorts of things were falling on those trying to listen to Jesus. I'm not sure what I would do if, while I was preaching, some guys were tearing a hole in the roof above my head. Jesus, of course, handled it quite well.

When they had completed making a hole in the ceiling, these four men lowered the mat their friend was lying on. Notice what Mark says next: "When Jesus saw their faith, he said to the paralyzed man, 'Son, your sins are forgiven.'"

That's fascinating, for a couple of reasons. First of all, Jesus doesn't scold them for interrupting the meeting. That's amazing in itself. I doubt that any of us would have responded with so much grace, Second, this lesson is fascinating because of what Jesus says about faith. In other places Jesus tells people they were healed because they themselves had faith. But this man was healed BY HIS FRIENDS' faith. Think about that.

You are a fortunate person indeed if you have friends who are people of faith. Friends who are praying for you . . . friends who are encouraging you . . . friends you are assisting you. How much is a good friend worth?

One evening an alcoholic named Mark told an AA group that he often felt the need to have a drink in the middle of the night. Mark knew he had to find a way to keep from drinking, because his alcoholism was a matter of life and death. He sought the help of his fellow alcoholics.

"I'm going to pass my phone book around the room," Mark told the others in the room. "If any one of you wouldn't mind getting a call from me in the middle of the night, please jot down your name and phone number."

Mark emphasized to the attendees that if they had any misgivings, he didn't want them to put their phone numbers in his book.

"I want to be able to call you without feeling guilty," he explained, "and, of course, if you don't want to be disturbed during the night, I understand that too. You don't have to sign the book."

As the book circulated throughout the room, Mark saw people digging into their pockets and purses for pencils. The room was silent while he waited for the phone book to be returned to him. Mark couldn't help but wonder how many people would sign the book.

Moments later, the last man to sign the book handed it to Mark. When Mark opened the book, he began to cry. He discovered he had some really good friends—lots of them. Fifty-six people were at the meeting. Fifty-six of them signed his book. (2)

Do you think that Alcoholics Anonymous would have helped as many people as it has if it was simply a weekly educational meeting? It succeeds because of the dedication of its members to one another. How much is a friend worth?

Some of you may have been fans of the television show, The West Wing which ran for many years on NBC and starred Martin Sheen as President Jeb Bartlett.

In one episode Deputy Chief of Staff Josh Lyman, played by Bradley Whitford, has been shot and wounded when the presidential party was attacked by two gunmen. Josh's physical wounds were not as severe as his psychological wounds from having been shot. Some weeks after the shooting, he is behaving wildly and dangerously. The President orders him to be interviewed by a traumatologist—a person who specializes in helping people who have been through serious traumas. In that interview Josh allows his vulnerability to surface, but then fears losing his job because of what he has revealed.

After the lengthy interview he finds his boss, Chief of Staff Leo McGarry, who has himself battled alcohol addiction, waiting patiently for him outside. Josh hesitantly admits his extreme behavior brought on by the trauma of the shooting. This leads Leo to tell Josh a story: "This guy's walking down the street," says Leo, "when he falls in a hole. The walls are so steep he can't get out. A doctor passes by, and the guy shouts up, 'Hey, can you help me out?' The doctor writes out a prescription, throws it in the hole, and moves on. Then a priest comes along, and the guy shouts up, 'Father, I'm down in this hole. Can you help me out?' The priest writes out a prayer, throws it down the hole and moves on. Then a friend walks by. 'Hey Joe, it's me. Can you help me out?' And the friend jumps in the hole.

"Our friend says, 'Are you stupid!? Now we're both in the hole!' The friend replies, 'Yeah, but I've been down here before, and I know the way out.'" (3)

There is healing in having a friend you can count on—someone who not only knows the way out but who cares enough to jump into the hole with you. Of course, Jesus is that kind of friend to everyone who calls out to him.

This paralyzed man evidently had friends like that. They cared enough not only to bring him to Jesus, but also to do whatever it took to get him close enough to Jesus for him to be healed. And Jesus was impressed by that. "When Jesus saw their faith, he said to the paralyzed man, 'Son, your sins are forgiven.'"

Now that's also an interesting thing for Jesus to say. Jesus praises the man's friends' faith, but he heals the man by assuring him that he has forgiven his sins.

Evidently there is a link between health and sin. Often when Jesus heals someone, he does it by assuring them they are forgiven. What is this link between sickness and sin?

It certainly doesn't mean that sickness is a punishment for sin. The Book of Job dispensed with that notion long before Jesus' time. Sickness is not a punishment for sin, but in some cases it is a consequence. In any case, sin is always destructive, both to the body and to the soul.

The Bible never makes light of sin. Sin is that which tears down, that which destroys, that which causes pain to the heart and mind of God and humanity. Sin produces the negative emotions of guilt and resentment, anxiety and anger which eat away at our souls and our bodies.

Sin, by definition, is that which destroys the harmony between God and humanity, and between persons. In a world that was constructed for harmonious relationships, therefore, sin is always destructive. Even though we may not be aware of it at the time, sin does destroy. Perhaps this analogy will help.

Dr. Paul Brand was the first medical authority to say that the loss of fingers and toes from leprosy is not due to the leprosy itself but due to infections and injuries that lepers often fall prey to. For years, it had been assumed that some kind of decaying process caused these appendages to drop off. But Dr. Brand showed that major tissue damage occurs because the patient loses the warning of pain. Leprosy acts like a shot of Novocaine to the fingers or the toes or whatever portion of the body it attacks. It deadens that portion of the body to pain. So, if the person with leprosy injures a toe, he or she may be unaware of it until it is so infected that it falls off.

Dr. Marvin De Haan, a psychiatrist, has emphasized the remarkable parallel between leprosy and sin. He repeatedly stressed that pain is an expression of the grace and mercy of God. Sin is not to be hated primarily for the agony it brings into our lives, although that's part of it. But more important, it is to be hated because, like leprosy, it has a numbing effect. It deadens our sense of touch with God and lets us live without an awareness of the "injury and infection" that slowly damages the soul. (4)

We need to recognize the destructiveness of sin. That includes the memory of sins that were committed in days past. Another word for that is, of course, "guilt." Have you ever felt guilty about something?

Indeed, you are a remarkable person if you cannot remember some past deed or action that you would give almost anything to undo. Oh, to know the sweet grace and forgiveness of God.

Jesus was aware of the link between health and sin, the link between negative emotions and the overall wellness of the body. Evidently, the man who lay on the mat before Jesus lay there as the direct consequence of some secret sin, and Jesus healed him by assuring him that his sin was forgiven.

There is someone in this room who would leave here today a healthier person if you knew that you, too, are forgiven. "Be healed," Christ says to you. You are forgiven. "Go and sin no more."

But wait. There are some critics on the scene. Mark tells us that "some teachers of the law were sitting there, thinking to themselves, 'Why does this fellow talk like that? He's blaspheming! Who can forgive sins but God alone?'

"Immediately Jesus knew in his spirit that this was what they were thinking in their hearts, and he said to them, 'Why are you thinking these things? Which is easier: to say to this paralyzed man, Your sins are forgiven, or to say, Get up, take your mat and walk? But I want you to know that the Son of Man has authority on earth to forgive sins.' So he said to the man, 'I tell you, get up, take your mat and go home.'" At Jesus' words the man got up, took his mat and walked out in full view of everyone.

"This amazed everyone," Mark tells us, "and they praised God, saying, 'We have never seen anything like this!'"

It is still amazing even today what Christ can do with our lives. Christ can provide healing faith, healing forgiveness, healing victory over sin and death. Is there some secret sin in your life either current or in the past that is eating away at your soul? Is there some deep regret, some deep remorse that you are having difficulty resolving? He can help.

Christ can give us victory over both sin and guilt. That's the final thing we need to see. We are not talking about therapy here. Psychological therapists have their place. It can be very helpful to sit down with a counselor who can help us deal with the underlying emotions that have brought physical or mental misery into our lives. But Jesus didn't do therapy. Jesus forgave sins. This man needed forgiveness and that forgiveness facilitated his healing.

Is there some secret transgression in your life you would like to have forgiven? One woman says she regrets the way she treated her mother while she was alive. But there's no turning back the clock. It's too late for her to seek her mother's forgiveness. And so the guilt remains. A man thinks, if I hadn't betrayed my spouse. A younger man, perhaps, regrets the way he has poisoned his body with alcohol and drugs, as well as poisoning his relationships while under their demonic influence. The sources of regret are legion. Who will set us free? Only one has that power. And as your pastor I can say to you that he is ready and willing to forgive. You can leave here with a new heart and a new mind.

A writer says that when his little two and a half year old daughter was chastised for some little wrong, she used to say, "It was not I who did that; that was another little girl in me." St. Paul used a similar expression to describe the good within him, "I have been crucified with Christ and I no longer live, but Christ lives in me. The life I now live in the body, I live by faith in the Son of God, who loved me and gave himself for me" (Galatians 2:20).

And that is our hope. I hope everyone has friends who care enough about them to bring them to Jesus. Why? Because he is the only friend who can heal us and make us whole. It makes no difference what our distress is. He can make a difference.

Dr. Diane Komp is a pediatric oncologist; she specializes in treating children who are suffering from cancer. Through her work with suffering children, she has moved from being an agnostic/atheist to a Christian. One of her favorite quotes comes from a former patient: "For the Christian, the Big C is not cancer," she says. "The Big C is Christ." (5)

It is Christ. It is the fortunate person who has friends who care about them to bring them to Christ. Sin remains a big problem in our lives—producing guilt, fear, anger and a host of other negative emotions that eat away at our well-being. But Christ can heal us of our sin. He can take away our guilt. He can come into our lives and make us well again within. The big "C" in life is Christ. Won't you trust in him today?

1. The Associated Press.
2. Good Night, God! (Colorado Springs: Cook Communications Ministries, 2004), pp. 24-25.
3. Dr. Keith Wagner, http://www.bright.net/~coth/whenlove.htm.
4. M. R. DeHaan, "Latter Day Leprosy," Our Daily Bread, Feb. 1980.
5. Diane M. Komp, M.D. A Window To Heaven (Grand Rapids: Zondervan Publishing House, 1992), p. 18.

A Sinner's Prayer
Psalm 51:1-17

An ascription is found in many Bibles at the top of Psalm 51, our psalm for Ash Wednesday. It reads like this, "A psalm of David. When the prophet Nathan came to him after David had committed adultery with Bathsheba." What a somber introduction to a psalm. It refers, of course, to a sorry episode in the life of Israel's greatest king.

Bathsheba was the wife of Uriah, one of King David's most loyal soldiers. "One evening David got up from his bed and walked around on the roof . . ." That's how the story begins. Was David having trouble sleeping? Was he, like many middle age men, occasionally plagued by sleepless nights full of worries about who he really was and what his life was really worth? Did this put him in a more susceptible frame of mind when he spotted Bathsheba?

The Scripture writer hints that David was in Jerusalem with too much time on his hands when he should have been out in the field with his troops. Boredom has wreaked havoc in many people's lives.

Whatever the case, David saw Bathsheba out on her rooftop bathing and he saw that she was very beautiful. Though he knew she was married, he sent messengers to invite her to the palace. She came to him, and he slept with her.

What was Bathsheba doing out there bathing on her roof? She may have been engaged in a Jewish ritual bath, a mikvah, when David spotted her. The Bible makes it clear that she had just cleansed herself after her time of uncleanness (menstruation). Perhaps the reason the writer mentioned this was to prove that Bathsheba was not already pregnant before she slept with David.

We get no indication that Bathsheba was an unwilling partner in this relationship, though there was a definite imbalance of power, and David probably was exploiting his role as king. Power does that to people.

After their affair, Bathsheba returns home. Sometime later she sends a chilling message to the King: "I'm pregnant."

According to the Law, both David and Bathsheba could have received the death penalty for their sin (Lev. 20:10, Deut. 22:22). But David was the king. It is not unusual in any society for there to be two sets of rules—one for the common people and one for the power elite.

Let me remind you that Bathsheba was married to Uriah, one of David's most loyal soldiers. This makes their relationship even more odious. After David receives word of Bathsheba's condition, he summons Uriah to his palace. He makes small talk, then suggests that Uriah go home and relax after his hard work on the battlefield. He even sends along a gift of royal food, hoping this might put Uriah in a relaxed mood.

Obviously, he wants Uriah to go home and make love to his wife Bathsheba. But Uriah feels a loyalty to his troops and remains with the other soldiers and servants rather than going home. We can attribute this to his sterling character, or we might attribute this to some reluctance on Uriah's part to spend time with his wife. Maybe if he had been more attentive to Bathsheba . . . Who knows?

At any rate, Uriah's faithfulness to his men stands in sharp contrast to David's behavior. It is clear that adultery is a serious transgression, even for a king. David is getting desperate to cover it up. He gets Uriah drunk in the hopes that this will make Uriah forget his duties and return to his wife. But Uriah still insists on sleeping out in the fields with the soldiers. Finally, David draws up Uriah's death sentence. He writes an order to his commander, Joab, to put Uriah on the front lines of battle, and then to withdraw so that Uriah will be killed. Joab does as he is told. David has disposed of his problem but at a terrible cost.

After the acceptable period of mourning has passed, David marries Bathsheba, but, says the writer of II Samuel, "the Lord was displeased with them." David got what he wanted, but never again would his life be marked by God's blessings and peace.

The prophet Nathan confronts David about his sin. This bold prophet uses a parable about two men, a wealthy cattle owner and a poor man. The poor man had only a small lamb to care for, and it meant all the world to him. But the wealthy cattle owner selfishly took the poor man's lamb and killed it for a meal.

King David is incensed by this story. It isn't fair! It isn't right for the wealthy man to take the poor man's only lamb, and he demands justice for the poor man. At this point, Nathan reveals that the parable is about King David himself. God had given David abundant blessings. Yet David had taken Uriah's wife. Even though Uriah died in battle, Nathan makes it clear that David is guilty of murder.

And Nathan issues a prophecy from God (II Sam. 12:10): "Now, therefore, the sword will never depart from your house, because you despised me and took the wife of Uriah the Hittite to be your own." Nathan also prophesies that David's wives will be taken away and given to another.

David recognizes his sin right away and confesses it. Even though he deserves death according to the Law, Nathan informs him that God will not kill him. Instead, the child which Bathsheba carries in her body will die.

Can you imagine bearing that knowledge? Can you imagine knowing that you were responsible for the death of your own child? Like any of us, David probably would have preferred to die himself rather than face the knowledge that his sin had resulted in his child's death.

Now listen to the beginning of this psalm, written by King David: "Have mercy on me, O God, according to your unfailing love; according to your great compassion blot out my transgressions. Wash away all my iniquity and cleanse me from my sin.

For I know my transgressions, and my sin is always before me. Against you, you only, have I sinned and done what is evil in your sight; so you are right in your verdict and justified when you judge . . ."

Give David credit: he's honest. He confesses his sin. He acknowledges his responsibility. "Against you, you only, have I sinned and done what is evil in your sight." An Ash Wednesday service is a good time to take stock of our lives and to be honest about them. Have we done wrong? Guilt is a terrible thing to carry around.

Some of you will remember when actor Marlon Brando was one of Hollywood's brightest stars. Young, trim, handsome, winner of multiple Academy Awards, he had it all, as we like to say. Yet at his death in 2004 he weighed over four hundred pounds. As if to explain his unhappy plight, he told a friend, "I'm sorry for all the harm I've done and for all the troubles I've brought to others in my life. I've never been a good parent or a good husband. I've been too busy with my own life to have time for others. Now I'm a guilty old man who's ashamed of the kind of life I've led. There's nothing left for me . . . except eating." (1)

How very sad. That's what unresolved guilt can do to people. This guilt may be from something we've done as in David's case. It may be something we've said. How many of us can think of damage we've done to other people, perhaps even people very close to us, by a thoughtless word or action. Or perhaps something we didn't do.

One man grieves that he wasn't more patient with his mother during the last years of her life when she suffered from Alzheimer's. Some of you may have similar regrets.

Dr. Gregory Knox Jones tells about an experience he had several years ago when he went to Haiti. He visited an impoverished village where the children had bloated stomachs and little more to eat than sugar cane. While he was there, a small Haitian man who was missing most of his teeth, came up to him and said: "I heard that in America you have diet dog food. That's not true, is it?"

This poor man could not imagine that while his children were slowly starving, people in our country were feeding their pets diet food because they were so overweight. His question left Jones speechless. He could not tell the man that it was true. He said the man's words were like a knife piercing him and producing deep feelings of guilt because he knew that he should do more to help the hungry. (2)

Guilt can be an expression of our sins of omission or commission. The point is that the only healthy way to deal with guilt is to acknowledge it before God and ask for forgiveness. As we prepare ourselves for Lent, this is a good place to start—confession.

But notice what David does next. He asks God to change his heart. "Create in me a pure heart, O God," David writes, "and renew a steadfast spirit within me. Do not cast me from your presence or take your Holy Spirit from me. Restore to me the joy of your salvation and grant me a willing spirit, to sustain me."

It's one thing to confess your sin. It's quite another to ask God to so thoroughly change you that you never sin again.

Several years ago the Peanuts comic strip had Lucy and Charlie Brown practicing football. Lucy would hold the ball for Charlie's placekicking and then Charlie would kick the ball. But every time Lucy had ever held the ball for Charlie, he would approach the ball and kick with all his might. At the precise moment of the point of no return, Lucy would pick up the ball and Charlie would kick, and his momentum unchecked by the ball, which was not there to kick, would cause him to fall flat on his back.

This strip opened with Lucy holding the ball, but Charlie Brown would not kick the ball. Lucy begged him to kick the ball. But Charlie Brown said, "Every time I try to kick the ball you remove it and I fall on my back."

They went back and forth for the longest time and finally Lucy broke down in tears and admitted, "Charlie Brown I have been so terrible to you over the years, picking up the football like I have. I have played so many cruel tricks on you, but I've seen the error of my ways! I've seen the hurt look in your eyes when I've deceived you. I've been wrong, so wrong. Won't you give a poor penitent girl another chance?"

Charlie Brown was moved by her display of grief and responded to her, "Of course, I'll give you another chance."

He stepped back as she held the ball, and he ran with all his might to kick the ball. You know what happened. At the last moment, Lucy picked up the ball and Charlie Brown fell flat on his back. Lucy's last words were, "Recognizing your faults and actually changing your ways are two different things, Charlie Brown!" (3)

Well, they are two different things. King David knew that. He prayed not only for God to forgive him of his sins but that God would also give him a new heart so that he would not sin again.

That should be our prayer this night as we prepare ourselves for the celebration of Lent. May God not only forgive us for our sins, but may God also create within us a new heart. May God renew a right spirit within us and restore unto us the joy of our salvation. It should be the prayer of every sinner: "Create in me a pure heart, O God, and renew a steadfast spirit within me. Do not cast me from your presence or take your Holy Spirit from me. Restore to me the joy of your salvation and grant me a willing spirit, to sustain me."

1. Robert J. Morgan, Preacher's Sourcebook Creative Sermon Illustrations (Nashville: Thomas Nelson, 2007), p. 367.

2. http://www.chesterpres.org/osermons/s112402.htm.

3. The Timothy Report, http://www.timothyreport.com, August 21, 2006.

Looking For Rainbows
Genesis 9:8-15

Jack Coe was a popular evangelist in the first half of the twentieth century. Like many popular evangelists of the time, Coe held his services in a tent. Coe's tent was a massive structure which would hold ten thousand people.

One day Coe had a dream in which he saw a flood. The dream troubled him so much that he told his wife about it. Later, when he was conducting a crusade in Kansas City, he dreamed once again about a flood. Together these two dreams seemed so real that he felt that perhaps God was sending him a message.

A short while later, while in the midst of a crusade, Coe felt God speaking clearly to his heart, telling him directly to move his tent. He started packing up. The last hours of the removal of the giant tent were sheer panic. Many people mocked Coe as he and his helpers fled in their loaded trucks. However, they were just in time. We're told that the river rose twenty-two feet over the next few days, and the ensuing flood brought the worst disaster of its kind in North American history. (1)

In the book of Genesis a man named Noah has the same kind of experience, except God doesn't tell Noah to move his revival tent. God tells Noah to build a large boat. Noah built that boat and Noah was spared. His family was also spared, as were all the animals which he had gathered on his boat. It is a magical story that even our children know quite well.

The important part of the story, however, occurs when the waters begin to recede. God comes to Noah and his sons and makes a promise to them: "I now establish my covenant with you and with your descendants after you and with every living creature that was with you—the birds, the livestock and all the wild animals, all those that came out of the ark with you—every living creature on earth. I establish my covenant with you: Never again will all life be destroyed by the waters of a flood; never again will there be a flood to destroy the earth."

And God said, "This is the sign of the covenant I am making between me and you and every living creature with you, a covenant for all generations to come: I have set my rainbow in the clouds, and it will be the sign of the covenant between me and the earth. Whenever I bring clouds over the earth and the rainbow appears in the clouds, I will remember my covenant between me and you and all living creatures of every kind. Never again will the waters become a flood to destroy all life."

This is an important story. It tells us that every time we see a rainbow it is more than sunlight refracting through water vapor. It is a reminder of God's covenant. It is a reminder of God's love. It is a reminder that no matter how disappointed God may become with humanity, never again will the story of the great flood be repeated.

My guess is that, in our materialistic culture, most people who see a rainbow think of the pot of gold that supposedly is at the end of the rainbow rather than God's promise. And that is a shame. God's promise is worth far more than a pot of gold.

Besides, according to one popular legend, this pot of gold is guarded by a mischievous mythical creature, the leprechaun. If the treasure is ever in danger of being discovered by a mortal, legend has it, the leprechaun is to trick the human out of his prize!

There is an amusing story of a man who once tricked a leprechaun into revealing the whereabouts of his valuables. The treasure was located beneath a bush in a large field surrounded by other similar shrubbery. The man needed to go off and get a shovel with which to dig up the treasure, so he tied a red ribbon to the bush so he could identify it on his return. He made the leprechaun promise not to remove the ribbon. Convinced he was more clever than the leprechaun and had secured his gold, the man made off to get his shovel. On his return however, much to his dismay, he found that the little creature had tied a red ribbon on every bush in the field! (2)

That is why you never run into anyone who has ever found the pot of gold at the end of the rainbow. A leprechaun has tricked him out of it. I guess we better not include finding a pot of gold at the end of the rainbow in our retirement planning—though it does make as much sense as betting on the lottery. Nevertheless, in our planning for life, looking for rainbows makes a great deal of sense.

God has made a covenant with us. If you could remind yourself of that truth every time you see a rainbow, it will help you deal with every aspect of your life. God has made a covenant with us. The rainbow is but one symbol of that covenant. The cross is an even more important symbol of it.

On May 12, 1993 two slivers of an olive tree, said to have come from the cross on which Jesus was crucified, were sold for more than $18,000 in an auction in Paris. Accompanying the two slivers of wood were two certificates from the Vatican issued way back in 1855 that apparently authenticated those slivers of wood. (3)

Who knows what this woman's motive might have been in buying those two relics? Maybe she has more money than she knows what to do with, and bought them on a whim. Perhaps, on the other hand, she will reverently mount them in her home and display them in the same way we might display a precious stone. Or maybe, just maybe, if she really believes them to be authentic, she might forever carry those slivers with her, and each day touch them and remember what Christ has done in her behalf.

If so, she would not be the first to do that. Do you know where the expression "knock on wood" comes from? Maybe you have knocked on wood for luck at some time in your life. I read recently that the "knock on wood" superstition originated from an ancient practice that has nothing to do with luck at all. According to this ancient practice a person would touch wood whenever he or she experienced an act of good fortune. The reason he or she would touch wood was in gratitude to Christ who died on a wooden cross. (4)

Actually, this ancient practice sounds like a good idea. Don't "knock on wood" to change your luck. It won't work anyway. It's a mere superstition. However, when something good happens to you, knock on wood—or simply touch a piece of wood—and say thank you for all that Christ has given you—including his own life.

This is the first Sunday of Lent. We are preparing ourselves for the celebration of Christ's death and resurrection. Truly what happened in those three days in Jerusalem more than 2,000 years ago dwarfs even the rainbow that Noah saw in the sky. And yet, they are part and parcel of the same story—God's love for fallen humanity. Both declare this mighty truth: God is not interested in punishing humanity for its sin, but in saving humanity from that sin. You and I need to hold on to that promise. It's spelled out in John 3:17: "For God did not send his Son into the world to condemn the world, but to save the world through him." That has been God's intent since the beginning of time. That's what a rainbow in the sky means. Every time you see it give thanks. Knock on wood, if you will. God has made a covenant with humanity.

That's particularly good to know when the storm clouds are rising and you think there might be a flood.

The past few years have been devastating for many families—and I'm not just thinking of those who have been affected by actual floods like those that hit New England, or droughts and wildfires like those that hit Texas, or tornados like those that hit the South and the Midwest within recent years. I'm thinking about events like the flood of foreclosures and the flood of lost jobs. Studies show that children have been affected by the economic downturn more than any other segment of our population. It's been a slow recovery for most of us. It's been an outright depression for many families with kids.

But even when economic times are good, there are other calamities that come like the flood did on Noah's neighbors—sickness, death, divorce. Sooner or later the flood waters begin to rise for all of us. Some of us make it through life with relatively few storm clouds, but no one escapes altogether.

There is a Jewish legend. It is called the "Sorrow Tree." According to this legend, on the Day of Judgment everyone will be allowed to hang all of their unhappiness on a branch of a great tree. Each person then will walk around the tree and examine all of the troubles hanging in the branches. Anyone may freely choose someone else's unhappiness as their own. But, the legend concludes, no one will choose someone else's sorrows: everyone will reclaim their own over those of others.

This is a way of saying that sooner or later all of us will experience the flood waters of adversity. I dare say that some of you have already waded through those waters. Others will someday soon. We need to acknowledge that truth. TV evangelists sometimes give the impression that, if you trust Christ, your life will be one long stream of blessings. That's a lie. Your heart, your soul, your mind will be blessed—but the flood waters will still rise.

Pastor Jerome Cooper of Baltimore tells about a woman named Lynn. Lynn was a woman seeking for truth. Even though she had been a member of a Christian church, she began her intense search for truth in Buddhism. The reason she chose Buddhism is that Lynn was impacted by the suffering of the world and Buddhism deals a lot with suffering. She began that path toward Buddhism, seeking an answer on how to deal with the suffering of the world. However, it was through her seeking an answer in Buddhism, that she was led back to Jesus Christ.

As she thought more and more about suffering, she eventually looked back at Jesus in a new way, and saw that Jesus had also suffered. He had suffered pain of the heart, as well as pain of the body. She saw Jesus answering in a new way the questions she had been asking about suffering.

She could have come to this understanding of the suffering Christ much sooner, but the church as she had known it had painted an entirely different Christ— a Christ who was always happy, always positive. She realized that what had been presented to her was only a half truth. It was only the victorious Christ, without the suffering Messiah, and she didn't relate to that Jesus. (5)

We need to be honest about it lest anyone misunderstand. Sometimes some of the best people that God ever created suffer horribly. People who sing in the choir, people who teach Sunday School, people who serve for years on church boards—no one escapes completely. And the vexing part is that we do not know why.

A young minister was in his office when a lady—a stranger to him—came into the church and into his office.

"Are you the minister here?" she asked.

"Yes, I am," he replied.

"Come with me," she said curtly.

They went out to the front of the church where she had her car parked on the street. Stretched out in the back seat, the minister saw a twisted figure of a man. She waved her hand referring to that man, and said, "This is my brother. Paralyzed by an accident caused by a drunk driver. If you are a man of God, do one of two things: (1) heal him, or (2) explain this tragedy." He could do neither. (6)

Neither can I. I can't tell you why suffering comes. I can only point you to a rainbow and a cross and say to you: God has not forgotten us. God has promised that He will not forsake us when the flood waters of sorrow and suffering threaten. Hold on to that promise.

I read a story sometime back about Dr. Wayne Oates. You probably will not recognize that name. Wayne Oates was a psychologist and religious educator who coined the word 'workaholic.' Oats wrote fifty-seven books, many of them dealing with pastoral psychology. He was a great man who influenced many people, particularly thousands of pastors over his lifetime.

In his autobiography, which is titled The Struggle to be Free, Oates described his growing up years. Wayne Oates knew what it was to struggle. Born to a poor family in Greenville, South Carolina in June 1917, Oates was abandoned by his father in infancy and was brought up by his grandmother and his sister while his mother supported them by working in a cotton mill. His mother made $30 a week. They survived, says one source, on pinto beans, turnip greens, cornbread and molasses.

In his early school years, Oates discovered he had the ability to excel academically. And if he was ever going to get out of the mill town, out of poverty, that might be his way.

"The trouble was," says this source, "at age 14 everybody had to go to work in the mill and that meant you never graduated from high school. He was tempted to quit studying, but his grandmother told him to keep trying and to remember that life was like a funnel, and that if you started on the small end, the difficult end, the tough end [of the funnel] that then life began to broaden out. But if you started at the easy end, the broad end, life became more narrow all the time."

What an interesting philosophy!

Wayne Oates worked hard and he had an amazing break at the tender age of fourteen. He was one of a small number of impoverished but bright boys selected by a congressman to serve as a page in the United States House of Representatives. This was a life-changing experience, but it didn't keep Oates out of the mill forever. Sixteen is the highest age you can be a page and so he had to go back to Greenville and his work at the mill. But he had tasted something more in Washington and so he insisted on finishing high school. He worked his way through Wake Forest University then went on to Southern Seminary, the first of his family to get a higher education.

He writes in his book how difficult it was to leave that mill town and how much the peer pressure was to stay, not to leave. People were saying, "So you think you're too good to work in the mill, huh? Think you're better than we are, do you? Just don't want to have anything to do with hard working folks like us, is that it? I never thought you, Wayne, of all people would ever desert your family." (7)

But it wasn't that Wayne Oates felt better than his peers, nor that he wanted to desert his family and friends. It was simply that Wayne Oates was sustained by a promise, the promise of his grandmother that if he kept trying, he would eventually end up at the broad end of the funnel. He was also sustained by God's promise that whatever came, he would never be alone.

That promise has sustained millions of people through the centuries. Christians do not look at life through rose-colored glasses. We know there will be storms. We know the flood waters will rise, but God has promised us that they will never overwhelm us, and so, in the storm we look for the sign of a rainbow. And it's there . . . and it will always be there. Even more important, we can see that promise in the cross upon which Christ died. God has made a covenant with us and that covenant will not fail.

1. The Practice of Pentecost. Cited by David Pytches, Does God Speak Today? (Minneapolis: Bethany House Publishers).

2. http://www.colours-of-the-rainbow.com/legends.html.

3. Moody, April 1993, p. 13. Cited by Raymond McHenry, Something to Think About (Peabody, MA: Hendrickson Publishers, Inc., 1998).

4. Vergilius Ferm, Lightning Never Strikes Twice (New York: Gramercy Publishing Company, 1987), p. 131.

5. http://www.centralpc.org/sermons/2001/s011223.htm.

6. David Keller, http://www.gbgm-umc.org/southavenueumc/sermons/God's%20Blessing %20of%20Health%20and %20Wholeness%202005%20November%2013b.htm.

7. Dr. Peter James Flamming, http://www.fbcrichmond.org/sermons/11-28-99sermon.htm.

Acting On Faith
Genesis 17:1-7, 15-16

You've probably heard the ridiculous story about the man who was refused entry into a fancy dinner club because he wasn't wearing a tie. The doorman sent him away with instructions to return if, and only if, he had a tie wrapped around his neck.

The fellow rummaged through his car, but couldn't find a necktie. However, he did find a pair of jumper cables in the trunk. He decided to fashion a necktie from those jumper cables.

He returned to the door of the club. The doorman saw those jumper cables around the man's neck and realized that technically they could serve as a tie. So he said, "Well, I guess you can come in." Then he added, "Just don't start anything."

Bad joke, but here is where we want to begin today's message—the people in history who have most impacted our lives were people who were determined to start something.

Nearly two thousand years before the time of Jesus, God came to a man named Abram and gave him a command and a promise. He was to go from the land of his father to a land that God would show him and God would cause him to father a great nation. And then we read one of the most important statements in all literature: "So Abram went, as the Lord had told him . . ." (Gen, 12:1-40)

Did I mention that Abram was seventy-five years old when God first approached him? And yet, with God's leading, Abram started something—a new people, a new nation. This, by the way, is what faith is. God speaks, we obey.

God speaks, and we get into action. Sometimes that is all that is needed. Our biggest obstacle is often lethargy. We simply need to get moving.

Recently I read about Henry Brown, a slave in Richmond, Virginia, who decided he didn't want to be a slave anymore. But this was 1856. What was he to do? Runaway slaves could be hung. That's good motivation for doing nothing. But doing nothing was not an option for Henry Brown. He found a wooden crate just large enough for him to crawl inside, and postmarked it to an abolitionist in Philadelphia, which was free territory. He got inside the box, sealed the box from the inside, and mailed himself to freedom.

It took three weeks for the abolitionist to get the crate. How Brown survived we do not know. But when the abolitionist lifted the lid of that crate, Henry Brown stood up and said, "How do you do, sir. My name is Henry Brown and I was a slave. I heard about you being an abolitionist, so I'm entrusting my future to you." (1) Sometimes what is important is simply to get moving. God speaks and we act!

Today's lesson takes place nearly twenty-five years after God first called Abram. Abram is ninety-nine years old now. He's no "spring chicken." He has followed the Lord's leading from the time the Lord first called him, but the Lord has been slow to reward Abram's faith. He and his wife Sarai are still childless. How can Abram father a great nation when he and Sarai can't produce a single heir? That's faith, too. Patience. Persistence. Trust. Surely Abram and Sarai were ready to give up. Nearly twenty-five years and no return on their investment? When do you cut your losses? When do you say, it was all an illusion—the promise didn't pan out? That could have been their attitude, but, instead, they chose to trust God.

And the Lord appears to Abram again. The Lord reaffirms that promise of long ago, but this time it is stated more forcefully. "I will make you very fruitful; I will make nations of you, and kings will come from you . . ." And God changes Abram's name to Abraham and Sarai's name to Sarah. And of course God kept His promise. At ninety years of age, Sarah bore a son and from that son came countless heirs to Abraham, both physical descendants and spiritual descendants, of whom you and I are numbered. And those descendants have impacted the world in a mighty way. It is an amazing story. There are some lessons from Abraham and Sarah's life that you and I need to see.

The first lesson is that our timetable may not be God's timetable. As someone has put it, God's promises delayed are not God's promises denied.

Dr. Ray Pritchard gives us a humorous chronology of the 25 years between the first time God promised Abraham and Sarah offspring and the time when that promise was fulfilled:

At age 76, Abraham buys a crib

At age 78, they make a list of possible boy names

At age 80, they order a supply of super absorbent Pampers

At age 85, Abraham goes hunting while Sarah's friends give her a baby shower.

At age 86, they put up wallpaper in the baby's room

At age 90, they subscribe to New Parent magazine

At age 93, Abraham and Sarah start Lamaze classes

At age 96, Abraham drives a practice run to the hospital

At age 98, he packs the suitcase and sets it by the tent door

At age 99, Abraham scratches his head and says, "I wonder if God was just kidding." (2)

I think I would have decided that God was kidding. But I am not Abraham. I'm a bit impatient, and I suspect that so are you.

I read recently about a lawsuit in India which was filed in the year 1205. A man named Moloji Thorat filed this suit. Here is what is remarkable about this lawsuit. It was filed in 1205, but it was not settled until 1966—seven-hundred sixty-one years later. By the way, they ruled in Thorat's favor. Obviously it didn't do him any good but his descendants did receive an undisclosed amount of rupees. (3)

That's a long time for a family to wait for justice—761 years. Abraham and

Sarah only had to wait for twenty-five years, but that was surely a test of their faith. That's a test that many of us would have failed.

None of us like waiting. We grow impatient—even with God. And yet God is faithful to His promises. We shall yet be rewarded if we do not grow weary. Our timetable is not the same as God's timetable. God's promises delayed are not God's promises denied.

But there is a second thing that we need to see about Abraham and Sarah's life: God's purposes are grander than our imaginations can envision.

Abraham and Sarah had dreams for their lives just as you and I have dreams. They dreamed about where they would live and the kind of work they would do. They dreamed about children and grandchildren. That's a dream that they nearly missed out on, but still they dreamed. However, do you think that ever in a million years they dreamed that we would be sitting here today in this church nearly 3,000 years later telling their personal story? Not only that, do you think they imagined that more than a billion Christians and nearly as many Moslems and Jews would be telling their story all over this world, too? You see, they could not see that their lives were part of a grander purpose that existed in the mind of God, for it was through this elderly couple that God blessed the world in a unique and eternal way.

You and I think too small. If we could only imagine what God can do with our lives . . .

Way back in 1858 a Sunday School teacher in Chicago named Ezra Kimball became interested in the spiritual welfare of a young shoe clerk in his town. After debating what to do about it, Kimball started down toward Holton's shoe store where the young man worked. After walking by the store once, Kimball finally mustered up his courage and went in. Finding the young man in the stock room, Kimball proceeded to talk with the young man about his faith.

The shoe clerk Kimball showed such interest in that day was named Dwight L. Moody. Kimball got through to Moody, and Moody went on to become the greatest Christian evangelist of his day. But this is just the beginning of what God would do through that Sunday School teacher's witness.

Dwight L. Moody went on to preach a crusade in England and, in 1879, awakened the heart of Frederick B. Meyer, a pastor, then, of a small church. Meyer went on to become a renowned theologian.

In fact, later, Meyer was preaching in Moody's school in Northfield, Massachusetts. A young man in the back row heard Meyer say, "If you are not willing to give up everything for Christ, are you willing to be made willing?" Those words transformed the ministry of another young man, J. Wilbur Chapman. Wilbur Chapman became a YMCA worker, back when the Y was still a religious institution.

Among those whom Chapman recruited to help him in his ministry was a former professional baseball player. That baseball player was a remarkable figure named Billy Sunday. Billy Sunday went on to become the greatest evangelist of his generation.

Later at a revival in Charlotte, North Carolina, Billy Sunday so excited a group of local men that they began an ongoing prayer group. Later they engaged an evangelist named Mordecai Hamm to come to their town to keep the revival spirit alive. In the revival with Mordecai Hamm, a young man heard the gospel and made his profession of faith. His name? Billy Graham. (5)

Do you think that Sunday School teacher one-hundred-fifty years before—trying to get up his courage to share his faith with a young shoe clerk in Holton's shoe store—had any idea that his actions would one day touch millions of lives through Dwight L. Moody, Frederick Meyer, Wilbur Chapman, Billy Sunday, Mordecai Hamm, Billy Graham, and anyone who has been touched by Graham's ministry?

You and I think too small. God has imagined greater things for your life and mine than we can ever envision if we will but trust Him. God's timetable is not like our timetable. God's purposes are greater than our minds can possibly imagine.

But there is one thing more we need to see: It is in trusting God that our lives find their greatest fulfillment. Following Christ is not just about building God's kingdom. It is also about discovering the abundant life for ourselves.

Some of you will remember a man who once had an enormous impact on American television audiences. His name was Catholic Bishop Fulton J. Sheen. Sheen was known for his preaching and especially his work on television and radio. At one time his nationally televised show drew as many as 30 million viewers, making it one of the most popular programs on television. How did Sheen get to where he did?

The turning point in Fulton J. Sheen's life happened when he finished college. A national examination was given to college students. The prize was a three-year university scholarship. Sheen took the examination and won one of the scholarships. He was informed of this sometime during the summer and immediately went to St. Viator's College to see Father William J. Bergan, a very good friend.

Father Bergan was on the tennis court when he arrived. With great glee and delight Sheen announced: "Father Bergan, I won the scholarship!"

Father Bergan turned from his tennis playing, put his hands on Sheen's shoulders, and looked him straight in the eyes. Father Bergan asked: "Fulton, do you believe in God?"

Young Sheen replied: "You know that I do."

Father Bergan said: "I mean practically, not from a theoretical point of view." This time Sheen was not so sure. He said: "Well, I hope I do."

"Then tear up the scholarship," Father Bergan declared.

"Father Bergan," Sheen protested, "this scholarship entitles me to three years of university training with all expenses paid. It is worth about nine or ten thousand dollars." [This, obviously, was many years ago.]

Bergan retorted: "You know you have a vocation; you should be going to the seminary."

Sheen countered: "I can go to the seminary after I get my Ph.D., because there will be little chance of getting a Ph.D. after I am ordained, and I would like very much to have a good education."

Bergan repeated: "Tear up the scholarship; go to the seminary. That is what the Lord wants you to do. And if you do it, trusting in Him, you will receive a far better university education after you are ordained than before."

Listen to how Fulton Sheen describes that turning point in his life, "I tore up the scholarship and went to the seminary. I have never regretted that visit and that decision." (6)

What I am saying to you is this. When you follow God's leadership, you not only play a part in God's great plan for creation, but you find the most fulfilling life for yourself as well. Abraham and Sarah did as God commanded and God rewarded them far beyond their wildest dreams. Not as quickly as they might have thought . . . God's timetable is not our timetable . . . But God rewarded them far beyond anything they could ever have imagined. They became a blessing to the entire world. And they had a rich and fulfilling life as well. So can we, friend. So can we.

1. Anthony T. Evans, Tony Evans' Book of Illustrations (Chicago: Moody Publishers, 2009).
2. http://www.sermonnotebook.org/romans/Rom%204_18 25.htm.
3. Leland Gregory, Stupid History Tales of Stupidity (Kansas City, MO: Andrews McMeel Publishing, LLC, 2007), p. 246.
5. King Duncan, The Amazing Law of Influence (New Orleans: Pelican Press, 2001).
6. Fulton J. Sheen, Treasure in Clay (Garden City, NY: Doubleday & Company, Inc., 1980), pp. 31-32.

Responsible Living
Exodus 20:1-17

Jeanie Duck is a single mother with a three-year-old daughter. One day a friend gave Jeanie a two-pound box of See's dark chocolate nuts and chews. Being a chocolate lover, Jeanie was in heaven! As she was oohing and aahing over the box her daughter, Jennifer, joined in the excitement. This was a bad sign. If Jennifer was excited, it was because she expected to share in Jeanie's newly acquired bounty. Clearly the only way Jeanie could get rid of her was to share some of her precious chocolate, so she gave Jennifer a piece and sent her to bed. Then she had "just a few" pieces for herself, and went to bed.

Later that night, there was a terrible storm. Jeanie got up in the dark and went from room to room, closing the open windows. As she did, she stepped on something crunchy in the hallway. When she turned on the light, she saw that the floor was covered with little round pieces of dark brown paper. She followed the trail of candy wrappers and found a totally empty box of See's candy!

Jeanie was stunned. She thought, "She's only three, for goodness sake! How could she possibly polish off two pounds of chocolate?"

She found Jennifer sound asleep in her bed, looking angelic.

Waking her daughter she said sternly, "Jennifer Duck, you ate all my candy!"

"No, I didn't," Jennifer replied with a look of earnestness and fear on her face.

"Oh yes, you did." Jeanie said. "Only two people live here—you and me—and I didn't do it!"

Jennifer hung her head. Then, quietly, she mumbled, "I wish I had a baby brother!" (1)

Every child wishes she had a baby brother when she needs someone to take the blame. That would be convenient, wouldn't it? But children are not the only ones to play the blame game.

Sometime back, a Colorado man brought a "malparenting suit" against his mother and father. He sued them for $300,000 for "lousing up his life." He claimed that they had intentionally done a terrible job of parenting and had made him what he was.

The judge dismissed the suit by saying that there must be a "statute of limitations" on parenting. [Thank goodness for that.] The judge went on to say that there must come a time when an adult takes responsibility for his or her own life. If we don't, then next will come suits against brothers, sisters, teachers, and even friends. (2)

It's like an old Peanuts cartoon.

Peppermint Patty telephones Charlie Brown, "Guess what, Chuck . . . the first day of school, and I got sent to the principal's office. It was your fault, Chuck."

"My fault?" Charlie Brown replies surprised. "How could it be MY fault? Why do you always say everything is MY fault!"

"You're my friend, aren't you, Chuck?" Peppermint Patty responds, "You should have been a better influence on me!"

That's the spirit of the times, isn't it?

It's like a headline that appeared in a small-town newspaper: "State population to double by 2040; babies to blame."

I don't believe we can blame babies for being born.

An interesting book came out years ago by an author named Count Saint Exupery. The book was called Wind, Sand, and Stars. One incident in it is especially inspiring.

The author and his comrade, a man named Guillaumet, flew mail over the Andes for the government of Chile. One morning Guillaumet took off on a solo flight in the face of a fierce snow storm. A combination of ice on his wings, heavy snow and terrible winds kept him from rising over the mountains and forced him to land on a frozen lake in the wilderness.

When he was down, Guillaumet dug a shelter under the cockpit and surrounded himself with mail bags. There he huddled for two days and two nights. When the storm finally subsided it took him five days and four nights to find his way back to civilization, crawling on his hands and knees in temperatures twenty degrees below zero.

How did he ever make it? How did he overcome the desire to lie down and rest, which would have meant death for him? Well, he thought of his wife and his sons and how they needed him. He thought of his responsibility to get the mail through. And he survived, although his hands and feet were so badly frozen that they had to be amputated.

When Saint Exupery described his friend's bitter experience and his superhuman struggle to survive, he summed it all up in one sentence: "To be a [human being] is, precisely, to be responsible." (3)

There it is: a crucial theological statement—a statement so critical to our understanding of life that it often goes unspoken and unexamined. To be a human being is to be responsible.

When God placed Adam and Eve in the garden, they were given the responsibility for tending the garden and keeping God's one commandment: "Of the tree of the knowledge of good and evil you shall not eat, for in the day that you shall eat of it you shall die." (Gen. 2:17) Unfortunately they failed the test of responsibility.

Adam and Eve had two sons—Cain and Abel. Cain slew Abel in a jealous rage. When confronted with his crime, Cain cried out, "Am I my brother's keeper?"

In other words, he was asking if he was responsible for his brother. You know the answer to that.

A lawyer once asked Jesus a question very similar to that one. When Jesus said that we are to love our neighbor as we love ourselves, the lawyer asked, "Who is my neighbor?"

In other words, "How far does my responsibility extend? Am I responsible for my family, my immediate neighbors, the people in my own city, the people of Somalia? Where does it all end?"

Jesus' disciples struggled with this same question: Is the gospel just for Jews, or is it for the Gentiles as well? Am I responsible for people who respond positively to me, or am I even responsible for my enemies?

Our Old Testament text today contains the set of moral injunctions that we know as the Ten Commandments. And what are the Ten Commandments but an attempt to define human responsibility? Thou shalt not kill. Thou shalt not steal. Thou shalt not commit adultery. Honor thy father and mother. [It sounds more authoritative in King James English, doesn't it?]

What are my responsibilities to my neighbor? What are my responsibilities to God? The Ten Commandments seek to answer those questions. To be a human being is to be responsible.

We say to young people: "Be responsible." We say the same thing to married couples, to new drivers, to voters: act responsibly. Every facet of our life together depends on people acting responsibly. That is such a simple, obvious truth, and yet we so often fail to confront it. To be a human being is to be responsible.

That of course can be a problem. Are there any of us who want to have someone tell us to "act responsibly." Do you teenagers want to hear it from your parents? Do any of us want to hear it from our spouse, or even from our pastor? Responsibility is a heavy burden for many of us.

What we really long for at times is escape. Many of us want to flee from our responsibilities.

Just look at the numbers: how many alcoholics and drug addicts are chemically snared while seeking escape? How many extramarital affairs and other destructive activities are the simple product of people running away from responsibility?

Many of us resent responsibility. We act a lot like the fictional character José Jiménez. Perhaps a few of you will remember José. José Jiménez was a character created and performed by comedian Bill Dana on The Steve Allen Show way back in 1959. José became increasingly popular during the 1960s. However, Dana retired the character after protests by Hispanic groups.

In one very funny routine, however, José plays an astronaut being interviewed by newsmen just before his blast off to the moon. One reporter asks, "Tell me, do you have any grave doubts about your success?"

José responds, "Please don't use the word 'grave.'"

Another newsman asks, "How do you think you'll feel when you leave earth and pass on into space?"

José says, "Please don't use those words 'pass on.'"

Another asks, "Do you have any fear about this undertaking?"

José answers, "Please don't use the word 'undertaking.'"

José was not really excited about his job as an astronaut. If we had a job like that, we might be a bit reluctant, too.

Who among us would not rather escape from, rather than face up to our responsibilities? And yet, to be emotionally mature is to be responsible. To be a follower of Jesus Christ is to be responsible.

If you have read Dr. M. Scott Peck's very popular book The Road Less Traveled, you know the emphasis he places upon accepting responsibility. Dr. Peck is both a psychiatrist and a medical doctor. He tells about counseling a man who was a career sergeant in the army, stationed in Okinawa. This sergeant was in serious trouble because of his excessive drinking. In their sessions the sergeant denied that he was an alcoholic, or even that his use of alcohol was a problem. "There's nothing else to do in the evenings in Okinawa," he said in justifying his behavior, "except drink."

Peck asked him if he liked reading, and the sergeant said he loved to read. So the doctor asked him if he couldn't read a book instead of going out drinking.

"Nah," said the sergeant, "the barrack's too chaotic with all the guys."

"You could go to the library," Peck suggested.

No, the library's too far away was the response. Confronted with the fact that the library was no farther away than the bar the sergeant claimed he wasn't really that much of a reader after all. The doctor suggested fishing, which the sergeant liked, but said he wasn't available in the day and Okinawa didn't have night fishing. Peck came back with an offer to put the sergeant in touch with a number of people who were enthusiastic night fishers, and suddenly the sergeant wasn't much of a fisherman either.

"So," Dr. Peck said, summing things up, "There are things you could do here besides drink, but given the choice, you're going to choose drinking over any of them."

"Guess that's right," said the sergeant.

"But since it's getting you in all kinds of trouble, seems like you've got a pretty severe dilemma on your hands."

With a curse the sergeant answered, "This island would drive anyone to drink." (4)

Members of Alcoholics Anonymous learn that the first step out of their addiction is admitting that they have a problem. There was no hope for this sergeant if he refused to face that reality. That's true of all of us. If there is a problem in our life that is robbing us of our health, robbing us of our joy, robbing us of our relationships, robbing us of our peace of mind, we need to face up to it. To be a human being is to be responsible. To be a follower of Jesus Christ is to be responsible.

Ultimately, responsibility is just what the word suggests: it is our response to God's love as manifested in Jesus Christ. If we resent responsibility, it may be that we do not understand what responsibility is. Responsibility is our joyful response to what God has done for us in Christ Jesus. That is why the Ten Commandments and the Great Commandment are relevant to our lives. We read in 1 John 4:19, "We love because He first loved us." We take responsibility for ourselves and others because He took responsibility for us on the cross of Calvary. Responsibility is not a terrible weight we carry. Responsibility is the road we travel on our way to the abundant life Christ has provided for us.

Pastor John Jewell uses this analogy: A dear friend of his is a recovering alcoholic. One day his friend said to him, "If I heard once, I heard a million times that I needed to 'change'—as though I didn't know that. I decided to change almost every night of my drinking life. I would finish my bottle with the absolute promise to myself that the next day would be different. It would be a 'new' day. And it never was."

But his friend did change. He was able to overcome his addiction and take responsibility for his life. How did he do it? He did it by responding to God's love poured out in Jesus Christ. He quit fighting his addiction in his own strength and made a fresh commitment to give God the controls for his life.

"It may be weird," he said, "But it's like I handed over the remote." (5)

Let me ask the men in our congregation . . . is it easy to hand over the remote . . . any remote? How about the remote that controls your life? God created us to be responsible—responsible parents, responsible members of our nation, of our community and of our church. We can do that without Christ, but many of us will feel we are living in a straitjacket. There will be no joy in our lives, only a sense of duty. If we will make a fresh commitment to God—turn the remote of our lives over to God— if our lives are lived in response to the love poured out for us in Jesus Christ—then there can be a new dimension to our lives. We will be living out of grace—not simply doing good works, but enjoying abundant life in Christ Jesus.

To be human is to be responsible. Yes, but to know Christ is to walk in his joy.

1. Jeanie Daniel Duck, The Change Monster. Cited by Dr. Stephen C. Lien, http://www.bpcusa.org/Sermons/sermon11804.pdf.

2. David A. Seamands, Putting Away Childish Things (Wheaton: Victor Books, 1982).

3. Msgr. Arthur Tonne, Five Minute Homilies on the Gospels (Hillsboro, Kansas: M.B. Publishing House, 1977).

4. Dr. M. Scott Peck, The Road Less Traveled (New York: Simon and Schuster, 1978).

5. http://www.lectionarysermons.com/jan09-00.html.

The Handiwork Of God
Ephesians 2:4-10

In David Redding's book, Before you Call, I Will Answer, we get a vivid description of the power and destruction of war. We follow the Confederate and Union armies as they lock horns during the Battle of Fredericksburg. The Confederate army gained a stronghold atop a hill called Marye's Heights and slaughtered the Union army below with relative ease.

However, one young Confederate soldier, Sergeant Richard Kirkland wrestled with his conscience. He simply could not bear the carnage before him. Finally, he approached his superior officer and asked if he could he go out on the field and carry water to the suffering men, most of whom were members of the Union Army. The officer, though mystified by his sergeant's request, granted his permission. And thus Confederate soldier Richard Kirkland bravely stepped forward to assist the legions of dying men he saw on the battlefield. He knew the great risk he was taking as he entered the field of conflict, but his act of courage had a sobering effect on both armies.

As soon as Kirkland stepped on the battlefield, the intense gunfire suddenly ceased. The shock of an enemy offering aid to the opposition struck both armies with amazement. Back-and-forth Kirkland went from battlefield to water station, aiding every soldier along his path. Each time he stepped back on the field of battle, fighting ceased.

"Sergeant Kirkland earned a nickname that day," says Redding, "'The Angel of Marye's Heights.' Later, he would be killed in the war. Those who witnessed his death said that he died a hero, thinking of the men under his command up until the very end." (1)

Do you understand that this was why Christ came into the world? It was to create a world of Sergeant Richard Kirklands . . . people who know how to love . . . people who know how to put compassion before personal security . . . people who do not divide others into friends and enemies . . . but who see all people as children of God.

That is what the Gospel is about. That is what the kingdom of God is about. "For we are God's handiwork," writes St. Paul, "created in Christ Jesus to do good works, which God prepared in advance for us to do."

Let me ask you a question: How do you feel about yourself? Do you feel like you are the handiwork of God? Do you feel you have within yourself the ability to be heroic like Sergeant Richard Kirkland? Do you feel you could change the world? Or are you satisfied to just get by? Are you satisfied doing as little as you possibly can to justify your existence? I believe God created us for more than just getting by.

Do you know the story of Kit Summers? In the early 1980s Kit Summers was one of the finest jugglers in the world. He was the star attraction at a major casino in Atlantic City. One rainy night when visibility was near zero, Kit was on his way to do a show at that casino. He crossed a busy street when, suddenly, out of the downpour, a truck appeared. There was no time to get out of the way! The collision was inevitable. Kit was thrown onto the hood of the truck, broke the windshield with his head, rolled off to the side and tore off the side mirror with his body, then lay in a crumpled heap 30 feet away.

For 37 days, Kit lay in a coma. Then slowly he awoke. He was glad to be alive, but he soon realized that he would have to learn to do everything all over again, and I do mean everything. This included eating, talking, walking, and of course, juggling. Although he knew "how" to do these tasks in his mind, the connections from his brain to his nervous system had to be reestablished.

With amazing patience, dedication, and discipline Kit set out on the arduous road to recovery. And it paid off. On the one year anniversary of his accident, Kit performed again in public, and although his skill hadn't quite returned to its previous level, he was on his way to regaining his stature as one of the best jugglers in the world. In the meantime Kit has also become a world class motivational speaker, author and successful businessman. On the evening of his return to performing, Kit's friends threw a party in his honor. They called it a "We are glad we are all alive" party as a tribute to Kit. (2)

Do you think Kit Summers made his recovery by being satisfied with just getting by? Do you think he became a world class juggler in the first place with minimal effort?

The word is commitment. The word is dedication. The word is sacrifice. You and I have a choice to make about our lives. Will we settle for being lumps of clay who are here for a while and then return to the earth without leaving any lasting impression, or will we allow ourselves to be the handiwork of God fashioned by His hand for greatness?

St. Paul writes, "For it is by grace you have been saved, through faith—and this is not from yourselves, it is the gift of God—not by works, so that no one can boast. For we are God's handiwork, created in Christ Jesus to do good works, which God prepared in advance for us to do." St. Paul's words say three things to me.

First of all, they say we were created for greatness. Now it's important for you to understand what I mean by greatness. Greatness in God's eyes is different from what the world means by greatness.

Dr. Mark D. Roberts tells one of the most moving stories I've heard in quite a while. He tells about a phone call he received about bedtime one evening. He was the pastor on call that night at the First Presbyterian Church of Hollywood. The operator informed him that Mary, a member of the church, had asked for immediate pastoral assistance because her child had just died.

Jumping into his clothes, Roberts sped off in his car to a hospital several cities away. He was thankful that he had some idea who Mary was. In a church of over 4,000 members you couldn't count on this. But Mary had been involved in the young adult group, so he knew her enough to say "hello." Yet he couldn't ever remember seeing her with a child, so he was shocked to hear that her child had died.

When he got to the hospital, he was directed by the nighttime staff to a dark, quiet corridor. There he found Mary, just outside of her son's room.

"Thank you so much for coming," she said. "I really needed to pray with someone." As he and Mary sat in the hall, she told him the heartbreaking story of her son, Jimmy. Jimmy had been born with multiple physical and mental handicaps. His life of seven years had been marked with countless surgeries and therapies. Mary had spent much of her life in hospitals and long-term care facilities, comforting and encouraging Jimmy. He wasn't able to be around other people, so that's why Pastor Roberts had never seen Mary with him at church.

After they talked for a while, Mary and he went into the room where Jimmy's body lay. All the tubes and wires were still connected to him. Roberts was shocked by what he saw. Jimmy was tiny, much smaller than a normal seven-year-old boy. His little body was badly twisted and deformed. Roberts found it difficult even to look at him without wincing. But not Mary. She looked upon her son with eyes of uncompromised love. She touched his face and spoke quietly to him, even though he couldn't hear anymore. She tenderly kissed his cheek many times. Mary told Roberts how much Jimmy had meant to her, and how much she would miss him.

As Roberts stood there, he realized that Mary loved with kind of love that was far, far beyond any love he had ever given to anyone. It was the undeserved, unabashed, unquenchable love of a mother for her child. Whereas he saw Jimmy as someone marred in his appearance, almost beyond human semblance, Mary saw him as a beautiful, lovely human being. Jimmy had not earned her love with his handsomeness or his human achievements. Mary loved him simply, freely, graciously, all of Jimmy's life. Had she been able to do so, Mary would have exchanged places with Jimmy that night, dying so that he might live. Mary loved her precious son with all she had." (3)

Friends, that mother is the handiwork of God. That what I mean by being called to greatness. Some of us are called to be world-class parents. Some of us are called to be world-class employees or world-class employers. All of us are called to be world-class servants of God wherever our place in life may be. We are the handiwork of God.

The second thing that means is that this greatness does not come from us. It comes from God. Listen again to Paul's words: "For it is by grace you have been saved, through faith—and this is not from yourselves, it is the gift of God—not by works, so that no one can boast. For we are God's handiwork, created in Christ Jesus to do good works, which God prepared in advance for us to do."

Do you understand what grace is? Pastor Anthony Evans tells an unusual story about a man who took his girlfriend out for dinner and when they sat down, he laid an elaborate box on the table for her birthday. All the while they were eating dinner, she just kept thinking about this box, because it was a big box, and she wanted to know what was inside. She could hardly eat. The waiting to open the gift was killing her, but her boyfriend told her to open the gift after dinner. All she could think about was what was in the box.

Finally dinner was over. "Can I open the box now?" she asked.

"Yeah," he replied, "you can open the box."

She opened the box and pulled out . . . a pillow. "Oh, wow, I mean, this is a nice pillow," she said, "but it's a pillow." She turned the pillow over, thinking that something was taped to the backside. There was nothing. "Well, thank you." It was obvious she was disappointed that she got a pillow.

Her boyfriend got up, took the pillow from her, and laid the pillow on the floor. He got down on one knee, took her by the hand, and said, "Will you marry me?"

Immediately she forgot about the pillow. The one who gave her the pillow now became a lot more important. (4)

The Lord of all the universe has come to us on bended knee, as it were, to let us know how much we are loved, how much we are treasured. That's grace. He "humbled himself," says St. Paul. That's grace. However, he did not come on bended knee so that so that we could spend our lives just getting by. He did it so that he might fashion us into his handiwork. He did it so that we might become world-class parents, world-class spouses, world-class employees and employers, world-class servants of God.

I like to think that we have some world-class members of our church—people who give more, care more, help more. You can be a world-class member of a committee. You can be a world-class usher or a world-class choir member. That doesn't mean you'll be invited to sing at the Met. But it does mean that you're not a slacker, you give your very best in whatever ministry you're involved in. You are God's handiwork.

We become God's handiwork when Christ Jesus lives within us and we engage in acts of service in his name. "For it is by grace you have been saved, through faith—and this is not from yourselves, it is the gift of God—not by works, so that no one can boast. For we are God's handiwork, created in Christ Jesus to do good works, which God prepared in advance for us to do." Why have we been saved? "To do good works."

In a recent book author Max Lucado tells a wonderful story about a ship that is blown off course. It quickly comes across a group of uncharted islands.

The ship's captain orders the boat's anchor dropped at the first island and sets foot on it. What he discovers is a scene of total despair. Poverty and discord abound on this island. The people are dispirited and demoralized. The Captain and his crew move on to other nearby islands and they, too, reveal villages in the midst of blight, suffering from conflict, lack of food and illness.

Finally, the Captain enters the largest island of the chain and discovers a totally different world than he had encountered on the other islands. This island has plush irrigation systems, strong able bodied citizens and a bright outlook. When the Captain asks a local why this island is so far ahead of its neighbors, he is told that a Father Benjamin has educated the people of the island in everything from agriculture to health. The Father also assisted the town in building schools, roads, hospitals and irrigation systems.

Seeing such an amazing community led by one man, the captain asks to meet Father Benjamin in person. "Show me where he lives," he says. At first, the Captain is guided to various buildings that the Father was responsible for building. But the Father is not there. Then the locals bring him to a fishpond that Father Benjamin had constructed that helps to feed the community. Again, however, there is no sign of Father Benjamin.

The Captain is finally led up a mountain. "Aha," he thought, "Finally I will meet the amazing Father Benjamin." Once again, there is no sign of this good Father and the Captain grows frustrated. He asks the townsfolk why they have led him to many places which Father Benjamin made possible, but not to the gentleman himself.

Finally, the Captain is told that Father Benjamin has died. The Captain asks why they did not tell him up front that the priest was dead. "You didn't ask about his death," the chief explains. "You asked to see where he lives." (5)

Wow! You want to know where Christ lives? He lives within each person who is willing to open himself or herself to become the handiwork of God. He lives wherever a hospital has been built in Christ's name, or a homeless shelter, or a soup kitchen. Christ lives wherever anyone has given sacrificially to minister to any of "the least of these."

Being the "handiwork of God" is not for the fainthearted. It is not for those who are content to just get by in life. I can tell you that there is no joy in simply existing. But there is joy without end to those who desire to be world-class in serving him. Your Lord kneels on a pillow, hangs on a cross, says to you and to me, "You were created for good works, for making a difference in the world, not that you might boast but that others might glorify my Father." That's who we are and what we are about when Christ lives within us—God's handiwork.

1. (Old Tappan, NJ: Fleming Revell Company, 1985), pp. 141-144. Richard Nunn Lanier, The Angel Of Marye's Heights.
2. Michael J. Gleb and Tony Buzan, Lessons From the Art of Juggling (New York: Harmony Books, 1992).
3. http://www.markdroberts.com/htmfiles/sermons/5.9.04.htm
4. Tony Evans' Book Of Illustrations (Chicago: Moody Publishers, 2009).
5. Outlive Your Life: You Were Made to Make A Difference (Nashville: Thomas Nelson, Inc., 2010).

Yada, Yada, Yada
John 12:20-33

A man is watching television. His wife is trying to engage him in conversation: "Dear, the plumber didn't come to fix the leak behind the water heater today."
Husband: "Uh-huh."
Wife: "The pipe burst today and flooded the basement."
Husband: "Quiet. It's third down and goal to go."
Wife: "Some of the wiring got wet and almost electrocuted Fluffy."
Husband: "Darn it! Touchdown."
Wife: "The vet says he'll be better in a week."
Husband: "Can you get me a Coke?"
Wife: "The plumber told me that he was happy that our pipe broke because now he can afford to go on vacation."
Husband: "Aren't you listening? I said I could use a Coke!"
Wife: "And Stanley, I'm leaving you. The plumber and I are flying to Acapulco in the morning."
Husband: "Can't you please stop all that yakking and get me a Coke? The trouble around here is that nobody ever listens to me." (1)

Poor guy, nobody was listening.

It was six days before the celebration of the Passover. Passover was a massive celebration in Jerusalem. Josephus, the notable Jewish historian, estimated that over two million people were attracted to the great Passover Feast. Devout Jews from all around the Mediterranean came to offer their sacrifices to God and to pay their half shekel temple tax.

We're told that 256,500 lambs were slain at one such Passover and that each lamb represented at least ten worshippers, so you can see what a crowd was present. Among those who came for the celebration were Romans, Persians, Syrian, Egyptians, and Greeks.

As our lesson opens Jesus is in Bethany, where Mary and Martha and Lazarus lived. Bethany was a small village about one and a half miles from Jerusalem. This was some time after Jesus had raised Lazarus from the dead. In gratitude, Mary and Martha were throwing a dinner in Jesus' honor. Lazarus, of course, was there, alive and in the flesh, as we say.

A large crowd of Jews found out that Jesus was there and came, not only because they wanted to see him, but also to see Lazarus. Lazarus had become somewhat of a celebrity. We can imagine the tabloid headlines: "Bethany Resident First Man to Be Raised from the Dead." We've noted that since the beginning of his ministry Jesus had a rock star kind of following. The raising of Lazarus did nothing to discourage that. As one of the Pharisees said to a colleague, "Look how the whole world has gone after him!"

Among those who came to see Jesus were some Greeks. They approached Philip, who was from Bethsaida in Galilee. Philip's surname was Greek and his home village was known as a place where there were numerous Greek descendants. Maybe the visiting Greeks thought Philip would be more open to their inquiries than the other disciples. "Sir," they said to him, "we would like to see Jesus." Philip went to tell Andrew; and together they told Jesus.

Jesus was not impressed. He replied as he often did with a somewhat cryptic message about his coming death. He concludes his response to them by saying, "Now my soul is troubled, and what shall I say? 'Father, save me from this hour'? No, it was for this very reason I came to this hour. Father, glorify your name!"

Then a voice came from heaven, "I have glorified it, and will glorify it again."

Seemingly this was an audible voice, a voice which could be heard by anyone listening. But notice this: John tells us that the crowd that was there and heard the voice coming down out of heaven dismissed it as thunder; others said an angel had spoken to Jesus. In response to their reaction, Jesus said, "This voice was for your benefit, not mine . . ."

That's interesting, don't you think? God spoke from the heavens, but the people who heard the sound of God speaking simply dismissed it as thunder.

When I read about this reaction, I thought of that phrase that the television show Seinfeld introduced to the world, the expression, "yada, yada, yada." Yada, yada, yada is used by the person who doesn't want to go into boring, inconsequential details. "I saw him looking at me, yada, yada, yada . . ." The phrase "blah, blah, blah" fills the same purpose in today's vernacular.

To the crowd that day when God spoke, it meant nothing to them. It was "yada yada yada . . . blah, blah, blah." It was only the sound of thunder.

Dr. James B. Lemler was preaching one time about the Trinity. He told about a couple of parents who had gone home from his church and during Sunday lunch were talking about his sermon. In the midst of their conversation, their second-grade daughter sitting at the table chimed in. "Oh, Father Lemler's sermons, they're always the same," she said, "You know . . . blah, blah, blah, . . . love . . . blah, blah, blah . . . love."

Dr. Lemler said he was amused and thought to himself, "Hey, this little girl really got it . . . the message, the repetition, the core, the redundancy.

"And so it is with the Holy Trinity," says, Dr. Lemler, ". . . Over and over again . . . blah, blah, blah, love . . . blah, blah, blah, love . . ."

"God the Creator . . . I love you and give you life.

"God the Redeemer . . . I love you and embrace you in that love forever.

"God the Spirit . . . I love you and warm your heart and your soul with my love.
"Blah, blah, blah love . . ." (2)

I wish that is what the people heard that day when the voice spoke from heaven, "Yada, yada, yada love . . . ." But Mark described it like this: "The crowd that was there and heard the voice said it had thundered . . . "

Here's the truth of the matter: Many people are so disconnected from God, that if God were to speak to them, they would not hear His voice. All they would hear would be thunder. Jesus said to those who heard only thunder, "This voice was for your benefit, not mine," but they did not hear.

There is a rather obscure definition of sin in the Bible. It comes from a Hebrew word that means "a failure to listen." When we fail to listen, we are cut off from whoever is speaking to us. (3)

In George Bernard Shaw's play St. Joan, which is about Joan of Arc, Joan tells of hearing God's messages. She is talking to King Charles. Charles doesn't appreciate this crazy lady in armor who insists on leading armies. He's threatened by her. He says, "Oh, your voices, your voices, always your voices. Why don't the voices come to me? I am king, not you."

Joan replies, "They do come to you, but you do not hear them. You have not sat in the field in the evening listening for them. When the Angelus rings . . . you cross yourself and have done with it. But, if you prayed from your heart and listened to the trilling of the bells in the air after they stop ringing, you would hear the voices as well as I do." (4)

Joan heard the voice of God; the king, if he heard anything at all, heard only thunder. Why? Because she was listening for that voice. Some people are so disconnected from God that they never hear God's voice.

Other people are so preoccupied with their own pursuits that they're unaware when God speaks.

There is a time-honored story about an old farmer who was persuaded by his nephew to visit the big city. The young man proudly took the farmer on a tour of the large metropolis.

At one point as they walked down the street the old man suddenly stopped and asked, "Did you hear that?"

The young man looked at the milling pedestrians and the traffic and replied, "Hear what?"

"A cricket," the old man said as he walked toward a little tuft of grass growing out of a crack next to a tall building. Sure enough, there tucked in the crack was a cricket.

The young man was amazed. "How could you pick up the sound of a cricket in all this noise?" he asked.

The old farmer didn't say a word and just reached into his pocket, pulled out a couple of coins and dropped them on the sidewalk. Immediately a number of people began to reach for their pockets or look down at the sidewalk.

The old man observed, "We hear what our ears are trained to hear."

Psychologist Ellen Langer says that many people are so preoccupied with their daily tasks that they rarely listen to those around them. It's like that little game that children play:

What do we call a tree that has acorns? Oak.

What do we call a funny story? Joke.

What do we call the sound made by a frog? Croak.

What do we call the white of an egg?

How many of you said, in your mind "yolk"? The correct answer, of course, is "the white." But nearly everyone gets it wrong. They've become accustomed to words ending in the "oke" sound, and so they answer, "The yolk." (5)

How well do you listen to those around you? How well do you listen to God?

Author Mark Buchanan tells about a scene from the movie Ray which was based on the life of musician Ray Charles. Ray Charles went blind at age seven. He lived his childhood in poverty, in a one room shack at the edge of a sharecropper's field.

In this scene from the movie, we see Ray as a child run into his house and trip over a chair. He starts to wail for his mother. She stands at the stove, right in front of him, and instinctively reaches out to lift him. Then she stops . . . backs up . . . stands still . . . watches.

"Young Ray stops crying. He listens. He hears, behind him, the water on the wood stove whistling to a boil. He hears, outside, the wind pass like a hand through cornstalks. He hears the thud of horse hooves on the road, the creak and clatter of the wagon they pull. Then he hears, in front of him, the thin faint scratch of a grasshopper walking the worn floorboards of his mama's cottage. He inches over and, attentive now to every sigh and twitch, gathers the tiny insect in his hand. He holds it in his open palm. 'I hear you, too, Mama,' he says. She weeps with pride and sorrow and wonder."

Later he explains to someone, "I hear like you see." (6)

Ray Charles trained himself to listen. That would be wise for those of us who have our sight. Listen to your colleagues. Listen to your loved ones. Listen to God.

It is important to know that God does speak to those who listen. Not audibly, perhaps. We worry when somebody says they hear voices, as we should. The voice of God will be an inward voice, a silent voice, a voice within the mind. God may speak through a friend. God may speak through a strong emotion.

Someone says, "I felt God telling me that I should support that mission project." And I am confident God did. The greatest untapped source of power in this world is the unheeded voice of God in human affairs.

Jesus said, "This voice was for your benefit, not mine . . ."

Many of us were moved a few years back when the story came out about how the D.C. snipers were apprehended. Do you remember in October 2002 when those tragic shootings were being perpetrated in Washington, D.C., Maryland, and Virginia? Ten people were killed and three others were critically injured. Many citizens assisted police in solving this heinous crime. Among these was trucker Ron Lantz, a resident of Ludlow, KY.

Lanz was listening to a radio show when he heard a description of a car being sought by officials in connection with the sniper case. A short time later he noticed a car that matched the description, a Chevrolet Caprice, at a Maryland rest stop and called 9-1-1. He was one of several who called police that night, and not the first.

However, he did play an important part in capturing the two suspects. After calling 9-1-1, Lantz and another driver blocked the exits to the rest area, effectively trapping the suspects until police could arrive.

Here is what is special about Lantz' story, as verified by several trusted sources. About a week before he helped make this capture, Lantz was driving down the Interstate when he heard another report about the snipers. He decided somebody needed to pray about this situation. He got on his C-B radio and sent out a call to any other truckers who were nearby to join him at a certain rest area for a time of prayer about this situation. It was getting dark when Lanz pulled his rig into the rest area. There were about 50 other rigs already there. They all got out of their cabs and stood in a circle, holding hands, 60 or 70 of them, including some wives and children.

"Let's pray," Ron Lantz said. And for almost one hour they did just that. They prayed that these killings would come to an end. And one week later Ron Lantz spotted a Chevrolet Caprice at a Maryland rest stop.

Are the two related? Some will say, "Coincidence." Yada, yada, yada. Blah, blah, blah. All they will hear is thunder. And perhaps they are right. Perhaps it was coincidence. But I know this, if you are not daily communicating with God, making known your requests and listening for God's reply, you are missing out on the greatest resources life has to offer, the leading of God in an uncertain world.

Mother Teresa of Calcutta put it this way: "We need to find God and he cannot be found in noise and restlessness. God is the friend of silence. See how nature—trees, flowers, grass—thrive in silence; see the stars, the moon and sun, how they move in silence . . . The more we receive in silent prayer, the more we can give in our active life. We need silence to be able to touch souls. The essential thing is not what we say, but what God says to us and through us." (7)

God spoke but all most people heard was thunder. How about you? Do you hear God's voice today?

1. John C. Maxwell, Be a People Person (USA: Victor Books, 1989).
2. http://day1.org/1094-blah_blah_blah_blah_love.
3. Dr. Vance L. Shepperson & Dr. Bethyl Joy Shepperson, Tracks in the Sand (Nashville: Thomas Nelson, 1992), p. 85.
4. Bruce Larson, My Creator, My Friend (Waco: Word Books Publisher, 1986).
5. Richard C. Whiteley, The Customer-Driven Company (New York: Addison-Wesley Publishing Company, 1991).
6. Hidden In Plain Sight (Nashville: Thomas Nelson, Inc., 2002), pp. 30-31.
7. Cited by Malcolm Muggeridge, Something Beautiful for God.

After The Parade
Mark 11:1-11

Welcome to this celebration of Palm Sunday. Today we remember the crowds of people who lined the streets of Jerusalem to welcome our Master into their city. Ironically, today is also, of course, April Fools' Day. Maybe that is more appropriate than ironic. For, after all, didn't St. Paul teach us the Gospel is foolishness to those who do not believe? "A stumbling block to Jews and foolishness to Gentiles . . ." is the phrase he used (1 Corinthians 1:23). So perhaps April Fools' Day is an appropriate day to celebrate Palm Sunday.

I was reading recently about a truck driver named Cornelius. Cornelius specialized in hauling animals, especially cows. He hauled live cows, and he also hauled dead cows that needed to be disposed of. Sometimes, however, he was hired to haul other varieties of animals.

One April Fools' Day he received a phone call. "I have a dead elephant for you to pick up in Los Angeles," said the voice on the other end.

"Yeah right," said Cornelius. "You aren't going to get me on that one!"

The guy said to him, "No, seriously, I've got this dead elephant I need for you to pick up."

Cornelius again said, "Look, I know what day this is. You aren't going to fool me today of all days!"

The guy was insistent that this was a serious call, but Cornelius was equally determined that he wasn't going to be the object of an April Fools' Day prank. He told the guy that if he drove all the way out to Los Angeles and it was a joke, he would charge the caller double plus a fee for the extra tow truck that Cornelius would require.

The caller agreed and so Cornelius drove to Los Angeles and, indeed, there was a dead elephant waiting on him. He wouldn't believe it until he saw it with his own eyes. I mean, getting such a phone call on an April Fools' Day would make you suspicious. (1)

Many who witnessed Jesus riding into Jerusalem on that first Palm Sunday probably thought they were witnessing an April Fools' prank. They had come out to see what they thought was the leader of a new religious movement, and quite possibly the long-awaited Messiah. They had heard amazing stories about this man—about his feeding thousands of people with two fish and five small loaves, about his ability to heal, and even about his raising of Lazarus from the dead. Could this be, they wondered hopefully, the One they had long been awaiting?

"Here he comes," those at the front exclaimed as the procession drew near. Those at the back jostled for a better look. They stretched as high as they could on tiptoe and held up small children that they might have a view of the man they hoped would be their new king. And then their hearts sank. This man they had heard so much about, whom they hoped would deliver them from the iron grip of the Romans, wasn't riding on a mighty stallion as Caesar surely would have. Nor he was he riding on a mighty elephant, as Alexander the Great might have. Instead, he was riding on a humble donkey. The man the people of Jerusalem expected to lead them to victory over their enemies was riding a lowly beast of burden.

What kind of Messiah was this, they wondered to themselves? Where was his armor? Where was the pomp and grandeur that was expected out of a leader? Think if one of our candidates for president came to town this election year, not in a limousine with flags waving and polished chrome sparkling, but in a rusted-out Ford Pinto? What kind of credibility would he have?

It didn't occur to the people who were disappointed that day that the prophet Zechariah had foretold that the Messiah would indeed enter Jerusalem while riding on a donkey (Zechariah 9:9). Later, some of them might have remembered, but at the time it was happening it may have indeed felt like an April Fools' Day prank.

But there were others who were not put off by the Master's means of transportation. They had seen his miracles first hand. They had listened to his teachings in person and knew he taught not like the Pharisees but with an authority that could only have come from God. And so, as he made his entrance into their city they spread their cloaks and palm branches on the road in front of him.

Those who accepted him as the One they had been awaiting were exuberant in their welcome. They shouted, "Hosanna! Blessed is he who comes in the name of the Lord! Blessed is the coming kingdom of our father David! Hosanna in the highest heaven!" For them, it was a grand celebration, just as it is for us.

The story as told in Mark's Gospel, however, ends rather abruptly. After a brief description of the Palm Sunday parade, we read these words, "Jesus entered Jerusalem and went into the temple courts. He looked around at everything, but since it was already late, he went out to Bethany with the Twelve."

I would like to focus our attention for a few moments on these brief, final words from Mark's Gospel about Jesus' actions after the Palm Sunday parade. They help us set the stage for the celebration of Holy Week.

Jesus has made his triumphant entry into Jerusalem . . . exhilarating some while deflating others. Now it is evening. He is probably feeling a bit of a letdown after the day's busy activities. Soon he will retire with his disciples to Bethany, a small village just outside the city. But, before he goes, he has a few moments to kill. How shall he spend his time? Mark tells us he went to the temple courts and "looked around at everything."

I wonder what was on Jesus' mind as he surveyed the temple courts that Palm Sunday evening. Much that will happen over the last week of Jesus' life will be centered in or near the temple courts.

Was he already offended by thoughts of the moneychangers taking advantage of worshipers there in the temple? Was it then he decided to confront them the following day?

Or perhaps he looked around at the massive stones of the temple. Was it then it occurred to him to say to his disciples that this mighty temple would soon be destroyed? This was a prophecy that was fulfilled within 40 years of his death.

Or did his mind turn toward the curtain in the temple—the curtain which separated the Holy of Holies from the rest of the Temple—the curtain that would be mysteriously torn in two at his death?

Perhaps he was focused simply on what would happen to him in the next few days—the betrayal, the mockery of a trial, the scourging, the agony of crucifixion.

In Mark 10 we read that some days prior, while they were on their way up to Jerusalem, Jesus took the Twelve aside and told them what was going to happen to him. "We are going up to Jerusalem," he said, "and the Son of Man will be delivered over to the chief priests and the teachers of the law. They will condemn him to death and will hand him over to the Gentiles, who will mock him and spit on him, flog him and kill him. Three days later he will rise."

These were not words the disciples wanted to hear. In fact, in many ways they refused to hear them. They still cherished dreams that he would overthrow the ruling powers and set up a new kingdom in which they would have favored positions.

But they were in Jerusalem now, and his prophecy about his death was about to be fulfilled. The die was cast. There was no turning back. Jesus stood there in the courtyard of the Temple and surveyed the scene. We cannot know what was going through his mind. In fact, we know only a few things for certain about his final week on earth.

We know, first of all, about his courage. Jesus knew what lay ahead—the physical and emotional pain, a cruel and unjust death. He dreaded it with all his being, but he did not cut and run as many of us might have. With great bravery he moved toward his destiny. He was a man of great courage.

His courage evidently had an effect on his followers after Pentecost. We read in Acts 4:13 that when contemporaries of Peter and John noticed their courage they ascribed it to the fact that they "had been with Jesus." The courage which they possessed was not something which they had been taught by the Master, but something which they had caught from him. The courage of Jesus was contagious.

Edward Hughes Pruden once told of a picture which hung over the mantel in his study. It was Hofmann's picture of the boy Jesus at age twelve in the temple at Jerusalem, talking to the doctors of the law, answering and asking questions.

Pruden said he was intrigued by the picture because it told him not only a great deal about Christ but also about those who were standing around him there in the temple. The faces of these elderly authorities in Israel seem to indicate that they were thinking of Christ in terms of what he might become as he would grow into manhood.

"What a fine young Rabbi this boy is going to make. He has such a vivid imagination; such a scintillating personality; such a persuasive manner. We must see to it that he is called to one of our finest synagogues, for there he will fascinate large congregations with his brilliant messages. He will be highly honored in the community and live to a ripe old age to receive the esteem of all his fellow townsmen."

They could not see that Jesus would never be swayed by the lure of success. He was set on rattling the very gates of hell and nothing would stop him for he was a man who conquered fear. People with such courage invariably change the world.

We see his courage and then we see the level of his commitment. In a few days he will kneel in a garden and pray, "My Father, if it is possible, may this cup be taken from me. Yet not as I will, but as you will" (Matthew 26: 42). He didn't want to drink from the cup which was being offered him, but he was driven by one motivation—to do the will of his Father. Mark this well: ultimately, it was not blind courage that drove him; it was determination to do what God wanted him to do.

Christ's commitment reminds me of a Japanese social worker who lived before and during the Second World War named Toyohiko Kagawa. Kagawa was a devout Christian whose faith caused him to have an extraordinary impact on the working conditions of ordinary citizens in Japan. He was so well thought of in that land that he came on a mission to the U.S. before the beginning of the Second World War to seek to prevent that terrible conflict breaking out. Even though he failed in this effort, he gained international renown for his Christian witness and selfless work.

Years later Kagawa was on a lecture tour to the United States. Two college students were walking across their campus after hearing him speak. One of them confessed that he was disappointed in Kagawa's simple message.

After some reflection, the other student replied: "I suppose it really doesn't matter very much what a man says when he has lived as Kagawa has lived."

That is true. In today's vernacular, it is more important that Kagawa walked the walk and not just talked the talk. A consecrated life is far more eloquent and convincing than any well thought out argument. The world will not accept the way of Christ because we can out talk our spiritual opponents, but only because we can out live them. Such a demonstration of the superior quality of our faith will verify our witness more readily than any other effort in which we can engage. Kagawa did that superbly. His life, however, was simply a reflection of the life of his Master.

Jesus walked the walk more perfectly than anyone who has ever lived. He lived out the ethic which he taught. He was totally committed to doing his Father's will. He was a man of courage. He was a man of commitment.

And we see his absolute compassion. Above all else, during Holy Week, we see the love that took him to the cross. "Greater love has no one than this: to lay down one's life for one's friend," reads John 15:13. Those were Jesus' words and that is exactly what he did.

On January 13, 1982 an airliner crashed into the icy waters of the Potomac River near Washington, D.C. Seventy-nine people were aboard that ill-fated aircraft, and of that number, only five survived. Each of those survivors had something in common: they owed their life to another passenger, a 46-year-old bank examiner named Arland D. Williams Jr.

Workers on the rescue helicopter sent to the crash reported that Williams was one of only a half a dozen survivors clinging to twisted wreckage bobbing in the icy Potomac when they arrived. Life vests were dropped, then a flotation ball. Williams repeatedly spurned the safety line and passed it on to the five others floating in the bitterly cold water. One by one they were taken away to safety. By the time the helicopter crew could return for Williams, however, both he and the plane's tail section had disappeared beneath the icy surface. He had been in the water for twenty-nine minutes with five opportunities to be saved, but each time he deferred to another. His body was later recovered. According to the coroner, Williams was the only passenger to die by drowning; the rest died on impact. He did not so much lose his life as gave it.

When the helicopter pilot was interviewed later he described Williams as a brave and good man. "Imagine," said the rescue pilot, "he had just survived that horrible plane crash. The river was ice-cold and each minute brought him closer to death. He could have gone on the first trip but he put everyone else ahead of himself." The man was truly a hero. Later, the bridge the plane hit on its way into the icy water was renamed. Today it is the "Arland D. Williams Jr. Memorial Bridge." (2)

"Greater love has no one than this: to lay down one's life for one's friend . . ." That's what sent Jesus to the cross. His courage, his commitment, his absolute compassion as shown on the cross on which he died. Have you such courage, such commitment, such compassion? We don't know what was on his mind that first Palm Sunday evening as he surveyed the Temple Courtyard, but we know how his week ended. He gave himself for you and for me.

1. Rev. Brian D. Kuyper, http://www.crcna.org/pages/kuyper_john20.cfm
2. Rev. Ronald Botts, http://www.firstchurch.org/sermons/2003/2003070129.htm.

A Table Like No Other
1 Corinthians 11:23-26
(Maundy Thursday)

The earliest recounting of the event we commemorate this evening comes from the Apostle Paul. In 1 Corinthians 11, he writes, "For I received from the Lord what I also passed on to you: The Lord Jesus, on the night he was betrayed, took bread, and when he had given thanks, he broke it and said, 'This is my body, which is for you; do this in remembrance of me.' In the same way, after supper he took the cup, saying, 'This cup is the new covenant in my blood; do this, whenever you drink it, in remembrance of me.' For whenever you eat this bread and drink this cup, you proclaim the Lord's death until he comes."

What powerful words. "The Lord Jesus, on the night he was betrayed . . ." Notice who was at the table that sacred night. Judas the betrayer was there, already plotting his diabolical scheme . . . Selling the Lord for thirty pieces of silver . . . Designating him as the one to be captured and crucified with a kiss. And yet there Judas is at the table with Jesus. Could that happen here, this night? Could there be someone who comes to a Maundy Thursday service knowing in your heart that you are preparing to betray Christ, preparing to betray your own values, preparing to betray those who you love?

It would not be the first time that has happened. Surely it will not be the last. Some of us have become quite adept at compartmentalizing our lives. Our religion is in one compartment. Our relationship with our family is in another. Our work is in another. Our influence in the community is still in another. Sometimes they overlap. But sometimes they do not. So, the abusive father still occupies the same pew every week in church. The salesman with the shaky ethics, who often takes advantage of the weak, may still sing in the choir. The unfaithful spouse still may teach children in Sunday School. It happens. "On the night he was betrayed . . ." Notice who was at the table that sacred night—Judas the betrayer.

But notice something else even more important—the Master did not turn him away. The Lord's Table is a table of grace. Judas didn't deserve to be there at the Last Supper, but neither did Simon Peter. Peter denied Christ, and he was closer to Jesus than any of the disciples. If Simon didn't deserve to be there, who did? None of them. Neither do any of us. That's all right. This is the Lord's table. It is a table of grace.

In his book, Letters to a Young Evangelical, Tony Campolo shares a story about grace. He says that when he was very young, perhaps six or seven, he was sitting with his parents at a Communion service. He noticed a young woman in the pew in front of them who was sobbing and shaking. The minister had just finished reading 1 Corinthians 11:27. This verse, which follows our lesson from the Epistle, reads like this: "So then, whoever eats the bread or drinks the cup of the Lord in an unworthy manner will be guilty of sinning against the body and blood of the Lord." Evidently this young woman took Paul's words as an admonition directed at her—that somehow she was unworthy to take the bread and the cup.

As the Communion plate with its small pieces of bread was passed to the crying woman sitting in front of young Tony and his parents, she waved it away and then lowered her head in despair. It was then that Tony's father, a first generation Sicilian immigrant, leaned over the young woman's shoulder and, in broken English, said sternly, "Take it, girl! It was meant for you. Do you hear me?"

The young woman raised her head and nodded—and then she took the bread and ate it. Tony Campolo writes, "I knew that at that moment some kind of heavy burden was lifted from her heart and mind. Since then, I have always known that a church that could offer Communion to hurting people was a special gift from God." (1)

Jesus didn't even turn Judas away from the table. If there's room for Judas, friend, there's room for you and me. Jesus showed his table to be a table of grace.

He also showed it to be a place where we can be in his presence. Listen again to Paul's words: "The Lord Jesus, on the night he was betrayed, took bread, and when he had given thanks, he broke it and said, 'This is my body, which is for you; do this in remembrance of me.' In the same way, after supper he took the cup, saying, 'This cup is the new covenant in my blood; do this, whenever you drink it, in remembrance of me.'" In the bread and the cup we have access to Christ.

I love the imagery of Jesus breaking the bread. In the film Jesus of Nazareth, the bread is portrayed as a large, round flat disk of bread which Jesus reverently breaks and offers to his disciple. One six-year-old saw this and asked if Jesus was feeding his disciples pizza. Well, the unleavened Passover bread might have passed for a colorless, somewhat tasteless pizza. The point is that when he offered the bread and offered the cup, he was offering himself. Every time we take this sacrament, in the quietness of our own hearts we are able to reach out and touch the Master, we are able to receive him anew into our lives.

In his book The Body, Charles Colson tells about Pat Novak, a pastor who was serving his internship as a hospital chaplain several years ago. Pat was making his rounds one summer morning when he was called to visit a patient admitted with an undiagnosed ailment. John, a man in his sixties, had not responded to any treatment; medical tests showed nothing; psychological tests were inconclusive. Yet John was wasting away; he had not even been able to swallow for two weeks. The nurses tried everything. Finally they called the chaplain's office.

When Pat walked into the room, John was sitting limply in his bed, strung with IV tubes, staring listlessly at the wall. Pat was terrified; he had no idea what to do. But John seemed to brighten a bit soon as he saw Pat's chaplain badge and invited him to sit down. As they talked, Pat sensed that God was urging him to do something specific: to ask John if he wanted to take Communion. Chaplain interns were not encouraged to ask patients about such things as communion in this tax-supported hospital, but Pat did.

At that John broke down. "I can't!" he cried. "I've sinned and can't be forgiven."

Pat paused a moment, knowing he was about to break policy again. He asked John if he wanted to confess his sin. John nodded gratefully. To this day Pat can't remember the particular sin John confessed, nor would he say if he did, but he recalls that it did not strike him as particularly egregious. Yet it had been draining the life from this man. John wept as he confessed, and Pat laid hands on him, hugged him, and told John his sins were forgiven. Then Pat asked John a second time if he wanted to take Communion. He did. Pat gave John a Bible and told him he would be back later. Already, says Pat, John was sitting up straighter, with a flicker of light in his eyes.

Pat visited a few more patients and then ate some lunch in the hospital cafeteria. When he left he wrapped an extra piece of bread in a napkin and borrowed a coffee cup from the cafeteria. He ran out to a shop a few blocks away and bought a container of grape juice. Then he returned to John's room with these make-shift elements and celebrated Communion with him. John took the bread and chewed it slowly. It was the first time in weeks he had been able to eat solid food. He took the cup and swallowed. He had been set free. Within three days John walked out of that hospital. (2)

There is healing at this table. Why? Because here we can touch Christ, even if only symbolically. We can feast on him. This is his body. This is his blood.

But there's one thing more to be said. Listen again to the whole text: "For I received from the Lord what I also passed on to you: The Lord Jesus, on the night he was betrayed, took bread, and when he had given thanks, he broke it and said, 'This is my body, which is for you; do this in remembrance of me.' In the same way, after supper he took the cup, saying, 'This cup is the new covenant in my blood; do this, whenever you drink it, in remembrance of me.' For whenever you eat this bread and drink this cup, you proclaim the Lord's death until he comes."

Focus on the words, "For whenever you eat this bread and drink this cup, you proclaim the Lord's death until he comes." This table is linked to Christ's return.

What does that mean? We don't know completely. We're not sure as we read in scripture about Christ's return how much is symbolic and how much is to be taken literally. This much we do know. A time is coming when all people will be drawn to the Kingdom of God, when God's love and God's grace will live in every heart. I don't know how or when that will occur, but there will come a time when every knee shall bow and every tongue confess that Jesus Christ is Lord.

It's like a story that Pastor Bruce Rigdon, a Presbyterian pastor in Grosse Pointe, Michigan, tells. Rigdon once performed a large wedding in his church—the largest wedding he ever experienced. It was a beautiful Saturday night. The church was filled with people who were devoted to the young couple being married. Many of the people in the congregation were from different cultures and faiths. Included in the wedding ceremony was the celebration of the Lord's Supper.

After the exchange of promises, Pastor Rigdon says he moved to the communion table and invited all who had been baptized and who loved the Lord, to come forward to celebrate the sacrament. To his great surprise when he looked up from the table and out at the congregation, he saw virtually everyone—regardless of who they were or what their faith tradition was—coming forward. What was he to do? Say, "Stop! Only the baptized are invited to the table!" How totally absurd, he thought. What a travesty that would be to our Lord. And so he welcomed all to the table.

After the wedding a Jewish couple came up to him and explained that they were children of Holocaust families and that even though they had lived by a rule never to enter a Christian church, their love for the bride had brought them there that night. The gentleman said, "When you invited people to the table and everyone around us began to move, we couldn't remain seated. We know, Pastor, it's Jesus' table, not ours. But we were drawn . . . by some kind of love, so please, we hope we haven't offended you or your community. But we were received at the table tonight and were deeply moved."

Shortly after this confession, another couple came up to him, identifying themselves as Moustafa and Munir, originally from Lebanon. They said, "So you know what our life has been like . . . You know about the pain and bloodshed . . . We are, of course, Muslim." Then they told how their children rose to go to the communion table, and they were drawn inexplicably to follow them. "We know we shouldn't have been there," they said, "but somehow, for us tonight, the war has ended." (3)

Friends, that is a picture of how things will be at Christ's return. All will be drawn in love to him.

This is a table like no other. It is a table of grace. It is a table where we can touch Christ. It is a table that is linked to Christ's return and to his Kingdom of love. Won't you come to his table and allow him to make himself real to you once again?

1. Pete Kontra, http://oaklandchurch.org/pdf/sermontexts/OS-04-10-11-If%20You%20Share.pdf.
2. (Nashville: Word Publishing, 1992), pp. 139-140. Cited in Robert J. Morgan, Preacher's Sourcebook Creative Sermon Illustrations (Nashville: Thomas Nelson, Inc., 2007), p. 528.
3. Susan Warrener Smith. Cited Dr. Mickey Anders,
Nttp://www.pikevillefirstchristianchurch.org/Sermons/Sermon20020113.html.

Were You There?
John 18:1-19:42

There is an old spiritual that asks this very familiar question: "Were you there when they crucified my Lord?" It's a question that has been asked through the ages. And every generation has provided its own answer. You and I must answer it as well. Were we there? Were we there when they crucified our Lord?

We know the cast of the original Good Friday drama. They are listed in John's telling of the passion narrative.

Judas Iscariot was there. He definitely was instrumental in crucifying Jesus. John tells us that Judas came to the garden where Jesus went to pray, guiding a detachment of soldiers and some officials from the chief priests and the Pharisees. They were carrying torches, lanterns and weapons. Judas betrayed Jesus for 30 pieces of silver. Even worse, he betrayed him with a kiss. Was it greed that led Judas to such a desperate act? Perhaps. Greed is a powerful motivator, but 30 pieces of silver wasn't a lot of money. He may have had another motive.

Perhaps, on the other hand—as one popular interpretation declares—he wanted to force Jesus' hand. Judas wanted to hurry the coming of a kingdom in which he would be part of the inner circle, a kingdom in which he would have a high office. That is the unfortunate result of excessive ambition. It's happened before and it will happen again.

Bishop Fulton J. Sheen once told of a colleague in China, a Bishop Ford, who died a martyr's death in a communist Chinese prison in 1952. A nun who was imprisoned with Bishop Ford gives us a picture of Bishop Ford's last days: "His hair was long and white and his beard matted, his face emaciated and pale from torture . . . Whenever Bishop Ford was given a walk outside the prison, being unable to support himself, he leaned on two fellow prisoners. Then came the day of the death march. He was put in line between the two other prisoners. The Chinese Communist colonel who had seized the chapel tied a sack around Bishop Ford's neck weighing over twenty pounds. He tied it in such a way that the rope would tighten as the bishop walked."

How did Bishop Ford come to such a fate? "The Bishop's Chinese cook, who had served him for many years, and whom he regarded as a good friend and a good Christian, was the man who delivered [Bishop Ford] over to the Communist authorities and falsely accused him. Despite the fact that he knew how the Bishop had [brought solace to] the sick and buried the dead, he nevertheless delivered him over to suffering. The reward the [cook] received was to be made chief of police of that village."

After Bishop Ford's martyrdom, the former cook went back to the chapel, threw a rope over a rafter and committed suicide. (1) Betrayal happens. It happens in organizations, it happens in families. It happens in business. It happens in churches.

When it was all over, Judas also went and hanged himself. That's not surprising. Can there be any sin more grievous than betraying a friend? Judas was there when they crucified my Lord.

Simon Peter was there as well. When the soldiers came to take Jesus, Peter tried to defend him with his sword. He struck the high priest's servant, a man named Malchus, cutting off his right ear. Jesus commanded Peter, "Put your sword away! Shall I not drink the cup the Father has given me?"

When Jesus was arrested, Peter followed the Master and the soldiers at a distance. And then, before the cock crowed, Peter denied his Lord three times. Where was Peter when the crosses were raised on Golgotha? Nobody knew. Peter was not in sight. He was in hiding. But Peter was there just as surely as Judas was there.

It scarcely seems possible that Peter would have so disappointed the Master. Peter was present every time Jesus performed a miracle or spoke a parable or communed with God. When Jesus walked on the water, it was Simon Peter who tried to duplicate the feat, but faltered and had to be rescued by Christ. Peter was there with James and John on the Mount of Transfiguration when Jesus was revealed once and for all as the chosen one of God. How could Simon Peter deny he ever knew him?

Simon Peter's sin came about in a moment of weakness, while under intense stress. He was weak as sometimes you and I are weak. It's not that we go out seeking to do wrong. It's just that when temptation comes we simply are too weak to resist it. We don't like to admit we're weak, but we are.

Pastor John Ortberg tells how that growing up, he loved the comic book hero Superman because he was so strong. He disguised himself as mild-mannered Clark Kent, but his vulnerability was just an act. Underneath was the man of steel. Superman came to help people who were weak and needy; but he himself was never afraid, never confused. "Superman never joined a twelve-step recovery group," says Ortberg, "even though he had lost both his biological parents and the planet he had called home. He never joined a lonely hearts club, although he was always alone. He never got into therapy, even though he wore blue tights and a cape beneath his regular clothes." (2)

Superman didn't know what it was to be weak. But Superman was a fictional character. Clark Kent, his alter ego, fooled people sometimes into thinking he was a normal man, but his vulnerability was just an act. Underneath was the man of steel. Real people, on the other hand, try to be Superman on the outside showing no vulnerability, but underneath they are really just a weak and sometimes confused Clark Kent. Peter, for all his bluster, was a weak man. Peter was there when they crucified my Lord.

Pontius Pilate was also there. Pilate didn't want to be responsible for Christ's death. He tried to avoid sentencing Jesus to death by offering the crowd the choice of Barabbas or Jesus. Barabbas is Aramaic for "son of the father." Ironic. Jesus was the true Son of the Father. But that was the choice the crowd was given, Barabbas or Jesus, and they chose the false son of the Father. Barabbas was a small-time insurrectionist. He plotted against the government. He was probably popular with the people because of his opposition to Roman rule. So the crowd chose Barrabas to pardon and Jesus to execute. Pilate's ploy fails and so he washes his hands of the whole affair. He washes his hands of the chance to do the right thing. He washes his hands of the true Son of God, though deep in his heart he knew that Jesus was who he said he was.

Pontius Pilate was there when they crucified my Lord.

Here's someone that you may not have thought of who was there when they crucified the Master: Nicodemus. Do you remember Nicodemus? Nicodemus was there when they crucified my Lord. Nicodemus was a prominent Pharisee who had come to Jesus at night. He entered into a deep theological discussion with Jesus on matters such as the Kingdom of God, and God's sending his son into the world to save humanity from its evil ways. It was Nicodemus to whom the Lord spoke those words about not being able to see the Kingdom of God unless he was born again.

I find it heartening that Nicodemus was there. John 7 contains a wonderful story about Jesus' presence at the Feast of Tabernacles, not long before his arrest and crucifixion. The soldiers, at the urging of the religious elite, were already watching out for Jesus. But he slipped by them into the Temple and began teaching . . . and everyone was astounded at his teaching. This of course infuriated the religious authorities. They confronted the temple guards and asked them, "Why didn't you bring him in?"

"No one ever spoke the way this man does," the guards replied.

"You mean he has deceived you also?" the authorities retorted.

At this point Nicodemus, who was a member of the Jewish ruling council steps forward and asks, "Does our law condemn a man without first hearing him to find out what he has been doing?"

Can you imagine how courageous this was on Nicodemus' part? Notice how the Pharisees responded to his question. They replied, "Are you from Galilee, too? Look into it, and you will find that a prophet does not come out of Galilee." They were indirectly accusing Nicodemus of being one of Jesus' disciples.

It appears that Nicodemus got the hint. Like the disciples of Jesus he seems to fade into the woodwork during the rest of the Passion narrative. Fear probably got the best of him. Like Jesus' disciples he probably wished later he had done more. But he did do one thing: after Jesus was dead, it was Nicodemus, this wealthy and prominent Pharisee, who helped Joseph of Arimathea get Jesus' body to the tomb. According to John, Nicodemus procured a very large quantity of myrrh and aloes for Jesus' burial. These were expensive perfumes, which surely cost Nicodemus a small fortune. (3)

It was a small gesture performed too late, but it was undoubtedly a heart-felt gesture of a man who was on his way to being what the Master wanted him to be. Nowhere does the scripture insist that a person must be born again all at once. For many it is a journey of a lifetime. It was for Nicodemus. Tradition tells us that, like many others, Nicodemus was martyred sometime in the first century. But Nicodemus was there when they crucified my Lord.

There were many others there when Christ was crucified. Time will not permit me to tell their stories. Herod, that despicable monarch, was there … as were the soldiers who gambled for Christ's garments while he hung on the cross … and the thieves who died on either side of him … and the blessed women, including his mother, who wept at the foot of the cross. Only one disciple, John, the beloved disciple was physically there when Jesus died. Jesus assigned to John the care of his mother.

There were other minor characters who were also there when they crucified him including the mob that cried, "Crucify Him! Crucify Him!" Ignorant people, stirred to hatred by molders of public opinion who had their own selfish agenda. Those people, like those molders of opinion, are still around today crucifying Christ time after time with their anger, their hatred, their greed.

The question of the night is, of course, were we there when they crucified our Lord? And the answer is yes we were there, as was all humanity. Anyone who has ever been cowardly and given in to the crowd, anyone who has ever kept silent in the face of bigotry and persecution, anyone who has ever been weak when you know you should have been strong was there encouraging this … the most tragic crime in history.

Actor and director Mel Gibson has become a sad and controversial figure the past few years. Most tragic of all, his personal life now overshadows his remarkable accomplishment in producing the film, The Passion of the Christ. In the film, Gibson makes the point that all of us were there when Christ was crucified. None is exempt. Gibson, the actor, does not appear in the film, but his hand does. At the crucifixion he holds the nail to be driven in the hand of Christ, and holds the hammer that drives it in! He is saying: it is my sin that nailed Him to the Cross! (4)

We were all there. I don't know about you, but of all the characters who were there I identify most closely with Nicodemus. I confess my sin. I'm not all Christ wants me to be, but there is hope for me. Beginning with this Good Friday service, by the grace of God I can be a better person. I can begin now living more like the Master. How about you? You were there as well. Is this a time for a new beginning for you as well?

1. Treasure in Clay The Autobiography of Fulton J. Sheen (Garden City, NY: Doubleday, 1980), pp. 118-120.
2. Ortberg, John, The Life You've Always Wanted (Grand Rapids, MI: Zondervan, 2002), pp. 115-116.
3. The Expositor's Bible Commentary, Frank E. Gaebelein, ed. (Grand Rapids: Zondervan Publishing House, 1990), p.177.
4. http://www.gordonmoyes.com/sermon_archive/ministry/sermons/040406.html.

Crying At The Tomb
John 20:1-18

Al Smith was once governor of New York. He was doing his first tour of New York's Sing Sing Prison when the warden asked if he would address the inmates. The governor was taken by surprise, but he agreed. His awkwardness was revealed when he began like this, "My fellow citizens . . ." He stopped himself. He wasn't sure if inmates actually had the full rights of citizenship. So, he changed courses.

"My fellow convicts," he began again. Everyone laughed.

He tried once more. "Well anyhow, I'm glad to see so many of you here . . ." as if his audience had any choice.

Well, you had a choice and I'm glad to see so many of you here today. And where else would you be on Easter Sunday? On the golf course? In the comfort of your bed? Well, you could be, but I'm glad you chose to be in this sacred place to give God thanks for Easter.

We live in a strange world. Even Easter is not exempt from some of the fads that are sweeping through our land.

A soldier wrote recently to Reader's Digest to tell about an incident that took place on Easter Sunday in the chapel on their military base. The pastor called the children to the front and told them the story of how Jesus was crucified by the Romans, his body placed in a tomb, and the front covered by a stone.

"But on the third day," the pastor said, "the stone was rolled away, and Jesus was not there." Then the pastor turned to the children and asked, "Do you know what happened next?"

One kid shouted, "Jesus turned into a zombie and went after the Romans!" (1)

Well, that's not exactly how the story goes. I'll admit, that's how a modern storyteller might narrate it. But Jesus didn't become a zombie and he didn't go after the Romans. The real story is far more beautiful.

Early on the first day of the week, while it was still dark, a woman named Mary Magdalene came to Jesus' tomb. Mary was one of Jesus' most prominent converts. There were legends that she had been a prostitute. The Bible does not say that. It only tells us that Jesus had delivered her from seven demons. We don't know what those demons were. But we do know this: Mary Magdalene was thoroughly converted. Christ was Lord and Master of her life.

In fact, of all the New Testament cast of characters, Mary Magdalene is the only person mentioned by all the gospels as having been at the cross until the very end. She saw his agony, heard his cries, watched all hope drain from Christ's face. She heard his last words, his final gasp. The men disciples were mostly in hiding. Even Jesus' brothers and sisters were nowhere to be found at the end. But there at the foot of the cross, Mary stayed faithful to the very last.

Now it's the morning of the third day and it's Mary Magdalene, of course, making her way to Christ's tomb. She discovers that the stone has been removed from the entrance and the body of her Master is missing. We can only imagine the thoughts that ran through her mind. She ran to two of Jesus' closest disciples and reported to them that someone had taken the Lord's body. Notice that she doesn't even mention the possibility of resurrection. It's important to understand that Jesus' closest friends and followers, even Mary Magdalene, were totally taken off guard by his resurrection. Even though he had tried to prepare them, the idea was simply too big for them to entertain until they experienced it firsthand.

The two disciples ran to the tomb and confirmed what Mary had told them. The body was gone. Since there was nothing more that could be done, the men then went home.

Now Mary stands alone outside the tomb crying. As she weeps, she bends over once more to look into the tomb. This time she sees two angels in white, seated where Jesus' body had been, one at the head and the other at the foot. They ask her, "Woman, why are you crying?"

"They have taken my Lord away," she said, "and I don't know where they have put him." At this, Mary turned around and saw Jesus standing there, but she did not realize that it was Jesus. We can understand that. Her eyes were too full of tears.

He asked her, "Woman, why are you crying? Who is it you are looking for?"

Thinking he was the gardener, she said, "Sir, if you have carried him away, tell me where you have put him, and I will get him."

Jesus said to her, "Mary."

And at the sound of her name Mary Magdalene was brought back to reality. She turned toward him and cried out in Aramaic, "Rabboni!" (which means "Teacher").

Crying at the tomb. Many of you have been there, haven't you? A parent, a friend, perhaps even a child—you've stood there by a tomb and wept. Perhaps you wept so hard that you could not even sense the risen Master standing next to you seeking to comfort you. And now you are here, seeking as we all do, to hear your name called, to experience the kind of transformation Mary Magdalene experienced, to have the fog of doubt and fear lifted from your mind and heart and to know that the Good News really is true. Christ lives and because he lives, you and I can receive the gift of eternal life.

It is natural for us to have these yearnings. Even the most skeptical among us still have a glimmer of hope that the Easter story is true—that Christ has been raised from the dead.

There was a report sometime back in the The Futurist magazine. The Futurist is a magazine for people who seek to anticipate the changes that are taking place in our society. The subject of this particular report was "virtual immortality." What is virtual immortality? Some of you have already guessed it has something to do with computers. You're right.

Imagine that everything that there is to know about you—your appearance, your mannerisms, your voice, and even your knowledge and experience—were all digitized and dumped into a very sophisticated database. The computer churns all this information together and then begins bringing to life a virtual representative of yourself—an avatar, if you will. This virtual representative of yourself would preserve much of your personality, your preferences and your appearance for eternity. In a sense you would have a form of eternal life inside a computer. (2)

This may not sound very appealing to you, spending eternity as a computer avatar, but we are rapidly approaching a time when this is very much a possibility. Vastly improving information storage and processing and sophisticated virtual-reality graphics already create nearly lifelike experiences. Add the growing wonders of artificial intelligence into the mix, and who knows what is possible?

A few of you may be familiar with the name Ray Kurzweil. Kurzweil is a brilliant scientist, inventor, author and a man who is greatly influencing thought about humanity's future, particular as it relates to the rapid increases in the power of computers. He was featured recently on the cover of Time magazine with an article titled, "2045: The Year Man Becomes Immortal." Ray Kurzweil claims no religious affiliation; no belief in God. And yet Kurzweil hungers for immortality.

One of the motivations for his life's work is the dream of resurrecting his dead father. This is no joke. This is his dream. He hopes not only to avoid death himself, but also to reconnect someday with his dead father by somehow resurrecting him through the wonders of science.

It is a shame that Ray Kurzweil, this brilliant scientist and thinker, is not able to relax and believe the good news of Easter. Christ has provided a way for him to be reconnected with his dead father. And it has nothing to do with complex algorithms. There is nothing virtual about it. It is real, as real as life itself.

Crying by the tomb. Many of you have been there. Ray Kurzweil has been there. Even the most secular and the most skeptical among us, however, still have a glimmer of hope that the Easter story is true—that Christ has been raised from the dead.

Mary Magdalene was there—crying at the tomb. And the Master spoke her name. Note that—he spoke her name. It is when she hears Christ speak her name that the veil of doubt and dread is raised.

There is an enchanting myth from the time of the ancient Greeks. It is the story of the beautiful Helen of Troy. Do you remember the words used to describe Helen? Hers was "the face that launched a thousand ships."

But there is another legend about Helen of Troy from later in her life. Helen is captured and carried away. She becomes a victim of amnesia. She can't remember who she is. Neither can she remember that she is of royal blood. And because she can't remember and there is no one to remind her, Helen of Troy becomes a prostitute.

Meanwhile, back in her homeland Helen's friends didn't give up hope of finding her. One old friend in particular goes looking for her. One day he finds himself wandering through the streets of a strange city. He comes across a wretched woman in tattered clothes. It is Helen. Time has not been kind to her. Her face is deeply lined with wrinkles. Believing he recognizes her, however, this friend walks up to Helen and asks, "What is your name?"

She gives him a name, but it is another name and not Helen.

"May I see your hands?" he asks because he remembers some distinctive lines in Helen's hands. She holds her hands in front of his face. He can't believe his eyes. "Helen!" he exclaims. "I've found you! You're Helen!"

At the sound of her name, Helen's memory begins to return. The fog begins to lift from her brain. She recognizes her name and she senses something familiar in the manner of the one who has spoken her name. She falls into her friends' arms, weeping with gratitude. She is restored to the queen she was meant to be.

It's only a pagan myth, but it reminds us of Mary of Magdala's experience. Even though her grief had blinded her to his presence, when Christ spoke her name, she knew who he was.

Have you ever heard Christ speak your name? I believe he is speaking it right now. In Acts 14, Paul is trying to point pagan believers to the living God revealed in Christ. He speaks these words, "In the past, [God] let all nations go their own way. Yet he has not left himself without testimony: He has shown kindness by giving you rain from heaven and crops in their seasons; he provides you with plenty of food and fills your hearts with joy (vs. 16-17)." In other words, God is constantly revealing Himself to those who would see Him. And God is speaking our name to anyone who will listen. If you are crying on the inside this morning, wipe your tears for a moment and listen. God is here. Christ is alive. He's speaking your name. He's saying to you, "It's all real. I am with you. I have conquered death."

Mary was crying by the tomb. The Master called her name, just as Christ is calling your name. And something dramatic happened in Mary's life. Mary Magdalene will never be the same again, because she was the first human being, male or female, who knew for certain that Christ is alive. What a wondrous thing that would be!

You have heard me quote Pastor Tony Campolo many times in the past. Some of you are undoubtedly familiar with Campolo's famous sermon, "It's Friday, but Sunday's Coming," based on a sermon he once experienced in his home church, a black church in West Philadelphia. Campolo grew up in that church. He's the only white member of the 2,500 member congregation. African-American congregations and pastors have their own unique and wondrous approach to the Gospel message, notes Campolo. And Campolo himself has been deeply affected by that unique approach.

He says he remembers when he went to his first black funeral. He was seventeen years old. A friend of his named Clarence had died. The minister was magnificent. Campolo described that preacher like this: "He preached about the Resurrection and he talked about life after death in such glowing terms that I have to tell you, even at seventeen I wished I was dead just listening to him! He came down from the pulpit. Then he went over to the family and spoke words of comfort to them. Last of all, he went over to the open casket and for the last twenty minutes, he preached to the corpse. Can you imagine that? He just yelled at the corpse. 'Clarence! Clarence!' he yelled. He said it with such authority," says Campolo, "I would not have been surprised had there been an answer."

"'Well,'" this preacher said, "Clarence, you died too fast. You got away without us thanking you." He went down this litany of beautiful, wonderful things that Clarence had done for people. Then he said, "That's it, Clarence. When there's nothin' more to say, there's only one thing to say, good night!"

"Now this is drama," says Campolo. "White preachers can't do this! . . . [The preacher] grabbed the lid of the casket and he slammed it shut and he yelled, 'Good night, Clarence! Good night, Clarence!' As he slammed that lid shut he pointed to the casket and he said, 'Good night, Clarence, 'cause I know, yes, I know that God is going to give you a good morning!' Then the choir stood and started singing 'On that great gettin' up Morning we shall rise, we shall rise.' People were up on their feet and they were in the aisles hugging and kissing each other and dancing. I was up dancing and hugging people," says Tony Campolo. "I knew I was in the right church, the kind of church that can take a funeral and turn it into a celebration. That's what the faith is about. It's about the promise of eternal life . . . death doesn't threaten us any more." (3)

It can't be expressed any better than that. If in your heart for any reason you are weeping by a tomb this day . . . not just the tomb of a family member or a good friend. Maybe it's the tomb of a lifelong dream . . . the tomb of disappointment or despair . . . the tomb of heartbreak or rejection . . . the tomb of fear and frustration . . . if you're crying beside any tomb this day . . . hear the good news for the day. Jesus is calling your name. He's here with reassurance. The Gospel is true. Jesus is alive, and because he is alive, you can live, too. Mary heard the Master speak her name and through her tears she knew. He is alive. He IS alive. Today and forevermore.

1. Lou DelTufo, Livingston, New Jersey in Reader's Digest.
2. World Trends & Forecasts, July-Aug 2007, p. 12.
3. http://www.csec.org/csec/sermon/campolo_4604.htm

Victorious, But Not Unscarred
John 20:19-31

I'm sure someone looked at the title of today's message, "Victorious, But Not Unscarred" and thought, "Evidently the pastor just finished filling out [his] income tax form."

April 15th—it's not only income tax day as you may remember. It's also the day the Titanic sunk and the day Lincoln was shot.

Sometime back in California, a seventy-one year old grandmother pleaded not guilty to armed robbery, saying she had been driven insane by the Internal Revenue Service. That seems perfectly understandable to me.

Someone said the difference between death and taxes is that death doesn't get more complicated each year.

The ambivalence people feel toward the IRS even made it into a lawyer joke: If a lawyer and an IRS agent were both drowning, and you could only save one of them, would you go to lunch or read the paper?

Actually most tax people are honorable public servants, as are most employees of our federal and state governments. Most of us receive many benefits from our system of government—though sometimes we can all feel a little sympathy for the businessman who, while on his deathbed, called a friend. He said, "Joe, I want you to promise me that when I die you will have my remains cremated."

"And what," his friend asked, "do you want me to do with your ashes?"

The businessman said, "Just put them in an envelope and mail them to the Internal Revenue Service and write on the envelope, 'Now you have everything.'"

"Victorious, But Not Unscarred." Actually we are not dealing with tax matters today. We are dealing with an appearance of Jesus to his disciples after Easter.

It is interesting. A couple of years ago, the Reuters News Service carried a story about a Russian teenager who survived a lightning strike which was so powerful it vaporized a gold cross on her neck.

The bolt hit this young woman on the top of her head and seared through her body into the ground. The necklace she had been wearing was "atomized," leaving burns in the shape of a cross on her neck. Only a couple of links of the chain could be found.

A doctor at the local hospital who treated her over a period of two weeks said: "It is a miracle she survived." She did survive and is fine now but, says the report, "she will have deep scars on her neck where the cross was for the rest of her life." (1)

In a like way, after Jesus' resurrection from the grave, he still bore the scars from the cross. We read in John's Gospel, "On the evening of that first day of the week, when the disciples were together, with the doors locked for fear of the Jewish leaders, Jesus came and stood among them and said, 'Peace be with you!' After he said this, he showed them his hands and side . . ."

Then a few verses later we read, "Now Thomas . . . was not with the disciples when Jesus came. So the other disciples told him, 'We have seen the Lord!'

"But [Thomas] said to them, 'Unless I see the nail marks in his hands and put my finger where the nails were, and put my hand into his side, I will not believe.'

"A week later his disciples were in the house again, and Thomas was with them. Though the doors were locked, Jesus came and stood among them and said, 'Peace be with you!' Then he said to Thomas, 'Put your finger here; see my hands. Reach out your hand and put it into my side. Stop doubting and believe.'

"Thomas said to him, 'My Lord and my God!'"

Thomas said that unless he could see the nail marks in Christ's hands and put his finger where the nails were, and put his hand into Christ's side, he would not believe that Christ was alive. And that is exactly what he experienced. To me, it is significant that though Christ had been resurrected from the dead, his body still bore the scars from his crucifixion. Victorious, but not unscarred.

It is a reminder to me that no one ever achieves anything of lasting significance without getting a few scars along the way. No one makes a lasting contribution to the world who does not pay a price.

On this April 15th we might remember a well-known tax evader named Henry David Thoreau. Unlike modern tax evaders who are interested only in their own welfare, Thoreau willingly went to jail rather than pay taxes to support a war, the Mexican-American War, fought in the interests of slavery.

You will remember the famous exchange between Thoreau and his friend, Ralph Waldo Emerson. "Henry, what are you doing in there?" asked Emerson when he strolled by the jail one day.

"Ralph, what are you doing out there?" replied Thoreau.

The point was that there are some causes worthy of sacrifice, worthy of suffering, worthy of obtaining scars for. No one ever achieves anything of lasting significance without getting a few scars along the way. We need to understand that not all Christians have chosen the safe, secure life we enjoy.

We need to know about people like Dr. Eleanor Chestnut. After arriving in China in 1893 under the American Presbyterian Missions Board, Dr. Chestnut built a hospital, using her own money to buy bricks and mortar. The need for her services was so great, she performed surgery in her bathroom until the building was completed.

One operation involved the amputation of a common laborer's leg. Complications arose, and skin grafts were needed. A few days later, another doctor asked Chestnut why she was limping. "Oh, it's nothing," was her terse reply.

Finally, a nurse revealed that the skin graft for the patient, a coolie at the bottom of Chinese society, came from Dr. Chestnut's own leg, taken with only local anesthetic.

Sadly, during the Boxer Rebellion of 1905, Dr. Chestnut and four other missionaries were killed by a mob that stormed the hospital. (2)

Eleanor Chestnut knew the dangers of serving in China, but her faith was strong and her commitment to Christ and the Chinese people was complete. Today the Chinese Christian community is the fastest growing body of Christians in the world. But it would not even be there in that historically closed society if people like Eleanor Chestnut were not willing to bear on their own bodies the scars of commitment. Victorious, but not unscarred. The scars that Christ bore remind us that no one ever achieves anything of lasting significance without getting a few scars along the way.

Those scars are also a reminder of just how much Christ loves us.

Some of you are familiar with American Sign Language, the language which serves so many of our friends who are deaf. Do you know what the sign is for Jesus? I understand it is the tip of the middle finger of one hand touching the palm of the other. When deaf persons are worshipping, they will make this sign many times during their service: Jesus, the one with scarred hands. And when they touch the place where the scars were, they remember. (3)

The details of Christ's death have always had an impact on those who believe in him, though sometimes in ways that are not so healthy.

The New York Times Magazine carried a story some years back about a sect of American Indians who had been converted to Christianity. They were called "The Penitentes" and they once flourished in the Southwest. The centerpiece of their frightening rituals was a Good Friday re-enactment of the crucifixion—in which one of their members was literally nailed to the cross, while others scarred and mutilated themselves in the pattern of Christ's wounds. They were, in a sense, Jesus impersonators who carried the imitation of Christ to a bloody literal conclusion. (4)

That is a perversion of our faith. Christ does not want us to scar our bodies as a way of showing our devotion to him. However, who can help but be moved by the knowledge that the pure Son of God who knew no sin allowed himself to be brutalized and slain by sinful human beings? Why did he do it? He did it out of unadulterated love for you and me.

It's like a story that William Barclay once told about a young French soldier in the First World War who was seriously wounded. His arm was so badly smashed that it had to be amputated. He was a handsome young man, and the surgeon was grieved that he must go through life maimed. So he waited by his bedside to tell him the bad news when he recovered consciousness.

When the lad's eyes opened, the surgeon said to him: "I am sorry to tell you that you have lost your arm."

"Sir," said the lad, "I did not lose it; I gave it—for France."

In the same way, Christ did not lose his life; he gave it for you and me.

"What wondrous love is this," wrote the poet, "That caused the Lord of bliss/ To bear the dreadful curse/ for my soul, for my soul . . ." And that's what those scars say to us. This is how much God loves us. "Victorious, But Not Unscarred."

In a sermon on the web, the Rev. Christi O. Brown tells about a tennis friend who understands about scars. This friend is a highly fit 30-something-year-old. Yet she wears a brace on each knee. Brown once pointed to her friend's knee and asked if her scar was from knee surgery. She said, "No, it's from my son, and I actually have an identical scar on my other knee."

Here's the story: several years ago this young mother "scooped up her toddler son from the swimming pool and began to walk toward a lounge chair. As she stepped onto the tiled patio, her foot slipped on the wet slick surface. She was also seven months pregnant, and it was one of those moments where you feel like you're moving in slow motion but there's nothing you can do to stop the fall. Within a split second, she knew her momentum was toppling her forward, and she could either fall and land on top of both her son and her unborn child, or she could fall on her knees.

"Of course, as any loving parent would do, she chose to fall on her knees directly onto the unforgiving concrete. Her knees immediately burst open and blood went everywhere. She ended up needing stitches, which resulted in scars, but her son and unborn child were both unscathed.

"It is hard for me to tell this story," writes Christi Brown, "without tearing up, because to me, it serves as a miniscule example of the immense sacrifice and love of Jesus Christ for us. You see, we are the beloved children of God for whom Jesus took the fall. Christ suffered on the cross and endured unimaginable pain for us. His is the greatest scar story ever told." (5)

"Victorious, But Not Unscarred." The scars that Christ bore remind us that no one ever achieves anything of lasting significance without getting a few scars along the way. Those scars are also a reminder of how much Christ loves us.

This brings us to a final thing to be said: Christ's scars are a summons to us to commit ourselves more fully to his work. The saddest commentary on our lives is probably the fact that we bear so few scars for Christ and for his kingdom.

Doesn't it concern you that our faith really requires so little of us? Some of us tithe. That's a considerable sacrifice, but 10% is half of what some of us tip servers who bring us our food in restaurants. We're here in worship most Sundays, but usually only when something more pressing, like a family outing or a fishing trip or whatever, doesn't get in the way. No one will accuse us of being fanatics about our religion. That's sad.

Jim Congdon in Leadership Magazine tells about a jarring TV commercial that ran sometime back. The commercial featured no dialogue. It simply showed a series of people who have one thing in common—a nasty injury or scar. There's a cowboy with a huge scar around his eye, and something wrong with the eye itself; a fellow with a bulbous cauliflower ear; another with horribly callused feet. There's no explanation at all . . . except a Nike swoosh and the words, "Just Do It."

The ad has been analyzed and criticized widely as being incomprehensible and extreme. But the key to the controversial commercial lies in the background music, says Congdon. Joe Cocker sings, "You are so beautiful . . . to me."

To these athletes—the wrestler with the cauliflower ear, the surfer with a shark bite, the bull rider blind in one eye—their injuries are beauty marks from their commitment to their sport. And to their fans, these athletes are beautiful because of their scars. "Beauty is in the eye of the beholder," says Mike Folino, the ad's creator.

It reminds me of one last story about a Confederate general named John B. Gordon. Gordon directed the last official action against the Union Army on a Sunday morning in April, 1865, at Appomattox when Lee surrendered to Grant.

Later Gordon became a candidate for the United States Senate. However, a man who had once served under Gordon became enraged over some political incident. As a member of the legislature, he vowed to do all that he could to defeat Gordon.

At the convention, this man stormed down the aisle to present his vote against Gordon in order to stop his bid for election. As he neared the platform upon which Gordon sat, he happened to look up at his former commander. The once handsome face was now disfigured by battle scars. He recalled the actions in which Gordon had led the troops, actions which had left him permanently disfigured.

Overcome with emotion, Gordon's opponent had tears falling down his cheeks. He declared to the assembly that he could not vote against John Gordon. Then turning to Gordon, he asked the general's forgiveness. "Forgive me, General. I had forgotten the scars." (6)

Victorious but not unscarred. That is how we too will one day see our Lord and Master and it will remind us of his great love for us. I wonder if on that day when we see him face to face, he will examine us for scars too.

1. http://reuters.com.
2. Edward K. Rowell, 1001 Quotes, Illustrations, and Humorous Stories (Grand Rapids: Baker, 2008), pp. 255-256.
3. James S. Hewett, ed., Illustrations Unlimited, p. 165.
4. "Among the Believers," September 24, 1995, p. 62.
5. http://www.faithandleadership.duke.edu/sermons/scars- hope.
6. Dr. William P. Barker, Tarbell's Teacher's Manuel (Elgin, IL: David C. Cook Church Ministries, 1994).

How Odd Of God
Acts 3:12-19

There is a small poem that is often quoted in Christian Bible studies that goes like this: How odd/ Of God/ To choose/ The Jews. Jews often use the word Goyim to refer to non-Jews. And so an unknown Jew with a biting wit responded to "How odd/ Of God/ To choose/ The Jews" by writing these words: "Not odd/ Of God:/ Goyim/ Annoy Him."

I cite these little bits of creative poetry strictly in fun. Our Jewish friends are generally delightful people, and they have contributed to the advance of civilization far out of proportion to their numbers.

The New Testament is often called anti-Semitic, or anti-Jewish. I believe that is in error. There is no question that it has been used many times throughout history to justify persecution of the Jews. And that is unforgivable. After all, Jesus himself was a Jew as were all of the original Christians. To be anti-Jewish is to be anti-Christ. But a careful reading of the New Testament shows it to be anything but anti-Semitic.

Take, for example, today's lesson from Acts. It follows one of the most beautiful scenes in the scriptures. One day Peter and John were going up to the temple at the time of prayer. A man who was lame from birth was being carried to the temple gate called Beautiful, where he was placed every day to beg from those going into the temple courts. When he saw Peter and John about to enter, this lame man asked them for money.

Peter looked straight at him and said, "Look at us!" So the man gave them his attention, expecting to get something from them. Then Peter said, "Silver or gold I do not have, but what I do have I give you. In the name of Jesus Christ of Nazareth, walk."

Taking him by the right hand, Peter helped the man up, and instantly his feet and ankles became strong. He jumped to his feet and began to walk. Then he went with them into the temple courts, walking and jumping, and praising God.

When all the people saw him walking and praising God, they recognized him as the same man who used to sit begging at the temple gate called Beautiful, and they were filled with wonder and amazement at what had happened to him. While the man held on to Peter and John, all the people were astonished and came running to them.

When Peter saw this, he said to them: "Fellow Israelites, why does this surprise you? Why do you stare at us as if by our own power or godliness we had made this man walk? The God of Abraham, Isaac and Jacob, the God of our fathers, has glorified his servant Jesus. You handed him over to be killed, and you disowned him before Pilate, though he had decided to let him go. You disowned the Holy and Righteous One and asked that a murderer be released to you. You killed the Author of life, but God raised him from the dead. We are witnesses of this."

Now, if we were to stop right here, we could say, "Yes. Peter is calling the Jews Christ-killers." But listen to how the story ends. Peter is still talking, "Now, fellow Israelites, I know that you acted in ignorance, as did your leaders. But this is how God fulfilled what he had foretold through all the prophets, saying that his Messiah would suffer. Repent, then, and turn to God, so that your sins may be wiped out, that times of refreshing may come from the Lord . . ."

Listen carefully. Peter is basically saying four things to his Jewish listeners: 1) You did wrong; 2) But you acted out of ignorance; 3) God used what you did to fulfill the messianic prophecy; and 4) Repent and turn to God, so that your sins may be wiped out, that times of refreshing may come from the Lord.

Does that sound like a statement of hatred and condemnation from Peter toward the Jews? It sounds to me like the advice of one good friend to another. His words could be directed, not toward the Jews, but toward you and me. In fact, let's use these thoughts and apply them to ourselves.

You did wrong. Peter had no personal animosity toward the people he was addressing. He was simply speaking the truth. They had done wrong, just as you and I sometimes do wrong. As the politicians say, "Mistakes were made."

I make mistakes, you make mistakes. I have sinned, you have sinned. It happens.

There is a scary story about a babysitter who made a call to the police. Someone was making continuous, but anonymous, calls to the home where she was sitting and it was beginning to frighten her. To her dismay the police told her to get out of the house immediately. The trace they had placed on the phone revealed that these frightening calls were coming from inside the house where she was sitting.

"This reminds us," says writer Phil Munsey, "that this can become our own horror story; sometimes the enemy is in the house." And that's true. The greatest enemy we have in this world is sometimes in our own hearts. (1)

Is the enemy living in the house which is your heart? It might be a simple thing like envy.

Richard Layard in his book titled Happiness tells about something that happened in East Germany when they were reunited with West Germany after 1990. The living standards of the East German people soared after reunification. However, their level of happiness fell. Why? With reunification the East Germans began to compare themselves with their West German counterparts who were doing even better still. Prior to reunification the East Germans had compared themselves with the other countries in the former Soviet bloc, and they felt pretty good about themselves. But in comparison with West Germans, they suddenly realized how far they had to go. And they became depressed.

The same thing often happens in the business world in this country, says Layard. He gives the example of women, whose pay and opportunities have improved considerably in recent years relative to men. However, their level of happiness has not. Indeed, in the United States women's happiness has fallen relative to men's. Perhaps women now compare themselves more directly with men than they used to and therefore focus more than before on the gaps that still exist. (2)

Erma Bombeck captured the heart of envy in this humorous prayer: "Lord, if You cannot make me thin, at least make my friends look fat."

I have seen envy raise its ugly head in church. People get indignant if the pastor spends more time with one group than another. Soloists have been known to grow envious if someone else gets chosen for the plump parts in the church cantata.

So what's the problem with a little envy? Nothing unless it eats into our happiness. Nothing unless it leads to catty remarks about others. Nothing unless it leads to division in the body of Christ. Nothing unless it causes us to shun people we should be having fellowship with.

Our ancestors spoke of seven deadly sins: anger, greed, sloth, pride, lust, envy, and gluttony. Can you find yourself anywhere on that list? These sins are deadly because of the effect they can have on our soul, even if they do not lead to any overt actions. In many cases the real enemy is inside the house. We are sinners. That's the first thing Peter says to his fellow Israelites. But it wasn't just true of the Israelites. It's true of every person who has ever lived. We're sinners.

Here is the second thing Peter said to the Jews: "I know that you acted in ignorance, as did your leaders."

This is a remarkable statement. It echoes Jesus' words on the cross: "Father, forgive them, for they do not know what they are doing." (Luke 23:34)

First of all, well-meaning people sometimes do awful things. For example, we get upset about Moslem extremists. We need to recognize that they are not the only religious group that has persecuted others for their faith. For example, throughout history Christians have persecuted peoples of other persuasions. If you believe that you are the only true faith and you believe that all other religions are leading people to hell, it is easy to justify in your mind that these other people must be stopped by any means necessary. [Shucks], we don't have to even go outside our faith community. Historically, Catholic and Protestant Christians have delighted in persecuting one another. People can be stirred up so easily to hate others who are not like themselves. Peter said to the Jews: "I know that you acted in ignorance, as did your leaders." And that is what it is—blind ignorance. There are a lot of stupid people around who can easily be stirred up into a mob. There are a lot of ignorant people, even in positions of leadership, who would rather be right than be Christ-like.

A pastor tells of visiting the Holy Land recently. He visited the Church of the Holy Sepulcher in Jerusalem. The Church is the traditional site of the hill of Christ's crucifixion and burial. It was built during the time of Constantine, roughly 326 A. D.

The Church of the Holy Sepulcher has gone through many different owners in its life and now there are at least six faith groups with claims on it. The three main ones are the Greek Orthodox, the Armenian Orthodox and the Roman Catholic. Three other communities—the Egyptian Coptic Orthodox, the Ethiopian Orthodox and the Syrian Orthodox—also possess certain rights and small properties in or about the building. And—get this—the key to the church is owned by a Muslim family.

While there, this pastor saw a ladder resting on the church's ledge. The story goes that in 1860, a member of one of the factions claiming rights to the church noticed a broken window pane. The members of this faction put a ladder up in order to fix the window, but before they could do so, another faction pointed out that the window belonged to them. So since the broken window pane belonged to one faction and the ladder belonged to another, the end result was that the ladder was left leaning against the wall under the window pane. It's been there since1860; it remains there today. (3)

Talk about "acting in ignorance." But that is how people are—all people everywhere under some circumstances. Peter said to the people of Israel that they had done wrong in crucifying Jesus, but that they acted out of ignorance. Then he makes a statement that is breathtaking: "But this is how God fulfilled what he had foretold through all the prophets, saying that his Messiah would suffer." In other words, what they intended for evil, God used for good.

Peter was addressing the Jews. They had crucified God's own Son. On a scale of 1-10 where would you put that on a sliding scale of misdeeds? Pretty near to the top, wouldn't you? But Peter points out that God had taken this terrible event and used it to save humanity. Now, where would you rank it?

This is why we should never give up, no matter how badly we have messed up. God is in control of this universe, and God can take even our sins and bring something good out of them.

Peter's words echo some words found in the Old Testament. You will remember that Joseph, the Old Testament patriarch, was sold into slavery by his envious brothers. They told their father that he was killed by a wild animal. The slave traders take Joseph to Egypt where, through the force of his character, he rises from slavery to being the second most powerful man in the empire. Later, in the midst of a great famine, Joseph's brothers come searching for food. They end up in an audience with their brother Joseph, whom they do not recognize. Why should they? Who would expect their brother to be in the royal palace? When Joseph reveals himself to them, they react in fear. What will Joseph do to avenge their great act of treachery? And the answer is, not a thing. He forgave them. And then Joseph speaks words that could only come from one of God's very special people: "As for you, you meant evil against me, but God meant it for good, to bring it about that many people should be kept alive, as they are today" (Gen. 50:20).

Those are words very similar to what Christ could have said to his persecutors following his resurrection: what you intended for evil, God used for good.

When we have sinned, we should never make light of it. Sin is more serious than we realize. But don't give up on your life. The awareness of your sin can cause you to become a better person. You are no longer ignorant of your own weakness. It can help you have more compassion for others who have given into their weaknesses, so that you might help them back up. When you have sinned, give that sin to God and ask, "Lord, I have done this terrible thing. I pray that you will redeem it and use it somehow to your glory."

You've done wrong, says Peter to the Israelites. But God has taken that wrong and used it to save fallen humanity. Then Peter speaks these final words, "Repent, then, and turn to God, so that your sins may be wiped out, that times of refreshing may come from the Lord." In other words, turn your life around and God will wipe away your sins and refresh your spirit.

This, my friends, is what grace is all about. Even when we have been our worst, God can give us His best if we are willing to receive it. You can go out of this room a new person. But you have to choose it. You must be willing to hand over to God even the smallest of sins, for they are seeds of deep destruction if they are not eliminated from our hearts. Envy, anger, greed, lust, sloth, pride, gluttony, or any other sin—turn them over to God and feel a burden lifted from your soul.

Dr. Jacob Chamberlain, an early missionary to India, tells of preaching to a group of people who had come to bathe in the "sacred stream" of the Ganges. Among them was a man who had crawled many agonizing miles on his knees and elbows. He was trying to atone for his sins and to win the favor of the god of the Ganges. Exhausted, he breathed a prayer to his god, and then slipped into the water. When he came out of the water, says Chamberlain, he felt no better. He still felt the weight of his sins. The fear of death still tugged at his heart. Then he heard Chamberlain tell the wonderful story of God's grace and how Christ died on the cross to cleanse needy sinners. With new hope the man staggered to his feet, clasped his hands together, and cried, "Oh, that's what I need! Cleansing and peace!" The missionary soon led him to Jesus. (4)

Here is the Good News for the day. If you have done wrong, whether a small infraction or a major sin, there is no reason to give up. There is no sin that God will not forgive—no wrong that God cannot redeem. God will forgive your sin and refresh your spirit. We began our message by quoting that refrain, "How odd of God to choose the Jews . . ." It should read like this: "How odd of God to choose any of us." But He has, and for some reason that only God knows, He never gives up on us no matter what we have done. Why then should we ever give up on ourselves?

1. Legacy Now (Charisma House, 2008).
2. Happiness Lessons From A New Science (New York, NY: Penguin Group, 2005), p. 45.
3. http://www.the5tos.com/KT_documents/Ephesians%203_1-13%20-%20Sermon%20-%20rev2.pdf.
4. Rev. Adrian Dieleman, http://www.trinitycrc.org/sermons/jn13v1f.html.

No Other Name
Acts 4:5-12

We want to begin with a little trivia contest. Can anyone tell me the name of the 33rd President of the United States? The 33rd President of our country was Harry S Truman. Question number two: what was Truman's home state? That's right, Missouri. Last question. We remember him as Harry S Truman. What did the "S" stand for? Trick question: the middle initial of Harry S Truman's name did not stand for anything. Both his grandfathers had names beginning with S so he was given the bare initial S to avoid having to choose between them. (1)

Names are fascinating. Pastor Ray Stedman says he had a friend whose middle initial was "T." Once at a party another friend announced that he had discovered what that "T" stood for: It stood for "Theophilus," he said, because when he was born, the doctor said, "That's the awfulest baby I ever saw!"

An article appeared in the newspapers sometime back. The writer was researching the relationship between a person's name and the choices they make as they go through life. The writer included choices such as profession and even the choice of a spouse. The researcher indicated that there were statistical tendencies—not rules, but tendencies. There were more dentists, for example, named Dennis than could be explained just by random chance; more women named Louise living in St. Louis—things like that. There was a statistical correlation pointing toward people marrying other people whose first names started with the same letter as theirs—David and Denise, for example. The president of the Audubon Society, the famous bird watching organization, at that time was a fellow named John Flicker (and for those of you who may not be bird-watchers, a flicker is a kind of woodpecker.) (2) Names are fascinating. Sometimes people have funny reasons for choosing names.

Lino Piedra, the former Chairman of the Board of Diamond-Star Motors, an automobile manufacturing joint venture of Chrysler Corporation and Mitsubishi Motors Corporation, likes to tell a story about an effort that was made in his company to "anglicize" the first names of some of the Japanese managers. This was because their American counterparts had trouble with the Japanese names. So, for example, the public relations manager suggested to Osamu Itoh, the assistant general manager of human relations, that he might like to simply be known as Sam.

"No," Itoh replied, "I think I would like a different name."

"What would you like to be called?" the P.R. manager asked.

Itoh replied that he would like to be called, "Awesome." "I think Awesome Itoh is a very good choice," he said.

They had a similar problem with Mr. Watanabe of MMC International Corporation. He chose the name "Handsome," remarking that he had always wanted to be handsome. In the end, the Japanese managers at Diamond-Star retained their given names. (3)

Several years ago, when they were selecting a new Pope, a gentleman from Spain was given weighty consideration. His name was Cardinal Sicola. However the College of Cardinals decided against him in the end. Could you imagine the name, Pope Sicola? Actually I think his real name is Scola, but why mess up a good joke.

Some names are ridiculous. Our Puritan ancestors chose some absurd names for their children. For example, one man was afflicted with the name of "Kill Sin." Even worse, his full name was Kill Sin Pimple. Kill Sin lived in Sussex, Massachusetts in 1609. In the spring of that year, the record shows, Kill Sin served on a jury with some of his neighbors. These included others with names like More Fruit Fowler, God Reward Smart, Be Faithful Joiner and Fight the Good Fight of Faith White. "Poor men," noted a writer in Time magazine some years ago. "At birth, their parents had turned them into religious bumper stickers." (4)

Names are fascinating. Names are sometimes funny. Sometimes names are ridiculous. And sometimes names are significant. Some of you perhaps have seen the movie Cast Away starring Tom Hanks. It was a big hit a few years ago. Hanks' character finds himself alone on a tiny island in the South Pacific, the lone survivor after an airplane crash. Desperate for a friend, Hanks does something interesting. He paints a human face on a volleyball that has washed ashore. Then he begins to speak to the volleyball as if it were a human being. He even gives his volleyball a name, "Wilson." Once the volleyball has a name, he is able to relate to it as if it were human.

Names are important. Maya Lin, designer of the Vietnam War Memorial was explaining to a TV interviewer why her remarkable work has come to have such a strong grip upon the emotions of the American people. "It's the names," she said, "the names are the memorial. No edifice or structure can bring people to mind as powerfully as their names." (5)

There is a popular children's book by Yangsook Choi called The Name Jar. A young girl has just moved to the United States with her family from Korea. On the first day of school, the little girl is nervous about being accepted by the American kids, and she gets teased a little on the bus on the way to school. She is embarrassed by her Korean name, and instead of introducing herself on the first day, she tells the class that she will choose an American name by the following week.

Her new classmates are fascinated by this no-name girl and decide to help out by filling a glass jar with names for her to pick from. So the kids put names in the jar, and the little girl practices being a Suzy, a Laura, or an Amanda.

In the meantime, one of her classmates comes to her neighborhood and discovers her real name . . . and its special meaning. On the day of her name choosing, the name jar mysteriously disappears. Encouraged by her new friends, the Korean girl chooses her own Korean name and helps everyone pronounce it.

Her real name is Unhei [pronounced "yoon-hay]—and it turns out that in Korean Unhei means "grace." (6)

For Christians, that is a sweet name, Grace, for to us it signifies God's unmerited love for sinners. It would be hard to have a more significant name than Grace. There is only one name that is sweeter to the believer than Grace. It is the name Jesus.

Peter and John encountered a man, lame from birth, who was being carried to the temple gate called Beautiful, where he was placed every day to beg from those going into the temple courts. When he saw Peter and John about to enter the gate, the lame man asked them for money.

Peter looked straight at the man, as did John. Then Peter said, "Look at us!" So the man gave them his attention, expecting to get something from them.

Then Peter said, "Silver or gold I do not have, but what I do have I give you. In the name of Jesus Christ of Nazareth, walk." And the man leaped to his feet.

"The next day," says Dr. Luke as he continues his narrative, "the rulers, the elders and the teachers of the law met in Jerusalem. Annas the high priest was there, and so were Caiaphas, John, Alexander and others of the high priest's family. They had Peter and John brought before them and began to question them: 'By what power or what name did you do this?'

"Then Peter, filled with the Holy Spirit, said to them: 'Rulers and elders of the people! If we are being called to account today for an act of kindness shown to a man who was lame and are being asked how he was healed, then know this, you and all the people of Israel: It is by the name of Jesus Christ of Nazareth, whom you crucified but whom God raised from the dead, that this man stands before you healed. Jesus is the stone you builders rejected, which has become the cornerstone. Salvation is found in no one else, for there is no other name under heaven given to mankind by which we must be saved.'"

What a powerful statement: "there is no other name under heaven given to mankind by which we must be saved."

Many of us remember a question that comes from one of Shakespeare's plays. "What's in a name?" asks Juliet in one of the world's most famous dramas about young love, Romeo and Juliet. Juliet's family is sworn enemies with Romeo's family, and no matter how much the two young lovers may want to marry each other, it's just not going to happen. Young Juliet isn't yet hardened to the ways of the world, and she has a brilliant idea, a way through their dilemma: "Deny thy father and refuse thy name," she says to Romeo. "Or if thou wilt not, be but sworn my love, and I'll no longer be a Capulet." After all, she reasons, "What's in a name? That which we call a rose, by any other name would smell as sweet."

One writer notes, "That's a radical statement in [Juliet's] world, where your name is related to your family, your property, your honor—all the things that are supposed to matter. Romeo and Juliet learn that there is a lot in a name, and they end up being together only in death." (7)

Names are important—especially one name.

Bishop Woodie White tells about one of his role models, the late Howard Thurman, a beloved professor at the Boston University School of Theology. Thurman was a nationally recognized preacher, author, and lecturer. He served for many years as dean of the chapel at Boston University, bringing it international acclaim.

In his autobiography titled With Head and Heart Howard Thurman records a compelling experience on his first trip to India in 1935. He was invited to preach at an Anglican cathedral in South India.

Following the evening service, as he stood greeting the worshippers, there came a young man who appeared to be moved by his sermon. Expecting affirmation for his sermon, Dr. Thurman was surprised when the man spoke in a soft but broken voice these words: "You did my Master wrong tonight. It was a terrible thing: You preached your entire sermon and not one time did you call my Savior by name—not one time."

Howard Thurman, stunned by this observation and the reaction of this worshipper, went on to explain that his message was really the essence of the teaching of Jesus—his values, his witness—what he would describe as the kingdom on earth and the kingdom to come. "This was all Jesus," he said.

The young man agreed. Howard Thurman's sermon was all of that, he allowed, and then said, "Yes, but this is not the point. You did not call him by name, and it is important that his name be lifted up, that he might draw all men unto him." (8)

It is important to lift up the name of Christ. There is something powerful about that name. John W. Maccallum, an evangelical author from the nineteenth century, put it this way, "At the mention of His name I have known the drunkard to start from his frenzy, leap out of the galling chains in which he has been bound for twenty years, and, clothed in his right mind, go forth, breathing the testimony of divine saving to rescue thousands from death and illimitable woe. At the name of Jesus, spoken to him reverently, I have known the maniac to cease his wild ravings and become as a little child, tender and submissive. In a revival, not long since, a helpless stammerer was suddenly cured of his impediment as he named the name of Christ in praise. I have seen men who had been bitterest enemies for years, suddenly fall weeping into each other's arms, their spite and hatred buried forever, just by the power of the name of Jesus. Oh! It is a mighty Name! Jesus!"

What does that name mean to you? There are some settings in which the only time you will hear Christ's name used will be as a curse word. Heaven help people who use it like that. It is a precious name to us. It is a name we use each time we pray. When we serve the Lord's Supper or baptize or when we attend to any of the ministries of the church, we do it in Jesus' name. We have seen popular heroes—celebrities, politicians, business leaders, clergy—whose names have been sullied by time, but not this name. It is a name above all names. And as you leave this place today, my prayer is that you will take that name with you and treat it with reverence.

Well known evangelist Sam Kamaleson of India was preaching in an evangelistic crusade in Romania just as the Communist world of Eastern Europe was collapsing. His audience, so long deprived of God and His Word, was large and attentive. One night as he preached, Sam became conscious of an unexpected sound that swept across his audience. Slowly he recognized that the wave of sound came every time he used the name of Jesus. Then he realized that it was the women in the audience weeping. The sound increased, and he realized that the men were weeping as well. Sam said that by that time he found himself weeping every time he used the name of Jesus as well. Sam explained, "You know, when the last alternative option to Jesus has been exhausted and shown for its true bankruptcy, the name of Jesus takes on great power and allure." (9)

Yes it does. In the words of the Gospel song writer of long ago,

"Take the name of Jesus with you,

Child of sorrow and of woe;

It will joy and comfort give you,

Take it then where'er you go. Amen."

By no other name can we be saved. Jesus.

1. William Hartston, The Encyclopedia of Useless Information (Naperville, IL: Sourcebooks, Inc., 2007), p. 370.

2. Pastor David Hamilton, Http://www.napavalleylutheran.org/vsItemDisplay.dsp&objectID=E0150A7B-6B02-4202-A917 CB0DDD69CA4C&method=display.

3. Joseph E. Cappy in The Business Speaker's Almanac, Edited by Jack Griffin and Alice Marks (Prentice Hall, 1994).

4. Time, March 8, 1993, p. 76.

5. Rev. Barbara A. Kenley, http://www.firstpresbyterianrichmondindiana.com/serm0107.htm.

6. Rev. Brent Beasley, http://www.2ndmemphis.org/2004/pdfs/072504.pdf.

7. Reverend Rhonda Lee, http://www.calvaryepiscopal.org/rlsermon-01-01-06.html.

8. Bishop Woodie White, http://www.day1.net/index.php5?view=transcripts&tid=103.

9. Dr. Dennis Kinlaw, "This Day with the Master" December 2nd.

How Connected Are You?
John 15:1-8

It helps to have connections. Everybody knows it's true. It's not what you know, the cynic says, but WHO you know that makes a difference. Unfortunately in some regards that's also true. In this competitive world where it is so difficult to land a job, it does pay to know somebody who can help you on your way. Oh, your mother's friend is president of a company? Good for you. Being connected may not help you actually land the job, but at least you are more likely to be considered if you know the person in charge. And that is important. You can see how difficult this might make things for people who are not connected—who do not know people in strategic places. Nevertheless, there is no use fighting it. That's the way things are. It pays to be connected.

About thirty years ago there was a wonderful book which was later turned into a powerful motion picture titled Schindler's List. You may be interested in how that book was first published. A shopkeeper named Leopold Page was a survivor of the Holocaust. He survived through the efforts of one man, Oskar Schindler, a Roman Catholic, who saved not only his life but the lives of 900 of his fellow Jews. Page was determined to find a writer who would be interested in telling the story of Oskar Schindler.

One day a novelist, Thomas Keneally, came into Page's shop to buy a briefcase, and Page told him his story. Keneally was intrigued and agreed to commit Schindler's story to print. What resulted was a moving story of a man who helped hundreds of Jews escape certain death at the hands of the Nazis. The book was dedicated to Oskar Schindler and to Page's "zeal and persistence" in getting Schindler's story told.

But that's not the end of the story. Page, the zealous and persistent shopkeeper had some friends who had some friends . . . and somehow he was able to get his book to the attention of a director named Steven Spielberg. You've probably heard that name before. Spielberg was fresh from making the blockbuster film, Jurassic Park.

"Stop playing around with dinosaurs," Page told Spielberg when they first met. "I promise you, you'll get an Oscar for [telling] Oskar's story." And he did. Spielberg turned Schindler's List into a major motion picture. The book—and the movie, which won seven Oscars, including Best Picture—more than fulfilled Page's lifelong dream. "I did not know how I would do this," Page had said, "but I promised Oskar Schindler I would make him a household name." And he did. Leopold "Paul" Page was number 173, by the way, on Oskar Schindler's list. He was 173 of the 900 who were spared death at the hand of the Nazis thanks to Oskar. (1)

Leopold Page was a shopkeeper, not a writer. But his commitment to his friend led him to connect with people who could bring his dream to reality. It's important in life to have connections. If you don't HAVE connections, then it's important to MAKE connections. Don't fight it. Make prudent use of this adage—it's not what you know but who you know. And so today I want to ask you this important question, how connected are you?

Of course, when I ask the question about being connected, the younger members of our congregation probably think in terms of social media—Facebook, Twitter, LinkedIn, etc. This is a brave new world, and being connected has taken on a whole new meaning.

One woman said their new high-speed computer was in the shop for repair. Her son was forced to work on their older model with an obsolete black-and-white printer.

"Mom," he complained to her one day, "this is like we're living back in the twentieth century."

For some of us that is a reality check—BACK in the twentieth century. This IS the twenty-first century I may need to remind some of us.

A group of young children were sitting in a circle with their teacher. She was going around asking each of them questions.

"Davy, what noise does a cow make?"

He said, "It goes moo."

"Alice, what noise does a cat make?"

"It goes meow," she answered.

"Jamie, what sound does a lamb make?"

"It goes baaa," he said.

"Jennifer, what sound does a mouse make?"

Without hesitation she answered, "It goes click!"

Well, a computer mouse does go click. The question, "Are you connected?" means different things to different people. However, there is a danger associated with electronic connectedness. Despite all the hype about being connected through the Internet, a number of studies suggest that this technology is actually disconnecting many of us from those around us.

A study of the Stanford Institute found that: 13 percent of regular net users—that is, those who are on the web five hours or more a week—reported spending less time with family and friends; 8 percent said they were now attending fewer social events; and 26 percent said they talked less to friends and family by telephone. That's disturbing. (2) Being connected to family and friends is what gives life meaning.

As another prominent researcher noted recently, many people have a swarm of friends on Facebook. But "friending" is not the same as "befriending"—being a friend. Instead of creating a global village, the Internet has distracted and distanced us from each other. One impact is that lonely people have no one to turn to in hard times. (3)

Of course, not all or even most of our personal isolation can be blamed on the Internet. The average American today already has only a third as many friends as 25 years ago, and one-fourth have no close confidants at all, according to recent research. We are becoming a disconnected society.

This is troubling because staying connected is important to our health and general well-being. That is what medical studies are showing us. One study compared 12,000 Japanese men living in Japan with Japanese men who had moved to Hawaii or California. The researchers looked at smoking, diet, exercise, cholesterol levels, and social support (the maintenance of family and community ties). The group with the lowest social support (the California group) had a threefold to fivefold increase in heart disease. The researchers concluded that social networks and close family ties help protect against disease and premature death. (4) Stay connected to other people, the research shows, and you will be healthier.

But the effects of social isolation are not just medical. A British study suggests that social isolation is in part responsible for the fact that suicides among those under the age of 35 have risen at such a dramatic rate. In studying the lives of 148 young people who died of either suicide or natural causes, the researcher found that those who killed themselves were more likely to be living alone, single, unemployed and with few friends. In other words, they were socially isolated, disconnected. (5)

In his book, Real Age, Michael Roizen calculates how different factors affect one's life expectancy. For socialization he cites three factors: 1) being married, 2) seeing at least six friends at least monthly, and 3) participating in social groups. The "real age" for a 55-year-old man who meets all three criteria—married, has at least 6 friends, and goes to church—is 46 in terms of life expectancy. And you thought being married made you older. Not so, in terms of life expectancy, it makes you younger. If the 55-year-old man meets at least two of these criteria, his real age is 49. If he meets one criterion, his real age is 53. The real age of a 55-year-old man who meets none of these criteria is 63—eight years older than his chronological age. For a 55 year old woman the real ages are 49, 53, 59, and 61. Presumably, says researchers, the effect is a little stronger for men because women in our culture are better at social networking. (6)

Need more evidence? When a partner's spouse dies, his or her risk of illness or death skyrockets for the first year. Retirement also changes social networks and can be very stressful. The point is that it's very important at any age in life to stay connected.

Of course our most important connection is to Christ. In our lesson for the day from the Gospel, Christ says to us, "I am the vine; you are the branches. If you remain in me and I in you, you will bear much fruit; apart from me you can do nothing. If you do not remain in me, you are like a branch that is thrown away and withers; such branches are picked up, thrown into the fire and burned. If you remain in me and my words remain in you, ask whatever you wish, and it will be done for you. This is to my Father's glory, that you bear much fruit, showing yourselves to be my disciples."

"I am the vine; you are the branches . . ." Here is where staying connected is most vital. Christianity has two central foci—staying connected to our neighbor and staying connected to God—and without either of these, we are not whole people.

In his book, A Blue Fire, psychologist James Hillman describes a condition among "primitive" people which anthropologists call "loss of soul." In this condition a person is unable to make an outer connection to other humans or an inner connection to himself. He is unable to take part in society, its rituals, its traditions. They are dead to him, he to them. "Until he regains his soul he is not a true human."

Hillman tells about an experience he had one day in Burgholzli, the famous institute in Zurich where the words "schizophrenia" and "complex" were born. Hillman watched a woman being interviewed. She sat in a wheelchair because she was elderly and feeble. She said that she was dead for she had lost her heart. The psychiatrist asked her to place her hand over her breast to feel her heart beating: it must still be there if she could feel its beat.

"That," she said, "is not my real heart." She and the psychiatrist looked at each other.

"There was nothing more to say," writes Hillman. "Like the primitive who has lost his soul, she had lost the loving courageous connection to life . . ." (7)

We lose our heart, we lose our soul, when we lose our connection to God. "What good is it for someone to gain the whole world," said Jesus on one occasion, "yet forfeit their soul?" (Mark 8:36) We know the answer to that. Lose your connection to God, and nothing else you accomplish will have any real meaning. Lose your connection to God, and you lose the meaning to life.

Back during the days of the Cold War a woman named Svetlana Stalin, daughter of the cruel former Soviet dictator Josef Stalin shocked the world by immigrating to the United States seeking a new life. She explained her change of allegiance this way, "I found it was impossible to exist without God in one's heart."

Ms. Stalin was right. It is impossible to exist as a full human being without God in one's heart. How connected are you to Christ?

It's important to note that, if we lose our connection to God, it won't be God's doing. God's love for us is everlasting and unconditional.

The popular radio Bible teacher J. Vernon McGee once told about a little piece of wood that he kept on his desk. He explained that he took this small piece of wood from a vineyard in the San Joaquin Valley. The small piece of wood consisted of a section of a grapevine out of which grew a branch. The owner of the vineyard told McGee that if two people were to have a tug of war with this section of vine, it would break. However, it would never break where the vine and branch are joined together. The place on a grapevine where the vine and the branch are joined together is the vine's strongest point.

"Now if you pull on a branch that goes into a tree," the owner explained, "it will always break at the trunk of the tree—in a tree that is the weakest place. But in a grapevine that is the strongest point." (8)

No wonder Christ used the analogy of the vine and its branches to explain his relationship with us, his followers. The strongest place on a grapevine is where the branches are attached to the vine. In other words, we don't need to worry that our connection to Christ will be broken—at least not from Christ's side. That connection is a powerful one. Do you know anyone who needs to be connected to Christ and needs to be connected to others? I'll bet you do. They are all around us.

Author Max Lucado tells about a friend of his named Steve who worked at a pharmacy while attending college. Steve's primary job was to deliver supplies. One of his customers was an older woman, perhaps in her seventies, who lived alone in a small apartment in a building about fifty feet behind the pharmacy. Steve would deliver a jug of water to this woman twice a week, receive the payment, thank the woman, and leave.

Over the weeks Steve grew puzzled. He learned that the woman had no other source of water. She relied on his delivery for all of her washing, bathing, and drinking needs. However, she could have had municipal water. In fact, it would have been significantly cheaper. Why didn't she choose the less expensive source?

You have probably guessed the answer. The city sent only the water; they didn't send a person. His visits were the reason she was willing to pay more for her water. (9)

Are there people in our community who are that lonely? Of course there are. There are children, there are teenagers, there are adults and there are seniors who have somehow become disconnected. Isn't it interesting that when God wanted to save the world, God sent a person, Jesus of Nazareth, God's own Son. Christ says to us, "If you want to find life, be connected to me. I will never leave you or forsake you. Where you and I are connected is the strongest place on the vine."

And so I ask you one last time: how connected are you?

1. Randy Cassingham, www.thisistrue.com.
2. Donald M. Tuttle, http://www.first-christian-cc.org/images/sermons/Oct%201,%202000.htm.
3. Michael Bugeja, Interpersonal Divide (Oxford University Press, 2005).
4. American Journal of Epidemiology (1975): 102(6): 514-25. Cited by Walter L. Larimore M.D., 10 Essentials of Highly Healthy People (Grand Rapids: Zondervan, 2003), p. 140.
5. Donald M. Tuttle, http://www.first-christian-cc.org/images/sermons/Oct%201,%202000.htm.
6. Michael Brickey, Ph.D., Defy Aging (Columbus, OH: New Resources Press, 2000), p. 18.
7. James Hillman, A Blue Fire (New York: HarperPerennial, 1989), pp. 17-18.
8. The Best of J. Vernon Mcgee (Nashville: Thomas Nelson Publishers, 1988).
9. Traveling Light (Nashville: W Publishing Group 2001), pg. 105.

Love Each Other
John 15:9-17
(Mother's Day)

A little boy watched, fascinated, as his mother gently rubbed cold cream on her face. "Why are you rubbing cold cream on your face, mommy?" he asked.

"To make myself beautiful," said his mother.

A few minutes later, she began removing the cream with a tissue. "What's the matter?" he asked. "Are you giving up?"

Welcome on this Mother's Day 2012. It's not easy being a Mom. Those of you who have children know it's not easy, regardless of their age.

One Mom says that she's going to try something different next summer with their dog and with their kids. Next summer, she says, she's sending the dog to camp and the kids to obedience school.

That wonderful writer Erma Bombeck once said, "What mother has never fallen on her knees when she has gone into her son's bedroom and prayed, 'Please, God, no more. You were only supposed to give me what I could handle.'"

It's not easy. Or as someone has said, "The hand that rocks the cradle usually is attached to someone who isn't getting enough sleep."

Of course, sometimes it's not easy having a mom, either. Comedian George Wallace says, "I grew up hearing such stupid things. My mother would say, 'That's the last time I'm gonna tell you to take out the garbage.' Well," he adds, "thank God." (1)

Maybe Mom's advice sometimes seemed a little silly to us.

One mother, Pam Hodgskin tells about when her son arrived back in the United States after fighting with the First Marine Division in Iraq. She says she still couldn't help reacting like a mom when she saw him running across the base carrying a bayonet to give to some of his buddies.

"Kevin!" she shouted halfway across the base, before she could stop herself. "Don't run with that knife in your hands!"

Every mom has done it at some time or another, but let's face it: most of us would have been lost without our moms.

A couple was moving across the country. They decided to drive both cars. Their 8-year old son Nathan worried. "How will we keep from getting separated?"

Dad reassured him, "We'll drive slowly. One car can follow the other."

"But what if we DO get separated?" Nathan persisted.

"Well, then I guess we'll never see each other again," Dad joked.

Nathan quickly answered. "Then I'm riding with Mom." (2)

Smart young fellow. Actually, the situation can be summed up in the words of one mom when she said, "I'd like to be the ideal mother, but I'm too busy raising my kids." Touché!

Our lesson for the day from John's Gospel is perfect for Mother's Day because it is about love: "As the Father has loved me, so have I loved you. Now remain in my love. If you keep my commands, you will remain in my love, just as I have kept my Father's commands and remain in his love. I have told you this so that my joy may be in you and that your joy may be complete. My command is this: Love each other as I have loved you. Greater love has no one than this: to lay down one's life for one's friends. You are my friends if you do what I command. I no longer call you servants, because a servant does not know his master's business. Instead, I have called you friends, for everything that I learned from my Father I have made known to you. You did not choose me, but I chose you and appointed you so that you might go and bear fruit—fruit that will last—and so that whatever you ask in my name the Father will give you. This is my command: Love each other."

There are several thoughts we can draw from this lesson. Note, first of all, that love is a command. Jesus isn't giving us a suggestion that we love one another. This is a command. To be a follower of Jesus Christ is to love—love our families, love our friends, even love our enemies. "By this all men will know that you are my disciples," said the Master, "if you love one another" (John 13:35).

You can't be any more direct than that. There aren't many rules to the Christian faith, not really, but this rule is iron clad. We are to love. Of course, this was not the first time that the Master lifted up love as the great commandment.

In Matthew's Gospel an expert in the law tested Jesus with this question: "Teacher, which is the greatest commandment in the Law?"

Jesus replied: "'Love the Lord your God with all your heart and with all your soul and with all your mind.' This is the first and greatest commandment. And the second is like it: 'Love your neighbor as yourself.' All the Law and the Prophets hang on these two commandments," Jesus declared (Matthew 22:34-40).

A young boy in elementary school was given a test in English grammar. He was being tested on the perfect tense of verbs. One question had a column of verbs in the present tense, and he had to put the perfect form of each of these verbs in the opposite column. He came to the verb live, and in the opposite column for the perfect tense of the word live he wrote the word love.

Grammatically he was wrong, but from a Christian standpoint he was right on target. The perfect form of "to live" is to love.

John Ortburg talks about a friend of his who had a tough life. This man had virtually no father growing up and his mother was a difficult person. She married five times, none of the relationships lasting long. She had little time for her children and gave them little encouragement. This adult man still carries many wounds from her inattention.

However, late in life his mother developed a degenerative muscular disease and gradually lost almost every physical capacity. You can imagine how difficult she was to care for. None of her other children would have anything to do with her. Neither would any of the men she had married—no one except this son, Ortburg's friend.

Ortburg says, "My friend decided to love. He took her into his home and cared for her, feeding her by hand, combing her hair, and cleaning up after her messes . . . about all she could do was cry and moan incessantly."

Ortburg thought to himself about his friend, "How can he stand this? I've been given so many blessings—the church, Scripture, family—exponentially greater than this guy, and I don't know if I could love like this."

When his friend's mother died sixteen people came to the funeral. None of her other kids came. The son who cared for her had a little toy tape recorder his mother had gotten him one Christmas and he played a tape of he and his mom singing a Christmas carol. He talked about how she loved Christmas and how that when he was a kid he would play the guitar and she would sing with him.

Ortburg says, "He didn't love her perfectly, not by a long shot. But he loved her when loving was hardest. He loved her when no one else would love her, and he remembered her with kind words." (3)

That must have been difficult—loving her when she showed him so little love. But that's what Christian love is. That's the kind of love Christ gave us when we were undeserving. Love is a command.

Note, secondly, that love is sacrificial. Christ speaks of "laying down one's life for one's friends . . ."

For many of us love is a squishy emotion without any real content. "I love you for what you can do for me," is the basic rule of such love. "You meet my needs and so I have a warm feeling for you." We sing about such love, but in our hearts we know such love is horribly superficial. True love is sacrificial.

There is a story about two tribes in the Andes that were at war. One tribe lived in the lowlands and the other high in the mountains. The mountain people invaded the lowlanders one day, and as part of their plundering, they kidnapped a baby of one of the lowlander families and took the infant with them back up into the mountains. The lowlanders didn't know how to climb the mountain. They didn't know any of the trails that the mountain people used, and they didn't know where to find the mountain people or how to track them in the steep terrain. Even so, they sent out their best party of fighting men to climb the mountain and bring the baby home.

The men tried first one method of climbing and then another. They tried one trail and then another. After several days of effort, however, they had climbed only several hundred feet. Feeling hopeless and helpless, the lowlander men decided that the cause was lost, and they prepared to return to their village below.

As they were packing their gear for the descent, they saw the baby's mother walking toward them. They realized that she was coming down the mountain that they hadn't figured out how to climb. And then they saw that she had the baby strapped to her back. How could that be?

One man greeted her and said, "We couldn't climb this mountain. How did you do this when we, the strongest and most able men in the village, couldn't do it?"

She shrugged her shoulders and said, "It wasn't your baby." (4)

Every parent worth his or her salt understands. There is nothing that we will not do for our children. Of course, some of us are at that stage of life when it is our parents who need our sacrificial love. It's part of the circle of life. Our parents provided for our needs when we were young, but now it is they who have pressing needs. Who will be there for them? You may be part of what is often referred to as the "sandwich generation," caught between the needs of your children and the needs of your aging parents. That really is a difficult place.

A lady named Bev Hulsizer tells about a time years ago when her mother came to visit. Her mother asked Bev to go shopping with her because she needed a new dress. Bev confesses that she is not a patient person, and did not look forward to shopping with her Mom, but they set off for the mall together nonetheless.

They visited nearly every store that carried ladies' dresses, and her mother tried on dress after dress, rejecting them all. As the day wore on, Bev grew weary and her mother grew frustrated.

Finally, at their last stop, her mother tried on a lovely blue three piece dress. The blouse had a bow at the neckline, and as Bev stood in the dressing room with her Mom, she watched as her mother tried, with much difficulty, to tie the bow. Her hands were so badly crippled from arthritis that she couldn't do it. Immediately, Bev's impatience gave way to an overwhelming wave of compassion for her Mom. She turned away to try and hide the tears that welled up involuntarily.

Regaining her composure, she turned back to her mother to tie the bow for her. The dress was beautiful, and her mother bought it. Their shopping trip was over, but the event was etched indelibly in Bev's memory.

For the rest of the day, her mind kept returning to that moment in the dressing room and to the vision of her mother's hands trying to tie that bow. Those loving hands that had fed her, bathed her, dressed her, caressed and comforted her, and, most of all, prayed for her, were now touching her in a most remarkable manner.

Later in the evening, Bev went to her mother's room, took her Mom's hands in her own and kissed them. Then much to her surprise told her Mom that to her they were the most beautiful hands in the world.

Bev says she's so grateful that God let her see with new eyes what a precious, priceless gift a loving, self-sacrificing mother is. She prays that someday her own hands, and her heart, will have earned such a beauty of their own. (5)

Some of you can relate to that simple story. You remember the many loving sacrifices your Mom or your Dad made in your behalf. Now you watch sadly as your parents struggle with aging. Now it's your turn to make sacrifices. Again, it's not easy. Christ never promised that it would be easy. But love is sacrificial.

Love is what life is about. In I Corinthians 13 St. Paul summed it up like this: "These three remain: faith, hope and love. But the greatest of these is love."

Author J. Allan Petersen tells about a flight he once took on a 747 out of Brazil. He was awakened from sleep by a voice announcing, "We have a very serious emergency." Three engines had quit because of fuel contamination and the fourth was expected to go at any second. The plane began to drop and turn in the night, preparing for an emergency landing.

At first the situation seemed unreal to Petersen, but when the steward barked, "Prepare for impact," he found himself—and everyone around him—praying. As he buried his head in his lap and pulled up his knees, he said, "Oh, God, thank You. Thank You for the incredible privilege of knowing You. Life has been wonderful."

As the plane approached the ground, his last cry was, "Oh, God, my wife! My children!"

Petersen survived. As he wandered about the airport afterward in a daze, aching all over, he found he couldn't speak, but his mind was racing, What were my last words? What was the bottom line? As he remembered, he had his answer: relationship.

Reunited with his wife and sons, he found that all he could say to them over and over was, "I appreciate you, I appreciate you!" (6)

He discovered—as sooner or later we all discover—the bottom line of life is love. Love is what life is all about. God created this world so that He would have persons He could love. God sent His only begotten Son to die on the cross because of love. When one day we are gathered around God's throne with all those we love, we will discover that the final payoff for living is love. "These three remain: faith, hope and love. But the greatest of these is love." Today go forth from this place determined to live a life of love that you might perfectly fulfill the commandments of Christ.

1. Judy Brown, Squeaky Clean Comedy (Andrews McMeel, 2005).
2. http://1stpres.home.bresnan.net/Sermons/John%2020_19-31%20-%20Peace%20Be%20With%20You.htm.
3. Cited by Chuck Queen, http://www.ibcfrankfort.com/sermons/030908.pdf.
4. Meir Liraz, The 100 Top Inspirational Anecdotes and Stories.
5. Jack Canfield and Mark Victor Hansen, Chicken Soup for The Christian Soul 101 Stories to Open the Heart and Rekindle the Spirit (Deerfield Beach, FL: Health Communications, Inc, 1997), pp. 111-112.
6. God's Little Devotional Book (Tulsa: Honor Books, Inc., 1973), p. 153.

How Can I Know God's Will?

Acts 1:15-17, 21-26

Wesley D. Tracy tells about a woman whom he calls Kate Dowd. That is not her real name, but she is a real person. Kate, a dedicated wife and mother, volunteered at her church, helped with Cub Scouts, tatted lace, and knitted scarves. Then she discovered something that was more exciting than all the rest of her activities combined—riverboat gambling. Almost immediately her life was completely changed—and not for the better.

Kate would cross the river daily to Illinois and board either the Alton Belle or the River Queen riverboats to indulge in her new passion. Soon she had emptied the family bank account and pawned her wedding ring. She was still gambling when the house payment was 17 months behind.

"The day they came to repossess the house, gambling lost its charm. She drove her 1988 Oldsmobile to a mall parking lot, climbed into the back seat, put the muzzle of a .357 Magnum behind her right ear, and pulled the trigger. Kate Dowd, university graduate, loving mother, and faithful church worker left a note, 'To Whom It May Concern,' and died with $2.58 in her purse." (1)

Gambling can be a fatal disease. For most people it is certainly a losing proposition. We often hear about people who have gone to Las Vegas or Atlantic City and have won huge jackpots. We don't hear about the majority of people who go to these places and lose—sometimes just a little bit, but sometimes their house payment or their groceries. According to a report in the New York Times, gamblers in Las Vegas casinos lost $6.1 billion in one year alone. As someone familiar with the lure of gambling has said, the only way to double your money in Vegas is to fold it and put it in your pocket.

Of course you don't have to go to Vegas to lose money gambling. I'm not going to ask if any of you have ever bought a lottery ticket. Someone has called the lottery a tax on the poor because so many people look at the lottery as their only hope of coming out of life ahead. What it does, of course, is put them deeper in a hole.

In an article in Time magazine writer Ginia Bellafonte told about a man, about 60, waiting in line outside a stationery shop in Greenwich, Connecticut to buy lottery tickets. The temperature was at least 95 degrees. Within a short time he keeled over onto the sidewalk. An ambulance came, but the man, still conscious, refused to leave the line without first buying $15 worth of tickets.

In that same line was a 25-year-old father of three, who drove two hours from Brooklyn to Greenwich to spend $175—mostly crumpled up fives and 10s—on Powerball tickets. Could he afford it? "No comment," he replied.

More disturbing still was the fact that a 28-year-old waiter was also in that

line funneling all the money he had been saving for college—$3,000—into Power-
ball tickets. (2) It is a form of madness, and we ought to be more concerned about
it than we are. Television commercials tell us about the millions the lottery provides to education; nothing is said about the savings lost or the lives broken.

J. E. Bendenbaugh wrote to Reader's Digest to tell about his grandmother,
a staunch Southern Baptist, who had marched him off to Sunday School and
church regularly. So when he switched to the Episcopal Church after marriage
she challenged him: "What's wrong with the Baptist Church, son?" she asked.

"Well," he explained, "Carole and I flipped a coin to see if we would go to
her church or mine, and I lost."

"Serves you right," said his grandmother. "Good Baptists don't gamble."

I'm tempted to say neither do good [Lutherans, good Methodists, good Presbyterians, etc]. I know some people regard it as a harmless form of recreation. "I
can afford it," many will argue. Think how much better it would make you feel,
though, if you put that money to work, for example, feeding a hungry child.

Of course, some forms of gambling have always been with us. In the book
of Acts, when the disciples were faced with a choice between two men to replace
the disciple Judas after he had betrayed Christ and hung himself in despair, we
read that the disciples "cast lots" to choose his successor. Casting lots in that day
and time was a mild form of gambling. As I understand it, when used to decide
elections, they would write the names of the candidates on pieces of stone or
wood, etc., and put them in an urn. The names were then drawn at random and
this settled the case. It's certainly not a sinful way to go about making a decision.
It's not much different from flipping a coin. However, it seems a strange way for
the disciples of Christ to choose a successor to carry on his work. I guess they
couldn't find any other way to choose. Both men were equally qualified and this
was a quick, easy way to make a decision. So we should not be too critical. It just
seems strange that they would seek the will of God this way.

But, then, how do you know the will of God? This is one of the most vexing
questions in our faith. Many of us want to know God's will for our lives so that
we can make appropriate choices. A young man falls in love. "Is this the right
person for me?" he asks himself. "Is it God's will for me to marry?" Perhaps that
is a question that isn't asked much anymore. And maybe, from the looks of all
the statistics on marriage and divorce, just maybe it ought to be.

Talk about a gamble. A young couple meets at a vulnerable time in their
lives when hormones are bubbling, and their judgment has not quite matured,
and we expect them to make a decision about the person they're going to spend
the rest of their lives with. No wonder so many marriages do not survive. Would-
n't it be great if we could have God's input in the matter?

One of the spiritual giants of the Christian faith had this battle once upon a time. His name was John Wesley. It was under his leadership that the Methodists, the Nazarenes and so many other Christian groups sprang. Wesley, early in his ministry as an Anglican priest, spent time as a missionary in Georgia. This was during the 1700s. Wesley's ministry in Georgia was not a successful venture. For one thing, he was attracted to a young woman named Sophia Hopkey. They talked of marriage. Wesley struggled with this. Was it God's will? He prayed about it, he sought the counsel of friends, he searched the scriptures and, finally, when he could not resolve it any other way, he cast lots. Yes, just as the disciples did in choosing a successor to Judas, Wesley cast lots. One lot had on it "not to marry." One lot had on it "to marry." And a third lot said to break off the relationship altogether, which is what he eventually did. Some of you may know the rest of the story. Sophia turned around and married someone else, and young Mr. Wesley refused to serve them communion. The matter ultimately ended up in court and Wesley made the wise decision that Georgia was not the place God was calling him to be after all.

This should caution us that even spiritual giants may not have a clue as to the will of God in matters of the heart. It is very difficult to know the will of God. It humbles us all.

A couple wants to start a business. They are a very religious couple of a strong evangelical background. They want to do God's will. So they decide to "put out a fleece." The concept of putting out a "fleece" is found in Judges 6, where Gideon is given a difficult task by God. Gideon starts wondering if he heard God right, so he "tests" God by putting out a fleece.

Gideon says to God, "If you will save Israel by my hand as you have promised—look, I will place a wool fleece on the threshing floor. If there is dew only on the fleece and all the ground is dry, then I will know that you will save Israel by my hand, as you said." And that is what happened. Gideon rose early the next day; he squeezed the fleece and wrung out the dew—a bowlful of water. Meanwhile the ground around was dry.

Then Gideon said to God, "Do not be angry with me. Let me make just one more request . . . with the fleece, but this time make the fleece dry and let the ground be covered with dew." That night God performed another miracle. This time the fleece was dry; all the ground was covered with dew (6: 37-40).

What a wonderful story. Gideon asked God to give him a sign that he was really in the will of God. When God did exactly as Gideon asked, Gideon asked for another sign just to make sure.

I really wish knowing the will of God was that easy for us. This very religious couple that put out a fleece about whether God wanted them to start a business were very certain that they had gotten a sign from God that starting a business was God's will for them. They invested their life savings . . . and they lost their proverbial shirt. Can you imagine how devastating that was to them spiritually as well as financially?

Friends, it is very difficult to know God's will in specific circumstances. The disciples cast lots because they were in a situation where they could not lose. Both candidates fit the requirements for being a disciple. The disciples just needed to make a decision. And so they decided by casting lots. Either choice would have worked out fine because God was going to use whomever they chose to accomplish His purposes. It didn't matter if it was Matthias or Barsabbas, the other candidate. All that mattered was that God was involved. Still the question remains: How do you know the will of God? Let me suggest some better ways than casting lots.

First of all, be a person of prayer and a student of the scriptures. In other words, spend time daily with God. Do not wait until a moment of crisis or when you are facing a difficult decision. Pray daily to "have the same mind in you which was in Christ Jesus" as St. Paul writes in Philippians 2:5. It's a simple starting point, but it will put you on solid ground.

According to a nationwide study by George Barna, only 13% of adults turn to the Bible for help in making moral decisions. About 14% of people rely on their parents' advice and values when making a decision. And a full 25% of adults, 1 out of every 4 people, rely simply on their "feelings" to be their moral guide in a sticky situation. (3)

Friends, you can't disregard your feelings, but they are a poor guide to knowing the will of God. People are continually being led into bad decisions by their feelings. Pray and study that you will discover the mind of Christ. That way you're more apt to make better decisions in every situation, not just when you're confronting an especially challenging choice.

Secondly, if you have a really difficult decision to make, consult someone whose judgment you trust. Remember how Jesus said, "Whenever two or three of you agree, then it will be done" (Matthew 18:19). Sometimes we have too much invested in a decision personally to see clearly what God's will may be. We need someone else's viewpoint who is not as emotionally involved. If it is a matter of a relationship to a person of the opposite sex, do not ignore possible warnings of Christian friends or of parents or whomever. They can be wrong, but again I emphasize that feelings when you are head over heels in love cannot be trusted.

If you are starting a business, be diligent in your research. Do not act impulsively. Get the advice of people who understand how business works. Again the experts can be wrong, but at least listen to their input.

You know the old story about a person who bought a car that turned out to be a lemon. A friend who was very knowledgeable about cars asked, "Why didn't you ask me for advice?" And the person said, "I was afraid you would tell me not to buy it." That happens. The last thing some of us want to do is to ask for advice, particularly when our hearts are set on a certain course. But that is the very reason we need advice.

After you have done all that, pray that God will help you make the best decision possible. Then make your decision. Don't look for a sign. Don't consult the morning astrological forecast. Don't put out a fleece. Take the three steps which we have listed, make your decision, and then take one more step—the most important step of all.

After you have made your decision, trust God to help you turn that decision into the right decision. When we have to make a decision, the very reason it is difficult is that the future is unknowable. There is only one thing certain about the future and that is that God is in it. Even if your decision turns out not to be the best possible decision due to some unforeseeable circumstances, God will help you turn it into something good, even if it is only a necessary learning experience.

Remember, there are many desirable benefits that come only through failure. This is important. Everyone makes bad decisions sometimes. Don't assume that because you are successful that you are in the center of God's will. You may have only been lucky. Or maybe you are more talented or more intelligent than those who have not been so successful. And just because you fail at something doesn't mean you are outside God's will. The cross on which Christ died can hardly be considered a symbol of success. It is a symbol of love and sacrifice, not luxury and success.

It is no accident that so many successful people have failed miserably at some venture previously in their lives. They learned some things about themselves from that failure that made them successful later.

Leslie Weatherhead was one of the great preachers of the twentieth century, but sometimes things did not turn out as he hoped. Here is what he wrote about that, "I can only write down this simple testimony. Like all [people], I love and prefer the sunny uplands of experience when health, happiness and success abound but I have learned more about God, life, and myself in the darkness of fear and failure than I have ever learned in the sunshine. There are such things as the treasure of darkness. The darkness, thank God, passes, but what one learns in the darkness, one possesses forever."

If you're facing a difficult decision, here's what to do: Pray daily. Know the Scriptures. Consult with people whose opinion you respect and listen to their counsel. Pray over your specific decision and go ahead and make it. And finally, and most important, trust God to help you turn that decision into the right decision. Even if your decision turns out to be the wrong one, don't give up. Trust God. After all, God made the ultimate gamble when God sent His Son to die in

our behalf. Then God took that event—the rejection of his Son by sinful humanity—and used it to save the world.

So, follow these steps for all your decision making. They probably won't
help you at a Las Vegas roulette table—except perhaps to keep you away from
such gambling devices. What these steps will do is take much of the gamble out
of life. Remember, roulette tables are for losers. Living according to the will of
God always puts you on the winning side.

1. Herald of Holiness, July 1995, p. 2.
2. "The Lucky Thirteen" Aug. 10, 1998, p. 64.
3. "Poll Finds Church Scene 'Back to Normal' After Attack" by Jon Walker, Pulpit Helps, Feb.
2002, p. 9.

The Sound Of A Mighty Wind

Acts 2:1-21

(Day of Pentecost)

On April 27, 2011 the largest tornado outbreak ever recorded hit parts of the southern U. S. causing catastrophic destruction in five states—Alabama, Arkansas, Georgia, Mississippi, Tennessee, and Virginia. Four of the tornadoes which swept through the South on that terrible day were destructive enough to be rated EF5 tornadoes, which is the highest ranking possible. EF5 tornadoes are extremely rare and yet on this day alone there were four EF5 tornadoes killing an estimated 346 people.

Tornadoes, hurricanes and typhoons have always been with us, of course. However, there are disturbing indications that with the earth gradually warming they are becoming ever more violent. No one wants to be in the path of one of these freaks of nature.

Probably the most famous tornado of all time exists only in a work of fiction. Once there lived a little girl named Dorothy. Dorothy lived with her aunt and uncle in Kansas during the Depression. One day a violent tornado struck their house. This powerful storm takes Dorothy and her little dog Toto to an entirely new world. There is not one single thing in this new world that resembles the world in which she previously lived. In this new world there is immense beauty—beauty of which Dorothy had never dreamed. There is also danger. Along the way Dorothy develops friendships with a Scarecrow who needs a brain, a Tin Man who wants a heart, and a Cowardly Lion who desperately needs courage. Together these four, plus Toto, have a mighty adventure. By the time Dorothy returns home to Kansas she learns many lessons about life. (1)

Our lesson from the Epistle on this Pentecost Sunday begins with the sound of a violent wind. We have no reason to believe it was a tornado. No damage was recorded. Nevertheless this wind filled the room where the disciples of Jesus were gathered. The disciples did not realize it at the time, but this wind would carry them on an adventure that would last for the rest of their lives—an adventure both fascinating and frightening, delightful and dangerous, life-changing and life-surrendering.

You know the story. On the Day of Pentecost a violent wind filled the house where the disciples were gathered and what seemed to be tongues of fire came to rest on each of them. All of them were filled with the Holy Spirit and began to speak in other tongues as the Spirit enabled them.

The Day of Pentecost was a Jewish holy day, and the city was filled with Jews from every known nation on earth. When they heard the sound of this violent wind and the disciples speaking in various languages, a crowd gathered in bewilderment.

One reason they were bewildered was that each person in the crowd heard their own language being spoken. Remember they represented every nation known at that time—and yet each of them heard the disciples in their own language. It was like the United Nations General Assembly where a speaker is speaking in his or her own language and interpreters are translating the words and transferring them to the delegates through head-sets. Except there were no interpreters or head-sets when this happened on the day of Pentecost—only the Holy Spirit. Utterly amazed, people in the crowd asked: "Aren't all these who are speaking Galileans? Then how is it that each of us hears them in our native language? What does this mean?"

Well, what does it mean? Good question.

For one thing, it means that God was there. There is no other explanation for Pentecost. The wind, the tongues of fire, the crowd who heard the Gospel each in his own language—this was a world-changing event. God was giving birth to a new movement, a movement that was destined to sweep across the earth.

Do you think it was coincidental that this miracle occurred at a time when Jews from every nation were in Jerusalem? Of course not. This was in the plan of God. God was preparing the way for the Gospel to enter every land. We are a universal faith and that was exactly what God intended. One day "every knee shall bow" St. Paul tells us in Philippians 2:10—not just every Western knee nor every Caucasian knee nor every Bible-belt knee—but every knee on this earth will bow at the name of Jesus.

That's not just wishful thinking. It is a prophecy being fulfilled even as we speak. We mentioned a few weeks ago that even though the Christian movement has stalled for a while in America and Europe, it is exploding in many parts of the world. It's an exciting thing. Look at the record. In 1900 80% of all Christians lived in Europe or America. Today that statistic has been halved: only 40% of Christians live in Europe or America; and fully 60% live in the developing world.

Of the world's six billion people, more than two billion are now Christians— one-third of the world's population. There are 480 million Christians now in Latin America. There are 313 million in Asia. There are 360 million in Africa. Central and South America in the last generation have experienced an explosion of Christian converts. In Asia, China continues to be the big story. David Aikman in Jesus in Beijing estimates that there are currently 100 million Christians in China, most of whom worship largely in underground churches. (2)

We are a universal movement. It was no accident that the Spirit of God fell upon the church on this particular day when so many foreigners were present in Jerusalem. This was God's plan all along. All the world's people will someday be God's people. That's the promise of Scripture.

Notice the second miracle that took place that day: the change that occurred in the lives of the disciples. Remember, these men who were testifying had basically been in seclusion since Christ's crucifixion out of fear of the Roman authorities. The resurrection buoyed their spirits but it did not change them into flaming apostles of Jesus Christ boldly proclaiming his name and performing miracles that all the world could witness. Yet here they were witnessing in such a way that even strangers who spoke no Hebrew or Aramaic, knew what they were saying.

Of course some of the onlookers made fun of them. There are cynics in every crowd. "They have had too much wine," some of the onlookers said. But Simon Peter put them straight in a hurry. Think of it. Simon Peter spoke up and this time he got it right. Somehow his foot-in-the-mouth disease had been cured. That alone qualifies as a miracle. Peter is uncharacteristically eloquent. He raises his voice and addresses the crowd: "Fellow Jews and all of you who live in Jerusalem, let me explain this to you; listen carefully to what I say. These people are not drunk, as you suppose. It's only nine in the morning! No, this is what was spoken by the prophet Joel: 'In the last days, God says, I will pour out my Spirit on all people. Your sons and daughters will prophesy, your young men will see visions, your old men will dream dreams. Even on my servants, both men and women, I will pour out my Spirit in those days, and they will prophesy.'" Peter spoke and the crowd listened. Miraculous.

But it wasn't just Peter who was transformed. On this day Thomas the Doubter became Thomas the Dynamic. He later took the Gospel to India where he was martyred. Simon the Zealot whose name implies that he was more interested in politics than in religion became known not for his politics but as an effective preacher of the Gospel. There are no reliable records, but tradition says he was killed for his preaching.

Nearly all of these men who were testifying eventually paid the ultimate price for their devotion to Christ. John MacArthur in his book The Twelve Disciples tells about the price they paid. Peter was crucified upside down because he felt unworthy to die as his Lord had died. (This occurred under the persecutions of the Emperor Nero in about 65-67 A.D.) Andrew died lashed to a cross rather than being nailed to it—in order to prolong his suffering.

James wanted a crown of glory; Jesus gave him a cup of suffering. He was the first of the Twelve killed for his faith. Herod Agrippa I had him beheaded (Acts 12:1-3). Philip was martyred by stoning at Heliopolis (Asia Minor) 8 years after the death of James. Stephen, of course, was stoned to death as the apostle Paul, then known as Saul, looked on.

There is no reliable record of how the disciple Nathanael died; one report said he was tied in a sack and thrown in the sea; another says he was crucified. There is no doubt he was martyred. Early traditions say Matthew was burned at the stake.

Nothing is known about the fate of James the Less or Matthias, the disciple who was chosen by the casting of lots to replace Judas in Acts 1. They were rather obscure figures, but undoubtedly they paid a price as well.

Only one of the twelve disciples probably died a natural death—the beloved disciple John, the one to whom was given the care of Jesus' mother. It is said he died in 98 A.D. According to Jerome, John was so frail in his final days at Ephesus that he had to be carried into the church. One phrase was constantly on his lips: "My little children love one another. It is the Lord's command, and if this alone be done, it is enough." (3)

Can there be any doubt that something miraculous happened on the Day of Pentecost—something that could only have come from God? The writer of Acts tells us that three thousand people were added to the church that day. What an outpouring of the Holy Spirit that was!

Notice a third thing: these were ordinary people who were used by God in an extraordinary way. None of these men were high-powered executives, none were entertainment superstars or high government officials. They were very ordinary men with ordinary dreams until the Holy Spirit fell upon them on the Day of Pentecost.

Andrew Lloyd Weber and Timothy Rice got it right in their portrayal of the disciples in their 1971 rock musical Jesus Christ Superstar. Remember that one song sung by the disciples?

Always hoped that I'd be an Apostle,
Knew that I would make it if I tried.
Then when we retire we can write the gospels
So they'll all talk about us when we die.

The disciples were very much like you and me. Before Pentecost they were still looking out primarily for their own selfish interests. They were weak, confused men who were caught up in something they didn't really understand. But after Pentecost they were so transformed that they turned the world upside down.

Wouldn't you love to see such a miracle take place in this church today? It could happen, but every one of us would need to surrender ourselves to God like the disciples surrendered themselves to God. We would need to pray that whatever it costs, God would use us to touch our family members, touch our neighbors, touch our co-workers as the disciples touched the lives of people around them. We would need to become new people. We would need to pray that the Holy Spirit would work through us in such a way that we could make a real difference in our community.

Some of us would need to overcome things like our shyness and timidity to do that. Pastor Edward Markquart of Seattle, Washington tells about someone he knows who did just that. He was a young man named David Hughes and, at the time, he was a blocking back for the Seattle Seahawks professional football team. Hughes came to Markquart's church to the men's Bible study to speak publicly for the first time about Christ.

Hughes told the men gathered there that he was more scared of talking to them about Christ than he was of preparing for a professional football game.

"He was not a professionally groomed Christian speaker," says Markquart, "and that was what was good about him. He just quietly told what had happened in his life. He told of the time when he was eleven years old and his father, a policeman, was killed, and they had a huge police escort at his father's funeral. The eleven year old David was strong . . . or so he thought . . . and fought back all tears. Time passed. Years passed. Recently, a policeman in Seattle was shot to death, and there was an enormous police escort at this policeman's funeral. [Witnessing this event] David Hughes pulled his car off to the side of the road and started to cry intensely, after fourteen years. For fourteen years, the feelings from his father's own funeral had been bottled up in him, but now he was ready to talk. He talked about the importance of reading his Bible every day, of praying every day, of worshiping God every day."

Edward Markquart says, "I was so glad we heard this man before he got professional with his words, while he still had a nervous stomach, while he had not learned to be smooth in his delivery. God touched David Hughes' heart, spirit and tongue so that he spoke the right words to us." (4)

That's what happened on the Day of Pentecost more than two thousand years ago. The Holy Spirit fell on a group of untrained, uneducated Galileans and they started speaking with such sincerity and power that everyone who heard knew immediately what they were saying and were touched by their words. Could it happen again . . . in our church?

I pray that the Holy Spirit will take my words and translate them in your life so that you will know that Jesus Christ is your Savior. I pray that you will be led by that same Spirit to translate God's love to everyone you meet to the end that the day will draw nearer when everyone on earth will know himself or herself to be a child of God. If each of us could surrender ourselves to God's Holy Spirit, it will hasten the day when every knee will bow and every tongue confess that Jesus Christ is Lord to the Glory of God the Father. Wouldn't you like to see that happen? It can. God is here today just as he was there long ago. All God needs is for each of us to surrender to His leading. Are you ready for a mighty adventure today? We don't have to hear the sound of a mighty wind. God also speaks in a still small voice. Let us pray to hear God's voice today.

1. The Wizard of Oz, 1939.
2. Michael T. Parker,
http://www.unitedparishbowie.org/parker/sermon_unbelieving_thomas.html
3. Twelve Ordinary Men by John MacArthur, p. 198.
4. http://www.sermonsfromseattle.com/series_c_reluctant.htm.

Breaking Loose
Romans 8:14-17
(Trinity Sunday)

Charles Simpson of Mobile, Alabama tells of meeting a young man who dives for exotic fish for aquariums. This adventurous young man said that one of the most popular aquarium fish is the shark. He explained that if you catch a small shark and confine it, it will stay at a size proportionate to the aquarium. Sharks can be six inches long yet fully matured. But if you turn them loose in the ocean, they grow to their normal length of eight feet. (1)

Mother Nature is amazing. How does the shark know that it could outgrow its surroundings, I wonder, and by what mechanism does it quit growing?

Years ago Dr. James Dobson told about an interesting experiment that was conducted with wall-eyed pike, a fish commonly found in the northern U.S and Canada.

A pike was placed in a fish-tank with minnows (a food which wall-eyed pike dearly love). A pane of glass was inserted across the middle of the tank between the minnows and the pike. At first, the pike would bang into the glass time and time again trying to reach the minnows. Finally it gave up.

Here is what is interesting, however. When the glass was completely removed, the wall-eye pike still did not chase after the minnows. In fact, the minnows could swim around the pike, even bumping him on the mouth, and the pike would not try to eat them. What the researchers discovered was that, once conditioned, wall-eyed pike will starve to death without ever bothering to try to catch one of those minnows. You see, in its mind it has been taught it cannot get to them! (2)

It's a theme that you see time after time in nature.

A writer named Clarence Harvey tells about an experience he had as a boy. One summer he was packing to spend three months with relatives at a lake which was up north from where they lived. His dad said for him to take his pet gold-fish with him. His father said he didn't want to take care of a fish all summer.

So, one day after they got up to the lake, young Clarence decided to become a liberator. He went down to the dock with his fish bowl and gave his fish a little talk. "I'm going to throw you in this lake," he said. "You will be free. You can eat well here and grow up to be a big fish."

However, when Clarence put the gold fish in the water at the end of the dock, it stayed right there. He backed off, thinking, perhaps, that the fish was attached to his shadow. But when he moved back to be sure it was gone, it was still right there. He even threw a stone into the water to scare it away, but that gold fish just swam around the stone.

When he came back after lunch, the gold-fish was still there, swimming in the same spot. Clarence sat down and thought, "That fish should be free. It's got the whole lake to swim in." Suddenly he saw in the water a huge ripple. Whop! A big bass swallowed his little gold-fish.

Later in life someone told him that a gold-fish, "once it has lived in a circumference of a certain size, has been conditioned to think small. It will stay there until it dies—swimming around in that small circle." (3)

That's fascinating to me. Psychological conditioning can be powerful stuff, if you can call it that when speaking of sharks, wall-eyed pike and gold-fish.

Now what does our lesson for the day from Paul's letter to the Romans have to do with these creatures of the sea? Just this: St. Paul is writing to believers to tell them that they do not have to give in to the fear-induced limitations of their old lives any longer. They no longer need to be enslaved by petty thoughts and meaningless dreams. Christ has come so that they can be free. The Holy Spirit has come to take off the chains from their hearts and their minds that they may soar as they have never soared before. This is the Father's will for us, Paul declares to them, that we shall live in faith, not fear.

Listen to his words: "For those who are led by the Spirit of God are the children of God. The Spirit you received does not make you slaves, so that you live in fear again; rather, the Spirit you received brought about your adoption to sonship. And by him we cry, 'Abba, Father.' The Spirit himself testifies with our spirit that we are God's children. Now if we are children, then we are heirs—heirs of God and co-heirs with Christ, if indeed we share in his sufferings in order that we may also share in his glory."

Do you hear what St. Paul is saying to us? He's saying that some of us are letting our circumstances and not our faith dictate how we feel about life. We are letting our fears and our doubts enslave us. God's purpose is that we may not give in to our circumstances but they we might overcome them—that we might break loose from the bonds that keep us from being all God created us to be.

It is sad to see anyone who has been broken by life. Some people have bumped into obstacles for so long that they have quit trying. Life has been so painful for them that they have built a fence around themselves with the sole purpose of ensuring that they are never hurt again. They have been conditioned to accept limitations that may exist only in their own minds.

Dr. Walter Larimore says that one time he and his wife Barb were visiting friends whose neighbor had a young golden retriever which was confined to the yard by an electronic fence. The fence had a buried cable that would cause a probe in the dog's collar to lightly shock the dog if she got too close to the underground wire. So she stayed in the yard. Safe, never straying, but always looking longingly at the edge of the bay that lapped up next to the property.

The Larimores and their friends were sitting on the back porch one day when some people came down the beach with a set of puppies. Exuberant in their energy, the puppies were chasing sticks being thrown into the water.

Larimore watched the golden retriever's ears cock forward and her tail wag ferociously as she watched the pups frolicking in the surf. She slowly crept up to the buried wire of the invisible electric fence. The retriever knew where she was called to be, and it was not within the safety of the yard. Her heart longed to join the puppies in the water she loved—the waves where she was meant to play.

Larimore wondered if she would risk the momentary shock. Was the memory of the pain she had experienced in the past too scary? As the family slowly moved down the beach, the dog stayed in the yard. When the playful puppies were out of view, the retriever sunk down, Larimore declares, and literally moaned.

The next morning while out for a walk Dr. Larimore met the dog's owner and shared his observations from the evening before. The owner laughed. "You know," he said, "we've had that wire turned off for several weeks now."

Larimore says he felt a pang of sadness. It was the pain of the retriever's past that was keeping that dog imprisoned. If she had only known, she could have been free to be who she was created to be. (4)

That is sad. But it doesn't just happen to golden retrievers. It happens to Homo Sapiens as well. How many painful experiences can a person have before they just quit trying? How many rejections? How many failures?

Many people today without jobs are learning how cruel the world can be to you if you don't have the right connections, don't have an income, don't have a way of making your mortgage payment or providing for your family's basic needs.

Other people have had their hearts broken in relationships enough times that they have concluded that they are unworthy to be loved. It's sad to see anyone who has been broken by life, who is enslaved by negative emotions, who has given in to a spirit of fear and self-loathing. That is one of the reasons Christ came into the world. He came to deliver us from desperate, meaningless lives. He came to give us hope and a sense of well-being. How does that happen? Paul tells us in this passage from Romans.

First of all, he reminds us who we are. Listen again to his words, "For those who are led by the Spirit of God are the children of God. The Spirit you received does not make you slaves, so that you live in fear again; rather, the Spirit you received brought about your adoption to sonship. And by him we cry, 'Abba, Father.' The Spirit himself testifies with our spirit that we are God's children . . ."

You and I are God's children. Do you understand what that means? We have an innate dignity, a reason for being that should allow us to live with heads held high, knowing we are loved. It is a sad thing when a person loses sight of who he or she is.

Annette Simmons in her book The Story Factor tells a wonderful story about

Tipper Gore, the ex-wife of former Vice-President Al Gore. I suspect that most people were saddened to learn that Al and Tipper Gore divorced sometime back. Tipper was an asset to our country when Al was Vice President.

In those days Tipper volunteered regularly to aid the homeless around the Lafayette Park area of Washington, D.C. She helped to provide food, shelter, and other services. Annette Simmons tells about one particular homeless woman that Tipper helped. Her name was Mary. Mary was always in or around Lafayette Park.

The volunteers' goal one particular day was to transport the homeless people in the Lafayette Park area to a shelter for a healthy lunch. Mary would not leave the park. Why would she not leave? It was because she was convinced in her own mind that she was married to the president of the United States, Bill Clinton. And for this reason no amount of cajoling could convince her to leave the Lafayette Park area.

Tipper came up with an idea. She asked Mary if she would accompany her to the guardhouse next to the White House. As they approached, the guard immediately recognized Tipper. As the guard watched, Tipper stood behind Mary and shook her head, "no" to the guard. The guard looked puzzled but knew something was up so he followed her lead.

Tipper said to the guard, "I have Mrs. Clinton here." After the briefest pause, he nodded in deference. "Mrs. Clinton wants to come with us," Tipper continued, "to have some lunch. Could you give us a pen and paper and see that President Clinton gets our message that she is with us. We don't want him to worry."

The guard snapped to attention and said, "I most certainly will." Mary wrote her "husband" Bill a note and was then happy to leave the park and go to the shelter for lunch. This was a turning point for Mary. Ultimately, reports Annette Simmons, Mary was reunited with her family, given medication, and now has a full-time job and a home. (5)

Now obviously Mary was delusional. Still Tipper Gore's compassion made it possible for Mary to regain a sense of her own identity. Christ came, St. Paul tells us, and he sent his Holy Spirit to us, to help us know who we are: we are God's adopted children.

When Steve Jobs died last year much was made out of the fact that he had been deserted as a child and then adopted. One of the reasons it was suggested that he accomplished so much was that his adoptive parents emphasized to him that the fact of his adoption made him a special child. He was so special that they chose him out of all the rest of the children to be their son.

We're told by Bible scholars that St. Paul's words carried that same idea. To be adopted in the Roman world was to be specially selected to be a part of a household in order to carry on the family's name and to inherit their property. To be adopted was considered a great privilege.

Do you understand that you are God's adopted child specially selected to be part of His family and heir to life eternal? Don't ever get to the point that you get down on yourself and give up no matter how much hurt and pain you have experienced to this point in your life.

God's will is for you to overcome your circumstances, whatever they may be, by trusting in His love. Writes St. Paul, "The Spirit you received does not make you slaves, so that you live in fear again; rather, the Spirit you received brought about your adoption to sonship . . . The Spirit himself testifies with our spirit that we are God's children."

Comedian Charlie Chaplin once said that the greatest gift that his mother gave to him was a large view of life. When his mother was eighteen, she eloped with a middle-aged man and they went to live in Africa.

The marriage was a failure, so she returned to London and married a struggling artist who fathered Charlie, but then died at thirty-seven. Chaplin's mother, once a singer, lost her voice; she lived on the edge of poverty, but nevertheless entrusted to her son a precious gift—the belief he could adjust to any situation. Said Chaplin: "Mother was always able to stand outside her environment." (6)

That's what we must do sometimes—by the grace of God, live outside our environment. Someone asks us how we are doing and we reply, "Oh, all right, under the circumstances."

God's will is for us to get on top of our circumstances, not under them. Don't let life break you down. You are God's own child. You have not been given a spirit of fear but a spirit of sonship . . . or of daughtership, if I may coin a word. Take the chains off of your brain and your heart. You are free—free to be everything God created you to be.

I like the way Bruce Larson once put it: God has better things for us. Unfortunately, much of the time we're like the caterpillar, who watches a butterfly fly by and says to himself, 'You'll never get me up in one of those things.' God has a better dream for us than we can imagine. If we can shed our prison, our cocoon, we may even fly." (7)

Are you ready to fly? Nothing is impossible to the sons and daughters of God.

1. Pastoral Renewal, date unknown.
2. Dare to Discipline (Wheaton, IL: Tyndale House, Publishers, 1970).
3. Net Results, Feb. 1991. Cited in Parables, Etc, date unknown.
4. 10 Essentials of Highly Healthy People (Grand Rapids: Zondervan, 2003), p. 204.
5. Secrets of Influence from the Art of Storytelling (New York: Basic Books, 2001).
6. Edward Paul Cohn in James W. Cox, Editor, Best Sermons, Vol. 1 (San Francisco: Harper & Row Publishers, 1988).
7. The Presence (New York: HarperSanFrancisco, 1988), p. 63.

Toss Your Cap Over The Wall
Mark 3:20-35

Even though this is baseball season, I want to begin with a basketball story. It is about Michael Jordan, perhaps the greatest professional basketball player of all time. One night he scored sixty-nine points in a single game.

In that same game, rookie Stacey King made his inauspicious debut. He shot one free throw and made it. After the final buzzer, a reporter asked King for his thoughts on the game. Stacey King, with tongue planted firmly in his cheek, replied: "I'll always remember this as the night that Michael Jordan and I combined for 70 points."

Well, I guess that is one way to look at it.

Michael Jordan was a great basketball player. And yet John Eliot, in his book titled Overachievement, claims that Michael Jordan was not really a very gifted basketball player. For example, Jordan ranked ninth in the NBA for field goals made and eighteenth in total points. He never ranked first in any major NBA statistic. Even in his prime, Jordan was not the fastest or most accurate shooter; he certainly was not a rebounder or brilliant at defense. (1)

Yet Jordan is considered the greatest player of his era, and maybe the best ever. How did a poor defender and average shooter get to be a five time NBA MVP— not to mention earn the reputation as the best hoops player on the planet? Passion? Confidence? Determination? All of these were involved, of course. Michael Jordan, who famously was cut from his middle school team, simply set out to be the best he could be and the rest is history.

There is a part of almost everyone that is thrilled when someone attempts to reach lofty goals. The pioneer, the successful entrepreneur, the victorious athlete— all speak to us about the ability of the human spirit to achieve monumental accomplishments when properly motivated. Vicariously, we share in their achievements and find hope for our own lives in their successes.

President John F. Kennedy's hero was his grandfather, and he loved to hear stories about his grandfather's boyhood in Ireland. One of these stories concerned how Grandfather Fitzgerald used to walk home from school each day with a group of friends. Sometimes these boys would challenge each other to climb over the stone walls along the lanes of the countryside.

However, there were times when young Fitzgerald and the other boys were sometimes hesitant to dare the hazardous climbs. So they devised a way to motivate themselves to take the risk involved: they would toss their caps over the wall. You see, they knew that they dare not go home without their caps, so then they had to climb over the walls to get them. They tossed their caps over the wall as a way of motivating themselves to take a risk. The poet said, "A man's reach should exceed his grasp, or what's a heaven for?" And it is true.

There are times when all of us long to toss our caps over the wall. There are times when we hunger in our own way for the heroic—whether we want to change jobs, start our own business, go back to school, or whatever. There come those times in life when we feel the need to make a change.

I know of one young man in particular who decided to make such a change. He was thirty years old at the time, and he owned a successful small business which had been left to him by his father. He was secure, he was liked and respected by his friends and neighbors, and he was meeting his responsibilities. But he knew that this was not where he belonged. He felt called to a ministry—a ministry of teaching and preaching and healing. And so, he threw his cap over the wall.

At first he met with spectacular success, and his reputation spread with amazing speed. But as his popularity increased, so did the number of his critics, especially in his home town. Some of his closest friends tried to dissuade him from his insanity, and his family was also concerned for him. But he persevered in his new calling for three years, only to die an untimely death.

As he hung on a tree between two thieves—dying a cruel and unjust death, feeling forsaken by both God and man—no one would have judged his life to be a success. But it was. It was the most successful life ever lived. For all of this took place around Nazareth more than 2000 years ago. Jesus tossed his cap over the wall, and you and I are thankful that he did. He modeled for us what the life of adventure should truly be.

Early in the twentieth century the world thrilled as Colonel Charles Lindbergh flew his little sprucewood plane solo across the Atlantic. As he was leaving the last stretches of land in Nova Scotia and Newfoundland, he kept looking down on the forests and lakes and valleys and thinking that if an emergency arose he would land in that little clearing beside the river, or he would clear that little clump of trees and land in that lake. But soon there were no more clearings, no more clumps of trees—only ocean. His cap was over the wall.

James Freeman tells of touring Salt Lake City and visiting with his Mormon guide. The young man told him that his grandmother had come to Salt Lake City in the early days when the Mormons had first come to Utah. Apparently she had traveled all the way from Omaha on foot, pushing a handcart. Can you imagine that? Across deserts and mountains she pushed a handcart. But the people of her faith were waiting at the end of her journey. Her cap was over the wall.

Doesn't it make your blood run faster, to know that there are people who have charted a heroic course for their lives and seen it through? There are times in everyone's life when they need to toss their cap over the wall.

Of course, no one has ever accomplished anything of note without critics. Toss your cap over a wall and you learn very quickly who your true friends are.

Winston Churchill, truly a man of heroic stature, was one of the most criticized politicians who ever lived. But he knew how to handle his detractors.

Perhaps the most famous of Churchill's exchanges was one he had at a state dinner with Nancy Astor, whose own reputation for acid wit and instant repartee was considerable.

During this dinner Lady Astor was compelled to listen to Churchill expound his views on a great number of subjects, all of them at variance with her own strongly held views. Finally, no longer able to hold her tongue, she spat, "Winston, if you were my husband, I would flavor your coffee with poison."

To which Churchill immediately replied, "Madam, if I were your husband, I should drink it." (2)

No one accomplishes anything of note without critics. Certainly Jesus had his critics. In today's lesson from Mark's Gospel Jesus is still in the early part of his ministry. However, people are starting to take note of him. He has chosen his twelve disciples who will carry on the work after he is gone and the crowds are growing larger. Momentum is building toward a magnificent ministry.

But almost immediately he runs into opposition. First of all, it was from his own family. Mark tells us that when Jesus' family heard about what was happening, they went to take charge of him, for they said, "He is out of his mind."

Can you imagine that? Jesus' family wanted him to shut down his ministry and come home. Isn't this the way life is? Sometimes it is those closest to us who have the hardest time coming to grips with our dreams and aspirations. Often husbands and wives especially have problems because of this.

I like the story about the first grade teacher who was taking her pupils on a field trip to the local zoo. Each child was given a turn at guessing the names of the various animals. The camel, lion, giraffe, bear, and the elephant all were named correctly.

Then it got to be a little boy's turn. The teacher pointed to a deer and asked him if he knew what it was.

He hesitated for a long time, looking unsure of himself. So the teacher tried to prompt him by telling him to think of what his mother called his father at home.

The boy brightened up immediately: "So that's what a baboon looks like!"

I won't ask you if your spouse has ever called you a baboon. But I can assure you that anyone who seeks to make a dramatic change in their life is going to encounter criticism and tension. Sometimes it will come from your own family.

Or it may come from colleagues. In Jesus' case, it was the teachers of the law who had come down from Jerusalem. With a poisonous sneer they greeted his teachings like this, "He is possessed by Beelzebul! By the prince of demons he is driving out demons."

That's the way life is. Start to make waves and somebody will try to wrest the oars out of your hands by belittling your work. One author has called this the "Salk Theory."

Jonas Salk, that great doctor of medicine who pioneered polio research and discovered the Polio Vaccine, had a legion of critics he dealt with over the years. At one point, he made an interesting observation about the nature of criticism, which seems to hold true for any person who is successfully innovative.

"First," he said, "people will tell you that you are wrong. Then they will tell you that you are right, but what you're doing really isn't important. Finally, they will admit that you are right and that what you are doing is very important; but after all, they knew it all the time." (3)

We all have our critics. The best way to answer your critics is to do as the builder of the Panama Canal did. He had to endure carping criticisms from countless busybodies back home who predicted that he would never complete his great task. But the resolute builder pressed steadily forward in his work and said nothing. One of his subordinates, irritated by the flak they were receiving, asked the great engineer if he was ever going to answer his critics. "In time," he said, "when the canal is finished."

There comes a time when we toss our caps over the wall in spite of everything the critics have to say. Nothing is ever accomplished by people who value comfort and safety and acceptance above all else. There comes a time for what is often called a leap of faith.

Of course the greatest adventure that one can start out on—the most spectacular, and often the most courageous change that can be made in a life—is that of becoming a disciple of Jesus Christ.

Now it is unfortunate that, for the most part, that statement will fall on deaf ears. All too often we confuse discipleship with membership in the church. Or we confuse discipleship with respectability. But there is certainly no particular risk involved in being respectable or belonging to a church. But, to become a disciple of Jesus Christ, to move from a nominal belief to a radical conviction, to move from a nodding acquaintance with God to a complete commitment of one's life, that is more of a challenge for the human creature than digging a canal, or finding a cure for polio or being the best basketball player in the world.

I was reading about Noel Paul Stookey's conversion to Jesus Christ. Some of you might know of Stookey by the beautiful wedding song that he wrote:

He is now to be among you at the calling of your hearts
Rest assured this troubadour is acting on His part.
The union of your spirits, here, has caused Him to remain
For whenever two or more of you are gathered in His name
There is Love, there is Love. (4)

Others of you might know Paul Stookey as the second member of the 1960s folk singing trio, "Peter, Paul and Mary."

At one point in his life, Stookey was going through a time of searching and crisis. He was disturbed by the hypocrisy in his life. And he turned to an old Greenwich Village friend named Bob Dylan for advice.

Two things that Dylan said stood out in Stookey's mind: One, go for a long walk in the country, and two, read the Bible. Paul took the advice. He walked in the country, and it helped him sort out his priorities. And he read the Bible. Although his folk group had sung several spirituals and gospel tunes, Stookey had never opened a Bible before. But now he read through the entire New Testament and parts of the Old. He had a hard time with some of it: it was slow and often mysterious. But something real happened in Paul Stookey's life then, and today he is living as a disciple of Jesus Christ. (5) His cap is over the wall.

Isn't it time for some of us to toss our cap over the wall? A certain high jumper was referring to a world record he set in his sport. He said he threw his heart over the bar and the rest of him followed. Perhaps you and I need to throw our hearts over the altar, so that we may follow.

It is exciting to read about the early days of Jesus' ministry. He had his critics, of course. But he never let them detract him from his call. His life is a challenge to our lives. It is time for us to toss our cap over the wall as well.

1 The New Model for Exceptional Performance (New York: Penguin Group, Inc., 2004), pp. 118-119.
2. Leon A. Harris, The Fine Art Of Political Wit (E.P. Dutton.)
3. Michael and Donna Nason, Robert Schuller: His Story (New York: Jove Books, 1983).
4. Copyright 1971 by the Public Domain Foundation.
5. Fred Hartley, 100% Beyond Mediocrity (Old Tappan, N.J.: Fleming H. Revell Co., 1983).

The Awesome Power Of A Mustard Seed
Mark 4:26-34
(Father's Day)

A man was out on the golf course. He spotted another man who seemingly had four caddies. "Why so many caddies?" the first man asked the second.

The second golfer replied, "It's my wife's idea. She thinks I should spend more time with the kids."

Well, that's one way of doing it. I suspect he's the same Dad who was asked by his wife when they brought home their first baby to help with changing diapers.

"I'm busy," he said, "I'll do the next one."

The next time came around and she asked again. The husband looked puzzled, "Oh! I didn't mean the next diaper. I meant the next baby!"

If that doesn't make you laugh, it'll make you cry. Welcome on this Father's Day 2012.

We lost a very popular cartoonist a few years back—Bill Keane of the Family Circus cartoon strip. In one of his most memorable cartoons we see Dad relaxing in his easy chair trying to read the paper. He turns to see little Billy carrying his ball, bat and glove. Billy says, "Anytime you're ready, Daddy, I'll be sitting outside growing older."

Ooh, that hurts. It's not easy being a Dad just as it is not easy being a Mom. Of course, there are times when dads come in handy.

I read recently about a beautiful wedding in which a radiant bride processed down the aisle on the arm of her father. They reached the altar where the smiling groom stood waiting. The bride kissed her father and placed something in his hand.

It was . . . his credit card. Sometimes dads do come in handy.

Comic Robin Fairbanks says, "I have an 18-year-old; her name is Alexis. I chose that name because if I hadn't had her, I'd be driving one." (1)

It's not easy, particularly in today's world, to be a Dad. Kids today expect so much. I personally like comedian Phyllis Diller's comment. She said, "I want my children to have all the things I couldn't afford. Then I want to move in with them."

Just kidding, of course.

Our text for the day isn't designed specifically for fathers. It is designed, rather, for followers, followers of Jesus Christ. The Master is talking about the kingdom of God and he speaks hopeful words about the days ahead. He says, "What shall we say the kingdom of God is like, or what parable shall we use to describe it? It is like a mustard seed, which is the smallest of all seeds on earth. Yet when planted, it grows and becomes the largest of all garden plants, with such big branches that the birds can perch in its shade."

Some of us may have a misconception about the plant which comes forth from a mustard seed. There is no such thing as a mustard tree. If you're thinking of a tree like a mighty redwood emanating from a tiny mustard seed, you are mistaken. If Jesus had been teaching in California, he might have used a giant redwood and talked about the miracle of the acorn. The principle would have been the same. However, he was teaching in Palestine. And so he chose the mustard seed.

The mustard plant is a shrub, but in that part of the world it is the largest of all the shrubs. It is large enough for birds to nestle in its branches. The point of the parable is the same, however. From a tiny seed major accomplishments may emerge.

An example of that growth is the story of the early church. It began with only the Master and twelve disciples and an unknown number of women. We must not forget the women; they were there from the very beginning giving their support, sharing their witness. But look at how much that tiny group has grown.

It is estimated that there are now 2.1 billion (yes, billion) Christians in the world (about one third of the total population of the planet), and we are still growing. While it is true that churches in the West have slowed their growth, and some churches have actually declined, there are places, particularly in Asia and South America, where the Gospel is exploding. From the smallest of seeds, the mightiest of all plants has grown.

But the church is itself a seed. God planted us in the world to make a difference in the world. And even though we have been a flawed group of people through the ages, the influence that this group of people has had upon our world cannot be overstated.

Many of the values of Western civilization are rooted in Jesus and the Scriptures. For example, all the hospitals in America were originally Christian hospitals. All the colleges in America were originally Christian colleges. The civil rights movement had its origin in the Scriptures. We are continually reminded of how male-oriented the scriptures are, but tell me any religion on earth that has freed as many women as Jesus has.

As one observer has noted, even our system of government is a product of those values. Where did our Constitution come from? It was authored by Thomas Jefferson. Where did he get his ideas? The French Enlightenment. Where did the French Enlightenment get its ideas? The Renaissance. Where did the Renaissance get its ideas? The Reformation. Where did the Reformation get its ideas? From the Bible. (2)

A tiny seed planted more than two thousand years ago is slowly changing the world. Not as quickly as God would like. Sometimes Christian people are a barrier rather than a bridge to a better world. Still, that seed is growing until the day comes when every knee shall bow and every tongue confess that Jesus Christ is Lord (Philippians 2:8-11). There is indeed power in what we might call "mustard seed faith."

Of course, parents see the power of mustard seed faith all the time. A baby is born into a household. Can you imagine the significance of that event? Every baby born into this world represents hope for a new beginning.

It is said that Queen Victoria was fascinated by the brilliance of the scholars who made up England's Royal Society. On one occasion she whispered to Prime Minister John Bright, "Where do all these learned men come from?"

Bright replied, "From babies, your Majesty, from babies." Every time a baby is born into the world a potential mustard seed of greatness is planted.

It's like a small church in rural Kentucky which over the years has produced several outstanding clergy. While interviewing a new slate of pastoral candidates, a member of the search committee mentioned the former pastors from that small church who had gone on to serve in prominent church positions—one as president of a seminary and pastor of a large city church, another also as a seminary president, and a third as president of two denominational conventions and an international alliance.

"How in the world did you find that many potentially great men in this little church?" the astonished candidate asked.

"Find them!" said the committee member. "We didn't find them. We made them!" (3)

And of course that committee member was right. Our children are our most important product as a church. That is why we must make our ministry to both our children and our youth all that those ministries can possibly be.

Don M. Aycock in his book Symbols of Salvation tells of an Italian film with the unusual title, "Tree of the Wooden Clogs." This film portrays the plight of Italian peasants at the close of the nineteenth century. In one scene the village priest is shown talking with the parents of a 5-year-old boy. They are quite poor. The boy's father wants the boy to stay at home, work around the farm and help support the family. The priest tells him the family must send the boy to school since God has given the boy the gift of intelligence. He explains that the potential of the whole world is wrapped up in that fuzzy-headed boy. The parents agree, at first reluctantly, to send the boy to school. They know the priest is right . . . children hold the world's potential in their often dirty little hands. (4)

I love the way Pablo Casals, the world-renowned cellist, once described it: "What do we teach our children? We teach them that two and two make four and that Paris is the capital of France. When will we also teach them what they are? We should say to each of them: Do you know what you are? You are a marvel! You are unique . . . there has never been another child like you. Your legs, your arms, your clever fingers, the way you move. You may become a Shakespeare, a Michelangelo, a Beethoven. You have the capacity for anything. Yes, you are a marvel . . ." (5)

They are a marvel. Children are the primary mustard seed that our church is sowing. If we do our job right, they will be ambassadors of Christ making the King-dom of God ever more of a reality in a world which badly needs saving.

This is to say that one way we can serve God is by helping our young ones know who they are and what God can do through them.

I guess this is turning into a Father's Day message after all. But of course it's not just for fathers. It is for everyone in this room. You don't have to be a parent or a grandparent or an aunt or an uncle to influence a child's life. Everyone in this room directly or indirectly influences our children whether you are a parent or not. Some of the finest teachers in the history of the Sunday School movement have had no children of their own.

Dr. Fred Craddock, the eminent retired seminary professor who has influenced so many pastors across our land once told of the teacher who most influenced him.

Her name was, "Miss Emma Sloan." Miss Sloan was an elderly woman, single. She taught him in the primary department, and since there was nobody to teach his group as juniors, she went right on with them, and taught them for years. She gave him a Bible. She wrote in the front: "May this be a light to your feet, a lamp for your path. Emma Sloan." She taught the children to memorize the Bible; she never tried to interpret it. Craddock says he doesn't remember her ever explaining anything. She said, "Just put it in your heart, just put it in your heart."

She used the alphabet, and they'd go around the room saying verses. "A—A soft answer turns away wrath. B—Be ye kind, one to another, tenderhearted, for-giving each other, as God also in Christ has forgiven you. C—Come unto me, all you who labor and are heavy laden. D—Do unto others as you would have them do unto you. E—Every good and perfect gift . . . F—For God so loved the world . . ."

He says he can still remember those verses. Miss Emma didn't explain what the verses meant. She just sowed those seeds of Scripture from the King James Bible in their hearts. They learned those verses and then recited them before the adults on Sunday afternoon. "I can't think of anything, anything in all my life that has made such a radical difference as those verses," says Fred Craddock. "The Spirit of God brings them to my mind appropriately, time and time and time again." (6)

You don't have to be a parent to have an influence on children or youth. Every teacher, every adult who speaks a word of encouragement to a young person, every church officer who votes on the budget for our children's or youth ministry makes a difference on how effective we are in ministering to children and youth.

So many people ask, what great thing can I do for God? I can't be an overseas missionary. I don't have the resources to do much to feed the hungry. But every one of us can provide the proper environment for our children and our youth to grow in an atmosphere of love, support and spiritual guidance. Our children are the mus-tard seeds that God has provided us. We are to love them, nurture them and help them be all God intended them to be.

"What shall we say the kingdom of God is like, or what parable shall we use to describe it? It is like a mustard seed, which is the smallest of all seeds on earth. Yet when planted, it grows and becomes the largest of all garden plants, with such big branches that the birds can perch in its shade."

That is the story of the church. Someone summed up mustard seed faith like this: "The Son of Man grew up in a despised province; he did not appear in public until his thirtieth year; then taught for two or three years in neighboring villages, and occasionally at Jerusalem; made a few converts, chiefly among the poor and unlearned; and then falling into the hands of his enemies, died the shameful death of the cross; such, and so slight, was the commencement of the universal kingdom of God." (7)

A tiny mustard seed sown in the ground. But God brought Christ forth from the grave. And then those who had learned from him spread his story. And today two thousand years later here we sit telling that story, sowing the seed again and again. Chief among our duties is to make certain that our children and young people are well steeped in the story so that they might make it their own and pass it to their children. What a grand privilege. What a purpose that is for a life.

Some of you probably saw the movie some years back, Oh, God! starring George Burns and John Denver. Burns played God. Denver played a grocery store manager named Jerry. One day God decides to communicate his love to the world through Jerry. Jerry, with much reluctance, holds a news conference to deliver God's message. This lands him in a courtroom where God must take the stand in his defense.

Toward the end of the movie, the two evaluate the success of their mission. Denver, the manager, judges it to be a failure.

"Oh, I don't think so," says God. "You never know; a seed here and a seed there, something will catch hold and grow."

And that's the story of our faith—a seed here, a seed there. But the Kingdom is growing. One way it is growing is our ministry to children and youth. There is power, unlimited and everlasting power in a tiny mustard seed.

1. Reader's Digest

2. Edward F. Markquart, http://www.sermonsfromseattle.com/series_c_the_mustard_seed.htm.

3. Patricia Bolen, "Worshipping God in all the small places," Moody, September 1994, p. 54.

4. (Nashville: Broadman Press, 1982).

5. Dr. M. Norvel Young, Living Lights Shining Stars (West Monroe, LA: Howard Publishing Co., 1997).

6. Fred B. Craddock, Craddock Stories (St. Louis: Chalice Press, 2001).

7. R. C. Trench, Notes on the Parables of our Lord.

Why Are You So Afraid?
Mark 4:35-41

Karen Fair tells about her three-year-old daughter, Abby, who was having trouble sleeping through the night. She kept waking up because she was afraid. Each time Karen tucked her into bed again, she would remind her that Jesus was with her and that He would keep her safe.

The sleepless nights continued, with Abby seeking comfort in her parents' bedroom. Finally, one night Karen asked her daughter if she had prayed for Jesus to take her fear away and help her fall asleep.

"Oh yes," Abby assured her. "He told me to come and get you!" (1)

In our lesson for the day Jesus has been teaching by the lake. When evening came, he said to his disciples, "Let's go over to the other side." Leaving the crowd behind, they got in their boat and headed to the other side. Suddenly a furious squall came up, and the waves broke over the boat, so that it was nearly swamped. Jesus was in the stern, the back of the boat sleeping on a cushion. The disciples woke him and said to him, "Teacher, don't you care if we drown?"

Jesus got up, rebuked the wind and said to the waves, "Quiet! Be still!" Then the wind died down and it was completely calm.

Then he turned to his disciples and asked, "Why are you so afraid? Do you still have no faith?"

Then, says Mark's Gospel, they were terrified and asked each other, "Who is this? Even the wind and the waves obey him!"

That has always fascinated me. The disciples, including the sturdy fishermen that Jesus had called, were afraid of the storm, but when Jesus calmed the storm, then they really were terrified. They were terrified of his power over the wind and the waves. To me that adds so much credibility to the Gospel narrative. It shows the disciples in all their humanness. They didn't know how to take Jesus. "Who is this?" they asked. "Even the wind and the waves obey him!"

Before we deal with the question the disciples asked, we need to deal with the question Jesus asked them, "Why are you so afraid?" That is a question I could ask many of you. It is a question I could also ask myself: Why are you so afraid?

Fear is at the heart of most of the problems that human beings have. The opposite of faith is not doubt. The opposite of faith is fear. Think about it for a moment and try to tell me any problem in the human heart that is not based in fear.

Pastor Jon Walton tells about a commercial that was being shown a few years back. "There is a car that has been in an accident and it's on its side and the woman who's driving can't move," says Walton. "She's frightened and in shock. Three young black kids run to the scene and you just know what they're gonna do. They're gonna reach in that car and grab her purse and run as fast as they can and leave her bleeding inside that wrecked contortion of steel and glass. But no, that isn't what it's about at all. One of the kids sends the others for help and starts giving instructions to the driver. 'Don't move,' he says, 'everything's gonna be all right. We've gone to get help.' He knows what to do to prevent injury. It's a Shell gasoline commercial promoting safety instruction manuals on how to help in the event of an accident. And I thought," says Walton," it was another one of those portrayals of urban crime. You know, somebody's always out there to get you. What's that tell you about me? What's that tell you about you? Sometimes the greatest danger to us is not what's in the world but what's in our hearts." (2)

At the heart of bigotry and every other negative emotion is fear, fear of people who are not the same as we are, fear about our own adequacy and self-worth, fear about our ability to cope with life, fear concerning the future and the areas of life over which we have no control. At the heart of worry, resentment, hatred, guilt and almost every negative emotion—emotions that eat at our well-being and peace of mind—is fear. And so often our fears are out of proportion to reality.

Someone had made a recent trip to the beach. He said upon his return, "I discovered I scream the same way whether I'm about to be devoured by a great white shark or if a piece of seaweed touches my foot."

It's true of most of us, even if we're not aware of it. We have a tendency to turn molehills into mountains primarily because deep down we are afraid. Most of the problems we have are caused by fear. It may be the fear that someone's going to take advantage of us, it may be fear of failure, it may be fear of looking foolish, fear that we won't fit in, fear that we will be abandoned. Few people aren't driven by some fear or another. Jesus says to us, "Why are you so afraid? Do you still have no faith?"

That is to say, the way to conquer fear is through faith. Faith is the only true antidote I know of for fear.

Writer Gwendolyn Mitchell Diaz tells about a trip she took with her family one summer. They loaded up their van and headed north to visit friends and relatives. On the way home they stopped in Boone, North Carolina, and spent a few days sightseeing.

Gwendolyn says she will never forget the afternoon they spent at Grandfather Mountain, the highest peak in the Blue Ridge Mountains. They were told that if they dared cross a long suspension bridge called Mile-High Swinging Bridge, they could stand on a rocky ledge that offered a tremendous view of the valley thousands of feet below.

It was late afternoon when they arrived at the bridge, and a storm was blowing in. The wind was beginning to gust significantly. Gwendolyn took one look down the eighty-foot-deep ravine spanned by the bridge, clutched her baby Jonathan, and refused to set foot on it. Her older sons Zach and Matt took off running onto the bridge. They were about halfway across the swaying boards when the wind became so strong it made them stagger. But they loved the challenge and the thrill and fought their way to the other side. Three-year-old Ben had started running after them. However, he stopped suddenly and clung to the nearest post. He wasn't so sure he wanted to continue the dangerous trek.

Dad, seeing what fun Zach and Matt were having as they fought against the wind, reached for Ben's hand and said, "Let's go. I'll take care of you."

"It was obvious that all kinds of what-ifs started tumbling around inside Ben's mind as he stood glued to the post contemplating Dad's offer," says Gwendolyn. "But suddenly he reached up, grabbed Dad's big hand, and started skipping across the bridge into the gusting wind. Ben had obviously transferred all of his what-ifs to Dad and decided to let [Dad] worry about them. The swaying bridge, the extreme height, the blustery wind, the impending storm—these weren't his problems anymore. Whether or not he could handle the situation did not matter. It was completely Dad's responsibility." (3)

Maybe that's what Jesus meant when he said, "Unless you change and become like a little child you shall never enter the kingdom of God" (Matthew 18:3) To have that kind of trust, to turn it all over to Daddy, Abba—if we could live like that most of the things that keep us awake at night would simply disappear. Fear is the biggest problem in our lives. The best way to conquer fear is with faith.

But not just faith in anybody or anything. The only kind of faith that really matters is faith in Jesus Christ.

"Who is this?" asked the disciples about Jesus. "Even the wind and the waves obey him!" Suddenly they realized there was something about Jesus that was different. He could calm storms.

In one of the Chicken Soup for the Soul books there is a touching story about a young man, a veteran, ready to marry and settle down. But this young man had a problem—a problem directly caused by fear.

He was a responsible young man but he couldn't keep a job and he was discouraged. Why was he in such a state? It was because he stuttered quite badly.

He heard that a candy company in Plant City, Florida, was looking for a route driver. And he'd heard that the owner of the company, a man named Miller, was a former stutterer who had somehow learned to control his stutter. A fellow sufferer, this young man decided, would certainly understand and hire him. He set his heart on getting that job.

In his interview Mr. Miller asked him why he wanted the job. The young man said, "B-b-because I need the m-m-money."

For a long time, Mr. Miller didn't say anything. Then finally he looked him straight in the eye. [Young man]," he said softly, "I'm not going to give you a job."

The young man stared at him, dumbfounded.

"Oh, don't get me wrong," Mr. Miller said. "I think you'd do well. It's just that I don't have an opening right now." Then he reached into his desk drawer and pulled out a piece of paper, worn and tattered. "I'd like you to take this home and read it," he said. "Read it every night for a month."

Hardly hearing Mr. Miller's words, the young man reached out numbly, took the paper and stuck it in his pocket. Tears of disappointment burned his eyes. He turned his head away, told Mr. Miller goodbye and slumped out of the Miller Candy Company.

That night he felt totally dejected. Who wants a stutterer around? he asked himself in defeat. Nobody. And as long as he stuttered he would be a nobody. He had lived with this pain all his life. After the interview with Mr. Miller, he was prepared never to utter another sound. He took the piece of paper Miller had given him out of his pocket, ready to tear it to shreds. But something made him look at it. It was a prayer—a very well-known prayer, but one he didn't know at the time. It read like this: "God, grant me the serenity to accept the things I cannot change, the courage to change the things I can, and the wisdom to know the difference."

He read the words again. Then again. They were like the light at the end of a tunnel.

He pondered the first phrase: "Accept the things I cannot change." He could work at easing his stuttering, he knew, but he probably could never really change the way he talked. He would need to accept that.

Then he read the second phrase: "Courage to change the things I can." What he could change were his fears—fear of stepping out of his shell, fear of trying to be somebody, fear of thinking bigger than he had been doing.

Then he came to the third phrase, "God, grant me the serenity . . ." Here, he knew, was the key to the whole prayer. When, he wondered, was the last time he actually had reached out to God? Years earlier, when he was a kid, the young man had prayed that he would wake up one morning and talk differently. When it didn't happen, he forgot about God. But suddenly now he had the feeling that God hadn't forgotten about him.

Soon he was asleep—a deep and restful sleep. But though serenity came that night, it didn't hang around all the time. And change didn't come overnight either. He kept reciting that prayer, reminding himself of its words and their meaning, till he finally could place himself in God's hands, in trust, without fear of what might happen to him.

One thing he had learned as a young boy in church was that when he sang he did not stutter. It seems that when a stutterer speaks, air gets trapped in his throat. But when he sings, for some reason the breathing apparatus works normally and there is no stutter.

This young man loved to sing the songs he learned at church, and he discovered he had a gift for writing songs. And so one day he decided to exercise the courage that he had been praying about—the courage to change the things he could.

Armed with some of his songs, he went to Nashville in hopes of getting somebody to listen to his work. One door led to another, and one day he got an appointment to audition for Minnie Pearl, one of the biggest names in country music.

He was scared. As he went to the studio, he kept praying: "Your serenity, Lord. Your serenity."

The audition went well and Minnie Pearl hired him as a backup musician and a songwriter. He was grateful for this break, but he longed to be a solo performer.

Then, in 1970, singer Glen Campbell invited him to accompany him on his new television show. As they rehearsed for the show, they would swap jokes. Campbell discovered that this young man had a terrific sense of humor and his stutter only added to the humorous impact that he had. Campbell wanted him to start talking and singing on his show. The young man was terrified. He called his wife and told her he wanted to back out. She assured him that they were all behind him. "Don't be afraid," she said.

"Afraid," he thought to himself. That's what he was. When he hung up the phone, his mind went back to that scrap of paper. Its words by now were as clear in his memory as they must have been on that paper when Mr. Miller first wrote them. "God, grant me the serenity . . . ." (4)

Some of you know that this is the true life story of country music superstar Mel Tillis. He will tell you that without his faith in God he would have been defeated long ago, defeated not by forces on the outside, defeated not even by his stuttering, but defeated by his fear. "God, grant me the serenity to accept the things I cannot change, the courage to change the things I can, and the wisdom to know the difference."

"Why are you so afraid?" Jesus asked his disciples. He asks that same question of us. Are you letting your fear keep you from being all God created you to be? Fear is the biggest problem in our lives. The best way to conquer fear is with faith. But not just faith in anybody or anything—faith in God—faith in Jesus Christ.

"Who is this?" asked the disciples about Jesus. "Even the wind and the waves obey him!" Yes, they do. Nothing can stop the person whose faith is in the Lord.

1. Let My People Laugh.
2. http://jonwalton.org/sermons/1998/981108.htm.
3. Sticking Up For Who I Am (Colorado Springs: NavPress, 2003), pp. 97-98.
4. Copyright©1978 by Guideposts, Carmel, NY 10512. Cited in Jack Canfield, Mark Victor Hansen, Ron Camacho, Chicken Soup for the Country Soul (Deerfield Beach, FL: Health Communications, Inc., 1998), pp. 157-161.

I Want My Dollar Back!
2 Corinthians 8:7-15

David Russell, a pastor in Union City, Tennessee tells about Nathan, a precocious three-year-old in his church. Nathan's parents were trying to introduce him to what it means to be in church. One Sunday they gave him a one-dollar bill that Nathan was to place in the offering plate. When the plate moved down Nathan's pew, his parents held it in front of him and told him to place the dollar in the plate. Nathan balked. Finally his mother gently took the dollar from him. She placed it in the plate, and it was passed on down the pew.

Suddenly the stillness of the offertory was shattered by a voice demanding, "I want my dollar back! I want my dollar back!" In Nathan's eyes, he had been robbed and he wanted everyone to know it. His parents tried in vain to quiet their son, but he was insistent, "I want my dollar back!" Everyone in the congregation was fighting a losing battle against laughter. Throughout the remaining strains of the organist's meditative tune, the only thing most worshippers heard was, "I want my dollar back!" Eventually, his parents gave Nathan another dollar to hold and he was content enough so that the congregation could make it through the Doxology.

Pastor Russell says that as he stepped into the pulpit, he knew he needed to talk about what had happened. Looking out at the smiling faces he said, "We shouldn't laugh. It may be that Nathan is only voicing the feelings that some of us have after having given to God. We do so, not joyously but out of a sense of obligation. We do so unwillingly. We may not say it, but some of us think it, 'I want my dollar back!'" (1)

You may wonder why we are talking about money on the first day of July. We are not having a financial campaign. There is no special stewardship emphasis going on. It just so happens that today's text from the epistle of 2 Corinthians is about giving.

You know by now I am not a pastor who dwells on the subject of money. One of the most prominent pastors in our land, now deceased, said that he never, ever went into the pulpit without slipping in a reference to tithing. Think of that! Every sermon, three times a week because he was a Southern Baptist, for fifty years he slipped in a reference to tithing. I understand that his church did have more than its share of tithers—people who gave more than 10% of their income to the church. So I guess it worked.

I heard about one rural pastor who used a different approach. One Sunday he announced, "Now, before we pass the collection plate, I would like to request that the person who stole the chickens from Farmer Jones' henhouse please refrain from giving any money to the Lord today. The Lord doesn't want money from a thief!" The collection plate was passed around, and for the first time in months everybody gave. That approach might work, but stealing chickens is not a big problem around here.

Some of you remember the wonderful television host Art Linkletter. What you may not know is that Linkletter grew up in poverty. His father was an itinerant evangelist who sometimes preached on street corners. The family lived where they could, on such money as his father was able to collect from his "offerings." Once they occupied one room in an old folk's home. Most of the rooms they lived in were skimpy and bare. He says that Christmas and Thanksgiving would have been bleak if churches hadn't donated their dinners.

In fact, Linkletter's first public appearance was in a church. His father used him to help swell the Sunday offering. Dressed in neat, patched clothes, he would solemnly parade up and down the church aisles with an offering plate, while his father beamed down from the pulpit and encouraged everyone to "dig deep, brothers and sisters, for the good work." (2) Well, that's another way to raise money for the church, I guess.

None of these approaches to raising money quite fits me. I hope you appreciate that. It's not that I'm embarrassed to talk about money. Jesus, as you may know, talked more about money than any other one subject. He knew what money can do to people. And he knew the proper place of money in our lives.

Money is important. We spend much of our life working for money. Some of us spend even more time worrying about money. It's always been so.

Some of you have had a difficult year. Over the past decade people have suffered lost jobs, declining home values, drained savings. It's hard. In a free market society, money ebbs and flows. Bubbles form and they burst. You may think this is a recent phenomenon. It is not.

Nearly three hundred years ago the great scientist, Sir Isaac Newton, lost money in a similar financial bubble. "I can calculate the motions of the heavenly bodies," Newton commented ruefully, "but not the madness of crowds." (3) He could have said, "The madness of the financial markets." Economists tell us that things are improving, but there are still many people in pain from the financial woes of the past five years.

Losing funds set aside for retirement, watching our home equity drain away, losing our job, our source of income, can bring us much pain. However, money can bring us much pain when we have too much of it as well. For some people, money becomes their God. Nothing matters as much as holding on to their wealth.

In the 1890s there was a Turkish professional wrestler named Yousouf who competed in Europe and the United States under the name "The Terrible Turk." He insisted he be paid for his matches in gold. Following his retirement,

Yousouf headed back to Turkey with the gold he had won. On its second day at sea, however, the ship ran into a storm and started to sink. Yousouf jumped into the sea near a lifeboat, but the weight of the gold in his belt, estimated to be between $8,000-10,000, pulled him downward and he drowned. It's hard to say which is worse. To have money and lose it or to become so obsessed with money that it costs you your life and/or your soul.

St. Paul was writing to the church at Corinth. The church at Corinth was relatively well off, at least compared to some of the other churches that Paul had started. Some of these latter churches were struggling to survive. Some members of these churches were literally on the verge of starvation. Paul's message to the Corinthians was basically, "share the wealth!" He writes, "But since you excel in everything—in faith, in speech, in knowledge, in complete earnestness and in the love we have kindled in you—see that you also excel in this grace of giving." Further on he writes, "Our desire is not that others might be relieved while you are hard pressed, but that there might be equality."

You would think that the one place this message of equality would be acceptable would be in the church. After all, when the church first began, the members had all things in common. You would think that church people would say "Amen" to the idea of sharing resources. You would be wrong. I can hear some of the people at Corinth complaining, "Why should we help them? Nobody helped us when we were struggling." That's human nature—even in churches. St. Paul knows that and so he appeals not to their human nature but to the divine nature. He writes, "For you know the grace of our Lord Jesus Christ, that though he was rich, yet for your sake he became poor, so that you through his poverty might become rich."

Giving is the Christian's response to what God has done for us in Jesus Christ. The first person to share the wealth was Christ. He shared the riches of God's grace.

Whether it is giving to the local church or giving to foreign missions, or giving to United Way or giving to the homeless person on the street—there is one motivation for the Christian to give. Christ gave, first of all, to us.

Theologian Leonard Sweet speaks of four "rules" by which we live.

The first is what he calls The Iron rule— "Do to others before they do to you." We know people who live by that rule.

The second he calls The Silver rule— "Do to others as they do to you." In other words, if someone does something good for you, do something for them in return. Some people live by this rule. It is a good rule, but it's not the ideal.

The third we know as The Golden rule which Jesus gave us— "Do to others as you would have them do to you." This is a major step up from the Iron rule and the Silver rule. In other words, treat other people like you would like to be treated.

However, to these Sweet adds what he calls The Titanium rule— "Do to others as Jesus has done to you."

Jesus was the original giver. He gave to us the gift of salvation. Everything we give to his work or as an act of charity is in response to his gift to us. Giving is the Christian's response to what God has done for us in Jesus Christ.

Giving is also the Christian's recognition of the proper place of money in our lives. Donald Olson quips that "the average American is busy buying things he doesn't want with money he doesn't have to impress people he doesn't like." And that can happen. Some people are owned by their money. Money is their master rather than their servant. When we give to the work of God we are declaring our freedom from materialism. We serve God, not mammon.

The Rev. Bill Hayes tells a wonderful story about some college girls who were renting a house. One day an old man appeared at the back door that they were a little leery of. His eyes were glassy and his furrowed face glistened with silver stubble. They thought he was an alcoholic—and had no idea what else he might be. He clutched a wicker basket holding a few vegetables. He bid the girls a good morning and offered his produce for sale. They were uneasy about having what they thought was this old alcoholic at their doorstep and made a quick purchase to get rid of him.

To their chagrin, he returned the next day and introduced himself as Mr. Roth, a man who lived in the shack down the road. As their fears subsided, they got close enough to realize it wasn't alcohol but cataracts that marbleized his eyes. On subsequent visits, he would shuffle in, wearing two mismatched right shoes, and share his philosophy about life.

On one visit, he exclaimed: "The Lord is so good! I came out of my shack this morning and found a bag full of shoes and clothing on my porch."

"That's wonderful, Mr. Roth!" the girls said, "We're happy for you."

"You know what's even more wonderful?" he asked. "Just yesterday I met some people who could use those shoes and clothing." (4)

No wonder that old man was so happy. He owned his material goods, they didn't own him. The Bible doesn't say that money is the root of all evil. It says, of course, that the LOVE of money is the root of all evil. There are some things that only money can do—put food on the table and clothes on our back. Pay the mortgage and buy us fuel and medicine. There are some things that only money can do. What it can't do is buy us happiness or fulfillment or salvation. Giving is the Christian's response to what God has done for us in Jesus Christ. Giving is also the Christian's recognition of the proper place of money in our lives.

Mother Teresa once told of a young Hindu couple who came to her and gave her a large amount of money. She asked them, "Where did you get so much money?"

They answered, "We got married two days ago. Before we got married we had decided not to celebrate the wedding, not to buy wedding clothes, not to have a reception or a honeymoon. We wanted to give you the money we saved."

Mother Teresa knew what such a decision meant, especially for a Hindu family. She asked them, "But how did you think of such a thing?"

"We love each other so much," they answered, "that we wanted to share the joy of our love with those you serve." (5) This young couple understood better than most of us the place that money is supposed to occupy in our lives—we are to share it with those in need. It is in giving that we receive joy.

But there is one thing more to be said: giving is our declaration of faith in Jesus Christ. You may say something like, "I would give more to the church and to those in need, but I'm afraid that I won't have enough to meet my own needs." What does that say about your relationship to God? Do you trust God? Has God ever let you down? If you don't have enough to meet your real needs, then of course, do not give. But don't refuse to give simply because you are afraid.

Frances Ridley Havergal was a young English woman, daughter of an Anglican pastor. She was chronically ill most of her life, and she was not a woman blessed with wonderful gifts of any kind. Yet she desired to give what she had back to Christ. She had a passion for missions. One day she determined that she really had no need of her jewelry. She packed it all up, all save a couple of pieces with some sentimental value, and shipped it off to the Church Missionary Society, and asked them to dispose of it and use the proceeds for their work. "I had no idea I had such a jeweler's shop," she wrote to her friend. "Nearly fifty pieces are being packed off . . . I never packed a box with such pleasure."

Frances Havergal didn't say, "What if I need this jewelry some day to sell to pay my bills?" She could have. She wasn't a wealthy woman. But she didn't say that. She trusted God. Her simple desire was to give back to God in response to what God had given her. Of course, we remember Frances Ridley Havergal not because she gave her jewelry to church missions, but because of some verses she wrote about giving—words she meant from her heart. They went like this:

Take my life, and let it be Consecrated, Lord, to thee;
take my moments and my days; let them flow in ceaseless praise.
Take my hands and let them move At the impulse of thy love.
Take my feet, and let them be Swift and beautiful for thee.
Take my voice, and let me sing, Always, only, for my King.
Take my lips, and let them be Filled with messages from thee.

Take my silver and my gold; not a mite would I withhold.
Take my intellect, and use Every power as thou shalt choose.
Take my will and make it thine; It shall be no longer mine.
Take my heart, it is thine own; It shall be thy royal throne.
Take my love; my Lord, I pour At thy feet its treasure-store.
Take myself, and I will be Ever, only, all for thee. (6)

Giving is the Christian's response to what God has done for us in Jesus Christ. Giving signals our recognition of the proper place of money in our lives. Giving is our declaration of faith in Jesus Christ. There may be some among us who think in our hearts, as the offering plates are passed, like little Nathan, "I want my money back!" I suspect that most of us, however, are filled with gratitude for God's gift to us of Jesus Christ. Our desire is to give more, as Christ has given to us.

1. Rev. W. David Holwick, http://www.holwick.com/sermons/thanksgiving/thank5.html.
2. Art Linkletter, Kids Say the Darndest Things! (Berkeley: Celestial Arts, 2005).
3. Edward Cornish, Futuring: The Exploration of the Future (Bethesda, MD: World Future Society, 2004).
4. http://revbill.wordpress.com/2011/01/02/ephesians-13-14/
5. José Luis González-Balado, Mother Teresa: In My Own Words (Liguori, MO: Liguori Publications, 1996), p. 19.
6. The Rev. Richard O. Johnson, http://www.predigten.uni-goettingen.de/predigt.php?id=3007&kennung=20110731en.

When The Going Gets Tough
2 Corinthians 12:2-10

The golf course was crowded with golfers one pleasant fall morning. Bob was standing in front of a tee preparing to swing at his ball. He visualized hitting a beautiful shot that would carry hundreds of yards. As he was standing there lost in his thoughts, an announcement came over the public address system: "Would the gentleman standing at the women's tee please back up to the men's tee?"

Bob ignored the announcement. He continued his pre-shot routine.

Again, the announcement came across the PA system: "Would the gentleman on the women's tee please back up to the men's tee?"

This announcement seemed incredibly rude to Bob, particularly since it was directed at him. He turned toward the clubhouse and shouted, "Would the announcer in the clubhouse kindly shut up and let me play my second shot?"

My guess is that this was not going to be a great day for Bob, if his first shot got him no farther than where the women tee off. We all have days like that, don't we? Of course, some of those days are nothing to laugh about.

David Heller wrote a delightful little book from which pastors love to quote. It's titled, Dear God: Children's Letters to God. Inside that book are some witty observations from the lips of young children:

"Dear God, What do you do with families that don't have much faith? There's a family on the next block like that. I don't want to get them in trouble, so I can't say who. See you in church. Alexis (age 10).

Dear God, Want to hear a joke? What is red, very long, and you hear it right before you go to sleep? Give up? A sermon. Your friend, Frank (age 11).

Then there is one that is more thoughtful than humorous. It goes like this: "Dear God, I have doubts about you sometimes. Sometimes I really believe. Like when I was four and I hurt my arm and you healed it up fast. But my question is, if you could do this, why don't you stop all the bad in the world? Like war. Like diseases. Like famine. Like drugs. And there are problems in other people's neighborhoods too. I'll try to believe more. Ian (age 10)." (1)

Many of us struggle with the same questions as Ian. Any thinking person does. St. Paul certainly struggled with these questions. And yet it is evident that his faith allowed him to resolve many of these issues. And it wasn't because Paul had not known his share of suffering. He had. But rather than destroying his faith, suffering had deepened it.

Listen to his words in our lesson for the day beginning with the seventh verse: "Therefore, in order to keep me from becoming conceited, I was given a thorn in my flesh, a messenger of Satan, to torment me. Three times I pleaded with the Lord to take it away from me. But he said to me, 'My grace is sufficient for you, for my power is made perfect in weakness.' Therefore," Paul continues, "I will boast all the more gladly about my weaknesses, so that Christ's power may rest on me. That is why, for Christ's sake, I delight in weaknesses, in insults, in hardships, in persecutions, in difficulties. For when I am weak, then I am strong."

Not many of us could delight in insults, hardships, persecutions, and difficulties. But St. Paul could. Paul had had some unique spiritual experiences. He was proud of those experiences. They had nourished his faith in a wonderful way. He knew that because of those experiences he was tempted to be puffed up with pride. But Paul had a condition, probably a physical condition that carried with it some degree of humiliation and shame. Some scholars speculate that he suffered from epileptic seizures. We don't really know. Paul simply called it, his "thorn in the flesh."

Some of you are gardeners. Some of you grow roses. You know what it is to get a thorn in your hand or arm. It's uncomfortable, painful. You pull it out as quickly as possible. Scholars suggest that Paul's thorn was much more serious than one from a rose bush. Scholars say Paul's thorn was more like a large, sharpened wooden shaft jabbing into his flesh. This thorn caused him great distress. And there was no way that it could be removed.

Paul said that he asked the Lord three times to remove the thorn from him. In other words, the pain, whether physical or mental, had on three occasions nearly overwhelmed Paul to the point that he pleaded with God to help him. That says something about Paul's faith right there. You and I would plead with God far more than three times. Most of us would turn to God night and day. But not St. Paul. After three times of making his plea, Paul turned it over to God. And in the process, Paul discovered something quite wonderful. He heard the voice of the Lord say to him, "My grace is sufficient for you, for my power is made perfect in weakness."

What a powerful sentence. "My grace is sufficient for you . . . my power is made perfect in weakness." Paul discovered two things in suffering with his thorn in the flesh. First, he discovered that God's grace is sufficient. And, second, he discovered that God's power is made perfect in weakness. Let's talk for a few moments about the first of these: The sufficiency of God's grace.

Life is difficult. That is something about which all of us will agree. I read a humorous story recently. It was about an event that occurred one time in a production of the opera, Carmen, in a very prestigious theater crammed with thousands of theater patrons.

This particular night the singer playing the character Don José forgot to bring his stage knife for the stabbing scene in which he murders Carmen. Imagine that. He's on stage in front of hundreds of theatergoers. He is supposed to murder Carmen but he's forgotten his knife. What does he do? What would you do in such a situation? Here is what this resourceful actor did. Since he didn't have a knife, he decided to strangle her. That makes sense. However, he didn't have time to warn the singer playing Carmen. She didn't know what he was doing with his hands around her throat, so according to an eye-witness account, she fought back like a tigress. Here's what's amazing to me. Somehow, she managed to go on singing throughout a prolonged and somewhat muted strangulation! (2) In the process, the opera house patrons got a show they didn't expect

Sometimes life has caught me off-guard like that poor opera singer and I, too, have reacted with surprise and dismay, and maybe with anger. Sometimes I have been able to keep on singing. Sometimes I have not. But that's life. Sometimes it catches us off-guard. We didn't schedule sickness on our Day Planner, but there it is. Our smart phone didn't warn us that the company was down-sizing. We didn't see it coming that our teen-ager would have an accident. Life is sometimes very difficult.

Some people handle life's adversities better than others. Psychologists speak of resiliency. Some people are more resilient than other people even as children. By their very nature, some people take life in stride. No one knows why this is true of some people, but not others. As the old adage goes, the same sun that melts butter hardens clay. People differ in how they react to life, even in the same family.

Once there were two brothers whose last name was Bulger. These brothers grew up in an impoverished family in Boston. James Bulger drifted into crime, went to prison, escaped, and eventually was put on the FBI's Ten Most Wanted Fugitives list.

Meanwhile, his brother William went to college, then entered politics, and eventually became president of the University of Massachusetts.

How do you explain that? Same parents. Generally the same early experiences. But one was a stunning failure while the other was a stunning success. I must add this sad footnote, however. William was forced to resign as President of the University of Massachusetts in 2003 after being accused of concealing information that might lead to his brother's capture. (3) How sad that he had to pay for his brother's misspent life.

People differ in their reactions to life's difficulties. Some people are more resilient than others. Paul was one of those resilient people. But his resilience grew out of his faith in God. "My grace is sufficient for you . . ." Paul heard God say.

Pastor Chuck Swindoll tells of attending a memorial service for a friend several years younger than he who had died with liver cancer. Talk about a thorn in the flesh. This man's cancer certainly was more like a sharp wooden shaft. Swindoll compares it to an arrow piercing his friend's flesh.

However his friend did not let the disease defeat him emotionally or spiritually. He didn't curl up in a corner with a calendar and put Xs on days, says Swindoll. On the contrary, the news of his malignancy only spurred him on to drain every ounce out of every day.

His physician had told him he would probably be gone before Thanksgiving. "Says who?" his friend mused. Not only did he live through Thanksgiving, at Christmas he threw a party. The following Easter was delightful. A fun picnic on the Fourth of July was a gas and he had a special celebration in the planning stage for a second Thanksgiving. He didn't quite make that. However, a close friend of Swindoll's told him that the last time they talked, this friend had made an appointment to have his teeth fixed. A dying man doesn't make an appointment to have his teeth fixed, but this man did. He was resting in the sufficiency of God's grace. (4)

"My grace is sufficient for you," Paul heard God say to him. "I am with you," God was saying to him. "Whatever your need is, I will help you through." Then God adds, "My power is made perfect in weakness." What does that mean? God's power is made perfect in weakness.

It means at least two things. First of all, it means that adversity strengthens us for service. We grow by overcoming our weaknesses.

The story is told of a Renaissance artist who made the world's most prized vases. A visitor came to observe his method. After laboring for many weeks with one piece of clay—firing it, painting it, baking it—he placed it upon a pedestal for inspection. The visitor sat in awe at this thing of unspeakable beauty. But it appeared that the artist was not yet finished. In a shocking and dramatic moment, the artist lifted the vase above his head and dashed it against the floor, breaking it into a thousand shards. And then, quietly, he reconnected the pieces by painting the edges with a paint of pure gold. Each crack reflected invaluable gold. In the end, this magnificent, but imperfect, piece became the most valued piece in the collection. (5)

Some of you know what it is to have your life almost shattered. But with God's help you have picked up the pieces of your life and today you are stronger than ever. Adversity strengthens us in a way that a life of ease never can. But even more important is the effect that overcoming weakness has on those around us.

The power of God is never more apparent than when a believer is made strong by his or her relationship with God. When you are confronted with a situation which you know you cannot handle without God's help, then your life becomes a living testimony to God's presence in the world.

Some of you are old enough to remember Roy Campanella, a catcher for the Brooklyn Dodgers baseball team. Campanella won the Dodgers' Most Valued Player award many times; he played on baseball's All Star Team and in 1955 his Dodgers won the World Series.

In January 1958, Roy Campanella's baseball career was cut short after a car crash left him a quadriplegic. The unthinkable had happened to him. This is the point at which so many people would give up on God and life, but not Campanella.

After he was injured, he spent a lot of time in the Institute of Physical Medicine and Rehabilitation in New York City,

One day he stopped to read a gold plaque upon one of the walls. This plague resonated deeply with his Christian faith. Some of you will recognize these words:

I asked God for strength, that I might achieve.

I was made weak, that I might learn to humbly obey . . .

I asked for health that I might do great things.

I was given infirmity that I might do better things . . .

I asked for riches that I might be happy,

I was given poverty that I might be wise . . .

I asked for power, that I might have the praise of others.

I was given weakness that I might feel the need of God . . .

I asked for all things, that I might enjoy life.

I was given life that I might enjoy all things . . ."

In response to these words Roy Campanella wrote, "I got nothing I asked for, but I received everything that I had hoped for." (6)

Roy Campanella inspired more people off the field than he ever could have on the field. This is the mistake we often make. We think it is the perfect athlete who makes the best spokesperson for God . . . the glamorous actor . . . the polished speaker . . . the successful business person. People want to be just like them, we reason, including appropriating their faith. This leads us to think our witness is somehow inferior because we're not athletic, glamorous, polished or successful. Nothing could be further from the truth. The best witness for Christ is authentic Christian living in the face of daunting adversity. It is when we allow God to lead us through the rough times, and in all things we give God the praise, then people will see the power of God made manifest.

Paul prayed that the thorn might be removed from his flesh. He heard God say to him, "My grace is sufficient for you . . . my power is made perfect in weakness." That's all Paul needed to become one of the most powerful witnesses for God who ever lived. My friends, that's all we need as well.

1. Bantam, 1987. Cited by Dr. David E. Leininger,
http://lectionary.org/Sermons/Lein/Mark/Mark_06.14-29_WhenEvil.htm.
2. Hugh Vickers, Even Greater Operatic Disasters (London: MacMillan, 1982), p. 41.
3. Edward Cornish, Futuring: The Exploration of the Future (Kindle Edition).
4. Charles Swindoll, Day By Day (Nashville: W Publishing Group, 2000), p. 93.
5. Rev. Dr. Robert M. Franklin, http://day1.org/1328-strong_in_the_broken_places.
6. Gary Dennis, http://www.lacanadapc.org/transcripts/sm041104.html.

Adopted

Ephesians 1:3-14

A man in Wilton, Connecticut named Gary Klahr told a remarkable story in Guideposts a few years back. He said that one night in 1975 he made a new friend at a local restaurant. This new friend, Steve Barbin, happened to be seated at the next table and they got to talking. By the time they finished their burgers, they'd pushed their tables together and were well on the way to becoming best friends. They grew so close that they finished each other's sentences and shared belly laughs at jokes that no one else seemed to get.

Even the rhythms of their speech seemed identical. They were so close that, at Steve's wedding, Gary told Steve he was truly his brother. Of course, that was just a figure of speech. Gary said his parents had tried for years to have a child before he came along, and they called him their gift from God. Steve, on the other hand, was adopted. Steve had known this for many years, and told Gary of many positive experiences of being adopted. For some reason it surprised Gary that Steve was adopted.

Gary and Steve had been best buddies for 23 years when, out of the blue, in December 1998, Gary got a phone call from a woman with the Connecticut Department of Children and Families. She needed to confirm Gary's name and birth date.

"You should probably sit down before I tell you why I'm calling," she said. "Did you know that you were adopted?"

"Are you sure you have the right Gary Klahr." Gary asked.

She persisted. "Believe me," she said, "I wouldn't do this if I weren't sure. One of your biological siblings needs urgent medical information from his family."

Gary was floored. His parents had always treated him like he was their own biological child, never once saying he was adopted. He assumes they wanted to protect him somehow.

"In all of my years in this work, I've never seen a case like this," the lady from the State agency went on. "Your biological parents lived in Bridgeport. They had thirteen children, and nine of them were adopted by other families. Is there someone besides your parents you can talk to about this? Someone you're close to?"

"My buddy Steve is adopted, and he's okay with it," Gary said slowly. "So I guess I will be, too, once I have some time to get over it."

"What's Steve's last name." she asked.

"Barbin," he said.

"Gary," said the lady from the State agency, "Steve is your brother." (1)

What a wonderful story. Our lesson from the writings of St. Paul to the

Ephesians is about adoption. And the people who are adopted are you and me. Paul begins this lesson like this: "Praise be to the God and Father of our Lord Jesus Christ, who has blessed us in the heavenly realms with every spiritual blessing in Christ. For he chose us in him before the creation of the world to be holy and blameless in his sight. In love he predestined us for adoption to sonship through Jesus Christ, in accordance with his pleasure and will—to the praise of his glorious grace, which he has freely given us in the One he loves."

Think about those words, "In love he predestined us for adoption to sonship through Jesus Christ . . ."

Now don't stumble over that word "predestined." That's for another sermon. We're not going to deal with predestination here.

I do like something that Christian comedian Emo Phillips once said. "I'm not a fatalist," he said, "And even if I were, what could I do about it?"

Even if you and I were predestined by God in a narrow sense of that word, what could we do about it? There is a story pastor Mark Schaefer tells about a scene in the epic film Lawrence of Arabia that speaks to the question of predestination.

In the film British officer T.E. Lawrence is leading an Arab army in a surprise attack against the Turkish army at Aqaba. In order to do this, they must cross a dangerous and deadly desert. The most dangerous section of this desert is called "the Anvil." They cross The Anvil at night, because it is deadly during the day.

As they emerge from the desert, they discover that one man has been left behind. He had fallen off his camel somewhere back on the Anvil.

Lawrence turns his mount around and heads back out to find the man before the sun kills him. His Arab allies shout to him that there is no point—no one can survive the Anvil. "It is written," they say.

Sometime later, Lawrence emerges from the desert in the middle of the day carrying the ailing form of the missing man. As the man is lowered down and given water, Lawrence says to his men, "Nothing is written."

Sometime later they encounter another tribe whom they enlist to help them with the attack against Aqaba. Suddenly, there is a disturbance. One of Lawrence's group has murdered a man from the new group. The fragile alliance is about to fall apart, since the new group will be enraged if the man is not brought to justice, and the original group will be infuriated if the other tribe brings one of their own to justice. Lawrence declares that he will carry out the sentence—since he is a member of neither tribe. When they bring forward the guilty party, Lawrence discovers it is the man he had rescued from death in the desert. Pained and devastated, Lawrence executes the man.

When the leader of the new tribe asks why Lawrence was so upset, he is told that the man he killed was that same man that he saved from the Anvil.

"Ah," responds the leader of the new tribe. "It was written." (2)

We could spend many fruitless hours arguing over predestination, determinism and free will. The word "chosen" would better suit our purposes. Here is the good news for the day: God has chosen us to be His own adopted children.

Biblically the concept of adoption is an interesting metaphor. You won't find the word "adoption" anywhere in the Old Testament. Adoption was not practiced in the Old Testament world, at least not by the Jews. Neither was it a practice among Jews in New Testament times. Jesus never used the term adoption nor is the word used in the four Gospels.

Adoption is a concept that Paul introduced from his own background as a Roman citizen. He used the term at least five times. It was quite common in the Roman world for wealthy families who did not have sons to adopt one in order to have someone to inherit their property. Girls weren't adopted in that time since, under Roman law, they could not inherit property. (3) It was a very special thing in the Roman world to be adopted. It still is a special thing to be adopted today.

A little girl came home from school one day very sad. Her mother, sensing that something was wrong, tried to find out what the problem was. At first the little girl didn't want to talk about it but finally through tears she told how she had been made fun of at school by some of the other kids because she was adopted. "No one really loves you," the children taunted her.

So her adopted mother held her in her arms, slowly rocking her and telling her daughter how much she was loved. She explained to her daughter that mommies and daddies who have children of their own love them, but they have no choice about the children they will have. They simply get what they get.

"We, on the other hand," the mother explained, "chose you. We looked and searched and out of all the children we saw, we chose you. That's how much we loved you from the first time we laid eyes on you." It's a special thing to be adopted.

It's like one young mother who stayed with her parents for several days after the birth of their first child. One afternoon she remarked to her mother that it was surprising that her baby had dark hair since both she and her husband are fair. Without thinking, her mother answered, "Well, your daddy has black hair."

"But, Mama, that doesn't matter," the young woman protested, "because I'm adopted."

With a smile of embarrassment, her mother spoke the most wonderful words this young mother had ever heard. She said, "Oh, my. I always forget." (4)

It's a special thing to be adopted. The Apostle Paul says that you and I, through the death and resurrection of Jesus Christ, have been adopted by God. That is why we are heirs of every good thing God has. We are God's adopted children. We were specially chosen because God wants children with which to share His love.

But notice that there is a purpose to our adoption: We were adopted to be holy and blameless in God's sight. Paul writes, "For he chose us in him before the creation of the world to be holy and blameless in his sight. In love he predestined us for adoption to sonship through Jesus Christ . . ."

That's a word we don't use much in the church anymore, "holy." Oh, it's all right to say God is holy. In fact, we ought to take God's holiness more seriously. We're just uncomfortable applying those words to ourselves. Who wants to be a holy Joe? There was a time when it was common to make fun of some of our more enthusiastic fellow Christians as "holy rollers." Who wants to be called a holy roller? The most common place we see the term "holy" used is in the derisive phrase, "holier than thou." Nobody today wants to be called "holier than thou." That indicates that we look down on others, that we revel in a sense of moral superiority.

Because of the unfortunate connotations that the word "holy" has acquired, we might want to substitute the word "excellent." That is, Christians are called to live an excellent life—excelling in faithfulness, excelling in generosity, and most importantly, excelling in love. When we seek after excellence in these things, we do not feel ourselves to be superior to anyone. Indeed when we excel as Christ excelled, we seek to be a servant to others.

Several years ago there was an article in a national magazine about a number of religious conventions that were held in a certain Midwestern city that summer. The local citizens couldn't have been happier, according to this article.

Sgt. Hayden Kirk, a police traffic supervisor tells why. He said that he was impressed by a woman who, after getting out of her car, noticed that a facial tissue had fallen out. "She went back over and picked it up," Kirk commented. "Now when's the last time you saw that?"

He also said the trash collectors found that conventioneers had stacked refuse in neat piles next to containers when they became filled. And parking lot attendants didn't have to argue with delegates when they were asked to put their cars in certain spaces. Recalling how some other conventions turned into shouting matches because the visitors were unruly and demanding, Kirk summed it up, "But these folks were terrific!" (5)

These are small things, of course. But they represent a little of what we mean by excellence in living. We are to seek after excellence in all things.

St. Paul says we were predestined to be holy and blameless. But notice how he qualifies the words, holy and blameless. He writes, "For he chose us in him before the creation of the world to be holy and blameless in His sight . . ." What a beautiful statement. We could put it like this: In God's eyes, we look as if we have never done anything wrong.

How do we get those white robes that the writer of Revelation says we will wear when we surround God's throne in glory? They are white because they have been washed in the blood of the Lamb (Rev. 7:14). Holiness is not something we earn, but something that is bestowed upon us by God because of what Christ has done in our behalf.

Pastor Mickey Anders shares a story that was circulated on the Internet sometime back. The author is unknown. It is interesting because it is a true story.

It's a letter written to a man on death row. The letter was written by the Father of the man who was killed by the death row prisoner. The letter reads like this:

"You are probably surprised that I, of all people, am writing a letter to you, but I ask you to read it in its entirety and consider its request seriously. As the Father of the man whom you took part in murdering, I have something very important to say to you. I forgive you. With all my heart, I forgive you. I realize it may be hard for you to believe, but I really do.

"At your trial, when you confessed to your part in the events that cost my Son his life and you asked for my forgiveness, I immediately granted you that forgiving love from my heart. I can only hope you believe me and will accept my forgiveness. But this is not all I have to say to you. I want to make you an offer—I want you to become my adopted child.

"You see, my Son who died was my only child, and I now want to share my life with you and leave my riches to you. This may not make sense to you or anyone else, but I believe you are worth the offer. I have arranged matters so that if you will receive my offer of forgiveness, not only will you be pardoned for your crime, but you also will be set free from your imprisonment, and your sentence of death will be dismissed. At that point, you will become my adopted child and heir to all my riches.

"I realize this is a risky offer for me to make to you—you might be tempted to reject my offer completely—but I make it to you without reservation. Also, I realize it may seem foolish to make such an offer to one who cost my Son his life, but I now have a great love and an unchangeable forgiveness in my heart for you.

"Finally, you may be concerned that once you accept my offer you may do something to cause you to be denied your rights as an heir to my wealth. Nothing could be further from the truth. If I can forgive you for your part in my Son's death, I can forgive you for anything. I know you never will be perfect, but you do not have to be perfect to receive my offer. Besides, I believe that once you have accepted my offer and begin to experience the riches that will come to you from me, that your primary (though not always) response will be gratitude and loyalty. Some would call me foolish for my offer to you, but I wish for you to call me your Father. Sincerely, the Father of Jesus." (6)

And, friends, that's what it's all about. We have been adopted by God to become holy and blameless in God's sight. We've been called to excellence in living. Our city ought to be a better city, our family ought to be a better family, just because we are here. Why? Because we have a Heavenly Parent who looks at us with the eyes of love. God looks at us as if we have never in our lives done anything wrong. And in response to that love, we, in turn, give God our best.

1. Guideposts, Copyright (c) May 2002, http://www. guideposts. org
2. http://www.aumethodists.org/worship/sermons/2005-spring/freewill/.
3. Edward F. Markquart, http://www.sermonsfromseattle.com/books_ephesians_strong.htm.
4. The Rev. Jason E. Gamble, http://www.culvercitypres.org/sermons/Ephesians%201.3 14.htm.
5. Jim Davis, http://www.focusongod.com/security.htm.
6. http://www.mickeyanders.com/Sermons/Sermon19990905.html

Walls, Walls, Everywhere Walls
Ephesians 2:13-22

"Something there is that doesn't love a wall, That wants it down!" wrote poet Robert Frost. I wish that everyone shared that sentiment. Unfortunately most people do not. Most people love walls. They see walls as their security, even their salvation.

It is interesting that the largest construction project ever undertaken by humanity was the building of a wall. I'm talking, of course, about the Great Wall of China. It is said that enough stone was used in that 1,700-year project to build an 8-foot wall girdling the globe at the equator. The Great Wall snakes its way over more than one-twentieth of the earth's circumference. (1) It is the perfect metaphor for humanity's obsession of building walls to separate one people from another.

The Great Wall of China was built to keep out foreigners. Many of us can remember another famous wall that was built to keep people from fleeing their homeland. It was known as the Berlin Wall. It was constructed in 1961. It was only twenty-five miles long, but it divided a great city and it came to symbolize the failure of communism. Many of us have probably forgotten what a symbol of hatred and fear that wall became.

The Berlin wall was eleven feet high and was topped by barbed wire. Behind the wall was an area known as the "death area." Refugees who had reached that area were shot without warning. Beyond that was a trench to prevent vehicles from breaking through. Then there was a corridor with watchdogs, watchtowers and bunkers, and then a second wall. At least 100 people were killed trying to escape over the Berlin Wall. And it was a day of incredible rejoicing on November 9, 1989 when that wall came tumbling down. (2) But it is the story of humanity: walls, walls, everywhere walls.

We live in the time of the gated community. It's the sign of an exclusive neighborhood. High walls, a gate across the entrance; sometimes a guard. Most of the time it's for security. We understand that. Everyone wants to be secure. However, a pastor in Auburn, California asked one of his members who lived in a gated community what he liked best about it. Without hesitation the church member said that what he liked best about living in a gated community was the fact that only "certain" people could get in and the "rest" were kept out—and then he went on to characterize the "rest" as being those who he deemed to be less than "the cream of the crop." (3) Walls, walls, everywhere walls . . .

A journalist once asked the famous American writer, three times Pulitzer Prize winner, Carl Sandburg, "What is the ugliest word in the English Language?"

After a few minutes Sandburg replied, "Exclusive." Another way of speaking about walls.

There was a song in the 1960s. Maybe you've heard it. It's called "The In-Crowd."

The first verse went something like this: "I'm in with the in-crowd; I know what the in-crowd knows. I'm in with the in-crowd; I go where the in-crowd goes." Walls, walls, everywhere walls . . .

Even in churches there are walls. We don't like to admit it, but it's true. A pastor in a church in upstate New York tells about a man in his first parish named Jimmy. Jimmy was a well-known figure in town. No one knew Jimmy's age, but he walked the streets at all hours of the day and night carrying a large portable radio on his shoulder and singing to the music at the top of his tuneless voice. Sometimes Jimmy's elderly mother walked with him. When she did, they argued. Nights when the arguments got violent, Jimmy slept in the church doorway.

Jimmy and his mother began to come to church. The first Sunday they sat in someone else's accustomed seats. Jimmy enjoyed the hymns and sang lustily, but he talked during the sermon, walked up and down the aisles, and had no money for the offering. Regular worshippers began to wait to see where Jimmy and his mother would sit so as not to get too close.

After a few months Jimmy and his mother became an issue in the church. People said, "They're disruptive. They smell. They don't give any money to the offering." Jimmy and his mother were blessedly oblivious to this firestorm.

A year or so later, Jimmy and his mother found an independent church that had a bus ministry, so he and his mother began attending elsewhere. This pastor writes, "My congregation was relieved of coping with Jimmy. I however, was deeply shaken. The church, where people like Jimmy should have been welcome, was no different from anywhere else. Serious questions were raised in that church about telling Jimmy to stay away. And what if others like him began to attend?"

This pastor continues, "Didn't Jesus come to be among the Jimmies? Didn't Jesus extend hospitality to people who were otherwise outsiders? Didn't he heal when he wasn't supposed to and touch when no one else would?"

Twenty two years later, she says, "I am still ashamed, for we all—including myself—missed the point of holy hospitality." (4) Walls, walls, everywhere walls . . .

You know who doesn't like walls? Jesus. Listen to what the Apostle Paul says, "But now in Christ Jesus you who once were far away have been brought near by the blood of Christ. For he himself is our peace, who has made the two groups one and has destroyed the barrier, the dividing wall of hostility, by setting aside in his flesh the law with its commands and regulations. His purpose was to create in himself one new humanity out of the two, thus making peace, and in one body to reconcile both of them to God through the cross, by which he put to death their hostility. He came and preached peace to you who were far away and peace to those who were near. For through him we both have access to the Father by one Spirit. Consequently, you are no longer foreigners and strangers, but fellow citizens with God's people and also members of his household, built on the foundation of the apostles and prophets, with Christ Jesus himself as the chief cornerstone. In him the whole building is joined together and rises to become a holy temple in the Lord. And in him you too are being built together to become a dwelling in which God lives by his Spirit."

The wall St. Paul is referring to in specific is the wall between Jews and Gentiles. The first Christian congregation was all Jewish and most of the members would have preferred to keep it that way. But Simon Peter had a vision and St. Paul had a passion, and together they broke down the wall that kept Gentiles out. They began to understand that Jesus didn't like walls—any kind of walls—particularly walls that made some people feel inferior or rejected.

We sing the old spiritual, "Joshua fought the battle of Jericho, Jericho, Jericho, Joshua fought the battle of Jericho, And the walls came tumbling down!"

Joshua was an Old Testament Hebrew name. In the New Testament Greek, the name "Joshua" becomes "Jesus." Jesus fought the battle of Golgotha, and the walls came tumbling down—the wall between Jews and Gentiles, the wall between men and women, the wall between people of different colors, the wall between saints and sinners. It could have been Jesus, not Robert Frost, who first said, "Something there is that doesn't love a wall."

The first thing we need to see is that all forms of hatred are from Satan, not from God. I hope you already understand that. You cannot love God and hate your brother or your sister.

The little epistle known as I John puts it so clearly that surely none of us can misunderstand. We read, "Dear friends, let us love one another, for love comes from God. Everyone who loves has been born of God and knows God. Whoever does not love does not know God, because God is love." (4:7-8) There is no hatred in God. God is pure unadulterated love. Anyone who says they hate anyone for any reason cannot be filled with the Spirit of God. It is a logical impossibility.

Sometime back, we are told, the American Red Cross was gathering supplies—medicine, clothing, food, and the like for the suffering people of an African drought and civil war. Inside one of the boxes that showed up at the collection depot one day was a letter. It said, "We have recently been converted and because of our conversion we want to try to help. We won't ever need these again. Can you use them for something?" Inside the box were several Ku Klux Klan sheets.

For any of our younger members who may not be familiar with the Klan, in parts of our nation historically the Klan has been the very epitome of racial and religious hatred. The most interesting manifestation of their hatred was that they used a cross—a burning cross—as a means of intimidation. The truly sad thing is that, in their twisted minds some of them actually believed they were serving Christ with their hateful acts. They were serving Satan.

Anyway this particular group had come to know the love of Christ and had disbanded, and they sent their robes, their white sheets, to the Red Cross. Quite significantly, the Red Cross cut the white sheets into strips and eventually used them to bandage wounds—the wounds of suffering black people in Africa. (5) Now, that is a conversion that would thrill the heart of God.

All forms of hatred are from Satan, not from God. Nothing could be more evident from the New Testament. It is difficult to see how Christians can hate anyone in Jesus' name. In our lesson for today, St. Paul says that Christ came to break down the "wall of hostility." That is my prayer, too, that, if anyone is this room has any hostility in your heart toward any other person for any reason, or toward any other group of people, that you will ask God to deliver you from that hostility.

Years ago, beloved actor Dick Van Dyke wrote a little book titled Faith, Hope, and Hilarity.

In it he told about a Sunday School teacher who asked her class, "What do you think about when you see the church doors open to everyone who wants to worship God here?"

An African-American student answered, "It's like walking into the heart of God." (6) That young man was right. God's nature is love. Wherever love reigns, God reigns. Hatred is from Satan. Love is from God.

Here is the second thing we need to see: We all belong to one family.

Here again is a spiritual truth so evident that it is hard to see how so many persons have missed it. The biblical testimony is that we all belong to one family. We all descended from one set of parents. The Genesis writer called them Adam and Eve. We don't know how long ago that was. We only know that the first man was fashioned from the dust of the earth and at death his physical body returned to that earth. We don't know how God created Adam and Eve. We only know that God breathed into them His own Spirit. Then God told these new humans to multiply, which is the only commandment that humans ever fully obeyed. But scripture is clear—we had one set of parents.

You are my brother and my sister, but so is the man working long hours in a factory in China and so is the tired woman in the Sudan carrying her starving child across the desert, as well as the teenager in Pakistan seething at what he perceives as an unjust world. We need to be reminded of that from time to time, and where will that happen if not in church? We are all one family, the family of God. The only hope this world has is that someday we will reach across the walls of hostility between peoples and religions. When that day comes we will understand what the Kingdom of God is—that time when God will reign in every heart.

And this brings us to the final thing to be said: The coming of the kingdom of God will begin when each of us has the love of God living in our hearts.

There is a little chorus that many of us learned to sing in grade school: "Let there be peace on earth and let it begin with me ..." And that is the way peace always comes.

It is when we as God's people open our hearts to God's love and then pass that love on to others. We may not be able solve all the world's problems, we may not be able to speak to all the world's people, we may not be able to personally intervene to prevent the death of innocent people in places where hatred is strong and life is cheap. But what we can do is take responsibility for our lives, to pray for God's love to reside within us, and then live out that love on a day-to-day basis so that everyone we come into contact with is touched by that love.

Do you see any other hope for the world? I don't know of one. We need leaders and we need citizens who are committed to love, committed to peace and committed to justice in this world . . . or hatred will destroy us all. Surely, if we are totally committed to it, we can find new solutions to old problems.

Wallace Hamilton once told the story of a Christian farmer who raised sheep. But he had a serious problem. His neighbor's dogs would, from time to time, get into his sheep pen and injure or even kill one of the sheep. The farmer went to talk with his neighbor but his neighbor didn't do anything about it. So the farmer thought, the next dog that attacks my sheep will be a dead dog. But he knew that was wrong. His next thought was to sue the man. But Paul makes it clear in the 6th chapter of 1st Corinthians that Christians don't sue Christians. "I'll build a wall," he thought, but that would have been expensive. He didn't have that kind of money. And besides, walls are such ugly things.

Finally he prayed, "Lord, what should I do about my neighbor's dogs?" Then that night the answer came to him. The next morning he went out to his sheep. He selected two baby lambs and he took those lambs to his neighbor's house and gave them to his neighbor's daughters as pets. The girls were thrilled (there is nothing cuter than a little lamb). His neighbor was thrilled because his daughters were happy, and since he now had sheep of his own to protect, he started controlling his dogs. (7)

Wallace Hamilton told that story as an illustration of Christmas. When God wanted to make peace with the world he sent us the Lamb of God. But it speaks also to the heart of the Gospel message. Christ came to tear down the wall of hostility. Never has the world needed the peace that Christ brings more than it does today. There is hostility and hatred all about us. These come from the powers of wickedness, not from God. God's intent is that we all be one family. And we shall be when you and I surrender ourselves completely to the love of God through Jesus Christ.

1. ArcaMax - Trivia, http://tinyurl.com/9kf44

2. Dr. Mickey Anders, http://www.mickeyanders.com/Sermons/Sermon20030720.html.

3. Pastor David Wobrock, http://firstgoodshepherd.org/pdf/sermon-pd-9-27-09.pdf.

4. Cited by the Rev. Cynthia F. Reynolds, http://glenridgecong.org/sermon/092009_sermon_cr.pdf.

5. Rev. Adrian Dieleman, http://www.trinityurcvisalia.com/sermons/jn15v08.html

6. Faith, Hope, and Hilarity (New York: Doubleday, 1952).

7. Rev. John Fitzgerald, https://booneumcevents.org/uploads/Sermon2009_09_20.pdf.

Holy Smokes! God Is Here
John 6:1-15

The Rev. Thomas Bandy tells about a meeting his wife Lynne, also a pastor, once attended. The meeting was sponsored by a group in their denomination. To begin this meeting, they had a customary sharing time. Each person answered the question: "How did you experience God this summer?"

"Several people in the room told how they had experienced God in nature. At the cottage, in the woods, or on the lake, they saw a sunset, heard a loon's cry, or felt a summer's breeze." And as they listened, participants thought of their own experiences with God and nodded in agreement, "Yes, God was there."

"Several other people in the room told how they had experienced God in children. Since most of the people in the . . . meeting were over 55, they really meant grandchildren . . . They reflected on the innocent smile, the childlike laughter, the spontaneity of youth." And as they listened, participants thought of their own children and grandchildren and nodded in agreement, "Yes, God was there."

"A few people in the room told how they had experienced God in music. They had attended a concert, or purchased a new CD, and heard Tchaikovsky as they had never heard him before." And as they listened, participants thought of their own experiences with great music and nodded in agreement, "Yes, God was there."

"Finally, it came the turn of a woman who was a newcomer to the group. She was a lay person . . . about 35 years old. She looked very uncomfortable. She said hesitantly: 'One morning this summer I awakened with an incredible compulsion to go see my ex-husband. Normally I am not very spontaneous. In fact, I don't really like my ex-husband. We haven't spoken in over a year. But I was filled with such a compulsion to see him, that I literally could not resist it. So I gathered up my children, dressed hurriedly, and we drove to his house. We found him collapsed on the floor, having experienced a massive heart attack. We called 911 and saved his life.' The listeners were stunned. Some stirred uncomfortably in their chairs. This was an unexpected story. Finally, one whispered tensely: 'Holy smokes!'" (1)

This experience was a little different than seeing a sunset or an innocent child or listening to a grand piece of music. This particular experience reeked of a direct revelation of God. A woman feels a compulsion to see her ex-husband, a compulsion that is too strong to ignore, and she and the children go to his home and find him in the midst of a heart attack and save his life? How else do you explain it? Holy smokes! God was there!

Have you ever had what you felt in your heart of hearts was an experience of God? They happen far more often than we might want to admit.

Imagine you are a Jew in Palestine a little more than 2,000 years ago. You hear about a man named Jesus who is teaching and healing in a region around the Sea of

Galilee and you decide you want to hear him. Is he really a man sent from God? You don't know. You only know him by reputation. You want to find out for yourself.

You're self-employed as a farmer or a fisherman or a shopkeeper. It would be no big deal if you closed down the shop or left the boat or the farm for the day and went to where Jesus is teaching. It might be an inspiring way to spend some time.

But the meeting lasts longer than you expected. Jesus obviously doesn't realize it is written in stone that worship services should always conclude sharply at noon. He keeps teaching and healing people long into the afternoon. People are sitting there with their mouths open in awe at his wisdom and his acts of healing. It is a wonderful event. It's all you had hoped it would be and more. However, your stomach is beginning to growl. You had come expecting that the event would last an hour or so; you hadn't even thought to pack a lunch. Not a brilliant move. Is there a village nearby where you can grab a sandwich?

Then you begin to notice that you are not by yourself. There are at least 5,000 hungry men there and a scattered number of women and children as well, and you are not the only one who failed to pack a lunch. Even if there are a dozen fast-food shops on the road going into town, they will have difficulty feeding that many tired and hungry souls. You think to yourself, "What a frustrating ending to an otherwise wonderful day."

Then you notice the Teacher talking to one of his associates. You step a little closer so you can hear. The Teacher asks, "Where shall we buy bread for these people to eat?" Good question. At least the Teacher is aware of your situation. Little good that will do, however. About all he can do under these circumstances is to pronounce the benediction and tell everybody to go home.

One of the Teacher's associates, a man named Philip, can see how hopeless the situation is. "It would take more than half a year's wages to buy enough bread for each one to have a bite!" he says. You're thinking, "Look around guy, we're not near a supermarket. We're on top of a mountain. How are you going to get the food up here even if you had the funds to buy it? Be realistic. Say a benediction and get us out of here."

But then another of the Teacher's associates, a man named Andrew, speaks up. You see him nudging a small boy to the front of the crowd where the Teacher could see him. "Here is a boy with five small barley loaves and two small fish," he says, "but how far will they go among so many?"

Andrew is probably trying to make the boy feel important. Andrew was like that. Children are important to the teacher. Give the boy some attention and some praise. Besides, it's good that he came prepared. You wish you had done the same. But deep in your heart you're praying, "Let's wrap things up. I'm starving."

The Teacher's not ready to go home yet, though. "Have the people sit down," he says. "Oh, no," you think to yourself, "He's going to keep us longer. My blood sugar is starting to drop. I'm going to faint if he doesn't let us go before long."

But everyone starts sitting down. Then the Teacher does something unbelievable —no, unbelievable doesn't even begin to describe what you are witnessing. The Teacher takes the five small barley loaves that the boy had with him, says a prayer over them, and then starts passing the bread among the crowd. Is he crazy? Five thousand men, and no telling how many women and children? Five tiny barley loaves? Who's he kidding? Then he does the same with the small fish. "Hey," you want to shout, "pass it to me. I could consume that amount of food all by myself."

But something miraculous is happening. Something that cannot be explained. The more bread that is eaten, the more bread there seems to be. The same thing is happening with the fish. Five barley loaves and two small fish and thousands of people are being fed. "That's impossible," you think as you reach out hungrily for your share. "It's impossible. Fish and bread don't multiply. What's happening here?" Then the thought grabs your mind: "Holy smokes. Holy smokes. God is here. This is holy ground. I am standing in the presence of God." It is a day that will stay with you as long as you live.

When everyone has eaten their fill, they gather up what is left over, as the Teacher instructs, and they fill twelve baskets with the pieces of the five barley loaves which are not needed. And you and at least 5,000 other people sit there in stunned silence. Then somebody whispers, "Holy smokes. Surely this is the Prophet who is to come into the world." Someone else murmurs, "This is our long awaited king." And you begin to sense that the crowd is turning into a mob. Not a mob bent on destruction, but a mob intent on making Jesus their king. And you're one of them. But then you look around and the Teacher is gone. Just when you were going to volunteer to help lead the insurrection, he's gone. And you pause for a moment and think to yourself a little more soberly, "God was here. I have experienced the presence of God."

This is the impact Jesus had on people. They came to see a simple carpenter who built cabinets and kitchen tables and instead they found themselves in the presence of the One who created the universe. Make no mistake about it. Jesus was more than a wise teacher. We have always had wise teachers. Every faith has laid claim to wise teachers. And we should listen to them. The Lord knows we need all the wisdom we can gather. But Jesus was more than a great teacher.

He was more than a great physician. We prize people who can heal our bodies. We call them "Dr." and give them proper deference. But he was more than a physician. Here was a man to whom even the forces of nature were subservient. Not only could he give sight to the blind and hearing to the deaf without the benefit of MRIs and X-Rays, he could still the storm, walk on water, cause ordinary bread to multiply, and even raise the dead. What can we say in his presence, except this, "Holy smokes. Here is God."

Have you ever experienced God? Many of you tell me that you have. People still experience God today.

Many of you know the story of Captain Eddie Rickenbacker. It is one of the most remarkable wartime stories I know. In October of 1942 our entire nation held its breath when word came that Eddie Rickenbacker's B-17 Flying Fortress had run out of gas and gone down at sea. For three awful weeks Rickenbacker and his nine-member crew barely survived on three small rafts lost in the far Pacific. They battled storms. They ran out of food. Sharks, some ten feet long, would ram their nine-foot boats. When asked how they were able to endure that experience, Rickenbacker's answer was quite succinct. He said simply, "We prayed."

For days they drifted helplessly under the scorching tropic sun. The heat, the hunger, the exhaustion, brought Rickenbacker and his young, inexperienced crew to the breaking point. But Eddie Rickenbacker continued to pray.

Were his prayers answered? You decide. When he and his crew were almost at the end of their rope, a sea gull flew in from out of nowhere and landed right on Eddie Rickenbacker's head. He caught the sea gull and that day he and his crew had food. Not only did they have food for that day, they cut the intestines of the bird into strips of flesh so that they had bait for several more days for the two fishhooks they had. Then came their first rainstorm, and suddenly they had fresh water. The survivors were sustained and their hopes renewed by that lone sea gull, hundreds of miles from land.

Miraculously, nearly two weeks later they were spotted and rescued. Rickenbacker's explanation: "We prayed."

It is a powerful true story. Writer Max Lucado in one of his books adds a footnote to the story. He tells about James Whittaker a member of Rickenbacker's crew. "James Whittaker," Lucado reports, "was an unbeliever." Experiencing a plane crash didn't change his unbelief. Facing death didn't cause him to reconsider his destiny. In fact, Mrs. Whittaker, his wife, said her husband grew irritated with John Bartak, a crew member who continually read his Bible. But it was one morning after a Bible reading that the seagull landed on Captain Rickenbacker's head. And at that moment, his wife reports, Jim Whittaker became a believer. (2)

That makes sense to me. You're out at sea about to starve, hundreds of miles from shore, and a seagull drops right in your lap. Holy smokes. God was there.

The same God who fed the hungry multitudes with five small barley loaves and two small fish, the same God who plopped a seagull on Eddie Rickenbacker's head, is still alive in our world, still working miracles, still revealing Himself to people today.

I'm told there is a Methodist minister in Texas. There was a time, he confesses, when he was a confirmed atheist and a hateful, greedy person. But he suffered a massive heart attack in Paris, and died on a stretcher in the hospital. At that point he had what is often referred to as a "near-death" experience. In this experience he saw his body, knew it had died, and found himself in a dense gray fog-like state. He didn't know what to do, but he knew he couldn't get back to his body.

He heard his name called, and followed the sound of the voice until he was in a dark place, where creatures began to pull at him, prod, and shriek; they became more insistent as he became more resistant; he suddenly knew he was going to hell.

He despaired; but he suddenly remembered a song from his childhood, and in great sadness he began to sing: "Jesus loves me, this I know . . ."

At the name of Jesus, he says, the beings let go of him and screamed for him to stop singing. He repeated, "Jesus loves me . . ." And at every mention of Jesus, the beings moved farther away, until at length, he was alone. In that pitiable state, as he thought of his life, death, and now his future, he came to say a very brief prayer: "Jesus, I'm sorry. Please help me." And with those words, he saw a pinprick of light a great distance away—and then, just as suddenly as the light appeared, it was with him, and he was filled with warmth, and love and joy—and he knew he was with Jesus.

He wanted nothing more than to stay there, but Jesus told him he must return to earth. When the man said he could not go back and be as he was before, Jesus assured him he would not be. And he has not been. But he has preached and made known the powerful name and most loving person of Jesus ever since. (3)

Now some of you might be listening to this message with some skepticism. Skepticism allows us to keep Jesus at arm's distance. It keeps us from letting go and giving ourselves unreservedly to him.

Could it have been a coincidence that a woman felt a strong compulsion to visit her ex-husband at just the moment he was about to have a heart attack? It could have been.

Could it have been a coincidence that a seagull got blown off course and ended up hundreds of miles off shore and needed a place to rest its weary wings when it spied Eddie Rickenbacker's head bobbing around in that raft and decided that would make a good landing place? Anything's possible.

Are such things as a near-death experience such as this Methodist preacher described just a chemical reaction occurring in the brain as a dying person is about to succumb to death? If you say so.

Can 5,000 hungry men and an unknown number of women and children be fed with five barley loaves and two small fish? You tell me. All I can do is pass on the reports of people who were there. They saw it happen with their own eyes. They tasted it on their own lips. And they wanted to make him king. I hope you want to make him king of your life. I hope you look into the eyes of Jesus today and say something like this, "Holy smokes, God is here. I am experiencing God."

1. http://www.netresults.org/fileadmin/community/PDF_Files/Hearts%20Afire.pdf.

2. Max Lucado, The Lucado Inspirational Reader: Hope and Encouragement for Your Everyday Life (Nashville: Thomas Nelson, 2011).

3. Janet Fulmer, http://www.redeemermarin.org/Sermons/HolyName.html.

Where Is Your Pebble?

Ephesians 4:1-16

Some of you will remember country comedian Jerry Clower. Besides being a funny story-teller, Clower, who died in 1998, was a deeply religious man. He tells of an occasion when he invited Sue, his 14-year-old daughter, and one of her friends to go with him on a trip to the Country Music Awards show in Hollywood. He listed for Sue some of the celebrities she would meet if she went, some of the best-known entertainers at that time. Sue's response?

She said, "Daddy, I love you and I'm so glad that you would arrange it to where me and one of my friends could go on this trip, but Daddy, there's something going on at church . . . I don't want to miss. I won't be able to go with you this time."

Jerry Clower says tears welled up in his eyes and he wanted to sing the Doxology to think that a church activity was more important to his daughter than a trip to the CMA awards in Hollywood. Interesting. A church activity was more important than a trip to meet celebrities in Hollywood. (1)

Anglican Bishop James Cruckshank was once asked by a student, "What is the first thing we should do when we start with a new church?"

Bishop Cruckshank immediately replied. "Once you arrive, go to your office, sit down and remain there until you realize that what your church is doing is the most important mission in the community. And then give thanks that Christ has called you to be part of it." (2)

The "most important mission in the community"—I ask again: how important is church to you? Do you believe that God has a plan for our church? Do you believe that what we are doing, preparing this world for the coming of the Kingdom of God by proclaiming the Gospel of Jesus Christ, is the most important work any group of people can do? Do you believe that or do you look at the church as just another organization that you belong to because it is good for the children or, perhaps, good for business?

I believe that God has called this group of people to turn the world upside down.

I read a story recently about a circuit riding preacher during the frontier days of our land. He was a humdinger of a preacher named Jesse Lee. He once preached a sermon on Acts 17:6 that reads like this in the new King James Version: "These that turned the world upside down have come here also."

The thrust of his sermon was that sin has turned the world upside down, and the design of the gospel and the business of the ministry are to set the world right side up again. Well, the people of the town decided to have some fun with this passionate circuit rider and so the next day when he rode into town nearly everything looked ridiculous. Everything that could be turned upside down had been turned upside down: wagons, signs, gates, etc. (3)

The people of the town got a laugh at the preacher's expense, but at least they got the point. The purpose of the church is to turn the world upside down—or better—right side up. You and I have a tendency to take the church of Jesus Christ for granted. We see the church as a mere institution—as a club, as a place where we can make friends or business contacts. What we fail to see is the church as God's agent, Christ's body at work in the world.

Christ came into the world to save the world. John 3:17, "For God did not send his Son into the world to condemn the world, but to save the world through him." But how does Christ save the world? Certainly he saved the world through the cross. He gave his life and by his life we received life eternal. Certainly that is true.

What we fail to recognize however, is that Christ is still saving the world today by the giving of his body, the church, in service to the world. This is to say that you and I are central to the plan of God. If we fail to do what Christ has called us to do, if we fail to be what Christ has called us to be, then Christ's saving action will be incomplete.

In her bestselling book, Traveling Mercies, Anne Lamott explained why she made her son as a young person go with her to church. She says, "The main reason is that I want to give him what I found in the world, which is a path and a little light to see by. Most of the people I know who have what I want—purpose, heart, balance, gratitude, joy—are people with a deep sense of spirituality. They are people in community, who pray, or practice their faith . . . They follow a brighter light than the glimmer of their own candle; they are part of something beautiful . . . Our funky little church is filled with people who are working for peace and freedom, who are out there on the streets and inside praying, and they are home writing letters, and they are at the shelters with giant platters of food." Then she says, "When I was at the end of my rope, the people at St. Andrew tied a knot in it for me and helped me hold on." (4)

That's good— "they tied a knot in it for me and helped me hold on." The work of the church is important work. Indeed, it is critical work. If you do not understand that, you cannot appreciate the words of the Apostle Paul to the church at Ephesus. Paul is in prison. He knows his time is limited. And so he writes to the church at Ephesus with a real sense of urgency about the meaning of the gospel and about their mission as the people who are to convey the gospel. He conveys to them two important truths about the church. For God's plan to be realized, says the Apostle, two things are critical.

First of all, it is vital that our unity be maintained. St. Paul writes, "Make every effort to keep the unity of the Spirit through the bond of peace. There is one body and one Spirit, just as you were called to one hope when you were called; one Lord, one faith, one baptism; one God and Father of all, who is over all and through all and in all." In other words, it is vital that the church be unified.

I suppose there is nothing sadder than to see a church that is split with dissension.

A pastor was telling why he had resigned from his pulpit. He had hired a young minister to work with the youth of his church. The young minister said some rather radical things within the hearing of some of the young people. You know, when you're young, and you're searching, you can say some things that may make older people uncomfortable. Most of us understand that. But there were some people in that church who made a big issue of it, and the church became divided. The minister felt as a matter of integrity that he had to back up his young assistant. And that is when the trouble really began.

He said, "One Sunday my wife went up to sit in the choir and right in front of the whole congregation, two members of the choir got up and moved so they would not have to sit next to her. I couldn't take it any longer, the way some Christians can treat other Christians, and so I resigned."

My friends, if you believe that the Church of Jesus Christ is at the center of God's purpose for creation, if you believe that we are called to be the light unto the nations of the world, that will break your heart. If we are the hope that God has for this world, then the rest of the world is in trouble if we cannot love one another. Our unity is critical. We must work as a unit, as a team.

I heard about a pastor who gathered his congregation in a circle and told them to picture God at the center of the circle. Then he instructed them to move forward to God. The group complied but at one point they came shoulder to shoulder with each other and stopped. This pastor then said, "You can't get closer to God without at the same time getting closer to one another." (5) Maybe we ought to do that exercise some time to emphasize that we are a unit, we are the body of Jesus Christ. You cannot split a body asunder, and have that body carry out its task. We are called to be Jesus in earthly flesh to the world, and it is important that we work together and love one another. So St. Paul says that our unity is critical.

He says one other thing: he says each of us has a gift to be used in God's service. St. Paul notes that Christ gave gifts to some of us to be apostles, and some prophets, and some pastors and teachers. The purpose of those specific gifts is ". . . to equip his people [the church] for works of service, so that the body of Christ may be built up . . ."

These gifts which Paul lists are gifts of ministry, but all of us have gifts. Some of us are gifted as sales people, some as engineers, some as mechanics and farmers, but all of us are gifted in some way—and it is when we offer our gifts to be used of God that God's kingdom is brought nearer.

Some of our boys and girls may know Aesop's fable about an old crow who was out in the wilderness and was very thirsty. He had not had anything to drink in a long time. He came to a jug that had a little water in the bottom of it. The old crow reached his beak into the jug to get some of that water, but his beak wouldn't quite reach. So what did he do? Some of our boys and girls know. He started picking up pebbles one at a time and dropping them into the jug. What happened as those pebbles accumulated in the bottom of the jug? Why, of course. The water rose until finally the old crow was able to get a drink.

My friends, that is my understanding of the way God has chosen to work in this world. Each of us dropping in our own little pebble—teaching that Sunday School class, making that visit, working on the finance committee and on the church board, making that special gift to missions, serving as an usher, etc. Each of us serving in his or her own special ministry. Doing that little task that may not seem so important at the time, but those pebbles are accumulating in the bottom of that jug, and the water is rising, and one of these days God is going to bring in His own Kingdom. That is God's plan for creation. It is centered in this group of people.

Now the obvious question is: Are you dropping in your pebble? Are you using your gift to the glory of God?

You may say, "Pastor, what can I do?" Let me tell you about a little lady in a small church in Maryland many years ago. Her name, quite appropriately was Miss Fuss. And she really could fuss—particularly at her young pastor. But he knew and others knew she had a heart of gold.

Miss Fuss was severely handicapped by arthritis—one of the most thoroughly afflicted people you can imagine from this dread and painful disease. Her wrists and her knees and ankles were all swollen up. She could barely keep going, but she would not quit. Every Sunday morning when the doors of her church opened, there was Miss Fuss. She had to have a cane to get around; someone had to help her climb the church steps, but she said to herself and to others, "If I ever quit going, I'm afraid I'll die." So she was there for every service.

Miss Fuss' pastor stood up one Sunday morning and preached a sermon on the idea that each of us has a ministry—that each of us has a pebble we can drop in. Miss Fuss went up to him after the service and said, "Pastor, what can I do?"

Her pastor looked down at this little severely handicapped lady who could barely get down the aisle of the church each Sunday, and he had to admit that he was stumped. He said, "Miss Fuss, I don't have an answer for you right away, but I'll pray about it, and you pray about it, and I'll be by later this week and we'll talk about it."

Later that week the pastor went by to see Miss Fuss. She called for him to come in because it took her too long to make her way across the room to open the door. He went in and sat down with Miss Fuss. She was so happy to see him. Her face was alive with excitement. She said, "Pastor, I think I've discovered my calling."

The pastor, who had not been able to think of a specific calling for Miss Fuss was relieved. He said, "Well, tell me about it."

She said, "We have some shut-ins in this little town who have nobody to look after them. Some of them have family living miles away. They could die and it might be several days before anybody would know it. So I've started a program of calling each of these shut-ins and talking with them for five minutes each day."

Now Miss Fuss couldn't dial the telephone the way most people dialed a telephone back then—with her fingers—because of her arthritis. This was before the day of the touch-tone telephone. Miss Fuss had a rotary phone with a dial that had to be turned. And so, Miss Fuss had a little stick she placed in the dial of her rotary telephone to turn it with. Dialing each call was slow and tedious. She started this ministry of calling each of these shut-ins to make sure they were alright even though anyone else in her condition would be a shut-in themselves. She says, "I limit my calls to five minutes each day because I'm afraid that if I exceed that limit I might be tempted to tell them my problems rather than listening to their problems."

Miss Fuss had found her ministry. She found her gift. She found her pebble to drop in the jug. And friend, I have to say to you, if Miss Fuss could find a ministry in her condition, you and I have no excuse. That is how the kingdom of God is coming—one pebble at a time.

What is the pebble you have to offer? For you see the crisis of the church today is not one of belief. The Gallup survey shows that most American Christians still believe pretty much the same things they believed several years ago. The crisis of the church today is not one of resources. Most churches have more resources than Peter and Paul ever dreamed about in their lifetime.

The crisis of the church today is one of commitment. Jesus said, "If anyone would be my disciple, he must take up his cross and follow me." That is another way of saying that we must find that unique ministry that Christ has called us to offer to the world. It will not be preaching for most of us; it won't even be teaching or singing in the choir, or serving in a leadership capacity. Some of us will do our best work in quiet ways that few people will know about. But in order for the waters of God to rise, each of us must drop in our pebble, whatever that might be.

There is a time-honored story that many of you will remember that says the angel Gabriel approached Jesus in heaven after his time was finished on earth. Gabriel asked Christ, "Master, did you accomplish everything you set out to do on earth?"

"No," replied Jesus, "not yet. There is still much to be done."

Gabriel was perplexed. "Then what's next?"

Jesus said, "I've left it in the hands of my disciples. They will carry on the work I have begun."

Gabriel frowned and looked rather skeptical. He said, "Do you really think they will? What if the people somewhere along the way forget? Do you have a plan B?"

Jesus answered, "No. That's it. I'm counting on them. There is no plan B."

What a tremendous privilege it is to be the Church of Jesus Christ. We are Christ's own body, the light of the world. That means that our unity is critical. That also means that everyone one of us has a calling, a ministry—a pebble to drop in. And one day God will take all of those pebbles and build His Kingdom, and the day will come when "every knee shall bow and every tongue confess that Jesus Christ is Lord, to the glory of God the Father."

1. Jerry Clower, Let the Hammer Down! (Waco: Word Books, 1978), pp. 92-93.
2. James Love http://www.jameslove.com/sermons/ yeara_pentacost16_2002.htm.
3. Frederick E. Maser and Robert Drew Simpson, If Saddlebags Could Talk (Franklin, TN: Providence House, 1998), p. 58.
4. Anne Lamott, Traveling Mercies (New York: Anchor, 2001).
5. Rev. Donald Ng, http://www.fcbc-sf.org/sermons/srm092709.pdf.

Screaming At The Television
Ephesians 4:30-5:2

Have you ever been so angry that it caused you to do something really stupid? I mean, really stupid! One guy said he saw two men literally pummeling each other over a parking spot. Both cars had nosed into this particular parking spot. Fortunately they stopped just before colliding. Now the owners of both cars were violently swinging at one another. What amused the man observing these fisticuffs was a sign over the intended parking spot. It said . . . you guessed it . . . "No parking." (1)

I wonder if the guy who won the fight got a ticket for illegal parking. People get upset sometimes over the most trivial things and sometimes they act out their anger in strange ways.

One of the most bizarre stories from ancient history is told on the Persian military leader Xerxes who lived in the fifth century B.C. Xerxes sought to invade Greece with a huge army. His plan was to cross a narrow strait between Greece and Persia called the Hellespont. He purported to do this by building two pontoon bridges and using them to cross over the strait. It was quite an engineering feat. However a great storm came up and destroyed both of these pontoon bridges before his army could cross over them. This infuriated Xerxes to the point that he had those responsible for building the bridge beheaded.

If he had stopped there, we could deem him reasonably sane, though dreadfully cruel—but Xerxes didn't stop there. He also took out his fury on the body of water itself. He had fetters—the chains and shackles that prisoners normally wear—thrown onto the body of water upon which the pontoon bridges floated in order to punish the strait. Not satisfied with this he had his soldiers give the body of water—not a person or an animal, mind you—but a narrow body of water—300 lashes with whips—and then, as if that weren't enough, he branded the body of water with red-hot irons. We say, "How stupid! What a dumb thing to do!"

Meanwhile we perfectly rational people yell at our television set when a football coach makes what we regard as a dumb call and our team loses yardage. We scream at the television as if somehow the coach will hear us and change his strategy for the game. I know, nobody in this room would do anything like that, but anger sometimes causes us to do silly things.

There is an old Buddhist legend about a young farmer paddling his boat up the river feverishly seeking to deliver his produce to a nearby village so that he can get home before dark. Suddenly he spies another vessel coming downstream directly at him. It's as if the pilot of the other boat is deliberately trying to ram him. He begins screaming at the other vessel: "You idiot! Watch where you're going or you're going to ram me." But the other vessel continues coming directly at him and then suddenly there is a sickening thud as the other boat does indeed ram into his. He continues his tirade at the other vessel with even more vehemence: "You moron! Look what you've done now. The river's plenty wide. You could've gotten around me."

Then he happens to notice that there is no pilot in the other boat. The vessel is empty. A boat had broken loose from its moorings upstream. He has been screaming at an empty vessel. His ranting has been as futile as ours when we scream at our television during a football game. But the point of the legend is this, the boat is always empty. Our ranting and raving solve nothing. (2) But anger does that to people. It causes us to do really stupid things. Sometimes, of course, it causes us to do tragic things.

Stephen Arterburn tells a story about Dr. Benjamin Carson, one of the most famous surgeons in our nation. Dr. Carson is director of pediatric neurosurgery at Johns Hopkins Hospital in Baltimore, and he is much respected, particularly for the care he gives to children.

Early in his life, however, Dr. Ben Carson had a terrible problem with his temper. His parents divorced when he was eight years old. He says, "I adopted God as my earthly father as well as my Heavenly Father when I was fourteen." But that experience of adopting God did not cause his temper to magically disappear. He began running with some teenagers in his neighborhood.

One day he was involved in a scuffle with another boy. He let his temper get out of control and before anyone could stop him, he drew a knife and stabbed at the other boy. Fortunately his knife caught on the other boy's belt buckle and didn't do any real damage. But young Ben Carson was wise enough to realize how close he had come to doing something really tragic. He rushed home and fell to his knees and began to pray.

"I had tried to stab another teenager," he wrote later, "and I recognized that I had a personality defect with my terrible temper. I prayed for three hours and asked the Lord to take that defect away. I had been reading Psychology Today, and I knew it was difficult to change a personality defect, but God took it away from me. Since then," says Dr. Ben Carson, "I've never had a problem with my temper." (3)

What a fortunate person Ben Carson is. His life could've taken an entirely different turn if his prayer had not been answered. Anger can cause us to do tragic things.

In our lesson from the Epistle, Paul is writing from jail. In last week's lesson, you'll remember, he instructed the church at Ephesus to maintain their unity as a people and to develop the gifts God had given them. He reminded them that they were God's people doing God's work on earth. Today Paul is addressing individual Christians in their faith journey. Listen to his words: "And do not grieve the Holy

Spirit of God . . . Get rid of all bitterness, rage and anger, brawling and slander, along with every form of malice. Be kind and compassionate to one another, forgiving each other, just as in Christ God forgave you . . ."

Paul is telling the people at Ephesus—and he is telling us—to get rid of all of our feelings of hostility—to be kind, compassionate and forgiving. Most of us will agree that is easier said than done. But somehow Paul had managed to do it. If anybody had good reason to be angry it was Paul. After all he was writing from prison, a fate he did not deserve. He could've been bitter toward those who had put him there. He could have been equally bitter toward those in the church who were constantly criticizing him, slandering him, making all kinds of unjust accusations against him.

There was a time when Paul might have fought back at those who persecuted him like this. Remember he had been a fire-breathing reactionary at one time in his life, punishing people who did not conform to what he believed was the true religion. But Paul's heart had been changed. He truly became a new person on the road to Damascus when he was confronted by the risen Christ. Christ had performed a great work in his life and so, later in life, St. Paul was able to return hatred with love, anger with gentleness, and slander with words of kindness. Not many people reach that level of spiritual maturity.

There are some people we encounter whose hearts are filled with anger. We see it on the road—road rage it's call. We see it in our offices—people who tend to fly off the handle at the slightest provocation. Some of us live with someone like that at home.

Perhaps we have a spirit of bitterness and anger ourselves. It causes us much grief. Each New Year's we make resolutions that this year we will learn to control our temper. And after every tirade we apologize to our loved ones. We truly do regret that we have allowed ourselves to get out of control, but still we do not change.

Notice this: Paul says that we not only bring grief to our family members, friends and co-workers when we let our negative feelings get out of control. He says we also bring grief to God. "Do not grieve the Holy Spirit of God . . . Get rid of all bitterness, rage and anger . . . ." he writes. That's interesting, don't you think?

That says to me that anger is a spiritual problem. Anything that threatens our relationships with others is an enemy of God. You cannot be what God wants you to be when you are filled with rage. God is not able to use us as effectively to do His work, if we are filled with anger, bitterness, malice and slander. This is a spiritual problem that demands a spiritual solution. What is the solution to a foul temper? How do we escape from this prison of our own negative feelings?

On a human level, the best we can do with rage is to find an acceptable way of releasing it. The worse thing is to hold those feelings in.

I enjoyed reading about a hotel in Spain a few years ago that was making major renovations. Rather than getting a professional demolition company to do the job, however, they offered 30 "highly stressed out people"—a group selected by a team of psychologists—the chance to take up sledge hammers and battering rams and smash through the hotel's rooms. Wearing protective dust masks, goggles, white overalls, helmets and gloves—the amateur demolition crew swung hammers into television sets and bedroom walls and tossed beds and desks like hard-partying rock stars. Those picked for the stress-relieving smash-up were invited back to admire the hotel's new interior the following September. (4) I'm certain they felt better after releasing their pent-up rage. On a human level, that's about all we can do with anger.

Max Lucado tells about a man named T. D. Terry who understood that principle. Many years ago a stressful job caused Terry to perpetually carry around angry feelings within himself. His daughter, upon hearing him describe those feelings years later, responded with surprise. "I don't remember any anger during those years," she said.

He asked if she remembered a certain tree—the one near their driveway about halfway between the gate and the house. "Remember how it used to be tall?" he asked. "Then it lost a few limbs? And after some time there was nothing more than a stump?"

She remembered.

"That was me," T. D. explained. "I took my anger out on the tree. I kicked it. I took an ax to it. I tore the limbs. I didn't want to come home mad, so I left my anger at the tree." (5) On a human level, that's about all that we can do with anger—find a socially acceptable way of releasing it.

William Blake wrote a little poem titled "A Poison Tree." It went like this:
I was angry with my friend, I told my wrath, my wrath did end.
I was angry with my foe, I told it not, my wrath did grow.

Anger can only be bottled up for so long without manifesting itself in ways that may be damaging to ourselves and to others.

But there is another way to deal with anger. That is to do what Ben Carson did: turn it over to God. Because anger is a spiritual problem, there is a spiritual solution.

For one thing we need to ask where these negative emotions came from in the first place? What causes us to be angry? What causes us to be filled with bitterness? What is there about us that we are not able to overcome feelings of malice and all the other negative emotions Paul warns us about?

Don't most of these negative emotions grow out of our basic insecurity about who we are? There is a deep unrest within many of us that began in our earliest years. This unrest reflects a deep question about whether we can trust other people, whether we can trust ourselves and ultimately whether we can trust God.

Psychologists tell us that the first question we ask emotionally is—is the world a friendly place? Something happens to some of us early in our life that causes us to believe that the world is not a friendly place, that there is no one we can trust.

Somehow some of us got negative messages about ourselves, about the world around us and even about the God in whom we believe. And it left us with a terrible ache, an ache that expresses itself for some people through depression, and others through anger. There is only one solution to such a deep-seated emotion and that is to ask God to reach deep down into our souls and to pluck out that mistrust, that fear, that deep anger—and to make us new people. Spiritual problems demand spiritual solutions. We need to ask God's help in dealing with our anger.

And we need to go one step further: we need to ask God to help us convert our anger into love. This is where a spiritual solution really begins to take hold of us. It is when we are able to return good for evil.

The Rev. Curtis Goforth tells a story about his old Hebrew professor's experience one year on an archaeological dig in Israel. He said that there were a number of Ethiopians employed by the dig. Their job was to help them with the labor. However, said the old professor, they were really a strange bunch. He said most of them were Coptic Christians and that they do some things a little differently than we do.

He said that he had been up all day and most of the night trying to get everything done to wrap the excavation up and go back home, but he was distracted by the rather loud voice of one of the Ethiopians in the tent next to him. He yelled to tell him to be quiet, but it was no use. He said he finally ended up throwing one of his dusty boots at the tent which finally made the noise stop.

The old professor said that he learned later that the gentleman in the tent next to his had been praying aloud, as many Coptic Christians do. Imagine that. The old professor had thrown a boot at a man because he was praying. He said that he awoke the next morning to find the dusty boot he had thrown at the tent placed next to the entrance to his tent, and both his boots had been cleaned and polished as he slept.

"We throw dusty boots at one another all the time though, don't we?" asks Rev. Goforth. "How many times can we say that we have taken those dusty boots hurled at us and polished them and handed them back to the offending person?" (6)

It takes a remarkable person to do that. But that is exactly what God intends for us to be—remarkable people, people who have grown to resemble His Son, Jesus Christ.

Anger is a spiritual problem that requires a spiritual solution. It's good if you have a tree that you can take out your anger on. That's better than taking it out on your family and friends. But better still is to pray that God will reach into your soul and remove the deep insecurity which causes you to manifest anger and replace it with His Holy Spirit, the Spirit of love. Then perhaps you will be able to move to that highest level of spiritual maturity, that of returning hatred and anger with love.

1. Richard F. Shepard, In Enemy Waters (St. Louis: Bethany Press, 1962), p. 64.
2. Marshall Goldsmith, What Got You Here Won't Get You There (New York: Hyperion, 2007), pp. 63-64.
3. Flash Points (Wheaton, IL: Tyndale House Publishers, Inc., 2002), pp. 176-177.
4. Harold Heckle, The Associated Press.
5. A Love Worth Giving (Nashville: Publishing Group, 2002), pp. 82-83.
6. http://revgoforth.wordpress.com/sermons-on-john/john-131-17-31-35/.

Enough Foolishness!
Ephesians 5:15-20

Is there anyone in the room who has felt dumb in front of a computer? It's happened to all of us at one time or another, I suspect.

A technical support advisor received a call from a woman who had been told that her computer was infected by a virus! This alarmed her. She wanted to know how she could disinfect it. The tech advisor asked her what software she was using. She sounded a bit confused. What did he mean, software? After a few minutes on the phone, the tech support guy realized that she had dismantled her computer and was preparing to wipe everything down with Lysol, a disinfecting cleaner. It took him a minute to compose himself and tell her to stop before she ruined her computer. "You don't disinfect a computer virus with Lysol," he told her. He says he doesn't know if she stopped or not. He never heard from her again, but it took him ten minutes to stop laughing. (1)

Another support technician reported getting a call from another computer user. She told the support person that her computer was not working. She described the problem. The technician concluded that her computer needed to be brought in and serviced. He said, "Unplug the power cord and bring it up here and I'll fix it for you."

A short time later she showed up at his door . . . carrying only the electrical cord. (2) No computer, just the cord. Well, that's what the technician said, "Unplug the power cord and bring it up here . . ."

People are amazing, aren't they? Of course, some people don't need a computer in front of them to act stupid.

Longtime Washington, D. C. news correspondent Helen Thomas tells an incredible story that she says is true. She says that shortly after the inauguration of President George W. Bush, someone in Danville, Kentucky, managed to pay for a $2 order at a fast-food restaurant with a bogus $200 bill. This bill featured a picture of President George W. Bush on its face. There was also a picture of the White House with a sign in front of it that said, "We like broccoli" (harking back to Bush, Sr.'s admitted dislike for broccoli). On the back of the bill was a picture of an oil well.

Police said the cashier at the Dairy Queen not only accepted the bogus $200 bill for payment, she gave the culprit $198 in real money as change. (3)

People are amazing. And sometimes they act foolishly. I say "they," but actually all of us do foolish things at some time in our lives. It is partially in our behalf that St. Paul writes to the church at Ephesus, "Be very careful . . . how you live—not as unwise but as wise, making the most of every opportunity, because the days are evil. Therefore do not be foolish, but understand what the Lord's will is. Do not get drunk on wine, which leads to debauchery. Instead, be filled with the Spirit, speaking to one another with psalms, hymns, and songs from the Spirit. Sing and make music from your heart to the Lord, always giving thanks to God the Father for everything, in the name of our Lord Jesus Christ."

St. Paul was trying to give the Christians at Ephesus some very practical advice about how to live a fulfilling life. St. Paul had found great joy in living for Christ and he wanted others to experience that same joy. He had found meaning and purpose, a reason for being. He saw all around him people who were living lives of quiet desperation just as we see people today living lives of quiet desperation. He wanted them to know that there was more to life than what they were experiencing. And so he gave them three simple steps that they could take that would increase their joy, increase their sense of fulfillment and increase their ability to cope with the world around them.

The first step which he prescribed was to rid themselves of the spirit of the world. He writes, "Do not get drunk on wine, which leads to debauchery. Instead, be filled with the Spirit, speaking to one another with psalms, hymns, and songs from the Spirit. Sing and make music from your heart to the Lord . . ."

It is clear that people in Paul's day were abusing alcohol, just as people today abuse alcohol and drugs. Chemical abuse is an ancient ill that has taken a toll on many people. It has destroyed families, and it has destroyed the spiritual well-being of those who have become addicted. I realize that it is not fashionable today for a pastor to warn of the dangers of alcohol abuse. Drug abuse, yes—alcohol abuse, no. There was a time when pastors were guilty, perhaps, of preaching too often on the dangers of demon rum, as if that were the only sin worth discussing.

It's like the story of the little boy drawing a picture in Sunday School. His teacher asked him to describe his picture. He replied, "It's a cowboy going into a saloon."

The Sunday School teacher looked shocked.

"Oh, don't worry," the little boy said. "He's not going in there to drink. He's just going in to shoot somebody."

Some of you may have been brought up to believe it was worse to take a drink than to shoot someone. However, the dangers of alcohol abuse are very real.

There was a tragic story in the news sometime back about a teenager, Melissa Vinson, an honors student at Seminole High School in Sanford, Florida. It seems that Melissa was involved in a game called "Pass-Out." She was playing this game with two of her schoolmates. "Pass-Out" is a drinking game. It's a board game, but in this game, rather than landing on Park Place or Boardwalk, players land on squares that read, "Take a drink," or "Go to the bar," and they recite tongue-twisters on cards that are called "Pink Elephant" cards.

In a two-hour period of playing this game, Melissa consumed most of a liter bottle of vodka. Later that night she began to convulse. Finally she blacked out on her living room floor. She was pronounced dead at Florida Hospital in Orlando. Medical examiners concluded that possibly a reaction of the vodka to a prescription drug she was taking contributed to her death. (4)

What a tragic loss. But the story could be repeated hundreds of thousands of times over the ages. Abuse of alcohol and drugs has taken an enormous toll on human beings since the beginning of time. And alcohol and drug abuse are out of control in our land today. Recent surveys show that 38 million Americans, roughly one out of six adults, are so-called "binge drinkers" who over-indulge more than four times a month. The toll that takes in automobile accidents, the toll that takes on families, the toll that takes on people's minds and bodies is indescribable. "Do not get drunk on wine," Paul says.

I was quite surprised to read that binge drinking is not just a problem among college students, though, of course, it is. But among older people—retired people who are old enough to know better—binge drinking is becoming epidemic. When we are unrestrained in any of our personal habits, there is a price to be paid—in relationships with family members and friends, in the quality of our health, in our relationship with God. No one wants to hear a sermon filled with "Thou shalt nots . . ." but this is a matter that must be addressed.

"Be very careful . . . how you live—not as unwise but as wise, making the most of every opportunity, because the days are evil. Therefore do not be foolish, but understand what the Lord's will is. Do not get drunk on wine, which leads to debauchery. Instead, be filled with the Spirit, speaking to one another with psalms, hymns, and songs from the Spirit. Sing and make music from your heart to the Lord, always giving thanks to God the Father for everything, in the name of our Lord Jesus Christ."

What a beautiful picture of a joyful person: "Sing and make music from your heart to the Lord, always giving thanks to God the Father for everything, in the name of our Lord Jesus Christ."

The second thing Paul says is to be filled with the spirit of the Lord. This is the clear alternative to dependence on alcohol and drugs, and even to other dangers like materialism and pride. Be filled with the Spirit and the joy of the Lord. The happiest people on this earth are people who are filled with the Spirit of God. That is one of the best kept secrets in society.

Most of you are familiar with the name, William Wilberforce. Wilberforce, an Englishman, gave his life to fighting slavery. The battle consumed 46 years of his life. There was huge economic and political opposition to his work. Having slaves to do your back-bending work was very profitable for a great many successful people.

The cause of abolishing the slave trade was defeated eleven times before it was finally passed in 1807. Slavery itself was not defeated decisively in Britain until three days before Wilberforce died in 1833. On top of this huge opposition, Wilberforce had health issues. He had to deal with bad eyes, ulcerated bowels, and a curvature of the spine so bad that without a brace his head would have been sitting on his chest. Yet at his funeral, when people eulogized William Wilberforce, what they talked about over and over again was his joy. One man said, "He was always a most cheerful Christian; no gloomy atmosphere of melancholy moroseness surrounded him; his sun appeared to be always shining." Wilberforce himself believed that joy was an "injunction strongly enforced in the New Testament." (5)

The happiest people on this earth are people who are filled with the Spirit of God. If you are ever around genuinely devout religious people you know it's true. They have a great time together. I worry about Christians who go around with a sour expression all the time. Somehow they have missed out on the Good News of God's love.

Early Christian congregations were known for their joy. In the words of Markus Barth: "early Christian congregations were singing, jubilant, exulting assemblies." They were known not only for their love but for their joy. Such assemblies still exist in modern-day Christianity, but generally they exist in less affluent parts of the world.

Pastor Gerald Stephens gives us an example of exuberant worship in the Congo. He says he's been in evangelical churches where folks were well-trained to "act" joyous but in the Congo, it's no act. The most joyous time in the service, he says, is when the offerings are taken. Don't you think that's interesting? The singing reaches its loudest, the dancing and clapping are the most unbridled during the offering time. Usually, there are at least two offerings per worship service—one for the parish, the other for the poor. I wonder if having two offerings would engender joy in our congregation.

Stephens says the worshippers in these African services come forward dancing and singing to put their money into a box at the front of the worship place. He says he enjoys most "watching the older men dance to the front, chuck their money in the box, and then dance back to their places. They're dressed to the nines," he notes, "and do a kind of understated two-step while holding their arms outward and bent at the elbows ... Somehow their hips," he says, "take on a life apart ...." He challenges us to imagine one of our church officers or the chairperson of the finance committee dancing toward the altar with his or her offering like this. "It's great stuff!" he says, "It's especially great because it's so extraordinarily sincere, in no way contrived." (6)

We ought to try that some time. I'll bet some of you would look pretty cool dancing your way to the altar. The point is that being filled with the Spirit of the Lord ought to fill us with a corresponding joy. We are God's own people. We need fear neither life nor death. In all things, God is with us.

The final thing St. Paul says to us is to learn to give thanks for everything. "Sing and make music from your heart to the Lord always," he writes, "giving thanks to God the Father for everything, in the name of our Lord Jesus Christ."

We've talked before about the gratitude attitude. It is a wonderful thing when a person has a thankful spirit. It is so much better than grumbling all the time that life has been unfair to you. Let me give you an example of someone with that kind of attitude.

Dr. Tim Hansel tells about a friend of his who has no hands. How's that for being dealt a bad hand in life?—no pun intended. His friend has no hands. Instead, he uses hooks. He uses them so well that he is able to play tennis and ride a bicycle. This man named Mark, sometimes takes off his hooks and is still able to function using only his wrists.

One day Tim accompanied Mark to the grocery store. Mark didn't have his hooks on. Nevertheless he used both wrists to pick up items and drop them into his grocery shopping cart. As he was picking up some cereal, two boys about six or seven years of age watched in disbelief. And then they asked the inevitable question, "Mr. what happened to your hands?"

In mock surprise, Mark replied, "My goodness, where are they? I must've left them among the cereal boxes!"

The boys quickly joined him in searching for his missing hands. Mark was having fun with his disability. When the hands still did not turn up, Mark turned to the boys and said, "When I washed my hands this morning I must've left them lying on the edge of the sink." (7)

Mark had learned one of the great lessons in life. Everyone has some kind of disability. Even people who have lived a charmed life have a disability even if it is simply that they have never learned to cope with life. And that is a skill that everyone will need at some time or another. If you can learn to trust God to the extent that you can give God thanks even for those things in life that give you much distress, if you can say to God as St. Paul did on another occasion, "I don't know why I was given this thorn in the flesh, but help me to praise You and use it to Your glory," then you will be one of the most blessed people on this earth.

Here is the secret to a wondrous life: "Be very careful . . . how you live—not as unwise but as wise, making the most of every opportunity, because the days are evil. Therefore do not be foolish, but understand what the Lord's will is. Do not get drunk on wine, which leads to debauchery. Instead, be filled with the Spirit, speaking to one another with psalms, hymns, and songs from the Spirit. Sing and make music from your heart to the Lord, always giving thanks to God the Father for everything, in the name of our Lord Jesus Christ."

1. Teddi's Humor, teddi@alohabroadband.com.
2. Clean Laffs, http://www.gophercentral.com/sub/sub-jokes.html.
3. Thanks for the Memories, Mr. President (New York: A Lisa Drew Book/Scribner, 2002), p. 203.
4. Rev. David P. Nolte, http://www.holwick.com/sermons/joshua/joshua24.html.
5. Pastor Andy MacFarlane, http://media.lincolnberean.org/pdfdocs/Psalm126Trans_MacFarlane.pdf.
6. The Rev. Dr. Rick Dietrich, http://day1.org/502-hey_pay_attention
7. Nell W. Mohney, Just Choose Happiness: A Guide to Joyous Living (Nashville: Abingdon Press. 2009), p. 2.

Quitters
John 6:60-69

There is a time-honored story about a football game featuring two mismatched teams. One team was much larger than the other. The larger team was dominating the game, severely intimidating the smaller team in the process. The hitting was fierce.

The smaller team had one player, however, who might make a difference. His name was Calhoun and he was the fastest running back in the league. His coach felt that if Calhoun could get any blocking at all, he could easily break free and outrun the larger players. The coach talked with his quarterback about giving the ball to Calhoun and letting him run with it. The quarterback agreed.

However, the first play came and Calhoun did not touch the ball. The coach was mystified. Then the second play came, but once again Calhoun did not touch the ball. Now the game was in the final seconds with the smaller team's only hope being for Calhoun to break free and score the winning touchdown. The third play was executed and still Calhoun did not get the ball. The coach was furious. It was fourth down. He sent in word to the quarterback, "Get the ball to Calhoun." The ball was snapped and the quarterback pedaled backward and was sacked, ending the game. The coach was furious as he confronted his quarterback: "I told you four times to give the ball to Calhoun."

The quarterback stood tall and said, "Coach, you don't understand! Calhoun didn't want the ball!" (1) Calhoun may have been the fastest back on the team, but evidently, he wasn't the most committed.

One of the most vital qualities to a successful life is commitment, the willingness to carry the ball no matter how large the adversary. That's true in the workplace, that's true in marriage, that's true in caring for your health, that's true in being a responsible citizen, etc. Success in any endeavor begins with making a commitment. No commitment, no victory! It's true in all of life. But the most important commitment that we make in life, of course, is the one we make to Jesus Christ. Unfortunately, when it comes to making an authentic commitment to Jesus Christ, many people are like Calhoun. They don't really want to carry the ball.

In John 6, in one of the most amazing scenes in scripture, Jesus feeds the multitude. We talked about that a few weeks ago. Five thousand men and possibly an equal number of women and children were fed with five small loaves and two fish. The impact of that event on the multitude was enormous. They knew someone special was in their midst and they wanted to make him king.

When Jesus saw that they were getting carried away in their response to this event, he retreated across the Sea of Galilee to his home in Capernaum.

People came looking for him there. Jesus knew they had come to find him because they had been impressed with this miracle. And so he decided to separate the sheep from the goats, the highly committed from the casually interested. He began to discuss theology. Any preacher will tell you, if you want to clear a room quickly, just begin a deep theological discussion. Like rats fleeing a sinking ship the room will empty in a hurry.

What Jesus began discussing was what we know as the sacrament of the Lord's Supper. It was not a popular subject for an after dinner conversation. The people who heard him didn't know what he was talking about and they were repulsed by his imagery. After all, he seemed to be talking about his disciples eating his body and drinking his blood. What is this? the people wondered—the plot of a vampire movie? This sounds more pagan than religious—eating his body; drinking his blood?

They didn't get it and they were disappointed. They wanted him to set forth his economic policy as their new king, how he was going to give them everything they wanted and needed without raising their taxes. That's what they were looking for. They weren't much different than people today. They wanted the benefits, but not the cost. Jesus wanted them to know that the easy part was over. Now it was time to tackle the nitty-gritty of what a commitment to his kingdom meant. And most of the crowd would have nothing to do with it. In verse 66 we read these words, "From this time many of his disciples turned back and no longer followed him."

Those are important words. "From this time many of his disciples turned back and no longer followed him." Some of you have been through difficult times in recent years. Health problems, family problems, business problems. Life hasn't followed the rosy scenario you once thought it would. Some of you may have felt your faith weaken. Jesus understands. After he fed the 5,000, the people would have declared him king. Within a few days, however, their enthusiasm had cooled and they turned away. This was a turning point in Jesus' life and ministry. He knew, of course, that it would happen this way, but still it must have been disappointing.

The way of Jesus is not for everybody. You understand that, don't you? Jesus is for everybody, but not everybody is for Jesus. Even some of those who declare they follow Jesus don't really go with him all the way.

The Rev. Dr. David Galloway is an Episcopal priest. A while back, he told a story with which some of us can identify. He says that he had just finished playing a round of golf with his three best friends in Tyler, Texas. They had stopped into the 19th Hole, the men's grill at Willowbrook Country Club, for some refreshments. The room was full of people telling lies about their great round of golf—of spectacular shots made and of long putts that had dropped into the cup.

Into that room entered a man whom Galloway calls Hugh. Galloway says that Hugh was from central casting as to what a Texas oil man might look like—red-faced, large, and loud. Hugh always wanted you to know he was in the house. He was a back-slapping, heehawing fellow both on the golf course and in the town. It's not surprising that nobody wanted to play with him because he was so overbearing, so obnoxious.

Anyway, Galloway was sitting there in the 19th Hole when Hugh came in, a drink in one hand and a cigar in the other. He came up to Galloway's table and started talking loud, the only volume level he had. He was so loud that the attention of the whole room naturally turned to him. He bellowed at Galloway, "You Episcopalians don't believe in the Bible, do you?!" Rather than take the bait, Galloway just looked at Hugh and smiled weakly, hoping he would pass on by like an East Texas thunderstorm.

Hugh was referring to a recent decision by the Episcopal Church on some topic that was not to his liking. He went on. He called Galloway by name. "David," he said loudly, "I want to go to a church that is Bible-believing. Do you understand me? A place where the preacher is not trying to tippy-toe around the hard lessons of Jesus, a preacher who will lay it on the line, not try to water down the Gospel. I want a preacher who will be bold and put it out there, the full measure of the Bible, not hold back a lick. I want a preacher who will not let sinners slide and will call them out by name. I want the full Gospel. I don't want a preacher to pussy-foot around the message of Jesus."

Galloway says he doesn't know where his response came from, but he heard himself saying, "You want the full Gospel, Hugh? You mean the part about selling all you have and giving it to the poor?"

A pregnant silence fell over the room, after which Hugh responded, "Well, not that part!" Galloway says the room broke up in laughter and Hugh slunk out of the room as quietly as possible. (2)

We know that many of Jesus' so-called disciples would slink away if they were put on the spot about some of Jesus more difficult teachings. And before someone asks, Jesus didn't tell everyone to sell all they have and give it to the poor, but Jesus did tell us to be willing to do it in case we were ever called on to make that sacrifice. And he did tell us to have compassion for the poor and to do what we could to help. But the way of Jesus isn't for everyone.

Even those of us who are genuinely committed to him sometimes get distracted.

There was a story on the Internet recently by an unknown author. The story was titled, "The Day the Cricket Preached."

The author wrote that as a youth, he squirmed through many worship services. However, on one particular Sunday he was forced to contend with an added distraction. As soon as the pastor stood up to deliver his sermon, a cricket hopped onto the platform. The tiny dark creature probably came from one of the cracks in the old building. It looked dazed, and stumbled near the edge of the pulpit area.

The author says that he couldn't keep his eyes off of the cricket as it moved from one side of the platform to another. Whenever it would come near the edge of the platform the author would inwardly shout to the cricket, "Jump! Jump!" But alas, the cricket didn't jump. He just continued to move back and forth.

The author says he doesn't know if the sermon was any good that day, but the cricket was sure fun to watch. This was a Baptist church. And at the close of the service an invitation was given for anyone who wanted to follow Christ to come forward. When the invitation song began, the cricket began to move. He almost got stepped on when the song leader walked toward the microphone. Some others who had noticed the cricket began to laugh. Then, says the author, his own laughter turned to amazement. Someone had gone forward to receive Christ! It was his dad. His father had never before made a commitment to Christ. He and his mom had been trying for years to get his father to come to church with them, but to no avail . . . until today. Now the pastor was taking his dad back to baptize him.

"Dad," the author asked his father later. "What made you want to be baptized today?"

His father answered, "Didn't you hear how Jesus gave His life for us so that we could be saved?" The author said he hung his head in shame. He confesses that the beautiful message of the Bible did not reach him that day. He had been busy watching the cricket.

"To this day," he writes, "I believe that cricket was [talking] to me. He was saying, 'Watch me! Jesus isn't important. I'm more fun!'" Since then, he confesses, there have been many more crickets walk across the stage of his life that have distracted him from hearing Christ's message. (3) And that's true of all of us if we are not careful.

In fact, life is one big bundle of distractions. Our work, our family situation, life's many pleasures and responsibilities. It's not so much that we don't want to follow Christ. We're just so busy. There's so much to do, so much we want to experience. Watch out for the crickets, anything that would distract you from Christ's message.

"From this time many of his disciples turned back and no longer followed him." Some of them just weren't suited for the Christian life in the first place. Others, I suspect, got distracted by crickets.

But for the rest of us, those committed to follow Christ until the end, we can't imagine anything else. We have found in Jesus Christ everything we will ever need. We have found healing and hope and happiness in him that we never could have found any other place.

When the crowd had gone away and Jesus was left with the original twelve who had followed him since the early days in Galilee, Jesus turned to them and asked, "You do not want to leave too, do you?"

It was a logical question. The comparatively easy days of his ministry—the days of his immense popularity, the days of his wondrous miracles, the days when people hung on his every word—were drawing to a close. Jesus knew it and the disciples probably sensed it. Jesus wanted to give them a way out. "You do not want to leave too, do you?"

It was, of course, Simon Peter who spoke up, "Lord, to whom shall we go? You have the words of eternal life. We have come to believe and to know that you are the Holy One of God."

What a magnificent statement of faith! No wonder Jesus loved Simon Peter. Simon wasn't perfect. There would come a time when he would let Christ down. But isn't that true of all of us? No matter how intent we are on following Christ, no matter how hard we try to keep crickets from distracting us, there will be times when we will falter. We are not Christ, just as Simon Peter was not Christ. That does not mean, however, that deep in our hearts we do not want to serve Christ. He is our Lord. He is our Master. He is the one who has the words of eternal life. He is the one whom we believe is the Holy One of God.

Martin Copenhaver is a minister in the United Church of Christ denomination. United Church of Christ pastors have a reputation for being rather liberal in their theology, though that is not always the case. UCC pastors do tend to be advocates of a variety of social causes. And they tend to intellectualize their faith, which may seem to make them seem less passionate than pastors of some other denominations.

Martin Copenhaver probably fits most of these stereotypes. So it surprised the congregation of one of his churches when on his final Sunday there, he decided to be more personal. Here is how he closed his message that day: "I want to tell you what Jesus means to me," he said. "I want to share my belief that everything depends on him. I want to urge you to learn from him. I want to assure you that you can lean on him in times of trouble . . . you can entrust your life to him . . . He is Emmanuel, God with us, God with us all, whether we are together or apart. That's what it's all about. That's all I know."

One woman, he said, was so overcome with emotion after this sermon that she had to wait until everyone else had left before speaking. Her words haunted him, "Why," she asked, "didn't you tell us this before?" (4)

Perhaps he took it for granted that everyone already knew that he felt that way. Perhaps he felt that because he was a minister of Christ, people would assume that Christ was Lord of his life. He may have been wrong on both counts. This woman, at least, was surprised.

I don't want you to be surprised. I want to echo his words. I want to tell you this is what Jesus means to me as well: "... everything depends on him. I want to urge you to learn from him. I want to assure you that you can lean on him in times of trouble ... you can entrust your life to him ... He is Emmanuel, God with us, God with us all, whether we are together or apart. That's what it's all about. That's all I know."

Jesus turned to the twelve and asked, "You do not want to leave too, do you?"

Simon Peter answered, "Lord, to whom shall we go? You have the words of eternal life. We have come to believe and to know that you are the Holy One of God."

1. Rev. Donald Ng, http://www.fcbc-sf.org/sermons/srm092709.pdf.
2. The Reverend Gary Anholt, http://www.alutheranchurch.org/resources/SERMON09.27.09.pdf.
3. http://www.laughandlift.com/. Cited by MONDAY FODDER, http://family-safe-mail.com/.
4. Rev. Adolph Smith, http://www.raefordumc.net/2010/04/john-20-19-31-sermon.html.

How Many [Presbyterians] Does It Take
To Change A Light Bulb?*
Mark 7:1-8, 14-15, 21-23

Someone once asked the profound question, "How many [Presbyterians] does it take to change a light bulb?"

The correct answer is, of course, "Change the light bulb? Why, my grandfather donated that light bulb!" (1)

Well, [Presbyterians] are not the only ones who have trouble with change. Anytime change takes place in any institution, particularly the church, there is resistance.

Pastor Pete Kontra tells about a small-town church in upstate New York. They'd had a rector in that church for over thirty-five years. He was loved by the church and the community. After he retired, he was replaced by a young priest. It was his first church; he had a great desire to do well. He had been at the church for several weeks when he began to perceive that the people were upset at him. He was troubled.

Eventually he called aside one of the lay leaders of the church and said, "I don't know what's wrong, but I have a feeling that there's something wrong."

The man said, "Well, Father, that's true. I hate to say it, but it's the way you do the Communion service."

"The way I do the Communion service? What do you mean?" asked the priest.

"Well, it's not so much what you do as what you leave out," said the layman.

"I don't think I leave out anything from the Communion service," the priest answered.

"Oh yes, you do," the layman replied. "Just before our previous rector administered the chalice and wine to the people, he'd always go over and touch the radiator. And, then, he would . . ."

"Touch the radiator?" said the young priest, "I never heard of that liturgical tradition."

So the younger man called the former rector. He said, "I haven't even been here a month, and I'm in trouble."

"In trouble? Why?" asked the older man.

"Well, it has something to do with communion—something to do with touching the radiator. Could that be possible?" he asked. "Did you do that?"

"Oh yes, I did," said his predecessor. "Always before I administered the chalice to the people, I touched the radiator to discharge the static electricity so I wouldn't shock them."

It seems that some of his congregants had been getting shocked slightly when the communion cup touched their lips. For over thirty-five years, the people of his congregation had thought that touching the radiator was a part of the holy tradition. That church has now gained the name, "The Church of the Holy Radiator." (2)

The Pharisees and some of the teachers of the law who had come from Jerusalem gathered around Jesus one day and saw some of his disciples eating food without washing their hands. This wasn't a question of hygiene, but of tradition. The Jews had a ritual for washing hands as well as for the washing of cups, pitchers and kettles. I say it wasn't a matter of hygiene, but it would be interesting to know how many of these religiously prescribed traditions protected the Jews from an array of illnesses. Anyway, the disciples of Jesus neglected these ancient ceremonies.

So the Pharisees and teachers of the law asked Jesus, "Why don't your disciples live according to the tradition of the elders instead of eating their food with defiled hands?"

Jesus is somewhat harsh in his reply. He says, "Isaiah was right when he prophesied about you hypocrites; as it is written: 'These people honor me with their lips, but their hearts are far from me. They worship me in vain; their teachings are merely human rules.' You have let go of the commands of God and are holding on to human traditions." Jesus was a practicing Jew, yet he did not want his disciples to be slaves to Jewish tradition. We may wonder, why not?

Tradition is a powerful force in our lives. That is not only true in religion, but in all of society.

We have our family traditions. One woman tells about a banana loaf she was making. The loaf was in the oven when her 16-year old son came into the kitchen where the family had gathered. "That bread smells about done, don't you think, Mom?" he asked. His mother told him that she had set the timer and it was fine. A little later he passed through the kitchen again. He said, "Mom, I really think that loaf is done. I think you should check it." Always quick to her mom's defense, the woman's 13-year old daughter said, "Eddie, Mom's been burning that banana bread for 20 years, now. I think she knows when to take it out." (3)

Well, Mom's burned banana bread had become a tradition. We have traditions in our families, some of which are wholesome and some, perhaps not. But tradition shows up in everything we do.

You may have seen on the Internet a little item about how tradition played a role in the design of our transportation system, specifically in determining how far apart rails are for our trains. The official distance between rails in this country is four feet, eight and one-half inches. Why? Because that's the way they built them in England. Why did the English build them like that? Because the first rail lines were built by the same people who built tramways. Why did the builders of tramways space them like that, then? Because the people who built the tramways used the same jigs and tools that they used for building wagons, which used that wheel spacing.

Okay! Why did the wagons have that particular odd wheel spacing? Well, if they tried to use any other spacing, the wagon wheels would break on old rural roads, because that's the spacing of the wheel ruts. So who built those old rutted roads? The first long-distance roads in England were built by the Romans for their imperial legions. And the ruts? Roman chariots made the initial ruts, which everyone else had to match for fear of destroying their wagons and wheels. Since the chariots were made by the Roman Empire, they were all alike in the matter of wheel spacing.

Thus, we have the answer to our original question. The distance of four feet, eight and one-half inches derives from the original specification for an imperial Roman war chariot. But why did the Romans use that spacing? Their chariots were made just wide enough to accommodate the behinds of two war-horses. That's the ultimate answer to the question of how it was determined how far apart train rails should be spaced—the size of the behinds of two war horses. But wait . . . there's more.

When we see a space shuttle sitting on its launch pad, there are two big boosters attached to the sides of the main fuel tank. These are solid rocket boosters, or SRBs. These SRBs are manufactured in Utah. The engineers who designed the SRBs might have preferred to make them a bit fatter, but the SRBs had to be shipped by train from the factory to the launch site. The railroad line from the factory had to run through a tunnel in the mountains. The SRBs had to fit through that tunnel. The tunnel is slightly wider than the railroad track. So, the major design feature of what is arguably the world's most advanced transportation system was still determined by the width of two horse's rear ends. (4) That's hilarious to me, but tradition is important. Tradition has an impact on our daily lives.

Traditions give us our identity and, to a certain extent, set borders on our behaviors. We have traditions according to our cultural heritage. We even have traditions according to the region of the county we live in and which sports team we follow or what hobby we may have. Of course, traditions play a bigger role in some communities more than others.

Dr. G. Carswell Hughs, a Presbyterian pastor, says that people in Charleston, South Carolina pay more attention to tradition that any place he has ever seen. He says they pay particular attention to how long a family has lived in their city. The general assumption is that a family cannot claim to be native Charlestonians until they have lived in Charleston for at least three generations. And that means being born in Charleston and remaining in Charleston until "death do you part!"

He says that at a dinner party, he met a man whose accent was definitely that of Charleston. Never having met him before, he casually asked the man if he were a native Charlestonian. With a sad expression on his face, the man said, "No, I am not a native Charlestonian. I have lived in Charleston all my life. My father and mother were both born and lived in Charleston all their lives. The same is true of both sets of my grandparents, and their parents and grandparents. But I will never be a native Charlestonian." As the man spoke, Hughes was counting. It certainly sounded like more than three generations to him!

The man explained why he was still not a native Charlestonian like this: "I was born during the Second World War. My father was overseas. My mother visited relatives in Greenwood, South Carolina, and, by chance, I was prematurely born there." So, he could never be a real Charlestonian, even though his family had been there for generations because, due to a quirk of fate, he was born elsewhere. He said all of this at a dinner party, says Hughes, as if he were confessing his greatest sin. When he finished, Hughes said he was tempted to say, "God be with you. Go, and sin no more." (5)

That may sound silly to us, but traditions give us a sense of our identity. For the Jews this has always been important. They viewed themselves as set apart by God as a holy people, and their traditions helped them maintain their identity and set borders on their behaviors.

You remember that wonderful line that Tevye speaks in Fiddler on the Roof about tradition. "You may ask, why do we practice these traditions," he says, "Well, I'll tell you . . . I don't know. But they're traditions!" Tevye is the head of a Jewish family living in a small village in Russia. He continually struggles with traditions and values. In his small village, there were traditions for everything—how to eat, how to sleep, how to wear clothes. For instance, they always kept their heads covered and always wore a little prayer shawl to show their constant devotion to God. Because of their traditions, everyone knew who they were and what God expected them to do.

Tevye is molded by his adherence to tradition, but he is not a rigid man. He has the capacity to compromise . . . until his last daughter asks his approval to marry an atheist. This he cannot compromise. He loudly declares, "Some things I will not, I cannot allow—tradition!" (6)

In many ways traditions are a good thing. They were for the Jews. Considering the persecution the Jewish community has experienced throughout its history, it is doubtful that it would have survived without help from its traditions. However, traditions can get out of hand. In the eyes of the Pharisees and the teachers of the law, to eat with unclean hands was worse than how one treated one's neighbor. The traditions had taken over the religion. And this is the greatest danger of traditions.

Traditions may serve as a substitute for God. Traditions may tell us what was appropriate for our ancestors, but they may not be reliable indicators for how we should live today. Jesus was continually saying to his disciples, "You have heard it said . . . , but I say unto you . . ." Tradition is one guide for our behavior, but only one. Times change. Situations change. Far more important is the living Spirit of God moving in our midst now, guiding us in our present situation. Let me use an example.

Suppose we had a tradition in our church that only people who dressed in a certain way would be acceptable in our church. For example, men should only wear suits. On the surface, we might be able to justify that. We believe that the worship of God deserves our best, so why should we not dress in our very best to worship God? That sounds like a reasonable tradition, but is it where God would lead us?

Cornelia Lehn tells a story of a man, a smelly beggar dressed in rags, who visited a church. The congregation did its best to ignore him. When the usher finally showed him a seat, it was near the door where the breeze could dissipate some of the smell.

However, when the next Sunday came around, the same man came to the church. This time he was dressed in an expensive suit. The usher did not recognize him. Rather, he determined from the man's appearance that he was someone very important. He bowed to him, took him to the front of the church, and got him settled in a good pew. Indeed, there was a stir in the entire church as the congregation became aware of their distinguished visitor, and after the service the minister and his wife invited this man in the expensive suit to come to their home for dinner.

When they got to the house they made certain that they treated this finely dressed man like royalty. They wanted him to have nothing but the best. Then something quite peculiar happened. They sat down to dinner, but when the meat was passed around, their guest took a portion of meat and put it into his pocket! The hosts quickly looked away, but couldn't help notice the stain it made on the man's expensive suit. Then, when the potatoes were passed, the visitor calmly put them in his other vest pocket. And when the gravy came around, he poured it into another pocket!

Finally the host asked, "Why are you doing this?"

"Well," said the man, "you obviously did not invite me to dinner—you invited my suit. So I am feeding my suit!" (7)

Ridiculous story? Yes, but so is our tendency to elevate our traditions over Christ's love for all people. Suppose it were our tradition to have only people of a certain race in our church? Or a certain theology? Or a certain way of worshipping God? Can you see that there might come a time when God would say to us that it is time for us to move out of our comfort zone—to accept people we have previously shut out? This might be necessary for the sake of Jesus Christ.

The Pharisees and the teachers of the law were deeply religious people, but they had begun substituting their traditions for God. Their traditions told them who was acceptable and who was not. Even if God Himself came to them and tried to change their traditions, they would not listen. Indeed, God did come to them in the person of Jesus of Nazareth. They would not listen. Instead, they nailed him to a tree. Do you see that the same thing could happen to us? It has certainly happened to us in the past. Indeed, we might say one of our traditions is resistance to change. But God is a God of change. Let us open our hearts to the movement of the living God today.

1. http://www.tellicochurch.org/Sermons/990905.html.

2. http://oaklandchurch.org/pdf/sermontexts/OS-04-10-11-If%20You%20Share.pdf.

3. Mark Mail, http://mrhumor.net/

4. From Internet humor archives. Cited in John Mason, Believe You Can—The Power of a Positive Attitude (Grand Rapids: Revell, 2004).

5. http://www.fpcknox.org/sermons/25may2003.htm.

6. Robert H. Schuller, Don't Throw Away Tomorrow (New York: HarperCollins Publishers, Inc., 2005), p. 67.

7. "Show no Partiality," #68, I Heard Good News Today: Stories for Children. Cited by Don Friesen, http://www.ottawamennonite.ca/sermons/belonging.pdf.

*Change to your denomination, if it fits.

Rich Man, Poor Man
James 2:1-5

It is said that in Hollywood there is an exclusive school attended by children of movie stars, producers and directors. One day a teacher in that school asked her very privileged pupils to write a composition on the subject of poverty. One little girl started her literary piece like this: "Once there was a poor little girl. Her father was poor, her mother was poor, her nanny was poor, her chauffer was poor, her butler was poor. In fact, everybody in the house was very, very poor."

I don't think that little girl had ever been exposed to anyone who was truly poor.

It reminds me, though, of a "Peanuts" cartoon by Charles Schultz many years ago. Schultz was a devout Christian as many of you will remember.

In this particular cartoon Snoopy is shivering out in a snow storm beside an empty food dish. He looks longingly, expectantly, toward the house. Lucy comes out, and instead of putting anything in Snoopy's dish, Lucy simply says, "Go in peace, be warmed and filled." And then she turns, goes back into the house and slams the door.

In the last frame you see a confused Snoopy looking toward the house, shivering and hungry and utterly baffled. (1)

If that doesn't make you laugh, it will make you cry.

Last week we told a story about a man who came to a church dressed in smelly rags and was ignored by the congregation. The following week he came dressed in expensive clothes and he was treated like royalty. Our lesson from the little book of James carries much the same message. Listen carefully to its words:

"My brothers and sisters, believers in our glorious Lord Jesus Christ must not show favoritism. Suppose a man comes into your meeting wearing a gold ring and fine clothes, and a poor man in filthy old clothes also comes in. If you show special attention to the man wearing fine clothes and say, 'Here's a good seat for you,' but say to the poor man, 'You stand there' or 'Sit on the floor by my feet,' have you not discriminated among yourselves and become judges with evil thoughts?

"Listen, my dear brothers and sisters: Has not God chosen those who are poor in the eyes of the world to be rich in faith and to inherit the kingdom he promised those who love him?"

This is the one place where the teachings of Christ definitely clash with the ways of the world: how we view the poor. This discrepancy is apparent in a question we often ask about people—a question to which we apparently do not give much thought. We might ask of someone, referring to a third party, "How much do you think he or she is worth?"

What we are asking is, "How much money do you think he or she has?" But think about how we ask the question: "How much do you think he or she IS WORTH?" The truth of the matter is we do value a person of wealth more than we do a person without wealth. I wonder why we do that?

It may be because we aspire to wealth ourselves. This is only natural. We want the fine things of life ourselves and so we admire the people who have already attained them. And we want to associate with them, perhaps in the illusion that it will rub off.

Years ago Dr. Harry Emerson Fosdick of Riverside Church in New York City remarked: "Our grandparents were reared to say 'What shall I do to be saved?' This generation has been reared to say, 'What shall I do to succeed?'"

That's a common attitude in our time. Above all else, we want to be successful. We want to have nice things. And so we admire those who have climbed the ladder of success themselves. Of course, for many people of wealth, it was their grandfather who climbed the ladder and they have not had to earn it at all. But we disregard that. All that matters is that they have what we want. And so we value them.

Besides, sometime we may need to gain the favor of wealthy people to further our own ends. They can open doors for us and so we treat them with respect. The poor can do nothing for us and so we devalue them.

Perhaps we treat the poor differently because they make us feel guilty. Who hasn't had the experience of being approached by a homeless person asking for a hand-out and afterward feeling guilty for turning him away, or making him, in some way, feel inferior? I suspect we all have experienced that at some time or another.

And then we turn to the teachings of Jesus. In his first major public sermon, Jesus says, "Blessed are you poor. Blessed are you when you're hungry. Blessed are you who mourn. Blessed are you when people hate you."

And then we encounter Jesus' parable about the sheep and the goats: "When the Son of Man comes in his glory, and all the angels with him, he will sit on his glorious throne. All the nations will be gathered before him, and he will separate the people one from another as a shepherd separates the sheep from the goats. He will put the sheep on his right and the goats on his left.

"Then the King will say to those on his right, 'Come, you who are blessed by my Father; take your inheritance, the kingdom prepared for you since the creation of the world. For I was hungry and you gave me something to eat, I was thirsty and you gave me something to drink, I was a stranger and you invited me in, I needed clothes and you clothed me, I was sick and you looked after me, I was in prison and you came to visit me.'

"Then the righteous will answer him, 'Lord, when did we see you hungry and feed you, or thirsty and give you something to drink? When did we see you a stranger and invite you in, or needing clothes and clothe you? When did we see you sick or in prison and go to visit you?'

"The King will reply, 'Truly I tell you, whatever you did for one of the least of these brothers and sisters of mine, you did for me.'

"Then he will say to those on his left, 'Depart from me, you who are cursed, into the eternal fire prepared for the devil and his angels. For I was hungry and you gave me nothing to eat, I was thirsty and you gave me nothing to drink, I was a stranger and you did not invite me in, I needed clothes and you did not clothe me, I was sick and in prison and you did not look after me.'

"They also will answer, 'Lord, when did we see you hungry or thirsty or a stranger or needing clothes or sick or in prison, and did not help you?'

"He will reply, 'Truly I tell you, whatever you did not do for one of the least of these, you did not do for me.'" (Matthew 25:31-46)

That's a scary parable—especially in a society that determines a person's worth on the basis of his or her bank account. But this is where the teachings of Jesus clash quite definitely with the values of society—how we view the poor.

Scripture is clear: our closeness to God is reflected in how we treat those less fortunate than ourselves. This is true in both the Old and the New Testaments.

There is an ancient legend among the Jews that while the Israelites were wandering in the desert, they decided to ask God to dinner. Their leader, Moses, explained that God is not a physical being and so He does not eat. But when Moses went up on the mountain to talk with God, God said to him that He would accept the Israelites' dinner invitation.

All the next day, the Israelites prepared dinner for God. An old man, poor and hungry, arrived and asked for something to eat, but the Israelites were too busy to give the old man some food. That evening, the Israelites looked for God, but they didn't see Him. The next morning Moses went up on the mountain and asked God why He had not come for the dinner.

God replied, "I did come. If you had fed the old man, you would have fed Me." (2) Scripture is clear, Old Testament and New: our closeness to God is reflected in how we treat those less fortunate than ourselves.

Evangelist Jim Wallis has an interesting twist on this idea. He says that he often does a little Bible quiz for audiences he's speaking to. He asks this question: "What is the most famous biblical text in America about the poor?" He says that every time he asks this question, he receives the same answer: Jesus said, "You always have the poor with you, but you do not always have me."

Wallis notes that Jesus was speaking to his disciples. The reason Jesus' disciples will always have the poor with them, says Wallis, is that this is their job: to minister to society's rejects. "You will always have the poor with you because you are my disciples." Jesus assumed that his followers would be continually ministering to the poor and the down trodden. Oh, but that were true. (3)

Ray Stedman is a man with very clear credentials as a conservative, evangelical pastor. No one would dub him a starry-eyed liberal. And yet here is a prayer he once quoted while preaching on this passage. It is a prayer that says out loud what's often really going on in the hearts of Christian people when they think of the poor. Let me read you part of this prayer:

"We miserable owners of increasingly luxurious cars, and ever-expanding television screens, do most humbly pray for that two-thirds of the world's population which is undernourished; You can do all things, O God . . .

"That the sick may be visited, the prisoner cared for, the refugee rehabilitated, the naked clothed, the orphan housed, and that we may be allowed to enjoy our own firesides evening by evening, in peace; You can do all things, O God . . .

"O Son of God, we beg, we beseech, we supplicate, we petition, we implore You to hear us. Lord, be good to us. Christ, make things easy for us. Lord, deliver us from the necessity of doing anything [ourselves]." (4) Amen.

Do you get the satire in that prayer—praying for the poor, but praying that God will take care of them so we won't have to bother with them ourselves?

Our closeness to God is reflected in how we treat those less fortunate than ourselves. And the truth is that some of us are really not that close to either God or our fellow man. We will remember them in our prayers, perhaps, but not in our actions. This is where the teachings of Jesus clash quite definitely with the values of society—how we view the poor. Scripture is clear: our closeness to God is reflected in how we treat those less fortunate than ourselves.

And that brings us to the final thing to be said: The mark of a follower of Jesus is to be kind and compassionate to all people, regardless of their station in life. This is not a class warfare sermon. We are to treat ALL persons with love and respect, and to be servant to all. This is how we best show our love for Christ.

Pastor Alex Steveson tells an intriguing story that brings this point home:

Once upon a time there was a squire who longed to be a knight. He wanted to serve his king and be the most honorable and noble knight who ever lived. At his knighting he was so overcome by dedication that he made a special oath. He vowed to bow his knees and lift his arms in homage to his king and his king alone.

This knight was given the task of guarding a city on the frontier of the kingdom. Every day he stood at attention by the gate of the city in full armor.

Years passed. One day as he was standing at attention guarding his post a peasant woman passed by with goods for the market. Her cart turned over spilling potatoes and carrots and onions everywhere. The woman hurried to get them all back in her cart. But the knight wouldn't help the poor woman. He just stood at attention lest he break his vow by bending his knees to help pick up the woman's goods.

Time passed and one day a man with one leg was passing by and his crutch broke. "Good knight, sir, reach down and help me up," he begged. But the knight would not stoop or lift a hand to help lest he break his vow to bow only to his king.

Years and decades passed, the knight was getting old. One day his grandson came by and said, "Grandpa pick me up and take me to the fair." But the knight would not stoop to pick up his grandson lest he break his vow to the king.

Finally after years the king came to visit and inspect the knight. As the king approached, the knight just stood there at attention. He did not bow, but simply remained erect. The king inspected him, but then he noticed that the knight was crying. "You are one of the noblest knights I have ever seen," said the king. "Why do you cry?"

The knight responded: "Your majesty, I took a vow that I would bow and lift my arms in homage to you, but I am unable to keep my vow. These years have done their work and the joints of my armor are rusted. I cannot lift my arms or bend my knees."

With the loving voice of a parent the King replied, "Perhaps if you had knelt to help all those who passed by, and lifted your arms to embrace all those who came to you, you would have been able to keep your vow to pay me homage today." (5)

There are some of us who are in danger not just of rusted knees and rusted arms, but rusted hearts as well. Our hearts will make a pitiful offering to Christ someday, because we have not exercised them in acts of kindness and compassion for all people.

One day, Marlene Nance's little daughter, Emma, was playing with her Bible character paper dolls when she realized that the Jesus character was missing. Marlene and Emma looked all over the house, but they couldn't find Jesus anywhere.

Later that afternoon, Emma came running to her mother with some good news. She had found Jesus! He was in one of her Daddy's magazines. Emma proudly held out her new Jesus. Marlene gasped as she took the picture from Emma's hands. It was a picture of a tall, bearded homeless man dressed in rags. Because of his long hair and beard, he did resemble Emma's paper-doll Jesus. As Marlene reflected on Jesus' own words about the poor and powerless, she decided that her little girl had indeed found Jesus. (6)

"My brothers and sisters," writes the author of the little epistle of James, "believers in our glorious Lord Jesus Christ must not show favoritism. Suppose a man comes into your meeting wearing a gold ring and fine clothes, and a poor man in filthy old clothes also comes in. If you show special attention to the man wearing fine clothes and say, 'Here's a good seat for you,' but say to the poor man, 'You stand there' or 'Sit on the floor by my feet,' have you not discriminated among yourselves and become judges with evil thoughts?

"Listen, my dear brothers and sisters: Has not God chosen those who are poor in the eyes of the world to be rich in faith and to inherit the kingdom he promised those who love him?" Amen.

1. Dale Lykins, http://www.jacksoncumc.org/worship/3_os_openingdoors.htm.
2. James Fadiman and Robert Frager, Essential Sufism, pp. 11-12. Cited in David Bruce, 250 Anecdotes about Religion (Kindle edition).
3. Jim Wallis, God's Politics (HarperSanFrancisco, 2005). Cited by The Rev. Charles Booker-Hirsch, http://www.northsidepres.org/worship/sermons/sermon/96.
4. Quoting from He Sent Leanness—Book of Prayers for the Natural Man (Discovery Publishing). Cited by Stephen Muncherian, http://www.muncherian.com/s-ro13v8.html.
5. http://pastoralex.fortunecity.com/pent18.htm.
6. Marlene Nance, "Mommy, Jesus is Missing!" Decision magazine, December 2000, p. 36.

Did You Come Here To Die?

Mark 8:27-35

A man from the U.S. was on his first trip to Australia. He summoned a taxi at the airport. He was shocked when the taxi driver asked him in a strong Australian accent, "Did you come here to die?"

This was unexpected and disturbing—a cabbie asking him, "Did you come here to die?"

What kind of ride was he in for? The man wondered. He said, "Excuse me?"

The cabbie elaborated, "Did you come here to die, or yester-die?"

In today's Gospel lesson Jesus is breaking it to his disciples that he has come to die—and he's not speaking with an Australian accent. It's one of the most famous passages in the Word. Jesus and his disciples are in the vicinity of Caesarea Philippi when Jesus asks them, "Who do people say I am?"

They reply, "Some say John the Baptist; others say Elijah; and still others, one of the prophets."

"But what about you?" he asks. "Who do you say I am?"

Of course it was Peter who answered, "You are the Messiah."

And Jesus warned them not to tell anyone about him. Then Jesus began to teach them that he must suffer many things and be rejected by the elders, the chief priests and the teachers of the law, and that he must be killed and after three days rise again. This was horrifying to his disciples, as you might expect. They loved Jesus. He was not only their teacher, but he was their best friend. It was Peter, of course, who began to rebuke Jesus for even mentioning the possibility of dying. I can hear him now, "Don't say things like that, Master, it's discouraging to hear you talk like that."

Then Jesus turned and looked Peter in the eye and said to him, "Get behind me, Satan! You do not have in mind the concerns of God, but merely human concerns."

Then Jesus called the crowd to him along with his disciples and said: "Whoever wants to be my disciple must deny themselves and take up their cross and follow me. For whoever wants to save their life will lose it, but whoever loses their life for me and for the gospel will save it."

This passage ought to make us a bit uncomfortable. Jesus came to die—to die for us. That is how much he loves us. In the words of writer Max Lucado, "Nails didn't hold God to a cross. Love did."

Several years ago, the Red Cross in a small Oklahoma town posted signs all over town containing these words:

I gave my blood—Christ gave his. I gave a pint—He gave all.

The needle is small, sharp—The nails were large, dull.

The table soft, restful—The cross rough, painful.

The nurses kind, gentle—The soldiers cruel, mean.

The crowd applauds my sacrifice. "They that passed by reviled him."

Mine is for O Positive. His for positively all.

Mine, at best, will prolong a life for a while.

His, without doubt, can save all forever. (1)

Jesus died for us. What do we do in response to such love? The truth is, most of us could answer . . . not much.

There was an article in the news sometime back about a teacher's aide in Pennsylvania who had been suspended without pay for a year. It seems that she had worn a necklace with a cross on it to work. She knew that she was violating school policies when she wore the cross. She had been warned twice before. Still, this seems to be a little overkill to most of us—suspension for a year without pay.

What disturbs me far more, however, than a teacher wearing a cross to class in defiance of a school policy, is that so many people wear crosses that have no significance to them. They wear them as a mere decoration. It's one thing to wear a cross as a declaration; depending on the circumstances we might even salute that. It is another to wear it as a decoration. What does it mean to us when we wear a cross? Does it mean that we are willing to die for him as he died for us? For some, it may, but probably not for most. It would be interesting to interview people on the street. What does wearing a cross mean to you? Is it the same thing to wear a cross as it is to bear a cross?

Even in church we don't talk about the cross as much as we once did. It's a hard sell in our society to ask anyone to sacrifice—even Christians.

There was a marketing report in the Wall Street Journal that was quite revealing. It had to do with how thick pew cushions are becoming in America. Church suppliers note that 50 years ago there was virtually no market for pew cushions. None! People in churches sat on hard benches. But today 50% of their orders are about softening the seats of people in church. It has become a market share commanding hundreds of millions of dollars annually.

According to some of the pastors and church leaders weighing in on the subject, soft pews are an essential part of church life today. "Let's face it," says one, "soft seats are more inviting." Another says, "It's hard enough to find comfort in the world and church should be comfortable." And one more said, "I love the Lord, but there is absolutely no reason to hurt for an hour while doing so!" (2)

And I agree. I don't believe that a hard pew ever saved anybody. Still, cushioned pews might be a metaphor for what is happening to us in the church today. The idea of taking up a cross and following Jesus has been practically banished from our thoughts. Finding personal fulfillment and satisfaction has taken its place. In December we bemoan the fact that many people seem to be taking Christ out of Christmas. What we really need to be concerned about is the growing tendency throughout the entire Christian year to take the cross out of Christian living. Christ died for us. He died because he loved us so much. What have we given him in return?

University of Wisconsin historian Thomas Reeves is really put off by the state of religious belief and service in our land today. "Christianity in modern America," he writes "is, in large part, innocuous. It tends to be easy, upbeat, convenient, and compatible. It does not require self-sacrifice, discipline, humility . . . There is little guilt and no punishment, and the payoff in heaven is virtually certain." (3) Is he wrong?

Pastor Ed Markquart, a Lutheran pastor in Seattle, Washington tells about an encounter he had once with a pastor named Richard Wurmbrand. Some of you will recognize that name. Wurmbrand, who died in 2001, was a Christian minister of Jewish descent in Romania who suffered years of imprisonment and torture under the communists because of his faith.

Some years ago Markquart and some members of his church went to the Holy Land together. While there they took a cruise on a ship following the journeys of the Apostle Paul. One of the passengers on that cruise was Richard Wurmbrand.

One night Markquart and his wife found themselves sitting with Wurmbrand at an evening dinner table. Much to his surprise, Markquart found Wurmbrand to be witty, charming and intelligent as he told delightful stories at the table.

He was delightful until at the end of the dinner, when he learned over to Orlie, a layman from Markquart's church who was also making the trip, and asked him, "Is that pastor over there (referring to Markquart) a good pastor?"

Markquart says it bothered him that Orlie paused before his answer. Finally, Orlie answered, "Yes."

Wurmbrand asked another question, "Why is he a good pastor?"

Orlie responded, "Well, he makes good sermons."

Then, says Markquart, Wurmbrand looked right at him and asked Orlie, "Yes, but does he make good disciples?"

"In that moment," says Markquart, "there was a pause, a flash of embarrassment, and a little dagger went into my soul. He didn't say it but he could have said that the purpose of the church is not to make good sermons or good music or good youth programs or good sanctuaries, but the purpose of the church is to make disciples of Jesus Christ. Through the power of the Holy Spirit, does he make disciples?

"In that moment," Markquart continues, "Wurmbrand was the angel of the Lord to me . . . The purpose of God for all pastors and in all sermons is to make disciples of Jesus Christ. People who love Jesus Christ, who follow Jesus Christ, who call Jesus Christ their Lord. That is what we are all called to be: to make disciples of Jesus Christ. Not make church members. Not make Sunday schools. Not make buildings. These can all become ends in themselves. We are to make disciples of Jesus Christ. That is what it is all about." (4)

Richard Wurmbrand was right. Ed Markquart is right. This is why I have the privilege to stand before you each week. It is not to entertain you. It is to encourage you to walk in the steps of the Master; to help you be better disciples of Jesus Christ.

Discipleship is about self-denial. Jesus turned to his disciples and to the crowd around them and said, "Whoever wants to be my disciple must deny themselves and take up their cross and follow me. For whoever wants to save their life will lose it, but whoever loses their life for me and for the gospel will save it."

Many beautiful stories came out of the tragedy of the fall of the twin towers of the World Trade Center on Sept. 11, 2001—stories of sacrifice and heroism. None is more impressive than the story of Ron Fazio of Closter, New Jersey.

Fazio was Vice President of a company with offices on the 99th floor of Tower Two. When the plane slammed into Tower One, Ron Fazio made one of the best decisions of his life. He ordered his employees to evacuate the building. Even though the South Tower where their offices were had not been hit by the second plane, he insisted that employees get away from the windows, leave their desks and get out of the building. He stood there and held the door, yelling for everyone to hurry, and held the door open until everyone from his company had started down the stairs. They all made it down. So did he. But he remained outside Tower Two, helping others out of the building, talking on his cell phone. The last anyone saw of him, he was giving his cell phone to someone else, after which the tower collapsed and no one ever heard from Ron Fazio again.

Ron's wife Janet and their kids have started a foundation to honor their father's heroism. It's called "Hold the Door for Others, Inc." In son Rob's words, "My Dad was a quiet, humble man who died after holding the door open for others. As a family, we're trying to do the same thing, to help people move through the pain so they can begin to dream again." (5)

That's the difference between wearing a cross and bearing a cross—the willingness to give your life for others. Please understand. I'm not against wearing crosses. I'm against wearing them if you have never thought through the sacrifice represented by that cross. In a sense it represents Jesus holding the door open so that we can walk through to life. Discipleship is about self-denial.

Discipleship begins when you acknowledge Jesus as your Savior and Lord. It is so sad that so many Christians view a decision for Christ as the end of the journey. Now they're accepted. Now they can confidently say they will be able to walk through Heaven's door. Friends, the day you acknowledge that Christ is your Savior is only the day you begin the journey of faith. At that moment begins the process of remaking you in Christ's image.

Steve Brown tells the story about a British soldier during World War I who lost heart for the battle and in fear decided to desert and run away. As he left the field and headed for what he thought was the coast so he could catch a boat back to England the skies turned very dark. It was so dark that he became hopelessly lost.

In the darkness he came across what he thought was a signpost. It was so dark that he could not make out the top of the signpost so he started to climb up the post so he could read it. As he reached the top of the pole, he found himself looking squarely in the face of Jesus Christ! He realized that rather than running into a signpost, he had climbed a roadside crucifix! Suddenly this encounter with the crucifix reminded him of the one who had died for him, the Lord who had endured, who had never turned back!

The next morning he made his way back to the trenches. After staring into the face of Christ he got a second wind of strength to endure! (6) Have you ever stared into the face of Jesus? It will change your life if you have. We need to stare into the face of Jesus so that we might see the kind of person we can yet become.

Most of you probably remember Tom Landry, the longtime head coach of the Dallas Cowboys. Landry spent three decades in professional football. Before that he flew 30 combat missions for the U.S. Air Force in World War II and starred for the University of Texas football team. A man of physical strength and courage, Landry experienced many successes in athletics. Yet he once wrote, "I had a difficult time finding a purpose for my life. Football was my whole life—it was my religion. I slept it. I ate it, and I talked it."

Landry was an all-pro football player for many years before becoming a coach. He played in several Pro Bowl games and had a celebrated career as a player. But something was missing in his life. A friend met Landry on the street and invited him to a Wednesday morning Bible study. Tom was hesitant. He reasoned, "I don't need it." Since childhood, he had attended Sunday School and church services regularly. He felt he was morally sound. But he agreed to go to this Bible study because this man was a good friend. In the Bible study Landry learned about the challenge of following Jesus Christ and it changed his life. Says Landry, "When Jesus became real to me ... I found real happiness and the most satisfying purpose for living." (7)

Have you found God's purpose for your life? Have you acknowledged Christ as your Savior? Are you opening doors for others? "Whoever wants to be my disciple," said the Master, "must deny themselves and take up their cross and follow me. For whoever wants to save their life will lose it, but whoever loses their life for me and for the gospel will save it."

1. Dr. Mickey Anders, http://www.mickeyanders.com/Sermons/Sermon20040801.html.
2. Ronnie Adams, http://www.metrobaptistchurchnyc.org/reflections/where.pdf.
3. Douglas Harding, http://www.hickorytech.net/~sibumc/Sermons/pe16b06sep24sermon.pdf.
4. http://www.sermonsfromseattle.com/series_a_go_go_go.htm.
5. Dale Lykins, http://www.jacksoncumc.org/worship/3_os_openingdoors.htm.
6. Source Unknown. Cited by Rev. Dennis Markquart, http://www.nnedaog.org/sermons/sernofr5.htm.
7. James D. Kegel, http://www.lectionary.org/Sermons/Kegel/OT/Isaiah_06.1-8_Leader.htm.

Big Men In Little Planes
Mark 9:30-37

There is an interesting story that comes out of the Second World War. England and Germany both had state-of-the-art fighter planes. Germany had the Messerschmitt, which was considered to be the world's fastest fighter plane. The British had the Supermarine Spitfire. The Spitfire was slower than the Messerschmitt. Nevertheless, German pilots were envious of their British counterparts.

You see, the Messerschmitt had been designed to hold the perfect German. Who was the perfect German? Who else but Der Fuhrer, Adolf Hitler. Hitler was little more than five feet tall. However, the German pilots who guided the Messerschmitt were considerably taller than 5 feet. So the Germans had to fly in very cramped quarters. But who was going to tell Adolf Hitler that he was not the perfect German? The Messerschmitts were faster, but their pilots were not happy men. (1)

It is an amazing fact, but many leaders fail because of big egos. Big men in little planes. Big egos in little men. "Pride goeth before a fall," says the ancient adage. And it's true.

In the summer of 1986, two ships collided in the Black Sea off the coast of Russia. Hundreds of passengers died as they were hurled into the icy waters. News of this disaster grew even grimmer when an investigation revealed the cause of the accident. This tragedy was not the result of some sort of equipment malfunction or a technology glitch. The radar and other safety systems on each ship were working just fine. The collision was not caused by a blanket of thick fog or other dangerous weather condition. The cause . . . was human stubbornness. Each captain was completely aware of the other ship's presence. Either one could have steered clear, but according to news reports, neither captain wanted to give way to the other. Each captain was too proud to yield first. By the time they finally came to their senses, it was too late and the ships collided! (2)

Jesus and the disciples were passing through Galilee. They made a stop at Capernaum. It was there that Jesus asked his disciples what they had been arguing about while on the road. The Scripture says his disciples kept quiet. They didn't want Christ to know that they had been arguing about which of them was the greatest.

Surely men never do that . . . do they? Try to one-up one another? Boast about their accomplishments? Surely you don't know a man with a big ego.

We read that when the disciples refused to answer Jesus' question, he sat down. He also probably let out a loud sigh. He called his disciples to gather around and said to them, "Anyone who wants to be first must be the very last, and the servant of all."

Interesting words from the Master. If you want to come in first, you've got to be willing to come in last and you must be willing to serve. Let's begin with the very human desire of wanting to be first. I joked about men with their egos. Women have egos too. They're just a little more subtle about it.

There was a noted priest in Florence in the 15th century. One day he saw an elderly woman worshiping at the statue of the Virgin Mary which stood in his city's great cathedral. On the following day, he noticed the same woman again on her knees before the statue. With great interest, the priest observed that day after day, she came and did homage before the statue. "Look how she reverences the Virgin Mother," he whispered to one of his fellow priests.

"Don't be deceived by what you see," the priest responded. "Many years ago an artist was commissioned to create a statue for the cathedral. As he sought a young woman to pose as the model for his sculpture, he found one who seemed to be the perfect subject. She was young, serenely lovely, and had a mystical quality in her face. The image of that young woman inspired his statue of Mary. The woman who now worships the statue is the same one who served as its model years ago. Shortly after the statue was put in place, she began to visit it and continued to worship there religiously ever since." (3)

She had fallen in love with a likeness of herself. You don't have to be a man to have a big ego. Many of us are so afflicted.

However, please do not misunderstand. Having a big ego is not all bad. People with big egos get things done. People who want to be first, who want to be the greatest, often are doers. Adolf Hitler had a big ego. He was a monster, but he got things done. Given a few breaks here and there, he might have realized his dream to rule the world. As a person of faith, I believe those breaks may well have been determined by God . . . but still he got things done.

It's very rare to discover a successful person in any field who does not have a healthy degree of their own self-worth. Like any virtue, however, an overly developed ego can be detrimental. You could make the case that Mother Teresa had a strong ego. No one could deter her from her cause. She could confront powerful politicians and get what she wanted from them. The reason she was so effective, however, is that her ego was restrained by humility, the humility of understanding herself as a servant of Christ.

I have read that the home where Mother Teresa's nuns lived had no stoves, no washing machines, no electric fans, no air conditioners. Mother Teresa explained their absence like this, "I do not want them. The poor we serve have none."

When she first had the idea of starting her organization, the Missionaries of Charity, she even planned to allow the nuns to eat only the kind of food the very poorest people ate—rice and salt. However, she asked advice from another nun whom she respected. This nun wisely asked her, "How do you expect your sisters to work, if their bodies receive no sustenance?" As a result of this advice, Mother

Teresa allowed her nuns to eat well, but to eat only simple food. (4)

Mother Teresa had a very strong sense of servant-hood. Her ego was disciplined by her commitment to Christ and to the poor whom she served.

Those who serve Christ need a healthy sense of their own self-worth. Contrary to popular belief, Jesus doesn't need more wimps. Jesus doesn't need more people whose eyes are always downward because they don't feel worthy. Jesus doesn't need wimps, he needs warriors—people who understand their own value, who have a deep sense of their own self-worth, not because they think there's anything special about them, but because they understand that they are children of God.

Sometimes we put too much emphasis on the meek and mild Jesus. If he were that meek and that mild, why in the world would anybody ever crucify him? If he were that meek and that mild, would he have driven the tax collectors from the temple? Jesus came to be servant to all, but he wasn't a wimp. I think it's interesting that when they came to take him that night in the Garden of Gethsemane, they sent a whole brigade of soldiers. They didn't regard him as a wimp. They regarded him as a dangerous person.

In his own way Jesus was a warrior. He was a warrior intent on storming the very gates of hell. He was a strong man in every sense and he wants his followers to be strong. For life is difficult. And he wants followers who will set an example for other people in how to live victoriously. He wants followers who are up to the rigors of facing the evils of this world and preparing this world for the coming of his kingdom. So he said to his disciples, "Anyone who wants to be first must be the very last, and the servant of all."

In other words, he doesn't ask us to give up our strong egos. Rather he wants us to discipline those egos to serve him and to serve all those for whom he died.

Dr. Melvin Cheatham, a medical doctor, tells about a friend of his named Barb Peters. Barb was not a person with what most of us would call a big ego, but she was the kind of strong person who could be used of God. Barb went with Dr. Cheatham and his wife to Kenya in East Africa on a mission trip one time. What she experienced there greatly impacted her life.

From childhood, Barb wanted to become a doctor so she could serve God by working with people who were underprivileged. So in her fifties, she sold her home and moved into a humble abode in order to afford to go to medical school. That's a bold move to make when you are in your fifties. Barb says that, had her dream been realized, she would probably have been the oldest graduating doctor ever! Still, she believed that even if she was too old for medical school she might be able to get a doctorate in science and work in a mission hospital as a lab technician.

While in her first year of school, she supported herself by working a full-time job in real estate sales. She studied hard and made it through the first year. She wrote to Dr. Cheatham to tell him of her studies and her desire to serve in the mission field. She wrote in her letter, "In about six years I will be ready to serve in a mission hospital."

Cheatham replied, "How about now? You have two masters' degrees already and a background in teaching. Someone like you is badly needed at a mission school in Londiani, Kenya. The teachers there need the expertise you have to train them, and they need it now."

Now? Kenya? she gulped. Barb says that, being a person who is used to the finer things in life and who takes germs very seriously, she had visions of tribal warfare, genocide, natives on the rampage, AIDS, malaria, the Ebola virus, and all sorts of other things. Still, she managed enough courage to ask the next question: "Where is this Londiani?" She found Londiani was a small village in western Kenya. Another Christian missionary was already there and had started the school. She was now building a medical clinic and dreamed of starting a small hospital.

Barb decided this was where she needed to be. However, when she announced to her grown children, "I am going to the jungle this summer to work as a missionary," they were not encouraging. "You know, you're losing it, Mother," one said. Another commented, "I'm proud of you. Mom, but can't you do something nice and safe that is a little bit closer to home than East Africa?" Another questioned her wisdom. "I don't want you to die," said this offspring.

Barb finally blurted out, "I tried to teach you how to live, and now I am going to teach you how to die." (5)

Well, of course, not everyone who goes as a missionary to Africa ends up dying there. But Barb had settled in her own mind that, if this was required of her, she was willing to pay the price.

Barb wasn't a wimp by any stretch of the imagination. She was a woman of courage, the kind of woman, the kind of person that God is looking for. Jesus didn't scold his disciples for having great dreams, for wanting to be the best, the greatest. Ambition can be a very useful tool for motivating us to be all we can be. Christ wanted his disciples to understand that being greatest in the kingdom of God meant a total commitment to serving all God's children.

It is interesting that while they were still trying to digest this teaching, Jesus took a little child and placed that child before them. Taking the child into his arms, he said to them, "Whoever welcomes one of these little children in my name welcomes me; and whoever welcomes me does not welcome me but the one who sent me."

Part of serving Christ is helping create the kind of world that is safe for all the world's children—making sure that children in our own community and around the world get the kind of help they need, whether it is food or medicine or education, whatever they need to thrive. If you want to be the greatest, commit your life to serving the least and the lowest.

I like the way evangelist Bill Glass puts it. Some of you who are football fans may remember Glass. He was All-Pro defensive end for the Detroit Lions and the Cleveland Browns for many years. Since leaving football he has been involved in Christian ministry. He talks about what he calls "The Baseball Game of Life." He says that there are three bases which the Christian needs to touch before crossing home plate. The three bases are: First base—Salvation; Second base—Sanctification or growing into the likeness of Christ; and Third base—Service . . . Glass says that some of us try to touch only first base, salvation, without touching second and third.

It's like an example that pastor Gary Sanford uses. He recalls playing baseball as a boy. Sometimes his friends didn't have enough boys to play all the positions, so they played a game that they called "Chicken-Base Baseball." In Chicken-Base Baseball, the runner was not required to run around all the bases. He simply ran from home plate to first base and back. He skipped second and third base completely.

Gary comments that the church is saddled with lots of "Chicken-Base Christians." These Christians care only about their personal salvation. They run to first base salvation, skip second and third bases entirely (sanctification and service), and take the short trip back to home plate. (6)

In reality, that can't be done. Both Glass and Sanford are right. When we give our lives to Christ, when we are baptized, when we acknowledge that Jesus Christ is the Lord of our lives, that is not the end of the process. It is only the beginning. By the power of the Holy Spirit we are to continue to grow into the spiritual image of Christ. That doesn't mean that we will be perfect, but it does mean we will continue to grow in love, to grow in compassion, to grow in our ability to forgive and accept others. That is as much a part of the Christian life as salvation. You may think pretty highly of yourself as a Christian, but it is my responsibility as your pastor to tell you that if you are not a more loving, more accepting, more compassionate person than you were when you first began your Christian journey, you are still stuck on first base.

Salvation is only the beginning of the journey. Growing to be more like Jesus is the continuation of the process. And the crowning achievement, what makes you the greatest, is humbling yourself to serve those who are less fortunate, those who do not have the advantages that you and I have, those who do not know God's amazing grace.

Big men in little planes. Why were they in those little planes? Because of a big ego in a little man. God wants us to stand tall by humbling ourselves as he humbled himself and giving our lives as he gave his life to save and to serve the world. If you want to be No. 1, if you want to be the greatest, that is the blueprint. Make this a better world for all God's children. In the words of truly one of the greatest people of the last century, Dr. Albert Schweitzer: "I don't know what your destiny will be," he once said, "but one thing I do know, the only ones among you who will be really happy are those who have sought and found how to serve."

1. Leonard & Thelma Spinrad, Speaker's Lifetime Library (Paramus, NJ: Revised & Expanded, 1997, p. 526).

2. Pastor Dustin Bergene, http://www.trinityabita.org/home/180003585/180003585/docs/sermon%2010.4.09.pdf?sec_id=180003585.

3. Rev. Adrian Dieleman, http://www.trinitycrc.org/sermons/phil2v03.html.

4. Amy Ruth, Mother Teresa, pp. 55-56, 68. David Bruce, 250 Anecdotes About Religion (Kindle Edition).

5. Make a Difference: Responding to God's Call to Love the World (Nashville: Thomas Nelson, Inc., 2004), pp. 37-38.

6. Richard Niell Donovan, http://www.lectionary.org/Sermons/Dono/NTOther/James_02.01-17_ChickenBase.htm.

The Golf Shot That Destroyed An Airforce
Mark 9:38-50

A little girl had been naughty, so she was sent to her room for a quiet time. Afterward, all smiles, she returned to her family, saying, "I prayed to God."

"That's good," said her mother. "Did you pray that God would help you be a good girl?"

"No," she replied. "I prayed that God would help you put up with me."

Many of us are like that little girl. We do wrong, but rather than repenting of our sins, we pray that God will put up with us. And why not? It's our nature to sin; it's God's nature to forgive. Some of us have that attitude.

A prominent book a few years back asked the question: whatever became of sin? It's a good question. We don't really sin nowadays. Instead, mistakes were made, as our politicians remind us. And yet, when we look at some of the teachings of Jesus, we get an entirely different view of wrongdoing. Listen to these very stark words from the lips of the Master:

"If your hand causes you to stumble, cut it off. It is better for you to enter life maimed than with two hands to go into hell, where the fire never goes out. And if your foot causes you to stumble, cut it off. It is better for you to enter life crippled than to have two feet and be thrown into hell. And if your eye causes you to stumble, pluck it out. It is better for you to enter the kingdom of God with one eye than to have two eyes and be thrown into hell, where the worms that eat them do not die, and the fire is not quenched."

Pretty strong stuff. What shall we do with these teachings of our Master? Many Christians simply ignore them. They don't fit into their theology of grace. They're too harsh. After all, theology today is like a buffet line. You go down the line and pick what you find agreeable and leave the rest behind.

I was reading not too long ago that a recent Gallup poll indicated that 80% of Americans believe in God. And nearly as many believe that Jesus is God's son. And yet, only 40% believe that religion is important in life.

Now let me get this right. We believe that there is a personal God who created us and reigns over us. And we believe that Jesus is his very Son. And yet we do not take the words of Jesus seriously? We do not feel that those words apply to us? His words are not really important? I'm not certain that's a very wise approach to life.

Jesus says to us in today's lesson that we should take sin very seriously. "If your hand causes you to stumble, cut it off . . ." That sounds pretty serious to me. You and I live in a rather benign world. We are rarely confronted with absolute evil. If we were, we too would take sin far more seriously.

In his book, Descending into Greatness, Bill Hybels, the Senior Pastor of

Willow Creek Community Church, tells the story of a World War II soldier who was part of the liberation of the Nazi concentration camp at Dachau, Germany. If you don't know your WWII history, Dachau was one of the death camps where thousands of Jews were exterminated. The man told this story:

"A buddy and I were assigned to a boxcar. Inside were human corpses stacked in neat rows, exactly like firewood. The Germans, ever meticulous, had planned out the rows, alternating the heads and the feet, accommodating the different sizes and shapes of bodies. Our job was like moving furniture. We would pick up each body—so light—and carry it to a designated area.

"Some fellows couldn't do this part. They stood by the barbed wire fences retching. I couldn't believe it the first time we came across a person in the pile still alive! But it was true. Incredibly, some of the corpses weren't corpses. They were human beings. We yelled for doctors and they went to work on these survivors right away.

"I spent two hours in that boxcar; two hours that for me included every known emotion: rage, shame, pity, revulsion. Every negative emotion, I should say. They came in waves . . . all but the rage . . . it stayed, fueling our work.

"After we had taken the few survivors to a makeshift clinic, we turned our attention to the Nazis: the SS officers in charge of Dachau. Our captain asked for a volunteer to escort a group of a dozen SS officers to the interrogation center, and a guy named Chuck . . . his hand shot right up. Chuck claimed to have worked for Al Capone before the war, and not one of us doubted it.

"Well, Chuck grabbed his machine gun and prodded the group of SS prisoners down the trail. They walked ahead of him with their hands locked behind their heads, their elbows sticking out on either side. A few minutes after they disappeared into the trees, we heard the rattling burp of a machine gun and three long bursts of fire.

"Soon Chuck came strolling out, smoke still curling from the tip of his weapon. 'They all tried to run away,' he said with a kind of leer.

"It was that day that I felt called by God to become a pastor. First, there was the horror of the corpses in the boxcar: I could not absorb such a scene. I did not even know that such absolute evil existed! But when I saw it, I knew beyond a doubt that I'd spend my life serving whatever opposed such evil . . . serving God. Then came the Chuck incident. I had a nauseating fear that the captain might call upon me to escort the next group of SS guards; and even a more dreadful fear that if he did, I might do the same thing that Chuck had done! The beast that was in those guards was also in me. The beast within those guards, the beast within Chuck, the beast was also in me." (1)

To say that sin is not serious is naive. You and I have a beast within us. It may only reveal itself under the most dreadful of circumstances, but it is there.

Sin is serious because sin always hurts people. That is why God hates sin. Sin hurts the sinner, but sin also hurts innocent people.

Pastor David Holwick tells about two Baptist ministers named Don Saunders and Buddy Stride. They were inseparable friends, and had been since high school. Both had gone to Bible college and married within a year of each other. These two friends got their doctorates together and preached in the same church. They were soon to be formally installed as the pastor and assistant pastor of that church. They were so close that their families even shared the same house.

However, one drizzly Friday night in February Saunders and Stride left their home along with Stride's 2-year-old son to drive to the local grocery. They were picking up chocolate doughnuts and a videotape for a family night with the kids. They never made it back.

There was a driver on the road named Louis Serianni, Jr. Serianni shouldn't have been near a car. His license had been revoked in 1982 after the state labeled him a "habitual offender." But Serianni, 39, a mechanic, kept driving. "He'd forged an insurance card and racked up so many moving violations that his record runs 18 pages. He wasn't due to get his license restored until 2019."

"Serianni was steering his 1970 Oldsmobile Cutlass convertible in and out of traffic on a busy four-lane road, doing an estimated 60-70 mph in a 35 mph zone. His headlights were off and his blood alcohol level was more than twice the legal limit. At 7 p.m., witnesses told police, the big Olds crested a hill and slammed broadside into a small white car turning left." It was the car in which Saunders and Stride and Stride's small son were making their trip to the grocery.

Lois Stride was feeding dinner to her three girls when the police arrived. The first thing they said was, "The little boy's OK." Both men, however, were dead. (2)

Because of their deep religious faith the widows of Don Saunders and Buddy Stride were able to handle this deep tragedy. However, these two pastors were killed, not because they had done anything wrong, but because of the sinful actions of another.

Sin hurts people. It hurts the sinner. But it also hurts innocent people, people who have done nothing whatsoever to deserve being hurt. That's easy to identify in a situation like this one, of course, but it is also the case anytime we violate our sense of integrity, anytime we are guilty of wrongdoing. Somebody is likely to get hurt.

The problem is that actions have consequences and sometimes those consequences are far out of proportion to the actions themselves.

A young man goes to a party where there is much drinking. He takes only a few drinks, but then gets behind the wheel of an automobile. He has no intent of hurting anyone. He's just having a good time. But then . . .

The lonely housewife, suffering from low self-esteem, reaches out to a man who is not her husband. No big deal. It's only a harmless flirtation. But then . . .

The business man feels his corporation doesn't appreciate his hard work. Also, he's having more and more trouble keeping up with the lifestyles of his neighbors. And an opportunity comes to take a little extra out of an account that's under his guardianship. Just a little. It will never be missed. But then . . .

Few of us look down the road to see where our acts may be leading us. The tempter never slams us head on. He always begins with the tiniest transgression.

Leland Gregory in his book Stupid History tells about an amazing incident that took place in the Republic of Benin, a small nation in West Africa. Benin doesn't have a golf course, but a technicality like that never gets in the way of a dedicated golfer. A man in Benin named Mathieu Boya is a dedicated golfer.

Benin has five airfields within its borders, but only one has a paved runway; it was here at the Benin Air Base where Boya routinely practiced driving golf balls. Boya wasn't playing a round of golf that day in 1987. He was simply practicing driving the ball, but he did hit a birdie while he practiced driving, a real birdie. He struck a hapless passing seagull in mid-air.

The unconscious gull subsequently fell into the open cockpit of a French-built Mirage III fighter plane which was taxiing the runway. The gull landed on the pilot's lap. The bird regained consciousness and began flapping wildly, which startled the pilot, as you might imagine. The pilot lost control of the plane and crashed it into the four other Mirage fighter jets sitting on the tarmac. The pilot was okay, and the gull flew out of the cockpit before impact, but all five jets, the entire fighter defense force of the Benin nation, were completely destroyed. So an errant golf ball flew into a flying bird which landed on a pilot who lost control of his plane and thereby destroyed the Air Force of an African nation. (3)

Do you understand that life sometimes works that way—particularly when it comes to harboring sin in our life? Those simple vices like greed and envy and lust and sloth and anger can very quickly get out of hand. And sometimes the consequences of a sinful action are far out of proportion to the original action.

There was a crash several years ago of an Aeroflot jet in Siberia. All 75 people aboard the jet were killed. Before the crash you could hear their terrified voices on the flight recorder.

Apparently the pilot was giving his children a flying lesson at the time of the crash. You can hear a child sitting in the captain's seat ask, "Daddy, can I turn this?" Then came the voice of the captain shouting, "Get out! Get out!" It seems his son had "accidentally pushed the right pedal, sending the aircraft into an irreversible spin." (4)

It's not a big deal, is it? A pilot, a loving father, neglects his duty as an airline pilot for just a few moments to show his son what he does for a living. However, it becomes a very big deal in a hurry when the child pushes something he shouldn't have pushed. Seventy-five people lose their lives. Sin hurts. Actions have consequences, sometimes far out of proportion to the original act.

Christ came to save us from our sins. This is so important for us to understand. Christ did not come to condemn us for our sins. Christ came to save us from our sins. If there is something in your life, some wrongful behavior, some potentially damaging indiscretion, whatever it may be, that you know has the potential to hurt you or to hurt someone else, Christ wants to help you deal with that. That is the message of the cross. Christ loves you so much that he will go to any length to keep you from making a mess of your life. And if you have already made a mess of your life, he is waiting to forgive you of your sins and to heal you of your hurt. That's the Gospel. That's what it's all about. Why would Christ go to all that trouble? Why would he suffer all that pain? Because sin is serious business.

Donald Grey Barnhouse tells of an event that occurred at the Atomic Energy Commission laboratory in Oak Ridge, TN on November 20, 1959. On that day a small amount of solvent exploded and blew open the door of a processing cell. When that happened, about one-fiftieth of an ounce of plutonium was scattered into the air. Remember, only one-fiftieth of an ounce of plutonium was involved, but here's what the Atomic Energy Commission says resulted from this tiny spill:

All those who were within a four-acre area of the explosion turned in their laboratory-issued clothes to be decontaminated. Their urine was checked to insure that they had not inhaled or ingested any plutonium. The processing plant and a nearby research reactor were shut down. The buildings were washed with detergents, and the buildings' roofs were resurfaced. The surrounding lawn was dug up and the sod carted to a deep burial place. One hundred yards of surface was chiseled off a nearby asphalt road. To anchor any speck of plutonium that might have survived, the buildings were completely repainted. Final cost, including resodding, repaving, and reroofing: approximately $350,000. (5)

The AEC will go to all that trouble for a fraction of an ounce of plutonium.

Why? Because just a tiny amount of plutonium can do endless harm when released into the environment. Sin is like that. Even the tiniest sin has a way of getting out of hand and wreaking havoc in our lives. Sin destroys lives. Sin destroys families. Sin destroys churches and communities. And without the cross, sin would have destroyed all humanity.

"If your hand causes you to stumble, cut it off . . ." Not a very cheerful subject for a sermon, but it comes from the lips of the Master. And so we should listen. Sin is serious business. Get it out of your life. Keep it out of your life for your sake and for the sake of those around you. Let Christ help you get your life in order. Nobody loves you more than he does. Let him give you a new beginning today.

1. Bill Hybels, Descending Into Greatness (Zondervan, 1993), pp. 144-145.
2. Daily Record newspaper, Parsippany, NJ; "Widows Recall 2 Who Lived For Lord," by Jeffrey Brodeur, Associated Press, 1998. http://www.holwick.com/sermons/Job-book/job1_1.html.
3. Tales of Stupidity, Strangeness, and Mythconceptions . . . (Kansas City: Andrews McMeel Publishing, LLC, 2007), p. 172.
4. Daily Encounter, http://www.actsweb.org/. Cited by MONDAY FODDER, http://family-safe-mail.com/.
5. Timeless Illustrations for Preaching and Teaching (Peabody, MA: Hendrickson Publishers, Inc., 2004), p. 448

What Does The Bible Really Say About Divorce?
Mark 10:2-16

I enjoy humor about married couples.

Comedian Brian Kiley said recently, "I love being married. When I was single, I got so sick of finishing my own sentences."

A pastor was teaching on Proverbs 16:24 which reads like this: "Pleasant words are as a honeycomb, sweet to the soul, and health to the bones."

The minister then added, "In other words, you can catch more flies with honey than with vinegar."

One woman in the congregation put this advice to work immediately. She leaned over, put her head on husband's shoulder and whispered in his ear, "I just love to watch your muscles ripple when you take out the garbage."

Our lesson from Mark's Gospel is about marriage. It is also about the more painful subject of divorce.

A man tells about browsing in a Christian bookstore one day. He discovered a shelf of reduced-price items. Among these items was a little figurine of a man and woman, their heads lovingly tilted toward one another. The figurine was obviously designed to be a gift.

"HAPPY 10TH ANNIVERSARY" read the inscription. It appeared to be in perfect condition, yet there was a tag on it which said, "DAMAGED."

Examining it more closely, he found another tag underneath this tag that explained what was damaged. The tag said simply, "WIFE IS COMING UNGLUED." (1) Well, it's evident in our society today, that not only are some husbands and wives coming unglued, their marriages are, too.

I suspect the fragility of families today partially explains the nostalgia many people have for the 1950s. We live in a world very different from those seemingly innocent days of the '50s. Oh, in some ways things are better. Technology has added to our lives such things as HD-TVs, smart phones and other material goodies. With these changes, however, have come longer working hours, more stress, more meals away from home, more disposable income and less free time to enjoy it. One change has been particularly noticeable—the destruction of many families.

A few of you remember the days of black and white television when television networks carried shows like "Father Knows Best" and "Ozzie and Harriet." The norm for these programs was a family with a working husband and a wife who stayed at home lovingly devoted to her husband and her children. At least that was the image the media portrayed. Most families even then were not as idyllic as the sitcoms portrayed them.

Nevertheless, we live in an altogether different world today—a world of single parent families, two income families, blended families and latchkey kids. Divorce, almost unheard of during the 1950s now affects 60% of the children in America before they reach eighteen. (2)

Everyone is this room has probably been touched by divorce or a dysfunctional marital relationship in one way or another. You may have been through a divorce yourself. Or perhaps it's been your son or daughter, your sister or brother or a close friend. You may be a child of divorced parents, or perhaps you bear scars not from a divorce, but from a father and mother who maintained their marriage relationship but were so abusive to one another that it would have been better if their marriage had never taken place.

So Jesus' teachings on marriage and divorce are important to you even if you have decided to remain single. Perhaps, if you are divorced, Jesus' teachings have been used against you, and you have had pain added to the heartbreak of a broken marital relationship by the reaction of so-called Christian family members or friends. As someone has said, we are the only army that shoots its wounded. That's not altogether true, but let's wrestle with Jesus' teachings for a few moments, even though they may trouble some of us.

Some Pharisees came to test Jesus. They were not honest seekers who were coming to learn from him. They were enemies who were trying to catch him in violation of the Law of Moses. They tested him by asking, "Is it lawful for a man to divorce his wife?"

You need to understand that divorce was quite common in Jesus' time, just as it is today. It was a different social situation from our own, however. Women were basically property. Often they were sold by their families to men whom they thought would bring the family land and other real property. And as property, women were sometimes disposed of quite cruelly.

The beautiful picture from the first chapters of Genesis of woman created from man's side as an equal in the marital relationship had never quite been realized. Some say it still hasn't been realized. Notice that the Pharisees didn't ask, "Is it lawful for a man and woman to divorce?" They asked, "Is it lawful for a man to divorce his wife?" It would be unthinkable in that culture for a woman to divorce her husband.

Marriage was unequal. Still, it was about all the legal protection that a woman had. If her husband threw her out, a woman would probably be consigned to a life of abject poverty. If she had no family to take her in, she would starve, or turn to begging or prostituting herself to survive. She might even lose her children since the children too were property of their fathers.

These one-sided arrangements were protected by the religious establishment. Oh, to be sure, there was controversy in the religious community over reasons why husbands could divorce their wives. One prominent rabbi named

Shammi said that divorce was allowable only for adultery and infertility. However, another prominent rabbi named Hillel taught that anything the woman did that displeased her husband was grounds for divorce. Burn the toast? Scratch the bumper of the car? "You're outta here!" This was the historical situation. This helps explain Jesus' answer to the Pharisees.

"What did Moses command you?" Jesus asked, turning the question back to the Pharisees.

They said, "Moses permitted a man to write a certificate of divorce and send her away."

To this Jesus gave an interesting answer that surely shocked the Pharisees. "It was because your hearts were hard," he said, "that Moses wrote you this law."

What did Jesus mean by this? Think of it this way. In the time of Moses, men were abandoning their wives. And why not? If they were simply property, why not trade them in for the latest model? Human nature really has not changed much over the past 3500 years. In light of what was already happening among the people, Moses commanded the men to at least give the woman they were abandoning a certificate of divorce. That way she would at least be free to remarry. Without that certificate, technically she was still the property of her former husband. So Moses was trying in a small way to give women some protection. Not enough, quite obviously, but it was a step in the right direction.

However, Jesus wanted the Pharisees to know that Moses did not go far enough. What Jesus wanted them to see was that even the religious scholars had missed the whole point of the relationship between men and women. People are not property, regardless of their gender. People are not things to be used and then disposed of. Relationships are sacred, especially the marriage relationship. Jesus doesn't appeal to the Law of Moses as his authority. He goes farther back to the story of creation.

"It was because your hearts were hard that Moses wrote you this law," he says to them. Then he goes back to the second chapter of Genesis. "But at the beginning of creation," Jesus continues, "God 'made them male and female.' 'For this reason a man will leave his father and mother and be united to his wife, and the two will become one flesh.' So they are no longer two, but one flesh. Therefore what God has joined together, let no one separate."

Did you catch that? He's not talking about property rights. He's not talking about legalities. He's talking about two people merging not their real estate, but their hearts, their souls, their minds. Isn't that how most of us approached the marriage relationship —those of us who are married or have been married? We sincerely wanted to become one with our partner.

If that is not how you approached marriage, then shame on you. If you got married with the idea up front that, "Oh, well, if this doesn't work out, I can move on to someone else"—you're too immature and self-involved for marriage in the first place. We approach God's altar and ask God's blessing on our choice of a bride or groom with the idea that this is the one and this is forever. That's why the breakup of a marriage is so painful. So much hope, so much faith, so much love was invested in this relationship —for some people it is as if the very heart is torn out of them.

Jesus wants us to see that, right from the very beginning, this was what God wanted for His children. The marriage relationship is God's gift to us. It is God's way of providing a lover, a helpmate, someone who will always be there for us. God never intended for men to treat women like property—or women to treat men like that for that matter—even if it was encoded in the Mosaic Law. God has something much, much better in mind for us. "So they are no longer two, but one flesh. Therefore what God has joined together, let no one separate."

Considering the social mores of Jesus' time, when women still could be abandoned so easily, this was quite a shocking teaching. Even the disciples asked Jesus to clarify what he meant. His reply to his disciples was even more pointed, "Anyone who divorces his wife and marries another woman commits adultery against her. And if she divorces her husband and marries another man, she commits adultery." In other words, he was saying to his disciples, "Forget everything you've ever heard about marriage and divorce. Here is how it is. Marriage is a sacred event. Divorce is a sin."

Those are strong words. I know they make me uncomfortable. But notice this: if anybody ever asks you, "What does the Bible say about divorce?" tell them quite properly, it depends on where you look. Moses says in Deuteronomy 24:1, a man can give his wife a certificate of divorce and walk away, having fulfilled the law. Then Jesus says that, if you divorce and remarry, it is adultery. Then St. Paul, who, remember, wrote years after Christ's death and resurrection, in I Corinthians 7:10-16 suggests that it would be acceptable for a believer to divorce an unbeliever. So we have three different views on this important subject by the three leading lights in Scripture. Of course, Jesus is the one true light so we have to give his teaching priority.

But notice that St. Paul felt emboldened to amend Jesus' teaching. This says to me that he understood that Jesus was not giving us a legalistic formula for marriage and divorce when he gave this answer to the Pharisees. He was answering a specific question within a specific context. The Pharisees were looking for a loophole. "Is it legal for a man to divorce his wife?" Jesus didn't really worry that much about what was legal. He worried more about the effect of divorce on people. Good people were being damaged by the abuses of the marriage contract in his time. He wanted them to see that this was not what God intended marriage to be. Marriage is a gift God has bestowed upon human beings—the gift of sexuality, the gift of a lasting relationship, the gift of affirming love. Jesus wanted them to focus on the gift and not the law.

Divorce happens. It shouldn't happen, perhaps, but it does. Jesus knew that. He acknowledged that when he spoke of Moses and the hardness of human hearts. Moses gave his edict because he knew how people were. Some men were going to cast off their wives. And, given the chance, some women will cast off their husbands. Not every marriage is made in heaven. Some couples marry for all the wrong reasons. People sin. People fail. People fall. That's why we have forgiveness. That's why we have grace.

Does Jesus condemn divorced people? Is it adultery if a divorced person remarries? Well, even if you take it literally that it is adultery, remember that Jesus said that even to look upon a woman with lust in your heart is adultery (Matthew 5:28). Jesus wanted us to focus on the condition of a person's heart, not a legalistic approach to life. And listen again to his words in John 8 to the woman who was caught in the very act of adultery, "Woman, where are they? Has no one condemned you?"

"No one, sir," she said.

"Then neither do I condemn you," Jesus declared. "Go now and leave your life of sin."

So, even if we interpret Jesus' words literally to mean that remarriage of a divorced person is a sin, forgiveness is available—there is no condemnation—not by the Master. And if not by the Master, then who dares condemn the divorced person? If the tragedy of divorce has happened in your life, don't listen to the legalistic Pharisee who would kick you when you are down. Divorce is not God's plan for God's children, but divorced people are loved by God just as much as the purest saint.

But let's get back to Jesus' main point. Marriage is a gift from God. It is not intended to be a burden but a blessing. It can be the most wonderful thing that happens to us if our hearts are one with each other as marriage partners, and our hearts are one with God.

A few years ago, there was a man whose wife became seriously ill with Alzheimer's disease. She completely lost all of her memory and her ability to remember who she was or who anyone else was. She was in a nursing home and her husband came by to sit beside her bed and be beside her every day.

One of his sons told him that he didn't need to keep doing that because she didn't remember who she was and she didn't remember who he was. The man said: "I know she doesn't remember anything, but I do. I remember who she is and I remember who I am. I am the husband who said to her 55 years ago, I will love and cherish you for better or worse and in sickness and health. And I intend to do just that." (3)

What a gift that man was giving to his wife, a gift like unto one that many of us may one day be required to give to the person we love. Even more importantly what a gift God offers humanity—a lifelong partner to help us through life's joys and sorrows. It doesn't always work that way, even for the best of people. Divorce happens. It doesn't make God happy, but neither does it change God's love for the persons involved. And it shouldn't change our attitude toward them either.

1. Gayle Urban in Edward K. Rowell, 1001 Quotes, Illustrations, and Humorous Stories (Grand Rapids: Baker Publishing Group, 2008), p. 345.
2. Larry Davies, Sowing Seeds of Faith in a World Gone Bonkers (Amelia Court House, VA: ABM Enterprises, Inc., 1996), pp. 169-170.
3. Rev. Dr. William S. Shillady, http://www.parkavemethodist.org/sermon.php?s=16.

What God Has Joined Together
Mark 10:2-16

Our lesson from the Gospel of Mark today is on marriage. You may be familiar with the story of a pastor who was asked to talk with a class of boys and girls about marriage. He prepared his lesson carefully, entered the class and began with a question. "Boys and girls, I am here this morning to talk with you about marriage. Before I begin, can any of you tell me what Jesus had to say about marriage?"

After an awkward silence, little Johnny raised his hand eagerly. When the pastor nodded, he proudly gave his answer: "Jesus said, `Father, forgive them, for they know not what they do.'"

Well, no, that's not exactly what he said.

I want to ask those of you who are married a question: Is being married easy?

I heard about one woman with a rather sharp tongue who hired a medium to bring back the spirit of her dead husband. When he appeared, she asked, "Honey, is it really better up there?"

Without hesitation, he answered, "Oh, yes, it's much better here . . ." Then he added, "but I'm not up there!"

That little joke will either make you laugh . . . or make you cry. For some couples marriage is not easy. These marriages were definitely not made "up there."

A number of years ago Dr. Joyce Brothers spoke at a convention of the American Hospital Association. In her presentation Dr. Brothers stated that marriage is a "quiet hell" for over half of married American couples. She went on to state that four out of twelve marriages will probably end in divorce. Another six of those twelve marriages, she said, will become loveless "utilitarian" relationships to protect children, property, shared careers, and other goals. To put it another way, Dr. Joyce Brothers contended that only one out of six marriages in the United States can be called successful. The rest can be characterized as a quiet hell. (1) That is quite an indictment of the state of marriage in our time, if it is true. Unfortunately, other studies back up her contention.

Some years back, a report by the Detroit Free Press showed that 70% of all couples in the U.S. would not marry their same mates if they had the opportunity to marry again. Another study estimated that as many as 70% of retired couples who stay together do so in a state of mutual hostility. That's sad. One study reported that 80% of couples seriously consider divorce at some time or another. (2)

John W. Drakeford compares what is happening today to marriages to sinkholes in Florida. He tells about a Winter Park, Florida, family who came home from church one Mother's Day and discovered that their beautiful house had completely disappeared into a gaping hole: 1000 feet wide and 125 feet deep. Over the next few days the hole continued to widen, eating up a roadway, two businesses, and a public swimming pool. The owner of a luxury automobile, who had left his car at a shop for a tune-up, found that it was taking its turn down the hole. He chartered a large helicopter in a futile attempt to rescue the rapidly disappearing vehicle. Residents crossed their fingers as the hole slowly continued to widen. A city official projected the possibility that, if the hole were filled with water, it could become yet another Florida lake. (3)

Drakeford takes sinkholes like this one and draws a parallel between them and the collapse of marriages today. And it is an apt analogy. Marriage as an institution is rapidly sinking. That is why today's lesson from the Gospel of Mark is so important.

Some Pharisees came to Jesus. Their purpose was to try to test him with a question, "Is it lawful for a man to divorce his wife?"

"What did Moses command you?" Jesus replied.

They said, "Moses permitted a man to write a certificate of divorce and send her away."

"It was because your hearts were hard that Moses wrote you this law," Jesus replied. "But at the beginning of creation God 'made them male and female.' 'For this reason a man will leave his father and mother and be united to his wife, and the two will become one flesh.' So they are no longer two, but one flesh. Therefore what God has joined together, let no one separate."

That is the eternal ideal for marriage—a man and a woman becoming one flesh. Marriage has stood the test of time, and it also stands the test of Scripture. Jesus' first miracle was at a wedding feast in Cana of Galilee (John 2). The writer of Genesis, hundreds of years before the time of Christ, spoke from the heart and mind of God when he wrote, "It is not good for man or woman to be alone" (Gen. 2:8). And in this passage, Jesus states the matter succinctly: "Therefore what God has joined together, let no one separate." But marriage is not easy. There are three elements that are essential for a successful marriage. There are no shortcuts. All three must be present if a marriage is to work.

The first element is commitment. Commitment is almost a forgotten word in our culture. Remember Paul Simon's song? —"Fifty Ways to Leave your Lover?"

Just slip out the back, Jack/ Make a little plan, Stan

You don't need to be coy, Roy/ Just listen to me.

Hop on the bus, Gus/ You don't need to discuss much

Just drop off the key, Lee/ And get yourself free. (4)

Many people enter marriage with just about that level of commitment. And it just doesn't work!

Suzanne Britt Jordan wrote an article in Newsweek in which she said, "I think people should be upset about so serious a thing as divorce . . . I'm grown up; I have responsibilities; I am in the middle of a lifelong marriage; I am hanging in there, sometimes enduring, sometimes enjoying. For some reason, we assume that people can't stay married for life, but we make no such assumption about staying on the same job, keeping the same religion or voting the same ticket." (5)

"Married for life"—it doesn't always work that way, but a marriage should never be entered into with any other intent. Many of our mothers and fathers grew up, married, and raised families with the notion that divorce was unthinkable. And because it was unthinkable, they worked at their marriages and found fulfillment in them. Some of us have the idea that marriage was somehow easier back then. But it wasn't. Marriage has always been an imperfect institution because it is made up of imperfect human beings.

There's a story of a wife who went to the police station with her next-door neighbor to report that her husband was missing. The policeman asked for a description. She said, "He's 35 years old, 6 foot 4, has dark eyes, dark wavy hair, an athletic build, weighs 185 pounds, is soft-spoken, and is good to the children."

The next-door neighbor protested, "Your husband is 5 foot 4, chubby, bald, has a big mouth, and is mean to your children."

The wife replied, "Well yes, but who wants HIM back?"

There is no such thing as a perfect marriage because there are no perfect people. But, and this is important, most marriages can work if we are committed to them AND to each other. Commitment is the first element of a successful marriage.

Communication is the second. Redbook magazine reported that money and in-laws are no longer the major causes of divorce, though they once were. Studies today show that lack of communication is the leading cause of marriage breakup. It is not the only problem, of course. Changing goals and sexual difficulties are numbers 2 and 3. But communication heads the list.

According to a study done by the Family Service Association, 87 percent of the people interviewed said that communication was a major conflict in their marriages. One student of failing marriages reported that the average couple married ten years or more spends only 37 minutes a week in close communication. One family sociologist contends that openness of communication is virtually nonexistent between husbands and wives by middle age. (6) I suspect I am getting a silent "Amen" from many wives at this point. But you can see the problem.

Years ago there was a story about a man who had just installed a CB radio in his car and was trying it out as he drove down a country road. After he had fiddled with switches and dials, and shouted into his microphone for 10 or 15 minutes with no results, his wife said to him, "If you are so desperate to talk with someone, why don't you quit fooling with that thing and talk to me?"

Ouch, that hit the nail right on the finger for many of us—particularly for husbands. Most men have more difficulty communicating their feelings than do their wives. That's a generalization of course, but I think most of you will agree. I don't know why it is, but communication is hard work for most men. But it is a step that both husband and wife must make if a marriage is to work.

Let me say a personal word to husbands about this for a moment. This is an insight that comes from Tim and Bev LaHaye in their book, Spirit Controlled Family Living. They deal with the question of why the Bible commands husbands four times to love their wives and wives only one time to love their husbands. Their answer is this: First of all, women have a greater need to be loved. Some of you will quarrel with that stereotype, but like the communication difficulties of men, we have to admit the possibility of some truth there. Secondly, men have a harder time loving. Again, a stereotype, but still an important insight. For a marriage to be successful, most husbands will need to work harder at communication. Studies show that wives who become involved in extra-marital affairs do so, first of all, for someone who will talk with them! (7)

Marriages need Commitment and Communication. Even more important, a good marriage requires a covenant between a man, a woman, and God. If it is at all possible, marriage between two Christians should always take place in a church. I am aware that couples are getting married in hot air balloons and on water skis and in every imaginable location, but a Christian marriage is more than just a civil ceremony. It is a lot more than a legal contract. It is a sacred and holy covenant. There is a Trinity in the marriage ceremony: the husband, the wife, and God.

Pastor Ed Markquart reported the only statistics about marriage that really matter. What is the divorce rate of two people who love each other? He asked. Fifty percent. What is the divorce rate of two good people who love each other and believe in Christ? Fifty percent. What is the divorce rate of two good people, who believe in Christ and come to church on Christmas and Easter? Fifty percent. What is the divorce rate of two good people who believe in Christ, worship on Christmas and Easter AND are present 75% of the time in church . . . ? Two percent.

What does it take today to have a successful marriage? Commitment—for life, if at all possible; heart-felt communication; and a covenant—husband, wife and God together. Marriage does not have to be a quiet hell. It can be a foretaste of heaven with a commitment, good communication and a covenant.

---

(1) From an article by Pastor Anthony Bland, "Marriage Doesn't Have to be a 'Quiet Hell.'"
(2) Ibid.
(3) John W. Drakeford, The Awesome Power of the Listening Heart (Grand Rapids: Zondervan, 1982).
(4) © Universal Music Publishing Group, CARLIN AMERICA INC.
(5) Newsweek, June 11, 1979, p. 27.
(6) Bland.
(7) Tim and Bev LaHaye, Spirit Controlled Family Living (Fleming H. Revell).

Someone Bigger Than Phil
Hebrews 4:12-16

Several years ago, Carl Reiner and Mel Brooks did a comedy skit called the "2013 Year Old Man." In the skit, Reiner interviews Brooks, who is the old gentleman. At one point, Reiner asks the old man, "Did you always believe in the Lord?"

Brooks replied: "No. We had a guy in our village named Phil, and for a time we worshiped him."

Reiner was surprised: "You worshiped a guy named Phil? Why?"

Brooks replied: "Because he was big, and mean, and he could break you in two with his bare hands!"

Reiner asked: "Did you have prayers?"

Brooks answered: "Yes, would you like to hear one? O Phil, please don't be mean, and hurt us, or break us in two with your bare hands."

Reiner: "So when did you start worshiping the Lord?"

Brooks: "Well, one day a big thunderstorm came up, and a lightning bolt hit Phil. We gathered around and saw that he was dead. Then we said to one another, 'There's something bigger than Phil!'" (1)

Well, yes, there is something bigger than Phil. There is Someone bigger than the totality of our universe.

Daniel Benedict tells about a group of college students who were having a discussion about the nature of God. Some of the students did not believe in God . . . but most had a belief of some kind. The discussion was lively. One young woman said, "God is like a great big Teddy Bear who gives me a hug when I need it."

To this, a young man replied, "No Teddy Bear God for me! God is the Chief Justice of some kind of universal Supreme Court who's going to nail me to the wall when I show up for judgment!"

The discussion raged on for some time and finally someone offered up this idea, "God is whatever we think God is. One person's idea is as good as another person's idea. We shouldn't be judging other people's religious ideas."

This opinion seemed to gain traction with the group. Benedict, who had been mostly silent to this point, then asked a question. "What about Son of Sam's idea of God? He said God told him to kill some people. Is his idea of God okay?"

The group decided to modify their opinion just a bit. "People can have any idea they want of God as long as they don't hurt other people," they decided. "That really sounded like the most reasonable way to many of the students. Nobody gets hurt and everybody gets their own god . . . ." (2)

These young people were genuinely searching for a way to understand God. Most of us, however, would be uncomfortable with the idea that God is whatever people think that God is. We believe that God has revealed himself through Jesus

Christ. God is neither a Teddy Bear nor is God a Supreme Court justice who is going to nail us when we show up for judgment. God, we believe, is like Jesus.

The writer of Hebrews spells out our understanding of God and God's relationship to us in our lesson for today. He writes: "Therefore, since we have a great high priest who has ascended into heaven, Jesus the Son of God, let us hold firmly to the faith we profess. For we do not have a high priest who is unable to empathize with our weaknesses, but we have one who has been tempted in every way, just as we are —yet he did not sin. Let us then approach God's throne of grace with confidence, so that we may receive mercy and find grace to help us in our time of need."

Notice how we are to come to God's throne—we are to approach God with confidence. What is the first thing we learn about God from this passage? We learn that God is approachable.

This is important. Old Testament writers had an entirely different view of God. To approach the Old Testament God was to risk life and limb. The "throne of grace" of which the writer of Hebrews speaks is the New Testament equivalent of the Old Testament Ark of the Covenant.

In the book of Numbers, you may remember, when the ark was captured by the Philistines, numerous people, including some who merely looked at the ark, were killed by its power. Similarly, even some of the priests of the tribe of Aaron who served in the Temple were warned that viewing the ark would result in their immediate death (4:20).

And, in 1 Chronicles 13 we read about the time when David and his soldiers moved the ark from Abinadab's house. When they came to the threshing floor of Kidon, one of the soldiers named Uzzah reached out his hand to steady the ark, because the oxen stumbled, and he was struck dead simply and solely because he had put his hand on the ark (8-10). The Ark of the Covenant was so holy that only the high priest was to approach it, and he was to do so with fear and trembling, for any transgression against the Ark would have fatal consequences for him too. Since the ark was representative of God, the idea that God was unapproachable was the accepted norm.

But this is not so with the throne of grace. Our high priest, Jesus Christ, has already interceded in our behalf. And because he has, we can approach the throne of grace confidently and boldly. He has made us sons and daughters of the Most High.

You don't approach your parents with fear and trembling, do you? Our young people, you don't come crawling on your hands and knees with your face buried in the carpet and say, "O exalted and majestic father, please do me the honor of granting your humble servant, worm of the dust that I am, the high honor of borrowing the car tonight." You don't approach your father like that, do you? Well, some of us may.

Some of us may have grown up with a very strict father. I like the way one older comedian once described the changes in the modern family. He said, "When we were kids we were disciplined harshly. My father was very strict, but along came the electric razor and took away the razor strop. Then furnaces took away the old woodshed. And along came taxes and the worries of it took away my dad's hair and with that the old hair brush disappeared. And that's why kids today are running wild: the old man has run out of weapons!"

Some of you may have had parents who were quite harsh in their methods of discipline. Thankfully, parents have, for the most part, changed . . . For most of us, the image of "father" is one of kindness and accessibility. Not for all, unfortunately, but for most. And that is the image that the writer of Hebrews wants us to have of God. Jesus called God, Abba, "Daddy." That is the first reason the writer of Hebrews writes, "Let us then approach God's throne of grace with confidence . . ." Jesus showed us that God's nature is love and that God is approachable.

But why should we come to the throne of grace in the first place? The writer tells us why: "so that we may receive mercy and find grace to help us in our time of need." That is why we come. Life is hard. Sometimes it is cruel. Where do we turn at times like that? We approach the throne of grace. That is the second thing we learn about God from this passage. God is merciful; God understands our situation and cares.

Last year the world of women's basketball was stunned when Pat Summitt, long-time coach of the Tennessee Lady Vols and the winningest coach in the history of either men's or women's basketball announced she was stepping down as coach because she was battling early-onset Alzheimer's. She said she would fight this dread disease with determination and with faith.

Her situation reminds me of a pastor named Bob Davis. Some years ago Davis announced his retirement. His congregation was deeply shocked. Their eyes filled with tears as he told them he had Alzheimer's and would have to resign at age fifty-two. Listen to what he said to them: "As a Christian I belong completely to Christ. My life is not mine but Christ's. Today my ministry draws to a close and I can say with Paul, I have finished the race, I have kept the faith. Now I stand at the finish line in victory, because God set the distance I was to run . . . and I am finished at fifty-two!

"Pray for Betty, my wife," he said, "as I turn guardianship over to her. I will not suffer nearly as much as she will. Pray that I in no way inadvertently disgrace our Lord, this church or the people I love. Finally, when I get to that stage where my mind is gone, pray that the Lord will take me home quickly. The glory of being with Christ makes me gasp with joy."

When asked, "What about miracles?" Bob Davis said, "I am like Paul whose thorn in the flesh God did not remove and I don't expect God will remove my

Alzheimer's thorn . . . But I have made up my mind to find joy in my weakness because that means a deeper experience of the power of Christ." (3)

What a testimony of faith by this devoted pastor! Why do we come to the throne of grace? Usually, it is "so that we may receive mercy and find grace to help us in our time of need." That is what Christ teaches us about God's nature and character: God is approachable; God understands and cares about us in our time of need.

But there is one thing more to remember: We have access to that throne of grace only because of what Christ did for us on the cross. We did not receive God's grace because of any merit on our part. We received that grace because of what Christ did in our behalf.

The writer of Hebrews says, "Therefore, since we have a great high priest who has ascended into heaven, Jesus the Son of God, let us hold firmly to the faith we profess. For we do not have a high priest who is unable to empathize with our weaknesses, but we have one who has been tempted in every way, just as we are—yet he did not sin. Let us then approach God's throne of grace with confidence, so that we may receive mercy and find grace to help us in our time of need." We approach that throne confidently only because Christ gave himself for us to make it possible.

Henri Barbusse once wrote a novel with the French title, Le Fleu, or The Flower. In this novel there are two soldiers. One of the soldiers is a man of sterling character. His friend, however, whose name is Dominique has made many mistakes in his life.

In one passage the solder with the unblemished record has been wounded and is dying. He turns to Dominique and says: "It can't be long now. Listen, Dominique. You've lived a bad life. There are many convictions against your name. But there are no convictions against me. There's nothing on my name. Take my name. Take it—I give it to you. Straight off, you've no more convictions. Take my name, and give me yours—so that I can carry [all your past mistakes] away with me." (4)

That soldier truly cared about his friend. They would exchange names and he would bear forever his friend's misdoings. What if we had a friend like that— one who would take all our past mistakes upon himself? The Scriptures say this is indeed what Christ has done for us—given us his good name, as it were, and taken our name which is stained by sin. Isaiah writes: "Surely he took up our pain and bore our suffering . . . he was pierced for our transgressions, he was crushed for our iniquities; the punishment that brought us peace was on him, and by his wounds we are healed." (Isaiah 53:4-5)

Have you ever thought to yourself, "Ah, if I could only be 18 again and know what I know now! If only I could live my life over, I would do a much better job the second time around." Unfortunately, that is one luxury that is never given to any of us. Time marches relentlessly onward. Pontius Pilate spoke for all of us when he said, "What I have written, I have written."

We can't go back. We cannot undo the past. We can, however, do something about the future. Some of us are perhaps carrying a great deal of excess baggage with us from the past. If we could just forget the past—with its heartaches, disappointments and errors—if we could just somehow lay that burden down, the future would hold much more promise for us. Christ offers us that opportunity. "He was pierced for our transgressions, he was crushed for our iniquities; the punishment that brought us peace was on him, and by his wounds we are healed."

I understand that, on the edge of a lake in the North Carolina mountains, there is a cross that is about thirty feet high. The cross is placed so that its full image can reflect on the water. The cross is painted white and, at night, a spotlight floods it with light so that the reflection is even more brilliant against the darkness.

One night for devotions, a youth leader took a group of kids and their counselors down to the edge of that lake and had them stand behind the cross, so that the light was shining toward them and the lake stretched out before them.

Finally, the leader asked them to look up at the cross and tell the group what they saw. Wanting to sound scholarly and devout, the young people blurted out responses like, "forgiveness," and "salvation," and "sacrifice."

This counselor wanted them to see more. "What you should see when you look up at the cross," he said, "is God, on the other side, looking back down at you. Whenever God looks at us, he looks at us through the cross of his Son, Jesus. His victory over our sin, his victory over our chaos is what God sees." (5)

That's how God looks at us—through the prism of the cross of Christ. And because of that cross God sees us as if we were without blemish.

A father says to his son, "How much do I love you?" Then he opens his arms as far as he is able and says, "I love you us thiiiiissssss much." That's what we ought to see when we look at the cross.

The writer of Hebrews shows us God's character and God's relationship to us, God's children: "Therefore, since we have a great high priest . . . Jesus the Son of God . . . Let us then approach God's throne of grace with confidence, so that we may receive mercy and find grace to help us in our time of need."

1. Rev. Eldon Reich, http://www.aberdeenmethodist.info/Reichsermons/thanksgiving2007.pdf.
2. http://www.lectionarysermons.com/june_18_00.htm.
3. Rev. Robert W. Bohl, Day 1 http://day1.org/851-what_has_religion_done_for_you.
4. George E. Vandeman, I Met A Miracle (Nashville: Southern Publishing Association, 1971).
5. The Reverend Phillip W. Martin, Jr., http://eman.obroskyds.org/sermons/Sermon_20080914.pdf.

Blind Ambition
Mark 10:35-45

It's been more than twenty years, but I suspect most of us remember the case of the "Texas-Cheerleader-Murdering-Mom." Wanda Webb Holloway of Channelview, Texas wanted her daughter Shanna, 13 at the time, to be picked for the high school cheerleading squad. Her rival for this honor was a girl named Amber Heath.

Wanda Webb Holloway was the organist at the local Baptist church. She was a respected member of the community. However, that did not keep her from going to extreme measures to try to get her daughter on the cheerleading squad by eliminating her chief opponent. The first year, Ms. Holloway tried to have Amber disqualified from the competition on a technicality. The second year, she showed up at school and handed out promotional pencils and rulers imprinted "Shanna Harper cheerleader." This was a violation of school rules which got her own daughter Shanna disqualified.

If only she had stopped there, she would not have made national headlines. But her obsession only deepened. In 1991, Wanda Webb Holloway attempted to murder Amber Heath's mother just before the tryouts. She figured that, if her mother were killed, Amber would be too grief-stricken to compete in the cheerleading contest. Holloway had asked her ex-brother-in-law to arrange for a hit man to perform the murder, but he went to the police instead. He told the police Holloway toyed with the idea of killing both mother and daughter, but couldn't afford the $7,500 fee.

It was then that Wanda Webb Holloway became nationally known as the "Texas-Cheerleader-Murdering-Mom" and was sentenced to 10 years in prison. The school principal, James M. Barker explained it this way, "After all, it's the American way. We all want our children to achieve. There is a part of Wanda Holloway in all of us." That's probably true, but, hopefully, Ms. Holloway is an extreme example.

James and John, the disciples of Jesus, are more typical of you and me. James and John had dreams. They had ambition. Jesus called them "Boanerges," which means, "sons of thunder" (Mark 3:17). I am not sure what that means, but my guess is James and John were never shrinking violets.

There is one occasion told in Luke 9 that may give us a hint as to their character. Jesus and his disciples were on their way to Jerusalem. Jesus sent some messengers into a nearby Samaritan village to get things ready for him. But the people there did not welcome him, because he was heading for Jerusalem. Jerusalem was sacred to the Jews and that meant it was despised by the Samaritans, so the people of the village rejected Jesus' representatives. Luke tells us that when James and

John learned about this, they asked Jesus, "Lord, do you want us to call fire down from heaven to destroy them?"

That's seems to be an extreme reaction to a simple rejection, don't you think? Jesus rebuked James and John, of course, but maybe this is why he called them the sons of thunder. James and John had been fishermen when Jesus called them. They were probably strong, courageous men. Fishing wasn't a sport to them, it was their livelihood. And it wasn't an easy way to make a living.

James and John were among Jesus' first disciples, and they were closer to Jesus than any of the other disciples, except for Simon Peter. The three of them—Peter, James and John—were definitely the inner circle among Jesus' disciples. They are mentioned on five separate occasions as accompanying Jesus for significant events when the other disciples were not present.

They were the only witnesses to the raising of the Jairus' daughter (Mt. 9:18–26). And it was they who were chosen to go with Jesus up to the mountain top for the transfiguration, where Jesus was shown in the company of Moses and Elijah (Mt. 17:1-9). Later they were with Christ in the garden of Gethsemane when the soldiers took him to be tried and then crucified (Mt. 26:36-56).

Maybe it was because of their status as part of Jesus' inner circle that caused them to be a little proud. At least they seem proud in light of the request they made of our Lord. "Teacher," they said, "we want you to do for us whatever we ask." Uh-oh, those of you who are parents know that some kind of mischief is afoot. Beware when your children ask you to grant them something without specifying what it is. "We want you to do for us whatever we ask."

Jesus probably let out a sigh before answering, "What do you want me to do for you?"

They replied, "Let one of us sit at your right and the other at your left in your glory."

I'm sure Jesus anticipated their request, and at the same time I'm sure he was disappointed in James and John for making it. "You don't know what you are asking," he said. "Can you drink the cup I drink or be baptized with the baptism I am baptized with?"

"We can," they answered.

Their answer was probably sincere. James and John were quality individuals. They didn't always understand Jesus' mission, but they were loyal to Jesus and Jesus knew that. We don't know as much about James as we know about John, but we do know this: after Christ's resurrection and ascension, when Herod wanted to send a chilling message to the church, he did it by having James beheaded—the first of the disciples to die a martyr's death.

John, on the other hand, probably lived out his full life. But remember, it was John to whom Jesus entrusted the care of his mother. That shows his confidence in this one who is often called the beloved disciple.

That is probably why Jesus said to them, "You will drink the cup I drink and be baptized with the baptism I am baptized with, but to sit at my right or left is not for me to grant. These places belong to those for whom they have been prepared." It's important to note that Jesus didn't chastise them for their ambition. They were misguided, but he appreciated their drive and their courage.

The rest of the disciples became indignant when they learned of James and John's request. Jesus, however, used it as a teaching moment. He called all of his disciples together and said to them, "You know that those who are regarded as rulers of the Gentiles lord it over them, and their high officials exercise authority over them. Not so with you. Instead, whoever wants to become great among you must be your servant, and whoever wants to be first must be slave of all. For even the Son of Man did not come to be served, but to serve, and to give his life as a ransom for many."

We all want to be no. 1, don't we? We want it for ourselves and, those who are parents want it for their offspring.

There was an article in the Associated Press about a pregnant woman in West Palm Beach, Fla. This woman made the newspapers because she had doctors induce labor six days early. Why was it important to move up her child's birth? It was so that her newborn son could beat the Sept. 1 state enrollment deadline for kindergarten a few years hence. Now that's planning. When this mother realized six more days in the womb for her son could mean an extra year of preschool for him, she told her doctor to give nature a push. "Giving birth a few days early is worth it to me and my husband," she said before the birth. "It will mean a lot in school if my child has the necessary skills and maturity of other children his age." (1)

We can understand that. We live in a competitive world. That's the nature of our society. They're not playing football games all over our nation every weekend this fall just for the exercise. Winning is important to us. Pride is important to us. Prestige.

Two archaeologists, a Greek and Egyptian, were arguing over who came from the most advanced ancient civilization. The Greek bragged that it was obviously his country. He said, "While digging in Corinth, we found copper wires buried under the village. This proves we already had telephone wires in the sixth century BC!"

The Egyptian replied, "Well, we dug under one village that dates back at least that far and found no wires at all. This proves we had already gone wireless." (2)

Countries want to be number one, colleges want to be number one, individual people want to be number one. That is one of the most natural instincts that God has given us.

Maybe you remember the song from the Broadway musical, Annie Get Your Gun: "Anything you can do I can do better. I can do anything better than you." And the retort: "No, you can't!" "Yes, I can!" "No, you can't!" "Yes, I can! Yes, I can!"

We live in a competitive world. Companies compete. Colleges compete. Hospitals compete. Individuals compete. We turn all kinds of things into competitions.

I understand that, in 2002, German citizens celebrated the first ever Extreme Ironing World Championship. I'm not making this up—the Extreme Ironing World Championship. The goal of this competition is to perform the mundane task of ironing clothes, but in extreme locations and under extreme conditions. The five required locations were "Forest ironing, Water ironing, Rocky ironing, Urban ironing, and Freestyle ironing." Participants carried an iron, an ironing board, and a piece of clothing to various locations. Then they were timed how long it took them to successfully iron their particular fabric under extreme conditions. (3)

We live in a competitive world . . . and that's not all bad. The desire to get ahead, the desire to rise to the top, the desire to be number one has driven many people to live productive lives.

Our society is based on a healthy level of competition. Bill Gates and the late Steve Jobs were both very competitive. That is why we have two of the greatest technology corporations in the world. That is why we enjoy many innovative products. Many people have made major contributions to society primarily because they were hard driving, ambitious people.

Dr. Rachel Remen tells the story of the CEO of a highly successful company named George. George came to Dr. Remen's office six months after he had been diagnosed with terminal lung cancer.

George's company manufactured a medical device that George had patented. For George this had no particular significance. He was a business man. His goal was to make money. But now he was facing his own mortality. He told Dr. Remen he had wasted his life. "I have two ex-wives and five children," he said. "I support all of them, but I don't know any of them. I do not think they will miss me. I've left nothing behind me but a lot of money. What an old fool. A stupid old fool."

Ironically, another of Dr. Remen's patients at the time was a woman named Stephanie. What was ironic was that Stephanie used the device that George's invention had made possible. That medical device had changed Stephanie's life. Before, she was almost housebound. She was unable to work, unable to do much more than manage the symptoms of her medical condition. After she was fitted with this device, she had gotten a job, gotten married, and had a child. She had, in effect, been given another life.

Dr. Remen asked Stephanie if she would be willing to write George a letter about her experience. Stephanie did better than that. She invited George to her home for dinner. Stephanie's whole family—parents, siblings, aunts, uncles, nieces, nephews, cousins—were present, as well as many of her friends and neighbors. They each shared their perspective on Stephanie's life. George cried most of the time while this was going on. At the very end, Stephanie came to George and said, "This is really a story about you, George. We thought you needed to know."

George said, "And I did. I did." (4) George's life was a mixed bag, Dr. Remen admits. He had made many mistakes. But in his drive to reach the top of his company, he had also made a significant contribution.

God would not strip us of our ambition. Blind ambition can be destructive. Ambition under God's control can be used in a powerful way.

If you really want to be number one, says Jesus, be number one serving God and your neighbor. "Whoever wants to become great among you must be your servant," Jesus said to his disciples, "and whoever wants to be first must be slave of all. For even the Son of Man did not come to be served, but to serve, and to give his life as a ransom for many."

Author Max Lucado tells about some people in his church that he calls "The Society of the Second Mile." In one place he describes one of those second-mile servants. "By profession he is an architect," says Lucado. "By passion, a servant. He arrives an hour or so prior to each worship service and makes his rounds through the men's restrooms. He wipes the sinks, cleans the mirrors, checks the toilets, and picks up paper off the floor. No one asked him to do the work; very few people are aware he does the work. He tells no one and requests nothing in return. He belongs to the Society of the Second Mile."

"Another second-miler serves in our children's ministry," writes Lucado. "She creates crafts and take-home gifts for four-year-olds. Completing the craft is not enough, however. She has to give it a second-mile touch. When a class followed the theme 'Walking in the Steps of Jesus,' she made cookies in the shape of a foot and, in second-mile fashion, painted a toenail on each cookie." (5)

What an ambitious undertaking! We have ambitious servants like that in this church. They also are achievement-oriented people, though they probably would not call themselves that. The achievements that they seek simply grow out of their desire to serve. Of course, they serve because Christ first served them.

I like the way Bishop Fulton J. Sheen once put it. "Our Lord was not a superstar," said Sheen, "He was a Super-scar." He showed his disciples his feet and his riven side and he said to them: "As my Father sent me, so also I send you."

Jesus wants us to be number one. He wants us to serve our community and our world like no church or any community service organization has ever served. Then we will look over our lives with no regrets, but only satisfaction.

Someone once put it like this: "Life is a lot like the game of tennis. Those who don't serve well end up losing." And that's true. It's all right to be ambitious, but make sure you're ambitious about the right things. Be number one at serving God and serving your neighbor, then you'll never come to the end of your life and say, "What a waste." Neither will the Master say, "What a waste." Instead he will say, "Well done, thy good and faithful servant."

1. Copyright 1998 The Associated Press. All Rights Reserved.
2. Thomas Cathcart and Daniel Kline, Aristotle and an Aardvark Go to Washington (New York: Abrams Image, 2007), p. 28.
3. Guinness World Records 2004, edited by Claire Folkard, et. al. (Guinness World Records Limited, 2003), p. 268.
4. Rev. Nancy Alma Taylor, http://www.sonomacongregational.org/9.24.2006sermon.pdf.
5. Every Day Deserves a Chance (Nashville: Thomas Nelson Publishers, Inc., 2007), p. 109.

What Do You Want From Jesus?
Mark 10:46-52

I was tempted to have the ushers hand out 3x5 index cards this morning and ask you to write on that card one thing you would like Jesus to do for you. Now please understand. I don't believe in using our communication with God like a heavenly vending machine—asking God to fulfill our desires for wealth, good looks, victory for our alma mater in football, etc. God would doubtless fail to honor such trivialization of our faith. But all of us have needs, deep legitimate needs in our life.

Perhaps some of us may have a secret sin that we are struggling with. Yes, it happens even among church people. We probably wouldn't want to write that sin on a card here in public. But Jesus knows about it. And we know about it. And we know the possible harm that may result from that sin. Secretly, in our hearts if not on a card, we might say, Jesus, rip this sin out of my soul. See me free, Lord. Unfortunately, some of us don't have the moral strength to pray that prayer. Some day we will likely be praying that God will rescue us from the consequences of that sin. Too bad.

Maybe you are in need of a particular kind of healing, perhaps physical healing. Physical hurts are easy to identify. That sometimes makes them easy to cure. Some diseases, however, have no known cure. Jesus may be your last hope. And so you might write on that card, "Please heal me of my cancer, or please heal my failing heart." Jesus hears those prayers. Sometimes a miracle does indeed occur—a cancer will go away—a heart will grow stronger. We don't know why such miracles sometimes occur or why other times they do not. We'll find out some day, but for now "we see through a glass darkly," as St. Paul put it (I Cor. 13:12).

Maybe your request would be for someone you love. You might write on that card, "Lord, my son is struggling right now to overcome an addiction." Or, "Lord, my daughter's marriage is coming apart." The needs that people have seem almost endless sometimes. What would you have Jesus do for you or someone you love?

A man named Bartimaeus sat by the roadside begging. You and I don't like beggars. They make us uncomfortable. If we pass them by, we feel guilty. If we give them something, we wonder if we have been taken advantage of. But imagine if you had no other source of income for your family? Imagine there was no safety net—even for the poorest of the poor. Welcome to Bartimaeus' world. There was no Goodwill industry committed to helping the blind. No Lions' Club to buy you a cane and provide you with a guide dog. No Social Security Disability checks. You were on your own and you lived in a world of perpetual, impenetrable night.

You wouldn't like begging either, but you had no other option. So you sit there day after day totally dependent on the kindness of strangers. But not every stranger is kind. And the gifts are meager, but still you sit there because there is no other way to survive.

Until, one day you hear that a man named Jesus is passing by. For one precious moment a glimmer of hope enters your life. And so, even though there is a large crowd all around who have also been drawn to see the Master, suddenly you begin to shout, "Jesus, Son of David, have mercy on me! Jesus, Son of David, have mercy on me!"

Your friends are embarrassed by your behavior. They tell you to be quiet. You're making a spectacle of yourself. But you shout even louder with no idea whether Jesus can hear you at all, "Son of David, have mercy on me!"

Friend, have you ever been there where Bartimaeus was that day? "Lord, please hear my prayer. Lord, have mercy on me!"

Some of you have. You didn't have to worry about losing your sight, perhaps, but some other great problem had come into your life, something too big for you, something too big for your doctor, or your employer, or your pastor. The only one who could help you was Jesus, and so you prayed, "Lord, please hear my prayer. Lord, have mercy on me."

If you have never been where Bartimaeus was that day, some day you will be. I'm sorry to tell you that, but it's true. Life takes some strange twists and turns. Some of you have already learned that. The rest of us will sooner or later.

Bartimaeus was shouting over the din of this large crowd of people accompanying Jesus out of Jericho, "Son of David, have mercy on me!"

Then, Mark tells us, Jesus stopped. Wow, what wonderful words of hope. Jesus stopped . . . and said to those closest to him, "Call him." He was speaking of Bartimaeus. He not only stopped for Bartimaeus, but he called for him.

There have been times when Jesus has stopped for me. Not all the time, of course. There have been times when I've sung that old Gospel hymn, "Pass me not O gentle Savior . . ." And I know in my heart of hearts Jesus heard me, but it felt like he just kept on walking. That's how it felt. I knew he did stop and consider my plea, but he sees life much clearer than I do, and so, for the time, it felt like he passed on by. My prayer wasn't answered in just the way I had hoped. I am sure some of you have had the same experience. But there have been times when I have called out, and Jesus has indeed stopped and called for me.

Jesus stopped for Bartimaeus. People starting nudging Bartimaeus and saying with excitement, "Cheer up! On your feet! He's calling you."

I love these next words. Mark tells us that, "Throwing his cloak aside, [Bartimaeus] jumped to his feet and came to Jesus."

Bartimaeus was not going to let this opportunity pass him by. That's important. Some people let life beat them down to the point that they simply quit trying. That is the worst thing you can do.

I like something Erik Weihenmayer once said. Some of you will remember Erik. He is an amazing man who, though he is blind, has climbed some of the largest mountains in the world. After climbing El Capitan, the 3,000 foot sheer rock face in Yosemite, Erik said, "Someone told me that blind people need to realize their limitations; but I think it's more exciting to realize my potential." What an attitude!

A few years ago Guideposts magazine carried the story of Sabriye Tenberken, a young woman who has been blind since the age of 13. Sabriye does not let her impairment stand in the way of living a full life. She also loves to participate in outdoor activities like hiking and kayaking. On a visit to Tibet, Sabriye encountered a community in which there were few resources available to the blind. Blind children in Tibet have little chance for an education or meaningful work. Many families tie their blind children up during the day so they won't wander away and get hurt.

Sabriye knew that the blind children of Tibet, if given the right tools, could live out their full potential. So she established Braille Without Borders, a school for blind children in Tibet. At the school, the children learn computer skills, receive job training, and participate in outdoor sports, like mountain climbing. They also learn a Braille version of the Tibetan alphabet, which Sabriye created herself. (1)

Bartimaeus lived a much more limited life than these modern superstars like Erik and Sabriye, but I believe he shared their spirit. An opportunity came for him to be more and do more and he jumped at the opportunity. So many people let life beat them down until they quit trying. I am not being judgmental of them. I am simply imploring each of us not to do that. There is some truth to the expression, "where there is a will, there is a way."

There is a somewhat amusing story about Captain Horatio Nelson of the British navy who in 1801 was engaged in attacking French troops in Copenhagen, Denmark. The tide of the battle turned in favor of the French, and Nelson was ordered by the command ship to retreat. But Nelson wanted to continue fighting and ignored the command. A subordinate urged the captain to heed the commander's order, and Nelson picked up a telescope to verify the signal for himself. Then Nelson did something a little devious. He was blind in one eye, so he purposely held the telescope to his sightless eye and said truthfully that he "couldn't see" any signal of retreat. Nelson continued his attack and won. Says Leland Gregory in his book, Stupid History Tales, "This event left us with a phrase that means "to ignore something" and is still used today: "to turn a blind eye." (2)

Sometimes it pays us to turn a blind eye to our obstacles and to focus our one good eye on our opportunities. Jesus called for Bartimaeus and Bartimaeus threw aside his cloak, jumped to his feet and came to Jesus. He was not going to let this opportunity pass him by.

Jesus asked Bartimaeus, "What do you want me to do for you?"

Bartimaeus said, "Rabbi, I want to see."

"Go," said Jesus, "your faith has healed you."

Bartimaeus made a specific request of Jesus and Jesus granted that request. Bartimaeus wanted his sight and Jesus gave him his sight.

Ed Markquart, a Lutheran pastor in Seattle tells about an article that appeared in Time magazine some years back. The article was titled "Miracles."

The story was about a family from North Carolina. Their child was born some years ago with droopy eyelids. Sometime later, the family made an appointment with a neurologist. A scan was taken which revealed a brain tumor. A preliminary surgery was performed which revealed a type of malignancy that no human being had ever before survived. There was to be future paralysis and then inevitable death.

The family was devastated, as you might imagine. The grandfather of the child with droopy eyelids, a surgeon for thirty-nine years, prayed that the family would have good doctors. The father, a young attorney, prayed that the will of God would be done. The mother prayed that somehow she would be able to endure this tragedy. It came to seven days from surgery, and a friend came to visit—an Episcopal priest. This priest prayed for a miracle, a healing, and he anointed the child with oil.

Forty-eight hours before the impending surgery, the surgeon went into the child's brain and drew out some fluid. They decided to postpone the surgery for two more days. The doctor went into her brain the next day to examine the fluid again and this time there was nothing. Nothing. There were no lesions, no cancer, no tumor. The article in Time magazine said, "[The doctor] was . . . baffled . . . he was bewildered." And the mother? She was overwhelmed. She said, "If you ever see my thirteen year old Elizabeth running around, with a drooping left eye, do not feel sorry for her. I am astounded that my child is alive! I don't understand it but my child has experienced a miracle." (3)

I don't doubt that she did. I don't pretend to understand such miracles. I certainly don't know why she experienced healing when many children die every day of such tumors and other terrible diseases. I don't know why Jesus said to Bartimaeus, as well as many others, "Your faith has healed you." Too many people feel guilty about the death of someone they love. "If only they had more faith," they tell themselves, "my loved one would still be alive." I do not believe that. As a pastor I have seen too many wonderful Christian people go through too many tragedies to entertain that thought even for a second.

I believe that Bartimaeus' determination to get well gave him a better shot at healing, so in that sense his faith played a role. And his belief in Jesus certainly contributed as a psychological and spiritual tool. But many people have had great faith in Jesus, but experienced no such miracle. It is a mystery, but still I will pray for those who are sick that they will be made well. God works where He will. And I trust God.

Jesus asked Bartimaeus, "What do you want me to do for you?"

Bartimaeus said, "Rabbi, I want to see."

"Go," said Jesus, "your faith has healed you."

Immediately, Mark tells us, Bartimaeus received his sight and followed Jesus along the road. Here is the important miracle. After his healing Bartimaeus became a follower of Jesus. He was grateful for what Christ had done for him and he followed Jesus forever after. What's so miraculous about that? I'll tell you. There are many people who have been gifted by God in so many ways, and they have ignored God altogether.

Let me ask you a question. Which is better—to have been Bartimaeus who spent his growing up years blind and then received his sight as an adult or—like most of us—to have the precious gift of sight all your life and take it for granted? Who is the more fortunate—Bartimaeus or you and me? I believe you know the answer. Then why aren't we following Jesus with all kinds of gratitude for what he has done for us? Some of us are, but some of us are just going through the motions. You might say that some of us are Bartimaeus before Jesus healed him. We, too, are blind, spiritually blind.

I began this message asking what you would have Jesus do for you. Someone in this room needs to answer with Bartimaeus, "Rabbi, I want to see. I want to see my own sinful pride. I want to see my spiritual neglect. I want to see the person of gratitude and joy I could be if I surrendered myself to you. I want to see."

Fanny Crosby could see. Oh, not with her physical eyes. When Fanny was six weeks old, she had an eye infection. Her regular doctor was out of town, and a man posing as a doctor gave her the wrong treatment. Within a few days, she was totally blind. When she was only eight years old, she wrote this poem:

Oh, what a happy child I am, Although I can not see.

I am resolved that in this world, Contented I will be.

How many blessings I enjoy That other people don't.

To weep and sigh Because I'm blind, I cannot and I won't!

Instead of being bitter and feeling sorry for herself, instead of blaming the doctor for his "sin" against her and dwelling in spiritual and emotional darkness all her days, Fanny Crosby used the gifts that God had given her to write over

8,000 hymns and poems to praise and glorify God. (4)

Fanny Crosby saw things that other people do not. She saw God's love for her in spite of her infirmity. She saw that her life still had value and that she could be a productive member of society. Fanny Crosby could see more than many of us. My friend, what would you have Jesus do for you? How about helping you see how fortunate you really are, and to see all the productive and loving things you could be doing with your life?

1. Adam Hunter, "Unlimited," Guideposts, July 2004, p. 12.
2. (Kansas City: Andrews McMeel Publishing, LLC, 2007), p. 121.
3. http://www.sermonsfromseattle.com/easter_astounded.htm.
4. Rev. Richard J. Fairchild, http://www.rockies.net/~spirit/sermons/a-le04su-laughter.php.

A Rock Thrown—A Lesson Learned
Mark 12:28-34

Author Ron Dykstra tells about a young and successful executive who was traveling through a neighborhood, driving a bit too fast in his new Jaguar. Suddenly a brick smashed into the Jag's side door! The young executive slammed on the brakes and backed up to the spot where the brick had been thrown. He then jumped out of the car, grabbed the nearest kid and pushed him up against a parked car, shouting, "What was all that about and who are you? Just what the heck are you doing? That's a new car and that brick you threw is going to cost a lot of money. Why did you do it?"

The young boy was apologetic.

"Please mister . . . please, I'm sorry, but I didn't know what else to do," he pleaded. "I threw the brick because no one else would stop . . ."

With tears dripping down his face and off his chin, the youth pointed to a spot just around a parked car.

"It's my brother," he said. "He rolled off the curb and fell out of his wheelchair and I can't lift him up."

Now sobbing, the boy asked the stunned executive, "Would you please help me get him back into his wheelchair? He's hurt and he's too heavy for me."

Moved beyond words, the driver tried to swallow the rapidly swelling lump in his throat. He hurriedly lifted the handicapped boy back into the wheelchair, then took out a handkerchief and dabbed at the fresh scrapes and cuts. A quick look told him everything was going to be okay.

"Thank you," the boy said. Too shook up for words, the man simply watched the boy push his wheelchair-bound brother down the sidewalk toward their home.

It was a long, slow walk back to his car. Funny, he never bothered to repair that dented side door. He kept the dent there to remind him of this message: "Don't go through life so fast that someone has to throw a brick at you to get your attention!" (1)

In Mark 12, we discover the Pharisees, the Sadducees and some of the Herodians trying to trap Jesus. They knew he was stirring up the people. They viewed him as a trouble maker and they wanted to find some grounds by which they could bring him up on charges. However, what they discovered was a man who knew the Law better than they did. More importantly, he understood the heart of the Law rather than just a surface view. And some of them were impressed.

One of the teachers of the law heard them debating and asked Jesus, "Of all the commandments, which is the most important?"

"The most important one," answered Jesus, "is this: 'Hear, O Israel: The Lord our God, the Lord is one. Love the Lord your God with all your heart and with all your soul and with all your mind and with all your strength.' The second is this: 'Love your neighbor as yourself.' There is no commandment greater than these."

In the Jewish books of the law—Genesis, Exodus, Leviticus, Numbers and Deuteronomy—scholars have counted 613 laws. Of these laws, 248 are considered to be positive in nature, while 365 are considered to be negative. That is, some compel the righteous person to do certain things while others forbid certain activities. These 613 laws formed the basis for Jewish belief and practice. In his answer to this teacher of the law, Jesus boils all the Law, the Commandments and all the teachings of the prophets down into one word: Love. Love God; love your neighbor. (2)

What does it mean to love? One thing it means is that a person in need shouldn't have to throw a rock at our car to get our attention. Christians are called to do more than have warm feeling toward people. Followers of Jesus are called to seek out people who are hurting and minister to them.

It's easy to be a Christian if that means simply keeping the "thou shalt nots" of the law. "We don't smoke and we don't chew . . . and we don't go with the girls that do," as the little country ditty went. If that is what it means to be a Christian, then we've got it made. It would be hard to keep all 365 of those laws that prohibit certain behaviors, but most of them don't apply to us anyway.

And it is easy to be a Christian if all it means is coming to worship from time to time and putting some change in the offering plate. We've got that covered. Look at us. Whoopee! We're followers of Jesus.

I'm sorry to say that many of us who think we are following Jesus have missed the mark altogether. The most important thing Jesus told us to do was to love God and to love our neighbor. What is love to you? A squishy emotion? The way you feel about dark chocolate? A romantic whisper in your ear?

Let me tell you what love meant in one church. It's a story that Dr. Barbara K. Lundblad tells. It's about a friend of hers who's a pastor in New England.

"How's your building program going?" Dr. Lundblad asked her friend one day.

"Oh, we ran out of money before we got to the worship space," this pastor said.

Dr. Lundblad thought to herself, "What could be more important than the worship space?" But she kept her thoughts to herself.

"We renovated the basement," this pastor explained. "You know, we have a shelter there for homeless men. We put in new showers and renovated the old kitchen. The basement was so drab, and the showers—well, there was only one shower and it was lousy."

Then this pastor added these very moving words, "On the Sunday before the shelter opened, the worship service began as usual in the sanctuary. When it came time for communion, the people carried the bread and the cup downstairs to the basement. The whole congregation gathered around the empty beds. They passed the bread and the cup around the circle. The body of Christ given for you." Then this pastor concluded with these words: "That night the shelter beds were full, and the worship space still needed a lot of work." (3)

What does that story say to you about love? It says to me that this congregation didn't need a rock thrown through its window to get its attention concerning the people in their community who were hurting. Now I'm not saying that we ought to convert some of our space into a homeless shelter. I am saying that there are hurting people in our community. Some of them are lonely. Some of them have emotional problems. Some of them are single moms who are overwhelmed by the needs of their family. Some of them are being crushed by some form of addiction. We can be nice people and wait for them to come to us—if they ever do—and then apply a few band-aids. But friends, that is not love. I'm sorry. It's not.

Love requires that somehow we find out who the hurting are and go to them. Sometimes it's hard to identify those who are hurting.

I read an interesting story recently about a college student named Chris van Rossmann. Chris answered a knock at the door of his apartment in Corvallis, Oregon one day to find police and civil air patrol and search-and-rescue personnel standing there demanding to know why he was sending out a distress signal. Chris clearly wasn't in any apparent distress, and he was completely unaware that he was doing any such thing.

After a little investigation, the response team was surprised to discover that the signal was being emitted by Chris's year-old flat screen television. There was some freakish problem with the flat screen that was causing it to emit this weird signal that was very much like a distress call. This distress call had been picked up by a very sensitive satellite and routed to the Air Force Rescue Center at Langley Air Force Base in Virginia. "They'd never seen a signal come that strong from a home appliance," the 20-year-old told reporters. They had apparently expected to find a malfunctioning transponder on a boat or small plane, the usual problem in incidents such as this.

As the response team left, they told Chris not to turn on his TV set or he'd be facing a $10,000 fine for "willingly broadcasting a false distress signal." Fortunately, the manufacturer of the TV offered to provide him with a free replacement. (4)

It would be helpful if everyone who needed help emitted a distress signal that we could pick up here in the church. Then we would know where to go to share the love of Jesus. But they usually don't send out such signals. That means we will simply have to go to some of the most obvious places and find them.

That wonderful preacher and teacher Tony Campolo tells about a church deacon he knows of who did exactly that. This deacon wanted some place he could share the love of Christ. The youth in their church led a worship service once a month in a nursing home. One month this deacon went with them. He stood in the back of the room. The young people were performing and this old man in a wheel chair rolled his chair over to where this deacon was standing, took hold of the deacon's hand and held it all during the service. That was repeated the next month and the next month and the next month and the next month.

Then they went one Sunday afternoon and the man wasn't there. The deacon asked the nurse in charge, "What happened to that man?"

"Oh," she said, "He's near death. He's just down the hall, the third room. Maybe you should go in and visit him. He's unconscious, though."

The deacon walked down and went into the room. It was a typical nursing home setting. Sparse. There was a chair, a bed, and a man with tubes attached to him, near death.

The deacon went over and took hold of one of the old gentleman's hands. He felt moved to say a prayer. When he said "Amen," the old gentleman in the bed unexpectedly squeezed his hand in recognition. The deacon was so moved by that squeeze of the hand that he began to weep. He shook a little. He tried to get out of the room and as he was leaving the room, he bumped into this woman who was coming into the room. She says, "He's been waiting for you. He said he did not want to die until Jesus came and held his hand, and I tried to tell him that after death he would have a chance to meet Jesus and talk to Jesus and hold Jesus' hand. But he said, 'No. Once a month Jesus comes and holds my hand and I don't want to leave until I have a chance to hold the hand of Jesus once more.'" (5)

Where can you go, my friend, to show somebody the love of Christ? A nursing home? A Big Brother organization?

Here's what we need to see. Every time we perform an act of love we glorify Christ. The first commandment is, of course, to love God. When we love somebody in Jesus' name, we are showing our love for God.

Deacon Eric Stoltz tells about a report that was on "60 Minutes" about a group of New York City paramedics. A year before this broadcast the Kashmir region between India and Pakistan was hit by a gigantic earthquake. One hundred thousand people died in that earthquake. When these 13 paramedics heard about the disaster, they immediately decided to go help.

When they arrived, they discovered that they were the only foreign aid workers for miles around. No one else had come. That didn't stop them. They made some rudimentary tents and began treating the thousands of injured people who streamed to them. Parents carried injured children from destroyed villages, walking days to reach them. The 13 paramedics worked day and night. They estimated they saved one life every half hour for several months.

None of the people in that region had ever met an American. One of the paramedics told "60 Minutes": "We are not just healing people. We are inoculating an entire valley against Islamic fundamentalism." That's not why they went, but it's something they discovered by being there. (6)

If they had been Christian missionaries, they would have said, "We have been glorifying Christ by showing his love to those in need."

Wouldn't you agree with me that a lot of cynicism in our society toward organized religion would disappear overnight if we just carried the love of Christ out these doors?

Let me read you something that President Abraham Lincoln once said about religion. These are important words: "When any church," said Lincoln, "will inscribe over its altar as its sole qualification for membership, the Savior's condensed statement of the substance of both law and Gospel, 'Thou shalt love the Lord thy God with all thy heart and with all thy soul, and thy neighbor as thyself,' that church will I join with all my heart and all my soul." So would a lot of other people in our society with a negative view of religion.

A teacher of the law asked Jesus: Of all the commandments, which is the greatest? "The most important one," answered Jesus, "is this: 'Hear, O Israel: The Lord our God, the Lord is one. Love the Lord your God with all your heart and with all your soul and with all your mind and with all your strength.' The second is this: 'Love your neighbor as yourself.' There is no commandment greater than these."

"Well said, teacher," the man replied. "You are right in saying that God is one and there is no other but him. To love him with all your heart, with all your understanding and with all your strength, and to love your neighbor as yourself is more important than all burnt offerings and sacrifices."

When Jesus saw that he had answered wisely, Jesus said to him, "You are not far from the kingdom of God."

That's where I want to live, don't you, near to the kingdom of God? How do I do that? One answer: Love.

1. Ron Dykstra, Clean Jokes, Inspirational Stories and More (Kindle edition).
2. Alan Carr, http://www.sermonnotebook.org/new%20testament/Mark%2012_28-34.htm.
3. The Rev. Dr. Barbara K. Lundblad, http://day1.org/938-whe_pentecost_ends_too_soon.
4. By Gary Swanson, source unknown.
5. Tony Campolo, http://www.csec.org/csec/sermon/campolo_4519.htm.
6. http://www.stbrendanchurch.org/blogs/index.php?/archives/62-Twenty-third-Sunday-in-Ordinary-Time-B-Ephphatha!-Be-Open!-911.html.

The Truth About Warren Buffet's Secretary
Mark 12:38-44

The election is now far behind us. I guess it's safe for me to talk about Warren Buffet's secretary. In case you've been on a deserted island somewhere cut off from all media, Warren Buffet, one of the richest men on earth and a prominent Democrat, caused quite a stir sometime back when he said that his secretary pays a higher percentage of her salary in taxes than he pays. That is because wages are taxed differently than are investments, and wealthy people have a clear advantage in accumulating more wealth because of that inequity. Some people were horrified by his example. Others just shrugged their shoulders and said, "That's the way capitalism works."

But now that the election's long past, finally here's the real truth about Mr. Buffett's secretary: If Mr. Buffett's secretary is like most of the secretaries in this world, she probably gives more money to her church proportionally than her boss does. Now I know that Mr. Buffet is a very generous man. In fact, under the influence of Bill and Melinda Gates, Buffet has been giving away vast sums of money for a variety of good causes. But the principle remains—on a percentage basis, those in the lower echelons of society give more of their income to serve Christ than do the people who employ them. Income inequality is a big issue in our society. What I would like to talk about for a few minutes is generosity inequality.

Pierce Harris, a legendary pastor of the First Methodist Church in Atlanta, Georgia many years ago once did something that caused quite a stir in his church. He decided that once a year he would publicly post the annual contributions of his church members. Don't worry we're not considering that here, but that's what Pierce Harris did. Harris said, of course, that he had planned it so he would be in Europe for the two months following the posting. Discretion is the better part of valor. But on the bulletin board and in the church newsletter there was listed the name of every church member, and beside that name the amount of contributions for the last year.

He said a lot of people got mad. Some left the church. But, he pointed out, it was only those who did not tithe who walked away. Those who were faithful in their giving were not ashamed or threatened. The rest simply did not want everyone knowing just how stingy they really were. It was embarrassing, he said, for people to discover that a secretary gave more than her wealthy boss, that the man who rode around in an expensive automobile gave less than the widow who was sending her son through college on a pension. (1)

Now, in the words of an old joke, some of you are thinking, "Oh, no, he's quit preaching and gone to meddling." But that's what today's text requires of me.

Jesus and his disciples were in the temple courts where Jesus was teaching.

They were in an area near the treasury. Scholars tells us that the Temple complex was made up of various courtyards which became increasingly exclusive the closer one came to the religious heart of the Temple—the Holy of Holies: the place where God dwelt. This particular story is set in the Court of the Women—one of the outer, less holy areas. In this area stood 13 trumpet-shaped, brass receptacles. There were little signs on each of these receptacles denoting how the money thrown into that particular receptacle was to be used. One said, for example, building maintenance; another said rabbis' salary; another said widows and orphans fund, etc. The room would have been absolutely jammed with people who had come to offer sacrifices during the feast of Passover.

From their vantage point, Jesus and his disciples could see what people were putting into these receptacles. There was a long line of rich people. They loved making a show of their giving. And some of them did, indeed, throw in large amounts of money. However, Jesus' attention was drawn to a poor widow. She came and put in two very small copper coins, worth only a few cents.

Jesus called his disciples over to him and said to them, "Truly I tell you, this poor widow has put more into the treasury than all the others. They all gave out of their wealth; but she, out of her poverty, put in everything—all she had to live on."

Here's our first principle: When it comes to giving, people are impressed by how much you give; God is impressed by how much you have left over. God isn't impressed by a sham sacrifice. This poor widow gave everything she had. She didn't have anything left over. That's faith. She evidently didn't worry about tomorrow. She knew that God held the future and she trusted God to take care of her in the future just as He was taking care of her today.

When Dr. Scott Weimer first came to the church he is now serving, he received in the mail a very unusual financial gift for his church. The gift was a money order made payable to the church in the amount of $5, along with a personal note of gratitude.

At first he thought the note and the gift were some kind of a joke. Who sends a money order for $5 as a stewardship pledge to a Presbyterian church?

In the note, a woman named Lillian Hafer, from Washington, D.C., wrote of how much his church meant to her. She believed in the mission and ministry of his congregation, she wrote, and it gave her great joy to send her offering. The note was hand-written, clearly written by an elderly person who had difficulty writing.

No one in the church seemed to recognize Lillian Hafer's name. However, each year for ten years she sent a money order for $5 with a similar note of gratitude. Then, after ten years of faithful giving, Weimer received a phone call from a coroner's office in Washington, D.C. Lillian Hafer had died and had listed their congregation and him personally as her "next of kin." She had lived and died in a government-sponsored retirement home with no possessions or money to speak of. The coroner simply wanted to confirm that someone at the church knew who she was.

Dr. Weimer says he believes that Lillian Hafer was like the widow in the Temple. She owned very little. She lived simply. Yet, her life was characterized by the same genuine heart for God and grateful spirit that motivated her to give with a generous attitude of giving. He says he believes that Jesus would point to Lillian and say, "That's what I'm after! Follow her example!" (2)

The devotion of this widow is not an isolated example. Over the ages there have been many like this widow who only had a few coins to give, but they have given them gladly.

Do you recognize the name Oseola McCarty? Oseola was a washerwoman in Hattiesburg, Mississippi who was dirt poor by our standards. She took in bundles of dirty clothes, washed and ironed them. She started her work after dropping out of school in the sixth grade. She continued long into her eighties. McCarty never owned a car; she walked everywhere she went, pushing a shopping cart nearly a mile to get groceries. She rode with friends to attend services at the Friendship Baptist Church. She did not subscribe to any newspaper, considering the expense an extravagance.

Oseola never married and had no children. All through her life she rarely spent any money. She lived in her old family home and wore simple clothes. She saved what money she could until her life savings grew to an amazing $150,000.

Then to everyone's surprise in Hattiesburg, she gave her entire savings to the state's Black College Fund. She wanted to share her wealth with young people before leaving this world. Before her death in 1999 she was able to witness many of the students who were awarded scholarships graduate from college with the help of her financial support. (3)

Again, that is not an isolated example. There are many people with very limited means who give sacrificially to the Lord and do so joyfully.

Dr. Scott Weimer tells about a Kenyan woman who was a member of his church. Her name was Lydia. Weimer says this African woman loved the congregation of his church, but she really missed certain aspects of her home church, especially parts of the worship service. Weimer asked her what she missed the most, and she told him something he's never forgotten.

She said, "I miss the offering. In Kenya, we would sometimes dance down the aisles during the offering. We didn't have much to give, but what we did have we gave with much joy. What a privilege to give back to God!" she said. (4)

We've talked before about the custom of African people dancing to the altar to bring their gifts to God. The devotion of this widow to whom Jesus drew his disciples' attention is not an isolated example. The secretary who gives far more to her church than her wealthier boss is not an isolated example either. In fact, it is the rule, not the exception.

Prosperity and high income, as a rule, don't help people become generous. In fact, it generally works the other way. Wealth can be a narcotic; the more you have, the more you feel you need. The craving never stops.

Henry Ward Beecher, the father of novelist Harriet Beecher Stowe, warned that prosperity and high income could actually make people less likely to give. He said, "Watch lest prosperity destroy generosity."

Author John Maxwell notes that people in the United States live in the most prosperous country in the world during the most prosperous time in its history. Yet the average American donates only 2.5 percent of his or her income to charitable giving. That's lower than it was during the Great Depression (2.9 percent). And 80 percent of Americans who earn at least $1 million a year leave nothing to charity in their wills. (5) We've talked about it before, but is an insidious thing that each of us needs to watch out for. Money is like a recreational drug—the more you have, the more you crave. There is never enough, even when you have all you will ever conceivably need.

In The Lion, the Witch and the Wardrobe, C. S. Lewis told of boy named Edmund who sampled a drug which Lewis called Witch's Turkish delight. Then Edmund sacrificed all that was good in his life to get more of it—only to find that the more he gorged himself on it, the sicker and less satisfied he became. Randy Alcorn in his book, Money, Possessions and Eternity writes, "We fail to realize that the bait of wealth hides the hook of addiction and slavery." (6) In our materialistic society we don't like to think of wealth as a dangerous drug. But it can be, and it costs many people their soul.

Theologian John Piper helps us envision the final irony of materialism:

"Picture 269 people entering eternity in a plane crash in the Sea of Japan. Before the crash there is a noted politician, a millionaire corporate executive, a playboy and his playmate, a missionary kid on the way back from visiting grandparents. After the crash they stand before God utterly stripped of MasterCards, checkbooks, and Hilton reservations. Here are the politician, the executive, the playboy, and the missionary kid—all on level ground with nothing, absolutely nothing in their hands, possessing only what they brought in their hearts. How absurd and tragic the lover of money will seem on that day," says Piper, "like a man who spends his whole life collecting train tickets and in the end is so weighted down by the collection he misses the last train." (7)

This is all to say that the way we regard our possessions is a basic spiritual issue. This is why Jesus talked more about money than any other single issue. It wasn't because he and his disciples were trying to raise big offerings. Jesus had no need of offerings, but he saw what money could do to people. "It is easier for a camel to go through the eye of a needle than for someone who is rich to enter the kingdom of God," (Matthew 19:24) he said on one occasion. That's pretty pointed. That's hyperbole, of course. He didn't mean that literally a wealthy person doesn't have a chance to get through the pearly gates. We are saved by grace, not by how much or how little we have in our bank account. He was simply warning us of the dangers of wealth and reminding us that we do not fool God. Is our giving a real sacrifice or are we simply giving God an anemic tip for services granted?

An interesting item appeared many, many years ago in a church bulletin. You will know it was many years ago by the amounts cited. The author was an unknown agent from the I.R.S. It's whimsical, but it will make you think. I quote this I.R.S agent:

The other day I checked a [strange tax] return. Some guy with an income under $5,000 claimed he gave $624 to some church. Sure, he was within the 20% limit, but it looked mighty suspicious to me. So I dropped in on the guy and asked him about his return. I thought he'd become nervous like most of them do, but not this guy.

"Have you a receipt from the church?" I asked, figuring that would make him squirm.

"Sure," he replied, "I always drop them in the drawer." And off he went to get his checks and receipts.

Well, he had me. One look and I knew he was on the level. I apologized for bothering him, explaining that I have to check on deductions that seem unusually high.

As I was leaving he invited me to attend his church.

"Thanks, I belong to a church myself," I replied.

"Excuse me," the man replied, "that possibility never occurred to me."

As I drove home, I kept wondering what he meant by that last remark. It wasn't until Sunday morning when I put my usual dollar in the offering plate that it came to me.

All the wealthy men were lined up throwing large sums of money into the receptacles of the Temple. They knew they would never miss it and they enjoyed being in the spotlight. But there was a poor widow who had only two small coins, but gladly she gave those coins to God. Only one person noticed her gift, but that one is the only One who really matters. She was not a slave to material possessions as many people are. Now you know the truth about Warren Buffet's secretary.

1. Jamie Buckingham, (Lake Mary, FL: Creation House, 1991), p. 123.
2. http://day1.org/1555-what_god_values_in_stewardship
3. God's Little Lessons on Life for Women (Tulsa, OK: Honor Books, 1999).
4. The Rev. Dr. Scott Weimer, http://day1.org/1555-what_god_values_in_stewardship.
5. U.S. News and World Report, December 22, 1997. Cited in Today Matters (New York: Warner Books, 2004).
6. (Wheaton, Illinois: Tyndale House Publishers, Inc., 1989).
7. Desiring God (Portland, Oregon: Multnomah Press, 1987), p. 156. Cited in Alcorn, Money Possessions and Eternity.

You Provoke Me . . . And That's Good
Hebrews 10:11-14, (15-18), 19-25

A three-year-old boy opened a birthday gift from his grandmother. It was a water pistol. He squealed with delight and headed for the sink to fill it.

His father was not so pleased. Provoked, he turned to his own mom and said, "I'm surprised at you. Don't you remember how we used to drive you crazy with water guns?"

His mother gave him a wicked smile and replied, "I remember!"

Has anyone here ever heard one of your parents say, "Don't you provoke me!" Maybe it was when you had a water gun in your hand.

What were they saying? Basically they were saying, "You are making me very angry." So, you may have learned early on not to provoke your parents.

Actually, there is nothing in the Bible about children provoking their parents. However, it does say in the King James Version of Colossians 3:21, "Fathers, provoke not your children to anger, lest they be discouraged." What a great verse. "Provoke not your children to anger, lest they be discouraged." But that's another sermon.

I bring up this question about parents provoking their children and children provoking their parents because of a remarkable verse in today's lesson from Hebrews. Again I am reading from the King James Version. Hebrews 10:24 reads like this: "And let us consider one another to provoke unto love and to good works." That's an interesting use of the word "provoke," don't you think? I never thought of provoking someone to love and good works. Usually I think of "provoke" in a negative sense.

The NIV makes the meaning of this verse a little clearer. It reads like this: "Let us consider how we may spur one another on toward love and good deeds, not giving up meeting together, as some are in the habit of doing, but encouraging one another . . ."

Here is the first thing we need to see in this passage: The church of Jesus Christ is intended to be a community that encourages one another—that provokes one another to love and good works. We are to provoke one another to acts of love and kindness.

Is it all right if I tell a really bad joke? I'm really not asking for permission. I'm only giving you a warning.

A guy goes into a bar. He's sitting on the stool, enjoying his drink when he hears a voice say, "You look great!"

He looks around—there's nobody near him. He hears the voice again, "No really, you look terrific."

The guy looks around again. Nobody. He hears a voice again, "Is that a new shirt or something? Because you are absolutely glowing!"

He then realizes that the voice is coming from a dish of nuts on the bar.

"Hey," the guy calls to the bartender, "What's with the nuts?"

"Oh," the bartender answers, "They're complimentary." (1)

I warned you it was a bad joke. However, don't you enjoy being around someone who is complimentary? Someone who encourages and gives you praise? What is that likely to do for you? Doesn't it make you more apt to encourage someone else?

There is a commercial on television. I'm sure you've seen it. A man walking on a sidewalk sees a small child in a stroller drop a doll. The man picks up the doll and returns it to the child. The child's mom notices this gesture, and smiles at the man.

Later she is walking out of a donut shop. She sees a man who's reading a newspaper. She notices his cup of coffee is perilously close to the edge of the table. She quietly slides it back toward the center. Through the shop window another man notices this.

Later that man comes upon another man who has slipped and fallen down on the rainy sidewalk. "You all right" he asks? The fallen man waves and says, "Thanks," and a third man notices.

Later this third man is in the elevator as the doors are closing—and he sees a woman running to catch it. He pushes the "open" button to let the woman in. The woman smiles, and another man in the elevator notices.

Later this man is coming out of a grocery store, and he sees a pickup truck with a topper trying to parallel park—but the driver's about to hit a parked motorcycle. So this man bangs on the truck. "Hey, be careful." And a woman walking by notices, etc. (2)

You get the idea. One good deed leads to another, then another, then another. It's a commercial for an insurance company, but, in 60 seconds, it dramatizes the fact that kindness is contagious.

Kindness is contagious and you never know what kind of effect an individual act of kindness will have on others.

Columnist Leo Aikman of the Atlanta Constitution once told of a family of eight that had a nice plot with a vegetable garden bordered by lilac bushes. A tenement in back of their home was populated by people who would throw their trash—old shoes, socks, and an assortment of things—into that family's garden. The sons in the family with the garden thought that these people should be told off.

Their mother, though, had another idea. This woman who was an immigrant and had never gone beyond grammar school in the Old Country, and had never heard of "psychology," told the boys to go out and pick some lilacs from their bushes. Then, she directed them to give each of the dozen families in back a bouquet, and say, "Our mother thought you might enjoy these."

"Somehow, a miracle happened," said the son who told Aikman this story. "No more [items were thrown into our garden]." (3)

You never know where a simple act of kindness may lead.

Author and motivational speaker Mark Sanborn tells about a shy and self-conscious fifteen-year-old named Tony who spent three years sitting on the bench of his junior high basketball team. He evidently was not going to play. His coach, who also coached baseball, discouraged him from going out for the baseball team, to save him the embarrassment of being cut from that as well. In all, Tony was cut from seven different sports teams. His dream of being an athlete seemed impossible to attain.

Then one morning the doorbell rang. When Tony answered the door, there stood Frank Wethern, his fifty-something-year-old neighbor. Frank, a jogger, invited Tony to join him for a run. This was in 1973 shortly before the running boom began in the U. S. Up until this time running was a relatively obscure sport. Tony didn't particularly want to go running with Frank, but for some reason he said yes.

Frank used his stopwatch to time Tony for four laps around the high school track. It took him eight minutes. "Just twice as long as Roger Bannister," Frank explained. Frank suggested that Tony could be a pretty good miler himself someday, and maybe even break four minutes. He encouraged Tony to go out for the track team.

Coincidentally, the next Monday at school, Mr. Kafka, the track coach, pulled Tony aside in the hallway and also encouraged him to go out for track. Tony entered the mile run. He came in last place, but he kept at it. And he got better and better. In fact, Tony Schiller went on to enjoy a 33-year career as one of America's top endurance athletes. Now past the age of 50, he still races and holds his own against top triathletes half his age. Since turning 40 he's won 17 triathlons—outright—plus five national and two world master's championships. He has also become a motivational speaker, and the creator and director of the MiracleKids Triathlon, a major fundraiser for kids with cancer.

"I've often thought of how different my life would have turned out if Frank had simply jogged by the house that morning, as he had always done . . . ," Tony reflects. "But on that day . . . he felt a strong impulse to reach out to me . . . As is so often the case, the simple gesture done at just the right moment can be life-changing. It was for me that day. Those four laps gave a very troubled teen's life a completely new direction. And so I will always be grateful to Frank Wethern . . . For some reason, he and Coach Kafka . . . not only reached out to me at my biggest moment of need, they did it by zeroing right in on where my life-gift sat waiting to be discovered. I'm convinced the gift would have sat that way, too—at least for a very long time had either one turned away from the urge to help me." (4)

You never know where an act of kindness may lead. Jewish physician Boris Kornfeld was imprisoned in Siberia. There he worked in surgery, helping both the staff and prisoners. During this time he met a Christian whose name is unknown but whose quiet faith and frequent reciting of the Lord's Prayer had an impact on Dr. Kornfeld.

One day while repairing the slashed artery of a prison guard, Dr. Kornfeld seriously considered suturing the artery in such a way that the guard would slowly die of internal bleeding. The violence he recognized in his own heart appalled him, and he found himself saying a verse from the Lord's Prayer, "Forgive us our sins as we forgive those who sin against us." Afterward, he began to refuse to obey various inhumane, immoral, prison-camp rules. He knew his quiet rebellion put his life in danger.

One afternoon he examined a patient who had undergone an operation to remove cancer. He saw in the man's eyes a depth of spiritual misery that moved him with compassion, and he told this patient his entire story, including a confession of his new secret faith in Jesus Christ. That very night, Dr. Kornfeld was murdered as he slept. But his testimony was not in vain. The patient who had heard his confession became a Christian as a result. He survived the prison camp and went on to tell the world about life in the gulag. That patient was Alexander Solzhenitsyn, who became one of the leading Russian writers of the twentieth century. He revealed to the world the horrors of the prison camps and perils of Russian communism. (5)

You never know when an act of kindness, a word of witness to God's love as revealed in Christ, may lead. That is why the writer of Hebrews tells us to provoke or to spur one another on toward love and good deeds. . . encouraging one another . . ."

I want to read you something C.S. Lewis once said in his famous sermon, "The Weight of Glory." It is not an easy passage to grasp by simply listening to it, but I want to read it to you nonetheless. Lewis says: "It is a serious thing to live in a society of possible gods and goddesses, to remember that the dullest and most uninteresting person you can talk to may one day be a creature which, if you saw it now, you would be strongly tempted to worship; or else a horror and a corruption such as you now meet, if at all, only in nightmare. All day long we are, in some degree, helping each other to one or the other of these destinations. It is in the light of these overwhelming possibilities, it is with the awe and the circumspection proper to them, that we should conduct all our dealings with one another, all friendships, all loves, all play, all politics. There are no ordinary people. You have never talked to a mere mortal."

Did you grasp that? Lewis is saying that you can never tell what another person may become—an angel or a monster—and thus we need, in all things, to encourage one another in order to bring out the best in everyone we meet. Lewis is saying what the writer of Hebrews is saying: Let us "spur one another on toward love and good deeds."

A great Jewish rabbi named Abraham Joshua Heschel once wrote, "When I was younger, I used to admire intelligent people. Now that I am older, I admire kind people." Why do you think he said that? It is because he knows that kindness is contagious and kind people are truly building a better world.

Of course, Christ set the example of love and kindness for us. "We love because he first loved us," says I John 4:19.

Michael J. Gelb, in his book How to Think Like Leonardo da Vinci notes that da Vinci's "The Last Supper," one of the classic masterpieces in the history of art, was done in a circular motif. Everything on the table is round, such as the bread and the plates. Also, the disciples are arranged in a half-circle on either side of Jesus. There is a distinct purpose behind da Vinci's use of the circular theme. As Mr. Gelb writes, "Like a stone tossed into the still pond of eternity, Leonardo conveys Christ's influence rippling out to change human destiny forever." (6)

Da Vinci understood the power of Christ's example on those who follow him.

In 1990 in San Diego a conversation took place between Mother Theresa and Tony Robbins, the motivational speaker whose infomercials once told everyone how to be rich, popular and successful. Robbins is about 6'7" and Mother Theresa was about 4'2".

Robbins asked Mother Theresa: "How did you manage to become so successful and so famous?"

Mother Theresa looked up at him with a smile and said, "Jesus."

Tony Robbins said, "No, I mean, how is it that you run such a huge religious institution, serve the most desperate people, travel constantly, and yet touch so many people?"

"Jesus," she said again, with a big smile.

"No, I'm asking how you do it," he continued. "How do you carry on with this difficult, extraordinary life, how do you speak to millions, how do you win the respect of the world, how do you manage to be one of the greatest people in the world and in the history of the world?"

Mother Theresa looked up at him and said, "Jesus."

And, reports one observer, Tony Robbins was totally mystified. He had no idea what she was talking about. (7)

Do you know what she was talking about? You do if Christ has touched your life. And the way Christ will most likely touch your life is through the influence of someone whom he has also touched. That is why we are to provoke one another to love and good works. So that someday the whole world will know Jesus and his love.

1. The Good Clean Funnies List, good-clean-fun-subscribe@yahoogroups.com
2. A complete version of this commercial was compiled by Kenneth J. Hockenberry at http://www.beulahpresbyterian.com/sermonapr05_07.html. Or it can be viewed at http://www.youtube.com/watch?v=76h8jbjZqOI.
3. Stephen R. Covey, Everyday Greatness (Nashville: Rutledge Hill Press, 2006), p. 345.
4. You Don't Need a Title to Be a Leader (Colorado Springs: Waterbrook Press, 2006), pp. 100-102.
5. God's Little Devotional Book for the Class of 2000 (Tulsa: Honor Books, 2000), p. 81.
6. (New York: Dell Publishing, 1998), p. 29.
7. Father John Dear http://www.johndear.org/sermons_homilies/where_I_am.htm

Serving The King Of Kings
Revelation 1:4b-8; John 18:33-37

In 1957, Ben Michtom, president of the Ideal Toy Company, had a brainstorm: why not sell a Jesus doll? The majority of kids in America were Christian, so he figured parents would jump at the opportunity to make playtime a religious experience. Other Ideal executives were horrified, but Michtom consulted with some religious leaders, including most notably the Pope, and the Jesus doll was born. It had beautiful brown glass eyes and was wrapped in molded swaddling cloth. It came in a 12" x 16" package, brown with gold on the edges, made to look like a Bible.

As Sydney Stem describes the doll in Toyland, The High-Stakes Game of the Toy Industry, the Jesus doll was a horrible flop. Parents were horrified at the idea of their child undressing the Jesus doll, dragging it around, sticking it in the bathtub. Ordinarily, there is a no-return policy on products already shipped, but in this case it was such a horrible mistake that Ideal took the dolls back. It appears that what Ideal did with them was give each of its employees a doll and then ground up the rest and put them in landfills. (1)

If the president of Ideal Toys had asked you or me, we could have told him a Jesus doll or even a Jesus action figure wouldn't work. For one thing, you simply can't reduce Christ to the level of Barbie or Batman or a rock star, or a politician, or even a monarch. Jesus towers over every real or imagined figure that has ever graced the pages of literature or starred on the silver screen. Jesus is King of Kings and Lord of Lords.

In today's lesson from the Revelation, the writer calls him "the faithful witness, the firstborn from the dead, and the ruler of the kings of the earth." This is that day in the church year we celebrate Christ's reign in human life. There is none to whom Christ can be compared.

Oh, there have been attempts to elevate human figures to Christ's stature. I understand that there is now a First Church of Jesus Christ, Elvis. I'm not making this up, though surely the whole effort is tongue-in-cheek. The catchphrase of this particular church is, "For unto you is born this day in the city of Memphis a Presley, which is Elvis the King." This church's picture of Elvis is rather Catholic: the sacred heart is beating in his chest.

If you feel more Protestant, you could opt for The First Presleytarian Church of Elvis The Divine. Their picture of Elvis makes the furor sometime back of Madonna singing suspended from a cross in Russia look tame: Elvis is hanging on a cross made to look like a guitar. (2)

Surely someone has let their sense of satire run wild, but who knows? We live in a crazy world. When people fail to believe in Christ, they begin to believe in all kinds of foolishness. That's why this day is important. Today on this last

Sunday of the church year before we begin the season of Advent, we celebrate Christ the King of Kings.

In our lesson from Revelation the Apostle John writes to the seven churches in the province of Asia: "Grace and peace to you from him who is, and who was, and who is to come, and from the seven spirits before his throne, and from Jesus Christ, who is the faithful witness, the firstborn from the dead, and the ruler of the kings of the earth. To him who loves us and has freed us from our sins by his blood, and has made us to be a kingdom and priests to serve his God and Father—to him be glory and power for ever and ever! Amen."

Our lesson from the Gospel is from the Epistle of John in which we read of Christ's appearance before Pontius Pilate. Pilate is inside his palace. He summons Jesus and asks him, "Are you the king of the Jews?"

"Is that your own idea," Jesus asked, "or did others talk to you about me?"

"Am I a Jew?" Pilate replied. "Your own people and chief priests handed you over to me. What is it you have done?"

Jesus said, "My kingdom is not of this world. If it were, my servants would fight to prevent my arrest by the Jewish leaders. But now my kingdom is from another place."

"You are a king, then!" said Pilate.

Jesus answered, "You say that I am a king. In fact, the reason I was born and came into the world is to testify to the truth. Everyone on the side of truth listens to me."

It is a cryptic passage. There was no way that Jesus could explain to Pilate the nature of his kingdom. How do you explain to a person who is totally immersed in a material world what a spiritual kingdom is? It is like trying to explain color to a person who has never even seen light, or music to a person who has never heard a single sound.

"My kingdom is not of this world." How do we ourselves get our tiny brains around such a lofty concept? "My kingdom is not of this world." Let's begin here.

Christ's kingdom is about how you live rather than where you live. In this world, citizenship is determined primarily by geography. If you live in California, you are by definition a Californian. You may not look like a Californian, whatever a Californian looks like; you may not act like a Californian—that's a line I am not going to touch. I'm just kidding, of course. There are some nice, normal people who live in California. If you live in California, you are a Californian. You are also probably an American. Citizens of other countries may live in California, but if you were born in that state, you are an American. Citizenship in this world is determined primarily by where you live or at least where you were born. Citizenship in Christ's kingdom is determined by how you live.

The Rev. John H. Pavelko tells about a man named Tom. Tom was born and raised in Mobile, Alabama. As a high school student in the mid-sixties he opposed the desegregation of the public schools and eventually joined the Ku Klux Klan. By the age of 21, he was a designated terrorist in the White Knights of the Ku Klux Klan, once described by the FBI as the most right-wing terrorist organization in America. After a bloody shoot-out with the police and FBI, in which his partner was killed and he nearly died, Tom was arrested. He was eventually sentenced to thirty years in the Mississippi State Penitentiary, one of the worst in the nation at that time. A few months later, he escaped from prison, but was later apprehended by the FBI after another shoot-out in which one of his accomplices was killed.

While in prison Tom began reading as if for the first time about Jesus and his love for all people. After several weeks of reading and soul searching, Tom surrendered his life to the King of Kings. Slowly his animosity toward black people began to dissolve. He renounced the Klan and his past life of racial hatred. After eight years Tom was released from prison and he began a remarkable new life. Instead of going back to a life of hatred, Tom worked to promote racial reconciliation. He co-authored with Dr. John Perkins, a black minister, a book titled, He's My Brother. He's since been ordained into the ministry and has served as a campus pastor and parish priest in Washington D. C. He is now serving as the President of the C. S. Lewis Institute. (3)

This is to say that Tom has a new spiritual residence. Tom is now a citizen of the Kingdom of God, the Kingdom of Christ. Citizenship in that kingdom is not based on where you live, but how you live.

This is to say that citizenship in Christ's kingdom depends on where you place your ultimate allegiance. In the U. S. we place our hands over our hearts and say, "I pledge allegiance to the flag of the United States of America . . ."

Where do you pledge your ultimate allegiance? If you say, your country, that's noble. You are a loyal citizen of the United States of America, and I admire you. But it does not make you a citizen of Christ's Kingdom. Nations, any nation, are made up of people. People can as easily be stirred up to evil as well as to good. There may come a time when you might have to make a choice between the flag and the cross. This would be very difficult for many people. Some will resent that I even raise the possibility that our nation could do wrong. However, the Bible makes it very clear—we can have no other ultimate allegiance than our allegiance to Christ.

Our Jehovah's Witness friends understand this principle. They're the folks who ring our doorbells and want to drop off the Watchtower publication. We can learn from their commitment.

They refuse to serve in the Armed forces because of their religious convictions. Most of us believe that this is naive. We believe there are times when military force is necessary to stop the advance of evil in the world. However, we can disagree with them and still admire their commitment to their principles.

One woman confronted a Jehovah's Witness spokesman who was defending his refusal to bear arms. With passion she said, "My son was shot and killed defending your freedom."

The spokesman said calmly, "I'm sorry about your son's death. I can guarantee you, though, that it was not a Jehovah's Witness who shot him."

Again, we may disagree with this particular example, but the biblical principle is clear. If we should ever have to choose, the cross comes first if you live in Christ's kingdom.

Where is your ultimate allegiance? What is it that is most important in your life? Some of us will say, "My family matters most to me." And that is an admirable trait, but it will not get you into the kingdom. Members of the Mafia are said to put their families first. In fact, family is said to be everything to these mobsters. But they don't know a thing about the Kingdom of Christ.

Where do you place your ultimate allegiance? Theologian Paul Tillich called it our "ultimate concern." What is your ultimate concern? What is it in life that you value most—that you would not only die for, but also live for? Be careful how you answer. It is a most difficult question. Some people will say, "Why, Jesus is what matters most in my life." And yet, when the time of testing comes, we discover that it is not Jesus that matters most. It is the esteem with which our friends hold us that really matters most. We get along by going along with the attitudes of our friends.

Most of really don't guide our lives by the principle, "What Would Jesus Do?" We guide our lives by, "what would my friends do?" or "what is acceptable among my peers?" To whom do you owe your ultimate allegiance?

Citizenship in Christ's kingdom is ultimately determined by whom you worship. Who is it that you admire more than any other? Who is it you try to emulate in your daily life? Who is your ultimate role model?

We live in a celebrity-conscious world and it is amazing how much influence celebrities can wield in our culture. If a celebrity dresses a certain way, then her fans will soon follow suit. For a person with a weak sense of right and wrong, a celebrity can even be a role model for the cultivation of personal habits. Sometimes these role models are constructive; sometimes they are not.

A few years ago, before her tragic death, the biggest celebrity in the world was Princess Diana. She was a beautiful, fairy-tale princess who captured the imagination and even adulation of people all over the world. Diana was a remarkable person, but her legacy is mixed.

On the one hand, she had a remarkable concern for the least and the lowest. An American physician accompanied her on hospital rounds. There were no cameras to play to. And yet, he said she did not hesitate to caress and linger beside patients with disfigurements and symptoms that were distressing even to medical personnel. That capacity, the doctor emphasized, cannot be faked.

A pastor, William Boyer, tells about a man from India who sat in his office on the day after Princess Diana died and said, almost reverently, "She touched the lepers." It was, obviously, an important memory for him.

Evidently, on a trip to India, Diana had visited a leper colony and touched the patients, an apparently small thing. But it was as if, in her simple act of grace (for this man), the life of a beautiful young woman was summed up. You see, royals don't have to touch lepers. They can avoid such contact in a hundred ways, and who would blame them? But Diana did. She touched the lepers, put herself on the same level with them, and did it of her own free will. (4)

In that sense Princess Diana was a worthy role model, but she was not perfect—just as none of us are perfect. Every celebrity who has ever lived has fallen short in one area of their lives or another. Only one person has ever lived who merits our worship. And that is the man for others, the man who not only touched the lepers but gave his life for them as well as for us on the cross of Calvary.

Someone has described our Master like this:

To the hungry he is the Bread of Life.

To the sick he is the Great Physician

To the lonely he is the one who comes and sits beside, often in silence.

To the lost he is the Good Shepherd who goes out seeking his lost sheep.

To the Prodigals he is the parent waiting at home, watching—ready to throw a party in celebration of the return home.

To the anxious he is peace.

To the proud he is One who comes and makes us humble.

To the happy he is the One who enjoys our celebrations and parties. (5)

Does that describe Christ in your life? Do you live in his kingdom? That kingdom is determined not by where you live, but by how you live. That kingdom is determined by where you place you ultimate allegiance. It is determined by your ultimate role model, by the One you worship. I love the way the late African-American preacher S. M. Lockridge once put it: "The Pharisees couldn't stand Him. But they found out they couldn't stop Him. Pilate couldn't find any fault in Him. Herod couldn't kill Him. Death couldn't handle Him, and the grave couldn't hold Him. Yea! That's my King."

Is he your King? If not, will you make him your King today?

1. Uncle John's Ultimate Bathroom Reader (The Bathroom Readers' Institute, Bathroom Readers' Press, Berkeley, California 1996.

2. Dave Faulkner, http://bigcircumstance.com/2006/09/16/sermon-discipleship-according-to-elvis-mark-827-38/.

3. http://www.crossroadspc.org/thebarrel/20031123.htm.

4. http://www.oakchapel.com/Sermon/04_05_98.html

5. From a sermon by Pastor Dennis Plourde, http://firstbaptist-mtlkterr.org/Worship/2009sermons/Sermon090913.pdf.

Cycle C

Open The Window, Aunt Minnie, Here It Comes!
Jeremiah 33:14-16

Before the advent of television, baseball broadcasts depended on colorful announcers to captivate a listening audience. One of the best of these announcers was named Rosey Rowswell. Rowswell was the radio voice of the Pittsburgh Pirates.

The star slugger with the Pirates at the time was Ralph Kiner. Rowswell got his audience to imagine a little old lady with an apartment window facing Forbes Field. Whenever Ralph Kiner would connect with a potential home run, Rowswell would yell, "Open the window, Aunt Minnie, here it comes!" Then, as the ball left the park, he would smash a light bulb near the microphone. (1)

Rosey Rowswell knew how to create excitement.

We ought to enter Advent with a level of excitement. It is a shame that Advent hymns tend to be slow and almost mournful. Sometimes I think that shopping malls do a better job of promoting this season of the year than houses of worship. That's a pattern I would like to break. And so on this first Sunday in the Advent season, I want to shout with great enthusiasm, "Open the window, Aunt Minnie, here comes Advent!"

Children understand that kind of excitement. Just wait until Christmas gets a little closer. Some of them are already making lists of things they want Santa to bring them.

Pastor John Jewell tells about a young boy a few years ago who at one of their Christmas Eve candlelight services expressed his excitement. Immediately after the benediction, this four year old broke out at the top of his lungs with, "Hooray! Hooray! Hooray! Jesus is born! Jesus is born! Let's get going!"

It seems the boy's parents had told the lad that he could not open his gifts until after the church service. Waiting was difficult for him so just as soon as the service was over, he was thrilled that he could get on to the things that mattered most to him. (2) That lad didn't understand the true meaning of Christmas, but he certainly caught its excitement. "Hooray! Hooray! Hooray! Jesus is born! Jesus is born! Let's get going!"

The prophet Jeremiah understood that kind of excitement. He writes in our Old Testament lesson for today: "'The days are coming,' declares the LORD, 'when I will fulfill the good promise I made to the people of Israel and Judah. In those days and at that time I will make a righteous Branch sprout from David's line; he will do what is just and right in the land. In those days Judah will be saved and Jerusalem will live in safety. This is the name by which it will be called: The LORD Our Righteous Savior.'" Jeremiah is known to many students of the Bible as "the weeping prophet." Often he was the purveyor of bad news. He gave bad news because he was a prophet of God and the people of Israel were living outside of God's favor. Jeremiah knew the people's sins and he knew of God's justice. He knew that God would not protect the people of Israel from the consequences of their own bad choices forever. Israel had been unfaithful to the laws of the covenant and had forsaken God by building high altars to Baal. Some of them even offered up their children as a sacrifice to Baal. Consequently Jeremiah prophesied the destruction of Jerusalem by invaders from the North. He also prophesied that the nation of Israel would be faced with famine, be plundered and taken captive by foreigners who would exile them to a foreign land. That was not a popular message, as you might imagine. Jeremiah was persecuted for his prophecies. People don't like to hear that their nation is under judgment by God. They didn't like to hear it then. We don't like to hear it now.

But Jeremiah spoke the truth, no matter how distasteful—and everything he prophesied came true. The nation fell; the population was dispersed; the people were in despair. However, just when everything looked totally bleak and hopeless, God gave Jeremiah a new message. Jeremiah finally gets to tell his people good news. All is not lost. The exiles will come home. God is faithful to His promises. God will "make a righteous Branch sprout from David's line . . ." This was exciting news for the people. Open the door, Aunt Minnie, the children of Israel are coming home.

For Christians, this is, of course, a prophecy of Jesus—he who "will do what is just and right in the land . . ." and by whose life and death Israel and Judah and all the peoples of the earth will be saved. This is the very heart of the Gospel message.

God always fulfills His promises. That's the first thing we need to see this day. God always fulfills God's promises. Jeremiah writes, "'The days are coming,' declares the LORD, 'when I will fulfill the good promise I made to the people of Israel and Judah . . .'"

Jewish psychiatrist Victor Frankl was arrested by the Nazis in World War II. He was stripped of everything—property, family, possessions. He had spent years researching and writing a book. When he arrived in Auschwitz, the infamous death camp, his manuscript, which he had hidden in the lining of his coat, was taken away.

This was devastating to Frankl. He called it the loss of his "spiritual child." He found himself confronted with the question of whether under such circumstances his life was ultimately void of any meaning. He was still wrestling with that question a few days later when the Nazis forced the prisoners to give up their clothes.

In place of his own clothes Frankl inherited the worn-out rags of an inmate who had been sent to the gas chamber. Instead of the many pages of his manuscript which were now lost, he found in the pocket of his newly acquired coat a single page torn out of a Hebrew prayer book. Only a single page of that prayer book remained—yet on that page were words that turned Victor Frankl's life around. That single page contained the most holy prayer of the Jews, the Shema Yisrael—what Jesus called, the great commandments: "Hear, O Israel! The Lord our God is one God. And you shall love the Lord your God with all your heart and with all your soul and with all your might."

Was it a coincidence that a page such as this would find its way into Frankl's seeking hands? He did not think so. He interpreted it as a sign of God's faithfulness. Frankl sums up the meaning of his experience like this: "How should I have interpreted such a 'coincidence' other than as a challenge to live my thoughts instead of merely putting them on paper?" (3)

That is the best way to interpret any experience: resolve to live your thoughts instead of merely putting them on paper. God is faithful. You can trust His promises.

Martin Luther King, Jr. trusted God's promises. He, too, was a prophet of God speaking words of judgment to people who were blind to the sin of racial injustice. As a young pastor, King's intent was not to be a civil rights activist. His intent was to be a shepherd to the flock that had called him to be their pastor. However, after Rosa Parks captured national attention by refusing to move to the back of the bus, the civil rights movement exploded in Montgomery, Alabama. And King was thrust into leadership almost without his consent. Immediately afterward, he was thrown in jail for driving only five miles over the speed limit, and he began receiving threatening phone calls.

Late one night, according to writer Philip Yancey, King sat in his kitchen, his wife and young daughter asleep in the next room. And he found himself wrestling and murmuring with God. He was unsettled, scared, angry, and he felt very distant from God. And then he found himself praying: "Lord, I think what I am doing is right. But I'm weak. I'm faltering. I'm losing my courage." And at that point—a moment of brutal honesty and need—King heard a voice, the voice of God: "Martin, stand up for righteousness. Stand up for justice. Stand up for truth. And lo, I will be with you even until the end of the world."

Yancey says it was the crystallizing moment of King's life. "And even three nights later, when a bomb exploded on his front porch, Martin never forgot the power of those words, the reassurance of that Voice, a Voice that echoed again and again and again in his soul through all the dark days of his crusade. God had promised never to leave him, never alone, never to leave him alone." (4)

It has been the anchor of every soul committed to the work of God through history: God always fulfills His promises. No matter how dark the night, no matter how harsh the critics, no matter how violent the enemy—God will not forsake us. That is the first thing Jeremiah reminds the people of Israel. God will fulfill His promises.

But Jeremiah said something else. He prophesied the coming of the Messiah. Jeremiah wrote: "a righteous Branch [will] sprout from David's line; he will do what is just and right in the land. In those days Judah will be saved and Jerusalem will live in safety. This is the name by which it will be called: The LORD Our Righteous Savior."

Jeremiah undoubtedly believed in a messiah who would unite a divided nation and restore it to its former glory. He could not foresee that God had a much grander plan in mind. He could not foresee the manger in Bethlehem. He could not foresee the coming of one who would rise above nationalistic dreams and be the Savior not only of Judah but of the entire world.

Jeremiah knew that God was faithful. He knew that God had promised that, from the line of David there would come a Savior. However, he could not know that this Savior would come—not as a conqueror—but as one who would allow himself to be crucified on a cruel cross. He could not know that the Messiah would be a humble carpenter from Nazareth whose name would one day be held in reverence by people of every race and nation. He knew God would send a Messiah; he could not know this Messiah would be the kind of Messiah Jesus turned out to be.

Rev. Bill Hayes tells about an event that occurred several years ago when the community of Spencer, South Dakota was devastated by a tornado. Six people died in that tornado. Among the structures that were devastated was St. Matthew's Lutheran Church.

The day after the tornado the pastor of St. Matthew's Lutheran Church walked through the devastation. She writes that it was an unbelievable sight—a grain elevator twisted and fallen, a water tower toppled, vehicles and other heavy items strewn around like toys, whole buildings gone from their foundations.

When she got near the site of the Church someone called out: "Look! There He is! There's Jesus!"

"Sure enough," this pastor writes, "there was the statue of Jesus that had stood at the altar of the Church. There it was—a beacon to what had been the site of a 100-year-old congregation's place of worship." The pastor later wrote that it was so fitting to look up from the chaos around her and see Jesus—arms outstretched, welcoming, and loving His people. She wondered how the statue had survived the devastation—and later learned that two young girls, helping clean up for a family member in a nearby home had taken time to come over to where the Church had been and found the statue in the rubble. They decided that everyone in Spencer needed to see that Jesus was still there, so they stood him up for all to see. (5)

Those young girls were right. Whether times are good or bad, in times when things seem hopeful and times when they seem hopeless, people need to see Jesus. He is our hope. He is the Savior of the world.

You have heard me mention before the name Anne Lamott. Lamott is a Christian author, though somewhat unconventional in her approach to the faith. Perhaps for that reason, she is helping so many Christians rediscover their faith.

What you may not know is that Ann Lamott has a tattoo on her ankle—I told you she was unconventional. The tattoo reads like this: "Trust the Captain, trust the crew."

Lamott points out that those words are not her own. The phrase came from the title of an episode of The West Wing, the TV series from a few years ago.

The episode was about a U.S. submarine that was in trouble in North Korean waters. The president is faced with a dilemma. If he does nothing, their situation might deteriorate and lives would be lost. On the other hand, if he or any navy personnel were to radio the sub to gather more information, the boat and its crew would be discovered immediately by the North Koreans, not only putting their lives at risk, but also provoking an international incident, perhaps even sparking war.

Wrestling with this dilemma, the President finally decides that the best thing to do is to let the captain and the crew of the sub handle the crisis on their own. The President chooses to trust the captain, trust the crew.

Lamott latched onto the phrase because, as a Christian, she knows it is a marvelous statement about keeping faith in God and the Christian community. It resonates with her so well that she has "Trust the Captain, trust the crew," tattooed on her ankle. (6)

Some of you have learned the same lesson. We can trust the Captain. He always keeps his promises. Among those promises is the promise that he will never forget us or forsake us. And we trust the crew. We are a family, the family of Christ. We begin this Advent season as one body, his body. That is reassuring to know. And that brings us to the final thing to be said: we need to spread the excitement.

This is an exciting time of the year. It's very busy, I know, but it is exciting as well. Some of you will undoubtedly view the wonderful operetta, "Amahl and the Night Visitors," this Advent season. Amahl, hearing the description of the Christ child, cries in joy, "For such a king I've been waiting all my life." You and I have been waiting all our lives for such a king as well, even if we aren't always aware of it. It is an exciting time of the year.

I hope you will use the Advent season as an opportunity to invite a friend to worship with you. The most powerful form of advertising any church can do is word of mouth. When people are excited about their faith, they spread that excitement to others. Are you excited? Do you have the same excitement as that little boy when he shouted, "Hooray! Hooray! Hooray! Jesus is born! Jesus is born! Let's get going!"

Maybe you're not quite that excited. At least maybe you will be just as determined to spread the good news of Christ as the two young girls who lifted up Christ after the storm swept through their town so that everyone could see their Savior.

God always keeps His promises. Jesus is the Savior of the world. That's exciting. Watch out, Aunt Minnie, here comes Advent!

1. Saul Wisnia with Dan Schlossberg, Wit and Wisdom of Baseball (Lincolnwood, IL: Publications International, Ltd., 1999), p. 181.

2. http://www.lectionarysermons.com/ADV3-98.html

3. Cheryl A. Bourne, http://www.prinevillepc.org/Beyond_Suffering.pdf.

4. Soul Survivor (New York: Doubleday, 2001), pp. 20-21.

5. Rev Bill's Sermons, http://revbill.wordpress.com/2009/11/29/jeremiah-3314-16-luke-2125-36/.

6. Charles Grant, "Trust the Captain, Trust the Crew," May 1, 2011. Cited by Gregory Knox Jones, http://www.wpc.org/uploads/sermons/pdf/May8Jones2011.pdf.

A Road Straight To Your Heart
Luke 3:1-6

Somewhere I read about a meeting of a group of software designers. They were using typical technical jargon to discuss a data exchange interface with a vendor.

One engineer said the programming that had been ordered was delayed because the vendor was suffering from a "severe nonlinear waterfowl issue."

Curious, the team leader raised his eyebrows and asked, "What exactly is a severe nonlinear waterfowl issue?"

The engineer replied, "They don't have all their ducks in a row."

On this second Sunday of Advent, John the Baptist comes to ask us if we have a severe nonlinear waterfowl issue. Do we have all our ducks in a row for the coming of the Messiah? Luke tells us that the coming of John the Baptist is the fulfillment of the prophecy of Isaiah, "A voice of one calling in the wilderness, 'Prepare the way for the Lord, make straight paths for him. Every valley shall be filled in, every mountain and hill made low. The crooked roads shall become straight, the rough ways smooth. And all people will see God's salvation.'"

Whenever a king was going to enter a city, the people who lived there would build a special entrance that was always straight and smooth. According to Dr. Craig Barnes, one of the most exciting archeological digs going on in Israel today is in Beit Shean which is uncovering a great Roman City. If you go there, you can see the main entrance into the city which is a wide, straight, even road, with magnificent columns on either side. That city is located at the juncture of the Jezreel and Jericho valleys.

John the Baptist must have been by this impressive road all the time. Anyone traveling from Galilee to Jerusalem would have seen it. Everyone knew that a wide, straight even road was what you made when a king was coming. (1)

We're experts at building roads, are we not? Our land is covered with ribbons of concrete designed for our cars. And we have miles and miles of road projects underway in every nook and cranny of our republic. The most expensive highway project in our nation's history was known as the Big Dig. It is in Boston. It involved building a buried highway through the heart of the city. It is about 3.5 miles in length and, by the time it was finished, it cost a staggering twenty-two billion dollars.

Rep. Barney Frank, a congressman from the area, said it would have been cheaper to raise the city instead of lowering the road. (2)

John the Baptist wanted his people to build a road for the coming King—

not a road made of asphalt, bricks or concrete, but a road built out of righteousness, repentance and justice. His goal was to prepare the people of Israel for the coming Messiah. He went into all the country around the Jordan, preaching a baptism of repentance for the forgiveness of sins. On this Second Sunday of Advent, as the celebration of Christ's birth comes near, John the Baptist confronts us with this critical question: have we built a straight highway into our hearts for Christ's coming?

For some of us, it is very difficult to focus on the meaning of Christ's coming, especially during this season of the year. The sheer busyness of the season is daunting—the presents to buy, the parties to attend, the attention to so many details.

One chaplain was talking about the common practice today of replacing the Christ in Christmas with an X—Xmas. He said that when people use Xmas, they really mean Xhaustion, Xcuses, Xchanges, Xcesses, Xtravagances, Xasperations, Xhibitions, and worldly Xcitement. (3)

It is significant that the secular world begins the celebration of the Christmas season the day after Thanksgiving with a bonanza of holiday sales. The day, of course, is appropriately named Black Friday. This ominous name seemed even more appropriate in November 2008 after a Long Island Wal-Mart store employee was crushed to death in a stampede of early morning shoppers. (4)

I'm told that before the beginning of the Christmas season many retailers hold anger management seminars for their employees, and conflict management training to deal with difficult customers; some stores now keep their top selling items off the shelves on Black Friday so people don't fight over them.

The secular world has almost taken over the celebration of Christ's birth. It is difficult for us to stay focused on the real meaning of Christmas. I'm glad you're in worship this morning. This is a time for you to take a deep breath and relax. Tune out all the responsibilities, all the busyness, all the claims on your time and attention of this hectic season and listen to the voice of God. Are you prepared internally to properly celebrate the birth of the Messiah into our world?

Preparation is the key to success in almost every endeavor. You wouldn't invite friends to your house for a Christmas celebration without making adequate preparations, would you? The house must be clean, decorations hung, the food and beverage prepared, the silverware polished, etc. You know that preparation is the key to the success of your party. That's true in all of life.

When baseball legend Casey Stengel was managing the Boston Braves, he spotted a speedy rookie during the spring training. The kid couldn't play very well, but he could run like a deer, so Casey carried him along for use in an emergency.

The emergency came during a game with the old Brooklyn Dodgers. The score was tied going into the ninth and Boston had a runner on second. Casey waved the rookie in to run for the batter. The next man up slammed a hard single between third and short. Stengel heaved a sigh of relief; the fast-running kid could make it easily. As he rounded third, though, the rookie started stumbling and slipping, and he just barely made it back to the bag. Because the young ball player failed to score the game went 23 innings and ended in a tie.

When it was all over, Stengel asked the youngster how he happened to stumble and to turn the game into a tie and one of the longest games on record. The rookie was heartbroken. "Casey," he said, "I figured I wouldn't get to play anyway and I wore shoes without spikes so I'd be comfortable." (5)

How sad, but how human. He didn't think he would get to play anyway, so he didn't do what he needed to do to get ready for his big moment. "Spectacular achievement," someone has said, "is always preceded by unspectacular preparation."

Speaking of being prepared, former President Jimmy Carter in his book, Living Faith, tells about our friends of the Amish faith and what preparation means to them.

The Amish do not believe in an ordained ministry. All their religious services are held in private homes. Whenever a worship service is held, a big black wagon full of benches is driven to the designated home, and the worshipers gather. No one knows in advance who will preach the morning sermon; the leader for the day is chosen by lot or by last-minute consensus.

Carter asked an Amish bishop how people could prepare a sermon if they didn't know when they would be called on, and he replied, with a genuinely modest attitude, "We always have to be prepared." (6)

Wow! Imagine coming to worship never knowing when you may be called on to give the sermon. It's hard enough to prepare yourself to listen to a sermon, but what if I unexpectedly called on you to deliver the message for the day? You would probably come to worship better prepared. So, let's do a check list and ask once more, are we prepared internally to celebrate Christ's birth?

Is your relationship with God intact? John the Baptist came preaching a baptism of repentance and forgiveness of sin. Sin has to do with our relationship with God. Have you kept your relationship with your heavenly Father as strong as you long for it to be?

John the Baptist spoke of building a straight road. The opposite of a straight road, I suppose, would be a maze. Have you ever been in a maze? Author Max Lucado has. In one of his books he tells about a trip his family took to the United Kingdom. They visited a castle. In the center of the castle garden sat a maze with row after row of shoulder-high hedges, leading to one dead end after another. If you successfully navigate the labyrinth, you discover the door to a tall tower in the center of the garden.

He says that if you were you to look at their family pictures of the trip, you'd see four of their five family members standing on the top of the tower. Hmmm, someone is still on the ground. Guess who? Lucado says he was stuck in the foliage, lost in the maze. He couldn't figure out which way to go. But then he heard a voice from above. "Hey, Dad." He looked up to the top of the tower to see his daughter Sara, peering through the turret. "You're going the wrong way," she explained. "Back up and turn right."

Do you think he trusted her? He didn't have to, he points out. He could have trusted his own instincts, consulted other confused tourists, sat and pouted and wondered why God would let this happen to him. But do you know what he did? He listened. Her vantage point was better than his. She was above the maze. She could see what he couldn't. (7)

Are you lost in a maze this Advent season? Isn't it time you paused for a moment and listened to God's voice? God's perspective on your life is flawless. There are several things God probably would ask you about if you were to listen: your relationships with your family and friends; your priorities with regard to your use of your time and money. Maybe that secret sin that you run to every time you're feeling bad about yourself. We don't like to talk about sin at Christmas time, but sin always complicates our lives. It drags us down. It causes us shame when God is trying to nudge us toward our highest potential. It causes us to drift out of range of God's voice.

The people of Israel were not the only ones who needed to repent to make ready for the coming King. We need to take stock of our lives, particularly our relationship with God.

Are your relationships with others what they ought to be? We can't build a straight road into our hearts if we have to veer around lots of obstacles caused by deteriorating relationships with our family and friends.

One of the things we love about Christmas is how it brings families and loved ones together. One of the things many people dread about Christmas is that broken relationships become even more painful. For parents who live with the hell of having a son or daughter held prisoner by drug or alcohol addictions, Christmas is a painful remembrance of earlier times of innocence and love. For those whose families that have been torn with tragic conflicts, Christmas is a painful reminder that something very dear and sacred has been torn asunder.

A young man in the Air Force said that he and his dad were very, very good pals. His father loved him and they would play and have fun together. But one day in the heat of an argument he slapped his father, something he never dreamed he could ever do, and something his father could never, ever tolerate.

Immediately he saw the anguish, the pain and the hurt in his father's face. His father's countenance changed. And that father who had looked upon him with compassion in the past, looked upon him now in desperation. His father went out of control. He was so out of control that he tried to kill his own son. His mother pleaded and wrestled and tussled with the father for almost thirty minutes to try to calm him down, to keep his father from destroying him.

At the end, his father said, "I will let him live for your sake, but as far as I am concerned he is no longer my son. No son of mine is going to hit me and live."

And this young man, years later with tears in his eyes said to a friend, "I have never been able to make up with my father. My father is cold and distant to me. And I can never go back to where I was before with him." (8)

Can you imagine the pain this young man feels when he hears the sounds of, "I'll be home for Christmas, you can count on me; Please have snow and mistletoe And presents under the tree"? Christmas is a particularly difficult reminder of broken family relationships. Is there someone in your family with whom you need to be reconciled this Advent season?

What is it that you need to do to straighten that road into your heart that the Christ child may be born anew in you? Is your relationship with God intact? Are your relationships with others as they ought to be?

Are you focused this year on the true meaning of the Savior's coming? Charles Schultz, the wonderful creator of the Peanuts cartoon could always see to the heart of things. Charlie Brown's younger sister Sally is sitting in a beanbag chair watching television while Linus tries to read to her about the real meaning of Christmas from a scholar's point of view:

"Listen to this, Sally. It says here the census that brought Mary and Joseph to Bethlehem which is said to have been to all the world probably just means the Roman Empire at the time. And listen to this. When we read that there was no room in the inn, the word "inn" is better translated 'guest room.' The intention of course is to contrast a place of human lodging with a place for feeding animals. Not only that, Sally, listen to this—the name Bethlehem itself is interesting. It means 'house of bread' or it can mean 'house of fighting.' That's fascinating. What do you think, Sally?" asks Linus.

At this, Sally stands up, looks at Linus and says, "I think if I don't get every single thing I want for Christmas this year, I'm going to totally gross out." (9)

It's clear that Sally wasn't ready for the Messiah to take residence in her heart. Christmas obviously meant something entirely different to her. How about you? Has your preparation so far this Advent season been pretty much superficial? You're getting your shopping under control. Your calendar is full, but you're starting to get a handle on all of the busyness of the season. Now it's time to deal with the bigger issues. How's your relationship with God? How about your relationships with those closest to you? A voice of one calling in the wilderness, "Prepare the way for the Lord, make straight paths for him. Every valley shall be filled in, every mountain and hill made low. The crooked roads shall become straight, the rough ways smooth. And all people will see God's salvation.'"

Has the road been made straight for the coming of the King into your heart?

1. http://www.natpresch.org/sermon.php?d=1997-12-14%200000
2. The Rev. Dr. B. Wiley Stephens, http://day1.org/1610-uncluttering.
3. Dr. Daniel Lioy, Tarbell's Lesson Commentary, September 2004- August 2005, (Colorado Springs: Cook Communications).
4. Michael Slaughter, Change the World: Recovering the Message and Mission of Jesus (Kindle edition).
5. Sam Molen, They Make Me Laugh (Philadelphia: Dorrance & Company, 1947), p. 43.
6. (New York: Random House, Inc., 1996), p. 260.
7. The Lucado Inspirational Reader: Hope and Encouragement for Your Everyday Life (Kindle edition).
8. Dr. John McNeal, When Black Preachers Preach, Vol. 2 (Kindle edition).
9. Rev. Charles Schuster, http://www.fcfumc.net/sermons/docs/12-16-07-ChristmasCouldDisappointUs.pdf.

Made For Joy
Philippians 4:4-7

I want to give you some good news. It is good news anytime of the year, but especially so at Christmastime. Here is that good news: You were made for joy. You weren't made to fret and worry and think dark thoughts. You were made for peace and love and light and joy.

The story is told of a woman who dreamed of traveling to England and riding a train through the English countryside. One day her dream came true. She flew from the U.S. to London and after a good night's sleep she boarded a train. However, after a short time on her excursion she began fretting about the windows and the temperature. She complained about her seat assignment, rearranged her luggage, and so on. To her shock, she suddenly reached her journey's end. With deep regret she said to the person meeting her, "If I'd known I was going to arrive so soon, I wouldn't have wasted my time fretting so much." (1)

That is the story of so many of us. We get to the end of our lives and realize that we spent time fretting over so many things, complaining about this and that—yet life was passing by so quickly. So let me say it again: You were made for joy. You weren't made to fret and worry and think dark thoughts. You were made for peace and love and light and joy.

Poet Carl Sandburg understood that. He once wrote about children:
You were made for joy, child.
The feet of you were carved for that.
The ankles of you run for that.
The rise of rain,
The shift of wind,
The drop of a red star on a far water rim . . .
An endless catalogue of shouts and laughters,
Silent contemplations —
They made you—from day to day—for joy, child, for joy. (2)

St. Paul understood that. He writes in our lesson from Philippians: "Rejoice in the Lord always. I will say it again: Rejoice! Let your gentleness be evident to all. The Lord is near. Do not be anxious about anything, but in every situation, by prayer and petition, with thanksgiving, present your requests to God. And the peace of God, which transcends all understanding, will guard your hearts and your minds in Christ Jesus."

The amazing thing is that St. Paul wrote these words from prison while he was, in effect, on death row. We are told that when he penned this epistle he was literally chained to a Roman soldier and guarded day and night. And yet he could say, "Do not be anxious about anything . . ."

Wow! I think I would have been anxious under such circumstances. But not St. Paul. He tells us to rejoice. It takes a special kind of faith to proclaim joy in such dire circumstances—the kind of faith that comes from living in the center of God's will and love. You and I were made for such joy.

What is it that robs you of your joy? Is it worry about the future? That's the root of much of our anxiety, isn't it? We're worried about our future.

We're told that advice columnist Ann Landers used to get about 10,000 letters a month about people's problems. She was asked, what is the number one problem that people have? She said the number one concern of most people is anxiety. She said people are afraid of losing their health, afraid of losing their wealth, afraid of losing loved ones. She said people are afraid of life itself.

A man was lying in bed one night. He found himself worrying. He thought to himself, "It is very strange. Here I am lying in bed, and I don't have a worry in the world. Then the thought came, 'That worries me.'"

Do you know of anyone like that—someone who would worry about the fact that they didn't have anything to worry about? You know who you are. Some of us fret over such minor things. As some unknown poet put it:

"It's the little things that bother us and put us on the rack,

you can sit upon a mountain but you can't sit on a tack."

It is the little things that tie us up in knots, usually little things that are easily fixable with time. Is that what is robbing you of your joy—anxiety about your future?

The insightful writer Isak Dinesen said, "God made the world round so that we would never be able to see too far down the road." And that's true. We can't see down that road. That itself is the cause of anxiety for many of us. And sadly there is something within us that causes us to look down that road with fear rather than with faith.

Pastor John Ortberg tells us an interesting fact about the wonderful motion picture, It's a Wonderful Life. Have you watched that film yet this Christmas season? Most of you know the story. It is about a young man, George Bailey, who dreams of doing great things such as traveling and making his father proud. But none of his dreams are realized. He ends up trapped in a small town with a two-bit savings and loan company, wondering whether his life is worth anything. Of course he discovers that his life is very valuable because of the impact he has had on others.

John Ortberg says he saw an article that said this movie is now much more popular than it was when it first came out. In 1946 its box-office performance was a bit of a disappointment. The writer of the article suggested that one reason for its resurgence is that it resonates with so many disappointed baby boomers who feel, like George Bailey, that life did not turn out the way they planned. They want to know that they matter, that what they have done is worthwhile after all. They want reassurance that when all is said and done, their overriding feeling will not be disappointment. (3)

Is that the source of your anxiety—that your life will be a disappointment? Some people lose their joy because they are continually comparing their lives with others, and so they focus not on their blessings, but on their shortcomings.

Futurist Faith Popcorn says that one possible downside of the Internet is the development of what she calls Comparative Anxiety. She says the Internet has created a networked world that allows everybody to compare everything, instantly. How much money are you making compared to people your own age who graduated from the same college you did? How many words does your baby know versus millions of babies her exact age, around the world? She predicts that this ability to benchmark yourself in seconds with others will create an increasing epidemic of comparative anxiety—a national wave of insecurity. (4)

Is that what is robbing you of your joy—comparing yourself with others? There may be someone who is already worrying because a neighbor's child will be getting more toys under the tree this Christmas than your child. Or that Uncle Bob will be able to give the family more treats than you can afford.

Comedian George Gobel found one way to deal with this particular anxiety. Some of the older members of our congregation will remember "Lonesome George" and his signature phrase, "Well, I'll be a dirty bird."

George Gobel lived across the street from Lou Costello of "Abbott and Costello" fame. Costello really got into Christmas each year, setting up an elaborate Christmas display with angels, music, reindeer, and many hundreds of Christmas lights. Gobel did nothing for Christmas except to put up a sign. The sign said, "See our display across the street." (5)

That's one way to deal with comparative anxiety at Christmastime—with humor. Are those the sort of things that are keeping you from rejoicing—fear about the future, fear that you do not measure up to others?

Do you remember what the first thing that the angel said to the shepherds watching over their flocks that first Christmas night? The first thing the angel said to them was, "Fear not." That's an important word for us as we approach this year's celebration of the holy event. Don't be afraid. Don't be afraid of the future with its uncertainties. God holds the future in His Almighty hands. God will not let you down. And don't be afraid that somehow your life doesn't measure up. God loves you just as you are.

Toward the end of the 15th century, all of Europe was caught in the lull of despair and hopelessness. There was such dismay that people widely believed that the end of the world was coming very soon.

In the year 1492 a German author produced a book titled The Nuremberg Chronicle. It was a compendium of all the calamities that had befallen the human family up to that moment. Then, with a climax of dejection, the author invited the reader to use blank pages at the end of the book to record any further catastrophes that would occur before the not-too-distant end of the world.

The next year there sailed into the harbor of Lisbon a battered little sailing ship. It had come through storms in the Atlantic. At the helm was a man whose story was too amazing to be true. He spoke, not about the end of the world, but about a new world of endless possibilities. Of course, you know his name—Christopher Columbus. Just when things looked their worst, something happened which changed despair to hope. (6)

The first thing that the angel said to the shepherds was, "Fear not." The second thing the angel said was, "For, behold, I bring you good tidings of great joy . . ."

Christmas was never intended to be a season of anxiety, but of joy. That's why St. Paul's words from Philippians are so appropriate for the third Sunday of Advent, "Rejoice in the Lord always. I will say it again: Rejoice!"

In his book Talking to Ducks, James A. Kitchens explains there are two major types of joy: internal joy and external joy. Internal joy comes from within, but external joy comes and goes with whatever is happening in our environment. It is extrinsic because it arises from the outside. When the circumstances change in one direction, joy comes. When fortune reverses, joy leaves. Internal joy stays with us regardless of our external circumstances. (7)

Pastor Anthony Evans tells about the night that darkness descended on New York City during the blackout of 2003. It was a chaotic night, you may remember. Evans happened to be there that night. Manhattan, including Wall Street and the United Nations, was completely shut down, as were all area airports and all rail transportation including the subway.

There was one exception to that darkness. Evans happened on a restaurant where people were lined up to get hot food. He reports that in this dark situation there was this one place with all this light and joy and music and laughter and excitement. He went over to the assistant manager and said, "Mister, I don't understand. It's dark everywhere. The airport is right over there and it's dark. My hotel is right over yonder and it's dark too. Everything is dark, and yet you are lit up like a Christmas tree. How can this be?"

The manager said, "It's really fairly simple. When we built this [place], we built it with a gas generator. We've got power on the inside that is not determined by circumstances on the outside. Even though there's nothing happening out there, there's plenty happening in here."

Anthony Evans goes on to say, "When you accepted Jesus Christ, He came into the inside. So what's happening on the outside shouldn't determine whether or not you've got a lighthouse on the inside. What's happening out there shouldn't determine your joy. God has given us a generator of life and liberty in our souls through our relationship with Jesus Christ. We don't have to live our lives determined by life's circumstances." (8)

"Fear not," said the angel to the shepherds, "For, behold, I bring you good tidings of great joy which shall be to all people. For unto you is born this day in the city of David a Savior, which is Christ the Lord. (Luke 2:10-11)

Here is the reason we have light and hope during December's darkness. Here is how we can have internal joy in the midst of external despair. A Savior has been born.

Do you know the story of Isaac Watts? Watts was one of the most prolific hymn writers of all time. He had a great internal peace in the midst of truly difficult external circumstances.

Isaac Watts was sickly as an infant. He barely survived childhood. His health was so frail throughout his life that he often could not stand. He became the pastor of a large independent chapel in London in his twenties because of his outstanding training and abilities. There he found himself in the position of helping trainee preachers, despite his poor health. His health began to fail seriously in his early thirties and during this time he developed a fever that shattered his constitution. His delicate condition frequently prevented him from serving his congregation as he wanted. Because he could not make pastoral calls as he wished, he wrote long, hope-filled letters to encourage the ill, bereaved, or discouraged members of his church.

Watts wrote hymns because he felt the church music of his day was mostly dull and depressing. He penned the words for over six hundred hymns and practically revolutionized church congregational singing. Isaac Watts had many reasons to be afraid, but he had a joy that never failed him. This season, we sing one of his most outstanding pieces, "Joy to the World, the Lord Is Come!" Some authorities maintain that this great hymn is the most widely sung of all Christmas carols. (9)

Isaac Watts' example would be a good one for us to follow. "Fear not," said the angel to the shepherds, "For, behold, I bring you good tidings of great joy which shall be to all people. For unto you is born this day in the city of David a Savior, which is Christ the Lord." (Luke 2:10-11)

Don't worry about your future this Advent season. God is in control. Don't worry about disappointing your family or your friends. Let them know you love them. That is the greatest gift you can give them. That is the gift God gave us in the stable of Bethlehem. In the words of St. Paul, "Rejoice in the Lord always. I will say it again: Rejoice! Let your gentleness be evident to all. The Lord is near. Do not be anxious about anything, but in every situation, by prayer and petition, with thanksgiving, present your requests to God. And the peace of God, which transcends all understanding, will guard your hearts and your minds in Christ Jesus."

1. http://preceptaustin.org/philippians_illustrations_4.htm

2. Rev. Scott W. Alexander, http://www.rruuc.org/index.php?id=191&sermon=070722.

3. John Ortberg, If You Want to Walk on Water, You've Got to Get Out of The Boat (Grand Rapids: Zondervan, 2001), p. 114.

4. With Adam Hanft, Dictionary of the Future (New York: Hyperion, 2001), p. 249.

5. Bob Thomas, Bud & Lou: The Abbott & Costello Story. Cited by David Bruce, The Funniest People in Comedy (Kindle edition).

6. From a sermon by the Reverend David Rogne.

7. Rev. Dr. Benjamin Reaves, http://www.csec.org/csec/sermon/reaves_4807.htm.

8. Tony Evans' Book Of Illustrations (Chicago: Moody Publishers, 2009).

9. Tarbell's KJV & NRSV Lesson Commentary (Colorado Springs: Cook Communications Ministries, 2003).

Mary's Song
Luke 1:39-45

I want to make my annual public service announcement to the men in our congregation. Guys, it's time to do your Christmas shopping. I hope our men have this task already out of the way. But just in case, please heed my announcement.

I understand that a [certain couple in our church] slipped off to [a nearby city] to do their Christmas shopping and somehow they got separated for several hours. Fortunately they had their cell phones with them.

"Honey, where are you!?" [the woman] asked.

"Darling," [he] says, "do you remember when we were first married the jewelry shop where you saw that diamond necklace you loved? But we didn't have enough money at the time, so I said, 'Someday I'll come back to this shop and buy that necklace for you.' Do you remember?"

"Yes!" she shouts, excitedly.

"Well," [he] says, "I'm in the Home Depot next door to that jewelry shop getting some supplies." ***

The big day is almost here. We have experienced another exhausting Advent season. So many things required our attention.

Maula Powers is a storyteller. In an issue of Catholic Digest some years ago Ms. Powers told about a creature called the "Advent Teufel." Teufel is a German word for devil. According to an old German folktale it is the Advent Devil who tries during the Advent season to keep people so busy in outward affairs that they lose sight of the real meaning of Christmas. The Advent Devil doesn't want people to have time to experience the rebirth of Christ within themselves. The temptations of the Advent Devil are diabolically clever. He makes it so easy for us to go along with the flow of seasonal celebrations. The Advent Devil's business is to keep us so busy with holiday obligations that we forego daily prayer, Scripture study, and church services.

Some of us have been fighting the Advent Devil this year. Hopefully, we now have him under control. Just a couple more days. I hope you are in a position to use that little bit of time that's left to focus on the real meaning of it all.

Our lesson from Luke's Gospel takes place some months before the birth of Christ. In fact, Mary has only recently learned from the angel that she will bear a child, a child conceived of the Holy Spirit. Almost immediately, Mary decides to visit her older cousin Elizabeth. This meant she had to travel about 100 miles south to the hill country of Judah. This would be about a five day journey, an amazing trip for a young teenage pregnant girl. It's disconcerting to realize that Mary would have been in about the 9th, maybe the 10th grade when all this happened to her.

Perhaps the awkwardness of her situation played a role in her decision to visit her cousin. After all, for having a child out of wedlock, she could be stoned for adultery. At the very least, she could be rejected by Joseph, her parents, her village. She could spend the rest of her days in poverty, struggling to keep herself and her child fed outside the safety of a marriage and community. We accept an out-of-wedlock pregnancy much more casually in our society, but this would have been a big deal in biblical times.

Elizabeth herself was married to a priest named Zechariah. Elizabeth was a descendant of the Hebrew people's first high priest, Aaron. They were a deeply religious couple. Luke describes them as being righteous. Elizabeth was also pregnant for the first time. She would also face ridicule. The source of Elizabeth's social torment, however, would be age. There would be those who would whisper to their friends, "Isn't she too old to have a baby?" Elizabeth was far beyond normal childbearing years, yet she was six months pregnant. In fact Gabriel came to her long before he came to Mary to announce her son's coming. Elizabeth's son was not divinely conceived any more than you and I were, but his birth was still significant. He would be the forerunner of the Messiah. We know him as John the Baptist.

Elizabeth and Mary were quite a pair. As Dr. M. Craig Barnes has noted, "One of them is too old to be a mother and the other is too young. But both are in the hands of God."

In that culture and at that time and place, it normally would have been appropriate for Mary to pay homage to the elder Elizabeth, but this is not a normal situation. Elizabeth, through the Spirit, recognized that she was in the presence of the mother of the Messiah. Luke tells us that as soon as Elizabeth heard Mary's greeting, the baby leaped in her womb, and she was filled with the Holy Spirit. So she praised Mary and pronounced her blessed. In a loud voice she exclaimed: "Blessed are you among women, and blessed is the child you will bear!"

That's interesting, don't you think? Elizabeth's unborn son announced the coming of God's son. Elizabeth asks with humility, "But why am I so favored, that the mother of my Lord should come to me? As soon as the sound of your greeting reached my ears, the baby in my womb leaped for joy. Blessed is she who has believed that the Lord would fulfill his promises to her!"

At this Mary breaks out in a song, a song we know as the Magnificat. She sings, "My soul glorifies the Lord and my spirit rejoices in God my Savior, for he has been mindful of the humble state of his servant. From now on all generations will call me blessed, for the Mighty One has done great things for me—holy is his name. His mercy extends to those who fear him, from generation to generation. He has performed mighty deeds with his arm; he has scattered those who are proud in their inmost thoughts. He has brought down rulers from their thrones but has lifted up the humble. He has filled the hungry with good things but has sent the rich away empty. He has helped his servant Israel, remembering to be merciful to Abraham and his descendants forever, just as he promised our ancestors."

The Magnificat echoes several Old Testament biblical passages, but the most pronounced allusion is to the Song of Hannah, from 1Samuel 2:1-10. The Magnificat is radical and revolutionary. The humble and the hungry are lifted up but the wealthy are sent away empty. William Temple, Archbishop of Canterbury, warned his missionaries to India never to read the Magnificat in public. Christians were already suspect in that country and they were cautioned against reading verses so inflammatory. (1)

In our land, Mary would be accused of "class warfare." It's dangerous to talk about the greed of the wealthy and powerful and the oppression of the least and lowest.

What is it that we need to take away from Mary's song so close to Christmas? Three things. First of all we need to see that Jesus came to turn the world right side up.

Jesus didn't come to maintain the status quo. Jesus came to bring righteousness and justice. The message of God's love for all people regardless of who they are or what they have is the most liberating message in the world.

Some of you recognize the name, Harriet Tubman. Before the Civil War Harriet was one of the most courageous leaders of the Underground Railroad, leading at least 300 slaves to their freedom in the North. At one point in her courageous journeys, Harriet had a premonition that her three brothers, all still slaves, were in trouble. She decided then and there that her brothers would be with her on the next Underground Railroad to the North. With the help of a literate friend, she sent a coded letter to her three brothers. In those days, the authorities often read the mail of influential black people, looking for any suspicious anti-slave activity. So Harriet's code to her brothers that they should follow her to freedom was as follows: "Read my letter to the old folks, and give my love to them, and tell my brothers to be always watching unto prayer, and when the good old ship of Zion comes along, to be ready to step on board."

One of Harriet's Underground Railroad stops was at her parents' cabin. She and her fellow travelers would hide out in the barn. Because Harriet's mother was given to outbursts of screaming and crying whenever she was happy, it was impossible for them to let her mother know they were there. Instead, they subtly alerted Harriet's father to their presence. Before Harriet's father entered the barn, he put a blindfold over his eyes. He knew the authorities would come to ask him if he had seen Harriet, and he wanted to be able to say "no" truthfully. (2)

One reason that Harriet's coded messages contained biblical references is that African-American slaves could relate to the message of freedom that the Bible proclaims. Remember that the very first message the adult Jesus preached was based on the words of the prophet Isaiah and went something like this: "The Spirit of the Lord is on me, because he has anointed me to proclaim good news to the poor. He has sent me to proclaim freedom for the prisoners and recovery of sight for the blind, to set the oppressed free, to proclaim the year of the Lord's favor" (Luke 4:18-19).

Jesus was not a revolutionary. He was sent to be the Savior of the world. However, his message was revolutionary. Once you accept that God is the Father of all people, once you accept the fact that Christ died for all people, once you accept the fact that everyone on earth is our brother and our sister, it becomes impossible to justify the oppression of one people by another. It becomes impossible to justify that some would live in absolute luxury while others go to bed each night with hunger pangs gnawing at their insides. Jesus came to turn the world right side up.

Jesus also came to give dignity to those whom society does not value. The Christmas story shows those in government palaces in the worst possible light. Meanwhile members of society's least prestigious vocation, shepherds, hear the message of "Peace on earth, good will toward men." That is no accident.

Dr. Craig Barnes, pastor of the National Presbyterian Church in our nation's capital, tells of walking downtown several years ago. It is Christmas time and he was late for an appointment. He rushed past a small group of young teenagers who were singing carols on the sidewalk.

He should have kept running, he says, but for some reason he stopped for just a moment. It was then that he noticed all of these teenagers had some kind of developmental disability. One young lady with Down syndrome had the job of playing the triangle. Whenever the director pointed to her, her face would light up, she would smile from ear to ear, and give her triangle a whack. Barnes says he was riveted by her. He says she became his priest. As his eyes teared up something inside him leapt for joy. He noticed the stressed-out leaders of business and government around him who had also been captivated by this moment, dabbing their eyes. What was happening? He wondered. "Something deep inside," he writes, "something planted by God, was touched as they sang, 'the hopes and fears of all the years are met in thee tonight.' That holy thing God had started leaped up to our hearts and every one of us wanted to join that group of singers saying, 'I have disabilities, too. My spirit and heart have been disabled by cynicism, hurt, and anger. I would love to have your innocence and purity leap out of me as it does your little choir.'" (3)

It is only right that at Christmas we should be mindful of those for whom life is a struggle. It is only right at Christmas time that we should be reminded of our bounty and the world's need. Sometimes it seems that Christmas is homage to Mammon and not to God. Whose birthday is it anyhow? Jesus came to turn the world right side up. Jesus came to give dignity to those whom society does not value.

Jesus came to give hope to the hopeless, peace to those who hearts are in turmoil, love to those who are broken.

In an issue of Good Housekeeping magazine some years back, Sheryl Van Vleck-Wells tells her favorite Christmas story, a true story that happened many years ago in the life of Sheryl's mother, Phyllis.

Phyllis grew up in a very poor but very happy family. One year, just before Christmas, Phyllis contracted diphtheria. Diphtheria was a serious and highly contagious illness, so the whole family had to be quarantined for many weeks. Every Christmas Phyllis' mother had sold baked goods in order to buy Christmas presents for the children. But this year, due to the quarantine, her mother wasn't allowed to sell any baked goods. But seven-year-old Phyllis' biggest concern was that the quarantine would keep Santa from coming to their house. The poor little girl spent the weeks leading up to Christmas in a depression.

On Christmas morning, Phyllis' father went up and brought his daughter down so she could see her surprise. Under the tree was the most beautiful doll Phyllis had ever seen. For years she would recall that doll as the best gift she'd ever been given.

Years later, Phyllis learned the secret of the doll's origins. Phyllis' mother had taken one of Phyllis' old, ragged dolls and washed and painted it. Then she took her one and only dance gown, the prettiest dress she owned, and cut it up to make a dress and booties for the doll. Finally, she cut off a length of her own beautiful hair and fashioned a wig for the doll. Her mother's sacrifice resulted in a Christmas memory that will be passed down through many generations. (4)

What that mother did for her daughter, God wants to do for each of us this Christmas season. He wants to take our lives and transform them. He wants to take our misplaced values and put them more in line with His divine purpose. He wants to take our broken dreams and broken hearts and replace them with dreams that are ever new and a heart that will never fail.

In "Family Circus" sometime back we see little Billy. He's spent the afternoon wandering through various stores where he's seen signs that say, "Don't forget Christmas Candy; don't forget wrapping paper, don't forget to visit Santa, don't forget last minute gifts."

Billy goes home and draws a picture of Mary, Joseph and Jesus and the star and writes on it simply, "Don't forget." (5)

Among the things we will want to remember is the song the gentle maiden sang as she awaited the birth of her son, God's son. The song was about her son and his mission in the world. Jesus came to turn the world right side up. Jesus came to give dignity to those who society does not value. Jesus came to give hope to the hopeless, peace to those who hearts are in turmoil, love to those who are broken. Jesus came to give you the greatest gift of all.

[***Note: this joke works well if you choose a real couple in your church who are good sports, and a real nearby city.]

1. Bruce Larson, The Communicators Commentary, Vol. 3, Luke (Waco: Word Books, 1983), p. 39.
2. "Free For Christmas," by Lerone Bennett, Jr., Ebony, December 1994.
3. http://www.natpresch.org/sermon.php?d=2000-12-17%200000.
4. "The Miracle Doll," by Sheryl A. Van Vleck-Wells, Good Housekeeping, December 1994, p. 78.
5. Source unknown.

Victory Over Darkness

(Christmas Eve)

Isaiah 9:2-7

Tonight is an exciting night—particularly for the younger members of our congregation. As they grow in their understanding of the true meaning of Christmas, I hope they do not lose the pure, unadulterated joy that Christmas brings them.

A grandmother was reading the Christmas story to her granddaughter. The little girl was just a toddler and grandmother was reading from the King James Version of the Bible. The granddaughter was baffled by the phrase, "Mary was great with child." Grandmother did her best to explain.

When the little granddaughter finally understood the phrase, she clapped her hands excitedly and said, "Oh, goody! I hope it's a girl."

What children lack in understanding, they make up for in enthusiasm. What would we do without them?

Today, though, we want to look a little deeper into the meaning of Christmas.

Chuck Colson and several other Christian leaders had a meeting with the President of Ecuador sometime back. Their purpose was to discuss a ministry in Ecuadorian penitentiaries. They had barely begun to speak when the President interrupted the conversation with a story—the story of his own imprisonment.

President Borja had been involved in the struggle for democracy in Ecuador. The military cracked down, and he was arrested. Without trial, they threw him into a cold dungeon with no light and no window. No one knew where he was, and for three days he lived in solitary darkness.

Just when the situation seemed unbearable, the huge steel door to his cell opened, and someone crept into the darkness. He heard the person working on something in the opposite corner. Then the figure crept out, closed the door, and disappeared.

Minutes later the room suddenly blazed with light. Someone, perhaps taking his life into his hands, had connected electricity to the broken light fixture. The darkness of the dungeon was gone. "From that moment," said the President, "my imprisonment had meaning because at least I could see." (1)

CHRISTMAS EVE IS ABOUT DELIVERANCE FROM DARKNESS. What better way to describe the utter despair in so many lives? What better way to describe the confusion and uncertainty that grips so many in our society?

There was a sad story in the press sometime back. It was about a man named John Casole who for ten years each December decorated his entire yard in Lindenwold, New Jersey with a magnificent Christmas display. It included a room-sized Nativity scene dotted with waterfalls, thousands of Christmas lights, 100 Santa Clauses, 117 snowmen, 51 angels, and 46 flickering candles.

There were enough lights to rack up an average electric bill of $1,000 for the month. The Lindenwold Police Department had to turn Casole's suburban street into a one-way road to control traffic brought by fans of the light display.

Thirty-one years of lights, however, were dimmed and finally extinguished by a divorce settlement between Casole and his wife of 40 years. The final Christmas display was during December 1986. Now the lawn and house are dark at Christmas. (2)

What a sad story, but what a common story. There are families in distress during this Christmas season—married couples as well as parents and children groping around in the darkness trying somehow to connect.

And there are solitary individuals living in darkness as well. Lonely people. Frightened people. People on the edge of despair. Even little children.

There was a report in Time magazine several years ago about East Palo Alto, California. It seems that, at that time, East Palo Alto suffered one of the highest homicide rates in the nation. It was so bad that teachers in the Ravenswood Elementary City School District there often found themselves chipping in as much as $500 to help defray the funeral expenses of a student caught in the crossfire.

Since minimum expenses for funerals tend to run as high as $1500, the district was facing a grim decision. The school board was discussing whether to buy life insurance for its students in order to make sure that funerals were covered. Since most of the students in the district are poor, district superintendent Charlie Mae Knight was seeking outside contributions to finance the insurance. Said she: "We have a community under siege. We have to take some action." (3)

What a horrible thought. Funerals for elementary children caught in the crossfire. Yet, as Dan Rather used to say, it is a part of our world tonight. As someone has said, "After thousands of years, western civilization has advanced to where we bolt our doors and windows at night while jungle natives sleep in open huts." Many people live in darkness.

FOR SOME, DARKNESS IS A CHOICE. There are people who seem to enjoy the dark. No question about that. The Greek philosopher Plato talked about people turning to and from the light and living with relative degrees of darkness and light, truth and error. He acknowledged that some people don't want to face the truth or the light.

Others have lived in the darkness for so long that they would not leave it if they could. They are like the convict who was brought out of the Bastille in Paris where he had been confined in one of its gloomy cells for many years. But instead of joyfully welcoming his liberty, he begged to be taken back. It had been so long since he had seen the sunshine that his eyes could not endure its brightness. We ask, how can some people keep making the same mistakes time after time? They have become captives of the dark.

CHRISTMAS EVE REMINDS US THAT CHRIST IS THE LIGHT OF THE

WORLD. We so take for granted this faith that we embrace. Suppose we lived under a government that would not allow us to celebrate Christmas or Easter or even Sunday Morning worship, then there would be a hole in our lives, a longing that could not be satisfied. There would be darkness. There have been times in history when people were not allowed to celebrate their faith.

Take the candles that so brighten our room this evening. The custom of placing lighted candles in the windows at Christmas was brought to America by the Irish. The historical background of this custom is interesting. When religion was suppressed throughout Ireland during the English persecution, the people had no churches. Priests hid in forests and caves and secretly visited the farms and homes to say Mass there during the night. It was the dearest wish of every Irish family that at least once in their lifetimes a priest would arrive at Christmas to celebrate Mass on this holiest of nights. For this grace they hoped and prayed all through the year. When Christmas came, they left their doors unlocked and placed burning candles in the windows so that any priest who happened to be in the vicinity could be welcomed and guided to their home through the dark night. Silently the priest would enter through the unlatched door and would be received by the devout inhabitants with fervent prayers of gratitude and tears of happiness that their home was to become a church for Christmas.

To justify this practice in the eyes of the English soldiers, the Irish people explained that they burned the candles and kept the doors unlocked, that Mary and Joseph, looking for a place to stay, would find their way to their home and be welcomed with open doors and open hearts. The English authorities, finding this Irish "superstition" harmless, did not bother to suppress it. The candles in the windows have always remained a cherished practice of the Irish, although many of them have long since forgotten the earlier significance. (4)

Think of that. All year long they hoped and prayed that on this one night a priest would visit their home. In the same way Israel, for centuries, prayed for a Messiah to enter their dark and hostile world. That is why Isaiah the prophet wrote: "The people who walked in darkness have seen a great light." Isaiah was announcing the coming of Christ. Christmas Eve reminds us that Christ is the light of our world. It is his love that is the hope of this dark, sometimes cruel world. When we celebrate the manger and Mary and Joseph, and the wise men and the shepherds, and the angels singing in the heaven, we are celebrating light coming into a darkened world. Christ is the only light sufficient for this world.

But what is our place in all of this? To what does Christ call us this Christmas Eve? To sing our carols? Certainly. To worship the newborn babe? Of course. But more. IN THE WORDS OF THE SPIRITUAL, OUR PLACE IS TO LET OUR LITTLE LIGHTS SHINE IN THE DARKNESS TOO.

Back several years ago there was a news story that caught my eye. Surrounded by police on a Virginia highway, accused drug dealer Alfred E. Acree, Jr., fled on foot. Diving into a dark wood at night, Acree was no doubt amazed by the swiftness of his apprehension by county sheriff's deputies. He did not realize that he had signaled his presence brilliantly with his brand-new L.A. Gear Light Gear athletic shoes. These are shoes that are battery powered so as to illuminate the wearer's every move. Officers found $800 worth of cocaine in Acree's pockets. We might say that Alfred was letting his light shine. (5)

We hope that our light will be more constructive. Our light is the light of God's love as revealed through Bethlehem's babe. Obviously, it would be a mite expensive if we tried to outfit everyone in this congregation with a pair of glow-in-the-dark athletic shoes. But the symbolism of each of us taking a light from this place to shine in the world's darkness is very powerful. It reminds me of a very thought-provoking story.

A man had built a prosperous business. As he advanced in age, he felt concerned about the future of his enterprise because he had no close relatives except three nephews. One day he summoned the young men and said, "I have a problem, and whoever comes up with the best solution will inherit all that I possess." Giving each of them an equal sum of money, he instructed them to buy something that would fill his large office. "Spend no more than I've given you," he directed, "and be sure you're back by sunset."

All day long his nephews sought to fulfill their mission. Finally, when the shadows lengthened, they obediently returned to make their report. Their uncle asked to see their purchases. The first dragged a huge bale of straw into the room. When it was untied it made a pile that nearly hid two of the walls. After it was cleared away, the second brought in two large bags of thistledown, which when released, filled three-fourths of the room. This was even better than the first.

The third nephew stood silent and forlorn. "And what have you to offer?" asked his aged relative. "Uncle, I spent half of my money to feed a hungry child and gave almost all the rest to the church. With the little I had left, I bought these matches and a small candle." Then he lit the taper, and its light filled every corner of the room! The kindly old man blessed him for making the best use of his gift and gave him all his possessions. (6)

It is amazing how the glow of a tiny candle can light an entire room. Light enough candles and we could set the entire world aglow. That is our job. We live in a world of darkness. Christ is the light of our world. We are to let his light shine through us.

1. Ronald W. Nikkel, Washington, D.C., Leadership, Summer 1993, p. 60.
2. Dr. William P. Barker, Tarbell's Teacher's Guide (Elgin, IL: David C. Cook Publishing Co., 1988).
3. Time, Jan. 25, '93, p. 15.
4. Francis X. Weiser, The Christmas Book (New York: Harcourt, Brace and Company, 1952).
5. Time, April 19, 1983, p. 23.
6. Contributed by Wayne Long. Source: Biblical Illustrator.

The Difference A Baby Makes
Isaiah 9:2-7; Luke 2:1-14, (15-20)
(Christmas Day)

Emailsanta.com receives more than a million emails every year, and each one gets a response. Here are some samples of the emails they receive:

Dear Santa, I'm sorry, but I don't have a chimney . . . I'll leave the cat flap unlocked for you, but please watch out for the litter box! — Jon, (aged) 4

Dear Santa, Do you have elves that help or elves that sit on the sofa all day long? — Jenny, 8

Dear Santa, Mommy & Daddy says I have not been very good these past few days. How bad can I be before I lose my presents? — Christian, 7 (Many adult Christians ask that question, don't they?)

Dear Santa, Did you really run over my grandma? — MacKenzie, 11

Dear Santa, I'm sorry for putting all that Ex-lax in your milk last year, but I wasn't sure if you were real. My dad was really mad. — Bri, 7

Dear Santa, You really don't need to send me the motor home. I know that you won't be able to fit it in your sleigh. I know that the elves won't be able to reach the pedals, and anyway, my mom said I can't get my driver's license yet. — Kyle, 5

Dear Santa, Pleease! Don't bring me any new clothes. — Kayla, 9

Dear Santa, Thank you for the remote control car last year, even though it broke the day after. I know you tried, and that's what counts. — Alex, 8

Dear Santa, Do you know Jesus is the real reason for the Christmas? Not to be mean, but he is. — Rosanne, 11 (1)

Rosanne is right, of course. Jesus is the reason for the season.

A few years ago, Roberta Messner was browsing through a local flea market when she came upon an antique Christmas creche, or manger scene. The price was too good to be true. When Roberta questioned the owner, she verified that it was the correct price. "You can have it for a dollar," she said. "It's all there except Jesus."

No wonder the price was so low! A Christmas creche is worthless without the figurine of the Christ child. That's the centerpiece, the most important part. Suddenly, Roberta realized that she was just like that Christmas creche. She was going through that whole Christmas season without making Jesus the centerpiece of her activities. (2)

That says it all, doesn't it? That's what Christmas is all about. That is why we read with so much eagerness that wondrous story about shepherds living out in the fields, keeping watch over their flocks at night. An angel of the Lord appeared to them, and the glory of the Lord shone around them, and they were terrified. But the angel said to them, "Do not be afraid. I bring you good news that will cause great joy for all the people. Today in the town of David a Savior has been born to you; he is the Messiah, the Lord. This will be a sign to you: You will find a baby wrapped in cloths and lying in a manger."

Suddenly a great company of the heavenly host appeared with the angel, praising God and saying, "Glory to God in the highest heaven, and on earth peace to those on whom his favor rests."

When the angels had left them and gone into heaven, the shepherds said to one another, "Let's go to Bethlehem and see this thing that has happened, which the Lord has told us about."

So they hurried off and found Mary and Joseph, and the baby, who was lying in the manger. When they had seen him, they spread the word concerning what had been told them about this child, and all who heard it were amazed at what the shepherds said to them. But Mary treasured up all these things and pondered them in her heart.

Someone has called it the greatest story ever told, and it is.

When they laid the first transatlantic cable across the bed of the Atlantic Ocean to Europe they wondered: What should be the first message sent over this cable to see if it is working? Finally, they chose these words spoken first by the angels: "Glory to God in the highest, and on earth peace, good will toward men."

Christmas began in the heart of God. That's the first thing we need to see. "Love came down at Christmas," wrote the poet, and it's true—God's love came down to us in the manger of Bethlehem. Christmas began in the heart of God.

There is a time-honored story about a grandfather who was babysitting his four-year-old grandson. He read him a story and tucked him into bed. Then he went downstairs to watch television.

A storm came up, a big thunderstorm, lightning, thunder. The little boy was scared. "Grandpa, I'm scared. Come up here and help me."

Grandpa didn't want him to be afraid, and said to him, "Don't worry, you'll be all right. You know God loves you."

The little boy answered down the steps, "I know God loves me, I just need something with skin on it." We look into the manger and we see God comes to us with skin, the word made flesh. (3) That is why Christmas brings out the best in us. The New Testament teaches us that the very nature of God is love. In the glow of Christmas, we know ourselves to be loved and we are led to love others.

Several years ago a woman in California took into her home over Christmas a family evacuated from a severely flooded area. Since she had six children of her own and a comparatively small house, a friend asked her why she felt it was up to her to assume this responsibility.

This woman explained that at the end of World War II, a family in her home town in Germany was left destitute. On Christmas Eve the mother of this family said to her children, "We are not able to have much for Christmas this year, so I have just one present for all. Now I will go get it." She returned with a little orphan girl and announced, "Here is your present."

This generous California mother went on to tell how the children in this family welcomed the little child with affection. She grew up as a full member of that family—as their sister. Then she added, "I was that Christmas gift." (4)

She gave to this family of evacuees what she had once been given. The Bible says, "We love because God first loved us" (I John 3:19). Christmas began in the heart of God.

Christmas is about hope. It is no accident that Christmas comes at the darkest time of the year. We don't know the date when Jesus was actually born, so when the date was set for Christmas it was to symbolize the words of Isaiah that the people who sat in darkness have seen a great light. Christmas represents hope. There is no finer symbol of hope than the birth of a child. As Carl Sandburg wrote: "A baby is God's opinion that life should go on . . ."

In his autobiography Long Walk to Freedom, Nelson Mandela tells about the impact a baby had on his life.

Mandela had been a political prisoner for fourteen years doing hard labor in a rock quarry on infamous Robben Island, South Africa. However, in 1978, Zeni, his second-youngest daughter married a prince—a son of the king of Swaziland. There was a tremendous advantage in Zeni's becoming a member of the Swazi royal family: she was immediately granted diplomatic privileges and could visit Mandela virtually at will. This was amazingly good news for Mandela. For just about his entire imprisonment he had been cut off almost entirely from his children.

That winter, after they were married, the young couple came to see Mandela, along with their newborn baby daughter. Because of his son-in-law's status as a prince, Mandela and his family were allowed to meet in the consulting room, not the normal visiting area where one is separated from one's family by thick walls and glass.

Mandela reports that he waited for his daughter and her family with some nervousness. It was a truly a wondrous moment when they came into the room. He stood up, and when Zeni saw him, she practically tossed her tiny daughter to her husband and ran across the room to embrace him. He had not held his now-grown daughter since she was a baby. It was a dizzying experience, says Mandela, as though time had sped forward in a science fiction novel, to suddenly hug one's fully grown child. He then embraced his new son, Zeni's husband, the prince.

Finally, his son-in-law handed Mandela his tiny granddaughter. Mandela says he did not let go of this precious child for the rest of the visit. To hold a newborn baby, so vulnerable and soft in his rough hands, hands that for too long had held only picks and shovels, was a profound joy. He says that in his mind, no man was ever happier to hold a baby than he was that day.

The visit, however, had a more official purpose and that was for Mandela to choose a name for the child. It is a custom in their culture for the grandfather to select the new child's name, and the one he chose was Zaziwe—which means "Hope." The name had special meaning for Nelson Mandela, for during all his years in prison, he says, hope never left him—and now it never would. He was convinced that this child would be a part of a new generation of South Africans for whom apartheid would be a distant memory—that was his dream. (5)

A baby named Hope. Jesus could have been named Hope, for he represented humanity's most profound hope. Instead he was named Jesus—Deliverer, Savior. Isaiah gave him other names: Wonderful Counselor, Mighty God, Everlasting Father, Prince of Peace. Christmas comes from the heart of God. Christmas is about hope.

This is to say that Christmas is the best news this world could ever receive. An angel had the privilege of first announcing the news to the shepherds. "Today in the town of David a Savior has been born to you; he is the Messiah, the Lord." What a powerful message.

Years ago Chuck Swindoll pointed out the difference that a baby can make. He wrote of Napoleon sweeping through Austria in 1809. That was the big news that transfixed the world of that time. Looking back, however, the really important news of that year was not the battles that were fought, but the babies that were born: William Gladstone, for example, one of the finest statesmen that England ever produced. Alfred, Lord Tennyson, the extraordinary poet. Oliver Wendell Holmes, Edgar Allen Poe, Charles Darwin, and perhaps most notably, Abraham Lincoln.

Swindoll writes, "If there had been news broadcasts at that time, I'm certain these words would have been heard: 'The destiny of the world is being shaped on an Austrian battlefield today.' Or was it?

"Funny, only a handful of history buffs today could name even two or three of the Austrian campaigns. Looking back, you and I realize that history was actually being shaped in the cradles of England and America as young mothers held in their arms the shakers and the movers of the future . . ." (6)

History was certainly being shaped as Mary held her newborn son in her arms. Not only the history of the world, but your history and mine. Let us give God thanks this day. Christmas comes from the heart of God. Christmas is about hope. Christmas is the best news this world could ever receive.

1. From the Internet. Source unknown.
2. Roberta Messner, Daily Guideposts 2000 (Carmel, N.Y.: Guideposts, 1999), p. 369.
3. Rev. Charles Schuster, http://www.fcfumc.net/sermons/docs/12-16-07-ChristmasCouldDisappointUs.pdf.
4. Reader's Digest. Date unknown.
5. Charles R. Swindoll, Growing Deep in the Christian Life (Portland: Multnomah Press, 1986).
6. Nelson Mandela. Long Walk to Freedom: The Autobiography of Nelson Mandela (Kindle edition).

When Your Parents Don't Understand
Luke 2:41-52

The Rev. Rosemary Brown tells of something that happened in a church she once served. One night she received a phone call that two of the little boys from her church were missing. The boys' family lived across the street from the church. It was already pitch dark. Mom and Dad were in a panic. They searched everywhere and couldn't find the boys.

Rev. Brown opened the door to the church and was going to use the phone in her office to call for more help. As she passed through the darkened sanctuary, she heard somebody say, "Ssshhhhhhhh," and she looked down front and she could see the outline of two little heads. Those little boys were sitting down front in that darkened church. As Rev. Brown approached them, she asked, "What are you doing here?"

"We were waiting for the Holy Ghost," one of them said. The little guys had been studying the Holy Ghost, or the Holy Spirit, in Sunday School, Brown explains, and there they were in God's house waiting for that very same Holy Ghost to appear. (1)

Obviously that is one Sunday School lesson these boys had taken to heart.

It is Luke who tells us of the time when the boy Jesus went missing. His parents, Mary and Joseph, had made their annual pilgrimage to Jerusalem for the Festival of the Passover. Mary and Joseph were devoted to their Jewish faith. Adult Jewish males who lived within twenty miles of Jerusalem were required to attend Passover annually, but males living farther away might make the pilgrimage once in a lifetime. Women were not required to make the pilgrimage at all, which says something about Mary's devotion. The journey from Nazareth was about 80 miles and would have taken considerable travel time. (2)

Luke is the only one of the four Gospel writers who tells this story, by the way. The other three Gospels are silent about Jesus' childhood years. That may be because so many legends were already being spread about the young Messiah. That often happens with great figures. It's like the story of Washington chopping down the cherry tree in our own folklore.

In these apocryphal tales about Jesus, Jesus made birds out of clay and breathed into them and they flew away. The neighborhood bully tried to pick a fight with Jesus, but when he went to punch him his hand just withered up and fell off. The robe Jesus wore as a baby magically grew longer on him as he grew taller, etc. In one such story, Jesus strikes down some children and raises them up again. Exaggerated stories like these always grow up surrounding great figures, and here was the most amazing life ever lived. The Gospel writers were very concerned with separating fact from fiction. Luke, a meticulous historian, felt this story of Jesus in the Temple was authentic enough to include it in his account of Jesus' life.

It is a very human story. You know it well. Jesus is twelve. His parents take him on their pilgrimage to Jerusalem. As they are returning home, they discover Jesus is missing. Now, before we continue our story, we need to remember the significance of his being twelve. In Jewish culture, he is on the verge of being a man. We don't know when the Jewish rite of the Bar Mitzvah was initiated—probably much later in Jewish history. Today, when a Jewish boy reaches the age of 13, he is declared to be a man and a "Son of the Covenant" or a "Son of the Law." A Bar Mitzvah is held as a celebration of this significant step in his life. After the Bar Mitzvah he is expected to 1) keep the Law, 2) learn a trade, and 3) attend a great Jewish feast. (3) Jesus was nearly of that age.

To be twelve was to be on the verge of manhood. In that time and in that culture a twelve-year-old boy was expected to shoulder more responsibilities than we might expect out of a boy of that age today. To put matters into perspective, if Jesus had been a girl, he might already be betrothed. In many ways it was a very different world.

You may remember a story that appeared in the newspapers sometime back. It concerned Etan Patz—the first missing child to be pictured on a milk carton. He vanished on May 25, 1979, after leaving his family's apartment for a short walk to catch a school bus. He was six years old at the time. It was the first time his parents had let him go off to school alone. And he vanished. Not too long ago, thirty-three years later, after receiving a tip, a man confessed to murdering Etan Patz.

Someone asked what Etan's mother was thinking of letting him walk that distance by himself. Someone else explained that back then, in 1979, you didn't worry so much about a child walking by himself on a city street. But after Etan's abduction, society changed. People started being much more careful about leaving children on the own. Times change. Worries change.

Mary and Joseph lived in a different time. There was perhaps just as much crime as there is today, but it was a different kind of crime than that which stains our world. Parents certainly didn't worry so much about a twelve-year-old boy being on his own. Still, it is shocking that it took almost a day for them to miss him. Part of this was due to the nature of Mary and Joseph's excursion.

Part of the journey from Nazareth to Jerusalem was through hostile country—through Samaria. It was a difficult trip, with some danger involved. This is why Mary and Joseph traveled in a group with family and friends. In those days, women and children traveled in front, while men followed behind.

Thinking Jesus was probably playing with his friends somewhere in the midst of this large company of pilgrims, Mary and Joseph traveled for a day. Then they began looking for him. It was then they discovered, much to their dismay that Jesus was not with them. When they failed to find him, they went back to Jerusalem to look for him.

After three days they found him in the temple courts. Three days. That number may be significant. It is certainly a long time to have your child missing. When they found their son, he was sitting among the teachers, listening to them and asking them questions. Luke tells us everyone who heard him was amazed at his understanding and his answers. When his parents saw him, they were astonished, but their astonishment was tempered by their exasperation. Mary said to him, "Son, why have you treated us like this? Your father and I have been anxiously searching for you."

Here the boy Jesus seems a little insensitive. "Why were you searching for me?" he asked. "Didn't you know I had to be in my Father's house?" Then Luke adds these interesting words: "But they did not understand what he was saying to them."

Is there anyone in this room who has not felt at some time in your life that your parents did not understand you? Of course not. All of us have had times when we felt like our families didn't understand us. Conflict within families, particularly between the generations, is as old as time.

It's not easy being a parent—at any age.

A teenager who had just received her learner's permit offered to drive her parents to church. After a hair-raising ride, they finally reached their destination.

When the mother got out of the car she said emphatically, "Thank you!"

"Anytime," her daughter replied with a smile.

As her mother headed for the church door, she said, "I wasn't talking to you. I was talking to God."

It's not easy being a parent. Particularly of a twelve or thirteen-year-old.

One woman said, "Doctor, I'd like you to evaluate my 13 year-old son."

"OK," said the doctor, "He's suffering from a transient psychosis with an intermittent rage disorder, punctuated by episodic radical mood swings, but his prognosis is good for full recovery."

The woman was surprised. "How can you say all that without even meeting him?" she asked.

The doctor said, "I thought you said he's 13?" (4)

It's not easy being a parent. And it's not easy being a young person. Nature has constructed us so that young people go through sometimes radical hormonal and physical changes as they enter puberty. They start distancing themselves from their parents and they begin establishing their own identity.

The writer Adair Lara has an interesting way of describing these changes.

She says young children behave like dogs. That is, they're affectionate and love being around you. But when they hit the teen years, says Ms. Lara, they start acting like cats—distant and finicky. They make you feel unneeded. (5)

That goes with the territory for many teens. Nothing could be more normal. Don't panic when it happens in your family. There are times when all of us feel like our family does not understand us.

Remember, even as an adult, Jesus' family did not understand him. Once, when he was at least 30 years of age, Mary, his mother, and his brothers came to him and pleaded with him to leave his ministry and come home. They were concerned about him and felt that perhaps he was going off the deep end (Mark 3:20-34).

Anybody in your family ever think you were getting a little too far out there? It happens. If it could happen to Jesus, the only perfect man who ever lived, it could happen to anyone. People worry about their children, regardless of their age. As time passes, children worry about their parents, particularly aging parents. That's part of life together in families. Jesus' family finally did come around, of course. Acts 1:12 indicates they were a vital part of the church after Christ's resurrection, but there was a time when they didn't understand him at all.

Jesus' family didn't always understand him, but they were always committed to him and he knew it. That's what was important. Parents and young people need one another. Young people particularly need to know that their parents are committed to them and that nothing will ever break that commitment.

A tired mom opened the front door of her home to find a young minister from the neighborhood. The pastor said, "I'm collecting donations for the new children's home we're building. I hope you'll give what you can."

"To be sure," said the beleaguered woman, "I'll give you two boys, two girls, OR one of each." (6)

Some of you know how that tired mom felt. You also know she was just kidding. There is nothing she would take in exchange for her children. Children may bring all kinds of heartaches, particularly during adolescent years, but they need to know that your love is a constant in their lives. They need to know they will never cease being your son or daughter.

Writer Richard Foster tells about a father who was walking through a shopping mall with his two-year-old son. The child was in a particularly cantankerous mood, fussing and fuming. The frustrated father tried everything to quiet his son, but nothing seemed to help. The child simply would not obey. Then, under some special inspiration, the father scooped up his son and holding him close to his chest, began singing an impromptu love song. None of the words rhymed. He sang off key.

And yet, as best he could, this father began sharing his heart. "I love you," he sang. "I'm so glad you're my boy. You make me happy. I like the way you laugh." On they went from one store to the next. Quietly the father continued singing off key and making up words that did not rhyme. The child relaxed and became still, listening to this strange and wonderful song. Finally, they finished shopping and went to the car. As the father opened the door and prepared to buckle his son into the car seat, the child lifted his head and said simply, "Sing it to me again, Daddy! Sing it to me again!" (7) That's the love of a parent for his child, a love like unto God's love.

Jesus' family was bound together by mutual love and respect. We can tell that by how the story ends.

"Why were you searching for me?" Jesus asked. "Didn't you know I had to be in my Father's house?" But they did not understand what he was saying to them. Then, says Luke's Gospel, "He went down to Nazareth with them and was obedient to them. But his mother treasured all these things in her heart. And Jesus grew in wisdom and stature, and in favor with God and man." Jesus knew he was loved and that Mary and Joseph were committed to him.

Mother Teresa believed in strong family ties. "Only when love abides at home can we share it with our next door neighbor," she said. "Then it will show forth and you will be able to say to them, 'Yes, love is here.' And then you will be able to share it with everyone around you."

She told about the time she found a little girl in the street. She took the child to their children's home. There at the home they gave the little girl clean clothes and they made her as happy as they could. After a few hours, however, the little girl ran away. Mother Teresa looked for her, but she couldn't find her anywhere. Then after a few days, Mother Teresa found her. And, again, she brought her to the children's home. This time she told a sister to follow the child if she should leave again.

The little girl did run away again. But the sister followed to find out where she was going and why she kept running away. She discovered that the girl had gone to find her mother. Her mother lived under a tree on the street. The mother had placed two stones there and did her cooking under that tree.

The sister sent word to Mother Teresa and Mother Teresa went to where the child was. Mother Teresa reported that there was joy on that little girl's face, because she was with her mother, who loved her and was making special food for her in that little open place.

She asked the little girl, "How is it that you would not stay with us? You had so many beautiful things in our home."

The girl answered, "I could not live without my mother. She loves me."

That little girl was happier to have the meager food her mother was cooking in the street than all the things Mother Teresa and all her nuns had given her. (8)

That's the way things should be in a family. Material blessing are not the only things that matter in a home. There will be misunderstandings, but there should also be a bond of love that nothing can break. Mutual love, mutual respect and the ability to accept and forgive will usually be enough to bind those basic bonds of human love for the entirety of our lives.

1. http://www.faithandvalues.com/viewer/text.asp?URL=http:%2F%2F
www.faithandvalues.com%2Ftx%2F00%2F00%2F01%2F16%2F1673%2Findex.html
2. http://www.bibletruthonline.com/Luke%202%2041%2052sermonfortheweekof
January1st.htm.
3. http://www.neverthirsty.org/pp/series/Life/LH015/LH01.html
4. www.mikeysFunnies.com.
5. http://www.allprodad.com/pod/playoftheday.php
6. www.mikeysFunnies.com.
7. http://www.karlcoke.com/Jesus_Bar_Mitzvah.htm
8. Mother Teresa, No Greater Love (Novato, CA: New World Library California, 1989), pp. 121-123.

The Glow Of A Star
Isaiah 60:1-6; Matthew 2:1-12

A young man sitting in church one day made a startling discovery. He was a pre-med student, only nineteen years of age. The sermon that day was probably a dull one. There are such things I understand, dull sermons. Of course, you wouldn't know about such things.

Anyway, instead of listening to the sermon, this young man's attention was drawn to the altar lantern swaying back and forth, back and forth, back and forth. ["You are getting very sleepy . . ." If I could hypnotize all of you, I could stop now and go home.] This young man, however, did not get sleepy. Instead, he started timing the swings of the lantern, using his own pulse as a clock. And he made a discovery, a discovery that changed his life, and to a certain extent, changed our world. For, after this experience, this young man dropped the study of medicine and began studying mathematics and physics. His name, of course, was Galileo. According to Stephen Hawking, Galileo probably bears more of the responsibility for the birth of modern science than anybody who has ever lived. In fact, Albert Einstein called Galileo the father of modern science.

Galileo revolutionized how people kept time. At the time of Galileo's discovery the very best clocks in the world easily lost—or gained—fifteen minutes a day. A few decades later, after Galileo, all the best clocks were using pendulums and they were losing or gaining only ten seconds a day! No doubt hundreds of people had sat in that church watching that lantern sway—back and forth, back and forth—but Galileo saw much more. Whereas others simply saw an old oily lantern swaying back and forth, Galileo thought, Aha! There's more here than meets the eye. (1)

When was the last time you had an Aha! experience? There's a word for an Aha! experience, of course. It is epiphany. When we have an epiphany, we discover something new, something exciting. As we begin this New Year in worship we hope to have some Aha! experiences regarding our understanding of God. Impossible, you say? You believe you already know as much about God as you're ever going to know? How sad.

It reminds me of a Calvin & Hobbes cartoon years ago in which Hobbes, Calvin's stuffed tiger, asks, "Did you make any resolutions for the New Year?"

Calvin becomes highly indignant and shouts, "NO! I'm fine just the way I am! Why should I change? In fact, I think it's high time the world started to change to suit ME! I don't see why I should do all the changing around here. If the New Year requires resolutions, I say it's up to everybody else, not me! I don't need to improve! Everyone ELSE does!" After he finishes his tirade Calvin asks, "How about you? Did you make any resolutions?"

Hobbes says, "Well, I had resolved to be less offended by human nature, but I think I blew it already." (2)

It's true. Some of us think we have arrived, that we don't have any more growing to do. And we think we know everything about God we're ever going to know. That would be our loss if it turns out to be true.

At the beginning of each New Year, Howard Thurman, a professor at Boston University, would write down his understanding of God's nature. Each year, he compared last year's journal entry about the nature of God with that current year's description. And if there was no real change in his understanding of God's nature, then Professor Thurman was disappointed. He expected to grow in his knowledge and understanding of God, and if he didn't notice any spiritual growth in himself, then he considered that past year to have been wasted. (3)

Thurman, a professor of theology, didn't think he knew everything he needed to know about God. To paraphrase the popular song, "He wanted to see God more clearly, love God more dearly." How about you? Is that the sincere desire of your heart?

Famed Bible teacher J. Vernon McGee once asked, "What is your ambition in life today? Is it to get rich? Is it to make a name for yourself? Is it even to do some wonderful thing for God? Listen to me, beloved. The highest desire that can possess any human heart is a longing to see God." (4)

That is the meaning of Epiphany. That is the desire that drove the wise men to Bethlehem. Epiphany is the twelfth day after Christmas. According to tradition this is the day we celebrate the arrival of the wise men to worship the one who was born to be King of the Jews. The wise men followed a star until it came to the place where the young child lay. On coming to the house, they saw the child with his mother Mary, and they bowed down and worshiped him. Then they opened their treasures and presented him with gifts of gold, frankincense and myrrh. It is a wonderful story, one of the best known stories of our faith.

The prophet Isaiah anticipated the coming of those wise men hundreds of years before. He wrote, "Arise, shine, for your light has come, and the glory of the Lord rises upon you. See, darkness covers the earth and thick darkness is over the peoples, but the Lord rises upon you and his glory appears over you. Nations will come to your light, and kings to the brightness of your dawn . . . Herds of camels will cover your land . . . And all from Sheba will come, bearing gold and incense and proclaiming the praise of the Lord."

These were words of prophecy. However, even Isaiah did not understand the full import of what would happen when his prophecy was fulfilled. He only prophesied what God laid on his heart. "Arise, shine, for your light has come . . ."

What do those words mean to you—your light has come? For the magi, these words represented the birth of a king. What do they mean for you?

Doesn't the coming of light imply that the world was in darkness? "Arise, shine, for your light has come, and the glory of the Lord rises upon you. See, darkness covers the earth and thick darkness is over the peoples . . ."

Isaiah first spoke these words to the people of Jerusalem during a time of great travail for the nation. They were a captive people. Their homes and fields were ravaged and abandoned, laid desolate by the power of the Babylonian empire. But God would not abandon His people forever, counseled Isaiah. God would act in their behalf.

Darkness is a powerful metaphor. Pastor Thomas Hilton tells about a significant event that took place on July 11, 1991—a total eclipse of the sun. Though not visible in the northern United States, on this date more than twenty years ago several major cities, including Mexico City were plunged for a few moments into total darkness in the middle of the day. It was an eerie experience according to those who were there. And tens of thousands of people were there. Some of them traveled thousands of miles in order to personally experience this once-in-a-lifetime event. (5)

Darkness, however, usually signifies all the things we most dread. Criminals are more likely to prefer the dark than the light. Fear is more prevalent. Ignorance is associated with darkness. But here's what's disturbing. There will come a time, says the Bible, when people will love the darkness more than the light. Is that time closer than we think?

There was an article in Time magazine a few years back about a new trend in fine dining that was appearing in which people really did prefer the dark. This trend was termed, "dinners in the dark." It explained that some restaurants had begun turning out all the lights and serving meals in the dark. The diners were not told what they were eating. This practice of eating in the dark was supposed to allow the diner to focus on the flavor of the food. Waiters in these restaurants wore night-vision goggles so as to minimize the risk of trips or spills. The story by Lisa McLaughlin was titled, "The Ultimate Blind Date." (6)

Well, if you were a rather plain looking person on a date or if you had offensive eating habits, dining in the dark could have its advantages. Usually when we think of darkness, however, it has negative connotations.

A rabbi tells of hearing a ten-year-old boy who was studying the events that are recorded in the book of Exodus. He was perplexed by the third plague which God sent—darkness over all the land. Why, this child wanted to know, didn't the Egyptians simply light lamps so that they could see? After all, we must assume this is what they normally did each evening when darkness fell. They simply lit their lamps. Why, he wondered, when it became dark over all the land, didn't the Egyptians simply light their lamps?

The teacher explained to the youth that the darkness in Egypt didn't affect the eyes. It affected the heart. Physically the Egyptians could see, but in their hearts they didn't recognize the misery that their intolerance and persecution were causing other people. The Egyptians were blind to the suffering of others. That is what is meant by the plague of darkness. (7)

No one wants to be kept "in the dark" unless they are doing evil. Darkness hides our misdeeds; light reveals our misdeeds in all their ugliness.

King Herod lived in perpetual darkness. He was ruthless: murdering his wife, his three sons, his mother-in-law, brother-in-law, uncle, and many others. His crowning cruelty of course was the murder of the infant boys in Bethlehem of Judea in a vain attempt to slaughter the newborn King of the Jews.

The philosopher Plato once wrote, "We can easily forgive a child who is afraid of the dark: the real tragedy of life is when [adults] are afraid of the light." Herod was afraid of the light. And so he sought to slaughter the one about whom John would say, "In him was life, and that life was the light of all humankind. The light shines in the darkness, and the darkness has not overcome it" (1:2-4).

The world was in darkness. Ignorance and evil were both ascendant, as they are even today. But darkness will never have the last word. That is the message of Epiphany. Light has come into our world.

A student, asked to summarize all the gospel in a few words, responded like this: "In the Bible, it gets dark, then it gets very, very dark, then Jesus shows up."

That says it all. The world was in darkness, deep darkness, but Jesus showed up.

In his book The Gulag Archipelago, Aleksandr Solzhenitsyn tells a story about how, as a political prisoner in a labor camp in the USSR, he was forced to live in a cell without any lights, and with windows that were painted so he couldn't see outside. But one day a little fleck of paint fell off the window, and in the darkness Aleksandr saw a tiny ray of sunlight shine its beam of hope in to his dark cell. This light is what gave him strength to continue on, the light to know that he was still alive and a part of the created order. It was enough for him to know that the world was still progressing. (8)

More than two thousand years ago a tiny babe was born in Bethlehem of Judea. It may have seemed that it, too, was a tiny ray of light in a dark world, but that tiny ray of light was exactly what the world needed. And even today that light is still lighting people's lives, helping them to move out of the darkness.

A man named Jim Birchfield once gave a powerful illustration of a person moving from darkness into the light. He told about Father Greg Boyle, a Jesuit priest who works with gang members in East Los Angeles.

Father Boyle has put together a team of physicians trained in tattoo removal using laser technology. The team is part of a program that removes the tattoos of ex-gang members and wipes the slate clean. For many, it is as crucial a service as it is merciful.

To a former gang member, the gang tattoo fosters the attitude that the gang's claim on that person's life is permanent. It is a mark of ownership as much as identity. The process of tattoo removal is extremely painful. Patients describe the laser procedure as feeling like hot grease on their skin. Yet the waiting list grows of those who will put up with whatever pain it takes to receive a new identity. (9)

"Arise, your light has come." What does that mean to you? Biblically it means that without Christ, the world is a dark and lonely place. It is a world of conflict and injustice. It is a world of ignorance and fear. But that is not the end of the story. "It gets dark, then it gets very, very dark, then Jesus shows up."

But there's one thing more to be said. If the darkness of this world is going to be pushed back any further, you and I will need to let our little lights shine. Christ is the light of the world, but we who are followers of Christ are called to reflect in our lives that we have been in his presence. We do that by continuing to shine the light of his love into our dark world.

Henry Van Dyke wrote one of the most famous fictional accounts of the coming of the magi to Bethlehem which he called The Story of the Other Wise Man. In this story Van Dyke speaks of a fourth wise man who searched for years for the Christ child, but was never able to catch up with the others. This wise man had three jewels, a gift of great wealth which he intended to give to the newborn king. But in his journey to find the newborn king he came across people who had great needs. He could not pass them by without trying to help. He ended up using the three jewels he had intended to offer the Christ child to care for the needs of these persons he found in want.

This fourth magi searched for Jesus for the rest of his life, only to realize at the end of his life that he had both found him and worshipped him each time he gave himself and his gift to one who was in need. Through his compassion this fourth wise man pushed back some of the world's darkness. And that is our task as well. We are to live in the presence of Christ so that with time we will be able to reflect his light through the service we give to others.

A traveling man bought his wife a little souvenir—a phosphorescent match box which was supposed to glow in the dark. However, when he turned out the light to demonstrate its use, there was not even the faintest glow. Disgustedly, he concluded that he had been cheated.

The next day his wife examined the box more closely, and found an inscription in tiny letters, "If you want me to shine in the night, keep me in the sunlight through the day." She did as directed; and that night after dinner it was a pleasant surprise for her husband when she turned out the light and the match box shone with a brilliant glow. (10)

What was true of that match box is true of us. Any light we shine in this dark world is but reflected light. It is the light of Christ's love. When we live in his presence and seek to show his love to our neighbors, then the darkness is pushed back—until the day comes when we all live in his love and eternal light.

1. Mikey's Funnies. To subscribe: http://www.mikeysFunnies.com/sub/.
2. Don Friesen, http://www.ottawamennonite.ca/sermons/aha.htm.
3. Martha Graybeal Rowlett, Responding to God (Nashville: Upper Room Books, 1996), pp. 30-31.
4. "Feasting on the Word," Christianity Today, Vol. 37, no. 7.
5. The Clergy Journal, March 1995, p. 26.
6. Time, April 7, 2003.
7. Rabbi Emeritus Arthur Rulnick, http://www.thewjc.org/sermons/tolerance.htm.
8. http://matthewmoore.wordpress.com/2009/06/14/sermon-mark-426/.
9. John A. Huffman Jr., http://www.preaching.com/sermons/11600669/page-4/.
10. Arthur P. Ciaramicoli, and Katherine Ketcham, The Power of Empathy (New York: Penguin Putnam Inc., 2000).

The Baptism Of Jesus

Luke 3:15-17, 21-22

Our lesson for this First Sunday after Epiphany is the baptism of Jesus. Speaking of baptism, I understand that it was so dry in Texas this past summer that the Baptists were starting to baptize by sprinkling, the Methodists were using wet-wipes, the Presbyterians were giving out rain-checks, and the Catholics were praying for the wine to turn back into water. Now that's dry!

We are in our series of messages on "Discovering God." One place we discover God most powerfully is in remembering our baptism. You know the story of Christ's baptism. John the Baptist was baptizing people in the River Jordan. People were flocking to hear him and responding to his invitation. Among those who came to John to be baptized was a young carpenter from Nazareth who happened to be John's cousin. John knew who Jesus was of course. He also knew that Jesus ought to be baptizing him. But when the appropriate time came Jesus stepped into the water and was baptized by John. After he was baptized Jesus began to pray and as he prayed, heaven was opened and the Holy Spirit descended on him in bodily form like a dove. And a voice came from heaven: "You are my Son, whom I love; with you I am well pleased."

There are a couple of interesting things to note about Jesus' baptism. Notice, first of all, that when Jesus was baptized, the Holy Spirit alighted on him as a dove.

Pastor Randy Ott tells a delightful story about a family with young children that had started bringing their children to his church's preschool and kindergarten program. This was a new family in the area without much of a church background.

Soon after going to the church the mom told Pastor Ott of pulling into a McDonald's restaurant and the kids were all excited. Well, what kid isn't excited about going to McDonald's, but that is not why they were excited. They were excited because a seagull landed on the hood of their car. Tell me, when is the last time or any time in your life when you were excited because a seagull landed on your hood? But they were excited because this little 4-year-old or 5-year-old in the car said, "Look Mom! It's the Holy Spirit in the form of a dove!" (1)

Obviously that young tyke was learning something in the church's preschool. You might remember that the next time you see a seagull or a dove land somewhere close by. It may be the Holy Spirit trying to say something to you.

In the case of Jesus, the symbolism of the dove is profound. Remember, this was the King of Kings and the Lord of Lords, the Messiah who so many hoped would be a warrior-king. Yet the Holy Spirit, which is characterized as a mighty wind or tongues of flame in other parts of the Bible, came upon Jesus in the form of a dove, a symbol of peace and meekness. (2)

It is also worth noting that doves were the minimum sacrifice that a poor person could bring to the temple to be sacrificed for his or her sins (Luke 2: 24). This may have symbolized Jesus' coming as a sacrifice for our sins, even for the very poorest and least of us. (3)

And then recall that it was a dove that Noah sent out to find signs that the water from the great flood was receding. When the dove returned in the evening, there in its beak was a freshly plucked olive leaf! Then Noah knew that the water had receded from the earth (Genesis 8:11). The dove, then, was a symbol of hope and salvation.

So, from the beginning Jesus gave every indication that he was a different kind of Messiah. He came not as conqueror but as a peace maker; not as a master, but as a servant; not as a judge, but as a Savior. The symbol of Christ is not that of an eagle or a hawk, but a dove.

It is also interesting to note that Christ was baptized by his cousin John. John was Elizabeth and Zechariah's boy. This humble couple were righteous people in the best sense of the word. Zechariah was a priest and Elizabeth was of a priestly family. John was born to them in their old age and his birth was foretold by God. Elizabeth and Zechariah had great dreams for their boy and he already was the most successful preacher in the land. Still John knew that Jesus was someone special—someone far greater than he himself. John did not mince words: "I baptize you with water. But one who is more powerful than I will come, the straps of whose sandals I am not worthy to untie. He will baptize you with the Holy Spirit and fire. His winnowing fork is in his hand to clear his threshing floor and to gather the wheat into his barn, but he will burn up the chaff with unquenchable fire."

John was talking about Jesus, of course, but it sounds more like he is talking about himself. John the Baptist was a preacher of judgment. He was concerned that people live as they should according to the Law.

It is significant that, even though Jesus came as a bringer of grace, he in no way repudiated John's message. Righteousness is an important characteristic of the follower of Jesus. People who are baptized ought to live differently than people who are not. They ought to be kinder, they ought to seek after justice, they ought to be more forgiving and tolerant. John's baptism was a baptism of repentance and baptized persons ought to live on a higher plane than those who are not baptized.

The Reverend Jeffrey Smead, an Anglican pastor, tells a beautiful story about a woman pastor in Chicago, a Reverend Sarchet.

A 10 year-old boy in Rev. Sarchet's congregation named Cameron, walked into her office one day and said he needed to talk to her. Cameron was fresh from soccer practice. He was wearing his Cincinnati Reds baseball cap. But Cameron had a request for his pastor. "I'd like to be baptized," he said. "We were learning about Jesus' baptism in Sunday School. The teacher asked the class who was baptized, and all the other kids raised their hands. I want to be baptized too."

Using her best pastoral tone of voice, Rev. Sarchet said, "Cameron, do you really want to be baptized just because everyone else is?"

His freckles winked up at her and he replied, "No. I want to be baptized because it means I belong to God." His pastor was touched by his understanding.

"Well, then," she said, "How about next Sunday?"

His smile turned to concern and he asked, "Do I have to be baptized in front of all those people in the church? Can't I just have a friend baptize me in the river?"

She asked where he came up with that idea.

"Well," he said, "Jesus was baptized by his cousin John in a river, wasn't he?"

Caught off guard, she conceded, "You have a point. But," she asked, "if a friend baptized you in the river, how would the church recognize it?"

Realizing this was a teachable moment, she climbed up on her foot stool to reach for her Book of Orders that was located on the highest shelf. But before she placed her hand on the book, Cameron responded with these unforgettable words: "By my new way of life," he said.

Rev. Sarchet nearly fell off the foot stool. She left the Book of Orders on the shelf. She realized that Cameron's understanding was far from childish. It was profound. (4)

Baptism—whether it occurs as an infant, a youth or an adult—ought to signify a new way of life. If there is one thing that is hurting the church's witness today it is that church people are indistinguishable from the general population. If people do think of us as different from everyone else, it is usually in a negative sense—as coming across as close-minded or judgmental or intolerant. John's baptism was a baptism of repentance.

There is an old story of a machinist years ago at the Ford Motor Company plant in Detroit who became a Christian and was baptized. He decided he needed to make restitution for some parts and tools he had stolen from the company prior to his conversion. The next morning he brought all the tools and parts back to his employer that he had pilfered over the years. He explained that he had just been baptized and asked for his foreman's forgiveness.

This was such an amazing turn of events that the foreman immediately sent a telegram to Henry Ford, who was visiting a plant in Europe at the time. Ford immediately returned a cable with this message: "Dam up the Detroit River, and baptize the entire city."

Can you imagine a world where the whole city or the whole country or even the whole world was baptized and everyone lived out his or her baptism? Then the Lord's Prayer that our Master taught will have been fulfilled: "Thy kingdom come, thy will be done, on earth as it is in heaven."

This is to say that baptism is more than a religious rite; it is a rite of passage to a new life.

The truth of the matter is that many of us take our baptism for granted. [Many of us have our babies baptized without truly thinking of it as a binding commitment on our own part to bring up our children as committed followers of Jesus Christ.] As youths we are sometimes baptized because we have reached a certain age and our friends have been baptized. Even as adults, many are baptized with little recognition of what it means to walk in the footsteps of Jesus. For some of us, baptism is simply one of the rituals we go through as we make our way through life.

That would not be true if we lived in many parts of the world. In many parts of the world being baptized requires immense courage. In countries like Nepal it once meant imprisonment. For Soviet or Chinese or Eastern bloc believers, it was like signing their own death warrant. (5) In many Islamic countries it is still a truly risky enterprise.

That is the way it was for those who were baptized into the early church. It meant that, at the risk of their lives, they were becoming part of this group of people who were despised by the greater culture.

When you say, "I have been baptized," that ought to mean something quite significant. I like the simple way that Pastor Tony Evans explains the meaning of baptism. He says, "When a lady gets married, she puts on a ring. That ring does not make her married. She could be married without a ring, just like you could be saved without being baptized. But what the ring does do is serve as a sign that she is married.

Many times when you see a guy talking to a girl," Evans continues, "you will see his eyes go south as he is looking at the left hand to see whether or not she has already been spoken for and belongs to another.

"I am certain that a wife who refused to wear her ring would insult any man. He would probably take that as a rejection of him. [And a man who had a wedding band and refused to wear it would probably insult his wife.] The ring is more than a piece of jewelry. This piece of jewelry represents an institution and a covenant. Like a ring is symbolic for marriage, baptism is a sign of our covenant with God." (6)

Even though Jesus came as a bringer of grace, he in no way repudiated John's message. John's baptism was one of repentance. It was more than a mere religious rite; it was a rite of passage to a new life. And so baptism should be today. There one more interesting thing about Jesus' baptism.

It concerns a question that is often asked: Why was Jesus baptized in the first place? He certainly did not need to repent. He had no sins that needed washing away. And the answer, of course, is that he did it as a sign of the grace of God.

Some of you may have seen a movie titled Tender Mercies. In this movie, Robert Duvall plays Mac, a down-on-his-luck country singer with a drinking problem. With the help of a young widow Mac turns his life around, and both Mac and the widow's young boy, Sonny, decide to get baptized.

Driving home after the baptism, Sonny says to Mac, "Well, we done it Mac, we was baptized." He stares at himself a moment in the rearview mirror, then says, "Everybody said I'd feel like a changed person. Do you feel like a changed person?"

"Not yet," replies Mac.

"You don't look any different, Mac. Do you think I look any different?"

"Not yet," answers Mac. (7)

"Not yet was a good answer." We need to understand that there is nothing magical about baptism. Baptism is a sign of grace. Baptism is a sign of God's great love for us and Christ's sacrifice for us. It is as we reflect on our baptism and focus on what it should mean for our lives that we are changed. Jesus was baptized as a sign of God's grace and he wants his followers to be baptized as a sign of that grace as well. There's nothing special about the water; nothing special about the ceremony, but it can be the most important event in our life as the Holy Spirit works in our life following that simple ceremony.

Max Lucado, in his book, Six Hours One Friday, tells the story of a missionary in Brazil who discovered a tribe of Indians in a remote part of the jungle. They lived near a large river. The tribe was in need of medical attention. A contagious disease was ravaging the population. People were dying daily.

A hospital was not too terribly far away—across the river, but the Indians would not cross it because they believed it was inhabited by evil spirits. To enter the water would mean certain death. The missionary explained how he had crossed the river and was unharmed. They were not impressed. He then took them to the bank and placed his hand in the water. They still wouldn't go in. He walked into the water up to his waist and splashed water on his face. It didn't matter. They were still afraid to enter the river. Finally, he dove into the river, swam beneath the surface until he emerged on the other side. He punched a triumphant fist into the air. He had entered the water and escaped. It was then that the Indians broke out into a cheer and followed him across. (8)

Jesus entered the Jordon River to be baptized by John not because he needed it, but because we need it. Baptism is a sign of God's grace. It is an initiation into the family of Christ. It is the beginning of a new life in him. It is Christ's dream for the world that all the world's people will experience God's grace and love and all persons will be baptized into his family. As members of his family, that should become our dream too. He has plunged into the water. Friends, let's follow.

1. http://www.mzluth.org/Sermons/2006-09-24.pdf.
2. Myron S. Augsberger, The Communicator's Commentary, Vol. 1 (Waco: Word Books, 1982), 46.
3. Frederikson, Roger L. The Communicator's Commentary, Vol. 4 (Waco: Word Books, 1982), 56.
4. http://www.sermoncentral.com/sermons/by-my-new-way-of-life-j-jeffrey-smead-sermon-on-baptism-163584.asp.
5. Charles Colson and Ellen Santilli Vaughn, The Body: Being Light in Darkness (Waco: Word Publishing, 1992), page 137.
6. Anthony T. Evans, Tony Evans' Book Of Illustrations (Chicago: Moody Publishers, 2009).
7. Pastor Glenn Schwerdtfeger, http://maynardav.org/sermons/BaptismSermon.htm.
8. Don Hawks, http://www.sermoncentral.com/sermons/why-we-share-communion-don-hawks-sermon-on-church-practices-47226.asp?page=2.

The Bride Of Jesus
Isaiah 62:1-5; John 2:1-11

Rev. Julie Ruth Harley tells about a couple in Manhattan who got hitched after meeting in a rather unusual way. They were in a car accident.

They say love is blind but, according to a report in the New York Times, Joanna Greenwald really did have her eyes closed when she first met Christopher Masters. The reason she had her eyes closed was that a pickup truck had just crashed into the back of her BMW. She then sideswiped Chris' Dodge, ricocheted onto the median and headed toward oncoming traffic.

When she opened her eyes, Joanna's car was totaled and she expected to see a great white light. Instead, she crawled out of the wreckage and saw the man of her dreams. While the two talked at the accident scene, Joanna barely thought about the damage to her car, the shards of glass in her clothes and hair, or the fact that she had almost died. When her mother arrived, in a state of panic, Joanna said, "I'm fine, Mom, I'm fine. Get away from me, now." Her eyes were evidently fixed on Chris.

Chris and Joanna exchanged business cards, ostensibly for insurance reasons, and the next day Chris called and asked Joanna out. At their wedding reception, the couple did not place flowers or chocolates at each place setting. Instead, they posted copies of the accident report. (1)

If I were to ask some of you, how did you meet your mate? I would get some interesting stories. I would also get some interesting stories if I asked about your wedding.

In his book, Hustling God, Dr. Craig Barnes tells about a wedding that started as a real disaster. First, the weather was atrocious. Some of the main streets had to be closed due to flooding which meant that some of the out-of-town guests never made it to the ceremony. Also, for some strange reason, about half the candles on the candelabras wouldn't light. The flowers didn't arrive on time so the church's wedding hostess put together something from the previous week's sanctuary flowers . . . which had a lovely brown tint around the edges. The real flowers showed up15 minutes into the ceremony. Undaunted the florist marched down the center aisle and arranged the new flowers right in front of the bride, groom, and soggy guests. It was unbelievable. There are usually a few tears at weddings but at this particular wedding they weren't tears of happiness.

Wisely Barnes made a few adjustments to his wedding homily. He talked about how fitting it was to have an imperfect wedding for what was always going to be an imperfect marriage, just like every marriage. Even as he talked, however, he says he could still see anger and hurt in the eyes of the bride and groom. They had worked so hard to get everything right for their wedding.

Nevertheless, the moment they turned and faced each other to say their vows, everything changed. Barnes writes, "The groom's eyes watered up with tears of joy as, for the first time on that day of mishap after mishap, he really SAW his beautiful bride. All of his frustration melted away as he finally beheld the joy of his life. That got her crying," Barnes concludes, "which made me cry as well." (2)

There is something about a wedding, isn't there? Whether things are perfect, or even very imperfect, there is something about weddings that touch us.

Throughout the Bible the relationship which God has with His people is compared to the love a bridegroom has for his bride. It is the predominant theme of the book of Hosea. In Hosea 2:19 we read, "I will betroth you to me forever . . ." Hosea's wife was unfaithful to him just as Israel was unfaithful to God, but still Hosea was committed to her just as God is committed to His people. And that set the tone for his book.

The theme of the bride and the divine wedding is carried over into the New Testament. It is not surprising that Christ's first miracle was at a wedding. After all he referred to himself on one occasion as the bridegroom (Matthew 9:15). This same imagery is present in many of the parables that Jesus taught. We are his beloved. And one day we will join him at the wedding feast.

Paul used this imagery in advising couples about their own marriages in Ephesians 5: 25-33. The last words of that passage go like this: "For this reason a man will leave his father and mother and be united to his wife and the two will become one flesh." Then Paul adds these words, "This is a profound mystery—but I am talking about Christ and the church."

The imagery of the Divine wedding continues all the way to the book of Revelation. We read in verse 19:7: "Let us be glad and rejoice and honor him; for the time has come for the wedding banquet of the Lamb, and his bride has prepared herself." Who is the Lamb? Christ. Who is the bride? The church. This theme continues right up until the end: "I saw the Holy City, the new Jerusalem, coming down out of heaven from God, prepared as a bride beautifully dressed for her husband . . ." (Rev. 21:2)

Then, in the very last chapter of our Bible, we read, "The Spirit and the bride say, 'Come!' And let him who hears say, 'Come!'" (Rev. 22:17)

So, in the last chapter of scripture, describing the end of time, we have this magnificent picture of Christ with his bride saying to all, "Come, come to the wedding feast. Come, all who would, and receive what has been prepared for you from the beginning of the world." As someone has said, human history began with a marriage ceremony in the Garden of Eden and human history will end with the marriage ceremony between the bride and groom, between Christ and his church.

In our lesson for today from the Old Testament, Isaiah the prophet uses this same imagery. Israel is in a bad way. Time after time, they had been defeated by their enemies. They were recovering from exile in Babylonia. The land is deserted and desolate. Jerusalem has been torn down and the temple has been destroyed. There is a phrase that is often used about the prophets—that they afflict the comfortable and comfort the afflicted. Isaiah is in his comforting mode in this passage and here is the word he gives Israel in God's behalf: "You shall no more be termed Forsaken, and your land shall no more be termed Desolate; but you shall be called My Delight Is in Her, and your land Married; for the Lord delights in you, and your land shall be married. For as a young man marries a young woman, so shall your builder marry you, and as the bridegroom rejoices over the bride, so shall your God rejoice over you." (62:4-5)

This is a beautiful passage. Israel has gone through a difficult time. Things were so bad that Jerusalem was called "Abandoned" and the land was called "Desolate." But God had not forgotten them. They had forgotten Him, but God had not forgotten them. A new day was coming. No longer would they be called "Abandoned" and "Desolate." God would give them new names, "My delight is in her" and "Married."

The word "married" is important. There were negative cultural connotations to a woman who was not married in those ancient times. An unmarried woman was often an outcast, and widows lived an uncertain existence. Since women could not own property, if a woman had no family, it was almost impossible for her to provide for herself above the most meager of existences without resorting to prostitution. So, once Israel was abandoned and desolate, says Isaiah, but now she has two significant new names "My delight" and "Married." It is a beautiful way of expressing God's love and God's grace.

Why are Israel's problems of concern to us? Some of us, without doubt, have gone through a difficult time when our name could easily have been, "Abandoned" and "Desolate." Maybe we, like Israel, have gotten ourselves into a bad way because of some moral failure or some bad decision. That happens. Or maybe it was through no fault of our own. Life can be hard in any event.

There was an interesting item in Reader's Digest recently about Stefan and Erika Svanstorm of Stockholm, Sweden. Stefan and Erika packed their suitcases for a four-month honeymoon in December 2010. That's exciting—a four-month honeymoon. Except these honeymooners encountered six natural disasters on this, their first trip together. In Munich, Germany they were caught in one of Europe's worst blizzards ever. Then they flew to Australia where they weathered a cyclone, were evacuated, and spent 24 hours on a cement floor. Later, still in Australia, they were stuck in a flood and later narrowly escaped a series of brushfires. In Christchurch, New Zealand they arrived shortly after a 6.3-

magnitude earthquake hit. They then flew to Tokyo where they survived the horrific earthquake that hit that nation a couple of years back. Somehow they returned to Stockholm with their lives and their marriage still intact.

Most of us will never have a run of bad luck quite that long. Or maybe we will. Life can be cruel.

Pastor Ed Markquart tells a heartbreaking story about a woman in her mid-forties visiting an elderly woman at a nursing home. The younger woman asks the older one, "How are you?" There is a long pause.

"Just fine," says the older woman. There is another long silence.

The older woman then asks, "Where did the leaves go?"

The woman in her forties responds, "It's fall; the leaves have fallen." Another long silence. For two hours, this pattern continues. A short comment punctuated by long periods of silence.

The older woman asks, "Do you have a daughter?"

The younger woman answers, "Yes, she's twelve years old." Long silence.

"Do you have any sons?" the old lady asks.

"Yes, our boy is sixteen." Long silence.

"What is his name?"

"Mark. He is such a tall boy, almost six feet four."

"My, he is a tall boy." These two women talk back with long periods of silence in between.

It finally comes time to leave. The younger woman says, "I must be going now."

The older woman asks, "Do you live far away?"

"O yes," is the reply, "almost three hundred miles away."

The two of them go together to the outside door, the older woman being pushed in her wheel chair by the younger woman. The old woman says, "This has been nice. You are pretty. Come see me again. But, but, but I don't know your name."

The middle-aged woman chokes back the tears and says, "My name is Lorraine." And then for a moment, there is a blinding flash of recognition in the old lady's mind, then shame, then sorrow, then nothing. The younger woman turns and runs to her car, tears streaming down her face, glad that her mother had called her "pretty." (3)

Life can be like that. Desolate. Abandoned. Maybe you've gone through a difficult time when your name could easily have been, "Abandoned" and "Desolate."

I trust that in those experiences you found what Isaiah found—that God was with you. That is what has sustained believers through the centuries in good times and bad. We are God's beloved. God is married to us. God will never forsake us, no matter what we do or what our circumstances may be.

I like the way Pastor Daniel Habben has put it. He writes, "Have you ever been to a downtown that has seen better days? Where there once were people and activity there is nothing but broken glass and litter. Banks and stores have moved to the suburbs leaving behind grand brick buildings that have become canvass to neighborhood punks and their graffiti. It's not just depressing to go through such a desolate place; it can be dangerous. But then developers move in enticed by low taxes and before you know it, empty warehouses turn into expensive loft apartments. Cracked sidewalks are repaired and flowers planted. Restaurants and galleries open in those brick buildings scoured clean of their graffiti. What was desolate is now a delight again to inhabitants and visitors." (4)

That is the kind of transformation that Isaiah is promising Israel. It is the same promise God makes to each of us. If you are going through a difficult time, hang in there. God has not forgotten you.

A farmer once had an unusually fine crop of grain. Just a few days before it was ready to harvest, there came a terrible hail and wind storm. The entire crop was demolished.

After the storm was over, the farmer and his small son went out onto the porch. The little boy looked at what was formerly the beautiful field of wheat, and then with tears in his eyes he looked up at his dad, expecting to hear words of despair.

All at once his father started to sing softly, "Rock of Ages, cleft for me, let me hide myself in Thee."

Years after, the little boy, grown to manhood said, "That was the greatest sermon I ever heard." (5)

That farmer knew that whatever the circumstances God was not going to forsake him. His name would never be Abandoned or Desolate regardless of how grim things might appear.

Dr. Anton DeWet tells about an aunt of his in South Africa who has had a difficult life. Her daughter, two weeks before she was to write her final paper before qualifying as a medical doctor, committed suicide. Can there be a more devastating blow to two parents than this one? His aunt and his uncle struggled through this loss with great difficulty, as you might imagine. They regained enough balance that with time his uncle was chosen to serve a term as South Africa's ambassador to Poland. But this is not the end of the story. His uncle was on a safari with a Polish guest when he lost his footing on a cliff overlooking a beautiful canyon and fell to his death 300 feet below. As someone very close to his aunt, DeWet says he has had the opportunity to see her deal with two tragedies in her life that have left her deeply wounded. When he asks her how she copes, her answer always remains the same: "Only by God's grace." (6)

Friends, that is the only ways any of us cope. Life happens. Sometimes great things happen and we thank God for them. And then there are those times when we feel abandoned and desolate. But God comes to us and whispers our name and tells us we are not alone. In the words of Isaiah, our names have been Abandoned and Desolate, but they shall be, "My Delight is in You" and "Married." Married to Christ.

1. http://www.uchinsdale.org/worship_sermons_rites/sermons/20050731.htm.

2. Mark Adams, http://www.redlandbaptist.org/sermons/sermon19990411.htm.

3. http://www.sermonsfromseattle.com/series_a_making_the_deserts_bloom.htm.

4. http://www.sermoncentral.com/sermons/from-desolate-to-delight-the-lord-will-glorify-his-church-daniel-habben-sermon-on-assurance-of-salvation-101507.asp.

5. The Timothy Report, http://www.timothyreport.com.

6. http://uccportland.org/sites/default/files/Sermon%2008-28-11.pdf.

The Joy Of The Lord
Nehemiah 8:1-3, 5-6, 8-10

There is an ancient Egyptian myth which says that, after death, every individual is confronted with two questions that have to be answered honestly. First, did you find joy? And second, did you bring joy?

Evangelist Billy Graham says that "Joy is one of the marks of a true believer. This is not a gushy emotion or a forced grin, but the security of knowing God's love."

Graham tells about a news story concerning soldiers in the Persian Gulf years ago watching videotapes from their families back home. In a gloomy tent, sipping coffee to ward off the morning chill, the soldiers listened in silence as one wife held herself erect and sang a gospel hymn that her husband could think of whenever he felt alone.

"Joy is not just jumping up and down whenever your team makes a touchdown," says Graham. "It's that deep, abiding emotion that gives a lonely soldier's wife the ability to reach out to an equally lonely man and touch him with God's presence. The ability to rejoice in any situation is a sign of spiritual maturity." (1)

G. K. Chesterton once said, "Joy . . . is the gigantic secret of the Christian."

C. S. Lewis put it this way, "Joy is the serious business of heaven."

Dorothy Sayers said, "The only real sin a Christian can commit is to be joyless."

Brother Lawrence said it like this: "Joy is the surest sign of the presence of God."

Our lesson for the day from Nehemiah tells us, "The joy of the Lord is our strength." What a great affirmation: "The joy of the Lord is our strength."

Nehemiah voiced this memorable phrase under some remarkable circumstances. Jerusalem had been destroyed under the Persians in 586 B. C. The temple was destroyed, the walls of the city were torn down, the gates burned. Thousands of people were transported to Babylon as captives and slaves. A generation passed, and then another. As time went on, the children and grandchildren of these captives and slaves rose to positions of responsibility in Persia. One of them was a man named Nehemiah.

Nehemiah had spent all of his life in Babylon, but his heart belonged to Jerusalem. He had never been there, but he knew the stories of his people. When he learned that Jerusalem still lay in ruins, he grieved. He asked the king of Persia to whom he served as cup bearer for permission to go to Jerusalem along with some men to rebuild the walls. The king granted his permission and appointed Nehemiah governor.

The story of Nehemiah's return with the exiles, how he and his co-workers rebuilt the walls—and the obstacles and opposition they overcame—are recorded in the first seven chapters of Nehemiah. It is an amazing story. They had no heavy equipment. They were under threat of attack at all times. Only half of the men could work at any one time. The other half was needed to stand guard. Those who worked still wore their swords. Often they held a spear in one hand while they worked with the other. But the entire project was finished in 52 days. It was a remarkable feat.

Now it was time to worship God. Chapter eight begins with all the people gathered in the square before what was known as the Water Gate. Ezra the priest brings out the five scrolls of the Law of Moses. He stands on a high wooden platform built especially for this occasion. He opens the scrolls and as he begins reading, the people all stand. They remain standing the entire time. Nehemiah reads aloud from daybreak till noon. And all the people listen attentively and they weep as Ezra reads. When he is finished, Ezra praises the Lord and all the people lift their hands and respond, "Amen! Amen!" Then they bow down and worship the Lord with their faces to the ground.

Then we come to this wonderful phrase. Nehemiah and Ezra and the Levites who were helping them say to the people, "This day is holy to the Lord your God. Do not mourn or weep."

Then Nehemiah adds, "Go and enjoy choice food and sweet drinks, and send some to those who have nothing prepared. This day is holy to our Lord. Do not grieve for the joy of the Lord is your strength." Do not grieve . . . do not mourn, says Nehemiah, for the joy of the Lord is your strength.

Nehemiah was a remarkable leader. Others would have said the task he undertook, rebuilding the walls of the city even as he fended off enemy attacks, was an impossibility. But he and those he led completed it in record time. What a testimony to both his leadership and his faith. When Nehemiah said "the joy of the Lord is our strength," I believe he was talking about a kind of joy that grows out of a particular attitude toward life—an attitude that made Nehemiah an effective leader.

First of all, Nehemiah approached life with a positive attitude. A positive attitude grows out of joy and reinforces joy in the believer's heart.

Joe Gordon says a pessimist is someone "who can look at the land of milk and honey and see only calories and cholesterol." That's how Nehemiah could have approached his return to his ancestral home—as a pessimist or even as what some would call a realist. If he had, he would have failed. He began his mission with the belief that with God's help, he would succeed. And he did.

Pastor James Moore tells a story about a woman who went to see her doctor with a whole list of complaints. The doctor could find no physical ailment. He suspected the woman's negative outlook on life was the real problem. He got up from his desk and pointed to a shelf filled with bottles. He said to her, "Look at these bottles. All of them are empty. I can take one of them and fill it with poison, enough poison to kill a human being. Or I can take that same bottle and fill it with medicine, enough medicine to cure a headache or bring down a fever or kill bacteria. The important thing is that I make the choice. I can fill each bottle with something hurtful or with something helpful."

Then the doctor looked her straight in the eye and said, "Each day that God gives us is like one of those empty bottles. We can choose to fill it with positive thoughts that lift us and other people; or we can fill it with negative thoughts that depress us and everyone else. The choice is ours." (2)

The ability to choose the attitude with which we confront life can be powerful. Let me give you example of that power at work. It is a true story about a French poet named Robert Desnos. During World War II, Desnos was an active member of the French Resistance network. Because of his work with the resistance he was captured by the Nazis and was deported to a Nazi concentration camp.

One day Desnos as well as some other prisoners were taken away from the barracks of this camp. Leaving the barracks, the mood among Desnos and his fellow prisoners was somber. The prisoners rode on the back of a flatbed truck. Everyone knew the truck was headed for the gas chambers. When the truck arrived no one could speak at all. Even the guards fell silent. Suddenly Robert Desnos interrupted the silence. He energetically jumped into a line of condemned prisoners. He grabbed the hand of the woman in front of him and began to read her palm.

"Oh," he said, "I see you have a very long lifeline. And you are going to have three children." He was exuberant. And his excitement was contagious. A person nearby offered his palm to Desnos. Here, too, Desnos foresaw a long life filled with happiness and success. Other prisoners quickly joined in and offered up their palms to be read and the prediction for each one was for longevity, more children, abundant joy.

As Desnos read more palms, not only did the mood of the prisoners change,
the guards became visibly disoriented. They were so disoriented by this sudden change of mood among those they are about to kill that they are unable to go through with the executions. So all the prisoners, along with Desnos, were packed back onto the truck and taken back to the barracks, their lives spared for yet a little longer. (3)

I am sad to report that Robert Desnos did die in a concentration camp. But it was after the camp was liberated. He died of typhoid. He did not die at the hands of the Nazis directly—though the ravages of the camp did weaken him. What kept him alive for so long? His attitude. His determination. In a sense, his faith. The joy of the Lord really was his strength.

As you read the story of Nehemiah working against great odds and encouraging his men to persevere, you have to be struck by his attitude—the attitude that—because God was with him—he would not be defeated.

Nehemiah had a positive attitude. And Nehemiah had a powerful purpose. Some of you who have read those first seven chapters of his story will remember that scene when his enemies were scheming to harm him. They sent him a message, "Come, let us meet together in one of the villages on the plain of Ono."

Nehemiah knew they were up to no good. So he sent messengers to answer them with this reply: "I am carrying on a great project and cannot go down. Why should the work stop while I leave it and go down to you?" Four times they sent him the same message, and each time he gave them the same answer, "I am carrying on a great project and cannot go down." He was telling the truth. He was carrying on a great project. Nehemiah had a powerful purpose.

What is your life's purpose? There is a story about Albert Einstein, the brilliant scientist who won the 1921 Nobel Prize. Einstein was known to be absent minded.

One day he was traveling by train. After he boarded the train, he couldn't locate his ticket. He checked his coat pockets, the pockets in his pants—nothing. About that time the conductor came along and said, "Mr. Einstein, what is the problem?"

Einstein answered, "I can't find my ticket."

The conductor replied, "Mr. Einstein, I know who you are. You don't need a ticket!"

Within a few minutes the conductor noticed Mr. Einstein on his hands and knees looking under the seats. "Mr. Einstein, I said you don't need a ticket, I know who you are."

"Yes, I know who I am, too," said the great scientist, "but I don't know where I'm going!"

That's a sad place to be—when you don't know where you're going. I like something that Welch poet David Whyte once wrote: "I don't want to have written on my tombstone, when finally people struggle through the weeds, pull back the moss, and read the inscription there: 'He made his car payments.'"

Do you hear what he was saying? We need a reason for living beyond meeting a mortgage or a car payment. We need a purpose that gets us out of bed and gets us going in the mornings.

Author Steve Chandler in his book 100 Ways to Motivate Yourself notes that during times of war suicide rates go down. Experts believe it is because many people during times of war begin to feel useful and challenged.

In the 1970s the economist Tibor Scitovsky wrote a book called The Joyless Economy. Tibor tried to explain why so many people today are unhappy, even though they have plenty of money. His explanation is boredom. People have chosen comfort instead of stimulation. They have failed to find active interests that would engage them outside their work.

His diagnosis has an important element of truth. Even though many people feel under tremendous pressure, the average American still finds three and a half hours a day to watch television. People no longer have to struggle to stay alive, as human beings have done for most of our history. So we have more choice over our goals. Getting those choices right is the problem. (4)

Recently journalist David Brooks, author of the bestseller, Bobos in Paradise, wrote a fascinating article for the Atlantic Monthly titled, "Kicking the Secularist Habit." The word secularist refers to someone who makes decisions with indifference to religion and religious considerations. It is a dominant theme in our land today. Here is what David Brooks has to say about Secularism. He says it is a big mistake. He writes, "Secularism is not the future; it is yesterday's incorrect version of the future." It's not really economics that drives human behavior, Brooks continues. "People everywhere," Brooks says, "long for meaning, purpose, and righteousness beyond economics. . . . Human beings yearn for a world that reflects God's will in many cases as strongly as they yearn for money or success." (5)

Brooks is saying that if you do not have a meaningful purpose for your life, life will not have much zest, and you will not be as happy as God intends for you to be. The happiest people on this earth are people who have a Godly purpose for life. When Nehemiah told the people that "the joy of the Lord is our strength," he was speaking of the joy of a positive attitude and the joy of a powerful purpose. He was also speaking of one more thing.

Nehemiah had the presence of God in his life. This is where he got his great attitude. This is where he got his great purpose. This is where he got his joy. This is why he never got discouraged, never drowned himself in despair. God was present with him. God was working though him.

Young William Wilberforce was discouraged one night in the early 1790s after another defeat in his 10-year battle against the slave trade in England. Tired and frustrated, he opened his Bible and began to leaf through it. A small piece of paper fell out and fluttered to the floor. It was a letter written by John Wesley shortly before his death. Wilberforce read it again.

Here is what Wesley had written to William Wilberforce: "Unless the divine power has raised you up . . . I see not how you can go through your glorious enterprise in opposing that (abominable practice of slavery), which is the scandal of religion, of England, and of human nature. Unless God has raised you up for this very thing, you will be worn out by the opposition of men and devils. But if God be for you, who can be against you? Are all of them together stronger than God? Oh, be not weary of well-doing. Go on in the name of God, and in the power of His might." (6)

If a friend of Nehemiah's had been writing to him in his gargantuan task of rebuilding the walls of Jerusalem, might he not have said the same thing? "Unless God has raised you up for this very thing, you will be worn out by the opposition of men and devils. But if God be for you, who can be against you? Are all of them together stronger than God? Oh, be not weary of well-doing. Go on in the name of God, and in the power of His might."

Nehemiah had a positive attitude, a powerful purpose, and the presence of the living God within. He had the joy of the Lord in his soul. That was his great strength. Do you have that joy? If not I hope you will claim it today.

1. Hope for the Troubled Heart (Dallas: Word Publishing, 1991), p. 106.
2. http://www.preaching.com/sermons/11642680/page-3/.
3. Whole Earth Review, Sausilito, California, 1989. Jill Oglesby Evans, http://www.emorypresbyterian.org/sermons/Acts1v1-8_CanYouImagine.pdf.
4. Richard Layard, Happiness Lessons from a New Science (New York: Penguin Group, 2005), p. 74.
5. John M. Buchanan, http://www.fourthchurch.org/%202003/040603sermon.html.
6. Daily Bread, June 16, 1989.

Extreme Love
1 Corinthians 13:1-13

Our lesson today is on love. Now, obviously we're not talking about romantic love, though sometime we might talk about romantic love. After all, it's an important part of our lives. I read something funny recently. It was an announcement that was made in the chapel of a very conservative church college some years back. It went something like this: "On this campus there is to be absolutely no physical contact of any kind between male and female students. There is only one legitimate exception to this rule. If a male student happens to see a female student about to fall to the ground, it is permissible to touch her to break her fall. However," the announcement continued, "we shall not tolerate any young woman making a practice of falling." (1)

Yes, young people, there have been colleges that have been that strict.

Our lesson for today is about love. In fact, it's called the love chapter. Many of us probably first heard it read in weddings. It is the highest expression of love in all of literature. It was composed by St. Paul, obviously under the guidance of the Holy Spirit. I consider it one of the most extreme, radical chapters in all the Bible. And I believe that, by the end of this service, you will too because here is the basic message of this chapter: You can be more Christian than Christ himself, but if you are not committed to living a life of love, you've missed the whole message of the gospel. Think about that for a moment. You can be more Christian than Christ himself, but if you are not committed to living a life of love, you've missed the whole message of the Gospel.

I have time today to deal with only the first few verses of this wonderful chapter in depth, but these few verses are life-changing. I Corinthians 13, one of the most beloved chapters in all literature, begins like this: "If I speak in the tongues of men or of angels, but do not have love, I am only a resounding gong or a clanging cymbal."

Let's pause here for a moment: "If I speak in the tongues of men or of angels . . ." This is a letter to the Corinthians. Corinth was in Greece. Greeks prized the spoken word. Their orators received wide public acclaim. Remember the legendary orator Demosthenes who is said to have filled his mouth with pebbles to improve his diction.

The Greeks prized the gift of oratory. Four hundred years before Paul a man named Aristotle wrote a work which he called Rhetoric. Aristotle's Rhetoric spelled out rules for public speaking that are still being studied by students of public speaking today.

The Corinthians valued eloquence of speech highly. And so Paul begins by saying it is wonderful to be a fine speaker, to "speak in the tongues of men or of angels," but if your heart is not filled with love, your eloquent speech sounds like "a resounding gong or a clanging cymbal."

People in Paul's time were also familiar with the monotonous tone of a gong or the clashing sound of a cymbal. Scholars tell us there was a big gong or cymbal hanging at the entrance of most pagan temples. When people came to worship, they hit these noisy percussion instruments in order to awaken the pagan gods so they would listen to their prayers. So Paul is saying it's all right if you're a fine speaker, or teacher or even a fine preacher. However, your fine words are as futile as the act of striking a gong or a cymbal to awaken a pagan idol if you are not committed to a life of love.

St. Paul continues, "If I have the gift of prophecy and can fathom all mysteries and all knowledge, and if I have a faith that can move mountains, but do not have love, I am nothing . . ." Friends, that's radical. That's extreme. Paul is saying that love is even more important than faith. "If I have a faith that can move mountains, but do not have love, I am nothing . . ." This is revolutionary. Think about those people in our society who call themselves followers of Jesus, but they hate Moslems, they hate Jews, they hate Mormons, they even hate other Christians who do not believe exactly as they believe. And they do it in the name of Jesus. Amazing! Could it be that these Christians who hate people of other faiths are more apt to end up in hell than the very people they despise? That could be true if love is more important than faith.

You say, Pastor, you've gone too far. It's not me—it's St. Paul. If you're not convinced, look at how he ends the chapter, "And now these three remain: faith, hope and love. But the greatest of these is love." Love is more important than faith? How you live is at least as important as what you believe? It's a good thing we're saved by grace. Neither our faith nor our works alone would do the job. We are saved by God's extreme love for us—a love God intends for us to pass on to others.

Now please do not misunderstand. Faith is important. It is essential. You are not going to love as Jesus loved if Christ does not live in your heart. Faith is important. So is hope. But Paul says that love is even more important than faith or hope.

But he's not finished, "If I give all I possess to the poor . . ." You mean you can give your money to charity or stand on the streets handing out money to homeless people and do it with an unloving spirit? Amazing, but true!

"If I give all I possess to the poor and give over my body to hardship . . ." That's the NIV translation. Many of us remember the King James Version: "though I give my body to be burned . . ." Some of you remember the Vietnam War when Buddhist priests would pour gasoline all over their bodies, then set themselves on fire.

You mean you can be seized with that kind of religious extremism, and it will profit you nothing without love? Let me say it again so that no one can misunderstand. You can be more Christian than Christ himself, but if you are not committed to a life of love, you've missed the whole message of the gospel.

Of course, St. Paul is only expounding on the teachings of Jesus. It was Jesus who first said that the great commandment was to love . . . to love God and to love one's neighbor (Matthew 22:36-40).

The religious Jew in the first century was committed to the keeping of more than 600 commandments. Jesus summarized all these duties in one teaching: "A new command I give you: Love one another. As I have loved you, so you must love one another. By this everyone will know that you are my disciples, if you love one another" (John 13:34-35).

Did you hear that? This is how the world will know that you follow Jesus—not by how many Bible verses you can quote; not by your perfect attendance in worship; not by giving a million dollars to the church—well, you could always try that one. These are wonderful acts of devotion, but none of them matter if you have let your life be taken over with malice and resentment and hate.

This is to say that love is the central task of the Christian. If this is how people will know that we are followers of Jesus, isn't this what we should be doing every hour of every day—showing love to others of God's children?

Bill Wilson pastors an inner city church in New York City. His mission field is a very violent place. He himself has been stabbed twice as he ministered to the people of the community surrounding the church. Once a Puerto Rican woman became involved in the church and was led to Christ. After her conversion she came to Pastor Wilson and said, "I want to do something to help with the church's ministry."

Wilson asked her what her talents were and she could think of nothing—she couldn't even speak English—but she did love children. So he put her on one of the church's buses that went into neighborhoods and transported kids to church. Every week she performed her duties. She would find the worst-looking kid on the bus, put him on her lap and whisper over and over the only words she had learned in English: "I love you. Jesus loves you."

After several months, she became attached to one little boy in particular. The boy didn't speak. He came to Sunday School every week with his sister and sat on the woman's lap, but he never made a sound. Each week she would tell him all the way to Sunday School and all the way home, "I love you and Jesus loves you."

One day, to her amazement, the little boy turned around and stammered, "I—I—I love you too!" Then he put his arms around her and gave her a big hug. That was 2:30 on a Sunday afternoon. At 6:30 that night he was found dead. His own mother had beaten him to death and thrown his body in the trash . . . (2)

"I love you and Jesus loves you." Those were some of the last words this little boy heard in his short life. The reason he heard them was because an immigrant woman from Puerto Rico was committed to love people in Jesus' name. But here's what we need to remember: when she held that child on her lap and whispered, "I love you. Jesus loves you," she was fulfilling all the law and the Prophets. When she held that child in her arms and whispered those words, her witness was more authentic than all those who strut their piety around and claim to be righteous. Love is the central task of the Christian.

That is to say the love Jesus wants to place in our lives is proactive—it seeks out people who need loving. Authentic love is not passive. Authentic love always looks for people who need loving.

There was a missionary named Doug Nichols who went to India to be a missionary. In 1967 while he was just starting to study the language he became infected with tuberculosis and had to be put in a sanitarium to recuperate. This was not the kind of clean and wholesome sanitarium you and I might expect here in the U.S.

While in the sanitarium Doug unsuccessfully tried to reach some of the patients for Christ. He was handicapped by his inability to communicate in their language. When he offered them tracts or pamphlets, they politely refused. It was obvious that the patients wanted nothing to do with him or his God. Doug grew discouraged and wondered why God had allowed him to be there since no one would listen to him.

One night around 2:00 in the morning, Doug woke up coughing. Across the aisle, he noticed an old man trying to get out of bed. The man was too weak to stand, and he fell back crying and exhausted. Early the next morning the same scene repeated itself. Later in the morning, the smell that began to permeate the room revealed the obvious. The old man had been trying to get to the bathroom and had not made it. The other patients made fun of the old man. The nurses who came to clean up his bed weren't kind to him either. In fact, one of them slapped him in the face. Nichols said that the old man just laid there and cried.

The next night this scene was repeated. The old man tried in vain to get to his feet. Although sick himself and as weak as he had ever been, Doug got out of bed. He placed one arm under the old man's neck and the other under his legs. With all his strength Doug lifted the sick man and carried him down the hall to the filthy, smelly bathroom and he gently held him while the man completed his task. Then he carried him back to his bed. The old man kissed

Doug on the cheek and said an Indian word meaning, "Thank you."

The next morning, when Doug Nichols woke up, one of the other Indian patients was waiting to serve him a hot cup of tea. After the patient served the tea, he made motions indicating that he wanted one of Doug's tracts. Doug said, "All throughout the day, people came to me asking for Gospel tracts. This included the nurses, hospital interns, the doctors, until everyone in the hospital had a tract, booklet, or Gospel of John." Over the next few days, he adds, several told him they had come to trust Christ as their Savior as a result of reading these materials! To think, Doug Nichols says, "I simply took an old man to the bathroom. Anyone could have done that." (3)

Yes, anyone could do that, but none of them did. How did the people in the sanitarium know that Doug Nichols was a follower of Jesus—by the pamphlets and tracts that he passed out? You know the answer to that question. They knew he was a follower of Jesus because of the love he showed this pitiable old man.

Paul finishes up this chapter with these inspiring words: "Love is patient, love is kind. It does not envy, it does not boast, it is not proud. It does not dishonor others, it is not self-seeking, it is not easily angered, it keeps no record of wrongs. Love does not delight in evil but rejoices with the truth. It always protects, always trusts, always hopes, always perseveres. Love never fails. But where there are prophecies, they will cease; where there are tongues, they will be stilled; where there is knowledge, it will pass away. For we know in part and we prophesy in part, but when completeness comes, what is in part disappears. When I was a child, I talked like a child, I thought like a child, I reasoned like a child. When I became a man, I put the ways of childhood behind me. For now we see only a reflection as in a mirror; then we shall see face to face. Now I know in part; then I shall know fully, even as I am fully known. "And now these three remain: faith, hope and love. But the greatest of these is . . ." What? You know the answer, "Love."

Pastor Ray Pritchard gives us a wonderful way of grasping what Paul is saying. Suppose you multiply 1,000,000 X 1000, says Pritchard. You end up with one billion, don't you? What comes after a billion? A trillion. What comes after that? A quadrillion. After that is a number called a quintillion, which is one followed by 18 zeroes.

Now, says Pritchard, let's do it the way children might do it. Let's start with the biggest number in the world times the biggest number in the world. Now whatever that number is, let's multiply it by zero. What do you get? Zero. It doesn't matter what you start with on the left. If the number on the right is zero, the answer will always be zero.

Pritchard says: "God is saying that life without love is zero. You can pile up all the good deeds, all the education, all the spiritual gifts, and all the noble works that you like. Without love, it still equals zero. You can be smart, beautiful, strong, wealthy, educated, multi-lingual, rich and famous but without love it still equals zero. (4)

In other words, you can be more Christian than Christ himself, but if you are not committed to a life of love, you've missed the whole message of the gospel. Of course, the greatest example of self-giving love is the cross on which Christ died. "God so loved the world that He gave His beloved Son . . ." (John 3:16). "In this is love, not that we loved God, but that he loved us and gave us his son for the expiation of our sins but not for ours only, but for the sins of the whole world . . ." (1 John 4:10). "We love because He first loved us . . ." (1 John 4:19). How will people know that we are followers of Jesus? By our love. "And now these three remain: faith, hope and love. But the greatest of these is . . ."

1. Wayne Brouwer, Wedding Homilies (Seven Worlds).
2. http://www.sermoncentral.com/illustrations/illustrations-about-palm-sunday.asp.
3. http://www.lesliepuryear.com/2011/04/doug-nichols-story.html.
4. Pritchard credits Pastor Leith Anderson with this example. Cited at http://www.keepbelieving.com/sermon/2000-11-26-The-Greatest-of-These/.

The Ultimate Mountaintop Experience
Exodus 34:29-35; Luke 9:28-36, (37-43)
(Transfiguration)

In 1976, by the invitation of the President of Mexico, Mother Teresa opened a home in a very poor section outside of Mexico City. The Sisters who visited in the homes of these very poor people were surprised when, despite their poverty, these impoverished people did not ask for clothes, medicine, or food. They only said, "Sisters, talk to us about God." (1)

Today is the last Sunday in the season of Epiphany. Our theme has been "Discovering God." The Scriptures have shown us many epiphanies during this season. We saw the star lead the magi to Bethlehem so that they could see and worship the child who was born King of the Jews. Then on the second Sunday we had the epiphany of a dove and a voice from heaven, "You are my Son, whom I love; with you I am well pleased." Then we had the epiphany of God's people as His bride. On the fourth Sunday we had the epiphany of joy—the joy of the Lord which is our strength. Last Sunday we had an epiphany about the Christian life—that it is all about love. And finally, today we go up on a mountain to discover Christ in all his glory.

We are told that the occasion of the transfiguration of Christ probably took place on Mt. Hermon, which rises to an elevation of 9,166 feet and is located in the area of Caesarea-Philippi. The story begins like this, "About eight days after Jesus said this, he took Peter, John and James with him and went up onto a mountain to pray . . ."

You might rightly ask, "Eight days after saying what?" This is most interesting. It was eight days after Simon Peter had his own significant epiphany. Remember, Jesus had asked the disciples who people were saying that he is? And Simon Peter answered, "God's Messiah."

In Luke's telling of the story, Jesus immediately warned them not to tell this to anyone. He said to them, "The Son of Man must suffer many things and be rejected by the elders, the chief priests and the teachers of the law, and he must be killed and on the third day be raised to life." This in itself is an epiphany. He is telling them that he must suffer, die and then be resurrected. This is followed with another epiphany as to what their life is to be like after his resurrection: "Then he said to them all: 'Whoever wants to be my disciple must deny themselves and take up their cross daily and follow me. For whoever wants to save their life will lose it, but whoever loses their life for me will save it. What good is it for someone to gain the whole world, and yet lose or forfeit their very self? . . .'" Then he concluded this section by saying, "Truly I tell you, some who are standing here will not taste death before they see the kingdom of God" (20-27).

This is a very important chapter in the Bible where much is revealed and, in a sense, it is all leading up to this high moment here on Mount Hermon. But let's continue the story: "About eight days after Jesus said this, he took Peter, John and James with him and went up onto a mountain to pray . . ."

Don't you think that it is significant that Christ felt the need from time to time to go off by himself or in the company of a few select friends and pray? After all, he was Christ! Surely he was in constant communion with God. His thoughts and God's thoughts were one and the same. And yet, he felt the need for a time of prayer. Doesn't that say something to us about how we spend our time?

Peter Story, an Anglican priest, who served in South Africa, tells a story about Archbishop Desmond Tutu and their fight together against apartheid many years ago. He said that often those fighting against apartheid would come into Johannesburg and rent a room for the night, where several people would stay. There might be as many as ten of these fighters in a room.

One night, Peter Story says he was awakened about 4:00 in the morning by a shuffling sound over in the corner. He looked and he saw someone sitting in the corner with a white sheet covering him. It was Archbishop Tutu, retreating from the world for a few minutes, beginning his day in prayer. And then he said that every month, Tutu would leave the work and go away for two days for a contemplative, silent retreat.

One day, Reverend Story decided to confront Desmond Tutu: "There were young men and women dying. How could he leave the movement for two days a month?"

Desmond Tutu answered, "I leave and go on retreat for two days a month, so that I can do the work God has called me to do the other 28 days." (2)

We don't know why Jesus felt the need to go off and spend time in prayer. Maybe it was because his ministry was so draining. Anyone who works with people, meeting their needs, consoling them in times of heartache, helping them find healing in a time of distress, will understand. After all, we believe that while on earth Jesus was fully human as well as fully divine. Human beings need to recharge. We need to spend time with God to renew our sense of God's presence in our lives.

I love something that Billy Graham once wrote. "I watched the deck hands on the great liner United States," he wrote, "as they docked that ship in New York Harbor. First they threw out a rope to the men on the dock. Then, inside the boat the great motors went to work and pulled on the great cable. But, oddly enough, the pier wasn't pulled out to the ship; but the ship was pulled snugly up to the pier. Prayer," says Graham, "is the rope that pulls God and us together.

But it doesn't pull God down to us; it pulls us to God. We must learn to say with Christ, the master of the art of praying: 'Not my will; but Thine be done.'" (3)

Maybe that's why Christ spent time in prayer. Maybe the events that accompanied being continually in the public eye pulled his focus and his energy away from God. So he took time to be in the Father's presence simply as a way of energizing his ministry once again. As Desmond Tutu put it, "I leave and go on retreat for two days a month, so that I can do the work God has called me to do the other 28 days."

The story continues: "As [Jesus] was praying, the appearance of his face changed, and his clothes became as bright as a flash of lightning. Two men, Moses and Elijah, appeared in glorious splendor, talking with [him]. They spoke about his departure, which he was about to bring to fulfillment at Jerusalem. Peter and his companions were very sleepy, but when they became fully awake, they saw his glory and the two men standing with him. As the men were leaving Jesus, Peter said to him, 'Master, it is good for us to be here. Let us put up three shelters—one for you, one for Moses and one for Elijah.'" Luke tells us that Simon Peter "did not know what he was saying."

"While he was speaking, a cloud appeared and covered them, and they were afraid as they entered the cloud. A voice came from the cloud, saying, 'This is my Son, whom I have chosen; listen to him.' When the voice had spoken, they found that Jesus was alone. The disciples kept this to themselves and did not tell anyone at that time what they had seen."

Here on the Mount of Transfiguration we have the highest epiphany of all. We see Christ in all his glory. We see his appearance changed, both his face and his clothing. They were "as bright as a flash of lightning." And we see him in the company of the two leading lights of the Old Testament, Moses and Elijah. And we hear the voice of God: "This is my Son, whom I have chosen; listen to him."

Let's begin with Christ in all his glory. Peter has already announced that Jesus is the Messiah. The other disciples probably were still unconvinced. So, at least for James and John, this experience on the mountain provided confirmation that Peter was right. "As he was praying, the appearance of his face changed, and his clothes became as bright as a flash of lightning." This was God's way of showing us that Jesus was one of a kind. There is no one else who can compare.

There is a famous story about the eighteenth century German sculptor Johann Heinrich von Dannaker. Dannaker is known for his carving of Greek goddesses, as well as one of John the Baptist. But his finest sculpture was one he did of Christ.

For two years he worked on this sculpture. When he felt he was finished he called to some children playing outside his studio and asked one of them to come in and evaluate his work. "Who is that?" he asked.

A little girl promptly replied, "A great man."

Dannaker instantly knew his impression of Christ had failed. So he undertook the project again. For the next 6 years he toiled with his chisel to recreate the masterpiece. When he was finished, he tested his work again. He asked a little girl to identify the statue. "Who is this?" he asked her.

This time the child replied: "It's Jesus."

And thus, Dannaker declared his powerful work ready for the world. The sculptor later confessed to a friend that during those six years Christ revealed himself in a vision. Dannaker said he simply transferred his vision to the marble statue. He did a magnificent job. It was said by one who was familiar with his work that his portrayal of Christ's face "was so tender and beautiful that strong men wept as they looked upon it."

Later, Napoleon Bonaparte asked Dannaker to make a statue of Venus, the Roman Goddess of love. Dannaker refused. "A person who has seen Christ," he said, "can never again employ his gifts in carving a pagan goddess. My art is a consecrated work for my Savior."

Peter, James and John experienced Christ in all his glory. If there had been any doubt in their minds whatsoever that he was the one who was to come, it would have been gone in a flash after what they experienced on this mountain.

They also saw him in the company of Moses and Elijah. This is significant. I love the way Barbara Brown Taylor describes it, "To see him standing there with Moses and Elijah was like seeing the Mount Rushmore of heaven—the Lawgiver, the Prophet, the Messiah—wrapped in such glory it is a wonder the other three could see them at all."

You might remember that Moses and Elijah had their own mountaintop experiences. In our lesson from Exodus, when Moses came down from Mount Sinai with the two tablets of the covenant law in his hands, he was not aware that his face was radiant because he had spoken with the Lord. When Aaron and the rest of the Israelites saw Moses, they were afraid to come near him. That's how brightly Moses' face shown. When Moses finished speaking to them, he put a veil over his face. Eventually the radiance faded from Moses' face, but that's what being in the presence of God did to him.

We read about Elijah's experience with God on Mount Horeb in I Kings 19. Remember he had fled the wrath of Queen Jezebel. He was feeling sorry for himself as he hid in a cave on Horeb, which was called the mountain of God. The writer describes his experience like this: "Then a great and powerful wind tore the mountains apart and shattered the rocks before the Lord, but the Lord was not in the wind. After the wind there was an earthquake, but the

Lord was not in the earthquake. After the earthquake came a fire, but the Lord was not in the fire. And after the fire came a gentle whisper. When Elijah heard it, he pulled his cloak over his face and went out and stood at the mouth of the cave. Then a voice said to him, 'What are you doing here, Elijah?'"

The Scriptures don't say that Elijah's face shown, but it is clear his life was changed. You can't come into God's presence without something important happening in your life. You may or may not look different, but you cannot help but act different. The disciples saw Jesus' appearance transformed, they saw him in the presence of Moses and Elijah.

One final thing: They heard the voice of God saying, "This is my Son, whom I have chosen; listen to him." This is why Christ brought them up on the mountain. This was the ultimate epiphany he wanted them to grasp. He was doing the will of his Father. Even more importantly, he and the Father were one. "This is my son, whom I have chosen; listen to him."

This is one of the holiest moments in Scripture. This is epiphany at its best. Christ is revealed to the disciples in all his glory. Christ is revealed as God's own Son. It is the kind of scene that makes us want to take off our shoes because we are on holy ground. That is the kind of experience that is missing in today's secular world.

Pastor Quintin Morrow tells about a cartoon that appeared in Christianity Today magazine sometime back. It depicted three scenes in three boxes. The first showed the Reformer Martin Luther, quaking with fear and sweating. He says, "In the pages of Holy Scripture I encountered an utterly holy God. And there I learned that I was completely unable, through my own good works, to acquit myself and quiet my conscience before Him."

Scene two shows John Wesley, the great revival preacher and father of Methodism, with arms outstretched to heaven, crying, "God's holiness, revealed in His holy Word, convicted my sinful heart and there I discovered that I was undone. And after reading Luther's commentary on the Book of Romans my heart was strangely warmed."

The final box shows a modern, 21st century woman with frizzy hair, big spectacles and big earrings. Her smiling face is saying, "In Skip and Jodi's Bible study I discovered that I needed a check-up from the neck up! I don't need another diet. What God wants me to do is learn to love me." (4)

I wonder if it is even possible to talk about an experience of the holiness and majesty of God in today's world? We have reduced the Gospel to a check-up from the neck up. Is it even possible to talk about God's glory, God's majesty, God's holiness? Jesus went off on a mountain with his disciples to pray. Even though he was God's son, Jesus needed to pray, just as you and I need to spend time each day in prayer. While he was praying, "the appearance of his face changed, and his clothes became as bright as a flash of lightning. Two men, Moses and Elijah, appeared in glorious splendor," talking with him. Finally a cloud appeared and covered them, and a voice came from the cloud, saying, "This is my Son, whom I have chosen; listen to him."

Are you listening to him? Do you sense his presence? Can you feel his glory, his majesty, his holiness? The impoverished people of Mexico City did not ask for food, medicine, or clothing from the nuns who had come to minister to them. Instead, they said to them, "Sisters, talk to us about God." Are we as wise as they? Is that the yearning of our hearts as well?

1. José González-Balado, compiler, Mother Teresa: In My Own Words (Liguori, MO: Ligouri Press, 1996), p. 43.
2. Drema's Sermon, http://www.fairlingtonumc.org/sermons_2003/sermon08032003.htm.
3. Source unknown.
4. http://www.sermoncentral.com/sermons/wholly-holy-lord-god-almighty-quintin-morrow-sermon-on-descriptions-of-god-54070.asp.

When We're Estranged From God
Matthew 6:1-6, 16-21
(Ash Wednesday)

It's an old story, but it bears repeating. An armed robber accosted a French priest on a dark, back street in Paris and demanded his wallet. As the priest opened his coat to reach for his wallet, the thief caught sight of his clerical collar, and immediately apologized. "Never mind, Father, I didn't realize you were a priest. I'll be on my way."

The priest was relieved, of course, and good-naturedly offered the man a cigar. "No, thank you, Father," the robber said, "I gave up smoking for Lent." (1)

One of the hallowed traditions of Lent is to that we should give up something, something we enjoy, for the duration of this sacred season. Usually it means something like chocolate, or beer, or some other alleged vice. This, of course, has opened us to a multitude of lame jokes.

One civic-minded individual said he gave up taxes for Lent. Another said he had given up his New Year's resolutions for Lent. Comedian Stephen Colbert—who, I understand, is a Sunday School teacher at his local Catholic church—joked that he was giving up being Catholic for Lent.

People laugh at the idea of giving up things for Lent, but the idea, originally, was to share experientially in the sufferings of Christ. Christ gave his life for us. We ought to give up something to show our devotion to him. However, even under the best of circumstances, this practice has never worked very well.

Dean Snyder, the senior minister of Foundry United Methodist Church in our nation's capital said that he was doing some research on religion and eating. One little factoid he ran across was that in medieval times, monks gave up butter and lard and fat for Lent. They had an Ash Wednesday ceremony called "Burying the Fat" in which they would put butter in a casket, hold a funeral service, and bury the casket.

They gave up butter, lard and fat, because this made them constipated, and this— they felt—was their way of sharing in the sufferings of Christ.

Snyder said he shared that in a staff meeting, and one of his staff members responded by saying, "Well, I guess." (2)

I guess there are all kinds of ways to share in Christ's suffering.

A serious response to this idea of making a sacrifice during Lent has been for many Christians to fast during Lent. Medical experts are divided today on the wisdom of fasting. However, many saints have reported that fasting has brought them closer to God.

According to John Maxwell, in his book Partners in Prayer, fasting played a major role in the Great Awakening that swept both America and England in the 1800s. John Wesley, father of the Methodist movement and his brother Charles and other fellow believers regularly fasted and prayed. John Wesley so believed in this practice that he urged early Methodists to fast and pray every Wednesday and Friday. He felt so strongly about fasting those two days a week that he refused to ordain anyone in Methodism who wouldn't agree to do it. I suspect there are many Methodist pastors who are happy this is no longer a requirement for ordination.

Maxwell lists several Christian greats for whom fasting was a regular part of their lives: Martin Luther, John Calvin, John Knox, Jonathan Edwards, Matthew Henry, Charles Finney, Andrew Murray, and many more. (3)

Many people have benefited spiritually from this practice. But even a good thing like fasting can be abused.

In our lesson from the Gospel we hear our Lord say, "When you fast, do not look somber as the hypocrites do, for they disfigure their faces to show others they are fasting. Truly I tell you, they have received their reward in full. But when you fast, put oil on your head and wash your face, so that it will not be obvious to others that you are fasting, but only to your Father, who is unseen; and your Father, who sees what is done in secret, will reward you."

Jesus was not saying, "Do not fast." In fact, he appears to be explicitly endorsing the practice of fasting. He even gives directions for how to go about it. "When you fast," he says, "put oil on your head and wash your face . . ." In other words, fasting is good—but not if it is an idle show of your religiosity.

I've always appreciated the words of one of the church fathers, St. John Chrysostom, when it comes to fasting: "Do you fast?" he asked. "Give me proof of it by your works. If you see a poor man, take pity on him. If you see a friend being honored, do not envy him. Do not let only your mouth fast, but also the eye and the ear and the feet and the hands and all the members of our bodies.

"Let the hands fast, by being free of avarice. Let the feet fast, by ceasing to run after sin. Let the eyes fast, by disciplining them not to glare at that which is sinful . . . Let the ear fast . . . by not listening to evil talk and gossip . . . Let the mouth fast from foul words and unjust criticism. For what good is it if we abstain from birds and fishes, but bite and devour our brothers?" That's hitting the nail squarely on the head. Even a good thing like fasting can be abused.

The central purpose of lent is to bring us back to God. That is the message of our lesson from the epistle. If fasting or making small personal sacrifices brings you closer to God, that's all to the good. But it's important not to lose sight of why we fast or why we make personal sacrifices. St. Paul writes to the church at Corinth, "We are therefore Christ's ambassadors, as though God were making his appeal through us. We implore you on Christ's behalf: Be reconciled to God. God made him who had no sin to be sin for us, so that in him we might become the righteousness of God . . ."

The point of Ash Wednesday, indeed the point of Lent, is that we shall be reconciled with God, that we who have wandered away from Him might come home. We may indicate our desire for reconciliation by fasting or by making a sacrifice during the Lenten season, but that is peripheral. We are here this night confessing that we need to come back to God.

To say we need to be reconciled to God, of course, is to confess that all of us to some degree are estranged from God.

There are some members of this congregation who live very close to God. I am in awe of your spiritual commitment. But let's not kid ourselves. None of us is perfect. We're all sinners. There are gaps in our lives—emotions that will not heal, resentments that still fester, prejudices that come to the surface under stress.

In a sense we are like snowflakes. Snowflakes are so beautiful and white and look so pure, but every snowflake has a tiny piece of dust at its core. And so do we. That is why Ash Wednesday and Lent are so important for us—they help us deal with that tiny particle of dust that keeps us from perfectly reflecting Christ's image.

C.S. Lewis once noted that there are two central truths about human nature. "First," he writes, "that human beings, all over the earth, have this curious idea that they ought to behave in a certain way, and cannot really get rid of it. Secondly, that they do not in fact behave in that way. They know the Law of Nature; they break it. These two facts," he continues "are the foundation of all clear thinking about ourselves and the universe we live in." (4)

And that's true. It may not be fashionable to use the word sin. To many it is archaic. Still, it is the central fact of human nature. No matter who we are, no matter how hard we try, we have not arrived at perfection.

Children sing the little nursery rhyme, "Humpty Dumpty sat on a wall, Humpty Dumpty had a great fall; All the king's horses, and all the king's men, Couldn't put Humpty together again." And it is true of our lives. We are broken people and the only hope we have of being put back together again is for God to touch our lives. We can't put ourselves back together again, but God can.

There was a young man in Wisconsin named John. John was kind of scary. He was in his early twenties and was very active in MMA, or Mixed Martial Arts. He liked to fight.

One day his family went to a church event, a community picnic, held by a church in his community. The pastor of that church talked with John and invited him to church. John didn't seem very interested.

Some time went by, and one day John showed up at church, accompanied by his 3-year-old son. And something happened to John in that church . . . something quite beautiful. The word of God took root and grew in John's heart. He went to church some more. He took some instructional classes. Finally, he joined the church!

One Sunday John walked into church late—really late—almost at sermon time. After the service his pastor asked him why he was so late. John said he got up that morning and his car would not start. He tried to fix it but he couldn't. So John got out his 10-speed bike, bundled up his kid, and peddled 5 miles in freezing Wisconsin temperatures because nothing was going to stop him from being in worship. (5)

I've seen that happen in people's lives. John had something missing in his life. He could not put himself back together again. But God did. John is not perfect, but he is growing. He is growing in the same way that you and I hope to grow this evening as we submit ourselves to the ashes and ask God to more completely fill our lives.

Of course, if we are reconciled with God we shall more easily be reconciled with one another. Reconciliation with our neighbor always goes with reconciliation with God.

Anthony Robinson in his book What's Theology Got To Do With It? tells a story about the Palestinian Christian priest Elias Chacour. It is said that Chacour tired of presiding at the sacrament of communion in his congregation. The reason was that he knew that many of his parishioners hated each other. Some had not talked with one another in years, even decades, and bore grudges dating back to the previous generation.

One Sunday Father Chacour locked and barred the doors to the church. Then he told the congregation that he had no intention of presiding at the service and sacrament or of unlocking the doors until those at odds with one another confessed their sins, offered forgiveness, and made peace.

What followed, after a stunned silence, was nothing short of remarkable. A policeman got to his feet, confessed his misdeeds and asked forgiveness. Others followed. When the Lord's Supper was finally celebrated, it was no longer a mockery. It was a sacrament in which members of the congregation recognized one another as the body of Christ. (6)

At the end of this service I will be applying ashes to your forehead. There was a time when I would have cautioned you against making a show of those ashes. I would have warned you, as Jesus did, not to make a show of your religion. What I prefer to say to you tonight, however, is do not wear those ashes in vain.

Our world hungers for an authentic sign of Christian devotion. If you wear those ashes home tonight, do not snap at your family. If you stop at a fast-food facility on the way home, do not be impatient with the server. Show genuine Christian love and goodwill in action. Be reconciled to God. Be reconciled with your neighbor. When we have the ashes on our heads, it is not a sign that we think ourselves better than others. Exactly the opposite. We are sinners dependent upon God's grace. Fast in the way that St. John Chrysostom recommended. Fast by your good works.

1. http://www.boydspc.org/sermons/20070304Philippians3,17-4,1.pdf
2. http://www.foundryumc.org/sermons/3_1_2006.htm.
3. (Nashville: Thomas Nelson Publishers, 1996), pp. 125-126.
4. C. S. Lewis, Mere Christianity (New York: MacMillan Publishing Co., 1943), p. 7.
5. Pastor Phil Huebner, http://ctkpalmcoast.wordpress.com/2010/01/24/sermon-on-nehemiah-81-3-5-6-8-10/.
6. Cited by Rev. Alice M.C. Ling, http://www.fpc-ucc.org/sermons/2007/03/second-sunday-in-lent.html.

When We Are Tempted
Luke 4:1-13

Pastor John Jewell tells about a 20/20 episode sometime back in which some children of about four years of age were forced to deal with the ancient scourge of temptation. They were left alone in a room. Sitting in front of them was two or three M&Ms. They were told they could have a whole package of M&Ms if they would wait five minutes for a bell to ring before devouring the two or three M&Ms in front of them. The struggle of temptation was recorded through a two way mirror. The result was hilarious, says Jewell, as these poor kids twitched, fidgeted, wiggled and twisted their faces up in knots trying not to grab those M&Ms. About half made it and half said in effect, "To heck with it, I want what I want when I want it!" (1)

We all know about that struggle, don't we? Maybe not for M&Ms, but all of us have our weak spot. Even Jesus had to struggle with the Tempter.

After his baptism, Luke tells us, Jesus, full of the Holy Spirit, left the Jordan and was led by the Spirit into the wilderness, where for forty days he was tempted by the devil.

Note that. Jesus had just come off of a spiritual high. He had just been baptized by John the Baptist. He was full of the Holy Spirit. And that's when the Tempter came. That is so true to life. You go off to a church retreat. You have a spiritual mountaintop experience. You're feeling closer to God and closer to others than you have ever felt before. Beware! That is the time when you may be the most vulnerable to temptation.

Jesus was led by the Spirit into the wilderness, where for forty days he was tempted by the devil. He ate nothing during those days, and at the end of them he was hungry. Here, too he was vulnerable. A physical need needed to be met. And so the devil said to him, "If you are the Son of God, tell this stone to become bread."

It was a reasonable response to Jesus' hunger. He had power over nature. The stilling of the storm proved that. And stones were abundant there in the wilderness. He could use his extraordinary gifts to meet his physical needs. But Jesus knew that was not what he was sent to do. His gifts were to be used to do the work of his Father. So Jesus answered, "It is written: 'Man shall not live on bread alone.'"

And that's true. Many people today have their physical needs met but they are shriveling and dying on the inside. Physical needs have an urgency, but spiritual needs are every bit as critical.

Having failed to tempt Jesus with his stones to bread routine, the devil takes a different tact. He leads Christ up to a high place and shows him in an instant all the kingdoms of the world. And he says to him, "I will give you all their authority and splendor; it has been given to me, and I can give it to anyone I want to. If you worship me, it will all be yours."

Who could resist being handed the power and the status that would come with ruling over all the kingdoms of this world? It is every politician's dream. And you have to wonder how many politicians have been willing to bow down to Satan in order to achieve such dreams.

Jesus was offered all the kingdoms of this world and all he would have to do would be to bow down to the devil. But it was too high a price for him to pay. Jesus answered, "It is written: 'Worship the Lord your God and serve him only.'"

The devil thinks to himself, "Rats! Foiled again!" But he has one more weapon in his arsenal.

The devil leads him to Jerusalem and has him stand on the highest point of the temple. "If you are the Son of God," he says, "throw yourself down from here. For it is written: 'He will command his angels concerning you to guard you carefully; they will lift you up in their hands, so that you will not strike your foot against a stone.'"

And Jesus answers, "It is said: 'Do not put the Lord your God to the test.'"

You do understand, don't you, that this was exactly what Satan was doing? He was testing Jesus. That is what temptation is. It is a test. Fail the test of temptation and you become even weaker spiritually. Pass the test and you become infinitely stronger.

Jesus passed the test with flying colors. Then note Luke's words, "When the devil had finished all this tempting, he left him UNTIL AN OPPORTUNE TIME." Satan wasn't finished with Jesus. None of us ever gets to the point where we are beyond being tested. Even Jesus did not reach that point. His struggle in the Garden of Gethsemane proved that.

In Mel Gibson's controversial film, The Passion of The Christ, we see the nature of the Tempter quite vividly. This isn't a scene from the Bible. It is a fictional account, but it is quite powerful. Jesus is shown at Gethsemane, agonizing over his betrayal, arrest, and crucifixion. A shadowy figure appears and says to him, "No one was meant to save so many. No one can. It is too much. You cannot." The presence whispers these words over and over, trying to split Jesus from his relationship with God. Finally, Jesus gets up, steps on the head of a snake the tempter has dropped near him, and goes off. The Tempter is unable to turn Jesus from his destiny and calling. There would be other temptations later. But for now the Tempter had been defeated. (2) But even Jesus was tempted—tempted without sinning.

There are some things about temptation we need to see. The first is that temptation is universal. We joke about temptation, because it is part of the human condition. Everyone has to deal with temptation.

An unknown wit once said, "Most people who fly from temptation usually leave a forwarding address."

"Opportunity only knocks once," someone else has noted. "Temptation leans on the doorbell."

One student of the human dilemma put it like this, "I've noticed that women generally flee from temptation while us men kind of crawl away from it in the cheerful hope that it might overtake us." There's probably a lot of truth in that observation.

Temptation goes all the way back to the first man and the first woman according to the first chapters of Genesis. I like the way an old spiritual tells it,

"Long came a serpent six foot three. Dem bones gonna rise again.

Wrapped himself around that tree. Dem bones gonna rise again.

He wrapped himself around that trunk. Dem bones gonna rise again.

And his eye at Eve he wunk. Dem bones gonna rise again.

My those apples sure look fine. Dem bones gonna rise again.

Take one, the Lord won't mind. Dem bones gonna rise again."

But, of course, Eve did take one and paradise was lost. Temptation is one inescapable fact of life upon this earth. And it is no joking matter.

Peter Gomes, popular author and one-time pastor at Harvard's Memorial Church, once stated that "temptation is the single greatest source of human anxiety." That is quite a dramatic statement. He further stated that in the thousands of people with whom he had counseled over the years of his ministry, he had found the problem of temptation to be at the heart of their personal anxiety. (3)

Think about it for a while and you will see that what he says is true. Think of the tests you and I face every day—at work, in our family life, among our friends. We are constantly making decisions. At heart many of these are moral decisions. Should we speak the truth when a falsehood would serve our purposes better? Ought we to cut corners in order to maximize our profits? What is the harm in a seemingly innocent flirtation? Can we stay on our diet? The list goes on and on, but many of these decisions represent one temptation or another. And should we give in to temptation, much can be lost.

The Greek philosopher Plato once told a story of a carriage drawn by a pair of young and spirited steeds. In the vehicle, the driver holds the reins and guides the horses on the straight and smooth road.

One day a heavy drowsiness comes upon the driver and he falls fast asleep. The horses, not feeling the restraint of the reins, go off the right path, and soon they are bouncing over bush and brush, to the edge of a deep pit, a bottomless abyss. A man standing nearby, seeing the threatened danger, calls out to the driver in a loud and mighty voice: "Wake up! Save yourself!"

With a start, the driver suddenly awakens. In a moment he realizes his peril. Pale and trembling, he hastily grasps the reins, and, exerting almost superhuman effort, he succeeds in swerving the horses to one side, thus saving his own life and those of his animals. Plato says the moral of the story is this: the fiery steeds are the appetites, desires, lusts, and passions to which the heart of the human inclines from youth. The driver is the wisdom, understanding, and intelligence with which God has endowed human life that we might rule over our appetites and desires and have dominion over our self-destructive impulses. (4)

Woe to us if we never hear the voice of conscience, the voice of God, telling us to wake up before we destroy our lives. Temptation is universal and potentially deadly.

Here's the second thing we need to see. With God's help temptation is resistible. The biggest lie that the Tempter tells us is that we are helpless when faced with temptation. We do not have the strength that Christ had to resist temptation, but it can be done, although sometimes we do need help.

Many of you basketball fans are familiar with former all-pro basketball player Charles Barkley. Barkley is now a popular sports commentator, but at one time he played for the Philadelphia 76ers where he was known as "The Round Mound of Rebound."

When Pat Croce became the physical therapist for the Philadelphia 76ers he instituted a new diet and exercise program for the team. At 6' 5" and 300 pounds, Charles Barkley resisted. He had no desire to pay the price to lose weight and get in shape. After all, he was a phenomenal player, even with the extra flab.

Croce is famous as a motivator; it didn't take him too long to coax Barkley into an exercise program. But Charles' eating habits were another story! He had been known to eat a one-pound bag of M&Ms in one sitting. He had a serious love affair with pizza. So Pat Croce decided to take some drastic steps to get Charles in shape.

He waited outside Charles' mansion one night and ambushed the pizza delivery man. The delivery man had two pizzas for Charles. Pat took one and one-half of the pizzas away. He also threatened to do serious bodily harm to the delivery man if he ever delivered more than one-half of a pizza to that address in the future. Charles got the message. That season, he lost fifty pounds. (5)

Wouldn't it be great if all of us had a Pat Croce in our lives, someone who would be there for us each time we are tempted?

That, of course, is the genius of Alcoholics Anonymous. They are there for each other in times of temptation. Many times in the middle of the night a member of this group will be called to sit with a buddy and help him fight the cravings that would destroy him. Members of Alcoholics Anonymous also know what it is to rely on God. They know that the key to turning their lives around is admitting their weakness, admitting that they were, are, and always will be powerless over alcohol. But they believe that a Power greater than themselves can restore them to sanity, and so they make a decision to turn their will and their lives over to the care of God.

No one knows how many lives have been saved by this organization. Hundreds of thousands? Millions? How many families have been saved? How many potentially abused children have been spared? How many battered spouses? No one will contend that any temptation can be resisted without a terrible struggle, but if you are willing to reach out to a friend, and if you are willing to throw yourself in complete surrender on the grace of God, the Tempter can be resisted.

Of course, the ultimate key to lessening temptation's hold on your life is to love God with all your heart and with all your mind.

Pastor and author David Jeremiah states it like this: "Over time I believe I've discovered that temptation isn't so much a matter of what we do but of whom we love. Knowing Christ—really knowing Him, not simply knowing about Him—changes everything. More often than not, power in the time of temptation comes because we've filled our minds with His magnificence, and there's not room for the world's shabby offerings. There's power in the name of Christ, and there's power in His presence as well. Worship and fellowship with God in the morning actually make it difficult to walk right out into the world and commit some transgression. Knowing that we've just been in the presence of the Lord of creation, and that we're carrying Him with us, makes it very difficult to sink to our lowest levels. The best escape Jesus provides is His own embrace." (6)

David Jeremiah is right. The best escape from temptation is to turn your gaze toward Jesus.

Leslie Dunkin once told about a dog he had when he was a boy. This was an unusually obedient dog. Periodically his father would test the dog's obedience. He would place a tempting piece of meat on the floor. Then he would turn toward the dog and give the command, "No!" The dog, which must have had a strong urge to go for the meat, was placed in a most difficult situation—to obey or disobey his master's command.

Dunkin said, "The dog never looked at the meat. He seemed to feel that if he did, the temptation to disobey would be too great. So he looked steadily at my father's face."

Dunkin then made this spiritual application: "There is a lesson for us all. Always look up to the Master's face." (7)

That dog was smarter than most people I know. Temptation is universal, and some temptations are deadly if they are not reined in. But with God's help, and some-times with the help of a really close friend, temptations are resistible. "Turn your eyes upon Jesus, look full in his wonderful face; then the things of earth will grow strangely dim in the light of his glory and grace." (8)

1. http://www.lectionarysermons.com/zun1l.html.
2. Dan Fowler,
http://www.fortbraggpresbyterian.org/html/sermons/sermon2-13-05.html.
3. Quoted in The Minister's Manual for 2000, p. 167. Cited in a sermon by Dr. Mickey Anders.
4. http://www.boydspc.org/sermons/20070304Philippians3,17-4,1.pdf.
5. Pat Croce, with Bill Lyon. I Feel Great, and You Will Too! (Philadelphia: Running Press, 2000), pp. 97-98.
6. MONDAY FODDER, http://family-safe-mail.com/.
7. Rev. Adrian Dieleman, http://www.trinitycrc.org/sermons/jam1v13-18.html.
8. Lyrics by Helen H. Lemmel.

When We Are Uncertain About The Future
Genesis 15:1-12, 17-18

A young man tells of visiting a college, which had a series of security call boxes every few hundred feet or so. If you were wandering around the campus at night and felt uneasy about somebody following you, for instance, you could hit the button and have a security officer come investigate immediately.

On one of these phones hung a sign that said, "Out of Order."

Underneath it someone had scrawled. . . "Keep Running!" (1)

Fear is a powerful emotion, isn't it?

It's like the story of the Bishop who had an irrational fear that his legs were going to become paralyzed. One night while he was at a dinner party he reached down and pinched his leg. He couldn't feel anything. He was alarmed. Out loud he exclaimed, "Oh, no. It is just as I feared. I am totally without feeling below my waist."

A lady sitting next to him turned and smiled. "If it's any comfort your grace," she said, "the leg you pinched was mine." (2)

All kinds of things can hit our panic button. We've commented before on how many times the words "Fear not!" appear in the scriptures. It is one of the most common expressions in the sacred Word. The very first time God says "Fear not" to anyone in the Bible is in our lesson for today from Genesis. It comes at an interesting time.

Abram, or Abraham as he would later be known, has returned from a tremendous military victory over four kings from Mesopotamia. These kings had banded together for the purpose of military conquest and had kidnapped Abram's nephew Lot. Abram is not only successful on the battlefield against these four kings and their armies, but he is beginning to acquire both wealth and stature in this new land to which God has called him. Still, in spite of all his accomplishments, his heart is uncertain—uncertain about his future and uncertain about the God who had called him.

Do you know what that is like? Is anyone here uncertain about your future, maybe even downright worried? It is not unreasonable in today's world. Some of you have been saving for your retirement. You've known that Social Security would not provide enough income to take you for the rest of your life. So you have been saving. You have been investing. But the rates on Money Market accounts have been almost nonexistent the last few years. And the Stock Market has been wildly erratic. The value of your home equity took a tremendous hit a few years back and it still has not made it back to the plus side of the ledger. And so you are becoming fearful. How will you ever keep up with the pace of inflation? Does anybody know what I'm talking about?

One reason Abram was uncertain was because he and his wife were childless. Some of you know that heartache. It is a very difficult human condition to go through at any time in history. But for people in the ancient world, childlessness was particularly difficult. This was an agrarian society. Children were needed many times to help gather crops or tend animals. Children were the means of carrying on the family line and preserving the family inheritance. Even more important, not having children made people very vulnerable in their old age with no one to care for them. And there would be no one to look after the funeral rites when you died, rites that were seen to secure your soul's rest in the life to come. Not having a child and thus an heir weighed heavily on Abram and his wife, Sarai. Some of you know their pain.

Of course, some of you HAVE children and that weighs on you in its own way. It's not easy having a family in today's world.

A man, submitting information to his income tax preparer, was asked how many dependents he had. "Eight," he replied.

The preparer asked, "Would you mind repeating that?"

The man replied, "Not if I can help it." (3)

Children are a source of many joys. They are also a source of many sleepless nights. What kind of future will our children have? Will they be safe? Will they resist certain temptations? What kind of world will they inherit?

Abram was uncertain about his future. Everyone in this room can relate to him, regardless of your age or station in life. For teenagers, it might be the uncertainty of moving to a new school. Will the students there accept me? For those getting near to the end of high school, it might be, "Will I get accepted at the college of my choice?" And for those getting ready to enter the work force, "What kind of job can I possibly get in today's economy?"

It doesn't get any easier in adulthood. "What if the company lays me off? The people I'm working with seem to get younger and younger. Do they look at me as an old fossil, no longer able to hack it? My family seems to be coming apart. What if I end up alone?"

And then there are the trials of the aging. "How long will my health hold out? Can I make it without being a burden to my children?"

I had better quit before all of us are depressed, but this is life. Abram was uncertain about his future, and all of us have been there or will be there, sooner or later.

Every person of every age and station knows what it is to be afraid. Anxiety has been called "the official emotion of our age" and it can be an awful emotion.

The word "anxiety" comes from the Greek word ananke, meaning "throat" or "to press together." Ananke was the name of the Greek god of constraint who presided over slavery. Ananke was the word used for the yokes or rings on the necks of slaves.

The connection between the words ananke and anxiety are obvious. Anxiety can hold us back, take us by the throat, and chain us like a slave. Other words from the same root include the German word "angst" which means a general dread and the Latin word "angere" which means to choke or strangle, as well as the English word "angina" which means the tight sensation in the chest that accompanies dread. (4)

Fear is a universal emotion. Of course, some people have more to fear than others.

Mother Teresa once told about a child she picked up from the street. She could tell from the child's face that she was hungry. Mother Teresa didn't know how many days it had been since that little one had eaten. So she gave her a piece of bread, and the child took the bread and, crumb by crumb, started eating it.

Mother Teresa said to her, "Eat, eat the bread. You are hungry."

And the little one looked at her and said, "I am afraid. When the bread will be finished, I will be hungry again." (5)

Compared to that little girl, most of our problems are inconsequential. You know that, don't you? Most of the fears that most of us have are really overblown. Most of us are not going to end up homeless. We're not going to starve to death. Over eating is our major concern. Most of us are not going to contract a fatal illness anyway soon.

Knowledge, however, is not always a cure for fear. I can give you all kinds of accurate information about the things of which you are afraid, but it might not help you overcome your fears.

For example, neuroscientist Richard Restak notes that the odds are 94,900,000 to 1 that a shark will attack you. The odds for drowning are much worse, 225,000 to 1. In other words, it is hundreds of times more likely that you will drown compared to getting bit by a shark. However, when you go to the beach, which do you worry most about—drowning or a shark attack? Some of us still hear the theme from the motion picture Jaws whenever we venture out deep. Even when we know that our fears are overblown, many of us are afraid. Of course, a little bit of knowledge can even increase our fears.

I understand this was true of the great scientist Louis Pasteur. Once Pasteur discovered the germ theory of disease he began to realize that germs are in the air and on everything you touch. And, in Pasteur's time there was no such thing as antibiotics.

Through pasteurization, the process Pasteur developed, he discovered he could remove bacteria from milk. However, humankind was still at the mercy of invisible killers like strep and staph infections, and the bacteria and viruses that cause diseases like anthrax, cholera, and rabies. Extensive use of antibiotics was still a century away.

Pasteur's discovery that germs were everywhere haunted him. He became obsessed with contamination and cleanliness. He compulsively washed and re-washed his hands—he even washed the bar of soap! He refused to shake hands with anyone. If anyone managed to grab his hand to shake it, Pasteur immediately rushed to a sink. His fear of germs became almost a paranoia. It affected his eating habits and it was a constant problem for his family.

During the Franco-Prussian War, Pasteur's son, Jean-Baptiste served in the French army. Jean-Baptiste was stationed in an army hospital. Pasteur actually wrote to his son's commanding officer requesting that Jean-Baptiste be sent to the frontline and away from the contagion in the hospital. In Pasteur's mind, flying bullets on the frontline were safer than sleeping beside all those germ-ridden sick and wounded men.

Of course, he may have been partly right. Even today people in hospitals are at risk from bacteria, especially super-bugs. Pasteur's fears were not totally groundless. (6)

I would like to say that knowledge is a powerful weapon against fear, but that is not altogether true. Actually I know of only two ways to deal with fear.

The first is to face up to your fears. That is what researchers have discovered in trying to help people with phobias. They call it Exposure Therapy—carefully exposing people to the very thing they most dread can help them overcome their fears.

The problem is that so few people seek help; most of us prefer trying to avoid the thing that awakens terror within us. "Your instincts tell you to escape or avoid," says one psychologist who has done extensive work in this field, "but what you really need to do is face down the fear." (7)

Have you ever known someone who was afraid of going to the doctor because of fear they were sick and they didn't want to have their fears confirmed? How counter-productive. Get into the doctor's office. You may not be nearly as sick as you think and if you are, for heaven's sake, begin treatment. Running away from your fears is a terrible way to cope with them.

In 1972 David Miln Smith spent a night alone in St. Michael's Cave on the island of Gibraltar as a test of his courage. In his book Hug the Monster he tells of hearing strange sounds all around him as he lay there in the pitch-black, damp, deserted cave. Most frightening was the fear that he was not alone!

His fear turned to panic. He was afraid he was losing his mind. Then suddenly, as he was approaching his psychological breaking point, Smith thought to himself, "Whatever the monster looks like, I will hug it." "That simple, almost silly thought brought great relief to his restless mind. He soon fell into a deep and peaceful sleep until morning. He learned that embracing his fear, literally or figuratively, allowed him to subdue it."

The next time you're afraid, try "hugging the monster," says author Steve Goodier. "Face that fear head-on, whatever it is, and embrace it. You may be surprised at how quickly it slips away and at how confident you begin to feel. Like . . . Eleanor Roosevelt once said, 'You gain strength, courage, and confidence by every experience in which you stop to look fear in the face.'" (8)

That's the first way of conquering your fear: face it. The second is, fall back on your faith. "The word of the Lord came to Abram in a vision: 'Do not be afraid, Abram. I am your shield, your very great reward.'" After hearing Abram's statement of uncertainty over his childless state, God takes him outside and says, "Look up at the sky and count the stars—if indeed you can count them." Then he said to him, "So shall your offspring be." And the writer of Genesis records, "Abram believed the Lord . . ." That's a life-changing statement of faith: "Abram believed the Lord . . ."

Do you believe the Lord? Do you trust Him? Sometimes mistaken ideas about faith and about God can cause us to be afraid.

A pastor recounted how as a child he sat through many long and boring worship services. He says he couldn't help envying his unchurched friends.

One Sunday, he slipped out of church and went to the local candy store where he spent his offering on Tootsie rolls. He returned to church just in time to hear the sermon about Ananias and Sapphira. Do you remember that story? In the book of Acts we're told how Ananias and Sapphira lied about their offering and were struck dead because of it.

Going home this little boy prayed fervently and passionately for forgiveness for spending his offering on candy. He stayed up all night chanting, "I love Jesus, I love Jesus," in hopes that this would convince God to spare his life. (9)

It is sad that our faith, rather than giving us comfort, can sometimes add to our distress. As a child that pastor had not yet experienced the love and comfort that God would one day bring into his life. So he was afraid. A mature faith understands that though life is difficult, we are never beyond God's loving and gracious care.

Dr. Thomas G. Long tells of talking to a minister of a church in a dangerous part of the city. This pastor said he was always amazed by a certain woman, a member of his church, who seemed to have no fear about coming to meetings and services at the church at night, even though she had no car and would have to walk home through the dark and frightening streets.

One night, after a prayer service at which this woman had been present, the minister was locking up the church, and he happened to see her walking from the church down the street toward her apartment. As she walked, she was holding her hand out, as if some unseen companion were walking with her and holding her hand, and as she walked, she was humming a familiar spiritual, "Precious Lord, take my hand, lead me on. Hold my hand, lest I fall. Take my hand, precious Lord, lead me home." (10)

Was she afraid? Yes, she was. Did she let her fear defeat her? No! She faced her fear and fell back on her faith. She trusted God. Perhaps she looked up, as Abram did, and counted the stars. Of course, not very many stars show up over a large city. But there are enough, enough to remind us that God is with us. It's a good song for all of us to sing as we walk through life: "Precious Lord, take my hand, lead me on. Hold my hand, lest I fall. Take my hand, precious Lord, lead me home."

1. MONDAY FODDER, http://family-safe-mail.com/

2. Denn Guptill, http://www.sermoncentral.com/sermons/forget-it-denn-guptill-sermon-on-new-years-day-100382.asp?page=3.

3. Mikey's Funnies, subscribe at http://www.mikeysfunnies.com/sub/index.html.

4. Peter L. Steinke, Congregational Leadership in Anxious Times: Being Calm and Courageous No Matter What [Kindle Edition].

5. No Greater Love (Novato, CA: New World Library California, 1989), p. 97.

6. Uncle John's Bathroom Reader Plunges into Great Lives (San Diego: Portable Press, 2003), p. 272.

7. Stephen Arterburn, Flash Points (Wheaton, IL: Tyndale House Publishers, Inc., 2002), p. 167.

8. (Kansas City: Andrews and McMeel, 1996). Cited by Steve Goodier, http://www.lifesupportsystem.com.

9. Jerry Ruff, http://www.sumcnj.com/sermons/srm2003/Sermon07.13.03.htm.

10. http://day1.org/481-called_by_name.

When The Drought Gets Really Bad
Isaiah 55:1-9

In a book titled God's Little Devotional Book there is a delightful story of a great drought that struck Baghdad during the reign of Abdullah the Third. Moslem leaders in the land issued a decree that all the faithful should offer prayers for rain. Still, the drought continued.

The Jews were then permitted to add their prayers to those of the Moslems. Their prayers didn't seem to do the job either.

Finally when the drought resulted in widespread famine, the Christians in the land were asked to pray. Almost immediately, the heavens opened and rain began falling.

The leaders of the Moslem Conclave were alarmed that the rain started when it did. Feeling that some explanation was necessary, they issued this statement to the masses: "The God of our Prophet was highly gratified by the prayers of the faithful which were as sweet-smelling savors to Him. He refused their requests in order to prolong the pleasure of listening to their prayers; but the prayers of those Christian infidels were an abomination to Him, and He granted their petitions the sooner to be rid of their loathsome importunities." (1)

Well, that's one explanation, I suppose.

In a book called, Blame It on the Weather there is another delightful drought related anecdote. This happened at the beginning of a major drought that extended all over North America in 1988. A meteorologist at the brokerage firm Smith Barney Inc. in Chicago, Jon Davis, inadvertently created quite a stir on the Chicago Stock Exchange when he wore his trench coat outside for a cup of coffee. Davis told The Wall Street Journal that he had to walk past the traders on the exchange floor to get out of his office at Smith Barney. When the traders saw the company's meteorologist wearing a trench coat, they figured this was some kind of secret signal that the weather would break and start raining, so they started selling the market. In fact, Davis explained, it was a cool day in May and he'd put the coat on because it was chilly. (2) It's a crazy world.

One more drought-related story, but this one has a serious point to it.

Bestselling author Andy Andrews tells about a tribe of Aboriginal rainmakers in Australia who were 100% successful in making it rain. Now, Aboriginals are known for their rain dances, but some tribes were more successful than others, and word got around that this particular tribe was always able to make it rain. When the white communities were in trouble due to drought, they began to call this particular tribe to do their rain dance.

On one such occasion, the leader of the white community went to the king of this renowned group and asked, "Why is it that every single time you dance, it rains?"

The king replied, "It's very simple, actually. We dance until it rains." (3)

That's a good lesson, not in magic, but in perseverance.

Droughts have always been with us. The worst famine in recorded history occurred in China from 1876-1879. This drought destroyed food crops, resulting in the deaths of approximately 13 million people. (4)

Droughts will always be with us. Much of our nation was afflicted with a terrible drought in 2012 and climatologists tell us this is only the beginning of many more weather related adverse events which we will experience in the future. These droughts will be accompanied by severe shortages of drinking water. Experts warn us that stealing water is set to be one of the defining crimes of the twenty-first century. Half the world's population is likely to be living in water-stressed regions by 2025 and some countries could be in very serious trouble. (5) That's scary if you think about it. What happens if we run out of water?

The people of Israel knew about droughts. They lived in a land where water was a precious commodity. So Isaiah the prophet spoke to a receptive audience when he wrote, "Come, all you who are thirsty, come to the waters; and you who have no money, come, buy and eat! Come, buy wine and milk without money and without cost. Why spend money on what is not bread, and your labor on what does not satisfy? Listen, listen to me, and eat what is good, and you will delight in the richest of fare. Give ear and come to me; listen, that you may live . . ."

Isaiah is speaking to Israel in behalf of God. He's not writing about physical thirst, of course. He is writing about spiritual thirst, and he gives the people some clues why their lives are spiritually parched.

On a more contemporary note, author Joseph Campbell once said about his friends, that they were living what he called "Waste Land lives . . . that they just are baffled; they're wandering in the Waste Land without any sense of where the water is—the source that makes things green." Spiritual thirst didn't end in Isaiah's time. It is still with us today.

Isaiah says that the people become spiritually thirsty, first of all, when they have misplaced values. "Come, buy wine and milk without money and without cost," he writes. "Why spend money on what is not bread, and your labor on what does not satisfy? Listen, listen to me, and eat what is good, and you will delight in the richest of fare." That is at the heart of the people's problem, says Isaiah. They are spending their money and their time on that which will never permanently satisfy them. That's true of people in every generation.

In one of her books, Annie Dillard writes of the ill-fated Franklin expedition. In 1845, Sir John Franklin and 138 officers and men embarked from England on two large sailing vessels to find the Northwest Passage across the high Canadian Arctic to the Pacific Ocean. Each vessel carried an auxiliary steam engine and a twelve-day supply of coal for the entire voyage, which was projected to take two or three years. Instead of additional coal each ship made room for a 1,200 volume library, a hand organ playing fifty tunes, china place settings for officers and men, cut-glass wine goblets, and sterling silver flatware. The expedition carried no special clothing for the Arctic, only the uniforms of Her Majesty's Navy. (6) That was a sad, sad mistake.

Not long after the expedition entered the Arctic waters, the two ships became trapped in ice off King William Island. Many of the crew members perished onboard ship, including Franklin. The remaining crew began walking on the ice toward the Canadian mainland. They did not make it. They all perished including two officers who set out pulling a large sled. They traveled more than 65 miles across the treacherous ice with this heavy load in tow. When rescuers found their bodies, they discovered that the sled was filled with table silver.

They gave their lives for a sled full of forks, knives and spoons! How absurd. No matter how much that sled was worth it wasn't worth their lives. But people make that mistake. Parents neglect their children in search of the almighty dollar. Spouses neglect one another. We trade our health, we trade our integrity, we lose our souls searching after that which can never really satisfy.

Reverend Jim Pye tells a contrasting story about a lady in Northern Ireland who was much wiser than this. She was having a series of prayer meetings at her house. She invited her neighbor who was of a different faith to come. The neighbor felt she couldn't come. However, after the first meeting the neighbor inquired how the prayer service had gone. The woman replied, "Oh wonderful. We had thirty-five in my little cottage and it was full."

A week later they had a similar conversation. "We had fifty-one in my little cottage," said the woman this time, "and it was full. The final meeting is next week. You would be welcome to come."

The neighbor did not come, but still inquired how the final meeting had gone. "Marvelous. We had sixty-two and my little cottage was full."

The neighbor said, "You know this is impossible. How can you have had 35 the first week and it was full, 51 the next week and it was full, and 62 yesterday and it was full again?"

"Oh, it's quite simple," said this lady, "We simply got rid of every piece of furniture and put them in the garden. We emptied the house of everything that cluttered it up, and it was filled with people." (7)

Furniture wasn't important, in this lady's estimation, people were. Table silver wasn't important, but two officers of a frozen ship gave their lives trying to take it with them. People become spiritually thirsty when they have misplaced values.

People also become spiritually parched when they betray their values. The

Bible's way of saying this is that people become spiritually thirsty when they sin. A few verses further on in this passage we read, "Seek the Lord while he may be found; call on him while he is near. Let the wicked forsake their ways and the unrighteous their thoughts. Let them turn to the Lord, and he will have mercy on them, and to our God, for he will freely pardon . . ."

We don't use the word "wicked" much anymore or the word, "unrighteous." That doesn't mean that people no longer do wicked or unrighteous things, we just use different words to describe them. In today's vernacular, "mistakes were made" or people "were confused." It might help us during this Lenten season to acknowledge that what we are doing is "sinning"—sinning against our family, perhaps, sinning against our neighbor, sinning against ourselves, and ultimately sinning against God.

During the early years of his ministry not long after becoming a Christian, Keith Miller traveled around the country speaking to lots of men's gatherings about the adventure of life with Christ. At one meeting—on impulse—he said, "I have the darndest feeling that I came here to talk to one of you guys." As soon as he sat down he said to himself, "You stupid jerk! Why did you say that?"

After the meeting, a handsome, distinguished man named John came forward. He had tears in his eyes. "I'm the one," he said. They began to talk.

"How did you get here?" Miller asked.

"I'm an attorney," John said. "I travel a lot. I'm married. I don't live in this town . . . but my mistress lives here. I was going to see her. When I got out of my car at her apartment I ran into three guys from my home town. 'Hey, John. What are you doing here?' one of them said.

"Inside I was paralyzed," said John. "I didn't know what to say so I shrugged and said, 'Just passing through.'

"'Fine,' he said, 'Why don't you come with us to hear this Christian businessman named Keith Miller?'

"'Sure,' I said, 'I haven't got anything else to do.' That's how I got here. I heard what you said about being frustrated, pushing your life too hard, and how God is helping you. I realized my life is out of hand and I'm scared."

Keith had a plane to catch, but didn't want to just leave the man. "Would you like to commit your life to Christ, leave this woman and learn to live again?"

"Yes," John said.

"Then tell God where you've been and who you are," said Keith Miller. "Confess. Then tell Christ, 'I give up. Show me how to live because I don't know how anymore.'"

"I'm not sure I can do that," John said.

"Well, can you tell God you want to want to do that?" asked Miller.

"Yes, I can," said John. The two prayed and Keith Miller left.

They kept corresponding over the next year. John was changing. He was doing loving things for his family, church, and community. He was talking to people about what was happening in his life. John lived in a town of 10,000 people. He wrote one day and asked Keith to come and give a talk to some of his friends about Christianity.

John picked Keith up at the airport. "People keep asking me how I became a Christian," John told Keith. "I don't know what to say."

"I don't know what I can do, but I'm glad to see you, and we'll give it a try." Keith said.

As they entered the church and approached the sanctuary, he heard the muffled sound of singing. The minister met them and said, "I want to tell you, Mr. Miller, I don't know what you did for John, but he has changed my life."

Keith was taken aback by those words, but not as much as by what he saw when he entered the sanctuary . . . the faces of John's friends who wanted to know what happened to him . . . all 800 of them. (8)

John's life was changed in a dramatic and beneficial way. But first he had to acknowledge his sin. He had to ask God's help in beginning again. "Let the wicked forsake their ways and the unrighteous their thoughts. Let them turn to the Lord, and he will have mercy on them, and to our God, for he will freely pardon." People are thirsty because of misplaced values. People are thirsty because they have betrayed their values.

Finally, people are spiritually parched because they depend on their own resources. Listen again to the words of Isaiah: "Come, all you who are thirsty, come to the waters; and you who have no money, come, buy and eat! Come, buy wine and milk without money and without cost."

Those words are echoed in Revelation 22:17, "The Spirit and the bride say, 'Come!' And let the one who hears say, 'Come!' Let the one who is thirsty come; and let the one who wishes take the free gift of the water of life."

The resources of God are available to all of us, regardless of who we are or what we've done. They are available and they are free. All we have to do is ask.

There is an old story about a ship that was sailing in those days before radio beacons and it floundered in a hurricane on the coast of South America. The crew began to run out of water. All around was water, but it was salt water and drinking it could be fatal to them. One-by-one they died. The tragedy of this situation was that unknown to them they had travelled into the region of the mouth of the mighty Amazon river. The Amazon River is the largest river in the world. The mouth is 90 miles across. There is more water flowing out of the Amazon than the Yangtze, Mississippi and Nile Rivers combined. So much water comes from the Amazon that they can detect its currents 200 miles out in the Atlantic Ocean. All around these unsuspecting sailors was fresh water. All they had to do was reach down and drink all they needed.

My friend, does that describe your situation? Is your life materially rich but spiritually parched? "Come, buy wine and milk without money and without cost," writes Isaiah. "Why spend money on what is not bread, and your labor on what does not satisfy? Listen, listen to me, and eat what is good, and you will delight in the richest of fare." You will live in a Waste Land no more.

1. (Tulsa: Honor Books, Inc., 1973), p. 163.

2. David Phillips, Michael Parfit, Suzanne Chisholm (San Diego: Advantage Publishers Group, 1998), p. 203.

3. Mastering the Seven Decisions that Determine Personal Success (Nashville: Thomas Nelson, 2008).

4. Guinness World Records 2004, edited by Claire Folkard, et. al. (Guinness World Records Limited, 2003), p. 70.

5. Richard Watson, Future Files: A Brief History of the Next 50 Years (Kindle edition).

6. Annie Dillard, Teaching a Stone to Talk (New York: Harper and Row, 1988) pp. 24-26

7. http://www.sermonsplus.co.uk/Ephesians%205.15 20.htm

8. Rev. David Bibbee, http://www.eccob.com/sermons/1997/sr970803.htm.

When We Feel Lost
Luke 15:1-3, 11b-32

A certain aged Catholic priest had become deaf. So members of his parish would write out their sins on a piece of paper before going to confession.

One day, a parishioner slipped a piece of paper to the priest which read, "Two loaves of bread, a gallon of milk, a box of detergent and a pound of bananas."

The puzzled priest scanned the note, then passed it back to the parishioner. The parishioner looked at the note, then exclaimed with horror, "Oh, no! I've left my sins at the grocery store."

Well, where did you leave your sins? Where should we leave them? How can we be rid of our sins forever? The answer, of course, is repentance, which means, in essence, "turn around; go home." Repentance is what the prodigal son did. He turned around and went back home. That's the best way to rid yourself of sin.

George Buttrick, one of the greatest preachers America has produced, has said that Jesus' parable of the Prodigal Son captures "the essence of the Christian faith." It is a story of repentance and forgiveness and grace. It is also, however, a story of self-righteousness, resentment and anger. It has a very familiar beginning, "There was a man who had two sons." So, from the beginning, we are introduced to three characters.

The first, of course, is the prodigal. He's the younger boy. Adventurous. Rebellious. Determined to learn life's lessons by making his own mistakes. Some of you can identify with him. You've been there.

In Jesus' story the younger son says to his father, "Father, give me my share of the estate." So the father divides his property between his two sons and the younger one sets off for a distant country and there squanders his wealth in wild living. After all his wealth is gone there's a severe famine in the country, and this young man's in trouble. He's hungry. So he hires himself to a local farmer who sends him to his fields to feed pigs, which is the worst job in the world for a good Jewish boy. He is so hungry, Luke tells us, he would gladly have eaten the pods that the pigs are eating.

Finally, Luke tells us, "He comes to himself." He heads back home with his tail between his legs. He is hungry and hurting. Home is starting to look awfully good. However, is he truly penitent or is he simply posing, play-acting, so he can worm himself back into his father's good graces? We don't know. Since this is a parable and not a real life incident, there is no follow-up. We can only imagine that he is heading home for good.

Or maybe not! Some of you may know a young person who has become involved with drugs. The first thing to go is their truthfulness. Many parents today know what it is to have a young person on drugs come back home, confess their sins, vow to do better, and then not only leave again but steal money on the way back out the door. In these cases, a parent asks, "How many times am I supposed to forgive? How many times do I let him come back home?"

Some prodigals repent many times, but never really come home.

It's like one of Garrison Keillor's stories from Pastor Ingfest's Lutheran Church in Lake Wobegon. "Larry Sorenson was back at the Lutheran Church," Keillor writes. "Larry the Sad Boy, who was saved twelve times in the Lutheran Church, an all-time record. Between 1953 and 1961, he threw himself weeping and contrite on God's throne of grace on twelve separate occasions—and this in a Lutheran Church that wasn't evangelical, had no altar calls, no organist playing 'Just as I am without one plea' while the choir hummed. Larry Sorenson came forward weeping buckets and crumpled up at the communion rail, to the amazement of the minister, who had just delivered a dry sermon on stewardship, and who now had to put his arm around this limp, saggy individual and pray with him and see if he had a ride home. Twelve times. Granted," says Garrison Keillor, "we're born in original sin and are worthless and vile, but twelve conversions is too many. There comes a point where you should dry your tears, and join the building committee and start grappling with the problems of the church furnace and the church roof and make church coffee and be of use, but Larry just kept on repenting and repenting." (1)

Let's assume the young man in Jesus' parable is truly penitent. Let's assume he's ready to "join the building committee and start grappling with the problems of the church furnace and the church roof and make church coffee and be of use . . ." We can sympathize with him. He's learned some hard lessons, but at least he is back home. Most of all, he's learned how lonesome it can be when you turn your back on those who love you. He is headed home. He has done wrong. He has repented. Now he is headed toward the safety of his father's house. The prodigal is the first character in this remarkable story.

The second character is his father.

The young man has rehearsed what he is going to say to his father. "I will set out and go back to my father and say to him: 'Father, I have sinned against heaven and against you. I am no longer worthy to be called your son; make me like one of your hired servants.' So he got up and went to his father. But while he was still a long way off, his father saw him and was filled with compassion for him; he ran to his son, threw his arms around him and kissed him.

"The son said to him, 'Father, I have sinned against heaven and against you. I am no longer worthy to be called your son.'

"But the father said to his servants, 'Quick! Bring the best robe and put it on him. Put a ring on his finger and sandals on his feet. Bring the fattened calf and kill it. Let's have a feast and celebrate. For this son of mine was dead and is alive again; he was lost and is found.' So they began to celebrate."

The father, of course, represents God. God in all His grace and love. Helmut Thielicke says this parable ought to be called the Parable of the Waiting Father rather than the Parable of the Prodigal Son. Everything depends on God's grace.

In the magnificent Hermitage, the palace of Catherine the Great in St. Petersburg, Russia, there is a fascinating painting by the Dutch artist Rembrandt called, "The Return of the Prodigal Son." Some have called this work the greatest picture ever painted.

In Rembrandt's painting based on Jesus' parable, the son has returned home after wasting his inheritance and falling into poverty and despair. He kneels before his father in repentance, wishing for forgiveness and a renewed place in the family. Standing at his right is his older brother, who crosses his hands in judgment.

The most fascinating aspect of this painting is the portrayal of the father's hands as he bends over to embrace his penitent son. It is said that the hands of the father were one of the last things Rembrandt painted just before he died.

The father's left hand is not surprising. It is a strong, masculine hand, the kind of hand that you expect this farmer/father to have. But the right hand is much different. It is smaller. It is the soft feminine hand of a woman. Think of the significance of that—one figure but with noticeably different hands—one masculine, the other feminine.

Father Henri Nouwen noticed the difference between these two hands. He wrote a book also titled, Return of the Prodigal Son, in which he comments on Rembrandt's painting. He writes: "As soon as I recognized the difference between the two hands of the father, a new world of meaning opened up for me. The Father is not simply a great patriarch. He is mother as well as father. He touches the son with a masculine hand and a feminine hand. He holds, and she caresses. He confirms and she consoles. He is, indeed, God, in whom both manhood and womanhood, fatherhood and motherhood, are fully present. That gentle and caressing right hand echoes for me the words of the prophet Isaiah: 'Can a woman forget her baby at the breast, feel no pity for the child she has borne?'" (2) We moderns are conscious of masculine and feminine images of God, but Rembrandt was hundreds of years ahead of us.

I thought of Father Nouwen's analysis of this great painting when I read evangelist Franklin Graham's story about his own return home after living as somewhat of a prodigal. He tells his story in his book Rebel with a Cause.

Franklin Graham is, of course, the son of the world's most famous evangelist Billy Graham. By his own admission, Franklin was a rebel; in fact, he openly opposed every value and every virtue his parents stood for, including the Christian faith. He smoked, he drank, he cursed, he caroused; he did it all. But no scene in his book is more poignant than the day that Franklin Graham was kicked out of a conservative college in Texas for taking a co-ed off campus for the weekend and piloting a rented plane to Florida. He writes: "The drive home from Texas was dreary. Maybe by driving slow I was prolonging the inevitable; I would have to face my parents. I knew they had to be disappointed in me—I was! They had invested a lot of money in my education, and now I'd messed up.

"I drove through the gate and started up the road to our home, imagining the lecture my parents would give me. So many other times when I had come home I could hardly wait to say hello to everyone. But no joy this time. I felt so badly when I finally reached the house. Then I saw mama standing on the front porch and I wanted to run and hide in the nearest hole. It was one of the few times I can remember not wanting to look her in the eye.

"When I walked up to her, my body felt limp. I barely had the nerve to lift my head or extend my arms for a hug. But I didn't need to. Mama wrapped her arms around me, and, with a smile, she said, 'Welcome home, Franklin.'" (3)

Rembrandt knew that a gracious God could be portrayed as a loving mom or dad.

There has been a long-running controversy in Christian circles over inclusive language, especially for the person of God. Is God a male? Of course not! Is a God female? No. God is spirit. Maleness and femaleness are characteristics of physical, created beings. God encompasses the best characteristics of both sexes. Most important of all, however, God's character is one of unconditional love.

But there is a third character in the story, the elder brother. His story is so different from that of his brother. The elder brother didn't go into the far country. He didn't lose his inheritance, didn't live among pigs. He stayed home . . . did what was expected of him. He was obedient to a fault. But listen to how he responds to his brother's return: "Meanwhile, the older son was in the field. When he came near the house, he heard music and dancing. So he called one of the servants and asked him what was going on. 'Your brother has come,' he replied, 'and your father has killed the fattened calf because he has him back safe and sound.'

"The older brother became angry and refused to go in. So his father went out and pleaded with him. But he answered his father, 'Look! All these years I've been slaving for you and never disobeyed your orders. Yet you never gave me even a young goat so I could celebrate with my friends. But when this son of yours who has squandered your property with prostitutes comes home, you kill the fattened calf for him!'"

Notice how he refers to his relationship with his father. He says, "All these years I've been slaving for ,you . . ." Those are revealing words. Not "working for you" or "serving you" or "helping with the family farm." No, he says he was "slaving for his father." Pastor Tim Keller calls this "duty without beauty." Notice how he refers to his brother: "But when this son of yours . . . comes home." He can't ever refer to him as his brother, but as "this son of yours."

The father seeks to set him straight. "My son," his father says, "you are always with me, and everything I have is yours. But we had to celebrate and be glad, because this brother of yours was dead and is alive again; he was lost and is found." Notice that the father reminds the elder son, first of all, that the prodigal is his brother! Sometimes that happens to those who are so eager to condemn those who are weaker and have given into temptation. They are still our brothers and sisters.

The elder son peers with critical eyes and a cold unforgiving heart at both his brother who has broken all the rules and his father, so eager to welcome his wayward son back home. The elder brother is spiteful, angry, resentful. And some of us understand that. We sometimes wonder why God bends over backward to welcome back the wayward and seems to ignore those of us who have always played by the rulebook. It is hard for us to accept that Jesus sees more hope in the much-deserved humility of the prodigal than the self-righteous indignation of his brother. And yet it is important that we do hear Jesus' message.

We sometimes read this parable and consign the elder brother to the supporting cast, a minor character in the narrative. The truth is, Jesus may have intended for him to be the central character in the story. Remember who Jesus is telling this parable to. It is the religious leaders of the day. The first two verses of the chapter tell us that. We read, "Now the tax collectors and sinners were all gathering around to hear Jesus. But the Pharisees and the teachers of the law muttered, 'This man welcomes sinners and eats with them.'"

The story of the prodigal is intended to give hope to the tax collectors and the sinners. But it is a devastating judgment on the attitudes and actions of the scribes and Pharisees. For you see, they are the elder brother in Jesus' parable—keeping the Law, but looking with disdain upon those not as righteous as they. And friends, that is how the church appears to many people in our society today.

Joseph Stowell, President of Moody Bible Institute, began a message on the parable of the Prodigal Son with these words: "I have never known a time when Christians have been more mad about more things than we are now . . . We're angry about values, politics, television, media, education, the violation of the unborn, condoms and criminals . . . We're shouting more . . . we're shooting at doctors of abortion clinics . . . Publicly we are perceived to be long on madness and short on mercy . . . We've become grumbling warriors instead of committed seekers."

You know what he's talking about, don't you? And such attitudes are making it more and more difficult for us to reach people, especially young people, with the message of Christ.

Three characters: the penitent prodigal; his loving and gracious parent representing God; and his smug, self-righteous brother. If you are the prodigal, come home. It's not too late. If you are the elder brother, also please come home. I know it is harder for you to see your sin than it is for your weaker brother or your sister, but your sin of self-righteousness may be the most deadly sin of all. Come home to the waiting arms of the Father.

1. George F. Woodward, http://www.saintedmunds.org/sermons/doc/Dec17th2006.htm.
2. (New York: Doubleday, 1992).
3. Steven Molin, http://www.lectionary.org/Sermons/Molin/OT/Isaiah%2043.01-7,%20We'rePrecious.htm.

When We Don't Know God
Philippians 3:4b-14

In one of his books, writer Bruce Wilkinson reminds us of the story of the late Howard Hughes. Wilkinson says that, if there was one word that would describe Hughes' ambition, it was the word more. "He wanted more money, so he invested his enormous inheritance and increased it in just a few years to a billion dollars. He wanted more fame, so he went to Hollywood and became a filmmaker and a star. He wanted more sensual pleasure, so he used his fabulous wealth to buy women and any form of sensual pleasure he desired. He wanted to experience more excitement, so he designed, built, and piloted the fastest aircraft of his time.

"Hughes could dream of anything money could buy—and get it. He firmly believed that more would make him happy." But, of course, it did not. In Wilkinson's words, Hughes confused the pleasure of having more for oneself for the greater joy of giving oneself to something bigger than oneself. "His Dream," says Bruce Wilkinson, "was not significant enough to bring meaning to his life."

And so, in his old age, Hughes became withdrawn. News reports portray him at the end of his life as drug addicted, emaciated and unkempt with decaying teeth and long, twisted fingernails. "But until his death he held onto his destructive dream that more possessions would bring more fulfillment." (1) His misguided quest for more made him one of the most pitiable men on earth.

Let me tell you about another man in search of more. His name was Saul of Tarsus. Does anybody remember him? Of course you do. Saul of Tarsus became St. Paul the Apostle, but before his conversion on the road to Damascus, he also was in quest of more. In his case, his quest was more religion.

Listen to his words in our lesson for today: "If anyone else thinks he has reasons to put confidence in the flesh, I have more: circumcised on the eighth day, of the people of Israel, of the tribe of Benjamin, a Hebrew of Hebrews; in regard to the law, a Pharisee; as for zeal, persecuting the church; as for legalistic righteousness, faultless . . ."

Before his conversion, Saul was the epitome of religiosity. "If anyone else thinks he has reasons to put confidence in the flesh," he writes, "I have more . . ." Then he goes on to list his superlative religious qualifications: Circumcised on the eighth day as a part of the people of Israel, the most religious people on earth, God's own people. And of the Israelites Paul was the most religious of the religious. In his own words, "a Hebrew of Hebrews; in regard to the law, a Pharisee; as for zeal, persecuting the church; as for legalistic righteousness, faultless." Saul was super-religious—even to the point of persecuting early Christians. Do super-religious people ever persecute people who don't think as they think? Boy, do they! Saul was super-religious. But it is clear, something important, indeed something critical, was missing from his life.

Saul sounds somewhat like John Wesley, the founder of the Methodists, in his early years. Following his studies at Oxford, Wesley, the son of an Anglican pastor, became a pastor himself. He was a rigorous student, careful in his orthodoxy. He lived a devout life, a life of good works. He and his friends visited prisons, provided slum children with food, clothes, even an education. They observed Saturday as the Sabbath as well as Sunday. They gave alms, studied diligently and fasted regularly. At Oxford they were known as the Holy Club. Then, as if that were not enough, Wesley became a missionary to save the heathen in Georgia. [This was 200 years ago.]

But John Wesley wondered inwardly if anyone would ever save him. At this point in his life he was super religious and smugly self-righteous, but deep in his heart he knew something was missing from his life too. At a place called Aldersgate, however, Wesley felt his heart "strangely warmed" and he began to trust not his diligent good works but Christ alone for his salvation.

As for Saul of Tarsus, he met Christ on the road to Damascus, but he also suddenly realized that all of his religiosity meant nothing. Later he would write in our lesson for today, "I consider everything a loss compared to the surpassing greatness of knowing Christ Jesus my Lord, for whose sake I have lost all things. I consider them rubbish, that I may gain Christ and be found in him, not having a righteousness of my own that comes from the law, but that which is through faith in Christ— the righteousness that comes from God and is by faith. I want to know Christ and the power of his resurrection and the fellowship of sharing in his sufferings, becoming like him in his death, and so, somehow, to attain to the resurrection from the dead."

Saul's experience leads us to two critical questions: first, what is the difference between being religious and knowing God. And secondly, how can we know God today? Obviously, these are huge questions to address in one brief message, but let's go with them as far as we are able.

First of all, what is the difference between being religious and knowing God? We ask this only because of the experience of devout believers like St. Paul and John Wesley and many, many other devoted saints down through the ages who came to a point in their lives when they realized that, in the words of Isaiah, their religion and their righteousness were like filthy garments (Isaiah 64:6).

When Dr. Jack McKinney was pastor of First Baptist Church of Bethesda, Maryland, he preached a sermon on our lesson for the day in which he paraphrased Paul's words. He saw a parallel in his own life and used contemporary terminology. He interpreted Paul's word like this:

"If anyone thinks they have a birthright in the church, let him come talk to me. I was born in the church. Cradle roll from day one. I wasn't a week old when

I attended my first church potluck . . . I memorized the Ten Commandments when I was six. I memorized the Beatitudes when I was seven. I memorized the Sermon on the Mount when I was ten. I not only knew the rules at an early age, I kept them. No drinking, no chewing, no dancing. I had perfect Sunday school attendance for seventeen straight years, and it would have been longer if the doctor hadn't insisted that the flu was not something I needed to share with my sisters and brothers in Christ.

"(But) I woke up one day and realized that . . . my strict adherence to the rules meant little to me. I was always striving to be good, to be the best, to be righteous, but I was constantly frustrated with my failures . . . Everything that I have tried to do in my life to make God like me now seems so worthless. I was striving to will myself into being a person worthy of God's love and all the while God was trying to tell me that I was already loved.

"I've thrown away the rulebook and stopped keeping count of my wins and losses as a Christian. I'm trying to live in a free, loving relationship with Christ my Lord, who calls me to follow him, not just a set of commandments . . ." (2)

Dr. McKinney's discovery was an honest one. When you seek to be religious, you have a tendency to focus on rituals, rules and regulations, not upon the more pressing business of your relationship with your neighbor and your relationship with God. Rituals, rules and regulations can be helpful in living out your faith, but they can also become an idol in themselves, so that they actually cause you to despise your neighbor and to ignore the prompting of God toward a deeper sense of God's presence.

Let me give you a concrete example of this, though this may burn just a little.

In his book The Call, Os Guinness tells a story about Dr. Arthur Burns, the former chair of the Federal Reserve Board. Although he was Jewish, Dr. Burns agreed to join a White House Bible Study. Since he was Jewish, the other members of the study were afraid to ask him to pray at the end of their time together.

One day they had a guest leader who didn't know about this unwritten rule. He asked Dr. Burns to pray. To everyone's surprise, Arthur Burns stood up and began to pray, "O God, may the day come when all Muslims will come to know Jesus and when all Jews will come to know Jesus, and when all Christians will come to know Jesus." (3) Oooo, that hurts, doesn't it? But it is true. There are many Christians who do not know Jesus.

Would it surprise you if I said that there have been many super-religious people who have done terrible damage in our world? Think Inquisition. Think Salem witch trials. Think 9-11. How do you know if you know God? Just being religious is not enough. The very best place to hide from God is religion, especially religious fanaticism. So, how do you know? Here is the best answer I can give you: Are you trying your best to live like Jesus? The formula is much maligned—WWJD? What would Jesus do?—but we have no other reliable guide.

What is the best guard against doing horrible things in the name of Jesus? Focus on his character. Can you imagine Jesus condemning someone else because they look different, or talk different, or act different, or even believe different from how you believe? The only times I can think of that he outwardly condemned anyone were his reaction to the moneychangers in the temple who were taking advantage of people in the name of God and his reaction to many of the super-religious Pharisees who professed love for God, but looked down on others.

We sing around the campfire, "They will know we are Christians by our love." Are you Christ-like in how you live your life?

Of course, there were other components to Christ's character besides compassion for the least and the lost. There was Christ's dependence on prayer and his attendance in the synagogue as well as his knowledge of the scriptures. And, of course, his willingness to lay down his life as a sacrifice for all. WWJD covers a lot of territory. However, if there is anything in your life that you cannot imagine being part of Christ's life, then no matter how much scripture you have memorized, how faithful your attendance in church, how sincere your prayer life, probably you do not know God. Particularly, if your heart is filled with hatred and resentment, there is probably not much room there for Christ.

This brings us to our second question: how can you and I come to know God today? And the answer is simple—just say "yes" to God. That's it. There is nothing else you need do. Indeed, that is nothing else you CAN do! Just say yes.

If you want to read your Bible, that's well and good. If you want to get involved in acts of social justice, that's wonderful. If you want to spend hours on your knees, terrific. If you want to make a gift of $100,000 to the church, praise the Lord! [I thought I would just throw that in.] All these are time-honored ways of showing that you love God. But they are not prerequisite to knowing God. Knowing God is simply a matter of saying yes.

Faith is a gift. To know God is simply to say yes to God. God is already running down the driveway, moving through the briars and the brambles of the wilderness, knocking at the door. Just say yes. Pray, "Lord Jesus, come into my life and make me like you." Isn't that what St. Paul is seeking? He writes, "What is more, I consider everything a loss compared to the surpassing greatness of knowing Christ Jesus my Lord, for whose sake I have lost all things. I consider them rubbish, that I may gain Christ and be found in him, not having a righteousness of my own that comes from the law, but that which is through faith in Christ—the righteousness that comes from God and is by faith. I want to know Christ and the power of his resurrection and the fellowship of sharing in his sufferings, becoming like him in his death, and so, somehow, to attain to the resurrection from the dead."

Paul wants to be like Jesus, even to the point of suffering like Jesus. And he did suffer for his faith. Most of us will not have that privilege. It amuses me to hear affluent, middle-class American church-goers saying with great piety, "Oh, yes, if you follow Jesus, you will be persecuted." How we cheapen the sufferings of the saints when we say that. Oh, you mean you might not get invited to a neighbor's party because they're worried you will embarrass them with your opinions? That's persecution? Your neighbors might speak critically of you? The truth of the matter is that modern day Christians are more apt to persecute than to be persecuted. That's because we do not know Jesus.

How can you and I come to know God today? Just say yes to Him. Then seek to live as Jesus lived.

Some of you are familiar with a delightful song from the 1970s, the chorus of which goes like this, "To see thee more clearly, love thee more dearly, follow thee more nearly day by day."

The song is from the musical, Godspell. In the musical, which is based upon the Gospel of Matthew, the cast acts out the parable of the unforgiving servant. To refresh your memory, a servant owes an enormous debt to his master. The master forgives the debt. However, a much smaller debt is owed to this servant by a fellow servant. The servant who has been forgiven this enormous debt by his master refuses, however, to forgive the much smaller debt owed him by his fellow servant (Matthew 18:23-35).

After Jesus explains that his followers must forgive each other from their hearts, the cast sings a beautiful prayer that asks God for three things: "To see thee more clearly, love thee more dearly, follow thee more nearly day by day." (4)

Is that your prayer?

Do you know God or are you just religious? What's the difference? Is your faith about following rules and regulations or is it about relationships—relationships with your family, friends and all God's children, as well as God Himself? Do you want to know God better? Do you want to see God more clearly, love God more dearly, follow God more nearly day by day? Simply say "yes" to God. Invite Christ to take up residence in your life and to fill you with his love. Soon you will know that you know God . . . for the grace of God will be evident in your life.

1. Bruce and Darlene Marie Wilkinson, The Dream Giver For Parents (Sisters, OR: Multonomah, 2004), pp. 45-46.
2. Sermon posted on PRCL, 10/3/1999. Cited by Dr. Mickey Anders,
http://www.mickeyanders.com/Sermons/Sermon20010325.html.
3. The Rev. Dr. M. Craig Barnes, http://day1.org/669-could_you_be_wrong_about_god.
4. Godspell, Stephen Schwartz, 1973. Cited in Robert Schnase, Five Practices of Fruitful Congregations (Kindle Edition).

When We Feel Unwanted
Psalm 118:1-2, 19-29; Luke 19:28-40

Is there any pain that stays with us longer than that of not being wanted, of being rejected? This rejection may come from our family, our friends, colleagues or even the greater society.

An older man was recounting his teenage years. He said, "Back when I was a boy, we played spin-the-bottle. We played it this way, we spun the bottle and if it landed on you, the girls were supposed to kiss you, or if they chose to, they could give you, instead of a kiss, a quarter." He said, by the time I was 18 I had accumulated enough quarters to pay my way through college.

Well, a quarter's all right, but it's poor compensation for a girl not wanting to kiss you. It's hard to be rejected, to be unwanted.

There was a heartbreaking story in the Associated Press a couple of years back. It was about the plight of unwanted girls in India.

You already know about China, where the government enforces a one child policy. Every family is supposed to have only one child to keep the population under control.

Let me ask you a question: If you could have only one child, which would you prefer? You and I say, well, it wouldn't matter. We would love a little girl or a little boy just the same. That's easy for us to say in a modern technological society. However, in a poor, agricultural society where help on the farm is crucial, it is believed that a typical male baby will, over a lifetime, contribute more to the household than a typical girl baby. This idea has led to perhaps millions of girl fetuses being aborted in China. This has produced a wildly skewed gender gap between the number of little boys born in that society and little girls. As young people move into cities, this skewing of genders may very well lead to some other dire issues. Time will tell.

A similar phenomenon takes place in India, though the reasons are slightly different. Part of the reason Indians favor sons is the enormous expense of marrying off their daughters. Families often go into debt arranging marriages and paying for elaborate dowries to marry off their girls. A boy, on the other hand, will one day bring home a bride and a dowry as well. And so, there too, there are many abortions. The problem is so serious in India that hospitals are legally banned from revealing the gender of an unborn fetus in order to prevent sex-selective abortions, though evidence suggests the information somehow gets out.

Some female infants who are not aborted are treated with such neglect that they do not survive. Many of those who do survive are given a name, "Nakusa" or "Nakushi," which, in Hindi, means "unwanted." Can you imagine naming a child unwanted? Activists say the name "unwanted," which is widely given to girls across India, gives them the feeling they are worthless and a burden. That is why one district in India has started conducting ceremonies in which Indian girls are able to officially erase their names. Those who are named "Nakusa" or "Nakushi" are allowed to replace that name with a name of their own choosing, a name that tells them they are worthy and accepted. (1)

Is there any emotion more devastating than feeling unwanted, rejected—especially by those who are supposed to love you? Jesus knew what that was like. His own people rejected him. One who was closest to him betrayed him, another denied him, and, when he needed them most, almost all of his friends turned their back on him. He knew what it was to have those who once showered him with praise reject him and even shout, "Crucify him, crucify him, crucify him . . ." All this, of course, was foretold in the Old Testament. For example, in today's lesson the psalmist writes: "The stone the builders rejected has become the cornerstone . . ."

Welcome on this Palm Sunday 2013. Palm Sunday is intended to be a day of celebration. On this day we remember how the people of Jerusalem welcomed Jesus into their city. You know the story.

Jesus has been making a slow steady journey accompanied by his disciples and some other supporters to Jerusalem. As he approached Bethphage and Bethany at the hill called the Mount of Olives, he sent two of his disciples on ahead to a village where, he said, they would find a colt of a donkey which no one had ever ridden. He told them to untie it and bring it to him.

If anyone asked, "Why are you untying it?" They were to say, "The Lord needs it."

Some background might be helpful here. We are told that donkeys were valuable. Because many of the people were quite poor, donkeys were often cooperatively owned by several families. This system seemed to work fairly well. However, property laws were not absolute. There was an ancient law that required citizens to render to any king or one of his emissaries any item or service needed by the king. If the king needed a donkey, they were obligated to give it to him. That is why in our story Jesus tells his disciples to procure the colt of a donkey and if the owner asked what they were doing, they were simply to respond, "The Lord needs it."

And so, the disciples brought the young donkey to Jesus, threw their cloaks on the colt's back and put Jesus on it. Notice what comes next. As he went along, people spread their cloaks on the road. This again was based on an ancient custom. Spreading clothing to carpet the pathway was a way to honor royalty. We read in 2 Kings 9 that when the people became aware that Jehu had been anointed king of Israel, "They hurried and took their cloaks and spread them under him on the bare steps. Then they blew the trumpet and shouted, 'Jehu is king!'"

In like manner, Luke tells us the people spread their cloaks down before Jesus. It is in John's Gospel that we read that people came out to meet Jesus with palm branches. (2) When the procession came near the place where the road goes down the Mount of Olives, the whole crowd of disciples began joyfully to praise

God in loud voices for all the miracles they had seen. They shouted out, "Blessed is the king who comes in the name of the Lord!" and "Peace in heaven and glory in the highest!"

Obviously this did not set well with some of the Pharisees in the crowd. They said to Jesus, "Teacher, rebuke your disciples!"

Jesus replied, "I tell you, if they keep quiet, the stones will cry out."

This would have been a great place to end Luke's Gospel. Jesus was receiving the welcome he richly deserved. He had taught the kingdom of God faithfully, he had healed those who were sick or otherwise infirmed, he had set an example of living at its very best. Now he was being welcomed into Jerusalem as a king. That could have been how the story ended. But of course it was not to be.

In a recent book titled The Last Week, theologian Marcus Borg tells about another parade that was occurring on the opposite side of the city even as Jesus entered the holy city. Pontius Pilate, the Roman governor was entering Jerusalem at the head of a column of imperial cavalry and soldiers. Jesus' procession proclaimed the kingdom of God; Pilate's proclaimed the power of empire. Pilate was there with his soldiers in case there was trouble. That was a common occurrence in Jerusalem, especially at Passover, a festival that celebrated the Jewish people's liberation from an earlier empire.

"Imagine the imperial procession's arrival in the city," writes Borg. "A visual panoply of imperial power: cavalry on horses, foot soldiers, leather armor, helmets, weapons, banners, golden eagles mounted on poles, sun glinting on metal and gold. Sounds: the marching of feet, the creaking of leather, the clinking of bridles, the beating of drums. The swirling of dust. The eyes of the silent onlookers, some curious, some awed, some resentful."

Pilate's procession displayed not only imperial power, but also Roman imperial theology. According to this theology, the emperor was not simply the ruler of Rome, but the Son of God. This pagan heresy began with the greatest of the emperors, Augustus, who ruled Rome a couple of decades before Christ. His father was said to be the son of the god Apollo. Inscriptions referred to Augustus as "son of God," "lord," "savior," one who had brought "peace on earth." After his death, he was seen ascending into heaven to take his permanent place among the gods. Underscore this: Pilate's procession into Jerusalem embodied not only a rival social order, but also a rival theology. (3)

Pilate on one side of the city; Jesus and his disciples on the other. The stage was being set for an inevitable clash between the mightiest kingdom of this world and the kingdom of God. And when that clash reached its climax, crushed in between the might of Rome and the will of God, was the broken body of the crucified Jesus.

In the words of Isaiah, "Surely he took up our pain and bore our suffering, yet we considered him punished by God, stricken by him, and afflicted. But he was pierced for our transgressions, he was crushed for our iniquities; the punishment that brought us peace was on him, and by his wounds we are healed. We all, like sheep, have gone astray, each of us has turned to our own way; and the Lord has laid on him the iniquity of us all. He was oppressed and afflicted, yet he did not open his mouth; he was led like a lamb to the slaughter, and as a sheep before its shearers is silent, so he did not open his mouth. By oppression and judgment he was taken away. Yet who of his generation protested? For he was cut off from the land of the living; for the transgression of my people he was punished. He was assigned a grave with the wicked, and with the rich in his death, though he had done no violence, nor was any deceit in his mouth. Yet it was the Lord's will to crush him and cause him to suffer, and though the Lord makes his life an offering for sin, he will see his offspring and prolong his days, and the will of the Lord will prosper in his hand." (Isaiah 53:3-10)

So Palm Sunday was a celebration, but it was short lived. And very soon the innocent Galilean was being tried before this same Pontius Pilate and he was being turned over to the people to be crucified. Unwanted. Rejected by his own people.

But that is not the end of the story, as you well know. Next Sunday we will be celebrating Christ's resurrection. Jesus Christ who was dead was made alive by the power of Almighty God. The stone was rolled away. The tomb was empty. The risen Christ began making appearances to those who believed in him. We'll talk more about that next week. For now let's be content with the words of the Psalmist: "The stone the builders rejected has become the cornerstone . . ."

Pastor Wayne Brouwer tells a wonderful story about the Irish poet, Sir Thomas Moore. Moore had a beautiful, radiant wife. She had flaming red hair, and warm green eyes, and people in that part of the world said they'd never seen a lovelier bride. Moore and his wife loved each other madly. They loved each other fully. They were the best of friends: Two hearts, beating in just one mind! as a popular song puts it.

But one year, when Sir Thomas was called away for a long time, his wife came down with smallpox. There were no medicines for it. Most who got it, died. Those who survived became ugly with scars and sores. Mrs. Moore hung onto life. But when the fevers subsided, and she looked in her mirror, she wished she wouldn't have made it. The most beautiful bride in the world had become deformed and grotesque.

She couldn't stand to see herself anymore. She hid in her bedroom, and ordered the servants to hang heavy curtain over the windows. She refused to let anyone see her.

And then Sir Thomas returned. The servants warned him at the door: Your wife had smallpox! Her face is a horrible mess! She's locked herself in her room! He went up to see her. But when he opened the door, the room was gloomy and dark. And from the bed came the voice of his wife: "No, Thomas! Come no nearer! I have resolved that you will never again see me by the light of day!"

He hesitated, and then turned slowly from the room. That night he wrote one of his most memorable poems. As the sun began to light the eastern sky the next morning, he went back upstairs. From the hallway outside her room, he read these words to his wife: "Believe me, if all those endearing young charms, which I look on so fondly today, were to pass in a moment, and flee from my arms like fairy dreams fading away, thou would'st still be adored, as this moment thou art. Let thy loveliness fade as it will; and around the dear ruin, each wish of my heart would entwine itself verdantly still."

Having finished reading his poem to her, Sir Thomas Moore strode across the room to the window, and threw back those heavy curtains. And as the first rays of the morning sun flooded the room, he turned to his wife, kissed her disfigured face, and drew her into his arms. And from that moment she began to live again! (4)

Friends, that is what happened on Easter Sunday. Jesus who had been unwanted, rejected by his own people, lay in a lonely tomb, but as the first rays of the morning sun flooded the sky, God strode into that tomb and brought forth his beloved son raised from the dead. And now Christ reigns at the right hand of his Father. "The stone the builders rejected has become the cornerstone; the Lord has done this," writes the Psalmist, "and it is marvelous in our eyes. The Lord has done it this very day; let us rejoice today and be glad . . ."

And we do rejoice and we are glad. For that stone that was rejected and is now the cornerstone is our Lord and Master. And the new life God breathed into him on that first Easter Sunday is the life that has been promised to those who believe on him.

We shall rejoice and be glad all our lives until that day comes when we witness the heavenly choirs gathered around the throne of God taking up the song sung by a fickle crowd that first Palm Sunday, "Hosanna, Hosanna, blessed is he who comes in the name of the Lord." But this time, there will be no rejection, no not being wanted. "The stone the builders rejected has become the cornerstone; the Lord has done this and it is marvelous in our eyes. The Lord has done it this very day; let us rejoice today and be glad . . . Blessed is the king who comes in the name of the Lord! . . . Peace in heaven and glory in the highest!" Amen.

1. Chaya Babu, The Associated Press, 10/22/2011.
2. Dr. Ralph F. Wilson, http://www.jesuswalk.com/lessons/19_28-40.htm.
3. Kindle edition.
4. Wayne Brouwer, Wedding Homilies (Seven Worlds).

The Servant Leader
John 13:1-17, 31b-35
(Maundy Thursday)

Actress Mae West produced many memorable quotes, some of them quite naughty. It was she who said, "Between two evils, I always pick the one I never tried before" and, "Any time you've got nothing to do and lots of time to do it come on up." Her most revealing quote however is the theme of many celebrities today, "I never loved another person the way I loved myself." That is a typical celebrity attitude. However it is not true of every celebrity.

Veteran television star Tom Selleck seems to have avoided the self-worship that characterizes most Hollywood personalities. He says that whenever he gets full of himself, he remembers the nice, elderly couple who approached him with a camera on a street in Honolulu one day. When he struck a pose for them, the man said, "No, no, we want you to take a picture of us."

The truth of the matter is that many people consider a big ego to be prerequisite for success in today's world. Without a big ego it is almost impossible to become a celebrity and being a celebrity is very profitable in our star-struck society. People who depend on celebrity are constantly looking for ways to push themselves to the forefront.

Old-time comic artist Harry Hershfield was a pro at self-promotion. Whenever he was in a group photograph for a newspaper he always made it a practice to stand on the group's right side. That way, his name always appeared first in the newspaper caption.

That's a pretty slick trick if you want to make certain people know who you are.

When you are in a position of leadership, it's easy to let your ego take over. Maybe that is why the Lord gave some of us spouses—to keep us humble.

The story is told of the head of a large company who with his wife was waiting in line to get his driver's license renewed. He was frustrated at how long it was taking and grumbled to his wife, "Don't they know who I am?"

She replied, "Yeah, you're a plumber's son who got lucky."

It was just before the Passover Festival. Jesus knew his time with his disciples was drawing to a close. They were enjoying the meal that has become memorialized as the Last Supper, the final meal they would share together before his crucifixion. Judas had already set into motion the events that would bring about his death. How could the Master impress upon his disciples what he needed from them? How could he get across to them what his kingdom was really all about?

Welcome to this Maundy Thursday celebration. I suspect that many of us have been coming to this service for years without having any idea where the word "Maundy" comes from. Maundy comes from the Latin word "maundatum," which means "commandment." This day is called Maundy Thursday because at the end of this scene at the Last Supper, Jesus gave us a new commandment. In verses 34 and 35 we read this commandment, "A new command I give you: Love one another. As I have loved you, so you must love one another. By this everyone will know that you are my disciples, if you love one another."

At the Last Supper Christ gave us a new commandment—that we should love one another. Even more important, he demonstrated how this new commandment is to be lived out. John tells us that while the meal was still in progress, Jesus stood up, took off his outer clothing, and wrapped a towel around his waist. After that, he poured water into a basin and began to wash his disciples' feet, drying them with the towel that was wrapped around him. This, quite obviously, was the last thing the disciples were expecting.

Christ knelt before Simon Peter. "Lord, are you going to wash my feet?"

Christ replied, "You do not realize now what I am doing, but later you will understand."

"No," said Peter, "you shall never wash my feet."

The Master answered, "Unless I wash you, you have no part with me."

"Then, Lord," Simon Peter replied, "not just my feet but my hands and my head as well!" That is SO Simon Peter!

When he had finished washing the feet of all those who were present including the feet of Judas who would betray him, Jesus put on his clothes and returned to his place. "Do you understand what I have done for you?" he asked them. "You call me 'Teacher' and 'Lord,' and rightly so, for that is what I am. Now that I, your Lord and Teacher, have washed your feet, you also should wash one another's feet. I have set you an example that you should do as I have done for you. Very truly I tell you, no servant is greater than his master, nor is a messenger greater than the one who sent him. Now that you know these things, you will be blessed if you do them."

What an amazing story this is. A little background might be helpful. The washing of feet was part of the hospitality which people in this part of the world offered their guests. Usually it was done by a servant. It was not a pleasant task. People went barefoot or they wore sandals. Not only were the streets dusty and dirty, but they usually contained garbage and the waste from the animals that traveled up and down the same streets. And so the task of washing the feet of guests was usually relegated to the person of the lowest rank. Since none of the disciples felt they fit that description they all had come to the meal with unwashed feet.

This was unacceptable. Remember, they didn't take a meal sitting in chairs around a table as we do. Rather they reclined on the floor with the food spread out before them. Imagine the scene in your mind. They were reclining on the floor in a circle. That meant that one person's feet were in someone else's face— not the most appetizing way to consume a meal. The rite of washing feet was therefore essential. The problem was that each of the disciples felt they were too good to perform this ritual.

Remember this is the same group that on at least one occasion had argued about who among them was the greatest (Luke 22:24). Instead of serving one another, the disciples were jealous of one another and were competing for the best place. As someone has put it, "They were ready to fight for a throne, but not for a towel." (1)

How could the master teach them that greatness comes through service? How could he teach them that it is in laying down your life that you will find it? He did it with this astounding object lesson. He took off his outer garments, wrapped a towel around his waist and began washing his disciples' feet. The Lord of all the universe humbled himself before his disciples and took on the role of the humblest servant. What an example he gave his disciples. What an example he gave to us.

Gene Wilkes, in his book, Jesus on Leadership, writes these very meaningful words: "Jesus did not come to gain a place of power. He did not come to defeat his human enemies. He did not come to overthrow an unjust government. Jesus came to show us the heart of God. His entire message and ministry on earth was to show selfish, power-hungry people like you and me what love looks like. As he knelt before Judas, Jesus showed us a love that no human can conceive on his own: a love that is brutally honest about what is going on but still kneels before us to lay down his life so we can be free from the sin that infects us. Jesus loves you as he loved Judas. If you miss that, you have missed eternal life." (2)

The love that led Jesus to kneel down and wash his disciples' feet is beyond our comprehension. We don't see many examples of this kind of servant-hood today. Indeed, there are many who believe that choosing to be a servant is for losers. Arrogance and aggressiveness are the attitudes that strut down most corridors of power. But not always.

One of the most obvious examples of the power of servant-hood was a young Albanian girl named Agnes. At the age of 18 Agnes gave in to the tugging on her heart that she had felt for many years. She became a nun.

When she announced her intention to enter a convent to her brother who was a soldier, he reacted with disbelief because his sister was such a vivacious young woman. Agnes had the perfect answer for him. She replied that he was proud as a soldier to be serving a king who ruled over a few million subjects.

She, on the other hand, would be serving the King of the entire world. Agnes entered a convent where she remained for 17 years.

In 1948, after 17 years living this cloistered life, Agnes decided to walk away from the convent taking nothing with her except three Saris to go over her white habit. She left the convent and went into the street to serve the least and the lowest. She had no building for her ministry. She had to beg for money to support what she was doing. She said the goal of her life was "to be a pencil in God's hand." She said she was called to care for the sick, the poor, the dying, and the dispossessed, to show them the love that God had for them. She spent the rest of her life picking up dying people off the street and carrying them to shelter. She cleaned infected wounds, lovingly washing and providing basic care for people on the verge of death. And she did it all with a beautiful smile. We know Agnes, of course, as Mother Teresa, a true saint of God and one of the great people of the twentieth century.

She was the perfect example of the kind of greatness Dr. Martin Luther King, Jr. once talked about: "Everybody can be great," he said, "because anybody can serve. You don't have to have a college degree to serve. You don't have to make your subject and verb agree to serve . . . You only need a heart full of grace, a soul generated by love."

Dr. King was correct. Everybody can be great and you don't have to put on the habit of a nun to do it. Pastor Don Friesen tells of a successful executive on the rise in his profession who every Tuesday night volunteered at a foot clinic for homeless people. He wore nice clothes, says Friesen, and wore his success comfortably, but at the clinic he would sit on a stool before a homeless guest, take the guest's feet and place them in a basin of warm water. After washing them, he took a towel and dried the feet, applying ointment to their sores. When asked why he did this, the man answered, "I figure I have a better chance of running into Jesus here than most places." (3) That's a pretty good explanation. And it is a challenge to the rest of us.

I love the way Ruth Harms Calkin put it in a poem, titled I Wonder:
You know, Lord, How I serve You
with great emotional fervor in the limelight.
You know how eagerly I speak for You at a Women's Club.
You know my genuine enthusiasm at a Bible study.
But how would I react, I wonder,
if You pointed to a basin of water
and asked me to wash the calloused feet
of a bent and wrinkled old woman
day after day, month after month,
in a room where nobody saw and nobody knew? (4)

Does that challenge you? It does me. Maundy Thursday is that day in the church year in which we take the bread and the cup in remembrance of Christ. But let's not forget why it was called Maundy in the first place. It was at the Last Supper that Jesus said to the disciples and to us: "A new command I give you: Love one another . . ."

The bread and the cup are important to us as followers of Christ. But so are the towel and the basin. Christ has called us to a life of serving others. That is how the world will know that we are his followers.

1. Merrill C. Tenney, John: The Gospel of Belief (Grand Rapids: Eerdmans Publishing Co., 1948), p. 199.
2. (Lifeway Press, 1998), p. 168.
3. http://www.ottawamennonite.ca/sermons/silence.htm.
4. Biblical Illustrator.

Pilate's Dilemma

John 18:1-19:42; Luke 22:14-23:56

(Good Friday or Passion Sunday)

Pilate was a politician. That says it all, doesn't it?

I read recently that 53 percent of Americans can't name their representative in Congress. That doesn't keep Congress from being highly unpopular. As someone once asked, "If pro is the opposite of con, is progress the opposite of Congress?"

Someone else has said that the reason a person in Congress try so hard to get re-elected is that they would hate to have to make a living under the laws they've passed.

I heard about one southern Congressman who had been working desperately throughout his district for reelection. He was relaxing one evening, following a speech, in the home of a friend.

"I have heard your speeches," his friend said, "but the real question is what will you do if you are reelected?"

"No," said politician, "the real question is what will I do if I am not reelected?"

Pontius Pilate could sympathize with that Congressman. Pilate married into a political family. His wife Claudia was the granddaughter of Caesar Augustus. So, Pilate was a member of the Emperor's family by marriage, not merit.

Pilate served as the Roman prefect of Judea for ten years, from A.D. 26-36. A prefect is like a governor. It is a position of power, but not absolute power. Pilate took his orders from Rome and for that reason, he was insecure in his position. He ruled at the whim of his wife's family. Being appointed prefect of Judea was a mixed blessing in itself. Judea was a hotbed of insurrection. The Jews were a restless people, ready to begin a rebellion at the drop of a hat.

Pilate got in bad with the Jews from the very beginning. As soon as he took office in 27 AD, he needlessly provoked the pious folks in Jerusalem by riding into the city with his troops bearing their standards in full view. On the top of every flagpole that the soldiers bore was a carved image of Caesar. For the Jews this was a transgression of the commandment to have no graven images. Even more grievously, because of the Roman custom of emperor worship, Pilate's action smacked of blatant idolatry. This thoughtless action provoked a riot. So Pilate was in trouble from the beginning of his reign.

There were some skirmishes in which Pilate proved himself a brutal ruler. Luke 13 mentions one of these—an occasion where Pilate's soldiers killed some Galileans. To compound their crime, however, the soldiers then took the Galileans' blood and mixed it with sacrifices to their pagan gods. It was a despicable act.

Pilate's brutality probably grew out of his fear of being deposed. He was caught between a Roman government which had little respect for him and a civilian population that was known for its intractability. And then he had to deal with Jesus.

It was the religious leaders who brought Jesus to Pilate's palace. It's interesting. They brought him to Pilate, but they refused to enter Pilate's palace. Why? Because this would make them ceremonially unclean by entering the residence of a lowly Gentile. Jews believed that if you took two steps over a Gentile threshold you defiled yourself. So they wanted Pilate to do their dirty work, but they wanted to keep their distance from him while he did it.

To show you how afraid Pilate was of offending the religious authorities, he agreed to come out to them. The dialogue is intriguing. Pilate asked the religious authorities, "What charges are you bringing against this man?" referring to Jesus.

"If he were not a criminal," they answered defensively, "we would not have handed him over to you." That alone tells us what we need to know about the charges brought against Jesus. They were totally unsubstantiated.

Pilate knew of no Roman law Jesus had broken. He tried turning him back over to the religious leaders: "Take him and judge him according to your law."

That didn't work. "We are not permitted to put anyone to death," they said.

And it was true. The only man in the city who had the authority to pass a death sentence was Pontius Pilate. And the religious leaders were determined that Christ be put to death.

Pilate then went back inside the palace, summoned Jesus and asked him, "Are you the king of the Jews?"

"Is that your own idea," Jesus asked, "or did others talk to you about me?"

"Am I a Jew?" Pilate replied. "Your own people and chief priests handed you over to me. What is it you have done?"

Jesus answered somewhat cryptically, "My kingdom is not of this world. If it were, my servants would fight to prevent my arrest by the Jewish leaders. But now my kingdom is from another place."

"You are a king, then!" said Pilate.

Jesus answered, "You say that I am a king. In fact, the reason I was born and came into the world is to testify to the truth. Everyone on the side of truth listens to me."

And it is here that Pilate cynically asked, "What is truth?"

Listen to political debates on television and you will ask the same thing: "What is truth?" Truth is whatever is left over after the politicians spin the facts.

Then the religious leaders hit Pilate's weak spot: "If you let this man go, you are no friend of Caesar. Anyone who claims to be a king opposes Caesar."

There is no question Pilate was frustrated by Jesus. It was also clear to him that Jesus posed no threat to the empire. He said himself that his kingdom was not of this world. Pilate went out again to the religious authorities and said, "I find no basis for a charge against him."

Pilate tried to reason with them. Then he tried to bribe them. He remembered that the Jews had a tradition that they would release one prisoner at Passover. He offered to release a notorious political prisoner named Barabbas! Still they would not be appeased. "Crucify him, crucify him," they shouted, referring to Jesus.

At this point, Pilate had Christ flogged, hoping that would appease the mob, but it did not. He had his soldiers mock Christ. They put a purple robe on him and thrust a crown of thorns on his head, and called out in derision, "King of the Jews." That still wasn't enough.

He tried turning Jesus over to Herod. But that didn't work either. Pilate was getting desperate. The mob was determined for Jesus to die, while Pilate's sense of justice told him the man was innocent. According to Matthew's Gospel, even Pilate's wife Claudia wanted Pilate to have nothing to do with Jesus. Matthew 27:19 states, "While Pilate was sitting on the judge's seat, his wife sent him this message: 'Don't have anything to do with that innocent man, for I have suffered a great deal today in a dream because of him.'"

Pilate simply didn't know what to do. He couldn't in good conscience find Jesus guilty, but it was not politically expedient to set him free. Three times, Pilate tried to release Jesus, fully convinced of Jesus' innocence, but the mob would not listen. "Crucify him, crucify him," they shouted.

It is Matthew who reports that when Pilate saw that he was getting nowhere, but that instead an uproar was starting, he took water and washed his hands in front of the crowd. "I am innocent of this man's blood," he said. "It is your responsibility" (27:24).

And with that Pilate handed Jesus over to be crucified. It was a cowardly act, one that has stained Pilate's record for more than 2,000 years.

Oh, one thing more: Pilate had a notice prepared and fastened to the cross on which Christ died. The notice read like this: "Jesus of Nazareth, the King of the Jews."

Many of the residents of Jerusalem read this sign, says Luke, for the place where Jesus was crucified was near the city, and the sign was written in Aramaic, Latin and Greek. The chief priests of the Jews protested to Pilate, "Do not write 'The King of the Jews,' but that this man claimed to be king of the Jews."

Pilate answered, "What I have written, I have written."

If Pilate had only known how those words would haunt him. He was the man who had the innocent Son of God put to death. And this time, it wasn't because he was brutal. It wasn't because he was trying to rob Jesus of his life. He was not. Pilate's only crime was, he was weak.

And friends, that is true of so many of us. If we do wrong, it will probably never be because we are brutal, or greedy or even hard-hearted. It will probably be because we are weak—morally weak, spiritually weak. We keep quiet when we should speak up, we give in when we should walk away, we strike a bargain when we should remain true to our values.

You know about weakness, don't you—moral weakness, spiritual weakness? The kind that wrecks families and ruins lives. The kind that refuses to speak out in the face of evil? Weakness sometimes takes the form of sexual temptation. Sometimes it entraps us in chemical dependency.

In his novel, The Testament, John Grisham paints a powerful word portrait of one man's weakness and his subsequent surrender to God.

Nate O'Reilly, a disgraced corporate attorney, is plagued by alcoholism and drug abuse. After two marriages, four detox programs, and a serious health crisis, Nate acknowledges his need for God. Grisham describes the dramatic transformation in these words: "With both hands, he clenched the back of the pew in front of him. He repeated (his) list, mumbling softly every weakness and flaw and affliction and evil that plagued him. He confessed them all. In one long glorious acknowledgment of failure, he laid himself bare before God. He held nothing back. He unloaded enough burdens to crush any three men, and when he finally finished Nate had tears in his eyes. 'I'm sorry,' he whispered to God. 'Please, help me.' As quickly as the fever had left his body, he felt the baggage leave his soul. With one gentle brush of the hand, his slate had been wiped clean. He breathed a massive sigh of relief, but his pulse was racing." *

I wonder if Pilate ever experienced that kind of release from the baggage of his wrong doing? It's possible. After all, he spent considerable time in the presence of the Messiah. He is one of the few people on earth to have a one-on-one interview with the Son of God.

Pilate asked, "What is truth?" Here's the truth: After Pilate had scorned Christ and had him flogged, mocked and crucified, if Pilate had confessed his weakness, Christ would have forgiven him. He, too, would have experienced the grace of Jesus Christ.

And that is true of each of us. If we have been weak, if we have some time or another, betrayed our values, if we have ever followed the crowd rather than voicing our convictions, if we have committed some grievous sin, not because we are mean, not even because we are bad, but simply because we are weak, there is room at the foot of the cross for us.

Archbishop Desmond M. Tutu once put it this way: "We tend to turn the Christian religion into a religion of virtues, but it is a religion of grace. You become a good person because you are loved. You are not loved because you are good."

There is hope for weak persons like you and me. There was even hope for Pontius Pilate if he was willing to accept it. But, to the best of our knowledge, he did not. Friend, do not make that same mistake. Accept the grace of God today.

*The Rev. Dr. Leslie Holmes, http://day1.org/1060-quitting_aint_an_option.

Surprise In A Graveyard
John 20:1-18 or Luke 24:1-12

On February, 27, 1991, at the height of Desert Storm, Ruth Dillow received a very sad message from the Pentagon. It stated that her son, Clayton Carpenter, Private 1st Class, had stepped on a mine in Kuwait and was dead.

Ruth Dillow later wrote, "I can't begin to describe my grief and shock. It was almost more than I could bear. For 3 days I wept. For 3 days I expressed anger and loss. For 3 days people tried to comfort me, to no avail because the loss was too great." Every parent here can relate to her grief. But 3 days after Ruth Dillow received that message, the telephone rang. The voice on the other end said, "Mom, it's me. I'm alive."

Ruth Dillow said, "I couldn't believe it at first. But then I recognized his voice." Ruth's son was alive. The earlier message she had received was a mistake! She said, "I laughed, I cried, I felt like turning cartwheels, because my son whom I had thought was dead, was . . . alive . . ." (1)

Surprise, Ruth Dillow, the son you thought was dead is alive.

A two-year-old girl could hardly wait for Easter to come. She had a new dress to wear and new shoes to go with it, but her father wondered whether she knew the true meaning of Easter. "Kara," he asked, "do you know what Easter means?"

"Yes, I do," she smiled.

"What does it mean then?" her father asked.

With a smile on her face and her arms raised, she cried, "Surprise!" (2)

There is no better word for Easter. "Surprise!"

That was the clear reaction of Christ's disciples and closest friends that first Easter day. In Luke we read that Jesus' disciples were distraught after his crucifixion. Early on Sunday morning, some of the women took spices to the tomb. They found the stone rolled away from the mouth of tomb. When they went inside Christ's body was not there. Suddenly two men in gleaming white clothes stood beside them. The women bowed down their faces with fright, but the men said to them, "Why do you look for the living among the dead? He is not here; he has risen! Remember how he told you, while he was still with you in Galilee: 'The Son of Man must be delivered over to the hands of sinners, be crucified and on the third day be raised again.'" Then they remembered Christ's words. When the women came back from the tomb, they told the disciples what had happened. But none of the men believe them. Their words seemed like nonsense.

Surprise, doubting men, he is alive!

John, in his telling of the story, focuses on Christ's appearance to Mary

Magdalene. Mary comes to the tomb and sees that the stone has been rolled away. So she runs to Simon Peter and John, and says, "They have taken the Lord out of the tomb, and we don't know where they have put him!" Evidently the thought had not occurred to Mary that Christ could be resurrected from the grave.

Peter and John start for the tomb. When they, too, find it empty, what do they do? They simply go back to the house where they were staying. There was no celebration, no cries of, "He's alive. He's alive." You might expect those who knew Christ best to be bubbling over with excitement that first Easter Sunday morning, because he had been delivered from the tomb, just as he said. Instead, they were totally mystified that his body was gone. They didn't expect him to be alive any more than Ruth Dillow expected her son to be alive.

As for Mary, she stands outside the tomb crying. She bends over to look into the tomb and sees two angels in white, seated where Jesus' body had been, one at the head and the other at the foot. They ask her, "Woman, why are you crying?"

"They have taken my Lord away," she explains, "and I don't know where they have put him." At this, she turns around and sees Jesus standing there, but she doesn't recognize him.

"Woman," he says, "why are you crying? Who is it you are looking for?"

Thinking he's the gardener, she says, "Sir, if you have carried him away, tell me where you have put him, and I will get him."

Jesus calls her name, "Mary."

She turns toward him and cries out in Aramaic, "Rabboni!" (which means "Teacher"). Surprise, Mary! Surprise! Your Master is alive. Surprise, Peter. Surprise, John. Surprise, all those who thought Jesus was dead. Surprise, world, Jesus is alive!

The story of Easter is no carefully contrived story designed by Jesus' followers to convince us of something that isn't so. The story of Easter is the honest reporting of baffled believers who had no idea where Christ was leading them until he appeared to them beyond the grave. Surprise, everyone!

Easter is such an extraordinary day. No wonder people gather in such numbers all over the world to celebrate the event of the resurrection. Jesus Christ who was dead is alive!

Pastor Michael Slaughter tells of traveling to Moscow with a group of church leaders in April 1992 just as the Cold War was ending. These Christian leaders were there to celebrate Russia's first Easter after the fall of the Iron Curtain. A large banner proclaiming "Christ has risen" loomed over Red Square. Slaughter says he couldn't help noticing that less than twenty-five yards away stood the tomb of Vladimir Lenin, the father of the Soviet Revolution. It struck him as ironic that the banner with "Christ has risen" on it overshadowed the tomb of the Communist leader who had once proclaimed that God was dead.

It also struck Slaughter that Lenin lay entombed in a granite and marble mausoleum, his body sealed in a glass sarcophagus while Christ's tomb was empty. (3) Surprise! Lenin is dead. Stalin is dead. Communism is dead. But Christ lives on!

Chuck Colson, in his book The Good Life, tells us of one man who believed strongly in Christ's resurrection. His name was Edward Bennett Williams. Williams, now deceased, was one of the great lawyers and Washington power brokers of our age, an extraordinarily gifted man, says Colson. "For one full generation, he was the man to go to if your life was on the line. His client list reads like a who's who of American celebrities over a thirty- or forty-year period, starting with Joe McCarthy and Jimmy Hoffa, through Frank Sinatra, and a series of senators and high government officials.

"Although Williams was quiet about it," says Colson, "he was a deeply religious man, a daily communicant in the Roman Catholic Church. He fought a long and valiant fight against cancer. As he struggled on his deathbed and as it became clear that he was losing the battle, his son showed him an article that named him one of the most powerful men in Washington. The Washington Post, for whom Williams was counsel, wrote that he 'waved the magazine away.' He then said, 'They don't realize what power really is . . . I'm about to see true power. Fighting death is selfish. It's time to let go and see what real power is.' Williams died peacefully," notes Colson, "as unshakable in his conviction about the resurrection as he had ever been in the cases he argued so brilliantly in court." (4)

Christ is alive. In 1 Corinthians 15:3-7 the Apostle Paul wrote, "For what I received I passed on to you as of first importance: that Christ died for our sins according to the Scriptures, that he was buried, that he was raised on the third day according to the Scriptures, and that he appeared to Cephas, and then to the Twelve. After that, he appeared to more than five hundred of the brothers and sisters at the same time, most of whom are still living, though some have fallen asleep. Then he appeared to James, then to all the apostles . . ."

Did you catch that? Paul was telling about a shared experience of the Christian community. The risen Christ had appeared to more than five hundred believers, most of whom were still alive when Paul was writing. All it would have taken to shake Paul's witness would have been one of those 500 who had encountered the risen Christ to refute his testimony, but none of them did. To their minds, there was no doubt. Christ is alive. Nothing in the ancient world refutes that testimony. The tomb was empty. The body was missing. Even more importantly, hundreds of lives were changed by the appearance of Jesus after his death.

Nothing in the ancient world refutes that testimony. Nothing in the modern world refutes that testimony either. It always has been fashionable in some circles to doubt Christ's resurrection. The critical mind cannot accept what cannot be proved or, at least, that's what we say. And yet we are not always so resistant to alternative ideas. We accept many things that cannot yet be proved.

If I were to tell you, for example, that some scientists entertain the hope that someday it might be possible to take a strand of DNA and recreate, or reformulate, or resurrect, if you will, a living human being in a laboratory—would you agree that such a thing might indeed be reasonable? I'm not saying that it is possible. But imagine it were true. If you were to read such a statement in tomorrow's newspaper, I predict that many of you would give a yawn and turn to your spouse and say, "Gee whiz, hon, scientists are telling us that they will one day resurrect people using only their DNA." Many of us would have no problem accepting the possibility that science might indeed perform such a miracle. After all, modern science is producing miracles all the time.

The extraordinary question is, how can we possibly believe that scientists are capable of such miracles, while our rational, critical mind supposedly tells us that God is incapable of resurrecting His Son? Is there not something demonic about that? Science is capable, but the God that created science is not? That's absurd. Christ is alive. Nothing in the modern world refutes that testimony. Science does more to reinforce our faith than refute it.

For example, science has been telling us for some time that nothing in this world is ever lost forever. It is only transformed into something else. This pulpit looks solid. If I pound it from time to time (how long has it been since you've seen a preacher pound the pulpit?), it would feel solid, too. I could bruise my hand on it, it seems so solid. Our ancestors would have fought us if we told them that this pulpit is not as solid as it looks. Science tells us that what we call matter is actually made up of whirling centers of energy; nothing is static; all is bewildering motion.

Scientists would also tell us that everything is powered and transformed by energy—light becomes heat, heat becomes motion but in all these changes of form nothing is ever lost, only transformed. It is interesting to read that scientists are looking for what they call the God-particle that supposedly will explain how it all began in the first place. I can tell you how it all began and I don't have to spend billions of dollars building a laboratory under the Swiss Alps to do it. "In the beginning God created the earth and all that is in it . . ."

And I can tell you what evolution is all about. It is about creating the only being who is conscious of being part of this magnificent creation and who can interact with his Creator—a being created in the image of God. Now I ask you, if the universe is so constructed that no form of energy is ever lost, does it not make sense that nature's greatest creation, the human spirit, with its ability to think and love and will, will also be preserved? When the evolutionary process reaches its apex does it suddenly reverse itself and begin to destroy that for which it was engineered in the first place? The answer is, no! The universe conserves energy and it also conserves spirit. Christ is alive. Does your mind not tell you that? Does not your heart? (5)

Deep within our souls the very spirit of God testifies with our spirit, he is alive!

A man named Robert E. Smith once told of hearing the "Hallelujah Chorus" sung by five hundred trained voices. The "Hallelujah Chorus," of course, is the triumphant part of Messiah composed by George Frederic Handel after he was stricken with blindness in 1751. Handel claimed he had a vision and that this chorus is that vision set to music. Smith wrote that he could not for an instant doubt Handel's claim, not after having his soul lifted into paradise by those 500 inspiring voices.

The "Hallelujah Chorus," said Smith, is a magnificent expression of two thoughts: first that Christ reigns over all, and second that his reign is eternal. About the middle of the chorus the bass voices begin singing, "And he shall reign for ever and ever." Then the tenor voices join, "And he shall reign for ever and ever." Then the alto voices follow with, "And he shall reign for ever and ever." Then, still higher, the soprano voices add, "And he shall reign for ever and ever." Then bass, tenor, alto, and soprano all unite, and in a burst of melody which seems to come from heaven itself they blend in the grandest of all refrains, "And he shall reign for ever and ever, King of kings and Lord of lords! Hallelujah, hallelujah!"

Here is how Bob Smith expressed the experience of being swept up by the sound of those 500 voices: "I frankly confess that my soul was stirred profoundly, my mind was quickened spiritually and my imagination carried me beyond things earthly, beyond the stars, into the very midst of the paradise of God. I saw a great chorus which no [person] could number assembled before the shining white throne. Most intently did I listen to the song which they sang. It was a song of triumph to the King of kings, telling of his wondrous achievements and of the universality and permanency of his reign. In the midst of their song I heard the voices of the patriarchs peal forth, 'For he shall reign for ever and ever.' Then I heard the voices of the prophets add, 'For he shall reign for ever and ever.' Then the voices of the apostles and church fathers followed, 'For he shall reign for ever and ever.' Then the voices of the martyrs triumphantly sang, 'For he shall reign for ever and ever'... Then the patriarchs, prophets, apostles, church fathers, martyrs ... with the angels of God and all the redeemed of the ages, joined in one grand chorus, and my spirit was lifted to bliss supernal, to ecstasy supreme, as they pealed forth the blessed, the glorious, the triumphant strain, 'For he shall reign for ever and ever, King of kings! and Lord of Lords! Hallelujah! Hallelujah!'" (6)

Most of us couldn't express it that well, but we've experienced that same emotion. It is the music of Easter. It is the joyous surprise of Mary, and Peter and those other 500 believers to whom the risen Christ appeared. And it is the song that rings in our hearts this day, "For he shall reign for ever and ever, King of kings! and Lord of Lords! Hallelujah! Hallelujah!"

1. Melvin M. Newland, http://www.sermoncentral.com/sermons/easter—what-a-difference-melvin-newland-sermon-on-easter-resurrection-33346.asp.

2. Dr. Daniel Lioy, International Bible Lesson Commentary (Colorado Springs: David C. Cook, 2008), p. 270.

3. Change the World: Recovering the Message and Mission of Jesus.

4. Edward Bennett Williams, quoted in Christopher Buckley, "The Case for Edward Bennett Williams," Washington Post, November 3, 1991, X1. (Wharton, IL: Tyndale House Publishers, 2005, pp. 341-342).

5. This is an argument most notably advanced years ago by Roy A. Burkhart.

6. Modern Messages from Great Hymns (New York: The Abingdon Press, 1916).

Blessed Are Those Who Believe
John 20:19-31

Comedian Bob Hope—whom most of you will remember quite fondly as a wonderful entertainer—was married to his wife Dolores for 69 years, the longest Hollywood marriage on record. Bob lived two months past his hundredth birthday. Dolores died at 102.

Dolores was a devout Catholic. Bob loved to tell about the time she got on a plane in which two priests were seated in front of her. Three nuns were seated behind her. One of Hope's writers named Charlie Lee was also on the flight. Lee asked Hope, "Why can't she take out regular flight insurance, like the rest of us?" (1)

I doubt Dolores believed that being surrounded by those people of faith would keep the plane in the air. But she no doubt knew being surrounded by other believers would keep her faith up in the air. She could have learned that lesson from the central character in our story from today's lesson from the Gospel of John.

He was known to his friends as Thomas Didymus, Thomas the Twin. Jews in the first century were typically known by two names—one Hebrew and one Greek. For example, Peter was also known as Cephas. Cephas is Hebrew; Peter is Greek. Thomas is Hebrew; and Didymus is Greek. Didymus is Greek for Twin. (2) Thomas evidently had a twin brother.

Thomas was no villain by any means. In fact, Thomas was very much like you and me. He was a realist. For him, seeing was believing. Both his experience and his common sense told him that people who have been crucified, dead and buried don't come back to life. No one had ever called his cell phone from a sealed tomb. Dead people only walk around in Hollywood movies. Yet that was what his friends were saying about Jesus. They were saying that Jesus, whom he knew had been put to death by the Romans, was alive! And Thomas just wasn't buying it.

It is true that Thomas had seen Christ work miracles. He had also heard him teach with great authority on the Holy Scriptures. There was no question Jesus was no ordinary man. Thomas had hoped he was the Messiah, the one who would come to redeem Israel. But how could the Messiah be put to death? How could he who was to save the Jews be rejected by those he came to save? It made no sense. Jesus died on a cross between two thieves. Many of Thomas' hopes and dreams died there on that cross as well. Now doubt and disillusion had set in.

Thomas took no pride in his skepticism. Some people do. Doubt and skepticism are convenient tools for avoiding commitment. I can say I doubt the truth of the resurrection and avoid doing the unpleasant things one must do as a follower of Jesus—like sharing the Gospel with my friends, like serving meals to the homeless, like taking up a cross daily and following Jesus. That's not true of Thomas. Thomas wanted to believe. It's just that he was afraid of being made a fool.

Have you ever had someone let you down? Isn't it hard, really hard, to trust in that person again? Fool me once, we say, shame on you. Fool me twice, shame on me. Thomas had been willing to die for Jesus and the kingdom Jesus proclaimed. But now Jesus was dead. What Messiah? What Kingdom? He dared not allow himself to be suckered in again.

Besides, he was not alone in his doubting. The other disciples had trouble believing Christ was alive too. When the women returned from the tomb and testified about the empty tomb and the angels who had told them that Christ had risen as he said, the other disciples—all males—dismissed it as an idle tale. They did not believe it. That first Easter evening they were still cowering behind locked doors. They were still living in fear, not faith. Then Christ burst through those doors and revealed himself to them. Only then did they begin to believe.

Now it was a week later. For some reason Thomas had not been there behind those locked doors when Christ appeared to the others on that first Easter Sunday evening. He really should be remembered as Absent Thomas rather than Doubting Thomas. It's always dangerous to miss church. You never know when Jesus is going to make an appearance.

Thomas had not been there, but his friends had. Why he could not accept their testimony we do not know, but he didn't. Well, it was incredible. "Unless I see the nail marks in his hands and put my finger where the nails were, and put my hand into his side," he said to them defiantly, "I will not believe."

Now they were behind locked doors once again. Even though they testified that Christ was alive, they still had not unlocked the doors. I've known Christians like that, haven't you? They say, "Oh, yes, I believe in the resurrected Christ," but their lives are a mess. If they believe with their brains that he is alive, they haven't told it to their hearts. No, Thomas wasn't the only one who was slow in accepting the good news.

Then suddenly Christ was present in their midst once again. And he came directly to Thomas. He said to him, "Put your finger here; see my hands. Reach out your hand and put it into my side. Stop doubting and believe."

Thomas didn't need to reach out. He was stricken to his very soul when he saw Jesus' scars. Thomas' response was one of utter sincerity, "My Lord and my God!"

Then Jesus told him, "Because you have seen me, you have believed; blessed are those who have not seen and yet have believed." These words were directed at you and me, for we are in the same boat as Thomas before his personal experience of the risen Christ. "Blessed are those who have not seen and yet have believed."

We are more than two thousand years removed from that room with locked doors. We have the same resistance that Thomas had, the same natural skepticism.

How can we believe even though we were not there to see the scars and to hear the words of reassurance the risen Christ spoke to those who were his followers? What can we learn from Thomas about keeping our faith vital and strong so that we are not forever cowering in fear with locked hearts and locked minds?

The first thing we can learn is to stay in the company of fellow believers. Even if it were only coincidental, Dolores Hope was right to fly surrounded by people of faith. That's the only way to travel.

Rev. Dr. Jana Childers is Professor of Homiletics and Speech Communication at San Francisco Theological Seminary. She tells about preaching at Allen Temple Baptist Church in nearby Oakland during a traditional African-American Good Friday service.

This was an interesting service. The men of the congregation, including some younger males who were not quite teenagers, were providing the special music that day while the seven last words of Christ were being preached by seven women preachers, Dr. Childers being one of those preachers.

The men were clearly getting a kick out of it. Dr. Childers knew she would get a kick out of it too because she knew her sermon would be followed by her favorite baritone, Deacon Sellers, singing a song. She says it's all she can do to keep from swooning each time she hears Deacon Sellers sing "The Holy City," and this time she was glad he was singing after she preached. It might be too much for her to preach after hearing him sing.

Of course, there weren't seven male soloists of the stature of Deacon Sellers who could get off from work on a Friday afternoon—even at a large, flourishing church like Allen Temple—and so it was that some of the young baritones-in-training were given their first outing at this service.

She says there was one young man who seemed to be eleven or twelve years old. His voice wavered through the first few bars of the assigned song a good two blocks from the key the organist was in. The congregation was with him, though. "All right, now," said voices from the congregation. "That's right. Sing, child."

Gradually, she noticed that the young man's voice begin to strengthen. And then he appeared to finally find the right key. The young voice was encouraged by the congregation's support, but there was something else. The boy's voice was being shadowed, it seemed to Dr. Childers, by a steady, stealthy voice. She looked around. In the choir loft a few yards behind the soloist sat Deacon Sellers, his face and eyes averted. He just happened to be there, you know. Waiting his turn. She looked again. Deacon Sellers was singing. Quietly, steadily, surreptitiously singing that green twelve-year-old into key. Gradually, she realized that there were four or five men scattered through the large loft, also looking very casual, also singing. (3)

That young man wasn't on his own. He was being undergirded by these experienced men of faith. What a grand example of what the church is meant to be,

notes Dr. Childers. If you want to keep your faith strong, if you want to have a support group that will be there in your time of need, this is where you will find it. Surround yourself with people of faith. That's one way to ensure that doubt and
skepticism don't sap you of your confidence in God. Here's the second.

Remember that a locked mind is a far bigger obstacle than a locked door.
Thomas may have sounded like a firm skeptic when he stated that he would not believe unless he saw with his own eyes and touched with his own hands, but why was
Thomas there with the others if he no longer wanted anything to do with Christ? He
could have stayed home and watched Sunday Night Football, but he was there with
his friends. You know why he was there. Thomas wanted to believe.

There are plenty of other people who would have stayed home. There are
some people who have locked their minds firmly against faith. Sometimes this is
the result of unfortunate past experiences. Sometimes this is a guard against having
to make any kind of commitment. For some people this is a genuine intellectual decision. People reject Christ for all kinds of reasons.

What we need to see is that Christ will always honor their decision. He will
not force himself on anyone. He will allow us to go our own way. But believe this.
He will leave a light burning in the window so that when we come to ourselves, we
can come home.

Bishop William Willimon tells about the early life of the well-known writer
Annie Dillard. Dillard grew up in Pittsburgh. She was a bright, well-read child and
teenager with many questions about God including the age-old question about why
there was suffering in the world. Finally all her questions led her away from God.
One day at the grand old age of fifteen she took it upon herself to make an appointment with her aging pastor at the Shadyside Presbyterian Church. She said to him,
"I want my name off the roll. I don't believe in God anymore."

The pastor said, "Okay."

Annie Dillard said, "You're not going to try to argue me out of it?"

And he said, "No, no, no. You're too smart for me. There's no way I could argue
you back in."

So she said, "I want my name off the roll."

He said, "It's off the roll."

She said, "Okay." She walked out of the minister's office and on her way down
the hall she heard him mutter to himself out loud, "She'll be back!"

Young Annie Dillard wheeled around, went back into the office and said,
"What did I hear you say?"

He said, "Oh, I said I presumed that you'll probably be back."

And she said, "Look, this is my life. I live my life like I want to live my life. I'm
not coming back!"

Well, Annie Dillard wrote in her life story, "As I write this I'm 48 years old and I'm back." (4)

Most people, if they are presented with a healthy expression of the Gospel and a loving environment when they are young, they will come back. But it is a matter of a personal decision. Christ respects our freedom. He will burst through locked doors of a room where his disciples are hiding, but he will not burst into a locked mind.

Still Christ wants us to know that we are loved. Just because Thomas doubted the Gospel did not mean that Christ had stopped loving him. And Christ wants you and me to know that, if we have a difficult time believing the Gospel, he hasn't stopped loving us either. To me, that is what's beautiful about Christ's scars.

In her book, The Fourth Instinct, Arianna Huffington tells an ancient fable of an Indian healer who cured a man of leprosy. He took away all the disfiguring marks of the disease, but left the man with one small scar. What was the scar for? The healer answered, "So he will always remember." (5)

Have you ever wondered why God left the risen Christ with wounds still on his body—the scarred hands and feet and the wounded side? After all, the New Testament teaches us that when God gives us new life beyond the grave, we are given a new body, one that is whole and perfect and never dies again. We know that Christ had this new spiritual body because he entered the room without the doors being unlocked. Why then did his body still retain the scars?

I believe it was to remind us of God's great love for us. We may doubt, we may deny, we may even betray God and every good value that God would have us embrace, but God never stops loving us.

When Thomas saw Christ's scars, he cried out, "My Lord and my God!" Those scars told Thomas how much he was loved.

Hymn writer Isaac Watts put it like this:

See from His head, His hands, His feet, Sorrow and love flow mingled down! Did e'er such love and sorrow meet, Or thorns compose so rich a crown?

Were the whole realm of nature mine, that were an offering far too small; love so amazing, so divine, demands my soul, my life, my all.

Christ loves you. Christ died for you. Christ rose from the dead and now he welcomes all who would come into his Father's kingdom. Are you ready to take that step?

1. Bob Hope, The Road to Hollywood, p. 38.
2. http://www.calvarycsd.org/sermons/john-111-16-lessons-when-a-friend-dies/.
3. Chicago Sunday Evening Club. http://www.csec.org/csec/sermon/childers_4421.htm.
4. Bishop William Willimon, http://www.csec.org/csec/sermon/willimon_5316.htm.
5. (New York: Simon & Schuster, 1994), p. 99.

A New Kind Of Authority

Acts 9:1-6, (7-20)

Former President George H. W. Bush, the elder Bush, was speaking to an appreciative audience some years back, immediately after leaving office. He explained what it was like to go from being Vice President for eight years and President for four years, to being a private citizen.

"The first day I woke up," he said, "I reached over to push the button to get somebody to bring me some coffee, but there was no button, and there was nobody to bring any coffee." Then he added, "Barbara said, 'Get out of bed and make the coffee yourself.'" (1)

That would be quite a shock. One moment you are the leader of the most powerful nation in the world. The next you are an average everyday American. That's the beauty of democracy. We spread the privilege of serving. Our theme today is leadership, authority.

There is an old Peanuts comic strip. Linus is upset over the news that one of his school teachers is about to be fired. He turns to Lucy and says, "They can't fire Miss Othmar! I'll write a letter of protest! I'll blow this thing wide open! I'll write to someone in authority! Someone who can really do something!"

Linus composes himself for a moment as he prepares to set his pen to his paper. It is obvious he doesn't know anyone of authority. Finally he asks Lucy, "How does one go about getting a letter to the Apostle Paul?"

Well, the Apostle Paul did have a certain kind of authority. Think how closely we study his words in the church today. There was a time, however, when he had a different kind of authority, an authority that sent chills down the spines of Christian believers.

As you well know, before his conversion Paul had a different name, Saul, and he was a man to be feared, especially if you were a Christian. Saul seemed to take delight in persecuting the followers of Jesus. That was because of his fierce devotion to the faith in which he was nurtured. Saul was Jewish. He called himself a Hebrew among Hebrews, so fervent in the faith and traditions of his own people that he stood by and watched over the cloaks of the mob that dragged Stephen off and stoned him to death. Stephen's crime? Preaching the good news of Jesus Christ (Acts 7:55-Acts 8:3).

Later on, Saul had risen to such prominence and respect with his own people that he could go see the high priests of the Sanhedrin and receive from them letters that gave him the authority to persecute and arrest any Christians he came across. Saul was a big, self-righteous man with big, ambitious plans. He probably felt very special, very important as he rode along, tall in the saddle on the way to Damascus.

Luke, the author of our lesson from the book of Acts describes the situation like this: As Saul neared Damascus suddenly a light from heaven flashed around him. He fell to the ground and heard a voice say to him, "Saul, Saul, why do you persecute me?"

"Who are you, Lord?" Saul asked.

"I am Jesus, whom you are persecuting," the voice replied. "Now get up and go into the city, and you will be told what you must do."

The men traveling with Saul stood there speechless; they heard the sound but did not see anyone. Saul got up from the ground, but when he opened his eyes he could see nothing. So they led him by the hand into Damascus. Suddenly Saul didn't seem all that big and fearsome, did he? That can happen in life.

A pastor writing on the Internet tells about a man he knew, a very proud man who was well off financially. He had an attractive young wife, a good job, lived at the beach, and all the rest. He came to church sometimes and was always friendly and supportive.

One day this man read in the newspaper that one of his sons was being sought for committing murder. The man talked to his pastor, at first convinced that his son didn't do it. As the years went on, the son went to trial and was convicted and sentenced to life in prison without parole. The father continued to support him, always convinced of his innocence. The father didn't want his son to be alone at the other end of the country so he found a church of his denomination near the prison and the church folks began to minister to the son. When the father visited the son, he attended that church himself. He said to his pastor that nothing had ever humbled him like the shame of having a son in prison and at the same time finding more love from God than he had ever known. (2)

Saul could have related to that father. He had been riding high. Now he was brought low. Luke tells us that for three days Saul was blind, and did not eat or drink anything. But then Saul experienced the love of God. This love came through an ordinary Christian disciple living in Damascus named Ananias. This is the only time this particular Ananias is mentioned in scripture except a little later on when the Apostle Paul is giving his testimony and he describes Ananias as "a devout observer of the law and highly respected by all the Jews living [in Damascus]" (Acts 22:12). Other than that we know nothing. But the little we know of him is sufficient. Ananias didn't need Paul's impressive credentials and connections to be used of God. As Saul lay blind and helpless Ananias had a vision in which the Lord called to him, "Ananias!"

"Yes, Lord," he answered. That's always the response of faith, "Yes, Lord."

The Lord told Ananias, "Go to the house of Judas on Straight Street and ask for a man from Tarsus named Saul, for he is praying." Evidently being stricken as he was had humbled Saul to the point that he was calling on God for help. The

Lord continues with his instructions: "In a vision [Saul] has seen a man named Ananias come and place his hands on him to restore his sight."

"Lord," Ananias answered, "I have heard many reports about this man and all the harm he has done to your holy people in Jerusalem. And he has come here with authority from the chief priests to arrest all who call on your name."

But the Lord said to Ananias, "Go! This man is my chosen instrument to proclaim my name to the Gentiles and their kings and to the people of Israel . . ."

Then Ananias, probably quite reluctantly, went to the house where Paul was staying. Placing his hands on Saul, he said, "Brother Saul, the Lord Jesus, who appeared to you on the road as you were coming here has sent me so that you may see again and be filled with the Holy Spirit."

Immediately, something like scales fell from Saul's eyes, and he could see again. He got up and was baptized into the very faith he had set out to destroy, and after taking some food, he regained his strength. Then Luke adds these very descriptive words, "Saul spent several days with the disciples in Damascus. At once he began to preach in the synagogues that Jesus is the Son of God."

I believe you will agree, this was quite a transformation. Saul could sing quite literally, "I once was lost but now I'm found, was blind but now I see."

So Saul, the ambitious man with big plans, has an experience that brings him to his knees. And he realizes that his whole life has been one big mistake. And through the touch of an ordinary man named Ananias, Saul's life is radically changed, and he becomes an Apostle of Jesus, whose followers he had persecuted.

Do such things happen to people in the real world—that kind of radical life-change? Sometimes.

Some of you will remember the name Eldridge Cleaver. At one time Eldridge Cleaver was the much maligned leader of the Black Panthers, the violent militants of the early 1960s. But something significant happened in Eldridge Cleaver's life.

Pastor Ray Stedman tells of a conversation he had with Cleaver sometime back. In that conversation Cleaver gave one example from his former life. He said that while he was a Black Panther he was filled with a terrible feeling of hatred and violence against any law enforcement agency. He couldn't help himself. Every time he would get near an officer of the law he would feel this terrible sense of anger and murder and rage within him. But one night in the south of France, in a balcony overlooking the Mediterranean Sea, Eldridge Cleaver had a vision, an inner view, of the face of Jesus Christ, coming out of his boyhood to him. It drove him to reading the Scriptures. He read Psalm 23 over and over again. He said that ever since that time on the balcony, he had never had that feeling of hatred again. He has looked for it, and expected it, but instead, there has been a feeling of love for everyone he meets. (3) Again, what a transformation!

Even though we could never mention Eldridge Cleaver's name in the same company spiritually with St. Paul, nevertheless their experience of Christ shared some similarities. Both were delivered from feelings of hatred to feelings of love and acceptance by their experience of the risen Christ.

Here's what I find fascinating, however. Sometime after his experience in Damascus, Saul changes his name to Paul. What's fascinating about that?

Saul, the Hebrew name, means "asked for" or "prayed for." You'll remember that the people of ancient Israel asked God for a king. God gave them a king. Does anyone remember his name? That's right. His name was Saul. Saul was "asked for," "prayed for" by the people of Israel. Undoubtedly this New Testament Saul was named by his parents after this first king of Israel since they were both of the tribe of Benjamin.

There was just one thing wrong with King Saul—he was a big disappointment. He was driven by his ego and became desperate to maintain his position, finally being driven mad in his determination to destroy young David who, you'll remember, was becoming more popular than he was. Maybe Saul's name was part of the problem—"asked for," "prayed for." Such a name has to make you feel important.

The New Testament Saul, like his namesake the former king of Israel, was a man who became haughty in his power and authority enforcing Jewish Law and had to be brought low. So, Saul either chose or was given a new name, Paul. Now here's what's fascinating: Paul, a Latin name, means "Small"—as in tiny, little, insignificant. It is intriguing to me that the Apostle chose to identify himself in this way. The once "big man," identifies himself after his conversion, as "Small."

It happens sometimes in sports. A 300-lb. lineman will be called "Tiny" by his teammates. But it doesn't happen often and I believe it is significant in Paul's situation. He wanted people to know he wasn't the same man he had been. In fact, later Paul may have been making a pun on his name meaning small, when he refers to himself as the "least of the Apostles."

Sometimes as adults—even Christian adults—who are also parents or bosses or leaders in our churches or communities, we can let a little bit of authority or power or success go to our heads. We may think because we are used to making decisions that we are somehow in charge of our lives, running things, and we may forget that every job we do, every dollar we earn, indeed every step we take and every breath we draw, is all by the grace of God. A person may be anointed and commissioned to do a task for God, but if he or she ever forgets that it is God who empowers us and God to whom we should look to direct our steps, we run the risk of getting far off track.

Saul thought he knew what he was doing. He believed he was serving the God of Israel by carrying out his own hate-filled agenda. Saul thought he knew everything he needed to know about God. He had no idea that God had revealed so much more through Jesus of Nazareth. Saul thought he had power and authority, but God took away his autonomy and independence. God literally knocked him off his horse and blinded him in order that he might see more than he had ever seen before. Saul was brought low, forced to recognize not only the true Jesus but also the truth about his own actions. Instead of serving God, he was persecuting God's only Son. And now, upon realizing that Jesus is Lord, the one with true power and authority over everything, Saul was humbled to the point that he could become a magnificent ambassador for Christ.

Saul had a reputation . . . but he received a revelation—a revelation about himself and a revelation of God in Christ Jesus. From this day forward he would subject his reputation and his authority to the will and glory of Jesus Christ. The converted Saul who once thought he had it all figured out now sees himself as an unimportant and weak "vessel," and a mere slave to an all-important and all-powerful Lord (2 Cor. 12:5-10).

And the same thing can be true of us. Until we submit ourselves to the Lordship of Christ, each of us finds ourselves traveling a dangerous, difficult road. Up until we yield ourselves to God's leadership, we live our lives puffed up with an inflated sense of our own authority or power, and warped by our own selfishness and self-importance. Even though we may believe we mean well or see ourselves as good people, until we enter into a living relationship with Jesus, until the Lord introduces himself to us and enters in to live and love through us, then we are like Saul. We might think we are doing well, but sober reflection will reveal that our lives are empty.

Lee Strobel once knew that emptiness. Though he was a successful journalist, by his own account he was not a happy man. He describes himself at that stage in his life as "profane and angry." To prove his point he cites a time when he came home one night and kicked a hole in the living room wall just out of anger with his life. Can you imagine the impression his conduct made on his five-year-old daughter? But Jesus Christ came into Lee Strobel's life and changed his life radically. He says that five months after he gave his life to Christ, his little girl went to her mother and said, "Mommy, I want God to do for me what he's done for Daddy." It's hard to argue with a testimony like that. Strobel says that God changed not only him, God changed his family and changed his world. Today he is a well-known author and pastor.

Can you give the same kind of testimony? Saul was a big man with big plans. But he was an angry man who took out his anger on others. Christ humbled Saul and gave him a new name, Paul, a name that means small. Ironically, after becoming small, after becoming the least of the Apostles, Paul became the second most influential man who ever lived after Christ himself. After his blinding experience on the road to Damascus, he became a man who could see the purposes of God so clearly that to this day we study his words with rapt devotion. Even more importantly he became God's instrument. It was in dying to his former self that he became alive to God's plan for his life. And God used him in a mighty way. Friend, God can use us too if we will humble ourselves and believe the Gospel.

1. Gerhard Gschwandtner, Personal Selling Power, July/August 1994, p. 26.
2. http://www.raefordumc.net/2009/07/mark-1035-45-sermon.html.
3. http://www.pbc.org/files/messages/4754/3533.html.

Belonging To Christ's Flock
Psalm 23; John 10:22-30

A couple retired to a small Arizona ranch and acquired a few sheep. At lambing time, it was necessary to bring two newborns into the house for care and bottle-feeding.

As the lambs grew, they began to follow the rancher's wife around the farm. She was telling a friend about this strange development.

"What did you name them?" the friend asked her.

"Goodness and Mercy," she replied with a sigh. (1)

She was referring of course to a line in everyone's favorite Psalm, "Surely goodness and mercy shall follow me all the days of my life: and I will dwell in the house of the Lord forever" (KJV).

Our lessons for today from Scripture all refer to sheep or shepherds. It is probably the most familiar image in Scripture. God is a shepherd. We are God's sheep. Sheep were important to the agricultural lives of the ancient Hebrews. That is perhaps why sheep are mentioned more than 500 times in the Bible, more than any other animal.

For King David, who authored much of the Book of Psalms, the metaphor of the sheep and the shepherd was an obvious way to think of our relationship with God. He had vivid memories of life as a young shepherd before he became a warrior and a king. Thus he begins his popular and beloved Psalm 23 with, "The Lord is my Shepherd."

But David wasn't the only Old Testament writer to use this imagery. The Prophet Isaiah used sheep to illustrate the waywardness of God's people. Isaiah writes, "All we like sheep have gone astray; we have turned everyone to his own way." Now you're probably thinking, how did he know about us? He sure got us right.

And, of course, this descriptive language is carried over into the New Testament, concerning Jesus. He is the ultimate Shepherd of God's people as well as the unblemished, sacrificial Lamb of God.

Now, unless you've grown up on a sheep ranch or spent a lot of time at a petting zoo, you're probably not all that familiar with sheep. In any case, you probably wouldn't think that being described as a sheep is very flattering—although, the truth is, sheep have more right to be offended by the comparison than we do.

Most of us probably prefer to think of ourselves as mavericks, too smart, too free-spirited and individual to go along with any herd. It's natural, perhaps for Americans in particular, to celebrate qualities that are more characteristic of mules than of sheep. Sheep, unless someone is having a hard time getting to sleep, tend to be woefully under-appreciated.

When most of us think of sheep, we suppose them to be feeble-minded animals too stupid to think for themselves, and therefore apt to follow along with the rest of the herd, sometimes into dangerous or deadly situations. However, this image of the life of a sheep is based on a lack of understanding. When you really get to know a little bit more about sheep, you begin to realize that being a good sheep—that is, a sheep that sticks with its flock and tries to remain close to the shepherd—requires some basic qualities that are also essential to being a disciple or true follower of Jesus Christ. And, like the disciple of Christ, the sheep benefits greatly from belonging to the flock, gaining safety, guidance, nourishment, correction and care, as well as the opportunity to be useful and productive. Being part of the flock is the sheep's equivalent of American Express—membership has its privileges.

But membership also has its responsibilities. And in our more mule-like character, we are sometimes resistant to those responsibilities. It requires the work of the Holy Spirit to make us into the right kind of sheep to follow Jesus—especially those of us who, if you don't mind a bad pun, are seriously "hard-of-herding."

We need to ask ourselves, what does being a good sheep require? How can we make sure we're in the right flock, obeying the Good Shepherd instead of wandering off on our own or following a stray herd? What do we need to know and do as members of Christ's flock? Let's look at that for just a few moments.

Our lesson from John's Gospel is set during the Festival of Dedication at Jerusalem. The Festival of Dedication is what we know nowadays as Hanukkah or the Feast of Lights. It's celebrated for eight days in December.

Jesus is in the temple courts walking in Solomon's Colonnade. Solomon's Colonnade was a long covered walkway on the east side of the temple. As he walked, some inquiring Jews came up to him and asked, "How long will you keep us in suspense? If you are the Messiah, tell us plainly."

Jesus answered, "I did tell you, but you do not believe. The works I do in my Father's name testify about me, but you do not believe because you are not my sheep. My sheep listen to my voice; I know them, and they follow me. I give them eternal life, and they shall never perish; no one will snatch them out of my hand. My Father, who has given them to me, is greater than all; no one can snatch them out of my Father's hand. I and the Father are one."

Notice what Jesus says about his flock. First of all, he says that he knows them individually. This is a beautiful picture of our relationship with God, each of us is known by God.

There is an amazing story that comes from the Wycliffe Bible Translators. This story concerns a tribal people in Cameroon called the Hdi. [Nowhere could I find the proper pronunciation of this tribe's name or the other key words in this story, so bear with me.]

Translator Lee Bramlett, working with the Hdi people, discovered that verbs in the Hdi language consistently end in one of three vowels: i, a, or u. Even more interesting, the ending vowel determines the true meaning of the word. This appears to be true of every word in the Hdi vocabulary except for one—the word which means love. When it comes to the word love, the Hdi people use an "i or a," for the last letter. However, no word for love ends with "u." In other words, the two words for love are dvi, d-v-i and dva, d-v-a. There is no dvu, d-v-u.

Lee Bramlett asked the Hdi people for help in understanding this discrepancy concerning the word love. He asked, "Could you 'dvi' your wife, [d-v-i]?"

"Yes," they said. That would mean that the wife had been loved but the love was now gone.

Then he asked, "Could you 'dva' your wife, [d-v-a]?"

"Yes," they said. That kind of love depended on the wife's actions. She would be loved as long as she remained faithful and cared for her husband well.

Then Lee Bramlett asked the question that truly puzzled him, "Could you 'dvu' your wife, [d-v-u]?"

Everyone laughed. "Of course not!" they said. "If you said that, you would have to keep loving your wife no matter what she did, even if she never got you water, never made you meals. Even if she committed adultery, you would be compelled to just keep on loving her. No, we would never say 'dvu.' It just doesn't exist."

Lee sat quietly for a while, thinking about John 3:16, and then he asked, "Could God 'dvu' people?"

There was complete silence for three or four minutes; then tears started to trickle down the weathered faces of these elderly men. Finally they responded. "Do you know what this would mean? This would mean that God would keep loving us over and over, millennia after millennia, while all that time we rejected His great love. He is compelled to love us, even though we have sinned more than any people." (2)

Do I need to tell you that the word dvu was added to the Hdi translation of the Bible to express God's love for all the people of the world?

Christ knows his sheep by name. Christ dvus his sheep. He keeps loving us over and over, millennia after millennia, even when we reject his love. He is compelled to love us, even though we sin more than any people. That's the first thing Jesus says about our relationship with the Shepherd. He knows us individually. But listen to what comes next.

Jesus says the sheep listen to his voice. This relationship between the sheep and the shepherd is not one-sided.

A man in Australia was arrested sometime back and charged with stealing a sheep. But he protested that he owned the sheep and that it had been missing for many days.

When the case went to court, the judge didn't know how to decide the matter. Finally he asked that the sheep be brought into the courtroom. Then he ordered the plaintiff, the man who had accused the man of stealing his sheep, to step outside and call the animal. The sheep made no response except to raise its head and look frightened.

The judge then instructed the defendant to go to the courtyard and call the sheep. When the accused man began to make his distinctive call, the sheep ran toward the door and his voice. It was obvious that the sheep recognized the familiar voice of his master.

"His sheep knows him," said the judge. "Case dismissed!" (3)

Let me ask you a question: is this imagery descriptive of your relationship with Christ? Do you listen to the voice of Christ?

It reminds me of something Fred Rogers, "Mister Rogers" to many of you, once wrote. He said, "Listening is where love begins—listening to ourselves, and then to our neighbors." I believe Fred Rogers, in the proper context would have added, "As well as listening to God."

I believe you will agree that most of us are great talkers when it comes to our devotional life, but poor listeners. We give God our orders for the day, but we are not committed to reverently listening to the orders God has for us. Christ says he knows his sheep, but then he adds, "and they listen to my voice."

Then he says his sheep follow him.

Author Neal Andersen contends that those of us who live in the western world don't have a correct picture of what it means to be led like sheep. Western shepherds drive their sheep from behind the flock, often using dogs to bark at their heels. Eastern shepherds, like those in Bible times, lead their sheep from front.

Andersen tells about watching a shepherd lead his flock on a hillside outside Bethlehem. The shepherd sat on a rock while the sheep grazed. After a time he stood up, said a few words to the sheep and walked away. The sheep followed him. It was fascinating! Andersen says the words of Jesus in this passage suddenly took on new meaning for him, "My sheep hear my voice, and I know them, and they follow me." (4)

You can judge whether a person is a disciple of Christ by how well he or she follows. Many of us want the benefits of belonging to Christ's flock—to be known completely and intimately by God—without the responsibility of listening to Christ and following him daily. We want to know him as our Savior without having him as our Master.

Jesus is well aware of our weakness and our waywardness, so he adds this final word of Grace: Christ says that no one can snatch his sheep from him. In other words, God dvus us. Nothing in all creation can come between us and our Shepherd.

There is a story from yesteryear that says it beautifully. The year was 1850. On the prairies of the Midwest light snow was still falling in March. There was a little log cabin on the prairie in which a little boy, Timmy, was on the verge of death from diphtheria. A Methodist circuit rider came by to visit Timmy. He wanted to see if the boy was all right, since he had heard that he was not doing well. He came into the room to find little Timmy sick in bed.

The circuit riding preacher asked Timmy if he knew how to say the 23rd psalm. Timmy replied that he had learned it in the second grade at his Sunday school. He started reciting the Psalm, "The Lord is my shepherd, I shall not want."

The pastor told him he was reciting it much too fast. Timmy tried to say it again—this time more slowly. The pastor decided to teach him how to say the 23rd psalm in a different way. He asked him to count the words on his fingers, beginning with his thumb. "The Lord is my . . ." This way when he uttered the word "my" he would be holding the fourth finger of his hand. The preacher explained, "Your parents wear their wedding rings on the 4th finger of their hands. This is the finger of love. So, if each time Timmy recited "The Lord is My Shepherd," when he grabbed his fourth finger, it would be a reminder that the Lord is his personal shepherd, "The Lord is MY Shepherd." This pleased Timmy and he recited the psalm accordingly. Then the pastor bid Timmy farewell and went on his way.

When he came back to see Timmy it was springtime. He noticed that there was a mound of upturned earth with a cross on it in the backyard. He realized that Timmy had passed away. Timmy's parents spoke about what a good boy Timmy was. Then they described his final night. They had kissed Timmy good night. In the morning when his mother went to check on him, she realized that he had died. But there was something that caught her eye and she found it extremely strange. She noticed that Timmy was holding on to his 4th finger. She asked the pastor about it. The pastor could only answer her with tear-filled eyes. (5)

You and I know what it meant. "The Lord is My shepherd." Or as Jesus said, "My sheep listen to my voice; I know them, and they follow me. I give them eternal life, and they shall never perish; no one will snatch them out of my hand. My Father, who has given them to me, is greater than all; no one can snatch them out of my Father's hand. I and the Father are one."

Jesus, the Good Shepherd knows us by name. We are to listen for his voice and follow him, knowing that he will provide for every need. And nothing will every separate us from his love. This is his promise to his people, the sheep of his pasture.

1. Arizona Highways.
2. Dvu, Peter and Kate Nash in Monday Fodder.
3. http://www.visitgateway.org/Services/Messages/2011/03-27-11/I_Am_Gary_Gaertner_03_27_11.pdf.
4. Neil T. Anderson, Victory Over the Darkness (Ventura, CA: Regal Books, 1990), pp. 103-104.
5. Edward F. Markquart,
http://www.sermonsfromseattle.com/series_a_the_lord_is_my_shepherd.htm.

On God's Side Or In God's Way?
Acts 11:1-18

I want to go back for a few moments into TV history. Some of you grew up watching the hilarious Roadrunner cartoons. These cartoons featured a character named Wile E. Coyote. Wile E. Coyote's virtually endless quest in life was to capture his nemesis, the Roadrunner. The coyote was stubbornly persistent in this quest despite the fact that, not only did he fail time after time after time, but meanwhile he repeatedly plummeted from high cliffs, was blown up, and was continually getting flattened by numerous large, heavy falling objects.

On one occasion the coyote pursued the roadrunner into a long, dark tunnel, so dark that all that was visible of him were his eyes, shining in the blackness. Unable to see the roadrunner, the coyote paused, uncertain. Then he would see a light at the end of the tunnel and head for it, only to discover at the last minute—when it was too late—that the light he faced belonged to an oncoming locomotive. So the coyote got plowed down and flattened, again, and the object of his chase, yet again, eluded him. Perhaps the Roadrunner cartoons gave us the humorous expression about realizing that the light at the end of the tunnel is an approaching locomotive.

Normally we might think of the coyote's dilemma as an example of our lives when adversity strikes. I know there have been times in my life when I felt I had been flattened by a locomotive. At such times I have prayed for the ability to get back on my feet. Most of us can relate to such experiences.

But today I would like to apply the metaphor of the oncoming locomotive to the coming of the kingdom of God. And the question I would like to pose is this—are there times when we find ourselves like Wile E. Coyote standing in the way of God's oncoming kingdom?

In our lesson today from the book of Acts, the early disciples of Jesus are confronted with a critical turning point. All the members of the early Christian community had been Jewish. This was important to many of them. The Jewish faith had drawn much of its strength from its exclusivity. Jews viewed themselves as set apart to be a holy people. Even those Jews who had become Christians clung to this belief that Gentiles were in some way unclean, unfit to belong to the body of Christ.

Then something quite unsettling occurred. Word was spreading throughout the community that Gentiles were being accepted into the faith. It was being whispered that even the Apostle Peter, the most influential of the first Apostles was part of this movement. So when Peter went up to Jerusalem, those Christians who prided themselves on their Jewish backgrounds criticized him. They had heard reports about him. They heard that he had not only entered the houses of uncircumcised Gentiles, but he had actually eaten with them. "Tell us, Peter," they cried, "that it's not so!"

But it was so. So, starting from the beginning, Peter explained how he had come to this position of accepting Gentiles. "I was in the city of Joppa praying," he said, "and in a trance I saw a vision. I saw something like a large sheet being let down from heaven by its four corners, and it came down to where I was. I looked into [this sheet] and saw four-footed animals of the earth, wild beasts, reptiles and birds. Then I heard a voice telling me, 'Get up, Peter. Kill and eat.'

"I replied, 'Surely not, Lord! Nothing impure or unclean has ever entered my mouth.' But the voice spoke from heaven a second time, 'Do not call anything impure that God has made clean.' This happened three times, and then it was all pulled up to heaven again.

"Right then," Peter continues, "three men who had been sent to me from Caesarea stopped at the house where I was staying. The Spirit told me to have no hesitation about going with them. These six brothers also went with me, and we entered [a man's house, named Cornelius. Cornelius] told us how he had seen an angel appear in his house and say, 'Send to Joppa for Simon who is called Peter. He will bring you a message through which you and all your household will be saved.'

"As I began to speak," Peter concludes, "the Holy Spirit came on them as he had come on us [on the Day of Pentecost]. Then I remembered what the Lord had said: 'John baptized with water, but you will be baptized with the Holy Spirit.'" So, Simon Peter says with finality, "if God gave them the same gift [of the Spirit] . . . who was I to think that I could stand in God's way?"

What a wonderful passage of scripture. It is a passage that you and I should be mighty thankful for, or else we who are from non-Jewish backgrounds would not be in the church today. "Who was I," said Simon Peter, "to think that I could stand in God's way?" Peter understood that it was God's will to throw open the doors of the church to all who would be saved, including Gentiles, and he wasn't going to oppose God or, in his words, "stand in God's way."

I want you to think of possible times in our history when Christians actually stood in God's way. Are there times in the church when we have behaved like Wile E. Coyote? Perhaps, for example, when we persecuted Galileo for his scientific discoveries? Or perhaps when many Christians opposed the Civil Rights movement? I'll leave it to you to fill in the blanks of all the places we as an institution or as individuals might have been standing in God's way.

I don't know why some religious people have such an affinity for the status quo—why do we have such fear of change? Not all, of course. The church has been at the forefront of many of the positive changes that have occurred in society. However, to be fair, I don't know of any significant progress that has taken place in human society that some religious group or another hasn't been against it.

Over two hundred years ago, in Gloucester, England, a man named Robert Raikes started a movement which was to have a far-reaching impact on the moral and religious life of the Western world. He began the Sunday School movement. He selected four women who gathered a group of children together on Sundays to instruct them in reading and in the church catechism.

Believe it or not, the Sunday School movement was strongly resisted by the established church. The ruling classes, who had much influence in the church of that day, feared that such a program would lead to popular education which in turn would lead to revolution. And then there was a legalistic wing of the church that believed strongly that the Sabbath day was for worship and rest only, not for recreation or for school. One Scottish preacher feared that such Sunday Schools would "destroy all family religion." (1) Imagine that. Sending children to Sunday School would destroy family religion. Every progressive step that has ever been made in human society has first of all been opposed by somebody in the name of Christ.

During the early days of the Salvation Army, General William Booth and his associates were bitterly attacked in the press by certain religious leaders. Can you imagine religious people opposing a group that has no other reason for existence except to help the down and out? When his son Bramwell showed General Booth a newspaper containing an attack on the Salvation Army, the General replied, "Bramwell, fifty years hence it will matter very little indeed how these people treated us; it will matter a great deal how we dealt with the work of God."

Some of you saw Steven Spielberg's movie on the life of Abraham Lincoln. There is a story told on Lincoln that reminds me of General Booth's words. In the midst of the Civil War a certain pious minister told Lincoln, "I hope the Lord is on our side."

The president responded, "I am not at all concerned about that . . . But it is my constant anxiety and prayer that I and this nation should be on the Lord's side."

It is amazing that Abraham Lincoln should be a better theologian than many who call themselves ministers of the Gospel.

Some of you grew up in the days of segregation in this land. I know it sounds like ancient history to our young people. But some of you can remember a few decades back when even many religious people were guilty of overt racism. Racism is still alive in our land. In fact, some recent surveys show that it might even be increasing. Heaven help us if it is, but at least it is not the law of the land like it was just a few decades ago.

In a collection of sermons which he titled Strength to Love, Dr. Martin Luther King Jr. described the beginning of the 1956 Montgomery, Alabama bus boycott. For those of you who weren't even a gleam in your parents' eye in 1956 let me give you a little background.

On December 1, 1955, Rosa Parks, an African American woman, was arrested for refusing to surrender her bus seat to a white person in Montgomery, Alabama. So, the African-American community and their supporters struck back by boycotting the Montgomery bus system. For eleven months Civil Rights workers operated a voluntary car pool to get people to and from their jobs. One of the leaders of that boycott was a young Baptist pastor by the name of Dr. Martin Luther King, Jr.

The boycott was a substantial blow to the city's financial health. So the mayor of Montgomery, a man named W. A. Gayle, went to court to seek to crush it and it looked very much like he might succeed. Dr. King tried his best to keep the spirit of his discouraged troops alive. "We have moved all of these months," he told them, "in the daring faith that God is with us in our struggle. The many experiences of days gone by have vindicated that faith in a marvelous way." Nevertheless, he could tell their hopes were flagging. "The night was darker than a thousand midnights," he wrote. "The light of hope was about to fade and the lamp of faith to flicker."

Ironically it was while Dr. King and his attorneys where in the courtroom awaiting the ruling about the legality of their boycott that the word came that the United States Supreme Court had ruled unanimously that bus segregation in Montgomery, Alabama was unconstitutional. Dr. King wrote, "My heart throbbed with an inexpressible joy. The darkest hour of our struggle had become the first hour of victory." (2)

Over the months ahead America discovered how complete that victory was. Jim Crow, the spirit of segregation, like Wile E. Coyote, had been flattened by the unstoppable locomotive of God's purpose. It is absurd to think you can defeat God. Mark it down, my friend, there is a time coming when every child on this earth will live in freedom and dignity. This is God's will, and we should either help make it happen or get out of the way.

Jesus taught us that there is a kingdom at work in this world—a kingdom that will someday result in all people living freely and joyfully as God's own people. We can fight it by the strength of our sinful natures, we can delay it by our lack of faith, but we cannot stop it—anymore than we can stop an oncoming locomotive by standing in the middle of a track and putting out a defiant hand. And so, you and I have a decision to make—are we on God's side or are we in God's way?

Dr. R. Steven Hudder tells about a legislator in Georgia, Donald Ponder, who decided he wanted to be on God's side. A representative to the state legislature he stood on the House floor of this conservative Southern state and implored his colleagues to pass a bill that would impose extra penalties for hate crimes committed against ethnic and racial minorities, as well as against gay and lesbian people.

He confessed to the state Legislature that all his ancestors in the nineteenth century owned slaves and that his great-grandfather had fought in the Civil War for the Confederacy. He told his fellow legislators of how his college fraternity had ostracized six members because they were gay. He told of his nanny, an African-American woman who had raised him from birth, who had taught him more than anyone else the difference between right and wrong. He told of how one day when he was a boy about to leave for school, she had leaned over to give him a kiss on the cheek, and how he had averted his head because he had been taught all his life that black people were not supposed to kiss white people. He spoke of the shame that he had carried since that day.

Then Representative Donald Ponder spoke these unforgettable words: "The day came not long ago when we buried the magnificent woman who had raised me. I pledged to myself that day that never again would I look in the mirror and know that I had kept silent and let hate, prejudice, and indifference negatively impact another person's life. I finally have figured it out. The only way we are ever going to make progress in this world is when somebody gets up and takes a stand. And so I stand before you today, my distinguished colleagues, and I urge the House of Representatives of the State of Georgia to pass this hate crimes bill." And you know what? They did. (3)

God is at work in this world anytime someone is willing to be used of God. If we will be used of God, we can see miracles occur. The way will open in front of us and we will see God's victory.

It reminds me of a story that an African-American preacher tells. He was driving his car one time traveling north, trying to get to Fredericksburg, Virginia. Suddenly his lights went out while he was driving in North Carolina. His alternator had quit working. There he was, hundreds of miles from his destination on a dark night with no way to see where he was going. He prayed, "I don't have an alternator, Lord, but I want to get back."

After that, he says, a Greyhound bus came by just flying. He thought to himself, "There's my ticket to Fredericksburg." He got right behind that big bus and laid right on the bumper of that bus and it carried him all the way to Virginia.

About that experience, he says, "I just believe God. You say, weren't you afraid of the highway patrol? No. Because the highway patrol should have been concerned about the bus as fast as it was going. They didn't need to be concerned about me." He concludes by saying, "Have faith in God! And believe that God is able." (4)

God is able. And God will do what he has promised. When it comes to justice and righteousness, we are either on God's side or in God's way.

I heard somebody ask a humorous question. The question was based on archaic language in our legal system. The question was, "Can a church be insured against acts of God?" Maybe it's not so humorous after all. A church that stands in God's way will be flattened like Wile E. Coyote. No insurance policy in the world can protect a church or a nation that chooses to ignore the oncoming locomotive of God's Kingdom.

1. Warren Wiersbe, The Wycliffe Handbook of Preaching (Moody Press, 1984), p. 185.

2. (Minneapolis: Fortress Press, 2010).

3. http://www.christ-congregational-church.org/Sermons/Life%20Light%20and%20Love.htm.

4. When Black Preachers Preach: Leading Black Preachers Give Direction & Encouragement to a Nation That Has Lost Its Way, Vol. 2 (Kindle Edition).

Coincidence Or Providence?
Acts 16:9-15

Way back in 1669 a most unusual occurrence took place. The entire village of Runswick, England, slipped into the sea. Yes, such tragedies occur from time to time. The entire town was swallowed up in the raging tides. Here's what is interesting, though—not a single inhabitant of Runswick drowned! Why? All the residents of the town were attending a funeral in a neighboring village at the time of the catastrophe. (1) Amazing!

Now, if you had been a resident of that village where not a single life was lost in that terrible catastrophe because they were all at a funeral in another town, would you say that was providence or would you say it was simply a co-incidence? In other words, was it the hand of God that all members of the community—men, women, even little babies—were at that funeral when this tragedy occurred, or was it a matter of simple happenstance? Interesting question.

Dr. Steve Land tells about a seminary student during World War II who was preparing himself to enter the war as a military chaplain. One day this student found a used book at a bookstore on the subject of "How to Speak Russian." This student was somewhat of an introvert. He preferred to remain in his room reading rather than going out to socialize with his friends. He decided that this little book on how to speak Russian would be a nice, quiet way to spend his evenings. From then until his graduation he studied that Russian language book whenever he had a chance.

After graduation the young man was inducted into the Army as a chaplain. He was sent to Europe where his battalion was involved in heavy fighting. One night as he lay on his bedroll, staring up at the stars, he became depressed. Every day and every night he was constantly giving comfort to wounded and dying soldiers. Seminary didn't prepare him for this. In fact, he did not feel prepared for anything he was being asked to do.

Just then, while those thoughts were troubling him, a medic came running up to him. "Chaplain," he said, "we have a man who is seriously wounded, he is scared and panicking but we can't understand what he is saying to us. Can you come help us?"

Upon arriving at the scene, he realized that it was a Russian soldier who had evidently gotten separated from his company. As he knelt beside the man he suddenly recognized he could understand much of what the soldier was saying. For the rest of the night he stayed by the soldier's side speaking words of comfort to him in broken Russian and praying with him the best he could until the man died from his wounds.

As he returned to his bedroll and lay down under the stars once again, the young chaplain felt that somehow the stars were brighter and the load he was carrying was a little lighter. He now knew that God was at work even in this awful war. This little Russian language book had fallen into his hands and God used it to comfort a dying soldier through him. (2)

Now, was this a coincidence or was it providence? Did God lead this young soldier to study Russian just for this particular moment in his life? Or was it just coincidental? I guess it depends what you believe about the universe. I guess it depends on what you believe about God.

The Apostle Paul had many unusual experiences that brought him into contact with a wide assortment of people. He was shipwrecked, jailed, he traveled all over to countries on the rim of the Mediterranean Sea. Sometimes he didn't know exactly where he would be going or why—or who he was supposed to meet when he got there. Nevertheless, when the Lord prompted him to go he went, because he trusted God to show him what to do.

One night Paul had a vision of a man from Macedonia. This man was standing and begging to Paul, "Come over to Macedonia and help us." Paul believed this was a call from God. He and three of his friends embarked at once for Macedonia. However, the trip to Macedonia wasn't easy. They traveled by boat and were forced to make stops along the way. One of those stops was at Philippi, the leading city of the district of Macedonia. Paul and his friends stayed there several days.

Evidently there was no synagogue in Philippi. So when the Sabbath came, they went down to the river to find a place to pray. It seems that the river was a favorite place for pious people to gather on the Sabbath. There was a group of women by the river who had also come to pray. Paul and his companions began talking with the women.

One of the women was named Lydia. Visualize Lydia as a successful business woman—slender, smartly dressed—carrying her attache case and her smart phone which she consulted quite regularly. Lydia would be quite comfortable in our world.

Lydia was a dealer in purple cloth and probably quite wealthy. Purple was the color of the Roman elite. Indeed, the emperor, and only the emperor, would wear a toga made entirely of purple cloth. Purple dye was quite expensive. It was made from a juice found in minute quantities in shellfish. It took thousands of these small crustaceans to make a yard or two of purple cloth. Purple dye was rare and purple fabric was worth its weight in silver. Franchises for dealing in purple were highly coveted.

That Lydia was a woman of considerable means is also evidenced by the size of her house. At the conclusion of this short vignette, she invites Paul and those who are with him to stay at her house. What makes this impressive is that

Lydia did not live alone. There were others in Lydia's household, probably servants as well as children, if she had children. Lydia seems to have been the head of her household. No husband is mentioned. Perhaps she was a widow. We simply do not know. There could have been extended family. Anyway, to house four traveling evangelists in addition to the rest of her household and servants indicates that Lydia's house was quite large for the time.

It's important to note that Lydia was not a Jew, but she did worship God. We'll talk more about that in just a few moments. As Lydia listened to Paul's message, Luke tells us the Lord opened her heart to the message of Jesus. And right there on the spot, she and all the members of her household were baptized into the Christian faith. Afterward, she invited Paul and his friends to her home. "If you consider me a believer in the Lord," she said, "come and stay at my house." And they accepted her kind hospitality. Incidentally, Lydia was Paul's first convert in Europe. It's a beautiful story.

Now, if you had asked Lydia, "Did you just happen to be there when the Apostle Paul came down to the river to pray?" how do you think she would have answered? Was it providence or coincidence? God's hand or mere happenstance? Obviously you could make a case either way. But I believe that Lydia would have said, "It was providence. God brought me to that spot just so I could hear the Gospel."

I believe that Lydia would say her encounter with Paul was providence because Lydia was a person of faith even before she was exposed to the Gospel. This is important. There is a tendency on the part of some religious people to divide the world into the saved and the unsaved, the righteous and the unrighteous. If you're not a baptized believer, in these people's eyes, then you are somehow inferior, unacceptable, probably immoral, too.

Interestingly enough, the New Testament isn't that narrow. In the New Testament there are Jews and there are Christians and there are people who are referred to as God-Fearers. Lydia fits the description of a God-Fearer. Luke refers to Lydia simply as a worshiper of God. In today's church parlance, we might call her a "seeker," someone who is outside the traditional faith community, but is seeking after God.

There's a man in Acts 10 who also fits the description of a God-Fearer. His name was Cornelius. Cornelius was an officer in what was known as the Italian Regiment of the Roman army. Cornelius commanded a hundred men whose main job was to maintain order in Caesarea. Cornelius was not a Jew. Neither was he a Christian. Here is how Luke describes him, "He and all his family were devout and God-fearing; he gave generously to those in need and prayed to God regularly." Do you get this? Can there be someone who is outside the mainstream of Judeo-Christian faith and still be devout and God-fearing? Of course there can. In fact, according to the book of Acts, you can be outside the mainstream of the faith community and still be used of God.

Cornelius is a great example of this. One afternoon about three o'clock Cornelius has a vision. He sees an angel of God. This angel comes to him and says, "Cornelius!"

Whoa, Cornelius is not prepared for this. He stares at the angel and he is afraid. "What is it, Lord?" he asks timidly.

The angel says to him, "Your prayers and gifts to the poor have caught God's attention. He has a job for you. You are to send some of your men to Joppa to bring back a man named Simon who is called Peter. He is staying with Simon the tanner, whose house is by the sea."

When the angel had gone, Cornelius called two of his servants and another devout soldier. He told them everything that had happened and sent them to Joppa.

Now here's what's important. All this was happening about the same time Peter was having his famous dream of the sheet being lowered from heaven—the sheet with all the animals on it. Peter had been taught to consider some of the animals on the sheet unclean. But God told Peter that nothing which He created was unclean. It was this dream that caused Peter to understand that it was all right for him to break bread with Gentiles. It was to Cornelius' house that God summoned Simon Peter. This was a life-changing experience for Peter and it was a life-changing experience for the early church, and it came through this non-Jewish, not yet Christian, man named Cornelius.

In New Testament terms Cornelius was a God-Fearer. Lydia also was a God-Fearer. She was a Gentile but she was a worshipper of God. She was seeking after God. So it was no accident that she was down at the river engaged in a prayer meeting when she encountered the Apostle Paul. Lydia was hungry for God.

I've belabored this point for this reason—our land is filled with people like Lydia and Cornelius. There are fine, decent people, particularly young people, in our society today who are seeking God. They have little or no church background. They may have been turned off by the church at some time in the past. They may have even been hurt by the church sometime in the past, but they hunger for God. Maybe they hunger for God because they've seen the bankruptcy of other approaches to life. They're disgusted by the hedonism and the materialism of our greater society. They want values—solid, life-changing values. They want something they can depend on as they wend their way through life. And we, the church of Jesus Christ, need to reach out to them. We need to encounter them where they are and share genuinely and generously what God has done in our life. If we do that, God will use our witness in a marvelous way.

I love a story that Dr. Elizabeth Kubler-Ross tells about a woman she encountered when she was writing her famous book on death and dying. Part of Dr. Kubler-Ross' research involved interviewing dying patients in the hospital, trying to find out how they felt and what they thought as they faced death. As she went from room to room in the hospital, she began to notice a remarkable pattern. Sometimes she would go into a dying person's room and the person would be calm, at peace, and tranquil. She also began to notice that often this was after the patient's room had been cleaned by a certain hospital orderly.

One day, Dr. Kubler-Ross happened to run into this orderly in the hospital corridor. The doctor said to her, "What are you doing with my patients?"

The orderly thought she was being reprimanded by Dr. Kubler-Ross. She said, "I'm not doing anything with your patients."

"No, no," responded the doctor. "It's a good thing. After you go into their rooms, they seem at peace. What are you doing with my patients?"

"I just talk to them," the orderly said. "You know, I've had two babies of my own die on my lap. But God never abandoned me. I tell them that. I tell them that they aren't alone, that God is with them, and that they don't have to be afraid." (3)

Now, let's imagine that you are a patient in that hospital. And you have reached a low point in your life. A gentle and caring hospital worker comes in to your room and while she cleans your room, she listens to your concerns. And quietly this orderly shares with you that she was once in your situation and she reached out to God and God was there and God helped her through a bad situation. And you are helped by this genuine act of caring and sharing. In fact, you come out of that hospital experience a stronger person than you went in. It changes how you deal with life.

Later you look back on that experience. How do you explain it? Was it just a coincidence or was it providence you encountered this woman in your hour of need? In truth, it was both. It may indeed be happenstance that you were assigned to that particular room where that woman was working. But it was also providence because she had yielded herself to God and God was working through her, reaching out to anyone who would heed her calming and reassuring message.

You see, this is how St. Paul looked at his life. He had many adventures, not all of them pleasant, but he knew that wherever he was God could use him. And so, when there was no synagogue in Philippi where he could worship, he and his friends looked for a place down by the river where they could at least join in prayer.

And when they encountered these women and realized that the women were seeking after God, they knew that God had brought them to this place and so they shared from their heart. And this smart, successful woman named Lydia responded to their message. She and all her household were baptized and became followers of Jesus Christ. And if you had later heard Lydia tell her story, my guess is she would say, "I was so fortunate. One day I was praying with my friends and God sent me a messenger, a man named Paul, and God changed my life."

Friend, the Lydias of this world are all around us. They are waiting for you and me to reach out to them with the love of Jesus Christ. We can be a tool of God's providence and grace if we yield ourselves to be used of God—if we look at every conversation we have as potentially a God-sent opportunity to make a difference in someone's life. Then we will realize that there are actually very few real coincidences in life. Many of these so-called coincidences are acts of providence in disguise.

1. Julie Mooney, et. al., Ripley's Believe It Or Not! Encyclopedia Of The Bizarre Amazing, Strange, Inexplicable, Weird and All True! (Black Dog & Leventhal Publishers, 2002), pg. 21.
2. Mark Beaird, http://markbeaird.org/steph/pdf/sermons/mark_beaird/nothing_will_be_wasted.pdf.
3. The Rev. Dr. Thomas G. Long, http://day1.org/3822-whats_the_gift.

Jailhouse Rock

Acts 16:16-34

I'm not certain that I have ever titled a sermon after a song by Elvis Presley before. That may be surprising to you considering the timeless quality of some of his early hits like "Hound Dog," "All Shook Up," "Blue Suede Shoes," and "Hard-Headed Woman." I guess I could have derived a sermon from some of those, but somehow it seemed a stretch. Today's lesson from the Book of Acts, however, is a different story. The story really does at least fit the title of Presley's 1957 hit record "Jailhouse Rock."

Perhaps you may remember "Jailhouse Rock." It's about a group of convicts who throw a party in the county jail with good 'ole rock-and roll music, and they have so much fun they don't want to leave. The song featured some memorable lyrics like, "Number forty-seven said to number three: You're the cutest jailbird I ever did see. I sure would be delighted with your company, Come on and do the jailhouse rock with me." (1) It's an absurd song, of course, but maybe it can help us focus on the most important jail house rock in history.

Paul and Silas are in Philippi where they have been savagely beaten and thrown into jail. This is not an unusual circumstance for these early disciples of our Lord. They knew what it was to face all kinds of adverse circumstances for their faith. But they learned to handle these circumstances in a magnificent way. You and I can learn from how they deal with this particular situation. I want you to notice three things that can help us when we find ourselves in adverse situations. I want you to notice their attitude, their actions and the impact they had on those who observed them. Even though I've given this message a somewhat frivolous title, this passage of Scripture is life-changing.

Let's begin with their attitude. Let me add a few more details to our story thus far. Paul and Silas had delivered a slave girl from some kind of an evil spirit that had allowed her to operate as a fortune teller. We honestly don't know what kind of spirit this was, but we do know that her owners had been making income off of this girl's strange gift. Now, nobody cares if you go about doing Christian things, as long as it doesn't interfere with commerce. Then they have a tendency to get quite testy.

When the slave girl's owners realized that they could no longer make money off of her, they seized Paul and Silas and dragged them into the marketplace to face the authorities. A mob gathered supporting the owners. At this sign of unrest, the not-so-courageous town magistrates ordered Paul and Silas to be stripped and beaten with rods. After they had been severely flogged, they were thrown into prison, and the jailer was commanded to guard them carefully. So he put them in an inner cell and fastened their feet in stocks.

That is their situation—unfairly accused, stripped, beaten, severely flogged, thrown into jail, and now in chains. Life in the early church was not easy. Now how do Paul and Silas respond to this adverse situation? Quite nicely as it turns out.

The writer of Acts tells us that about midnight Paul and Silas were praying and singing hymns to God, and the other prisoners were listening to them.

Can you imagine what kind of attitude, what kind of faith you would have to have to have been beaten and thrown into prison and then break out that evening in song? I don't know about you, but I suspect that if that had been me, I would have been on my cot in a fetal position whining to God to rescue me. But not Paul and Silas. They were singing hymns.

I wish I could do that, don't you? My life is much easier than theirs. Nevertheless my faith is much shakier. I worry like you do when sickness strikes or when someone I love is in distress. I look at the condition of our economy and I wonder with fear what lies ahead. Will we have the resources we need to make it to the end? I have to confess there are times when my fears and my doubts put me in chains.

Do you know what I'm talking about? Maybe you've had your own prison experience—worry about a marriage that is falling apart, a teenager who's fallen in with the wrong crowd, a job that has disappeared thanks to a weak economy. There are all kinds of prison experiences in this world. I don't know what yours might be—failing grades in school, an oppressive environment in your workplace, rising costs and diminishing assets?

In the middle of your prison experience, are you able to sing? Maybe you should. I know that neither Paul nor Silas had ever read a book on bio-feedback, but experts in that field tell us when we express a positive action it produces a positive emotion. Experts tell us that people don't smile because they feel good, they feel good because they smile. According to a study at Wake Forest University, singing aloud is one of those positive actions that can increase a feeling of well-being. So, when you are in prison, when you're depressed, when it seems everything you try is a failure, when you are about to lose hope, force yourself to break out in a song, especially a song of hope and joy. See if it doesn't make you feel better.

I doubt that this is why Paul and Silas were singing. They were such people of faith that their songs were probably a statement of their confidence in God. However, those songs were also a witness to the other prisoners. In fact the writer of Acts makes a point of telling us that the other prisoners were listening to them. Could that be one reason they were singing, as a witness?

On a perilous sea voyage from London to the British colony of Georgia, two young Anglican preachers found themselves trapped on a small ship in a big storm. They, along with the rest of the passengers and the crew, feared for their lives. There was only one exception to the panic on board—a band of Moravians who spent the entire storm singing hymns and praising God. These two Anglican preachers were so impressed by the faith of these Moravians that they sought them out and spent time with them. When the two returned to London, they began to worship with the Moravian community there. One night at a service on Aldersgate Street, one of those young men experienced what he called a "warming of the heart." His name was John Wesley, and he became one of the most effective evangelists of the 18th century. He founded the Methodist movement that has brought millions of people into a relationship with Jesus Christ. All because Wesley had been inspired by the singing of some Moravians. (2) Singing in a storm, or in prison, or in a bad marriage or wherever it might be is a witness!

Let's continue our story. Paul and Silas are singing hymns in a prison. That's their attitude. "Suddenly," says the writer of Acts, "there was such a violent earthquake it rocked the foundations of the prison. At once all the prison doors flew open, and everyone's chains came loose." Now there's a jailhouse rock to remember.

Notice that nowhere does the story say that God caused this earthquake. You and I may believe that God did cause this earthquake, after all it liberated these holy men. But the Bible doesn't say that. The fact that the earthquake came just as Paul and Silas were singing may have been entirely coincidental. I mean earthquakes do happen all the time. That's not important.

What is important is Paul and Silas' actions when the earthquake occurs. They didn't try to escape. They didn't try to run like you or I may have. Paul and Silas had a radical faith. They believed that God was with them regardless of their circumstances. They didn't panic when the earthquake occurred. Neither did they take off running when the cell doors flew open.

Maybe they were concerned about the jailer. The jailer had been ordered to keep a close eye on them. They were his responsibility. If they escaped he was in serious difficulty. We see this in the story. With all the racket and commotion of the earthquake, the jailer woke up, and when he saw the prison doors open, he drew his sword and was about to kill himself because he thought his prisoners had escaped. But Paul shouted, "Don't harm yourself! We are all here!"

Now this isn't typical behavior for prisoners in jail. This is the behavior of people who are at peace with God. Sometimes we are prevented from improving our situation simply because we are in such a panic that it skews our thinking.

James Brown of Wildsville, Louisiana, tells of taking flying lessons some years back. His instructor told him to put the plane into a steep and extended dive. Brown says he was totally unprepared for what was about to happen. After a brief time the engine stalled, and the plane began to plunge out of control. It soon became evident that the instructor was not going to help him at all. After a few seconds, though—which seemed like eternity to him—Brown says his mind began to function again. He quickly corrected the situation.

Immediately he turned to the instructor and began to vent his fearful frustrations on him. He recalls the instructor speaking very calmly and saying, "There is no position you can get this airplane into that I cannot get you out of. If you want to learn to fly, go up there and do it again."

James Brown says, "At that moment God seemed to be saying to me, 'Remember this. As you serve me, there is no situation you can get yourself into that I cannot get you out of. If you trust me, you will be all right.'" (3)

That's the faith that Paul and Silas had. They didn't panic. They didn't run. And out of their concern for the jailer who had the responsibility of keeping his eye on them, they stayed where they were, though where they were was not where they would have chosen to be.

We've seen in this adverse situation the disciples' attitude, singing in jail. We've seen their actions. Trusting God, they stayed where they were. Now we're going to see their impact on others.

The jailer woke up, and when he saw the prison doors open, he drew his sword and was about to kill himself because he thought the prisoners had escaped. But Paul shouted, "Don't harm yourself! We are all here!" At this, the jailer called for lights, rushed in and fell trembling before Paul and Silas. He then brought them out and asked, "Sirs, what must I do to be saved?"

The jailer had seen their attitude in this adverse situation, he had seen their actions, the actions of men of integrity and great faith, and the jailer obviously said to himself, "Hey, I want what they've got!" This is evangelism in its purest form.

The jailer brought them out and asked them, "Sirs, what must I do to be saved?" But it wasn't because they had knocked on his door in an evangelistic campaign. It wasn't because the disciples had confronted him and asked, "If you were to die tonight, would you go to heaven?" It was because he saw that Paul and Silas not only talked the talk, they walked the walk. He could see by their attitudes and by their actions they were special people. They were God's people. And he wanted to be one of God's people too. He cried out, "Sirs, what must I do to be saved?"

Paul and Silas replied, "Believe in the Lord Jesus, and you will be saved—you and your household." Then they spoke the word of the Lord to him and to all the others in his house. And that very night the jailer took them and washed their wounds; then immediately he and all his household were baptized. Then the jailer brought Paul and Silas into his house and set a meal before them; he was filled with joy because he had come to believe in God—he and his whole household.

Notice the difference between Paul's conversion and this jailer's conversion. When Paul was converted there was a blinding light and Paul heard the very voice of Christ speaking to him. It was a dramatic and somewhat traumatic experience. This poor jailer didn't have that kind of experience at all. In his case he was simply exposed to the attitudes and actions of two genuinely Christian people and that was enough for him to decide to become a Christ follower.

Friends, that is how most people come to Christ. They don't come to Christ because they have had some dramatic experience. They come to Christ because some other ordinary Christian's faith "went viral." These ordinary Christians lived their faith in such a way that people around them were infected.

This is Mother's Day. Many of us are here today because of the impact our mothers had on us.

Some years back a lady named Ruth Simmons became the president of Smith College, one of the country's most elite institutions of higher learning for women.

Simmons is the great-great-granddaughter of slaves. She began her journey to the presidency of Smith College on a cotton farm in Grapeland, Texas, where her parents were sharecroppers. Later the family moved to a poor section of Houston. There her father went to work in a factory, and her mother scrubbed floors for white families.

How did such humble beginnings spawn a career that led to the top of academia?

"I had a remarkable mother," says Simmons. "She would sometimes take me with her to work when I was a little girl, and the thing I remember vividly is how good she was at what she did. She was very demanding in terms of her own work. 'Do it well, do it thoroughly,' she'd say, 'whatever you do.'"

At her inauguration President Smith carried a Bible her mother had given her father on the day they were married. "I know the Smith Board of Trustees thinks I'm trying to live up to the standards they set for me, and that's okay," she says. But she is aiming toward a higher standard. "Every day that I'm here," Simmons says, "I try to be the kind of person my mother wanted me to be." (4)

Some of you had a mother like that. Even if you didn't, most of you are here because you were exposed to someone who did their best to live like Jesus. You saw something in their attitudes and actions that made you say, "I want what they have." That's the way it works. So let me ask you. Would your attitudes and actions cause someone to want to be a follower of Jesus Christ? Being an effective witness of Jesus isn't brain surgery. Live your faith regardless of your circumstance. Talk the talk and walk the walk and sooner or later you will be having an impact on those who are listening and watching.

1. Song by Mike Stoller and Jerry Leiber.
2. Rev. Russell B. Smith, http://thirdmill.org/newfiles/rus_smith/NT.smith.colossians.1.1-13.html.
3. Discoveries, Fall, 1991, Vol. 2, No. 4.
4. "A Higher Standard," Sara Rimer in New York Times, "Personal Glimpses," Reader's Digest, March 1996, p. 38. \

Filling The Hole In Our Hearts
Acts 2:1-21

A Sunday School teacher taught her class to recite the Apostles Creed by giving each child one phrase to learn. When the day came for the class to give their recitation, they began beautifully.

"I believe in God the Father Almighty, maker of heaven and earth," said the first child.

"I believe in Jesus Christ, his only Son our Lord," said the next.

And so it went perfectly until they came to the child who said, "He ascended into heaven, and sitteth at the right hand of God the Father Almighty: from thence he shall come to judge the quick and the dead."

At that point an embarrassed silence fell. The next line was to be, "I believe in the Holy Spirit . . ." but there was only silence. Finally, a little girl spoke up and said, "Uh, the little boy who believes in the Holy Spirit is absent today."

Welcome to this celebration of Pentecost, the day when the Holy Spirit descended upon the church. We might conclude by looking at the state of many churches today, that people who believe in the Holy Spirit are largely absent from the church. The church hardly resembles the church at Pentecost. And yet the Holy Spirit is just as relevant to our lives as it was to first century believers, for the Holy Spirit is the presence of God in our lives.

British newspaper columnist Bernard Levin wrote an op-ed piece sometime back. I find it quite descriptive of our situation. Levin wrote, "Countries like ours are full of people who have all the material comforts they desire, together with such non-material blessings as a happy family, and yet lead lives of quiet . . . desperation, understanding nothing but the fact that there is a hole inside of them that however much food and drink they pour into it, however many motor cars and television sets they stuff into it, however many well balanced children and loyal friends they parade around the edges of it . . . it aches." (1) Do you know what he's talking about? Do you have that same ache at the center of your life—that same void that needs filling?

Deepak Chopra, the popular writer and dispenser of new age wisdom, recently said almost the same thing. He said, "There seems to be a hole in the middle of everyday life, as if a rock had been thrown through a plate glass window. But instead of a physical hole, one could call this a 'meaning,' hole . . ."

Does that describe your life? Do you have a meaning-hole?

This is what the Holy Spirit is about—filling that void, that hole in our lives.

The Holy Spirit came upon the church on the day of Pentecost. The first disciples of Jesus were all Jewish and they celebrated the holy days of the Jewish people. One of those holy days was called Pentecost. Pentecost was a feast day that celebrated the giving of God's Law to His people through Moses on Mount Sinai. For Christians Pentecost became the celebration of the gift of God's Spirit to His people.

You know the story. Before his ascension, Jesus told his disciples to wait in Jerusalem for the Spirit to come upon them. They probably didn't have a clue what he was talking about, but they didn't question it. After all, they had already watched him die and then come back to life. All the questions they might have had about his Lordship had pretty much vaporized. If the Lord said wait, they were going to wait.

Now it was Pentecost, fifty days after Christ's resurrection. The city was full of visitors who had come to celebrate this sacred festival. Jesus had not told the disciples exactly when the Spirit would come. The scripture says, "When the day of Pentecost came, they were all together in one place." Probably they were together simply because they were good Jews and they were celebrating a Jewish event. Suddenly, however, a sound like the blowing of a violent wind came from heaven and filled the whole house. And they saw what seemed to be tongues of fire that separated and came to rest on each of them. Then, says the author of Acts, "All of them were filled with the Holy Spirit and began to speak in other tongues as the Spirit enabled them."

Notice that they were not speaking in unknown tongues, a practice we sometimes think of as being "Pentecostal." They were speaking in known tongues, known languages of other nations. The really miraculous thing is they were speaking in these languages, but they had neither studied nor spoken in these languages before. This was an amazing event. If I were to suddenly burst out speaking in an unknown tongue, some of you would be disturbed, since we don't normally do that in our church. A few of you might be freaked out. One or two of you would question my sanity. Somebody might react like some outsiders reacted on that first Pentecost, "Hey, the pastor's drunk. Listen to him carry on." And you might go home telling jokes at my expense.

But imagine that you heard a mighty wind and the room shook and then I started speaking in flawless German or Italian or Arabic, some known language I had never studied. Wouldn't that impress you even more? Wouldn't you go home saying that you had experienced a miracle? I know I would. That's what happened on the Day of Pentecost.

God arranged for the Holy Spirit to come down on these early Christian believers on the very day that thousands of Jews from all over the known world were collected in Jerusalem for this celebration. When they heard the sound of the wind blowing and the disciples speaking, the crowd was totally bewildered, because each one heard his or her own language being spoken. Utterly amazed, they asked: "Aren't all these who are speaking Galileans? Then how is it that each of us hears them in our native language?" They were witnessing a miraculous event. No wonder thousands of them responded to the Gospel message and were baptized.

Pentecost is sometimes known as the birthday of the Church. However, this celebration is different from the other Christian celebrations such as Christmas and Easter. These other celebrations are focused on God's gift to us of his Son, Jesus Christ, and on Christ's life, death and resurrection. Meanwhile, Pentecost has at its center the coming of the Holy Spirit.

The Holy Spirit is sometimes described as the most misunderstood person of the Trinity, and this is not without reason. After all, it is somewhat easier to visualize God the Father, creator and author of all goodness, and Jesus Christ, the son, firstborn of the many children of God who would be known as joint heirs with him in glory, as well as their Good Shepherd. After all, the Father and the Son are described in familiar, human terms to which practically any person who has experienced any sort of family or community life can relate.

The Holy Spirit, however, is often described through comparisons with natural objects or forces. The Holy Spirit is compared to the invisible wind that "blows where it will," sometimes violently, as a "rushing, mighty wind." Elsewhere it is compared to tongues of flame, or to a dove descending from heaven, and so on.

Here is what we need to know about the Holy Spirit—it is God present with us today. It is that part of the Godhead that fills the empty hole in our lives.

It is the Holy Spirit that helps us make sense out of our lives and helps us understand God's purpose for us.

Life is confusing. Sometimes life doesn't make sense. We have good days when we think that everything is going to work out beautifully, and then suddenly, out of the blue, we get a phone call, and our world is turned upside down. We go to the Bible and we try to get some guidance there but sometimes it's like it is still written in Greek. The words are so confusing. We have difficulty concentrating. And even when we are able to understand all the words, we have difficulty relating to them.

But we linger with the text, and we pray, "Lord, what is it you are trying to say to me?" All of a sudden the meaning sometimes becomes crystal clear. It's like God whispered the meaning into our ear. That is the working of the Holy Spirit.

That amazing preacher of the Gospel, Dr. Tom Long gives us a wonderful illustration of this aspect of the Holy Spirit's work.

Long was a member of a rock-and-roll band in high school and he was fascinated with the music of the great blues master Jimmy Reed. Reed was a legend in the 50s and 60s. Playing the harmonica and guitar Reed, a share-cropper's son, brought the rhythm-and-blues music of the Mississippi Delta to the popular rock-and-roll mainstream. He had a significant impact on such stars as Elvis Presley and the Rolling Stones.

There's an interesting story behind the Jimmy Reed records, says Long. "If one listened very carefully [to these records], there could sometimes be heard, ever so faintly in the background, a soft woman's voice murmuring in advance the next verse of the song. The story that grew up around this . . . was that Jimmy Reed was so absorbed in the blues beat and the guitar riffs of his music that he simply could not remember the words of his own songs. He needed help with the lyrics, and the woman's voice was none other than that of his wife, devotedly coaching her husband through the recording session by whispering the upcoming stanzas into his ear as he sang." (2)

This, for the Christian, is the task of the Holy Spirit. It is God whispering to us, giving us comfort and encouragement and helping us to make sense of our lives. As Paul writes in Romans 8:16, "The Spirit of God testifies with our spirit that we are children of God . . ." In other words it is the Holy Spirit that quietly whispers into our heart reminding us who we are. It is the Holy Spirit that interprets Scripture for the believer and relates it to our daily lives. The Holy Spirit helps us make sense out of our lives and helps us understand God's purpose for us.

Furthermore, it is the Holy Spirit that gives us the power to accomplish what God has called us to accomplish. Jesus had given the disciples a commission. We call it the Great Commission. They were to go into all the world and "make disciples of all people baptizing them in the name of the Father and of the Son and of the Holy Spirit, and teaching them to obey everything [Christ] had commanded them." What an impossible task. How could they possibly accomplish this assignment? Well, of course they couldn't accomplish it relying only on their own abilities. But Christ made them a promise, "And surely I am with you always, to the very end of the age" (Matthew 28:16-20). Christ would be with them through the presence of the Holy Spirit working in their lives. This is why they were still in Jerusalem on the Day of Pentecost awaiting the gift of the Spirit.

In Acts 1 we read, "Do not leave Jerusalem, but wait for the gift my Father promised, which you have heard me speak about. For John baptized with water, but in a few days you will be baptized with the Holy Spirit." Then a few verses later we read, "But you will receive power when the Holy Spirit comes on you; and you will be my witnesses in Jerusalem, and in all Judea and Samaria, and to the ends of the earth" (1:5, 8). It is the Holy Spirit that gives us the power to accomplish what God has called us to accomplish.

I like the way Corrie ten Boom described the work of the Holy Spirit. Corrie was a Dutch Christian whose family sheltered Jews from Hitler's forces during World War II. Corrie and her family ended up in one of Hitler's death camps—but Corrie managed to survive. She later became famous as a Christian author and speaker, because she was so obviously filled with the Spirit of God.

Listen to what Corrie ten Boom said to one of her audiences. She said: "I have a glove here in my hand. The glove cannot do anything by itself, but when my hand is in it, it can do many things. True, it is not the glove, but my hand in the glove that acts. We are gloves. It is the Holy Spirit in us who is the hand, who does the job. We have to make room for the hand so that every finger is filled." (3)

That is our main task if we want to do anything great for God—we need to make room for the hand of the Holy Spirit. The Holy Spirit fills the hole in our life. It helps us make sense of life and helps us understand God's purpose for our life. And the Holy Spirit gives us the power to accomplish what God has called us to accomplish.

To sum it all up, the Holy Spirit helps us become all God has created us to be. One of the images used in Scripture to help us understand the work of the Holy Spirit is that of fire. You'll remember that tongues of fire appeared above the heads of the disciples on the Day of Pentecost. Some denominations use a flame to indicate the presence of the Holy Spirit in their church logo. The symbol of fire represents the work of the Spirit helping us become what God intends for us to become.

There is a story that comes from frontier days about three women who were members of a Bible study. One day they were reading in their lesson for the day that the Spirit was a refining fire. They didn't understand what that meant—a refining fire.

One of them volunteered to go to a nearby silversmith and see what that meant. When she went to see the silversmith, she didn't tell him why she was really there.

The silversmith explained the process of refining silver this way. He said you want to be sure you put the silver in the hottest part of the fire. That is so all the impurities in the silver will be burned away. He also said that you had to watch it at all times to make sure it was not in there too long. If it were there too long, it would be ruined. The woman was fascinated by his explanation. She asked, "How do you know when it is done?"

His answer was, "That's easy: when you see your reflection in it."

God desires to see His reflection in our lives. Scripture tells us that we were created in God's image. When we went astray, he sent His Son to save us from our sin-distorted lives. After Christ's death, resurrection and ascension, God sent us the gift of the Holy Spirit to work in us, bearing witness with our

Spirit, to help us be restored to a right relationship with God. When that work is accomplished, God will be able to see His reflection in our lives.

All of this is what we mean when we say, "I believe in the Holy Spirit." It is God attempting to fill the hole in our lives. It is God helping us to make sense of our lives and understand God's purpose for us. It is God giving us the power to accomplish what God has called us to accomplish, and it is God working in our lives, all our lives, helping us to become what God has created us to be, persons in whom He, and others, can see God's reflection. Pray for the gift of the Holy Spirit in your life today.

1. http://www.westminster-bflo.org/sermonrepository/aug1703.pdf.
2. http://www.gbgm-umc.org/saintpaulumc/sermons/Sermon%2805-13-2007%29%28John14-23-29%29.pdf.
3. Very Rev. Sherry Crompton, http://sermons.trinitycoatesville.org/.

What The Trinity Does
Romans 5:1-5

Welcome on this Trinity Sunday, 2013. Tomorrow you can start taking down all the decorations that you put up for this special day in the church year. You did put up decorations, didn't you? I know the children have been counting down the days in joyful anticipation of this day. I can hear them now, "Mommy, how many days is it until Trinity Sunday?" It is an exciting time. I hope each of you got what you wanted for Trinity Sunday. This is the last day we will sing all the Trinity carols that we have been enjoying for the past month. Some of you are already saying, "Why we can't we keep the Trinity spirit around all year long."

Oh, you didn't give Trinity presents this year? You didn't decorate your home? What do you mean you didn't even know it was Trinity Sunday until you looked at the bulletin this morning?

O. K., I'll have to accept the fact that Trinity Sunday isn't a very big event in the average Christian's life. Did you know that Trinity Sunday isn't much fun for preachers, either? Each year, on the Sunday after Pentecost, we are given the task of explaining the unexplainable—God, in three persons, blessed Trinity.

Roughly 100 years ago there lived an American choreographer named Isadora Duncan. Ms. Duncan is considered by many to be the creator of modern dance. Once, when asked about the meaning of a performance she had given, she made a profound statement. She said, "If I could say it, I wouldn't have to dance it." (1)

That's how I feel about the Trinity. If there were a Trinity dance, I would be better at dancing the Trinity than explaining it. [Wouldn't that be a pretty sight?]

The Trinity is a mystery. God manifests himself in three forms—Father, Son, and Holy Spirit—the Creator, the crucified one and the comforter who lives in our hearts. What does it all mean? It's a mystery. The best we can do is use metaphors to try to explain it.

I like a metaphor that Dr. John Pavelko uses. He compares the Trinity to our current obsession with multi-tasking. He points to some of the multi-tasking products we use, like the 3-in-1 Laser Pointer, Stylus, and Ball point pen he saw advertised. This 3-in-1 pen allows you to work faster and easier, according to the ads. You can enter your data into your PDA with the stylus, then rotate the top and sign a contact with the Ball point pen. When your work is all done you can use the laser to torment your dog.

Then there's the 3-in-1 Cooler, Fan and Ionic Air Purifier by Whirl Wind-

Air. It will cool your air through a water sprinkling system, while at the same time freshening the air by releasing negative ions. It also uses a washable strainer to purify the air of all those microscopic particles that plague your allergies.

Finally, to put all your work into a hard copy, there is the Dell Photo All-In-ONE Printer. It will make copies of your photos, print, fax, scan and photo-copy your documents with up to a 50-page auto feeder.

Dr. Pavelko asks, "With all of these multi-tasking devices, why do we have such difficulty accepting the notion that one God can exist as three persons?" (2)

Good question. Why as human beings, whose finest minds still can't cure the common cold, do we think we will ever have the ability to understand the workings of God, who is so far greater than we are that we could never fathom His nature?

If you really want an explanation of the Trinity, the best one possible comes from the great mind of C. S. Lewis who undertook that task in his book Mere Christianity seventy years ago. He writes, "An ordinary simple Christian kneels down to say his prayers. He is trying to get into touch with God. But if he is a Christian he knows that what is prompting him to pray is also God: God so to speak, inside him. But he also knows that all real knowledge of God comes through Christ, the Man who was God—that Christ is standing beside him, help-ing him to pray, praying for him. You see what is happening. God is the thing to which he is praying—the goal he is trying to reach. God is also the thing inside him which is pushing him on—the motive power. God is also the road or bridge along which he is being pushed to that goal. The whole threefold life of the three-person Being is actually going on in that ordinary act of prayer." (3)

That's as good an explanation of the Trinity as you and I are apt to get—and it is still too complicated for most of us.

Interestingly enough, the word Trinity doesn't even appear in the Bible. But the formula of Father, Son and Holy Spirit appears several times, including in today's epistle from St. Paul to the Romans. Paul, however, doesn't try to ex-plain this great mystery. What he does is to show its relevance to our lives, which is good, because that's what we need anyway. We don't really need to under-stand the Trinity. What we need is to see how God-in-three-persons helps us live as disciples of Christ.

Paul begins like this: "Therefore, since we have been justified through faith, we have peace with God through our Lord Jesus Christ . . ." Let's stop there. "We have peace with God through our Lord Jesus Christ . . ."

Now you may say flippantly, "Peace with God? I didn't know I had ever been at war with God." Maybe you haven't, but a lot of people do struggle with God without even knowing it.

I read something interesting about animals, at least male animals. If you place a mirror next to most male animals, they will immediately react aggressively, even attacking the mirror. The image causes the male animal to defend its territory. Scientists tell us that is because these animals lack awareness of who they are. They don't realize they are seeing themselves in the mirror. If you go higher on the evolutionary chain—to monkeys, elephants, dolphins, and some birds—they quickly realize that the image in the mirror represents themselves and they cease to attack it. (4)

But why do these male animals go into a fighting mode in the first place? It's in their DNA. It is a survival tool. Some of that same drive is within every human being, especially males. The most natural thing in the world is our drive for survival. This causes us to lash out against anything or anyone that threatens us. What an amazing transition it is for us to grow spiritually and emotionally to the point that we are able to regard every person as a brother or sister in Christ and not as a threat. That kind of growth rarely comes without struggle. It is part of what Paul would regard as our war with God. But when we are able to enlarge our ability to love, there comes with it great peace. Jesus, the bridge-builder between God and humanity and between people and their neighbors, brings us that peace.

I read about an old saint who was dying. He was visited by a friend who asked him, "Have you made your peace with God?"

The man replied, "No, I haven't."

To that his friend said, "What! Oh you must make peace with God."

"I'm sorry, I cannot do that." replied the dying man.

His friend said, "But you must! Don't you know that it is dangerous to die without making peace with God?"

To this, the dying man said, "But how can I make peace with God? My Lord made peace with me 2,000 years ago when He died on the cross, and I accepted it. I have had peace ever since!" (5)

Peace is the work of Christ. He lay down his life to reconcile us to one another and to God. He is the bridge, in C. S Lewis' words, that crosses the chasm between who we are and who God wants us to be.

Winston Churchill was honoring members of the Royal Air Force who had guarded England during the Second World War. He recounted their brave service and he declared, "Never in the history of mankind have so many owed so much to so few."

A similar sentiment appears on a memorial plaque in Bastogne, Belgium. That is the location of the famous Battle of the Bulge, one of the bloodiest conflicts of World War II. The inscription, in honor of the U. S. 101st Airborne Division, reads: "Seldom has so much American blood been shed in the course of a single action. Oh, Lord, help us to remember!" (6)

We need to remember the sacrifice of those soldiers, especially on this Memorial Day weekend, but it is even more important that we remember the sacrifice that Christ made to earn us permanent peace with ourselves with our neighbors and with God. Paul writes, "Therefore, since we have been justified through faith, we have peace with God through our Lord Jesus Christ, through whom we have gained access by faith into this grace in which we now stand." Then he adds, "And we boast in the hope of the glory of God." Sometimes Paul is a little hard to understand. What do these words mean—"boast in the hope of the glory of God?"

Let me ask you a question—where is your hope? Is your hope in the stock market? Good luck with that. Is it in the value of your home? How about your good health? Where is your hope? Your youth? Is it your personal ingenuity? Where is your hope? Is it in our political system, in free markets, in our health care system? Be careful where you place your hope.

This, of course, is the joy of youth. When you're young you have such a long horizon. You can dream dreams, make plans, come up with ideas, and with a reasonable amount of luck you'll be able to see them through. But as you get older, you become a little wiser, and you begin to realize that if you put your hope in any man-made construct, you're apt to be disappointed.

A feeble old millionaire, confined to his bed with the infirmities of age, pointed out the window at a husky teenager who was having an obviously enjoyable conversation with a pretty girl. "I wish I was as rich as he," remarked the old man.

"But he has no job," the rich man's nurse commented, "his family has ten mouths to feed, and he doesn't even know whether he'll be able to go to college."

"Yes," said the rich man, "but he has health and youth and hope—he's rich in all the things that money can't buy." (7) Most young people have no idea how rich they really are. Even when you're young, however, you soon learn there are limitations. Everyone who has ever lived has had limitations.

Some of us regard Albert Einstein as perhaps the smartest man who ever lived. Did you know that when Einstein died, he left an unfinished manuscript? This manuscript was to be his crowning achievement, his attempt to create a "theory of everything," an equation that would unlock the secrets of the universe and perhaps allow him to "read the mind of God."

But, if he had truly discovered those secrets at the heart of the universe, he died with them still locked within him. The night of his death, the newspapers printed a picture of his office, with that unfinished manuscript on his desk. The caption read that the greatest scientist of our era could not finish his greatest masterpiece. (8) All of us have limitations. Where is your hope?

The director of a medical clinic told of a terminally ill young man who came in for his usual treatment. A new doctor who was on duty said to him casually and cruelly, "You know, don't you, that you won't live out the year?"

As the young man left, he stopped by the director's desk and wept. "That man took away my hope," he blurted out.

"I guess he did," replied the director. "Maybe it's time to find a new one." (9) The new hope he was talking about is the only hope worth having—hope in God. All of us have to put our hope somewhere. Why not invest our hope in that which is eternal?

So Paul speaks of the peace that Christ brings, and the hope God gives. Then he moves on to that third part of the Trinity. He writes, "And hope does not put us to shame, because God's love has been poured out into our hearts through the Holy Spirit, who has been given to us."

Christ brings us peace. God gives us hope. And the Holy Spirit fills us with love.

Every once in a while someone comes to prominence for a while, a celebrity, if you will. But they're different from most celebrities and they remind us of what life is all about. Before he fades from public consciousness, I want to remind you of a young man named Kurtis.

Kurtis, a deeply religious young man, worked in a supermarket where he fell in love with a woman named Brenda. Kurtis was the stock boy and Brenda was the check out lady. He was twenty-two and she was twenty-six. Kurtis was attracted to Brenda and asked her out. She refused, saying she was divorced and had two children. She had "baggage." Kurtis persisted anyway.

A date was arranged and Kurtis arrived at the door. Brenda met him and again cancelled the date; the baby sitter had gotten sick. Finally, Brenda let Kurtis into her apartment to meet her two children. The little girl was as cute as a bug. The little boy was in a wheel chair, was a paraplegic, and had Down syndrome. Kurtis said, "There is no reason all four of us can't go out tonight."

Time went by and Kurtis became fast friends of the family, learning to lift the little boy out of the wheelchair to go to the bathroom. Eventually, Kurtis and Brenda fell in love, married and had two more children. Today, they are just as committed to one another as they were as young people, even though Kurtis left the super market and eventually became one of the biggest football stars in our land. Some of you have already guessed that Kurtis is better known as Kurt, Kurt Warner, the star quarterback for many years for the St. Louis Rams. Kurt Warner won two Most Valuable Player awards in the NFL as well as the MVP award in Super Bowl XXXIV. (10)

Kurt is retired from football today, but he has not retired from being a follower of Jesus Christ. If you ask Kurt Warner where he learned to love his family like he does, he would unashamedly tell you that it is the Holy Spirit working within his life.

Paul says to us, "God's love has been poured out into our hearts through the Holy Spirit, who has been given to us."

So, what is the Trinity about? I can't explain it as well as C. S. Lewis did, but I can tell you what it means in our life. Christ provides us with peace through his sacrifice on the cross; God gives us hope even in the darkest hour; and the Holy Spirit fills us with God's love. I can't explain what the Trinity is, but that is what the Trinity does.

1. http://charismanglican.com/2010/05/29/dancing-with-the-trinity-a-trinity-sunday-homily.

2. http://www.crossroadspc.org/thebarrel/20060611.htm.

3. (Macmillan Publishers, 1952).

4. Michio Kaku, Physics of the Future: How Science Will Shape Human Destiny and Our Daily Lives by the Year 2100 (Kindle version).

5. Alan Carr, http://www.sermonnotebook.org/romans/Romans%205_1-5.htm.

6. Dennis Davidson, http://www.sermoncentral.com/sermons/god-demonstrates-his-love-dennis-davidson-sermon-on-gods-love-159565.asp.

7. Leonard & Thelma Spinrad, Speaker's Lifetime Library (Paramus, NJ: Revised & Expanded, 1997), p. 283.

8. Kaku.

9. Our Daily Bread, December 19, 1996.

10. Edward F. Markquart, http://www.sermonsfromseattle.com/series_a_here_come_the_clowns.htm.

Keys That Unlock Miracles
Luke 7:1-10

H. L. Mencken was for a long time the editor of the American Mercury magazine. One day he startled his employees by suddenly shouting, "It's coming in the doors!" Everyone stopped what they were doing and looked at their boss.

"It's up to the bottom of the desk!" Mencken continued, "It's up to the seats of our chairs."

"What are you talking about?" asked one of his confused colleagues.

"It's all around us. Now, it's to the top of our desks," shouted Mencken as he jumped to the top of his desk.

"What do you mean?" inquired the newsroom staff.

"Mediocrity. We're drowning in mediocrity!" Mencken shouted as he jumped from his desk and exited, never to return. (1)

I know how he felt. We live in a time of moral and spiritual mediocrity. All around us are mediocre institutions and mediocre leaders—and often we lead mediocre lives ourselves.

So did many characters in the Bible. There are few shining heroes in the scriptures. The Bible is honest in its portrayal of human nature—all who have ever lived, except Christ, are flawed. As the Scriptures say, "For all have sinned and fallen short of the glory of God" (Romans 3:23).

There are few episodes in the Scriptures that reveal every participant at his best, but our lesson for today is one of them. Jesus has just finished teaching and he enters the town of Capernaum. He is surely tired. He had just finished giving the address we know as the Sermon on the Mount. Perhaps he had come into Capernaum for refreshment and relaxation.

But there was a delegation there to meet him. It was a group of Jewish elders. They had a request for him. This is interesting. So often the New Testament spotlights conflicts between Jesus and the religious establishment. But in this story, even the Jewish elders are cast in a positive light.

The elders had come to Jesus concerning a Roman centurion in their town—a man who was much respected by them all. The centurion had a servant for whom he had great affection. This servant was suffering a painful affliction and was near death. The centurion asked for Jesus to come to heal his servant.

For the moment Jesus forgot his fatigue. Some soul was in distress and needed his attention. He went with the elders. They were nearing the centurion's house when the centurion sent friends out to them with an amazing message. The message the centurion sent out went like this: "Lord, don't trouble yourself, for I do not deserve to have you come under my roof. That is why I did not even consider myself worthy to come to you. But say the word, and my servant will be healed . . ."

Luke tells us that when Jesus heard this message from the centurion he was amazed at the centurion's faith. There are only two times in the New Testament when Jesus was said to have been amazed. The first time was when he began his public ministry in his hometown of Nazareth. Do you remember what happened there? Jesus was rejected by those who knew him best. The Gospel of Mark tells us that Christ "was amazed by their lack of faith." (Mark 6:6).

The second time the word "amazed" is used is this encounter with the Roman centurion. This time Jesus is amazed not by a lack of faith but by how genuine this Gentile's faith was. Jesus turned to those who were with him and said, "I tell you, I have not found such great faith even in Israel."

Evidently that faith had an impact, for Luke tells us that "when those who had been sent by the centurion returned to the house, they found the servant well."

What happens in this story that made it possible for this centurion's servant to be made well? Of course this healing occurred because Jesus willed it, but there is more here than that. There are three elements in this story that are always helpful to the healing process—whether it is personal healing or the healing of a family or the healing of a society. There are three keys here that are present in every miracle.

The first is the power of caring. Where people truly care, there is healing. Where people care, miracles take place.

We see the centurion's love for his servant. Probably the servant had been a trusted member of the centurion's household for many years. Actually, "servant" is too nice a term. The Greek word used in this story is doulos which literally means "slave." The man about whom the centurion cared was a slave.

Dr. Leith Anderson notes that in Roman times slavery could often be quite cruel. Under Roman law slaves were considered to be property, giving the owner complete rights to do whatever he wanted without legal jeopardy. If he wanted to, he could kill a slave without getting into any trouble.

"Sick slaves and old slaves were especially at risk. It was a frequent practice to just 'put them out' when they couldn't work any longer. This did not set them free; it let them die in desperation.

"That the centurion so highly valued his slave and wanted to take the best care of him in his sickness is a most unusual expression of voluntary kindness." This does not in any way condone slavery, but it does show this man in a comparatively good light within an otherwise evil system. (2) The centurion cared about his servant.

Just as important, someone had cared enough about the centurion to tell him about Jesus. Otherwise he wouldn't have known where to turn in this time of need. How fortunate we would all be if more people were more open in talking about Jesus.

Open sharing of our faith and our friendship will always yield benefits.

Have you ever thought of how powerful a word spoken at just the right time is? It is said that on some of the Alpine slopes at certain times in the year guides forbid travelers to speak a word. They fear that the mere tremor of the human voice will loosen and bring down a deadly avalanche. But the human voice can be powerful in other ways. It can bring healing to broken hearts, help to those in despair.

It was a mere human voice that sent the centurion to the source of healing for his servant. Someone cared enough for the centurion to tell him about Jesus. The centurion, in turn, cared enough about his servant to call in the Jewish elders and ask them to bring Jesus to him.

In the same way, the Jewish elders cared enough about the centurion to overcome their prejudices. Can't you imagine that it was difficult for them to request Jesus to come to heal the servant? Can you imagine a delegation of clergy from the finest churches in our town going to an itinerant faith healer in a run-down store front mission and asking his assistance in healing someone in the mayor's household? That took a lot of humility. They cared enough to swallow their pride and go to Jesus.

And, of course, Jesus cared enough to go with them to the servant.

When people care that much, something good has got to happen. I wonder how many people occupy hospital beds today simply and solely because they believe nobody cares about them. I wonder how many young people end up in gangs because they think that nobody cares for them. There is healing in knowing that somebody is praying for you, looking in on you, telling others about you. That is what the church ought to be—a caring community of persons who seek to lift one another's burdens.

We see the power of caring. We also see the power of character. Where there are people of character, miracles take place.

We are not told of the servant's character, but may we not assume that it was of the highest order? How could a servant win the high esteem of his master if the servant had not proven himself a reliable and trustworthy steward of his master's property?

We do know the centurion's character. He was sent by Rome to command a garrison of soldiers at Capernaum. It is not easy to mix soldiers with an oppressed civilian population. But somehow this centurion had carried out his orders in such a way that he had the respect of the Jewish elders. They report to Jesus about the centurion. "He is worthy to have you do this for him, for he loves our nation, and he built us our synagogue."

So we know he was a generous man and a charitable man. We know that he was concerned about the well-being of the people over whom he ruled and the servants in his own household. He was a man of character. Such character seems rare in our present world, but it does exist.

For some of us the late Nelson Mandela of South Africa came to represent this kind of character. Pastor John Ortberg tells us that when Mandela was imprisoned on Robbins Island for his opposition to South Africa's system of apartheid, he was issued a pair of shorts—not long trousers—but shorts. His captors kept him in shorts so that they could think of him, and he would think of himself as a "boy" rather than as a "man." This would cause most people to burn with a deep, unrelenting anger, but not Mandela.

"During twenty-seven years in prison, he suffered and learned and grew. He called his prison 'the University.' He became both increasingly committed to justice and opposed to hate, and by the end of his captivity, even his guards were won over by his life. The final official charged to watch him used to cook Mandela gourmet meals."

When Mandela was finally released from prison he became a healing influence in South Africa. As President he sought to lead the country to peace through the Truth and Reconciliation Commission, established on the biblical principle that 'the truth shall make you free.'" (3)

Mandela was a man of character just as the centurion was a man of character. Wherever such character exists there is healing. Part of the centurion's character was his great humility: "Lord, don't trouble yourself, for I do not deserve to have you come under my roof. That is why I did not even consider myself worthy to come to you . . ."

How easy it is for some persons of authority and even of widely acknowledged virtue to allow their position in the community to cause them to esteem themselves more highly than they ought. Not this centurion. He was a good man in every sense of the word. Jesus undoubtedly loved him. "The prayer of a righteous person is powerful and effective," writes James in his epistle (5:16). There is healing in such character.

So we have these two powerful elements—caring and character. But there is a third element we dare not ignore: it was the centurion's confidence in Christ. Where people have confidence in Christ, miracles take place. That is another term for faith. The centurion was so confident that Jesus could heal his servant that he had his messenger say, ". . . do not trouble yourself to come under my roof . . . but say the word, and let my servant be healed."

Just a word from the Master would be sufficient—that was the centurion's faith. There is power in that kind of confidence. You can move mountains if you have that kind of faith.

Clarence Forsburg tells about a mother with five children years ago who became so desperate because of health and financial problems that she decided that life was not worth the struggle. She took her youngest child, a preschool girl, into the bedroom of their tiny house. Carefully she cinched the windows with rags and newspapers, and then turned on the gas heater without lighting it. She lay down on the bed with her arm around her small daughter. She could hear the gas escaping.

She could also hear another sound, however. Suddenly it occurred to her that she had forgotten to turn off the radio in the next room. For some reason it seemed important to her. She got up to do so. Someone on the radio was singing an old gospel hymn: "Oh what peace we often forfeit, O what needless pain we bear. All because we do not carry everything to God in prayer."

In that instant she realized the mistake she was making. She had forgotten the resources of her own faith. She rushed back into the bedroom, turned off the gas, and opened the windows wide. Then she picked up the little girl and held her tight. When she spoke about it later she said, "I began to pray. I did not pray for help. I prayed a prayer of gratitude to God for his blessings. I thanked him for life. I thanked him for five wonderful children. I promised him that I would not forget my faith again." Then she added as an afterthought: "and so far I have kept that promise." (4)

We began this message talking about the moral and spiritual mediocrity that is seeping into our life as a nation. There is not a single case of mediocrity in this story of the Roman centurion. It is a beautiful story that features a caring community; it features character and humility; it features confidence in what Jesus can do for us when we remember to pray. When you have those three elements at play all in one place—caring, character and confidence in Christ—miracles take place. You can heal a body, you can heal a family, you can heal a community, you can heal a world.

No wonder the centurion's servant was healed. With such forces at work in our lives, no battle would be too great for us.

1. Glenn Van Ekeren, Speaker's Sourcebook II (Englewood Cliffs, NY: Prentice Hall, Inc., 1994), pp. 142-143.
2. http://www.higherpraise.com/outlines/woodvale/Luke7a.htm.
3. John Ortberg, The Me I Want To Be: Becoming God's Best Version Of You (Grand Rapids: Zondervan, 2010), p. 26.
4. From a message by Dr. Joe Harding.

A Matter Of Trust
Galatians 1:11-24

One of the questions that is becoming more a matter of concern all the time is this one—who can I trust? We live in a strange world. Did you know that you can now buy trust in a bottle? All of you aspiring politicians listen up ... all you guys who want to win over a member of the fairer sex ... all of you who have a questionable product to sell to an unsuspecting public. A New York City lab claims to have put trust in a bottle.

According to their ads, "After showering in the morning simply spray a squirt or two of odorless Liquid Trust onto your skin, and then the people you meet during the next few hours will trust you without their knowing why they trust you."

One satisfied customer writes, "My boss is rather distant, but on days I wear Liquid Trust he includes me in conversations and jokes that he doesn't on days I don't wear Liquid Trust ... I get less hassle and sell more product on days I wear it, no lie. And my kids behave better when I wear it also. It isn't a cure-all but it makes my life easier on many days." There it is. Just what you needed. Solve all your problems with Trust in a Bottle.

What's in Liquid Trust? Allegedly it is the hormone oxcytocin [ok-si-toh-suhn]. The makers claim that oxcytocin is the actual scientifically proven elixir of trust—that it's a naturally occurring human hormone that "plays a significant role in childbirth, breast-feeding and romantic love."

How do we know they're telling us the truth? Good question, and since it retails for something like $50 a bottle, maybe, just maybe a little old-fashioned skepticism is in order. (1)

Let's deal with the issue of trust for a few moments. It's one of the most important issues with which all of us have to deal. It affects our life as a people, it affects our life together as families, it affects our individual happiness. Surveys today indicate that trust for other people and trust for institutions is at an all-time low.

Some of you remember when the journalist and television news anchor Walter Cronkite was often referred to as "The most trusted man in America." In this day and age, in a culture that is politically, racially, economically, and in countless other ways divided and polarized, trust is not an abundant commodity.

For example, we used to trust the financial community. I mean, if you can't trust your bank, who can you trust? If you can't trust Wall Street, what hope is there?

Can you believe it? Forbes magazine carried an article that suggested that most Americans no longer trust people on Wall Street. Seventy-one percent of those surveyed in a Harris poll said that "most people on Wall Street would be willing to break the law if they believed that they could make a lot of money and get away with it." Only 26% of respondents believe that Wall Streeters are generally "as honest and moral as other people." Even more depressingly, thirty-nine percent think Wall Street does more harm than good, a new record. (2) Who do you trust?

How about the press? A recent Gallup Public Confidence poll revealed that only 29 percent of Americans express a great deal of confidence in newspapers. That's down from 51 percent in 1959. Television news fared just a little better with 35 percent.

I won't even bother to cite statistics about how much trust people have in their government, particularly Congress. Here's a shocker: even scientists are suspect nowadays, as the controversy over climate change would seem to indicate. People nowadays don't trust their doctors, their bankers, or, I hate to say it—even their clergy.

The rapid rise in divorce rates indicates that even within the family trust is in short supply. The institution of the family has been in decline for the past 40 years leading many people to demand such things as prenuptial contracts or at least a long period of living together before jumping into something that may or may not work.

As for trusting your employer? It seems to be a thing of the past. Employees, even of large and stable corporations, view themselves increasingly as independent contractors ready to move at a moment's notice to greener pastures. Why? Because they feel that their employer would be equally eager to shed them if it would improve the bottom line. Corporate loyalty has gone the way of the Dodo.

Young people with huge education loans hanging over their heads are questioning whether our entire economic system can be trusted to give them the kind of future that their parents have enjoyed.

Trust in friendships, the economy, products, government, religion, and science—all has declined. This is a big deal! Our world was designed to run on trust.

Trust is essential to everything we do. We trust the other drivers on the road to stop when the light turns red. We trust the builders of bridges to get it right when they build a long span across a wide waterway. We trust the doctor to be accurate in her diagnosis and the hospital to provide the equipment and the sterile environment we need to survive a disease. We have to trust the banks, the government, yes, even Wall Street to guard our funds for our declining years. We trust that when we stand at an altar the person we are pledging ourselves to will fulfill their vows.

Trust is a very big deal. When journalist Eric Weiner traveled the world to discover what made some countries happier places than others to live, he found one primary common denominator among the happiest societies. The essential ingredient was trust. The happiest countries are those in which people feel they can trust their government, trust their social institutions, and trust their neighbors. (3) Trust is a very big deal indeed.

It is evident that one problem the apostle Paul had at the beginning of his ministry was that many in the early church did not trust him. We see in our lesson for today from Galatians that some in the church in Galatia had questions about Paul's credentials. They challenged his authority as a church leader and raised doubts about the authenticity of his calling.

In Galatians we find Paul taking great pains to assert the validity of his apostleship. After all, he recognizes that his background and his past could potentially raise reasonable questions. The apostles chosen by Jesus before his crucifixion had the advantage of being people who actually walked and talked with Jesus. Paul, on the other hand, had come along and announced his apostleship well after Christ's death and after his own notorious past as a persecutor of Christians. It was little wonder if some believers wanted to know such things as "Who is this man? Where is he coming from, and why should we trust him?"

Paul confronts these questions head on. He writes, "For you have heard of my previous way of life in Judaism, how intensely I persecuted the church of God and tried to destroy it. I was advancing in Judaism beyond many of my own age among my people and was extremely zealous for the traditions of my fathers."

When you think about it, it is amazing that people in the early church ever trusted Paul at all. Suppose we had somebody show up at our church who was known for his religious hatred, known for his proclivity for violence, was even known to have participated in the murder of a dear friend of ours, a highly respected member of our church. Would you ever trust him? Or would you say, "I'll never trust him. You can't change human nature." It had to be difficult for early Christians to accept Paul. Particularly, there had to be a lot of resentment in the part Paul played in the martyrdom of Stephen.

It reminds me of a story Rabbi Joseph Telushkin tells on Billy Wilder, the famed Hollywood director who was Jewish. Wilder served with the United States Army Psychological Warfare Division during World War II.

After the war, some Germans wrote Wilder for permission to put on a play depicting the crucifixion of Christ. After investigating the Germans, Wilder discovered that each of them had been either a storm trooper or a member of the Gestapo. So, he said, he would give them permission to put on the play depicting the crucifixion of Christ—as long as they used real nails. (4) Evidently Billy

Wilder wasn't eager to forgive and forget the sins of the German people.

It took time for Paul to win people's trust. We might get the idea that once Paul was converted he was accepted almost at once by the entire church and then he went sailing merrily off on his missionary journeys. Not true. Listen to his words: "But when God, who set me apart from my mother's womb and called me by his grace, was pleased to reveal his Son in me so that I might preach him among the Gentiles, my immediate response was not to consult any human being. I did not go up to Jerusalem to see those who were apostles before I was, but I went into Arabia. Later I returned to Damascus. Then after three years, I went up to Jerusalem to get acquainted with Cephas and stayed with him fifteen days. I saw none of the other apostles—only James, the Lord's brother. I assure you before God that what I am writing you is no lie."

What did Paul do during his time in Arabia and those three years in Damascus? And why did he go there rather than Jerusalem? Could it be that these were the only places he was accepted? Maybe this is why his missionary journeys were so extensive. Perhaps he needed to find places where people would not hold his past against him. That happens in the church. We have trouble accepting people who have done wrong, even when they are sincerely penitent. As someone has said, "We are the only army that shoots its wounded." When Paul wrote these words to the church at Galatia, it may have been twenty years after his conversion experience. Still, there were people who did not trust him, even after twenty years of ministry.

Pastor Scott Hoezee tells about an interesting study on forgiveness conducted by the Templeton Foundation in cooperation with the University of Michigan and the National Institute for Mental Health. According to this study, 75% of Americans are "very confident" that they have been forgiven by God for their past offenses. Surprisingly this is true even of those who are not regular church attendees. They don't have much to do with God otherwise, but they have few doubts about God's penchant to let bygones be bygones.

"The picture was less bright, however, when it came to interpersonal relations," says the author of the study. Only about half of the people claimed that they had completely forgiven others. God may forgive, but ordinary folks struggle. "It's difficult to forgive other people with whom you are angry. It's even difficult to forgive yourself sometimes. But where forgiveness does take place, the study found a link between forgiveness and better health. The more prone a person is to grant forgiveness, the less likely he or she will suffer from any stress-related illnesses." (5)

The New Testament church had the same problem many of us have. We accept the forgiveness that God offers us, but it's difficult to apply that same forgiveness to others. And, even if we do say that we forgive those who have hurt or betrayed us, we vow never to trust them again.

Paul understood this. He is very transparent about his past. He had done wrong in his prior life of persecuting the early church. There was only one way he could ever win back their trust and that was to live a Christ-like life from that day forward. And he did. That is the only way any of us who have done wrong can ever really make things right. That is to make a new start with God's help.

Andrew Jackson was the 7th president of the United States. Some people regard him as a fine president. His face is on the $20 bill, if that is any indication. But he was also tough. They called him "Old Hickory" and in some cases he was ruthless. He was the president who ordered the infamous "Trail of Tears" for the Cherokee Indians. His former ally Chief Junaluska said, "I would have killed him myself . . . if I had known what he was going to do to my people." Andrew Jackson had many enemies.

Jackson loved his wife, Rachel. They lived together at the Hermitage near Nashville, Tennessee. Rachel was a devout Christian. Jackson had a chapel built for her on the Hermitage grounds. Anyone who questioned Rachel's virtue (and evidently there were many) Jackson challenged to a duel. When Rachel died, part of Andrew Jackson died with her. They said that he would sit in the chapel for hours just to remember.

One day a minister came to visit and Jackson said: "I would like to be baptized and I would like to become a Christian."

The minister said, "Mr. President, there is nothing that would please me more. But in order to be baptized, you will need to repent, to seek forgiveness for your sins, and to forgive those who have sinned against you. Are you willing to do that, Mr. President?"

Andrew Jackson said, "I can forgive my enemies in battle, I can forgive my enemies in politics, but I will never forgive those who slandered Rachel." Old Hickory was not willing to bend. And that was the way that they left it.

Sometime later there was a knock on the minister's door. It was late at night and it was raining. There on the doorstep, soaked from the rain, was the former president of the United States. In a voice barely audible, Jackson said: "I'm ready to forgive."

The minister said, "Excuse me, Mr. President, I'm hard of hearing. What did you say?"

And Old Hickory broke down in tears and said: "I forgive them all." (6)

That pastor probably went too far in requiring Jackson to forgive others before he was accepted into the fellowship of the church. But friends, this is the only way that a person can ever really be trusted again—if they totally and completely repent of their sin and resolve with God's help never to make the same mistake again.

That is what St. Paul did. I love the way this story ends. Our lesson for today from Paul's letter to the church at Galatia reads like this: "Then I went to Syria and Cilicia. I was personally unknown to the churches of Judea that are in Christ. They only heard the report: 'The man who formerly persecuted us is now preaching the faith he once tried to destroy.'" Then he writes, "And they praised God because of me."

Paul's life was an open book. Once he had been Saul who had persecuted the church; now he was Paul who preached the Gospel, and everyone who got to know him could tell that he was not the same man he had been. This is how you rebuild the bonds of trust—forgiveness and repentance—becoming a new person in Christ.

1. Dr. Justin Imel, http://justinimel.com/mark/uncommonscents.html.
2. http://www.forbes.com/2009/03/23/hating-wall-street-intelligent-investing-trust.html.
3. Renee Garfinkel, Ph.D. http://www.psychologytoday.com/blog/time-out/201105/who-can-you-trust.
4. Rabbi Joseph Telushkin, Jewish Humor. Cited in David Bruce, 250 Anecdotes About Religion (Kindle version).
5. http://www.calvincrc.org/sermons/2002/matthew18.html.
6. From a sermon by Rev. John C. Fitzgerald, https://booneumcevents.org/uploads/Sermon2009_07_12.pdf.

Two Sinners

Luke 7:36-50

To learn how Americans feel about prayer, Life magazine once interviewed dozens of people. One person they talked to was a prostitute, age twenty-four, in White Pine County, Nevada.

"I don't think about my feelings a lot," she said. "Instead I lie in my bed and think [about God]. I meditate because sometimes my words don't come out right. But he can find me. He can find what's inside of me just by listening to my thoughts. I ask him to help me and keep me going. A lot of people think working girls don't have any morals, any religion. But I do. I don't steal. I don't lie. The way I look at it, I'm not sinning. He's not going to judge me. I don't think God judges anybody." (1)

That's an interesting take on God, don't you think? God doesn't judge anybody. It is an attitude that many people today find appealing. The last thing we want is a God who judges. Some people say that prostitution is a victimless crime. It is an argument advanced by those who would legalize what is called "the world's oldest profession." If it is true that prostitution is a victimless crime, why then do police reports show that the suicide rate of prostitutes is at least 45 times greater than for non-prostitutes? (2)

If prostitution is not harmful to its clients, who are at least in danger of contracting sexually transmitted diseases, it is certainly harmful spiritually and emotionally to the women who practice it. It is no coincidence that so many prostitutes come from backgrounds in which they were abused as children or youths. Something is broken within many of these women, something that deserves our compassion more than our condemnation. That was certainly true of the woman in our lesson for today.

Jesus was dining at the home of a Pharisee named Simon. They were reclining at Simon's table for the evening meal. They were not seated in straight back chairs as we might do. They were probably reclining on their side on something like short sofas, probably elevated at one end, with their elbow propping up their head.

There was a woman, a resident of their community, who was there uninvited. The Bible doesn't say that she was a prostitute, though it is generally assumed that she was. Luke simply tells us she "lived a sinful life." Prostitution was a common occupation in biblical times for women. There weren't many ways for an unmarried woman to survive financially. Some turned to prostitution. It may have been an act of dire circumstance that forced this woman to earn her living as she did. That did not keep the profession from inflicting great damage on her soul.

When she learned that Jesus was eating at the house of Simon the Pharisee, she decided to crash the party. Evidently Jesus' reputation for compassion preceded him. Why else would this desperate woman have sought him out? She came bearing an alabaster jar of perfume. She stood behind Jesus at his feet and she was weeping. Her weeping was so profuse that her tears were falling on Jesus' feet. She bent down and wiped Jesus' feet with her hair, then she kissed his feet and poured perfume on them.

This was more than the host, Simon the Pharisee, could bear. With a silent sneer he said to himself, "If this man were a prophet, he would know who is touching him and what kind of woman she is—that she is a sinner."

Jesus knew exactly what Simon was thinking. He said, "Simon, I have something to tell you."

"Tell me, teacher," Simon said.

And so Jesus proceeded to tell Simon a parable. "Two people owed money to a certain moneylender. One owed him five hundred pieces of silver, the other fifty. Neither of them had the money to pay him back, so he forgave the debts of both. Now," asked Jesus, "which of them will love him more?"

Simon replied, "I suppose the one who had the bigger debt forgiven."

"You have judged correctly," Jesus said. Then he turned toward the woman and said to Simon, "Do you see this woman? I came into your house. You didn't give me any water for my feet, but she wet my feet with her tears and wiped them with her hair. You didn't give me a kiss, but this woman, from the time I entered, has not stopped kissing my feet. You didn't put oil on my head, but she has poured perfume on my feet. Therefore, I tell you, her many sins have been forgiven—as her great love has shown."

Then Jesus came to the punch line: "Whoever has been forgiven little loves little." Think about that little gem for a moment: "Whoever has been forgiven little loves little."

Could that be why many of us are so tepid in our love for God? We have never really thought of ourselves as sinners. We have never hungered for forgiveness. "Whoever has been forgiven little loves little." We may love the song but we have never felt the emotion: "Amazing Grace, how sweet the sound that saved a wretch like me; I once was lost but now am found, was blind but now I see." When did we ever feel ourselves to be a wretch? When did we ever feel we were lost or blind?

A Presbyterian pastor was in his first year at a certain congregation. The congregation had traditionally had a Confession of Sin as part of their worship liturgy. This pastor's predecessor had eliminated this prayer of confession from the service. He tried to reinstate it. But resistance to the proposed change was fierce. Some members thought that a confession of sin was too morbid a thing to do in church, where one's spirits were supposed to be lifted up. During the heat of the debate, one woman—an elder in the church—exclaimed, "But I don't need to apologize to God for anything!"

The pastor was dumbfounded. "My seminary training hadn't prepared me for this," he said. "I thought everyone knew we had to confess our sin." (3)

Here's the problem: what if you have no consciousness of sin? What if pride has blinded you to your need for God's forgiveness and grace? That was the situation of Simon the Pharisee. He was blind to his need for God. And because he did not feel a need for God even though he was quite religious, he would never know the joy of being bathed in God's love. To see this, notice what happens next in our story.

Jesus says to the woman, "Your sins are forgiven."

Then, Luke tells us, the other guests in Simon's house began to say among themselves, "Who is this who even forgives sins?"

This is quite telling. The other guests, and probably Simon himself, missed the whole point of Jesus' parable. They were hung up on the fact that Jesus professed to forgive sins. That is probably because these guests were also Pharisees, as Simon was, or they were at least pharisaical in their attitudes. When Jesus gave his punch line, "whoever has been forgiven little loves little," he wasn't talking about the woman. He was talking about Simon, and everyone who is like Simon. We don't feel as much love for God that the forgiven prostitute feels, because we have never felt the need she felt.

There were at least two sinners involved in Jesus' parable—the woman and Simon the Pharisee. And in Jesus' eyes it was easier to forgive a prostitute who mourned in her heart that she had sinned than it was to forgive this Pharisee who thought he was so superior and didn't really need to be forgiven. She at least recognized her need, while he was oblivious to his shortcomings. This is the constant temptation of church people—this feeling that we are somehow superior to other people.

A young pastor was visiting in a very humble home in the mountains of East Tennessee. The home was really not much more than a shack. A layman was with this pastor. This layman was a pillar of the church, a middle-aged man of some means. They had come to the home to deliver a Christmas basket which was obviously much needed. There were several children in the family. They obviously were on welfare. Their home showed much neglect both inside and out.

The young pastor tried in every way to show the love of Christ to this family, to show acceptance and to epitomize the Christmas spirit. But just before he and his layman left this home, the layman showed how he really felt about this family by walking over to the television set and drawing his finger across the top of that set and displaying to all in the home the layer of dust that was on his finger. Then he shook his head somberly in disapproval. The young pastor wanted to sink through the floor. All the good intentions he had for showing the grace of Jesus Christ was completely undone by his ungracious layman.

We need to understand that there were two sinners at Simon's table that night, one a prostitute and the other a Pharisee. It is easy to recognize the prostitute's sin. She was selling her body and deadening her soul. The body is intended to be the temple of the Holy Spirit. Any use of the body that degrades the spirit is repulsive in God's sight. Jesus was not in any way condoning the prostitute's behavior. Even more reprehensible, however, in Christ's eyes was the smug, self-righteous spirit of the Pharisee. There was very little hope for him because he saw no need for change. The prostitute knew she was missing the mark; Simon was blind to the entire target. Even worse was his attitude toward this woman. Instead of having compassion for her, he turned up his nose at her.

Some of us like to play judge and jury when it comes to the behavior of others. That is what Simon was doing. "If this man were a prophet," he sneered, "he would know who is touching him and what kind of woman she is—that she is a sinner." Yes, she was a sinner, but that was not for Simon to decide. That was for God alone to decide.

The great evangelist and author F.B. Meyer once said that when we see a brother or sister in sin, there are two things we do not know: First, we do not know how hard he or she tried not to sin. And second, we do not know the power of the forces that assailed him or her. But there is another thing we do not really know: We don't know what we would have done in the same circumstances. (4)

Indeed, Christ seems to be indicating there was more hope for the woman than there was for Simon. Christ tells her that her sins are forgiven. Nowhere does he say that Simon's sin is forgiven—and that should trouble us.

Some of us come from comfortable situations where we have been loved, and from the beginning have been taught right from wrong. That is not true of everybody. Most of us have had a strong support system. We have had role models. We have had a Christian family and Christian friends and Christian teachers who have helped mold our behavior. Do we not realize that many people have not been as fortunate as we are?

Remember Ann Richards, the colorful Texas politician who suggested of a prominent political candidate that he had been born on third base and thought he had hit a triple? She was talking about many of us, at least spiritually. Do you really think that God judges us by the same standards He uses to judge those who were raised under less desirable circumstances? If God grades on a curve, as I suspect He does, we had better learn to be grateful for God's grace because you and I are in big trouble otherwise. "To whom much is given," says the Master, "much is expected" (Luke 12:48).

This is to say that it is our job to love people and to leave judging to God. This is how we best witness for Christ—by reaching out to others in the same way Christ reached out to us. "While we were yet sinners Christ died for us . . ." writes St. Paul (Romans 5:8). And that is the same attitude we should have in our relationships with others, loving them and not judging them. Simon felt no need to show compassion toward this woman or to help her to a better life. His only attitude toward her was one of cold condemnation. And Jesus hated that.

Dr. Robert Dunham tells a story that he heard on NPR sometime back. It was about a 31-year-old New York City social worker named Julio Diaz. Diaz customarily followed the same routine each evening. He got off the subway to the Bronx one stop early, just so he could eat at his favorite diner. But one night as Diaz stepped off the No. 6 train and onto a nearly empty platform, his evening took an unexpected turn.

He was walking toward the stairs when a teenage boy approached and pulled out a knife and asked for his money. So Diaz gave the boy his wallet. As his assailant began to walk away, Diaz said, "Hey, wait a minute. You forgot something. If you're going to be robbing people all night, you might as well take my coat to keep you warm."

The young man looked at him like he was crazy, and asked, "Why are you doing this?"

Diaz replied, "Well, if you're willing to risk your freedom for a few dollars, then I guess you must really need the money. I mean, all I wanted to do was get dinner . . . and if you want to join me . . . hey, you're more than welcome."

"I just felt maybe he really [needed] help," Diaz said later. Remarkably, the boy agreed, and the unlikely pair walked into the diner and sat in a booth.

Shortly the manager came by, the dishwasher came by, the waiters came by to greet Diaz. "The kid was like, 'You know everybody here. Do you own this place?'"

"No," Diaz replied, "I just eat here a lot."

The boy responded, "But you're even nice to the dishwasher."

"Well, haven't you been taught that you should be nice to everybody?" Diaz asked.

"Yeah, but I didn't think people actually behaved that way," the boy said.

The social worker saw an opening. He asked the boy what he wanted out of life. "He just had almost a sad face," Diaz said. He couldn't answer—or he didn't want to.

When the bill arrived, Diaz told the teen, "Look, I guess you're going to have to pay for this bill 'cause you have my money and I can't pay for it. But if you give me my wallet back, I'll gladly treat you."

The teen "didn't even think about it" and handed over the wallet. Diaz gave him $20 . . . he figured maybe it would help him. But Diaz asked for something in return, and the boy gave it to him. It was the knife which the boy had used to rob him. (5)

Two sinners were present at Simon's house when Jesus went to Simon's house for dinner. One was a woman who had lived a sinful life. The other was a Pharisee, one of the most respectable men in his community. Only one found salvation that evening. The other only marinated in his own smug self-righteousness. I hope God's grace will be sufficient for Simon on the Last Day when all of us will stand before the judgment seat of God, because there's too much of Simon in me . . . and probably in you. God's grace is our only hope unless we pray this day that God will help us to love other people without reservation and leave the judging to Him.

1. Craig Brian Larson, ed., Contemporary Illustrations for Preachers, Teachers, & Writers (Grand Rapids: Baker Books, 1996), p. 123.
2. The Houston Post, 1/10/94, p. A-10. Cited in In other Words.
3. Miroslav Volf, "Is It God's Business?" The Christian Century. Cited by Brian K. Jensen, http://www.meadvillefpc.org/2005_sermons_august_-_december.htm.
4. Stephen Brown, Christianity Today, April 5, 1993, p. 17.
5. As reported by Michael Garofalo on Morning Edition, March 28, 2008. Cited by Dr. Robert Dunham, http://day1.org/1759-which_comes_first_grace_or_repentance.

No Substitutes
Galatians 3:23-29

A church organist sent the following note to his minister: "I am sorry to say that my wife died last night. Could you please find a substitute for me for the weekend?"

Well, I'm certain he meant a substitute organist not a substitute wife.

Speaking of substitutes, there was an award ceremony years ago for the legendary baseball player Joe DiMaggio at the Lotos Club of NY. At that event, DiMaggio's former teammate, Phil Rizzuto, told the audience that one time DiMaggio, who was wildly popular, was supposed to speak at a church in New Jersey. But he couldn't make it. And so he asked Rizzuto to substitute for him.

The crowd at the church didn't know ahead of time that DiMaggio, the scheduled speaker, wouldn't be there and they were furious. They took it out on Rizzuto his substitute. Rizzuto said the priest told him later, "It was the first time anyone has ever been booed at a Communion Breakfast." (1)

Some of the churches that the Apostle Paul wrote his epistles to were a mess. They would probably have booed a speaker at a communion breakfast.

In today's lesson, Paul is writing to the church in Galatia. The Galatians had a controversy going on about adherence to the Hebrew Law. Some of them were still observing the Law of Moses rather than experiencing the freedom that Christ brings. Paul warns them about accepting any substitute for authentic faith. This is how he begins: "Before the coming of this faith, we were held in custody under the law, locked up until the faith that was to come would be revealed. So the law was our guardian until Christ came that we might be justified by faith. Now that this faith has come, we are no longer under a guardian. So in Christ Jesus you are all children of God through faith, for all of you who were baptized into Christ have clothed yourselves with Christ. There is neither Jew nor Gentile, neither slave nor free, nor is there male and female, for you are all one in Christ Jesus. If you belong to Christ, then you are Abraham's seed, and heirs according to the promise."

Paul was troubled by how some of the Galatians still clung to the Law. In his own life the Law had brought him so much pain. He found it impossible to live up to the demands of the Law and felt condemned for even trying to do so. Christ had brought such a feeling of freedom into his life that he couldn't even imagine going back to his old life. He had been freed from his prejudices against Gentiles, against women, against people of other nationalities and other stations in society. Why would anyone who had experienced such freedom ever want to cling to oppressive ways of the past?

Accept no substitute, Paul is saying to the people, for an authentic experience with the living God. Accept no substitute for freedom in Christ. With all his heart, Paul wanted the church at Galatia to escape their outdated form of thinking and to experience living under the guidance of the Spirit of Christ, not the Spirit of the Law.

Now we should understand, there was nothing wrong with the Law. The Law was God's gift to the Jewish people. It helped them establish civilized relations with their neighbors, and with God. For many Jews the law was a delight.

It was obedience to the Law that had kept the children of Israel together as a people through the destruction of their homeland, through their dispersal among surrounding pagan peoples, through their domination by the heavy hand of Rome.

There was nothing wrong with the Law. The Law served the Israelites well throughout their history. It gave them a way of life that was superior to any other culture on earth. In many ways the Jewish law strengthened the faith of the Jews in the coming Messiah. Dr. Warren Wiersbe has put it this way, "In the Old Testament, we have preparation for Christ; in the gospels, the presentation of Christ."

There was nothing wrong with the Law. The only problem was with those who turned the Law into a set of demands which one had to meet before one was acceptable to God. The only problem was with Christians for whom biblical laws had become not a source of guidance and inspiration, but an instrument whereby to oppress oneself and others.

You may have heard of the woman in Dayton, Tennessee who tried living by the Hebrew Law for one year and wrote a book about it. Her name is Rachel Held Evans and the book is titled A Year of Biblical Womanhood. The book is an attempt to take a look at real women in the Bible and how they are similar to women of today.

"I've long been frustrated," Evans said in a press release, "by the inconsistencies with which 'biblical womanhood' is taught and applied in my evangelical Christian community. So, inspired by A.J. Jacobs' [book], A Year of Living Biblically, I set out to follow all of the Bible's instructions for women as literally as possible for a year to show that no woman, no matter how devout, is actually practicing biblical womanhood all the way."

Evans temporarily changed her entire way of life in order to gain a better understanding of the teachings in the Bible that are geared toward women. For example, she wore a scarf over her head whenever she was in public and she called her husband, Dan, "master." She even stood on the side of a road with a sign that said, "Dan is awesome" in her extreme attempt to show her devotion as a biblical wife.

The book was written for both entertainment and educational purposes. Would you be surprised that the book hasn't been well received by some members of the Christian community? One of the largest Christian book store chains [which I will not name] has refused to sell the book. (2) Could it be that some Christians today are just as afraid as the church in Galatia about the meaning of the freedom Christ brings?

There is always a tendency among many people to set in concrete values and standards of the past—to deny the living reality of God now. For a number of people in

Paul's time the Law had become a substitute for God.

I wonder if that hasn't happened to many people today. Oh, I am not thinking about obedience to Jewish ceremonial law. Only a few small sects are still pulled in that direction. But there are other substitutes that we are tempted to set up in God's place and the effect of those substitutes can be just as deadening.

One substitute that I am thinking about is scientific law. I suspect that there are many faithful Christians, pillars of our churches, who are Deists at heart, believing that, Yes, God created the world, but then God left this world to run itself under the guardianship of the laws of nature.

This is one of the hurdles that former Chicago Tribune journalist Lee Strobel had to clear on his journey from being a skeptic, a self-described atheist, to being a follower of Christ. "How could miracles disobey the basic laws of nature?" he questioned. "Doesn't scientific reasoning dispel belief in the supernatural?" There are many people who have stumbled over the question of the relationship between Christianity and science.

Now please do not misunderstand me. I believe we live in a lawful universe. Our whole scientific and technological society is based upon predictability of the laws of nature. We give God thanks for His lawful works and the wonders of modern science. But I wonder if there are not many Christians who have lost the joy of praying because somehow someone has convinced them that God is a helpless captive of his own laws.

We trust the physician to manipulate the laws of nature to enable the healing process to take place—but we deny God, the creator of all the laws by which the universe is governed, the same privilege. For many Christians scientific rationalism has replaced a sense of a dynamic relationship with the Source of life. Scientific law can be a substitute for faith for many people.

What we might call the "sociological norm" can be another. It is always interesting to read the advice columns in the newspaper. It is there that we find out what is fashionable in morality. Isn't that how many of us set our standards nowadays? We let society dictate what is right and wrong for us. If 69% of married men confess to having extra-marital affairs then it must be all right. If everybody else's mom is allowing their 14-year-old to see "R" rated movies, then we dare not go against the norm.

Captain William Westy wrote an article titled "The Right to Be Different." Here is what he said: "Psychologists attempt to help persons adjust to society. Big business and big labor try to fit the individual into the organization pattern. Advertising extols the virtues of conformity . . . This same sort of logic should have convinced Columbus that the world was flat and the Wright brothers that man could never fly. Thank God that some [people] of all ages have dared to dispute the majority opinion when it was in error."

Do you get what he is saying? There is tremendous pressure in our society for us to conform, for each of us to be like everyone else. Now I am not arguing for us to become crackpots or eccentrics. But, thank God, there are some people who do not take their values and standards from the crowd. Our sense of right and wrong, our sense of duty and justice should flow not from the sociological norm but from a dynamic relationship with the living God. We dare not ever allow mob rule to become a substitute for the inner testimony of the Spirit of God.

Scientific law—the sociological norm—these are but two of the substitutes that we employ in place of faith in a living God.

Mood altering chemicals might be another. "I can't make it through the day without my valium—I need a drink—I have to have something to relax me at night so I can go to sleep—a few energy drinks to give me the energy I need for the day"—the list goes on and on. We are a society that runs on pharmaceuticals.

A young doctor stood before a group of pastors. "I developed a chemical dependence," he said, "while I was doing my residency. I was working unbelievably long hours. I started taking uppers—amphetamines—in order to keep up the pace. Then I needed a downer to help me go to sleep at night. Before long I noticed that it was taking more of each to do the job. I was caught in a vicious cycle. I was on a merry-go-round and there didn't seem to be any way off. My dependency on drugs was destroying my health—my work—my career. Finally I checked myself into a hospital that specializes in chemical dependency. And I started reaching out to God. I had noticed how successful Alcoholics Anonymous had been in helping persons regain control of their lives by surrendering them to God. I did the same thing."

That young doctor was smarter and luckier than most persons who get caught on the merry-go-round of drug and alcohol abuse. It is far too easy in our society today, and far too acceptable, I am afraid, to hide from our problems behind a glass of liquor or a mood-altering drug than to open ourselves to the presence of the living God and to allow God to help us cope with life.

Chemical dependency is another substitute. But there is one more which I would mention. For many of us, materialism has become our primary substitute for God. Who needs God in a world of I-pads and smart phones, and High-Def TVs, and spacious homes and luxury automobiles? It is difficult for a pastor to deal with any of these gods without sounding judgmental. And particularly in our affluent society today, when there are so many things to give us pleasure, so many status symbols to give us a sense of importance, so many tangible assets to give us a sense of security, anyone who warns against the dangers of materialism is truly a lonely voice crying in the wilderness.

There are television evangelists who tell us that God wants us to have all these things. Indeed, we are led to believe that the key to even greater riches is to simply follow their leadership. They have much louder voices and much flashier sets than the local pastor trying faithfully to proclaim the word.

But maybe, just maybe, there was a reason Jesus said that you cannot worship both God and mammon. Maybe there was a reason that Jesus gave his strongest warning to the possessors of great wealth.

My friends, I love nice things as much as anyone else. I want my family to have the opportunities that other families have. But I am also aware that there are persons today whose every thought is dominated by the desire to obtain more wealth. Every family conversation is dominated by a discussion of money. Every important value is determined by the price tag it carries. There are many of us who are in danger of bowing down at the altar of mammon. And like all idols, mammon can never satisfy our deepest needs. Only the real thing—only God himself can satisfy those needs.

As a pastor, I don't have the same problem as the Apostle Paul had. I don't have to worry about most of you living too biblically. Few of the women in this church are in danger of calling their husband "master" and following their husband's every dictate. But there are other idols that some of us substitute for an authentic relationship with God. It may be scientific rationalism. It may be devotion to the sociological norm. It may be chemical mood altering substances. It may be the lure of materialism. But, my friend, over the long haul there is no satisfying substitute. At the center of life, we need God. He is the source of our life, our strength, our hope.

Steve Rubell is one of the founders of the famed Studio 54 nightclub. At its height in the '70s, Studio 54 was the hottest nightclub in the country. Studio insiders recall wild parties and endless supplies of drugs. But in the late '80s, Steve Rubell reported that he saw all the old clientele of Studio 54 in a new place—coming out of a church. They had been attending an Alcoholics Anonymous meeting. (3)

I see that happening again. There are people in all walks of life who are rejecting many of the false idols of our society and are reaching out to God. Some of them are coming back to church. And no wonder. These other idols are inferior. No chemical, no beverage can satisfy your deepest need. There is no toy you can buy regardless of the size of your bank account. There is no substitute, my friend, for the real thing. Put God first in your life and everything else will fall in place.

1. The Jokesmith.
2. http://www.christianpost.com/news/woman-living-biblically-for-one-year-writes-book-rachel-evans-life-changing-experience-photo-83515/.
3. John Whitcomb and Claire Whitcomb, Great American Anecdotes (New York: William Morrow and Company, Inc., 1993), p. 160.

But First . . .
Luke 9:57-62

A lady was taking her time browsing through everything at a yard sale. In a conversation with the homeowner she said, "My husband is going to be very angry when he finds out I stopped at a yard sale."

"I'm sure he'll understand when you tell him about all the bargains," the homeowner replied.

"Normally, yes," the lady said. "But he just broke his leg, and he's waiting for me to take him to the hospital to have it set." (1)

Some things in life cannot be delayed. But we do delay them. Not for any sinister reasons, but because we don't attach any real urgency to them.

Pastor Gene Sikkink calls it the "But-First Syndrome." The American Medical Association hasn't recognized the "But-First Syndrome" as a disease yet, but that doesn't mean that many people are not suffering from some of its symptoms. Here are some examples of this ailment that Pastor Sikkink has noticed in his own life. He says:

I decide to do the laundry. I sit down with the intention of doing just that and notice the newspaper on the table. I will do the laundry, but first I'm going to read the paper. After that I notice some mail on the table. I'll stick the newspaper in the recycle bin, but first I'll look through the mail to see if there are any unpaid bills. As I leaf through the mail, I notice the empty glass on the coffee table from yesterday. I am now going to look for the checkbook to take care of those unpaid bills, but first I need to put that empty glass in the sink. I head for the kitchen with the glass, but then I notice through the window that our poor flowers need some water. I put the glass in the sink and see that the TV remote and the portable phone are both lying on the countertop. I don't know how they got there, but I do need to put them away, but first I need to water those plants . . ."

You get the idea. By the end of the day, he says he manages to get some of the laundry done, the newspapers are still on the floor by the table, the glass is now in the sink. However, the bills never got paid, the checkbook was never found, and the dog ate the remote control . . . (2) There was so much he meant to do, but he got sidetracked by the "But-First Syndrome."

As Jesus was walking along the road, he encountered three men. The first man said to him, "I will follow you wherever you go." We've all probably felt like that at some time or another. We've had some mountaintop experience or we were at a youth conference or some other inspiring situation and we felt so close to Christ that we said in our hearts, "I'll go wherever you want me to go. I'm yours. Do with me as you will."

But time has gone by, and the truth of the matter is that we have lived pretty ordinary lives since then. There have been plenty of instances where we could have served Christ better, but somehow other things got in the way.

Some of you remember when Billy Graham crusades were a big deal. Crowds as large as 100,000 would pack stadiums to hear Billy's sermons, and thousands would go forward as the choir sang, "Just as I am without one plea . . ." to make decisions for Christ.

Recently I read that only between 2% to 4% of those who went forward on such occasions are still actively observing the Christian life now. This is not to say that these crusades had no impact. There are people whose lives were touched in a beautiful way in these crusades, but, for most of those who went forward, it didn't last. The point is, in some situations, we might say, "Yes, Lord, I am yours," but Christ knows you're just caught up in the moment. This was obviously the way it was with this first man who said to him, "I will follow you wherever you go."

Notice Jesus' response to him, "Foxes have dens and birds have nests, but the Son of Man has no place to lay his head." Jesus seems to be saying to him in a gentle way: You don't know what you're saying. Following me is not for the faint of heart. It's not for people who are concerned about material possessions or comforts. It's for people who are ready to put it all on the line. It's not for people who get excited on one occasion, who respond for an hour to a nice, warm, spiritual feeling. It's for people who are ready to be Christ's man, Christ's woman regardless of their current circumstance or how they happen to be feeling at the moment. "Foxes have dens and birds have nests, but the Son of Man has no place to lay his head."

Notice Jesus' encounter with the second man. Jesus says to him, "Follow me." This man replies, "Lord, first let me go and bury my father."

Ah, here is a man suffering from the "But-first" syndrome. We might wonder what the man's doing talking to Jesus if his father had just died? In the first century, the Jews buried the dead almost immediately, usually the same day. There weren't well-equipped mortuaries to handle such needs back then. He was obviously needed back home.

And why does Jesus give him such a hard time? The man makes a perfectly normal request: "Lord, first let me go and bury my father."

Jesus' answer is a little harsh, "Let the dead bury their own dead, but you go and proclaim the kingdom of God." What's that about?

Commentators differ over whether the man's father had just died, whether he was near death, or whether he had a few years yet to go.

G. Campbell Morgan refers to a traveler in the Middle East who was trying to enlist a young Arab man as his guide. The young Arab replied that he could not go because he had to bury his father. When the traveler expressed his sympathy, he learned that the young man's father had not died, but that this was just an expression meaning that his father was getting up in years and he felt responsible for him. (3)

Some of you can identify with that. Your parents, too, are aging. You feel responsible for them. "As long as my Mom and Dad depend on me," this man is saying, "I better stay home."

The third man makes a request that is just as reasonable, "I will follow you, Lord; but first let me go back and say goodbye to my family." Hey, these are nice guys and they want to follow Jesus, but they've got responsibilities.

And so they say to him, "Yes, but first . . ." Jesus is just as short with this third man as he is with the others. Jesus says to him, "No one who puts a hand to the plow and looks back is fit for service in the kingdom of God." Obviously Jesus regarded the statement of the first man that he would follow him anywhere as superficial and the replies of the second two as mere excuses. He didn't need any more half-hearted disciples. He wanted people who were ready to make a commitment.

Jesus wasn't looking for fans; he was looking for followers. He wasn't looking for people to "like" him on Facebook, but to emulate him in their daily lives. Fans are easy to come by. Show the world that you are a winner, as the world defines a winner, and the world will regard you with adulation.

Of course, some of those fans will be fickle.

One year when the Houston Astros were not enjoying their best baseball season, their fans got a bit frustrated. We're told that a woman left her season tickets on the dashboard of her locked car—two of them. While she was in the store shopping, someone broke into her car. When she returned she found FOUR season tickets on the dash. (4)

The Astros aren't the only team with fickle fans. We're told that a sports fan in Cleveland, Ohio was strolling along a beach area in Cleveland when he spotted a bottle floating in Lake Erie. He fished the bottle out of the Lake and opened it, and out popped a Genie.

"Master," the genie said, "you have released me from my bondage in this bottle, ask any three wishes and I will grant them to you."

The man thought for a moment and said, "I would like the following three things to happen this year: The Cleveland Browns win the Super Bowl, the Cleveland Indians win the World Series and The Cleveland Cavaliers win the NBA title."

The Genie thought about this for a moment . . . and jumped back into the bottle.

It's hard to be a sports fan.

One man tells about his father who, he says, is an avid football fan. During a recent season his team got off to a poor start. Almost every Sunday afternoon Dad sat depressed, ranting at the TV screen.

One day, after shouts of disgust, silence fell. Puzzled, his wife went into the living room to find him quietly watching a World War II movie.

"I just switched over to something that I knew our side would win!" his Dad explained. (5)

Jesus doesn't want more fans. Fans are with you win or tie. Jesus has all the fans he needs. Jesus wants people who will walk in his footsteps daily regardless of their circumstances. Jesus wants people who will be with him whether he ascends to a throne or is crucified on a cross. Jesus wants people who mirror his compassion and his love, even when such love and compassion are unpopular.

Bishop William Willimon tells about a baptism ceremony he participated in when he was in campus ministry at Duke University. A fellow campus minister asked him to participate in a baptism of a graduate student. The grad student was from China. He had been attracted to the Christian faith while a student at Duke.

Willimon had met the young man once or twice before and joyfully participated in his baptism. He thought it a bright idea to bring his camera and take a few pictures after the baptism.

"You can send these pictures to your family back in China," Willimon said to the grad student. "You can share your baptism day with your friends at home," he said as he maneuvered everyone into place for the snapshots. He noticed that the group looked a little shy and awkward, but they all stood together as he took his pictures.

After the baptism the campus minister said to him, "Oh, that was embarrassing, you with your camera and all."

"Embarrassing?" Willimon asked, "Why?"

"Well, because now that he's baptized," his colleague explained, "his life has been ruined. His parents say that they will disinherit him. The government will probably take away his scholarship. He can't show those pictures to anybody back home. His life as he knew it is over; he's been baptized into Jesus." (6)

That young graduate student was making a decision that would cause him much pain. He was making a decision to be more than a fan of Jesus Christ. He was making a decision to be a follower. He was making the decision to walk in Christ's footsteps.

When we read the accounts of Jesus' life in the gospels we find him giving this command on many occasions: Follow me! He went to those fishermen—Peter, Andrew, James and John—and said, "Follow me, and I will make you fishers of men" (Matt 4:19). When the rich young ruler asked what he must do to have eternal life, Jesus answered, "One thing you lack: Go your way, sell whatever you have and give to the poor, and you will have treasure in heaven; and come, take up the cross, and follow me" (Mark 10:21). And we read in all three of the Synoptic Gospels the command: "If anyone desires to come after me, let him deny himself, and take up his cross, and follow me."

Jesus doesn't want fans. He wants followers. Jesus wants people who will do more than simply sit in a pew and clap and cheer. He wants people who will take up a cross daily, the cross of service and love.

Some of you may know the story of Rich Stearns. When Rich Stearns was a young man and new Christian, he got engaged. His fiancee like many young brides wanted to register for china at the local department store. But he said to her, "As long as there are children starving in the world, we will not own china, crystal, or silver."

What a wonderful statement of discipleship. His answer reminds me of that first man in our lesson who said, "I will follow you wherever you go."

However, as Rich entered the corporate world and started climbing the ladder, he found he had a really good head for business. Twenty years later he was the CEO of Lennox—ironically, the top producer of luxury tableware—fine china—in the country.

One day Rich received a phone call from an organization called World Vision, asking if he would consider getting involved with them. So Rich went to Rakai, Uganda —an area considered ground zero for the AIDS pandemic. In that village he sat in a thatched hut with a thirteen-year-old boy with the same first name as his—Richard. A pile of stones outside the door of the hut marked where they had buried Richard's father, who had died of AIDS. Another pile of stones marked where they buried his mother, who also died of AIDS. That kind of thing happens every day in Africa.

Rich talked for a while with young Richard—now the head of the household trying to raise his two younger brothers—and asked him at one point, "Do you have a Bible?"

Yes, the boy said, and he went into the other room and brought back the one book in their house.

"Are you able to read it?" Rich asked, and at that the boy's face lit up. "I love to read the gospel of John because it says Jesus loves children," the boy said.

And suddenly Rich Stearns knew what he had to do. He needed to follow Jesus full-time. He left his job and his house and his title. Today he's working for God. (7)

Rich Stearns is the kind of man Christ is looking for. Christ is not looking for people who'll get excited for a few moments on Sunday morning and then forget all about their good intentions. He's not looking for people who are suffering from the "But-first" syndrome and who are continually making excuses about why now is not a good time for them to make a commitment. Jesus is looking for followers—people who will wake up each day with a determination to live as Christ would have them live. Can he count on you?

1. Cybersalt Digest.
2. The Pastor's Story File, vol. 17, No. 8, June 2001.
3. (Old Tappan, NJ: Fleming H. Revell, 1931), p. 133.
4. Leith Anderson, Dying for Change (Bloomington, MN: Bethany House Pub, 1990).
5. Laugh & Lift, http://www.laughandlift.com/.
6. http://day1.org/1474-good_news.
7. John Rich Stearns, The Hole in Our Gospel (Nashville: Thomas Nelson, 2009). Cited in John Ortberg, The Me I Want To Be (Grand Rapids: Zondervan, 2010).

Are You In Labor?

Luke 10:1-11; 16-20

A woman goes to her doctor. The doctor verifies that she is pregnant. This is her first pregnancy. The doctor asks her if she has any questions. She replies, "Well, I'm a little worried about the pain. How much will childbirth hurt?"

The doctor thinks for a moment then says, "Well, that varies from woman to woman and pregnancy to pregnancy and besides, it's difficult to describe pain."

"I know, but can't you give me some idea?" she asks.

"Well, he said, "Grab your upper lip and pull it out a little . . ." "Like this?" the woman asked.

"A little more . . ." he said. "Like this?" she asked. "No. A little more . . ." "Like this?" she asked again. "Yes." The doctor said. "Does that hurt?" "A little bit," she replied. "Now," he said, "stretch your lip over your head!" (1)

Sounds to me like that would hurt. Some of you are nodding as if this doctor knew what he was talking about.

Today, we are not going to talk about those who are in labor, but we are going to talk about laborers. Jesus is looking for laborers, people who will labor for his kingdom.

In Luke 10:1-2 we read these words, "After this the Lord appointed seventy others and sent them on ahead of him in pairs to every town and place where he himself intended to go. He said to them, 'The harvest is plentiful, but the laborers are few; therefore ask the Lord of the harvest to send out laborers into his harvest.'" (RSV)

This is an interesting and important chapter. Notice that Jesus appointed seventy disciples to prepare the way for his ministry. Some manuscripts say seventy-two were appointed. It really doesn't matter which number is correct; the number is probably symbolic. Jesus obviously had a large number of followers. Certainly he had more than the twelve with whom we are familiar. On this occasion he sent the seventy out in pairs, undoubtedly for mutual encouragement and help.

Jesus saw a tremendous need, a need so great that a great corps of witnesses was needed. "The harvest is plentiful," he said, "but the laborers are few; therefore ask the Lord of the harvest to send out laborers into his harvest."

Christ's words ring just as true in this generation as in that day long ago. The harvest is still plentiful. People today still need what Christ has to offer.

People today are spiritually hungry. Many people in our society are lost . . . however you define that word. People have their lives as messed up as any generation has ever messed up their lives before. The world is crying out to us, "We need a Savior more than we ever have!" Jesus says, "The harvest is plentiful."

Christ's call for laborers, by the way, is based on human need. It is not based on a desire to build the biggest church in town. It is not based on the desire to cram our values down someone else's throat. The world desperately needs what only the church can give it—a Savior.

Someone has said that the church is not a museum for the saints, but a hospital for the hurting. If you understand that the church above all else is a place for people who have problems, then you can easily see what Jesus meant when he said the harvest is plentiful. Pastor Jeremy Houck put it this way:

The church is designed for the single mother who works two jobs to support her kids. The church is for the drug addict who can't stop his habit. The church is for the young person who struggles with self-esteem. The church is for the young couple who lives together and has never been exposed to the best way to build a home. The church is for the man who does not respect his boss, so he steals from the company and from his coworkers. The church is for the housewife who goes out searching for some excitement in the arms of a man who belongs to someone else. The church is for the alcoholic who is ready to admit he needs help. (2)

You do see, don't you, why many churches don't grow? They're seeking after the wrong audience. They're looking for people who have got it altogether, not those who are falling apart. They're looking for the up-and-ins, not the down-and-outs. They're looking for saints not for sinners. We're looking right over the great harvest and not even seeing it. What did Jesus say? "Those who are well have no need of a physician, but those who are sick; I have come to call not the righteous but sinners" (Mark 2:15). How did we get it so wrong?

"The harvest is plentiful," if you know where to look.

Many of you are familiar with the Celebrate Recovery programs popping up around the country. Celebrate Recovery services are designed to reach those who have had problems with alcohol or drugs, but also people who are hurting because as children they were abused, or they're suffering after a divorce or the loss of a spouse.

One man tells about visiting a Celebrate Recovery service in a city in the South on a Thursday evening. He says, "It was a loud service. The band, though, was great. But here's what impressed me. More than 400 people, primarily younger people in their 20s and 30s were gathered in one place. Some of them had been through rough times. At least half of them were men . . ."

Imagine that! Who says the church can't reach people in their 20s and 30s? Who says the church can't reach men?

"In this service," he reports, "more than 400 young and middle adults, more than half of whom were men were lifting high the name of Jesus."

Why? Because the church was meeting them at the point of their need.

There are many, many people in the world today who desperately need what Christ has to offer. No, let me amend that. ALL people need what Christ has to offer.

Some people, though, have a buffer zone around them—good health, numerous material possessions, people who love them. They still need a Savior. But the good life that our affluent society provides them keeps them from realizing the most important need they have. But don't kid yourself. They still need Christ. Jesus was speaking directly to our generation when he said, "The harvest is plentiful."

What Christ needs is laborers who will go out into the fields. Do you understand that? This is the church's primary reason for being—to be reaching out in love as Jesus reached out to a hurting and dying world.

The last thing Jesus did before he left this earth was give us the great commission: "Therefore go and make disciples of all nations, baptizing them in the name of the Father and of the Son and of the Holy Spirit, and teaching them to obey everything I have commanded you" (Matthew 28:19-20a). That is our primary purpose.

It is not our only purpose to be sure.

We are to be a charitable organization. We are to provide for those who cannot provide for themselves, remembering how Jesus said, "I was hungry and you gave me nothing to eat, I was thirsty and you gave me nothing to drink, I was a stranger and you did not invite me in, I needed clothes and you did not clothe me, I was sick and in prison and you did not look after me" (Matthew 25:42-43).

We are also to be responsible members of our community. We are to support community organizations and to work for peace and justice in the world.

And we are to maintain a house of worship and gather each week to worship God and to teach the sacred Word.

But, as vital as these things are they are not our main business. Our main business is to introduce the world to Jesus to the extent that people become his disciples, living the Christ life in such a way that the whole world is touched. That is not an easy thing for most of us to do—particularly if it means sharing our faith with a stranger.

Perhaps you've heard the hilarious story about the man who prayed the same prayer every morning: "Lord, if you want me to share my faith with someone today, please give me a sign to show me who it is."

One day he found himself on a bus when a big, burly man sat next to him. The bus was nearly empty but this guy sat next to our friend who was praying for a sign that he should share his faith. Having this burly man next to him made our friend nervous. He anxiously waited for his stop so he could exit the bus. But before he got to the next stop, the big guy burst into tears and began to weep. The burly man then cried out with a loud voice, "My life is such a mess. I need to find Christ. I need the Lord. Won't somebody tell me how to know the Master?"

The burly man finally turned to our timid friend and asked, "Can you tell me about Jesus?"

Our nervous friend immediately bowed his head and prayed, "Lord, is this a sign?" (3)

Most of us are not very comfortable sharing our faith with a stranger. It is easier to do if we do it with a friend. Maybe this is why Jesus sent these witnesses out in pairs.

There was a time when churches would send people out two by two to evangelize the community. Our Jehovah's Witness and Mormon friends still do it that way. It's not very effective. In fact, it's a good way to get shot in today's world. People don't seem to want strangers knocking on their door.

A woman who worked at home invited a friend over for coffee. She told her, "Ignore the sign on the door. It's just for drop-ins and salespeople."

The sign read, "Bell does not work." Then penciled underneath were these words, "Knocking won't, either." My guess is she didn't get many visitors.

One guy says there was a knock at his front door one cold and rainy day. He opened it and there stood two Jehovah's Witnesses, damp and shivering in the cold. They asked if they could come inside. He couldn't leave them standing there, so he said okay. He brought them into his living room and offered them a chair. They were quiet for a long time so he asked, "What happens now?"

The older one said, "We don't know. We never got this far before."

Going out two by two was once an effective strategy for reaching people. It is not today. We need to find new ways of extending the call of Christ to a new generation of seekers.

There are some things we know about this new generation of young adults. We know that they value relationships. As someone has put it, they are not looking for a friendly church; they're looking for friends. And we know that they despise phoniness. They want people to be genuine. And they like informality, including casual dress.

One writer tells about a friend of his, a woman perhaps 50 years of age. He's never seen her in anything but blue jeans and a somewhat sloppy blouse which she probably got at Goodwill. That's because he's never seen her anywhere but church.

Recently he discovered quite by accident that she comes from a very wealthy family. She grew up living in a prominent family on a multi-million dollar estate.

Why is she so under-dressed? He wondered. Is she that frugal with her money? No, it's because she doesn't want anyone to come to her church and feel that they won't be accepted because they can't afford nice clothes. This is a commitment she made years ago. She wants everyone to know that you don't have to belong to a certain economic group to be welcome in the family of God.

It's a new world, a more casual world. Even the doctor who treats you might be wearing blue jeans. We might look at our church and ask what we can do to make our worship and our life together as a church family more appealing to those who need what Christ has to offer but might have been turned off at some time by the church. Perhaps we need to be more relational, more genuine, less formal, more casual.

Sometimes a simple invitation is all people need. Surveys show that, if you invite a friend to church, 50% of the time they will respond with a "yes." That percentage goes up substantially with a second, third, or fourth invitation. (4)

The problem is that most of us are reluctant to even ask. Why is that? Are we ashamed of the Gospel? Are we ashamed of our church? Is there something we could do to make you so excited about our church that you would invite a friend to worship with you?

You may know the story of Garrison Keillor, host of the popular program on public radio, Prairie Home Companion.

Keillor was brought up in a fringe group of the Plymouth Brethren Church.

Finding the church's heavy legalisms and dullness off putting, Keillor stopped going to church. From then on people would ask him, "Do you go to church?" And he would say, "No." Then they would say, "Why don't you go to church?" And he would tell them.

That ritual exchange served him well for many years until, sometime back, a Lutheran friend—yes, some Lutherans do evangelism—engaged him in those same two stock questions, "Do you go to church?" and "Why don't you go to church?" But then this person surprised him with a third question: "Why don't you come with us?"

Never having been asked that before, Keillor didn't have a stock answer. And before he knew it, he found himself saying yes. And that's all it took and he was back in the fold once again. (5) Wouldn't it have been a shame if no one had ever asked?

The fields are ready for the harvest. That's what Christ teaches us. People today need Christ as much as they have ever needed him. Christ's greatest need is for laborers, people who are willing to share their faith openly and boldly with their friends and neighbors. Christ needs people who are sensitive to the needs of others in this fast-changing world. Sometimes all that is needed is a simple invitation. Can Christ count on you to give that invitation?

"The harvest is plentiful," says Christ, "but the laborers are few; therefore ask the Lord of the harvest to send out laborers into his harvest."

1. http://jokes.christiansunite.com/Mothers/Childbirth.shtml.
2. http://www.sermoncentral.com/sermons/i-want-the-church-to-grow-but-do-i-want-any-more-people—6-jeremy-houck-sermon-on-evangelism-fear-of-55342.asp.
3. Raymond McHenry, Something to Think About (Peabody, MA: Hendrickson Publishers, Inc., 1998).
4. Mike Slaughter, Momentum for Life, Revised Edition (Nashville: Abingdon Press, 2008).
5. Leonard Sweet, Faithquakes (Nashville: Abingdon Press, 1994).

The Two Ultimate Questions Of Life
Luke 10:25-37

Someone has made a list of what she calls "The World's Worse Questions." Are you ready for these?

No. 1 is, Will you promise not to get mad it I ask you something? Have you ever been asked that before?

No. 2. Do you have any statistics to back up that statement?

3. You don't honestly expect me to believe that, do you?

4. Haven't you any sense of humor?

5. You don't remember me, do you?

6. Have I kept you waiting?

7. NOW what's the matter?

8. You asleep?

9. So what?

And 10. WHEN are you going TO GROW UP? (1) The World's worst questions.

A friend once asked Isaac Isidor Rabi, a Nobel prize winner in science, how he became a scientist.

Rabi replied that every day after school his mother would talk to him about his school day. She wasn't so much interested in what he had learned that day, but she always inquired, "Did you ask a good question today?"

"Asking good questions," Rabi said, "made me become a scientist." (2)

Another Nobel winner said this: "You can tell whether a person is clever by his answers. You can tell whether a person is wise by his questions."

And the philosopher Voltaire said: "Judge a person by his questions rather than by his answers."

On one occasion an expert in the law stood up to test Jesus. "Teacher," he asked, "what must I do to inherit eternal life?" If we were to judge this expert in the law by his question, we would be deceived. He was not seeking to discover some profound secret about life. He was not even trying to discover the way to God. His purpose was to test Jesus, to trip him up, to lead Jesus to discredit himself by giving some unorthodox answer that would arouse the people against him. Still, Jesus used this experience to open the door of life for all who would enter.

Actually the expert in the law asked Jesus two questions. Let's deal with the first question: "Teacher," he asked, "what must I do to inherit eternal life?"

Note, first of all, that the lawyer's question stressed doing something. "What shall I DO to inherit eternal life?" What good action could he take to insure that God would accept him? It is evident that he had no concept of the part that God's love and grace played in the process of salvation. He simply wanted to know if there was some act he could perform that would guarantee that he would be accepted behind the pearly gates.

He's no different from many of us. We, too, want to make sure we meet the minimum standards. Believe in Jesus? Check. Been baptized? Check. Show up in worship at least on Christmas and Easter? Check. Nothing profound here—the man just wants to make certain all the bases are covered. But note how cleverly Jesus leads the conversation to open the man's eyes to new realities.

First, he shows this lawyer that he already knows everything he needs to know to find life. He's an expert in the law. Everything he needs is contained in the Law of Moses.

"What is written in the Law?" Jesus replied to him. "How do you read it?"

Everywhere he went this expert in the law carried with him a little leather box called a phylactery. Several passages of Scripture were in this phylactery, two of which were Deuteronomy 6:3 and Deuteronomy 6:11. These are the two verses which he quotes in response to Jesus' question. The expert in the law answers, "'Love the Lord your God with all your heart and with all your soul and with all your strength and with all your mind;' and, 'Love your neighbor as yourself.'"

"You have answered correctly," Jesus replies. "Do this and you will live."

What did Jesus mean when he said, "Do this and you will live?" The lawyer was already alive physically. Was there more to life than what he was experiencing? Was he missing something? Is there an aliveness that goes beyond simply existing?

The great missionary and writer E. Stanley Jones once said he was alive in the ALIVE. The second alive was spelled in capital letters. Alive in the ALIVE! Jones meant that he was not only existing but that he was truly alive through Jesus Christ.

Jesus promised, "I have come that they might have life, and have it more abundantly" (John 10:10, RSV). To find Christ is to become ALIVE, with capital letters—both in this world and the world to come.

So many people live such dreary lives. Country singing star Tim McGraw has an interesting twist on this idea. He has a song titled, "Live Like You Were Dying."

The song tells the story of a man in his forties who is told by his doctor that he has a very short time to live. And so this man changes his style of living. In the chorus, the man says to his friend: "I went sky diving, I went Rocky Mountain climbing, I went 2.7 seconds on a bull named Fumanchu And I loved deeper and I spoke sweeter. And I gave forgiveness I'd been denying. Someday," the refrain concludes, "I hope you get the chance to live like you were dying."

Good advice. So many people live dreary pointless lives. Someone has noted that the average American spends three years in business meetings, 13 years watching TV, makes 1811 trips to McDonalds, is involved in 6 motor vehicle accidents, is hospitalized 8 times (men) or 12 times (women), spends 24 years sleeping, about five years dreaming, and six months waiting at red traffic lights. So much of our lives is spent accomplishing humdrum tasks; yet so little time is spent being truly alive.

You've probably heard the story about when life really begins. It's a question theologians have bantered about seemingly forever.

A Catholic priest was asked when life began and he answered, "Life begins at conception."

A Jewish rabbi was asked when life began and he responded, "Life begins at birth."

A Protestant minister was asked, and she said, "Life begins when the last child goes off to college and the dog dies." (3)

When does life begin? What does it mean to be alive—really alive? The lawyer already had the answer in the Hebrew Law. Jesus answers the lawyer's question with a question of his own, "What is written in the Law? How do you read it?"

The lawyer replies, "'Love the Lord your God with all your heart and with all your soul and with all your strength and with all your mind;' and, 'Love your neighbor as yourself.'"

"You have answered correctly," Jesus replies. "Do this and you will live."

From Jesus' answer to the lawyer it is clear that new life is possible only through the power of love: love for God and love for neighbor.

As Sam Shoemaker once put it: "In the triangle of love between ourselves, God, and other people is found the secret of existence and the best foretaste, I suspect, that we can have on earth of what heaven will probably be like."

No one is more alive than when he or she is in love. Do you remember your first experience of being in love? Poets and songwriters have employed millions of words and melodies to celebrate the transforming power of love. "It's love, it's love, it's love that makes the world go 'round." Or as a popular song put it a generation or so ago, "If you ain't loving, then you ain't living. . . ." Poor grammar, but great theology!

Love is at the center of our lives. The power of love has driven persons to climb mountains, cross oceans, start wars, give up thrones. Love brings a glow to the face, a twinkle to the eye, a lightness to the step. No other force in this world can do that. Withhold love from a small baby and it will be sickly and perhaps die—no matter how many vitamins and minerals he or she may be fed.

Without love we cannot survive, not emotionally, not spiritually. We were made for community, for sharing, for belonging. There is no force in the world that moves us and motivates us as does love. Love tells us who we are. Love tells us we belong.

Many years ago the psychologist Kinch described an amusing experiment conducted by a group of five male graduate students. They chose as their subject, or shall we say "victim," a very plain-looking girl who was a fellow graduate student.

The boys' plan was to begin in concert to respond to the girl as if she were the best-looking girl on campus. They agreed to work into it naturally so that she would not be aware of what they were up to. They drew lots to see who would be the first to date her. The loser, under the pressure of the others, asked her to go out. Although he was not drawn to the girl, he was a good actor and by continually saying to himself "She's beautiful, she's beautiful . . ." he got through the evening.

According to the agreement it was now the second guy's turn and so it went. The dates were reinforced by similar responses in all contacts the young men had with the girl. In a matter of a few short weeks the results began to show.

At first it was simply a matter of more care in her appearance: her hair was combed more often and her dresses were more neatly pressed; but before long she had been to the beauty parlor to have her hair styled, and was spending her hard-earned money on the latest fashions in women's campus wear.

By the time the fourth young man was taking his turn dating the young lady, the job that had once been undesirable was now quite a pleasant task. And when the last guy in the conspiracy asked her out, he was informed that she was pretty well booked up for some time in the future. It seems there were more desirable males around than those "plain" graduate students who were conducting this mischievous experiment. (4)

The power of love. It is love that brings us alive, for it is love alone that affects us in heart, soul, strength and mind. Love demands our all—our emotions as well as our reason. To love is to live. To love God is the beginning of life. But what does it mean to love God?

There has been an erroneous notion in the Christian community that the Jews feared God but that Christians love him. Such a statement is far too simplistic. That lawyer who confronted Jesus and quoted the great commandment was quoting from the Hebrew Bible, which we call the Old Testament. We dare not forget that. The ancient Jew may have known more about the love of God than many of us ever will.

Samuel Taylor Coleridge once reminded us that the good Jew would not tread upon the smallest piece of paper in his way for possibly that piece of paper might have written on it the name of God. Can you imagine such a regard for God? Can you imagine such a regard for holiness? Maybe the Jew did fear God, but such an attitude is closer to love than the casual, irreverent way we use God's name today.

The name of God is not to be trampled upon. When we love God, we treat with reverence and respect everything that is God's—including other people. That brings us to the second critical question that the lawyer asked: WHO IS MY NEIGHBOR?

Jesus answered the lawyer with one of his most famous stories: "A man was going down from Jerusalem to Jericho, when he was attacked by robbers. They stripped him of his clothes, beat him and went away, leaving him half dead. A priest happened to be going down the same road, and when he saw the man, he passed by on the other side. So too, a Levite, when he came to the place and saw him, passed by on the other side. But a Samaritan, as he traveled, came where the man was; and when he saw him, he took pity on him. He went to him and bandaged his wounds, pouring on oil and wine. Then he put the man on his own donkey, brought him to an inn and took care of him. The next day he took out two denarii and gave them to the innkeeper. 'Look after him,' he said, 'and when I return, I will reimburse you for any extra expense you may have.'

"Which of these three," asked Jesus, "do you think was a neighbor to the man who fell into the hands of robbers?"

Authentic love for God always leads to love for people. All people. Samuel Taylor Coleridge goes on to say: "Trample not on any; there may be some work of grace there, that thou knowest not of. The name of God may be written upon that soul thou treadest on; it may be a soul that Christ thought so much of as to give his precious blood for it; therefore, despise it not." In short, Samuel Taylor Coleridge was saying, "Love your neighbor as you love yourself."

For many of us such an answer is idealistic—it will not work. That was the view of Sigmund Freud, the father of psychoanalysis. In his book Civilization and Its Discontents, Freud wrote that love is a valuable thing and must not be thrown away. Love imposes obligations and sacrifices. The loved person must be worthy of love.

Freud wrote that it is understandable for one to love a person who is like himself because he loves himself in that person. It is understandable, too, to love a person who is better than oneself or a person who happens to be the son of a friend. But, Freud adds, if there are no specific reasons for loving, to love will be difficult and will be an injustice to those who truly deserve to be loved.

As for loving a stranger, Freud states, "Not merely is this stranger on the whole not worthy of love, but, to be honest, I must confess he has more claim to my hostility, even to my hatred." (5) Sigmund Freud and Jesus were in two different camps.

Is it possible for me to love my neighbor if he is somehow different from me? Freud said no. But Jesus says, "Yes." The boundaries of our love can be extended.

"Do this and you will live." Do what? Love God and love every person you meet. This is how you have life abundant in this world as well as the world to come.

Jesus gave the lawyer the answer to both his questions. Want life abundant in this world and the world to come? Love God and love your neighbor. Who is my neighbor? Everyone on this earth.

1. Jane Goodsell, Reader's Digest.
2. Arno Penzias, Ideas and Information: Managing in a High-Tech World (Simon & Schuster, Inc., 1989).
3. Thomas Cathcart and Daniel Klein, Heidegger and a Hippo Walk Through Those Pearly Gates (New York: Penguin Books, 2009), p. 58.
4. Contributed. Source unknown.
5. Silvano Arieti and James A. Arieti, Love Can Be Found (New York: Harcourt Brace Jovanovich, 1977).

What Really Matters?
Luke 10:38-42

A joke appeared on the Internet recently that many of you women can relate to. A man was praying, "Oh Lord, please have mercy on me, I work so very hard, meanwhile my wife stays at home. I would give anything if you would grant me one wish. Please, switch me into my wife. She's got it easy at home and I want to teach her a lesson about how tough a man's life is!"

As God was listening he felt sorry for this poor soul and granted his wish. So . . . the next morning this man wakes up at dawn . . . as a woman. This new woman takes a quick shower and also takes care of the rest of her grooming quickly so that she can make coffee for herself and her spouse, feed the cat, make lunch boxes, prepare breakfast for four, wake up the kids for school, prepare clothes for the littlest one, put a load of clothes in the washer, take the meat out of the freezer, drive the kids to school, on the way back, stop at the gas station for a fill-up, cash a check at the local bank, stop by to pay the electricity and phone bills, pick up some clothes from the cleaners, quickly go to the grocery store for this week's essentials, and on the last leg home, stop at the post office to pick up a package.

By the time she gets home, it's 1:00 p.m. already, so she makes the beds, takes the clothes out of the washer, puts them into the dryer and puts another load in to wash, folds and puts away the clothes that don't need ironing, vacuums the house, boils some rice for a late lunch, goes to pick up the kids from school and argues with them while driving.

As soon as she gets home, she feeds the kids a snack, puts the dirty dishes in the dishwasher and starts it, takes out a second load of damp clothes to put into the dryer, helps the kids with their homework, finally feeds the dog, watches some TV while ironing some clothes from the first load, prepares and serves dinner, empties the dishwasher to load some more, cleans the stovetop and puts away leftovers, prepares the trash to be taken out, gives the youngest kid a bath, reads them each a story to put them to sleep, and pays some loving attention to her husband . . .

The next morning this man who had prayed to become a woman prays to God once again: "Oh Lord, what was I thinking when I asked you to grant my wish, I can't take it anymore. I beg you please switch me back to myself, please oh please!"

Then he heard God's voice speaking to him, saying: "Dear son, of course I'll switch you back into yourself now that you are wiser, but there's one minor detail. It'll be nine months before I can comply. I'm afraid you're pregnant." (1)

What did folks say in previous generations? "A man's work is from sun to sun, a woman's work is never done."

Well, some things haven't changed, while some things have. Women now are also in the workplace. So now, women also work from sun to sun, but for many women, when they get home, the day has just begun. That is why the biblical story of Mary and Martha is a little tricky for some women.

Most of you know the story. Jesus and his disciples are making a journey and they come to the village of Bethany. And a woman named Martha opens her home to Jesus. It has been speculated that Martha was a widow. It was still relatively rare in those times for a woman to own her own home, and this was a home evidently large enough to accommodate many guests. Certainly Martha was an industrious woman. It may be that she had made her own way in the world. It did happen in the ancient world. Think of Lydia, the seller of purple cloth. But it was still rare.

Martha shared her home with her sister Mary and their brother Lazarus. Yes, this is the same Lazarus that Jesus would later raise from the dead. Jesus developed quite a warm friendship with Mary, Martha and Lazarus. Remember how in John's Gospel Jesus wept at Lazarus' tomb. Actually, the Greek language says "Jesus sobbed" at Lazarus' tomb. Jesus loved Mary, Martha and Lazarus.

Most commentators assume that Mary was the younger sister. The scriptures don't actually tell us that either. Some interpreters have assumed that Mary was younger because Martha owned the home. Or perhaps the supposed birth order of Martha and Mary has been deduced from their behavior. We often stereotype the older sister as being more responsible; the younger more free-spirited. Whether you buy into this stereotype probably depends upon your experience with your sister or with sisters you have known.

When our story opens Jesus is teaching in Martha's home and free-spirited Mary is sitting in rapt attention at Jesus' feet listening to his every word. It was customary in the Middle East for students to sit at the feet of their teacher. However, it was not customary in first-century Palestinian Jewish society for a woman to be included among those students. Normally in the ancient world, all of the adult women would have shared in the responsibility for preparing a meal, but it appears that Mary chose not to help.

It says a lot about Jesus that he doesn't encourage Mary to help Martha. In patriarchal societies, there was (and still is) a strict division of labor along gender lines. Jesus was continually startling people with his disregard for cultural customs, especially within the family, and this is just one more. Of course, it should not surprise us that Jesus would not restrict the privilege of sitting at his feet according to gender. Jesus did more to liberate women than any man who ever lived. Just because some of his followers through the centuries have not been as enlightened as he was doesn't change the fact that Jesus did not discriminate.

Jesus was full of surprises. Even today people try to put Jesus in a box. We think, "Here's what Jesus would do." Be careful when you do that. Jesus would be just as upsetting to our cultural expectations as he was to that of the first century.

While Mary is sitting happily at Jesus' feet, Martha is working like crazy. Luke puts it like this: "Martha was distracted by all the preparations that had to be made."

Some of you women, particularly, know what that's like. It's not easy entertaining guests in your home. There is so much to be done. Particularly when you're entertaining a group of first-century men who are accustomed to having women treat them like masters. And it's even worse if you have a good-for-nothing sister who lollygags with the men and refuses to help. Excuse me. Am I taking sides?

Martha is thoroughly disgusted with Mary and she makes her displeasure with her sibling known. She comes to Jesus and asks, "Lord, don't you care that my sister has left me to do the work by myself? Tell her to help me!" Some of you are inwardly thinking to yourself, "Go, girl. Mary ought to be helping. It's only right." But, as usual, Jesus surprises us.

"Martha, Martha," Jesus answered, "chill out." Well, he didn't exactly didn't say, "Chill out." But it amounts to the same thing. He says something like, "Martha, you are worried and upset about many things, but only one thing is really important right now and Mary has chosen it."

This was not the reply Martha expected. And here, of course, is the message of our text for the day. There are many things that are important in life, but only one thing is of ultimate importance—that is sitting at the feet of Jesus.

Martha was not in the wrong in going about her duties. We all know that. Jesus knew that. There would have been a house full of hungry men if Martha had not been so conscientious in seeing after all the details of entertaining her guests. This was probably the focal point of her life—caring for her home—caring for her family. Martha was a responsible person. She did the things she believed were important and she did them well. We've all known Marthas, and we give God thanks for them. Some of them make all kinds of good things happen in our homes and in our church. But there is another dimension to life besides doing. There is more to life than simply keeping busy—even keeping busy doing good, looking after others.

Many scholars have suggested that it may not be accidental that Luke placed the story of Mary and Martha immediately after the story of the Good Samaritan.

Think about that for a moment. What is the significance of the story of the Good Samaritan? It's a call to action, isn't it? It's a call for us to care for the needy and to get busy ministering to their needs.

You know the story. A man has fallen among robbers who strip him of his clothes, beat him and go away, leaving him half dead. There he is lying beaten, bruised and probably dying beside the road. A priest and a Levite pass by and they do nothing. But a lowly Samaritan comes by, binds up the man's wounds, puts him on his donkey, takes him to a nearby inn and tells the landlord to take care of the man and put it on his tab. It is one of Jesus' best known stories and it is a call to action. It is a call to duty. It is a summons to take care of your neighbor, whoever that neighbor may be. And for two thousand years Christians have been building hospitals and looking after orphans and widows, feeding the hungry and doing all kinds of good works.

And that's good. Those are things we ought to be doing . . . and more! I am grateful that Christians are in the forefront of every movement designed to make this world a better place. That is exactly where Jesus wants us to be.

Former President Jimmy Carter in his book Living Faith tells about a group of Christian laymen who were doing missionary work. They approached a small village near an Amish settlement. Seeking a possible convert, they confronted an Amish farmer and asked him, "Brother, are you a Christian?"

The farmer thought for a moment and then said, "Wait just a few minutes." He wrote down a list of names on a tablet and handed it to the lay evangelist.

"Here is a list of people who know me best," he said. "Please ask them if I am a Christian." (2)

I love that story. Ask my neighbor if I am a Christian. That would be a good test for all of us to take. The clear implication is that you ought to be able to tell a Christian by what he or she does. And I am sympathetic to that perspective as are most of you, I suspect. However, that is not all of what it means to be a follower of Jesus. It is not even the better part of being a follower of Jesus. If it were, there would have been no need for Jesus to lovingly correct Martha.

We need to take time to sit at the feet of Jesus. It is good to be a responsible person going about doing all the good we can. It is important for us to take care of our families, and to feed the homeless and to serve our fellow men and women wherever they may be. But, in the process, we need to feed our own souls. This is where worship comes into the picture, and Bible study and prayer. We need to take time each day sitting at the feet of Jesus. That is where the fuel comes from for doing good works, meeting our responsibilities. Otherwise we run the risk of either burning out or resenting the tasks we are responsible for. We need the refreshment of seeking God's presence. We need to study the scriptures and to reflect on their meaning for our lives.

There is a wonderful story in one of the Chicken Soup for the Soul books that says it all. A father lay staring up at the ceiling. Beside him, his wife was fast asleep, exhausted after the long drive back home. The drive was made even longer by the emotional strain of returning home without their only daughter. It was her first day at the university. It was her first time away from them.

The father reminisced about his own first day of college. It seemed like a lifetime ago, riding in his father's rickety old truck with his whole life packed into the back.

The drive was incredibly long. He remembered a stop by a stream and eating lunch. But the similarities to his daughter's experience ended there. His daughter had a much larger dorm, stuffed full of electronics he could've only dreamed of at her age.

When his father left him, he looked him in the eye, shook his hand and said, "I have no real advice I can give. I was never smart enough to go to college myself. I don't have much money even now to give you, but here is a checkbook. If you get in a bind, write yourself out a small check and I'll do my best to make sure the money is there." He pulled the checkbook out of his pocket and handed it to his son.

He then reached down and pulled out his old and worn Bible. There was never a night he didn't see his father reading this Bible. He was a simple man, but he was a man of great strength and faith. Handing it to him, his father didn't tell him to read it every morning or every night. He just said, "This can help you, if you will let it."

Now lying in his own bed, decades later, this father felt a twinge of regret. He knew he gave his daughter all he could give, but despite all the wealth and prosperity he achieved in his own life, it amounted to nothing compared to what his own father gave him.

Quietly climbing out of bed, he made his way to the attic. He found the dusty old box his father's Bible was in. He pulled it out and smiled. It was exactly as he remembered it.

He carried the Bible down into his office where he found a large, padded envelope and set it inside. He grinned as he wrote a note. "This can help you," he wrote, "if you will let it." (3)

And it can help you, my friend, if you will let it. But you need to read it regularly and you need to read it prayerfully.

Martha was a fine person. She was a wonderful homemaker and host. But, in her busy-ness, just as in ours, she ran the risk of missing what was most important in life—sitting at the feet of Jesus. It's an easy mistake to make. Do all the good, responsible things God wants you to do—but don't forget to spend time in God's presence.

1. http://jokediary.com/2007/02/a-man-was-complaining-to-God.html.
2. Phillip Gunter, Leadership, Vol. 20, no. 2.
3. Chicken Soup for the Christian Family Soul (Deerfield Beach, FL: Heath Communications, Inc., 2000), pp. 95-97.

The Keys To Effective Praying
Luke 11:1-13

I want to begin with a true but incredible story. Back in September 1996 a man named Edouardo Sierra, a citizen of Spain, was on a business trip to Sweden. He was driving through the Swedish countryside when he came upon a Catholic church. He decided to stop in for a few moments to say a prayer. The church was empty except for a coffin with a body lying at rest inside it. Edouardo decided to take a few moments to stop and pray for the man who lay in the coffin. Then he signed a book of remembrance left by the coffin. Apart from his signature, the book was empty.

Some weeks later, Edouardo received a telephone call telling him he was a millionaire. The body was that of a Swedish businessman, with no close relatives, who had left his fortune "to whoever prays for my soul first." (1)

This morning we are going to talk about the keys to effective prayer. I wish that I could promise you that if you pray using these keys you will receive the kind of return on your prayer that Edouardo received. That would be far better than the stock market. Pray for just a few minutes and become a millionaire. As you have probably already discovered, it really doesn't work that way. Unfortunately, often times, just the opposite is true.

Recently I read about a man named Jack who is employed at his church's denominational headquarters. It was customary in this particular denominational office for all employees to pause for prayer each morning at 9:00. A "prayer bell" signaled the beginning and ending of this daily routine.

Occasionally, though, employees would find themselves on the phone during prayer time. Even though they wanted to end the phone call, it was not possible and so the entire office, now quiet, would overhear their conversation.

One morning, Jack reports, during prayer time, a co-worker named Paul could be heard in the quiet of the prayer time shouting from his desk, "Hello? Hello? I can hear you. Can you hear me?" (2)

We've all been there at some time or another. We've prayed and it seemed like no one was there to hear us. We know that's not true, but that is the way it seemed.

One day Jesus was praying in a certain place. When he finished, one of his disciples said to him, "Lord, teach us to pray, just as John taught his disciples."

The disciples were very much aware of what an important role prayer played in Jesus' life. The references to Jesus praying are numerous just within the opening chapters of the Gospel of Luke. Jesus prayed at his baptism (Luke 3:21). He prayed during his temptation (Luke 5:16). On one occasion he prayed all night (Luke 6:12). On the day when he asked the disciples, "Who do the people say that I am?" he had been praying alone (Luke 9:18). Afterward he went up onto a mountain to pray (Luke 9:28). And now, on this occasion, Luke tells us, "He was praying in a certain place."

Prayer was important to Jesus just as it ought to be to us. Martin Luther King, Jr. once said, "To be a Christian without prayer is no more possible than to be alive without breathing."

The disciples saw how important prayer was to Jesus and so they asked him to teach them to pray. At that point Jesus taught them the most famous prayer ever prayed. Luke's version of the prayer is a little shorter than the Lord's Prayer that we use, but it gets right to the heart of what prayer ought to be. Here is what Jesus taught them.

"When you pray, say: 'Father, hallowed be your name, your kingdom come. Give us each day our daily bread. Forgive us our sins, for we also forgive everyone who sins against us. And lead us not into temptation.'"

Note how the Master begins by focusing our attention on God. "When you pray, say: 'Father . . .'" This is important.

When we pray it is tempting to hop right in with our needs, our concerns. It is as if God is a peripheral player in our universe. Our focus is on the almighty me. That is the spirit of our times. Jesus began his prayer by focusing upon God.

"Father," he began. What a revolutionary statement of faith that was, of course. Only Jesus would be bold enough to call the Creator of all the universe Father. "Father, hallowed be your name . . ."

That's an antiquated word— "hallowed." A dictionary definition of hallowed would be "Sanctified, consecrated, highly venerated." Not only do we not use the word hallowed anymore, very few things in our world are regarded as sanctified, consecrated or highly venerated.

Many of us remember when our national institutions and flags were hallowed. Now it is impossible even to quiet some crowds while the national anthem is being played. We remember when the Sabbath was hallowed. Now it is the biggest shopping day of the week in many communities. We remember when civil authority was hallowed. Now we have to gag and handcuff ruffians to keep them quiet in the courtroom. Such hallowedness is gone forever.

Of course, not all of it is to be mourned. The Bible gives clear warning that any man-made institution—even laws regarding the Sabbath—can become idolatrous. One of the prime arguments that they used to crucify Jesus was that he broke the Sabbath.

Still, there is something wrong in a society where nothing is hallowed. If for no other reason, it keeps us from appreciating the wondrous awe that Bible characters felt in the presence of God.

Isaiah fell down in the presence of God and cried out, "Woe is me for I am a man of unclean lips and I dwell in the midst of a people of unclean lips, for my eyes have beheld the Lord" (6:5). Isaiah understood the meaning of hallowed.

Jesus evidently shared Isaiah's sense of awe. I suspect that Jesus would never have referred to God as "the man upstairs." He could call God "Father," but still do it with reverence. God is God. He is still "I am that I am."

Jesus taught his disciples to pray, "Father, hallowed be your name . . ." He told us to begin our prayer by focusing on God and Who God is.

Notice what he says next: "Your kingdom come." When Christ refers to God's kingdom, he is referring to any place God reigns in human affairs. Some of the ancient manuscripts like Matthew's gospel (6:10) include the words, "May your will be done on earth as it is in heaven." That is why we include those words when we say the Lord's Prayer. But, again, the focus is on God and His eternal purpose for life.

Here is the chief problem in our prayers oftentimes. We want to focus on our kingdom and our will. Jesus understands that. In the Garden of Gethsemane, remember how he prayed that the cup of suffering would be taken away from him. Nevertheless, when it came crunch time, he prayed, "Not my will, but yours be done."

All prayer is based in the goodness of God. We can pray "your kingdom come, your will be done" because we believe God's will is always for our best good. Notice how Jesus illustrates this truth later in this passage. He tells about a father whose son asks for fish and an egg. Will the father give him instead a stone, a serpent, or a scorpion? Of course not. Jesus begins with God because all prayer is based in the nature of God. He is Creator, Sustainer, and Father of all that is. And His nature is Love.

We need to see that, if God's will is done, we will receive everything we need. "Seek first his kingdom and his righteousness," said Jesus, "and all these things will be given to you as well" (Matthew 6:33). Sometimes we do not see that because we do not see life from God's perspective. But God knows our needs and God will provide.

A boy once said to God, "I've been thinking, and I know what I want when I become a man." He proceeded to give God his list: to live in a big house with two Saint Bernards and a garden . . . to marry a blue-eyed, tall, beautiful woman . . . to have three sons—one a senator, one a scientist, and one a quarterback. He also wanted to be an adventurer who climbed tall mountains and drove a red Ferrari.

As it turned out, the boy hurt his knee one day while playing football. He no longer could climb trees, much less mountains. He married a beautiful and kind woman, who was short with brown eyes. Because of his business, he lived in a city apartment, not a big house with a garden, and he took cabs, and rode subways, not a sleek, expensive Ferrari. He had three loving daughters, not three sons—a nurse, an artist, and a music teacher. They adopted, not two St. Bernards, but a fluffy cat.

One morning the man awoke and remembered his boyhood dream. He became extremely depressed. He called out to God, "Remember when I was a boy and told You all the things I wanted? Why didn't You give me those things?"

"I could have," said God, "but I wanted to make you happy." (3)

It is a wise person who realizes that the kindest thing God does for some of us is to not answer all of our prayers. When you pray, trust God. He knows your needs.

Jesus begins with God. That is where we too must begin. God knows our needs. He is the source of our life. He is our hope for a better life. He is the Lord of all creation. Only after Christ has focused our attention on God and His kingdom and His will does he turn to our needs.

"Give us each day our daily bread." It is interesting how much Jesus had to say about our physical needs—only one line. That's all.

Here again is why so much of our prayer life is ineffective. You and I probably spend most of our prayer time on our physical needs. Yet Jesus devoted four times as much time on our spiritual needs as upon our physical needs.

A young man was going blind. "You might as well shoot me," he was heard to say. "I could never cope without my eyes."

But many people do cope without their eyes. Many cope without limbs. Many cope in dire poverty. Many cope with the loss of everyone and everything they hold dear. How do they do it? They do it because they discover there is something more important in this world than that which is physical.

Fanny Crosby was blind. Yet she contended that she was the happiest person alive. She saw an inner beauty, and that is so much more important than any beauty that our physical eyes can behold.

This is not to say that daily bread is unimportant. Jesus taught us to pray for it. God's will is for our physical needs to be met. How can we be effective servants if our daily physical needs are not met? It is perfectly legitimate for us to share with God the pressing concerns of our life—whether it be making the house payment, or the baby's fever, or our own aches and pains. It is God's will that we share our physical concerns with Him. But our physical well-being is just part of our deepest needs. Focus on God and His kingdom. Begin your prayer by asking that God's kingdom will come and that his will be done. Give priority to His priorities, then he will provide the rest. Seek first His kingdom, then all these other things will be added. "Give us each day our daily bread." Our physical needs are important. Take them to God.

"Forgive us our sins, for we also forgive everyone who sins against us." Wow! That is a hard one. Forgiving someone who has wronged us is tough. Can you not see, however, that no matter how eloquent your prayers, you cannot be spiritually whole until you are able to forgive those who have wronged you? No matter how many physical blessings you have, if you are still carrying around anger and bitterness and resentment in your heart because someone has done you some wrong, you are carrying a cancer in your soul.

An expert on Divorce Recovery says that the major breakthrough for persons recovering from the brokenness and the pain of divorce is the willingness to forgive their former spouse, even if that former spouse doesn't think they need any forgiveness. Forgiving others is one of the most therapeutic exercises in which we can engage.

Once in a small church, in a small town, toward the conclusion of the service, a trembling woman came forward and sat on the front pew, asking forgiveness. She had not been in that church for several years. The woman who sat directly behind her looked shocked. She grew pale and nervous. Several people in the congregation looked bewildered and wondered if trouble would start all over again; for there had been trouble, lots of it, tragic and heart-breaking trouble—two murders, court trials with opposing families, and one death in the electric chair.

The trembling woman was the mother of the murderer. The woman behind her . . . it was her husband and son whose blood had been shed. What would the second woman's reaction be? Would she be able to forgive? Fortunately she was able. She reached forward to the trembling woman, clasped her hand, and said, "I'm glad you have come back to be with us in the church." This woman whose husband and son had been murdered later commented, "I feel better than I have felt in years. Now I feel free." (4)

Don't you see? You don't forgive the other person for their sake, but for your own. It's easy to obtain God's forgiveness. If you're sincerely repentant, God will surely forgive. But forgiving yourself and forgiving others, that is what is hard.

"And lead us not into temptation." Well, maybe a little temptation. I mean, nobody likes a saint. On and on we go with our meaningless evasions. When will we acknowledge our basic situation and need? We are sinners—sinners with infinite possibilities for good, but sinners still. All of us need to wash daily in God's cleansing streams. We need God's help to escape the temptations that are forever with us.

"Lead us not into temptation . . ." It is Matthew who adds, "But deliver us from evil . . ." You know He will deliver us from temptation if we ask, don't you? If you really want Him to. Many of us, however, are quite happy to be tempted.

Are you being tempted? Pray for His help. His main concern is your best good.

What are the keys to effective prayer? Focus on God and His goodness and His love. Ask for your physical needs, but remember your spiritual needs as well—your need for forgiveness, but also your need to forgive and your need to be kept from temptation.

"When you pray," said Jesus, pray like this: "Father, hallowed be your name, your kingdom come. Give us each day our daily bread. Forgive us our sins, for we also forgive everyone who sins against us. And lead us not into temptation."

It was the early church that added those last lines with which we complete the Lord's Prayer. But they represent the culmination of everything we believe about this loving God: "For thine is the kingdom, and the power, and the glory forever. Amen."

1. William Hartston, The Encyclopedia of Useless Information (Naperville, IL: Sourcebooks, Inc., 2007), p. 281.
2. The Lame Humor List, http://absoluterobeo.com.
3. God's Little Devotional Book (Tulsa: Honor Books, Inc., 1973), p. 105.
4. Leroy Brownlow, Making the Most of Life (Brownlow, 1988), p. 35.

Financial Planning
Luke 12:13-21

A woman who lost her husband several years ago developed a friendship with a man who had also lost his spouse. They seemed a perfect match. All their children agreed they should get married. So a date was set and invitations were sent out. The invitations read like this: "Phil, Richard, Karen, Allison, John, Matt and Steve request the honor of your presence at the marriage of their mother and father. Because they are combining two households, they already have at least two of everything. So please, no presents! Reception and garage sale immediately following the ceremony." (1)

We do accumulate a lot of stuff nowadays, don't we? What will happen to all that stuff when we die?

Jesus was teaching one day and someone in the crowd said to him, "Teacher, tell my brother to divide our father's inheritance with me."

Now there is a battle even Jesus didn't want to get in the middle of. Have you seen how people act when it comes to dividing up estates? Even nice people sometimes go years without speaking to their siblings because one family member got some family heirloom that someone else thought that she should get when mama's estate was divided. Sometimes these things even go to court. Such things happened in Jesus' time, too. That is why Jesus said, "Man, who appointed me a judge or an arbiter between you?"

Then Jesus decided to turn this family squabble into a teaching opportunity: He said to them, "Watch out! Be on your guard against all kinds of greed; life does not consist in an abundance of possessions."

And he told them this parable: "The ground of a certain rich man yielded an abundant harvest. He thought to himself, 'What shall I do? I have no place to store my crops.'

"Then he said, 'This is what I'll do. I will tear down my barns and build bigger ones, and there I will store my surplus grain. And I'll say to myself, "You have plenty of grain laid up for many years. Take life easy; eat, drink and be merry."'

"But God said to him, 'You fool! This very night your life will be demanded from you. Then who will get what you have prepared for yourself?'

"This is how it will be," Jesus concluded, "with whoever stores up things for themselves but is not rich toward God."

This is an important parable. And yet, the sad truth is that most of us don't see ourselves in this story. In our eyes we're not rich and we're not foolish. Well, maybe not rich, anyway. Actually we have more in common with the rich fool than any of us would like to admit. There are few of us whose lives are not dominated in one way or another by the pervasive materialism of our age. The desire for bigger houses, nicer cars, a boat, a swimming pool, a large screen television, a camper, new furniture, designer clothes—the list goes on ad infinitum.

Modern advertising is carefully designed to increase our need to acquire. We buy a certain perfume because, after all, "I'm worth it." Such advertising is even aimed at our children. I suppose it reached its epitome a few years ago with "Cool Shopping Barbie." If you don't remember that particular doll, it came with Barbie's own MasterCard and a cash register with a MasterCard logo on it. It even had a terminal through which Barbie could swipe her card. Of course, MasterCard has always been adept at pushing their product. Who in this room has never heard, "There are some things money can't buy. For everything else, there's MasterCard." And before that, there was the seductive lure of, "I bought my sombrero in Rio de Janeiro . . . so worldly, so welcome . . . MasterCard."

Because it hits us where we live, it is difficult to approach the subject of materialism without the risk that many of you will simply tune me out. Many of us already feel guilty about our affluence. We know that most of the world's people do not live as we do. It bothers us and yet, like the rich young ruler, we don't want to give up what we have. The last thing we need on a Sunday morning is a moralistic tirade on the sin of affluence.

There is another problem, too. Some of us may not be as affluent as we may appear. One man was asked, "What would you do if you had all the money in the world?"

He replied, "I'd apply it to all my debts as far as it would go."

Many, many families are in serious financial trouble today. We are told that the average American family operates just three weeks from bankruptcy.

Indeed, one survey by the U.S. Bureau of Labor and Statistics discovered that the average family spends each year $400 more than it earns. Who do we think we are—the government?

No wonder that another survey reveals that 70 percent of all our worries these days are about money.

As Adlai Stevenson once put it, "There was a time when a fool and his money were soon parted, but now it happens to everybody." No wonder it seems like meddling when the pastor feels obligated to talk about money.

There are some principles in the story of the rich fool, however, that are critical to our lives. Like most of the stories that Jesus told, the emphasis here is on practical application. The rich fool had devoted his life to acquiring goods. Now it was time for him to die. What would happen to the goods? Would they go on the auction block? Would they go to ungrateful relatives? What was the point of his life? He thought his wealth had bought security—but it could not protect him from the grim reaper. Of what use was it then? Of what ultimate benefit is wealth to us? What is its proper place in our lives?

In the first place, we need to see that the tragic thing about this man's life was not his wealth but his lack of commitment to anything else in life. There was nothing in the world that he was committed to except making money. All his thoughts, all his energies, all his ambitions had to do with the accumulation of wealth. Now he had come to the place where he had all the money he would ever need. What's next? Of course—more money! When you get to where you are going, where will you be? The tragedy of this man's life was not the abundance of his wealth but the poverty of his values. He had counted material success as the greatest goal in his life.

Did you know that the word "success" does not even appear in the Bible? The word is so important in our society. Indeed, for many persons it may be the most important word in their vocabulary. To be a financial success is their chief goal.

Could I challenge you to make a list of the things you are committed to besides making a living? Your family, your community, your church, the American Cancer Society, a scout troop—these are some possibilities.

At the same time let me challenge you to make a list of the things you do for your family besides simply supporting them. Do you take time for your spouse, for your children? Patricia Clafford once said, "The work will wait while you show the child the rainbow, but the rainbow won't wait while you do the work." What are the ways that you give of yourself, not simply your money, but of yourself to the things you believe in?

What I am trying to do is to help each of us avoid the snare that this rich man fell into of living only for accumulating wealth. Mammon is an insatiable god. There is never enough to satisfy him. And yet Mammon can never give us peace within, only external trappings. Mammon never built a happy family or a loving heart.

Be careful that you are not saying, "Oh, sometime I will have time for these things—but first I have a mortgage to pay off, an orthodontist to support, college to save for." For those whose lives are dominated by wealth—who are forever putting off more important things because they are so busy seeking after financial security—tomorrow never comes. Make certain that you know what your priorities are. Decide that you will be committed to more than simply making money.

In the second place, it is important for each of us to have a plan by which we manage our resources. I said that many of us have more in common with the rich fool than we might care to admit. Our problem is not money—its managing the money we do have. It is amazing how much money goes through our hands in a lifetime. A few years ago the website smartmoney.com reported that the average American will spend $2.9 million in a lifetime if he or she lives to the age of 81. Two point nine million dollars! That's a lot of money. Of course, most of us let that $2.9 slip right through our fingers. For many of us the problem is not money; the problem is management.

One man said it is true that money talks. Usually it says good-bye.

If we do not have a plan for the wise management of our financial resources, our money will continually say good-bye to us.

The question that God asked the rich man, "Then whose will these things be?"

indicates that the man had made no provision for the disposal of his wealth after his death. It is amazing how many persons never get around to making a will. Probably we don't like to face the fact that one day we will be leaving this world's possessions behind. But it is true that we cannot take it with us.

Somebody asked, "I wonder how much money a certain billionaire left at his death?"

A wise friend replied, "He left it all."

Someday so shall we. Wouldn't it be smart to make sure that the money we leave behind us will be put to good use?

If we do not plan for the disposal of our earthly possessions when we go to be with God, Uncle Sam will do it for us. Or greedy relatives will take care of the task. It might cause a few family feuds as it did in our lesson for today. Why not sit down and make a plan? That is what a will is—a plan for the management of our financial resources when we go to be with God.

Jesus knew the wisdom of good management and good planning. Remember some of his teachings: "No one builds his house upon the sand . . ." And on another occasion, "No one builds a tower without first sitting down and counting the cost . . ."

Jesus wanted his followers to be wise managers of their resources. He wants you and me to have a financial plan for our lives—a budget, if you will—that we can live within. That is the second principle in the story of the rich fool—we need a plan for the management of our resources.

In the third place, it is obvious that the rich fool never discovered the joy of generosity—the joy of using his money to bring happiness to other people.

His name is not as well-known as that of the Rockefellers, the Vanderbilts or Andrew Carnegie, but once there was an American philanthropist named Dr. Daniel K. Pearson. Daniel Pearson had a lasting impact on colleges throughout this land.

Pearson grew up in poverty. He worked his way through college, living in an attic and cooking his own frugal meals. He was a school teacher, studied medicine, and afterward was a farmer. Later he engaged in the lumber business where he was quite successful. He was blessed with a wife, of whom Dr. Pearson has said, "She wanted me to make money to give it away."

Pearson had a great knack for making money. But he didn't keep it. He used it to help young people who were struggling for an education. He provided endowments to forty-seven colleges, particularly in Appalachia.

Here is how he described his life: "I have had more fun than any other rich man alive. They are welcome to their automobiles and yachts. I have discovered that giving is the most exquisite delight in the world. I intend to die penniless."

And he did. As one biographer said, he died a poor but happy man. By the dawn of the twentieth century Dr. Daniel K. Pearson had given away more than $6,000,000. I can't even imagine how much that would be in today's dollars. Pearson knew the joy of living for others. We could truly say that he "laid up his treasure in heaven."

You and I will probably never have six million dollars to give away, but we can learn the joy of generosity. There are worthy, often wonderful, people who need our help. And we need to give. Not for their good as much as for our own. The rich fool lived only for himself, he never learned the joy of generosity.

And finally Jesus tells us that the rich man was a fool because he neglected his responsibilities to God.

Bruce Larson, in his book Believe And Belong, tells about a very wealthy Christian businessman who was asked back to his church to speak to the Sunday school class he attended long years ago. The children were curious about this man now worth millions and asked him to tell how it all began. He said, "Well, it all began right here in this church. Those were hard times. I was a young man with no job and very poor. We had a guest preacher who said, 'Give your life and all that you have to Jesus and He will bless you.' I had $3.54 in my pocket. It was all I had in the world, and I put the whole thing in the plate. I gave my life to the Lord that day and He has blessed me ever since."

He closed his talk with a time for questions, and the first hand up was that of a little boy in the front row. "Mister," he said, "Could you do it now?" (2)

Wow! There is the hard question, isn't it? It's easy to trust your resources to God when they total $3.54, but it is different when you have millions. Perhaps that is why Jesus so often warned against the danger of wealth. On the basis of disposable income, it ought to be easier to tithe when you make $80,000 a year, than when you make $20,000 a year. But somehow it doesn't work that way, does it? Somewhere along the way our money quits serving us and we begin serving it. "Thou fool," says Jesus. Learn from this rich man that there is no lasting security in wealth. Take to heart these four principles:

1. Make sure that you are committed to more than just making a living.

2. Have a plan for the management of your financial resources for both now and when you go to be with God.

3. Learn the joy of generosity. Find persons with whom you can share. You will find that it IS more blessed to give than to receive.

4. Finally, when you are making your financial plan, begin with your responsibilities to God. "What does it profit a man," Jesus asked, "if he gains the whole world and loses his soul?"

1. Top Greetings. Cited in WITandWISDOM(tm)
2. (Waco: Word Books).

Go Hard Or Go Home!
Luke 12:32-48

Dr. Randy L. Hyde tells about a wealthy family from Massachusetts who used to take a month's vacation every summer to the coast of Maine, taking their maid with them.

The maid had an annual ritual at the beach. She wore an old-fashioned bathing suit, complete with a little white hat, and carried enough paraphernalia to stock Wal-Mart. She would settle herself on the beach, cover every inch of her exposed flesh and journey down to the water's edge. There she would hesitate while taking deep breaths. Slowly she would work up her courage to enter the icy-cold water.

Finally, she would daintily extend one foot and lower it slowly into the water until she barely had her big toe submerged. Then she repeated the act with the other foot. Then, having satisfied her minimal urge for a swim, she would retreat to her chair and umbrella and spend the remainder of the vacation curled around a book. (1)

She reminds me of many Christians I have known. They have the stuff of greatness in them, but they never really wade into the waters of Christian discipleship. Maybe a toe. Sometimes an ankle, but rarely do they become so stirred up with the spirit of God that they venture anything great for God.

They are like a car whose transmission is locked in neutral. The sound of the motor is impressive. The lights and the radio work fine. The tread on their tires is brand new. They are shiny and they are attractive. The only problem is that they are not going anywhere. They settle for being only nominal followers of the Master.

Clarence Jordan, the great activist saint of God who inspired the musical, The Cotton Patch Gospel, believed such people violated the Third Commandment, "Thou shalt not take the name of the Lord your God in vain." He said taking the Lord's name in vain was not something you do with your lips (by uttering a profanity), "but with your life. You take the name of the Lord in vain when you accept the name of Jesus Christ but don't do anything with it."

Such people remind me of something baseball player Luis Gonzales once said. Gonzales played outfield for the Houston Astros. He had a personal motto which he once shared with a group of sports writers. His motto was, "Go hard or go home!" (2)

Time and time again Jesus said basically the same thing to his disciples: "Go hard or go home!"

One of the great unspoken commandments of the Scriptures is that we are to make our lives count for something. We are accountable for our actions. We are called to have dominion over our own destinies.

In the very first chapter of the Bible Adam was to have dominion over his world, and so are we. We are not to be reeds blown by every wind, or rocks unmoving and unmovable. We are to be responsible men and women who recognize that God has entrusted us with the precious gift of freedom. With that freedom God has given us opportunities untold to alter our circumstances, adjust our situations and to improve our lives. We are free to make our life count for something!

Jesus wants his followers to be productive. That's the first thing we need to see. In today's lesson he tells a parable about a wise and faithful servant whom his master left in charge of his household. How happy the master will be, Jesus tells us, if he returns and finds the servant living up to his responsibilities. And that is what Christ desires of each of us—to live up to our responsibilities—to make productive use of our time.

It is the productive person whom Jesus lauded time and time again. Jesus closed this particular parable by adding, "To whom much is given, much is expected."

That is the basic message of the parable of the talents. Those who put their talents to work were praised and their talents were increased, but the poor fellow who buried his talent in the ground had even the one talent taken from him (Matthew 25:14-30).

In another parable, there is even an unscrupulous servant who found out he was being fired and used his master's money to buy friends. To his disciples' surprise, Jesus lauded the man's ingenuity (Luke 16:1-18). At least he didn't sit around whining that life had been unfair to him. He took charge of his situation and Jesus praised him.

There is a rather amusing scene in the Book of Exodus. The children of Israel are up against the Red Sea. The army of Pharaoh is hot on their heels. Moses is exhorting the people to trust in God—that God will not forsake them. God breaks in on Moses' exhortation. As the Living Bible paraphrases it, God says to Moses, "Quit praying and get the people moving forward, march!" (Exodus 14:15)

There is a time for praying, but there is also a time for moving forward. There is no virtue in standing still.

"What good is a tree," asks Jesus, "if it does not bear good fruit?" (Matthew 7:19) "Why do you call me, 'Lord, Lord,'" he asks in Luke 6:46, "and do not do what I say?" Jesus calls his people to be productive. He wants us to use our brains and use our energies. He wants us to dream dreams and to move mountains.

Bill Borden, son of the famous and wealthy Borden family, went to China as a missionary. There he died of an oriental disease. At his bedside they found a note he had written while he was dying. On it were these words: "No reserve, no retreat, and no regrets."

I'm sure Jesus loved Bill Borden. "No reserve, no retreat, no regrets."

Jesus wanted his disciples to be productive. He knew what can be done with those who are ready to take charge—those whose lives radiate power.

That is the meaning of faith. Faith is not belief based on an intellectual premise. Faith is action based on an eternal promise.

That is the message of Hebrews 11. The writer begins with Cain and Abel as he shows how by faith the great men of old received the blessings of God. From Abel to Abraham he shows how God is faithful to those who walk according to His purpose.

One of the names included in that list is that of Enoch. Missing is the name of Enoch's son Methuselah. Methuselah, you will remember, lived 969 years. That's all we know about him. He lived longer than anyone has ever lived. But as far as we know his life made no other impact than that he lived a long time.

God calls his people to be productive, to be powerful. He calls us to make our lives count. To take charge. Go hard or go home!

Another word people like to use nowadays is "passionate." What is your passion? Motivation speakers tell us we will be successful if we will follow our passion. And that is true.

I was reading recently about the prolific writer of Western novels, Louis L'Amour. At one time L'Amour was one of the world's most popular writers. He wrote 89 novels, over 250 short stories, and sold more than 320 million copies of his work. His writings were translated into over 20 languages.

Such production didn't come out of a half-hearted effort. L'Amour constantly searched for factual material to fill his novels. Once, he found an abandoned cabin whose occupants seventy years earlier had used newspaper to insulate the structure against frigid winds. He spent days removing this home-made insulation. He took the newspapers home and gleaned enough facts for two stories.

This was not an isolated incident. By the time L'Amour started a novel, he was armed with copies of every topographical map, relief map, and mine chart that existed on the area covered in his story. "My descriptions must be right," he insists. "When I tell my reader about a well in the desert, he knows it's there, and that the water is good to drink."

Once, for $3 a day, he agreed to help an 80-year-old trapper who had been hired to skin all the dead cattle on a rancher's spread. "There were 925 of them, and some had been dead for a while," L'Amour remembered later. "Nobody else would come near the place," he said. "But the old man had a story to tell: he had been kidnapped by Apaches when he was seven years old and had been brought up as one of them. He had ridden with the great chiefs Nana and Geronimo." L'Amour concludes, "I had him all to myself for three months and got a lot of material for books I wrote later: Hondo, Shalako, and The Skyliners." (3)

That's passion. Would you be willing to skin 925 cattle, some of them dead for some time, in order to glean a few good facts? That's why Louis L'Amour was at the top of his profession. What is it that you have a passion for?

Pastor and author Rick Warren says one time he typed the phrase "a passion for..." into Amazon.com and found a couple hundred books with that title. "There's a book call A Passion for Birds, A Passion for Books, A Passion for Cactus, A Passion for Chocolate...A Passion for Fashion...for Fishing...for Flying...for Gardening ...for Needlepoint, Pasta, Ponies. There's a book called, A Passion for Potatoes... There's even a book called A Passion for Steam. I can't figure out," says Warren, "what that one's all about! I don't know why you'd get passionate about steam."

Then Warren adds this observation, "But in our culture it's ok to be passionate about anything except your religion, except your faith, except your relationship with God. I can go to a rock concert, or a political rally or a baseball game and I can shout my head off. I can get excited. I can get hoarse from yelling so loud. When my team loses I could cry. Nobody thinks that's a big deal. When my team wins I can jump up and dance around and wave my hands in the air. If I do that at a game people go, 'He's a real fan!' If I do that in church people say, 'He's a fanatic! He's a nut case.' You don't want to get too emotional about your faith. It's ok about anything else but not that." (4)

I think we all can relate to that, and it is a crying shame. That is what is missing in many of us. We have no great driving passion for God. It is not that we are bad people. Indeed, we desire to be better than we are. But we would rather not get too excited about it. We are not all that happy with our lives, but then why rock the boat? No passion—no power. Productive, powerful, passionate people—that is what God seeks.

There is one more descriptive word we should add, however, and that is "prepared." The Master leaves the servant in charge until he returns. He expects the servant to be prepared to give an accounting of his stewardship.

My friend, if the Master were to return today and were to ask you to give an accounting of your life, would you be prepared? There are some people—good people—salt of the earth people—who will have nothing to show the Master. They were nice enough. They didn't get into any real trouble. But they made no real contribution to their world, to their community, to their church. They just kind of blended into the landscape for their three score and ten years. The words of the Master, "Unto whom much is given, much is required," will come as an awful judgment to them.

Pastor Eric Ritz draws our attention to a book titled, Trouble Doesn't Happen Next Tuesday. It was written by a Salvation Army worker, who started a coffeehouse in a Chicago slum. She poured her whole life into helping troubled youngsters. She wanted them to turn their lives around, through God's grace in Christ.

In her book, she tells about a young African-American teenaged boy who became a close friend of hers. At first he seemed to be responsive to her ministry, but then he got into trouble. The boy's name was Terry. He had big hands—the hands of an athlete. In fact, several universities were interested in him as a football prospect.

She tells a moving story about how she and Terry met after he had been arrested. She said, "I took Terry's hands, hands that one day might carry a football for the Chicago Bears, and tried to put my hands around them. Then I asked the Lord to accept those hands, and use them for his glory. Then Terry prayed his own prayer—something like this: 'Help me, not to be using my hands for bad things but good things for people—like old folks and little children, people I like to help. Make my hands stronger, so that I can be a big help in the world. Amen, God.'" That Salvation Army worker was trying to help Terry prepare for a good life—a meaningful life and a productive one.

Most of us have had far more advantages than Terry, but how little we have done with those advantages. It is at the end of today's lesson that Jesus speaks those haunting words, "Unto whom much is given, much is required." Do you measure up? Are you using your hands to be a big help to the world? Here is what Christ wants out of each of us—productive, powerful, passionate, prepared. Such the Father wants to serve Him. Go hard or go home!

1. http://www.lectionary.org/Sermons/Hyde/Acts/Acts%2002.01-21,%20TimeDeliver.htm.
2. Raymond McHenry, Something to Think About (Peabody, MA: Hendrickson Publishers, Inc., 1998).
3. John G. Hubbell in Stephen R. Covey, Everyday Greatness (Nashville: Rutledge Hill Press, 2006), p. 240.
4. http://www.sermoncentral.com/sermons/reigniting-your-passion-for-god-rick-warren-sermon-on-attitude-general-127082.asp.

Real Heroes
Hebrews 11:29-12:2

I want to alert any of you who are into Xtreme sports that there is now a camera that will allow you to film your exploits. You have probably seen ads for this camera. It is specially designed for bikers, surfers, snowboarders, scuba divers, dirt track drivers, skiers, auto racers or participants in any other action sport. The name of this camera is the HD GoPro HERO camera. You can mount the HERO camera to your helmet, handlebar, windshield, car bumper or any other place you can think of where you might capture your adrenaline-pumping exploits. That's neat—a high definition Hero cam.

I wish there had been a high definition HERO cam in the first century AD. For then we might have had live action footage of real heroes—heroes whose lives changed the world. Since he didn't have a HERO cam the writer of Hebrews tries to capture these heroes with the written word. Listen to his words. Imagine you are seeing these scenes in high definition:

"By faith the people passed through the Red Sea as on dry land; but when the Egyptians tried to do so, they were drowned.

"By faith the walls of Jericho fell, after the army had marched around them for seven days.

"By faith the prostitute Rahab, because she welcomed the spies, was not killed with those who were disobedient.

"And what more shall I say? I do not have time to tell about Gideon, Barak, Samson and Jephthah, about David and Samuel and the prophets, who through faith conquered kingdoms, administered justice, and gained what was promised; who shut the mouths of lions, quenched the fury of the flames, and escaped the edge of the sword; whose weakness was turned to strength; and who became powerful in battle and routed foreign armies. Women received back their dead, raised to life again."

You want action heroes? Those were action heroes. And they were real people. Of course, not all of them tasted victory in this world. In fact, many of them were crushed because of their endeavors. The writer continues: "There were others who were tortured, refusing to be released so that they might gain an even better resurrection. Some faced jeers and flogging, and even chains and imprisonment. They were put to death by stoning; they were sawed in two; they were killed by the sword. They went about in sheepskins and goatskins, destitute, persecuted and mistreated—the world was not worthy of them. They wandered in deserts and mountains, living in caves and in holes in the ground . . ."

Can you sense what it means to be a hero in these words? Talk about an Xtreme lifestyle. These were men and women who looked into the face of torture and death and did not flinch. As we said, they were not always victorious—not in this world—

but they were heroes just the same, real-life heroes.

Hebrews 11 is sometimes called "The Faith Chapter." When you think about it, faith by its very nature is heroic. You and I in our daily lives don't know what tomorrow may bring, but we march forward trusting that an unseen God will be with us. Hebrews 11 gives us example after example of such courageous, uncompromising faith even in the face of incredible odds.

The epistle to the Hebrews was written to a group of Roman Christians during the time of Nero (around 66 AD). During this time, there was a terrible fire that burned for almost one week, decimating most of Rome. Remember the old expression, "Nero fiddled while Rome burned." Well, Nero did worse than that. Many of the citizens of Rome believed that Nero himself started this fire. In order to divert attention from himself, Nero laid the blame for the fire on Christians. As might be expected, this unleashed a wave of persecution that threatened to destroy the tiny band of believers.

New Testament scholar William Barclay gives this graphic description: "Nero wrapped the Christians in pitch and set them alight, and used them as living torches to light his gardens. He sewed them in the skins of wild animals and set his hunting dogs upon them to tear them to death. They were tortured on the rack; they were scraped with pincers; molten lead was poured hissing upon them. . ." (1)

It was during this time that the Christians began using the symbol of the fish as their identifying symbol. Some of you know the story. The Greek word for fish, Icthus, is an acronym for the biblical phrase, "Jesus Christ, Son of God, Savior," and was a kind of secret password among these terrorized Christians. The way you revealed yourself to a fellow Christian was to draw half the fish sign in the dirt with your foot as you talked. If the other guy completed the drawing with a swipe of his own foot, you could safely acknowledge your true beliefs. Today we see fish symbols on the back of expensive SUVs. That is a far cry from the conditions under which this symbol was born. The persecution under Nero was an unbelievably horrid chapter in the life of the church. It cost many believers their lives. It cost many other less committed believers their faith. (2)

Persecution caused many of weak or immature faith to leave the church. Most of the earliest members of the Christian community had been Jews. They had left the Jewish synagogue to worship instead as Christians in the church. With the persecution under Nero, however, many began returning to the synagogue. They couldn't reconcile their newly attained faith with the persecution that they were experiencing. After all, they had been taught growing up that God always rewarded right behavior. Now, under Nero's persecution, they began thinking to themselves that they had been wrong to turn away from the faith their parents had handed down to them. It would appear that they no longer had God's blessing since they had become Christians.

And who can blame them for thinking that way? Isn't that what many of us believe deep in our hearts? If I am a follower of Jesus, God will bless my life and protect me and those I love from all harm. Indeed, more than that, don't many of us believe that if we follow Jesus, God will prosper us in every good thing? According to a very immature view of life and faith, that's the way life ought to work. But it doesn't work that way, regardless of what some of the television preachers may say. In their theological studies, these preachers must never have gotten as far as Hebrews. The idea that if we follow Jesus God will automatically prosper us is nonsense; you might say it is heresy, but it is being preached every week on television. It is the content of the preaching of some of the most popular preachers in America. And it is a lie! Don't you believe it!

The fact that you are prospering does not mean that God favors you, and if you are going through a difficult time it does not mean that God has forgotten you. Many of God's most beloved people can be found in prison, can be found wandering around in rags, can be found among those who have been violently persecuted.

There was an article sometime back in Decision magazine about a man named Skender Hoti. Skender Hoti grew up in Kosovo. As a child Skender learned that in his culture toughness was valued above all other qualities. And so Skender proved his toughness by making trouble whenever he could. He got what he wanted through threats and force.

When Skender learned that his younger brother, Enver, was attending a Christian church, he gave Enver a good beating. But as Skender was hitting his younger brother, Enver looked up and said, "I love you, Skender, and God loves you."

Skender wanted to know what kind of place taught people to love those who beat them, so he decided to check out this church. The pastor gave him a New Testament, which Skender read in the hopes of finding some loopholes. But after reading it through three times, Skender Hoti gave his life to Christ. All of Skender's friends abandoned him when he did this, and his father threw him and Enver out of the house. But eventually the boys brought their father and the rest of their household to Christ.

A few years later, Skender became a pastor in his town. A group of military men kidnapped him and beat him because of his faith. But as they were beating him, Skender told the men about Jesus. Later, the commander of that military group came to Christ, and today he attends Skender's church. (3)

You know, don't you, that there are Skender Hotis all over this earth? Good people, people of deep faith, who are not only suffering IN SPITE OF their faith, but are suffering BECAUSE of their faith. Do you think that God loves us in our affluence more than God loves them in their affliction? What kind of god would God be if that were so? The writer of Hebrews says this about suffering saints of God, they are people "of whom the world is not worthy." And it's true. Don't you ever confuse your life situation with questions about whether you have God's blessing and love. God loves you regardless of where you are on the scale of life's fortunes or misfortunes.

Read the Bible sometime and you will see there is a conspicuous absence of the trappings of earthly material success as a reward for faith in the lives of many of the Bible's greatest heroes. And the greatest hero of all, of course, our Savior died a tortuous death upon a cross.

No wonder that some churches don't want a cross at the center of their worship. If the truth were known some of them should have a dollar sign at the center. They are mere baptizers of the materialistic culture of which we are a part. Let me repeat, the fact that you are prospering does not mean that God favors you, and if you are going through a difficult time, it does not mean that God has forgotten you. God loves you regardless of your situation.

The secret to a great life is to hold on to God and to prepare yourself for whatever life may send. Jesus said very clearly that God "causes his sun to rise on the evil and the good, and sends rain on the righteous and the unrighteous" (Matthew 5:45). In other words, good people prosper, bad people prosper. Good people suffer, bad people suffer. All sorts of tragic events can happen to the most blessed of saints. Expect the best, but—should life deal you a crippling blow—be prepared for it and hold on to God. Believe me when I say, God will never let go of you.

Pastor Ray Pritchard tells about a professor who, along with his son, went on a 1,000-mile backpacking trip from British Columbia to southern California.

They hiked through the mountains of Washington, Oregon and California. They faced every sort of discouragement—lack of food and water, danger from wild animals, from robbers. They experienced days of rain and mud, incredible physical exhaustion, the very real possibility of physical injury.

Before leaving on the trip, the professor discovered that over 90% of those who set out to hike more than 500 miles never make it. He discovered that those who succeeded versus those who failed understood that the biggest block was mental. They knew that their real enemy lay within, not without. Those who succeeded make two important decisions: First, they decided they would finish the trip no matter what happened, and second, they expected bad things to happen and decided they would not be surprised or dismayed.

So when the rains turned the trail into a quagmire, they didn't quit because they weren't surprised. When black clouds of mosquitoes descended, they didn't quit because they weren't surprised. "They knew that the key was simply putting one foot in front of the other. You take a step and hit the mud. You take another step and see a bear. You take another step and your legs begin to cramp. You take another step and the crazy people come out of the woods. Doesn't matter. You aren't surprised because you knew the crazy people would show up sooner or later. So you just keep putting one foot in front of the other and eventually your journey is finished." (4)

What a wonderful analogy of the Christian life. This text from Hebrews reminds us that the fact that we are believers does not protect us from experiencing life's "slings and arrows." We are more fortunate than those early followers of our Lord. Not only did their faith not protect them from suffering. They suffered because of their faith. We are not apt to ever be thrown into a gladiator's pit or torn to death by wild dogs because we are a follower of Jesus. But life is tenuous. It can be terrifying. Hold on to God and prepare yourself for whatever life may send.

Remember, you are not alone in life's struggle. It is beautiful how the writer of Hebrews concludes this passage. Remember he has just afflicted his readers with a long list of persons who had remained faithful to God even after suffering horribly. Then he writes these stirring words, "Therefore, since we are surrounded by such a great cloud of witnesses, let us throw off everything that hinders and the sin that so easily entangles. And let us run with perseverance the race marked out for us, fixing our eyes on Jesus, the pioneer and perfecter of faith. For the joy set before him he endured the cross, scorning its shame, and sat down at the right hand of the throne of God."

The metaphor that the writer uses is that of a race, a marathon that lasts the duration of our lives. We are running this race called life, and sometimes we climb steep hills and other days it is somewhat easy going as we traverse a level plain, but regardless of the terrain, we are not alone. There are people cheering us on—a "great cloud of witnesses" is how the writer describes them. Who are those witnesses? It is that list of heroes contained in the eleventh chapter of Hebrews, and it is also those of every age who have given their all for God. We draw our strength and our inspiration from them. They did not give up and neither shall we.

In every generation there are people from all walks of life who deserved to have their lives captured on a HERO cam. Some of them are in this congregation. What does it take to be a hero? It means whatever your background or your circumstances walking in the footsteps of Jesus. It means never giving up whatever life may throw at you. It means serving God and serving humanity and giving your all to make this a better world. "Therefore, since we are surrounded by such a great cloud of witnesses, let us throw off everything that hinders and the sin that so easily entangles. And let us run with perseverance the race marked out for us, fixing our eyes on Jesus, the pioneer and perfecter of faith. For the joy set before him he endured the cross, scorning its shame, and sat down at the right hand of the throne of God."

1. The Gospel of Matthew (Louisville: St. Andrew Press, 2001) p. 112.
2. Henry Chadwick, The Early Church (New York: Penguin Books, 1993).
3. "Hearing the Truth of Jesus Christ" by Skender Hoti, Decision Magazine, Sept. 2000, pp. 4-5.
4. Ray Pritchard, http://www.keepbelieving.com/sermon/2003-08-24-Finishing-Well/

Cure For An Aching Back
Luke 13:10-17

One Sabbath day, Jesus was teaching in a synagogue. A woman was there who was severely disabled. Her body was all bent over—so bent over that her head was nearly even with her waist. Dr. Luke tells us she could not straighten up at all. That strikes me as an unbelievably sad situation. Forgetting the pain and the inconvenience of not being able to straighten one's body, imagine what that would do to your self-image. Imagine not just the physical pain, but the emotional pain of this kind of obvious deformity of the entire body.

Dr. Ralph F. Wilson suggests that this woman's problem was probably what physician's today would call Ankylosing Spondylitis, or Marie-Strümpell Disease, a disease that causes bones in the spine to fuse together. It is a disease that usually affects young men, though women are susceptible too. It begins with inflammation and stiffness. "Early in the course of the disease, sufferers often find that the pain is relieved somewhat when they lean forward. So they often go through the day leaning slightly forward, and gradually their spine begins to fuse. The more they lean in order to relieve the pain, the greater the angle, until a patient might be bent almost double, as the lady in our story." Treatment focuses on relieving back and joint pain, and preventing or correcting spinal deformities. Even today, notes Dr. Wilson, we don't have any medicines that can actually cure this condition. (1)

If you have any compassion at all or any ability to empathize with another human being, you can't help but hurt for this woman. She was so terribly disabled. But you also have to admire her. She did not allow her physical condition to keep her from worshipping God.

Notice how our story begins, "One Sabbath day, Jesus was teaching in a synagogue. A woman was there who was severely disabled. Her body was all bent over." Even with her pronounced deformity she was in the synagogue on the Sabbath. I admire her. I wonder if I would have that kind of courage—to be in public with that kind of condition.

Even more important she had not allowed her physical condition to impair her relationship with God. She had been this way for eighteen years—all bent over and unable to rise up. The pain was sometimes severe. Yet, her habit was to be in worship to praise her Maker. Friends, that's faith. That's devotion.

I know people who will miss church if they have a slight headache. Or if there is a threat of a little rain—or the threat of sunshine for that matter—for there are so many other things you can do when the weather is nice. But here was this woman where she was supposed to be on this particular Sabbath: in worship. And because she was there, she received a very special blessing from God.

Now I know I'm preaching to the choir about being in worship. You believe in worship or you wouldn't be here today. And nobody forced you to be here. Well, maybe a spouse or a parent . . . However, I'm glad we don't live in earlier times when missing worship was a punishable offense.

You may be familiar with Jamestown, VA, the first permanent settlement in the new world. Some of their religious practices were rather interesting. For instance, they had two hour church services every day, and for five hours on Sunday, and everybody had to attend. Missing church was considered a sin and was dealt with severely.

The penalty for missing a service was the loss of food rations for a whole day. A second absence resulted in a public whipping. And the penalty for missing three times was to be placed in the stocks daily for six months! Historians tell us that research has not revealed anyone in Jamestown Colony ever missing church three times. (2)

Well, I imagine not. I believe we could improve our attendance if we instituted such a system. Obviously we would never do that even if we could. But missing worship really is serious business. Attendance in worship is a witness to our faith in Christ. Attendance in worship encourages others. Nothing is more discouraging to a first-time visitor than a half-empty church. But just as importantly, God is waiting in this place to bless you, to heal you, to strengthen you. This woman would have missed the healing touch of Jesus if she had not been in worship that day.

The Psalmist understood such devotion. "Surely goodness and mercy shall follow me all the days of my life: and I will dwell in the house of the LORD forever," he wrote in the beloved 23rd Psalm (23:6). And again, "I was glad when they said unto me, Let us go into the house of the LORD" (122:1). And in another place the Psalmist writes, "For a day in thy courts is better than a thousand [elsewhere]. I had rather be a doorkeeper in the house of my God, than to dwell in the tents of wickedness" (84:10). This sorely afflicted woman was in the synagogue on the Sabbath. This is where she was supposed to be, and because she was there, Jesus healed her.

From Luke's description we have to wonder whether the disease that crippled this woman could have been psychological in origin. Notice how Luke describes her condition: "On a Sabbath Jesus was teaching in one of the synagogues, and a woman was there who had been crippled by a spirit for eighteen years . . ." [emphasis added] What does that mean, crippled by a spirit?

In pre-scientific times, of course, it was quite common for people to attribute all disease to the presence of demons. This may be the simple explanation for this wording. Demon possession is certainly a recognized condition in the scriptures.

Or, in modern terms, maybe Luke is saying to us that this woman's problem was caused by something that was troubling her mentally or spiritually.

One of the Psalms attributed to David is very interesting. David writes, "I am bowed down and brought very low; all day long I go about mourning. My back is filled with searing pain; there is no health in my body. I am feeble and utterly crushed; I groan in anguish of heart" (Psalm 38:6-8).

If you read the rest of the Psalm, it is clear that David attributes at least part of the fact that he is bowed down to his own guilt. He writes, "Because of your wrath there is no health in my body; there is no soundness in my bones because of my sin. My guilt has overwhelmed me like a burden too heavy to bear" (38:3-4). Of course David had a lot to feel guilty about.

I would not be at all surprised if there were someone in this room today who has spent time in bed because of an aching back. And the cause of that aching back the doctor told you was stress. What did she give you for the aching back? Muscle relaxers. To have a healthy back is sometimes to have a healthy mind. Psychological problems can cause us to feel bowed down. We see someone who is deeply troubled and we say, "He seems to be carrying the weight of the world on his shoulders . . ." Before long we even start to see it in his posture. Not as badly as this woman, of course, but we see the shoulders slump and the back bend.

Low self-esteem can cause a person to shrink into himself or herself. We tell our children, "Throw your shoulders back and stand proud . . ." But some children seem incapable of doing that and so a kind of life-long deformity of slumping shoulders and, even more tragically, a slumping spirit begins forming.

All kinds of things in life can cause souls as well as backs to be bent or bowed down: humiliation and shame, lack of education, loss of a loved one through divorce or death, accident, disease, a problem with our appearance or personality.

We don't know if any of these applied to this poor woman. Maybe her problem was genetic. Or perhaps it was bacterial. All we know is that she was bent over and could not straighten up at all. When Jesus saw her, he called her forward and said to her, "Woman, you are set free from your infirmity." Then he put his hands on her, and immediately she straightened up and praised God.

It is a powerful thought: Jesus can heal those who are bowed down, whatever the reason is for their condition.

There is a verse, again in the Psalms that speaks to this. In the King James Version it reads like this: "The Lord openeth the eyes of the blind: the Lord raiseth them that are bowed down . . ." (Psalm 146:8).

This woman, whatever the origin of her spirit of infirmity was in worship on the Sabbath; when Jesus told her to step forward, she obeyed, and this terrible burden was lifted from her body and her soul. Says Dr. Luke, "Immediately she straightened up and praised God."

Jesus can do that for you, my friend. If there is some burden that is weighing you down, give it to Jesus. Some secret sin, some sense of inferiority, some smothering anxiety, some lingering illness—give it to Jesus whatever it may be. You don't have to carry it alone. Jesus is here to heal and make whole.

Unfortunately this wonderful story of the healing of this woman doesn't stop here. For there is another character in the story, a man with a different kind of spirit, a spirit of legalism and condemnation.

Immediately after reading that this woman straightened up and praised God, Luke tells us about this second character. Listen to these words: "Indignant because Jesus had healed on the Sabbath, the synagogue leader said to the people, 'There are six days for work. So come and be healed on those days, not on the Sabbath.'"

Oh, man, where do people like this come from? They throw cold water on every good event. And for some reason they seem to be drawn to the church and synagogue.

Pastor Lee Strobel is fond of quoting the reply Homer Simpson's fundamentalist neighbors gave when Homer asked them where they'd been: "We went away to a Christian camp," they said, "We were learning how to be more judgmental." (3)

This man who criticized Jesus must have attended one of those camps. He was the leader of the synagogue. God had done a great work in his presence. Wouldn't you think that he would be jumping up and down, giving God praise? But all he can do is criticize.

Someone has noted that this was the last time it is recorded that Jesus was ever in a synagogue. For one thing, from this point on he was such a controversial figure that no synagogue would allow him in the pulpit. But you have to wonder if the legalism of this synagogue leader drove him away. If so, he wouldn't be the first or the last person to have been driven away from a religious assembly by a legalistic spirit.

It reminds me of the time-honored story of a knight who returned to the castle at twilight. He was a mess. His armor was dented, his helmet skewed, his face was bloody, his horse was limping, he was listing to one side in the saddle. The lord of the castle saw him coming and went out to meet him, asking, "What hath befallen you, Sir Knight?"

Straightening himself up as best he could, the bedraggled knight replied, "Oh, Sire, I have been laboring in your service, robbing and burning and pillaging your enemies to the west."

"You've been WHAT?" cried the startled nobleman, "but I haven't any enemies to the west!"

"Oh!" said the knight. "Well, I think you do now."

I am convinced that many blessed saints with the spirit of legalism and condemnation have created enemies for God where previously there had not been any. Maybe you can understand why such people are that way. I do not.

This man was a leader of the synagogue. This is a good warning to me as a pastor. I remember a bulletin blooper I saw years ago, "Please welcome Pastor Don, a caring individual who loves hurting people."

Well, of course, you can read that two ways. He loves people who are hurting, or he himself enjoys hurting people. I've known pastors of both persuasions.

But lay people also can be of both persuasions.

In a sermon on the Internet, pastor David C. Fisher tells about a time when he was in graduate school doing doctoral work and serving as minister of a small, rural congregation in southern Indiana. This was a church in which no pastor in its one hundred ten year history had stayed longer than two and half years. They regarded ministers as outsiders to be mistrusted and kept at arm's length.

To make matters worse the congregation had suffered a recent and ugly split. The previous pastor and half the congregation walked out during a congregational meeting to start a rival church. "The memory of those who remained," says Fisher, "was the sound of the door slamming behind the dissidents. [Those left behind] were hurt, angry, and nursing old wounds."

Pastor Fisher, young and brimming with confidence figured he'd come in, do his thing, and things would turn around. Surprise. He got no response from this group of people—nothing. No matter what he tried, the people were determined not to accept him. In his words, this congregation raised passive-aggression to an all-time record high! They kept him and his wife at a distance and treated them with veiled hostility.

He says he learned a lot in the time he was pastor there. One lesson he learned is that in public life you receive a lot of other people's mail. What he means is this: much of the reaction to ministers of the past and especially his predecessor who split the church was unjustly visited on him. He received their mail. He writes, "It was horrible. At school I was trying to earn some acceptance and respect. At work [in that small church] I seemed a failure. It was so bad, one Sunday after church Gloria and I stood in our house looking out the window at a field and we held each other and cried. 'Is God here or not?' That was our question. 'Is God here or not?'" (4)

We can understand it if it is true that Jesus never taught in a synagogue again after his encounter with this particular synagogue leader. And we can understand why some people who have been hurt by the church never darken its doors again. That's not what church is about.

But it is sad. This is a place where people still come today for healing and acceptance. This a place where people still come today to find help for their hurting hearts. This is a place where persons with a disability can find His ability to heal. Imagine someone coming in the doors of our church who is bent over either figuratively or literally like this poor woman in today's story. Is she going to encounter the spirit of Jesus or is she going to encounter the spirit of this synagogue leader? The answer to that question is up to each of us—every one of us. Will they discover here a spirit that heals or one that hurts? Let's make certain that we are a church family that always seeks to heal—a church family that surrounds people with the love and grace of Jesus Christ.

1. www.jesuswalk.com.
2. http://www.sermoncentral.com/sermons/father-forgive-them-melvin-newland-sermon-on-easter-resurrection-33337.asp.
3. John Ortberg, The Life You've Always Wanted (Grand Rapids: Zondervan, 2002).
4. http://www.plymouthchurch.org/news/PCsermon051808.pdf.

The Narrow Door
Luke 13:22-30

Some of you remember George Foreman. Foreman is a two-time former heavyweight boxing champion of the world. He is also an Olympic gold medalist, ordained Baptist minister, author and entrepreneur.

Foreman is a colorful character who is probably better known today for his George Foreman Grill. When he won his second heavyweight world championship, at age 45, he became the oldest man in the world to win the heavyweight title. It's quite a remarkable story. In his book, God in My Corner, he tells about that second title.

He says that when he started his comeback, he had to get rid of what he called "some excess George." He was extremely overweight. In the nearly ten years he had been out of boxing, he had ballooned from 220 to 315 pounds. And it wasn't muscle that he gained!

To get back into an exercise regimen, he started with the basics—running every day. He was so out of shape that he couldn't go far. At first, he couldn't even make it around the block, which was about a mile. He had to stop a few times to catch his breath, huffing and puffing.

"Just imagine a big, fat guy," he writes, "gasping for air, barely able to jog around the block, who claims that he will be the heavyweight champion of the world again! I looked ridiculous to everyone who saw me. I'm sure they laughed as they peeked through their curtains early in the morning while I slowly shuffled past their houses. Only two people on this entire planet believed I could recapture the title—my wife and me."

But he had to get his weight down. He would walk and run, walk and run. Finally, he was able to run the whole time without walking. Then he began running longer distances, and with the combination of a proper diet and regular exercise, the fat continued to melt away. He kept running for the next eight months, until he finally got down to his fighting weight—229 pounds. The flab was fun to put on, he says, but hard to take off. Some of us know what he's talking about. However, he contends, he wouldn't have won the championship title if he first hadn't gotten rid of that extra weight. (1)

I admire George Foreman. I admire anyone who sets a lofty goal and then gives his or her best to attaining that goal.

A few years ago Karen Phelps, a distance runner, wrote these challenging words, "On this particular day, I didn't feel like running at all, but I made myself because running is a sport you have to practice every day. I wanted to win races, so I had a set plan for training.

"1. Run daily, even if you don't feel like it.

2. Run daily, even if you sometimes have to skip fun and pleasure.

3. Run daily, even in bad weather—even if people think you're weird.

4. Run daily, even when it gives you aches and pains and you feel like quitting.

5. Run daily, even if you don't feel it's doing you any good."

"One day," she continues, "as I jogged along on my training run, it came to me that daily practice-training was what my spiritual life needed. Do you know what I've learned? Sometimes you may not feel like praying or reading the Bible or going out of your way to help others. But if you're in training—physical or spiritual—you'll do it." (2)

Karen Phelps is right on target.

A strong spiritual life takes work. Too many Christians today take their spiritual life so casually that it is almost non-existent.

I normally don't tell bar jokes, but there is a really terrible joke going around that reminds me of too many believers.

A guy walks into a bar, orders three shots and downs them all. "What's up with the three shots?" asks the bartender.

"My two closest buddies and I have gone our separate ways, and I miss them terribly," says the guy. "See, this glass here is for Tom, this one's Bob, and this one's mine. I feel like we're all drinking together, just like old times."

So every day the guy comes in and the bartender sets up three glasses. Until one day, the guy asks for just two shots.

"I hate to ask," says the bartender, "but did something happen to one of your friends?"

"Nah, they're okay," says the guy. "I myself just decided to quit drinking."

I told you it was terrible. But I doubt that this guy really has decided to quit drinking, don't you?

Jesus was on his way to Jerusalem. As he made his way through the various towns and villages on his route, he stopped and taught those who came out to hear him. He was becoming quite a celebrity. Sometimes thousands came out. Yet he knew that most of these folks were merely curious. They were not truly seekers after the truth. In fact, someone along the way asked him, "Lord, are only a few people going to be saved?"

My guess is that this was a serious question. Maybe this person assumed that he or she was safely in and asked the question in a somewhat smug, self-righteous way. Or maybe this person asked because he or she was worried about being left out. Either way, it was probably asked in earnest. Luke usually tells us if he believes the questioner is trying to trip Jesus up.

Of course, Jesus rarely answered a question directly. He doesn't this time either. He turns the question back on the questioner. He says, "Make every effort to enter through the narrow door, because many, I tell you, will try to enter and will not be able to." What does he mean by that—enter by the narrow door?

Thinking about the narrow door always reminds me of the announcement that appeared in a church bulletin: "Weight Watchers meets next Tuesday night at the church. Please use the wide double doors at the back."

What does Jesus mean by the narrow door? Does he mean that the number of people who will get into heaven is limited? That's interesting because according to most polls, most Americans not only believe in heaven, they believe that they someday will be there. For example, a poll conducted by USA Today sometime back showed that 72 percent of the people polled rated their chances of getting to heaven as good to excellent. Interestingly enough, these same people said that only 60 percent of their friends will go to heaven. I wonder why the discrepancy. Eighty percent said they believe in heaven, but only 67 percent said they believe in hell. (3)

Here's what interests me: By what authority do they assume that they are likely candidates for heaven? Particularly if they are only nominally interested in religion as are most Americans? And, for that matter, by what authority do they believe in heaven but not in hell?

We can't definitively say what Jesus meant when he said that the door is narrow, but we do know that anything worth having in this world requires work. You want a strong body, you work for it. You want a strong marriage, you work at it. You want a strong company, you work at it. Why should it be any different in our spiritual life? We are so obsessed by the notion of salvation by faith that we totally ignore an entire body of Jesus' teachings that call for commitment and sacrifice.

St. Paul compared the Christian life to an athlete training for a race. What did he mean by that? Now, please do not misunderstand. The Bible is clear that we are not saved by our works, but neither is our faith sustained apart from good works.

Someone has compared the balance of faith and works to two wings on a bird. For the bird to fly smoothly both wings are required. We give our lives to Christ, then we submit ourselves to serving him through his body, the church. We serve him by caring for the down-and out. We serve him by showing our love to our neighbors. We serve him by using our influence in the community. My reading of the New Testament is very clear—we cannot say we belong to Christ if we are not obedient to his teachings.

Jesus says, "Make every effort to enter through the narrow door, because many, I tell you, will try to enter and will not be able to . . ." The Greek word for "Make every effort . . ." is agonisma. That's the same root found in the English word "agonize." When we say somebody is agonizing, we would say they're in an intense struggle. But agonisma was a technical term for athletics. It was used of athletes in competition, like at the Olympics. They "agonize" to win the prize.

What I'm trying to deal with is the idea that seems to be prevalent in the church today, that the Christian life is easy. That it requires only a minimal output of effort. We can turn it over to our pastor or our priest and focus on our secular affairs with little or no thought of God. What an absurd idea.

Think I'm exaggerating? George Gallup of the Gallup Poll contends that fewer than ten percent of Christians in this land could be called deeply committed. The majority who profess Christianity do not know basic Christian teachings and do not act differently because of their Christian experience. As a Lutheran pastor put it, "Ninety percent of our parishes across the country require less commitment than the local Kiwanis club." (4)

This is disturbing, yet who could deny it is true? Let me ask you a question that was popular a few years back and is still relevant today, "If you were put on trial for being a Christian, could enough evidence be presented to convict?" The narrow door suggests that Christ loves us whoever we may be and whatever we have done, but Christ expects that we will not stay where we are. Christ expects us to agonize, to strive mightily to live according to the standard he has established for us.

Some of you are undoubtedly familiar with the movie Coach Carter. Coach Carter is the true story of Kenneth Carter, an inner-city Richmond basketball coach who took a ragtag group of high school players and shaped them into a tightly disciplined and almost unstoppable team of athletes. "To accomplish that, he was brutal. He pushed the boys, always to the edge of their endurance, and then a little further. Any insolence was immediately reprimanded with a crackdown of grueling drills. The slightest lateness was penalized. Backtalk was squelched beneath a mounting regimen of workouts. To show you that Carter meant business, he made headlines in 1999 for benching his entire undefeated high school basketball team due to poor academic results. When was the last time you heard of a coach doing that? Under Coach Carter's taskmaster harshness, the boys at first withered, then flourished. (5)

Why did Carter put his players through such agony? Was it because he hated them? No, it was because he loved them and wanted the best for them. His desire was that they should be more than they were. And that is Christ's desire for us. He wants us to be fit to share eternity with him.

William Willimon once told of the Methodist Bishop of Angola who came to Evanston, Illinois to speak to a group of young Christians. This bishop was asked, "What is it like to be the church in a Marxist country? Is the new Marxist government supportive of the church?"

"No," the Bishop responded, "but we don't ask it to be supportive."

"Have there been tensions?" they asked.

"Yes," said the Bishop. "Not long ago the government decreed that we would disband all women's organizations in the church."

"What did you do?" they asked.

"Oh, the women kept meeting," he commented. "The government is not yet strong enough to do much about it."

"But what will you do when the government becomes stronger?" they asked.

"Well," he said, "we shall keep meeting. The government does what it needs to do. The church does what it needs to do. If we go to jail for being the church, we shall go to jail. Jail is a wonderful place for Christian evangelism."

Then the bishop said this: "Our church made some of its most dramatic gains during the revolution when so many of us were in jail. In jail, you have everyone there, in one place. You have time to preach and teach. Sure, twenty of our Methodist pastors were killed during the revolution, but we came out of jail a much larger and stronger church."

And, as if seeing the drift of their questions, the bishop said, "Don't worry about the church in Angola, God is doing fine by us. Frankly, I would find it much more difficult to be a pastor in Evanston, Illinois. Here, there is so much, so many things, it must be hard to be the church here." (6)

It is hard to be the church in Evanston, Illinois just as it is hard to be the church in [this community]. Not because we are being persecuted, but because we have it so easy that we have no sense of urgency about entering by the narrow door. Let me say it again: we can't definitively say what Jesus meant when he said that the door is narrow, but we do know that anything worth having in this world requires work. Why should it not be true with the life of faith? The narrow door suggests that Christ loves us whoever we are and whatever we have done, but Christ expects that we will not stay where we are. Christ calls us to a new way of living. Christ calls us to a life of loving God and loving our neighbor. God calls us to train ourselves spiritually as an athlete might train himself physically for a major contest. In such a way we glorify God.

"Lord," someone asked, "are only a few people going to be saved?" Jesus answered, "Make every effort to enter through the narrow door . . ."

1. George Foreman, God in My Corner (Nashville: Thomas Nelson, 2007), p. 169. Cited at www.kentcrockett.com.
2. Contributed. Source unknown.
3. Glenn Van Ekeren, Speaker's Sourcebook II (Englewood Cliffs, NY: Prentice Hall, Inc., 1994), p. 326.
4. Wayne Pohl, Leadership (Winter, 1982), p. 95. Cited by Steven J. Cole, http://www.fcfonline.org/content/1/sermons/011799m.pdf.
5. Mark Buchanan, Hidden In Plain Sight (Nashville: Thomas Nelson, 2002), p. 60.
6. Cited by Don Gordon, http://www.yateschurch.org/clientimages/41513/sermons/strippedbeat-enimprisonedandfree5-11-08.pdf.

Re-Thinking Our Mission
Luke 14:1, 7-14

A science fiction story is told about a planet which earth was attempting to colonize. This was a harsh planet with terrible weather and hostile inhabitants. Earth's best men and women were gathered into teams and sent to do the job. Expedition after expedition came home broken, each one having failed.

Finally a new manager was charged with the responsibility of making the colonization work. But something surprising happened. This new executive did not look for the strongest and most qualified people he could find to send for establishing this colony. Instead, he went to the waterfronts, to the slums, to the darkest places on earth and got together a contingent of thieves, prostitutes, indigents, and sent them off to this harsh planet. And, quite remarkably, where the able had failed, the disabled succeeded.

Why? Well, for several reasons. First of all, they already had learned to survive in a hostile environment. Second, they had no place to go but up. (1)

The Pharisees grumbled about the kind of people who came to hear Jesus. Those who gathered around the Master were uneducated persons who had little use for pomp and circumstance in religion. The Sadducees and Pharisees held them in contempt. They regarded Jesus' followers as the scum of the earth—fishermen, tax-collectors, prostitutes. It particularly galled the Pharisees when Jesus said that these persons of low social stature would go into the kingdom of God before they, the religious elite, would. This was a bizarre teaching to many of Jesus' listeners. Yet Jesus made it clear that this was the heart of the Gospel.

"When you give a luncheon or dinner," he says in today's lesson, "do not invite your friends, your brothers or sisters, your relatives, or your rich neighbors; if you do, they may invite you back and so you will be repaid. But when you give a banquet, invite the poor, the crippled, the lame, the blind, and you will be blessed. Although they cannot repay you, you will be repaid at the resurrection of the righteous."

Obviously Jesus had never been to a Church Growth seminar. One of the major tenets of the modern church growth movement has been that successful churches, like successful businesses, should choose a target audience, preferably a homogeneous audience where everyone pretty much fits the same demographic.

For example, in his best-selling book, The Purpose Driven Church, Rick Warren, the Senior Pastor at Saddleback Church in southern California, writes about their "target market." He writes: "Our Target: Saddleback Sam. He is well educated. He likes his job. He likes where he lives. Health and fitness are high priorities for him and his family.

"He'd rather be in a large group than a small one. He is skeptical of 'organized' religion. He likes contemporary music. He thinks he is enjoying life more than he did five years ago. He is self-satisfied, even smug, about his station in life . . ."

That's the kind of person Saddleback Church is geared up to reach. And what church wouldn't want members like that? Good job, strong family, healthy, well-educated—gather enough people in that demographic and your church is going to be extremely successful as the world terms success.

Now, to be fair, Saddleback Church is also the home of the Celebrate Recovery movement that reaches out to those who have hurts, destructive habits and self-defeating hang-ups. But still, I have yet to meet a church growth advocate whose target audience is "the poor, the crippled, the lame, the blind . . ."

Yet those are the people whom Jesus told us to target. Those are the people Jesus himself targeted.

On one occasion he declared, "I have come to seek and save that which was lost" (Luke 19:10). And on another occasion he declared, "The well have no need for a physician, but those who are sick" (Mark 2:17)

When he stood up to preach his first sermon he announced his mission: "He has anointed me to preach good news to the poor; He has sent me to proclaim release to the captives and recovering of sight to the blind, to set at liberty those who are oppressed" (Luke 4:18, RSV).

It is ironic, don't you think, that this is where Jesus placed his emphasis—the poor, the blind, those who were oppressed and captives—and yet these are the last people on earth that the average church is geared up to reach?

As one author has put it: "Church culture in North America is a [mere] vestige of the original Christian movement, an institutional expression of religion that is in part a civil religion and in part a club where religious people can hang out with other people whose politics, world-view, and lifestyle match theirs." (2)

That description of the church hits the nail squarely on the thumb. We want to be around people who are like us. That's only natural, but it does not make it Christian.

The Rev. Bob Stump tells about camping with his family. He says that one of his favorite parts of camping is sitting by the camp fire late into the evening. Its circle of light provides a wonderful setting for quiet conversation and warm fellowship.

"Most of the other campers have their fires, too," he notes. "They sit and have quiet conversation and warm fellowship in their own private circles of light. Rarely do the campers leave their circles of light and venture out into the darkness. And almost never do they venture from their own circles of light to invade another circle. Each camping group is content in its own circle of light, safe from the darkness and secluded from outsiders in its own exclusive fellowship." (3)

What a wonderful metaphor for the average church, "content in its own circle of light, safe from the darkness and secluded from outsiders in its own exclusive fellowship."

"When you give a luncheon or dinner," says the Master, "do not invite your friends, your brothers or sisters, your relatives, or your rich neighbors . . . when you give a banquet, invite the poor, the crippled, the lame, the blind, and you will be blessed."

What is the Master saying to us in this strange teaching? Is he not saying, first of all, that the church is the one institution in our society that does not exist for the benefit of its own members? Yes, it's natural to want to be around people who are like us, but Christ wants us to do something that is very unnatural—reach out to those who may not be like us, but who need us.

Larry Sarver tells about the days when he was a police officer. He notes that as an officer he was required to respond to several traffic accidents, some of them with very severe injuries. He noticed that at the scene of those accidents there were three groups of people, each with a different response toward those involved in the accident.

The first group was the bystanders and onlookers. They were curious and watched to see what happened but had little active involvement.

The second group was the police officers, of whom he was one. The response of the police was to investigate the cause of the accident, assign blame, and give out appropriate warnings and punishments.

The third group was the paramedics. They are the people usually most welcomed by those involved in the accident. The paramedics could care less whose fault the accident was and they did not engage in lecturing about bad driving habits. Their response was to help those who were hurt. They bandaged wounds, freed trapped people, and gave words of encouragement.

Three groups, notes Larry Sarver—one is uninvolved, one is assigning blame and assessing punishment, and one is bandaging wounds, freeing trapped people, and giving words of encouragement. (4)

Now many people in every society like to be mere spectators. Their mantra is, "I don't want to get involved." They're useless and unworthy of our consideration.

The scribes and the Pharisees whom Jesus confronted saw themselves as the police—assigning blame and assessing punishment. They were quick to criticize those who violated the Law of Moses and dealt out punishment where they felt it justified. They even tried to police Jesus. Notice how this chapter begins: "One Sabbath, when Jesus went to eat in the house of a prominent Pharisee, he was being carefully watched . . ." He was being watched to catch him doing something wrong. And when Jesus refused to conform to the religious leaders' understanding of what is lawful, it was they who assigned him the cruel punishment of the cross.

They loved being the police. Such behavior is not confined to the synagogue, of course. It can happen and often does happen in the church.

David Kinnaman of the Barna Group reports that unchurched people often have the perception that if they go to a church for help, they will be judged rather than being helped. (5)

Dan Kimball wrote a book sometime back titled, They Like Jesus But Not the Church. In his book Kimball focused on the perception in today's culture by many young people that church people have the tendency to be judgmental. This critical spirit becomes a turn-off in any attempt to reach young people for Christ.

In Larry Sarvers's metaphor of spectators, police and paramedics, the scribes and Pharisees saw themselves as police, enforcers of the Law.

Jesus, however, wants his followers to identify, not with the police, but with the paramedics—bandaging wounds, freeing trapped people, and giving words of encouragement. The church is the one institution in our society that does not exist for the benefit of its own members. Jesus is very clear on this point. We are to be his body reaching out to those in need.

There is one thing more we need to see, however. Reaching out is not easy. It is much easier to be a spectator or to sit back and pass judgment on others than it is to get our hands dirty seeking to minister to the needs of others. But that is not what Jesus wants from us. He wants us to reach out to those "who cannot pay us back."

Pastor Don Friesen tells a wonderful story about a children's worker named April McClure. April teaches a Wednesday Bible study for boys and girls in her church.

One day a nine-year-old boy named Brandon turned up for April's class. Immediately she could see he was going to be a troublemaker. Within 30 seconds of entering the room, he had pulled a chair out from under a girl, punched the only other boy in the class in the arm, and used a four-letter word rarely heard in that church.

Brandon's family history was not a pretty one. His father was in jail for the third time. He had been abused by his mother, who was no longer allowed to see him, and so he was living with his grandmother. She worked afternoons and evenings. The woman who provided childcare for him while the grandmother worked was not available until 6 p.m. The principal of Brandon's grade school had heard that April's Bible study lasted until 7:30, and so, for at least one night a week, Brandon would not be on his own for three hours.

Imagine being a children's teacher and having Brandon in your class. Imagine him constantly changing the subject to talk about things that he had heard from his 20-year-old uncle about girls. Think about listening with apprehension as he told the other children stories he had heard about his father in jail.

April McClure did her best to reach out to Brandon. She set him right next to her in the Bible class and she let him help with passing out papers when he behaved himself. She helped him try to control his anger, to keep him from striking out at other children.

Even during recreational times, though, Brandon acted up, hitting and pinching the other children. During music, he goofed around and carried on conversations; during meal time, he was an absolute terror—throwing food, spitting at people, and making the little kids cry.

April and the other leaders didn't know what to do. They secretly hoped that his grandmother would make other arrangements for him. The other kids missed an occasional Wednesday but not Brandon. He was there every single week.

After about seven months of this, however, April noticed a change in Brandon. He started giving her a hug when he left for the evening with his babysitter. One day, she saw him in the grocery store, and he ran up to her, and pulled her over to meet his grandmother who was one of the cashiers. April told her pastor about this rare breakthrough and her pastor reported that the same thing had happened to her.

Another woman who was his substitute teacher at school reported that Brandon had introduced her to the class on the day she subbed like this: "Mrs. Leman goes to my church with me on Wednesday nights."

"One day toward the end of the school year, the Bible study class was discussing hospitality, and the teacher asked the kids to think about the place where they felt most secure, most at home. Some said their bedrooms, or some other place in their homes. One kid mentioned the playroom at his grandpa's house. When it came to Brandon, he said, 'Man, I've lived in a million places.' They all laughed and waited for him to go on. He asked, 'You mean the place where we feel happy and safe?' The teacher said yes. 'Oh,' he said matter-of-factly, 'That's right here in my church.'" (6)

My friend, that's what Jesus wants for every person in this world—rich and poor, seeing and sightless, athlete and physically disabled. He wants them to find a safe place, a secure, happy place in his family. He doesn't want anyone to feel left out.

Friends, I have to tell you most churches don't really want people who have problems. Why? People who have problems sometimes cause problems. Like Brandon when he first came to April's Bible Study. Yet these are the persons for whom God's heart aches. And these are the people whom he has called us to reach out to.

"When you give a luncheon or dinner," says the Master to his church, "do not invite your friends, your brothers or sisters, your relatives, or your rich neighbors . . . when you give a banquet, invite the poor, the crippled, the lame, the blind, and you will be blessed."

1. Madeleine L'Engle, Walking on Water (New York: Bantam Books, 1980).
2. Reggie McNeal, The Present Future: Six Tough Questions for the Church (San Francisco: Jossey-Bass, 2003).
3. Tim Zingale, http://www.sermoncentral.com/sermons/mountain-faith-tim-zingale-sermon-on-transfiguration-88525.asp?page=2.
4. http://www.sermoncentral.com/sermons/the-3-things-needed-for-reaching-the-lost-larry-sarver-sermon-on-evangelism-how-to-49316.asp
5. David Kinnaman and Gabe Lyons, UNChristian (Baker Books, 2007), p. 181.
6. http://www.ottawamennonite.ca/sermons/impractical.htm.

A One Sentence Legacy
Luke 14:25-33

I heard recently about a guy named Bob. Bob was single and lived with his father. Bob worked in the family business, a very successful family business.

When it became apparent that his father would not live much longer, and that he would soon inherit quite a fortune, Bob decided to find a wife with whom to share his soon-to-be abundant wealth.

One evening, at an investment meeting, Bob spotted the most beautiful woman he had ever seen. Her natural beauty took his breath away.

"I may look like just an ordinary guy," he said to her, "but in just a few years, my father will die and I will inherit $200 million."

Impressed, the woman asked for his business card. Three days later, this beautiful woman became Bob's stepmother. (1)

There's a woman who had a plan for success. Everybody needs a plan in today's fast changing world—though marrying a wealthy widower may not work for everybody. But the world is changing and we need to be prepared.

Dan Miller, in his book No More Dreaded Mondays, tells about many of the changes that are taking place in the American workplace. He enumerates the many jobs being lost because of technology or as the result of foreign competition. You already know this, but still it is jarring when you are confronted with the harsh reality of it all. Did you realize as you pick up your cash at your bank's ATM that these convenient devices are doing the work of 179,000 former bank tellers? It makes life easier for the rest of us, but those are nice people losing their jobs.

Even with the continuing problems of the U. S. Postal Service, did you know that sight-recognition machines have replaced 47,000 postal workers? That's startling, but it is a phenomenon faced by an increasing number of workers.

As for foreign competition, did you realize that many apparel workers and financial analysts have been coerced into training their foreign counterparts who will work for a fraction of the hourly wage expected in America? (2)

The world is changing. None of us can count on lifetime security from a job any more. So we better be prepared. Experts tell us that a person between ages eighteen and forty-four will have an average of 10.8 different jobs over the period of his or her lifetime. Many people are losing well-paying jobs and having to settle for careers in lower paying situations. Some counselors are telling us that today's workers, particularly younger workers, need to think like entrepreneurs. We need to take responsibility for our own careers and not leave that to our employer.

Making a living has always required diligence. Jesus knew what it took to succeed in the world. We forget that for about half of his life he was a carpenter. There are some scholars who think he might have been quite successful at his work—perhaps on the order of a contractor or an architect rather than simply a hired worker.

Today's story from Luke's Gospel reflects Jesus' business background. There were many who were starting to follow him. Did they know what they were getting into? Unbridled enthusiasm has its place, but it must be tempered with reason. So Jesus uses an analogy. "Suppose one of you wants to build a tower. Won't you first sit down and estimate the cost to see if you have enough money to complete it? For if you lay the foundation and are not able to finish it, everyone who sees it will ridicule you, saying, 'This person began to build and wasn't able to finish.'"

Jesus then moved to another analogy. "Or suppose a king is about to go to war against another king. Won't he first sit down and consider whether he is able with ten thousand men to oppose the one coming against him with twenty thousand? If he is not able, he will send a delegation while the other is still a long way off and will ask for terms of peace. In the same way, those of you who do not give up everything you have cannot be my disciples."

Jesus was stating a solid spiritual principle in practical and recognizable terms. People fail in business. People also fail in life. And the reasons are often the same.

One guy said sadly, "I started out on the theory that the world had an opening for me. I was right. Today I'm in a hole."

We know what he was talking about, don't we? For the person who does not sit down and count the costs—whether building a tower or conducting a military campaign or building a life—can find himself or herself deep in a hole.

Successful living begins with a plan. It is amazing how many people fail to plan. The old saying is true: people who fail to plan, plan to fail.

I was reading about an Englishman named Lionel Burleigh. In the 1960s Burleigh decided to become a newspaper man. He was unhappy with the depth of reporting in British newspapers at the time, so he decided to publish his own paper. He called his paper the Commonwealth Sentinel.

Burleigh worked diligently for weeks writing articles, promoting the newspaper on billboards, selling advertising space, and printing up 50,000 copies. He was determined to make the first edition a success.

On February 6, 1965 after the newspaper had left the printers, an exhausted Lionel Burleigh was resting in his hotel room when he was interrupted by a call from the London police. "Have you anything to do with the Commonwealth Sentinel?" the officer asked. "There are 50,000 of these newspapers on the outside entrance to Brown's Hotel and they're blocking Albemarle Street."

With the hundreds of details to attend to when publishing a newspaper, Burleigh had overlooked one critical detail: He never got a distributor. Nobody was out delivering his newspapers. They were sitting in the middle of the street blocking traffic. The Commonwealth Sentinel folded the following day. (3)

Poor foolish Lionel Burleigh. He was probably a fine man. He may have even been a smart man in many ways. But his plan was not completely thought out. Like the man who ran out of money building a tower or the king who brought too few soldiers into battle, Lionel simply didn't take all the necessary contingencies into consideration.

How much time do you spend planning for the future? Some people spend more time planning for a vacation than they do planning for their life. We are so busy with so many things in our lives, we may not even think about the things that really matter. I want to ask you two questions that all of us must answer at some time or another.

Let's begin here: what kind of legacy do you hope to leave to those you love and to the world? One of these days you will be leaving this earth. How will people remember you? In what ways will the world be a better place because you've been here?

Stephen Covey in his Seven Habits of Highly Effective People suggests that we begin with the end in mind. We've talked about this before, but, if you were to die tomorrow, what would you leave behind? Which of your values would you want to pass on to your heirs? Are you living out those values right now? When you get to the end of your life, will you do so with a lot of regrets? What will your friends say about you? Your family? Will you have the resources to meet the challenges of your final years, not only financial resources, but emotional resources, relational resources, spiritual resources? Those are big questions. But they must be answered if we are going to have anything close to a successful life.

Author and business guru Peter Drucker says his life was shaped by a teacher who once asked, "What do you want to be remembered for?" Drucker was only 13 when he heard this question, and he really didn't have an answer.

"I didn't expect you to be able to respond," the teacher continued. "But if you still can't [answer this question] by the time you're 50, you will have wasted your life." That was a wise teacher.

Phil Munsey, in his book Legacy Now, notes that there are seventy-eight million baby boomers in America. One of them turns sixty every six seconds, and the youngest are quickly turning fifty. This has created a huge interest among people in that age range in what he calls midlife evaluation. Boomers are feeling that it is time to make a change.

This evaluation, says Munsey, is bringing a transition from "me" to "we" and from "take" to "give." That's a healthy transition. By necessity, perhaps, boomers are moving from a "more-is-less" to a "less-is-more" world-view. (4)

German psychologist Erik Erikson called this shift the developmental stage of "Generativity vs. Stagnation." This is when people become aware of the need to live beyond themselves and begin the difficult task of leading a meaningful and useful life.

Of course, we don't have to wait until we are a boomer or beyond to adopt this perspective on life. It is the kind of worldview that Jesus encouraged among his followers. What kind of legacy do you hope to leave to those you love and to the world?

In 1962, Clare Boothe Luce, one of the first women to serve in the U.S. Congress, offered some advice to President John F. Kennedy. "A great man," she told him, "is a sentence." Abraham Lincoln's sentence was: "He preserved the union and freed the slaves." Franklin Roosevelt's sentence was: "He lifted us out of a Great Depression and helped us win a world war." Luce feared that Kennedy's attention was so splintered among different priorities that his sentence risked becoming a muddled paragraph. (5)

As you contemplate your purpose for being, your plan for life, begin with the big question: What's your sentence?

Former pro football great Bubba Smith came face-to-face with his sentence many years ago, and he didn't like it. Do you remember Bubba? He first came into prominence at Michigan State University as an All-American defensive end. The first selection of the 1967 NFL Draft, he played nine years in the pros. He was named to two Pro Bowls and was a First-Team All-Pro in 1971.

After football, Smith was recruited to appear in commercials for Miller Lite beer. He and fellow NFL veteran Dick Butkus were cast as inept golfers and polo players in the TV spots.

In one of the most memorable ads, Smith recited the virtues of the beer, beaming into the camera, "I also love the easy-opening cans," while ripping off the top of the can.

But Smith walked away from the job because he didn't like the effect drinking had on people and he realized that he was contributing to a significant social problem. In a magazine article about his life, Bubba Smith said that neither beer nor any other alcoholic beverage had ever been part of his life. But he advertised Lite beer and felt good about his job. It was an easy job. It was an enjoyable job, it paid a good salary.

Until one day when he went back to Michigan State, his alma mater, as the Grand Marshal of the Homecoming Parade. As he was riding in the limousine at the head of the parade, he heard throngs of people on both sides of the parade route shouting. One side was shouting, "Tastes great!" and the other side was shouting, "Less filling!"— the slogans Miller Lite used to promote their products. Bubba Smith suddenly realized that he and the beer commercials that he made had had a tremendous impact on the students at Michigan State.

Later, Bubba was in Ft. Lauderdale during Spring Break, and he saw drunken college kids up and down the beaches, shouting "Tastes great! Less filling!" And when it came time to renew his contract, he refused to sign because he said that he didn't want his life to count for something like that. He said that there was a still, small voice in his mind that kept saying, "Stop, Bubba. Stop." Bubba Smith didn't want the sentence he would leave as his legacy to be "Tastes great! Less filling!" So he walked away. (6)

What sentence will one day summarize your life? "He was a great father." "She kept a spotless home." "He had a bad temper." "She wore the cutest outfits." How about if that sentence was, "He or she was a genuine disciple of Jesus Christ."

Jesus was addressing people who were considering becoming his disciples. He wanted them to understand what was involved. He didn't need half-hearted saints. He wanted people who were willing to leave everything they considered important—if that were ever needed—in order to follow him. Would you measure up to that standard?

Years ago there was a remarkable village in southeastern France called La Chambon. What made this village remarkable is that the residents of that village, as a community, risked their lives to protect Jews during World War II. In later years documentaries were made about them; a wonderful book titled Lest Innocent Blood Be Shed was written about them by Philip P. Hallie. But the villagers tended to be irritated by questions that made their risks sound noble or praiseworthy. "What else would you do?" they responded. "You do what needs to be done." (7)

That would be a good one-word legacy: They did what needed to be done.

Former Secretary of State Madeleine Albright once told a most moving story shortly after the horror of 9/11. It involved a passenger on United Flight 93, which went down in Pennsylvania. That passenger, Tom Burnett, called his wife from the hijacked plane, having realized by then that two other planes had crashed into the World Trade Center.

"I know we're going to die," he said. "But some of us are going to do something about it." And because they did, many other lives were saved.

"I know we're going to die," is a wholly unremarkable statement. Each of us here could say the same. But those other words, "Some of us are going to do something about it," is an inspiring one sentence legacy.

What will be your legacy? What one sentence would you want to define your life? Are you living right now so that legacy may be achieved? "Suppose one of you wants to build a tower. Won't you first sit down and estimate the cost to see if you have enough money to complete it? . . . Or suppose a king is about to go to war against another king. Won't he first sit down and consider whether he is able with ten thousand men to oppose the one coming against him with twenty thousand? In the same way, those of you who do not give up everything you have cannot be my disciples."

What is your plan for your life? Are you living according to that plan today?

1. Fred Miller, MONDAY FODDER, http://family-safe-mail.com/
2. (New York: Broadway Books 2008).
3. Leland Gregory, Stupid History Tales of Stupidity, Strangeness, and Mythconceptions Through-out the Ages (Kansas City: Andrews McMeel Publishing, LLC, 2007), p. 173.
4. (Charisma House, 2008).
5. Daniel H. Pink, Drive: The Surprising Truth about What Motivates Us (New York: Penguin, 2009).
6. Melvin Newland, http://www.sermoncentral.com/sermons/love-divine-melvin-newland- ser-mon-on-christmas-40903.asp.
7. John Ortberg, The Me I Want to Be: Becoming God's Best Version of You (Grand Rapids: Zon-dervan, 2010), p. 75.

Lost, But Not The TV Show!
Luke 15:1-10

A marine tells about a field exercise he was participating in at Camp Lejeune, N.C. His squad was on a night patrol making their way through some thick brush. Halfway through, they realized they'd lost their map. The patrol navigator informed the rest of the squad that their odds were 1 in 359 that they'd succeed in getting back to their base of operations.

"How did you come up with that figure?" someone asked, "one chance in 359?"

"Well," he replied, "one of the degrees on the compass has to be right." (1)

Those marines were lost. One chance in 359 is not very good. Fortunately it was just a training exercise, but they were lost just the same. We've all been lost at one time or another. That's part of the human condition.

An 86-year-old man, Anthony, and his 85-year-old wife Viola lived in New Jersey. They got in their car to go to the store. But as Anthony was driving he took a wrong turn and they got lost. He kept driving but he could not find his way back. He drove and drove and drove over 800 miles. Two times he had to stop and fill up with gasoline. But he would not ask for directions. It was over 24 hours later that they returned home.

How did they finally find their way home? Anthony had an accident and ran into another car. The police came and helped them get back home. (2)

Can you imagine that—a man, of any age, who would not ask for directions? Amazing! People get lost for all sorts of silly reasons.

Luke 15 is one of the most important chapters in all the Bible. It includes three of the most famous parables ever told. Each of the parables deals with something that is lost—a sheep, a coin and a young man. The lost sheep may have been nibbling at the grass with its head down and wandered far from the flock and the shepherd. The lost young man rebelled against his father and went into a far country and indulged in destructive behavior that nearly destroyed him. It didn't matter to Jesus how those who were lost came to be where they were. All Jesus cared about was bringing them home.

I love how the chapter begins. "Now the tax collectors and sinners were all gathering around to hear Jesus . . ." We could derive an entire sermon from that one phrase. Tax-collectors and sinners were all gathering around Jesus. This shows two things. First of all, the tax-collectors and sinners were hungry for Christ's message. They were not coming out of idle curiosity, or to merely observe, or to find fault with him; they were coming out of a deep spiritual need. They needed his message of salvation.

And secondly, they were acknowledging that need. That may be the most surprising part of this story. Many people need to come to Christ; relatively few are willing to admit it. Publicans, that is, tax-collectors, worked for the Roman government, the nation that had conquered Israel. And they had a reputation for being unscrupulous. They were considered traitors to both Israel and God. Consequently, they were despised by the people and were cut off and shut out by the religious authorities.

The tax-collectors and the sinners . . . Those lumped together as sinners were the immoral and unjust who did not keep the Law, such as prostitutes, liars, thieves, murderers. Because of their waywardness they also were rejected by society. So when Christ came along preaching deliverance from sin and hope of the Kingdom of God, they also flocked to hear him.

The tax collectors and sinners were all gathering around to hear Jesus, says Luke. But listen to what he says next, "But the Pharisees and the teachers of the law muttered, 'This man welcomes sinners and eats with them.'" Think how different the narrative might be if we read that the Pharisees and the teachers of the Law rejoiced that the tax-collectors and the sinners gathered to hear Jesus' teachings. That's the way the story ought to read, but there was something dark in the heart of the Pharisees and the teachers of the Law, just as there was something dark in the heart of the tax-collectors and the sinners. At least, the tax collectors and sinners were aware of their need.

The Pharisees and the teachers felt it was beneath the dignity of any respectable person to associate with persons who did not obey the Law, and they were offended by Jesus' actions. Rather than having a heart for reaching out to those whom society had rejected, they wanted to keep them at arm's distance. We shouldn't have any difficulty understanding their attitude. They weren't much different from you and me. The Pharisees and the teachers of the Law wanted to associate with people who shared their values, people who were like them. Nothing could be more human than that. That is the way all humans design their society. People want to stay in their own comfort zone. But Jesus won't allow us to stay where we are comfortable.

He told them these parables: "Suppose one of you has a hundred sheep and loses one of them. Doesn't he leave the ninety-nine in the open country and go after the lost sheep until he finds it? And when he finds it, he joyfully puts it on his shoulders and goes home. Then he calls his friends and neighbors together and says, 'Rejoice with me; I have found my lost sheep.' I tell you that in the same way there will be more rejoicing in heaven over one sinner who repents than over ninety-nine righteous persons who do not need to repent.

"Or suppose a woman has ten silver coins and loses one. Doesn't she light a lamp, sweep the house and search carefully until she finds it? And when she finds it, she calls her friends and neighbors together and says, 'Rejoice with me; I have found my lost coin.' In the same way, I tell you, there is rejoicing in the presence of the angels of God over one sinner who repents."

These two parables and the one that follows them, the parable of the prodigal son, defined Christ's mission in the world. Jesus came to save that which is lost.

That is the heart of the Gospel. Earlier in Luke's Gospel Jesus sees a tax collector by the name of Levi sitting at his tax booth. "Follow me," Jesus said to him, and Levi got up, left everything and followed him.

Then Levi held a great banquet for Jesus at his house, and a large crowd of tax collectors and others were eating with them. But the Pharisees and the teachers of the law who belonged to their sect complained to Jesus' disciples about the Master's conduct. They asked, "Why do you eat and drink with tax collectors and sinners?"

Jesus answered them, "It is not the healthy who need a doctor, but the sick. I have not come to call the righteous, but sinners to repentance" (5:30-31).

That is Jesus' target audience—everyone who has ever gone astray.

St. Paul writes in his letter to Timothy, "Jesus Christ came into the world to save sinners." That is the heart of the Gospel, and it is great good news.

Why is it good news? Because we are all sinners. The tax collectors and the murderers and the prostitutes were sinners. The Pharisees and the teachers of the Law were sinners. And you and I are sinners. We look at ourselves and think to ourselves we're pretty good folks, and compared to some people, maybe we are. But that doesn't mean we've arrived. At heart we still have a problem, a flaw, a weakness. St. Paul once described his own situation: "I do not understand my own actions," he wrote. "For I do not do what I want, but I do the very thing I hate" (Romans 7:15). He's describing us.

The Bible is very realistic about the nature of humanity:

Abraham was the father of the Hebrew people, but he was far from perfect. Read the story and you will find him willing to give his wife to Pharaoh in order to save his own skin.

Jacob found favor with God and his name was changed to Israel. That is well because his earlier name meant "conniver" or "supplanter," and he lived up to it, or down to it, as the case may be.

David was a man after God's own heart, and yet David was an adulterous murderer.

Peter was Jesus' closest disciple and most outspoken friend, yet Peter denied him with a curse.

Even St. Paul, as he writes words of encouragement to Timothy and gives God thanks for finding him worthy to serve God, confesses to Timothy that he himself is the chief of sinners (I Timothy 1:15).

My friend, you and I, like the Pharisees and the teachers of the Law and the tax collectors and the sinners who gathered around Jesus are flawed creatures. We have become so adept at rationalizing our basic nature that we may not be conscious of it.

Dr. Menninger wrote a book years ago with the title, Whatever Happened to Sin? That's a good question. We shelved the concept of sin long ago. We minimize our adulteries as petty and meaningless affairs. We compromise our business ethics with the conviction that everyone is doing it. We fill our lives with the cheap and the trivial while the call to take up a cross and follow Jesus goes unheeded and unanswered.

There is a deep flaw within us and that is what the Bible calls sin.

A reporter once asked the great evangelist of an earlier age, Dwight L. Moody, what people gave him the most trouble. Immediately he answered, "I've had more trouble with Dwight L. Moody than any other man alive."

He was speaking for you and me, was he not? We are sinners in need of a Savior.

It is easy, like the Pharisees, to divide the world into saints and sinners, the lost and the found and to conveniently place ourselves among the saintly, those who have been found. But that is not the way the world shapes up. As someone once said, "There is so much good in the worst of us, and so much bad in the best of us, that it hardly becomes any of us to talk about the rest of us." And it's true. We take comfort in the fact that we are baptized believers in Jesus Christ, and we should, but that does not give us license to reject those who may not be as fortunate as we.

In fact, Jesus wants us to care for our brothers and sisters who are lost as much as he cares for them. How much does he care for them?—every bit as much as he cares for us.

There was an article in the 1965 edition of Life magazine about a Lieutenant Dawson who went missing in action when the reconnaissance plane he flew went down in Vietnam. When his brother Donald heard about this, he sold everything he had, left his wife with $20, and went to Vietnam to look for his brother.

He equipped himself with soldier's gear and wandered around the guerilla-controlled jungle looking for his brother. He carried leaflets in Vietnamese picturing the plane and offered a reward for news of the missing pilot. For nine long months, Dawson risked his life looking for his brother in the war-torn jungles of Vietnam, until he obtained proof from the Viet Cong that his brother died in captivity. (3)

The Pharisees and the teachers of the law took great pride in their righteousness. They worked very diligently to keep themselves separate from those who were not as fastidious as they. But this is not what Jesus wants out of his people. He wants us to reach out to the sinner, to embrace those who have wandered into the far country, as if they were our long lost brother or sister, for that is indeed who they are.

A pastor, Dr. John W. Yates, tells of the heart-breaking images which came across our TV screens a few years ago when a terrible tsunami swept across the coast of Asia. Perhaps the most heartbreaking of all were the scenes of mothers and fathers weeping over lost children. Yates writes, "I can't get out of my mind the image of one gentleman who, having lost his parents, his wife, his three children, after nearly three weeks of searching, hope against hope, found his youngest daughter, a little three-year old girl. She had been rescued and sheltered and was safe against all odds. The joy and the uncontrollable sobs of delight and gratitude were caught by a cameraman. It was deeply moving . . ." as you might imagine. (4)

Do you understand that God weeps over His lost children just like those parents who lost their children to the tsunami? Listen again to how Jesus ends each of these parables:

"Suppose one of you has a hundred sheep and loses one of them. Doesn't he leave the ninety-nine in the open country and go after the lost sheep until he finds it? And when he finds it, he joyfully puts it on his shoulders and goes home. Then he calls his friends and neighbors together and says, 'Rejoice with me; I have found my lost sheep.' I tell you that in the same way there will be more rejoicing in heaven over one sinner who repents than over ninety-nine righteous persons who do not need to repent.

"Or suppose a woman has ten silver coins and loses one. Doesn't she light a lamp, sweep the house and search carefully until she finds it? And when she finds it, she calls her friends and neighbors together and says, 'Rejoice with me; I have found my lost coin.' In the same way, I tell you, there is rejoicing in the presence of the angels of God over one sinner who repents."

God weeps over any of His children who are lost. That is why it is important that we should reach out to those who are lost as well. It makes no difference whether people are lost to various addictions or to prostitution or to various betrayals of character or to self-righteousness and pride. We are all sinners and God longs for all of us to come home.

Imagine how the sinners and tax collectors felt as they listened to Jesus tell these stories. Because of their position in society, they were outcasts and estranged from family and "polite" company. Imagine their joy, comfort, and relief in knowing that someone loved and accepted them, that God was eagerly searching them out. No wonder the tax collectors and sinners gathered around to hear Jesus. They knew what it's like to be lost and have no one looking for them. Society told them that they were too unworthy to stand in the presence of the Father. Then here comes Jesus telling them that they are deeply loved and valued, precious in His sight, and that God is eagerly seeking them to bring them back home. It must have sounded too good to be true. Yet that is the Gospel. Jesus came to save the lost. There was a time when we were lost. Now we are those who are called by Christ to reach out to others who are lost and help them find their way back home.

1. Reader's Digest.

2. Lance Webb, How Bad Are Your Sins? (Nashville: Abington Press, 1955).

3. Pastor Robert Barnett, http://faithepchurch.org/files/Documents/Sermons/08-09-09%20Good%20Enough%20for%20God.pdf.

4. Rev. Dr. John W. Yates II, http://www.thefallschurch.org/templates/custhefalls/details.asp?id=29455&PID=233349&Style=.

Work Like The Who?
Luke 16:1-13

Dan Miller in his book No More Dreaded Mondays tells a delightful story about a farmer many years ago in a village in India who had the misfortune of owing a large sum of money to the village moneylender. The old and ugly moneylender fancied the farmer's beautiful daughter, so he proposed a bargain. He would forgive the farmer's debt if he could marry the farmer's daughter.

Both the farmer and his daughter were horrified by the proposal, but the cunning moneylender suggested that they let providence decide the matter. He told them that he would put a black pebble and a white pebble into an empty money bag. The girl would have to reach in and pick one pebble from the bag. If she picked the black pebble, she would become his wife and her father's debt would be forgiven. If she picked the white pebble, she need not marry him and her father's debt would still be forgiven. If she refused to pick a pebble, her father would be thrown into jail until the debt was paid.

They were standing on a pebble-strewn path in the farmer's field. As they talked, the moneylender bent over to pick up two pebbles. The sharp-eyed girl noticed that he had picked up two black pebbles and put them into the bag. He then asked the girl to pick a pebble. Now, imagine that you were the girl standing in the field. What would you have done? If you had to advise her, what would you have told her?

Careful analysis would produce three possibilities: (1) the girl could refuse to take a pebble—but her father would then be thrown in jail. (2) The girl could pick a black pebble and sacrifice herself in order to save her father from debt and imprisonment. Or (3) the girl could pull out both black pebbles in the bag, expose the moneylender as a cheat, and likely incite his immediate revenge.

Here is what the girl did.

She put her hand into the money bag and drew out a pebble. Without looking at it, she fumbled and let it fall onto the pebble-strewn path, where it immediately became lost among all the other pebbles. "Oh, how clumsy of me," she said. "But never mind, if you look into the bag for the one that is left, you will be able to tell which pebble I picked." Since the remaining pebble was black, it would have to be assumed that she had picked the white one. And since the moneylender dared not admit his dishonesty, the girl would have changed what seemed an impossible situation into an extremely advantageous one. (1)

Don't we all love stories where the good guy uses his or her wit and cunning to defeat a villain? It may disturb us when a villain uses that same wit and cunning. And yet Jesus once told his disciples a parable about a dishonest man who did just that.

Remember that a parable is a story that has just one point. Jesus, of course, told many parables, many of them designed to disturb those who heard them. These parables were designed to get people to think outside the box of their upbringing. That's hard for most people to do. It's much easier to view life as you've always been taught.

In this case, Jesus told a parable about a rich man who had a manager who was accused of wasting the rich man's possessions. So he called him in and asked him, "What is this I hear about you? Give an account of your management, because you cannot be manager any longer."

Now this is understandable. The guy has been loose with his boss' money. So the boss has no choice but to give him a pink slip. But, evidently he doesn't fire him at once.

Do you remember when employers routinely gave their employees two weeks' notice before firing them? That day's gone. In today's corporate environment, the employer is more apt to approach an unsuspecting employee about 4:00 p.m. on Friday afternoon and instruct the fired employee to clean out his desk immediately, turn in his company credit card and office keys, and then have security walk the fired employee to the elevator where he would be told never to come back. (2)

Ah, yes, the good old days. Of course, today's employers would argue that there are good reasons for this change in policy—some employees can't be trusted. They could do lasting damage to the company if they were allowed to stay on the job and have access to company assets. And that's exactly what this dishonest manager did.

He says to himself, "What shall I do now? My master is taking away my job. I'm not strong enough to do manual labor, and I'm embarrassed to go on welfare. I know what I'll do. I'll use my remaining time and some of my boss' resources to insure my future."

So he called in two of his boss' customers who still owed his boss money. He asked the first one, "How much do you owe my boss?"

"Nine hundred gallons of olive oil," the man replied.

The dishonest manager told him, "Take your bill, sit down quickly, and make it four hundred and fifty gallons."

"Then he asked the second, "And how much do you owe?"

"A thousand bushels of wheat," he replied.

The dishonest manager told him, "Take your bill and make it eight hundred."

The unscrupulous manager was being dishonest, of course, but he was insuring that he would have some friends who would be indebted to him when he no longer had a job.

Now for the shocker: Jesus concludes this parable by having the manager's boss praise him because he had acted so shrewdly.

That's very troubling to many people. Jesus seems to be giving approval to a shady character. This parable has been troubling to people ever since Jesus told it—a fact that has probably given the Master a chuckle over the centuries. After all, Jesus often seemed to have a twinkle in his eye when he told his stories. He knew they were upsetting.

Theologians have puzzled long over this parable. Preachers have puzzled over it. Some Bible scholars believe that even Luke was embarrassed by it, because he hurriedly supplies some alternative explanations from others of Jesus' teachings to apply to the parable. What do you suppose the Master was trying to do with this parable?

A popular explanation today is that this is chiefly a parable about forgiveness. Jesus was praising the dishonest manager for forgiving his boss' debtors. And this makes some sense. After all, Jesus was all about forgiveness and grace. This parable comes right after the story of the prodigal who came home and was graciously welcomed and forgiven by his father even though he had acted disrespectfully toward his father as well as irresponsibly in squandering his inheritance. Yet the father, much to the chagrin of some of Jesus' listeners, welcomed the boy home unconditionally. Such is the extravagant forgiveness and grace that Christ has made possible for us. That is one interpretation of this parable, and it has its appeal.

A little girl, coming home from her first day at school, asked her mother where the marks on the blackboard went when they were rubbed out. The mother answered that they disappear. "But where do they disappear to?" the little girl questioned.

"They vanish," her mother told her.

"But where do they vanish to?" the child insisted. The mother used all the words she knew to explain but she could not make it clear to the child.

This story, says Donald Grey Barnhouse, illustrates what God has done with our sins. God goes so far as to say that He will remember our sins against us no more. (3)

God's forgiveness is extravagant.

In one of his novels Frederick Buechner depicts a scene in which a man is begging his pastor to declare God's forgiveness to a deeply disturbed woman whose life has recently fallen apart because of adultery.

The pastor says, "Well, she already knows that I have forgiven her."

To which the man replies, "But she doesn't know that God forgives her. That's the only power you have, pastor—to tell her that. Not just that God forgives her for her poor adultery, but that God forgives her for all the faces she can't bear to look at now— all the eyes whose glances she cannot meet. Tell her that God forgives her for being lonely and bored, for not being full of joy with a household full of children. Tell her that her sins are forgiven whether she knows it or not. Tell her that, pastor, because it's what we all need to know more than anything else. Tell her she's forgiven. What else on earth do you think you were ordained for?" (4)

And the message of God's grace does meet our deepest need, and it's one possible explanation of why Jesus would praise the dishonest manager. He forgave his master's debtors.

Another possible explanation is that this is chiefly a parable about money. Dr. Luke seems to interpret the parable in this way, for he attaches some of Jesus' other teachings about money right after this parable.

"I tell you," Jesus says, "use worldly wealth to gain friends for yourselves, so that when it is gone, you will be welcomed into eternal dwellings. Whoever can be trusted with very little can also be trusted with much, and whoever is dishonest with very little will also be dishonest with much. So if you have not been trustworthy in handling worldly wealth, who will trust you with true riches? And if you have not been trustworthy with someone else's property, who will give you property of your own?

"No one can serve two masters. Either you will hate the one and love the other, or you will be devoted to the one and despise the other. You cannot serve both God and money."

This explanation, too, has its appeal. Jesus had more to say more about money than any other topic, particularly in the Gospel of Luke. You've probably noticed that as we have been preaching on the lessons from Luke over the past several weeks. There are more passages in the Gospel of Luke about money than there are about death, marriage or family values. Jesus warned time after time about the dangers of riches. And we know it's true—we cannot serve God and money.

Money may be our number one national obsession. One estimate has it that close to one-half of the nation's divorces are due to differences of opinion on how to handle the family finances. And those couples are comparatively lucky. A sociological study in Chicago found that some 40.2 percent of all desertion cases were rooted in monetary tension between the husband and wife—as were 45 percent of the reported cases of cruelty. (5) So it makes sense that this was one more of Jesus' warnings about the danger of loving money.

However, there is a third alternative that we need to consider: Perhaps Jesus actually was praising the man for doing something about his situation. Notice how Jesus ends this parable. In verse eight we read, "The master commended the dishonest manager because he had acted shrewdly. For the people of this world are more shrewd in dealing with their own kind than are the people of the light."

Jesus was not praising his dishonesty, but his ingenuity and his initiative. That's the plain meaning of this parable. This man took hold of his life and got himself out of a tight situation. He didn't sit around flogging himself saying, "What shall I do? What shall I do?" He didn't spend all his time on his knees praying, "O Lord, please get me out of this." Jesus was praising this man for getting into immediate action.

Jesus had little sympathy for persons who always expected God to do things for them that they were perfectly capable of handling themselves. Jesus said, "For the people of this world are more shrewd in dealing with their own kind than are the people of the light." Those are important words that we ought to study. The people of light are good people, moral people, religious people, but they are also apt to be somewhat reserved people, almost apathetic people. Worldly people are more apt to head where the action is.

Remember to whom Jesus was directing this parable. It was to his disciples. It wasn't to the Pharisees or the multitudes. He was speaking to those closest to him. I think he was saying, "Look, guys, I know you are a nice people, and that's well and good, but I need you to be more than nice. I need for you to get out there and make a difference in the world. You're going to be called trouble-makers, and radicals and every other name in the book. That's all right because you are going to be turning the world on its head."

I believe that is what Jesus is saying to his church even today. O.K., we're nice people. Jesus likes nice people. But what Jesus really appreciates are people who are making a difference.

Are you familiar with the expression, "work like the dickens"? "Dickens" is an archaic way of saying, "the devil." The idea is that the devil is always at work in the world seeking to tempt people and to destroy them. The devil never lets up. What Jesus may have been saying with this colorful little parable is that he needs people who go beyond being nice. He needs people who work like the devil to bring his kingdom into being.

Jesus was not commending this manager for his deceit. He was commending him for his concern about the future and his dedication and energy. The manager was sold out to pursuing a goal, and that's what Christ needs from us. He needs us to be sold out to righteousness and justice and love and peace. He needs us to be sold out to changing the world.

It's a strange little parable. Maybe it is a call to radical forgiveness. Maybe it is one more of Jesus warnings about the corruptive power of money. Or maybe, just maybe, it is a summons to those who follow Jesus to step it up a bit and to sell out for serving him.

1. (New York: Broadway Books, 2008).
2. Dr. Mickey Anders, http://www.lectionary.org/Sermons/Anders/Luke/Luke_16.1-13_Dishonest.htm.
3. Timeless Illustrations for Preaching and Teaching (Peabody, MA: Hendrickson Publishers, Inc., 2004), pp. 218-219.
4. Scott Hoezee, http://calvincrc.calvin.edu/sermons/topics/heidCatechism/ld31MtJn.html.
5. Dan Benson, The Total Man (Wheaton, IL: Living Books, 1982).

You Never Noticed
Luke 16:19-31

"I used to think I was poor," says one comedian. "Then they told me I wasn't poor, I was needy. Then they told me it was self-defeating to think of myself as needy. I was deprived. (Oh, not deprived but rather underprivileged.) Then they told me that underprivileged was overused. I was disadvantaged.

"I still don't have a dime," this comedian concludes, "But I have a great vocabulary." Maybe that comedian was laughing to keep from crying, because whatever you may call it, being poor isn't any fun.

"There was a rich man," said Jesus, "who was dressed in purple and fine linen and lived in luxury every day. At his gate was laid a beggar named Lazarus, covered with sores and longing to eat what fell from the rich man's table. Even the dogs came and licked his sores.

"The time came when the beggar died and the angels carried him to Abraham's side. The rich man also died and was buried. In Hades, where he was in torment, the rich man looked up and saw Abraham far away, with Lazarus by his side. So he called to him, 'Father Abraham, have pity on me and send Lazarus to dip the tip of his finger in water and cool my tongue, because I am in agony in this fire.'

"But Abraham replied, 'Son, remember that in your lifetime you received your good things, while Lazarus received bad things, but now he is comforted here and you are in agony . . .'"

If there ever was a parable of Jesus that should keep us awake at night, it is the story of the rich man and Lazarus. Why? Because, compared to most of the people in the world, we are quite rich. That is why most of us would prefer not to think too much about this parable.

"We're saved by grace, not by works," we rationalize to ourselves, so we skip over this parable and other teachings of Jesus much like it concerning our responsibility to the disadvantaged of our world. Indeed, we are very much like the rich man in our ability to see only those teachings of the Master that we want to see.

Bible teacher William Barclay titles this passage, "The Punishment of the Man Who Never Noticed." That's us. How many of us have ever noticed how often Jesus talked about our responsibilities to the poor and the down-trodden?

"For I was hungry," the Son of Man will say on the Last Day, "and you gave me nothing to eat, I was thirsty and you gave me nothing to drink, I was a stranger and you did not invite me in, I needed clothes and you did not clothe me, I was sick and in prison and you did not look after me.

"They also will answer, 'Lord, when did we see you hungry or thirsty or a stranger or needing clothes or sick or in prison, and did not help you?'

"He will reply, 'Truly I tell you, whatever you did not do for one of the least of these, you did not do for me'" (Matthew 25:42-45).

This passage, too, we might call, "The punishment of the people who never noticed." "Lord, WHEN DID WE SEE YOU hungry or thirsty or a stranger or needing clothes or sick or in prison . . ." And that is the problem. Jesus was there in a person who was hurting and we didn't even notice.

How many of us ever really notice the problems of the poor in our society?

Eleanor Roosevelt, the wife of President Franklin D. Roosevelt, remembered that before they were married, she was working at University Settlement in New York City. Franklin called for her there late one afternoon. She wasn't ready because there was a sick child at the Settlement and she had to see that the child was taken home. Franklin said he would go with her.

They took the child to an area not far away and Franklin went with her up the three flights to the tenement rooms in which the family lived. It was not a pleasant place and Franklin Roosevelt looked around in surprise and horror. It was the first time that he had ever really seen a slum. When he got back to the street he drew a deep breath of fresh air. "My God," he whispered, "I didn't know people lived like that!" (1)

Obviously that experience had an enormous impact on the man who would be our longest serving president. But he's not alone. Most of us are unaware under what miserable conditions many people in our world live.

Pastor Edward F. Markquart tells how some years back he watched a political advertisement for a presidential candidate. The candidate's name was Ross Perot. Remember Perot? He had those big, wide ears that political cartoonists just loved to draw. Markquart notes that on that paid political advertisement, Ross Perot brought out several charts that described economic life in America. One of those charts showed the level of poverty of our nation's children compared to the levels of poverty of children living in European democracies.

"What percentage of the children who lived in European democracies were poor? About five to seven percent. What percentage of American children were poor? About 20% . . . No industrialized democracy was even close to the high number of 20% of American children living in poverty.

"Then Ross Perot said, with his big ears wagging, 'It ain't right, folks.'" (2)

And, pardon my grammar, friends, but Perot was correct: it ain't right. And many of us who follow Jesus close our eyes and refuse to even acknowledge the problem. Like the rich man in Jesus' parable we are the people who refuse to notice.

The rich man in this parable, of course, is not alone, or Jesus would not have told this story. All over the world in every generation, those who have much in terms of the world's goods turn a blind eye to those who have practically nothing. How else could we live with ourselves if we did not?

According to a report released by the World Bank, nearly 2.8 billion people—almost half the population of the planet—still live on the equivalent of two dollars a day or less. Of these, some 1.1 billion survive in extreme or absolute poverty on less than one dollar. Does anybody care? A few do, but it is still amazing to what lengths some people will go to not notice.

Brazil is a country with an even wider gap than the U.S. between the haves and the have-nots. I read recently that in Sao Paulo, Brazil, police have stopped seeking to remove beggars and other unsavory people from their streets. They've decided rather to concentrate on geographical containment of the problem. They're seeking to wall off the poor from the rest of the population. The city's rich have literally risen above it all by using helicopters to bypass poorer areas. There are now 240 helicopter landing pads in Sao Paulo, Brazil compared to just ten in New York City. (3)

Well, I guess that's one way to ignore the problem. That is one way not to notice. Get a helicopter and fly over it all. The rich man in our story would probably have bought himself a helicopter if they had been available back then. He probably settled for a gilded carriage with thick curtains so he would not have to look at Lazarus lying there helplessly at his gate.

Notice that Jesus said in his parable that Lazarus "was laid" at the rich man's gate. He didn't walk there or drive there. He was an invalid who had to be laid there. Lazarus was totally helpless. There were no welfare programs. He obviously had no family to care for him. All he could do was beg, but the rich man couldn't be bothered even to share a few coins. He refused to even acknowledge Lazarus' existence. He was the man who refused to notice.

But, friend, there was one who did notice. God noticed. Luke tells us that the time came when Lazarus died. And what happened then? Jesus tells us, "The angels carried Lazarus to Abraham's side." What a beautiful image. This time it wasn't friends or concerned neighbors who carried Lazarus home at the end of a long day of begging. It was the angels. God knew Lazarus' situation. God cared about Lazarus.

I was tempted to call this parable, "The man who made a name for himself, and the man who did not." That would have made a nice twist on the parable. It would demonstrate how differently we see the world from the way God sees the world. For you see, in Jesus' story it is Lazarus who made a name for himself. It is the rich man who is anonymous. The rich man is sometimes called Dives. Dives simply means "rich man." We know Lazarus' name, but not the name of the man who ignored him.

Jesus identified Lazarus; Lazarus was named. That is significant. When giving a parable, Jesus never named a character—not even once. The rich man was nameless, but Lazarus was named. The difference is ever so big. It is the difference between being known and honored by God and not being known or honored by God. Lazarus knew God and was known by God. His very name, Lazarus, means God is my Help or Helper.

"By naming Lazarus and not the rich man, Jesus' story completely contrasts with worldly understandings of who's who," writes Sarah K. Bunge. "As was his style, Jesus reminds us that heaven is the opposite of this world in many respects, especially when it comes to rating an individual's worth in society."

Ms. Bunge asked her high-schoolers to name some rich people in our society. "Bill Gates, Donald Trump, the Middle Eastern oil guys, and Oprah" were some of the names they listed. Then she asked them for names of the people in their town who beg, or are homeless. The students made vague references to "that one guy who sleeps behind [a local store]" and "that crazy lady always asking for change when I come out of McDonalds."

Bunge writes, "We all understood what Jesus was saying: God cares about everybody, even and especially those that society would rather not notice and definitely not name." (4) God noticed Lazarus and cared about him.

God also noticed the actions of the rich man who refused to notice the poor man at his gate. Luke tells us, "The rich man also died and was buried. In Hades, where he was in torment, the rich man looked up and saw Abraham far away, with Lazarus by his side. So he called to him, 'Father Abraham, have pity on me and send Lazarus to dip the tip of his finger in water and cool my tongue, because I am in agony in this fire.'

"But Abraham replied, 'Son, remember that in your lifetime you received your good things, while Lazarus received bad things, but now he is comforted here and you are in agony . . .'"

Why do you suppose the rich man was in Hades? It was because God noticed him as well. But why did God deal with him so harshly? There is no record of a vicious, glaring sin; no record of a vulgar, public sin. He was not cruel, as far as we know. He never ordered Lazarus from his gate or refused Lazarus the crumbs from his table. He was not a tyrant; not an oppressor of the poor, not a monstrous member of society. Rather, he may well have been a socially responsible, upright citizen, respected and well liked. No earthly court would ever think of arresting or condemning him. In society's eyes he was honored and highly esteemed. People liked him and spoke well of him. What then was his sin? It was the sin of not noticing.

How often do you and I take time to notice the people around us—their needs, their concerns? Not just the homeless people asking for handouts on a city street, but the lonely teenager who lives down the street or the young mother trying to keep her family together after her husband has abandoned her. How often do we notice the elderly person whom no one visits; the jobless guy who is being left behind by a culture that no longer values his talents? How often do we notice the person sitting just a short distance from us in the congregation who has just received a devastating report from a doctor? Do we even notice what other people around us are going through?

It is a sin that afflicts all of us to one degree or another, and yet we rarely talk about it. It is the sin of self-absorption. It is the sin of being so preoccupied with our own cares and concerns that we give no thought to the problems of those about us.

Professor Robert Wuthnow once conducted some research about why some people are generous and compassionate, while others are not. He found out that many compassionate people at some point in their lives had someone act with compassion toward them. This experience of having someone show compassion toward them had transformed their lives.

For example, Wuthnow tells the story of Jack Casey. "All I ever learned from my father is I didn't want to be like him," Jack Casey once said. He was raised in a tough home. His father was an alcoholic. But something happened to Jack when he was a child that changed his life. Jack needed to have surgery and was terrified. But there was a nurse who remained by his side, holding his hand, reassuring him that everything would be okay. "I'll be right here, no matter what," she told him. And she kept her word; she was there and greeted him with a smile the moment he opened his eyes.

Years later, Jack became a paramedic and he was called to the scene of an accident. A man was pinned upside down in his pickup. Jack did his best to free the trapped man even as gasoline dripped down on them. The man was afraid that he was going to die as the rescuers worked to free him. One spark and the whole scene would go up in flames.

Jack remembered back to that time when he was a child and the nurse who never left. He took the man's hands and squeezed them as he said, "Don't worry! I'm right here with you! I'm not going anywhere!"

Days after the rescue, the two men embraced as the driver said to Jack, "You know, you were crazy to stay there with me. We both could've died."

Jack smiled. "I just couldn't leave you," Jack said. (5)

Here is the point of today's message. There was a time, spiritually, when each of us was a beggar lying at the gate totally helpless, and Christ noticed us and Christ loved us just as we are. As we remember that truth, that compassion, that grace, Christ calls us to look around and see someone who needs our attention, our compassion, our love. And what the research shows is that this person might just remember our generous attention when he or she is in the position to help someone else. And so that original act of kindness and love is extended perhaps forever. But you can't be part of this chain of love if you never take time to look beyond you own cares and concerns. Don't be like the rich man who will forever be remembered as the person who refused to notice. Look around you today, to someone who needs your love.

1. Leonard & Thelma Spinrad, Speaker's Lifetime Library (Paramus, NJ: Revised & Expanded, 1997), p. 228.
2. http://www.sermonsfromseattle.com/series_c_money_and_wise_investments_for_the_future.htm.
3. Richard Watson, Future Files: A Brief History of the Next 50 Years (Boston: Nicholas Breasley Publishing, 2010).
4. http://www.thefreelibrary.com/Proper+21%3A+September+26,+2004.-a0120526513.
5. The Rev. Dr. Thomas G. Long, http://day1.org/1051-meeting_the_good_samaritan.

Series: Dynamic Faith for a Dying World
A Faith To Move Mountains

Luke 17:5-10

(Dynamic Faith for a Dying World, #1)

A man named Adrian Plass authored what he calls his Sacred Diary. In it, he tells how he once bought a book on faith that told him that real Christians should be able to move mountains by faith. So he decided to try it. He practiced with a paper clip. He put it on his desk and willed it to move. Nothing happened. He tried commanding it in a loud voice. Still nothing happened.

He tried it again the next day. The paper clip still wouldn't budge. He even promised God he would change his life if the clip would move just a little. Still nothing.

A few days later he got up early in the morning to have one last go at that paper clip. He concentrated as hard as he could and ended up hissing loudly at the paper clip, but nothing worked. He was a failure. How would he ever move a mountain with his faith if he couldn't move a mere paper clip?

Finally giving up, he opened the door of his study to find his wife and son outside listening in their night-clothes, looking quite distressed. His wife said, "Darling, why didn't you tell that paper clip you'd straighten it out for evermore if it didn't get its act together?" (1)

People are amazing, aren't they? Someone needs to explain to this dear brother the difference between faith and telekinesis. Telekinesis is the alleged ability to move and bend objects with your mind. In days past it was a favorite tool of would-be psychics and mediums. Examined closely, it was revealed to be nothing more than a magic trick.

There seems to be no such thing as telekinesis, in case any of you want to try it for yourself when you get home. By the way, you can go on the Internet and find sites that will supposedly teach you how to perform telekinesis. It works to one extent. Magically they will remove money from your wallet. There is a difference between telekinesis and faith.

Where did this idea come from that if you have enough faith, you can move mountains? It comes, of course, from a teaching of Jesus. We find it just after the strange little story of Jesus cursing the fig tree.

Matthew tells us that it was early in the morning. Jesus was on his way back to the city and he was hungry. There was no fast food place where he could run through a drive-through. Seeing a fig tree by the road, he went up to it but he found nothing on it except leaves. Then he said to it, "May you never bear fruit again!" Immediately the tree withered.

When the disciples saw this, they were amazed. "How did the fig tree wither so quickly?" they asked.

Jesus replied, "Truly I tell you, if you have faith and do not doubt, not only can you do what was done to the fig tree, but also you can say to this mountain, 'Go, throw yourself into the sea,' and it will be done" (Matthew 21: 19-21).

Hey, why settle for moving a paper clip when you can move a mountain? That, of course, was Jesus' metaphorical way of saying that with faith you can do amazing things. The disciples saw Jesus do amazing things. Now he was instructing them in the things he needed them to do after he was gone. This worried the disciples. How could they possibly do any of the things that he was telling him to do? Maybe he had faith to move mountains, but certainly they did not. They were still spiritual infants. Metaphorically, they couldn't move a paper clip much less a mountain.

And so in Luke's gospel we read that the apostles came to the Master and said, "Increase our faith!" It sounds to me almost like a desperate plea. "Hey, Lord. You're asking us to love people we would normally hate. You're asking us to forgive people who have hurt us time and time again. You're asking us to feed the hungry and to work for justice in the world. Master, we're not you. How can we move the mountains all around us when we haven't got a thimble full of faith among us all?

Jesus replied, "If you have faith as small as a mustard seed, you can say to this mulberry tree, 'Be uprooted and planted in the sea,' and it will obey you."

What did Jesus mean by "faith as small as a mustard seed?" The mustard seed was known for its small size, yet it grew to be one of the largest bushes. Picture a mustard seed lying in your hand. It is very small. Yet imagine the potential for growth. Faith is like that, said Jesus.

I recently read a story about Olga Deane, a famous Australian entertainer, socialite and show business personality. Her scrapbooks are in the Australian National Museum as a significant part of that country's show business history.

Olga Deane was known as "The Mustard Seed Lady." Throughout the last 30 years of her life she was so transformed by faith in Jesus Christ that she made it a habit to write cards to prominent public persons in Australian society, and she would tape a mustard seed to each card! She wrote to those people whenever they were facing problems or difficulties with these words of promise from the Master: "If you have faith as small as a mustard seed . . ." (2)

What is this faith that has so much power?

Someone has defined faith as believing the dentist when he says it isn't going to hurt. Well, yes, but the faith that Jesus was describing is so much more than that.

J. G. Stipe once said that, "Faith is like a toothbrush. Every man should have one and use it regularly, but he shouldn't try to use someone else's." Well, that's kind of a yucky analogy, but there is truth there as well.

But really what is faith? Is it an attitude? Is it the same thing as positive thinking?

Attitude is important. Our attitudes can change our perception of reality and they can help us deal with reality in a more effective way. By changing our attitude, we can change our level of confidence, which can help steady us when we're facing a difficult assignment.

Coaches understand that. The story's told about much-beloved basketball coach Jim Valvano who was seeking to lead his North Carolina State team to the 1983 championship of the ACC. Freshman Lorenzo Charles was going to the free throw line in the closing seconds. Valvano called time out. "After Lo hits these two free throws," Valvano said to his team, "I want us to guard the inbound pass . . ."

The team broke from the huddle and walked toward the free-throw lane. At the last second, Coach Valvano is rumored to have pulled point guard Sidney Lowe aside and whispered, "If Lo misses these two shots . . ." and he proceeded to tell him what to do in that case.

It is clear that Valvano did not want to plant the idea in Lorenzo Charles' mind that he might miss—even though Charles was only a 67% shooter. He knew the freshman needed a shot of confidence. And so he said, "After Lo hits these two free throws . . ."

Well, Charles' first attempt missed the rim—it wasn't even close. But his second shot fell through the net. N. C. State won the game and went on to win the national championship. (3)

Maybe his coach's positive affirmation helped Lorenzo Charles at that critical moment. Who knows? Studies have shown that attitudes are powerful. Attitudes can be life-changing—even when they are misguided.

There is an old story about a man who walked with a cane. One time some of his mischievous friends snuck his cane away from him and cut about 1/4" off of it. When he didn't seem to notice, they kept doing it—1/4" off of it each day. They kept doing this for a month or so. One day they saw him and they noticed he was real restless. He finally got up the courage to say, "You guys may think I am crazy, but I think I am getting taller!"

Well, he wasn't getting taller. His cane was simply getting shorter. His perception had been changed, but not his reality. Jesus was talking about something much more powerful than a changed attitude . . . Though having a changed attitude is an important part of authentic faith.

Pastor Lee Barstow tells a wonderful story about a man who was driving home from work one day. He came upon the crest of a hill and beheld the most beautiful sunset he'd ever seen. He was so moved by the sight that he pulled over and got out of his car to better take it in.

A couple of minutes later, another driver was also captivated by the beauty of the sunset, and he too stopped his car to sit and drink in the beauty. Emerging from his car he remarked to the first man that the sight was amazing.

The first man agreed and they sat there for a few minutes in rapturous wonder.

"This is happening because the sun is low," said the second man, "and so the light has to make its way through more atmosphere. As it does, it refracts into colors, kind of like a rainbow."

The first man was annoyed by the second man's explanation. "Actually," he said, "It's not really refraction. The water droplets in the air act like prisms, and this is what causes the colors."

"But I read about this last year in National Geographic," said the second man, "and it called it refraction. The article said the atmosphere acts like a colored filter covering a stage light in a theater."

The two went on like this for some time. By the time they looked up again, the glory of the sunset had passed.

How different that story would have been, says Pastor Barstow, if the two had avoided talking about the external facts about rainbows and had instead focused on their own internal experience. Imagine the second man saying, "Boy, I really needed this. I had an awful day at work, and this is reminding me there is more to life than that argument I had with my co-worker just before I left."

"Yeah," says the first man, "I was not looking forward to going home, and the sunset made me think of an amazing sunset my wife and I saw during our honeymoon. Now I'm looking forward to telling her about it." They could have then turned to watch the sunset slowly fade, and leave each other with fond goodbyes. (4)

In Pastor Barstow's two scenarios we have the same sunset, but in the first one it leads to a mild argument. In the second, it leads to some positive feelings and perhaps some positive changes in life situations. Positive attitudes are important.

But what is it that makes positive attitudes sustainable? Positive attitudes ultimately are the result of a confidence about life that comes from one source— being grounded in faith that the universe is friendly, because behind this universe there is a loving God.

In the book 450 Stories for Life, Gust Anderson tells about visiting a church in a farming community of eastern Alberta, Canada, where there had been 8 years of drought. The farmers were deep in debt, and their economic situation looked hopeless. In spite of their poverty, however, many of them continued to meet together to worship and praise God.

Anderson was especially impressed by the testimony of one of these farmers. Dressed in overalls and an old coat—the best clothes he had—this man stood up and quoted Habakkuk 3:17-18. With deep meaning he recited the words from the Hebrew Bible: "Although the fig tree shall not blossom, neither shall fruit be in the vines; the labor of the olive shall fail, and the fields shall yield no food; the flock shall be cut off from the fold, and there shall be no herd in the stalls; yet I will rejoice in the Lord, I will joy in the God of my salvation."

That dear saint, thought Anderson, has found the secret of real joy! (5)

Joy comes from more than a positive attitude. Can a positive attitude be sustained through endless years of poor crops? I doubt it. Sooner or later we will, as we say, have to face reality. But faith in a loving God is reality. If we are grounded in the knowledge that, regardless of our circumstances, God will not forget us or forsake us, we can endure any hardship, overcome any obstacle. And should we feel called by God to turn the world upside down, then we will discover what real faith and real power is.

Martin Luther King, Jr., a man who did turn this world upside down, understood that. In his last address before his death he issued this triumphant statement of faith, "And I've seen the Promised Land. And I may not get there with you. But I want you to know tonight that we as a people will get to the Promised Land. So I'm happy tonight. I'm not worried about anything. I'm not fearing any man. Mine eyes have seen the glory of the coming of the Lord. I have a dream this afternoon that the brotherhood of man will become a reality. With this faith I will go out and carve a tunnel of hope from a mountain of despair. . . .With this faith, we will be able to achieve this new day, when all of God's children—black men and white men, Jews and Gentiles, Protestants and Catholics—will be able to join hands and sing with the Negroes in the spiritual of old, 'Free at last! Free at least! . . . Thank God almighty we are free at last.'"

Some of you who remember the days of segregation in this country know what an enormous mountain that was. Dr. King and the other civil rights workers did not think that mountain out of existence, someone has said, they prayed it out of existence. It was their faith in God not their faith in themselves that proved triumphant.

Jesus wanted his disciples to understand that faith is a powerful force. The disciples, though, felt their faith was too weak to ever accomplish all the things Jesus was asking them to accomplish. Jesus assured them they did have enough faith—they simply needed to exercise their faith and trust God. What really mattered was not the size of their faith, but the size of their God. A little faith in a great God will change the world.

Faith is a matter of aligning our lives with the purposes of God in the same way that a free-hanging bar magnet will align itself with the magnetic pulls of the

North and South Poles. What kind of world does God want? Deep in your heart you know—a world where everyone lives in peace and harmony and dignity together. And that is the kind of world we will one day have. It is inevitable. God's kingdom is coming—the kingdom of justice and righteousness, the kingdom of peace and love. If you want to see mountains moved, or mulberry trees thrown into the sea, align yourself with the purposes of God. Again, it has nothing to do with the size of our faith, but the size of our God.

The apostles said to the Lord, "Increase our faith!"

Jesus replied, "If you have faith as small as a mustard seed, you can say to this mulberry tree, 'Be uprooted and planted in the sea,' and it will obey you."

How about it, my friend? Could you have just a little bit of faith in the God of Jesus? If so, then get ready for miracles. Mountains, mulberry trees, even paper clips if that is what God desires, will one day be moved.

1. Derek Frank, http://www.ebcg.ch/sermons/070826.htm.
2. Gordon Moyes,
http://www.gordonmoyes.com/sermon_archive/ministry/tra/2003/030504.html.
3. Eddie Jones, My Father's Business: 30 Inspirational Stories for Finding God's Will For Your Life (Kindle edition 2012).
4. http://www3.amherst.edu/~bcbarstow/blog/Sermon2009-09-27.pdf.
5. Illusaurus.

The Healing Power Of Faith
Luke 17:11-19
(Dynamic Faith for a Dying World, #2)

There is an old, old story about a traveling evangelist who also advertised himself as a faith healer. In one of his crusade services he jumped on the platform and said, "I have faith that two people will be healed tonight. Where are you?" he asked. "Who would like to be healed?"

A man ran down the aisle, named Harry. Asked what his ailment was, Harry said he had a lisp. He explained sadly, "I can't talk wite." He was instructed to go behind a curtain.

Another man hobbled down on crutches. His name was Frank. He said, "I haven't walked in 20 years without crutches."

He was told to go behind the curtain with Harry. Then the healer said "Frank, you've been healed. Slide those crutches out under the curtain one at a time." Slowly the crutches appeared under the curtain, and the crowd went crazy. The healer held up the crutches and broke them over his knee. Everyone cheered!

Then dramatically he declared that Harry was healed of his speech impediment too. The evangelist said: "Harry, the next sentence you speak will be the first you've ever said normally." Then he said, "Usher, take him a microphone." After he was certain Harry had the microphone the evangelist asked, "What would you like to say, Harry?"

There was a moment of silence. Then, from behind the curtain came these words, "Fwank fell down!"

I don't know how you feel about faith healing. I suspect that as a business, a very profitable business, God despises it. Showy crusades and shallow evangelists have brought a deep stain on the authentic work of Christ in the world. Yet healing is very much a part of the story of the church. Long before there were MRIs and the miracles of modern medicine, there were humble pastors as well as devoted lay people bowing their heads in prayer asking God to bring healing to someone who was afflicted with illness and broken with pain. Sometimes they watched as healing would come. Not every time, of course, but often enough so that the tradition has continued from the early days of our faith until the twenty-first century.

Our lesson for today from Luke's gospel is a case of the healing power of faith.

Jesus was on his way to Jerusalem. He was traveling along the border between Samaria and Galilee. As he was going into a village, ten men who had leprosy met him. They stood at a distance and called out in a loud voice, "Jesus, Master, have pity on us!"

Notice how desperate these men were. Leprosy was the most terrible disease of Jesus' day; it was greatly feared. It was disfiguring and sometimes fatal. People in Bible times associated leprosy with sin. Surely the person thus afflicted, or perhaps his parents, had done something terrible to deserve acquiring such a dread affliction.

The leper himself was considered utterly unclean—physically and spiritually. He could not approach within six feet of any person including his own family members. We read in Leviticus 13:4 : "His clothes shall be rent, and his head bare, and he shall put a covering upon his upper lip, and shall cry, 'Unclean, unclean.'"

The person with leprosy was judged by society to be dead—the living dead, sort of like today's fascination with zombies. However, the person with leprosy was alive. Nevertheless he had to wear a black garment so he could be recognized as from among the dead.

He was banished as an outcast, totally ostracized from society—earthly and heavenly. Again from Leviticus, "All the days wherein the plague shall be in him he shall be defiled; he is unclean; he shall dwell alone; without the camp shall his habitation be" (13:46). He could not live within the walls of any city; his dwelling had to be outside the city gates.

He was thought to be polluted, incurable by any human means whatsoever. Leprosy was thought to be curable only by God. One reason people believed in Jesus as the Messiah was that he healed people with leprosy.

Imagine the anguish and heartbreak of these people with leprosy, completely cut off from family and friends and society. Imagine the emotional and mental pain. Ten men with leprosy met Jesus as he was entering the city, coming in from a long journey. The lepers had no idea where Jesus was going. He could have been heading for an important meeting, or he could have been tired and exhausted, or he could have had no time for interruptions; but the lepers didn't care. They were so desperate they would interrupt him no matter what.

They stood at a distance as the law demanded and called out in a loud voice, "Jesus, Master, have pity on us!"

Have you ever been that desperate for Christ's healing touch, either for yourself or for someone you love? Some of you have. This can be a cruel world.

Good people can be afflicted in terrible ways. The pain is not always physical. Sometimes it is mental or emotional pain.

Did you know that suicide takes the lives of nearly 30,000 Americans every year? Between 1952 and 1995, suicide in young adults nearly tripled in this land. Over half of all suicides occur in adult men, ages 25-65. Would you say these men and women who take their own lives are in pain? Yes they are, but most of them probably are not in physical pain.

Emotional pain can be more devastating than physical pain. We can reach the level of desperation that these men with leprosy reached from a variety of causes. I know parents who are desperate over their inability to reach a son or daughter with an alcohol or drug problem. I know couples who are desperate to heal their marriage.

When we talk about healing faith, this faith covers a multitude of situations. A multitude of people in this community, in this city, around this world are crying out like these ten men with leprosy, "Jesus, Master, have pity on us!"

Notice, in the second place, that Jesus healed the ten men.

Jesus did more than have pity. When he saw them, he said, "Go, show yourselves to the priests." And as they went, they were healed. They were cleansed of their leprosy. This is a word of hope for us in our seasons of desperation. Christ hears our pleas as well as theirs. Christ is available to us as well as to them. And Christ still heals.

There was a woman who was in despair in the final stages of a terminal illness. A kind visitor from the church would come to see her from time to time.

One day, the ill woman stood in front of her living room window and said, "It feels like God is completely shut out from my life." And, in symbolic nature, she slammed the curtains closed.

Her friend kindly responded, "Just because you closed the curtains, doesn't mean that the sun isn't still shining." Just because we do not experience God's presence does not mean God has forgotten us.

Peter Marshall, whose dynamic preaching attracted crowds of people in the 1940s and whose life was chronicled by his wife Catherine in the best-selling book A Man Called Peter, died suddenly of a heart attack on the morning of January 25, 1949, at the age of 46. In one of his sermons he had said: "When the clock strikes for me, I shall go, not one minute early, and not one minute late. Until then, there is nothing to fear. I know that the promises of God are true, for they have been fulfilled in my life time and time again. Jesus still teaches and guides and protects and heals and comforts, and still wins our complete trust and our love." (1)

Peter Marshall was right. It doesn't matter whether you die at 46 or 106, the promises of God are sure. God knows our needs and heals us according to those needs.

Healing faith is the conviction that even though our circumstances are dire, there is a loving God who watches over us—and if we will trust Him, healing will come. It may not come as quickly as we would desire. It may not even come in the way we desire, but if we are steadfast we will see the salvation of our God.

This is a statement of mature faith. How many times have you looked back over your life and realized that situations you thought were hopeless were not hopeless at all? Even though you could not see a solution at the time, life worked out and you realize now that God used that supposedly hopeless situation in a wonderful way to make you what you are today. With the help of God, your mess became a masterpiece. Your burden became a blessing. You thought you were at the end of your rope, but you were only at the beginning of a new reality.

Dr. Steve Stephens tells about the writer Karen Blixen. Blixen, he says, had three loves in her life. Yet each left deep wounds. Her father committed suicide when she was ten. Her husband was continuously unfaithful and gave her syphilis, which had no treatment at the time. After eleven years in an unhappy marriage, they divorced. Then she fell in love with a man who was gay. For thirteen years he was her best friend, yet unable to return her love. When she was forty-six, he was killed in an airplane crash.

In spite of these tragedies, Karen kept a hopeful attitude. She wrote many books under her pen name, Isak Dinesen—books such as Out of Africa and Winter Tales. In reflecting on her life she wrote, "I think these difficult times have helped me to understand better than before how infinitely rich and beautiful life is in every way." (2)

Some of you can give the same testimony. You've experienced the pain, the despair, the heartbreak that life can sometimes throw at us. But you've kept your faith intact and you've grown emotionally and spiritually. God has given you a victory. God has given you healing. It did not happen overnight. It may not have happened in a way that you would have prescribed. But today you testify to the goodness of God.

The key is to hold on to God's promises. Jesus instructed the men with leprosy to show themselves to the priests. This was to witness to their healing. But it was also key to their healing. They were cleansed as they obeyed Christ's command. Christ tells us to trust him, to continue living a life of faith. By doing so we, too, will experience his healing power at work.

Dr. Joe Harding once told about astronaut Alan Shepard who in 1961 became the first American, to travel into space. It was Shepard who was asked by reporters what he thought about as he sat atop the Redstone rocket, waiting for liftoff. He answered with a quip that has become immortal. He said he thought about the fact that every part of the rocket on which he sat was built by the lowest bidder.

Later he said that on that first space flight—as the Redstone rocket began to gather speed—it began to vibrate more and more. It was as if the whole rocket would come apart. Shepard knew what was happening. He had been a test pilot. He knew that just before you break through the sound barrier the air resistance is tremendous, almost like hitting a wall. When Shepard reached that point in the flight his body was shaking all over. He couldn't read the instruments. He started to report what was happening to mission control, but then he realized that, if he did, "Someone would panic and abort the mission." So he held on. Within 30 seconds all the vibrations were gone, and he knew he was going supersonic. No longer any noise. No longer any sense of motion. He was flying in space.

"When we experience a little turbulence," wrote Dr. Joe Harding, "we are tempted to abort the mission too soon. Hang on . . . You may never walk upon the moon, but you will walk more confidently and gladly upon the earth."

And that's true. That is what true faith healing is all about. It is not about a circus tent with sawdust on the floor and a carnival-like atmosphere where pitiable people are called upon to come on stage to experience a mystical experience. Healing faith is about holding on and trusting God and waiting for God's salvation.

And one thing more: It is about developing a sense of gratitude along the way. You know how this story ends.

One of the ten men whom Jesus healed of this terrible disease, when he saw he was healed, came back to where Jesus was, threw himself at Jesus' feet and thanked him. Luke notes that this grateful man was a Samaritan.

Jesus asked, "Were not all ten cleansed? Where are the other nine? Has no one returned to give praise to God except this foreigner?"

Note the word "foreigner." The man who had the most reason to feel rejected was the most thankful. The man was a Samaritan, or in Jesus' description, a foreigner. "Foreigner" comes from a Greek word that means he was not only a foreigner within the bounds of a country to which he did not belong, but he was also, in the eyes of the Jews, a foreigner "from the covenants of promise, having no hope, and without God in the world" (Ephesians 2:12). Perhaps this is why he was the only one of the ten who returned. His was the greater gratitude. He had felt his need more keenly and deeply than the rest. He knew he needed to be saved, genuinely saved—spiritually as well as physically. Despite the fact that he had never known the real promises of God and that he had been without God in this world, he now knew God, and it was more than his heart could contain. He broke forth in joy to give glory to God. Jesus had saved him from so much.

It is then Jesus says to him, "Rise and go; your faith has made you well." Notice those words: "your faith has made you well." Here is what healing faith is all about. The words "your faith has made you well" means literally, "your faith has saved you." In other words, Jesus was pronouncing that the man was not only physically healed but emotionally and spiritually healed as well. This is the meaning of salvation. It means being made whole in every respect.

Ten desperate men with the most dreaded disease of that day. One was more desperate than the others, for he was a foreigner. All were healed physically. Perhaps they all were spiritually healed as well. We only know for certain that one was spiritually well, the one who came back to Jesus to say thanks.

How about you this day? Do you have need for healing—healing for your body, healing for your marriage, healing for your emotions? A good place to begin is to thank Jesus for the good things he's placed in your life already. And to go forth from this place holding onto his promise that he will never forsake you. And eventually, I don't know when, I don't know where, I don't know under what circumstances, but eventually, if you walk with God and trust Him, someday you will be made whole.

1. Landon Winstead, Redefining Success.
2. The Wounded Warrior (Sisters, OR: Multnomah Publishers, Inc., 2006), p. 96.

A Faith That Does Not Quit

Luke 18:1-8

(Dynamic Faith for a Dying World, #3)

On August 3, 1970, sixty-two-year-old Miriam Hargrave of Yorkshire, England, finally passed her driving test. It was her fortieth attempt. After so much struggle and perseverance, one would assume she started driving right away. But unfortunately, after spending so much money on driving lessons—$720—she couldn't afford to buy a car. (1)

Maybe it's just as well. How comfortable would you be knowing that the driver coming at you had failed the driving test forty times?

Another Brit, the Rev. David Guest required 632 lessons over a period of 17 years before he passed his driving test. "When I was told I passed I bent down on my knees and thanked God," he said after passing the test. The 33-year-old cleric spent $11,000 on lessons, wore out eight instructors and crashed five cars before that momentous accomplishment. The secret to his turnaround; he finally switched to a car with an automatic transmission. His problems stemmed from an inability to distinguish between the clutch and the brake while driving a car with a standard transmission. (2)

We admire people who refuse to give up, who refuse to cut their losses even when they are pursuing such mundane tasks as passing a driver's test.

Of course, there are some people we wish would give up. I was reading about a woman in Doylestown, PA, who didn't want to buy any magazines but couldn't get a magazine salesman to leave. Finally she agreed to give him $1 for every 10 push-ups he could do on her doorstep. He did 200 and she gave him $20. (3)

Well, he did make a sale. Maybe not for any magazines, but at least his return on 200 pushups was all profit.

Writer Ted Loder tells a story about a salesman named Barry, who was having a bad day. It was noon. He was in his favorite diner where he was forced, by the overcrowded noon crowd, into sharing his table with a very large woman who was wearing a loud print dress and green gloves which went to her elbows. After some initial superficial conversation Barry asked Angela, the lady at his table, her profession.

"I'm a messenger," said Angela proudly.

"A messenger? From whom?" asked Barry out of curiosity.

"From Her." replied Angela.

Barry wanted to know, "Her who?"

"You know," said Angela, "Her . . . God."

After a lot more disbelieving questioning on Barry's part he finally said to

Angela: "OK . . . suppose you are a messenger from . . . uh . . . Her . . . then what's the message?"

"The Message," says Angela without batting an eye, "is: 'Hang in there!'" (4)

Maybe that's the message from God you need to hear this day, whether God is a Him or a Her. I don't know what you're going through right now in your life. I don't know what dreads or dreams you are currently nurturing. I don't know what frustrations, failures or fears. But oftentimes God's simple message to us is simply "Hang in there. Don't give up. Keep going. You're going to make it."

Often the secret to successful living is, "Don't give up."

Jesus told a story once about an unjust judge. This judge, said Jesus, had no fear of God and cared even less about what other people might think of him. He took bribes and gave favors to persons who held position and authority. He didn't worry about conscience or law, about morality or justice. He was out to fill his pockets and to gain honor and recognition from those who held position, power, and wealth.

But there was widow who needed his help. She was poor. She had no money to bribe him even if that were her inclination. She was a widow, a woman all alone in a man's world. She had no man and no money to secure legal counsel to plead her case. She held no position or authority, none of the necessary clout to commend her to the judge. But she was being persecuted, being taken advantage of and abused by an unknown adversary.

Still, she let none of this stop her. Time and time again she kept coming to the judge with her plea, "Grant me justice against my adversary."

At first the judge responded with silence. He didn't make a move to help her. His heart was hard and harsh; he had no interest in helping anyone who would not benefit his career or fill his pockets.

But the poor widow kept on coming and coming, pleading and pleading. She would not let the judge rest. And notice what happened. The judge did not fear God, did not regard man's opinions, yet he finally gave in to the widow and gave her the justice she was seeking.

Why? Because she would not give up. He could not get rid of her. She would not accept silence or take no for an answer. She kept coming and coming.

The judge finally said, "Even though I don't fear God or care what people think, yet because this widow keeps bothering me, I will see that she gets justice, so that she won't eventually come and attack me!"

Some versions of the scripture translate the words, "so she won't eventually come and attack me" as "so she won't wear me out." But the words of the NIV are closer to the original which literally means, "unless she gives me a black eye."

Imagine that—a judge, a man of power in the community, but he was finally cowered by this poor widow.

This widow was persistent. She refused to let this corrupt judge go! It's one of those quirky little parables that Jesus loved to tell. But he adds a very serious moral to it: "And will not God bring about justice for his chosen ones, who cry out to him day and night? Will he keep putting them off? I tell you, he will see that they get justice, and quickly."

These words were designed for people who were suffering unjustly for their faith. "Hang in there," he was saying to them. "God hears your prayers. Hang in there and trust Him and you will not be disappointed."

We talked about this last week—how important it is to keep trusting God, no matter what your situation. This is a major part of the meaning of faith.

Having faith is more than simply saying, "I believe in God." Faith is trusting God whatever your circumstance.

Pastor Tony Evans tells an amusing story about a businessman who had to travel to a small town for a meeting. He invited his wife to accompany him. She was excited about the trip . . . until she learned her husband was going to be flown to the town in a small twin-engine Cessna plane.

"Honey, I've decided not to go," she said to him unexpectedly.

"What!" he exclaimed in disbelief. "Why not?"

She declared with some firmness, "I am not going on a little-bitty, twin-engine Cessna."

Her husband smiled and knowingly said, "Honey, your faith is too small."

She replied, "No, the plane is too small."

The businessman really wanted his wife to go with him, so he canceled the Cessna and booked travel on a major airline. His wife went with him because, as she put it, "her faith grew because the size of the plane grew." (5)

Some of you can relate to her concern. It's difficult to feel secure in a plane that seems too small. Even more defeating, however, is the belief that your God is too small to look after you.

J. B. Phillips once wrote a book with the title, Your God is Too Small. And he was right on target. Many people have a God who is simply too small.

Jeannette Strong learned that lesson when her son was a toddler. She says that washing her son's hair was always a problem. The little boy would sit in the bathtub while she put shampoo on the boy's hair. Then, when she poured on the water to make a lather, the little fellow would tip his head down so that the shampoo ran into his eyes, causing pain and tears.

She tried to explain to her son that if he just looked straight up at her, he could avoid getting the shampoo in his face. He would agree; then, as soon as she started to rinse his hair, the boy's fear would overcome his trust, and he would look down again. Naturally, the shampoo would run down his face again, and there would be more tears.

During one of their sessions, while she was trying to convince her son to lift up his head and trust her, she suddenly realized how this situation was like her own relationship to God. She knows that God is her Father. She is sure God loves her. She believes she does trust God. But sometimes, in a difficult situation, she confesses, she panics and turns her eyes away from God. This never solves the problem, she says. She just becomes more afraid, as the "shampoo" blinds her.

Jeannette Strong concluded, "Even though my son knew I loved him, he had a hard time trusting me in a panicky situation. I knew I could protect him, but convincing him of that wasn't easy, especially when all he could see was water coming down. His lack of trust hurt me, but it hurt him more. He was the one who had to suffer the pain.

"I'm sure my lack of trust hurts God very much, but how much more does it hurt me? Often in the Bible, we are told to lift up our head to God when problems come. He knows how to protect us if we remember to listen to Him. Now, when I find myself in a situation where it would be easy to panic, I picture my son sitting in the bathtub, looking up at me, learning to trust me. Then I ask God what I should do. Sometimes the answer may seem scary, but, one thing I'm sure of—He'll never pour shampoo in my face!" (6)

That's a simple analogy, but a powerful truth. The greatest problem that most of us have is either an insufficient faith or an inadequate God. Trust God and hang on. Trust God and keep going. Trust God and keep coming back demanding justice until God gives you a victory.

Many people experience defeat in life because they simply give up too soon.

Years ago an old man approached the famous 19th-century poet and artist Dante Gabriel Rossetti. The old man showed Rossetti some paintings. He asked, "What do you think, Mr. Rossetti?" Rossetti studied them. After the first few, Rossetti knew the paintings were worthless; they did not display the least hint of artistic talent.

But Rossetti was a kind man, and he told the elderly man as gently as possible that the pictures showed little talent. He was sorry, but he could not lie to the man. The visitor was disappointed, but seemed to expect Rossetti's judgment.

He then apologized for taking up Rossetti's time, but asked if Rossetti would look at just a few more drawings—these done by a young art student?

Rossetti looked over the second batch of sketches and immediately became enthusiastic over the talent they revealed. "These," he said, "Oh, these are good. This young student has great talent. He should be given every help and encouragement in his career as an artist. He has a great future if he will work hard and stick to it."

Rossetti could see that the old fellow was deeply moved. "Who is this fine young artist?" he asked, "Your son?"

"No," said the old man sadly. "It is me—40 years ago. If only I had heard your praise then! For you see, I got discouraged and gave up—too soon." (7)

What is it the poet says? "Of all sad words of tongue or pen, the saddest are these, 'It might have been.'" Don't let that be said of your life. Hang in there. Don't give up. Trust God. Don't miss out on a possible blessing because you became discouraged.

That is particularly important in serving Christ. Some people get their feelings hurt in a church meeting, and suddenly they're missing from the fellowship. Others get burned out, because the results of their labors for Christ seem negligible or non-existent. Christ is speaking directly to you. Hang in there. The results of your labors are not in vain. You are building up treasure in heaven.

In his book, A Home Forum Reader, Glenn Wasson relates a simple experience that had a profound effect on his life. He had been clearing brush in the mountains when he took a lunch break. He sat on a log by a rushing stream, woods all around him, and bit into his sandwich.

Suddenly a persistent bee began tormenting him, buzzing around his head, as if it intended to sting him. Glenn waved it off, but it quickly returned. This time he swatted it to the ground and stepped on it. He thought his problem was solved, but to his amazement, the bee emerged from the sand to renew its attack.

Before it had a chance to get airborne again, Glenn ground the insect into the sand. That should do it, he thought. He resumed his lunch. As he finished his lunch, out of the corner of his eye he noticed the bee burrowing out from its sandy grave. Glenn, intrigued, bent over to watch.

The bee's right wing seemed all right, but the left one was "crumpled like a piece of paper." Nonetheless, the bee with great patience stretched and tried its damaged wing, moving it slowly up and down. It ran its legs along the length of the wing, trying to straighten it out. The damage, though, seemed irreparable. Glenn, being a veteran pilot, knew a good deal about wings. As he knelt down watching the bee, he concluded that the bee would never fly again.

The bee, however, had other ideas. It furiously stretched out the damaged wing and increased the tempo of its fluttering. Then the bee attempted valiantly to fly. It managed an elevation of three inches before crashing back to earth. It tried again, and again. Each effort was a little more successful, though sometimes the bee would fly erratically this way or that. At last, the bee took off, buzzed over the stream, and was gone.

"As the bee disappeared," Glenn later wrote, "I realized that I was still on my knees, and I remained on my knees for some time." (8)

Friends, that bee demonstrated a faith that you and I can only envy. Some of us quit even before we really get started. When that happens remember that bee. When that happens remember the woman whom Jesus told about who kept demanding justice until she wore a crooked judge down. Don't miss out on one of the real secrets of life: Hang in there! Keep stretching that damaged wing until you can fly.

1. Leland Gregory, Stupid History Tales of Stupidity, Strangeness, and Mythconceptions Throughout the Ages (Kansas City, MO: Andrews McMeel Publishing, LLC, 2007), p. 71.
2. The United Church Observer, April 1995, p. 55.
3. The Oregonian, June 26, 2002, http://www.oregonian.com/.
4. Pastor Dan Mangler's Sunday Sermon.
5. Anthony T. Evans, Tony Evans' Book of Illustrations (Chicago: Moody Publishers, 2009).
6. Submitted by John R. Trammell, Savannah, GA.
7. Author Unknown, http://www.motivational-well-being.com/motivational-stories-9.html.
8. Cited by Alan Stewart,
http://sermons.pastorlife.com/members/UploadedSermons/sermon_2352.pdf.

A Faith That Leaves A Legacy

2 Timothy 4:6-8

(Dynamic Faith for a Dying World, #4)

What would you like to have as your epitaph some day? Have you ever given that any thought? What will people say about you after you're gone? It's always interesting to me to read some of the humorous inscriptions that have appeared on tombstones in days gone past. For example, here is one that should have been edited:

Here lies Col. Brown . . . Shot in battle by an enemy soldier.

"Well Done Thou Good and Faithful Servant."

A tombstone in Girard, Pennsylvania carries an epitaph that probably would be the source of a good lawsuit. It tells of Ellen Shannon, twenty-six, "Who," according to her epitaph, "was fatally burned March 21, 1870 by the explosion of a lamp filled with 'R. E. Danforth's Non-Explosive Burning Fluid.'"

Sounds ready-made for a class action lawsuit. I can hear the television commercial now: "Have you lost someone you loved in an explosion caused by R. E. Danforth's Non-Explosive Burning Fluid? Contact our law firm."

Some of you can sympathize with this etching on the tombstone of a lady named Margaret Daniels of Richmond, Virginia. It reads like this:

"She always said her feet were killing her . . . but nobody believed her."

Our lesson for today from Paul's letter to Timothy, though too lengthy for a normal epitaph, could have been inscribed on Paul's tombstone. They are inspiring words that challenge us to this day. He writes these words,

"For I am already being poured out like a drink offering, and the time for my departure is near. I have fought the good fight, I have finished the race, I have kept the faith. Now there is in store for me the crown of righteousness, which the Lord, the righteous Judge, will award to me on that day—and not only to me, but also to all who have longed for his appearing."

Here is the scene in which Paul is writing: He is sitting in the drab dungeon of a Roman prison. He is facing the capital charge of insurrection against the Roman government. He has had his preliminary hearing before Nero. Soon he will stand in his final trial and hear the fateful verdict: "Execution." How soon? We do not know, but these verses indicate that it will be quite soon. Paul knows that the end of his life upon earth is near.

This is the reason he had just passed the banner of the gospel over to Timothy—the reason he had just given Timothy the awesome charge of preaching the Word of God to a lost and dying world. Note how Paul encourages Timothy even in discussing his own coming death. He wants Timothy to look ahead to the end of his own life and to be able to bear the same testimony.

Paul begins by expressing his view of death. "For I am . . . being poured out like a drink offering," he writes, "and the time for my departure is near." Paul saw his death as an offering and sacrifice which he was presenting to God.

The Greek word for offering or sacrifice (spendomai) is striking: it refers to an offering called a drink offering that was sometimes presented to God. When a person wanted to make a sacrifice to God, he often took a cup of wine or oil and poured it out. The drink offering symbolized the Lord Jesus pouring out his soul—dying for us.

Paul is saying, "I am laying down my life as an offering to Christ Jesus my Lord—laying it down in the supreme act of sacrifice. I am dying for him."

Bible scholar William Barclay describes the scene like this: "Paul did not think of himself as going to be executed; he thought of himself as going to offer his life to God. His life was not being taken from him; he was laying it down. Ever since his conversion Paul had offered to God his money, his scholarship, his strength, his time, the vigor of his body, the acuteness of his mind, the devotion of his passionate heart. Only life itself was left to offer, and gladly Paul was going to lay life down." (1)

What a wonderful statement of commitment! It's hard for us to even imagine such dedication. It's hard to find a faith like that in our modern world.

A woman named Lila Moore tells about her days working at a card-and-gift shop. A young woman came in one day, and spent several hours looking through the books of wedding invitations. Finally she selected just the right one. She filled out the forms, and put in her order so that the invitations to her wedding might come on time.

Two weeks later, the phone rang, and Lila answered it. It was the same young woman calling. "Is it too late to make a few changes to my invitations?" she asked.

"Well," said Lila, "I'll have to check with the printer, and see if he's done your order yet. Why don't you tell me what you want changed, and I'll call you back?"

"Okay," says the young woman. "It's a different date, and a different church and, oh yes, a different guy!" (2)

I'm not certain that this young woman was ready to make the kind of commitment to have a successful marriage.

The reason that St. Paul made such an impression on the world, an impression that lasts to this day, is that he was totally committed. He offered up his life to God with nothing held back in reserve.

Of course, this was not unusual in the early days of our faith. The Greek words for martyr (ieromartyras) and witness (martyria) come from the same root word. In those early days of the church the commitment to be a witness for Christ could not be separated from the possibility of becoming a martyr for Christ. Throughout his ministry Paul understood the risk he was taking. He saw other leaders of the church offer up their lives. A sentence to death was always a possibility when you committed your life to Jesus; now it was a reality for Paul, and he was prepared.

"I am already being poured out like a drink offering," he writes, "and the time for my departure is near."

The Greek word for "departure" is also striking in its meaning. According to Dr. W. E. Vine in his dictionary of New Testament words, the word "departure" suggests three possible scenarios.

To depart is the picture of a ship hoisting the anchor and loosening the mooring ropes and departing one country for another country. Paul had been anchored and tied to this world, but the anchor and ropes of this world were now being loosed, and Paul was about to set sail for the greatest of all ports— heaven itself. That's one meaning of depart.

To depart is also the picture of "breaking up an encampment." Paul had been camping in this world, like some of us might camp at the beach or in the mountains. Many times the opposition to his preaching had been so violent, he had been forced to break camp and move on, sometimes fleeing for his life. But now, Paul was to break camp and depart for the last time.

And finally, to depart is the picture of the unyoking of an animal from the burden of the cart, plough, or millstone which it had been pulling to grind the grain. Paul was to be released from the yoke and burden of labor and toil in this life. He was being released and set free to depart for the pastures and still waters and rest of eternity. (3)

Matthew Henry says: "Observe . . . with what pleasure [Paul] speaks of dying. He calls it his departure: though it is probable that he foresaw he must die a violent bloody death, yet he calls it his departure, or his release. Death, to a good man, is his release from the imprisonment of this world and his departure to the enjoyments of another world; he does not cease to be, but is only removed from one world to another." (4) Paul begins by describing his death as an offering. Then he describes his life.

The way Paul describes his life is also full of meaning. He quickly glances back over his life and uses three pictures to describe it—the pictures of a soldier, an athlete, and a steward or manager.

Paul says. "I have fought a good fight." In other words, he had lived life like a faithful soldier: he had responded to the call of the Christ. He had suffered through the threats, scrapes, and wars launched by the enemies of Christ. He had done his time, stuck to the mission of Christ to the very end. Now he was being released from his service as a soldier for the King, released to go home to live at peace in the kingdom of his Lord forever and ever. "I have fought a good fight." That's one picture.

Then he says, "I have finished the race . . ." Paul had completed the race of life just like the athlete runs and finishes the course of his race. This is powerful, for it means that Paul disciplined and controlled his life to the utmost—just like an Olympic athlete. He controlled his thoughts and his actions. He focused upon the course of life, how he ran it. He could not run the risk of being distracted by the things of the world lest he become a castaway and be disqualified from running the race.

Barry J. Farber in his book, Dive Right In, tells about the Olympic athlete Michael Johnson. Johnson earned his reputation as the fastest human on earth at the Olympic trials in 1996.

Dr. Phil Santiago, official chiropractor to US. Olympic athletes, was there when Johnson pulled off this feat. Santiago was impressed and amazed by both Johnson's attitude and his willingness to do whatever it took to win the gold and break the world record. During the trials, Santiago asked Johnson how he was feeling. "Fine," the athlete replied. "I'm going to break the world record today." He did break the world record—but there was a technical problem with the timer and the officials would not count that race.

Afterward, Santiago commiserated with Johnson on his bad luck. "No problem," Johnson replied. "I'll break it again tomorrow." And he did.

Johnson also had the opportunity to win four gold medals in the games. He qualified to run the relays as well as the individual two-hundred-meter race. But he was so focused on destroying the Olympic and world records, he didn't care about winning the rest of the medals. "He selected the goal he wanted," says Santiago. "He knew that in order to break these records, he'd probably rip his muscles and be unable to run the relays. That was okay with him."

And that's what happened. Immediately after the race, his legs were packed in ice and he was out of commission for a week and a half. He'd known that would happen, but he had the discipline and the focus, the mental strength to go even beyond his body's limits. (5)

Johnson was running to win a gold medal and the recognition that goes with it. Paul had run his race in devotion to Christ. "I have finished the race," he said.

Finally, Paul says that he had kept the faith. He had looked after the faith just like a good steward looks after the estate of his master. The Lord had entrusted the faith to Paul, and he had kept the faith. He had proven faithful; he had faithfully managed the faith for his Master, the Lord Jesus Christ. The idea is that of a trust, of a management contract between Christ and Paul. Paul is saying that he had kept the terms of the contract; he had managed and looked after the trust faithfully and well.

Now Paul could look forward to his reward. This is an aspect of our faith that we don't talk about much anymore. We don't want our service to Christ to appear self-serving. That's understandable. But, at the end of life, there is a reward to those who have been faithful to Christ. Paul writes, "Now there is in store for me the crown of righteousness, which the Lord, the righteous Judge, will award to me on that day—and not only to me, but also to all who have longed for his appearing." We don't work for the reward, but still it comes.

I heard recently about a businessman who was telling his secretary about an award he was going to receive. She asked, "What exactly does this award do?"

He said, "It doesn't DO anything."

She said, "Then they're giving it to the right person." (6)

That couldn't be said about Paul. He wasn't receiving an award for doing nothing. Paul was receiving what he called "the crown of righteousness." But he didn't look at this crown as an exclusive award. It was the award that all who serve Christ will one day receive.

I love the way Joni Eareckson Tada once described that day when she will fully be in the presence of the Almighty. Joni, as you know, was left quadriplegic by a diving accident, unable to use her legs or her arms. She writes, "I can't wait to be clothed in righteousness. Without a trace of sin. True, it will be wonderful to stand, stretch, and reach to the sky, but it will be more wonderful to offer praise that is pure. I won't be crippled by distractions. Disabled by insincerity. I won't be handicapped by a ho-hum half-heartedness. My heart will join with yours and bubble over with effervescent adoration. We will finally be able to fellowship fully with the Father and the Son. For me, this will be the best part of heaven." (7)

It will be the best part of heaven. And the best thing of all is that it is free. It is a gift. No one understood that better than Paul. The crown of righteousness is not something you earn, something you achieve by your own striving, but something that God bestows upon you. Paul was to receive the crown of righteousness because he had given his life to be a soldier for Christ, because he had been an athlete for Christ, and because he had been a steward or manager for Christ and his faith, but Paul, more than anyone who ever lived, realized that even his striving was a gift from God. God had chosen him for His service and now Paul would enjoy the rewards that go with that calling.

Think about it: Paul was to be given a crown of righteousness that makes a person perfect before God—righteous and perfect so that he can live before God forever and ever. What a contrast with the fading and deteriorating crowns and trophies given by this world. And here is the good news for the day: That is our reward as well. As the Greek scholar Kenneth Wuest says: "To those who have considered precious His appearing and therefore have loved it, and . . . are still holding that attitude in their hearts, to these the Lord Jesus will also give the victor's [crown] of righteousness." (8)

What a fitting epitaph for every believer in Jesus Christ: "I have fought the good fight, I have finished the race, I have kept the faith. Now there is in store for me the crown of righteousness . . ."

What message will appear on your tombstone? It's not too late to make a change. It's not too late to make your life a living sacrifice to God.

1. The Letters to Timothy, Titus, and Philemon, p. 240.
2. Wayne Brouwer, Wedding Homilies (Seven Worlds).
3. W. E. Vine, Expository Dictionary of New Testament Words.
4. Matthew Henry's Commentary, Vol. 5, p. 849.
5. (New York: Berkley Books, 1999), p. 97.
6. Robert Orben, Current Comedy.
7. Heaven: Your Real Home (Grand Rapids: Zondervan, 1995), p.41.
8. The Epistles of Paul the Apostle to Timothy and Titus, p. 371f.

A Faith That Will Transform You
Luke 19:1-10
(Dynamic Faith For A Dying World, #5)

The news service Reuters carried a story sometime back about a man in Poland who was up a tree—literally. He was trying to avoid paying a cab driver. The man jumped from the cab with the driver in hot pursuit. The fleeing man must have been amazingly athletic. After climbing a tall tree, he jumped from branch to branch and hurled bananas from a shopping bag at a crowd which had gathered at the scene.

More than a dozen firefighters were called in. They spread out an airbag under the tree as a police psychologist was sent up in a ladder-bucket to negotiate with the man.

After a two-hour stand-off, he agreed to come down. However his attempt to evade paying the cab fare is likely to cost him far more than the fare itself. The fire brigade was planning to send him a $4,300 bill for the rescue operation.

It's not often that you see a grown man up in a tree. It's kind of a ridiculous position to be in. The most famous example of such behavior is found in our lesson for today from Luke's Gospel. It is, of course, the story of Zacchaeus.

The story is set in Jericho. Jesus is passing through the city when he spots Zacchaeus peering at him from the branches of a sycamore-fig tree. What makes this scene particularly fascinating is that Zacchaeus is the town's chief tax collector.

This is the only time in scripture the title "chief" is used with the title "tax collector." Its meaning is not known exactly. It probably refers to the head of the local tax office. If so, Zacchaeus was probably responsible to the Roman government for the management of the local tax-collectors and their monies. This means that Zacchaeus was without doubt a very wealthy man. Jericho was an important customs station and agricultural center. The position of chief tax collector would have provided exceptional opportunities for the accumulation of wealth.

Zacchaeus' wealth is important for two reasons. First of all, Zacchaeus had all the pleasures and comforts of life which money could buy. As entertainer Sophie Tucker once said, "I've been rich and I've been poor; rich is better." Nevertheless, Zacchaeus' wealth did not satisfy his deepest needs. Despite his wealth and the pleasures and comfort he enjoyed, he was apparently empty and lonely within. Why else would he have climbed a tree to see an itinerant teacher and preacher named Jesus?

Luke tells us that Zacchaeus was a short man. That's generally a disadvantage in our world. Studies show that even to this day, society rewards men according to their physical height. That's absurd, of course, and there have been many great men who have been diminutive in stature, but regardless, it can sometimes be a disadvantage. It was certainly a disadvantage for Zacchaeus in his attempt to see Jesus over the crowd. When there was no other way for him to see the Master, this man of position and wealth humbled himself and climbed a tree. He was determined to see the Lord, and nothing was going to stop him.

More than likely, Zacchaeus was experiencing the beginning of faith stirring within his heart. So he wanted to know more about this man who was causing such a stir in his society. He had perhaps heard reports about Jesus being the Messiah. Maybe he heard about Jesus calling Matthew, another tax collector, to be one of his disciples. Zacchaeus may have begun to believe these reports and to hope that they were true. His efforts to see Jesus and his resulting response to Jesus are evidence that there was some strong impulse driving him toward spiritual growth.

So, as Jesus is proceeding through the city he looks up and spots Zacchaeus in this tree. We shouldn't be surprised that Jesus noticed Zacchaeus. Jesus sees every person, no matter where he or she may be . . . but there is one person in particular whom Jesus sees. He sees the person who is seeking him. Jesus knows our need and reaches out to meet that need.

Zacchaeus was desperate to see Jesus, so he struggled against the odds and found a place where his view would be unimpeded. The place he chose meant humiliating himself in front of his neighbors, but he was willing to do whatever it took to get a look at the Savior. And, because Zacchaeus sought so diligently to see Jesus, Jesus saw him.

Even more wonderfully, Jesus knew and called him by name. "Zacchaeus," Jesus called to him, "come down immediately. I must stay at your house today." This was bound to strike Zacchaeus quite dramatically. When anyone, especially a stranger, calls us by name, our ears perk up and our senses become more alert. Jesus knows every person's name. He wants to address every one of us like he addressed Zacchaeus, but we must do as Zacchaeus did: seek to find a place where we can see Jesus; then Jesus will see us and call us by name.

"Zacchaeus," Jesus called to him, "come down immediately. I must stay at your house today." Jesus asked to be received with haste. He was set for Jerusalem and must not delay too long. There was no time to waste. Jesus wanted to spend some time with Zacchaeus; but Zacchaeus had to act then and there. Jesus had only a couple of hours before he had to move on to fulfill his purpose. The moment of opportunity was then and there, that day. The next day the grand opportunity would be gone.

Luke tells us that Zacchaeus came down at once and welcomed Jesus gladly. It is a beautiful picture of a person seeking faith and that search being rewarded.

But Jesus and Zacchaeus are not the only two characters in our story. Also present were the other residents of Jericho and they were unhappy. Luke tells us that "all the people saw this and began to mutter, 'He has gone to be the guest of a sinner.'"

It's interesting that the stories of Jesus' wondrous acts of grace are almost always accompanied by a chorus of the self-righteous decrying those very acts.

That brilliant thinker C. S. Lewis once dealt with the tendency of people to be self-righteousness. In one of his books, he wrote that religious people are most scandalized by sins of the flesh. There are sins involving the body, such as adultery, assault, drunkenness, murder. "Jesus [however] was most scandalized by sins of the spirit. The sins of the flesh are bad, but they are the least bad of all sins," said Lewis. "All the worst pleasures are purely spiritual: the pleasure of putting other people in the wrong, of bossing and patronizing . . . the pleasures of power, of hatred . . . That is why," according to Lewis, "a cold, self-righteous prig who goes regularly to church may be far nearer to hell than a prostitute." (1)

That states it pretty strongly, but it seems to accurately represent the attitude of Jesus toward people who are self-righteousness and judgmental.

This is not to say that Zacchaeus was without blame. As we noted Zacchaeus was a tax collector—the chief tax collector. As you know, tax collectors were bitterly hated by the Jewish people. Tax collectors served the Roman conquerors. Most tax collectors were Jews, but in the people's eyes they had denied their Jewish heritage and betrayed their country. They were thus ostracized, completely cut off from Jewish society and excommunicated from Jewish religion and privileges.

In addition, the tax collectors were usually cheats, dishonest and unjust men. The Roman government compensated tax collectors by allowing them to collect more than the percentage required for taxes. Tax collectors greedily abused their right, adding whatever percent they felt could be extorted. They took bribes from the wealthy who wished to avoid taxes. They fleeced the average citizen. They even swindled the government when they could. This is how most tax collectors became extremely wealthy.

It was an affront to the law abiding Jews of Jericho that Jesus would be visiting in the home of such a man. Eating supper with someone in biblical times meant you were willing to call that person your friend. So when Jesus said that he wanted to stay with Zacchaeus, and later ate with him, the religious people couldn't believe it. Doesn't Jesus know what this man did for a living?

If these self-righteous critics could only have known what was about to happen to Zacchaeus. When Jesus entered his home, Zacchaeus repented of his sins and changed his whole life. He said to Jesus, "Look, Lord! Here and now I give half of my possessions to the poor, and if I have cheated anybody out of anything, I will pay back four times the amount."

Imagine that—four times what he had taken. Restitution became a way of life for Zacchaeus after that. Think of the people he had cheated. Imagine how long it would take to track them down. This is an amazing act of contrition and conversion.

Some of you may remember the story of Mickey Cohen, a Los Angeles gangster in the late 1940s who supposedly became a Christian through Billy Graham's ministry. There was just one problem. After his so-called conversion Mickey Cohen didn't change his behavior or his mob connections. J. Edwin Orr, a revivalist and historian, was with Billy Graham when Cohen made his alleged conversion. When confronted about his lack of apparent repentance, Cohn responded, "You didn't tell me I would have to give up my work!" He meant his rackets. "You didn't tell me that I would have to give up my friends!" He meant his gangster associates.

Says Edwin Orr, "[Cohen] had heard that so-and-so was a Christian cowboy, so-and-so was a Christian actress, so-and-so was a Christian senator, and he really thought he could be a Christian gangster . . . ." (2)

To his credit Zacchaeus knew better than that and he was willing to do better than that. "Look, Lord! Here and now I give half of my possessions to the poor, and if I have cheated anybody out of anything, I will pay back four times the amount."

Jesus said to him, "Today salvation has come to this house, because this man, too, is a son of Abraham. For the Son of Man came to seek and to save the lost."

What a beautiful statement of hope for those who are broken of heart and of spirit. "The Son of Man came to seek and to save the lost." It makes no difference if your home is a mansion or a rescue mission—if your skin is black, brown, yellow or white. It doesn't even matter if you are a saint or a sinner, if your heart is empty, and you will let him, Jesus wants to come in and make his home there.

Years ago, a broken, unkempt homeless man found his way into one of our nation's greatest churches—Marble Collegiate Church, Fifth Avenue at Twenty-ninth Street, New York City. This great church would later be made famous by the ministry of Dr. Norman Vincent Peale.

A Dr. Burrell was the pastor of Marble Collegiate Church at the time of our story. It was he who welcomed this homeless man, named Billy, into this great church.

A life of alcoholism had befuddled Billy, but one thing was clear in his hazy mind. He believed that Dr. Burrell could help him. He had known Dr. Burrell a third of a century before, in better days. Now the two men came together under far different circumstances—the pastor of this great church and a broken man from the streets.

Dr. Burrell knew immediately, of course, that Billy needed help. He vowed to do what he could as he heard the story of Billy's wrecked life. The next Sunday Billy sat in a far-away seat in the great sanctuary of this church. On later Sundays he came early to get a seat nearer to the pulpit. For six months, Billy sat with upraised face, listening to Dr. Burrell's every word. At the end of that time, Billy came into Burrell's study and said: "Dr. Burrell, I want to take communion and join your church." And within a few weeks that once broken man took part in the communion service and stood before the congregation to be admitted to membership in that famous and rich old church.

But immediately afterward—without warning—Billy disappeared. Every pastor has seen this happen. People join the church and then kind of disappear—until Christmas or Easter. But this time the story was a little different. Billy disappeared . . . never to be seen in that great church again.

Two years later Dr. Burrell received a telephone call. The call came from the Hadley Rescue Hall in the Bowery. "Dr. Burrell," said John Callahan, the head of that mission, "can you come down here this evening and conduct a funeral? The man who is dead said he knew you very well."

When Dr. Burrell entered the mission that evening its seats were filled. Before the platform stood a casket and as Dr. Burrell looked at the face, he knew at once that it was Billy. He turned to John Callahan and asked, "What's he been up to, John? How did you find him? How did he come down here to the mission?"

"He came down here with his face shining," answered Callahan. "We didn't find him. He found us. Billy isn't one of those we picked off the streets. The night after you took him into your church he came here, and he's been here ever since. He patrolled the waterfront to find down-and-out men. And he found them. They'll tell us about it themselves, this evening."

The greater part of Billy's funeral service consisted of the tributes of people whose paths had crossed his. He seemed to have left a blessing wherever he moved. The landlady in the waterfront boarding-house where Billy had lived stood up with her beaming face covered with tears. "He taught God to me and to every person in the house. My house became full of Christians after Billy came there." That old boarding-house on the waterfront! It had become one of the happiest places in the big city. Billy had brought God to it, and out of it nightly went Billy, the landlady and the boarders to hunt for broken men and women and show them how they might become whole again.

One after another, people arose in the audience and, with happy but tear-stained faces, they told what Billy, the longshoreman, had done for them. Billy had earned his daily bread beside them. And all around him, as he worked, there had been a circle of song and happiness and prayer; he had held up the cross of Jesus to all he met. (3)

Such is the kind of complete change that happened in Zacchaeus' life. Paul Scherer, in describing this story, says that this meeting with Jesus "redeemed Zacchaeus' past, it transformed his present, and it re-directed his future."

We don't know what happened to Zacchaeus. There is a legend, and it is only a legend, that Zacchaeus later became bishop at Caesarea. Whatever became of him, we know his life was transformed by this experience with the Master, just as your life and mine can be transformed if we open ourselves completely and let Christ do his life-changing work in us. Jesus came to seek and to save the lost. If you find yourself feeling lost this day, whatever that may mean to you, won't you open yourself to his love?

1. I apologize, but I have misplaced the source of this quote.
2. Edwin Orr, "Playing the Good News Off-Key," Christianity Today, January 1, 1982, 24-25. Cited in Robert J. Morgan, Preacher's Sourcebook Creative Sermon Illustrations (Nashville: Thomas Nelson, Inc., 2007), pp. 662-663.
3. William G: Shepherd, Great Preachers As Seen By a Journalist (Fleming H. Revell, 1924).

A Faith That Will Bring You Alive
Luke 20:27-38
(Dynamic Faith for a Dying World, #6)

Brian Rice of Maple Grove, Minnesota writes that recently his wife asked the question men most dread: "Honey, do you think I look fat in my new dress?"

Brian was up to the test. Pointing to what he was wearing, he replied, "Do I look stupid in this shirt?" (1)

It's not easy to be married.

Comedian Wendy Liebman says she went through a messy divorce. She says, "My divorce was messy because there was a child involved. My husband."

I expected to hear an "Amen" from some of the women.

One of the surprise off-Broadway hits this year was titled Old Jews Telling Jokes. It boasted an interesting story line—old Jewish people who tell jokes. Here's one of them: During a bank robbery, the robber's mask falls off. He puts it back on, turns to a man, and says, "Did you see my face?"

The customer says, "Yes, I did." The robber shoots him.

He turns to a woman, "How about you?"

She says, "No. But my husband did." (2)

One woman says that her husband went back to school after they were married and had children. They didn't have much money for their family of seven.

At a friend's wedding, her four-year-old daughter was sitting next to her when the minister asked, "Do you take this man for better or worse, for richer or poorer, in sickness and in health?"

At that point she said her daughter turned to her and whispered loudly, "You chose poorer, didn't you Mommy?"

There are worse things than choosing "poorer." Marriage is tough nowadays. Maybe we can learn something from our Russian friends. I understand that in Russia the best man in a wedding must sign the marriage register guaranteeing that the union will last at least six months or he'll pay a fine of 150 rubles. That sounds like a pretty good incentive for a friend to help a friend stay married. Unfortunately that's only $4.80 in U.S. dollars. I doubt if any best man would intervene in his friend's marriage for $4.80.

In our lesson for today a group of religious figures ask a very interesting question about marriage. It's a little unique but that's what makes it interesting.

The question is posed to Jesus by a religious sect called the Sadducees. The Sadducees were the religious conservatives of Jesus' time. They accepted only what was written in the Torah, the books of Moses, also known as the Pentateuch, the first five books of the Bible. For the Sadducees, the Torah was regarded as many conservative Americans regard the U. S. Constitution. If it's not in the Constitution, according to these patriots, it won't fly. That is how the Sadducees regarded the Torah. If it was not in the first five books of the Bible in their estimation, then it was not crucial to the faith.

For example, the first five books of the Bible say nothing about eternal life or resurrection or immortality; therefore, such things should not be taught as part of the faith, according to the Sadducees. Accordingly, they did not believe in Heaven or Hell.

Because their faith was restricted to the first five books of the Bible, they did not have the benefit of such writings as the book of Job which contains this witness: "Oh, that my words were recorded, that they were written on a scroll, that they were inscribed with an iron tool on lead, or engraved in rock forever! I know that my redeemer lives, and that in the end he will stand on the earth. And after my skin has been destroyed, yet in my flesh I will see God; I myself will see him . . ." (Job 19:23-27) According to the Sadducees, there was no such thing as life beyond the grave.

So the question they posed to Jesus is quite surprising. "Teacher," they said, "Moses wrote for us that if a man's brother dies and leaves a wife but no children, the man must marry the widow and raise up offspring for his brother. Now there were seven brothers. The first one married a woman and died childless. The second and then the third married her, and in the same way the seven died, leaving no children. Finally, the woman died too. Now then," they asked, "at the resurrection whose wife will she be, since the seven were married to her?"

Now, that's a pretty grim story—in fact it could be a Grimm's fairy tale. We could call it "A Bride for Seven Brothers." Forgetting for a moment the absurdity of the Sadducees who did not even believe in the resurrection posing this question about "whose wife she will be at the resurrection?" think what this example says about the place of women in society. In that culture, women were no better than property to be passed along to keep the family estate intact. Think about it. When a man dies, if he did not leave a male heir, his eldest brother was to marry his widow. This would continue the man's name and keep his property "in the family." In this scenario, the woman was passed among seven brothers. She outlives them all, but then she dies. "Whose bride will she be at the resurrection?" asked these Sadducees.

It was, of course, a trick question. These Sadducees had no interest in the intricacies of life after death. They didn't even believe in such a thing. They simply wanted to get Jesus in trouble with the people. But Jesus was accustomed to scholars attempting to trip him up. Jesus, however, knew the Scriptures better than they did. Even more important, he saw beyond the Scriptures to the heart of the One who inspired the Scriptures, so he was never trapped by those who would discredit him. Notice his answer here. Jesus replied, "The people of this age marry and are given in marriage. But those who are considered worthy of taking part in the age to come and in the resurrection from the dead will neither marry nor be given in marriage, and they can no longer die; for they are like the angels. They are God's children, since they are children of the resurrection. But in the account of the burning bush, even Moses showed that the dead rise, for he calls the

Lord 'the God of Abraham, and the God of Isaac, and the God of Jacob.' He is not the God of the dead, but of the living, for to him all are alive."

Notice that Jesus does three things here. First of all, he met the Sadducees where they were. Secondly, he spoke to an uncertainty that many good people have about marriage. Finally, he answered the most pressing question of all of life—is there life beyond the grave? Let's consider each of these for just a few moments.

First of all, he met the Sadducees where they were. The Sadducees were people of the Torah, as we have already noted. If something wasn't in the Torah, it could not be part of their faith. So Jesus answered them from the Torah. He turns to the third chapter of Exodus, the story of Moses and the burning bush. You remember that wonderful story. Moses was tending the flock of Jethro, his father-in-law, the priest of Midian. Moses led the flock to the far side of the wilderness and came to Horeb, the mountain of God. There the angel of the Lord appeared to him in flames of fire from within a bush. Moses saw that, though the bush was on fire, it did not burn up. So Moses thought, "I will go over and see this strange sight—why the bush doesn't burn up."

When the Lord saw that he had gone over to look, God called to him from within the bush, "Moses! Moses!"

And Moses said, "Here I am."

"Do not come any closer," God said. "Take off your sandals, for the place where you are standing is holy ground." Then he said, "I am the God of your father, the God of Abraham, the God of Isaac and the God of Jacob."

It is a wonderful story of faith. However, notice that God does not say, "I WAS the God of Abraham, Isaac and Jacob." Remember, when Moses wrote these words the three patriarchs had been dead for centuries, yet God refers to them in the present tense. This, says Jesus to the Sadducees, is evidence right there in the Torah that life after death exists. God says, "I am . . . the God of Abraham, the God of Isaac and the God of Jacob." "God is not the God of the dead," Jesus insists, "but of the living."

Jesus answered the Sadducees in a way that they could understand. Jesus always meets people where they are. This is to say that none of us has an excuse when it comes to things of faith. If we are unsophisticated in our understandings, he will come to us with simplicity and patience. If we come from another faith, he will show us how the teachings that we prize most in our old faith point the way to him. If we come from a background of abuse, he will wrap his arms around us and gently bring us to a pure and wholesome relationship with him. Jesus always comes to us where we are if we will but open our hearts to him.

That is the first thing he did for the Sadducees, he came to them where they were.

Secondly, Jesus answered an uncertainty that many good people have about marriage. This poor woman outlived seven husbands. [Maybe, if we are mystery fans, we might be wondering what kind of secret poison she employed to get rid of each of these husbands. Just kidding, of course.]

"Whose wife," asked the Sadducees, "would she be in the afterlife?"

Now I doubt that many of us lie awake at night wondering about whether we will still be married in heaven. We're sophisticated people. We understand that marriage in this world is primarily defined as a physical relationship. In fact, the breaking of that relationship—adultery—is strictly defined in physical terms.

Heaven is not a physical place, but a spiritual one. We don't know what our spiritual bodies will be like, but evidently they will not require us to live as husbands and wives. We even say in our vows, "Till death do us part." That might be a relief to somebody in the room. I hope not, but it's possible.

There was a survey sometime back that said that, if they had it to do over again, 70% of men said they would marry the same woman, but only 50% of women said they would marry the same man. Something to think about.

There are many good people who outlive their spouses. In fact, if we are married, half of us will outlive our spouses. We don't want to be morbid about it. But death is simply a part of life. And half of spouses will one day be left behind. For most of us it will be a day of deep grief.

Eventually, however, the question may arise, "Should I take a new partner? Would that be a betrayal of the great love my spouse and I shared?" It is an emotional question. For some of you who have already dealt with this question, you may have discovered it was more emotional for other family members than it was for you. Sometimes children, particularly, can make their parents feel very guilty for all the wrong reasons.

The biblical answer to this question would be, by all means re-marry—if that is where your heart leads you. Marriage is only for this world. Your beloved former spouse who is now with God lives in a different kind of world that knows no marriage, only pure and unrestricted love. You need feel no guilt, no sense of betrayal if someone else fills the loneliness you now find in your heart. Remember those vows, "till death do us part."

And this brings us to Jesus' most important teaching. In this lesson Jesus answered unequivocally the most pressing question in life—is there life beyond the grave? And the answer he gave is, "Yes, there definitely is life beyond the grave." He not only gave us that answer with his lips, he also gave it with his own life. "He is alive!" reported the women on their return from the empty tomb, and he was alive and he still lives—this Jesus our Lord. I know, to some of us this seems too good to be true.

The great preacher of yesteryear, C.H. Spurgeon, once addressed our natural skepticism about such things. He pointed to one of the most common technologies of his time. The reference he made is dated, but the principle is still relevant:

"The electric telegraph," he said, "would have been as hard to believe in a thousand years ago as the resurrection of the dead is now. Who in the days of pack horses would have believed in flashing a message from England to America?

"Everything," he said, "is full of wonder till we are used to it, and resurrection owes the incredible portion of its marvel to our never having come across it in our observation—that is all. After the resurrection we shall regard it as a divine display of power as familiar to us as creation and providence now are." (3)

Spurgeon's language is archaic, but his rational is right on target. Of course living more than a hundred years ago he definitely would not believe in some of the marvels we take for granted today. What was considered impossible yesterday is now a reality. Life calls for intellectual humility. Just because you have not experienced a resurrection, do not assume that it is impossible. The best advice I can give is wait and see.

Of course, some of us have experienced a resurrection already in our spiritual lives. As the old Gospel song testified, "You ask me how I know he lives, he lives within my heart." That's the best evidence of the risen Christ.

Dr. Ray Pritchard tells about the funeral of Sir Winston Churchill, the former prime minister of England. "Most of us know [Churchill] as the man who single-handedly rallied the British people in the darkest days of World War II when the armies of Hitler were poised to cross the English Channel. By the power of his words he gave courage to an entire country.

"Before he died he planned his own funeral service at St. Paul's Cathedral in London. The service itself was magnificent in every way, filled with biblical liturgy and great hymns. Just as the benediction was pronounced, an unseen bugler hidden in one side of the dome began to play Taps, the traditional melody signaling the end of the day or the death of a soldier. As the mournful notes faded away, another bugler on the other side of the dome began to play Reveille, the traditional melody signaling the coming of a new day. 'It's time to get up, it's time to get up, it's time to get up in the morning.'

"It was Sir Winston's way of saying that though he was dead, he expected to 'get up' on the day of the resurrection." (4)

I have that expectation, too, and I hope that you do as well. It is Jesus' most important teaching—a teaching he conveyed by his lips and his life. Life beyond the grave is a reality. Because he lives, we, too, shall live. After all . . . "God is not the God of the dead, but the living for all are alive in Him."

1. Reader's Digest (Reader's Digest USA).
2. Ibid.
3. Charles H. Spurgeon in the Metropolitan Tabernacle Pulpit (Vol.18). Christianity Today, Vol. 33, No. 6. Cited by Daniel D. Meyer, http://www.cc-ob.tv/search.php? series_id=40&category=Sermon.
4. http://www.keepbelieving.com/sermon/2000-04-23-Whats-Your-Problem-with-the-Resurrection/..

A Faith That Works

2 Thessalonians 3:6-18

(Dynamic Faith For A Dying World, #7)

Someone visited an office and saw these signs hanging on the wall:

"Work fascinates me," said one, "I can sit and watch it for hours!"

"I don't mind going to work," said another. "But that 8-hour wait to go home is awful!"

"Hard work may not kill me," another said, "but why take a chance?"

People have all kinds of attitudes about their work.

Actor Robert Benchley said, "Anyone can do any amount of work provided it isn't the work he is supposed to be doing at that moment." That one may hit close to home.

An anonymous muse has said, "A perfect summer day is when the sun is shining, the breeze is blowing, the birds are singing and the lawn mower is broken."

Someone else has said, "The worst day of fishing is better than the best day of working."

However, most of us can relate to the bumper sticker that says: "I owe, I owe, so off to work I go."

St. Paul had difficulty with the church at Thessalonica. Some of the members were refusing to do their share of the work. He writes, "In the name of the Lord Jesus Christ, we command you, brothers and sisters, to keep away from every believer who is idle and disruptive and does not live according to the teaching you received from us. For you yourselves know how you ought to follow our example. We were not idle when we were with you, nor did we eat anyone's food without paying for it. On the contrary, we worked night and day, laboring and toiling so that we would not be a burden to any of you. We did this, not because we do not have the right to such help, but in order to offer ourselves as a model for you to imitate. For even when we were with you, we gave you this rule: 'The one who is unwilling to work shall not eat.'

"We hear that some among you are idle and disruptive. They are not busy; they are busybodies. Such people we command and urge in the Lord Jesus Christ to settle down and earn the food they eat. And as for you, brothers and sisters, never tire of doing what is good."

What do you do with people who refuse to do their share of the work? It's true in every organization. Some people do not do their share. Indira Gandhi once said, "There are two kinds of people, those who do the work and those who take the credit. Try to be in the first group—there is less competition."

Did you realize, by the way, that among rich countries people in the United States work the longest hours? Americans work much longer than Europeans, for example. This difference is quite surprising because productivity per hour worked is the same in the United States as it is in France and Germany, and it is growing at a similar rate.

In most countries and at most times in history, however, as people have become richer they have chosen to work less. In other words they decided to "spend" a part of their extra potential income on a fuller private life. Over the last fifty years Europeans have continued this pattern, and hours of work have fallen sharply. (1) But not in the United States. We seem to choose acquiring more things as opposed to having more leisure. Of course, the recent decline in the European economy may be related to their more relaxed view of work.

It's an interesting difference in attitude. Still, even with this American work ethic, there are many people who avoid doing their share. I won't ask if there are any slackers in your office. It would be surprising if there is not at least one.

Paul had that difficulty in the church at Thessalonica. Some people were faithful at work serving Christ, and others were not. Oh, this group had many good excuses. Some of them looked down on plain everyday work because of their upbringing. Some of those from Jewish backgrounds, for example, believed in hard work . . . but they believed that spiritual work was superior to physical work. They believed that only those who studied Scripture like the scribes were doing really worthy work, but not those who did manual labor. Some of those from Greek backgrounds didn't like to work, either . . . they felt it demeaning, and left most of their work to their slaves and servants. And then there were some from the Thessalonian congregation who believed work was no longer necessary because Jesus was going to return any moment.

They had many excuses for not working . . . Ask many people today. It is amazing how creative people can be in making excuses.

Abraham Lincoln was asked once about the size of the Confederate army. Lincoln said, "The Confederates have 1.2 million men."

One of his aides politely expressed doubt about that figure, so Lincoln said, "They have 1.2 million, there's no doubt. You see, all generals when they get whipped say the enemy outnumber them at least three to one. We have 400,000 men, so the Confederates must have 1.2 million."

Lincoln knew that it is part of human nature to make excuses when our performance is not up to par.

It is said that during World War II, the allied leaders Roosevelt, Stalin, and Churchill met for discussions of strategy and negotiation. In some of these meetings, Stalin would not approve of some strategy that Roosevelt and Churchill had planned out. When they asked why, Stalin would give some answer or another. Each time they would say, "That is no reason for you to refuse!"

Finally, Stalin told the two men a story about two Arabs. One Arab man asked his friend if he could borrow a rope. His friend said that he was unable to lend him his rope because he needed it to tie up his camel. The would-be borrower retorted, "But, friend, you told me that you do not own a camel."

His friend answered, "Yes I know. But if I don't want to lend you my rope, then one excuse is as good as another."

The members of the church at Thessalonica had many good excuses, just as you and I do when there is work to be done. Churches are a living testimony to Paretto's principle that 20% of people do 80% of the work. It's human nature.

Some of you are among that 20% that is responsible for the 80% of the work in this church. I am grateful for you. We could not make it without you.

Noted pastor and author Rick Warren asks, "Do you know what the worst sin is for Christians? It is not adultery. It is not murder. It is not some sort of sexual perversion. God tells us in Revelation 3. He says it's 'lukewarmness.' No passion."

These people have the attitude says Warren that "God is just one of the things in my life. I have my social life and my career life and my sexual life and my family life and over here is a little piece of the pie called church. God says, 'How dare you! I love you this much. I love you passionately. I made you, created you, planned you, purposed you, saved you, have a place for you in heaven, and you would treat that with half-hearted indifference saying, Excuse me but there's a good TV show on tonight.'

"Jesus says, 'I'd rather have you hot or cold. Lukewarmness makes me sick to my stomach.'" (2)

Certain members of the church at Thessalonica, like any church, were guilty of "lukewarmness." They were refusing to carry their share of the burden of the mission of the church.

Even worse, some of these lukewarm Christians brought a negative spirit into the fellowship. They were not only idle, but they criticized those who did work. Paul called these negative idlers, busybodies. And Paul had little use for these people. They did more harm than good. As Warren Wiersbe puts it, "They had time on their hands and gossip on their lips . . ."

Have you ever known anyone like that?

Chuck Swindoll describes these people like this: "Busybodies flit from house to house, taking little nectared drops of gossip with them and leaving behind their own residue of irritating pollen." Swindoll adds, "There's a vast difference between putting your nose in other people's business and putting your heart into their problems."

I like that way of putting it: "There's a vast difference between putting your nose in other people's business and putting your heart into their problems." Busybodies.

An unknown author said he met the strangest man on his way to church. Here is how he described this man:

"He said he believed in the Bible, but he never reads it.

"He said he thought well of the church of which he is a member, but he never attends or invites others to share in its ministry.

"He said a person should be honest with God in money matters, but he never tithes.

"He said the younger generation needs the Lord, but he isn't leading them in that direction.

"He said the church needs dedicated Christian members, but he isn't one.

"He offered some 'constructive' criticism of some of the workers—but he never works.

"He said the church should do more in ministering to people, but he doesn't help.

"He is critical of the way the church is 'run,' but he never participates.

"He says he believes in the Second Coming, but he lives as though the Lord will never return.

"He says prayer will change things, but he never prays.

"He was," says this author, "a strange man, indeed!" (3)

Not so strange. Their number in the church is legion. St. Paul called such people busybodies. They are busy, but not with constructive behavior. What we tend to overlook is this: the mind is always active; it is never still. It is either thinking positive thoughts or negative thoughts. A person may have an idle body, but not an idle mind. An idle brain is the devil's playground, as the old expression goes. This is the reason why so many idle persons—regardless of their age—get into trouble. The trouble can range all the way from becoming a busybody to murder. It is dangerous business to be idle.

Too many believers at Thessalonica had become idle busybodies, that is, poking themselves into other people's affairs, tattling, gossiping, and spreading all kinds of talk and rumors. Why? Because it is easier to be a busybody than it is to minister to the needs of those within the community who are hurting, lonely, desperate, dying, and lost.

Some of you are familiar with a little book that came out several years ago called Life's Little Instruction Book. It was compiled by H. Jackson Brown, Jr. As his son was packing for his freshman year in college, Brown retreated to the family room and wrote down 511 observations and words of counsel for his son. The result was Life's Little Instruction Book: 511 Suggestions, Observations, and Reminders on How to Live a Happy and Rewarding Life. Among his suggestions was no. 115: "Give yourself a year and read the Bible cover to cover." Here are some others: "Compliment three people everyday . . . Have a dog . . . Stop blaming others . . . Eat prunes . . . Lend only those books you never care to see again . . ." Here's an interesting one: "Avoid any church that has cushions on the pews."

But there are more: "Spend less time worrying who's right, and more time deciding what is right . . . Keep secrets . . . Remember that all news is biased . . . Just to see how it feels, for the next 24 hours refrain from criticizing anybody for anything . . . Don't use time or words carelessly. Neither can be retrieved . . . Don't gossip." (4)

That's good advice for all of us, but especially for anyone tempted to be a busybody.

Of course, the strongest argument against being idle or being a busybody is that we have a world to save in Jesus' name.

Look all about you at the people who need Christ. The lonely teenager, the shut-in, the single Mom struggling to keep her family afloat, the angry man with hate in his heart, the depressed woman looking for love in the wrong man's arms, the children who are never exposed to God or Jesus except in a curse. Tell me that you have nothing to do except criticizing those who are trying to make a difference. Tell me that you are a follower of Jesus but that these people don't matter.

Pastor Ron Hutchcraft suggests to us that Jesus wants us to "go M.A.D." That's an interesting way of putting it. Of course mad is spelled capital M period, capital A period, capital D period—M.A.D. Don't look for that in the original Greek, by the way. M.A.D. is an acrostic. When Hutchcraft says that Jesus wants us to "Go M.A.D.," he's saying that Jesus wants us to "go make a difference." If you make a constructive difference in people's lives, you won't have time to be a busybody.

Dr. Tom Long tells about a friend of his who was telling him about taking a church youth group on a mission trip to Jamaica. "On their trip they visited one of the local elementary schools, and they spent some time observing in a classroom seriously overcrowded with children, most of them very poor, all of them needy and wiggly and noisy and unruly. It was a difficult, sometimes even chaotic, learning environment; but the youth group marveled to see that the teacher carried herself with great calm and patience, treating all of the children with love and respect, despite the poverty and the chaos. They decided that the only way she could do this was that she must really love being a teacher. But they were surprised to hear her say, 'Oh, I don't come here every day mainly because I love teaching. I come here every day because I love Jesus, and I see Jesus in every one of these children.'" (5)

That saint of God will never be idle, never be a busybody. She'll never be among the 80% who want a free ride in the church. She loves Jesus. That says it all.

1. Richard Layard, Happiness Lessons From A New Science (New York: Penguin Group, 2005), p. 50.
2. http://www.sermoncentral.com/sermons/reigniting-your-passion-for-god-rick-warren-sermon-on-attitude-general-127082.asp.
3. The Timothy Report, http://www.timothyreport.com.
4. From a sermon by Dr. Robert Kopp.
5. Rev. Dr. Thomas G. Long, http://day1.org/1052-mary_and_martha..

A King Like No Other
Luke 23:33-43

WWJD—remember when those letters were the rage? There for a while, they were everywhere: bracelets, key rings, and just about anything that can be marked with the logo, WWJD: "What Would Jesus Do?"

Later, when the WWJD bracelet rage really started to catch on, people came up with some alternative bracelets: WWPMD for quarterbacks: "What Would Peyton Manning do?"

Or WWMSD for homemakers, What would Martha Stewart do?

Or DYWFWT for Liberal Arts graduates: "Do You Want Fries with That?"

For teens, there was a bracelet with simply a W: "Whatever" or "Whatsup," take your pick.

[There was even one for those of us who are aging—NWDIPOTB: "Now Why Did I Put On This Bracelet?"] (1)

If Christians of the first century had worn a bracelet, it would have said, "WDJDC? Why did Jesus die on a cross?" This was the question they had to struggle with. How could the Messiah be put to death?

Our text for today might seem strange to you for this season of the year. This Thursday is Thanksgiving. Next Sunday begins Advent. Yet our Gospel lesson focuses on Jesus on the cross. That is because this is the last Sunday in the Church Year. On this day we celebrate the meaning of Christ's journey among us.

We began last Advent. We celebrated his birth. Then at Easter we celebrated his resurrection. At Pentecost we celebrated the coming of the Holy Spirit and the birth of the church. Now we are ready to start the cycle all over again, but first we want to consider what it all means. Who was this man who walked among us? He was a man . . . yes, but he was more than that. This Sunday is called Christ the King in some churches. Some churches simply call this Sunday the Reign of Christ. Today we return to the scene of his crucifixion where we see most starkly what his kingship was all about.

The lesson begins like this: "When they came to the place called the Skull, they crucified him there, along with the criminals—one on his right, the other on his left."

Let's stop there. He was crucified between two criminals. That is the first clue to Christ's reign as king. He was crucified between two criminals. The Gospel writers use different words to describe these criminals. Matthew and Mark call them thieves. Luke uses a different word—a word that means "members of the criminal class, professional criminals, members of the underworld." (2) These men were hoods, thugs, perhaps cutthroat killers . . . They were anything but saints.

Some people are horrified that the Son of God should die in the presence of such men. I say that it is the most appropriate thing in the world. Friends, these criminals were the people Jesus came to save. On one occasion he declared, "I have come to seek and save that which was lost" (Luke 19:10). And on another occasion he declared, "The well have no need for a physician, but those who are sick" (Mark 2:17)

These are the people Jesus gave his life for. We need to remember that. Jesus didn't come to benefit good people. He came to benefit those who have difficulty being good. Maybe that includes you. I know it includes me. And I need to remind myself of that every time I am tempted to look down on another human being. Jesus doesn't look down on them. Jesus looks upon them as a lost brother or sister who needs help.

Some of you may remember the well-known British actor Michael Caine. Caine wrote a book several years ago in which he described how he fought his way out of a poor South London neighborhood to pursue his dream of becoming an actor.

In the '60s and '70s, Caine became a major star in Great Britain and the U.S. But on a visit back home in London, Caine was saddened by the news that his younger brother, Stanley, had not been heard from in months. So Michael Caine began searching out Stanley's old friends, hoping for some clue to his brother's whereabouts. No luck.

Not long afterwards, Caine went to a local furniture store to buy a luxurious new sofa. His chosen sofa was brought out by two workmen in dirty, shabby clothes. Caine recognized one of the workmen as his brother, Stanley. Stanley had fallen on hard times. Michael took his brother home and helped Stanley get back on his feet. (3)

That's what you do for a brother or sister you love—help them get back on their feet. Friends, that's the way Jesus regards everyone on earth—as his brother, his sister. And if one of these brothers or sisters has fallen on hard times, it is not in Jesus' nature to judge. Rather it is his nature to reach out a hand to save. "For God did not send his Son into the world to condemn the world, but to save the world through him" (John 3:17).

And that's what he expects out of us who call ourselves by his name. We are not here to judge our brothers and sisters who fall upon hard times, whatever the cause. Our calling is simply to reach out a helping hand. And we don't wait until they deserve such help. Christ didn't wait until we were worth saving. Paul put it this way, "God shows his love for us in that while we were yet sinners Christ died for us" (Romans 5:8, RSV).

What does our text say, first of all, about this man Jesus? What kind of king was he? "When they came to the place called the Skull, they crucified him there, along with the criminals—one on his right, the other on his left."

But look what it says next: Jesus said, "Father, forgive them, for they do not know what they are doing." Who was Jesus asking forgiveness for? It was, of course, for those who put him on that cross.

He was, for example, praying for the soldiers who cruelly tortured him and crucified him and who were preparing to gamble for his clothes. Even as he hung on the cross the soldiers mocked him, "If you are the king of the Jews, save yourself."

He also was praying for the crowd who was deriding him. "He saved others," they taunted, "let him save himself if he is God's Messiah, the Chosen One."

Then there were the religious leaders who, from their own jealousy and spiritual blindness, instigated his crucifixion. Pilate, finding no guilt in Jesus wanted to release him. But the religious authorities led the crowds in chants, "Crucify him! Crucify him!"

But there were others for whom Jesus was praying. After all, he could have spoken these words silently. This is a prayer. God would have heard a whisper. But he chose to pray these words aloud—loud enough for others to hear him and record his words. Jesus had a wider audience in mind when he prayed, "Father forgive them, for they know not what they do." I believe he was praying for everyone in history who has ever acted cruelly, who has ever lashed out in anger, who has ever caused anyone else pain.

What is there in the human heart that causes us to lash out in hatred and violence even within our own household? Why do husbands and wives abuse one another? Why do parents slap, scold and belittle their own precious children? What is there in the human heart that causes us to act with such cruelty?

Why has every generation in history demonstrated time and time again man's inhumanity to man? Why did Hitler have to exterminate 6,000,000 Jews before the rest of the world rallied to stop him? Why did Germany, an allegedly Christian nation allow the Nazis to come to power in the first place?

For that matter, in this country, why were Native Americans forced to march across our land in the infamous Trail of Tears? Why did the evils of cruel slavery in the South require a senseless slaughter of innocent young men from the North and the South in our nation's most costly war before slavery was made illegal? Why were four little African American girls slaughtered in a church bombing in 1963 in Birmingham, AL?

Why have innocent people been persecuted even in modern times because of their color, their gender, their sexual orientation? Why are we even now forced to put armed guards in our public schools? For that matter why is bullying a matter of concern in nearly every school today?

Why is it always that way—that the innocent have to experience extreme cruelty before the will and the way of the guilty is broken? Will it ever change? (4)

There is something wrong in the human heart, friends. But it's not just in the heart of the Romans or the religious authorities, or the crowds, or the Nazis or the white supremacist or the school bullies. There is something wrong in the heart of every person who has ever lived on this earth. Any of us given the right conditions are capable of unspeakable wrong-doing. Any of us given the right circumstances might have been in the crowd yelling, "Crucify him, crucify him, crucify him," if we felt our religion threatened, our rights threatened, our economic well-being threatened, our personal self-image threatened. The old spiritual rings out, "Were you there, were you there, were you there when they crucified my Lord?" And the truth of the matter is that all of us were there.

Isaiah said it 550 years before Jesus was born: "He was wounded for our transgressions, he was bruised for our iniquities: the chastisement of our peace was upon him; and with his stripes we are healed."

Who was Jesus praying for when he prayed, "Father, forgive them for they do not know what they are doing"? He was praying for us—all of us. "All have sinned and fallen short of His glory" (Romans 3:23).

That is the second thing this text tells us about the reign of Christ: he forgave his enemies. He, of course, was simply living out that which he taught: "You have heard that it was said, 'Love your neighbor and hate your enemy.' But I tell you, love your enemies and pray for those who persecute you, that you may be children of your Father in heaven" (Matthew 5:43-44). Jesus said, "Father, forgive them, for they do not know what they are doing." But let's finish our lesson:

"And they divided up his clothes by casting lots.

"The people stood watching, and the rulers even sneered at him. They said, 'He saved others; let him save himself if he is God's Messiah, the Chosen One.'

"The soldiers also came up and mocked him. They offered him wine vinegar and said, 'If you are the king of the Jews, save yourself.'

There was a written notice above him, which read: this is the king of the Jews.

One of the criminals who hung there hurled insults at him: 'Aren't you the Messiah? Save yourself and us!'

"But the other criminal rebuked him. 'Don't you fear God,' he said, "since you are under the same sentence? We are punished justly, for we are getting what our deeds deserve. But this man has done nothing wrong.'

"Then he said, 'Jesus, remember me when you come into your kingdom.'

Jesus answered him, 'Truly I tell you, today you will be with me in paradise.'"

Here's the third thing our lesson says about Christ: he made us a promise. There he hung on the cross while the soldiers and the crowd mocked him. They placed a notice above his head which read derisively "this is the king of the Jews." Even one of the criminals being crucified with him mocked him, but the other criminal rebuked him. Then this second criminal turned to Jesus and made a request: "Jesus, remember me when you come into your kingdom."

To me this is amazing. As pastor Ray Pritchard has noted: "Somehow this man saw Jesus bleeding and naked and hanging on a cross beside him and yet he believed that he would someday come into his kingdom. No man ever looked less like a king than Jesus did that day, yet this man saw him as he really was, the son of God.

"This is made more amazing when you consider that this man had none of the advantages the disciples had. He never heard Jesus teaching by the seashore, he never saw Jesus heal the sick or raise the dead. He knew nothing of Jesus' great parables and never saw any of his miracles. This man missed all the outward signs of Jesus' kingship. Yet he believed.

"He knew nothing of the virgin birth, the Old Testament prophecies or the raising of Lazarus. The coming miracle of the resurrection was unknown to him. All the things we take for granted, he knew nothing about.

"Yet there on the cross, he came to understand the heart of the gospel. In the crucified Jesus, beaten, mocked, forsaken, his life blood ebbing away, this thug saw a king. He saw obviously another crown than the crown of thorns. (5)

The second criminal says, "Jesus, remember me when you come into your kingdom." And that's our prayer. None of us deserves to enter Christ's kingdom, not on our own merit. We have only one hope, our connection to Christ. "Remember me, Lord, when you come into your kingdom."

And at this point Jesus made him a promise, but not to him only, but to all who call out to Christ for salvation: "Truly I tell you, today you will be with me in paradise."

The meaning of that phrase is quite self-evident. The moment this criminal died he would be in the presence of God—not because he deserved it, but because of God's free gift of eternal life. It is the promise that you and I cling to every time we ponder our own mortality or as we stand beside the grave of a loved one. It is that promise that allows us to carry on with our lives when life crashes in on us with its worst. "Today you will be with me in paradise."

In the musical Godspell, after Christ's resurrection, Mary Magdalene didn't want to let go of Jesus. She sang to him, "Where are you going? Where are you going? Can you take me with you? For my hand is cold, and needs warmth. Where are you going? Far beyond where the horizon lies . . . And the land sinks into mellow blueness/ Oh please, take me with you . . ."

And that is the refrain sung through the ages by everyone who loves Jesus. What kind of king is he? He's the kind of king who leaves his throne to die between two criminals. He's the kind of king who forgives his enemies. He's the kind of king who makes a promise to all who will turn to him no matter what we may have done in the past, "Truly I tell you, today you will be with me in paradise." What kind of King is Jesus? He is King of Kings and Lord of Lords. He loves us more than our own parents. He forgives us even as we sin against him and drive nails into his hands. And he has made it possible for us to live with him forever in his Kingdom of love. Don't you want him to reign in your life today?

1. http://home.roadrunner.com/~lyndale/Pentecost%2015B.htm.
2. Ray Pritchard, http://www.keepbelieving.com/sermon/1991-02-10-Last-Second-Salvation/.
3. Michael Caine, What's it All About? (New York: Turtle Bay Books, 1992), pp. 216-217.
4. From a sermon by Dr. Philip Ware Zebley.
5. Pritchard.